CULTURAL HERITAGE LAW AND POLICY

Series Editors

PROFESSOR FRANCESCO FRANCIONI

Professor of International Law and Human Rights and Co-Director of the Academy of European Law at the European University Institute in Florence

PROFESSOR ANA VRDOLJAK

Professor of Law at the University of Technology, Sydney

Intangible Cultural Heritage in International Law

CULTURAL HERITAGE LAW AND POLICY

The aim of this series is to publish significant and original research on and scholarly analysis of all aspects of cultural heritage law through the lens of international law, private inter national law, and comparative law. The series is wide in scope, traversing disciplines, regions, and viewpoints. Topics given particular prominence are those which, while of interest to academic lawyers, have significant bearing on policymaking and current public discourse on the interaction between art, heritage, and the law.

Intangible Cultural Heritage in International Law

LUCAS LIXINSKI

OXFORD
UNIVERSITY PRESS

OXFORD
UNIVERSITY PRESS

Great Clarendon Street, Oxford, OX2 6DP,
United Kingdom

Oxford University Press is a department of the University of Oxford.
It furthers the University's objective of excellence in research, scholarship,
and education by publishing worldwide. Oxford is a registered trade mark of
Oxford University Press in the UK and in certain other countries

First Edition published in 2013

Published in the United States of America by Oxford University Press
198 Madison Avenue, New York, NY 10016, United States of America

British Library Cataloguing in Publication Data
Data available

Library of Congress Cataloging in Publication Data
Data available

ISBN 978–0–19–967950–8

To
Antoine, Jannis, Martin, Mats, and Pablo,
brothers in arms.
And to
Carolina, Mariana, and Matheus,
the indestructible core.

Acknowledgements

An intellectual endeavour is to a large extent a collective one. No man is an island, after all. In this sense, I must thank the large number of people who have contributed to this book. First of all, I would like to thank Francesco Francioni, who supervised the PhD thesis that formed the basis of this book, for his guidance, support, and thoroughly insightful feedback every step of the way. More than a supervisor, he has been a true master, creating opportunities, supporting ideas and initiatives, believing in me, and I am deeply grateful for that.

I am thankful, too, to my first great master, Claudia Lima Marques, who has veered me into the ways of academic research in law and has continuously nourished me even after I was no longer formally her student. Thank you for the support, for the opportunities, for the imparted wisdom.

I would also like to thank the many other people who gave me their time by reading and giving comments on different parts of this book (or sometimes the whole of it). I am thankful to Ana Filipa Vrdoljak, Kathy Bowrey, Ben Boer, Martin Scheinin, Tullio Scovazzi, Karen Engle, Federico Lenzerini, Rob Howse, Barton Beebe, Jane Anderson, Adriana Dreyzin de Klor, Marjan Ajevski, Angelos Dimopoulos, Marija Bartl, Pierre-Marie Dupuy, Rosemary Coombe, Fernando Lusa Bordin, Maitê Schmitz, Jules Lombay, Mats Ingulstad, Jannis Panagiotidis, Antoine Vandemoortele, Henio Hoyo, Rainer Bauböck, Daniel Rodriguez, Jaime Lluch, Ruth Rubio Marin, Louise Buckingham, among others to whom I apologize for my forgetfulness. I am also thankful to the members of the EUI Working Group on Cultural Heritage (Adriana Bessa, Alessandro Chechi, Amy Strecker, Andrzej Jakubowski, Jeanne-Marie Panayotopoulos, Robert Peters, and Valentina Vadi); and the members of the NYU School of Law JSD Forum whose activities I took part in during the autumn of 2009. I would also like to thank the many audiences in multiple conferences that have been exposed to parts of this book and given me their anonymous yet valuable feedback.

A special thanks is also due to the Oxford University Press team behind the production of this book: Merel Alstein, Anthony Hinton, Olof Eyjolfsdottir, and Prabhavathy Parthiban. My thanks also to Mariana Lixinski Zieba for her keen insight and spatial intelligence in ensuring that the flowchart in the appendix made sense to people other than myself.

Finally, and most importantly, I would like to thank my family, Carolina, Edima, Mariana, Matheus, and Neri, for their continuous support throughout the years, to Darragh O'Keeffe for his incredible support in the final stages of this project, and the many friends I was infinitely lucky to make along the way.

Table of Contents

Table of Cases xi
Table of Legislation xv
List of Abbreviations xix

1. Introduction 1
1.1 'Cultural Property' versus 'Cultural Heritage' 5
1.2 Definition of Intangible Cultural Heritage 7
1.3 Nationalist versus Cosmopolitan Approaches to ICH Protection 10
1.4 The Challenge of Commodification 14
1.5 Tangible versus Intangible Heritage 18
1.6 Western versus Non-Western Heritage 22
1.7 Book Structure 25

PART I INSTITUTIONAL RESPONSES

2. International Framework 29
2.1 UNESCO 29
2.2 WIPO 56
2.3 International Trade and Intangible Cultural Heritage 58
2.4 The Convention on Biological Diversity and Traditional Knowledge 63

3. Regional Responses 67
3.1 Political Regionalism 67
3.2 Economic Regionalism 86

4. National Responses 105
4.1 Constitutional Responses 106
4.2 Intellectual Property Responses 120
4.3 *Sui Generis* Regimes 122
4.4 Policy-level Responses 126
4.5 Fragmented/Plural/Non-specific Responses 133
4.6 Multiplicity in National, Regional, and International (Institutional) Responses 141

PART II SUBSTANTIVE MEASURES TO SAFEGUARD INTANGIBLE HERITAGE

5. International Human Rights and Intangible Cultural Heritage 145
5.1 Bridging Intangible Cultural Heritage and Human Rights 146
5.2 Using Human Rights to Protect Intangible Cultural Heritage 152

6. Intellectual Property and Intangible Heritage 175
6.1 IP Tools and Intangible Heritage 176
6.2 The Public Domain and 'Cultural Commons' 197

7. Contractual Approaches 205
7.1 Creating a Structure for Contracting Out the Commons 206
7.2 Agency and Representation 210
7.3 Free, Prior, and Informed Consent 223
7.4 Financial Issues 229

8. Conclusions 233

Appendix The Flowchart of Living Heritage 243
References 247
Index 271

Table of Cases

African Commission on Human and Peoples' Rights

Social and Economic Rights Action Centre (SERAC) and Another v Nigeria (2001), 2001 AHRLR 60 212

Australia

George Milpurrurru, Banduk Marika, Tim Payunka and the Public Trustee of the Northern Territory v Indofurn Pty Ltd, Brian Alexander Bethune, Raymond King and Robert James Rylands [1994] 54 FCR 240 .... 6, 96, 121, 187

John Bulun Bulun v R & T Textiles Pty Ltd (1998) 41 IPR 513 .... 121, 188

Mabo v Queensland (1992) 121

Brazil

Civil Appeal No 70001422948 134

European Court of Human Rights

Arrowsmith v United Kingdom (Application No 7050/75), Comm Rep 1978, 19 DR 5 .... 166 167, 168

Anheuser-Busch Inc v Portugal (Application No 73049/01), judgment of 11 January 2007 192

Cha'Are Shalom ve Tsedek v France (Application No 27417/95), judgment 27 June 2000 .... 166 168

Ireland v United Kingdom (Application No 5310/71), judgment of 18 January 1978 171

Lee v United Kingdom (Application No 25289/1994), judgment of 18 January 2001 .... 164 165

Leyla Şahın v Turkey (Grand Chamber) (Application No 44774/98), judgment of 10 November 2005 167

López Ostra v Spain (Application No 16798/90), judgment of 9 December 1994 .... 147, 163

European Court of Justice

Case C-350/92, Spain v Council [1995] ECR I-1985 94

Human Rights Committee

A B et al v Italy, Communication No 413/1990, UN Doc CCPR/C/40/D/413/1990, 5 November 1990 149

Apirana Mahuika et al v New Zealand, Communication No 547/1993, UN Doc CCPR/C/70/D/547/1993, 15 November 2000 .... 148, 149

Carl Henrik Blom v Sweden, Communication No 191/1985, UN Doc CCPR/C/32/D/191/1985, 4 April 1988 161

CLD v France, Communication No 228/1987, UN Doc CCPR/C/33/D/228/1987, 26 July 1988 .... 155, 163

FH Zwaan-De Vries v The Netherlands, Communication No 182/1984, UN Doc CCPR/C/29/D/182/1984, 9 April 1987 .... 160, 161

Francis Hopu and Tepoaitu Bessert v France, Communication No 549/1993, UN Doc CCPR/C/60/D/549/1993/Rev/1, 29 December 1997 164

George Howard v Canada, Communication No 879/1999, UN Doc CCPR/C/84/D/879/1999, 4 August 2005 .... 155, 157, 158

HK v France, Communication No 222/1987, UN Doc CCPR/C/37/D/222/1987, 8 December 1989 .... 155, 163

Ibrahima Gueye et al v France, Communication No 196/1985, UN Doc CCPR/C/35/D/196/1985, 6 April 1989 ... 161
Ilmari Länsman et al v Finland, Communication No 511/1992, UN Doc CCPR/C/52/D/511/1992, 8 November 1994 ... 155, 156, 157
Ivan Kitok v Sweden, Communication No 197/1985, UN Doc CCPR/C/33/D/197/1985, 10 August 1988 ... 155, 156
Jarle Jonassen v Norway, Communication No 942/2000, UN Doc CCPR/C/76/D/942/2000, 12 November 2002 ... 155, 159
JB and HK v France, Communication Nos 324 and 325/1988, UN Doc CCPR/C/34/D/324/1988, 26 October 1988 ... 155, 163
Jouni E Länsman et al v Finland, Communication No 671/1995, UN Doc CCPR/C/58/D/671/1995, 22 November 1976 ... 155, 156, 157
Jouni Länsman, Eino Länsman and the Muotkatunturi Herdsmen's Committee v Finland, Communication No 1023/2001, UN Doc CCPR/C/83/D/1023/2001, 15 April 2005 ... 155, 156, 157
Lubicon Lake Band v Canada, Communication No 167/1984, UN Doc CCPR/C38/D/167/1984, 10 May 1990 ... 149, 155, 156
O Sara et al v Finland, Communication No 431/1990, UN Doc CCPR/C/50/D/431/1990, 24 March 1994 ... 155
RL et al v Canada, Communication No 359/1989, UN Doc CCPR/C/43/D/358/1989, 28 November 1990 ... 155
RT v France, Communication No 262/1987, UN Doc CCPR/C/35/D/262/1987, 3 April 1989 ... 155, 163
Sandra Lovelace v Canada, Communication No 24/1977, UN Doc CCPR/C/13/D/24/1977, 30 July 1981 ... 155, 156
Shirin Aumeeruddy-Cziffra et al v Mauritius, Communication No 35/1978, UN Doc CCPR/C/12/D/35/1978, 9 April 1981 ... 160
SR v France, Communication No 243/1987, UN Doc CCPR/C/31/D/243/1987, 5 November 1987 ... 155, 163
TK v France, Communication No 220/1987, UN Doc CCPR/C/37/D/220/1987, 8 December 1989 ... 155, 163
X v Australia, Communication No 555/1993, UN Doc CCPR/C/57/D/557/1993, 1 August 1996 ... 155

Inter-American Commission on Human Rights

Case 9.615, 5 March 1985 ... 114

Inter-American Court of Human Rights

Caballero-Delgado and Santana v Colombia. Merits. Judgment of 8 December 1995. Series C No 22 ... 171
Cesti-Hurtado v Peru. Merits. Judgment of 29 September 1999. Series C No 56 ... 171
Fermín Ramírez v Guatemala. Merits, Reparations, and Costs. Judgment of 20 June 2005. Series C No 126 ... 171
Juridical Condition and Rights of the Undocumented Migrants. Advisory Opinion OC-18 of September 17, 2003. Series A No 18 ... 158
López Álvarez v Honduras. Merits, Reparations, and Costs. Judgment of 1 February 2006. Series C No 141 ... 148, 162
'Mapiripán Massacre' v Columbia. Merits, Reparations, and Costs. Judgment of 15 September 2005. Series C No 134 ... 148
Mayagna (Sumo) Awas Tingni Community v Nicaragua. Merits, Reparations, and Costs. Judgment of 31 August 2001. Series C No 79 ... 169
Moiwana Community v Suriname. Preliminary Objections. Merits, Reparations, and Costs. Judgment of 15 June 2005. Series C No 124 ... 169, 171

Myrna Mack-Chang v Guatemala. Merits, Reparations, and Costs. Judgment of 25 November 2003. Series C No 101 148
Plan de Sánchez Massacre v Guatemala. Merits. Judgment of 29 April 2004. Series C No 105 148
Saramaka People v Suriname. Preliminary Objection. Merits, Reparations, and Costs. Judgment of 28 November 2007. Series C No 172 .... 169, 215
Sawhoyamaxa Indigenous Community v Paraguay. Merits, Reparations, and Costs. Judgment of 29 March 2006. Series C No 146 169
Suárez-Rosero v Ecuador. Merits. Judgment of 12 November 1997. Series C No 35 171
'The Last Temptation of Christ' (Olmedo-Bustos et al) v Chile. Merits, Reparations, and Costs. Judgment of 5 February 2001. Series C No 73 148
Yakye Axa Indigenous Community v Paraguay. Merits, Reparations, and Costs. Judgment of 17 June 2005. Series C No 125 .... 158, 159, 162, 169
Yatama v Nicaragua. Preliminary Objections. Merits, Reparations, and Costs. Judgment of 23 June 2005. Series C No 127 169

United States

Eldred v Ashcroft, Supreme Court of the United States, 537 US 1 (2003) 178
Penn Central Transportation Co v New York City, Supreme Court of the United States, 238 US 106 (1978) 138

World Trade Organization

GATT Dispute Panel Report on U.S. Restrictions on Imports of Tuna, Sept. 3, 1991, GATT B.I.S.D. (39th Supp.) (1993) 62
WTO Appellate Body Report on U.S. Import Prohibition of Certain Shrimp and Shrimp Products, WT/DS58/AB/R (12 October 1998) 62
WTO Dispute Panel Report on Dispute DS291 European Communities Measures Affecting the Approval and Marketing of Biotech Products (29 September 2006) 62

Other

Czechoslovak Language of Minorities Case, 3 Ann Dig of Pub Intl L Cas 314 (1925 26) 162

Table of Legislation

NATIONAL LEGISLATION

Bolivia

Bolivia Constitution 2009 ..... 110, 117, 118, 119, 120
Bolivia, Decreto Supremo No 12626 del 9 de junio de 1977 Normas sobre Patrimonio Etnográfico, Música Folklórica, Danzas Folklóricas, Literatura Folklórica y Arte Popular 122
Jurisdictional Division Act 119, 120

Brazil

Brazil Constitution 1988 ...... 112, 113, 114, 134, 135
Decree 3.551, of August 2000 .... 135, 136
Federal Law No 9.610, of 1998 136
Brazilian Civil Code 1916 112
Brazilian Civil Code 2002 112
Brazilian Indian Rights Act, Statute 6.001, of December 1973 ... 112, 113, 114, 115
Statute 5.371, of 5 December 1967, authorizing the institution of the 'National Indian Foundation' 113

China

Intangible Cultural Heritage Law of the People's Republic of China.......... 128, 129

Ecuador

Ecuador Constitution 1998 117
Ecuador Constitution 2008 .... 110, 117

Germany

German Civil Code (BGB) 197

Guatemala

Guatemala Constitution 1945.......... 109

Laos

Laos Constitution 130

Mexico

General Law on Linguistic Rights of Indigenous Peoples 111

Panama

Executive Decree no 12 of 20 March 2001 123
Law on the special intellectual property regime upon collective rights of indigenous communities, for the protection of their cultural identities and traditional knowledge, Law No 20 of 26 June 2000 ..... 123, 124, 125, 126

Philippines

Indigenous Peoples Rights Act of 1997 140
Philippines Constitution 140

Romania

Ordinance No 19 of 31 January 2007 on the immaterial cultural heritage protection 127, 128

United States

American Folklife Preservation Act 139
Endangered Species Act 139
Executive Order 12898.......... 139
Federal Records Act 139
National Environment Policy Act 139
National Historic Preservation Act......... 139
Religious Freedom Restoration Act 139
United States Constitution.......... 106, 138
Visual Artists Rights Act (VARA).......... 182

Uruguay

Uruguay Constitution 110

Viet Nam

Implementing decree for the Law on Cultural Heritage 131
Law on Cultural Heritage 2001 131

INTERNATIONAL INSTRUMENTS

African Union

African (Banjul) Charter on Human and Peoples' Rights (1981) 85, 159, 170
African Union, Assembly of Heads of State and Government, Resolution on the Return of the Pillaged African Monument the Obelisk of Axum.

AHG/Dec. 184 (XXVIII), 8 July 2002 ... 82
African Union, Charter for African Cultural Renaissance, adopted by the Sixth Ordinary Session of the Assembly, in Khartoum, Sudan, 24 January 2006 ... 83, 84, 85, 86
African Union, Executive Council, Decision on the Formulation and Establishment of an International Convention on Cultural Diversity and an International Convention on the Safeguarding of Intangible Cultural Heritage, Third Ordinary Session, 4 8 July 2003, Maputo (Mozambique), EX/CL/ Dec.67(III) ... 83
Constitutive Act of the African Union (2000) ... 81
Organization of African Unity, Cultural Charter for Africa, concluded during the Thirteenth Ordinary Session of the Organization of African Unity in Port Louis, Mauritius, 5 July 1976, Entry into force: 19 September 1990. Number of Parties as of January 2006 (when it stopped being open for ratification): 34 ... 83, 84, 85
Protocol to the African Charter on Human and Peoples' Rights on the Establishment of an African Court on Human and Peoples' Rights (1998) ... 170

Andean Community of Nations

Decision 391 of the Andean Community (Common Regime on Access to Genetic Resources, July 1996) ... 100
Decision 486, 2000 ... 101
Decision 523, July 2002 ... 101

Council of Europe

Convention for the Protection of Human Rights and Fundamental Freedoms, CETS 005, opened for signature on 4 November 1950. Entry into force: 3 September 1953. States Parties as of November 2012: 47 ... 147, 154, 159
Council of Europe, Convention for the Protection of the Architectural Heritage of Europe. Granada, 3 October 1985. ETS no 121. Entry into force: 1 December 1987. Parties as of November 2012: 41 ... 78
Council of Europe, European Convention for the Protection of the Archaeological Heritage (Revised). Valetta, 16 January 1992. ETS no 143. Entry into force: 25 May 1995. Parties as of November 2012: 42 ... 78
Council of Europe, European Landscape Convention, Florence, 20 October 2000. ETS no 176. Entry into force: 1 March 2004. Parties as of November 2012: 37 ... 78
Council of Europe, Framework Convention on the Value of Cultural Heritage for Society, Signed in Faro on 27 October 2005. ETS no 199. Entry into force: 1 June 2011. Parties as of November 2012: 13 ... 76, 78, 79, 80, 81
Council of Europe, Summit on Heritage and Communication, Declaration of Opatija on Intercultural Dialogue and Conflict Prevention, Adopted at the Regional Summit Forum on Communication of Heritage on 1 June 2006 ... 80

European Union

Council Directive, 93/7/EEC of 15 March 1993 on the Return of Cultural Objects Unlawfully Removed from the Territory of a Member State ... 92
Council Directive 93/83/EEC of 27 September 1993 on the coordination of certain rules concerning copyright and rights related to copyright applicable to satellite broadcasting and cable retransmission, Official Journal L248, 06/10/1993 P 0015-0021 ... 94
Council Regulation (EEC) 3911/92 on the Export of Cultural Goods ... 92
Decision 2228/97/EC of the European Parliament and of the Council of 13 October 1997 establishing a Community action programme in the field of cultural heritage (Raphael), OJ L 305, 8 November 1997, 31 ... 89
Directive 96/9/EC of the European Parliament and of the Council of 11 March 1996 on the legal protection of databases, Official Journal L 077, 27/03/1996 P 0020-0028 ... 94
Directive 2001/29/EC of the European Parliament and of the Council of 22 May 2001 on the harmonization of certain aspects of copyright and related

rights in the information society, Official Journal L 167, 22/6/2001 P 0010-0019 94
Directive 2001/84/EC of the European Parliament and of the Council of 27 September 2001 on the resale right for the benefit of the author of an original work of art, Official Journal L 272 13/10/2001 P 0032-0036 94
Directive 2006/115/EC of the European Parliament and of the Council of 12 December 2006 on rental right and lending right and on certain rights related to copyright in the field of intellectual property (codified version), Official Journal L 376, 27/12/2006 P 0028-0035 94
EU Charter of Fundamental Rights 97
European Neighbourhood and Partnership Instrument (ENPI) 91
'Television without Frontiers' Directive 61
Treaty Establishing the European Community . . . 87, 88, 89, 90, 93, 94, 95
Treaty of Lisbon 87, 88, 90, 93, 95, 96, 97
Treaty on the Functioning of the European Union 87, 90, 91, 95

Organization of American States (OAS)

American Convention on Human Rights 'Pact of San José, Costa Rica' (1969) 154, 158, 159
Charter of the Organization of American States 68, 69
Declaración de México sobre Cultura y Desarrollo 71
Draft Declaration on the Rights of Indigenous Peoples 25, 69, 73, 74, 75

Secretariat of the Convention on Biological Diversity

Akwé: Kon Voluntary Guidelines for the Conduct of Cultural, Environmental and Social Impact Assessments Regarding Developments Proposed to Take Place on, or which are Likely to Impact on, Sacred Sites, and on Lands and Waters Traditionally Occupied by Indigenous and Local Communities (2004) . . 217, 218, 219, 220
Bonn Guidelines on Access to Genetic Resources and Fair and Equitable Sharing of the Benefits Arising out of their Utilization (2002) 215, 216, 217, 227, 228, 230, 231
Convention on Biological Diversity 29, 33, 63, 64, 65, 100, 101, 215, 217, 226
Kari-Oca Declaration 65
Nagoya Protocol on Access to Genetic Resources and the Fair and Equitable Sharing of Benefits Arising from their Utilization (2010) 64, 65, 215, 216, 217, 228, 230

UNESCO

1989 *Recommendation on the Safeguarding of Traditional Cultures and Folklore* 30, 31, 32, 35, 51
Convention Concerning the Protection of the World Cultural and Natural Heritage (1972) 5, 16, 29, 30, 34, 35, 36, 37, 40, 42, 50, 55, 56, 57, 85
Convention for the Protection of Cultural Property in the Event of Armed Conflict (1954) 5, 16, 85, 86
Convention for the Safeguarding of the Intangible Cultural Heritage (2003) 3, 8 10, 17, 19, 22, 29 59, 63 5, 80, 82, 83, 85 6, 93, 102, 126 9, 135, 146 7, 150 2, 162, 169, 172, 175 6, 181, 195, 209, 216, 221, 235 9
Convention on the Means of Prohibiting and Preventing the Illicit Import, Export and Transfer of Ownership of Cultural Property (1970) 16, 85
Convention on the Protection and Promotion of the Diversity of Cultural Expressions, adopted by the UNESCO General Assembly on 20 October 2005. Entry into force: 18 March 2007 . . . . 58, 59, 60, 61, 62, 73, 85
Convention on the Protection of the Underwater Cultural Heritage (2001) 16
Draft Treaty for the Protection of Expressions of Folklore Against Illicit Exploitation and Other Prejudicial Action (UNESCO/WIPO, 1984) 57
General Assembly of State Parties to the Convention for the Safeguarding of the Intangible Cultural Heritage, *Operational Directives for the Implementation of the Convention for the Safeguarding of the Intangible Cultural Heritage (June 2008)* 38, 39, 43, 45, 48, 50
General Assembly of State Parties to the Convention for the Safeguarding of the

Intangible Cultural Heritage, Third Session (UNESCO Headquarters, 22 24 June 2010) Resolutions, resolution 3.GA 5, Doc.ITH/10/3. GA/CONF.201/RESOLUTIONS, of 24 June 2010 .... 54, 55
Intergovernmental Committee for the Safeguarding of the Intangible Cultural Heritage, First Extraordinary Session (Chengdu, China, 23 27 May 2007), Decision 1.EXT.COM 4 39
Intergovernmental Committee for the Safeguarding of the Intangible Cultural Heritage, Second Session (Tokyo, Japan, 3 7 September 2007), Decision 2. COM 5 .... 39, 40
Intergovernmental Committee for the Safeguarding of the Intangible Cultural Heritage, Second Extraordinary Session (Sofia, Bulgaria, 18 22 February 2008), Decision 2.EXT.COM 5 .... 39, 40
Intergovernmental Committee for the Safeguarding of the Intangible Cultural Heritage, Second Extraordinary Session (Sofia, Bulgaria, 18 22 February 2008), Decision 2.EXT.COM 9 50
Intergovernmental Committee for the Safeguarding of the Intangible Cultural Heritage, Second Extraordinary Session (Sofia, Bulgaria, 18 22 February 2008), Decision 2.EXT.COM 16 39
Intergovernmental Committee for the Safeguarding of the Intangible Cultural Heritage, Second Extraordinary Session (Sofia, Bulgaria, 18 22 February 2008), Decision 2.EXT.COM 17 45
Model Provisions for National Laws on the Protection of Expressions of Folklore Against Illicit Exploitation and Other Prejudicial Action (UNESCO/WIPO, 1982) 57
Tunis Model Law on Copyright for Developing Countries (UNESCO/ WIPO, 1976) 57
UNESCO Universal Declaration on Cultural Diversity (2001) 85
Universal Copyright Convention 30, 180, 185, 198, 240
World Heritage Committee, *The Yamato Declaration on Integrated Approaches for Safeguarding Tangible and Intangible Heritage*, adopted during the Seventh Extraordinary Session of the World Heritage Committee, Doc. WHC-04/7 EXT.COM/ING.9, of 25 November 2004 37

United Nations

International Covenant on Civil and Political Rights (1966)......... 111, 148, 149, 154, 155, 156, 157, 158, 159, 160, 161
International Covenant on Economic, Social and Cultural Rights (1966) 148, 153, 154, 170, 180, 181, 240
Optional Protocol to the International Covenant on Civil and Political Rights (1966) 154, 158
Optional Protocol to the International Covenant on Economic, Social and Cultural Rights (2008) 153, 170
United Nations Declaration on the Rights of Indigenous Peoples (2007) 73
Universal Declaration of Human Rights (1948) 79, 153, 154

WIPO

Berne Convention for the Protection of Literary and Artistic Works 30, 184, 188, 189, 190
Convention for the Protection of Producers of Phonograms Against Unauthorized Duplication of Their Phonograms (1971) 184
International Convention for the Protection of Performers, Producers of Phonograms and Broadcasting Organizations (1961) 184
WIPO Intergovernmental Committee on Intellectual Property and Genetic Resources, Traditional Knowledge and Folklore, *Decisions of the Nineteenth Session of the Committee* (July 2011).... 57
WIPO Performances and Phonograms Treaty (1996) 186

World Trade Organization

General Agreement on Tariffs and Trade 62, 63
General Agreement on Trade in Services 61
TRIPS agreement 58, 190, 194

List of Abbreviations

ACHR	American Convention on Human Rights
ACmHPR	African Commission on Human and Peoples' Rights
AU	African Union
CBD	Convention on Biological Diversity
CH	Cultural Heritage
CoE	Council of Europe
CPR	Civil and Political Rights
EC	European Communities
ECHR	European Convention on Human Rights
ECtHR	European Court of Human Rights
ESCR	Economic, Social and Cultural Rights
EU	European Union
FAO	United Nations Food and Agriculture Organization
FPIC	Free, Prior and Informed Consent
GATS	General Agreement on Trade in Services
GATT	General Agreement on Tariffs and Trade
GDP	Gross Domestic Product
HRC	Human Rights Committee
IACtHR	Inter American Court of Human Rights
IACmHR	Inter American Commission on Human Rights
ICCPR	International Covenant on Civil and Political Rights
ICESCR	International Covenant on Economic, Social and Cultural Rights
ICH	Intangible Cultural Heritage
IP	Intellectual Property
MFN	Most Favored Nation
NAFTA	North American Free Trade Area
NEPA	National Environmental Policy Act
NGO	Non Governmental Organization
NIAAA	National Indigenous Arts Advocacy Association
OAS	Organization of American States
OAU	Organization of African Unity
SIA	Social Impact Assessment
TK	Traditional Knowledge
TRIPS	Trade Related Aspects of Intellectual Property Rights
UDHR	Universal Declaration of Human Rights
UN	United Nations Organization
UNCTAD	United Nations Commission on Trade and Development
UNEP	United Nations Environmental Programme
UNESCO	United Nations Educational, Scientific and Cultural Organization
WHC	World Heritage Convention
WIPO	World Intellectual Property Organization
WTO	World Trade Organization

1

Introduction

The protection of cultural heritage, especially of the intangible type, is of growing international concern. International legal instruments and policy initiatives on the protection of cultural heritage are multiplying worldwide, and we are experiencing 'heritage fever'.[1] This book is about mechanisms for safeguarding intangible cultural heritage (ICH), with special emphasis on international law. It tells a story about how the law works and ought to work towards protecting communities, as those from whom ICH stems, and to whom benefits of its exploitation must return. The concept of 'intangible cultural heritage' will be discussed in more depth shortly. For the time being, it suffices to say that 'intangible heritage' refers to traditional forms of cultural expression, passed from one generation to the next, and that constitute an important part of a given community or group's identity.

The central thesis of the book is that the mechanisms for safeguarding intangible heritage will vary depending on the instrumental use one hopes to make of heritage. I explore a wide range of these possible mechanisms and goals, highlighting their potential and pitfalls, in an attempt to map this somewhat under-explored and under-theorized legal field. I do this in a way that takes into account the surrounding theory but is focused primarily on the practical possibilities.

This book is thus more of a 'law book' than it is a 'book about the law'. While I am sensitive to and aware of much of the critique of the patches of law exposed here, and I myself join much of the critique, my chief concern is to create a critique-informed body of law from many fragments, as opposed to a critique-oriented analysis of a body of law that, I argue, does not quite exist.

The legal solutions to the safeguarding of intangible cultural heritage depend, to a large extent, on the interests at stake when protecting it. The objective that is to be promoted by legal regimes (at least as a matter of official rhetoric) decisively influences the tools that are to be used in the legal instrument. The use of human rights mechanisms, for instance, looks at the protection and promotion of cultural identity as the primary interest at stake. But the use of intellectual property (IP), or trade law mechanisms, for instance, will put the economic/development interest at the forefront. This is one of the central concerns of the book. While I do have some personal preferences of prioritizing some interests over others when it

[1] David Lowenthal, for example, opens the first chapter of his book with the following sentence: 'The world rejoices in a newly popular faith: the cult of heritage'. David Lowenthal, *The Heritage Crusade and the Spoils of History* (Cambridge University Press, 1998), 1.

comes to protecting intangible cultural heritage, I acknowledge the plurality of interests and the importance of that plurality. My argument is that the protection of intangible cultural heritage can be best achieved through multi-level protection. This is despite the fact that there are many risks involved, including specifically the risks of fragmentation and dispersion of protection. This multi-level protection happens not only at the substantive level, but also at the institutional level.

This introduction aims to discuss some of the theoretical aspects of the legal safeguarding of intangible cultural heritage. Many of these 'theoretical tensions', as I choose to call them, are more often than not framed in the form of dichotomies: 'property v. heritage', 'tangible v. intangible' and 'western v. non-western' are just a few of them. As I will try to demonstrate, many of these dichotomies do not hold up to close scrutiny. This debate concerning the theoretical tensions associated with intangible heritage plays out repeatedly throughout this whole book. What will be seen in this chapter, thus, must be considered as only a prelude, a first approximation of the nature of these issues, which will be successively reframed in the context of more concrete legal initiatives.

I suggest an approach that distinguishes between the tangible and the intangible that offers more comprehensive protection to cultural heritage. This approach, reflecting the normative overlap of different treaty regimes, may be summarized as follows. To the extent the regime for the protection of tangible cultural heritage does not cover manifestations of heritage that are not deemed worthy of protection based solely on their external aspects, the international regime for intangible heritage, more nuanced and culturally sensitive, should step in and undertake the task of offering protection. This should be so at least to the extent that manifestations of heritage can be considered to be intangible and to fall under the regime. As all manifestations of heritage have an intangible element, what is left is to see whether they should fall under the current regime for the safeguarding of intangible heritage. I argue that not all heritage should be treated as intangible in international regimes, even though intangible values and aspects of all heritage must be taken into account when devising schemes for the protection of cultural heritage. As following chapters will show, several organizations have adopted regimes that do not look at heritage in light of the 'intangible/tangible' dichotomy, but rather as a holistic subject-matter, in which tangible and intangible elements have an essential interplay.

Before getting to the tensions specific to intangible heritage, however, it is necessary to place the development of intangible cultural heritage law within the broader context of international cultural heritage law. A good part of this evolution can be seen in the discussion of the conceptual shift from 'property' to 'heritage', explained below, but there are also other elements that merit separate discussion. The protection of intangible cultural heritage marks an important conceptual shift in international cultural heritage law, especially when it comes to the role of the State in safeguarding this heritage.

Protection of cultural heritage in international law was traditionally made in favor of the State, often regarded as the guardian of the interests of the (present and future) population. The protection of intangible cultural heritage challenges this view. Because it deals with living cultures (and as it is impossible to dissociate communities from their heritage), communities themselves rather than objects and sites are entitled to protection under the Convention for the Safeguarding of the Intangible Cultural Heritage (ICH Convention). This 'post-State' posture is one that drew a lot of attention during the negotiations of the ICH Convention.[2] States tried to contain interest by erecting new walls of sovereignty around this heritage. However, at least in its conception, intangible heritage implicitly challenges traditional ideas about State sovereignty and State entitlement to cultural heritage, moving closer to communities and to the human dimension of cultural heritage.[3]

There are several rationales for protecting ICH, and they ultimately boil down to the importance given to heritage and the perspective from which one seeks a use for it. Heritage must be protected, according to one commentator, for two fundamental reasons: first, because heritage forms an essential part of humanity's common past, and creates cultural identity; secondly, more often than not instances of heritage also represent important art forms that enrich people's lives because of their aesthetic value.[4] These are important values which essentially justify the protection of cultural heritage.[5]

However, heritage has no intrinsic value,[6] especially intangible heritage, in the sense that it should not be valued for its own sake, but rather in reference to the way people relate to it (in a way that is much more apparent than in other property-like claims, in which what is owned generally has its own, autonomous value). The value of heritage arises from the meanings placed upon the material artefacts and other forms in the present, and also from the representations created from them.[7] Heritage's value is therefore relational, rather than intrinsic. One notable exception is aesthetic value, but that is of relatively low importance in heritage (at least to the extent it is not what makes something 'heritage', it is what makes it 'art'). This is particularly so in the context of intangible heritage, which strives to be more 'representative' of a certain culture than an aesthetically appealing manifestation of heritage. Any such appeal is only incidental.

[2] Convention for the Safeguarding of the Intangible Cultural Heritage, Paris, 17 October 2003. Entry into force: 20 April 2006. States parties as of November 2012: 146 (hereinafter 'the 2003 UNESCO Convention', or 'ICH Convention').

[3] Francesco Francioni, 'La Protección del patrimonio cultural a la luz de los principios de Derecho Internacional Público', in Carlos R. Fernández Liesa and Jesús Prieto de Pedro (eds), *La Protección Jurídico Internacional del Patrimonio Cultural: Especial Referencia a España* (COLEX, 2009), 13 34 at 31 2; and Francesco Francioni, 'The Human Dimension of International Cultural Heritage Law: An Introduction', *EJIL* 22(1) (2011), 9 16.

[4] John Henry Merryman, 'Thinking about the Elgin Marbles', *Mich L Rev*, 83 (1984 85), 1881 1923 at 1895. Merryman is actually speaking of three reasons why one should care about the Parthenon Marbles. The first two reasons are those pointed out above, and the third is the concern over the depletion of the collections of major western museums in case all property should be repatriated to their countries of origin.

[5] Sarah Harding, 'Value, Obligation and Cultural Heritage', *Ariz St LJ* 31 (1999), 291 354 at 340.

[6] Harding, 'Value, Obligation and Cultural Heritage'; and a corroborating response by James W Nickel, 'Intrinsic Value and Cultural Preservation', *Ariz St LJ* 31 (1999), 355 61.

[7] GJ Ashworth, Brian Graham, and JE Tunbridge, *Pluralising Pasts: Heritage, Identity and Place in Multicultural Societies* (Pluto Press, 2007), 3.

Because heritage has no intrinsic value, other reasons for its protection that instrumentalize heritage and give it value, must therefore be sought. One of the most-often cited rationales for the protection of heritage is the preservation of cultural identity. Heritage in this sense is meant to provide a physical representation of the ephemeral concept of identity, and heritage is thus understood as a vehicle for promoting identity.[8] But at the same time one must bear in mind that communities, groups, and individuals often do not align themselves with one single identity, and individual identity is rather built upon several layers, leading to communities that are made up of several sub-communities.[9] So, a multiplicity of identities must be taken into account when considering identity as a goal to be protected through heritage, in order to avoid 'essentializing' culture and community perceptions of it.

Other compelling rationales include the creation or preservation of national identity (in the sense of political national identity);[10] the protection of a certain polity (minoritarian or majoritarian);[11] the enhancement of tourism;[12] the discovery of someone's values, social practices, and even legal rules (pertaining particularly to anthropology);[13] the strengthening of worldviews and political agendas of people not belonging to that heritage originally (that is, to 'bring the past into the

[8] Laurajane Smith, *The Uses of Heritage* (Routledge, 2006), 48.

[9] Smith, *The Uses of Heritage*, 53.

[10] A particularly interesting case study is the declaration of Macao religious figure carving as intangible heritage. This type of woodwork creates religious figures related to the Chinese ancestry, and their promotion through a recent exhibition in the Macao Museum can be constructed as promoting a perennial intangible heritage that survived in Macao despite the Portuguese control of the peninsula. As Macao has been reincorporated into China, there is obviously an interest in promoting a surviving political national identity that can relate Macao to 'mainland China'. See *Trabalhos com Engenho: Escultura de Ídolos Sagrados de Macau* (Museu de Macau, 2008) (book of the exhibition of the same title, which is proclaimed as national intangible heritage. The exhibition has run from December 2008 through April 2009).

[11] On the importance of heritage for minority protection, *see* Lowenthal, *The Heritage Crusade*, 81 7.

[12] Derek Gillman, *The Idea of Cultural Heritage* (Institute for Art and Law, 2006), 1. For a critique of how tourism homogenizes heritage, being in the long run harmful to it, see Brian Graham, Gregory John Ashworth, and John E Tunbridge, 'The Uses and Abuses of Heritage', in Gerard Corsane (ed), *Heritage Museums and Galleries: An Introductory Reader* (Routledge, 2005), 26 37 at 31 (arguing that 'tourism is parasitic upon culture, to which it may contribute nothing'). Laurajane Smith, on the other hand, presents a more nuanced view. Cf Smith, *The Uses of Heritage*, 71 (adding a more balanced perspective, by saying that '[w]hile the sense of experience often created in tourism has been criticized for its tendency to commodify or Disneyfy the past, or for its tendency to transform identities "through pernicious vogue storylines" [. . .] it nonetheless demonstrates the importance of "doing" and "being" at a "place"').

[13] For examples of how cultural practices and folklore can be used as a means to determine legal practices, see the collection of essays Alison Dundes Rentel and Alan Dundes (eds), *Folk Law: Essays on the Theory and Practice of* Lex Non Scripta (University of Wisconsin Press, 1995). See particularly Hermann Baltl, 'Folklore Research and Legal History in the German Language Area', in Dundes Rentel and Dundes (eds), *Folk Law: Essays on the Theory and Practice of* Lex Non Scripta, 397 407; Paul G Brewster, 'Traces of Ancient Germanic Law in a German Game-Song', in Dundes Rentel and Dundes (eds), *Folk Law: Essays on the Theory and Practice of* Lex Non Scripta, 407 16; John C Messenger, Jr, 'The Role of Proverbs in a Nigerian Judicial System', *Southwestern Journal of Anthropology* 15(1) (1959), 64 73; and Durica Krstić, 'Symbols in Customary Law', in Dundes Rentel and Dundes (eds), *Folk Law: Essays on the Theory and Practice of* Lex Non Scripta, 439 54.

present');[14] social inclusion;[15] education;[16] or even protecting heritage just for the sake of its aesthetic importance (even if this latter reason is of secondary significance).[17] When these justifications are translated into legal regimes, one can see that identity prevails as a rationale for protecting intangible heritage, and that other reasons become accessory, even if they are the formal justifications for triggering certain mechanisms within certain normative environments (for instance, using the enhancement of tourism, therefore an economic justification, to trigger economic integration processes and their machinery to protect intangible heritage).

1.1 'Cultural Property' versus 'Cultural Heritage'[18]

To better understand the object of this study, it is important to highlight the origins and reach of the term 'cultural heritage'. Early international legal instruments protecting projections of culture came about through international humanitarian law (particularly the 1954 Hague Convention for the Protection of Cultural Property in the Event of Armed Conflict), protecting cultural goods in times of conflict, and referring to them as 'cultural property'.[19] However, developments in the field reached a point at which the values attached to property needed to be modified in order for other social goals to be secured. While 'property' as a legal category offers interesting advantages, as it is often viewed as a near-absolute bundle of rights once conferred, its use implied the setting up of a social policy to protect the possessor of the cultural object. This approach, however, came into conflict with the fundamental goal of heritage protection, as there was a shift from protecting individual interests to protecting the interests of society in the preservation of cultural goods.[20]

[14] In this sense, David Lowenthal tells the story of how Chief Seattle's famous '*Brother Eagle, Sister Sky*' letter, which spurred the environmentalist movement in the United States by announcing the deep connection between the indigenous person and nature (a model of cooperation and respect that was taken to serve as an example to the whole of society) was actually never written by Chief Seattle, but rather by a Hollywood scriptwriter. Lowenthal, *The Heritage Crusade*, 150 1. See also Sally Yerkovich, 'Linking the Present with the Past through Intangible Heritage in History Museums', *Intl J of Intangible Heritage* 1 (2006), 44 52.

[15] See eg Viv Golding, '*Inspiration Africa!* Using Tangible and Intangible Heritage to Promote Social Inclusion Amongst Young People with Disabilities', *Intl J of Intangible Heritage* 1 (2006), 84 93.

[16] See eg Maria Vlachaki, 'Crossing Cultures through the Intangible Heritage: an Education Programme about Migration in Greece', *Intl J of Intangible Heritage* 2 (2007), 94 102.

[17] Gillman, *The Idea of Cultural Heritage*, 12.

[18] This section is partly extracted from Lucas Lixinski, 'World Heritage and the Heritage of the World Review of The 1972 World Heritage Convention: A Commentary', ed Francesco Francioni and Federico Lenzerini, *Eur J of Legal Studies* 2 (2008), 371 86.

[19] This development is outlined by Janet Blake, 'On Defining the Cultural Heritage', *ICLQ* 49 (2000), 61 85 at 61 2. For a pre-World War II evolution of the idea of cultural property in international law, see generally Ana Vrdoljak, *International Law, Museums and the Return of Cultural Objects* (Cambridge University Press, 2006).

[20] Lyndel V Prott and Patrick J O'Keefe, '"Cultural Heritage" or "Cultural Property"?', *Intl J of Cultural Property* 1 (1992), 307 20 at 309.

The law had evolved to deem the value to be protected by norms to be present and future generations, or society as a whole, rather than the particular possessor of a certain object.[21] This idea of protecting the interests of future generations gradually led to a change in terminology, and the term 'cultural heritage' began to be used in the English-language literature.

A critique of the use of the term 'property' goes beyond criticizing the ultimate value to be protected. After all, in one way or another, the protection of objects is one of the aims of property law, with the difference that property law does not question who is to benefit from such protection. It protects the interests of the possessor. For the purposes of the critique outlined above, it may well be said that the owner (of heritage as property) is society as a whole, and thus 'cultural property' would still work as a concept.

Several scholars, particularly in the field of legal anthropology, have raised the point that 'property' is a 'Western' concept, which does not necessarily address the needs of all peoples. There are several examples of societies that do not recognize 'property' as a social possibility; rather than owning something, individuals belonging to these societies believe that they are owned by the environment around them, which is in certain cases nothing short of the embodiment of the deities that they worship. It seems natural that a religion does not allow one to own one's object of worship, lest the reason for it (namely, that you worship some entity mightier than you) would cease to exist. If everything around me is a deity, and I cannot own a deity, I do not own anything.[22] This argument is closely related to the critique that using the term 'property' implies a commodification of cultural aspects of life, which should not be treated as goods in the marketplace.[23] Further, the use of the term 'property' also reinforces the idea that cultural values can be captured and frozen.[24]

The use of the term 'property' in the context of the protection of cultural heritage is thus misleading, to the extent that it is, in the end, associated with things whose value transcends their physical existence. One compelling example of this is that one of the fundamental aspects of property as a right, *ius abutendi*, cannot be exercised when dealing with cultural goods. *Ius abutendi* is the faculty that the owner of a thing has to destroy the object; this is rather difficult to accept when speaking of cultural heritage.[25]

Likewise, the use of 'cultural heritage' as a legal concept is not free from difficulties. One of the problems that the use of the concept poses derives from it having been imported from other disciplines without incorporating the necessary theoretical background of these disciplines, such as anthropology or cultural studies. This has led to 'cultural heritage' being one of the most problematic legal

[21] Prott and O'Keefe, 'Cultural Heritage', 309.

[22] A real-life example is given by Prott and O'Keefe, 'Cultural Heritage', 310 (mentioning a famous Australian case, *Milirrpum v Nabalco Pty Ltd*, to which I return in Ch 6).

[23] Blake, 'On Defining the Cultural Heritage', 65 6.

[24] Smith, *The Uses of Heritage*, 101.

[25] Prott and O'Keefe, 'Cultural Heritage', 310. See also Joseph L Sax, *Playing Darts with a Rembrandt: Public and Private Interests in Cultural Treasures* (University of Michigan Press, 1999).

concepts dealt with today.[26] In addition, the fact that 'heritage' as a legal concept tries to embrace features such as national patrimony, regional and ethnic legacies, and a commonly shared global heritage is also part of the challenge, as these features often translate into incompatible aims.[27]

All things considered, the concept of 'heritage' is most important for our purposes precisely because of its capacity to include notions beyond economics and ownership that are typical of property. But, more importantly for the present purposes, one must highlight the meaning of the shift in international legal discourse from 'property' to 'heritage'.[28] This shift means an acceptance that the protection of heritage goes beyond the protection of the actual sites, objects, and artifacts; instead, what is to be protected is the relationship between these sites, objects, and artifacts and human beings.[29] In this sense, what is protected is precisely the element of intangibility behind all heritage. This focus on the relationships implies the articulation of the idea that cultural heritage belongs to the whole of humankind, and must be protected to favour those communities more connected to it, as opposed to the individuals in possession of the items.

1.2 Definition of Intangible Cultural Heritage

Defining 'cultural heritage' implies defining 'culture'. Definitions of culture are broad, which makes it difficult to give them legal force. The 'relevant type of culture', for the purposes of protecting cultural heritage, is the one that contributes to the formation of identity. 'Heritage' as a qualifier to 'culture' implies that the type of culture identified will be the one that is relevant for the perpetuation of a given social group. It is this symbolic relationship between cultural heritage and culture-as-society that is important for understanding the concept of cultural heritage.[30] It is very difficult to define heritage in definite terms, and it has been stated that defining it is as difficult as defining beauty or art; heritage appeals to people's senses and emotions, and is therefore unfathomable.[31]

Despite all the complexity in defining cultural heritage, a working definition is needed. Cultural heritage can thus be defined as the elements necessary for the

[26] Blake, 'On Defining the Cultural Heritage', 63.

[27] Blake, 'On Defining the Cultural Heritage', 64 (citing Lowenthal, *The Heritage Crusade*, 227).

[28] Regina Bendix, 'Héritage et patrimoine: de leurs proximités sémantiques et de leurs implications', in Chiara Bortolotto (ed), *Le patrimoine culturel immaterial: Enjeux d'une nouvelle catégorie* (Éditions de la Maison des sciences de l'homme, 2011), 99 121.

[29] This shift was also mirrored in general debates about property law. Property has shifted from being a legal protection of an object (or the exclusive rights of the owner to its property towards non-owners) to the relationship between non-owners and the property, to the extent some rights can also be granted to non-owners. For a discussion and reconceptualization of property law, see generally David Kennedy, 'Some Caution about Property Rights as a Recipe for Economic Development', *Accounting, Economics and Law* 1 (2011), 1 62.

[30] Blake, 'On Defining the Cultural Heritage', 68.

[31] Robert Lumley, 'The Debate on Heritage Reviewed', in Gerard Corsane (ed), *Heritage Museums and Galleries: An Introductory Reader* (Routledge, 2005), 15 25 at 16.

maintenance over time of a certain cultural identity, important for the survival of a social group.

Cultural heritage may be tangible or intangible, the latter being the type in which I am most interested. Tangible cultural heritage refers to statues, monuments, architectural works, and other materialized forms of cultural expression. Intangible cultural heritage, by contrast, can be defined in two different ways. On the one hand, as a concept that is *dependent* on tangible cultural heritage, it acts as the underlying culture to any given expression, encompassing the processes, skills, and beliefs leading to the creation of tangible works. In a way, the term expresses the relationship of a people with their tangible cultural heritage. On the other hand, as an *independent* type of heritage, the term encompasses story-telling, songs, dances, among other forms of expression that cannot be ordinarily fixated in material ways.

During the drafting of the 2003 UNESCO ICH Convention, Francesco Francioni, Chair of the drafting meeting held in Turin (2001), presented a comprehensive report on issues that should be taken into account when drafting a definition of ICH. The report outlined the possibility of legally protecting 'non-material' goods using the example of IP rights (to be analysed in comparison with ICH in Chapter 6), but also drawing a line distinguishing between ICH and IP, in that IP focuses on the end product of the creative process, whereas ICH is the process itself. The report then outlined definitions of cultural heritage in existing international instruments, concluding that elements could be drawn from all these definitions that would be relevant for the formulation of a legal definition of intangible heritage, such as its significance, the importance of a broad definition with a non-exclusive typology, criteria that could be operationalized by the organ eventually in charge of administering the Convention, and the fact that intangible heritage should focus on the 'internal' cultural manifestations, and not on the products of it. A definition was proposed, and much of it made it to the final instrument.[32]

The 2003 UNESCO Convention thus defines intangible cultural heritage as follows:

Article 2 Definitions. For the purposes of this Convention, 1. The 'intangible cultural heritage' means the practices, representations, expressions, knowledge, skills as well as the instruments, objects, artefacts and cultural spaces associated therewith that communities, groups and, in some cases, individuals recognize as part of their cultural heritage. This intangible cultural heritage, transmitted from generation to generation, is constantly recre ated by communities and groups in response to their environment, their interaction with nature and their history, and provides them with a sense of identity and continuity, thus promoting respect for cultural diversity and human creativity. [...]

Intangible heritage, like indigenous heritage, must be seen as holistic.[33] This holistic understanding is both dependent on and independent from tangible

[32] UNESCO, *International Round Table: 'Intangible Cultural Heritage Working Definitions'*, meeting held in Turin Piedmont (Italy) on 14 17 March 2001.

[33] Amanda Kearney, 'Intangible Cultural Heritage: Global Awareness and Local Interest', in Laurajane Smith and Natsuko Akagawa (eds), *Intangible Heritage* (Routledge, 2009), 209 26 at 217.

heritage. To be more accurate, the Convention makes several tangible elements dependent on the intangible expressions from which they derive, and not the other way around. In other words, it protects objects because they derive from a larger cultural practice, and not the other way around, which would be the traditional response of museums, for instance, in protecting the objects themselves and hoping, perhaps, to indirectly protect the culture behind them.

Other important elements of the UNESCO definition include the precedence of group rights in the context of intangible heritage (since the rights belong primarily to the community, and only 'in some cases' to individuals), and the importance given to universalist conceptions of human rights, by affirming that those cultural practices that are incompatible with internationally recognized human rights do not fall within the scope of application of the Convention. The UNESCO definition is very broad, but this is necessary in such a comprehensive area of law, which tries to bring together interests which can at times be incompatible.

It is also interesting to notice that the definition of intangible heritage is 'forward-looking', in the sense that it protects manifestations of heritage necessary for the continuation of a certain community. Heritage studies have traditionally looked at heritage as escapist and 'backward-looking',[34] primarily because of their connection to tangible heritage and archaeology, where the object necessarily predated its discovery, turning these objects into sites for the exploration of 'lost' history. However, it is important to notice the shift in discourse when it comes to the protection of intangible heritage, which aims at defending living cultures.

The definition of the UNESCO Convention stresses that '[t]his intangible cultural heritage [. . .] provides [the communities] with a sense of identity [. . .]'. It is precisely *because* intangible cultural heritage provides a sense of identity that it is worthy of protection. Heritage connects each person to the community they stem from, and creates a sense of shared experience, and thus identity. Protecting this shared identity, and, ultimately, a shared humanity, is perhaps the most important goal behind heritage safeguarding. Thus, by protecting identity in general, one is also indirectly protecting intangible cultural heritage. Identity and culture can be protected by international human rights mechanisms, which are one of the possible tools for remedying misappropriation of intangible heritage, as I will argue in Chapter 5.

Further, heritage here is seen as the cultural processes behind certain objects, and not the objects themselves (which are a commodified version of these processes, as discussed below). In this sense, any attempt to indirectly protect intangible heritage through protecting the end-results of these cultural and social processes must necessarily take into account that they are protecting mummified manifestations of heritage, and not heritage itself, and necessarily fall short of fully protecting heritage.[35]

I will return to the issue of the definition of intangible heritage in Chapter 2, when analysing the relevant UNESCO Convention and the controversies

[34] Lumley, 'The Debate on Heritage Reviewed', 17.
[35] Smith, *The Uses of Heritage*, 54.

surrounding its drafting. For now, it suffices to say that the definition of ICH is multi-faceted and complex, and looks at heritage as an integral part (rather than a product) of a living culture, and an essential part of the maintenance of this culture through time.

Before moving on to analyse other theoretical tensions, a few words are needed on the use of 'intangible cultural heritage' as the preferred terminology. Many expressions have been used in the past to describe intangible heritage, including 'folklore', 'traditional cultural expressions', 'indigenous culture', 'traditional or popular culture', among many others.[36] While the use of 'intangible cultural heritage' is a term that can be criticized (for creating an apparent opposition to tangible heritage, for instance), it is the one for which it was possible to find consensus when drafting the UNESCO Convention, and it is the term I will use here.

1.3 Nationalist versus Cosmopolitan Approaches to ICH Protection

A cultural heritage relationship involves several actors at different levels, depending on the way one chooses to look at the relationship. Peter Howard speaks of the 'heritage cube', which is comprised of the different types of heritage, the people who are concerned with it, and 'the levels of identity at which the [heritage] activity takes place'.[37]

Regarding the second face of the cube, that is, the people who are concerned with it, the 'heritage relationship' can be described as involving the custodial communities (that is, the communities from whom manifestations of heritage come), the public at large and several 'bridge actors' that connect custodian communities and the general population, including media, museums,[38] tourism-promotion agencies, etc.

The academic community can be seen to a certain extent also as a 'bridge actor', depending on the role attributed to academics' work. But, generally speaking, they constitute a category of their own, that does not necessarily play the same instrumental role that other 'bridge actors' do. At the same time, though, academics set their own agenda when depicting heritage, in an attempt to provide the epistemological frameworks through which heritage will be subsequently discussed by policy- and law-makers, which can be seen as an attempt to perpetuate the importance of the academy and maintaining its privileged position with respect to knowledge and the meaning of the past and relevance of heritage.[39]

36 UNESCO, *International Round Table*.

37 Peter Howard, *Heritage: Management, Interpretation, Identity* (Continuum, 2003).

38 Patrick J Boylan, 'The Intangible Heritage: a Challenge and an Opportunity for Museums and Museum Professional Training', *Intl J of Intangible Heritage* 1 (2006), 54 65; and Matilda Burden, 'Museums and the Intangible Heritage: the Case Study of the Afrikaans Language Museum', *Intl J of Intangible Heritage* 2 (2007), 82 91.

39 Smith, *The Uses of Heritage*, 51.

The debate on the role of academics highlights the issue of stakeholders. For whom does heritage exist? One can look at heritage as existing for the sake of the custodial community itself. But even this seemingly intuitive answer raises two different sets of rather difficult questions: (1) what about the interests of the world community in cultural diversity and their enjoyment of the cultural treasures of the world?; and (2) who represents the interests of the custodian community?

The first question looks outside of this facet of the cube, and will be dealt with shortly. But the second question raises several issues of extreme relevance when speaking of heritage protection, particularly the issue of agency, which is intrinsically connected to 'authenticity'.[40] Who is entitled to 'control' heritage? To whom should third parties refer when looking for the quintessential format of a certain manifestation of heritage? In some circumstances, the answer is easy, such as when the manifestation of heritage has been created recently, and by an identifiable organization (such is the case with Kwanzaa),[41] or when the custodian communities experience a certain cultural isolation that allows the designation of community leaders. Such is the case with, potentially, indigenous heritage,[42] and also with some forms of intangible heritage in smaller cities in Japan,[43] for instance, even though in the latter case it is actually community leaders who are elevated to the status of heads of an organization created specifically for the protection of a certain manifestation of heritage.

One of the criticisms regarding the control of heritage is raised by Laurajane Smith, who, in her powerful critique of what she calls the 'authorized heritage discourse', indicates that heritage programmes, when they try to include communities and society at large, tend to do so in assimilationist terms, in which people are 'invited' to 'learn' about and 'discover' authorized meanings of heritage.[44] In speaking of 'heritage as identity', Laurajane Smith also discusses the role of the State in maintaining a certain view of heritage to the prejudice of communities and the bearers of heritage (which nevertheless is sometimes subsequently appropriated by the communities in their favour). Certain archaeological knowledge, produced by experts, is used as the foundation to protect heritage, particularly indigenous,

[40] See for instance Puente Calderón and Cecilia María, 'Protección Durable', *ICOMOS 15th General Assembly and Scientific Symposium (2005)*, available at <http://www.international.icomos.org/xian2005/papers.htm> (accessed 29 November 2012).

[41] Kwanzaa is a week-long celebration of African-American culture and identity in the United States, going from 26 December to 1 January each year. See Regina Austin, 'Kwanzaa and the Commodification of Black Culture', in Martha M Ertman and Joan C Williams (eds), *Rethinking Commodification: Cases and Readings in Law and Culture* (New York University Press, 2005), 178 90 and Susan Scafidi, *Who Owns Culture? Appropriation and Authenticity in American Law* (Rutgers University Press, 2005), 56 60.

[42] Scafidi, *Who Owns Culture?*, 56 60.

[43] Voltaire Garces Cang, 'Defining Intangible Cultural Heritage and its Stakeholders: the Case of Japan', *Intl J of Intangible Heritage* 2 (2007), 46 55.

[44] Smith, *The Uses of Heritage*, 44. There is much to be said on whether one can even speak of 'authentic' intangible heritage, inasmuch as one can speak of 'authentic' culture. For the sake of argument, I give 'authenticity' a lighter meaning throughout this book, to indicate a strong cultural connection to custodial communities and the cultural and social practice from which the manifestation of heritage stems.

becoming the dominating legal and political discourse through which this heritage is protected. These heritage resources become eventually items in power struggles over autonomy in wider political negotiations.[45] I will come back to these issues in Chapter 7.

The 'external' dimension of heritage deals with the level of institutionalization to which one hopes to connect identity, which can be international, regional/continental, national, regional/sub-national, local, and even private/home.[46] One of the most prominent voices in the debate regarding cultural nationalism and cultural cosmopolitanism is John Merryman, who argues for cultural cosmopolitanism.[47] Even if his concern was with tangible heritage (more specifically, the Parthenon Marbles), to the extent that it is also a broader discussion on the connection between heritage, national identity, and international concern, it is also valid for the purposes of safeguarding ICH.

Merryman argues that to see heritage as essentially national or local creates an unnecessary divide between source and market nations.[48] In his seminal article discussing the Parthenon Marbles,[49] Merryman points to three factors that must be taken into account when trying to decide whether a manifestation of heritage (for his purposes, a tangible cultural object) should be protected locally or put under some sort of 'international guardianship' (in his example, British guardianship). These are: preservation, integrity, and distribution.[50]

Preservation refers to the possibility of perpetuating a certain manifestation of heritage so that it may be enjoyed in the future. Merryman argues that this takes precedence even over context, since the value of having heritage present in its original context loses its meaning if there is no heritage to speak of due to its destruction for lack of preservation.[51] To the extent that heritage is constantly re-contextualized every time it is experienced, context moves to a secondary position over the paramount interest of preservation, which seems to be a sensible argument.

The second interest, integrity, applies only to disassembled property,[52] which is the case with the Parthenon Marbles. The suggestion is that the Marbles should be all in the same place, and it is for the other interests to determine where that place should be. However, it can also be read as meaning the contextualization of the heritage, since heritage only makes sense when connected to a context, otherwise it cannot be considered to be 'whole'. The same argument made above regarding the prevalence of preservation therefore applies.

[45] Smith, *The Uses of Heritage*, 50.

[46] Howard, *Heritage Management*, 148.

[47] See for instance John Henry Merryman, 'Two Ways of Thinking About Cultural Property', *AJIL* 80 (1986), 831 53.

[48] As discussed in Gillman, *The Idea of Cultural Heritage*, 28 9.

[49] Merryman, 'Thinking About the Elgin Marbles'. To refer to these marbles as the 'Elgin Marbles' already indicates a position in favour of British possession, whereas calling them 'Parthenon Marbles' seems more historically accurate and politically neutral, being thus the denomination I prefer.

[50] Merryman, 'Thinking About the Elgin Marbles', 1917 21.

[51] Merryman, 'Thinking About the Elgin Marbles', 1917.

[52] Merryman, 'Thinking About the Elgin Marbles', 1918.

The third argument, distribution, clearly favours cultural internationalism, as it allows the greater knowledge and appreciation of heritage by larger parts of the world population, as opposed to only the community of origin.[53] In the long run, this is also beneficial to the custodial community, which is bound to feel more pride over its own heritage upon the realization of its appreciation by others.

Nationalism, on the other hand, focuses on the significance of heritage to the national polity, and defends that this attachment is precisely what justifies the predominance of local interests over those of the international community. Culturally located practices are important to form identity, and local control over heritage is instrumental for the formation of this identity.[54] Supporters of the cosmopolitan approach reject this position, affirming it is unsustainable,[55] and often refer to the destruction of the Bamiyan Buddha statues in Afghanistan to support their claims.[56]

Cultural internationalism has been criticized for being used as a tool to enable western museums in possession of looted cultural artifacts to remain in possession of such items. Beyond the political debate, though, there is also the concern with the preservation of the common heritage of mankind, which is a legitimate concern in international fora.[57]

When it comes to the debate on cultural nationalism and internationalism in the specific context of intangible heritage, the debate gains a new dimension, at least to the extent that intangible cultural heritage is seen much more as a connection to a certain localized community than is the case with tangible cultural heritage.[58] International approaches are seen as failing to reconcile the international aspiration to view ICH as 'universal heritage of mankind' and the special interest of the State, people, or group to a particular element.[59] Cultural internationalism, then, can be read as having 'the power to override local and indigenous claims to self-determination and autonomy'.[60]

At the same time, though, cultural internationalism can be seen as a powerful counterpart to exclusively national accounts of heritage. At least to the extent that local heritage discourse is controlled by the State, the internationalization of it is a

[53] Merryman, 'Thinking About the Elgin Marbles', 1919 21.

[54] Ana Sljivic, 'Why Do You Think It's Yours? An Exposition of the Jurisprudence Underlying the Debate Between Cultural Nationalism and Cultural Internationalism', *GW J Intl L & Econ* 31 (1997 98), 393 438 at 401 2 and Gillman, *The Idea of Cultural Heritage*, 36.

[55] Gillman, *The Idea of Cultural Heritage*, 34.

[56] See for instance Roger O'Keefe, 'World Cultural Heritage Obligations to the International Community as a Whole?', *ICLQ* 53 (2004), 189 209; Francesco Francioni and Federico Lenzerini, 'The Destruction of the Buddhas of Bamiyan and International Law', *EJIL* 14(4) (2003), 619 51; and Francesco Francioni and Federico Lenzerini, 'The Obligation to Prevent and Avoid Destruction of Cultural Heritage: From Bamiyan to Iraq', in Barbara T. Hoffman (ed), *Art and Cultural Heritage: Law, Policy and Practice* (Cambridge University Press, 2006), 28 40.

[57] Sljivic, 'Why do you Think it's Yours?', 415 16; and Vrdoljak, *International Law, Museums*.

[58] Harding, 'Value, Obligation and Cultural Heritage', 300.

[59] Harding, 'Value, Obligation and Cultural Heritage', 353; and Kearney, 'Intangible Cultural Heritage', 220.

[60] Kearney, 'Intangible Cultural Heritage', 222. See also Rodney Harrison, *Heritage: Critical Approaches* (Routledge, 2013), 110.

tool through which local communities can be given a voice to go against their own States, much in the same way as international human rights law works as a tool to give voice to individuals' claims against the States in which they reside or which exercise jurisdictional control over them.[61] Therefore, while the cultural internationalist discourse is a tool of empire, it can also be subverted to favour challenging State-centric accounts of heritage by creating a backdoor. To the extent that heritage moves beyond a concern with the actual location of objects, sites, and artifacts to a struggle primarily over their meaning and significance (which is the case most notably with intangible heritage), cultural internationalism seems to be justified, even if for reasons different from those suggested by Merryman.

1.4 The Challenge of Commodification

The commodification discourse is important to the heritage debates because, by offering legal protection to heritage, one necessarily exposes it to the market. When speaking of intangible heritage, that is, living cultures, the stakes of commodification are much higher, as commodification can mean the ossification and ultimately the death of the culture. The discourse entered the legal arena through the Chicago-developed theory of Law and Economics. According to more radical advocates of this school of thought, everything should be treated as objects in the marketplace for the purposes of legal regulation, thus making it possible that law becomes an exercise of weighing and comparing things to which monetary values can be attributed. This school is far from finding general acceptance, however, and the question posed to lawyers everywhere is to what extent this commodifying trend should be legally limited.[62]

Commodification implies broadly the attribution of economic value to goods (here broadly understood, meaning tangible and intangible things, or anything that is capable of enhancing human happiness).[63] But in most contemporary uses, commodities are seen as manufactured goods or services, therefore typical of capitalism.[64] While economics in general tries to constantly expand commodification (at least to the extent that commodifying culture means including culture in the domain of economics), culture seems to attempt to restrict this.[65] This implies a

[61] Supporting this claim, see Chidi Oguamanam, 'Protecting Indigenous Knowledge in International Law: Solidarity Beyond the Nation-state', *L Text Culture* 8 (2004), 191 230; and John Henry Merryman, 'Cultural Property, International Trade and Human Rights', *Cardozo Arts & Ent LJ* 19 (2001), 51 68.

[62] Margareth Jane Radin and Madhavi Sunder, 'Introduction: the Subject and Object of Commodification', in Martha M. Ertman and Joan C. Williams (eds), *Rethinking Commodification: Cases and Readings in Law and Culture* (New York University Press, 2005), 8 33 at 10 11.

[63] This was the view expressed by Marie Louise Sorensen during her keynote address at the 9th Cambridge Heritage Seminar ('Packaging the Past: The Commodification of Heritage') at the University of Cambridge in April 2008 (copy on file with author).

[64] Arjun Appadurai, 'Introduction: Commodities and the Politics of Value', in Arjun Appadurai (ed), *The Social Life of Things: Commodities in Cultural Perspective* (Cambridge University Press, 1986), 3 63 at 7.

[65] Appadurai, 'Introduction', 17.

duality through which heritage can be seen as a resource of both cultural and economic capital. 'This is less a dialectic than a continuous tension', as commentators have highlighted.[66]

From one perspective, commodification in general is empowering and liberating;[67] from another, it implies reducing a person (subject) to a thing (object) or an object of exchange through which surplus value is extracted.[68] This latter approach goes against one of the basic tenets of human rights law, the Kantian imperative (according to which people should never be the means to an end, but ends in themselves). Translating this to law, it means that people should not be the object of legal regulation, but only its subjects.

This idea extends to cultural heritage law, as what often happens is that cultural heritage is commodified in violation of people's sensitivities, invariably affecting religious feelings, among other equally relevant concerns. This debate on whether heritage should or should not be commodified plays out particularly when one thinks of legal tools for protecting cultural heritage, especially intangible cultural heritage.

When one thinks of the relationship between commodification and culture, two competing views emerge. On the one hand, commodification tends to homogenize culture, which can be seen as helpful in creating commonalities and a sense of shared identity (a concern which will emerge often when discussing regional initiatives in Chapter 3). But, at the same time, it can strip away local meanings and contexts, making the culture of a certain group common, rather than unique. However, if commodification is understood as introducing something to 'the market', preventing a cultural expression from entering the market may impede cultural evolution, as it would preclude the exposure of a certain culture to other cultures, which is one of the most common means of cultural change.[69] Commodification becomes a challenge to the authenticity of culture and cultural heritage, and is a double-edged sword.[70] Therefore, if on the one hand commodification can ossify culture, on the other the non-commodification can lead to the same result. In this sense, Radin and Sunder note that 'the diverse and shifting cultural life of things is an expression of human life, not its rejection'.[71]

When it comes to the commodification of cultural objects, commodification is seen as an inevitable step in the 'social life of things',[72] and one that, once it has happened, cannot be undone.[73] Nevertheless, the communities from which these

66 Graham, Ashworth, and Tunbridge, 'The Uses and Abuses', 32.

67 Regina Austin, for instance, has argued that the commodification of black culture through the creation of the Kwanzaa holiday has led to the empowerment of black identity. See Austin, 'Kwanzaa and the Commodification', 178.

68 Radin and Sunder, 'Introduction', 9 (discussing how the first wave of commodification scholars led precisely to the realization that turning people into commodities harmed them, such as in the case of slavery).

69 Radin and Sunder, 'Introduction', 12.

70 Howard, *Heritage*, 203 4.

71 Radin and Sunder, 'Introduction', 13.

72 Appadurai, 'Introduction'.

73 Sarah Harding, 'Culture, Commodification and Native American Cultural Patrimony', in Martha M Ertman and Joan C Williams (eds), *Rethinking Commodification: Cases and Readings in Law and Culture* (New York University Press, 2005), 137 55 at 146 8.

cultural objects originate can benefit greatly from this commodification. To attempt to undo the commodification means to place communities in the position of passive victims, seeing as how all efforts will be put into returning to the pre-commodification state of affairs, which is not always possible. On the other hand, embracing commodification empowers communities, and more often than not enhances the value of heritage within the communities themselves, as their members feel some sort of pride over their own heritage once it has been valued by others, and what the community could potentially gain from fully putting their heritage on the market.[74]

Legal protection requires that what is being protected be defined and delimited, at least to some extent. Without the object of protection being 'graspable', it is very difficult to offer any concrete type of protection. In the field of cultural heritage law, this need for definition is often met without much difficulty; for instance, the World Heritage List offers a list of cultural heritage sites that need protection, and the description of each site is very precise in delimiting the exact area that is subject to protection, and the elements contained therein.[75] The same applies to the other core instruments on cultural heritage protection, such as the 1954 Hague Convention,[76] the 1970 Convention on the Return of Cultural Property,[77] and the 2001 Convention on Underwater Cultural Heritage.[78]

When one speaks of intangible heritage, however, heritage becomes less 'graspable', as the definition of intangible heritage outlined above indicates. Intangible heritage is a much more fluid concept, one that focuses on social and cultural practices underlying certain manifestations of heritage, which must be allowed to freely evolve, and must thus not be confined to a single, ossified format.

The idea of 'heritage as experience' means precisely that heritage is not frozen in time, but that it is a process that constantly recreates values each time heritage is experienced. The notion of heritage as experience significantly challenges conservationist ethics, which tries to fixate heritage in time so as to better 'control' it and determine its meaning. Heritage as experience challenges commodification, at least in its most absolute form,[79] as well as the Western legal concept of property, discussed above.

[74] Harding, 'Culture, Commodification', 151 2.

[75] Convention Concerning the Protection of the World Cultural and Natural Heritage, Signed in Paris on 23 November 1972. Number of States Parties as of November 2012: 190. The relevant provision on definitions is Art 1. For an extensive commentary to the World Heritage Convention and the lists created by it, see Francesco Francioni (ed), *The 1972 World Heritage Convention: A Commentary* (Oxford University Press, 2008).

[76] Convention for the Protection of Cultural Property in the Event of Armed Conflict, Signed in the Hague on 14 May 1954. Number of States Parties as of November 2012: 126. The relevant provision on definitions is Art 1.

[77] Convention on the Means of Prohibiting and Preventing the Illicit Import, Export and Transfer of Ownership of Cultural Property 1970, Signed in Paris on 14 November 1970. Number of States Parties as of November 2012: 123. The relevant provision on definitions is Art 1.

[78] Convention on the Protection of the Underwater Cultural Heritage, Signed in Paris on 2 November 2001. Number of States Parties as of November 2012: 41. The relevant provision on definitions is Art 1.

[79] Smith, *The Uses of Heritage*, 48.

There is hence an interest in not mummifying intangible heritage and freezing it in time, in order to let it evolve and remain meaningful to communities, rather than a memento from the past to which custodial communities do not feel connected. On the other hand, one wonders how to offer protection to something that is not defined beforehand. At the same time, some degree of commodification, through 'repackaging' heritage, can be seen as beneficial, because it makes heritage more easily understandable by people outside the custodial communities, which may in the long run reverse in favour of the custodial communities, who may feel more strongly attached to their own heritage. After all, external recognition can enhance internal pride and efforts towards preservation.[80]

A related tension is that of the notion of 'authenticity' in heritage in general, and intangible heritage in particular. While the very notion of intangible heritage challenges the assumption that there is such a thing as 'authentic' heritage, at the same time authenticity is an important bridge between the idea of heritage as experience and its market value. But, because heritage experiences are more focused 'on sincerity, rather than facts', it is understandable that this consumer sensibility will exert pressure for some notion of authenticity to come into play.[81]

A loss of authenticity becomes a price to be paid for repackaging heritage, but one must ask whether repackaging necessarily means compromising authenticity: if cultural encounters lead a community to change their heritage in a certain way, are we not promoting cultural evolution through exchange, rather than ossification and loss of authenticity? Is it not possible to think that the meaning of authenticity, to the extent one can speak of 'authentic' intangible heritage, for that particular manifestation of heritage is simply being redefined in light of a community's desire to attract more tourism? As long as the main stakeholders in the process are satisfied with the outcomes, maybe a paternalistic approach to authenticity and preservation should be re-thought.

This tension will play out particularly in the chapters on remedies (Chapters 5 7), but it is also an important issue to consider in my critique of the approach of the UNESCO ICH Convention (Chapter 2). For instance, perhaps the strongest currently existing trend is to use IP mechanisms to address cultural heritage concerns. Such an approach necessarily presupposes some degree of commodification of cultural heritage, but some will argue that commodification under certain conditions can be a valuable strategy for economic and cultural growth, or at the very least the lesser of two evils. In other words, to the extent commodification translates to an assertion of control, communities are better off if they are the bodies to assert control over their own heritage, as opposed to having to fight third parties after they have attempted to appropriate their culture.

One must take into account, then, whether one type of commodification (effective tools of legal protection) can at least partly correct the harm caused by

80 For a case study of this in the South African context, see Leslie Witz, Ciraj Rassool, and Gary Minkley, 'Repackaging the Past for South African Tourism', in Gerard Corsane (ed), *Heritage, Museums and Galleries: An Introductory Reader* (Routledge, 2005), 308 19.

81 Harrison, *Heritage*, 88.

another (that is, the giving of monetary value to religious beliefs and concepts of the sacred), and whether commodification thus becomes a desirable trade-off. In commodification studies, early theorists saw commodification as a necessary evil, while more contemporary approaches look at the ability to commodify as an empowering expression of freedom.[82]

If commodification is deemed acceptable, further questions to its limits are posed, referring to the exercise of these rights (or 'who controls the meaning of the commodity'),[83] and to the risks of 'mummification' of culture, whose living and ever-evolving character law is supposed to protect in the first place. A dilemma is evident from the concerns at stake here: if too much commodification can ossify culture and prevent its full enjoyment, at the same time too little of it can make culture an easy prey to 'Western' corporate culture or appropriation and control by others.

One should no longer speak of the 'enclaving' that protects certain things from commodification, but should accept that commodification, even by diversion (that is, the turning into commodities of things that were not originally meant to be so, which is often what happens in the context of cultural heritage), is inevitable today.[84] To the extent that diversion is a sign of crisis,[85] one must accept the cultural crisis of post-modernity as the triggering factor behind the commodification of heritage, and that commodification is a mixed blessing for the general public and custodial communities alike, but one we must inevitably deal with.[86]

These concerns seem to address, therefore, a question different to 'to commodify or not to commodify?'. Instead, the most pressing concern is what has been referred to as 'semiotic democracy', or the right of cultural groups to make their own cultural worlds and assign meaning to their own cultural expressions.[87] Commodification is thus an inevitable step, especially if one thinks of legal protection. The issue at hand is how to control the commodification process so as to ensure that the affected communities are not excluded in the process, and actually benefit from it.

1.5 Tangible versus Intangible Heritage

The linkage between tangible and intangible cultural heritage has been analysed by several scholars.[88] More often than not, manifestations of cultural heritage contain

82 Radin and Sunder, 'Introduction', 14 15.
83 Austin, 'Kwanzaa and the Commodification'.
84 For a contrary view, see Appadurai, 'Introduction', 26.
85 Appadurai, 'Introduction', 26.
86 Scafidi, *Who Owns Culture?*, 10 11.
87 Radin and Sunder, 'Introduction', 20.
88 See eg Margaret Hart Robertson, 'The Difficulties of Interpreting Mediterranean Voices: Exhibiting Intangibles Using New Technologies', *Intl J of Intangible Heritage* 1 (2006), 26 34; Nobuo Ito, 'Intangible Cultural Heritage Involved in Tangible Cultural Heritage', *ICOMOS 14th General Assembly and Scientific Symposium (2003)*, available at <http://www.international.icomos.org/victoriafalls2003/papers.htm> (accessed 29 November 2012); Charlotte Andrews, Dacia Viejo-Rose, Britt Baillie, and Benjamin Morris, 'Conference Report: Tangible-Intangible Cultural Heritage:

elements of both which are not in conflict or separation, but in a sort of symbiotic dialectic. While the intangible only receives expression by means of the tangible, the tangible only has meaning because of the intangible elements. This relationship has been explored in the context of cultural objects and the role of museums in the safeguarding of tangible and intangible heritage,[89] but little attention has been given to it with respect to manifestations of cultural heritage that cannot really be touched.

This dichotomy between tangible and intangible heritage is often not discussed openly, and it is possible that many heritage authors do not even consciously take a stance on it,[90] but rather that the stance is taken by them depending on the type of heritage they work with. The tensions of this dichotomy can be perceived differently depending on the focus of the person presenting them: people whose work focuses on tangible heritage will look at intangible elements as accessories to their work, whereas intangible heritage advocates will tend to look at tangible heritage as nothing but the embodiment of intangible heritage. I will briefly examine these claims, and try to offer solutions to reconcile this dichotomy.

From the outset, it must be stated that the discussions surrounding this tension do not concern all forms of cultural heritage. The discourse I analyse concerns primarily cultural objects, since these have a permanent physical existence. It is thus very difficult to undertake this discussion when dealing with forms of heritage that do not traditionally have a permanent physical existence, such as performed manifestations of heritage (theatre, dance, music, and so on). Nevertheless, the debate indirectly affects these 'ethereal' forms of heritage, at least to the extent that it affects the 'physical' elements associated with them (some examples are costumes, masks, and musical instruments). The fact that the UNESCO ICH Convention includes in its definition of intangible heritage the objects and artifacts associated with cultural practices evidences this point.

Further, to talk about whether manifestations of heritage should be deemed predominantly tangible or intangible relates to the importance attributed to heritage, and the rationale behind its protection. If one thinks of heritage as important for protecting cultural identity, for instance, the emphasis seems to be greater on the intangible aspect; conversely, if one aims at protecting heritage for the developmental opportunities that can be brought by it, especially through cultural tourism, then one thinks more of the tangible aspects at least to the extent that much of cultural tourism is done 'in a rush', just looking at manifestations from the aesthetic point of view, not necessarily taking into account the underlying cultural aspects.[91] It is important to highlight, moreover, that this relationship affects the integrity and

A Sustainable Dichotomy? The 7th Annual Cambridge Heritage Seminar', *Intl J of Intangible Heritage* 2 (2007), 124 9; and Smith, *The Uses of Heritage*, 53 7.

89 See eg Burden, 'Museums and the Intangible Heritage'.

90 See generally Andrews, Viejo-Rose, Baillie, and Morris, 'Conference Report'.

91 For a criticism of 'fast food' and 'red carpet' tourism, and how it alienates the intangible elements of cultural heritage, see Robertson, 'The Difficulties of Interpreting'.

authenticity of manifestations of heritage, and is thus more than a theoretical endeavour.[92]

1.5.1 The tangible side of the story

As I have mentioned, heritage scholars and professionals working with tangible heritage more often than not have problems acknowledging the importance of the intangible.[93] The 'tangible side' of heritage work considers, at the extreme end of the spectrum, that cultural objects have an intrinsic value that does not require any knowledge of their intangible values. In other words, for a cultural object to be appreciated it is not necessary that it be connected to a certain cultural group, or that such connection be at all known. Those who defend the protection of heritage primarily (or solely) for heritage's aesthetic values seem to endorse these views, even if not openly. Another similar view argues that, because intangible culture is 'destined to be lost or changed', it is pointless to preserve it, and one should focus precisely on the tangible elements.[94]

A more nuanced version of the 'tangible discourse', usually defended by museum curators,[95] and seemingly predominant in academic discourse, argues that there are intangible values to cultural objects to the extent that these values are useful to enhance the appreciation of a certain object. This attributes an instrumental value to the intangible elements of manifestations of cultural heritage, but it does not necessarily make these elements the central values to be protected in the conservation of heritage. The intangible element is an accessory, and an object will more often than not still be of interest more for aesthetic and scientific reasons than for its significance to the community of origin (at least to third parties external to the communities, which is usually the case with museum curators and patrons). Naturally, the scientific reason is often connected to the intangible values, as these arguably give meaning to the object and contextualize it in a way that makes the object useful for scientific studies in the fields of anthropology and archaeology.

While the case for intangible heritage appears to be strong, though, intangible heritage seems to suffer from a shortcoming when compared to tangible heritage inasmuch as the former can only deal with living heritage.[96] This is because tangible heritage is capable of referring to cultures that no longer exist. In this regard,

[92] Guo Zhan, 'Setting Factors and Judging Standards of World Cultural Heritage', *ICOMOS 14th General Assembly and Scientific Symposium (2003)*, available at <http://www.international.icomos.org/victoriafalls2003/papers.htm> (accessed 29 November 2012).

[93] See generally Andrews, Viejo-Rose, Baillie, and Morris, 'Conference Report'.

[94] Ito, 'Intangible Cultural Heritage'.

[95] This was for example the position of a curator of the British Museum, expressed during the 6th Cambridge Heritage Seminar (2006). See Andrews, Viejo-Rose, Baillie, and Morris, 'Conference Report', 125.

[96] This is the position adopted by an UNESCO official in discussing the tangible/intangible dichotomy during the 6th Cambridge Heritage Seminar (2006). See Andrews, Viejo-Rose, Baillie, and Morris, 'Conference Report', 125.

sometimes tangible objects can only be ascribed a meaning that is at best fragmented and speculative.

Even this more nuanced version of the dichotomy as seen from the tangible perspective does not give prominence to the intangible significance of cultural heritage. In fact, tangible heritage is seen as making heritage overall more convincing and powerful.[97] This has brought about reactions from people in the field of heritage studies whose focus is on intangible heritage.

1.5.2 The intangible version

Scholars focusing on intangible heritage more often than not look at intangible heritage as the only truly important goal of study, and at cultural objects and other physical manifestations of heritage as nothing but precisely the manifestation of an intangible heritage they try to understand and reconstruct through examining these objects. In this sense, tangible heritage becomes instrumental for the study of intangible practices, and any aesthetic value deriving from tangible objects is only incidental.

Accounts of cultural heritage based on intangibility tend to be more nuanced, and to more aptly reconstruct the meanings of heritage. Intangible heritage as a category, in a lot of ways, goes beyond more 'traditional' categories of heritage, based on the monumental and physical aspects of heritage, thus being a broader and more encompassing category.[98]

An extreme version of the case in favour of intangible heritage argues that all heritage is in fact intangible,[99] since manifestations of heritage will only make sense if one takes into consideration the specific context into which they have been created. Without this context, a cultural object will only have its aesthetic value to rely on, and it then becomes more of a work of art, instead of a manifestation of cultural heritage.[100] As far as all heritage is deemed intangible, one can leave aside the distinctions between tangible and intangible, and simply focus on the construction of identity and memory that can only be possible through the intangible values associated with heritage.[101]

While as a theoretical conception this idea has a certain appeal, such understanding is problematic for two reasons. The first reason, of a theoretical nature, is the reality that cultural objects and manifestations of heritage in general exist in the real world independently of any knowledge that the observer may have of the intangible

[97] Smith, *The Uses of Heritage*, 61.

[98] Andrews, Viejo-Rose, Baillie, and Morris, 'Conference Report', 126 (discussing a presentation by Emma Waterton).

[99] Smith, *The Uses of Heritage*, 56; and Andrews, Viejo-Rose, Baillie, and Morris, 'Conference Report', 126 (discussing a presentation by Laurajane Smith).

[100] Andrews, Viejo-Rose, Baillie, and Morris, 'Conference Report', 126 (discussing a presentation by John Carman).

[101] Giancarlo Nuti, 'Cultural Values: Intangible Forms and Places', *ICOMOS 14th General Assembly and Scientific Symposium (2003)*, available at <http://www.international.icomos.org/victoriafalls2003/papers.htm> (accessed 29 November 2012); and Andrews, Viejo-Rose, Baillie, and Morris, 'Conference Report', 126 (discussing a presentation by Laurajane Smith).

elements behind them. Whether a manifestation in these circumstances can still be called heritage, or should be referred to just as 'something beautiful', or 'something interesting', is the question to be answered. This is an extreme case, in which there is no information, but there are many instances in which there is only fragmentary knowledge of the intangible elements of a certain manifestation. While this knowledge may not in itself suffice to turn the manifestation into heritage, this fragment of information, coupled with aesthetic value and/or scientific interest, may still guarantee protection for a manifestation. Fragmentary knowledge is especially important (and sometimes the only knowledge available) in the cases of ancient or 'dead' cultures (as opposed to the 'living' cultures to which the reach of intangible heritage is restricted). Also, the tangibility of heritage, or its encapsulation in tangible objects and artifacts, helps resolve jurisdictional issues, since heritage objects are subject to the territorial jurisdiction of the State, while immaterial manifestations of heritage may easily escape any such jurisdiction and be far more difficult to regulate and protect.

The second reason, more related to bringing this theoretical framework into positive legal practice, does not seem to take into account the potential problems of overlapping legal regimes, and it suggests that the current regime for the protection of intangible heritage can 'take over' the other existing regimes. It is thus necessary to draw a boundary between the tangible and the intangible, even if only for practical purposes of choosing a regulatory regime. While I do agree that there should be some fluidity in applying these concepts, I strongly believe some separation is necessary for the purposes of offering legal protection.

In advancing this 'choice of regime' argument, one has to take into account the limitations of the regimes protecting exclusively tangible heritage. These regimes, according to critics, focus excessively on the 'monumental' aspect of protected manifestations, and thus fail to take into account less grand or less aesthetically impressive manifestations of heritage.[102] This is arguably a 'Westernized' understanding of cultural heritage, which might help explain why the early ratifications of the 2003 UNESCO ICH Convention were all by developing countries of the global south.[103]

1.6 Western versus Non-Western Heritage

The tensions between 'western' and 'non-western' heritage play out simultaneously in the discussion on 'tangible' and 'intangible' heritage, in terms of the following:

[102] A criticism of this 'monumentalized' approach, in the context of ICOMOS, is made by Andrzej Tomaszewski, 'Intellectual Context of Monuments and Sites in their Setting', *ICOMOS 15th General Assembly and Scientific Symposium (2005)*, available at <http://www.international.icomos.org/xian2005/papers.htm> (accessed 29 November 2012).

[103] Fu Chao-Ching, 'Cultural Sensitivity Towards Intangible Values in Monuments and Sites A Comparison between Eastern Asian and Western Countries', *ICOMOS 15th General Assembly and Scientific Symposium (2005)*, available at <http://www.international.icomos.org/xian2005/papers.htm> (accessed 29 November 2012); and Andrews, Viejo-Rose, Baillie, and Morris, 'Conference Report', 128 (reporting on a round-table discussion).

'tangible' is associated with the 'west', and 'intangible' with the rest of the world. The criticism of the World Heritage List as representing only European and western manifestations of heritage is vital in this sense.[104] The perception of a European legacy is reasserted and recreated through the World Heritage List, because 'listing is a process in which certain national narratives and values become authorized'.[105] In terms of legal protection, it means the exclusion of manifestations of heritage that, although representative of cultures and peoples, do not check the boxes of Western understandings of heritage, and are therefore altogether excluded from legal protection.

The same tension plays out in the debates over indigenous and non-indigenous heritage, to the extent that indigenous heritage is also seen as 'non-western'. But in the indigenous context the debate gains a new dimension, related to claims for autonomy and political struggles within western nations. The ability of indigenous peoples to control their own symbolic heritage is important to lend support to their cultural claims, which are the basis upon which their political claims for autonomy are built.[106]

When it comes to indigenous peoples, heritage and their control is still the prerogative of the State, which significantly impairs indigenous peoples' ability to control their own heritage.[107] The different perceptions of certain values important for heritage preservation also play a role. For instance, while traditional 'western' understandings of heritage law speak of 'rights', 'property', 'title', and 'entitlement', indigenous accounts (based on documented customary law) more often than not speak of 'responsibilities', 'obligation', 'authority', and 'privileges', which puts indigenous peoples in a much different position, one that usually is not fully grasped in the design of policies and laws regarding heritage protection.[108] However, it is also possible to find elements of 'non-western' understandings of law and heritage in western societies, and western conceptions in some indigenous groups. This makes the dichotomy false, and thus easily reconcilable.[109]

[104] See for instance José de Nordenflycht, 'El Culto Postmoderno a los Monumentos: Patrimonio Local en Contexto Global', *ICOMOS 15th General Assembly and Scientific Symposium (2005)*, available at <http://www.international.icomos.org/xian2005/papers.htm> (accessed 29 November 2012).

[105] Smith, *The Uses of Heritage*, 100.

[106] Smith, *The Uses of Heritage*, 282. On how indigenous culture has been translated as heritage, and what this means in terms of the weakening of their political claims, see Karen Engle, *The Elusive Promise of Indigenous Development: Rights, Culture, Strategy* (Duke University Press, 2010), 141 61; Chidi Oguamanam, 'Documentation and Digitization of Traditional Knowledge and Intangible Cultural Heritage: Challenges and Prospects', in Kono Toshiyuki (ed), *Intangible Cultural Heritage and Intellectual Property: Communities, Cultural Diversity and Sustainable Development* (Intersentia 2009), 357 83 at 370 1 (arguing there to be a difference between indigenous peoples in the North, more concerned with claims of self-determination, and the South, more concerned with development and economic benefits that can arise from the exploitation of their heritage).

[107] Ashton Sinamai, 'Cultural Shifting-Sands: Changing Meanings of Zimbabwe Sites in Zimbabwe, South Africa and Botswana', *ICOMOS 15th General Assembly and Scientific Symposium (2005)*, available at <http://www.international.icomos.org/xian2005/papers.htm> (accessed 29 November 2012); and Kearney, 'Intangible Cultural Heritage', 209.

[108] See for instance Martin Skrydstrup, 'Symposium Report: Only in America? Athnographic Archives, Communities of Origin and Intangible Cultural Heritage', *Intl J of Intangible Heritage* 2 (2007), 132 6 at 136.

[109] Harding, 'Value, Obligation and Cultural Heritage', 307.

The so-called 'authorized heritage discourse' plays a role here, and reinforces the need for indigenous peoples to be able to control their own heritage and meanings. Indigenous heritage and meanings have been constructed by States within a colonial discourse of authorized heritage meanings, and as such any indigenous cultural claims that fall outside of this authorized discourse tend to be disregarded as irrelevant or illegitimate.[110] As ICH is the key form of indigenous culture, and culture is a key strategic tool for indigenous claims, an international system for safeguarding intangible heritage gains an important emancipatory dimension.

Further, the very notion of thinking of indigenous or 'non-western' knowledge as being necessarily heritage, or 'traditional' knowledge, may have harmful consequences for these communities, in that it freezes knowledge in the past and impairs these communities' ability to pursue their own development.[111] Much of the evolution towards intangible heritage is associated with the idea of protecting living cultures, but the very notion of 'heritage' is charged with a connection to the past that is difficult to overcome.

By the same token, the relationship between heritage and sustainability also imposes some of this 'past-oriented' pressure on heritage holders. The connection between sustainability and heritage seems to play into the hands of one of sustainable development's unintended consequences. Communities, under the guise of sustainable development and cultural heritage safeguarding, can be stripped of the capacity to control their own development.[112] This removal of agency is complicated and, while the goals of sustainable development and heritage preservation are laudable, this requirement should ideally happen in terms that do not deprive communities of their agency.

The ability to control cultural identity and heritage is thus also the ability to control political identity and to advance political claims, and negotiating the ways in which indigenous peoples will appear before national, regional, and international political fora.[113] Intangible heritage is thus a tool for the empowerment of local communities,[114] and this feature must be borne in mind, alongside the other theoretical issues discussed above, when thinking about the legal strategies for safeguarding intangible cultural heritage.

[110] Smith, *The Uses of Heritage*, 295. For a discussion of western takes on indigeneity in the context of the environmental movement and the clash between environmental concerns and local or indigenous communities' interests, see Antonio Carlos Diegues, *O Mito Moderno da Natureza Intocada* (HUCITEC, 2000).

[111] Jane E Anderson, *Law, Knowledge, Culture: The Production of Indigenous Knowledge in Intellectual Property Law* (Edward Elgar, 2009), 9 11.

[112] For this critique with respect to development, see Engle, *The Elusive Promise*.

[113] Smith, *The Uses of Heritage*, 295.

[114] Manyanga Munyaradzi, 'Intangible Cultural Heritage and the Empowerment of Local Communities: Manyanga (Ntaba Zi Ka Mambo) Revisited', *ICOMOS 15th General Assembly and Scientific Symposium (2005)*, available at <http://www.international.icomos.org/xian2005/papers.htm> (accessed 29 November 2012).

1.7 Book Structure

This book is divided in two main parts. The first part of the book, dealing with institutional mechanisms for the safeguarding of intangible cultural heritage, addresses one of the facets of this multi-level protection. I will first look at international institutional responses to intangible heritage protection. I will examine primarily the work of three organizations: the United Nations Educational, Scientific and Cultural Organization (UNESCO), the World Intellectual Property Organization (WIPO), and the World Trade Organization (WTO). UNESCO's work is more oriented towards offering protection based on inventorying and funding for conservation initiatives; the WIPO, as its name suggests, looks at the prospects for IP protection; and the WTO (which is not an autonomous level of protection, but rather an incidental type of protection deriving from rules on the free movement of goods and services) will be analysed within the larger context of the 'trade and culture' debate.

Next, I will analyse the potential of regional initiatives, looking at both economic and political regional integration. On the economic integration side, I look at the possibilities of protection within the EU and the Andean Community of Nations, considering the extent to which culture can be regulated within an environment that aims primarily at protecting market interests and economic freedoms. In terms of regional political integration organizations, I will focus particularly on the Organization of American States (OAS), which is a noteworthy example as it is currently negotiating its own Declaration on the Rights of Indigenous Peoples. I also look at the Council of Europe and the African Union, the latter being in many ways both an economic and political integration organization.

The third chapter of the first part will look at different national solutions. The analysis of national solutions to the matter, important not only to inform the construction of an international framework, but mainly because it is when the topic can ultimately be dealt with efficiently, is essential. Such study requires the analysis of Foreign and Comparative Law, as well as regional solutions to the matter, when they exist. The study of comparative law in this sense should be centred not only on the mainstream legal systems of the countries studied, but also, whenever possible, on data portraying customary legal practices. Once again, resort to the accounts of anthropologists will be very important, especially in the analysis of *sui generis* schemes.

The second part of the book is 'remedy-oriented', that is, it looks at solutions for cases in which intangible heritage is misappropriated and custodial communities are harmed. I first look at the possibilities of using international human rights tools and institutions for the protection of intangible cultural heritage. I explore how intangible heritage may be protected with regard to one of its specific goals of protection, more specifically, the protection of cultural identity. Cultural identity is a value among others to be protected by intangible heritage protection. If one takes this value into account at the forefront of heritage protection, the use of human rights mechanisms for the protection of cultural identity seems perfectly suitable for offering an adequate international adjudicatory and quasi-adjudicatory framework for addressing grievances from individuals and communities based on harm to their identity as expressed by their heritage. In this sense, I analyse how several rights protected by international instruments have been reshaped and expanded to protect cultural identity, including the right to equality, the right to private life, freedom of religion and freedom of expression, among others.

The next chapter deals with the potential and pitfalls of IP protection for intangible cultural heritage. IP mechanisms have been suggested by several organizations, most notably the WIPO, but its use is not without problems. I will look at the several criticisms raised against the use of IP mechanisms, and use them as a basis to discuss contractual approaches in the following chapter. In this chapter, I will attempt to integrate the features of the multi-level protection schemes examined, and stitch together a coherent proposal for a unified system for ICH protection, which takes into account past experience and tries to conciliate different interests in ICH protection.

This book, by offering this comprehensive analysis of the foreground and background norms surrounding intangible heritage, attempts to mediate multiple tensions happening at multiple levels. It relies upon critiques of law as a tool for protecting culture, even if it is an eminently legal book. The book takes these non-legal critiques into account in order to re-shape law, and offers tools that can be valuable to people in a variety of disciplines related to heritage matters when understanding the different means for safeguarding intangible heritage.

PART I
INSTITUTIONAL RESPONSES

2

International Framework

After an initial assessment of some of the theoretical tensions regarding the legal safeguarding of Intangible Cultural Heritage (ICH), the next logical step is to look at the international framework on the matter. It has been at the international arena that intangible heritage has received most attention and gained momentum as a legal concern.

This chapter will look at the multiple international avenues for dealing with the issue. First of all, the United Nations Educational, Scientific and Cultural Organization (UNESCO) has concentrated efforts in the area. Its 2003 Convention for the Safeguarding of the Intangible Heritage, although conceived as a complementary instrument (as shown below), has quickly become a critical mechanism for the safeguarding of ICH. The instruments and initiatives preceding this instrument will also be analysed, inasmuch as they help shed light on the meaning and purpose of the 2003 Convention.

Next, the chapter will look at other complementary initiatives, including those under the World Intellectual Property Organization (WIPO), and the debate on trade and culture under the auspices of the World Trade Organization (WTO), and also the object of a major UNESCO instrument. Finally, this chapter will look at the Convention on Biological Diversity as the central instrument for the regime for the protection of Traditional Knowledge (TK), a type of knowledge that is part of the concept of ICH, and therefore relevant for our purposes.

2.1 UNESCO[1]

This section will analyse the initiatives under UNESCO to safeguard intangible cultural heritage. Starting from early initiatives more or less contemporaneous to the 1972 World Heritage Convention, the concern with protecting intangible heritage has always been a topic in UNESCO's agenda, even though the momentum for creating a specific legally binding regime for it was only achieved at the turn of the century.

I will first look at some of the historical developments that have paved the way for the 2003 Convention. But this analysis will not be exhaustive, as it is not my

[1] A reduced version of this section has been previously published in Lucas Lixinski, 'Selecting Heritage: The Interplay of Art, Politics and Identity', *EJIL* 22(1) (2011), 81 100.

intention to provide a complete evolution of the international treatment of the matter; rather, the goal is to look at the elements that have been important for the development of the current regime, the first comprehensive, legally binding one.

Next, I will analyse this instrument and the regime it creates, with its achievements and shortcomings. These will be considered not only in light of the conventional text and its drafting history (and therefore contrasting intentions and outcomes), but most importantly in light of the early practice of the organs created by the Convention and the guidelines for implementation produced by these organs.

2.1.1 Early initiatives

The international concern with the protection of intangible heritage dates back well over 50 years. As early as 1952, the Universal Copyright Convention (drafted under the auspices of UNESCO) gave rise to one of the core dichotomies in the work of UNESCO regarding ICH protection: the relationship between copyright and folklore.[2]

This relationship was further developed by the 1967 Stockholm Conference of the Berne Convention, which added a provision (Article 15.4.a) relative to the protection of folklore. It is interesting to note, however, that the word 'folklore' does not appear in this provision, as a means to avoid conceptual controversies. But the provision refers to the protection of 'unpublished works where the identity of the author is unknown', and determines that competent national authorities must be designated to protect such works. In 1971, UNESCO prepared a document called 'Possibility of Establishing an International Instrument for the Protection of Folklore'.[3]

In 1973, immediately after the adoption of the World Heritage Convention, Bolivia proposed an international instrument to protect folklore and other forms of indigenous heritage that were not covered by the 1972 instrument, which was focused on monuments, buildings, and sites.[4] And in 1976 UNESCO officially launched a 'Comprehensive Program on the Intangible (non-physical) Heritage', aimed at promoting appreciation and respect for cultural identity.[5]

In 1978 UNESCO and the WIPO formally agreed to jointly examine the question of the protection of folklore. But, while UNESCO would look at the

[2] This is pointed out as the first moment of phase one of international efforts to protect intangible heritage. See Samantha Sherkin, 'A Historical Study on the Preparation of the *1989 Recommendation on the Safeguarding of Traditional Culture and Folklore*', in Peter Seitel (ed), *Safeguarding Traditional Culture: A Global Assessment* (Smithsonian Institution, 2001), 42 56 at 43.

[3] Sherkin, 'A Historical Study', 43 4.

[4] Richard Kurin, 'The UNESCO Questionnaire on the Application of the 1989 *Recommendation on the Safeguarding of Traditional Culture and Folklore*: Preliminary Results', in Peter Seitel (ed), *Safeguarding Traditional Culture: A Global Assessment* (Smithsonian Institution, 2001), 20 35 at 20; and Federico Lenzerini, 'Intangible Cultural Heritage: The Living Culture of Peoples', *EJIL* 22(1) (2011), 101 20 at 103 4.

[5] Sherkin, 'A Historical Study', 44.

issue from a multidisciplinary and holistic perspective, the WIPO participation would be restricted to the intellectual property (IP) aspects of this protection.[6]

This dichotomy between IP and holistic protection persists to this day,[7] and the main focus of international attention has shifted throughout time. For instance, in the early 1980s the focus was on the IP aspects of folklore, until UNESCO created, in 1982, a Committee of Governmental Experts on the Safeguarding of Folklore.[8]

The activities of this Committee culminated with the adoption, in 1989, of the *Recommendation on the Safeguarding of Traditional Cultures and Folklore* (the '1989 Recommendation'). This Recommendation primarily addresses research scholars and governmental officials, and it has been criticized for not being sufficiently inclusive.[9]

An evaluation of the 1989 Recommendation was promoted in 1999 by the Smithsonian Institution, in cooperation with UNESCO. The results of this assessment were published in a volume that looked at the Recommendation and the possibilities for future action.[10] The Recommendation was evaluated as a success in that volume, if anything for increasing the interest of States in the protection of intangible heritage.[11] One of the difficulties of the 1989 Recommendation is that it does not specify the means of implementation or the obligations of Member States regarding its subject-matter.[12]

In response to this particular shortcoming, in 1993 UNESCO organized a conference the product of which was guidelines for the Intangible Cultural Heritage Program of the organization. The Guidelines speak of several concerns related to intangible heritage, including the danger of commodification, the concern with authenticity, and the need for a different methodology for intangible heritage protection (as compared to the methodology for tangible heritage protection).[13]

Despite its several shortcomings, the 1989 Recommendation was deemed a success by UNESCO officers, precisely for raising international awareness about the issue of ICH protection and building momentum for more aggressive forms of international law-making. For instance, in 1997 intangible heritage had become one of the highest priorities in UNESCO's cultural field, according to Member States gathered at the General Conference.[14]

[6] Sherkin, 'A Historical Study', 45.

[7] Noriko Aikawa-Faure, 'From the Proclamation of Masterpieces to the *Convention for the Safeguarding of Intangible Cultural Heritage*', in Laurajane Smith and Natsuko Agakawa (eds), *Intangible Heritage* (Routledge, 2009), 1 44 at 21.

[8] Sherkin, 'A Historical Study', 47.

[9] Anthony McCann et al, 'The 1989 Recommendation Ten Years On: Towards a Critical Analysis', in Peter Seitel (ed), *Safeguarding Traditional Culture: A Global Assessment* (Smithsonian Institution, 2001), 57 64 at 58.

[10] Peter Seitel (ed), *Safeguarding Traditional Culture: A Global Assessment* (Smithsonian Institution, 2001).

[11] Noriko Aikawa, 'The UNESCO *Recommendation on the Safeguarding of Traditional Culture and Folklore (1989)*: Actions Undertaken by UNESCO for Its Implementation', in Peter Seitel (ed), *Safeguarding Traditional Culture: A Global Assessment* (Smithsonian Institution, 2001), 13 19 at 13.

[12] Aikawa, 'The UNESCO Recommendation', 13.

[13] Aikawa, 'The UNESCO Recommendation', 14 15.

[14] Aikawa, 'The UNESCO Recommendation', 16.

The evaluation of the 1989 Recommendation was essential to the development of further normative action in the field. It indicated, for example, that States saw as a priority national/local normative action (77 per cent of responding States), instead of international efforts (66 per cent).[15] It also highlighted some important avenues of action for future developments, such as the need for an holistic approach to heritage protection,[16] and several participants spoke of the potential for protection of traditional culture and folklore via IP law.[17]

Some other ideas that came out of this evaluation effort include the concern with commodification of intangible heritage, its 'freezing' through a system of protection, the compliance with human rights standards, the respect for community-based systems of assessing agency (that is, in communities where communitarian approaches to rights prevailed, 'westernized' conceptions of individualism should not be used to measure agency).[18]

At the same time, the 1989 Recommendation was criticized for being biased towards the research community (as opposed to the custodial communities as the true bearers of ICH), the global public as the 'consumers' of intangible heritage, and manifestations of heritage that have been fixed by some means and have therefore been removed from their cultural context.[19] The definition of folklore given by the Recommendation, it was argued, was too product-oriented (and therefore dependent upon physical means), overlooking the fact that the real object of protection was the social practices and cultural contexts from which the products derived (therefore, intangible heritage as an independent type of heritage).[20] As I will argue below, many of these concerns have been addressed by the 2003 Convention, but its text (or its early practice) shows that not all of these criticisms have been heard.[21]

[15] Kurin, 'The UNESCO Questionnaire', 24.

[16] Robyne Bancroft, 'Everything Relates, or a Holistic Approach to Aboriginal Indigenous Cultural Heritage', in Peter Seitel (ed), *Safeguarding Traditional Culture: A Global Assessment* (Smithsonian Institution, 2001), 70 4 at 74.

[17] Preston Thomas, 'The 1989 UNESCO Recommendation and Aboriginal and Torres Strait Islander Peoples' Intellectual Property Rights', in Peter Seitel (ed), *Safeguarding Traditional Culture: A Global Assessment* (Smithsonian Institution, 2001), 89 96; Kamal Puri, 'Protection of Traditional Culture and Folklore', in Peter Seitel (ed), *Safeguarding Traditional Culture: A Global Assessment* (Smithsonian Institution, 2001), 97 103; Manuela Carneiro da Cunha, 'The Role of UNESCO in the Defense of Traditional Knowledge', in Peter Seitel (ed), *Safeguarding Traditional Culture: A Global Assessment* (Smithsonian Institution, 2001), 143 8; and Bradford S Simon, 'Global Steps to Local Empowerment in the Next Millennium: An Assessment of UNESCO's 1989 *Recommendation on the Safeguarding of Traditional Culture and Folklore*', in Peter Seitel (ed), *Safeguarding Traditional Culture: A Global Assessment* (Smithsonian Institution, 2001), 111 42 at 122 33.

[18] Lyndel V Prott, 'Some Considerations on the Protection of the Intangible Heritage: Claims and Remedies', in Peter Seitel (ed), *Safeguarding Traditional Culture: A Global Assessment* (Smithsonian Institution, 2001), 104 10 at 108 9.

[19] Simon, 'Global Steps to Local Empowerment', 121.

[20] Dawson Munjeri, 'Following the Length and Breadth of the Roots: Some Dimensions of Intangible Heritage', in Laurajane Smith and Natsuko Akagawa (eds), *Intangible Heritage* (Routledge, 2009), 207 42 at 217; and Aikawa-Faure, 'From the Proclamation of Masterpieces', 21.

[21] In the study that served as the basis for the ICH Convention, Janet Blake warned against these dangers. See Janet Blake, *Developing a New Standard-Setting Instrument for the Safeguarding of Intangible Cultural Heritage: Elements for Consideration* (UNESCO Publishing, 2001), 83.

In 1997, a small meeting took place in Marrakech, attended by a total of 16 experts on intangible heritage. The meeting aimed at exploring possible mechanisms through which UNESCO could raise international awareness about the importance of protecting oral heritage.[22] This interest by UNESCO was prompted by several factors: (1) the criticism raised against the World Heritage Committee for being geographically unbalanced and reflecting only European and North-American perspectives on the value of heritage; (2) the recognition of indigenous knowledge triggered by the Rio Earth Summit of 1992 (which culminated in the Convention on Biological Diversity, analysed below); and (3) the general normative neglect towards intangible heritage, despite it being a well debated issue for several decades.[23]

One of the proposals during this meeting was the creation of a prize system for oral heritage, bearing in mind the idea that award systems impact on world consciousness and are quick and easy to implement, thus generating awareness of the problem in the short term.[24] Marc Denhez, the main proponent of this idea, highlighted three main objectives to such a programme: (1) to officially recognize 'cultural spaces' where ICH and oral traditions are concentrated; (2) to encourage safeguarding and community and governmental participation in safeguarding actions; and (3) to raise awareness to the importance of ICH.[25]

Two main selection criteria were put to this programme: universal value as a general cultural criterion, and organizational criteria. The latter included the participation of the communities concerned with that particular manifestation of ICH in its protection.[26] The exact meaning of 'outstanding value' when it came to intangible heritage, however, was questioned by several States during the first meeting of the jury to select these masterpieces, in 2001. The jury responded by offering three criteria for defining the 'outstanding value' of ICH: (1) outstanding value to the custodial community and for cultural diversity; (2) being a long-lived practice; and (3) specific creation linked to a specific cultural space.[27]

The programme of Proclamation of Masterpieces of the Oral and Intangible Heritage of Humanity was active from 2001 to 2005, and it selected masterpieces three times, in 2001, 2003, and 2005, being an important precursor to the 2003 Convention.[28] With the entry into force of the 2003 Convention in 2006, the programme was cancelled, and the 90 proclaimed masterpieces were incorporated into one of the lists created by the 2003 Convention. But I will come back to this issue shortly, after delineating the main features and conceptual background of the 2003 Convention.

[22] Aikawa-Faure, 'From the Proclamation of Masterpieces', 14.
[23] Aikawa-Faure, 'From the Proclamation of Masterpieces', 15.
[24] Aikawa-Faure, 'From the Proclamation of Masterpieces', 16.
[25] Aikawa-Faure, 'From the Proclamation of Masterpieces', 17.
[26] Aikawa-Faure, 'From the Proclamation of Masterpieces', 18.
[27] Aikawa-Faure, 'From the Proclamation of Masterpieces', 32.
[28] Janet Blake, *Commentary on the UNESCO 2003 Convention on the Safeguarding of the Intangible Cultural Heritage* (Institute for Art and Law, 2006), 3.

2.1.2 The 2003 Convention for the Safeguarding of the Intangible Cultural Heritage

The 2003 Convention for the Safeguarding of the Intangible Cultural Heritage is in many ways a remarkable instrument[29] that offers a holistic approach to heritage protection.[30] It was drafted within two years,[31] and just nine years after its approval it has been ratified by 147 States.[32]

This section will look at the regime created by this instrument in light of its basic principles or tenets, the idea of complementarity of the Convention, and the features of the protection system created by it. Finally, I will offer a critique of this system, highlighting some of its shortcomings.

2.1.2.1 Basic tenets

The drafting of the UNESCO Convention was relatively short, but by no means uncontroversial. There were several meetings held for the drafting, including meetings in Turin (2001), Rio de Janeiro (2001), and Paris (2002). The Turin meeting focused primarily on the definition of intangible heritage, whereas the Rio meeting seems to have focused more on the development of the essential features of the regime (including the choice to follow the model of the World Heritage Convention, discussed in more detail below).[33] The Paris meeting was the meeting in which the 'Restricted Drafting Group' met and made important decisions regarding the text of the Convention and the model to be adopted.

One important definitional issue in the 2003 Convention is the idea that ICH refers not to the cultural objects, but rather to the social and cultural processes of which these objects are but the products. This was an important change of focus that happened gradually in heritage studies, and one that was decisively pushed into the 2003 Convention by the Organization of African Unity (later replaced by the African Union), alongside the group of experts responsible for the initial drafting of the Convention.[34]

The choice of the term 'intangible cultural heritage' has been criticized by some scholars. The term makes sense within the administrative logic of UNESCO,

[29] Janet Blake, 'UNESCO's 2003 Convention on Intangible Cultural Heritage: The Implications of Community Involvement in "Safeguarding"', in Laurajane Smith and Natsuko Akagawa (eds), *Intangible Heritage* (Routledge, 2009), 45 73 at 45.

[30] Mounir Bouchenaki, 'A Major Advance Towards a Holistic Approach to Heritage Conservation: The 2003 Intangible Heritage Convention', *Intl J of Intangible Heritage* 2 (2007), 106 9.

[31] Blake, *Commentary*, 15.

[32] *Status of Ratifications to the Convention for the Safeguarding of the Intangible Cultural Heritage (2003)*, available at <http://www.unesco.org/culture/ich> (accessed 29 November 2012).

[33] UNESCO, *Final Report on the International Meeting of Experts on Intangible Cultural Heritage: Priority Domains for an International Convention* (Rio de Janeiro, Brazil, 2002); and UNESCO, *Preparation of a Preliminary Draft International Convention on the Intangible Cultural Heritage, Meeting of the 'Restricted Drafting Group' (RDG) in Paris, 20 22 March 2002 Outline Work Plan*, para.5. See also UNESCO General Conference, *Oral Report of the Chairperson of Commission IV*, Doc. 31 C/INF.24, of 12 November 2001.

[34] Aikawa-Faure, 'From the Proclamation', 23.

precisely because of its opposition to tangible cultural heritage, which was addressed in other UNESCO instruments. However, to conceive of this type of heritage as 'intangible' in theory weakens its worth, rendering it disconnected and conveying the impression that its existence is ethereal or irrelevant. Further, the term 'intangible heritage' arguably weakens the status of traditional culture in legal practice, and can lessen the possibilities of protection.[35]

This seemed to be the best option, though, despite criticism. 'Folklore' was a term already charged with the product-oriented connotations of the 1989 Recommendation, as well as being perceived to imply banality within sacred traditions, ways of life, and cultural identity generally.[36] 'Treasures', on the other hand, was seen as being too paternalistic (and too oriented towards a 'westernized' conception of heritage shaped after the World Heritage Convention). Further, 'oral heritage' was considered too narrow in scope,[37] while 'traditional culture' seemed to obliterate the fact that ICH is about living cultures being constantly recreated.[38]

What exactly falls under the definition of 'intangible cultural heritage', however, was the object of much debate during the meeting of the Restricted Drafting Group in 2002. Three difficulties were identified: (1) that any such category of intangible heritage would be too broad; (2) conversely, that a list would run the risk of being too specific and restrictive; and (3) that the different views of States should be harmonized with respect to their perceptions of what ICH is. The (eventually adopted) flexible approach was identified as being necessary, taking into account UNESCO Member States' views on the topic, but at the same time avoiding overlaps with the mandates of other international organizations (most notably the WIPO and the WTO), while attending to the concerns of experts and facilitating legal protection.[39] Ultimately, the definition seems to have taken these factors into account, by weaving an open definition, with a non-exhaustive list of examples, and avoiding using examples from the area of IP law (out of respect for the division of work with the WIPO, but also with the consequence of autonomizing intangible heritage beyond the domains of IP).

Another important basic conceptual pillar of the Convention is its stress on the survival of ICH and its importance for cultural diversity and sustainable development.[40] The survival of ICH depends on the survival of the way of life of a certain community or group, and therefore on its economic viability.[41] There is thus a much closer connection between ICH and development than the normal connection between 'general' cultural heritage and development: while the latter

[35] McCann et al, 'The 1989 Recommendation', 60.

[36] Blake, *Commentary*, 22 and 32.

[37] Aikawa-Faure, 'From the Proclamation', 27.

[38] Richard Kurin, 'Safeguarding Intangible Cultural Heritage: Key Factors in Implementing the 2003 Convention', *Intl J of Intangible Heritage* 2 (2007), 10 20 at 12.

[39] UNESCO, *Preparation of a Preliminary Draft*, paras 30 1.

[40] On the connection between intangible heritage and sustainable development, see Toshiyuki Kono, 'UNESCO and Intangible Cultural Heritage from the Viewpoint of Sustainable Development', in Abdulqawi A Yusuf (ed), *Standard-Setting in UNESCO Volume 1: Normative Action in Education, Science and Culture* (Martinus Nijhoff and UNESCO Publishing, 2007), 237 65.

[41] Blake, *Commentary*, 25.

connection is based on external elements, and the development brought by the exploitation of that heritage is not necessarily directed at the preservation of that heritage, in the former connection development is a necessary element for the very survival of ICH.[42]

It is in this sense that economic alternatives for the exploitation of ICH must be considered as a powerful tool for the preservation of ICH. Naturally, economic exploitation must not mean a total commodification of heritage. At the same time it might be considered that commodification is what can keep intangible heritage alive. 'Banalization' as a result of mass tourism and staging shows of ICH is an important threat, and the Spanish delegation proposed that a warning against this threat was included in the Preamble of the 2003 Convention (the proposal ultimately did not make it into the final text).[43] It is important that economic viability is taken into account, but that concern must never risk emptying manifestations of ICH of any significance or modify meanings in a way that makes the heritage at issue unrecognizable to the custodial community.

The connection between human rights and ICH is also a fundamental element of the 2003 Convention. This was stated in the Preamble, by making reference to the international covenants on human rights, and also in the definition of ICH. Regarding the definition of ICH, human rights are evident in the fact that ICH can only be recognized as such when the social practices in question are in accordance with internationally recognized human rights.[44] The human rights dimension is also present in the domains of ICH, particularly the one referring to rituals and other social practices, since this necessarily interacts with rights such as freedom of association, freedom of religion, and privacy.[45] But I will come back to these issues in Chapter 5. Here, it was important to mention this connection and its relevance for the regime created by the 2003 Convention.[46]

Finally, another core tenet of the Convention is the idea of 'representativeness'. This will be analysed in detail below, when discussing the listing mechanisms of the Convention, but it is important to note here that, contrary to the World Heritage Convention, where the core value was the 'outstanding' quality of a certain manifestation of heritage, in the intangible heritage convention what is valued is the representativeness of the manifestation of heritage and consequently its contribution to cultural diversity.[47] I shall come back to this issue shortly, after analysing

[42] Blake, 'UNESCO's 2003 Convention', 48.

[43] Blake, *Commentary*, 26.

[44] Blake, *Commentary*, 35.

[45] Blake, *Commentary*, 38.

[46] On the connection between human rights and cultural heritage generally, see Francesco Francioni, 'A Dynamic Evolution of Concept and Scope: From Cultural Property to Cultural Heritage', in Abdulqawi A Yusuf (ed), *Standard-Setting in UNESCO Volume 1: Normative Action in Education, Science and Culture* (Martinus Nijhoff and UNESCO Publishing, 2007), 221 36 (pointing out that this is one of the factors behind the shift from 'cultural property' to 'cultural heritage'). See also UNESCO, *Preparation of a Preliminary Draft*, para 20.

[47] For the complete debate over the shift from 'masterpieces' to 'representativeness' during the drafting of the ICH Convention, see Valdimar Tr Hafstein, 'Intangible Heritage as a List: From Masterpieces to Representation', in Laurajane Smith and Natsuko Akagawa (eds), *Intangible Heritage* (Routledge, 2009), 93 111.

the complementarity of the Convention and the basic architecture of the safeguarding system created by it.

2.1.2.2 Complementarity and participation of non-State actors

The system created by the 2003 Convention was meant to be, from the very beginning, complementary to regimes that could be created by other specialized agencies.[48] The commitment to complementarity is true particularly regarding IP protection, which was, and still is, being developed by the WIPO. States participating in the negotiations of the 2003 Convention were well aware of the WIPO efforts, and wanted to avoid any possible overlaps between the work of the two organizations.[49] This is one of the reasons why, for instance, there was resistance in referring to 'individuals' in the text of the Convention, since this might suggest a possible crossover with the IP regime (which includes rights ascribed to individuals).[50]

The idea behind Article 3 of the 2003 Convention is also that of complementarity. This provision determines that the ICH Convention is not to be interpreted in any way contrary to other international obligations, particularly those undertaken under the 1972 World Heritage Convention (Article 3.a) or other IP and environmental agreements (Article 3.b).[51] The World Heritage Committee produced a document before the entry into force of the 2003 Convention outlining the need for integrated approaches for the safeguarding of cultural heritage, marking another point of distinction from the World Heritage Convention. The Yamato Declaration on Integrated Approaches for Safeguarding Tangible and Intangible Cultural Heritage calls upon UNESCO to, among other things, adopt integrated approaches in all its heritage programmes, taking into account the complementarity of the regimes created by the different instruments and the idea that all stakeholders can take better advantage of the regimes if integrated approaches are adopted.[52]

Complementarity is also an important element in the Convention when it speaks of the safeguarding of intangible heritage at the national, regional, and international levels, alongside the local (community-based) level. This feature of the different levels of protection, particularly the national and international levels, will be explored below, in the analysis of the safeguarding system.

Community involvement is an important part of the system created by the 2003 Convention.[53] It is in fact one of the basic purposes of the Convention, and it is

[48] UNESCO, *Final Report on the International Meeting of Experts.*
[49] Blake, *Commentary*, 11.
[50] Blake, *Commentary*, 29.
[51] Blake, *Commentary*, 42 3.
[52] World Heritage Committee, *The Yamato Declaration on Integrated Approaches for Safeguarding Tangible and Intangible Heritage*, adopted during the Seventh Extraordinary Session of the World Heritage Committee, Doc.WHC-04/7 EXT.COM/INF.9, of 25 November 2004, paras 13 and 15.
[53] Blake, 'UNESCO's 2003 Convention', 62; and Aikawa-Faure, 'From the Proclamation of Masterpieces', 37.

related to complementarity in the sense that the Convention sees communities as not only the bearers of ICH entitled to assistance, but also the primary responsible parties for the safeguarding of intangible heritage. The use of the term 'communities' raised several issues during the drafting of the 2003 Convention. It was unclear what the word meant as a legal term. Also, it raised the possibility of claims for group rights, which was not something all the drafters were supportive of or willing to accept.[54]

Doubt persists to this day in the implementation phase of the Convention, but the Intergovernmental Committee adopted the position that a definition of community was not necessary, and the one adopted by each State Party was sufficient to indicate community participation in the inscription of manifestations of heritage in the lists, for instance.[55] According to the Operational Directives of the Convention, States Parties should consult not only communities, groups, and individuals who are bearers of ICH, but also experts and research institutes. States Parties are encouraged to create consultative bodies to bring together communities and experts to help in the identification of ICH, the drawing of inventories, and the preparation of nomination files, among other activities.[56]

This is an important shift from the original text of the Convention, which did not really speak about expert participation in the implementation of the Convention. It is an important element, since one of the great shortcomings of the Convention is precisely the lack of expert knowledge on intangible heritage. The Subsidiary Body on modalities of participation has studied the matter, and concluded that communities must be returned the research results of work on ICH.[57]

Another important element of community participation is that States Parties commit to efforts to sensitize communities to the importance and value of their heritage. This is a means to ensure that the bearers of ICH may fully benefit from the Convention as a standard-setting instrument.[58] Naturally, if one of the core goals of the Convention is to raise awareness as to the importance of ICH, awareness should be raised primarily at the local level. This is because it is only by creating a sense of 'pride' that binds a community to its heritage that ensures its survival.

Also on the topic of participation of non-State actors in the implementation of the Convention, the Operational Directives contain rules for the participation of NGOs at the national and international levels. The rule on the participation of NGOs at the national level was not in the original draft of the Operational

[54] Blake, *Commentary*, 29.

[55] *Form ICH-02 (2009) Representative List*, Explanatory Note.

[56] General Assembly of States Parties to the Convention for the Safeguarding of the Intangible Cultural Heritage, *Operational Directives for the Implementation of the Convention for the Safeguarding of the Intangible Cultural Heritage (June 2008)*. Rule 77.

[57] Intergovernmental Committee for the Safeguarding of the Intangible Cultural Heritage, *Report of the Rapporteur of the Subsidiary Body on the Modalities for the Participation of Communities or their Representatives, Practitioners, Experts, Centers of Expertise and Research Institutes in the Implementation of the Convention*, presented at the Second Extraordinary Session (Sofia, Bulgaria, 18 22 February 2008), Doc.ITH/08/2.EXT.COM/CONF.201/INF.4, of 12 February 2008, para 12.

[58] General Assembly, *Operational Directives*, Rule 78.

Directives as submitted by the Intergovernmental Committee,[59] it was added by the General Assembly. In fact, it represents the only significant change made to the Directives after the Committee submitted its final draft to the General Assembly. This rule determines that States Parties must involve NGOs in the implementation of the Convention, as they may play an important role in the identification and definition of ICH, as well as in safeguarding activities, in cooperation and coordination with the States and communities, groups, and individuals.[60]

As to the participation of NGOs at the international level of implementation of the Convention, the Operational Directives determine that NGOs may be accredited to participate in the meetings of the Intergovernmental Committee and General Assembly, as long as they fulfil certain requirements: (1) proven competence, expertise, and experience in the safeguarding of ICH; (2) have a local, national, regional, or international nature; (3) have objectives in conformity with the spirit of the Convention; (4) cooperate with communities, groups, and individuals involved in the creation, transmission, and practice of ICH; and (5) possess 'operational capacities' to take part in the meetings.[61] Their accreditation is determined by the Operational Directives,[62] as well as by a specific form attached to the Directives.[63]

Among the NGOs accredited to participate in the meetings of the Intergovernmental Committee are the International Council of Museums,[64] the Mediterranean Diet Foundation,[65] the NGO Traditions for Tomorrow,[66] the World Martial Arts Union,[67] the International Council for Traditional Music,[68] the Federation of

[59] Intergovernmental Committee for the Safeguarding of the Intangible Cultural Heritage, Second Extraordinary Session (Sofia, Bulgaria, 18 22 February 2008), *Decision 2.EXT.COM 16.*

[60] General Assembly, *Operational Directives*, Rule 87.

[61] General Assembly, *Operational Directives*, Rule 88.

[62] General Assembly, *Operational Directives*, Rule 94.

[63] *Form ICH-09 (2009) Request from an NGO for Accreditation.*

[64] Intergovernmental Committee for the Safeguarding of the Intangible Cultural Heritage, First Extraordinary Session (Chegdu, China, 23 27 May 2007), *Decision 1.EXT.COM 4*; and Intergovernmental Committee for the Safeguarding of the Intangible Cultural Heritage, Second Session (Tokyo, Japan, 3 7 September 2007), *Decision 2.COM 5.*

[65] Intergovernmental Committee for the Safeguarding of the Intangible Cultural Heritage, First Extraordinary Session (Chegdu, China, 23 27 May 2007), *Decision 1.EXT.COM 4*; Intergovernmental Committee for the Safeguarding of the Intangible Cultural Heritage, Second Session (Tokyo, Japan, 3 7 September 2007), *Decision 2.COM 5*; and Intergovernmental Committee for the Safeguarding of the Intangible Cultural Heritage, Second Extraordinary Session (Sofia, Bulgaria, 18 22 February 2008), *Decision 2.EXT.COM 5.*

[66] Intergovernmental Committee for the Safeguarding of the Intangible Cultural Heritage, First Extraordinary Session (Chegdu, China, 23 27 May 2007), *Decision 1.EXT.COM 4*; Intergovernmental Committee for the Safeguarding of the Intangible Cultural Heritage, Second Session (Tokyo, Japan, 3 7 September 2007), *Decision 2.COM 5*; and Intergovernmental Committee for the Safeguarding of the Intangible Cultural Heritage, Second Extraordinary Session (Sofia, Bulgaria, 18 22 February 2008), *Decision 2.EXT.COM 5.*

[67] Intergovernmental Committee for the Safeguarding of the Intangible Cultural Heritage, Second Session (Tokyo, Japan, 3 7 September 2007), *Decision 2.COM 5*; and Intergovernmental Committee for the Safeguarding of the Intangible Cultural Heritage, Second Extraordinary Session (Sofia, Bulgaria, 18 22 February 2008), *Decision 2.EXT.COM 5.*

[68] Intergovernmental Committee for the Safeguarding of the Intangible Cultural Heritage, Second Session (Tokyo, Japan, 3 7 September 2007), *Decision 2.COM 5*; and Intergovernmental Committee

Associations of Traditional Music and Dance,[69] the Conservatory for Mexico's Culinary Heritage, and the Intangible Cultural Heritage Encyclopedia,[70] among others. The participating NGOs may help shape the type of manifestations of heritage that are inscribed in the lists in the future,[71] so it is important to be aware of the areas of activity of NGOs participating in the implementation of the Convention at the international level. It is particularly noteworthy that no indigenous groups seem to be in this list, even though associations allegedly representing indigenous peoples, such as the Brazilian National Association of Indigenous Action (*Associação Nacional de Ação Indigenista* Anaí), are accredited NGOs.[72]

After this analysis of some of the basic tenets of the Convention, as well as of complementarity as an overarching idea within it, it is now necessary to analyse the system created by the Convention. Bearing the core tenets in mind, I will now proceed to an examination of how the system designed by the Convention can accommodate these core values and concepts.

2.1.2.3 The safeguarding system

The purposes of the Convention, as determined in Article 1, are four: (1) to safeguard ICH; (2) to ensure respect for the ICH of communities, groups, and individuals; (3) to raise awareness; and (4) to provide international cooperation and assistance. This provision lays down the foundations of the safeguarding system created by the Convention. And there are two organs for this, the Intangible Heritage Committee and the General Assembly of States Parties. I will look at each of these organs in turn.

The General Assembly of States Parties is created by Article 4 of the 2003 Convention, and it represents a substantial shift from the 1972 World Heritage Convention, which does not contain provisions for a similar organ. This is symptomatic of a greater concern among States participating in the drafting over their sovereignty, especially when dealing with matters as sensitive as culture (living cultures, to be more specific) and claims by communities and groups. It was felt that sovereignty (a central feature of the instrument, explored in further detail below) should be strengthened, and one of the tools for that purpose was to create

for the Safeguarding of the Intangible Cultural Heritage, Second Extraordinary Session (Sofia, Bulgaria, 18 22 February 2008), *Decision 2.EXT.COM 5.*

[69] Intergovernmental Committee for the Safeguarding of the Intangible Cultural Heritage, Second Session (Tokyo, Japan, 3 7 September 2007), *Decision 2.COM 5.*

[70] These latter two took part only in the latest meeting. See Intergovernmental Committee for the Safeguarding of the Intangible Cultural Heritage, Second Extraordinary Session (Sofia, Bulgaria, 18 22 February 2008), *Decision 2.EXT.COM 5.*

[71] For an account of NGO participation in the shaping of the List of Masterpieces, see Anthony Seeger, 'Lessons Learned from the ICTM (NGO) Evaluation of Nominations for the UNESCO *Masterpieces of the Oral and Intangible Heritage of Humanity*, 2001 5', in Laurajane Smith and Natsuko Akagawa (eds), *Intangible Heritage* (Routledge, 2009), 112 28.

[72] For a full list of accredited NGOs, see *Non-Governmental Organizations accredited to provide advisory services to the Committee*, available at <http://www.unesco.org/culture/ich/index.php?lg=en&pg=00331> (accessed 29 November 2012).

an Assembly of Parties to be the supreme authority on most matters regarding the intangible heritage convention.[73]

The Intangible Heritage Committee, on the other hand, was created with the idea that intangible heritage is an area that requires a high level of expertise, due to its complexity, and that this level of expertise could only be reached by a Committee, inspired by similar experiences in the area of international environmental law.[74] Article 5 of the 2003 Convention determines that the committee shall be composed of representatives of 24 States Parties to the Convention, elected by the General Assembly. It is yet another intergovernmental organ, but one with reduced participation of States Parties. In this sense, then, the Committee is yet another layer of sovereignty imposed upon the regulation of ICH concerns.

The functions of the Committee are provided for in Article 7. Among these is the function to provide guidance on best practices for safeguarding and making recommendations in this sense. This provision was inserted in the text in light of the lack of municipal and international experience in the safeguarding of ICH, and thus the need to collect best practices as a means to offer guidance to States and UNESCO itself. It is closely connected to the first objective of the Convention, that of safeguarding ICH.[75]

Article 8 of the ICH Convention determines the working methods of the Committee. Article 8(1) clearly indicates the subordination of the Committee to the General Assembly,[76] and Article 8(4) suggests the possibility for the involvement of NGOs, communities, and practitioners in the meetings and work of the Committee (an idea further elaborated in Article 9).[77] Finally, Article 10 determines that the Committee will be assisted by the UNESCO Secretariat, which has the role of bringing further expertise into the committee's work in relation to the safeguarding of intangible heritage.[78]

The Intergovernmental Committee has established two subsidiary bodies. The first one, on the design of an emblem for the Convention, worked from September 2007 to June 2008, when the emblem of the Convention was chosen.[79] The second subsidiary body, also created in September 2007, deals with modalities for the participation of communities and others. I have already analysed some issues regarding the substantive work of this subsidiary body on community involvement, and will come back to them below, but it is important to notice at this point that the Intergovernmental Committee has the powers to create such bodies, and has already used them to tackle practical issues regarding the implementation of the Convention, one of them of great complexity and still unresolved.

The 2003 Convention also provides for the safeguarding of intangible cultural heritage at the national level. In fact, the creation of national systems of safeguarding, including awareness-raising, education, and a participatory approach are

[73] Blake, *Commentary*, 46.
[74] Blake, *Commentary*, 45.
[75] Blake, *Commentary*, 52.
[76] Blake, *Commentary*, 55.
[77] Blake, *Commentary*, 56 7.
[78] Blake, *Commentary*, 58.
[79] The emblem, alongside information about the process leading to its choice, is available at <http://www.unesco.org/culture/ich> (accessed 29 November 2012).

central to the Convention's success.[80] Article 11 imposes the core obligations in terms of safeguarding, and it determines that States shall take the necessary measures to ensure the safeguarding of ICH, including ensuring the participation of communities, groups, and NGOs in the process of identification and definition of the intangible heritage in each State's territory. This latter provision reflects the concern with the fact that the most important obstacle to the safeguarding of intangible heritage is precisely the lack of knowledge by each State of the knowledge present in their territories.[81]

This issue is addressed by the obligation imposed upon States Parties to make an inventory of the manifestations of intangible cultural heritage in their territories (Article 12). These inventories must be prepared by each State, periodically updated, and are an important part of the reporting that each State Party has to undertake and produce to the ICH Committee (Article 29).

There are also other forms of safeguarding required from States Parties (Article 13). These include policies to promote ICH in society as an important functional part of the social and cultural fabric, the establishment of competent bodies to deal with ICH and the adoption of other measures, legal, technical, administrative, and financial to foster ICH and ensure access to it while respecting communities and customary practices on the matter.

One criticism of this provision is that it determines that States Parties 'shall endeavour to' adopt the measures listed in this Article. This of course has the effect of weakening this provision and the measures mandated by it, making them subsidiary to the obligation of creating national inventories.[82] In this sense inventorying becomes the main safeguarding tool in the Convention's system, at least inasmuch as national measures are concerned.

Article 14, also determining that States 'shall endeavour' to adopt certain measures, speaks of measures aimed at education, awareness-raising, and capacity building. This provision, with its strong emphasis on the educational component of ICH, is an important innovation with regard to the 1972 World Heritage Convention, and one that illustrates the important shift in focus between the two instruments.[83] To the extent that ICH refers to living cultures, the perpetuation of ICH as a living culture requires that younger generations are educated to become future bearers of these traditions. This is the sense given to educational measures in this Article.

Finally, Article 15 determines that, at the national level, communities, groups, and individuals concerned with ICH shall participate in policy-making about, and management of, their own intangible heritage. This provision is distinct precisely to emphasize the importance of the role attributed to communities.[84] While this is a valuable development, I will argue below that this inclusion is limited to the national level (where there is much less international control, and less uniformity of practice). Furthermore, it does not necessarily compensate for the overall exclusion

[80] Blake, *Commentary*, 59.
[81] Blake, *Commentary*, 61 2.
[82] Blake, *Commentary*, 66.
[83] Blake, *Commentary*, 74.
[84] Blake, *Commentary*, 76.

of community input during the drafting of the Convention and its safeguarding system.

The safeguarding of intangible heritage at the international level happens primarily through intangible heritage lists. One of them is the 'Representative List of the Intangible Cultural Heritage of Humanity' (Article 16), while the other is the 'List of Intangible Cultural Heritage in Need of Urgent Safeguarding' (Article 17). It is important to note that only the first list is called a 'representative' list, while the other includes, at least in theory, all forms of intangible heritage in grave risk of disappearance.

The listing mechanism was opposed by some States, notably Norway, during the negotiations of the Convention. Norway was of the opinion that a list-based mechanism would create a hierarchy of manifestations of heritage (the 'listed', which would somehow be 'better', and the 'unlisted'). Norway thought that a catalogue of best practices alone would suffice to accomplish the objectives of the Convention. India, on the other hand, thought that the listing approach was an effective one, even though it should be approached carefully so as not to create any sort of hierarchy. This was generally the accepted argument, as the listing would help in the awareness-raising that was necessary for the achievement of the Convention's objectives. Further, as highlighted by the Brazilian delegation, the listing mechanism at the international level mirrored the national obligation of inventorying, thus being also a desirable means to implement the Convention.[85]

The criteria for the inscription of manifestations of heritage in these lists have been the subject of discussion of the Intergovernmental Committee. A first set of criteria has already been approved into the operational directives for implementation of the Convention and revised twice, in 2010 and 2012.

There are several criteria imposed for a manifestation of heritage to be inscribed on the list of intangible heritage in need of urgent safeguarding and all of them must be met: (1) heritage must be intangible heritage in accordance with Article 2 of the Convention; (2) it must be in need of urgent safeguarding 'because its viability is at risk' or 'because it is facing grave threats as a result of which it cannot be expected to survive without immediate safeguarding'; (3) there must be a plan of safeguarding measures elaborated to enable the element to be practised and transmitted; (4) free, prior, and informed consent must be obtained from the concerned community, group, or individuals; (5) the element must be in the national inventory of intangible heritage of the concerned State Party; and (6) the State must give the authorization for such inscription.[86]

These requirements are verified through standardized forms for inscription, annexed to the Operational Directives.[87] The explanatory notes to these forms indicate that the safeguarding measures that must be included in the request for

[85] Blake, *Commentary*, 79.

[86] General Assembly, *Operational Directives*, Rule 1.

[87] *Form ICH-01 (2009) Urgent Safeguarding List*; *Form ICH-01 (2010) Urgent Safeguarding List*; and *Form ICH-01 (2011) Urgent Safeguarding List*. These forms are identical, except for the timeframe they propose, as the first form refers to the first round of inscriptions in the urgent safeguarding list, while the other form refers to the second round.

inscription must be a detailed plan within a timeframe of approximately four years. These measures must be described so as to indicate the objectives of the safeguarding measures and results expected, the key activities to be carried out, the mechanisms for participation of communities, groups, and individuals, and the timetable and budget.[88] Also, the forms require that States prove that the concerned communities, groups, or individuals are willing and committed to the preservation of the intangible heritage the protection of which is sought.[89] And the free, prior, and informed consent of the community, group, or individuals must be proven. According to the wording of the explanatory note, this consent 'may be demonstrated through written or recorded concurrence, or through other means, according to the legal regimens of the State Party and the infinite variety of communities and groups concerned'.[90] This is so because the Committee has chosen to leave the door open for demonstrations of consent in accordance with the cultural traditions of the parties concerned rather than imposing a single format. Free, prior, and informed consent was highlighted by scholars as a necessary element for dealing with ICH from the very beginning of the process leading to the adoption of the 2003 Convention, even though many States opposed the idea of involving communities.[91]

During the first round of inscriptions 12 manifestations of intangible heritage were inscribed in the list of intangible heritage in need of urgent safeguarding, and four during the second round.[92] Four additional manifestations of intangible heritage were added to this list in 2010, and 11 in 2011. Of the manifestations of heritage inscribed in the first round, the Suiti Cultural Space in Latvia is noteworthy.[93] The Suiti is a small Catholic community in a predominantly Lutheran part of Latvia. The cultural space, comprising some 400 square kilometres, has a population of about 2,000 people, down from 10,000 at the beginning of the 20th century. The once flourishing community was deeply affected by World War II and the following Soviet occupation, and this led to the near-disappearance of Suiti culture, which is currently mastered by roughly 60 members of the community. Safeguarding measures proposed included not only the immediate preservation of the culture, but also the creation of a more favourable economic environment that would prevent younger generations from leaving the region in search of better employment.

[88] *Form ICH-01 (2009) Urgent Safeguarding List*; and *Form ICH-01 (2010) Urgent Safeguarding List*, Explanatory Note, para 4.b.

[89] *Form ICH-01 (2009) Urgent Safeguarding List*; and *Form ICH-01 (2010) Urgent Safeguarding List*, Explanatory Note, para 4.c.

[90] *Form ICH-01 (2009) Urgent Safeguarding List*; and *Form ICH-01 (2010) Urgent Safeguarding List*, Explanatory Note, para 5.b.

[91] Simon, 'Global Steps to Local Empowerment', 113.

[92] UNESCO, *The Intangible Heritage Lists*, available at <http://www.unesco.org/culture/ich/index.php?pg=00011&inscription=00003&type=00003> (accessed 29 November 2012).

[93] Intangible Heritage Convention, *Nomination Form for Inscription on the Urgent Safeguarding List Suiti Cultural Space*, available at <http://www.unesco.org/culture/ich/index.php?USL=00314> (accessed 29 November 2012).

The State has been endeavouring to increase awareness of the Suiti heritage (including vocal drone singing performed by Suiti women, wedding traditions, traditional costumes, the Suiti language, cuisine, religious traditions, celebrations of seasonal traditions, and a large number of songs and dances)[94] for the past several years, mostly through educational activities in schools and cultural festivals. It has also created a website inventorying the Suiti heritage, and has set up a weaving workshop to encourage traditional Suiti craftsmanship. A five-year framework has been designed for the revitalization of the Suiti heritage, including educational activities and the restoration of religious buildings, among other initiatives.

Local communities have been consulted about whether this manifestation of heritage should be proposed for inscription in the list, as well as in the design of the safeguarding measures, through workshops aimed at gathering ideas for specific safeguarding needs and planning of activities. The free, prior, and informed consent of the communities was established by a show-of-hands vote during a community meeting. It has also been established through motions approved by city council bodies of the cities within the cultural space.[95]

The criteria for inscription on the representative list are slightly different,[96] and in many ways impose a lesser burden on States seeking inscription. The criteria for inscription on the list of representative intangible heritage, all of which must be met by States seeking inscription, are: (1) that the manifestation of heritage falls within the concept of Article 2 of the Convention; (2) that the inscription will contribute to the visibility and awareness of the significance of ICH and will encourage dialogue, thereby entangling cultural diversity and being a testimony to human creativity; (3) that safeguarding measures are elaborated to protect and promote the element; (4) free, prior, and informed consent of the affected communities, groups, and individuals; and (5) that the element is present in one of the inventories required from States Parties.[97] Also, communities must be involved in the preparation of the nominations for this list.[98]

The manifestation of the heritage to be inscribed must be described in reference to the significant features of it at the present (this is because the Committee is aware that the element may, and probably will, change in the future),[99] also including the discussion of the social and cultural functions played by it. The

[94] 'Latvian Suiti Cultural Space Included in the UNESCO Intangible Cultural Heritage List', *Latvian Institute Factsheet No 88* (22 October 2009), available at <http://www.li.lv/images new/files/2009 10 02 %20No88-Suiti%20Cultural%20Space%20in%20UNESCO%20List.pdf> (accessed 29 November 2012).

[95] Suiti Cultural Space, *Documentation on Consent of Communities*, available at <http://www.unesco.org/culture/ich/doc/src/00314-Community%20consent-EN.pdf> (accessed 29 November 2012).

[96] For a comparison, see Intergovernmental Committee for the Safeguarding of the Intangible Cultural Heritage, Second Extraordinary Session (Sofia, Bulgaria, 18 22 February 2008), *Decision 2.EXT.COM 17* (*Report of the Intergovernmental Committee for the Safeguarding of the Intangible Cultural Heritage on its activities between the first and second sessions of the General Assembly of the States Parties to the Convention*, paras 11 19).

[97] General Assembly, *Operational Directives*, Rule 19.

[98] General Assembly, *Operational Directives*, Rule 21.

[99] UNESCO, *Report on the Expert Meeting on Criteria for Inscription on the Lists Established by the 2003 Convention for the Safeguarding of the Intangible Cultural Heritage* (Paris, 5 6 December 2005).

history of the element is not a required element.[100] The free, prior, and informed consent of the communities, groups, or individuals must also be secured and proven, in the same fashion as the consent for inscription in the urgent list.[101]

Seventy-six manifestations of heritage have been inscribed during the first round of inscriptions in October 2009. Among these, a few are noteworthy, including Tibetan Opera (see below), the Tango, Chinese sericulture and silk craftsmanship, an Afro-Uruguayan cultural practice called 'Candombe' and the cultural space associated with it (which is but a few blocks in a neighbourhood in Montevideo), and a traditional dispute settlement mechanism for water disputes in southern Spain, among many others.[102] These first inscriptions indicate that the range of safeguarding initiatives to be adopted under the Convention is very wide, and can go from the preservation of tangible elements necessary for the perpetuation of the activity, the enactment of specific laws, the institution of national holidays aimed at celebrating the cultures that served as the source for the manifestations of heritage inscribed, to educational and awareness-raising activities. Traditional norms of the involved communities have been taken into account when discussing community involvement, and also as important starting points for the preservation of the practices themselves.

In the second round of inscriptions (2010), an additional 49 elements were inscribed, some of which were more controversial than others. The Mediterranean Diet, for instance, was successfully inscribed (after a first failed attempt in 2009) jointly by Greece, Italy, Morocco, and Spain. The element was successfully inscribed as a result of its focus on the social practices behind the diet rather than the diet itself. Specifically, the ritual of eating as a social/communal event was at issue. The unsuccessful attempt at inscription, it seems, focused more on the actual staples of the diet, and was the target of much criticism because it was seen as a manipulation of the UNESCO listing mechanism for the sake of enhancing tourism, in order to allow restaurants to cater to tourists under some sort of 'UNESCO seal of approval' for their menus. The focus on the social practices seems to have largely remedied that, even if critical voices can still be found.

Another inscribed element is the Wayúu Normative System, applied by the Pütchipü'üi (*palabrero*), the first time a normative system was inscribed on the list.[103] The Wayúu is an indigenous people living in the La Guajira peninsula, between Colombia and Venezuela. The Wayúu normative system is a normative system that revolves around the Pütchipü'üi (the *palabrero*), who is the person 'in charge of administering the words' (in Spanish, *palabras*, or, in Wayúu,

[100] *Form ICH-02 (2009) Representative List*, Explanatory Note, para 2.

[101] *Form ICH-02 (2009) Representative List*, Explanatory Note, para 5.b.

[102] All the documents referring to these inscriptions are available at UNESCO, *The Intangible Heritage Lists*.

[103] For a more detailed discussion of the Wayúu normative system and implications of its inscription for indigenous advocacy, see Lucas Lixinski, 'Falling Short: The UNESCO Intangible Cultural Heritage Regime, Indigenous Heritage and the UN Declaration on the Rights of Indigenous Peoples', in Sarah Sargent (ed), *A New Millennium for Indigenous Rights: Challenges and Changes* (Buckingham University Press, forthcoming 2013).

pütchikalü).[104] This figure arises historically from a need to resolve disputes within the community, and it is a figure of authority. The *palabrero* is chosen on an ad hoc basis, taking into account an individual's social and economic status within the community. It is this status (including social connections) that creates and legitimates the authority of the *palabrero*. Gradually, the administration of justice role of the *palabrero* imposed that the *palabrero* proved stronger cultural connections and awareness of how their decisions impact on the social status of the group as a whole (which is connected to knowledge of history and a form of precedent within the community). Elder councils in the communities have a bearing on the activities of *palabreros*. Elder councils are the precedent library from which the *palabrero* draws. The Wayúu normative system collectivizes law, as traditionally the decisions of the *palabrero* have effects not only on the individual who is found guilty of misconduct, but on the individual's entire family or clan (Eirukü).

While it is commendable that a normative system can receive protection through a heritage listing mechanism, perhaps some of the criticisms against the listing mechanism in general (more specifically, the danger of commodification) are even more pressing here. The element was inscribed because of its promise of cross-cultural dialogue. The implications of inscribing a sophisticated system of dispute resolution in a necessarily less-nuanced cultural heritage list include the risk that the listing mechanism enables a kind of packaging of 'the other', and of compressing foreign legal systems into the boxes of 'mainstream' law. While this process is common to all of comparative law, and to some extent all of international law, it gains a special dimension in the case of cultural heritage lists, because the goal here is not to apply the normative system, but rather to be able to appreciate it.

Article 18 provides for programmes, projects, and other activities for the safeguarding of intangible heritage, and determines that the Committee (upon approval by the Assembly) shall select the ones that best reflect the objectives of the Convention. In this way, an inventory of best practices, so important for the implementation of the Convention for the reasons listed above, can be created.[105] One of the issues raised regarding this repository of best practices was whether it should be a selective listing, or a more inclusive one.[106] It was early decided, in the

[104] Most of this account is drawn from interviews with *palabreros* available on YouTube. See <http://www.youtube.com/watch?v=XnWuldfC-0w> (first of a three part series of an interview with a *palabrero*, accessed 18 January 2013); <http://www.youtube.com/watch?v=fojEsmitk8M> (interview with a historian specialized in Wayúu history, accessed 18 January 2013); and <http://www.youtube.com/watch?v=V vM i4yorA> (a video prepared to support the UNESCO nomination, accessed 18 January 2013). Another important source is an audio interview with the *palabrero* Guillermo Ojeda Jayariyu (also coordinator of the main body of *palabreros*, the Junta Mayor Autónoma de Palabreros Wayúu) on the Colombian National Radio's website, highlighting the risks and advantages of inscription on the UNESCO list. See <http://www.fonoteca.gov.co/index.php/home/actualidad/item/134-%C2%A1que-venga-el-palabrero> (accessed 29 January 2013).

[105] Blake, *Commentary*, 86 8.

[106] Intergovernmental Committee for the Safeguarding of the Intangible Cultural Heritage, First Extraordinary Session (Chengdu, China, 23 27 May 2007), *Discussion on the Implementation of Article 18 of the Convention for the Safeguarding of the Intangible Cultural Heritage*, Doc.ITH/07/1.EXT.COM/CONF.207/11, of 20 April 2007.

first draft of this part of the Operational Directives, that the listing should be selective.[107]

The Operational Directives determine the criteria that must be met for the selection of a best practice: (1) the programme involves safeguarding, as defined in Article 2(3) of the Convention; (2) the programme coordinates efforts for safeguarding at the regional, subregional, and/or international levels; (3) the programme reflects the principles and objectives of the Convention; (4) it has demonstrated effectiveness in contributing to the viability of the ICH concerned; (5) it counts on the participation of the community, group, or individuals with free, prior, and informed consent; (6) it can serve as a subregional, regional, or international model for other safeguarding initiatives (that is, it can be 'transplanted' or emulated in other contexts); (7) the involved State(s), communities, groups, or individuals are willing to cooperate with the dissemination of best practices; (8) it is possible to assess the results of the programme, project, or activity; and (9) the programme 'is primarily applicable to the particular needs of developing countries'.[108] These criteria are further developed in a standardized form attached to the Operational Directives, accompanied by explanatory notes.[109]

The first round of nominations of best practices selected three programmes for inscription as a best practice to promote the goals of the Convention (and none were nominated in the second round).[110] Of these, one is particularly noteworthy. The project called 'Safeguarding the intangible cultural heritage of Aymara communities in Bolivia, Chile and Peru' is a sub-regional project, involving more than one State Party to the Convention. It aims at promoting initiatives in primary schools 'aimed at ensuring the viability of endangered cultural expressions and which constitute the cultural identity of Aymara communities of Bolivia (La Paz-Oruro-Potosí), Chile (Tarapacá-Arica-Parinacota-Antofagasta) and Peru (Tacna-Puno-Moquegua)'.[111] The project has a strong focus on the importance of preserving the Aymara language as a vehicle to enable the transmission of intangible heritage related to agricultural methods, textile techniques, and traditional music and dance. The project involves the ethnographic study of the involved communities, as well as teacher-training programmes and the production of manuals. It also involves, at a latter phase, regional artistic contests, and the exchange of experiences amongst involved policy-makers.[112]

As to the actors involved in the process, the nomination form highlights that the project creates a network of 'individuals, communities, groups, cultural managers,

[107] Intergovernmental Committee for the Safeguarding of the Intangible Cultural Heritage, Second Session (Tokyo, Japan, 3 7 September 2007), *Preliminary Draft Directives for Implementing Article 18 of the Convention for the Safeguarding of the Intangible Cultural Heritage*, Doc.ITH/07/2.COM/CONF.208/12, of 30 July 2007.

[108] General Assembly, *Operational Directives*, Rule 7.

[109] *Form ICH-03 (2009) Programmes, Projects and Activities*.

[110] UNESCO, *The Intangible Heritage Lists*.

[111] Intangible Heritage Convention, *Nomination Form for Best Practice Safeguarding the Intangible Cultural Heritage of Aymara Communities in Bolivia, Chile and Peru*, available at <http://www.unesco.org/culture/ich/index.php?Art18=00299> (accessed 29 November 2012).

[112] Intangible Heritage Convention, *Nomination Form for Best Practice*.

specialists, indigenous organizations, research centers, NGOs and government among others, promoting the permanent exchange of experience, information and training in order to strengthen capacities in the region, achieving this way a wide participation of all the concerned actors'.[113] The project has secured the consent of a governing body of Aymara communities in all three involved countries, and has committed itself to guaranteeing Aymara participation in all stages of the project. Thus, by involving the community the way it does, the States give the Aymara control over their heritage, and act as facilitators for the strengthening of this intangible heritage. At the same time, the States benefit from having a prime example of a well-developed initiative that gives credence to their claims associated to indigeneity (being an indigenous or plurinational country, or simply one that respects its indigenous minorities).

Article 19 determines international cooperation for the safeguarding of intangible heritage, including the exchange of information and joint initiatives by States Parties. Article 20 determines the purposes of international assistance, while Article 21 outlines the forms of international assistance. Of these, 'standard-setting' is a particularly relevant one, and one that refers to the establishment of international standards to be subsequently translated into regional and national legislative initiatives.[114] In this sense, the Convention is not a product of input from previous national initiatives, but it is created to be precisely the catalyst of national measures for the safeguarding of intangible heritage.

States may further request international assistance for the safeguarding of intangible heritage in their territories (Article 23). This international assistance may be financial in nature, with money drawn from the fund created by the Convention. And any funds allocated shall generally be met by the State Party as a means to prove interest also from the State Party in protecting its intangible heritage (Article 24.2).[115] One important feature of these requests is that only States can ask for such assistance, in the same way that only States can propose manifestations of heritage to the lists created by the Convention. This is yet another feature of the strict sovereignty upon which the Convention system is built.[116]

The 'Fund for the Safeguarding of the Intangible Cultural Heritage' is created by Article 25 of the Convention. The resources of the fund come from contributions made by States Parties to the Convention, voluntary contributions from States (whether a party to the Convention or not), organizations from the UN system, private organizations and individuals, any other income deriving from the fund itself (investments, for instance), and specific fund-raising activities (Article 28). Article 26 offers a creative compromise to the difficult negotiation of the financial commitments of States, as it creates a duty of contribution to which States can submit opt-out declarations (Article 26.2). And, even when a State does deposit a declaration to such effect, it is still under an obligation to 'endeavour' to withdraw the declaration and contribute fully to the system (Article 26.3).

[113] Intangible Heritage Convention, *Nomination Form for Best Practice*.
[114] Blake, *Commentary*, 95. [115] Blake, *Commentary*, 102.
[116] Blake, *Commentary*, 99.

The mandatory contributions by States Parties may be of not more than 1 per cent of the contribution each State normally makes to the UNESCO budget (Article 26.1). While this seems to be a small amount of money, the budget for the first years of operation of the Convention has risen from about U$1.3 million to U$5.6 million per year, a significant amount.[117] It is unclear how much of this money comes from these mandatory contributions, and how much comes from voluntary contributions (regulated by Article 27) or other sources, but the fact is that, similar to the World Heritage Fund,[118] this seems to be fast evolving into a successful means of promoting the objectives of the Intangible Heritage Convention.

One final important feature of the system created by the ICH Convention is the transitional clause about the incorporation of the items listed in the Proclamation of Masterpieces of the Oral and Intangible Heritage of Mankind into the international lists created by the Convention. Article 31 provides that this list be incorporated, and that the incorporation of these items does not interfere with the criteria for inscription of other manifestations of heritage in the list.

While this clause is an important statement of the idea that the Masterpieces programme was a useful precursor of the 2003 Convention, it is also a reminder that the 2003 Convention has moved away from that model.[119] The Convention has moved away from the 'masterpieces' approach, which, as seen above, was closer to the World Heritage Convention model of outstanding value, towards a model of 'representativeness' and fostering of cultural diversity, rather than exceptional aesthetic (or other) value.[120]

The Operational Directives for the implementation of the Convention determine that the incorporation is automatic into the Representative List, immediately following the adoption of the Directives.[121] States with proclaimed Masterpieces that are not parties to the Convention[122] assume rights and obligations under the Convention only with regard to those items of the Representative List.[123] These States have been notified by the Director General of UNESCO about the inscription, and the ensuing change in the legal regime of the safeguarding programmes.[124] The UNESCO Office of International Standards and Legal Affairs

[117] Intergovernmental Committee for the Safeguarding of the Intangible Cultural Heritage, Second Extraordinary Session (Sofia, Bulgaria, 18 22 February 2008), *Decision 2.EXT.COM 9* (decision submitting draft budget for approval by the General Assembly for the period from September 2008 to June 2010); and General Assembly of the States Parties to the Convention for the Safeguarding of the Intangible Cultural Heritage, Fourth Session (UNESCO Headquarters, Paris, 4 8 June 2012), *Use of the Resources of the Intangible Cultural Heritage Fund*, Doc.ITH/12/4.GA/INF.7.1, of 15 May 2012.

[118] For a comment on the Fund, see Federico Lenzerini, 'Articles 15 16: World Heritage Fund', in Francesco Francioni (ed), *The 1972 World Heritage Convention: A Commentary* (Oxford University Press, 2008), 269 88.

[119] Blake, *Commentary*, 118.

[120] Blake, *Commentary*, 119.

[121] General Assembly, *Operational Directives*, Rule 34.

[122] As of November 2012, these States are: Malaysia, Palestine, and Russia.

[123] General Assembly, *Operational Directives*, Rule 35.

[124] States were given the opportunity to express their consent (within one year) to be bound to the new regime in what regards the items on the Representative List. In case this consent was not

states that the items incorporated in the list do not automatically generate any rights or obligations upon the States where the manifestations of heritage are located, and that additional steps are required to create this regime (in this case, the notification to the Director General to be bound to the Convention's regime).[125]

After discussing the system created by the Convention, and its early practice, it is important to recall some of the criticisms that can be raised against it, and that prevent it from becoming the central piece of the international machinery for the safeguarding of intangible heritage. To this criticism I move next.

2.1.2.4 Criticism of the Convention

One of the important features of the Convention is the resistance to create a system of 'legal guarantees' for safeguarding intangible heritage. There seemed to be resistance among the drafters of the Convention in establishing specific obligations to create systems of legal protection to intangible heritage. For instance, 'legal protection' was seen by an expert meeting on the implementation of the 2003 Convention as a potential complementary form of protection for ICH, but not one that was required, nor warranted the status of a separate element of safeguarding activities.[126]

This is in part a reflection of the 1989 Recommendation, examined above. In evaluating that Recommendation, the Smithsonian Institution found that only 17 per cent of the States had taken up legal measures as a form of policy aimed at protecting intangible heritage.[127] And only 3 per cent of States at the time thought that an international convention was suitable to enhance the legal protection of intangible heritage.[128] This may help explain why the obligations in the 2003 Convention are not to create a legal system of protection, but rather a system based on listing and 'policy-oriented' protection, including educational programmes and awareness-raising generally.

It was also said at the time of the 1989 Recommendation that the role of law in the efforts for protecting ICH should not be overestimated. Because law in this field could run counter to prevailing social and political processes (such as globalization, commodification, and economic interests related to the exploitation and misappropriation of ICH), one should not expect ICH law to be the sole tool to protect intangible heritage. Rather, ICH law should be seen in this context as one of several

demonstrated, the Committee had the right to withdraw these manifestations from the List. All manifestations were kept on the Representative List, which means that either all States have consented to the new regime, or, in the cases where that did not happen, the General Assembly decided to still keep the manifestations on the List. See General Assembly, *Operational Directives*, Rules 37 and 39.

125 Intergovernmental Committee for the Safeguarding of the Intangible Cultural Heritage, *Note by the Office of International Standards and Legal Affairs on the Incorporation of Masterpieces into the Representative List under Article 31 of the Convention for the Safeguarding of the Intangible Cultural Heritage*. Doc.ITH/07/2.COM/CONF.208/14, of 23 July 2007, para 14.

126 UNESCO, *Report on the Expert Meeting on Criteria for Inscription on the Lists Established by the 2003 Convention for the Safeguarding of the Intangible Cultural Heritage* (Paris, 5 6 December 2005).

127 Kurin, 'The UNESCO Questionnaire', 24.

128 Kurin, 'The UNESCO Questionnaire', 29.

social controls, including education and awareness-raising. Law's role, alongside these other initiatives, would be to empower custodian communities.[129]

Another criticism that can be raised against the ICH Convention is its excessive focus on sovereignty. This strongly sovereignty-based approach may have been the necessary compromise to approve the Convention, and may explain why the instrument was ratified so quickly, relatively speaking. At the same time the approach substantially weakens the reach of the instrument. Plus, it does not protect intangible heritage from being harmed by the State in which it originates, at least to the extent that the ultimate control over what constitutes intangible heritage and what may be worthy of protection, for the purposes of the Convention, still rests with the States Parties (the Tibetan Opera case below is a prime example of this problem). In this sense, then, the Convention is incapable of offering remedies against misappropriation by third parties, particularly when the third party is the State.

One example of this State-centrism is the fact that the General Assembly is the controlling body behind the Convention, as explained above. If States Parties choose to overlook the recommendations of UNESCO (done in the framework of the UNESCO Secretariat's role of assisting the operation of the Intergovernmental Committee), then there is really very little anyone can do about it. Intangible heritage, then, becomes a highly politicized matter, as are most matters related to identity.

Part of this excessive focus on sovereignty stems from the same justification used to explain the international initiative that led to the drafting of the Convention. According to commentators, there was deep concern about the protection of ICH at the international level, and what it might imply. States were concerned that, by elevating local cultures to international status, an instrument might give rise to claims against the State, including eventual claims for statehood. Most importantly, though, there was a concern expressed by several scholars and some States that to elevate intangible heritage to an international concern would necessarily take the heritage outside of its original cultural context, destroying intangible heritage by the very act of attempting to give it international protection. This paradox was solved by the affirmation that intangible cultural heritage is *not* the heritage of mankind; rather, it is the interest in the protection of local cultures and the intangible heritage associated with it that is an international concern.[130] The international concern is thus an instrumental, rather than a substantive, one. This compromise of sorts is reflected in the Preamble and Article 19(2) of the Convention, the latter determining that 'States Parties recognize that the safeguarding of intangible cultural heritage is of general interest to humanity'. The interest is the safeguarding, not the heritage per se.

Further, the internationalization of intangible heritage can also be beneficial for the very perpetuation of it. There have been instances (the Argentinean Tango being one of the most prominent)[131] in which communities only felt pride in their heritage after its exposure to the 'outside world', where it was well-received and

[129] Prott, 'Some Considerations on the Protection', 109. [130] Blake, *Commentary*, 90.

[131] The Tango made it to the Representative List through the first round of inscriptions.

praised.[132] In this sense, 'heritage loses its territorial identity, loosens its material ties in order to survive'.[133]

This scholarly concern seems to be present also in the actual practice of the Convention. For instance, China has successfully inscribed Tibetan Opera in the Representative List of Intangible Heritage. This inscription can be read as a laudable outreach initiative aimed at including Tibetan culture as part of the national Chinese culture, ultimately giving it legitimacy that is denied in domestic political fora. At the same time, however, a more critical reading indicates that, by inscribing Tibetan cultural manifestations in this list (and consequently in the national inventory), the Chinese government actually asserts control over the cultural manifestation, and the culture as a whole, subordinating its political caveats to tourism promotion and other economic interests, as well as to a larger national Chinese identity, ultimately diminishing the political strength of the Tibetan culture and all political claims of Tibetans.[134]

Another sovereignty-related issue is that of the participation of communities. Janet Blake, in her study that served as the basis for the drafting of the ICH Convention, highlighted the importance of involvement of communities in the implementation of the Convention.[135] According to the Convention and the early practice under it, however, community participation is restricted to the national level, and communities seem to not have a space at the international level of implementation of the Convention. Instead, it seems that communities are gradually being replaced by experts at the international level. Bulgaria has warned against this shift, and the need to preserve communities as the essential non-State actor in terms of ICH safeguarding.[136]

Such a shift refers back to the criticism of Laurajane Smith, analysed in Chapter 1, in what she calls the Authorized Heritage Discourse is perpetuated by the prominent role of heritage professionals over that of heritage bearers. This differentiation between communities and experts has been supported by several States, most notably Norway. According to the Norwegian delegation during the

132 For the account of how Tango was 're-appropriated' by Argentineans and became their national intangible heritage after being praised abroad, see Susan Scafidi, *Who Owns Culture? Appropriation and Authenticity in American Law* (Rutgers University Press, 2005), 28 31.

133 Ahmed Skounti, 'The Authentic Illusion: Humanity's Intangible Cultural Heritage, the Moroccan Experience', in Laurajane Smith and Natsuko Akagaway (eds), *Intangible Heritage* (Routledge, 2009), 74 92, at 76.

134 See in this regard Helaine Silverman and D Fairchild Ruggles, 'Cultural Heritage and Human Rights', in Helaine Silverman and D Fairchild Ruggles (eds), *Cultural Heritage and Human Rights* (Springer, 2007), 3 22 at 11 12 (using a different example of subordination of the Tibetan culture, involving a road construction project that created a cultural route). A similar situation happens in Burma, where identities and manifestations of intangible heritage that are ethnically Burman and Buddhist are given preferential treatment by the government, at the expense of minority groups. On the Burma example, see Janette Philp, 'The Political Appropriation of Burma's Cultural Heritage and its Implications for Human Rights', in Michele Langfield, William Logan, and Máiréad Nic Craith (eds), *Cultural Diversity, Heritage and Human Rights: Intersections in Theory and Practice* (Routledge, 2010), 83 100.

135 Blake, *Developing a New Standard-Setting Instrument*, 70.

136 Intergovernmental Committee for the Safeguarding of the Intangible Cultural Heritage, *Report for the Participation of Communities*, Annex 1.

negotiations of the 2003 Convention, communities must be excluded from participation at the international level because they lack the required expertise to contribute effectively to international cooperation, and should thus have the primary role to perform, maintain, and distribute ICH, but at the local/national level.[137] Further, experts would have roles to play both at the national and international level, while communities would be restricted to the national level.[138]

This was the adopted text of modalities of participation of communities and experts.[139] Communities, groups, and individuals play a role in the following instances: (1) consultation for the inscription in one of the Lists; (2) evaluation and selection of best practices; (3) provision of experts and practitioners to evaluate requests for international assistance; (4) evaluation of status of safeguarding of elements concerning them; (5) preparation of documents on manifestations of ICH concerning them; and (6) the establishment of operational directives for the implementation of the convention.[140]

On the other hand, the role of experts includes the following functions: (1) evaluation of nomination files for inscription on the lists; (2) evaluate and select best practices; (3) provide experts and practitioners to evaluate requests for international assistance; (4) examination of reports of implementation of safeguarding measures; (5) examination of requests for international assistance; and (6) examination of the periodic reports by States Parties and the Intergovernmental Committee.[141]

Not all is gloomy in the domain of community participation, however. A new set of operational directives for raising awareness about intangible heritage was approved in June 2010, which advances much stronger forms of community involvement. It uses much stronger language in referring to States' obligation to involve communities. Even though these rules refer to an apparently harmless aspect of the Convention, they can be read as a backdoor through which stronger views about the legal bite of the Convention and more effective means of community involvement are snuck into the system. These revised directives include principles on awareness-raising, which require not only that free, prior, and informed consent be sought, but also that control over the uses of heritage be ultimately given to the communities, rather than the State seeking an eventual nomination.[142]

[137] UNESCO, *Extracts of States Parties Comments on Possible Modalities for the Participation of Communities or their Representatives, Practitioners, Experts, Centers of Expertise and Research Institutes in the Implementation of the Convention for the Safeguarding of the Intangible Cultural Heritage*, Working document prepared by the Secretariat of the Intergovernmental Committee for the Safeguarding of the Intangible Cultural Heritage (January 2008), para 62.

[138] UNESCO, *Extracts of Comments on Modalities for the Participation of Communities*, paras 76 and 82.

[139] Intergovernmental Committee for the Safeguarding of the Intangible Cultural Heritage, *Report on the Modalities for the Participation of Communities*, Annex 2, paras 1.2 and 1.3.

[140] Intergovernmental Committee for the Safeguarding of the Intangible Cultural Heritage, *Report on the Modalities for the Participation of Communities*, Annex 2, para 3.1.h.

[141] Intergovernmental Committee for the Safeguarding of the Intangible Cultural Heritage, *Report on the Modalities for the Participation of Communities*, Annex 2, para 3.2.3.

[142] General Assembly of the States Parties to the Convention for the Safeguarding of the Intangible Cultural Heritage, Third Session (UNESCO Headquarters, 22 24 June 2010), *Resolutions, Resolution 3.GA 5*, Doc.ITH/10/3.GA/CONF.201/RESOLUTIONS, of 24 June 2010, paras 100 2.

Also, for the first time, the operational directives specifically mention the financial side of ICH, that is, the tension between safeguarding and commercialization of intangible heritage. This acknowledgment of the economic value, largely unseen in the first set of operational directives, is a very welcome step forward, especially because it determines that communities be taken into account at all times, and are ultimately empowered by all attempts at economic exploitation of their heritage.[143]

There are then two different levels of implementation of the Convention: when it comes to the relatively high profile listing mechanism, control still rests on the States. When it comes to other safeguarding activities, the Convention has within a little over one year of the publishing of its first set of operational directives moved from a State-centric to a more community-oriented approach (thanks to the work of the Committee). This situation mirrors some of what happened with the World Heritage Convention (through the work of the World Heritage Committee), but it is happening at a quicker pace here.

Overall, therefore, it seems that communities are once again placed on the backseat of international standard-setting and safeguarding of cultural heritage. There are positive steps forward, but they still fall short of fully empowering communities to control their own heritage and influence decision-making regarding it internationally.[144] Communities must be able to control the meaning of their heritage, and the different uses of it. It is in this sense that commodification can be positive, to the extent that it means empowerment. This type of commodification should be promoted by the UNESCO system, but it looks like the many layers of sovereignty imposed by the system may be an obstacle to this pursuit of cultural local empowerment.

Inventorying implies mummification and commodification of heritage (even though the early practice of the Committee is aware of these concerns and seems to be trying to avoid them). However, it was felt, during the drafting of the Convention, that the need of granting some form of legal protection to ICH overcame the potential downsides of commodification, as it would raise awareness to this heritage and thus avoid some other, more pressing, problems related to ICH, most importantly its total disappearance for lack of support to its continuation.[145]

When thinking of drafting what became the 2003 Convention, the experts involved in the process had three alternatives: (1) to draft an instrument based on IP solutions and *sui generis* mechanisms adapted from IP tools (which was soon seen as limited in reach and generally inappropriate for intangible heritage protection);[146] (2) to draft an instrument based upon the model of the 1972 World Heritage Convention; or (3) to draft an instrument in between these two

[143] General Assembly, *Resolution 3.GA 5*, paras 116 17.

[144] For a more positive outlook on the matter, see Richard Kurin, 'Safeguarding Intangible Cultural Heritage: Key Factors in Implementing the 2003 Convention', *Intl J of Intangible Heritage* 2 (2007), 10 20 at 15.

[145] Blake, *Commentary*, 7.

[146] Blake, *Commentary*, 13.

alternatives. Early thinkers on this process thought that the hybrid would be the best alternative.[147]

However, in the end the choice was made by intergovernmental experts (with the support of a large number of States)[148] to follow the model of the 1972 World Heritage Convention, as a means to guarantee immediate acceptance of the Convention and fast ratification, and also because the listing model of the 1972 Convention had proven to be an effective tool in raising awareness to cultural heritage and stimulating the development of policies aimed at the protection of heritage.[149] This choice offered several advantages, as it would promote awareness to ICH, it created a financial mechanism to foster ICH, and it created a necessary machinery to oversee the implementation of the treaty. There was a concern with the idea that the listing would create an unnecessary hierarchy by safeguarding only a limited number of manifestations of intangible heritage.[150] It must be highlighted that, even though the initial draft as proposed was in many ways a copy of the 1972 Convention, the experts who worked in the drafting of the Convention managed to move away from it in many respects, highlighted above. The effort of the experts is noteworthy, as it produced a document that was easily recognizable and acceptable to States, while at the same time moving away from such a model in important ways.

Be that as it may, the fact is that the main goals of the model (to raise awareness and stimulate the development of protective policies) were achieved. One must wonder, however, whether the price paid for it (that is, the lack of a more fitted international instrument, or one with more 'legal bite') was worth it, in the long run.

2.2 WIPO

There has been a long-lasting dichotomy between 'holistic' approaches to ICH protection (falling within UNESCO's mandate), and IP solutions to the matter.[151] The latter, internationally, fall outside of UNESCO's mandate, but are well within the WIPO's scope.

While the discussion of the substantive aspects of the use of IP tools and mechanisms for the protection of intangible heritage will be dealt with in Chapter 6, it is important to briefly look at relevant activities and programmes

[147] Prott, 'Some Considerations on the Protection of the Intangible Heritage', 110; and Blake, *Commentary*, 6.

[148] UNESCO General Conference, *Oral Report of the Chairperson of Commission IV*, Doc.31 C/INF.24, of 12 November 2001.

[149] UNESCO, *Final Report International Meeting of Experts on Intangible Cultural Heritage: Priority Domains for an International Convention* (Rio de Janeiro, Brazil, 2002); and Blake, *Commentary*, 4.

[150] Blake, *Commentary*, 13.

[151] Sherkin, 'A Historical Study', 50 1.

within WIPO to highlight the international concern with IP approaches to ICH protection, and the recent obfuscation of these ideas in light of the 2003 UNESCO Convention.

The work of WIPO in the field of folklore protection was typically conducted jointly with UNESCO. In 1976, the two organizations adopted jointly the Tunis Model Law on the use of copyright for the protection of folklore.[152] In 1982 the two organizations adopted Model Provisions for National Laws on the Protection of Expressions of Folklore Against Illicit Exploitation and Other Prejudicial Action.[153] And in 1984 a Draft Treaty on the matter was elaborated, but it was never approved, having been rejected by industrialized nations who objected to protecting community-based cultural expressions.[154]

During 1998 and 1999, the WIPO appointed experts to conduct nine fact-finding missions to assess and identify the IP needs of holders of folklore and TK, and as a result it created an Intergovernmental Committee on Intellectual Property and Genetic Resources, Traditional Knowledge and Folklore in 2000.[155] The Intergovernmental Committee is still at work, and, at the time of writing, it is negotiating the Draft Provisions for the Protection of Traditional Cultural Expressions/Expressions of Folklore. In July 2011, during its 19th session, the Committee negotiated an extension of its mandate to 2012 13, and it expects to approve the Draft Provisions by 2013, according to its divulged timeline.[156]

At the time of writing, the Draft Provisions propose an IP registration system along the lines proposed in Chapter 7. There are still many points of contention, the most important of which being the subject-matter of protection, beneficiaries, and the actual scope of protection (more specifically, whether it covers both moral and economic rights, or only one or the other). The draft text seems to struggle to find a proper tone between deference to domestic solutions/national law and a stronger international model/system. It is even unclear at this stage whether these articles will become a binding international instrument or a set of model provisions, even if there are indications on the part of the WIPO to conclude a binding international instrument on the matter.

A binding instrument seems to be the hope of indigenous and traditional communities, who, through NGOs, compose a 260-strong body of accredited organizations observing the work of the Committee. There have been calls for expansion of their role in the negotiating process, but, at the time of writing, it is

[152] Tunis Model Law on Copyright for Developing Countries (UNESCO/WIPO, 1976). Article 6 refers to folklore. See Blake, *Commentary*, 2.

[153] Model Provisions for National Laws on the Protection of Expressions of Folklore Against Illicit Exploitation and Other Prejudicial Action (UNESCO/WIPO, 1982).

[154] Draft Treaty for the Protection of Expressions of Folklore Against Illicit Exploitation and Other Prejudicial Action (UNESCO/WIPO, 1984). See Blake, *Commentary*, 10.

[155] Blake, *Commentary*, 3. Some of the Committee's latest work is the Draft Objectives and Principles. See WIPO Intergovernmental Committee on Intellectual Property, Genetic Resources, Traditional Knowledge and Folklore, *The Protection of Traditional Cultural Expressions/Expressions of Folklore: Draft Objectives and Principles*, WIPO/GRTKF/IC/10/4, of 2 October 2006.

[156] WIPO Intergovernmental Committee on Intellectual Property and Genetic Resources, Traditional Knowledge and Folklore, *Decisions of the Nineteenth Session of the Committee* (July 2011).

unclear whether they will be given a stronger position. On the other hand, States seem to favour more flexibility, which is not a surprise, considering the State-centric nature of the system created by the 2003 UNESCO Convention (which is naturally a reference point to international treatment of intangible heritage).

The WIPO is one of the most prominent actors in the regulation of intangible cultural heritage, even if it is lagging behind organizations such as UNESCO and its Draft Provisions are still at an alarmingly early stage of development. Be that as it may, an eventual WIPO regime must interact in conjunction with other international initiatives, and UNESCO's regime appears front and centre. Besides the work of the WIPO, the relationship between international trade law and culture is also worth mentioning, and I will analyse this interaction next.

2.3 International Trade and Intangible Cultural Heritage

To the extent that intangible heritage is constantly commodified, and that there is in fact an interest in advancing development through the sale of manifestations of intangible heritage, it is important to look at how the legal regime for international trade sees culture generally, and intangible heritage more specifically. Interestingly, heritage (and culture more generally) is considered a special type of product or service, and one that should not necessarily obey trade liberalization rules, at least when it comes to its existence in internal markets.

This is what is known as the 'cultural exception' to international trade, and it is the object of this section, which will look at it from two different perspectives. First, I will consider the perspective of the UNESCO Convention on the Diversity of Cultural Expressions (2005), which has been associated with heritage protection (wrongly, in my opinion, for the reasons I will outline below). Secondly, I will examine the general WTO rules on the matter.

On the WTO activities, the TRIPS agreement would also potentially be a part of this analysis. I will, however, reserve any considerations related to the TRIPS agreement for the discussion on substantive aspects of IP protection, in Chapter 6. Additionally, there is also a wide array of bilateral treaties about trade in cultural products, some of which may be more restrictive than the provisions of the TRIPS or other WTO agreements. Even if these agreements may qualify as 'strategic fragmentation' (that is, the creation of multiple and often divergent norms outside multilateral fora as a means to 'fly under the radar', as it were),[157] they also fall outside the scope of the present analysis of international regimes, which is oriented solely at multilateral arrangements.

[157] Eyal Benvenisti and George Downs, 'The Empire's New Clothes: Political Economy and the Fragmentation of International Law', *Stanford L Rev* 60 (2007), 595 631. See also Nico Krisch, 'International Law in Times of Hegemony: Unequal Power and the Shaping of the International Legal Order', *EJIL* 16(3) (2005), 369 408.

2.3.1 UNESCO Convention on the Diversity of Cultural Expressions

The UNESCO Convention on Cultural Expressions[158] looks precisely at the issue of safeguarding these expressions in light of mass culture and mass media. This instrument relates to cultural heritage in that it protects the fixation of cultural heritage by 'modern means', such as sound and video recordings.[159]

The Cultural Expressions Convention is in some ways related to its immediate antecessor in the law-making activities of the UNESCO, the UNESCO Convention for the Safeguarding of the Intangible Cultural Heritage. It takes a markedly distinct approach to cultural expressions, though while the intangible heritage instrument presents heritage as an entitlement,[160] the latter instrument takes a more utilitarian perspective, saying that cultural expressions and the heritage aspects they convey are to be protected because they are useful to the development of mankind, without there being an entitlement to such culture.[161]

Some of its core norms include: the reference to a clear linkage between culture and development;[162] the need to respect human rights in the implementation of the Convention;[163] the equitable access to cultural expressions;[164] the idea that cultural expressions are regarded as such independently of the means and technologies employed in fixation;[165] and the norm authorizing the use of a 'cultural

[158] Convention on the Protection and Promotion of the Diversity of Cultural Expressions, adopted by the UNESCO General Assembly on 20 October 2005. Entry into force: 18 March 2007. Number of Parties as of November 2012: 126 (125 States and the EU) (hereinafter the 'UNESCO Convention on Cultural Expressions').

[159] Michael F Brown, 'Heritage Trouble: Recent Work on the Protection of Intangible Cultural Property', *Intl J of Cultural Property* 12 (2005), 40 61 at 47.

[160] Blake, *Commentary*, 35.

[161] For this, and for an analysis of the drafting history of this instrument, see Yvonne Donders, 'The History of the UNESCO Convention on the Protection and Promotion of the Diversity of Cultural Expressions', in H. Schneider and P. Van den Bossche (eds), *Protection of Cultural Diversity from a European and International Perspective* (Intersentia, 2008), 1 30. See also Christopher M Bruner, 'Culture, Sovereignty, and Hollywood: UNESCO and the Future of Trade in Cultural Products', *NYU J Intl L & Pol* 40 (2008), 351 436.

[162] '**Art. 1**: The objectives of this Convention are: [...] (d) to foster interculturality in order to develop cultural interaction in the spirit of building bridges among peoples; [...]'

[163] '**Art. 2: Guiding principles** 1. Principle of respect for human rights and fundamental freedoms. Cultural diversity can be protected and promoted only if human rights and fundamental freedoms, such as freedom of expression, information and communication, as well as the ability of individuals to choose cultural expressions, are guaranteed. No one may invoke the provisions of this Convention in order to infringe human rights and fundamental freedoms as enshrined in the Universal Declaration of Human Rights or guaranteed by international law, or to limit the scope thereof. [...]'

[164] '**Art. 2: Guiding Principles** [...] 7. Principle of equitable access. Equitable access to a rich and diversified range of cultural expressions from all over the world and access of cultures to the means of expressions and dissemination constitute important elements for enhancing cultural diversity and encouraging mutual understanding. [...]'

[165] '**Art. 4: Definitions** For the purposes of this Convention, it is understood that: 1. Cultural diversity. "Cultural diversity" refers to the manifold ways in which the cultures of groups and societies find expression. These expressions are passed on within and among groups and societies.

Cultural diversity is made manifest not only through the varied ways in which the cultural heritage of humanity is expressed, augmented and transmitted through the variety of cultural expressions, but also

exception' to free trade norms.[166] The latter is the most important norm of the Convention, and it deserves further commentary. I will reserve the comments on 'cultural exception' rules to the following section, though, given the close relationship of the clause to the WTO rules.

Another important tension that relates to the trade-related goals of the UNESCO Convention on Cultural Expressions is the relationship between IP rights and the free circulation of cultural goods and services. The core problem here is the concern (still popular in liberal circles) that a lack of IP protection harms cultural industries. The UNESCO has responded to this through the Anti-Piracy section of the UNESCO Global Alliance for Cultural Diversity.[167] This is just one of any number of international 'anti-piracy' initiatives, however there remains significant debate over the norms associated with anti-piracy in a digital age. There is a concern that this agenda does not trump other goals such as education, development, and freedom of communication. For this reason UNESCO and WIPO anti-piracy initiatives lack bite and I will not explore them further.

2.3.2 The WTO system

The cultural exception and the 2005 UNESCO Convention as a whole aim at defending local cultures by validating the right of States Parties to control the importation of alien cultural products such as TV shows, movies, and magazines.[168] This rule is not original to this instrument, however. One of its first

through diverse modes of artistic creation, production, dissemination, distribution and enjoyment, *whatever the means and technologies used.* [...]' (emphasis added).

[166] '**Art. 6: Rights of parties at the national level** 1. Within the framework of its cultural policies and measures as defined in Article 4.6 and taking into account its own particular circumstances and needs, each Party may adopt measures aimed at protecting and promoting the diversity of cultural expressions within its territory. 2. Such measures may include the following: (a) regulatory measures aimed at protecting and promoting diversity of cultural expressions; (b) measures that, in an appropriate manner, provide opportunities for domestic cultural activities, goods and services among all those available within the national territory for the creation, production, dissemination, distribution and enjoyment of such domestic cultural activities, goods and services, including provisions relating to the language used for such activities, goods and services; (c) measures aimed at providing domestic independent cultural industries and activities in the informal sector effective access to the means of production, dissemination and distribution of cultural activities, goods and services; (d) measures aimed at providing public financial assistance; (e) measures aimed at encouraging non-profit organizations, as well as public and private institutions and artists and other cultural professionals, to develop and promote the free exchange and circulation of ideas, cultural expressions and cultural activities, goods and services, and to stimulate both the creative and entrepreneurial spirit in their activities; (f) measures aimed at establishing and supporting public institutions, as appropriate; (g) measures aimed at nurturing and supporting artists and others involved in the creation of cultural expressions; (h) measures aimed at enhancing diversity of the media, including through public service broadcasting.'

[167] UNESCO, *The Global Alliance for Cultural Diversity*, available at <http://www.unesco.org/new/en/culture/themes/cultural-diversity/2005-convention/global-alliance-for-cultural-diversity/> (accessed 29 November 2012).

[168] Véronique Guèvremont, 'Industries culturelles et négociations internationals: portrait d'une dynamique multidimensionelle. L'exemple des pays de la zone euro-méditerranéenne', *EUI Working Papers RSCAS 2007/33* (2007), 2.

appearances was in the US-Canada Free Trade Area, and it came as an imposition from Canada to protect its rather fragile cultural industries from being driven into bankruptcy by free competition with American products. This rule was an attempt to recast a concern over identity in economic terms, and it shows the limitations of translating identity concerns into economic rules (the limitations of this strategy will become even more evident when discussing the EU's activities with respect to heritage in Chapter 3). This cultural exception rule was put into place as part of trade law-making and, as the NAFTA does not completely succeed the US-Canada agreement, this rule is still valid.[169]

At the World Trade Organization level,[170] the cultural exception came as an imposition of the European Communities (EC) when negotiating the General Agreement on Trade in Services (GATS). The rule, as it is put in the GATS, creates an exception to the Most-Favored Nation (MFN) clause, which is one of the pillar principles of free trade. The exemption imposed by the European Communities is actually to trade in audiovisual services, in agreement with its 'Television without Frontiers' Directive.[171] In fact, the cultural exception may be regarded as being in the eyes of the beholder, and is not a general rule, but rather a transitory arrangement.

However, the current status of this issue is far from settled. While cultural products have been successfully excluded from the GATS (at least for the time being), subsequent agreements on e-commerce push for liberalization of trade in cultural products transmitted digitally, defeating substantially the goal of the cultural exception.[172] The United States pushed for the inclusion of digital cultural products in e-commerce agreements (thus limiting cultural exceptions in the mass media age) and this threatens to defeat all that has been gained under the GATS. It is hoped that the implementation of the UNESCO Convention on Cultural Expressions may provide States with means to counter these advances.

Sadly, the UNESCO Convention on Cultural Expressions contains two clauses on the relationship of that instrument with other instruments and regimes.[173]

[169] Therese Anne Larrea, 'Comment: Eliminate the Cultural Industries Exemption from NAFTA', *Santa Clara L Rev* 37 (1997), 1107 50; Stephen R Konigsberg, 'Think Globally, Act Locally: North American Free Trade, Canadian Cultural Industry Exemption, and the Liberalization of the Broadcast Ownership Law', *Cardozo Arts & Ent LJ* 12 (1994), 281 305; and generally Ralph H Folsom, *NAFTA* (West Group Publishing, 1999).

[170] On the cultural exception at the WTO level, and its relationship to the 2005 UNESCO Convention, see Jan Wouters and Bart de Meester, 'The UNESCO Convention on Cultural Diversity and WTO Law: A Case Study in Fragmentation of International Law', *J of World Trade* 42(1) (2008), 205 40.

[171] World Trade Organization, *Services: Schedules of Commitments and Lists of Article II Exemptions*, available at <http://www.wto.org/english/tratop e/serv e/serv commitments e.htm#commit exempt> (accessed 29 November 2012). See also Guèvremont, 'Industries culturelles et négociations internationals', 3 7.

[172] For an outline of this debate, Jane Kelsey, 'How Trade Trumps Culture', in *Toward Freedom*, available at <http://www.towardfreedom.com/home/content/view/514/55/> (accessed 29 November 2012).

[173] The relevant provisions are the following: '*Article 20 Relationship to other treaties: mutual supportiveness, complementarity and non-subordination.* 1. Parties recognize that they shall perform in good faith their obligations under this Convention and all other treaties to which they are parties.

While the first part of Article 20 is a very promising instrument in terms of promoting mutual supportiveness between this instrument and the WTO regime, the second paragraph, a standard conflict clause of international treaties, undermines the efforts proposed by the first paragraph, by stating, in a literal interpretation, that the obligations under the UNESCO Convention shall not modify pre-existing obligations under the WTO. This makes the Convention a rather weak instrument within the WTO system, where it was expected to play the larger role.

Another factor that has contributed to weakening the 2005 UNESCO Convention is the reluctance of the WTO Appellate Body to apply outside instruments as legitimate defences to WTO obligations.[174] Importantly, the WTO signalled towards accepting the idea that instruments foreign to the WTO system could play a role in assessing the reach of obligations under WTO instruments in the *Shrimp-Turtle* and *Tuna-Dolphin* disputes. In these matters it looked at multilateral environmental agreements as relevant sources to interpret trade obligations. This led at least one commentator to point at the hope of coordination between separate but interrelated systems of international law at the WTO level.[175] The decision of the Appellate Body in the *Biotech* dispute, however, reversed this hope.[176] In this dispute, the WTO said that an instrument external to the WTO system would only be relevant for WTO dispute settlement if it has been ratified by all members of the Organization. Given the impracticality of this rule, it is very likely that the WTO will not take the 2005 UNESCO Convention into account should any issue of cultural diversity be presented to its dispute settlement mechanism.

One possibility is that the Convention be internalized by a Member State to the WTO, and then invoked as being part of its domestic law (under the Article XX(d) defence that restrictions on trade are permissible when necessary to ensure compliance with domestic law that is not inconsistent with the GATT).[177] But for this the Member State would have to prove that not complying with the mandates of the UNESCO Convention (as implemented domestically) would mean a breach of said instrument, with Article 20.2 imposing a high threshold for such argument to hold water.

Accordingly, without subordinating this Convention to any other treaty, (a) they shall foster mutual supportiveness between this Convention and the other treaties to which they are parties; and (b) when interpreting and applying the other treaties to which they are parties or when entering into other international obligations, Parties shall take into account the relevant provisions of this Convention. 2. Nothing in this Convention shall be interpreted as modifying rights and obligations of the Parties under any other treaties to which they are parties. *Article 21 International consultation and coordination.* Parties undertake to promote the objectives and principles of this Convention in other international forums. For this purpose, Parties shall consult each other, as appropriate, bearing in mind these objectives and principles.'

174 Tania Voon, 'UNESCO and WTO: A Clash of Cultures?', *ICLQ* 55 (2006), 635 51 at 649.

175 Francesco Francioni, 'WTO Law in Context: The Integration of International Human Rights and Environmental Law in the Dispute Settlement Process', in Giorgio Sacerdoti, Alan Yanovich, and Jan Bohanes (eds), *The WTO at Ten: The Contribution of the Dispute Settlement System* (Cambridge University Press, 2006), 143 54 at 148 9.

176 World Trade Organization, *Dispute DS291 European Communities Measures Affecting the Approval and Marketing of Biotech Products*, Panel Report of 29 September 2006.

177 Voon, 'UNESCO and WTO', 650.

A final note on the WTO system relates to the General Agreement on Tariffs and Trade (GATT). While the GATT does not have a cultural exception clause, Article XX, which indicates the general exceptions to the application of the MFN and non-discrimination clauses of the GATT, creates a general exception for measures designed 'to protect national treasures of artistic, historic or archaeological value'.[178] At the time of writing, no dispute has yet been brought specifically under this part of Article XX, so it is still difficult to grasp its full reach.[179] Given that the WTO panels have in the past significantly expanded the scope of the GATT, and even made it more sensitive to issues such as environmental concerns,[180] there is some hope for cultural industries and cultural heritage.

2.4 The Convention on Biological Diversity and Traditional Knowledge

It is important to look at the system for the protection of TK, as TK is necessarily a part of ICH. As far as TK refers to traditional practices that belong to indigenous cultures and have important implications for environmentalism and (most importantly for economic purposes) pharmaceuticals, not all ICH can be translated into TK. All TK, however, may be translated into ICH.[181]

Intangible cultural heritage is a broader concept than TK, precisely because TK is restricted to certain applications of the knowledge that can be of service for 'outsiders' to the concerned community (even if sometimes the rationale advanced may be the protection of TK for the community's sake, seen as they should be the ones to benefit from exploitation), whereas ICH refers to practices useful for the sake of the community's protection (regardless of whether it can be used by outsiders). Further, to a certain extent the system for the protection of TK operates within a 'controlled environment' of essentialized indigeneity, becoming to a certain extent less politicized a topic than intangible cultural heritage. Further, the fact that the framework for TK under the Convention on Biological Diversity (CBD) has existed for at least ten years longer than that for ICH (as embodied in the 2003 UNESCO Convention) means that a lot of the political tensions that

[178] '*Article XX: General Exceptions.* Subject to the requirement that such measures are not applied in a manner which would constitute a means of arbitrary or unjustifiable discrimination between countries where the same conditions prevail, or a disguised restriction on international trade, nothing in this Agreement shall be construed to prevent the adoption or enforcement by any contracting party of measures: [...] (f) imposed for the protection of national treasures of artistic, historic or archaeological value; [...].'

[179] World Trade Organization, *WTO Analytical Index Guide to WTO Law and Practice*, available at <http://www.wto.org/english/res e/booksp e/analytic index e/analytic index e.htm> (accessed 29 November 2012).

[180] José E Alvarez, *International Organizations as Law-Makers* (Oxford University Press, 2006), 468 73.

[181] Blake, *Commentary*, 11.

existed initially have already been negotiated to an equilibrium, and the system has had a chance to develop further.

There are many soft law initiatives aimed at protecting TK (under the auspices of organizations such as FAO, UNCTAD, WIPO, UNEP, to name but a few), but to analyse them all goes beyond the present purposes. Instead, I will look at the single binding instrument to make explicit reference to TK and offer means for its protection, the CBD.

Article 3(b) of the 2003 Convention states that the ICH Convention must not be interpreted as conflicting with other international obligations of States Parties, particularly those referring to 'the use of biological or ecological resources'. Even though not explicit, the drafting history makes it evident that this is a reference to the CBD.[182]

The CBD offers important principles to inform *sui generis* regimes. As a matter of fact, what the CBD proposes is that access to TK be regulated through *sui generis* arrangements with each custodial community; better said, it is a 'contractual' approach to ICH protection,[183] that will be better explored in Chapter 7. Commentators highlighted the importance of the CBD contractual approach for ICH protection even prior to the drafting of the 2003 Convention.[184]

The potential of contractual approaches resides precisely in the giving of control over ICH to the communities of origin, and so enabling them to ensure that the information and resources will be used in a way that is acceptable to the communities, and that any benefits will be shared with these communities themselves, if they so wish.[185]

The CBD determines, in Article 8(j), that each State Party should preserve and maintain the knowledge and practices of indigenous and local communities related to the preservation of biodiversity, promoting this application 'with the approval and involvement of the holders of such knowledge', and encouraging the sharing of benefits arising from the use of such knowledge. This provision is important to intangible heritage protection, as it ensures the protection of cultural diversity and promotes sustainable development, both of which are core tenets of the legal regime for ICH protection.[186] In this sense, the lessons learned by the CBD implementation in terms of 'free, prior and informed consent' and access and benefit-sharing are valuable tools to be explored in determining how to shape these ideas for the implementation of the ICH Convention.

Much of the thinking behind the CBD in terms of free, prior and informed consent, access, and benefit-sharing was crystallized in the Nagoya Protocol on Access to Genetic Resources and the Fair and Equitable Sharing of Benefits Arising

[182] Blake, *Commentary*, 42 3.

[183] Henrietta Marrie, 'The UNESCO Convention for the Safeguarding of the Intangible Cultural Heritage and the Protection and Maintenance of the Intangible Cultural Heritage of Indigenous Peoples', in Laurajane Smith and Natsuko Akagawa (eds), *Intangible Heritage* (Routledge, 2009), 169 92 at 182.

[184] Simon, 'Global Steps to Local Empowerment', 131 3.

[185] Simon, 'Global Steps to Local Empowerment', 132.

[186] Blake, *Commentary*, 8 9.

from their Utilization.[187] I will come back to the substantive provisions of this instrument in Chapter 7, but, for the time being, it suffices to highlight its introduction as a landmark international instrument to help guide the safeguarding of intangible cultural heritage.

The Conference of the Parties has explicitly recognized the importance of indigenous TK for the implementation of the Convention,[188] which can then be translated into greater community participation at all levels of the Convention. Plus, indigenous communities from all around the globe (that is, holders of ICH related to biological diversity) participated actively in the drafting of the CBD by their presence during the 1992 Rio Earth Summit (which has culminated in the Kari-Oca Declaration during that summit, signed by over 700 indigenous leaders), and have been subsequently involved in the implementation of the CBD (even if many of the texts that came out of the Conference of the Parties, including the Nagoya Protocol, are highly deferent to State sovereignty, thus throwing into question the effectiveness of indigenous participation).[189] The ICH Convention differs in this respect as it seems to have excluded community participation at the implementation stage (internationally). Such exclusion evidences a further layer of protection to shield State sovereignty from cultural claims and claims of control over a given community's heritage. The fact that the CBD does include communities shows that international fora can benefit from this modality of involvement; this in turn would allow the CBD to renew its usefulness for future practice on the safeguarding of intangible heritage.

We have seen that the possibilities for protection at the international level are many, and attend to different goals. They are also limited in that they are still very deferent to State sovereignty, and seem to place too much emphasis on the prerogatives of States to control the meanings and potentials of heritage. Further, some international concerns about heritage become closely connected with trade, and the logics of identity protection is thus translated into economics and commodified. One of the few initiatives that seem successful in including heritage holders is the CBD and its programme for the protection of TK, but even that is limited, because it assumes that heritage as TK is only important to the extent it can be economically exploited elsewhere. But these are only the first pieces of the institutional mosaic of ICH protection. The next chapter will look at another set of initiatives at the regional level.

[187] Nagoya Protocol on Access to Genetic Resources and the Fair and Equitable Sharing of Benefits Arising from their Utilization (2010). As of November 2012, the Protocol had been signed by 92 States, and ratified by eight of them.

[188] Marrie, 'The UNESCO Convention', 185.

[189] Marrie, 'The UNESCO Convention', 183.

3

Regional Responses

Regional responses complement the several international ones in important ways. Often they run parallel, advancing different goals and justifications for the protection of intangible heritage. In this chapter, I will look at two different forms of regionalism.

First of all, I will look at political regionalism, that is, regional organizations created for the advancement of non-economic goals, and goals connected to regional peace and security, and the protection of democracy and human rights. There are three organizations I will focus on: the Organization of American States, the Council of Europe, and the African Union. I have chosen these three for their degree of development in terms of institutional structure, and also for their representativeness. There are no similar organizations with such wide scope (that is, attempting to cover an entire continent) in Asia or Oceania/the Pacific. The African Union is a 'mixed' type of organization, as it has been created to be simultaneously an organization of regional political and economic integration. However, in practice its activities resemble much more those of a regional political organization, and thus I will look at the African Union as such.

The second group consists of economic regionalism processes, or processes aimed at the liberalization of trade and growth of markets. As some of these organizations have greatly expanded their roles beyond the advancement of purely economic goals, I will analyse the role that culture and cultural heritage play in the political agendas of economic integration, looking at the examples of the Andean Community of Nations and the EU. These two organizations have been chosen for being the two most highly evolved (at least in terms of 'law on the books') organizations, and therefore the ones that have moved closer to considering cultural matters as falling within their scope.

3.1 Political Regionalism

In this part, I will look at three different 'political' regional organizations, and their different approaches to cultural heritage generally and intangible heritage more specifically. The Organization of American States focuses primarily on indigenous culture and heritage; the Council of Europe looks at heritage primarily as built heritage and cultural landscapes, on the surface overlooking living cultures for the sake of preserving European history and ancestry for the future; and the African

Union conceives of heritage as the common living culture of African Peoples, which must be liberated from colonial ties to allow the African continent to blossom. These three very different perspectives give interesting insights into the possibilities for the protection of intangible heritage, and I will analyse each of them in turn.

3.1.1 Organization of American States

The Organization of American States (OAS) was created in 1948 to promote democracy, human rights, development, and the ideals of pan-Americanism in the continent.[1] Its activities extend through a wide range of areas, with a strong focus on the goals that led to the foundation of the Organization. Importantly, Article 48 of the OAS Charter indicates that '[t]he Member States will cooperate with one another to meet their educational needs, to promote scientific research, and to encourage technological progress for their integral development. They will consider themselves *individually and jointly bound to preserve and enrich the cultural heritage of the American peoples*' (emphasis added).[2]

The OAS's structure is complex, and there are organs designed to address the several areas of activity of the Organization and fulfil its mandate. Among these is the Inter-American Council for Integral Development ('*Consejo Interamericano para el Desarrollo Integral*' CIDI), which is one of the organs created by the OAS Charter (Articles 93 8). This organ is composed of ministers or equivalents of each Member State,[3] and it counts on the support of the Executive Council on Integral Development, which is the bureaucratic arm of the body, connected to the

[1] Regarding culture and development, more specifically, the OAS Charter states that: '**Article 47.** The Member States will give primary importance within their development plans to the encouragement of education, science, technology, and culture, oriented toward the overall improvement of the individual, and as a foundation for democracy, social justice, and progress.' On cultural heritage: '**Article 48.** The Member States will cooperate with one another to meet their educational needs, to promote scientific research, and to encourage technological progress for their integral development. They will consider themselves individually and jointly bound to preserve and enrich the cultural heritage of the American peoples.' On the role of cultural cooperation as a tool to strengthen Pan-Americanism: '**Article 52.** The Member States, with due respect for the individuality of each of them, agree to promote cultural exchange as an effective means of consolidating interAmerican understanding; and they recognize that regional integration programs should be strengthened by close ties in the fields of education, science, and culture.'

[2] Charter of the Organization of American States, 119 UNTS 3, entered into force 13 December 1951; amended by Protocol of Buenos Aires, 721 UNTS 324, OAS Treaty Series, No 1-A, entered into force 27 February 1970; amended by Protocol of Cartagena, OAS Treaty Series, No 66, 25 ILM 527, entered into force 16 November 1988; amended by Protocol of Washington, 1-E Rev OEA Documentos Oficiales OEA/Ser.A/2 Add.3 (SEPF), 33 ILM 1005, entered into force 25 September 1997; amended by Protocol of Managua, 1-F Rev OEA Documentos Oficiales OEA/Ser.A/2 Add.4 (SEPF), 33 ILM 1009, entered into force 29 January 1996. Number of Parties as of November 2012: 35.

[3] '**Article 93.** The Inter-American Council for Integral Development is composed of one principal representative, of ministerial or equivalent rank, for each Member State, especially appointed by the respective Government. In keeping with the provisions of the Charter, the Inter-American Council for Integral Development may establish the subsidiary bodies and the agencies that it considers advisable for the better performance of its duties.'

General Secretariat of the OAS, and responsible for the execution and coordination of projects approved by the Council.[4]

The Council has undertaken the objective of promoting cultural heritage as a means to enhance development, in fulfilling the mandate of Article 48 of the Charter. This is one of the perspectives through which the OAS addresses the topic. The other one is cultural heritage as a human rights concern. While this topic will be addressed more extensively in Chapter 5, it is important to highlight some of the specific work of the OAS that is not related to human rights adjudication on the matter (which is the focus of Chapter 5). More specifically, then, this section will look at the work on the Draft OAS Declaration on the Rights of Indigenous Peoples.

One of the remarkable features of the OAS treatment of cultural heritage generally, and intangible heritage in particular, is that such heritage is approached as if it were almost exclusively the concern of indigenous peoples. When it comes to tangible heritage, there has been some recognition of non-indigenous heritage, but most of the discussion on the protection of culture still refers only to indigenous cultures (here included populations of African ancestry, which are in many municipal systems treated in the same way as indigenous populations). The idea is that, in the linkage between culture and development, one must look at American cultures and their tangible and intangible heritage as the historical result of a series of interactions among different cultures, most of which are indigenous.[5] The conservation of indigenous cultural heritage must be a priority, it is argued, because pre-Columbian cultures are the common and shared heritage of American identity.[6]

[4] '**Article 98.** The execution and, if appropriate, the coordination, of approved projects shall be entrusted to the Executive Secretariat for Integral Development, which shall report on the results of that execution to the Council.'

[5] Orlando Albornoz (March 2007), 'Relaciones entre Cultura y Desarrollo, informe presentado al Programa Regional Interamericano de Cultura Oficina de Asuntos Culturales', *Workshop on Case Studies in the Protection of Cultural Heritage Central American Region*, available at <http://portal.oas.org/Portal/Topic/SEDI/Educaci%C3%B3nyCultura/Cultura/TemasPrioritarios/Preservaci%C3%B3ny Protecci%C3%B3ndelPatrimonioCultural/Activities/ProtegiendoelPatrimonioCultural/tabid/1447/language/en-US/Default.aspx> (accessed 29 November 2012).

[6] Rodolfo Stavenhagen, 'La Diversidad Cultural en el Desarrollo de las Américas: Los pueblos indígenas y los estados nacionales en Hispanoamérica', *OEA, Unidad de Desarrollo Social, Educación y Cultural, Serie de Estudios Culturales No 9* (2004), para 19. This is, however, highly debatable, as such discourse groups together indigenous civilizations as diverse as the Mayans, Incas, Aztecs, Guaranis and many other indigenous groups. It seems that the existence of a non-colonial culture is common to all peoples in the Americas, but not the same culture. If one is to think of a common heritage, it is much easier to find it in that of the colonizers. However, this would imply a huge step back in terms of recognition of indigenous rights. The 'essentialization' of indigenous culture and their *cosmovisión*, albeit very debatable and mostly inaccurate, is not really disputed by indigenous leaders themselves, as it is this falsified cultural unity that gives the most strength to the indigenous movement. Part of the justification for heritage protection in indigeneity also lies on the fact that many indigenous peoples are considered 'witness peoples' ('*pueblos testimonio*'), that is, the only witnesses of the whole history of the American continent. They are, in Stavenhagen's words, 'a great force that claims the recognition of their cultural rights and their legitimate place in the cultural constellation of Latin America' (Stavenhagen, 'La Diversidad Cultural en el Desarrollo de las Américas', para 59 (my translation)).

And this is not because there are no manifestations of non-indigenous heritage worth protecting, much to the contrary. National systems protect non-indigenous heritage, as Chapter 4 will demonstrate. But the OAS focuses more on indigenous culture, and I suggest this may be rooted in an attempt at finding a distinctive, 'genuine' American identity that is separate from the European colonizers, similar to the African Union, but with less of a political undertone (which can probably be connected to the fact that American States gained independence many decades before African States). This focus on pre-Columbian identity is closely connected to the set of ideas often referred to as Pan-Americanism.[7] In attempting to construct an identity distinct from that of European colonizers as a means to catalyse nation-building throughout (Latin) America, these States have endeavoured to promote their indigeneity, even if such indigeneity is only a fragment of the identities of the political elites in these countries (who, at least in the 19th century, were still predominantly white, even if this situation has changed in recent years, particularly in Andean countries, to be looked at more closely in Chapter 4).

3.1.1.1 Intangible Cultural Heritage and development in the Americas

The Executive Council for Integral Development undertakes the core of activities related to heritage protection under the OAS. While there is a relatively developed sector on culture within the Department of Education and Culture,[8] and heritage protection is considered a priority topic, most of the activities in this regard refer to the preservation of tangible heritage, with a special emphasis on the illicit trafficking of cultural objects.[9]

There is, naturally, some mention of intangible heritage or at least intangible values, inasmuch as tangible and intangible heritage are intrinsically connected. But, fundamentally, there are no specific programmes (at the time of writing) aimed exclusively at the protection of intangible heritage.

Faithful to its mandate, the Council connects the protection of culture and heritage to its usefulness in the promotion of development. Therefore, the goal the OAS looks at when protecting heritage is the promotion of development. It has been highlighted that development programmes must recognize the specific role of culture in their design, reflecting that in the inclusion of programmes for

[7] See eg Alonso Aguilar, *Pan-Americanism from Monroe to the Present: A View from the Other Side* (Monthly Review Press, 1968); and Herbert L Matthews and KH Silvert, *Los Estados Unidos y América Latina: De Monroe a Fidel Castro* (Editorial Grijalbo, 1967).

[8] *OAS Organizational Chart*, available at <http://www.oas.org/documents/eng/OASstructureENG.pdf> (accessed 29 November 2012).

[9] See for instance the proceedings of the *Workshop on Case Studies in the Protection of Cultural Heritage Central American Region*, available at <http://portal.oas.org/Portal/Topic/SEDI/Educaci%C3%B3nyCultura/Cultura/TemasPrioritarios/Preservaci%C3%B3nyProtecci%C3%B3ndelPatrimonioCultural/Activities/ProtegiendoelPatrimonioCultural/tabid/1447/language/en-US/Default.aspx> (accessed 29 November 2012).

development of intangible and tangible heritage. The preservation of heritage is thus an important goal of development.[10]

Several policy documents make the connection between culture and development, and it is in these documents that one can find the most relevant information regarding the possibilities for the protection of intangible heritage within the OAS. Culture, for instance, has been pointed out as one of the goals of development. That culture is a goal of development beyond its market-oriented commodification is certainly a welcome development in contrast to the WTO posture discussed in Chapter 2. More specifically, to think of culture as integral to development (what the OAS does), as opposed to a trade staple (what the WTO attempts to do), is a far better solution. Heritage becomes integral to development politics, and is both a commodity and a tool for development more broadly. Economics is thus not necessarily the enemy of heritage, it just depends on how one conceptualizes economics. An OAS document, in preparation of a meeting of Cultural Policy Experts, highlights the shift from considering culture an obstacle to development, to seeing culture as an integral part of development, and a contributor thereto.[11] Development is seen as culture-sensitive, and with great economic potential.[12]

The Mexico Declaration on culture and development of 2004 gives voice to these concerns.[13] This Declaration is centred on three topics: culture as a generator of economic growth, employment, and development; challenges to cultural and creative industries; and culture as an instrument of social inclusion and cohesion and to combat poverty. The Declaration reaffirms that the safeguarding of cultural heritage in all of its forms is important for the promotion of cultural diversity, and that places, objects, and living traditions are a permanent legacy that needs to be acknowledged and preserved. Even though it affirms the need of protecting living traditions, however, the Mexico Declaration only speaks of the strengthening of cooperation for the prevention of illicit trafficking, wilful destruction and illicit possession of cultural goods, not mentioning intangible heritage as a specific policy area. This is partly explained by the fact that this Declaration was largely driven by archaeologists, who then focus more on looting and its impact on the integrity of archaeological sites. Once again, a class of expert professionals dictates how heritage should be best protected, without much direct concern with communities that are actually connected to or practise that heritage.

These documents have always been concerned with indigenous culture as a special type of culture, and perhaps the one to which more attention should be

[10] See José Álvaro Moisés, 'Cultural Diversity and Development in the Americas', *OAS Unit for Social Development, Education and Cultural, Cultural Studies Series No 9* (2004).

[11] Organización de los Estados Americanos, *La Cultura como Finalidad del Desarrollo: Documento para el Seminario de Expertos en Políticas Culturales, Vancouver, Canadá, marzo 18 y 19 de 2002*, 1.

[12] Organización de los Estados Americanos, *La Cultura como Finalidad del Desarrollo*, 4 5.

[13] Organización de los Estados Americanos, Consejo Interamericano para el Desarrollo Integral, *Declaración de México*, aprobada durante la Sexta Sesión Plenaria celebrada el 24 de Agosto de 2004, durante la Segunda Reunión Interamericana de Ministros y Máximas Autoridades de Cultura. OEA/Ser.K/XXVII.2 REMIC-II/DEC.1/04 cor.1, 1 September 2004.

devoted. For instance, in 2006 Guatemala, collaborating with Mexico, issued a 'Concept Paper on the Ministerial Topic of Culture and the Role of Indigenous Peoples' ('*Documento Conceptual para el Tema Ministerial Cultura y el Rol de los Pueblos Indígenas*'). This document highlighted the importance of indigenous cultures on the American continent, and evaluated the contribution of the tangible and intangible heritage of indigenous peoples for the development of national cultures in American States.[14] The document highlighted the new constitutional phase of countries on the continent (to be analysed in more detail in Chapter 4). Also, it revealed that they were generally more receptive towards indigenous culture, and the contribution of indigenous peoples to law in the Americas, through their *cosmovisión* (worldviews), based on the respect for and life in harmony with all living creatures.

After highlighting the 'fundamental principles of indigenous peoples', that is, what the document considers the basic philosophical tenets of the *cosmovisión*, it goes on to say that the lack of historical recognition of these values justifies indigenous claims for autonomy, as it is the only means to secure their cultural survival. The document then highlights the importance of indigenous tangible and intangible heritage for the development of national cultures. In the case of intangible heritage, it mentions manifestations of intangible heritage recognized as the 'intangible heritage of mankind' by UNESCO, therefore relying on this organization's assessment.

The protection of heritage specifically was the subject of another concept paper, presented by the United States, in collaboration with the Dominican Republic. The paper highlights that the protection of tangible and intangible heritage is a growing concern among Member States, and that one of the key issues in this regard is the documentation and presentation of intangible cultural heritage (ICH). More interestingly for our purposes, though, the document criticizes the fact that the documentation on intangible heritage is mostly done by UNESCO or other foreign organizations, and that this documentation usually belongs to the organizations that conducted the research, arguing that living heritage, because it is so closely connected to local populations, would be best documented precisely by local stakeholders.[15] In this way, the document highlights the importance of national protection to give visibility to heritage at the local level and thus helps to create an environment that will keep the culture alive.

Therefore, regional and international cooperation will only be effective if it creates the conditions for the entrenchment of the manifestation of heritage locally.

[14] Organización de los Estados Americanos, Consejo Interamericano para el Desarrollo Integral, *Documento Conceptual para el Tema Ministerial Cultura y el Rol de los Pueblos Indígenas, presentado por la Delegación de Guatemala para la Tercera Reunión Interamericana de Ministros y Máximas Autoridades de Cultura, del 13 al 15 de noviembre de 2006 en Montreal, Canadá.* OEA/Sr.K/XXVII.3 CIDI/REMIC-III/doc.4/06, 25 October 2006.

[15] Organization of American States, Inter-American Council for Integral Development, *Concept Paper for the Ministerial Theme Preservation and Presentation of Cultural Heritage, presented by the Delegation of the United States for the Third Inter-American Meeting of Ministers of Culture and Highest Appropriate Authorities, on November 13 15, 2006, in Montreal, Canada.* OEA/Ser.K/XXVII.3 CIDI/REMIC-III/doc.5/06, of 26 October 2006.

The intangible heritage of humankind, then, must first and foremost be the intangible heritage of the custodial community, and must be protected as such, if the living connection that makes it relevant in the first place is to be preserved. On the other hand, though, aiming to defend cultural identity and diversity, or the democratic use of intangible heritage, makes little sense if this use is restricted to the territory of each single nation (particularly if one considers that indigenous peoples do not necessarily fit neatly within current territorial States).[16] A balance must thus be struck between international recognition and protection and local initiatives aimed at entrenching intangible heritage into local communities, while simultaneously promoting international interest in protection.

Cultural diversity is also mentioned several times as an object of protection, rather than cultural heritage. More specifically, during the same ministerial meeting of 2006, Jamaica presented a Concept Paper highlighting the importance of cultural diversity, as protected by the 2005 UNESCO Convention on the Diversity of Cultural Expressions, for the promotion of identity and dignity.[17]

3.1.1.2 The draft OAS Declaration on the Rights of Indigenous Peoples

The Draft OAS Declaration is not meant to be a binding instrument, but rather a guide to law-makers in drafting national legislation on indigenous rights. It may also serve as an interpretive aid to the activity of the Inter-American Commission and Court of Human Rights.[18] The Draft Declaration mainly speaks of indigenous cultural rights. While this is the topic of Chapter 5 generally, that chapter looks more at the recognition and protection of cultural identity in human rights adjudication, so it is important to consider it briefly here as well, taking into account the specific context of the American continent.

Rodolfo Stavenhagen, in a report prepared to the OAS, identifies 'heritage' to be one of the possible meanings to be attributed to culture. According to him, the

[16] Néstor García Canclini, 'Las Industrias Culturales y el Desarrollo de los Países Americanos', *Workshop on Case Studies in the Protection of Cultural Heritage Central American Region*, available at <http://portal.oas.org/Portal/Topic/SEDI/Educaci%C3%B3nyCultura/Cultura/TemasPrioritarios/Preservaci%C3%B3nyProtecci%C3%B3ndelPatrimonioCultural/Activities/ProtegiendoelPatrimonioCultural/tabid/1447/language/en-US/Default.aspx> (accessed 29 November 2012).

[17] Organization of American States, Inter-American Council for Integral Development, *Concept Paper for the Ministerial Theme Culture and the Enhancement of the Dignity and Identity of Our People, presented by the Delegation of Jamaica for the Third Inter-American Meeting of Ministers of Culture and Highest Appropriate Authorities, November 13 15, 2006, Montreal, Canada*. OEA/Ser.K/XXVII.3 CIDI/REMIC-III/doc.6/06, of 26 October 2006.

[18] Given the Inter-American Court's willingness to look at instruments other than the American Convention in determining the reach of this instrument, and the number of indigenous cases brought before the system, it is likely that the Draft Declaration, once approved, will play precisely this role, and quickly reach the status of customary law before the Court. On how the Inter-American Court uses 'foreign' instruments to expand its understanding of provisions of the American Convention, see Lucas Lixinski, 'Treaty Interpretation by the Inter-American Court of Human Rights: Expansionism at the Service of the Unity of International Law', *EJIL* 21(3) (2010), 585 604. Also on the Draft Declaration, it is interesting to note that at the time of writing there is no clause on the relationship between this Declaration and the United Nations Declaration on the Rights of Indigenous Peoples, approved in 2007.

right to culture in this sense means the right of access to the 'cultural capital' that is formed by heritage, tangible and intangible.[19] He criticizes this view for saying that it fails to distinguish among cultural contents, and that if focuses exceedingly on a 'universal culture', failing to acknowledge that different societies have different competing understanding of cultures, which may often clash, and that culture cannot thus be understood as an abstract right, but as the right of a social group to its own culture. What is a people's cultural heritage is to be determined by the people itself.[20]

The Draft OAS Declaration on Indigenous Peoples is a controversial document. Similarly to its counterpart at the UN level, the Declaration is a highly debated document, with wide participation of indigenous communities. The first Draft of the Declaration was proposed by the Inter-American Commission of Human Rights, and States were subsequently given the opportunity to comment upon the Draft and propose amendments. As a result, all controversial language from the Declaration was eliminated, and its force and reach were weakened overall. Indigenous organizations members of the Indigenous Peoples' Caucus of the Americas (heavily involved in the negotiations) are currently working in restoring the force of the document, and facing fierce State opposition.

Of the many provisions of this document, the two most relevant ones for our purposes are Articles XII (Right to Cultural Identity and Integrity) and XXVIII (Protection of Cultural Heritage and Intellectual Property). It is worth noting that these provisions are almost consensual in their essence, and that disagreement is currently over the use of terminology that permeates the whole of the Declaration.[21]

Article XII proclaims the right of indigenous peoples to their cultural integrity and their heritage, as important factors for the survival of the communities and the identity of their members, especially to the extent that heritage is connected to the indigenous *cosmovisión*.[22] And Article XXVIII, on cultural heritage rights, specifies

[19] Rodolfo Stavenhagen, 'La Diversidad Cultural en el Desarrollo de las Américas: Los pueblos indígenas y los estados nacionales en Hispanoamérica', *OEA, Unidad de Desarrollo Social, Educación y Cultural, Serie de Estudios Culturales No 9* (2004), paras 128 9.

[20] Stavenhagen, 'La Diversidad Cultural', para 130.

[21] One example of such disagreement is the use of the term 'indigenous peoples', which many States propose be replaced by the term 'indigenous populations', significantly weaker, to the extent it dilutes the strong shared identity component of 'peoples', and also the potential of the term for future autonomy and territorial claims, which seem to be the greatest obstacle towards reaching consensus in the drafting process, as many States still adopt a rather narrow view of self-determination, according to which the exercise of the right to self-determination implies claims to independent statehood. Interestingly, indigenous advocates involved in the process, like those involved in the UN-level process, have consistently affirmed that the contemporary understanding of the right to self-determination, as applied to indigenous peoples, means only some degree of autonomy, but not a claim to statehood. For this view of self-determination coming from an indigenous representative, see Nimia Aparo, 'Derechos fundamentales de los pueblos indígenas', in *Los Pueblos Indígenas y la Integración Andina Primer Foro de Intelectuales e Investigadores Indígenas* (2008), 56 8 at 58 (of the Pueblo Calla, in Argentina). See also Natalia Álvarez Molinero, *Pueblos indígenas y derecho de autodeterminación. ¿Hacia un derecho internacional multicultural?* (Universidad de Deusto, 2008).

[22] The text, as of May 2012, is the following: '**Article XII. Right to cultural identity and integrity.** 1. Indigenous peoples have *the right to their own cultural identity and integrity and to their cultural*

what counts as the heritage of indigenous peoples, including both tangible and intangible elements, speaking of indigenous peoples' right to control their heritage, as well as the duty of States to secure free, prior, and informed consent and consult with indigenous peoples in the design of laws and other regimes for the protection of heritage 'and intellectual property associated with that heritage'.[23] This provision is far stronger than the Commission's original proposal (then Article XX), which only declared the right of indigenous peoples to collective forms of intellectual property (IP) adapted to their cultural specificities, and extending IP tools to the protection of their traditional cultural crafts, referring then to manifestations of ICH.[24] In this sense, IP is now subordinated to heritage, as opposed to being the main means through which it is translated into law. It is a much welcome development in the OAS and, considering these provisions have actually been

heritage, both tangible and intangible, including historic and ancestral heritage; and to the protection, preservation, maintenance, and development of that cultural heritage for their collective continuity and that of their members and so as to transmit that heritage to future generations. (Approved on 20 January 2011 Thirteenth Meeting of Negotiations in the Quest for Points of Consensus). [2. Indigenous peoples have the right to *reparations, including the right of restitution, of any cultural heritage* of which they have been dispossessed without their free, prior, and informed consent. Should restitution not be possible, indigenous peoples shall have the right to fair and equitable compensation.] 3. Indigenous people have the right to the recognition and respect for all their ways of life, world views, spirituality, uses and customs, norms and traditions, forms of social, economic and political organization, forms of transmission of knowledge, institutions, practices, beliefs, values, dress and languages, recognizing their inter-relationship as elaborated in this Declaration. (Agreed upon by consensus on January 26, 2007 Ninth Meeting of Negotiations in the Quest for Points of Consensus)' (emphasis added).

[23] The text, as of May 2012, is the following: '**Article XXVIII. Protection of cultural heritage and intellectual property**. 1. Indigenous peoples have the right to the full recognition and respect for their property, ownership, possession, control, development, and protection of their tangible and intangible cultural heritage and intellectual property, including its collective nature, transmitted through millennia, from generation to generation. (Approved on April 20, 2012 Fourteenth Meeting of Negotiations in the Quest for Points of Consensus Ad referendum of the Delegations of Brazil, Costa Rica and Peru) 2. The intellectual property of indigenous peoples includes, inter alia, traditional knowledge, ancestral designs and procedures, cultural, artistic, spiritual, technological, and scientific, expressions, [genetic resources including human genetic resources,] tangible and intangible cultural heritage, as well as the knowledge and developments of their own related to biodiversity and the utility and qualities of seeds and medicinal plants, flora and fauna. 3. States, with the full and effective participation of indigenous peoples, shall adopt measures necessary to ensure that national and international agreements and regimes provide recognition and adequate protection for the cultural heritage of indigenous peoples and intellectual property associated with that heritage. In adopting these measures, consultations shall be effective intended to obtain the free, prior, and informed consent of indigenous peoples. (Approved on April 20, 2012 Fourteenth Meeting of Negotiations in the Quest for Points of Consensus).'

[24] The text, as approved by the Commission, is the following: '**Article XX. Intellectual property rights**. 1. Indigenous peoples have the right to the recognition and the full ownership, control and protection of their cultural, artistic, spiritual, technological and scientific heritage, and legal protection for their intellectual property through trademarks, patents, copyright and other such procedures as established under domestic law; as well as to special measures to ensure them legal status and institutional capacity to develop, use, share, market and bequeath that heritage to future generations. 2. Indigenous peoples have the right to control, develop and protect their sciences and technologies, including their human and genetic resources in general, seed, medicine, knowledge of plant and animal life, original designs and procedure. 3. The states shall take appropriate measures to ensure participation of the indigenous peoples in the determination of the conditions for the utilization, both public and private, of the rights listed in the previous paragraphs 1. and 2.'

approved (except for the bracketed parts), it is a firm step towards better safeguarding of heritage by this organization.

Intangible heritage is thus protected in the Americas as a reservoir of the 'pure commonly-shared culture' of the continent, in an apparent effort to promote pan-Americanism. While this move may be criticized on grounds of inaccuracy, it is also a significant rhetorical tool indicating the favouring of broader development and human rights issues in the continent, especially those of indigenous peoples. The fact that States are willing to bring the debate on the safeguarding of indigenous culture to the OAS can be read as a reflection of internal developments towards recognition of the cultural rights of indigenous peoples (to be looked at more extensively with regard to Latin American Constitutionalism in Chapter 4). It can on the other hand be seen as a claim for development tied down to culture. It is internationalized but at the same time includes the important fallback position of protection of local cultures and ways of life, which necessarily includes economics. The several concept papers demonstrate that, while States acknowledge the important connection between heritage (and culture more generally) and development as a concept, they are still reticent to take concerted regional action on the matter. But the way the topic has been entangled with human rights protection is indicative, in my view, of a willingness to effectively promote regional means for the safeguarding of intangible heritage.

I will now contrast this perception with that of other regional political processes, starting with the Council of Europe.

3.1.2 Council of Europe

The founding documents of the Council of Europe (CoE) spoke of the protection of the 'common heritage' of the European nations that created the Organization aimed at fostering human rights and democracy as a means to maintain peace in the continent. The meaning of the expression 'common heritage' did not necessarily refer to cultural heritage, but it was left undefined as, at that time, it was felt that the term was self-explanatory.[25]

The Council of Europe's work in the field of heritage looks at heritage holistically, deeming distinctions such as tangible/intangible irrelevant, when not harmful to the goal of heritage protection.[26] Speaking of it in terms of its political goals, heritage protection is a concern for the Council of Europe inasmuch as it protects a common European identity, and such identity offers the background against which further European integration and cooperation can be built. I will look at this assertion in further detail in the next section, and then will examine the latest

[25] Peter Wagner, 'From Monuments to Human Rights: Redefining "Heritage" in the Work of the Council of Europe', in *Forward Planning: The Function of Cultural Heritage in a Changing Europe* (Council of Europe, 2000), 9 28 at 13.

[26] See for instance Council of Europe, *Presentation to the Framework Convention on the Value of Cultural Heritage for Society* (2005).

Council of Europe instrument in the field of heritage protection, which brings into evidence the holistic approach towards heritage mentioned here.

3.1.2.1 Fostering a shared European identity

Cultural heritage protection is often justified within the Council of Europe on the basis of its importance for identity, heritage being referred to as 'a bearer of identity'.[27] Engagement with the idea of 'identity' is essential to create regional commonalities and a regional identity that is capable of fostering the ideals of integration and regional cooperation.[28] The 'heritage question', it is argued, should be seen 'as part of a *project* to establish a common European identity through and in a variety of themes/issues and policy fields'.[29]

Heritage within the Council of Europe was a highly politicized topic at first, precisely because of this attachment to the idea of a 'common heritage' as instrumental to the achievement of regional peace and the promotion of democracy. Later on, it was de-politicized,[30] in favour of an understanding that saw culture and identity as contingent upon each other.[31]

In light of this conception, several projects have been developed which are geared towards fostering a common European identity through heritage preservation. One of them is the 'Heritage from Elsewhere, Heritage of Others' project, which aims at 'rediscover[ing] a common thread through time and space that will enable identification today of the human capital and cultural potential of the territories and populations with widely varying cultural traditions which have come together and combined' by means of examining existing heritage and reconstructing their cultural meaning.[32]

This project covers heritage holistically, including buildings and objects on the one hand, but also 'crafts, techniques and skills', 'ideas and knowledge', 'beliefs', and 'forms of cultural expression',[33] on the other. The project is aimed at awareness-raising, and it involves national governments and local authorities as well as civil society.[34]

Civil society involvement is another important concern of the Council of Europe in heritage conservation. When speaking of the protection of crafts and cultural heritage, a Council of Europe Rapporteur has highlighted the importance of involvement of non-governmental organizations for the survival of heritage, being

[27] Council of Europe, Steering Committee for Cultural Heritage, *Heritage from Elsewhere, Heritage of Others: Outline of an Awareness-raising Project.* Doc. Symbol CDPAT (2004) 30 final, 29 April 2004, 2.

[28] Wagner, 'From Monuments to Human Rights', 9.

[29] Wagner, 'From Monuments to Human Rights', 9 (emphasis in the original).

[30] Wagner, 'From Monuments to Human Rights', 14.

[31] Wagner, 'From Monuments to Human Rights', 17.

[32] Council of Europe, *Heritage from Elsewhere*, 3.

[33] Including 'languages, stories and legends, music and dance, live performance, etc.' Council of Europe, *Heritage from Elsewhere*, 3.

[34] Council of Europe, *Heritage from Elsewhere*, 3.

more important even than governmental support.[35] This means in practice the involvement of local communities, or even the larger national community where a manifestation of heritage takes place. Local involvement causes the necessary entrenchment of heritage and its importance that is necessary for it to flourish and be sustainable and alive in the future, avoiding that heritage becomes a museum piece, to remain as a manifestation of living culture.

The focus, nevertheless, remains on the extent to which local heritage can promote the ideals of a commonly shared identity. This value, or the importance of heritage to society, is the topic of the following section.

3.1.2.2 The 2005 Faro Convention

There are several instruments within the Council of Europe dealing with heritage protection, but these instruments more often than not deal with specific forms of tangible heritage, such as architectural heritage,[36] archaeological heritage,[37] or landscapes.[38] While it has been argued that several of these instruments offer sometimes contradictory approaches in distinguishing between local and international interests (among other conceptual issues),[39] the fact is that these instruments have successfully proliferated and created a reliable framework.

The Framework Convention on the Value of Cultural Heritage for Society (Faro, 2005),[40] on the other hand, deals with heritage in a more abstract manner. It is the most important instrument for the purposes of intangible heritage protection in the Council of Europe system, because it addresses heritage in abstract terms, in line with the idea of intangibility. Its purpose is to create a 'European ideal' of social organization; instead of preserving difference, heritage is here used to create commonality.[41] The contribution of heritage to society is seen in terms of its development for economic purposes, on the one hand, while at the same time advancing the common European identity. The developmental aspect of heritage is heavily influenced by the action of the EU in the field, which will be explored in detail below.

[35] Baroness Hooper, *Crafts and Cultural Heritage Conservation Skills, Report to the Committee on Culture, Science and Education of the Council of Europe Parliamentary Assembly. Doc. 11761*, 23 October 2008, para 9.

[36] Council of Europe, Convention for the Protection of the Architectural Heritage of Europe. Granada, 3 October 1985. ETS no 121. Entry into force: 1 December 1987. Parties as of November 2012: 41.

[37] Council of Europe, European Convention on the Protection of the Archaeological Heritage (Revised). Valetta, 16 January 1992. ETS no 143. Entry into force: 25 May 1995. Parties as of November 2012: 42.

[38] Council of Europe, European Landscape Convention. Florence, 20 October 2000. ETS no 176. Entry into force: 1 March 2004. Parties as of November 2012: 37.

[39] For an analysis of these issues, see Claude Karnoouh, 'Europe: Common Heritage and Differences', in *Forward Planning: The Function of Cultural Heritage in a Changing Europe* (Council of Europe, 2000), 29 52.

[40] Council of Europe, Framework Convention on the Value of Cultural Heritage for Society, Signed in Faro on 27 October 2005. ETS no 199. Entry into force: 1 June 2011. Number of Parties as of November 2012: 13.

[41] Council of Europe, *Presentation to the Framework Convention.*

The Framework Convention was designed after a series of consultations were held with the aim of creating a new instrument, either a protocol to existing Council of Europe Conventions or a totally new treaty that could address the latest understandings of cultural heritage, particularly its intangible aspects.[42]

The Framework Convention is innovative in speaking openly of a right to cultural heritage. This right, in the Convention, is an inherent part of the right to participate in cultural life, as protected by the Universal Declaration of Human Rights.[43] Heritage is referred to as deriving directly from identity, and all references to heritage or culture as 'concrete entities' is avoided, thus also avoiding the commodification of heritage.[44] This is not, however, an enforceable right, because of the very nature of a framework convention (in that it does not create self-executing norms, and therefore enforceable rights), and also because of an explicit provision announcing that the Convention does not create subjective rights of any sort.[45] The 'right to heritage', therefore, is only declaratory in the Convention.[46]

Cultural heritage is defined as 'a group of resources inherited from the past which people identify, independently of ownership, as a reflection and expression of their constantly evolving values, beliefs, knowledge and traditions. It includes all aspects of the environment resulting from the interaction between people and places through time'.[47] This definition highlights several issues relating to intangible heritage, particularly the idea of 'constantly evolving values', which indicates a living culture.

The Convention also defines the 'common heritage of Europe', as 'all forms of cultural heritage in Europe which together constitute a shared source of remembrance, understanding, identity, cohesion and creativity', and 'the ideals, principles

42 Council of Europe, *Explanatory Report to the Council of Europe Framework Convention on the Value of Cultural Heritage to Society* (2005).

43 The relevant provisions are the following: '**Article 1—Aims of the Convention.** The Parties to this Convention agree to: a. recognise that rights relating to cultural heritage are inherent in the right to participate in cultural life, as defined in the Universal Declaration of Human Rights; [. . .]' and '**Article 4—Rights and responsibilities relating to cultural heritage.** The Parties recognise that: a. everyone, alone or collectively, has the right to benefit from the cultural heritage and to contribute towards its enrichment; b. everyone, alone or collectively, has the responsibility to respect the cultural heritage of others as much as their own heritage, and consequently the common heritage of Europe; c. exercise of the right to cultural heritage may be subject only to those restrictions which are necessary in a democratic society for the protection of the public interest and the rights and freedoms of others.' Please note that the right to heritage as protected in the Convention is a relative right, which can be limited subject to a proportionality analysis, like the rights to cultural identity and minority protection, as developed by adjudicatory bodies. See Chapter 5.

44 Council of Europe, *Explanatory Report*.

45 The relevant provision is the following: '**Article 6—Effects of the Convention.** No provision of this Convention shall be interpreted so as to: a. limit or undermine the human rights and fundamental freedoms which may be safeguarded by international instruments, in particular, the Universal Declaration of Human Rights and the Convention for the Protection of Human Rights and Fundamental Freedoms; b. affect more favourable provisions concerning cultural heritage and environment contained in other national or international legal instruments; c. *create enforceable rights*' (emphasis added).

46 This view is reinforced by the Explanatory Report to the Convention. See Council of Europe, *Explanatory Report*. There are ways through which a 'right to heritage' can be constructed in an enforceable manner. For these, see Chapter 5.

47 Article 2.a.

and values, derived from the experience gained through progress and past conflicts, which foster the development of a peaceful and stable society, founded on respect for human rights, democracy and the rule of law'.[48] The first part of this double definition is cultural heritage explicitly, whereas the second part refers to the original understanding of 'common European heritage' of the founding of the Council of Europe, a notion which in this Convention comes without the political charge originally attributed to it, but still falls short of being merged into the idea of cultural heritage. Rather, there is a distinction there between the *cultural* heritage of Europe, on the one hand, and the shared *intellectual* heritage, which looks at the ideal of how a society should operate.[49] These two elements are seen as being mutually-supportive, and a unifying idea in the Convention, which refers back to the Declaration on Intercultural Dialogue and Conflict Prevention (the Opatija Declaration).[50]

This focus on values, rather than the constitutive elements of heritage, can also be seen as a further step in avoiding the commodification of heritage, and it represents a difference in approach from that of the 2003 UNESCO Convention. Another difference is that heritage is not protected in the Framework Convention as a goal in itself, but rather as also being instrumental in contributing to the lives of people and communities in Europe.[51]

Cultural heritage is also addressed in its relation to economic activity in the Framework Convention. Cultural heritage is then seen as a factor in sustainable economic development, and economic policies must take into account cultural heritage and its integrity, which must not be compromised in what refers to its 'inherent values'.[52] This latest provision recognizes that cultural heritage has a value that goes beyond its utility at a particular time and place, and must therefore be protected regardless of the purposes it serves, to respect the rights of communities and particularly future generations, which may find other purposes for heritage which can be lost if heritage is preserved only to the extent that it serves economic purposes.[53]

Finally, and perhaps more importantly for the future action of the Council of Europe, the Convention imposes upon the parties the obligation to create a monitoring body through the Council of Europe, to oversee legislative practice and other policies regarding heritage.[54] The Committee of Ministers received the

[48] Article 3. [49] Council of Europe, *Explanatory Report.*

[50] Council of Europe, Summit on Heritage and Communication, *Declaration of Opatija on Intercultural Dialogue and Conflict Prevention,* Adopted at the Regional Summit Forum on Communication of Heritage on 1 June 2006.

[51] Council of Europe, *Explanatory Report.*

[52] The relevant provision is the following: '**Article 10—Cultural heritage and economic activity.** In order to make full use of the potential of the cultural heritage as a factor in sustainable economic development, the Parties undertake to: a. raise awareness and utilise the economic potential of the cultural heritage; b. take into account the specific character and interests of the cultural heritage when devising economic policies; and c. ensure that these policies respect the integrity of the cultural heritage without compromising its inherent values.'

[53] Council of Europe, *Explanatory Report.*

[54] The relevant provision is the following: '**Article 15—Undertakings of the Parties.** The Parties undertake to: a. develop, through the Council of Europe, a monitoring function covering legislations,

mandate to create this body or delegate authority to an existing one to oversee the application of the Convention.[55] The Steering Committee for Cultural Heritage and Landscape is in charge of overseeing the implementation of the Faro Convention. At the time of writing, it is unclear what concrete actions will be taken, but it seems that most action is targeted at creating an information system about national implementation of the instrument. It is to be hoped that further action will offer the means for effective protection of ICH, not only through preventive protection via educational programmes and awareness-raising, but also offering States the tools to create an enforceable right to heritage within their national legal systems.

Early agreements on this matter during the drafting of the instrument indicate that the European Heritage Network and the Compendium of Cultural Policies will probably be the starting points for putting into practice Articles 15 and 16 of the Framework Convention.[56] The Framework Convention also takes a new approach when it comes to the information by States Parties: instead of reporting, States are required to enter information in a shared database, which should speed up the process of collecting data and compiling repertoires of best practices for the protection of heritage. This is a laudable development, and one that takes into account the developments of the information society. Hopefully, this will help the Convention achieve its aims and offer better integrated protection to heritage, in its tangible and intangible aspects.

3.1.3 African Union

The African Union (AU) is a hybrid of political regionalism coupled with economic regionalism. As most of its policy programmes to date still fit more within the frame of what is expected from a political regional organization, I will deal with these programmes within this section. Part of the reason why the focus seems to be more on political initiatives is that the AU replaced the Organization of African Unity (through a 2001 Treaty),[57] which was essentially a political

policies and practices concerning cultural heritage, consistent with the principles established by this Convention; b. maintain, develop and contribute data to a shared information system, accessible to the public, which facilitates assessment of how each Party fulfils its commitments under this Convention.'

[55] The relevant provision is the following: '**Article 16—Monitoring mechanism**. a. The Committee of Ministers, pursuant to Article 17 of the Statute of the Council of Europe, shall nominate an appropriate committee or specify an existing committee to monitor the application of the Convention, which will be authorised to make rules for the conduct of its business; b. The nominated committee shall: establish rules of procedure as necessary; manage the shared information system referred to in Article 15, maintaining an overview of the means by which each commitment under this Convention is met; at the request of one or more Parties, give an advisory opinion on any question relating to the interpretation of the Convention, taking into consideration all Council of Europe legal instruments; on the initiative of one or more Parties, undertake an evaluation of any aspect of their implementation of the Convention; foster the trans-sectoral application of this Convention by collaborating with other committees and participating in other initiatives of the Council of Europe; report to the Committee of Ministers on its activities. The committee may involve experts and observers in its work.'

[56] Council of Europe, *Explanatory Report*.

[57] Constitutive Act of the African Union, Adopted by the Thirty-Sixth Ordinary Session of the Assembly of Heads of State and Government of the Organization of African Unity, on 11 July 2000, in Lome, Togo. Number of Parties as of November 2012: 53.

regional organization. Many of the mandates have been kept, and it seems reasonable to assume that the transition towards economic regionalism simply has not taken shape yet because the spirit behind the foundation of the AU has not been sufficiently economic, and somehow there has been no time for the transition, due to the continuing political and security turmoil in certain parts of the continent and a lack of institutional resources which pose more pressing challenges to the Organization.

The AU, like its predecessor, has been founded upon the idea of laying the foundations for a prosperous, post-colonial Africa, and to wipe out as much as possible of the damage done to the continent by colonialism.[58] Part of this break with the colonial past includes the promotion of African identity, and an identity that is distinct from that of the colonizers. This is what justifies much of the cultural policy in the AU, and its efforts towards the protection of cultural heritage.

Cultural resources must be protected, according to the AU, because they provide the stimuli for continental integration, socioeconomic development and durable peace and stability in Africa. Given the number of conflict situations in Africa, the impact of war on cultural heritage is also a great factor to be taken into account. Culture is seen as 'an important element of institutional transformation'.[59]

The need to promote cultural policies in Africa also stems from the fact that culture has not been taken into account in the past when designing programmes for social and economic development. It is necessary thus to pay attention to African cultures themselves, creating an environment in which they can flourish.[60]

The protection of heritage is also one of the major developmental objectives of the AU. For instance, in a report called 'Africa, Our Common Destiny Guideline Document', the AU highlights as its third most pressing objective the development of African culture, through the preservation of African identity and the promotion of cultural unity in Africa by the safeguarding of cultural heritage.[61]

When it comes specifically to cultural heritage, the AU has shown great concern with international restitution, through the Cultural Charters (examined below), and also through resolutions regarding specific cultural objects, such as the Obelisk of Axum.[62] And in the field of intangible heritage, the AU has supported the UNESCO efforts in the area, by encouraging States to ratify the 2003 UNESCO

[58] See for instance these provisions of the Constitutive Act's preamble: '[...] **RECALLING** the heroic struggles waged by our peoples and our countries for political independence, human dignity and economic emancipation; **CONSIDERING** that since its inception, the Organization of African Unity has played a determining and invaluable role in the liberation of the continent, the affirmation of a common identity and the process of attainment of the unity of our continent and has provided a unique framework for our collective action in Africa and in our relations with the rest of the world. [...]'.

[59] African Union, *Aide Memoire to the First Pan-African Cultural Congress, 13 15 November 2006, Addis Ababa, Ethiopia, General Theme: 'Culture, Integration and African Renaissance'.*

[60] African Union, *Aide Memoire.*

[61] African Union, *Africa, Our Common Destiny Guideline Document prepared by the Commission of the African Commission* (2004), 48.

[62] African Union, Assembly of Heads of State and Government, *Resolution on the Return of the Pillaged African Monument the Obelisk of Axum*, AHG/Dec.184 (XXVIII), 8 July 2002.

Convention.[63] Further, many efforts related to intangible heritage have been aimed at the protection of African languages. To be exact, 2006 was the 'Year of African Languages', and, in launching this year, the AU affirmed that 'African languages constitute the bulk of the common African intangible heritage, and [serve] as an umbilical cord between generations: past, present and future'.[64]

3.1.3.1 The Cultural Charter and African cultural renaissance

The Cultural Charter for Africa[65] is a Treaty that was finalized in 1976 and provides for the protection of the sets of cultural values that reflect the distinctive character and personality of human societies, as reflected in their traditions, languages, ways of life and thought.[66] This document first mentions cultural heritage as the responsibility of peoples with the State acting as a facilitator to this process.[67]

The Charter speaks of colonial domination, and the ensuing cultural domination that derived from it (alongside political, economic, and social domination). It blames cultural domination for the 'depersonalization' of African peoples, for the falsification of African history and the combat to African values and languages, which were gradually replaced by those of the colonizers ('Recalling that cultural domination led to the depersonalization of part of the African peoples, falsified their history, systematically disparaged and combated African values, and tried to replace progressively and officially, their languages by that of the colonizer'). It goes on to argue that the unity of Africa is founded upon its history ('Convinced that the unity of Africa is founded first and foremost on its History'), and that the affirmation of cultural identity must be a concern of all peoples of Africa, as well as the protection of cultural heritage, which is intrinsically linked to cultural identity ('Convinced that it is imperative to carry out a systematic inventory of the cultural heritage, in particular in the spheres of Traditions, History and Arts').[68]

63 African Union, Executive Council, *Decision on the Formulation and Establishment of an International Convention on Cultural Diversity and an International Convention on the Safeguarding of Intangible Cultural Heritage*, Third Ordinary Session, 4 8 July 2003, Maputo (Mozambique), EX/CL/Dec.67(III). This is also present in the Charter for African Cultural Renaissance, analysed below.

64 African Union, *Press Release No 29/2006, Launching of 2006 as the Year of African Languages*. Addis Ababa, 20 June 2006.

65 Organization of African Unity, Cultural Charter for Africa, concluded during the Thirteenth Ordinary Session of the Organization of African Unity in Port Louis, Mauritius, 5 July 1976. Entry into force: 19 September 1990. Number of Parties as of January 2006 (when it stopped being open for ratification): 34.

66 Preamble: 'CONVINCED that any human society is necessarily governed by rules and principles based on traditions, languages, ways of life and thought in other words on a set of cultural values which reflect its distinctive character and personality [. . .]'.

67 Preamble: 'CONVINCED that all cultures emanate from the people, and that any African cultural policy should of necessity enable the people to expand for increased responsibility in the development of its cultural heritage [. . .]'.

68 Preamble.

The protection of African cultural heritage is one of the aims and objectives of the Charter,[69] and cultural decolonization one of the principles guiding cultural cooperation.[70] Mirroring similar language in other regional organizations, the Charter also states that diversity expresses a commonly shared identity.[71] Different from other regional organizations, however, the Charter places a much stronger emphasis on collective creation and the communitarian approach that is typical of African human rights law.[72]

The specific chapter of the Charter relating to the protection of cultural heritage makes no mention of ICH, which is understandable if one thinks that the Charter was adopted in 1976, when international cultural heritage law and debates on ICH were still at the stage of inception. Rather, the Charter focuses on cultural property, and on the restitution of cultural objects removed from the continent by virtue of colonialism.[73]

The Charter for African Cultural Renaissance (African Renaissance Charter) was approved in 2006 with the goal of replacing the Cultural Charter,[74] which will be replaced for all States Parties when the African Renaissance Charter comes into force (even though the old Charter will still be applicable until all of its 34 States Parties have ratified the new instrument).[75] This document is explicitly inspired by

[69] The relevant provision is the following: '**Article 1.** The aims and objectives of this Charter are as follows: [...] (b) the rehabilitation, restoration, preservation and promotion of the African cultural heritage; [...]'.

[70] The relevant provision is the following: '**Article 2.** In order to fulfill the objectives set out in Article 2, the African States solemnly subscribe to the following principles: [...] (e) exchange and dissemination of cultural experience between African countries, in the field of *cultural decolonization* in all its forms' (emphasis added).

[71] The relevant provision is the following: '**Article 4.** The African States recognize that *African cultural diversity is the expression of the same identity*; a factor of unity and an effective weapon for genuine liberty, effective responsibility and full sovereignty of the people' (emphasis added).

[72] The relevant provision is the following: '**Chapter II—The Democratization of Culture. Article** 7. The African States recognize that the driving force of Africa is based more on development of the collective personality than on individual advancement and profit, and that culture cannot be considered as the privilege of an elite'. For the communitarian perspective in African human rights law, *see* Makau wa Mutua, 'The Ideology of Human Rights', *Va J Intl L* 36 (1996), 589 657; Rhoda Howard, 'Group Versus Individual Identity in the African Debate on Human Rights', in Abdullah An-na-im and Francis Deng (eds), *Human Rights in Africa, Cross-Cultural Perspectives* (1990), 159 83; and Vincent Orlu Nmehielle, *The African Human Rights System: Its Laws, Practice, and Institutions* (2001).

[73] The relevant provisions are the following: '**Article 28.** The African States should take steps to put an end to the despoliation of African cultural property and ensure that cultural assets, in particular archives works of art and archeological objects, which have been removed from Africa, are returned there. To this end they should, in particular, support the efforts exerted by UNESCO and take all other necessary steps to ensure the implementation of the United Nations General Assembly resolution on the restitution of works of art removed from their country of origin.'; and '**Article 29.** The African States should take steps to ensure that the archives which have been removed from Africa are returned to African governments in order that they may have complete archives concerning the history of their country.'

[74] African Union, Charter for African Cultural Renaissance, adopted by the Sixth Ordinary Session of the Assembly, in Khartoum, Sudan, 24 January 2006. As of November 2012, the Charter has been ratified by five States, and signed by 26. At the time of writing, it is not yet into force.

[75] The relevant provisions are the following: '**Article 1—Replacement of the 1976 Cultural Charter for Africa.** The Cultural Charter for Africa adopted in 1976 by the Heads of States and Governments of the Organization of African Unity is hereby replaced by the present Charter'; and '**Article 2—Relationship between Parties to the Revised Charter and Parties Bound by the 1976**

its predecessor, and draws on many of the values embodied in the Cultural Charter for Africa,[76] but it also takes into account several changes in regional and international discourse relating to culture, including the African Charter on Human and Peoples' Rights, the UNESCO Declaration on Cultural Diversity, the UNESCO Convention on Intangible Heritage, and the UNESCO Convention on the Diversity of Cultural Expressions.[77]

The African Renaissance Charter revisits many of the values behind its predecessor, including the past of cultural domination of the continent, including colonialism and slave trading.[78] And it is innovative in that it mentions intangible heritage openly, as a type of heritage that goes hand in hand with tangible heritage, and stems to a large extent from African languages.[79]

One of the objectives of the African Renaissance Charter is to preserve and promote African cultural heritage, and it looks at three aims to be promoted by cultural heritage: human rights, social cohesion, and human development. Also, it proclaims the entrenchment of knowledge and heritage with local communities as a necessary step for the understanding and preservation of heritage.[80] It states that cultural diversity is a factor for mutual enrichment of peoples and nations, and it contributes to national and regional identities, as well as to the building of

Cultural Charter for Africa. (a) Between parties which are bound by this Charter, only this Charter shall apply. (b) The relationships between Parties to the original Cultural Charter for Africa of 1976 and Parties to this Revised Charter shall be governed by the provisions of original Cultural Charter for Africa'.

[76] Preamble: 'Inspired by the Cultural Charter for Africa adopted by the Heads of State and Government of the Organization of African Unity meeting in its Thirteenth Ordinary Session, in Port Louis, Mauritius, from 2 to 5 July, 1976; [...]'

[77] Preamble: '**GUIDED BY** [...] The African Charter on Human and Peoples' Rights (1981); The Convention on the Protection of Cultural Property in the Event of Armed Conflict (1954) and its additional Protocols; The Convention on the Means of Prohibiting and Preventing the Illicit Import, Export and Transfer of Cultural Property (1970); Convention Concerning the Protection of World Cultural and Natural Heritage (1972); The UNESCO Universal Declaration on Cultural Diversity (2001); The Convention for the Safeguarding of the Intangible Cultural Heritage (2003); The Convention on the Protection and Promotion of Diversity of Cultural Expressions, (2005); [...]'

[78] Preamble: '**RECALLING** That despite cultural domination which during the slave trade and the colonial era led to the depersonalization of part of the African peoples, falsified their history, systematically disparaged and combated African values, and tried to replace progressively and officially, their languages by that of the colonize, the African peoples were able to find in African culture, the necessary strength for resistance and the liberation of the Continent[.]'

[79] Preamble: '[...] That it is imperative to resolutely ensure the promotion of African languages, mainstay and media of tangible and intangible cultural heritage in its most authentic and essentially popular form and also as a factor of development; That it is imperative to carry out a systematic inventory with a view to preserving and promoting tangible and intangible cultural heritage, in particular in the spheres of History, Traditions, Arts and Handicrafts, Knowledge and Know-how; [...]'

[80] The relevant provision is the following: '**Article 3.** The objectives of this Charter are as follows: [...] (d) To preserve and promote the African cultural heritage through preservation, restoration and rehabilitation; [...] (i) To promote in each country the popularization of science and technology including TK systems as a condition for better understanding and preservation of cultural and natural heritage; [...] (k) To develop all the dynamic values of the African cultural heritage that promote human rights, social cohesion and human development; [...]'

Pan-Africanism.[81] In this sense, it mirrors other regional initiatives in using heritage for the construction of a common identity and the strengthening of regional ties and cooperation.

The part of the Charter related to cultural development, when laying down the basic principles of cultural policies, states that African cultural values must be introduced and promoted in cultural policy, and that this happens through the protection and preservation of tangible and intangible heritage, among other tools.[82] The specific chapter on the protection of cultural heritage still keeps much of the language of the old charter, and it offers only one vague provision related to intangible heritage, which endorses the 2003 UNESCO Convention by asking States to ratify it.[83]

Regional organizations of a political character, then, all promote the safeguarding of cultural heritage, tangible and intangible, as part of their goals concerned with development, and, more importantly, a commonly shared identity that can lead to greater integration and closer ties. The goal of promoting identity and the language of rights are a constant in these organizations. Whether similar features can be observed in economic integration processes is the topic of the following section.

3.2 Economic Regionalism

This part of the book will look at two different processes of regional economic integration, the Andean Community of Nations and the EU. I have chosen these two processes because they are the most advanced ones in terms of recognition of supranationality and an autonomous role for the international organization in relation to the Member States, with autonomous law-making powers and competences that go beyond simply securing a free trade area or customs union.

Economic regionalism is worth looking at when it comes to the protection of intangible heritage because, even though these processes have long gone beyond the advancement of purely economic goals, and some even announce their constitutionalization,[84] they are still very much connected to these economic goals,

[81] The relevant provision is the following: '**Article 5.** 1. African States recognize that cultural diversity is a factor for mutual enrichment of peoples and nations. Consequently, they commit themselves to defend minorities, their cultures, their rights and their fundamental freedoms. 2. Cultural diversity contributes to the expression of national and regional identities, and more widely, to building Pan-Africanism.'

[82] The relevant provision is the following: '**Article 10.** 1. States will ensure the introduction of African cultural values and the universal principles of human rights in education, as well as in information and communication programmes. 2. States commit themselves to: protect and promote the freedom of artists, intellectuals and men and women of culture; protect and develop tangible and intangible cultural heritage; financially and materially support cultural initiatives in all strata of society; facilitate access to education and culture for all segments of the population.'

[83] The relevant provision is the following: '**Article 29.** African States should ratify the Convention for the Protection of Cultural Property in the Event of Armed Conflict and the Convention for the Safeguarding of the Intangible Cultural Heritage[.]'

[84] For a relatively recent collection of essays on the subject, see eg Nicholas Tsagourias (ed), *Transnational Constitutionalism: International and European Perspectives* (Cambridge University Press, 2007).

especially where regional development through cultural trade and tourism is central to economic plans. That is, different policies and law-making efforts in these organizations still have to be justified in relation to the market, and the advancement of economic goals. In this sense, these organizations offer an interesting insight into how market interests can be instrumental in justifying protection of ICH.

3.2.1 European Union[85]

Article 151 of the Treaty Establishing the European Community (now Article 167 of the Treaty on the Functioning of the European Union) laid down the provisions on the protection of culture and cultural heritage for the EC. It mentioned cooperation among Member States, and the special significance of a common European cultural heritage. The Treaty of Lisbon (2007, entered into force on 1 December 2009) makes only small changes to this provision, and the amended Treaty on the Functioning of the European Union keeps the provision that determines the exclusion of the harmonization of laws and regulations in the Member States in cultural matters from the reach of the EU.

This section will analyse the state of affairs of the EU cultural policy prior to the entry into force of the Lisbon Treaty in terms of protection of cultural heritage, and will assess whether the maintenance of the current policy under the Lisbon Treaty is positive. I argue that the EU, as an international player of great importance (an importance the EU hopes to re-affirm and expand in light of the changes to its external relations competencies in the Lisbon Treaty), should adopt a more aggressive posture towards the protection of cultural heritage. This posture should be aimed both at the internal and external dimensions of EU law and policy: in its internal dimension, the EU would address an issue of great importance and offer a solution for it in the bloc; externally, it would positively influence its partner States also to pursue solutions. The adoption of solutions internally also has a spillover effect over the external dimension, simply because it sets a good example towards the international community at large.

To the extent that heritage loses some of its 'local' dimension, and becomes more and more an international concern, through the concept of 'common heritage of mankind', it is essential that international organizations gain a greater role in this area.[86] Harmonizing laws that can be used for the protection of cultural heritage, besides being an important goal in itself,[87] is part of the aggressive posture I advocate.

[85] An earlier version of this section was previously published elsewhere. See Lucas Lixinski, 'The Future of the EU Cultural Policy in the Protection of Intangible Cultural Heritage', *The Prague Ybk of Comparative L* 1 (2009), 119 39.

[86] On the specific case of the EU, see Evangelia Psychogiopoulou, *The Integration of Cultural Considerations in EU Law and Policies* (Martinus Nijhoff Publishers, 2008), 33; on the cosmopolitan debate on cultural heritage generally, see Chapter 1 and Derek Gillman, *The Idea of Cultural Heritage* (Institute for Art and Law, 2006), 1 3.

[87] This is also advocated by non-lawyers concerned with cultural heritage protection. See Hristina Staneva, 'Heritage Legislation Challenges in the Context of European Integration', *ICOMOS 13th*

In the case of ICH, IP law, especially copyright, can be used as a particularly valuable tool. As harmonization of IP is a newly-created competence of the EU under the Lisbon Treaty, this may provide a means of protecting at least some aspects of cultural heritage within the framework of the EU.

I will pursue this discussion in two main parts here. In the first part, I will look at the protection of cultural heritage in the EU through policy initiatives, both before and after the entry into force of the Lisbon Treaty. In the second part, I will look at the prospects for legislative action on the matter of protection of cultural heritage, especially through the harmonization of IP laws. While this was not within Community competence (at least not explicitly), the Treaty of Lisbon opened the door for harmonization of IP regulation. As far as IP laws are compatible with protecting intangible heritage,[88] this is a possibility to be explored for the protection of folklore at the regional level.

3.2.1.1 The protection of heritage through policy programmes

Most of the EU action in terms of heritage protection happens at the policy level.[89] Article 151 of the EC Treaty,[90] dealing with cultural cooperation, restricted this field of activity to the policy level, as it precludes harmonization of legislation, leaving it up to each Member State to determine its own cultural legislation. I will in this part analyse how this action happens, both in the internal and external policy of the EU.

3.2.1.1.1 The state of play prior to the Lisbon Treaty

It is important to note that, while cultural cooperation at the policy level for the protection of cultural heritage is encouraged by the EC Treaty, not much seems to happen inside the EU, and most of the focus is on EU external relations. One of the

General Assembly and International Symposium, available at <http://www.international.icomos.org/madrid2002/actas/112.pdf> (accessed 29 November 2012).

[88] For further analysis of this topic, see Chapter 6.

[89] Psychogiopoulou, *The Integration of Cultural Considerations*, 30.

[90] 'TITLE XII. CULTURE. **Article 151.** 1. The Community shall contribute to the flowering of the cultures of the Member States, while respecting their national and regional diversity and at the same time *bringing the common cultural heritage* to the fore. 2. Action by the Community shall be aimed at encouraging *cooperation* between Member States and, if necessary, supporting and supplementing their action in the following areas: improvement of the knowledge and dissemination of the culture and history of the European peoples, *conservation and safeguarding of cultural heritage of European significance*, non-commercial cultural exchanges, artistic and literary creation, including in the audiovisual sector. 3. The Community and the Member States shall foster *cooperation with third countries* and the competent international organisations in the sphere of culture, in particular the Council of Europe. 4. The Community shall take cultural aspects into account in its action under other provisions of this Treaty, in particular in order to respect and to promote the diversity of its cultures. 5. In order to contribute to the achievement of the objectives referred to in this Article, the Council: acting in accordance with the procedure referred to in Article 251 and after consulting the Committee of the Regions, shall adopt incentive measures, *excluding any harmonisation of the laws and regulations of the Member States*. The Council shall act unanimously throughout the procedure referred to in Article 251, acting unanimously on a proposal from the Commission, shall adopt recommendations' (emphasis added).

few initiatives inside the EU is the Raphael Programme.[91] It was launched in 1997 and aimed to raise awareness, share information and best practices on heritage conservation, and fund rehabilitation projects. This project lasted from 1997 to 2000, and, while it promoted no legislative efforts on the matter, it achieved policy goals related to cultural heritage protection, at least to the extent the heritage under the programme was part of the 'common cultural heritage' of Europe, as enunciated in Article 151.[92]

Another group of initiatives puts cultural heritage in the context of information technologies. This has been positively evaluated as to the achievement of its socio-economic goals, which indicates a quite successful cultural heritage policy within the EU, even if not a high-profile one.[93]

The bulk of heritage programmes take place within the EU external relations policy. Partner countries of the Mediterranean region are the greatest beneficiaries of these programmes. In this sense, the rejection of cultural assimilationism is one of the goals of the Union, and informs the construction and operation of these initiatives.[94]

The rationale for identifying cultural heritage as a relevant sector in EU external relations is based on several arguments: enhancement of cultural solidarity and mutual knowledge amongst partner countries through the protection of heritage;[95] the economic dimension of culture and the potential for cultural tourism; and the importance of heritage as a factor of cultural enrichment.[96] Programmes created and promoted in accordance with this rationale have gradually shifted from the protection of monumental heritage to a focus on intangible heritage, which is more representative of the aims of cultural enrichment.[97]

[91] Decision 2228/97/EC of the European Parliament and of the Council of 13 October 1997 establishing a Community action programme in the field of cultural heritage (Raphael), OJ L 305, 8 November 1997, 31.

[92] A brief commentary on this project has been made by Allison Carter Jett, 'Domestic, Supranational and International Historic Preservation Legislation: Does it Protect our Cultural Heritage or Restrict Development? Exploring its Impact on Ancient Roman Monuments', *Ga J Intl & Comp L* 31 (2003), 649 80 at 671.

[93] Flavio Tariffi, Peter Holm Christensen, and Hervé Le Guyader, *Third Socio-Economic Evaluation of Cultural Heritage Projects under the IST 2001 Work Programme: Report of the Evaluation Panel* (European Communities, 2002).

[94] Evangelia Psychogiopoulou, 'Euro-Mediterranean Cultural Cooperation in the Field of Heritage Conservation and Management', *Eur Foreign Affairs Rev* 10 (2005), 237 55 at 240.

[95] European Communities, *Strategy for the Development of Euro-Mediterranean Cultural Heritage: Ppriorities from Mediterranean Countries (2007 2013)* (European Communities, 2007), 8.

[96] Psychogiopoulou, 'Euro-Mediterranean Cultural Cooperation', 242.

[97] Psychogiopoulou, 'Euro-Mediterranean Cultural Cooperation', 248. One example of such a programme focused on the protection of intangible heritage is the Mediterranean Voices project. The Mediterranean Voices Project was established within the framework of the EU's EuroMed (Europe-Mediterranean Partnership) Heritage II programme. It is an initiative coordinated by the London Metropolitan University in conjunction with 13 other partner institutions, aiming to identify 'the roots and the routes' of communities in the region, particularly through elements of intangible heritage. The project consisted of a series of museum exhibitions in several cities of the Mediterranean region, as well as a website that has been developed for the project, as a means to have a permanent record of it. For a commentary on this project, see Margaret Hart Robertson, 'The Difficulties of Interpreting Mediterranean Voices: Exhibiting Intangibles Using New Technologies', *Intl J of Intangible Heritage* 1 (2006), 26 34 at 26 7.

This rationale was applied in the Mediterranean region through the EUROMED Heritage programme. This programme has been conceived in three phases, involving 36 different projects in the Mediterranean Partner Countries (MPCs).[98]

The EUROMED Heritage projects have arguably failed to integrate the expertise of the Council of Europe and of UNESCO in cultural heritage conservation matters,[99] and they have even been accused of cultural superposition, as the orientation for many projects seemed to be in the sense of incorporating European cultural practices.[100] However, they have also been considered successful in preserving and promoting cultural heritage and the values of dialogue and mutual understanding (part of the rationale behind the initiative) in the region.[101]

This is a brief description of the state of affairs of heritage protection initiatives at the policy level within the EU prior to the entry into force of the Lisbon Treaty. It is important to see the influence, if any, of the Lisbon Treaty on this, and speculate about the future of EU policy in heritage protection.

3.2.1.1.2 Post-Lisbon effects

Upon entry into force of the Lisbon Treaty, the consolidated EU Treaties' equivalent provision to Article 151 has become Article 167,[102] which does not significantly alter the text, at least in what refers to the present scope of analysis. This means that, at least in principle, there should not be many changes at the policy level for heritage programmes.

[98] European Communities, *Strategy for the Development of Euro-Mediterranean Cultural Heritage*, 9. These countries are: Algeria, Egypt, Israel, Jordan, Lebanon, Morocco, the Palestinian Authority, Syria, Tunisia, and Turkey.

[99] Psychogiopoulou, 'Euro-Mediterranean Cultural Cooperation', 250.

[100] Psychogiopoulou, 'Euro-Mediterranean Cultural Cooperation', 251 2.

[101] European Communities, *Strategy for the Development of Euro-Mediterranean Cultural Heritage*, 9.

[102] 'TITLE XIII. CULTURE. **Article 167 (ex Article 151 TEC)**.

1. The Union shall contribute to the flowering of the cultures of the Member States, while respecting their national and regional diversity and at the same time bringing the common cultural heritage to the fore.
2. Action by the Union shall be aimed at encouraging cooperation between Member States and, if necessary, supporting and supplementing their action in the following areas:
   improvement of the knowledge and dissemination of the culture and history of the European peoples,
   conservation and safeguarding of cultural heritage of European significance,
   non-commercial cultural exchanges,
   artistic and literary creation, including in the audiovisual sector.
3. The Union and the Member States shall foster cooperation with third countries and the competent international organisations in the sphere of culture, in particular the Council of Europe.
4. The Union shall take cultural aspects into account in its action under other provisions of the Treaties, in particular in order to respect and to promote the diversity of its cultures.
5. In order to contribute to the achievement of the objectives referred to in this Article:
   the European Parliament and the Council acting in accordance with the ordinary legislative procedure and after consulting the Committee of the Regions, shall adopt incentive measures, excluding any harmonisation of the laws and regulations of the Member States,
   the Council, on a proposal from the Commission, shall adopt recommendations.'

The EUROMED Heritage programme, however, is expected to undergo changes at the policy level. The most important of these changes is the enactment of the European Neighborhood and Partnership Instrument (ENPI), which eliminates the regional element of EU external relations policies, and encompasses all countries within the EU neighbourhood area.[103]

Another important recent initiative is the 'Ljubljana Process', launched in May 2008 and aimed at ensuring funding for a series of heritage rehabilitation programmes in the Western Balkans. This programme is a joint initiative by the European Commission and the Council of Europe (thus responding to one of the flaws of the EUROMED projects, pointed out above) in the context of the EU enlargement process. Its aim is to restore heritage as a means of attracting public and private investment to the region.[104]

In line with this it is interesting to note how this project is connected to the enlargement process. One might even say it is concerned with the 'common European heritage' part of Article 167: if heritage preservation is being fostered in countries who aspire to membership, in a way the EU can be said to be paving the way into the formation of this common European heritage prior to these States' actual accession, since once accession is completed heritage conservation measures will be reserved to the internal domain of States. One can speculate, then, as to the selection process for the funded projects. Namely, whether the initiatives supported by the EU in the Ljubljana Process are only the ones reflecting the 'European elements of identity' the EU prefers.

In terms of cultural heritage programmes, the objective to be achieved is to enhance 'the appropriation of cultural heritage by people themselves and therefore [. . .] education and access to knowledge of cultural heritage'.[105] In this sense, there is not much difference from the heritage conservation objectives pursued until this point, except that now there is a clearer concern with the implementation of international instruments and enactment of national legislation for the protection and safeguarding of cultural heritage More specifically, the idea is to frame legislation for the creation of inventories of heritage, including background norms about urban land registers, copyright, and tax incentives. It also includes the comparison of legislation across EU Member States and Mediterranean countries, and 'integration and coherence with international rules concerning the illicit trafficking of cultural objects'.[106]

These initiatives generally translate into 'development aid', targeted at heritage conservation projects. This can be an important tool, but development aid in

[103] European Communities, *Strategy for the Development of Euro-Mediterranean Cultural Heritage*, 9 10.

[104] The Press and Communication Department of the European Commission, *Figel' launches landmark process for cultural heritage in the Western Balkans*, available at <http://europa.eu/rapid/pressReleasesAction.do?reference=IP/08/737&format=HTML&aged=0&language=EN> (accessed 29 November 2012).

[105] European Communities, *Strategy for the Development of Euro-Mediterranean Cultural Heritage*, 10.

[106] European Communities, *Strategy for the Development of Euro-Mediterranean Cultural Heritage*, 16.

general has been criticized as being incapable of actually accomplishing its objectives.[107] One of the great challenges of aid resources is their fungibility, or the idea that development aid monies are (1) used in other activities that bear some connection to the goals for which aid was granted, but that ultimately have very little impact on the promotion of those goals; (2) are used in activities that are not really connected to the goals of aid funds; or (3) are simply deviated or lost (corruption being reported a specific problem here).[108] Especially when dealing with 'non-priority' areas such as cultural heritage protection, the risks that development aid never accomplishes its goals are higher. This has been countered by monitoring mechanisms and indicators,[109] and also by the idea that local actors should be actively involved (and determinantly so) in the way aid resources should be used. In the field of aid for intangible heritage safeguarding, this goes hand in hand with the idea of promoting more community participation.

At the policy level not many changes are to be expected, except for a greater openness towards legal regulation. This means that new avenues for protection will be opened for the creation of a specific cultural heritage-oriented legal framework. While this is a welcome development, it is unclear whether this is applicable only to EU external relations in the field of heritage preservation, or if it also extends to the internal market. Having this in mind, I will in the following part analyse possibilities for legal protection within the internal market.

3.2.1.2 Avenues for legal protection

The EC has previously attempted to protect cultural heritage through its own legislation. The most remarkable examples of this are the Directive and the Regulation for the protection and return of cultural objects.[110] While these two pieces of legislation were important attempts to curb the illegal trafficking of relevant pieces of cultural heritage, even early commentators foresaw their ineffectiveness.[111]

[107] See for instance William Easterly, *The White Man's Burden: Why the West's Efforts to Aid the Rest Have Done so Much Ill and so Little Good* (Penguin Press, 2006).

[108] On fungibility of development aid, see Dominique van de Walle and Dorothyjean Cratty, 'Do Donors Get What They Paid For? Micro Evidence on the Fungibility of Development Project Aid', *World Bank Policy Research Working Paper 3542* (2005).

[109] The World Bank's DIME (Development IMpact Evaluation) Initiative is very important in this sense, even if it only applies to projects funded directly by the World Bank. See World Bank, *Development Impact Evaluation Initiative*, available at <http://web.worldbank.org/WBSITE/EXTERNAL/EXTDEC/EXTDEVIMPEVAINI/0,,menuPK:3998281~pagePK:64168427~piPK:64168435~theSitePK:3998212,00.html> (accessed 29 November 2012).

[110] Council Directive 93/7/EEC of 15 March 1993 on the Return of Cultural Objects Unlawfully removed from the Territory of a Member State; and Council Regulation (EEC) 3911/92 on the Export of Cultural Goods.

[111] See eg Victoria J Vitrano, 'Protecting Cultural Objects in an Internal Border-Free EC: The EC Directive and Regulation for the Protection and Return of Cultural Objects', *Fordham Intl LJ* 17 (1994), 1164 201 (arguing that the reason why these texts would not become effective as they indeed have not laid on the fact that they failed to conciliate differences in the laws of Member States with respect to the acquisition of property); and Andrea Biondi, 'The Merchant, the Thief and the Citizen: The Circulation of Works of Art within the European Union', *CML Rev* 34 (1997), 1173 95 at 1182 93 (arguing that this legislation promoted only 'minimal harmonization' of Member States' laws).

In this part, I will focus mainly on the protection of intangible heritage through IP mechanisms within the framework of EU legislation, even though I will also make reference to some other possible mechanisms. For the purposes of this discussion, I overlook the objections raised against the use of IP mechanisms for protecting intangible heritage,[112] and start from the premise that these tools can be effectively used.[113] An in-depth discussion of the potential and pitfalls of IP law is the subject of Chapter 6.

3.2.1.2.1 The state of play prior to the Lisbon Treaty

Legislation not specific to cultural heritage protection can arguably be used in the protection of aspects of cultural heritage. Specifically in the context of cultural landscapes as a form of intangible heritage, EU legislation in the areas of environmental protection and agriculture could arguably be used as a means to safeguard cultural landscapes.[114] To the extent that the UNESCO Convention includes in its definition the 'cultural spaces' associated with intangible heritage, EU legislation that can protect such spaces, be it agricultural or environmental, offers an important avenue for legal action.

Turning specifically to protection through IP tools, the EC Treaty had no specific provision granting competence to Community Institutions to enact legislation on IP. Instead, legislation was often based on Articles 47(2),[115] 55,[116] and 95[117] of the EC Treaty. Reading these articles together creates the impression that

[112] One of the key objections against the use of IP, namely, that sometimes custodial communities (that is, communities who are holders of intangible heritage) do not recognize the concept of property, is not applicable. This is so because even the indigenous peoples present in the European continent recognize property as a concept, and thus such objection cannot be convincingly raised in this context. As to the other objections, concerning the requirements of identifiable authorship and the existence of a term of protection, I will mostly overlook them for the purposes of this chapter. For the objections against the use of IP in the protection of intangible heritage, see Christine Haight Farley, 'Protecting Folklore of Indigenous Peoples: Is Intellectual Property the Answer?', *Conn L Rev* 30 (1997), 1 57; WIPO, *Consolidated Legal Analysis of the Legal Protection of Traditional Cultural Expressions (2003),* Doc. symbol WIPO/GRTKF/IC/5/3, Annex, at 34 et seq; and Paul Kuruk, 'Protecting Folklore under Modern Intellectual Property Regimes: A Reappraisal of the Tensions between Individual and Communal Rights in Africa and the United States', *Am UL Rev* 48 (1999), 769 849, among many others.

[113] For a collection of successful examples of application of IP to the protection of intangible heritage, see Terri Janke, *Minding Culture: Case Studies on Intellectual Property and Traditional Cultural Expressions* (Geneva, 2003).

[114] François Lafarge, 'Landscapes in International Law and European Law', in Monica Sassatelli (ed), *Landscape as Heritage: Negotiating European Cultural Identity* (EUI Working Papers RSCAS No 2006/03), 37 44 at 37 8.

[115] '**Article** 47. [. . .] 2. For the same purpose [of making it easier for persons to take up and pursue activities as self-employed persons], the Council shall, acting in accordance with the procedure referred to in Article 251, issue directives for the coordination of the provisions laid down by law, regulation or administrative action in Member States concerning the taking-up and pursuit of activities as self-employed persons. The Council, acting unanimously throughout the procedure referred to in Article 251, shall decide on directives the implementation of which involves in at least one Member State amendment of the existing principles laid down by law governing the professions with respect to training and conditions of access for natural persons. In other cases the Council shall act by qualified majority. [. . .]'

[116] '**Article** 55. The provisions of Articles 45 to 48 shall apply to the matters covered by this Chapter [on services].'

[117] This provision is on the harmonization of laws necessary for the functioning of the internal market. Due to its length, it will not be reproduced here.

the Community understands IP as including industries and services that create employment opportunities within Member States. Because they are perceived as critical to the functioning of the internal market, harmonization of IP laws is within the purview of the Community. Article 95 provides the legal basis for harmonization on the grounds that this would prevent the future emergence of obstacles to the realization of the common market.[118]

If the aim was not only harmonization, but also included the creation of new rights within the EC related to IP, the threshold was even higher. For the creation of new rights superimposing those of the Member States, the basis for legislative action was not Article 95, but rather Article 308, which requires unanimity within the Council, as opposed to the majority required by Article 95.[119]

This basis has been pursued in several pieces of legislation dealing with specific topics that have created a certain *acquis communautaire* in terms of IP (and more specifically copyright).[120] This is a welcome development as to enable the EC to enact legislation in IP shifts the basic territorial unity for the purposes of IP from each individual Member State to the Community itself.[121]

This shift is necessary to avoid conflicts between the fundamental economic freedoms upon which the Community is based and national IP laws, which often create exceptions to these rules. If exceptions are to be created, it is best that they are created at the Community level, so that clashes can be minimized or even conciliated.[122]

The current legislation, however, relates only to specific topics of IP law, often connected with technological advances and the information society, and does not necessarily offer harmonized laws that can protect relevant aspects of intangible heritage,[123] because to do so would imply dealing with the limitations of IP law to protect intangible heritage. To create specific rights related to intangible heritage would require an articulation of the limits of existing categories of IP, and thus probably trespass into the cultural field that is excluded from Union competence.

[118] Case C-350/92, *Spain v Council* [1995] ECR I-1985 at [35], among others. See also Guy Tritton, et al, *Intellectual Property in Europe* (Sweet & Maxwell, 2002), 29.

[119] Tritton et al, *Intellectual Property in Europe*, 31.

[120] Commission of the European Communities, *Commission Staff Working Paper on the Review of the EC Legal Framework in the Field of Copyright and Related Rights, 19 July 2004* (SEC (2004) 995).

[121] Paul Craig and Gráinne de Búrca, *EU Law* (Oxford University Press, 2003), 1119.

[122] In the specific context of harmonization of copyright law, see Bryan Harris, *Intellectual Property Law in the European Union* (William S Hein & Co, 2005), 72.

[123] See eg Directive 2001/29/EC of the European Parliament and of the Council of 22 May 2001 on the harmonization of certain aspects of copyright and related rights in the information society, Official Journal L 167, 22/06/2001 P 0010 0019; Directive 2006/115/EC of the European Parliament and of the Council of 12 December 2006 on rental right and lending right and on certain rights related to copyright in the field of intellectual property (codified version), Official Journal L 376, 27/12/2006 P 0028 0035; Council Directive 93/83/EEC of 27 September 1993 on the coordination of certain rules concerning copyright and rights related to copyright applicable to satellite broadcasting and cable retransmission, Official Journal L 248, 06/10/1993 P 0015 0021; Directive 96/9/EC of the European Parliament and of the Council of 11 March 1996 on the legal protection of databases, Official Journal L 077, 27/03/1996 P 0020 0028; and Directive 2001/84/EC of the European Parliament and of the Council of 27 September 2001 on the resale right for the benefit of the author of an original work of art, Official Journal L 272 13/10/2001 P 0032 0036.

This offers a rather gloomy scenario for those interested in protecting heritage through harmonized legislation.

3.2.1.2.2 Post-Lisbon effects

While the EC Treaty did not offer a clear legislative basis for the harmonization of IP legislation, the Lisbon Treaty introduced a totally new provision expressly delegating this task to the Parliament and the Council.[124] This seems to give the Union Institutions a carte blanche to pursue the harmonization of IP law. Under the EC Treaty, legislation had to be justified on a rather narrow basis for competence; now, only the functioning of the internal market has to be positively affected by the legislation for the Union to be competent. Further, previously legislative harmonization could not usually go beyond the harmonization of laws (unless unanimity could be reached in the Council); now, all it takes is that the ordinary procedure is followed for there to be harmonized legislation and the creation of centralized Union bodies to oversee IP.

Before going on to outline what I think should be some factors to be taken into account when designing Union legislation for the protection of intangible heritage through IP, it is necessary to provide reasons why this enterprise should be advanced in the first place. If Article 167 of the consolidated Treaty on the Functioning of the European Union (former Article 151 of the EC Treaty) expressly precludes the harmonization of legislation on the cultural field, one cannot argue for the harmonization of legislation protecting cultural heritage on the grounds of its cultural value; instead, one has to argue the importance of protecting cultural heritage within the legitimate legislative bases provided by the Treaty for harmonization in other areas.

Going back to the example of landscape protection mentioned above, one has to insert isolated clauses in environmental or agricultural legislative texts to regulate cultural landscapes, or expect to justify landscape protection totally on the grounds of its benefit for the environment and/or agriculture. For example, to prevent the construction of a power plant in a certain place because of the environmental harm it would cause indirectly protects the landscape of the area; however, it is a totally different thing to say that the plant should not be installed primarily because it would affect the landscape.

It is arguably possible to pursue this latter scenario. However, the fact that the Treaty lacks a specific provision on harmonization of cultural regulation (and indeed, actually expressly precludes it), is a great obstacle to overcome. Further, it

[124] '**Article 118.** In the context of the establishment and functioning of the internal market, the European Parliament and the Council, acting in accordance with the ordinary legislative procedure, shall establish measures for the creation of European intellectual property rights to provide uniform protection of intellectual property rights throughout the Union and for the setting up of centralised Union-wide authorisation, coordination and supervision arrangements. The Council, acting in accordance with a special legislative procedure, shall by means of regulations establish language arrangements for the European intellectual property rights. The Council shall act unanimously after consulting the European Parliament.'

makes one wonder whether there should be any legislation at all dealing with ICH directly, rather than having only indirect effects on it.

It is not necessary, though, to justify legislation on the grounds of its effects upon cultural heritage. Legislation can be justified for its effects on agriculture or the environment and still validly protect a cultural landscape. Conversely, IP legislation protecting intangible heritage does not need to (and it cannot) be justified on the basis of the importance of cultural heritage; rather, it has to be justified on the basis of the protection of the internal market, and the impact that trade in heritage would have on the functioning of the EU internal market.

As there are, however, specificities when it comes to the protection of cultural heritage through IP (in the sense that IP mechanisms have to be adapted to certain special features of intangible heritage), one cannot hope that general IP legislation will successfully address all the concerns related to protecting folklore. Rather, it is necessary to argue that intangible heritage must be directly protected through IP legislation for there would otherwise be harm to the internal market. The same could also arguably apply to landscape protection through environmental and agricultural legislation, but I will focus my discussion on IP.

The justification for protecting cultural heritage through IP is self-evident, once one connects intangible heritage and IP. Intangible heritage can be successfully protected by IP mechanisms because they empower the holders or creators of heritage to be able to control their tradition or creation and prevent it from being misused or even misappropriated by third parties, even if it can only protect specific forms of expression (a more detailed discussion is in Chapter 6).[125] By contrast, IP regulation within the EU is necessary to avoid Member States using their own national rules to distort the economic freedoms upon which the Union is based (and also, on the external dimension, to provide a counterweight to the WTO and other US-dominated fora). Since the importance of regulating IP under the EU (at least in the Lisbon Treaty) is considered a given, and IP is important for protecting intangible heritage, IP legislation can be enacted within the EU for the regulation of this type of heritage.

The lack of clear rules can lead to undesired results. If one Member State protects intangible heritage through its IP laws, and another lacks any form of protection, the freedom of circulation of goods within the Union will mean that legal protection restricted to the boundaries of a Member State will not be sufficient, precisely because to a large extent these boundaries can no longer be considered to be there.

[125] One example of this is what has become known as the '*Carpets Case*' (*M*(deceased) v Indofurn*). In the case, a group of well-known Aboriginal artists, among them Banduk Marika, produced several sacred paintings and exhibited them at the National Australian Gallery. A carpet factory located in Vietnam that produced carpets to an Australia company called Indofurn, copied one of these paintings from the exhibition catalogue, called 'Djanda and the Sacred Waterhole', painted by Ms Marika. This painting represents the origin of the world to her tribe, the Rirratingu clan, of which she was a traditional custodian responsible for the dreaming story. The reproduction of the painting could imply her losing her religious rights, and have severe penalties imposed. Despite the fact that the reproduction of her art would be walked on is totally opposed to the cultural use of the central imagery and underlying knowledge in her work. Indofurn was ordered to pay damages and compensation, as well as remove all carpets from commercialization. For further details, see Janke, *Minding Culture*, 8.

Hypothetically, then, if crafts produced by a Sami group in Finland are protected by Finnish copyright law, but then sold in Germany where ICH products are deemed to be uncopyrightable and in the public domain (and thus not much protection is given) then reproduced and the copies sold back to Finland for a lower price, this distorts the internal market and provides a ground for regulation based on price differentials, which is traditionally the grounds upon which the ECJ has dealt with IP matters under the exhaustion of rights doctrine.[126] Thus, because IP can protect certain products of manifestations of intangible heritage (for otherwise there would be the possibility of market distortion), the EU can enact IP legislation specifically aimed at protecting intangible heritage.

This legal avenue, of course, implies disregarding the argument that items of intangible heritage are *res extra commercium* in that some of them reflect religious practices or are produced with an exclusively religious purpose.[127] In the specific context of the EU Member States, I think it is safe to assume that, for the purposes of legal protection, all items of intangible heritage can be considered to be marketable goods.

Another possible argument would be to reshape the underlying logic for regulating IP within the Union in order to protect cultural heritage: IP will not be regulated only because otherwise consumers would be harmed, and competition distorted;[128] instead, IP has to be regulated to protect the interests of the holders of intangible heritage. To protect the interests of holders of cultural heritage creates a better functioning market, especially if one considers that, given the incorporation of the EU Charter of Fundamental Rights into the EU Treaties, the protection of individual interests is a *conditio sine qua non* for the correct functioning of the market. Thus, one has to look at the basis for enacting IP legislation not only in light of the market effects, but also in terms of the individual interests at stake. I do recognize this is a stretch of the current views concerning IP in the EU, but at the same time I suggest this is an argument worth considering in light of some of the new fundamental changes introduced by the Lisbon Treaty (even though any attempt at 'constitutionalizing' the EU has been skilfully avoided in the text of the Lisbon Treaty).

Once a possible basis for regulating intangible heritage through IP has been provided, it is important to offer some general guidelines as to what would be desirable regulation of certain IP features, in attendance to certain specificities of intangible heritage. First of all, one has to bear in mind the possibility of authorship even of copyrightable material by abstract collectivities, since more often than not it is not possible to attribute authorship to a single member of a custodial community. The matter is further complicated here if one factors in the distinction between the protection of works and neighbouring rights, such as performance rights.

[126] For a collection of the case-law, see Craig and de Búrca, *EU Law*, 1088 103.

[127] See, for further comments, Agnes Lucas-Schloetter, 'Folklore', in Silke von Lewinski (ed), *Indigenous Heritage and Intellectual Property* (Kluwer Law International, 2003), 259 340 at 312 14.

[128] Craig and de Búrca, *EU Law*, 1088.

Also, and still in the domain of copyright, one has to examine the possibility of regulating moral rights,[129] even though this has been deemed unnecessary in the past by the Commission.[130] Using moral rights has the particular advantage that some of these rights do not extinguish over time, such as the right of attribution. However, not only are moral rights less strong in countries in the 'copyright' system than they are in those countries which adopt the '*droit d'auteur*' system,[131] but they also require an identified or identifiable author, not compatible to the notion of intangible heritage.

Therefore, it is important that EU harmonized rules on intangible heritage and IP (particularly copyright) have differentiated requirements of authorship, and give special consideration to moral rights. Moral rights should be given emphasis because these can be effectively used to protect the integrity of the work, which is the most important concern when it comes to intangible heritage.

But IP protection is not the only 'market-based mechanism' available to regional economic integration processes. The next section will look at the Andean Community and its option for *sui generis* regimes.

3.2.2 Andean Community of Nations

The Andean Community of Nations was created in 1969 and congregates nations from the North-Western part of South America (Bolivia, Colombia, Ecuador, and Peru)[132] around several factors of cohesion, including their shared cultural heritage, material and intangible.[133] In many ways, it resembles the EU in its structure and competences, as the organization is clearly empowered with elements of supra-nationality, distinguishing it from other regional trade areas in the world, which are still inter-governmental and depend on the Member States for decision-making in most areas.

More importantly for our purposes here, the Andean Region is home to vast indigenous populations, which in some of the countries of the Community actually make up for the majority of the population. There is evidently a great concern with

[129] See eg Kuruk, 'Protecting Folklore under Modern Intellectual Property Regimes', 829 30; Silke von Lewinski, 'The Protection of Folklore', *Cardozo J Intl & Comp L* 11 (2003), 747 68 at 759; and Farley, 'Protecting Folklore of Indigenous Peoples', 47 8. See also Chapter 6.

[130] Commission of the European Communities, *Commission Staff Working Paper*.

[131] The 'copyright' system is present in common law countries, in which the main purpose of copyright is remuneration for the labour of the author, that is, there is a principal concern on the economic aspects of intellectual property. On the other hand, the '*droit d'auteur*' system is typical of civil law countries, where the main objective of legal protection to authors is the protection of their honor and incentive to their creativity. Even though the standards and degree of protection of moral rights differ slightly in these two groups of countries, protection is granted at a similar level. For the argument that moral rights are universally protected at a minimum standard, see Lucas Lixinski, 'O Direito Moral de Autor como Direito de Personalidade e a Universlidade de sua Proteção', *Revista Trimestral de Direito Civil* 27 (2006), 49 79.

[132] Venezuela became a Member State in 1973, but it decided to leave the Andean Community in 2006 and join MERCOSUR instead. Chile, an original Member State, left the Andean Community in 1976.

[133] Andina Comunidad *¿Quienes Somos?*, available at <http://www.comunidadandina.org/quienes.htm> (accessed 29 November 2012).

the preservation of cultural distinctiveness in the region.[134] This is coupled with yet another important feature of the region, it being the home to a great percentage of the world's biodiversity.[135] These factors decisively shape the attitude of the Andean Community towards cultural heritage generally, and intangible heritage in particular.

3.2.2.1 Biodiversity, indigeneity, traditional knowledge, and intangible heritage

The link between traditional knowledge (TK) and ICH is a constant in the activities of the Andean Community regarding heritage protection. As a matter of fact, it is possible to say that the real concern of the Andean Community is TK protection, and that intangible heritage is protected only to the extent that the two notions converge, even if only accidentally.

The Andean Community regards TK as an indissoluble part of culture, and of strategic value for the development of indigenous peoples, and the development of the Andean Countries.[136] The Andean Community groups together biodiversity, what it calls 'cultural aspects' and intangible heritage (referred to as 'folklore' by the Andean Community).[137]

Indigenous TK is characterized as the intangible elements that constitute collective intellectual patrimony of indigenous peoples and form part of the fundamental rights of indigenous peoples, particularly those types of knowledge associated with uses of biodiversity (pharmaceuticals come to mind).[138] The purpose of protecting traditional and indigenous knowledge is to enhance the uses of TK for the benefit of indigenous peoples.[139] More specifically, there are several reasons why TK should be protected. Among the general reasons are: the protection of human rights; the intrinsic value of TK, which is connected to cultural identity; equity, and a defence against misappropriation that uses IP rights.[140] Specific reasons are connected to indigenous views of the relationship between human beings and nature, also known as the *cosmovisión*.[141]

[134] Some of these examples will be further explored in Chapter 4, dealing with national experiences.

[135] Estimates range between 30% and 50%. See Comunidad Andina de Naciones, *Elementos para la protección sui generis de los conocimientos tradicionales colectivos e integrales desde la perspectiva indígena* (2005), 18.

[136] Comunidad Andina de Naciones, *Elementos*, 3.

[137] Comunidad Andina de Naciones, *Elementos*, 7.

[138] Comunidad Andina de Naciones, *Elementos*, 11.

[139] Comunidad Andina de Naciones, *Elementos*, 12.

[140] Comunidad Andina de Naciones, *Elementos*, 14.

[141] On the *cosmovisión*, see Julio Valladolid, 'Sabiduría en la crianza de la chacra', in *Los Pueblos Indígenas y la Integración Andina Primer Foro de Intelectuales e Investigadores Indígenas* (2008), 61 5; Fernando Huanucurú, 'Cosmovisión sagrada de la vida', in *Los Pueblos Indígenas y la Integración Andina Primer Foro de Intelectuales e Investigadores Indígenas* (2008), 66 8 (an Aymara Indian from Bolivia); and Róger Rumrrill, 'Cosmovisión amazónica', in *Los Pueblos Indígenas y la Integración Andina Primer Foro de Intelectuales e Investigadores Indígenas* (2008), 82 4. See also Comunidad Andina de Naciones, *Elementos*, 14 15.

Again, then, there is a close connection between heritage (both tangible[142] and intangible) and indigeneity in the Andean Community, similarly to the OAS. There is a close connection between indigenous peoples and their traditional sites, which are seen as 'ceremonial centers for the reproduction of cultural identity with a highly spiritual content'.[143]

This indigenous approach, and the fact that much of the intangible heritage to be protected within the bloc stems from biodiversity, has led the Andean Community to consistently consider using the framework of the Convention on Biological Diversity. It has also forced it to consider other prospects, such as traditional IP responses, particularly in light of international trade law. A key report has been produced by the Andean Community precisely trying to conciliate all these different approaches and offering some alternatives and elements for consideration in all different international fora.[144] In this way, the Andean Community has recognized the plurality of different responses to the matter, and has attempted to conciliate the values it aims at defending when speaking of TK and intangible heritage.

3.2.2.2 The option for sui generis *regimes*

Within the Andean Community, unlike the EU, it is not possible to successfully implement IP regimes, even if adapted, to many indigenous peoples, as there are many objections to the use of property as a legal category (not recognized as such by some communities). Therefore, the Andean Community defends the use of *sui generis* regimes, and the complementary use of IP when not in contravention to indigenous customary law.[145]

Decision 391 of the Andean Community (Common Regime on Access to Genetic Resources, July 1996) deals with some aspects of TK (and intangible heritage) protection. Even though not incorporated by all Member States (at the time of writing Peru is the only Member State to have incorporated it), it could be a useful framework for analysis, as it establishes the basis upon which TK may be protected within the Andean Community. However, this rule falls short of creating a comprehensive regime, only determining that in the future such a special regime or rule allowing for the harmonization of national laws on the matter should be enacted.[146]

142 'Comunicado sobre la Protección y Recuperación de Bienes del Patrimonio Cultural de los Países Miembros de la Comunidad Andina', in *Los Pueblos Indígenas y la Integración Andina Primer Foro de Intelectuales e Investigadores Indígenas* (2008), 96.

143 Comunidad Andina de Naciones, *Elementos*, 8.

144 Comunidad Andina de Naciones, *Negociaciones sobre acceso a recursos genéticos y conocimientos tradicionales* (2003).

145 Comunidad Andina de Naciones, *Elementos*, 8. See also Fabián Novak, 'Biotechnology and Regional Integration Systems: Legislation and Practices in the Andean Community Countries', in Francesco Francioni and Tullio Scovazzi (eds), *Biotechnology and International Law* (Hart Publishing, 2006), 403 38.

146 Comunidad Andina de Naciones, *Elementos*, 12.

A subsequent Decision, on the regional strategy for biodiversity protection (Decision 523, July 2002) lays down more specific rules. It highlights the importance of collective property rights, prior informed consent and benefit sharing when it comes to exploitation of TK and biodiversity resources.[147] In this sense, then, it is a much more relevant rule, and, more importantly, it adopts essentially the same regime as that proposed by the Convention on Biological Diversity (examined in Chapter 2).

Another decision, on a common regime of industrial property (Decision 486, 2000), states that industrial property protection shall safeguard and respect biodiversity and genetic resources, as well as TK of indigenous and local communities, as well as communities of African ancestry. It subjects the granting of patents to compliance with norms regulating specifically these collective rights of communities over their TK.[148]

One of the reasons for preferring the distinctiveness of *sui generis* regimes over IP is that indigenous peoples are against the use of IP because of its market orientation, and that it creates monopolies, while indigenous knowledge is perceived as a commonly shared resource by indigenous populations, who are more often than not, happy to share their knowledge as long as they receive some form of recognition.[149]

There are essentially four strategies defended by the Andean Community when it comes to the protection of TK and intangible heritage. One is the adoption of 100 per cent *sui generis* regimes; another one is the predominant use of *sui generis* regimes, but having IP tools as a fall-back mechanism (in requiring patentees to disclose the use of TK and voiding patent grants that fail to disclose, in which case heritage trumps over IP); the third one is leaving the matter up to national legislations; and, finally, the use of indigenous customary law, which seems to be the preferred alternative by indigenous peoples in the region.[150]

The goals of TK protection are essentially to promote cultural identity and the indigenous *cosmovisión*, as well as to increase the use of TK within communities themselves, as a means to entrench traditional culture and keep it alive. Further, one of the goals is to avoid patents being granted to third parties who misappropriate TK from communities. The principles that should guide the promotion of these goals are related to the promotion of cultural identity and interculturality, as well as the promotion of self-determination of indigenous peoples and the inalienability of intangible knowledge.

All in all, then, the main thrust of the Andean Community action is aimed at protecting biodiversity resources and the TK of indigenous communities associated with it. There is a considerable conceptual overlap between 'ICH' and 'TK', and it may even be said that TK is a specialized type of intangible heritage.[151] However,

[147] Comunidad Andina de Naciones, *Elementos*, 12.
[148] Comunidad Andina de Naciones, *Elementos*, 12 13.
[149] Comunidad Andina de Naciones, *Elementos*, 22.
[150] Comunidad Andina de Naciones, *Elementos*, 23 5.
[151] Comunidad Andina de Naciones, *Elementos*, 15.

the way in which protection is framed suggests that the regime for protecting intangible heritage is the one of biodiversity protection, and not the one of the 2003 UNESCO Convention. The Andean Community itself is concerned with the fact that different elements of traditional culture should require different tools for protection, thus opening the way for a different regulation of TK and more 'general' or 'artistic' manifestations of intangible heritage, such as cultural spaces, crafts, and artistic and literary creations.[152]

Because of this emphasis, then, any protection granted to other aspects of intangible heritage, such as crafts, performing arts, and music are only incidental to the protection granted to biodiversity resources. This 'specialization' within the Andean Community is understandable once one considers the reality of the region, which has overwhelming biodiversity and was presented with the CBD regime a decade before the specific international ICH regime was designed, meaning that they are already familiar with the taxonomy of the CBD and its mechanisms, have for the most part already transposed them into national legislation, and thus prefer them.

Further, the type of protection granted within the Andean Community seems to be solely in response to the market, or to the extent to which biodiversity can contribute to development.[153] While this is a realistic account in many ways, and falls well into the mandate of an economic integration organization, it may fail to capture more nuanced concerns over religious feelings and cultural harm by adopting this logic of protection that aims at development through the sharing of genetic resources. Free, prior, and informed consent to exploitation of TK by third parties may help prevent much harm, but perhaps an organization established with essentially economic goals is not the best venue to address the issue. Nevertheless, one must bear in mind that economic organizations do bring important considerations to the table, and must be seen as important allies in protecting intangible heritage.

Regionalism then widens the number of tools available to protect ICH, and makes it clear how the choice of tools is determined by the goals to be advanced in protecting intangible heritage and, perhaps most evidently, by the constitutional constraints of each regional organization. Protection through rights becomes evident in the work of the OAS and the Council of Europe, where also the notion of development (beyond trade) comes to the fore. Economic integration organizations focus instead on the impact of heritage on trade, or on the idea of heritage as a tradeable commodity, at least internally; externally, the EU reverts back to the fostering of a shared identity, which is a means to advance the goals of integration and constitutionalization of the Union. And the fostering of a common regional identity is a running thread throughout all these regional organizations, but it becomes particularly evident in the African Union context, where identity is seen as

[152] Comunidad Andina de Naciones, *Elementos*, 33.

[153] Comunidad Andina de Naciones, *Biocomercio en la subregión andina Oportunidades para el desarrollo* (2005) (exploring a series of developmental projects using biodiversity and genetic resources as tools to promote development in the region).

a means to move away from colonialism and generate stability in the continent, not only as a means to promote trade relations.

But these are only some of the goals and means through which to safeguard intangible heritage. The plurality of initiatives and goals grows exponentially at the national level. It is to the analysis of some of these possibilities that I move in the next chapter.

4

National Responses

While there are multiple international and regional ways of addressing the legal safeguarding of intangible heritage, the national responses also present a plethora of options. This chapter aims to analyse some of these responses, and the ways in which future action on intangible heritage protection can benefit from the examples set by other countries.

The idea that intangible heritage serves many different purposes, and that the purpose the law-maker has in mind directly affects the drafting of the legislation and the tools adopted still holds true when it comes to national responses. But, differently from international and regional organizations, where law-making in the specific field of (intangible) heritage is constrained by the constitutive instruments of the organizations, meaning that heritage goals need to be translated into the overall objectives of the organization, national frameworks are free to choose the goal they wish to advance through heritage legislation, seen as constitutions are (generally) much broader and cover the entirety of legal goods that can be protected or promoted through specific legislation. And at the same time there is an almost ubiquitous concern with the protection of identity within national responses, which is even stronger than the one experienced in other levels and fora (particularly trade-oriented fora such as the WTO and economic integration processes).

It is difficult to say that there is a country offering no protection at all to intangible heritage, even if there is no specific instrument on the matter. The very idea that all cultural heritage is ultimately intangible (discussed in Chapter 1) means that all legislation protecting heritage to a certain extent also protects intangible heritage. But that would be too much of a stretch for the present purposes. What I mean by saying that all countries protect intangible heritage in some way is that even instruments not designed specifically for the protection of intangible cultural heritage (ICH) can be used to protect this form of heritage by means of interpretation. This type of protection can be accomplished by interpreting instruments designed to protect other forms of cultural heritage, or even general instruments on indigenous or aboriginal rights.[1]

[1] Evidence of this fact is that UNESCO has catalogued 234 legislative texts under the heading of 'intangible cultural heritage' in its database of cultural heritage legislation. Few of these texts aim directly at protecting intangible heritage, but many of them are indirectly applicable, such as legislation regulating the profession of craftsman, or creating national cultural holidays, or even cinema protection legislation. See UNESCO, *Database of National Cultural Heritage Laws*, available at <http://portal.unesco.org/culture/en/ev.php-URL ID=33928&URL DO=DO TOPIC&URL SECTION=201.html> (accessed 29 November 2012).

The national responses analysed in this part are derived primarily from secondary literature and case studies written by others. I chose this approach because it gave me the opportunity to look into a larger number of countries. Some countries will be analysed in detail while brief references will be made to other national experiences as a means of reinforcing assertions regarding the more extensive analyses (and as an aid in stitching together this rich quilt of national solutions).

The national responses I will look at can be categorized according to the type of solution they offer. I will first look at constitutional responses to ICH protection, looking specifically at the relationship between multicultural constitutionalism and the protection of intangible heritage. I will then look at some countries which focus on intellectual property, and next countries which have developed *sui generis* regimes. The next step will be to look at countries which have given priority to policy-level or 'non-legal' systems of protection, largely emulating the UNESCO system. Finally, I will look at countries which offer a plural approach, either by mixing several types of solutions, or simply by relying on fragmented and creative uses of instruments aimed at the protection of other forms of cultural heritage or of indigenous rights generally. The choice of countries for the latter category was somewhat arbitrary, and guided by accounts available in secondary literature. Nevertheless, they all converge in that these countries have not chosen a single or principal means of legally safeguarding ICH.

4.1 Constitutional Responses

Constitutional responses to cultural heritage protection can occur on several different levels. At one end of the spectrum, there is the example of the United States. The United States constitutionally protects cultural heritage indirectly via several underlying constitutional principles.[2] This leads to a situation in which ICH-related interests related to indigenous grave repatriations, for instance, end up being litigated as freedom of religion or equal protection clause cases.[3]

At the other end of the spectrum, there are countries' constitutions that explicitly mention intangible heritage and these are generally more recent texts. In between there are countries that mention the protection of culture, or even the protection of heritage (without specifying intangible heritage), as duties of the State or individual or group entitlements in their foundational texts.

Far from being an attempt at exhaustively analysing constitutional references to cultural heritage, this section aims to look at a few frameworks developed in constitutionalism that can be of use. The emphasis of this section will be on the

[2] James AR Nafziger, 'The Underlying Constitutionalism of the Law Governing Anchaeological and Other Cultural Heritage', *Willamette L Rev* 30 (1994), 581 608 at 590 6 (mentioning the principles of federalism and libertarianism, judicial review, inherent powers over foreign affairs, and constitutional inferences to the treatment of Indians as constitutional foundations for cultural heritage law in the United States).

[3] Nafziger, 'The Underlying Constitutionalism', 598 600.

relationship between constitutional law, the protection of multicultural societies, and ICH as a staple of multiculturalism.

4.1.1 Multicultural and intercultural constitutions and the protection of heritage

'Cultural diversity', 'multiculturalism', and 'interculturalism'[4] have become some of the most appealing mottos of contemporary constitutionalism. As States increasingly realize that respect for cultural diversity does not run counter to national unity, and if anything actually reinforces it,[5] strategies have been developed in modern constitutions to protect and safeguard cultural distinctiveness, opening the way for the legal recognition of the multicultural character of modern national societies.

The recognition of interculturalism and multiculturalism at the Constitutional level can take many forms, which will vary according to each country's ethnic composition and political organization.[6] Civil society inevitably plays a large role in bringing the debate to popular fora, as it is commonly the case that countries which do not recognize interculturalism or multiculturalism are dominated by one particular cultural group, and thus blind to the needs of recognizing 'otherness',[7] or, in a more Machiavellian version, simply unwilling to share power with other groups who are likely to alter the comfortable status quo in which these elites find themselves.

Will Kymlicka discusses the foundations of what he characterizes as 'liberal multiculturalism', and argues that, while there are common demands by indigenous groups and other minorities (referred to as 'substate/national minorities'), there are also differences in the types of claims advanced. The common principles are the repudiation of the notion of the State being in possession of a single national group; the repudiation of assimilationist policies for the sake of nation-building policies; and the acknowledgment of historic injustice.[8] However, when comparing the policies adopted in response to these two different 'varieties' of multiculturalism, as he presents them, there are some differences, most notably connected with land

[4] 'Interculturalism' here refers to a step beyond 'multiculturalism', in that it moves beyond the State aspirations to multicultural ideals into their actual implementation as a factual matter (which is what receives the label of 'interculturalism'). The rhetoric of interculturalism has been adopted by some recent Constitutions, most notably the 2009 Bolivian Constitution. See Will Kymlicka, 'Multicultural States and Intercultural Citizens', *Theory and Research in Education* 1(2) (2003), 147 69.

[5] United Nations Development Programme (UNDP), *Human Development Report 2004 Cultural Liberty in Today's Diverse World*, 3 4.

[6] For a survey of European constitutional practice regarding minority protection, see Julie Ringelheim, 'Minority Protection and Constitutional Recognition of Difference: Reflections on the Diversity of European Approaches', in A. Verstichel, A. Alen, B. De Witte, and P. Lemmens (eds), *The Framework Convention for the Protection of National Minorities: A Useful Pan-European Instrument?* (Intersentia, 2008), 33 50.

[7] I borrow this expression, and its uses towards indigenous peoples, from Paul Keal, *European Conquest and the Rights of Indigenous Peoples The Moral Backwardness of International Society* (Cambridge University Press, 2003).

[8] Will Kymlicka, *Multicultural Odysseys* (2007), 65 6.

rights and customary law (for indigenous peoples) or recognition of international personality in some instances (for instance, to sit on international bodies) towards minorities.[9]

In any case, the heart of the matter is that constitutions increasingly recognize multiculturalism as an important part of the political struggle for social peace. As multiculturalism is recognized, multi-ethnic societies see the claims of oppressed minorities placated, and the road is paved for the construction of a 'new', 'brighter', future, or so goes the discourse, roughly. Intangible heritage then comes into play as an important means to show goodwill towards minorities: by protecting their culture, or what makes these groups distinct, the larger polity commits to gathering proof of this multiculturalism until recently ignored. To be recognized and taken as a 'legitimate' other, as opposed to a 'backwards', 'shameful' other, is what most of these minorities seem to want to achieve, at least as a first step.

The way to this level of commitment to minority culture recognition at the constitutional level has not been easy, however, and is still under construction as multi-ethnic countries draft new constitutions in response to the end of dictatorial periods, or simply to put down on paper a blueprint of social change. The evolution of Latin American Constitutionalism in terms of recognition of indigeneity and multiculturalism is remarkable in this sense, and the following subsection is devoted to it.

[9] Kymlicka, *Multicultural Odysseys*, 67 71. More specifically, the policies Kymlicka mentions for indigenous peoples are the following: (a) recognition of land rights or title; (b) recognition of rights to self-government; (c) the upholding of historic treaties and/or the signing of new treaties; (d) the recognition of cultural rights, involving language and traditional economic practices such as hunting and fishing; (e) recognition of customary law; (f) guarantees of representation or consultation in the central government; (g) constitutional or legislative affirmation of the distinctive status of indigenous peoples; (h) support for or ratification of international instruments on indigenous rights; and (i) affirmative action programmes for the members of indigenous communities. Kymlicka affirms that States that have adopted six or more of these policies can be considered to have 'decisively shifted towards a multicultural approach', while States that have adopted three to five of these policies have made modest but significant shifts, and States adopting less than three of these policies have barely shifted in the direction of multiculturalism. When it comes to substate minorities, the following factors are considered: (a) federal or quasi-federal territorial autonomy; (b) official language status, either in the region or nationally; (c) guarantees of representation in the central government or on constitutional courts; (d) public funding of minority language schools/universities/media; (e) constitutional or parliamentary affirmation of 'multinationalism'; and (f) the according of international personality for certain purposes, including for instance the right to sit on international bodies, or sign treaties, or have a separate Olympic Team. Even though the distinction between minorities and indigenous peoples seems intuitive, when one looks at the factors taken into consideration by Kymlicka when deciding whether a shift towards multiculturalism has taken place with regard to indigenous peoples or minorities, the distinction seems to blur in many aspects. For instance, the recognition of language rights, the affirmation of multiculturalism, and the rights to self-government are common to both sets of groups. As we will see in the recent examples of Bolivia and Ecuador, official language status has also become an indigenous claim, and this can be argued to further approximate the two categories. Further, the recognition of customary law may well fit into the concept of granting of federal or quasi-federal autonomy, as federalism implies the recognition of the capacity for instituting a relatively separate and autonomous legal order from that of the State, which is not unlike what recognizing customary indigenous law amounts to. Perhaps the core difference regarding this last feature is that the recognition of federal status applies territorially, whereas customary law applies according to personal status (that is, belonging to an indigenous group).

4.1.1.1 *Examples in Latin American constitutionalism*[10]

Latin America presents an ideal scenario for studying constitutional change with regard to multiculturalism. Home to a large percentage of the world's indigenous peoples, and overwhelmingly ruled by cultural, economic, and political elites of European descent, many countries in the continent have been faced with new social movements created to defend indigenous interests that have been neglected for many centuries by colonial powers and subsequent political elites, in the name of sheer ignorance, of maintenance of power, or of nation-building (which was seen as requiring a uniform, unified people at its foundation).

One of the reasons for the late development of the multicultural question in Latin-American Constitutionalism is the fact that most of the countries in the continent experienced military dictatorships between the 1960s and the 1980s (with the notable exception of Costa Rica, which had abolished its military in 1948 after a civil war, and was thus not 'victimized' by military governments). These military regimes, as a rule, advanced the idea of egalitarian societies, in which political divergence was to be quashed. As the advancement of indigenous causes involves political divergence, these movements have been largely ignored or even suppressed (the Guatemalan Civil War, where a majority of those killed or disappeared were indigenous people, many of whom were connected to indigenous causes, comes to mind as an example). The advancement of indigenous rights, therefore, was stalled on the continent for three decades, remaining stationary, or, as in the Guatemalan case, taking a step back. The Guatemalan Constitution of 1945 recognized the multicultural composition of the Guatemalan society, and took steps towards granting autonomy to indigenous peoples. This constitution was revoked after the military *coup d'état*, however, in favour of one promoting a uniform society.[11]

The constitutional regimes for minorities and indigenous peoples in Latin America tend to be one and the same in every country. A large part of the efforts towards the constitutional recognition of multiculturalism in Latin America seem to focus on indigenous peoples. The contribution of Latin American Constitutionalism to multiculturalism has been documented precisely through the constitutional strategies aimed at protecting indigenous peoples.[12] Even in those countries where there are large minorities, these are legally treated as indigenous peoples. Examples of this are the communities of African origin in Colombia (*afrocolombianos*), Ecuador (*afroecuatorianos*), Brazil (*quilombolas*), and Honduras (*garífunas*), to

[10] An earlier and longer version of this section has been published elsewhere. See Lucas Lixinski, 'Constitutionalism and the Other: Multiculturalism and Indigeneity in Selected Latin American Countries', *Anuario Iberoamericano de Justicia Constitucional* 14 (2010), 235 65.

[11] Ordóñez Cifuentes, José Emilio Rolando, 'Las Demandas Constitucionales en Guatemala y México', *Revista de Derechos Humanos* 1 (2003), 169 88 at 169 70.

[12] See for instance Donna Lee Van Cott, *The Friendly Liquidation of the Past: The Politics of Diversity in Latin America* (University of Pittsburgh Press, 2000) (reviewed by Carlson, Kirsten Matou, 'Notice: Premature Predictions of Multiculturalism?', *Mich L Rev* 100 (2002), 1470 87).

name a few.[13] They are usually given most of the same rights as indigenous peoples, and, even though they are not 'formally' indigenous, as they were not the original inhabitants of the land, they still share a past of European domination, as the European colonizers were the ones who forcibly brought them to the continent.

There are several different degrees of recognition given to indigenous peoples in Latin American Constitutions. Some constitutions, like Uruguay's, make no reference whatsoever to indigenous peoples. Other Constitutions attempt to promote assimilationist policies (fortunately, the number of such Constitutions is decreasing in the continent). Others (the majority) promote forms of protection of cultural distinctiveness, either by exclusion and isolation of indigenous communities from 'mainstream society', and others by incorporating them into mainstream society and granting them special political participation rights, or differing degrees of legal autonomy and self-governance.

Assimilationist policies have been promoted in all of Latin America during the period of colonial domination by Spain or Portugal. Assimilationism has continued to be the predominant strategy in several countries during the early stages of their independent constitutionalism. This has been facilitated by the omission of the early rulers of newly-independent Latin-American States. A crude version of this argument is simply that the elites that succeeded the Spanish and Portuguese authorities in Latin American countries did little to alter the *status quo*, as more often than not they were already the privileged social segments during colonial times. Bluntly put, these elites simply did not care about multiculturalism, and were blind to the existence of elements of cultural diversity. This explains the initial lack of constitutional recognition for cultural diversity.

In addition to the passive lack of interest in promoting ways of life other than those of the dominating elite, there was also the active concern with achieving cultural homogeneity and unity, seen as necessary to form a unified polity, which would support and justify the effort of nation-building. This has led to the promotion of several assimilationist policies, which were backed by solemn consti-

[13] Regarding Afro-Colombian, *quilombola* and Afro-Ecuadorian communities, the work undertaken by the Bernard and Audre Rapoport Center for Human Rights and Justice at the University of Texas School of Law is noteworthy. The reports produced by field missions undertaken by the Center in both countries are available at <http://www.utexas.edu/law/academics/centers/humanrights/publications/> (accessed 29 November 2012). A remarkable example of recognition of Afro-Descendant rights is the new Bolivian Constitution of January 2009. Its Article 32 states that: '**Article 32.** The Afro-Bolivian people enjoys, in all that it corresponds, the economic, social, political and cultural Rights recognized in the Constitution to the indigenous and original Peasant nations and peoples'. For a more detailed analysis of the new Bolivian Constitution and what it represents in terms of constitutional recognition of multiculturalism, see fnn 42 52 below and accompanying text. The 2008 Ecuadorian Constitution is also remarkable: '**Article 58.** In order to strengthen their identity, culture, traditions and rights, the collective rights of the afro-Ecuadorian people are recognized as established in the Constitution, the law and the pacts, covenants, declarations and other international human rights instruments'. In the specific Brazilian context, it can be argued that the equivalence in treatment is not total, as *quilombola* communities are not deemed to be completely dissociated from the rest of society, and its individual members are not subject to the system of tutelage of the federal government. Nevertheless, in many instances land claims are treated roughly in the same way, applying rules on indigenous demarcation of lands to *quilombola* communities by analogy.

tutional statements about the 'unity and indivisibility', as well as the 'equality' of the people of the nation, promoting an 'ethnically blind' constitutional structure.[14]

Mexico was one of the last countries to formally move away from assimilationism. There, assimilationism is attributable to the fact that indigenous individuals in Mexico have always been considered an integral part of the Mexican nation, within the tenet of equality before the law.[15] In nation-building, indigenous protection was simply wiped out. This represented a step back in Mexico and in most other Latin American countries who, in an effort to justify independent nationhood on the one hand and prevent excessive territorial fragmentation on the other, pursued the idea of single national identity, which required an absolute and formalistic understanding of equality as a constitutional value.

Reforms in the late 1990s, largely triggered by the Zapatista movement,[16] came alongside a long process of constitutional reforms in Mexico aimed at, among other objectives, promoting indigenous rights and preparing the Mexican legal system for the NAFTA.[17] Reforms were also undertaken in 2001, including provisions aimed at granting a certain degree of autonomy to indigenous peoples,[18] and in 2003, when Mexico adopted at the infra-constitutional level a General Law on Linguistic Rights of Indigenous Peoples, alongside a number of corresponding state-level laws.

Fortunately, the assimilationist model is no longer adopted by Latin American Constitutions, and all those that refer to indigenous peoples and indigeneity grant (or attempt to grant) some form of protection, either through actively recognizing

[14] 'Equality', incidentally, is the reason behind France's constitutional approach to cultural diversity, which essentially denies it. If the Republic is founded upon the tenets of liberty, equality, and fraternity, 'equality' necessarily implies that no one deserves special treatment, and that all are equal before the law. As French Enlightenment has had great influence on the revolutionary thinking that led to the movements of independence in several Latin American countries, and consequently also on early Latin American Constitutionalism, it is understandable why so many Constitutions refused to recognize the existence of indigenous peoples as a 'separate class' of citizens. This formal philosophical construction of equality is the reason why France has a reservation to the ICCPR excluding the application of Art 27 (on minority protection) from its territory and even the territory of French possessions overseas (including several Pacific islands upon which indigenous peoples clearly reside). This reservation will come up again in Chapter 5. For more on the French approach to multiculturalism, see Cécile Laborde, 'The Culture(s) of the Republic: Nationalism and Multiculturalism in French Republican Thought', *Political Theory* 29 (2001), 716 35.

[15] Kevin J Worthen, 'The Grand Experiment: Evaluating Indian Law in the "New World"', *Tulsa J Comp & Intl L* 5 (1998), 299 334 at 329; and Francisco López Bárcenas, 'Territorios, Tierras y Recursos Naturales de los Pueblos Indígenas en México', in Jorge Alberto Gonzáles Galván (ed), *Constitución y Derechos Indígenas* (Universidad Nacional Autónoma de México, 2002), 121 43.

[16] On the Zapatista movement's contribution to constitutional reform and indigenous recognition in Mexico, see Gilberto López y Rivas, 'Las Autonomías Indígenas', in Jorge Alberto Gonzáles Galván (ed), *Constitución y Derechos Indígenas* (Universidad Nacional Autónoma de México, 2002), 113 20. On the evolution of constitutional recognition of indigeneity in Mexico generally, see Diego Valadés, 'Los Derechos de los Indígenas y la Renovación Constitucional en México', in Jorge Alberto Gonzáles Galván (ed), *Constitución y Derechos Indígenas* (Universidad Nacional Autónoma de México, 2002), 13 20.

[17] Jorge A Vargas, 'Mexico's Legal Revolution: An Appraisal of Its Recent Constitutional Changes, 1988 1995', *Ga J Intl & Comp L* 25 (1996), 497 559.

[18] On this reform, see José Luis Cuevas Gayosso, 'La autonomía de los derechos de los pueblos indígenas en la constitución mexicana (reforma 2001). Análisis y propuestas para su ejercicio formal y real', paper presented at the *XIV Congreso Latinoamericano de Derecho Romano, Universidad de Buenos Aires, 15 17 November 2004* (on file with the author).

the autonomy of indigenous peoples, or by excluding indigenous peoples from the rest of society.

Brazil is a peculiar example of a country that has moved towards the recognition of indigenous peoples. The 1988 Brazilian Constitution mentions the recognition of indigenous social organization, customs, languages, beliefs, and traditions.[19] Prior Constitutions only recognized land rights,[20] but the 1988 Constitution recognizes the protection of indigenous identity as a whole. However, unlike the majority of other Latin American countries, where the constitutional provisions are self-standing and in many ways 'self-executing', in the Brazilian case there is comprehensive infra-constitutional legislation related to indigenous rights, which in practice is implemented without regard to the Constitutional provisions. The Indian Rights Act ('*Estatuto do Índio*') determines that indigenous individuals fall within the category of 'incapable' persons ('*incapazes*'), basically attributing them the same legal autonomy as that of a minor under 16 years of age, and considering them incapable of freely expressing their will,[21] reflecting societal perceptions and

[19] The relevant provisions are the following: '**Article 231**. The social organization, customs, languages, beliefs and traditions of Indians are acknowledged, as well as the original titles over the lands they traditionally occupy, being the role of the Union to delimitate them, and to protect and make all their property respected. Paragraph 1. The lands traditionally occupied by Indians are those inhabited permanently, those used for economic activities, indispensable to the preservation of environmental resources necessary to the wellbeing and those necessary to their physical and cultural reproduction, according to their uses, customs and traditions. Paragraph 2. The lands traditionally occupied by Indians are destined to their permanent possession, being the Indians entitled to the exclusive use of the wealth from the land, the rivers and the lakes existing therein. Paragraph 3. The enjoyment of water resources, including energetic ones, the research and extraction of mineral resources within indigenous lands can only be undertaken when authorized by the National Congress, after the affected communities are heard, and the participation in the benefits of the extraction is secured in favor of these communities, in terms established by law. Paragraph 4. The lands referred to in this article cannot be sold or disposed of, and the rights upon them are not subject to a statute of limitations. Paragraph 5. The removal of indigenous groups from their lands is forbidden, unless so decided by the National Congress, in case of a catastrophe or epidemics that endangers the population, or for the protection of national sovereignty, after deliberation by the National Congress, being secured, in any case, the immediate return after the cessation of the risk. Paragraph 6. All acts that deal with the occupation, domain and possession of lands referred to in this article, or the exploitation of natural resources of the land, rivers and lakes existing therein are null and void, except for hypotheses of public interest of the Union, according to what is provided for in complementary legislation, not generating nullity and the extinction of the right to compensation or actions against the Union, except for those relating to improvements deriving from good faith occupation, according to law. [...] **Article 232**. Indians, indigenous communities and organizations are legitimate parties to initiate lawsuits to defent their rights and interests, the Public Attorney ['*Ministério Público*'] being required to intervene in all phases of the procedure.'

[20] For a survey of these provisions, see Sérgio Leitão, *Os Direitos Constitucionais dos Povos Indígenas* (UNAM, 2003).

[21] The Brazilian Civil Code of 1916 also expressly included indigenous individuals in this category, and it is most likely in order to reflect this piece of legislation that the Indian Act also considers them as legally incapable. The new Civil Code of 2002 refrains from making any such categorization of indigenous individuals, simply stating, in Article 5 (single paragraph) that special legislation shall address the issue of legal capacity of indigenous persons. Article 5 refers to those considered only 'relatively incapable', and it is thus somewhat telling of a movement towards greater emancipation of indigenous persons within Brazilian Law. One is only to hope that the full recognition of indigenous legal capacity will happen soon.

prejudices regarding indigenous peoples.[22] This status can change, and indigenous persons can be given full legal capacity, as long as they demonstrate that they have successfully 'integrated into the national community'.[23]

Indigenous rights and interests in Brazil are managed by the National Indian Foundation (*'Fundação Nacional do Índio'* FUNAI), an organ established by the federal government[24] that represents indigenous interests before the government,

[22] Lisa Valenta, 'Disconnect: The 1988 Brazilian Constitution, Customary International Law, and Indigenous Land Rights in Northern Brazil', *Tex Intl LJ* 38 (2003), 643 62 at 647.

[23] *Brazilian Indian Rights Act* ['Estatuto do Índio'], Statute 6.001, of 19 December 1973. The relevant provisions are the following: '**Article** 7. Indians and indigenous communities not yet integrated to the national communion are subject to the tutelage regime established in this Act. Paragraph 1. To the possible extent, the principles and rules of the ordinary law of tutelage are applicable to the tutelage regime established in this Act, independently, however, from the exercise of tutelage in what regards immovable property in legal mortgages, as well as [credit guarantees]. Paragraph 2. This tutelage is the duty of the Union, which will exercise it through the competent federal organ of assistance to savages.

Article 8. The acts practiced among Indians not yet integrated and any person foreign to the indigenous community are null, when there has been no assistance from the competent tutelage body. Single Paragraph. The rule in this article is not applicable in case the Indian reveals awareness and knowledge of the practiced act, as long as the action is not harmful to the Indian [...].

Article 9. Any Indian can request the competent judge to be freed from the tutelage system provided for in this Act, becoming totally capable to exercise legal acts, as long as the following requirements are met: I minimum age of 21 years; II knowledge of the Portuguese language; III habilitation to the exercise of useful activity within the national communion; IV reasonable understanding of the uses and customs of the national communion. Single Paragraph. The judge will decide after summary proceedings, and after the body of Indian tutelage and the Public Attorney have been heard, and the conceding judgment will be transcribed into the civil registry.

Article 10. Once the requirements of the preceding Article are met, and through a written request by the interested party, the assistance body will be able to grant the Indian, through a formal declaration, the condition of integrated, no longer subsisting any restriction to capacity, as long as, after being legally homologated, the act is inscribed in the civil registry.

Article 11. Through a decree of the President of the Republic, the emancipation of an indigenous community and its members can be declared, as to the tutelage regime established by law; as long as requested by the majority of the members of the group and certified, in investigation undertaken by the competent federal body, the community's full integration into the national communion. Single Paragraph. For the effects of this article, the fulfillment of the requirements listed in Article 9 will be required by the requesting parties.'

See also Siegfried Wiessner, 'Rights and Status of Indigenous Peoples: A Global Comparative and International Legal Analysis', *Harv Human Rights J* 12 (1999), 57 128 at 75.

[24] Statute 5.371, of 5 December 1967, authorizing the institution of the 'National Indian Foundation'. The relevant provision is the following: '**Article 1**. The Federal Government is hereby authorized to create a foundation, with its own patrimony and legal personality in private law, according to civil law, called "National Indian Foundation", with the following goals: I to establish the directives and guarantee the fulfillment of the indigenous policy, based upon the following principles: a) respect to the indigenous person and the tribal institutions and communities; b) guarantee to the permanent possession over lands they inhabit and the exclusive use rights over all the natural resources therein; c) the preservation of biological and cultural balance of the Indian, in its contact with national society; d) safeguard of the spontaneous assimilation of the Indian, so that its social-economic evolution is processed safe from abrupt changes; II to manage Indigenous Patrimony, so as to conserve, increase and enhance it; III promote scientific assessments, analyses, studies and research about the Indian and the indigenous social groups; [...] V to promote the appropriate basic education of the Indian aimed at his/her progressive integration in national society; VI to raise, by the publicity instruments, the collective interest towards the indigenous cause; VII to exercise political power in reserved areas and in matters concerning indigenous protection. Single Paragraph. The Foundation will exercise the powers of representation or legal assistance inherent to the Indian's tutelage regime, in the form established by ordinary civil legislation or special legislation.'

the judiciary, and Brazilian society as a whole. This foundation has been heavily criticized for being composed primarily of bureaucrats and giving few opportunities for indigenous participation, and even of pursuing assimilationist objectives.[25]

The discrepancy between the level of protection suggested at the constitutional level and the implementing legislation is perhaps the reason why the Brazilian case is in this uncomfortable intermediary position: while the Constitution promotes a model of recognition, the infra-constitutional legislation, which still guides bureaucrats responsible for designing and implementing governmental policies to this day, is aimed at a model of assimilation. New legislation on indigenous rights, moving away from this model and fully embracing recognition, was proposed in August 2009 by the Ministry of Justice and is now under consideration by the Legislative chambers.[26]

Further, this discrepancy may be explained by looking at the origins of the Constitutional provision. The momentum for the recognition of indigenous identity during the constitution-drafting process was built not by civil society or an organized indigenous movement (to this day rather inexpressive in Brazil), but rather by international pressure from condemnation of Brazil by the Inter-American Commission of Human Rights in the early 1980s in a case concerning the Yanomami indigenous group.[27] This case shed light on the lack of adequate protection for indigenous peoples in Brazil and, because the Constitution of 1988 was meant to represent a full break with the dictatorial past during which the acts were perpetrated against the Yanomami, the provision was drafted and included. However, as there was no strong civil society movement to follow-up on the implementation, the Indian Rights Act, enacted under a previous Constitution, is yet to be amended or replaced to reflect the changes the new Constitution aspired to. Implementation fell into the hands of a bureaucracy that had already been established under the old Act, and this bureaucracy did not seem very interested in expanding protection to reflect constitutional changes. The lack of bottom-up pressure, then, at the very least helps explain if it does not completely account for the failure of the Brazilian Constitution in achieving more protection towards indigenous peoples.[28]

This model resembles in many ways the colonial idea of the establishment of 'an official policy of benevolent guardianship'[29] towards indigenous peoples, which was

[25] Wiessner, 'Rights and Status of Indigenous Peoples', 75.

[26] Brazilian Ministry of Justice, National Commission of Indigenous Policy, *Indigenous Peoples Statute Proposal of the National Commission of Indigenous Policy*, available at <http://www.funai.gov.br/ultimas/noticias/2 semestre 2009/agosto/imagens/Estatuto.pdf> (accessed 29 November 2012).

[27] IACHR, Case 7.615, 5 March 1985. For a commentary to this case, see Gail Goodwin Gomez, 'Indigenous Rights and the Case of the Yanomami Indians in Brazil', in Cynthia Price Cohen (ed), *The Human Rights of Indigenous Peoples* (Transnational Publishers, 1998), 185 200.

[28] Discussing the importance of civil society in the advancement of indigenous claims in Chile and the United States, see Kevin J Worthen, 'The Role of Indigenous Groups in Constitutional Democracies: A Lesson from Chile and the United States', in Cynthia Price Cohen (ed), *The Human Rights of Indigenous Peoples* (Transnational Publishers, 1998), 235 70.

[29] I borrow this expression from Guillermo Floris Margadant, 'Official Mexican Attitudes toward the Indians: An Historical Essay', *Tul L Rev* 54 (1980), 964 86 at 968.

adopted once the colonizers realized that indigenous peoples could not 'live alone as free subjects of the King', and needed to be looked after and kept within certain boundaries.[30] It then reinstates the Nation-State, instead of challenging it, being a less than ideal model of promoting multiculturalism. As a matter of fact, multiculturalism is not promoted, or at least not a model of multiculturalism in which the culturally distinct segments of a polity interact with one another. While it is the choice of certain communities to remain isolated from mainstream society, in this model the choice is not open to communities, but rather made for them by a paternalistic State.

The legal capacity of indigenous individuals (or lack thereof, to be more precise) is then the determining factor of this model, distinguishing it from others. Some aspects of exclusion, such as territorial exclusion, are also part of this model, but are not exclusive to it, at least in principle. The delimitation of indigenous reservations is a quintessential feature of the protection regimes, and common to both.

This model helps perpetuate a state of affairs reminiscent of the colonial model, under which the ways of life of autochthonous communities are preserved at the cost of depriving these communities from any benefits enjoyed by the rest of society.[31] According to the relevant legislation, indigenous individuals are given two alternatives: either they integrate into Brazil's mainstream society, or they remain in isolation.[32] The statute is not prepared to accommodate indigenous peoples who wish to remain indigenous and still interact with the rest of society.

[30] For an explanation of this model, see Worthen, 'The Grand Experiment', 301.

[31] Angel R Oquendo, 'Indigeneity and the State: Comparative Critiques: Indigenous Self-Determination in Latin America', *Fla J Intl L* 17 (2005), 625 46 at 626.

[32] Brazilian Indian Rights Act ['Estatuto do Índio'], Statute 6.001, of 19 December 1973, Arts 2 and 4. '**Article 2.** It is the duty of the Union, the States and the Municipalities, as well as the organs of the respective indirect administrations, within the limits of their competences, in order to protect indigenous communities and preserve their rights: I to extend to Indians the benefits of common legislation, whenever its application is possible; II to give assistance to Indians and indigenous communities still not integrated into the national communion; III to respect, by giving the Indians means for their development, the peculiarities inherent to their condition; IV to secure to Indians the possibility of freely choosing their ways of life and subsistence; V to guarantee to Indians the voluntary permanence in their habitat, giving them the resources for their development and progress; VI to respect, in the process of integration of the Indian to the national communion, the cohesion of indigenous communities, their cultural values, traditions, uses and customs; VII to execute whenever possible with the collaboration of Indians, the programs and projects aimed at benefiting indigenous communities; VIII to use the cooperation of initiative and the personal qualities of the Indian, having in mind the improvement of their life conditions and their integration into the development process; IX to guarantee to Indians and indigenous communities, in the terms of the Constitution, the permanent possession of the lands they inhabit, recognizing the right to the exclusive usufruct of the natural wealth and all the utilities existing in those lands; X to guarantee to Indians the full exercise of civil and political rights guaranteed to them by legislation.

Article 4. Indians are considered: I Isolated When they live in unknown groups or of which there are few and vague reports through random contacts with elements of the national communion; II On the way towards integration When, in intermittent or permanent contact with foreign groups, they conserve a larger or smaller part of their native life conditions, but accept some practices and ways of existence common to the other sectors of the national communion, of which they depend more and more for their own subsistence; III Integrated When incorporated into the national communion and recognized in the full exercise of their civil rights, even if they keep uses, customs and traditions characteristic of their culture.'

This model is therefore insufficient. Regardless of the efforts by the Brazilian government in mitigating this exclusion, this is what happens in practice. It is necessary to find alternatives through which communities have their rights to both equality and difference respected.[33]

Protection via recognition, on the other hand, is the model increasingly adopted by new Latin American Constitutions. This model draws on the contemporary constructions of the principle of self-determination as applied to indigenous peoples, in the sense of granting recognition attached to some degree of self-governance.[34] It creates what has been called 'systems of deviated citizenship', as it confers a special status to indigenous peoples different from that conferred to individuals generally.[35]

This recognition can happen in two different ways, which do not necessarily exclude each other. On the one side, there can be 'exclusionary recognition', in the sense of granting exceptions to the application of the general legal system to indigenous peoples, usually via the recognition of customary law or even the possibility of creating alternative, parallel systems for the administration of justice within indigenous communities. Better said, 'exclusionary recognition' consists of recognizing the faculty of indigenous peoples to form (and sometimes even enforce) their own legal systems.[36]

Besides this more 'conventional' form of exclusionary recognition, other strategies can be labelled as such, including the delegation of governmental authority to existing indigenous entities, through the creation of (semi-)autonomous territorial units for indigenous peoples. This strategy is not found in Latin America, however, but rather in the United States and Canada, so I will abstain from exploring it.[37]

The other possibility is 'inclusionary recognition', or the granting of special incentives or rights to enhance indigenous participation in public decision-making and law-making, either by quotas in legislative bodies, city councils, and other equivalent bodies, or simply by re-drawing the boundaries of electoral districts so as to give indigenous peoples the opportunity to elect their own representatives even for head executive offices.[38] This gradually empowers indigenous peoples and gives voice to indigenous concerns. Bolivia exemplifies a particularly successful use of this

[33] Oquendo, 'Indigeneity and the State', 626.

[34] For an analysis of the right to self-determination as applied to minorities and indigenous peoples, see Patrick Macklem, 'The Wrong Vocabulary of Right: Minority Rights and the Boundaries of Political Community', *University of Toronto Legal Studies Series Research Paper No XX-05* (2005); and Patrick Macklem, 'Militant Democracy, Legal Pluralism and the Paradox of Self-Determination', *University of Toronto Legal Studies Research Paper No 05-03* (2003).

[35] Van Cott, *The Friendly Liquidation*, 10.

[36] Worthen, 'The Grand Experiment', 324 7 (1998); and Bartolomé Clavero, 'Derechos Indígenas y Constituciones Latinoamericanas', in Mikel Berraondo (ed), *Pueblos Indígenas y Derechos Humanos* (Universidad de Deusto, 2006), 313 38 at 329 34.

[37] For a rather thorough exploration of this perspective, see Worthen, 'The Grand Experiment', 315 17.

[38] Raquel Yrigoyen Fajardo, 'Hitos del reconocimiento del pluralismo jurídico y el derecho indígena en las políticas indigenistas y el constitucionalismo andino', in Mikel Berraondo (ed), *Pueblos Indígenas y Derechos Humanos* (Universidad de Deusto, 2006), 537 67 at 557; and Worthen, 'The Grand Experiment', 319 24.

strategy. Prior to the 2009 Bolivian Constitution, gradual electoral reforms paved the way for greater indigenous participation in political life, culminating in the election of Evo Morales, the first indigenous President in the country's history.

Ecuador also applies a recognition model, and its 2008 Constitution presents very interesting features. Generally, Ecuador's recognition model focuses more on an exclusionary strategy, by giving great importance to the autonomy of traditional indigenous legal systems for the administration of justice. Through a constitutional reform in 1998, Ecuador for the first time granted constitutional status to indigenous peoples as rights-bearers.[39] In the Ecuadorian system prior to the new 2008 Constitution, the recognition of legal pluralism required the recognition of: the status of indigenous peoples as rights-bearers; the authorities of indigenous peoples; the existence of indigenous rules and procedures to solve internal conflicts and elect their own authorities; and the faculty to decide any disputes arising within each indigenous community and enforce such decisions according to the community's own rules and procedures.[40]

The new 2008 Constitution recognizes the diverse composition of the Ecuadorian State, and it goes on to affirm a series of collective rights to indigenous peoples, as well as the affirmation of several indigenous values as quintessential constitutional values.[41]

But it is the new Bolivian Constitution, approved by a national referendum in January 2009, that represents the most revolutionary advance in the protection of

[39] The relevant provision of the previous Ecuadorian Constitution is the following: '**Article 191**. The exercise of judicial power shall be the duty of the bodies of the Judiciary. Jurisdictional unity shall be established. According to law there shall be peace judges, charged with the resolution in equity of individual, community or neighbor disputes. Arbitration, mediation and other alternative dispute resolution mechanisms shall be recognized, according to law. The authorities of indigenous peoples shall exercise judicial functions, applying norms and procedures appropriate to the resolution of internal disputes according to their customs or customary law, as long as they are not contrary to the Constitution and the laws. A separate act shall bring these attributions and those of the national judicial system into compatibility.' The equivalent provision in the 2008 Ecuadorian Constitution is the following: '**Article 171**. The authorities of the indigenous communities, peoples and nationalities shall exercise jurisdictional functions, based upon their ancestral traditions and their own law, within their territories, guaranteeing the participation and decision of women. The authorities shall apply norms and procedures specific to the settlement of their internal disputes, and that are not contrary to the Constitution and the human rights recognized in international instruments. The State shall guarantee that the decisions of the indigenous jurisdiction are respected by public authorities and institutions. Such decisions will be subject to a constitutionality check. The law shall establish the mechanisms of coordination and cooperation between the indigenous and ordinary jurisdictions.'

[40] Raúl Llasag Fernández, 'Jurisdicción y competencia en el derecho indígena o consuetudinario', *Anuario de Derecho Constitucional Latinoamericano* (2006), 749 78 at 752. Agustín Grijalva, 'The Status of Traditional Indian Justice in Ecuador', *Tribal LJ* 2 (2001 02), 1 20; and Esther Sánchez Botero, 'Los Derechos Indígenas en las Constituciones de Colombia y Ecuador', in Jorge Alberto Gonzáles Galván (ed), *Constitución y Derechos Indígenas* (Universidad Nacional Autónoma de México, 2002), 69 88.

[41] The relevant provision is the following: '**Article 83**. The following are duties and responsibilities of all Ecuadorians, without prejudice to other ruties and responsibilities required by the Constitution and laws: [...] 2. *Ama killa, ama llulla, ama shwa. Do not be lazy, do not lie, do not steal.* [...] 10. To promote the unity and equality in Diversity and intercultural relations. [...] 14. To respect and recognize ethnic, nacional, social, generational, gender, sexual identity and orientation differences. [...]' (emphasis added).

indigenous rights in the Americas. Article 1 of the new Bolivian Constitution starts by proclaiming Bolivia a 'Unitary Communitarian Social Plurinational State under the Rule of Law', and also affirming the 'political, economic, legal, cultural and linguistic pluralism within the country's integrational process' as the very foundation of the Bolivian State.[42] These provisions reflect the tension between unity and pluralism in many Latin American Constitutions that recognize indigenous rights.

But the new Bolivian Constitution goes a step further, by proclaiming several indigenous languages as official languages of the country alongside Spanish,[43] and also by proclaiming, among State values, essentially indigenous values, referred to by their indigenous names.[44] These provisions are truly revolutionary, because they move indigenous peoples away from the periphery of the constitutional order and put them at the very centre of it.[45] Indigenous peoples are no longer mere weaker parties to which recognition is granted by a 'benevolent State'; rather, they are empowered subjects (who have been subject to colonial domination and deserve reparations for that) and a central part of the polity.

Several other provisions of the new Bolivian Constitution also help reinforce this view. In the part that deals with fundamental rights, for example, there is the option for indigenous individuals to have their indigenous identity (the denomination of the indigenous people they are a part of) in all their official identification documents issued by the State,[46] as well as the right of isolated peoples to remain in

[42] The full text of the provision is the following: '**Article 1**. Bolivia constitutes itself as a Unitary Communitarian Social Plurinational State under the Rule of Law, free, independent, sovereign, democratic, *intercultural*, decentralized and with autonomies. Bolivia is founded upon plurality and political, economic, legal, cultural and linguistic pluralism, within the country's integrational process' (emphasis added).

[43] The relevant provision is: '**Article 5**. I. The official languages of the State are Spanish [*castellano*] and all the languages of the indigenous peoples and original peasant nations, which are aymara, araona, baure, bésiro, canichana, cavineño, cayubaba, chácobo, chimán, ese ejja, guaraní, guarasu'we, guarayu, itonama, leco, machajuyai-kallawaya, machineri, maropa, mojeño-trinitario, mojeño-ignaciano, moré, mosetén, movima, pacawara, puquina, quechua, sirionó, tacana, tapiete, toromona, uru-chipaya, weenhayek, yaminawa, yuki, yuracaré y zamuco. II. The plurinational Government and departmental governments must use at least two official languages. One of these must be Spanish, and the other will be decided taking into account the use, convenience, circumstances, needs and preferences of the population in its totality or the territory in question. The other autonomous governments must use the languages corresponding to its territories, and one of these must be Spanish.'

[44] The relevant provision is: '**Article 8**. I. The State assumes and promotes as ethical-moral principles of the plural society: ama qhilla, ama llulla, ama suwa (do not be weak, do not be a liar nor be a thief), suma qamaña (good living), ñandereko (harmonious living), teko kavi (good life), ivi maraei (land with no evil) and qhapaj ñan (noble way of life). II. The State is supported by the values of unity, equality, inclusion, dignity, freedom, solidarity, reciprocity, respect, complementarity, harmony, transparency, equilibrium, equality of opportunities, social and gender equity in the participation, common well-being, responsibility, social justice, distribution and redistribution of the products and social goods, to live well.'

[45] López Bárcenas, 'Autonomías indígenas en América', 439 (indicating this to be an important element for the construction of real indigenous autonomy).

[46] The provision is the following: '**Article 30**. I. A peasant original indigenous people or nation is all human collectivity that shares cultural identity, language, historical tradition, institutions, territoriality and worldview, the existence of which is prior to the Spanish colonial invasion. II. Within the framework of State unity and according to this Constitution the peasant original indigenous peoples and nations have the following rights: [. . .] 3. That the cultural identity of each one of its members, if she or he so wishes, are registered alongside the Bolivian citizenship in the identity card, passport or other identity documents with legal validity. [. . .]'

this condition.[47] A chapter on culture proclaims cultural diversity as the foundation of the new Plurinational Communitarian State,[48] and it contains several provisions related to the preservation of indigenous cultural heritage, tangible and intangible.[49]

There is also a particularly interesting chapter on the 'original peasant indigenous jurisdiction'. This chapter outlines the existence of parallel systems of administration of justice specific to indigenous peoples, declaring the validity of these systems of administration of justice as long as they comply with fundamental human rights protected by the Constitution.[50] The jurisdiction of these parallel systems is triggered by several scenarios, all requiring a 'particular bond' with an indigenous or peasant community.[51] It is determined that the State will guarantee the enforcement of the judgments of these systems, if necessary, and that a

[47] The provision is the following: '**Article 31**. I. The peasant original indigenous nations in danger of extinction, in situation of voluntary isolation and not contacted will be protected and respected in their individual and collective ways of life. II. The indigenous nations and peoples in isolation and not contacted have the right to remain in this condition, to the legal delimitation and consolidation of the territory they occupy and inhabit.'

[48] The provision is the following: '**Article 98**. I. Cultural diversity is the essential foundation of the Communitarian Plurinational State. Interculturality is the instrument for the harmonious and balanced cohesion and coexistence among all peoples and nations. Interculturality will respect differences and will happen in equality of conditions. II. The State will take as fortitude the existence of peasant original indigenous cultures, depositories of knowledge, wisdom, values, spirituality and worldviews. III. It is the fundamental responsibility of the State to preserve, develop, protect and diffuse the cultures existing in the country.'

[49] The relevant provisions are the following: '**Article 99**. I. The cultural heritage of the Bolivian people is inalienable, and no legal burdens can be imposed upon it. The economic resources generated by it will be regulated by statute, to address with priority its conservation, preservation and promotion. II. The State will guarantee the inventorying, protection, restoration, recovery, revitalization, enrichment, promotion and diffusion of its cultural heritage, according to the law. III. The natural, archaeological, paleontological, historical and documental wealth, as well as that deriving from religious rites and folklore, is the cultural heritage of the Bolivian people, according to the law.

Article 100. I. It is the heritage of the peasant original indigenous nations and peoples the worldviews, myths, oral history, dances, cultural practices, traditional knowledge and technologies. This heritage is part of the State's expression and identity. II. The State will protect the knowledge and wisdom through the registration of intellectual property that safeguards the intangible rights of peasant original indigenous nations and peoples as well as that of the intercultural and Afro-Bolivian communities.

Article 101. The manifestations of popular arts and industries, in its intangible component, will enjoy special protection by the State. Moreover, this protection will be extended to sites and activities declared to be cultural heritage of mankind, in its tangible or intangible components.

Article 102. The State will register and protect the intellectual property, individual and collective, of works of art and discoveries of authors, artists, composers, inventors and scientists, in the conditions determined by law.'

[50] The relevant provision is the following: '**Article 190**. I. The peasant original indigenous nations and peoples shall exercise their jurisdiction and competence functions through their own authorities, and will apply their own principles, cultural values, norms and procedures. II. The peasant original indigenous jurisdiction respects the right to life, the right to defense and other rights and guarantees established by this Constitution.'

[51] The relevant provision is the following: '**Article 191**. The peasant original indigenous jurisdiction is founded upon a particular bond of the persons members of a respective peasant original indigenous nation or people. II. The peasant original indigenous jurisdiction will be exercised in the following personal, material and territorial scopes: 1. The members of peasant original indigenous nations or peoples will be subject to this jurisdiction whenever they appear as claimants or respondents, complainants, accused or appellants. 2. This jurisdiction will analyse the peasant original indigenous matters in accordance to the provisions of a Jurisdictional Division Act. 3. This jurisdiction applies to

'Jurisdictional Division Act' ('*Ley de Deslinde Jurisdiccional*') will be enacted to determine the specificities of this relationship.[52]

As Constitutions in Latin America and elsewhere move towards the accommodation of cultural difference, they recognize the importance of the protection of intangible cultural heritage. The 2009 Bolivian Constitution is a remarkable instrument in this sense, and one of the very first to give constitutional status to ICH protection (Article 101). But the bulk of legal protection to intangible heritage still happens at the infra-constitutional level. The following sections will look at some of these responses, starting with domestic intellectual property measures.

4.2 Intellectual Property Responses

Intellectual property (IP) responses are usually also not ICH-specific responses. Instead of devising a specific system for ICH protection, States instead utilize their pre-existing IP regimes and apply them to traditional cultural expressions and manifestations of intangible heritage.

These solutions, and their feasibility/applicability will be analysed at length in Chapter 6. Now it suffices to say that there are several objections to the use of intellectual property, one of the most important of which being that ICH interests are usually communal rights, whereas IP consists of individual rights. Several countries have made use of this possibility, notably Australia and Indonesia.[53] Australia is the leading country in using this type of solution, to be looked at in some detail below.

4.2.1 Australia

Australia, like other countries that use IP solutions to protect ICH, does not have specific legislation on the protection of intangible heritage.[54] Legislation about cultural heritage generally exists at the federal and state levels, even though the federal legislation usually trumps State legislation. Australia has remarkable experience in what concerns IP approaches to intangible heritage, and must

the legal relations or facts that are initiated or the effects of which are produced within the jurisdiction of a peasant original indigenous people.'

[52] The relevant provision is the following: '**Article 192.** I. All public authorities or persons will abide to the decisions of the peasant original indigenous jurisdiction. II. For the enforcement of decisions of the peasant original indigenous jurisdiction, its authorities may ask for the support of the competent State bodies. III. The State shall promote and strengthen the peasant original indigenous justice. The Jurisdictional Division Act shall determine the mechanisms of coordination and cooperation among the peasant original indigenous jurisdiction, ordinary jurisdiction, agricultural-environmental jurisdiction and all the constitutionally recognized jurisdictions.'

[53] PV Valsala G Kutty, *National Experiences with the Protection of Expressions of Folklore/Traditional Cultural Expressions* (WIPO, 2002), 31 2.

[54] See Stephen Harris, 'Cultural Heritage Protection in Australia Legislation and Some Comments', *Proceedings of the ICOMOS 13th General Assembly Madrid, 2002: Strategies for the World's Cultural Heritage, Preservation in a Globalized World, Principles, Practices, Perspectives*, available at <http://www.international.icomos.org/publications/ga madrid.htm> (accessed 29 November 2012).

hence be cited. Since the precedent of the *Mabo* case,[55] Australian courts have recognized the existence of customary rights for Aborigines and Strait Islanders, where this is consistent with Australian laws. Through the precedent of the '*Carpets Case*' (*M*(deceased) v Indofurn*),[56] Australian Courts, although recognizing the need of development of special regimes for the protection of folklore, have granted protection through IP mechanisms, such as trademarks, industrial design, nominations of origin, and, as in the *Carpets Case*, copyright.

Heritage protection in Australia, as in most countries, is a highly politicized topic, which naturally creates obstacles to the enactment of specific legislation on intangible heritage. This politicization might help explain the choice for the use of IP mechanisms when it comes to intangible heritage. The IP legal framework was already there, and could be applied without much difficulty to art produced within traditional communities. Further, and more importantly, it is a somewhat 'technical', and thus 'apolitical' area of law, which has the unintended consequence of requiring that tensions be either negotiated beforehand in other venues, or excluded altogether from the process.[57]

The application of IP law does not fully fit aboriginal understandings of ownership over cultural expressions, but at the same time, to the extent Aboriginal law is thought of as being simply part of a case's 'factual matrix', and not a body of law that can be applied by Australian Courts,[58] the courts in these cases saw little problem in using IP mechanisms, which was and is in any case a preferable solution to a refusal from adjudicating a case.

IP mechanisms thus offer a ready-made, previously available and cost-free (at least with respect to copyright) framework into which ICH issues can be (arguably) negotiated and resolved. The face appeal of this type of solution is very clear and very high, but, as briefly indicated here and as Chapter 6 will explain in detail, this type of solution is very problematic when considering the nature of ICH in relationship to the communities of origin. Bearing these obstacles in mind, several

[55] *Mabo v Queensland* (1992). For further information on the case, see Keal, *European Conquest and the Rights of Indigenous Peoples*, 124.

[56] In the case, a group of well-known Aboriginal artists, among them Banduk Marika, produced several sacred paintings and exhibited them at the National Australian Gallery. A carpet factory located in Vietnam that produced carpets for an Australia company called Indofurn, copied one of these paintings from the exhibition catalogue, called 'Djanda and the Sacred Waterhole', painted by Ms Marika. This painting represents the origin of the world to her tribe, the Rirratingu clan, of which she was a traditional custodian responsible for the dreaming story. The reproduction of the painting could imply her losing her religious rights, and have severe penalties imposed. Despite the fact that the reproduction of her art would be walked on is totally opposed to the cultural use of the central imagery and underlying knowledge in her work. Indofurn was ordered to pay damages and compensation, as well as remove all carpets from commercialization. For further details, see Chapter 6 and Janke, *Minding Culture*.

[57] See generally Kathy Bowrey, 'Indigenous Culture, Knowledge and Intellectual Property: The Need for a New Category of Rights?', in Kathy Bowrey, Michael Handler, and Dianne Nicoll (eds), *Emerging Challenges in Intellectual Property* (Oxford University Press, 2011), 46 67; and Kathy Bowrey, 'International Trade in Indigenous Cultural Heritage: An Australian Perspective', in Christoph Beat Graber, Karolina Kuprecht, and Jessica Lai (eds), *International Trade in Indigenous Cultural Heritage: Legal and Policy Issues* (Edward Elgar, 2012), 396 438.

[58] *John Bulun Bulun v R & T Textiles Pty Ltd* (1998) 41 IPR 513.

other countries have looked at different, *sui generis*, solutions. The following section will look at them.

4.3 *Sui Generis* Regimes

Sui generis solutions to ICH safeguarding are solutions tailored to the specific needs of a certain group, and, when dealing with indigenous or minority groups, more sensitive to their customary law, while still attempting to translate it into a mainstream legal format. The clear advantage of this model is that, at least in theory, these tailored solutions will be able to overcome objections to the use of IP. At the same time, they establish a framework that generates *erga omnes* effects towards third parties who would otherwise meet no legal impediment to misappropriate a given group's intangible heritage.

At the same time, however, this type of solution can be rather expensive as it requires the creation of implementing/supervisory bodies, in addition to all the studies necessary to ensure that cultural specificities are accounted for. Cost works as a disincentive to the implementation of *sui generis* regimes.

Several countries have implemented this type of regime, including Bolivia and Panama. Bolivia has one of the earliest pieces of legislation on the matter (which is no surprise considering their pioneering role before UNESCO, discussed in Chapter 2), a 1977 Decree regulating the uses of folk art, literature, music, and dance.[59] This decree establishes property rights over part of this material in favour of the State (with the notable exception of crafts). These rights may be seen as a means of placing these manifestations of heritage into the public domain, as the decree does not establish rules referring to the payment of royalties of any sort.

It requires that the customary law of the community whose art is sought after, for commercial and non-commercial purposes alike, is respected and taken into consideration. It also requires that any uses of art collected from these communities be authorized by a governmental agency. As the customary law of the community is to be respected, one can conclude that community authorization is also a necessary condition for the use of this art.

When it comes to crafts, the Decree creates a registration system and a seal of authenticity. Further, it determines that crafts lacking such a seal may not be allowed to leave the country. It also creates industrial design rights over these crafts, although for a shorter period of time (a renewable period of five years, as opposed to the renewable ten-year periods of international legislation).

The decree also creates a committee for the conservation, protection, and promotion of folklore ('*Comité para la Conservación, Protección y Difusión del Folklore*'). The committee is in charge of organizing awareness-raising activities and festivals, and, most interestingly, of seeking links with artistic societies in

[59] Bolivia, 'Decreto Supremo No 12626 del 9 de junio de 1977 Normas sobre Patrimonio Etnográfico, Música Folklórica, Danzas Folklóricas, Literatura Folklórica y Arte Popular', *UNESCO, Database of National Cultural Heritage Laws*.

neighbouring countries, so as to prevent Bolivian folk melodies from being registered in those countries as copyrightable material.

This legislation thus gives the control of manifestations of intangible heritage to the communities, and it adds the help of a governmental entity as a means to ensure that the community has not been deceived into giving such authorization or not been consulted. This double-tiered system of safeguarding seems very effective. However, the decree generally falls short of enabling communities to reap eventual economic benefits arising from the exploitation of their art. The Panamanian example tries to address this issue. It is dealt with next.

4.3.1 Panama

Panama has a very sophisticated piece of legislation creating a *sui generis* regime for the safeguarding of intangible cultural heritage. It created the 'Law on the special intellectual property regime upon collective rights of indigenous communities, for the protection of their cultural identities and traditional knowledge'.[60] With the support of an implementing Decree,[61] indigenous communities' customary law is applied. These communities express their views on the management of their heritage through their general congresses or traditional authorities, which, for legal purposes, are the holders of the rights over folklore.[62] This reflects a conception of cultural heritage which prioritizes human relationships above economic rights.[63]

The Law creates exclusive, collective, and perpetual rights over the intellectual and artistic creations of indigenous peoples. It was motivated by the *mola*, which is a specific type of craft developed by the Kuna indigenous communities in Panama.[64] Law No 20 is the product of a specificity of the Panamanian system, it has been argued, to the extent that it protects indigenous peoples' interests without taking into account the interests of other traditional and vulnerable communities, let alone the interests of the larger national society.[65] As the discussion on Latin American constitutionalism has shown, however, this characteristic is not unique to Panama, but it is a common feature of Latin American legal systems which, in an effort to compensate for past injustices towards indigenous peoples, create systems of protection that collapse all cultural difference (and the special legal measures required to protect it) into indigeneity and its protection. Thus, other traditional communities, such as peasant ('*campesino*') communities, are largely ignored within the constitution.

[60] Law No 20 of 26 June 2000. A complete translation is available in the article by Irma De Obaldia, 'Western Intellectual Property and Indigenous Cultures: The Case of the Panamanian Indigenous Intellectual Property Law', *BU Intl LJ* 23 (2005), 337 94 at 390 4.

[61] Executive Decree No 12 of 20 March 2001.

[62] WIPO, *Comparative Summary of Sui Generis Legislation for the Protection of Traditional Cultural Expressions*, WIPO/GRTKF/IC/5/INF/3, Annex, 5.

[63] See generally, for all, Silke von Lewinski, 'The Protection of Folklore', *Cardozo J Intl & Comp L* 11 (2003), 747 68 at 765 6.

[64] Obaldia, 'Western Intellectual Property and Indigenous Cultures', 338 9.

[65] Obaldia, 'Western Intellectual Property and Indigenous Cultures', 341.

Ignoring peasant communities is at least partly attributable to another feature of Panamanian indigenous struggles that can also be found across the continent: the political clashes between indigenous communities, on the one hand, and peasant and other traditional communities, on the other. The fact that these two groups are competitors in the struggle for land means that they are at odds in all other political issues, including the protection of artistic creations. This conflict creates divided legislative bodies, with legislators standing by one segment or the other, often incapable of reaching compromise and performing concerted action.[66]

Law No 20 was enacted as the culmination of a long series of legislative acts that gradually extended protection to the *mola*. The *mola* is a type of textile craft that consists of panels of often intricate design with unnoticeable stitching, creating a beautiful and impressive visual effect. The *mola* panels then become the front of shirts used in everyday activities by Kuna women. An important feature to be highlighted is that the art is produced exclusively by women and that the myth behind the craft mentions the resistance of men in allowing women to master and control this craft.[67] The gender dimension is thus very apparent and is partly responsible for the imbalances in the protection of the *mola* through Law No 20.

Law No 20 creates a system of registration and protection akin to IP, but at the same time substantially different. It allows for group rights over the creation, in the first place, and also for the use of customary law of the indigenous communities in determining issues of agency when it comes to representing these interests before the government and third parties. According to this piece of legislation, any manifestation of intangible heritage can be registered.

The main goals of the law are to protect the collective rights and intellectual property of indigenous communities, as a means of promoting economic development through the commercialization of the products of these rights. By advancing these goals, the Panamanian law moves away from traditional IP policy goals (which would be the protection of creation for the benefit of society or the rewarding of individual artists); instead, it promotes development in favour of a specific segment of society.[68] The goal of promoting development is reinforced by the fact that the subject matter of protection of the law is restricted to manifestations of heritage with potential commercial use.[69]

Registration of expressions of heritage are made before the government in the same manner as the registration of any other IP right. However, only the General Congresses or the Indigenous Traditional Authorities can perform this act, and only for collective rights. This means that it is the traditional indigenous authorities who will exert ultimate control over the communities' rights.[70] These rights are guaranteed as the legislation also creates rights for the community against the non-indigenous population, so as to avoid uses and misappropriation by third parties.[71]

[66] Obaldia, 'Western Intellectual Property and Indigenous Cultures', 361 2.
[67] Obaldia, 'Western Intellectual Property and Indigenous Cultures', 356 9.
[68] Obaldia, 'Western Intellectual Property and Indigenous Cultures', 365.
[69] Obaldia, 'Western Intellectual Property and Indigenous Cultures', 367 8.
[70] Obaldia, 'Western Intellectual Property and Indigenous Cultures', 366.
[71] Obaldia, 'Western Intellectual Property and Indigenous Cultures', 367 8.

Communities are also responsible for the enforcement of their rights, which is another exception to ordinary IP legislation in which the persecution of infringers usually is the duty of the State not of the rights-holders.[72] This enforcement mechanism was created partly through the initiative of a certification mark attesting to the authenticity of the craft.[73] Finally, a lawyer is not required for the process of registering a manifestation of heritage. This is intended to render the rights more accessible.[74]

Exceptions to the rights created by this regime are for educational uses and folkloric dance groups, as long as the latter include indigenous members in the performances or are authorized by the respective indigenous groups. Also, licensing is allowed, and is compulsory in the case of non-indigenous artisans who made indigenous-like crafts and were registered as artisans before the General Directorate of National Crafts prior to the entry into force of Law No 20.[75]

The implementation of Law No 20 was more difficult and met more obstacles than initially thought. At the time of writing, it seems that only one manifestation of heritage has been registered under this Law; that is, the *mola*, which was the motivator of it. Therefore, it may be that the reach of this piece of legislation is actually very limited.

Also, even in the single case of the *mola*, there have been problems with the group rights perspective involving the gender dimension. As mentioned earlier, the *mola* is a craft practised exclusively by women, and, according to the myth behind the *mola*, men initially opposed the craft's development. And, according to Law No 20, the management of the rights over the exploitation of the *mola* are held by the traditional indigenous authorities, which are organs dominated by men, in accordance with Kuna indigenous customary law. Hence, the concerns of women, who are the producers of the *molas*, are ultimately disregarded. As a result, there have been awkward clashes between the individual rights of the Kuna women and the collective rights of the tribe over the *molas*. Some women started teaching their craft to non-Kuna individuals in contravention of decisions of the indigenous authority. They produced *molas* to be sold in neighbouring Costa Rica for a lower price, and did not observe the procedure determined by the indigenous authority, which aims, among other things, at controlling the quality and particularly the quantity of *molas* produced. Ultimately, a meeting between Kuna women and the heads of the Kuna General Congress seem to have dealt with the situation and reached a suitable compromise in favour of collective rights.[76]

Another problem related to the *molas* is the fact, already mentioned, that Law No 20 seems not to take into account the interests of other segments of Panamanian society,[77] creating a super-protective haven for Kuna art that prevents the flow of ideas and the dissemination of the art as part of the common pool of knowledge of

[72] Obaldia, 'Western Intellectual Property and Indigenous Cultures', 369.
[73] Obaldia, 'Western Intellectual Property and Indigenous Cultures', 371.
[74] Obaldia, 'Western Intellectual Property and Indigenous Cultures', 366.
[75] Obaldia, 'Western Intellectual Property and Indigenous Cultures', 369.
[76] Obaldia, 'Western Intellectual Property and Indigenous Cultures', 371 4.
[77] Obaldia, 'Western Intellectual Property and Indigenous Cultures', 375.

society. If one considers that the technique employed for the production of *molas* was inspired by the French technique of *appliqué*, and then employed by the Kuna as a replacement of or addition to their body-painting tradition,[78] the Kuna claim for exclusive ownership on the basis of their own creation of the technique does not necessarily hold true. To protect their exclusive right to employ the technique would be to consider heritage as isolationist, which flies in the face of the idea of cultural flow. Also, if Law No 20 is applied to other forms of art, it may in the long term lead to the ossification of Panamanian indigenous culture, and prevent the evolution of this culture and its techniques and arts.

The Panamanian experience, as well as the introduction of *sui generis* regimes generally, is very promising, but still not a completely adequate response to safeguarding intangible heritage. First of all, the larger societal claims have to be taken into account more effectively, so as to avoid the propertization of culture in favour of a certain group and to the detriment of society at large. Secondly, even within the communities who benefit, problems may arise when customary rules regarding agency and representation clash with the interests of those within the community who actually engage in the production of the art (not to mention the questions arising from the need to regulate transborder trade in *molas*, which seems to fall beyond the scope of the Panamanian law). These questions will be addressed in more detail in Chapter 7, and the Panamanian experience is an important reminder of their importance and practical implications.

Besides the two 'legal' forms of protection looked at so far, many countries have chosen to address the protection of intangible heritage through softer, more flexible policy programmes. Some echo the restricted reach of the 2003 UNESCO Convention. I will now look at how some of these initiatives have played out in practice.

4.4 Policy-level Responses

The countries who adopt predominantly policy-level measures for the protection of intangible heritage do so for many reasons. One is to avoid the difficulties of creating property rights over intangible heritage, which, as seen in the previous sections (and as it will be further elaborated in Chapters 6 and 7), can be a very complicated process of mediation of interests among a large number of stakeholders.

Another reason could be that, by avoiding 'legal' protection, the politicization and polarization that naturally arises from any attempt at harder protection is also minimized. This strategy is part of the general effect of mediation among stakeholders mentioned above, but also one that takes its own, especially in relation to the political power of identity.[79] A policy solution can be perennial or intentionally

[78] Obaldia, 'Western Intellectual Property and Indigenous Cultures', 357.

[79] On the political power of identity and the protection of the ways of life of crofters in Scotland as an ICH concern, see Cynthia A Lohman, 'Crofting: Securing the Future of the Scottish Highlands through Legislative Challenge and Cultural Legacy', *Transnational L & Contemporary Problems* 16 (2007), 663 704.

transitory (that is, it may offer an apolitical solution at first and, when people get used to the idea, subsequently advance towards a stronger form of protection, which will then not be deemed so controversial).

Finally, States can also choose not to offer stronger legal mechanisms simply based upon a preference choice of other heritage values. Instead of protecting economic interests that may arise from manifestations of heritage, States can legitimately choose to treat it simply as another cultural field. In such a scenario, the main interest of the State would be not in creating rights and claims to the heritage by certain segments of society, but simply to ensure that everyone can partake in this heritage. In this way heritage becomes automatically a commonly shared resource. To accomplish this ideal, States then invest in education, promotion and awareness-raising.

To a large extent, these strategies echo the tenets of the 2003 UNESCO Convention, analysed in further detail in Chapter 2. And many countries who have more recently adopted legislation to protect intangible heritage have done so precisely in response to becoming parties to this instrument.

Romania is an example of adopting legislation in response to the 2003 UNESCO Convention. It passed legislation in January 2007 'on the immaterial cultural heritage protection [sic]'.[80] Besides offering its own definition of 'immaterial heritage' which is fairly similar to the UNESCO definition, the Ordinance also determines that protection measures should be aimed at conservation and enhancement of this type of heritage. It imposes several obligations on the Ministry of Culture and Religious Affairs related to the safeguarding of intangible heritage.

Interestingly, the Ordinance largely excludes corporate entities from its scope of protection. It determines that the entitlement to protection in the field of crafts extends only to natural persons or family enterprises (which may employ third parties only as apprentices). It also establishes a 'distinctive traditional trademark' to be displayed in products meeting the Ordinance's requirements, as a means to foster economic development through the exploitation of intangible heritage. The authorization for the use of this trademark is to be given by the Ministry of Culture and Religious Affairs, who will also inventory each regional, ethnographic trademark.

The Ordinance also creates a programme to support what it calls 'living human thesauruses', which is fairly similar to the Japanese idea of 'living human treasures',[81] also existing in South Korea.[82] These are individuals who are considered to be repositories of particularly valuable intangible heritage and who are, through these programmes, sponsored by the government to pursue their art and ensure its

[80] Romania, 'Ordinance No 19 of 31 January 2007 on the immaterial cultural heritage protection', *UNESCO Database of National Cultural Heritage Laws*.

[81] On the Japanese experience, see Yosihiko Tokumaru, 'Transmitting Music: Towards a Re-Evaluation of the Human Body', in Oscar Salemink (ed), *Viet Nam's Cultural Diversity: Approaches to Preservation* (UNESCO Publishing, 2001), 233 8 at 237; and Voltaire Garces Cang, 'Defining Intangible Cultural Heritage and its Stakeholders: The Case of Japan', *Intl J of Intangible Heritage* 2 (2007), 46 55.

[82] Darrell A Posey and Graham Dutfield, *Beyond Intellectual Property: Toward Traditional Resource Rights for Indigenous Peoples and Local Communities* (1996), 150 2.

transmission to younger generations so as to secure the continuity of intangible heritage practices.

The Ordinance finally creates archives and inventories for intangible heritage, as well as a National Commission for Safeguarding the Immaterial Cultural Heritage. Criminal penalties and fines apply to those who make unauthorized use of a distinctive trademark, be they natural or juridical persons.

The Romanian Ordinance, as well as the Japanese 'living human treasures' programme, created varied policy programmes aimed at protecting and safeguarding intangible heritage. Other countries, particularly in Asia, also do this, responding to specific material conditions. The examples of China, Laos, and Vietnam are particularly valuable, and will be examined in the following subsections.

4.4.1 China

China's relationship with heritage is closely connected to the idea of promoting its own national (political) identity, and thereby reaffirming its self-assigned leadership position in Asia. By invoking and narrating its own history through its heritage, China puts its economic and political rise in context, and endows it with deep and ancient roots.[83]

The Chinese legislation with respect to intangible heritage is a prime example of the risks associated with listing, and the idea of State control over heritage discussed in Chapter 2. Characterized as an implementation of the 2003 UNESCO Convention by Chinese culture officials (even if it had been in drafting since 2001, the process only gained momentum after China's ratification of the 2003 UNESCO Convention),[84] the February 2011 'Intangible Cultural Heritage Law of the People's Republic of China' was enacted '[i]n order to carry forward the fine traditional Chinese culture, promote the construction of [a] socialist spiritual civilization, [and] strengthen the protection of intangible cultural heritage'.[85]

Importantly, too, the law specifies that the 'protection of intangible cultural heritage, should pay attention to the authenticity, integrity and heritage, and help enhance the cultural identity of the Chinese nation, and is conducive to safeguarding national unity and ethnic solidarity, help to promote social harmony and sustainable development'.[86] The administrative process for listing of heritage within China is set up with a view of promoting these goals, which amounts to precisely the monopoly of the State over the meaning of heritage, how it can be

[83] For this discussion, and a discussion of heritage protection in China generally, see Stefan Gruber, 'Protecting China's Cultural Heritage: A Legal and Policy Approach', PhD Thesis (University of Sydney, 2012); and Stefan Gruber, 'Protecting China's Cultural Heritage Sites in Times of Rapid Change: Current Developments, Practice and Law', *Asia Pacific J of Envl L* 10(3), (4) (2007), 253 301 at 274.

[84] Xinhuanet, *China's First Law for Preserving Intangible Cultural Heritage Passed*, available at <http://news.xinhuanet.com/english2010/video/2011-02/27/c 13752622.htm> (accessed 29 November 2012).

[85] Quote from an unofficial translation from the Chinese text on *WIPO Lex*, available at <http://www.wipo.int/wipolex/en/text.jsp?file id=215504> (accessed 29 November 2012).

[86] *WIPO Lex*.

used, and who should benefit from it. The law even goes to the point of centralizing the control over heritage, placing the central government over provincial and local governments in matters related to intangible heritage.[87]

The law facilitates access to knowledge about heritage by creating a freely accessible database (but also indicating that, in accordance with the law, some heritage may be excluded from the openly accessible part of the database), and that local stakeholders should be involved in preserving the heritage.[88] As the sole arbiter of 'authenticity' of intangible heritage, though, the central government exercises a tight control over heritage. The law even determines that foreign organizations in the field of culture working on Chinese intangible heritage must seek authorization from and report to the government, under risk of fines.[89]

The law contains (somewhat vague) provisions on the relationship between itself and other statutes (particularly IP), stating that other legislation has to be interpreted in accordance with the intangible heritage law. It seems to therefore prioritize intangible heritage safeguarding to other goals, even if that happens at the cost of controlling heritage (and thus also indirectly allowing for greater governmental control over related areas of law). Nevertheless, the law has been criticized for focusing too much on administrative procedures, without enough regard for private law issues (such as IP and other arrangements about the economic exploitation of heritage).[90]

It is somewhat puzzling that the law will give so much emphasis to governmental control over heritage and its meanings, if one considers what happened during the Cultural Revolution, during which Chinese art and heritage were essentially remade so as to advance a political ideal.[91] The fact that the Cultural Revolution ultimately failed would seem to be a reminder of how heritage's meanings should not be determined by a central government, but, at the end of the day, the goal of advancing Chinese national (political) identity has prevailed in China; despite its failure, some of the spirit of the Cultural Revolution lives on.

The Chinese Law is a perfect example of how implementation of the 2003 ICH Convention can have unintended consequences and dark sides. By doing exactly what the ICH Convention requires of States (cataloguing and awareness-raising), it allows States to exercise near-total control over the meanings and uses of heritage.

4.4.2 Laos

The protection of intangible heritage in Laos involves the peculiarity that there is still fragmented knowledge as to what is there to be protected. This lack of

[87] *WIPO Lex.* [88] *WIPO Lex.*

[89] *WIPO Lex.* See also news report at Xinhuanet, *China Adopts First Law for Intangible Cultural Heritage Protection*, available at <http://news.xinhuanet.com/english2010/culture/2011-02/25/c 13750084.htm> (accessed 29 November 2012).

[90] Luo Li, 'Does Intangible Cultural Heritage Law Resolve Everything in China?', *J of Intl Commercial L and Technology* 7(4) (2012), 355 62 at 362.

[91] For an in-depth discussion of the Cultural Revolution, see Gruber, 'Protecting China's Cultural Heritage', 53 60.

definition is actually part of a much larger, systemic problem of human geography in Laos. Neither the government, nor any international or non-governmental agency has a full ethnographic map of the country.[92]

Another important factor in Laos is its dependence on foreign aid and foreign tourism for development. These two forces have the capacity to shape culture generally and it has been argued that this is a particularly grave concern in Laos, where traditions have been openly and deeply modified to cater to foreign tourist preferences.[93] Nevertheless, Lao minority culture still flourishes spontaneously and must accordingly be protected, according to at least one commentator.[94]

One of the core concerns in Laos is the protection of minority languages. According to (incomplete) governmental data, there are 47 languages spoken in Laos.[95] There has been an active effort at cataloguing these languages and the cultures they embody, but there is still a long way to go.[96] The Constitution of Laos makes a clear effort to 'apply a policy of solidarity and equality in regard to different ethnic groups'.[97] In 1983 the government created the Institute of Research in Lao Culture, as part of the Ministry of Information and Culture.[98]

Another concern is that of protecting textiles, which are deemed to be the quintessential manifestation of intangible heritage of Laos. The Lao culture has even been referred to as a 'cloth culture', where textiles represent each cultural group, telling stories ranging from the mundane to the ethereal, and thus offering tools for the understanding of different social systems.[99] Quite some effort has been put in cataloguing the different fabrics and patterns used by the different groups, and to ascribe them social meaning and context beyond that of the items of clothing themselves.[100] The same can be said

[92] Gábor Vargyas, 'The Bru: A Minority Straddling Laos and Viet Nam', in Yves Goudineau (ed), *Laos and Ethnic Minority Cultures: Promoting Heritage* (UNESCO Publishing, 2003), 159 62 at 161; Jacques Lemoine, 'Creating an Ethnographical Data Bank in the Lao PDR', in Yves Goudineau (ed), *Laos and Ethnic Minority Cultures: Promoting Heritage* (UNESCO Publishing, 2003), 275 82; and Thongphet Kingsada, 'Some Vulnerable Languages in the Lao PDR', in Yves Goudineau (ed), *Laos and Ethnic Minority Cultures: Promoting Heritage* (UNESCO Publishing, 2003), 43 4.

[93] Georges Condominas, 'Safeguarding and Promoting the Intangible Cultural Heritage of Lao Minority Groups', in Yves Goudineau (ed), *Laos and Ethnic Minority Cultures: Promoting Heritage* (UNESCO Publishing, 2003), 19 26 at 21.

[94] Yves Goudineau, 'Managing the Intangible Cultural Heritage', in Yves Goudineau (ed), *Laos and Ethnic Minority Cultures: Promoting Heritage* (UNESCO Publishing, 2003), 33 7 at 33.

[95] See a map of these groups and languages in Yves Goudineau (ed), *Laos and Ethnic Minority Cultures: Promoting Heritage* (UNESCO Publishing 2003), 14 15.

[96] See eg Phéng Lasoukanh, 'Overview of the Ko Ethnic Group', in Yves Goudineau (ed), *Laos and Ethnic Minority Cultures: Promoting Heritage* (UNESCO Publishing, 2003), 181 4.

[97] This quote from the first chapter of the Lao PDR Constitution can be found in Houmphan Rattanavong, 'A Multi-Ethnic Culture', in Yves Goudineau (ed), *Laos and Ethnic Minority Cultures: Promoting Heritage* (UNESCO Publishing, 2003), 27 32 at 28.

[98] Rattanavong, 'A Multi-Ethnic Culture', 29.

[99] H Leedom Lefferts Jr, 'Textiles for the Preservation of the Lao Intangible Cultural Heritage', in Yves Goudineau (ed), *Laos and Ethnic Minority Cultures: Promoting Heritage* (UNESCO Publishing, 2003), 89 110 at 90.

[100] See for instance Lytou Bouapao, 'Traditional Hmong Weaving and Embroidery', in Yves Goudineau (ed), *Laos and Ethnic Minority Cultures: Promoting Heritage* (UNESCO Publishing, 2003), 119 27.

about architecture[101] and music and musical instruments,[102] even though they have less importance for Lao cultures.

The efforts of cataloguing the Lao minority cultures are still underway, and are largely dependent on foreign aid and assistance.[103] The government has also made efforts in this direction, and coordinates international action.[104] The example of Laos is thus an important reminder of how intangible heritage policies serve not only the goal of safeguarding ICH, but also serve to build the very foundation of a country, through the acquisition of knowledge about its own human geography.

4.4.3 Viet Nam

Viet Nam, although a neighbouring country to Laos and facing many of the same issues, has had a rather different experience in developing its framework for safeguarding ICH. For one, Viet Nam has specific legislation on ICH protection. In 2001 the National Assembly of Viet Nam adopted the Law on Cultural Heritage. This law contains an entire chapter dedicated to intangible cultural heritage. This chapter affirms that the State shall, through policies, encourage the collection, compilation, and preservation of works of literature, art, oral tradition, and folklore, to be disseminated domestically and through international cultural exchange.[105]

The implementing decree to this law reinforces the policy-oriented mandate of the State by determining the means to safeguard intangible heritage, which include nationwide inventorying of ICH, actions to increase public awareness, increasing transmission skills to younger generations, and support for archiving activities. It also determines that intangible heritage must be safeguarded in a sustainable

[101] Sophie Clément and Pierre Clément, 'Architecture as an Expression of Minority Culture', in Yves Goudineau (ed), *Laos and Ethnic Minority Cultures: Promoting Heritage* (UNESCO Publishing, 2003), 137 52 at 138 (arguing that architecture is a quintessential manifestation of intangible heritage, through its aesthetic and functional traits).

[102] Bouthèng Souksavat, 'The Tunglung: An Alak Musical Instrument', in Yves Goudineau (ed), *Laos and Ethnic Minority Cultures: Promoting Heritage* (UNESCO Publishing, 2003), 133 6; and Suksavang Simana and Elisabeth Preisig, '"Kmhumu" Music and Musical Instruments', in Yves Goudineau (ed), *Laos and Ethnic Minority Cultures: Promoting Heritage* (UNESCO Publishing, 2003), 123 32.

[103] Bouabane Vorakhoun, 'Survey of Preservation and Promotion of Minority Cultures in the Lao PDR', in Yves Goudineau (ed), *Laos and Ethnic Minority Cultures: Promoting Heritage* (UNESCO Publishing, 2003), 247 50 at 249; and Yoshikuni Yanagi, 'Research on Textile Traditions', in Yves Goudineau (ed), *Laos and Ethnic Minority Cultures: Promoting Heritage* (UNESCO Publishing, 2003), 261 4.

[104] Lemoine, 'Creating an Ethnographical Data Bank'. For a view from a governmental official summarizing governmental efforts, see Siho Bannavong, 'The Lao Front for National Construction and Minority Cultural Heritage', in Yves Goudineau (ed), *Laos and Ethnic Minority Cultures: Promoting Heritage* (UNESCO Publishing, 2003), 255 61; and Kamtay Siphandone, '5th Party Congress Directive on Cultural Activities in the New Era: Ninth Meeting of the Administrative Commission of the Party Central Committee', in Yves Goudineau (ed), *Laos and Ethnic Minority Cultures: Promoting Heritage* (UNESCO Publishing, 2003), 289 92 at 290 (referring to intangible cultural heritage as 'the foundation of national security').

[105] Nguyen Kim Dung, *Intangible Cultural Heritage Safeguarding System in Vietnam*, available at <http://www.unesco.org/culture/ich/doc/src/00174-EN.pdf> (accessed 29 November 2012).

manner, and for that purpose it creates a programme very similar to the Japanese initiative to protect 'living treasures of intangible and oral heritage',[106] already mentioned above in comparison to the Romanian initiative.

The Ministry of Culture and Information is the organ in charge of promoting actions to safeguard intangible heritage, as well as to inspect the implementation of the law on the matter and settle any disputes regarding the implementation of cultural heritage law. Several institutions under the Ministry of Culture and Information cooperate to safeguard ICH, including a specific Committee for Intangible Cultural Heritage, the Research Institute of Musicology, and the Institute of Culture and Information. These last two organs have set up an ICH data bank.[107]

One of the main challenges currently facing ICH safeguarding in Viet Nam is again the definition of the country's intangible heritage. Just as in Laos, the cultural diversity of Viet Nam is quite remarkable: there are about 54 languages spoken in Viet Nam, and a plethora of ethnic groups.[108] Also like Laos, the tourism industry in Viet Nam is large, and corresponds to a sizeable portion of the country's GDP. As a result, the power exerted by the tourism industry is quite large, and has been channelled towards modifying the presentation of traditional and minority culture in Viet Nam, to better cater to tourists' tastes. This is aided by the modernization of the country, and the cultural flows that come from outside, which have also substantially altered the country's intangible heritage. For instance, traditional Vietnamese music has been modified to accommodate instruments that can be found in the majority of orchestras around the world. So that Viet Nam's traditional music could gain a wider audience, it has been modified, and now it is taught in this way. Over time, then, younger generations are only exposed to the 'modernized' or modified versions of their own intangible heritage.[109] According to some commentators, this evolution is a bad consequence of economic development; others, however, argue that the best way to defend ethnic minority culture is precisely for these minorities 'to open up to the modern world and accept reforms, while preserving the essential values of their culture'.[110] Also, the experience of Bali is interesting in this respect: there, traditional dance forms have been adapted and transformed to accommodate tourist tastes, and gradually found their way into temples and mainstream Balinese cultural life, revitalizing traditional

[106] Dung, *Intangible Cultural Heritage.*

[107] Dung, *Intangible Cultural Heritage.*

[108] Dang Nghiêm, Van, 'Preservation and Development of the Cultural Heritage', in Oscar Salemink (ed), *Viet Nam's Cultural Diversity: Approaches to Preservation* (UNESCO Publishing, 2001), 33 62 at 34 5.

[109] See in this sense Tô Ngoc Thanh, 'Protecting the Intangible Cultural Heritage of Minority Groups in Viet Nam', in Yves Goudineau (ed), *Laos and Ethnic Minority Cultures: Promoting Heritage* (UNESCO Publishing, 2003), 219 22 at 220. He uses a particularly interesting metaphor to explain this process. In the author's words: '[...] To use a metaphor: the totality of the traditional culture is a mass of gold, many tons in weight. We take a few kilograms from that mass and make rings to a Western design. We give these rings to the younger generation and say that they comprise the whole national cultural tradition. The younger generations will know nothing of the huge mass of gold, which will be sunk deep in the past, or even destroyed by the younger generation in the mistaken belief that it is only a mass of common clay'.

[110] Van, 'Preservation and Development', 57.

cultures on the verge of extinction.[111] One must not forget, therefore, the importance and positive effect of re-packaging and economic incentive to the preservation of living cultures.

The effort to catalogue Vietnamese culture is ongoing, and efforts have been made towards the inventorying of epic poetry,[112] dance,[113] and music,[114] among other manifestations of heritage. However, participants in the inventorying process have noted that this is a passive method, as it only allows the heritage to survive in a 'textual' form.[115] Concerted action is needed, and has been taken, towards promoting the continuation of the cultural practices that make up the intangible heritage being safeguarded. The bulk of these initiatives have focused on the education of younger generations about minority languages,[116] even though other initiatives, such as awareness-raising through posters and even postal stamps, as well as the 'living human treasures' programme mentioned above, have been put into practice.[117]

The Vietnamese and Lao examples teach us that policy initiatives, even though lacking legal 'bite', can be very effective in safeguarding intangible heritage, and through that achieve other larger objectives, such as stability in multi-ethnic countries, and even help attract foreign aid to complete the ethnographic maps of countries lacking resources. A different set of objectives can be accomplished through a different type of action, which consists of applying a multiplicity of sources to promote ICH objectives. Some examples of this will be analysed in the next section.

4.5 Fragmented/Plural/Non-specific Responses

This group of countries is very diverse. One example of a country of this sort is South Africa: there is no specific legislation on the protection of intangible cultural

[111] Grant Evans, 'Tourism and Minorities', in Oscar Salemink (ed), *Viet Nam's Cultural Diversity: Approaches to Preservation* (UNESCO Publishing, 2001), 277 80 at 279.

[112] Phang Dang Nhât, 'The Timeless Epics of the Ethnic Minorities of Viet Nam', in Oscar Salemink (ed), *Viet Nam's Cultural Diversity: Approaches to Preservation* (UNESCO Publishing, 2001), 85 104.

[113] Osamu Yamaguti, 'Harmony in Cultural Projects: Revitalization of the Music and Dance of the Vietnamese Minorities', in Oscar Salemink (ed), *Viet Nam's Cultural Diversity: Approaches to Preservation* (UNESCO Publishing, 2001), 229 32.

[114] Trân Van Khê, 'Safeguarding and Promoting the Traditional Musical Heritage of Minority Groups in Viet Nam', in Oscar Salemink (ed), *Viet Nam's Cultural Diversity: Approaches to Preservation* (UNESCO Publishing, 2001), 105 10.

[115] Tô Ngoc Thanh, 'The Intangible Culture of the Vietnamese Minorities: Questions and Answers', in Oscar Salemink (ed), *Viet Nam's Cultural Diversity: Approaches to Preservation* (UNESCO Publishing, 2001), 121 6 at 123.

[116] Oscar Salemink, 'Who Decides Who Preserves What? Cultural Preservation and Cultural Representation', in Oscar Salemink (ed), *Viet Nam's Cultural Diversity: Approaches to Preservation* (UNESCO Publishing, 2001), 205 12 at 210 12; and Gábor Vargyas, 'Intangible Culture of the Bru: Preservation, Promotion and Reassertion of Values', in Oscar Salemink (ed), *Viet Nam's Cultural Diversity: Approaches to Preservation* (UNESCO Publishing, 2001), 199 204 at 203 4.

[117] William Dessaint, 'Intangible Cultural Heritage: Tibeto-Burmese Peoples and Minority Groups in Viet Nam', in Oscar Salemink (ed), *Viet Nam's Cultural Diversity: Approaches to Preservation* (UNESCO Publishing, 2001), 239 54 at 252 3.

heritage in South Africa; however, intangible elements permeate the application of all cultural heritage legislation in the country, especially when speaking of projects that somehow affect the country's memory of apartheid. And all cases of architectural development affect this, and must take into account the delicate balance between contested or competing understandings of intangibility itself: what for some segments of society is a reminder of a tranquil way of life, for some can stand as a symbol of oppression and suffering. The conservation of intangible values in an emerging country is thus very problematic on all levels.[118]

Another interesting example is Ireland, which has used its environmental legislation on the protection of landscapes as a means to address intangible heritage concerns.[119] There are countries that apply a mixture of intellectual property and *sui generis* regimes; some others have so far not developed a specific framework, and rather rely on a multiplicity of different laws that can be used indirectly to protect intangible heritage; and several other countries are currently drafting their specific legislation, and trying to choose a path. Brazil is in the latter category, and will be the object of analysis of the next subsection.

4.5.1 Brazil

Until recently, very little had been done in Brazil in terms of legal action for the protection of intangible heritage.[120] Brazil is an extremely diverse country, of great dimensions, and each of its regions has a very distinctive heritage. The Brazilian Federal Constitution of 1988 only declares, in Articles 215 and 216, the need for protection of cultural heritage and culture in general. Article 216 does include (within the meaning of Brazilian cultural heritage) both tangible and intangible elements,[121] which means Brazil is a nice addition to the Latin American constitutional panorama analysed above.

[118] For the South African experience, especially with regard to development and housing projects, see Karel Anthonie Bakker, 'Preserving Intangible Heritage Resources: Examples from South Africa', *Proceedings of the ICOMOS 14th General Assembly and Scientific Symposium: Place, Memory, Meaning: Preserving Intangible Values in Monuments and Sites*, available at <http://www.international.icomos.org/victoriafalls2003/papers.htm> (accessed 29 November 2012).

[119] Joseph C Pettygrove, 'Canyons, Castles and Controversies: A Comparison of Preservation Laws in the United States and Ireland', *Regent J Intl L* 4 (2006), 47 99.

[120] The Brazilian judiciary has also avoided approaching the issue several times, see eg a recent case from the Rio Grande do Sul State Court of Appeals (Civil Appeal No 70001422948). In the case, a jewellery designer sued a jewellery company for misappropriating her designs based on indigenous folklore. No mention was made at any time concerning the interests of the indigenous peoples in the use of their intangible heritage, regardless of the fact the designer was not an indigenous person. The case is available at the Court's website, at <http://www.tjrs.jus.br> (accessed 22 January 2013).

[121] The text of this Article is the following: '**Article 216**. The Brazilian cultural heritage consists of the assets of a material and immaterial nature, taken individually or as a whole, which bear reference to the identity, action and memory of the various groups that form the Brazilian society, therein included: I forms of expression; II ways of creating, making and living; III scientific, artistic and technological creations; IV works, objects, documents, buildings and other spaces intended for artistic and cultural expressions; V urban complexes and sites of historical, natural, artistic, archaeological, paleontological, ecological and scientific value.

Civil society is rather well organized in terms of the protection of intangible heritage and, in 1951, the 'Charter of Brazilian Folklore' was written, during the first Brazilian Folklore Symposium.[122] Ever since, civil society has played a positive role in the development of intangible heritage protection in the country, a role that has continued in the implementation of federal legislation on the matter.[123]

In 2000 a Decree was passed instituting the inventories of Brazilian intangible heritage.[124] The Federal Decree reproduces the listing system ('*tombamento*') that already existed regarding built heritage. It protects knowledge, celebrations, and festivals, forms of artistic expression, and cultural spaces. For each of these categories there is a separate book where recognized manifestations of intangible heritage are to be registered. The governing authority also reserves the right to start new books for new categories that may emerge.[125]

There is a specific procedure for inscription in these lists, and the request can be made by the Minister of Culture; institutions connected to the Ministry of Culture; state- and city-level culture departments; and civil society groups.[126] It is important to note that civil society may directly request inscription. Even though this provision was implemented prior to the 2003 UNESCO Convention, it seems to be a more advanced strategy in comparison to international initiatives.

After the request, the National Institute for Historic and Artistic Heritage (IPHAN '*Instituto do Patrimônio Histórico e Artístico Nacional*') will have 30 days to give an opinion on whether the manifestation should be registered. Registration in one of these books is for renewable periods of 10 years, so as to ensure that the manifestations of intangible heritage listed are part of living cultures. Interestingly,

Paragraph 1 The Government shall, with the cooperation of the community, promote and protect the Brazilian cultural heritage, by means of inventories, registers, vigilance, monument protection decrees, expropriation and other forms of precaution and preservation.

Paragraph 2 It is incumbent upon the Government, in accordance with the law, to manage the keeping of the governmental documents and to make them available for consultation to whomever may need to do so.

Paragraph 3 The law shall establish incentives for the production and knowledge of cultural assets and values.

Paragraph 4 Damages and threats to the cultural heritage shall be punished in accordance with the law.

Paragraph 5 All documents and sites bearing historical reminiscence to the ancient communities of runaway slaves are protected as national heritage.

Paragraph 6. The States and the Federal District may allocate up to five tenths percent of their net tax proceedings to a State fund for fomenting culture, it being prohibited the use of these funds to pay for: I expenses with salaries and social duties; II interests of debts; III any other current expense not directly linked to the investments or activities supported.'

See also Rodrigo Vieira Costa, *A Dimensão Constitucional do Patrimônio Cultural: O Tombamento e o Registro Sob a ötica dos Direitos Culturais* (Lumen Juris, 2011).

122 The 14th edition of this symposium has taken place in October 2004 in central Brazil, and every year recommendations regarding policies towards intangible heritage are taken and implemented somewhat independently from governmental action.

123 See Cristina Leme Lopes, 'La Protection Juridique du Patrimoine Culturel Immatériel: Le Cas Brésilien', Mémoire presented for a Master's Degree at the Universities of Paris I and II (2008), 72.

124 Decree 3.551, of 4 August 2000.

125 Carlos Frederico Marés de Souza Filho, *Bens Culturais e sua Proteção Jurídica* (2008), 80 1.

126 Souza Filho, *Bens Culturais*, 81.

the Decree does not require the recording or fixation in any means of the manifestation of intangible heritage; instead, it only requires a description of the practice and its cultural and social context.[127] As of 2008, 14 manifestations of heritage had been registered in these books, and 15 were pending approval.[128]

In 1997 local governments started studying intangible heritage and protective possibilities.[129] As Brazil is a federal country and applies the principle of subsidiarity in cultural matters,[130] this is a very welcome development. After passage of the Federal Decree 3.551 in 2000, some States followed suit and enacted their own legislation on the matter.[131]

Besides the listing mechanism examined above, several other alternatives have been pursued in Brazil. One of them is protection through IP mechanisms. Brazilian IP legislation, nevertheless, does not deal with the issue as it merely excludes 'ethnic and traditional knowledge' from the scope of its application.[132] A bill or draft piece of legislation, however, is currently under consideration and may change this scenario. This bill was proposed in 2007, and it extends the protection of copyright law to ICH and the groups and communities that practice such heritage. The fact that the bill attempts to create group rights to IP is a noteworthy development.[133]

The bill reinforces the inventorying system, but it also goes beyond that in creating a system of IP rights to be administered by communities themselves, and not subject to time limitations common to IP rights. As to the conflict between group and individual rights, the bill tries to mediate it by still guaranteeing the protection of individual rights to the carrier of community traditional knowledge who produces an innovative work of his/her own. It guarantees moral rights to the community, and determines that any monies collected by the community under the title of royalties shall be invested in the community itself, particularly in projects aimed at safeguarding the community's intangible heritage. At the time of writing, the bill is awaiting public hearings before it goes to the Legislative Committees for a vote.

But this is by no means the only bill on ICH protection pending in Brazil at the time of writing. To the contrary, there are a large number of bills being negotiated to protect different aspects of intangible heritage. One of these bills is the new Indian Rights Act, mentioned above when discussing Brazil's position in the

[127] Souza Filho, *Bens Culturais*, 81 2.

[128] See Lopes, 'La Protection Juridique', 77.

[129] Souza Filho, *Bens Culturais*, 52 3.

[130] Souza Filho, *Bens Culturais*, 107 11.

[131] Souza Filho, *Bens Culturais*, 53. A compilation of State level legislation has been prepared with the assistance of UNESCO. See Maria Laura Viveiros de Castro Cavalcanti and Maria Cecilia Londres Fonseca, *Patrimônio Imaterial no Brasil: Legislação e Políticas Estaduais* (UNESCO Publishing, 2008).

[132] Federal Law No 9.610, of 1998, Article 45, II. See also Sherylle Mills, 'Indigenous Music and the Law: An Analysis of National and International Legislation', *Ybk for Traditional Music* (1996), 57 86 at 72 4.

[133] Bill No 518 of 21 March 2007, available at <http://www2.camara.gov.br/agencia/noticias/125093.html> (accessed 29 November 2012). For a commentary on this bill, see Lopes, 'La Protection Juridique', 94 7.

protection of indigenous rights. The Act contains provisions for the protection of the intangible heritage of indigenous communities.

Another bill extends the scope of application of a statute on cultural incentives (known as *Lei Rouanet*, after its drafter) from high culture projects to also include traditional, regional music.[134] If it becomes law, this bill has the potential to increase significantly the visibility of traditional music, and also to break the stigma of regional and traditional music as 'second-rate' art or 'low culture'.

There is also a bill that intends to create 'units of cultural preservation'. These may be roughly understood as 'cultural reservations' for peoples who have participated in the 'national civilization process' and are thus entitled to the protection of the territories they have traditionally occupied and that are essential for the safeguarding of their ICH. With the creation of these reservations, the explanatory note to the bill says, it is expected that a first step is taken towards safeguarding the ICH of these groups. The bill determines the creation of these reservations in observance of several principles, including many economic, social, and cultural rights and the principles of sustainable development and intergenerational equity. The communities to benefit from the creation of such reservations are to be involved in every step of the process leading to the demarcation of their territory, which will be done after an expert opinion is given by the National Institute of Historic and Artistic Heritage. Once the demarcation happens, the community is to create a Community Council, which will then act as representative of the community before the State and other public authorities. The bill also institutes tax breaks for projects related to the preservation of intangible heritage within these territories.[135]

Lastly, the most recent bill on the matter refers to a specific traditional community, the *jangadeiros*, or 'rafters'. A *jangada* is a traditional type of raft used in certain parts of the Brazilian northeastern coast, and the populations who use *jangadas* have developed a very specific lifestyle and culture. The project aims to protect this lifestyle and the tangible and intangible heritage associated with it. The bill determines that the protection of this heritage shall take place first through the inventorying and registration of items of historic, cultural, and artistic value to the *jangadeiros*. Further, the bill stimulates research on the lifestyles of *jangadeiros* as a means to also safeguard their intangible heritage.[136]

The large number of bills and legislative Acts in Brazil indicates that many different angles are being tried out to tackle the issue of ICH safeguarding. Legislation currently in force, coupled with civil society involvement, make awareness raising an important part of Brazil's perceived role in safeguarding its own intangible heritage. Other proposals, currently under discussion, extend this pro-

[134] Bill No 3238 of 9 April 2008, available at <http://www2.camara.gov.br/agencia/noticias/124796.html> (accessed 29 November 2012).

[135] Bill No 3056 of 18 March 2008, available at <http://www2.camara.gov.br/agencia/noticias/EDUCACAO-E-CULTURA/139542-COMISSAO-APROVA-CRIACAO-DE-UNIDADES-DE-PRESERVACAO-CULTURAL.html> (accessed 29 November 2012).

[136] Bill No 6741 of 4 February 2010, available at <http://www2.camara.gov.br/agencia/noticias/145247.html> (accessed 29 November 2012).

tection into more 'legal' forms of safeguarding, creating rights to the communities and individuals responsible for this intangible heritage. This wide array of bills currently under discussion is generally mutually reinforcing, and not exclusive, and it offers several different methodologies for addressing the various segments of Brazilian society that are bearers of intangible heritage. This avoids intangible heritage becoming exclusively indigenous.

While in Brazil there seems to be a lot of enthusiasm and promise to enact legislation protecting ICH, the same cannot be said of other countries. A very distinctive approach to intangible heritage safeguarding can be found in the United States, where there is resistance to enacting specific legislation on ICH, but other legislation on cultural heritage and fundamental rights has been used. This is the next example to be analysed.

4.5.2 United States

The United States has a very peculiar framework of fragmented protection to ICH. As seen above, its Constitution does not specifically speak of cultural heritage, but cultural heritage protection has a constitutional grounding nevertheless, based on constitutional principles. In addition to that, the United States is a federal State, and that naturally influences the capacity of the federal government to regulate cultural matters. The US Supreme Court has determined that the protection of cultural heritage is a legitimate use of police power, which is a state prerogative.[137]

Based on the example of the EU analysed in Chapter 3 and the Brazilian example analysed above, one must naturally expect subsidiarity to play a role in the enactment of cultural heritage regulation here as well, seeing as culture is a matter closer to the local sphere.[138] Analysing State-level law protecting intangible heritage would, however, greatly exceed the purposes of this chapter. Instead, I will look at the potential of federal law for the protection of ICH.

In the United States, intangible heritage receives relatively little legislative attention. Aside from IP law (to be analysed in detail in Chapter 6) and the critique of excessive propertization of culture in the United States,[139] one way in which federal law impacts upon intangible heritage is through Social Impact Assessments

[137] James K Reap, 'Selected Legislative, Administrative and Management Approaches for Protecting the Setting of Heritage Places in the United States', *Proceedings of the ICOMOS 15th General Assembly and Scientific Symposium: Monuments and Sites in their Setting Conserving Cultural Heritage in Changing Townscapes and Landscapes*, <http://www.international.icomos.org/xian2005/papers.htm> (accessed 29 November 2012) (citing *Penn Central Transportation Co v New York City*, 438 US 106 (1978)).

[138] On the importance of involving local levels of government and governance in ICH safeguarding, see Harriet Deacon, Luvuyo Dondolo, Mbulelo Mrubata, and Sandra Prosalendis, *The Subtle Power of Intangible Heritage: Legal and Financial Instruments for Safeguarding Intangible Heritage* (Human Sciences Research Council, 2004), 4 and 43, also published *Proceedings of the ICOMOS 14th General Assembly and Scientific Symposium: Place, Memory, Meaning: Preserving Intangible Values in Monuments and Sites*, available at <http://www.international.icomos.org/victoriafalls2003/papers.htm> (accessed 29 November 2012).

[139] On this topic, with specific regard to US Law, see Susan Scafidi, *Who Owns Culture? Appropriation and Authenticity in American Law* (Rutgers University Press, 2005).

(SIAs), which are required in the case of large development projects, alongside Environmental Impact Assessments.[140] The majority of SIAs is done under the umbrella of the National Environmental Policy Act, when considering, for instance, the impact of fisheries' policies upon the traditional way of life of indigenous peoples. Another important environmental instrument is the Endangered Species Act, which has roughly the same type of effect upon intangible heritage: environmental concerns examined through the prism of traditional ways of life.[141]

SIAs are governed by guidelines which require the involvement of all affected publics and populations. The guidelines also require that alternatives be sought for every step of the developmental project under scrutiny, and that all probable social impacts be addressed. Mitigation plans must also be developed, alongside an estimate of indirect and cumulative impacts. These guidelines, while important as a means to ensure the consideration of intangible heritage aspects of large projects, are not often attended to; instead, a general rubric of 'socioeconomic impact' gives a broader, less detailed picture of the social aspects.[142]

Another important piece of legislation is the American Folklife Preservation Act, which created the American Folklife Center to inventory the intangible heritage of the United States.[143] In 1980 a report was commissioned from the American Folklife Center to assess the needs for preservation of ICH in the United States. The result was a recommendation that ICH be taken into account in the implementation of all legislation on cultural resources and cultural heritage.[144]

Many other legal mechanisms can be used to safeguard intangible heritage elements. These include the Religious Freedom Restoration Act,[145] Executive Order 12898 (on environmental justice concerning minority populations),[146] the National Historic Preservation Act,[147] and the Federal Records Act,[148] among others.

The United States, then, presents a complicated, multi-fragmented scenario for ICH protection. On the one hand, its model of federalism makes it very difficult for the federal government to enact legislation on topics that are so much closer to the local level than to the federal one. It is probably even desirable to ensure that local regulation comes first, as it helps engage local partners in the conservation effort, thus sustaining the cultural context that keeps intangible heritage alive.[149] On the other hand, as the existing federal law is very fragmented only small sections of each Act can be applied. Environmental legislation has attained a certain degree of success in being federalized in the United States. The connection between the

140 Thomas F King, *Cultural Resources Laws and Practice* (AltaMira Press, 2008), 288.

141 Dean B Suagee, 'The Cultural Heritage of American Indian Tribes and the Preservation of Biological Diversity', *Ariz St LJ* 31 (1999), 483 538 at 515 21.

142 King, *Cultural Resources Laws*, 290 3.

143 King, *Cultural Resources Laws*, 289.

144 King, *Cultural Resources Laws*, 289.

145 King, *Cultural Resources Laws*, 295 6.

146 King, *Cultural Resources Laws*, 298 9.

147 Suagee, 'The Cultural Heritage of American Indian Tribes', 521 7.

148 King, *Cultural Resources Laws*, 314 17.

149 Reap, 'Selected Legislative, Administrative and Management Approaches'.

environment (which can be the object of federal legislation through the commerce clause); traditional or indigenous cultures (which are a federal matter as are all indigenous issues); and intangible heritage, has created a small back door through which ICH can be somewhat protected at the federal level.

Other countries have made attempts at protection through multiple sources without having to face the subsidiarity obstacle that the United States and, to a certain extent, Brazil face. The Philippines is one such example.

4.5.3 Philippines

The Constitution of the Philippines acknowledges the importance of protecting traditional culture for the promotion of national identity, especially indigenous traditional culture, traditions, and institutions.[150] The Philippines has implemented a very particular solution, in proposing the use of both *sui generis* methods and IP mechanisms, through the Indigenous Peoples Rights Act of 1997,[151] whose main feature is a 'shift of paradigm from individual private property ownership to community ownership'.[152]

In the Philippines basketry plays a similar role to textiles in Laos: they are badges of social roles and group affiliations, and therefore important elements of intangible heritage to be safeguarded.[153] The law determines that the free, prior, and informed consent of indigenous communities must be obtained prior to the use of their intangible heritage by third parties, this being defined as 'consensus of all members of the indigenous communities to be determined in accordance with their customary law and practices'.[154] This national scheme, although it provides for the use of IP mechanisms when providing for possible protection of ICH in the copyright statutes, gives precedence to *sui generis* methods. In other words, what the act does is to transpose IP solutions into the indigenous domain, but turns them into group rights. When these mechanisms for some reason do not fit into the affected community's worldviews, a *sui generis* solution is to be developed for each case, and negotiations with the community undertaken.

Many countries thus adopt solutions that tackle the issue of ICH safeguarding from many different sides. Some countries, like the Philippines, still attempt to legislate around the propertization of ICH. Being sensitive to the advantages of IP and also to its shortcomings, these issues are often met with *sui generis* solutions. Other countries, like the United States, have not as yet legislated on the matter, but contain extensive legislation in other areas that can be invoked to protect ICH. In the United States, as in Brazil, federalism plays a role (as it should, since ICH is best

[150] Esteban T Magannon, 'Philippine Indigenous Cultural Communities: A Historical Perspective', in Oscar Salemink (ed), *Viet Nam's Cultural Diversity: Approaches to Preservation* (UNESCO Publishing, 2001), 133 48 at 146.

[151] For a short commentary, see Henri-Philippe Sambuc, *La Protection Internationale des Savoirs Traditionnels: La Nouvelle Frontière de la Proprieté Intellectuelle* (l'Harmattan, 2003), 68.

[152] Kutty, *National Experiences*, 27.

[153] Kutty, *National Experiences*, 24.

[154] Kutty, *National Experiences*, 27.

promoted taking the principle of subsidiarity into account). And Brazil is still trying to find its way around ICH protection, but it seems willing to respond to concerns of all stakeholders involved in the process.

4.6 Multiplicity in National, Regional, and International (Institutional) Responses

National responses to ICH protection are as varied as the goals one can hope to achieve through intangible heritage. Some countries use ICH to acquire self-knowledge, such as Laos, which has been attracting foreign interest and aid in its extremely rich intangible heritage as a means to secure the ethnographic mapping it needs. Other countries look at intangible heritage more as an element to attract tourism and promote development (Viet Nam is one such example). Other experiences suggest a preference for development to work exclusively in favour of the communities from which the intangible heritage originates, with disregard to the interests of the population at large, such as Panama.

Naturally, the classification offered in this chapter is not watertight. Countries which have been classified as adopting one type of solution usually also employ mechanisms in other areas. Examples are Bolivia and Romania: even though Bolivia was analysed as establishing a *sui generis* regime, and Romania as a policy-level regime, they both also contain in their legislation IP mechanisms.

Ultimately, then, all countries protecting ICH should be thought of as establishing plural regimes, but such thinking would be counter-productive. The prominence of a type of solution over the others is what gave rise to the classification offered in this chapter, but the fact that the separation is not rigid serves as a helpful reminder that the plurality of solutions should be sought after not only internationally and regionally, as suggested in Chapters 2 and 3, but also at the national and local levels.

International (or regional) law has clearly served as the driving force in the drafting of legislation in Romania, for instance, but debates at the international level surrounding intangible heritage have also served as an impetus elsewhere. For instance, to the extent countries such as Laos and Viet Nam enact legislation to protect intangible heritage as a means to secure foreign aid, it seems safe to suggest that there would be less interest in enacting legislation had there not been international momentum. But in some countries where legislation precedes international law, it is less clear whether they were influenced by ongoing international debates (even if by then they had failed to crystallize into international instruments), or whether they were the driving forces of international (or regional) legislation instead.

The experience of federal countries such as Brazil, and particularly the United States, teaches precisely this: the importance of subsidiarity and connecting intangible heritage to the local levels of governance. It is important, however, at the same time to promote a broader nation-wide agenda. In this sense, Brazil's experience seems more interesting than the US experience, because Brazil, in addition to state-level programmes, has also been investing considerable effort in trying to find solutions at the national level. And these solutions are truly plural, attempting to tackle the issue of ICH protection from all possible sides, trying to cover the largest possible number of stakeholders, and harmonizing different interests and concerns.

Institutional responses, therefore, should mean a concerted effort at all levels: international (global), regional, national, and local. Civil society, as the representatives of the bearers of intangible heritage, should always be involved, and it is an unfortunate development that, as one moves from local towards global, the politics of heritage has prevented true and meaningful participation of communities and individuals, who are ultimately the most important stakeholders.

The types of solutions advanced by all these levels vary considerably, but there are a few common patterns. The following chapters are dedicated to analysing the protection of intangible cultural heritage through the substantive subject-matters, rather than the institutional framing.

PART II

SUBSTANTIVE MEASURES TO SAFEGUARD INTANGIBLE HERITAGE

5

International Human Rights and Intangible Cultural Heritage

The protection of cultural heritage, especially intangible cultural heritage, is intuitively associated, among other rationales, with the need to protect cultural identity. If intangible cultural heritage (ICH) is protected for the sake of humankind, it is of course necessary to protect the bearers of ICH, the custodial communities and their members. And this requires protecting their ways of life, so as to ensure that they keep on undertaking the practices leading to the perpetuation of the valued cultural heritage.

Cultural identity is an aspect of human rights protection, even if such a right is not explicitly mentioned in all relevant instruments. A right to cultural identity means a right to elements that surround a person's way of life and their relationship to the surrounding environment (natural or social). For legal protection, it means that human rights law should strive to guarantee the conditions for the existence of idiosyncrasies that arise from this relationship between a person and their way of life. Thus, by protecting human rights related to cultural identity, one can potentially protect ICH. The aim of this chapter is to discuss this relationship: how the protection of human rights related to identity can be effectively used as a means to safeguard intangible cultural heritage.

The tone of the chapter reflects this aim: while previous (and subsequent) chapters are a lot more intent on criticizing certain bodies of law and institutions, and showing how the flaws of that law get in the way of safeguarding intangible heritage, this chapter focuses primarily and selectively on means and tools that can be used in a positive manner to safeguard one aspect that is at the background of intangible heritage (identity). I will devote relatively little space to discussing the ways in which heritage is an obstacle to the enjoyment of human rights (the so-termed 'human rights exception' to heritage), or to discussing a right to heritage. These two discussions, while important on their own right, seem to me to not sufficiently engage with the possibilities of international human rights legal practice, and focus more on discourses than action. This chapter focuses more on the practice of human rights through adjudication of the right to cultural identity.

This chapter will be structured as follows: I will in the first part analyse the bridge between human rights and ICH, looking at how human rights are one of the possible rationales behind the protection of ICH, and a particularly compelling one. I will then discuss some of the possible obstacles that can be raised against the use of HR in this context. In the second part, I will outline how institutionalized human rights mechanisms have protected aspects of cultural identity under several provisions that are not specific to cultural identity, and the extent to which this can be connected to ICH concerns. Finally, I will discuss some general limitations to the use of human rights.

5.1 Bridging Intangible Cultural Heritage and Human Rights

Even though there is a rich array of reasons justifying the protection of ICH, my current focus on cultural identity (and hence human rights) is attributable to the fact that protecting human rights is one of the most compelling and often cited justifications in international legal discourse, as I argue below.

5.1.1 Connecting (Intangible) Cultural Heritage to human rights

The protection of identity is the most-often cited rationale for safeguarding ICH, and the protection of cultural identity is a human rights goal, to the extent that identity defines a person, and thus gives this person dignity, which is the core norm behind the protection of human rights.[1] The protection of human rights is a clear rationale behind the 2003 UNESCO Convention: according to one commentator of this instrument, the use of the term 'safeguarding' in the Convention is meant to embody human rights concerns as a whole.[2] In this sense, to protect cultural identity means to protect the right to cultural identity, and to protect distinguishing aspects of someone's culture.

Further, religious feelings also play an important role in ICH debates, as cases involving notions of the sacred to certain custodial communities are often the most contentious ones.[3] Religious feelings, naturally, are a human rights concern, and this helps reinforce, even if only with respect to part of intangible cultural heritage, the connection I defend.

This bridge between ICH and human rights, however, is by no means clear or undisputed. I will outline below some of the obstacles to the use of human rights in the protection of heritage interests. This chapter will look primarily at the positive relationships between human rights and ICH,[4] that is, the ways in which human

[1] Katja S Ziegler, 'Cultural Heritage and Human Rights', *Social Sciences Resource Network*, available at <http://ssrn.com/abstract=1002620> (accessed 29 November 2012); and Carol Weisbrod, *Emblems of Pluralism: Cultural Differences and the State* (Princeton University Press, 2002), 178 202 (discussing how identity is formed from a cultural context).

[2] Janet Blake, *Commentary on the UNESCO 2003 Convention on the Safeguarding of the Intangible Cultural Heritage* (Institute for Art and Law, 2006), 35.

[3] Derek Gillman, *The Idea of Cultural Heritage* (Institute for Art and Law, 2006), 13.

[4] There is already some literature on minority rights that takes a similar approach, inquiring into how international adjudicatory and quasi-adjudicatory bodies (particularly HR bodies) have been used to create an 'international judicial discourse' oriented towards minority protection. For this, see Gaetano Pentassuglia, *Minority Groups and Judicial Discourse in International Law: A Comparative Perspective* (Martinus Nijhoff, 2009).

rights provisions can be positively used to protect cultural distinctiveness manifested through intangible cultural heritage.

5.1.2 Obstacles to applying the human rights framework

The objections to the use of human rights in the context of intangible heritage can be connected to the nature of ICH, or to the boundaries of human rights. I will address these concerns, and try to respond to them, in view of my general claim in this chapter that human rights can be used for safeguarding intangible heritage.

The argument connected to intangible heritage opposes the use of human rights because it implies the acceptance of one single rationale behind the protection, as opposed to the rich array of possible reasons justifying the importance of ICH. However, I do not claim human rights to be a totalizing, single logic for the protection of intangible heritage; rather, I believe it is one alternative worth exploring, but that there are additional means of protection that can also produce effective results while responding to other interests.

On the other hand, the arguments about the boundaries of the human rights system are twofold: first, there is a general claim that to include cultural heritage concerns in human rights mechanisms would be a stretch of the human rights system, in that it would be exercising competence over areas it was not originally meant to interfere with (such as cultural matters, often left to national discretion, but also environment being a prominent example). To this, one could respond that this would not be the first time in which human rights systems, through an 'evolutionary interpretation' of their instruments, go on to widen their general scope, expanding the scope of circumstances covered by specific rights; one example of this is the protection of the environment, that has been made possible in the ECtHR by an expansive interpretation of the provision on the right to private and family life (Article 8 of the European Convention).[5] Various other examples include the protection of social rights, international humanitarian law, special rights to women, the protection of investors' rights, to name but a few.[6]

The second argument related to the boundaries and the structure of human rights relates to the tension between individual and group rights and interests.[7] The 2003 UNESCO Convention seems to give clear preference to group interests, when it enunciates that ICH means the practices 'that communities, groups, and,

[5] *López Ostra v Spain* (Application No 16798/90), judgment of 9 December 1994. For an overview of how the European Court of Human Rights has expanded its jurisdiction through systematic interpretation, see Vassilis P Tzevelekos, 'The Use of Article 31(3)(c) of the VCLT in the Case Law of the ECtHR: An Effective Anti-Fragmentation Tool or a Selective Loophole for the Reinforcement of Human Rights Teleology? Between Evolution and Systemic Integration', *Mich J of Intl L* 31 (2010), 621 90.

[6] For an evolution towards the protection of these areas of adjudication in the Inter-American System, see Lucas Lixinski, 'Treaty Interpretation by the Inter-American Court of Human Rights: Expansionism at the Service of the Unity of International Law', *EJIL* 21(3) (2010), 585 604.

[7] On this connection, see Francesco Francioni, 'Culture, Heritage and Human Rights: An Introduction', in Francesco Francioni and Martin Scheinin (eds), *Cultural Human Rights* (Martinus Nijhoff, 2008), 1 15.

in some cases, individuals recognize as part of their cultural heritage'. The fact that individuals are put last, and recognized only 'in some cases', seems to clearly indicate their secondary role in the ICH context.[8] This reflects a general anthropological consensus in the sense of thinking of intangible heritage as belonging to collectivities, rather than identifiable individuals. It also seems to be a move away from the individualism that has burdened earlier international heritage instruments, and in a way a return to the group perspective of the minority protection system of the League of Nations.[9]

The tension between individual and group rights exists both at the scholarly and adjudication levels. As to the latter, it can be argued that human rights mechanisms in the exercise of judicial or quasi-judicial functions are supposed to address only individual claims, and not claims of a larger group (prohibition of *actio popularis*). The *actio popularis* tension is always present in human rights adjudication, though, to the extent that in order to resolve an individual case it is often necessary to adopt measures that will have effects on the community at large, and benefit other people in situations similar to the victim's. This is at least the approach adopted by the Inter-American Court of Human Rights (IACtHR) in its jurisprudence on reparations, when it comes to determining 'other forms of reparation'.[10]

A related argument goes on to question the very justiciability of group rights' claims in international human rights adjudication. One of the few group rights provisions in international human rights instruments is the provision on the right to self-determination, contained in Article 1 common to the ICCPR and ICESCR. A survey of the Human Rights Committee's jurisprudence in cases involving Article 1 of the ICCPR shows that the Committee has repeatedly declared the non-justiciability of rights protected under Article 1, and at most has transformed these claims into claims under other, individual rights protected by the Covenant.[11]

[8] Blake, *Commentary*, 35.

[9] For this history, see Ana Vrdoljak, *International Law, Museums and the Return of Cultural Objects* (Cambridge University Press, 2006).

[10] This has been done in several cases before the IACtHR, in which several measures have been determined, as a means to ensure that similar violations do not take place again in the future. These include police training programmes (I/A Court HR, *Case of López-Álvarez v Honduras*. Merits, Reparations, and Costs. Judgment of 1 February 2006. Series C No 141), the construction of memorials (I/A Court HR, *Case of the 'Mapiripán Massacre' v Colombia*. Merits, Reparations, and Costs. Judgment of 15 September 2005. Series C No 134), medical centres (I/A Court HR, *Case of the Plan de Sánchez Massacre v Guatemala*. Merits. Judgment of 29 April 2004. Series C No 105), the creation of scholarship funds (I/A Court HR *Case of Myrna Mack-Chang v Guatemala*. Merits, Reparations, and Costs. Judgment of 25 November 2003. Series C No 101) and even the modification of internal legislation incompatible with obligations under the American Convention (I/A Court HR, *Case of 'The Last Temptation of Christ' (Olmedo-Bustos et al) v Chile*. Merits, Reparations, and Costs. Judgment of 5 February 2001. Series C No 73). The latter hypothesis derives from a specific obligation under the American Convention that requires a State Party to have its legislation in accordance with the standards of the Convention (Art 2). For more on the jurisprudence of the IACtHR on reparations, see Sergio García Ramírez, 'La Jurisprudencia de la Corte Interamericana de Derechos Humanos en Materia de Reparaciones', in *La Corte Interamericana de Derechos Humanos: Un Cuarto de Siglo 1979 2004* (Corte Interamericana de Derechos Humanos, 2005), 1 85.

[11] See for instance the decisions of the Human Rights Committee in: Human Rights Committee, Communication No 547/1993, *Apirana Mahuika et al v New Zealand*, UN Doc CCPR/C/70/D/547/

These adjudicatory tensions are a reflection of a much more nuanced scholarly debate. While it is not my goal to exhaust this debate, as it would go beyond the scope of this chapter, it is necessary to sketch some of it, and draw on the elements that can enlighten the present discussion.

On the side of criticism, it may be argued fundamentally that to protect cultural heritage through individual human rights implies accepting a liberal human rights framework centred on individual rights, and on the idea that group interests boil down to individual interests. Advocates of the idea of group rights contend that collapsing group rights into individual rights reduces a much more complex structure of social relations to the sum of its individual components,[12] or that certain rights cannot be exercised individually, and hence there must be group rights.[13] While these are good points, it must not be forgotten that group rights may also be read as collective dimensions of individual rights. This perspective avoids the necessity of creating an entirely separate category of group rights. Concerning the former argument, as philosophically and historically construed, the goal of rights is to protect individuals against oppressive groups. Thus, to protect group rights would necessarily bring into question the eventual clashes between the interests of groups and opposing interests of individuals belonging to such groups.[14] And several group interests have been protected as individual rights for a long time, and there does not seem to be much of a problem, in international legal practice, with translating group interests into individual rights,[15] especially if one considers that instruments protecting minorities focus on the language of individual rights.[16] Further, to the extent that the foundation of groups is to

1993, 15 November 2000 (concerning Maori fisheries); Human Rights Committee, Communication No 413/1990, *A B et al v Italy*, UN Doc CCPR/C/40/D/413/1990, 5 November 1990 (concerning the German minority in South Tirol), to name but two examples. The Human Rights Committee has, however, on at least one occasion transformed claims under the right to self-determination (Art 1) into claims under the right to minority protection (Art 27), in what seems to be an application of the principle of *iura novit curia*. See Human Rights Committee, Communication No 167/1984, *Lubicon Lake Band v Canada*, UN Doc CCPR/C/38/D/167/1984, 10 May 1990, para 13.4.

[12] Darlene M Johnston, 'Native Rights as Collective Rights: A Question of Group Self-Preservation', 2 *Canadian Journal of Law and Jurisprudence* 19 (1989), reprinted in Will Kymlicka (ed), *The Rights of Minority Cultures* (Oxford University Press, 1995), 179 201 at 180 2 (arguing that communitarianism can be an alternative to a rights-based ethics).

[13] Yoram Dinstein, 'Collective Human Rights of Peoples and Minorities', *ICLQ* 25 (1976), 102 20 at 115.

[14] Michael Hartney, 'Some Confusions Concerning Collective Rights', 4 *Canadian Journal of Law and Jurisprudence* 293 (1991), reprinted in Will Kymlicka (ed), *The Rights of Minority Cultures* (Oxford University Press, 1995), 202 27 at 203.

[15] Hartney, 'Some Confusions', 219; Johnston, 'Native Rights as Collective Rights', 185 (mentioning an argument according to which collective rights are meaningless and individual rights collectively asserted are a common phenomenon); and Chandran Kukathas, 'Are There Any Cultural Rights?', 20 *Political Theory* 105 (1992), reprinted in Will Kymlicka (ed), *The Rights of Minority Cultures* (Oxford University Press, 1995), 228 55 at 230.

[16] In this sense, see Art 27 of the ICCPR, as well as the Council of Europe's Framework Convention on the Protection of Minorities. As to the latter, it is interesting to note that the original recommendation leading to the adoption of this Convention adopted the language of group rights, and that this language was abandoned in favour of individual rights in the final text. For a commentary on

promote the well-being of individuals, group interests must be translated into individual interests.[17]

Another possible argument is that to protect minorities could lead to essentializing them, in that individual interests would be suppressed in favour of a certain understanding of the group's needs. This liberal individualist argument goes on to say that groups do exist, but as associations of individuals, and the interests of groups should not prevail over the interests of its individuals,[18] being the rights of individuals a *conditio sine qua non* for the protection of groups, a position recognized even by advocates of group rights.[19] While some defending this argument come to the point of denying communities the right to self-preservation, a position which I do not share,[20] their point is valid in saying that clashes between individual and group rights are in fact clashes between rights of individuals as members of a culturally distinct community on the one hand, and rights of individuals as part of the common political community on the other.[21]

Moreover, current debates over individuals' roles in society no longer dissociate the latter from the groups in which they live, and explore how an individual's presence within a group shapes their personality, aspirations, and ultimately rights pretensions.[22] That is to say, a nuanced view of individual human rights nowadays will necessarily take group-originated dimensions of an individual into consideration, referring to a 'socially-located individual', rather than merely an individual.[23]

Naturally, my defence of this position attains to a rather 'Westernized' conception of individuals and societies, and I grant it will not be applicable in all cases. However, as many cases can be addressed with this framework in mind, I strongly believe that individual human rights can play an important role in occupying the 'adjudicatory vacuum' of group rights, even if only as a temporary fix. In the specific context of ICH, according to one commentator on the UNESCO Convention, while the notion of collective cultural rights seems to come from the text of the Convention, such an interpretation would be erroneous, as the Convention clearly refers to universal human rights standards, obviously based on individual human rights.[24]

This interpretation is further reinforced by another point of view which aligns the 'individual versus group rights' tension with the discussion of the interests to be

this evolution, see Miodrag A Jovanović, 'Recognizing Minority Identities Through Collective Rights', *Human Rights Q* 27 (2005), 625 51 at 628 9.

[17] Hartney, 'Some Confusions', 208.

[18] Kukathas, 'Are There Any Cultural Rights?', 237.

[19] Jovanović, 'Recognizing Minority Identities', 646.

[20] While I do not think communities are entitled to a right to self-preservation, I believe individuals are entitled to pursue the preservation of the communities they belong to. This can in fact be one of the core concerns behind the protection of intangible heritage. For an argument in favour of the right to self-preservation, see Johnston, 'Native Rights as Collective Rights', 186.

[21] Kukathas, 'Are There Any Cultural Rights?', 240 1.

[22] Gillman, *The Idea of Cultural Heritage*, 19.

[23] Gillman, *The Idea of Cultural Heritage*, 4.

[24] Blake, *Commentary*, 35.

protected by heritage. According to one commentator involved in this debate,[25] to look at heritage from the perspective of groups means to favour the national interests at stake, which may not always be protective of heritage,[26] or may protect heritage at the expense of other people's heritage.[27] On the other hand, looking at it from the perspective of individual rights opens room for looking at heritage as a 'global common', or 'the common heritage of mankind', which gives it a truly cosmopolitan character, and enhances the desirability of its protection, precisely because it becomes part of everyone's identity, present and future, and not the identity of a certain group alone. This position seems to be the one adopted by the UNESCO Convention to a certain extent, in that individualism seems to be key for the construction of the idea of 'common heritage of mankind' which justifies internationalism in the field of cultural heritage, discussed in Chapter 1. But the Convention also trails away from referencing individuals, only referring to them subsidiarily after the references to 'communities'. In a way, the rhetorical move of the 2003 UNESCO Convention moves away from equating groups with 'Nation States', and opens the possibility for smaller collective entities worthy of having their rights protected (despite the shortcomings to that emphasized in Chapter 2).

The argument based on intergenerational equity as a grounds for protecting cultural heritage (that is, the idea that heritage must be safeguarded for the sake of future generations) is an argument that seems to favour a group perspective, as it is not possible to protect an individual that does not yet exist.[28] Intergenerational equity becomes an important principle for the protection of cultural heritage in general, and of intangible heritage in particular. One of the main ideas behind the articulation of cultural heritage as a 'common concern of mankind' is the idea that future generations are entitled to share in this heritage, and nothing short of concerted global action can guarantee that. And, when it comes to intangible heritage, the intergenerational aspect is part of the very concept of ICH, which is a living culture that must be transmitted from one generation to the next. Hence, the group perspective for the sake of future generations is an important factor to be considered in the design of legal mechanisms for safeguarding ICH. However, the protection of heritage in the interest of future generations is but one of the goals of ICH protection, and it is by no means a compelling argument against the use of individual rights, that can be even seen as indirectly protecting the interests of future generations, since by granting protection in the present one necessarily safeguards the good for the future.

Another argument generally advocating group rights, but that is particularly suitable to the heritage debate, is to say that what differentiates a group from the

25 Gillman, *The Idea of Cultural Heritage*, 1 3.

26 An example of this is the story of the Bamiyan Byddhas, destroyed by the Taliban regime of Afghanistan in 2001. One of the claims made at the time was that this was solely an Afghan domestic affair, and the international community had no say in the matter. For this account, see Gillman, *The Idea of Cultural Heritage*, 4 5.

27 David Lowenthal, *The Heritage Crusade and the Spoils of History* (Cambridge University Press, 1998), 230 41; and Gillman, *The Idea of Cultural Heritage*, 52.

28 Jovanović, 'Recognizing Minority Identities', 635.

mere sum of its individual components is heritage. The group has a separate existence from that of its members through commonly shared heritage, and thus it is precisely heritage that makes it impossible for group interests to be reduced to those of its members.[29] There is no way around this argument, I suggest. However, there is a means of articulating group culture in a way that also makes sense for individuals, and the debate on interculturalism is an example of this possibility. To the extent that multiculturalism is the official State policy of cultural inclusion, interculturalism represents how multicultural values are translated individually.[30] Furthermore, seeing that I am concerned primarily with adjudication in this chapter, and judicial practice in international human rights does not seem to have a problem with translating group claims into individual ones in a sufficiently nuanced way, the argument of heritage as the factor that prevents reducing a group to the sum of its parts still holds true; what is desired instead is that the individual be thought of as more than just an individual.

Of all the several objections that can be raised against the use of human rights for the protection of ICH, only the group rights argument makes a compelling point, in my view, but at the same time it is not a sweeping argument that precludes the use of human rights in any circumstance, and it is an argument to be used with caution if one wants to give heritage claims 'universal weight'. Therefore, human rights can, and should, be used for the protection of intangible cultural heritage in as far as ICH relates to ways of life forming part of one's identity. In the next section I will explore the feasibility of using human rights mechanisms for the protection of intangible heritage.

5.2 Using Human Rights to Protect Intangible Cultural Heritage

At the outset, some observations must be made about the relationship between cultural heritage and human rights. First, it is to be noted that the language of 'cultural heritage' does not appear in international human rights jurisprudence. This is easily explainable, as human rights mechanisms will protect 'culture', or even 'ways of life', but human rights instruments do not make reference to 'heritage', as the term classically refers to tangible assets, not to states of mind with no physical existence (which is one possible description of a human right). However, even though these features are important elements of cultural heritage, they form only part of it. If one possible goal of protecting cultural heritage is the protection of culture and ways of life, then human rights mechanisms are an intermediary step, while acting within their treaty-established mandates.

Secondly, as to the existing human rights that *can* be invoked, the most obvious option available would be the right to take part in culture, as protected under the

[29] Jovanović, 'Recognizing Minority Identities', 633 (citing Patrick Thornberry, *International Law and the Rights of Minorities* (Clarendon Press, 1991), 57).

[30] Will Kymlicka, 'Multicultural States and Intercultural Citizens', *Theory and Research in Education* 1(2) (2003), 147 69.

Universal Declaration of Human Rights[31] and the International Covenant on Economic, Social and Cultural Rights.[32] These are the two most important universal instruments protecting culture.

When referring to the link between cultural heritage law and human rights, the literature on cultural heritage usually makes the connection between cultural heritage and social and economic rights, particularly the right to the enjoyment of culture and cultural life.[33] As a matter of fact, a recent General Comment from the United Nations Committee on Economic, Social and Cultural Rights (responsible for implementing the ICESCR) focuses on the right to take part in cultural life, and makes the access to cultural heritage an essential part of this right.[34] As there is no international mechanism for adjudicating Economic, Social and Cultural Rights, and the institutional framework for these rights is not as developed as for civil and political rights, I will focus the discussion on Civil and Political Rights.[35]

The advantages of using the framework of civil and political rights are manifold. First and foremost, the human rights discourse offers a very appealing, powerful rhetoric; to align some idea with human rights, or better yet, to frame a discussion in terms of human rights is to make the discussion relevant, especially if one takes into account that States automatically assume that international human rights instruments are relevant sources of law, which does not necessarily happen with international instruments in other areas. Secondly, the human rights framework is well-established and readily available, with a large membership, which means that States are more likely to be parties to one of these mechanisms, thus creating a forum. Thirdly, many of these bodies are empowered to hear individual complaints, giving the victims a venue they can address directly. Fourthly, institutional bodies for human rights adjudication, when compared to other international judicial or quasi-judicial organs, are comparatively effective, as States seem to be very concerned with compliance with human rights decisions. Fifthly, using human rights avoids commodifying cultural heritage as assessments of culture by human

[31] Universal Declaration of Human Rights, Adopted and proclaimed by General Assembly resolution 217 A (III) of 10 December 1948 (hereinafter 'UDHR'). The relevant provision is the following: '**Article** 27. (1) Everyone has the right freely to participate in the cultural life of the community, to enjoy the arts and to share in scientific advancement and its benefits. [...]'

[32] International Covenant on Economic, Social and Cultural Rights, Adopted and opened for signature, ratification, and accession by General Assembly resolution 2200A (XXI) of 16 December 1966. Entry into force: 3 January 1976. States Parties as of November 2012: 160 (hereinafter 'ICESCR'). The relevant provision is the following: '**Article** 15. 1. The States Parties to the present Covenant recognize the right of everyone: (a) To take part in cultural life; [...]'

[33] See eg Janet Blake, 'On Defining the Cultural Heritage', *ICLQ* 49 (2000), 61 85 at 75 83.

[34] Committee on Economic, Social and Cultural Rights, *General Comment 21: Right of everyone to take part in cultural life (art 15, para 1(a), of the International Covenant on Economic, Social and Cultural Rights)*, 21 December 2009, paras 49 54.

[35] One must note that an Optional Protocol to the International Covenant on Economic, Social and Cultural Rights has been approved on 10 December 2008, giving the Committee on Economic, Social and Cultural Rights the competence to hear individual complaints. This Protocol is not into force at the time of writing, however, and therefore it is still unclear whether the Committee will be able to address cultural heritage disputes on the basis of the right to the enjoyment of cultural life.

rights bodies tend to look at culture as an 'open', 'fluid', construction, rather than something that can be catalogued.

Finally, and key for the purpose of protecting culture, many of these organs have been willing to expand the scope of the rights they supervise through the use of 'general' or 'open-textured' clauses.[36] I will focus my analysis on this last feature, and I will analyse the case-law of three bodies that bring particularly relevant examples of this practice: the United Nations Human Rights Committee (HRC), the European Court of Human Rights (ECtHR), and the Inter-American Court of Human Rights (IACtHR).

5.2.1 Rights protected: selected case-law

The literature on the topic refers to the possibility of using civil and political rights,[37] such as the rights to freedom of expression,[38] freedom of religion,[39] private and family life,[40] and freedom of association,[41] among other rights. I will consider how different jurisdictional organs have looked at the protection of cultural life aspects in the context of these rights.

5.2.1.1 Specific provisions on minority protection

The main provision of an international human rights instrument for the protection of cultural specificities is Article 27 of the ICCPR.[42] The HRC, created by the ICCPR, was given competence to analyse individual petitions by its optional protocol.[43] The HRC has approved a General Comment on the application of

[36] José E Alvarez, *International Organizations as Law-Makers* (Oxford University Press, 2006), 474 83 (discussing the impact of the supervisory organs of the European and American Conventions on Human Rights in shaping the content and reach of the instruments they supervise); and Tzevelekos, 'The Use of Article 31(3)(c) of the VCLT'.

[37] See eg Michael F Brown, *Who Owns Native Culture?* (Harvard University Press, 2004).

[38] The provisions in the relevant international instruments are the following: UDHR, Art 19; ICCPR, Art 19; ECHR, Art 10; ACHR, Art 13.

[39] The provisions in the relevant international instruments are the following: UDHR, Art 18; ICCPR, Art 18; ECHR, Art 9; ACHR, Art 12.

[40] The provisions in the relevant international instruments are the following: UDHR, Art 12; ICCPR, Art 17; ECHR, Art 8; ACHR, Art 11.

[41] The provisions in the relevant international instruments are the following: UDHR, Art 20; ICCPR, Arts 21 22; ECHR, Art 11; ACHR, Arts 15 16.

[42] International Covenant on Civil and Political Rights, adopted and opened for signature, ratification and accession by General Assembly resolution 2200A (XXI) of 16 December 1966. Entry into force: 23 March 1976. Number of States Parties as of November 2012: 167. '**Article 27.** In those States in which ethnic, religious, or linguistic minorities exist, persons belonging to such minorities shall not be denied the right, in community with the other members of their group, to enjoy their own culture, to profess and practise their own religion, or to use their own language.'

[43] Optional Protocol to the International Covenant on Civil and Political Rights, adopted and opened for signature, ratification, and accession by General Assembly resolution 2200A (XXI) of 16 December 1966. Entry into force: 23 March 1976. Number of States Parties as of November 2012: 114. The relevant provision is the following: '**Article 1.** A State Party to the Covenant that becomes a Party to the present Protocol recognizes the competence of the Committee to receive and consider communications from individuals subject to its jurisdiction who claim to be victims of a violation by that State Party of any of the rights set forth in the Covenant. No communication shall be received by

Article 27 of the Covenant. In this comment, the HRC stresses that the scope of the application of this provision relates to culture and the maintenance of a certain way of life.[44] The jurisprudence of the HRC was the source for this conclusion, but the jurisprudence is more nuanced than its portrayal in this General Comment at least for our purposes of searching for a connection to cultural heritage.

Of the cases decided by the HRC between 1977 (year of the first decision of the HRC under the individual complaints mechanism) and the time of writing, 17 cases involved Article 27 of the ICCPR. Out of these, ten were declared inadmissible,[45] all on the grounds of lack of exhaustion of local remedies. There is an underlying tension in the six cases involving France, due to a French reservation to Article 27 of the ICCPR. This reservation states that '[s]ince the basic principles of public law prohibit distinctions between citizens on grounds of origin, race or religion, France is a country in which there are no minorities and [. . .] Article 27 is not applicable as far as the Republic is concerned'.[46] This shows a rather formalistic understanding of equality, which is inconsistent with current readings of equality and non-discrimination in human rights adjudication.

Five cases were considered as non-violations of the Covenant,[47] and only in two cases did the HRC decide that the State Party (in both cases, Canada) had violated rights under the ICCPR.[48] A look at these cases will help shed light over the criteria adopted by the HRC in deciding cases under Article 27.

the Committee if it concerns a State Party to the Covenant which is not a Party to the present Protocol.'

[44] General Comment No 23, *The rights of minorities (art 27)*, 8 April 1994, para 3.2.

[45] Human Rights Committee, Communication No 942/2000, *Jarle Jonassen v Norway*, UN Doc CCPR/C/76/D/942/2000, 12 November 2002; Human Rights Committee, Communication No 557/1993, *X v Australia*, UN Doc CCPR/C/57/D/557/1993, 1 August 1996; Human Rights Committee, Communication No 431/1990, *O Sara et al v Finland*, UN Doc CCPR/C/50/D/431/1990, 24 March 1994; Human Rights Committee, Communication No 359/1989, *RL et al v Canada*, UN Doc CCPR/C/43/D/358/1989, 28 November 1990; Human Rights Committee, Communication No 220/1987, *TK v France*, UN Doc CCPR/C/37/D/220/1987, 8 December 1989; Human Rights Committee, Communication No 222/1987, *HK v France*, UN Doc CCPR/C/37/D/222/1987, 8 December 1989; Human Rights Committee, Communication No 262/1987, *RT v France*, UN Doc CCPR/C/35/D/262/1987, 3 April 1989; Human Rights Committee, Communications Nos 324 and 325/1988, *JB and HK v France*, UN Doc CCPR/C/34/D/324/1988, 26 October 1988; Human Rights Committee, Communication No 228/1987, *CLD v France*, UN Doc CCPR/C/33/D/228/1987, 26 July 1988; and Human Rights Committee, Communication No 243/1987, *SR v France*, UN Doc CCPR/C/31/D/243/1987, 5 November 1987.

[46] Office of the United Nations High Commission for Human Rights, *Declarations and Reservations to the International Covenant on Civil and Political Rights*, available at <http://treaties.un.org/Pages/ViewDetails.aspx?src=TREATY&mtdsg no=IV-4&chapter=4&lang=en> (accessed 29 November 2012).

[47] Human Rights Committee, Communication No 879/1999, *George Howard v Canada*, UN Doc CCPR/C/84/D/879/1999, 4 August 2005; Human Rights Committee, Communication No 1023/2001, *Jouni Länsman, Eino Länsman and the Muotkatunturi Herdsmen's Committee v Finland*, UN Doc CCPR/C/83/D/1023/2001, 15 April 2005; Human Rights Committee, Communication No 671/1995, *Jouni E Länsman et al v Finland*, UN Doc CCPR/C/58/D/671/1995, 22 November 1996; Human Rights Committee, Communication No 511/1992, *Ilmari Länsman et al v Finland*, UN Doc CCPR/C/52/D/511/1992, 8 November 1994; and Human Rights Committee, Communication No 197/1985, *Ivan Kitok v Sweden*, UN Doc CCPR/C/33/D/197/1985, 10 August 1988.

[48] Human Rights Committee, Communication No 167/1984, *Lubicon Lake Band v Canada*, UN Doc CCPR/C/38/D/167/1984, 10 May 1990; and Human Rights Committee, Communication No 24/1977, *Sandra Lovelace v Canada*, UN Doc CCPR/C/13/D/24/1977, 30 July 1981.

The first Article 27 case was *Sandra Lovelace v Canada*. In this case, Sandra Lovelace, an indigenous woman, married outside of her tribe, to a white man. According to Canadian law at the time, if an indigenous woman married a white man she lost her indigenous status. This did not apply in the case of an indigenous man marrying a white woman.[49] The HRC said that a restriction on the rights protected by Article 27 requires a reasonable and objective justification.[50] And, because the measure as applied to Sandra Lovelace was not reasonable or necessary to preserve the identity of the tribe, it was inconsistent with Article 27 of the Covenant.[51] The Committee, in a later case, phrased the decision of this case as meaning that restrictions on an individual member of a minority 'must be shown to have a reasonable and objective justification and to be necessary for the continued viability and welfare of the minority as a whole'.[52] The continuity of the community, thus, seems to be the State interest against which individual rights protected by Article 27 must be tested.

In *Ivan Kitok v Sweden*, the HRC suggested the possibility of applying a proportionality test for Article 27 cases. Ivan Kitok was a Sami reindeer breeder who did not practice reindeer breeding for a period of more than three years and so lost the entitlement to resume the practice, according to Swedish law (aimed at reducing the number of reindeer herders).[53] The Committee analysed the Swedish legislation, and concluded that its limitation on reindeer herding was not in violation of Article 27,[54] as the *ratio legis* for the limitation was the improvement of the living conditions of the Sami and the sustainability of reindeer breeding for the future.[55] The HRC said that the practice Kitok was engaged in is protected by Article 27, and in some circumstances can protect indigenous economic practices,[56] but it upheld the Swedish law, saying that the purposes behind the law (economic and ecological) are legitimate, even if it went on to 'express grave concern' as to the proportionality of the law.[57] In a way, the HRC creates a 'test' for Article 27 that is similar to that of other more traditional freedoms (expression, religion, association).

In the series of cases of *Länsman v Finland*,[58] the Committee perfected its methodology with respect to Article 27. These cases concern the impact of tree-logging licences

[49] Human Rights Committee, Communication No 24/1977, *Sandra Lovelace v Canada*, UN Doc CCPR/C/13/D/24/1977, 30 July 1981, para 1.

[50] *Sandra Lovelace v Canada*, para 16.

[51] *Sandra Lovelace v Canada*, para 17.

[52] Human Rights Committee, Communication No 197/1985, *Ivan Kitok v Sweden*, UN Doc CCPR/C/33/D/197/1985, 10 August 1988, para 9.8.

[53] *Ivan Kitok v Sweden*, para 2.1.

[54] *Ivan Kitok v Sweden*, para 9.5.

[55] *Ivan Kitok v Sweden*, para 4.2.

[56] This reading was later reaffirmed by the Committee in Human Rights Committee, Communication No 167/1984, *Lubicon Lake Band v Canada*, UN Doc CCPR/C/38/D/167/1984, 10 May 1990. The case is rather confusing in terms of its factual background, and the legal findings are not clear. Therefore, I will not discuss this case in this chapter.

[57] Human Rights Committee, Communication No 197/1985, *Ivan Kitok v Sweden*, UN Doc CCPR/C/33/D/197/1985, 10 August 1988, para 9.6.

[58] For an analysis of the first two cases in this series, see Martin Scheinin, 'The Right to Enjoy a Distinct Culture: Indigenous and Competing Uses of Land', in Theodore S. Orlin, Allan Rosas, and

in Finland upon the way of life and reserves of reindeer breeders in Lapland. In all these cases, no violation of the ICCPR was declared, but the HRC made substantive progress in its jurisprudence.

In the first case, the Committee said that the standard for determining whether Article 27 has been violated depends on the impact caused by the interference on the way of life of the individual members of a minority.[59] The case presented a rejection of the margin of appreciation doctrine, while embracing a test of 'measuring the impact'. According to the Committee, a 'limited impact' on the way of life does not amount to a violation.[60]

Ten months after this decision by the HRC, a new complaint was filed by the same applicants, on the grounds that circumstances had been aggravated, and that now there was a sufficient impact on the lives of people belonging to the Sami minority so as to constitute a violation of Article 27.[61] Even though in the previous case the HRC had rejected the margin of appreciation doctrine, in this case the Committee said that the domestic courts were in a better position to analyse claims under Article 27, and that the Committee would only exercise its functions so as to see whether Article 27 had been misinterpreted or misapplied.[62] This seems to have been a setback from previous case-law, because, even though the margin of appreciation doctrine was not explicitly embraced, the Committee was deferential to domestic courts.

In the third case, the Committee refined its 'impact test' developed in the first case, and determined that what it was to consider in Article 27 cases was the 'overall effect' of the State interference in that geographical area over time.[63] Again the HRC did not find a violation of Article 27 in this case.

The case of *George Howard v Canada*, another case of non-violation, added new elements to the 'overall effects' test. As it is the latest case decided with respect to Article 27, it is the high watermark of the matter before the HRC. In this case, the HRC analysed whether a conviction against a member of a 'First Nation' for fishing out of season amounted to a violation of his rights under Article 27 as fishing was an essential part of his traditional way of life.[64] The Committee said that essential elements of ways of life can be regulated, as long as the regulation does not amount to a '*de facto* denial' of traditional ways of life.[65] Further, the HRC reaffirmed that

Martin Scheinin (eds), *The Jurisprudence of Human Rights Law: A Comparative Interpretive Approach* (Turku Institute for Human Rights, 2000), 159 222 at 163 72.

[59] Human Rights Committee, Communication No 511/1992, *Ilmari Länsman et al v Finland*, UN Doc CCPR/C/52/D/511/1992, 8 November 1994, para 9.4.

[60] *Ilmari Länsman et al v Finland*, para 9.5.

[61] Human Rights Committee, Communication No 671/1995, *Jouni E. Länsman et al v Finland*, UN Doc CCPR/C/58/D/671/1995, 22 November 1996, para 2.7.

[62] *Jouni E Länsman et al v Finland*, para 10.5.

[63] Human Rights Committee, Communication No 1023/2001, *Jouni Länsman, Eino Länsman and the Muotkatunturi Herdsmen's Committee v Finland*, UN Doc CCPR/C/83/D/1023/2001, 15 April 2005, para 10.2.

[64] Human Rights Committee, Communication No 879/1999, *George Howard v Canada*, UN Doc CCPR/C/84/D/879/1999, 4 August 2005, para 2.2.

[65] *George Howard v Canada*, para 12.7.

national courts were in a better position to make any such assessment, and because they had not analysed the claims brought before the HRC the court was unable to find a violation of the Covenant.[66]

Therefore, even though Article 27 is given effect by the individual complaints mechanism of the Optional Protocol to the ICCPR, a great margin of discretion is still left to the States, and the latest decisions of the HRC have considerably weakened the provision. It is important, though, to consider that even economic activities can be protected under the title of 'traditional', and that individual rights seem to trump community interests to a large extent.

A specific provision on minority protection is a particular feature of the ICCPR. There seems to be a reluctance with declaring violations of this provision, and this could be related to the fact that the idea of protecting group interests (even if the language of Article 27 is that of individual rights) still sits uncomfortably with the liberal rights paradigm. I will now analyse how other rights common to a larger number of international human rights instruments have also been invoked to protect culture and ways of life.

5.2.1.2 Equality and non-discrimination

The IACtHR, in the absence of a provision on minority protection in the American Convention, adopted a different approach. The IACtHR chose to look at the general provision of the American Convention on the 'Guarantee and Safeguard of Human Rights' (Article 1.1).[67] The duty of non-discrimination contained in this rule, according to the Court, is an emerging *jus cogens* norm and has *erga omnes* effects.[68]

The IACtHR examined the implications of this obligation in the *Case of the Yakye-Axa Community v Paraguay*. The case involved the lengthy process of attributing property entitlement to an indigenous community for lands ancestrally occupied by members of the community.[69]

In analysing the general scope of human rights obligations imposed upon the State in the context of indigenous communities, the Court said, in *obiter dictum*, that the right to equality, as guaranteed by the general provision on the respect for human rights of Article 1.1, imposed on States an obligation to undertake measures

[66] *George Howard v Canada*, paras 12.10 and 12.11.

[67] American Convention on Human Rights 'Pact of San José, Costa Rica'. Adopted on 22 November 1969. Entry into force: 18 July 1978. Number of States Parties as of November 2012: 23 (hereinafter 'American Convention' or 'Pact of San José'). The relevant provision is the following: '**Article 1. Obligation to Respect Rights**. 1. The States Parties to this Convention undertake to respect the rights and freedoms recognized herein and to ensure to all persons subject to their jurisdiction the free and full exercise of those rights and freedoms, without any discrimination for reasons of race, color, sex, language, religion, political or other opinion, national or social origin, economic status, birth, or any other social condition. [...]'

[68] I/A Court HR, *Juridical Condition and Rights of the Undocumented Migrants. Advisory Opinion OC-18 of September 17, 2003*. Series A No 18, para 110.

[69] I/A Court HR, *Case of the Yakye Axa Indigenous Community v Paraguay*. Merits, Reparations, and Costs. Judgment of 17 June 2005. Series C No 125, para 2.

to accommodate cultural differences.[70] This is a construction of 'substantive equality', as opposed to a more rigid, 'formal equality' advanced by the French reservation on Article 27 of the ICCPR, mentioned above.

Given that equality is one of the foundations of modern human rights law, to use general provisions on equality contained in human rights instruments would seem to be an optimal solution, if one gives equality the same reading the IACtHR has. The HRC has tackled this possibility in the case of the *Riast/Hylling Reindeer Herding District v Norway*, in which a violation of Article 27 of the ICCPR in conjunction with Article 2 (a norm similar in language to Article 1.1 of the American Convention) was argued.[71] As the case was declared inadmissible on the grounds of non-exhaustion of local remedies,[72] though, it is difficult to grasp what reach, if any, the Committee would have given to this norm, even though the Committee has said that the claim was not rejected *prima facie* on the grounds that it was an alleged exercise of *actio popularis*.[73]

Even though using the right to equality seems to be a fairly good solution to be adopted in systems that do not have their own mechanisms for the protection of culture and ways of life, there is a potential shortcoming in the language in which the provisions on equality in most instruments are drafted. The provisions in the American Convention,[74] the European Convention,[75] the African Charter,[76] and even the International Covenant on Civil and Political Rights (in cases where

[70] *Yakye Axa Community v Paraguay*, para 51. This paragraph deserves to be quoted in full: '51. In view of the fact that the instant case addresses the rights of the members of an indigenous Community, the Court deems it appropriate to recall that, pursuant to Articles 24 (Right to Equal Protection) and 1 (1) (Obligation to Respect Rights) of the American Convention, the States must ensure, on an equal basis, full exercise and enjoyment of the rights of these individuals who are not subject to their jurisdiction. However, it is necessary to emphasize that to effectively ensure those rights, when they interpret and apply their domestic legislation, the States must take into account the specific characteristics that differentiate the members of the indigenous peoples from the general population and that constitute their cultural identity. The Court must apply that same reasoning, as it will do in the instant case, to assess the scope and content of the Articles of the American Convention, which the Commission and the representatives allege were breached by the State.'

[71] Human Rights Committee, Communication No 942/2000, *Jarle Jonassen v Norway*, UN Doc CCPR/C/76/D/942/2000, 12 November 2002, para 3.1.

[72] *Jarle Jonassen v Norway*, para 9.

[73] *Jarle Jonassen v Norway*, para 8.5.

[74] '**Article 1. Obligation to Respect Rights**. 1. The States Parties to this Convention undertake to respect the rights and freedoms recognized herein and to ensure to all persons subject to their jurisdiction the free and full exercise of those rights and freedoms, without any discrimination for reasons of race, color, sex, language, religion, political or other opinion, national or social origin, economic status, birth, or any other social condition. [. . .]'

[75] '**Article 14. Prohibition of discrimination**. The enjoyment of the rights and freedoms set forth in this Convention shall be secured without discrimination on any ground such as sex, race, colour, religion, political or other opinion, national or social origin, association with a national minority, property, birth or other status.' This is the reason why the ECtHR has not declared an isolated violation of Art 14, but rather only analyses violations of this provision in conjunction with another article.

[76] '**Article 2**. Every individual shall be entitled to the enjoyment of the rights and freedoms recognized and guaranteed in the present Charter without distinction of any kind such as race, ethnic group, color, sex, language, religion, political or any other opinion, national and social origin, fortune, birth or other status.'

Article 27 cannot be invoked, such as the French reservation)[77] talk about the right to equality in the enjoyment of the rights protected by the respective instrument, and not an all-encompassing protection of equality.

The international jurisprudence on equality and non-discrimination is also not clear as to whether the forbidden discrimination is related to all grounds or to discrimination about the enjoyment of the rights protected by the relevant instrument. Even when the relevant instrument has a sweeping provision on equality (such as the ICCPR), the jurisprudence may give a rather confusing reading of the reach of such provisions.

The HRC analysed the meanings of equality as protected by the ICCPR in several cases. In *Shirin Aumeeruddy-Cziffra et al v Mauritius*,[78] for example, the HRC was confronted with discrimination caused by a set of two statutes on immigration, which changed the residency status of foreign men married to Mauritian women, while keeping intact the status of foreign women married to Mauritian men.[79] This situation allegedly created two sets of victims, one of single Mauritian women (who were no longer free to marry foreigners if they wanted to keep their Mauritian nationality), and another of Mauritian women married to foreign men.[80] The case was brought by 17 unmarried women, and only three married women,[81] but the Committee rejected the application of the 17 single women and focused on the rights of the three married women.[82]

The Committee affirmed that the law was arbitrary, and its arbitrariness rests on gender discrimination. The HRC avoided the discussion of the reasons for the discrimination, and focused on the arbitrariness of it.[83] The HRC bundled Article 26 together with the general obligation to respect the rights without discrimination (Article 2).[84] It is not clear from this decision whether Article 26 has any independent meaning, or if equality only meant non-discrimination in the securing of rights.

In another case, *FH Zwaan-De Vries v The Netherlands*,[85] the Committee analysed the issue of discrimination based on a legislative provision granting a benefit not required by the ICCPR. In the Mauritius case, the benefit (protection

[77] '**Article 2.1.** Each State Party to the present Covenant undertakes to respect and to ensure to all individuals within its territory and subject to its jurisdiction the rights recognized in the present Covenant, without distinction of any kind, such as race, colour, sex, language, religion, political or other opinion, national or social origin, property, birth or other status. [...]' and '**Article 26.** All persons are equal before the law and are entitled without any discrimination to the equal protection of the law. In this respect, the law shall prohibit any discrimination and guarantee to all persons equal and effective protection against discrimination on any ground such as race, colour, sex, language, religion, political or other opinion, national or social origin, property, birth or other status.' As it will be explained below, these provisions have been interpreted jointly by the Human Rights Committee.

[78] Human Rights Committee, Communication No 35/1978, *Shirin Aumeeruddy-Cziffra et al v Mauritius*, UN Doc CCPR/C/12/D/35/1978, 9 April 1981.

[79] *Shirin AumeeruddyCziffra et al v Mauritius*, para 1.2.

[80] *Shirin AumeeruddyCziffra et al v Mauritius*, para 6.2.

[81] *Shirin AumeeruddyCziffra et al v Mauritius*, para 7.1.

[82] *Shirin AumeeruddyCziffra et al v Mauritius*, para 9.2.a.

[83] *Shirin AumeeruddyCziffra et al v Mauritius*, para 9.2.b.2.i.4.

[84] *Shirin AumeeruddyCziffra et al v Mauritius*, para 9.2.b.2.i.5.

[85] Human Rights Committee, Communication No 182/1984, *FH Zwaan-De Vries v The Netherlands*, UN Doc CCPR/C/29/D/182/1984, 9 April 1987.

of the family) was required by the Covenant. Thus, if the Committee kept its position of analysing equality only in the enjoyment of the rights protected by the Covenant, it would imply not analysing this case. In this case, unemployment benefits were denied to a woman on the grounds of her being married.[86] The Committee declared that the terms of Article 26 were substantially different from Article 2, and that Article 26 required equality in the application of a State's internal law.[87] The Committee went on to determine that there had been discrimination on the basis of gender, significantly broadening the scope of equality protection under the ICCPR.[88] This reading of the ICCPR provision on equality, which means that States need to enforce equal treatment in all of their laws, and not only those related to human rights protected by the Covenant, was confirmed in later cases.[89]

A construction of the law such as that of the Inter-American Court is not by itself sufficient to protect culture, unless the right to equality is given the autonomy in international human rights adjudication it has been given by the HRC. Limitations imposed by the language of other instruments, however, seem to prevent such a sweeping construction.

However, even if the right to equality is thought of in the narrower sense, one has to bear in mind that the IACtHR understanding offers a good background against which the argued violation of other rights can be measured. This construction of equality becomes an auxiliary tool, and another right must be brought into play. This other right can be any right protected by the instrument. This is advantageous because it opens the possibility of fitting the protection of ways of life into all aspects of life, and not necessarily a single aspect, such as the right to family life.

[86] *FH Zwaan-De Vries v The Netherlands*, para 2.1.

[87] *FH Zwaan-De Vries v The Netherlands*, para 12.3.

[88] *FH Zwaan-De Vries v The Netherlands*, para 15.

[89] Human Rights Committee, Communication No 191/1985, *Carl Henrik Blom v Sweden*, UN Doc CCPR/C/32/D/191/1985, 4 April 1988; and Human Rights Committee, Communication No 196/1985, *Ibrahima Gueye et al v France*, UN Doc CCPR/C/35/D/196/1985, 6 April 1989. In *Carl Henrik Blom v Sweden*, the case deals with financial assistance that the State provides to secondary school students in partially funding private school students. The HRC does not specify what the ground of the discrimination is, even though it points out that the interest at stake is education, but the classes of individuals being treated different are not defined by reference to a ground of discrimination mentioned in Art 26. This case is part of a tendency in the HRC jurisprudence on discrimination generally in that the HRC tends not to say why it includes other categories within the scope of Art 26, and often does not even say what the distinction between the two classes of people is. It just assumes that the distinction is under the umbrella of Art 26. The case of *Ibrahima Gueye et al v France* deals with Senegalese men serving in the French army. After the independence of Senegal, they continued to receive a pension from France for 14 years, when the levels of the pensions were frozen with respect only of the Senegalese soldiers (the French soldiers kept on receiving raises). The soldiers argued this to be discrimination on the basis of race, but the HRC found it to be discrimination on the basis of nationality. The case can be read as including 'current nationality' as a basis for discrimination (national origin would not work, as the soldiers were originally French, strictly speaking). The reason why the Senegalese soldiers were given the benefit in the first place was independent of their nationality, so France should not be entitled to take their benefits away on the basis of nationality.

5.2.1.3 Freedom of expression

This idea of using the general provision of equality in an instrument, as insinuated by the IACtHR in the *Yakye-Axa* case, was later developed in the case of *López Álvarez v Honduras*, which was the case of a Garífuna leader who was imprisoned and had rights denied while in custody. In this case, the Court gave full meaning to the confused expression of the earlier case (*Yakye-Axa v Paraguay*) to say that a right to the enjoyment of culture was indeed clearly contained within the general provision of Article 1.1. The Court analysed this issue in the context of the prohibition imposed on a leader of the Garífuna community of Honduras (an Afro-Caribbean community) to use the Garífuna language while in prison to communicate with his partner.[90]

The IACtHR, analysing this prohibition in light of the right to freedom of expression (Article 13), the general provision on equality (Article 1.1), and the specific provision on non-discrimination of the American Convention (Article 24), came to the conclusion that the requirements of equality imposed on the State an obligation to allow expression in a prisoner's mother tongue. The Court thus affirmed that measures preventing an individual from expressing himself in his indigenous language amounted to a violation of the right to freedom of expression in conjunction with the general provision.[91]

At this juncture it is important to note that language is an element of intangible cultural heritage, according to the UNESCO Convention,[92] and was identified in the past as an 'essential distinctive mark' of cultural groups.[93] When it comes to languages as an element of ICH, the drafting committee of the 2003 UNESCO Convention made a clear effort to say that languages specifically important for ICH are protected under the convention, and not all languages. What exactly this distinction means is yet to be evaluated, but I suggest it has to do with the costs of protecting all languages as part of heritage, while States have been unwilling to give them protection through other means. There was a concern here with 'back-dooring' language protection legislation and programmes, which would impose financial and political costs on States. At any rate, this qualification of language as an element of intangible heritage is a narrowing down of the significance of language to intangible heritage.[94]

There were several cases brought before the HRC under Article 27 (always in conjunction with Article 19, which is the provision on freedom of expression of the

[90] I/A Court HR, *Case of López-Álvarez v Honduras*. Merits, Reparations, and Costs. Judgment of 1 February 2006. Series C No 141, para 54.49.

[91] *López-Álvarez v Honduras*, paras 169 and 174.

[92] 2003 UNESCO Convention, Art 2(a). For an example of the practical application of this aspect of ICH, see Matilda Burden, 'Museums and the Intangible Heritage: The Case Study of the Afrikaans Language Museum', *Intl J of Intangible Heritage* 2 (2007), 82 91.

[93] Philip Vuciri Ramaga, 'Bases of Minority Identity', *Human Rights Q* 14 (1992), 409 28 at 417 18 (referring to the *Czechoslovak Language of Minorities Case*, 3 *Ann Dig of Pub Intl L Cas* 314 (1925 26)).

[94] Blake, *Commentary*, 37.

ICCPR) regarding specifically the use of Breton in France.[95] However, all of these cases were deemed inadmissible. Many of the cases were about linguistic minorities[96] trying to make their cases before local courts in their minority languages instead of French. While they alleged that the dismissal of their actions for not being brought in French before local courts in itself constituted a violation of rights under the Covenant, the fact that they were in all cases proficient in French decisively weakened their cases and can be read as a negative result for the safeguarding of intangible heritage through human rights mechanisms because the Committee overlooked cultural significance of the language in order to favour an easier, less cumbersome, and economical solution for the State (namely, to simply disregard minority languages within the French territory).

Even the Inter-American Court, when relying on its general provision to interpret the provision on freedom of expression so as to incorporate elements of cultural identity, referred to the provision on non-discrimination, in this way tying together the substantive meaning of equality it had built in its previous case-law to a stronger, more general provision on equal treatment (even if the exact reach of equality, or the role it plays in that specific decision, has not been made clear in the case). Not all systems can rely on such provisions, though, and other choices have been made in order to find ways to protect cultural identity. The right to private and family life is a particularly powerful clause in this respect, and will be analysed below.

5.2.1.4 The right to private and family life

The right to private life can be considered a 'blanket' clause in human rights regimes, as it has been used not only for the protection of cultural identity, but also, for example, for environmental protection.[97] There are two aspects of this right to be considered separately, even though more often than not this right is taken as a whole: on the one hand, there is the right to privacy, which relates closely to the interest of custodial communities 'to be left alone'. In this sense, one could even speak of something such as 'cultural privacy'.[98]

On the other hand, one can talk of an extended meaning of the expression 'family life', construed so as to mean a person's way of life in relation to other

[95] Human Rights Committee, Communication No 220/1987, *TK v France*, UN Doc CCPR/C/37/D/220/1987, 8 December 1989; Human Rights Committee, Communication No 222/1987, *HK v France*, UN Doc CCPR/C/37/D/222/1987, 8 December 1989; Human Rights Committee, Communication No 262/1987, *RT v France*, UN Doc CCPR/C/35/D/262/1987, 3 April 1989; Human Rights Committee, Communication Nos 324 and 325/1988, *JB and HK v France*, UN Doc CCPR/C/34/D/324/1988, 26 October 1988; Human Rights Committee, Communication No 228/1987, *CLD v France*, UN Doc CCPR/C/33/D/228/1987, 26 July 1988; and Human Rights Committee, Communication No 243/1987, *SR v France*, UN Doc CCPR/C/31/D/243/1987, 5 November 1987.

[96] Language is one of the possible defining elements of a minority within Art 27 of the ICCPR. An emblematic case of a linguistic minority is the case of *Belgian Linguistics* before the ECtHR. For a detailed analysis of this case, see Ramaga, 'Relativity of the Minority Concept', 112.

[97] *López Ostra v Spain* (Application No 16798/90), judgment of 9 December 1994.

[98] Brown, *Who Owns Native Culture?*, 27 42.

people, or even the way of life of a community (thus adding a group dimension to the individual right). Further, a construction of 'family' could be undertaken to encompass a non-Westernized concept. This has been the position taken by the HRC in *Francis Hopu and Tepoaitu Bessert v France*. This case involved the threat posed by a hotel-construction project to the traditional lands, including the traditional burial ground, of a Polynesian tribe.[99] The HRC accepted the petitioners' contention that the Committee should interpret the term 'family' in accordance with their traditions, by which 'family' would mean the entire population of the tribe. Ultimately it determined that the construction of the hotel complex as planned would interfere with the privacy and family life of the petitioners.[100]

The French reservation preventing the application of Article 27 explains why the HRC decided to broaden its understanding of family for this case, but this position was criticized by some of its members on the grounds that even a broadened understanding of family could not possibly encompass all the members of a certain ethnic group.[101] In any event, for the present purposes, it is sufficient to say that a provision of the ICCPR (other than the specific one on the protection of minority culture) was used to protect characteristics relative to a people's way of life.

The ECtHR, in interpreting the European Convention,[102] has followed a similar path in cases dealing with individuals of Roma origin and aspects of their culture. One example of such an approach is *Lee v United Kingdom*.[103] Thomas Lee brought an application against the United Kingdom alleging that certain environmental measures prevented him from settling with his caravan in the place he had chosen for such purposes, and he alleged that this was contrary to his right to respect for home, family, and private life.[104] As a Roma, he had a nomadic lifestyle, and because of it he had been repeatedly prosecuted for 'illegal encampment'. To rectify this situation, he bought a piece of land and decided to settle there permanently.[105] One year after he had settled on the piece of land he had purchased he received an eviction order as his lands were in an area of special zoning due to landscape preservation concerns.[106]

The Court found that the issues of the case fell under Article 8 of the European Convention, reasoning that Thomas Lee's choice to live in a caravan '[...] is an integral part of his ethnic identity as a gypsy [and that m]easures which affect the applicant's

[99] Human Rights Committee, Communication No 549/1993, *Francis Hopu and Tepoaitu Bessert v France*, UN Doc CCPR/C/60/D/549/1993/Rev/1, 29 December 1997, paras 2.2 and 2.5.

[100] *Francis Hopu and Tepoaitu Bessert v France*, para 10.3.

[101] *Francis Hopu and Tepoaitu Bessert v France*, Individual dissenting opinion by Committee members David Kretzmer and Thomas Buergenthal, cosigned by Nisuke Ando and Lord Colville, para 4.

[102] Convention for the Protection of Human Rights and Fundamental Freedoms, CETS 005, opened for signature on 4 November 1950. Entry into force: 3 September 1953. States Parties as of November 2012: 47.

[103] *Case of Lee v United Kingdom* (Application No 25289/1994), judgment of 18 January 2001.

[104] *Lee v United Kingdom*, para 3.

[105] *Lee v United Kingdom*, paras 10 11.

[106] *Lee v United Kingdom*, para 15.

occupation of his caravans [...] affect his ability to maintain his identity as a gypsy and to lead his private and family life in accordance with that tradition'.[107]

After deciding that the case fell under Article 8, the Court went on to analyse whether there was an interference with the rights under this provision, and, if this was confirmed, whether the interference was justifiable. After determining that there had been interference,[108] and that it was one of environmental law (urban planning),[109] the ECtHR said that States enjoy a wide margin of appreciation in dealing with environmental matters,[110] and therefore have a fair amount of discretion in striking a balance between the needs of the population at large (protected by environmental legislation) and those of a minority group (which would claim a culture-based exception to being subject to those general measures).

When responding to the argument concerning the protection of minorities, the Court accepted the contention that the Council of Europe Convention on Minority Protection was an indicator of an emerging consensus around the protection of minority rights.[111] However, according to the Court, the consensus was not such so as to reduce the margin of appreciation granted to States in imposing limitations upon Article 8 rights, as the language of the instrument was mostly open-textured.[112] Thus, the applicant's argument was rejected, and the interference with his family life was found to fall within the State's purview in relation to which the Court would play a 'strictly supervisory role'.[113]

With this reasoning, the ECtHR accepted that elements of the way of life of a certain culture fall within the private life of individuals belonging to such a culture. Even though leading to a similar result, the reasoning adopted by the Court is distinct from that of the HRC in a very significant way. The ECtHR did not expand the concept of 'family'; instead, it simply said that a way of life is an integral part of private life. This reasoning is more powerful than that adopted by the HRC, and far less controversial, at least if one accepts a liberal notion of human rights as individual rights to support the protection of cultural heritage (which, as noted above, has intrinsic collective dimensions).

Different, culturally-sensitive constructions of 'privacy', 'family', and 'family life' can also offer a significant degree of protection to manifestations of cultural identity. These readings seem to be open enough to encompass all aspects of culture within the terms of this right, thus creating yet another powerful tool for the protection of ICH. However, it is uncertain whether human rights regimes will maintain or expand the enlarged scope of protection guaranteed by the right to private and family life. Further, as there are other aspects of ICH with human rights implications worth protecting, it is important to keep on analysing other possible cuts.

[107] *Lee v United Kingdom*, para 75.
[108] *Lee v United Kingdom*, para 80.
[109] *Lee v United Kingdom*, para 84.
[110] *Lee v United Kingdom*, para 94.
[111] *Lee v United Kingdom*, paras 85 and 95.
[112] *Lee v United Kingdom*, para 96.
[113] *Lee v United Kingdom*, para 96.

5.2.1.5 Freedom of religion

Freedom of religion offers a particularly relevant dimension for the protection of ICH as many of the concerns surrounding intangible heritage are related to views of the sacred by custodial communities, and to harm experienced from disrespect to religious views. Religion is one of the identifying characteristics of a minority within Article 27 of the ICCPR. Furthermore, there is a group dimension inherent in the concept of religious freedom that helps accommodate much of the concern over granting protection for group interests via individual rights. If one considers that freedom of religion is already protected as an individual right, even though the exercise of religion is more often than not a collective endeavour, it seems easier to overcome the resistance to using individual human rights for the protection of group interests associated with cultural heritage. The relevance of freedom of religion jurisprudence is twofold: first of all, the current standards of protection open an exception to social conventions that would otherwise make religious rituals public. In this sense, to secure freedom of religion means to create the means to protect the secrecy of certain religious practices that form part of intangible heritage, thus constituting some form of negative protection. A second instance consists of allowing for the creation of exceptional regimes of safeguarding for religious practices, thus constituting an aspect of positive protection.[114]

One interesting example of this latter aspect is the *Case of the Jewish Liturgical Association Cha'Are Shalom ve Tsedek v France.*[115] This case, however, must be read in light of *Arrowsmith v United Kingdom,*[116] a case decided by the defunct European Commission of Human Rights which set the standard for the freedom of religion jurisprudence of the ECtHR. I will first then analyse the *Arrowsmith* case.

Pat Arrowsmith, a pacifist, was convicted of distributing leaflets urging British soldiers not to go for tours in Northern Ireland. She was prosecuted under the Incitement to Disaffection Act, and sentenced to 18 months' imprisonment. She then alleged a violation of her rights under Article 9 of the European Convention (freedom of belief and religion). The Commission accepted that pacifism was a belief, but it said that the leaflets were not a protectable manifestation of belief bacause: (1) the leaflets did not contain pacifist views, but the views of those opposed to a particular war (as opposed to war in general); (2) the leaflets advanced a political criticism to British policy in Northern Ireland, and not pacifist views (it was more of political speech, instead of advancement of a belief); (3) the leaflets were directed to soldiers, and not the population at large.

114 For a review on how municipal legislation in several countries creates general exceptions to members of certain religions, especially in the domains of family and inheritance law, see Henry J Steiner and Philip Alston, *International Human Rights in Context Law, Politics, Morals* (Oxford University Press, 2000), 491 511. Unfortunately, these materials have been excluded from the third edition (2007).

115 *Case of Cha'Are Shalom ve Tsedek v France* (Application No 27417/95), judgment 27 June 2000.

116 *Arrowsmith v United Kingdom* (Application No 7050/75), Comm Rep 1978, 19 DR 5.

This case created the 'Arrowsmith test', being reinterpreted to stand for a certain composition that is only found in the dissent's characterization of the majority's holding, but not in the majority's opinion. The minority interprets the majority's holding to mean that there needs to be an element of necessity to the activity before it is called a practice to be protected by Article 9. The belief system in question has to require the action almost as a duty, in order to be protected by Article 9.[117]

The religion or belief system must require the individual to act in that particular way, for it to fall under Article 9. If there is no rule requiring that the practice, or the rule exists but is only a permissive rule, the practice is not protected. Objective proof that the practice is required is necessary, and a subjective assessment of the necessity of the practice is not enough. In this case, evidence that pacifism required her distribution of leaflets was necessary, regardless of how Pat Arrowsmith felt about it. This test helps make a stronger case for some belief systems (traditional systems, hierarchical, centralized, and well-structured), but it poses obstacles to others (new religious movements, more specifically). It also becomes a task of the judicial system to ask what the requirements of each religion are.

The *Arrowsmith* decision creates then a negative test, as stated in *Leyla Şahın v Turkey* (Grand Chamber).[118] The *Arrowsmith* decision has enormous implications for Article 9 jurisprudence, bringing religious law into the very core of the meaning of Article 9. This idea is relevant for interpreting the *Cha'Are Shalom* case.

In the *Case of the Jewish Liturgical Association Cha'Are Shalom ve Tsedek v France*, the Court was faced with the problem of ritual slaughtering of animals. The practice is prohibited in France except under certain circumstances.[119] Animals have to be humanely killed, and this requires them to be unconscious before the slaughter. Ritual slaughter requires the opposite (in effect compelling the violation of French Law). In France there are ritual slaughterers who have authorization cards, and the authority to give the card is given to a particular committee of an association in Paris, which itself is part of the broader Jewish religious organization, and has a statutory basis to exist.[120] An ultra-orthodox group wanted to pursue stricter practices of ritual slaughter, but the committee refused to authorize it.[121]

A religious sub-minority then challenged a rule imposed on them by the broader religious community, alleging that the rule violated their freedom of religion (Article 9), alone and in conjunction with the prohibition of discrimination (Article 14), and linking it to the State in that it refused to interfere in the larger minority's actions.[122] The *Arrowsmith* test was met because the practice of consuming only kosher products is required by Judaism.[123] The actual act of ritual slaughter was not the practice the Court focused on (the Court focused instead on the system for

[117] *Arrowsmith v United Kingdom*, para 2 of Commissioner Opsahl's dissenting opinion.

[118] *Leyla Şahın v Turkey* (Grand Chamber) (Application No 44774/98), judgment of 10 November 2005, para 105.

[119] *Case of Cha'Are Shalom ve Tsedek v France*, paras 20 1.

[120] *Case of Cha'Are Shalom ve Tsedek v France*, paras 22 5.

[121] *Case of Cha'Are Shalom ve Tsedek v France*, paras 27 34.

[122] *Case of Cha'Are Shalom ve Tsedek v France*, paras 36 and 58.

[123] *Case of Cha'Are Shalom ve Tsedek v France*, paras 13 19.

certification of kosher meat, and whether a monopoly for the certification of observation of the ritual was an encroachment of freedom of religion). By not focusing on that practice it was able to find that there was no interference.[124] By focusing on a practice that did not lie at the heart of the belief, and focusing instead on the bureaucratic tools necessary to implement the core practice, the ECtHR missed an opportunity to make a statement about rituals that are an integral part of intangible heritage. It may have been the case that this judgment is the lesser of two evils, and, had the Court chosen to take ritual slaughter head-on, it would still have upheld the State's right to regulate (and even forbid) the practice, which would have been a much greater blow to religious heritage than this decision, which ultimately allowed for the continuation of the practice. Sidestepping the core of culture became a means to safeguard it.

Article 9 requires the State to treat religious communities differently to the general population when regulating the market. In regulating economic activity, the State is required to treat religious communities differently from the rest of the population.[125] There is a plausible argument that France is not only required to exempt, but also consult with the community who is entitled to the exemption, or let the community itself determine it.

There is also a compelling argument that Article 9 requires differential treatment, and delegation of this type of decision-making to the community. However, the delegation to the community does not violate equality, even to the extent that several instances of law-making authority are being given to an entity other than the State. This argument allows the creation of a system of protection to religious interests that may be used to protect many instances of intangible heritage, especially in cases where it is difficult to 'fit' elements of ICH into currently existing legal categories. The law protecting religious freedom opens room to create a system of exceptions to the general applicable law that allows for the building of specific systems moulded after the specific needs of custodial communities.

The greatest pitfall in this approach, however, is that not all ICH practices have a religious element attached to them (and, as the Arrowsmith test suggests, any such link would need to be strong). However, considering that at least a good part of the most problematic issues in ICH do indeed deal with religious harm, the possibilities of protection by using freedom of religion are a powerful tool to be borne in mind.

5.2.1.6 Other rights

There are many possibilities within human rights law for protecting various aspects of ICH. I have addressed above some of the most common, but there are other rights worth mentioning that can be invoked with the objective of safeguarding heritage interests.

[124] *Case of Cha'Are Shalom ve Tsedek v France*, paras 74 and 77.
[125] *Case of Cha'Are Shalom ve Tsedek v France*, para 84.

Among these rights are rights to a fair trial. These rights also have somewhat the character of a 'blanket' clause in human rights regimes.[126] As 'fair trial rights' refer to internal proceedings on any legal claims, and not necessarily claims related to the human rights protected by international instruments, fair trial rights offer an indirect avenue of international redress, since proceedings on ICH claims can be lengthy, ill-balanced, and even amount to a denial of justice, considering the frequent power imbalances between custodial communities and third parties. Fair trial rights are also particularly important in the example of the use of language in internal proceedings, as mentioned above.

The right to freedom of association may also be invoked. As this right protects the right of individuals to form groups, it is possible to protect entire communities, and the communality required by ICH practices, by utilizing this right.

Another category of rights that can be used for the protection of ICH interests involves the right to physical integrity, a right from which there can be no derogation, thus belonging to a 'superior' hierarchy of rights. This has been explored by the IACtHR in the *Case of the Moiwana Community v Suriname*. In this case, the Court considered that the failure of the State in guaranteeing the community members the title to their traditionally-occupied lands, which prevented them from observing their burial rites, amounted to a violation of their right to physical integrity as protected by Article 5 of the American Convention, and ultimately led the State to demarcate the area and give title to the Moiwana community.[127]

In other cases of its jurisprudence on indigenous peoples, the IACtHR has used the right to property to guarantee land entitlements to indigenous communities.[128] To the extent that the land is an essential element to the existence of several of these cultures, and the definition of the UNESCO Convention incorporates the 'cultural spaces' associated with ICH in its definition,[129] to protect indigenous land claims is also a seemingly viable means to protect indigenous cultural heritage.

Finally, Economic, Social and Cultural Rights (ESCR) can be used for the protection of culture and cultural identity. These include the right to the enjoyment

[126] An example of how fair trial rights may be used to defend indigenous land claims is within the European system. Martin Scheinin talks about the possibility of using Art 6 of the ECHR (Fair Trial Rights) as an 'open-textured' clause to advance indigenous claims. Although Scheinin mentions this possibility in the context of indigenous land claims, nothing prevents its use for the advancement of cultural claims. See Scheinin, 'The Right to Enjoy a Distinct Culture'.

[127] I/A Court HR, *Case of the Moiwana Community v Suriname*. Preliminary Objections, Merits, Reparations, and Costs. Judgment of 15 June 2005. Series C No 124, para 103.

[128] See eg I/A Court HR, *Case of the Mayagna (Sumo) Awas Tingni Community v Nicaragua*. Merits, Reparations, and Costs. Judgment of 31 August 2001. Series C No 79; I/A Court HR, *Case of the Yakye Axa Indigenous Community v Paraguay*. Merits, Reparations, and Costs. Judgment of 17 June 2005. Series C No 125; I/A Court HR, *Case of Yatama v Nicaragua*. Preliminary Objections, Merits, Reparations, and Costs. Judgment of 23 June 2005. Series C No 127; I/A Court HR, *Case of the Sawhoyamaxa Indigenous Community v Paraguay*. Merits, Reparations, and Costs. Judgment of 29 March 2006. Series C No 146; and I/A Court HR, *Case of the Saramaka People v Suriname*. Preliminary Objection, Merits, Reparations, and Costs. Judgment of 28 November 2007 Series C No 172.

[129] 2003 UNESCO Convention, Art 2(a).

of culture, and the right to enjoy the benefits arising from creation. The problems associated with this set of rights mainly focus on the lack of a well-established institutional framework for their protection. So far, the United Nations Committee on Economic, Social and Cultural Rights cannot receive individual complaints (even though an optional protocol to the ICESCR has already been approved, and is now awaiting the necessary number of ratifications).[130] Further, the only regional system to openly protect ESCR, the African regime,[131] lacks altogether an effective enforcement mechanism, even though the African Commission and the recently-established African Court[132] have the potential to become effective oversight organs.

However, to a great extent ESCR elements are incorporated in CPR case-law. This can be seen from the broadened constructions of equality undertaken by the Inter-American Court and the HRC, as well as by the doctrine of 'positive obligations' of the ECtHR.[133]

These are, broadly, the rights that may be invoked for the protection of culture and cultural identity, which may then address ICH and indirectly offer it protection. It is now necessary to look at the limitations that can be imposed on these rights.

5.2.2 Limitations on rights

In the previous part of this chapter I addressed obstacles that could be raised to the application of the human rights framework in the protection of ICH. These could be called 'external' limitations, as they referred to the use of human rights *a priori*, such as the reluctance towards using the individual rights framework to safeguard (inherently collective) heritage. I now move to discussing limitations within the rights themselves, or 'internal' limitations.

There are several limitations on the use of the human rights here indicated. A first general limitation is the proportionality test required in cases involving the

[130] As of November 2012, there have been eight ratifications to this Protocol, and there are 33 other signatories. Ten ratifications are necessary for the Protocol to enter into force, according to its Art 18.

[131] African (Banjul) Charter on Human and Peoples' Rights, Adopted 27 June 1981 by OAU Doc CAB/LEG/67/3 rev 5. Entry into force 21 October 1986. Number of States Parties as of November 2012: 53 (all Member States of the African Union). 21 ILM 59 (1982). Arts 15 18.

[132] Protocol to the African Charter on Human and Peoples' Rights on the Establishment of an African Court on Human and Peoples' Rights, Adopted in July 1998, entry into force January 2004. Number of parties as of November 2012: 26.

[133] For a detailed analysis of positive obligations in the European system generally, see Alastair R Mowbray, *The Development of Positive Obligations under the European Convention on Human Rights by the European Court of Human Rights* (Hart Publishing, 2004) (analysing the right to life, the prohibition of torture, the right to liberty and security, the right to a fair trial, the right to respect for private and family life, freedom of thought, conscience and religion, freedom of expression, freedom of assembly and association, the prohibition of discrimination, and the right to an effective remedy). See also Frédéric Sudre, 'Les "obligations positives" dans la jurisprudence européenne des droits de l'homme', *Revue Trimestrielle des Droits de l'homme* 23 (1995), 363 84 at 365 (arguing that the doctrine of 'positive obligations' incorporates elements of ESCR into the ECtHR's jurisprudence).

rights to freedom of expression,[134] freedom of religion,[135] the right to private and family life, freedom of assembly and, as discussed above, the provision on minority protection of the ICCPR, at least as construed by the HRC.

Another general limitation is the discretion granted to States in guaranteeing all these rights. To the extent a margin of appreciation is given to States in applying certain rights, and considering that this margin of appreciation is even greater when it comes to more 'controversial' issues, this is an important internal limitation to be taken into account.[136]

A specific limitation involves specifically the general clause on equality, as discussed above. The main concern relates to the autonomy on the clauses protecting equality in the relevant international and regional instruments for the protection of human rights. If the provision on equality is not sufficiently autonomous, the potential for invoking it in the defence of ICH concerns is significantly diminished.

A limitation against invoking fair trial rights exists in that they do not in any way have the aim of protecting the substantive rights infringed in the case. Fair trial rights claims constitute an entirely separate legal issue abstracted from the set of facts of the domestic case. This has been confirmed on several occasions by the IACtHR.[137] The implication of such a statement is that, arguably, any 'indirect' protection given to identity claims by means of protecting fair trial rights is not actual protection and will necessarily fail to address the identity (and therefore, the heritage) concerns of the case.

When it comes to the right to property, the main obstacle to be overcome is the fact that a connection to land is an essential requirement. Since this connection to land is not present in all ICH manifestations, and is mostly restricted to the heritage of indigenous peoples, the right to property can be validly invoked almost exclusively to the benefit of indigenous heritage, not protecting non-indigenous custodial communities. Finally, to invoke the right to physical integrity, as done by the IACtHR in the *Moiwana* case, involves a rather high threshold for proving the violation.[138]

134 Specific limitations on these rights also exist. For example, when it comes to the right to freedom of expression, one question to be asked is whether the expression being affected is protected speech.

135 When it comes to invoking the right to freedom of religion, one has to consider how this right is operationalized, since to invoke freedom of religion implies the recognition of a certain practice as religious, which necessarily plays with the concept of religion.

136 On the margin of appreciation doctrine, see Howard Charles Yourow, *The Margin of Appreciation Doctrine in the Dynamics of European Human Rights Jurisprudence* (Kluwer Law International, 1996).

137 I/A Court HR, *Case of Caballero-Delgado and Santana v Colombia*. Merits. Judgment of 8 December 1995. Series C No 22, para 60; I/A Court HR, *Case of Suárez-Rosero v Ecuador*. Merits. Judgment of 12 November 1997. Series C No 35, para 37; I/A Court HR, *Case of Cesti-Hurtado v Peru*. Merits. Judgment of 29 September 1999. Series C No 56, para 108; and I/A Court HR, *Case of Fermín Ramírez v Guatemala*. Merits, Reparations, and Costs. Judgment of 20 June 2005. Series C No 126, para 63.

138 This high threshold can be also seen in the ECtHR jurisprudence on torture. See eg *Ireland v United Kingdom* (Application No 5310/71), judgment of 18 January 1978.

Another interest to be taken into account is what would fall in a proportionality analysis under the heading of 'the rights of others'. The tension I am referring to is the clash between the right to scientific expression of researchers and anthropologists, and the ways in which it can clash with many religious and privacy concerns of custodial communities.[139] This is a tension that runs throughout UNESCO instruments, and the 2003 UNESCO Convention seems to privilege the right of researchers over concerns for 'cultural privacy', to the extent it requires the cataloguing and studying of intangible heritage before affording it any sort of international recognition.

All these limitations help balance the application of human rights for the safeguarding of intangible heritage, and can be used as arguments to 'pacify' critics of this approach. The fact that there are internal limitations to the use of human rights may serve to offer a counterpoint to a totalizing view that could aspire to applying solely human rights in ICH-related cases.

5.2.3 A human rights exception to intangible heritage protection

A lot of debate on the relationship between human rights and intangible heritage focuses on how human rights are a limit to the protection of intangible heritage; in other words, how the limits of human rights are connected to the manifestations of heritage that can be deemed worthy of protection.[140] The very fact that the definition of intangible heritage in the 2003 UNESCO Convention imposes human rights as a limit to what can be considered intangible heritage worth safeguarding is illustrative of this notion.[141] The imposition of limits on ICH through human rights can be described as a negative relationship between human rights and ICH.

There is tension between some universal human rights standards and particular manifestations of ICH. One obvious example, and often cited, is that of female circumcision, which is defended by some on cultural grounds. This practice, despite being a traditional cultural practice, violates human rights, and as such does not merit protection.

The objection to intangible heritage that affects human rights is related to the 'invisible asterisk', or the idea that cultural rights, and cultural distinctiveness, will be protected as long as they do not violate other human rights.[142] And, while the idea of the 'invisible asterisk' (or its critique, to be more precise) seems to lean towards cultural relativism, I would like to suggest here that the invisible asterisk

[139] For a series of case studies on this clash, see Brown, *Who Owns Native Culture?*, 11 42.

[140] For a collection of essays on this topic, see Helaine Silverman and D Fairchild Ruggles (eds), *Cultural Heritage and Human Rights* (Springer, 2007).

[141] '**Article 2—Definitions.** [. . .] For the purposes of this Convention, consideration will be given solely to such intangible cultural heritage as is compatible with existing international human rights instruments [. . .].'

[142] This idea is more fully articulated in Karen Engle, *The Elusive Promise of Indigenous Development: Rights, Culture, Strategy* (Duke University Press, 2010), 133 7; and Elizabeth A Povinelli, *The Cunning of Recognition: Indigenous Alterities and the Making of Australian Multiculturalism* (Duke University Press, 2002).

can indeed be a useful tool for communities. I suggest that, while at a first glance this limitation may be seen as an obstacle for the protection of culture, it can also be looked at as informing the debate about certain cultural practices as it opens communities, albeit forcefully, to cultural exchange. The colonial imprint is noticeable in this argument, to the extent it suggests that communities can be 'civilized' or 'change their ways' towards more universally acceptable standards based on contact with other groups. However, if one is to advance a position of protecting intangible heritage that adds to cultural diversity, it may be permissible to essentialize communities, at least if these communities are willing to open their heritage to the appreciation of the outside world. It is not about imposing a colonial morality or mentality, but rather the non-negotiable core of human rights connected to a culturally-sensitive universalist orientation, to which I am aligned. Human rights as a limitation to heritage therefore functions as another stream in the 'cultural flow' that constantly transforms and gives new meanings to heritage.

Naturally, this 'positive' look at this 'asterisk' must be balanced by the idea that, inevitably, pressures for recognition and international aid can force communities to abandon their practices altogether, without going through any sort of debate as to the actual human rights implications of their practice. But mechanisms on community participation, further elaborated on in Chapter 7, can help address this concern.

As a justification for the use of human rights to protect cultural identity and the human right to a cultural identity the use of institutional human rights mechanisms seems only logical. But human rights adjudicatory and quasi-adjudicatory schemes have not in general been given the power to analyse cultural rights, which is why they have developed a rich case-law focused on other human rights aspects, such as the right to private and family life, the right to equality and non-discrimination, and freedom of religion, among other rights.

Protecting heritage through the protection of identity seems in many ways a detour, but it can also be thought of as cutting out the middle man, that is, protecting identity directly, without having to protect the manifestations of that identity. Heritage is protected because it has an impact on identity, to protect identity directly, and then use heritage as an evidence of identity.

A 'right to heritage' is fairly established as an offshoot of the right to cultural identity, and an important and instrumental part of it. It is usually translated as an individual right, but this fails to take into account the essential group aspect of cultural heritage in general, and of intangible heritage in particular. In this sense, international human rights adjudication is a helpful, but by no means complete, tool to safeguard intangible heritage at the international level.

6

Intellectual Property and Intangible Heritage

This chapter explores the use of intellectual property tools for safeguarding (ICH). This use was one of the most common topics discussed in literature on ICH protection prior to the entry into force of the 2003 UNESCO Convention, and it is still a very common topic.

Such focus on intellectual property (IP) may be attributed to the fact that the debate on the protection of intangible heritage was first framed as an IP issue (as discussed in Chapter 2). Plus, if one takes into account the most common manifestations of intangible heritage (dances, song, storytelling, crafts), they seem to fit nicely within the IP domain, in particular copyright. Much of the discussion in this chapter will focus on copyright protection, and the concepts surrounding copyright, understood here as the foundation for larger IP protection.

A lot of criticism has been directed at the use of IP in the ICH context, and this criticism will be taken into account throughout the chapter. The chapter starts with a discussion on the commodifying effect of IP protection and considers this against the need for cultural exchange and the fluidity of the concept of ICH. Next, the chapter examines specific IP mechanisms that can be (and often have been) successfully used to protect manifestations of intangible heritage.

The chapter will examine these IP tools in light of the criticism raised against each of them specifically within their own limitations, but it will also bear in mind the ideas of 'cultural commons' and the public domain, which advocate against proprietary claims over ICH. These ideas will be discussed in depth in the following section of the chapter. The last section will explore the central argument of the chapter, namely, that IP can be used as a means to (1) foster economic development of certain communities;[1] and (2) to prevent cultural harm through misappropriation. IP should be used very carefully, however, so as not to harm the cultural exchanges necessary to cultural diversity.

One must always bear in mind that IP is not capable of directly protecting intangible heritage. IP protection is limited to ideas, methods, and systems that can be translated into material objects or applications, and as such it can hardly be said to protect the 'non-pragmatic' culture (or culture with no immediate practical application) underlying these objects. However, it seems to be the constant assumption of literature on the topic, and an assumption I share, that by protecting the end results of

[1] On the relationship between heritage and economics, see Xavier Greffe, *Arts and Artists from an Economic Perspective* (UNESCO Publishing, 2002), 137.

ICH practices, that is, the products of manifestations of heritage, one indirectly protects the heritage itself, creating the conditions for its perpetuation.

6.1 IP Tools and Intangible Heritage

This first section will look directly at the issue of IP as applied to ICH protection. It was stated in Chapter 2 that the discussion on IP mechanisms predates discussions resulting in the 2003 UNESCO Convention. The 2003 Convention makes specific reference to a future IP regime as a complementary regime to the listing mechanism. Further, the debate on IP tools for safeguarding ICH has never been abandoned in other fora, more specifically the World Intellectual Property Organization (WIPO), which, at the time of writing, is close to completing a set of articles in this regard.

This section draws on this international debate, as well as several national experiences with the use of IP (most notably in Australia). But it also has in mind scholarly concerns, some of which have been raised before international fora, as to the suitability of using IP at all in the first place, in addition to objections to specific mechanisms. I will first look at the general objections against the use of IP in this context.

6.1.1 Commodification, cultural exchange, and the flow of ideas and creativity

It is important to bear in mind that IP law (particularly copyright) protects an idea translated into a given format, whereas cultural heritage law protects the expression of community beliefs, practices, and values.[2] This is an important difference, and outlines one of the core shortcomings of IP protection.

The debate on commodification has already been undertaken in Chapter 1, so it is unnecessary to revisit all of it here. It must be said, however, that to translate manifestations of intangible heritage into the language and categories of IP law is perhaps the most extreme form of legal commodification intangible heritage can be subject to. Setting aside the requirement of fixation in material form for IP protection (which, as seen below, is not uniform across jurisdictions or even in the international system), the fact of the matter remains that IP protection requires that the manifestation of heritage be translated into a format within certain parameters, from which there cannot be as much deviation as one can observe in cultural manifestations more broadly. To be more specific, while IP allows for certain fluidity in the fixation of the elements to be protected, it still requires that some claims be made over the basic parameters, especially in light of claims over authenticity of manifestations of heritage. And this requirement can be very

[2] Susan Scafidi, *Who Owns Culture? Appropriation and Authenticity in American Law* (Rutgers University Press, 2005), 31.

harmful to ICH, which is by definition an open and always-evolving type of heritage.

It is essential that intangible heritage changes, be adapted and transformed continuously. This transformation is, after all, the result of normal evolution. Intangible heritage is but an expression of culture, and culture cannot be captured or frozen in one static moment.

Further, the crystallization of intangible heritage in a static snapshot would also prevent cultural exchange, which is if anything the precursor to the development of new intangible heritage elsewhere. It has been documented, for instance, that the famous Venetian carnival masks have originated from similar masks that Marco Polo brought from one of his trips to what is now Iran. In Iran, these masks were a precursor to the Burka; in Italy, they became the icon of a quintessential cultural event in Italian life.[3]

Many authors have warned against the use of IP in society at large. Tales, song, and dance should form a common pool from which all should be able to draw inspiration for creative work in most circumstances (cultural harm, to be analysed below, being one clear exception). Further, to many, creative work is not something to be owned. Being creative works the product of a person's genius, or a person's gift, it should be treated precisely as such, as a gift.[4] This opinion has been espoused by one of the earlier opponents, in the Common Law system, of the right to exclusive monopoly over intellectual creations. Justice Joseph Yates in England, in justifying a fixed term for copyright protection, stated that the act of publication is a gift to the public, and that a published book was 'like land thrown into the highway'.[5]

Further, IP creates limited monopolies over products of human creativity and ingenuity. But if these monopolies create the right to appropriate something, and prevent others from using it unless a licence is paid, in the long run the biggest loser is society at large, because the imposition of licences can create overall a chilling effect upon society, at least to the extent to which all culture is based upon derivative works.

The example of the song 'Happy Birthday to You' is telling. A little known fact is that this song is copyrighted, at least in the United States. And this copyright protection, thanks to the Copyright Term Extension Act,[6] now goes until 2030.

[3] This is stated in a documentary by Roxana Pope, titled '*A Burka Vermelha*' ['The Red Burka'], sponsored by the Calouste Gulbenkian Foundation. See Fundação Calouste Gulbenkian, *Newsletter*, 99 (January 2009).

[4] Marcel Mauss, *The Gift: The Form and Reason for eExchange in Archaic Societies* (Routlege, 1990); and Lewis Hyde, *The Gift: Creativity and the Artist in the Modern World* (Vintage Books, 2007).

[5] Mark Rose, 'Nine-Tenths of the Law: The English Copyright Debates and the Rhetoric of the Public Domain', in James Boyle (ed), *Collected Papers: Duke Conference on the Public Domain* (Center for the Public Domain, 2003), 75 88 at 79.

[6] This Act has been referred to as 'the Mickey Mouse Act', as it is largely the result of lobbying by Walt Disney Inc lawyers to prevent Mickey Mouse from entering into Public Domain. Disney has pursued very aggressive policies of suing all those who unauthorizedly use the image of Mickey Mouse or any other major Disney character. The constitutionality of the Copyright Term Extension Act has been questioned on freedom of speech grounds. The US Supreme Court, however, has found that the provision in the US Constitution protecting copyright interests, in being balanced with the provision

The implication is that no one in the United States is entitled to publicly sing 'Happy Birthday to You' without paying royalties. This awkward situation, coupled with a series of lawsuits brought by the copyright holders, has led several restaurants to either forbid the singing of the song within their premises, or to developing alternative (and less catchy) songs for this purpose.[7] Society loses out here.

Alternatively, another idea in defence of IP is that preventing the free borrowing of ideas and creative works from others forces artists and other creators to be more original. This notion is countered by the argument that the resulting originality is more concerned about being original than about being artistically relevant.[8] Immortalized authors such as William Shakespeare have borrowed heavily from pre-existing mythology for their creation,[9] and this does not lead to the necessary conclusion that they are second-rate creators or copycats. Rather, it means that they could use ideas that belonged to the everyday culture of their time and elevate them to the status of perennial classics. While they have not been entirely original, their imprint is still very clear in their work.

Despite all the criticism against the overuse of IP (particularly copyright) in the information society, one must not overlook some of the benefits that can be gained from IP protection. Generally, IP protection does indeed foster creativity, at least to a certain extent. While excessive IP protection can stifle creativity, some of it, which allows benefits to be reaped by creators, creates the conditions for further creation.[10] As James Boyle put it, 'enclosure of the information commons clearly has the potential to harm innovation as well as to support it'.[11]

In the specific context of ICH protection, for instance, communities who are the bearers of intangible heritage with clear and direct economic potential should be entitled to reap the benefits of the commercial exploitation of their craft, or at least to prevent third parties from reaping these benefits alone (and forcing these third

on freedom of speech, still warranted the constitutionality of the Act, based on the idea that the constitutional protection to copyright incorporated 'its own speech-protective purposes and safeguards', and legislation enacted under it would not therefore be subject to the same high thresholds of the 'strict scrutiny' test under the First Amendment. See Supreme Court of the United States, *Eldred v Ashcroft*, 537 US 1 (2003); Jones, Michael, 'Eldred v. Ashcroft: The Constitutionality of the Copyright Term Extension Act', *Berkeley Technology LJ* 19 (2004), 85 106; and Peter K Yu, 'International Rights Approaches to Intellectual Property: Reconceptualizing Intellectual Property Interests in a Human Rights Framework', *UC Davis L Rev* 40 (2007), 1039 149 at 1099.

[7] Kembrew McLeod, *Owning Culture: Authorship, Ownership and Intellectual Property Law* (P Lang, 2001), 50 4.

[8] Negativland, 'Two Relationships to a Cultural Public Domain', in James Boyle (ed), *Collected Papers: Duke Conference on the Public Domain* (Center for the Public Domain, 2003), 239 62 at 242.

[9] This has been documented by Thomas Bulfinch, *The Golden Age of Myth & Legend* (Wordsworth Editions, 1993) (documenting references to mythology in literature, and how 'foreign' mythology has come to enrich storytelling in English language literature).

[10] On this balancing, see for instance the graph presented by Jakob Cornides, 'Human Rights and Intellectual Property, Conflict or Convergence?', *The J of World Intellectual Property* 7(2) (2004), 135 67 at 156; and Robin Gross, 'Intellectual Property Rights and the Information Commons', in Rike Frank Jorgensen (ed), *Human Rights in the Global Information Society* (MIT Press, 2006), 107 20 at 116 17.

[11] James Boyle, 'The Second Enclosure Movement and the Construction of the Public Domain', in James Boyle (ed), *Collected Papers: Duke Conference on the Public Domain* (Center for the Public Domain, 2003), 33 74 at 44.

parties into some benefit-sharing agreement).[12] Accruing financial benefits for communities is only possible through commodification, as commodification in this sense implies bringing the intangible heritage into a 'Western' legal framework that attributes monetary value to culture through IP.[13]

However, when it comes to the reaping of economic benefits, the fact is that currently most economic benefits are reaped not by creators or authors, but by the corporations who own the copyright and control distribution of copyrighted materials.[14] In the specific case of manifestations of intangible heritage, it would be hard to say who would benefit in fact from economic exploitation, since not many traditional communities have the resources to invest in IP protection in the first place (such as the fees necessary for registering trademarks), or to market their commodified heritage. This means that more often than not corporate partners will seek these communities out or will be sought by them, and eventually corporations will be the highest financial beneficiaries.

More important than the economic potential, the creation of monopolies by IP law can also be used to exclude others from using manifestations of intangible heritage, especially in instances where such use by unauthorized third parties can cause cultural harm. Commodification in this sense is translated into empowerment and control, which is very important in the prevention of misuse and cultural harm.[15]

As some traditional communities (particularly indigenous communities) are more interested in protecting their ways of life than in making money out of their intangible heritage, the possibility of excluding others from use is appealing.[16] But one must not forget that this is still not an ideal situation, since this commodification is imposed upon traditional communities as the lesser of two evils: either they commodify and create specific social norms for the purposes of asserting control over their intangible heritage, or they reject commodification and remain at the mercy of third parties who wish to commodify their heritage.[17]

[12] McLeod, *Owning Culture*, 49 (arguing that what many communities want is not monetary protection, but rather control over their creation so as to regulate, for instance, the use of sacred music).

[13] Johanna Gibson, 'Knowledge and Other Values Intellectual Property and the Limitations for Traditional Knowledge', in Guido Westkamp (ed), *Emerging Issues in Intellectual Property: Trade Technology and Market Freedom: Essays in Honour of Herchel Smith* (Edward Elgar, 2007), 309 18, 312 13.

[14] Gross, 'Intellectual Property Rights', 107; and Anupam Chander and Madhavi Sunder, 'The Romance of the Public Domain', *Calif L Rev* 92 (2004), 1331 73 at 1339.

[15] Victor Tolefo Llancaqueo, 'El nuevo régimen internacional de derechos de propiedad intelectual y los derechos de los pueblos indígenas', in Mikel Berraondo (ed), *Pueblos Indígenas y Derechos Humanos* (Universidad de Deusto, 2006), 509 36 at 533.

[16] As stated by Coenraad Visser in Hugh C Hanse, Michael Blakeney, Linda S Lourie, Paul E Salmon, and Coenraad Visser, 'Symposium: Global Intellectual Property Rights: Boundaries of Access and Enforcement: Panel II: The Law and Policy of Protecting Folklore, Traditional Knowledge, and Genetic Resources', *Fordham Intell Prop Media & Ent LJ* 12 (2002), 753 803 at 795.

[17] Robert K Paterson, and Dennis S Karjala, 'Looking Beyond Intellectual Property in Resolving Protection of the Intangible Cultural Heritage of Indigenous Peoples', *Cardozo J Intl & Comp L* 11 (2003), 633 70 at 634 5.

6.1.2 The potentials and pitfalls of IP

A lot of work has been done questioning whether the protection of IP rights amounts to a human rights issue.[18] The protection of interests over intellectual creation is mentioned in several human rights documents, including the Universal Declaration of Human Rights (UDHR), the International Covenant on Economic, Social and Cultural Rights, the American Declaration on the Rights and Duties of Man, and the San Salvador Additional Protocol to the American Convention on Human Rights in the Area of Economic, Social and Cultural Rights.[19] The drafting history of the provision in the UDHR in particular suggests that the main concern in the original drafting of the provision was with the protection of authors' moral rights.[20] This idea has been re-translated in subsequent debates, with some delegations holding on to the idea of individual human rights to the moral rights' control over creation, while other delegations re-interpreted moral rights to mean a public interest in the integrity of creation that should be protected.[21] The issue of moral rights, especially as applied to intangible heritage, will be discussed in detail below, but it is important to note that up to this day much of the literature connecting the protection of IP to human rights is still supported by the notion of moral rights.[22]

As debates progressed in the drafting of international instruments, however, this provision came to mean an attempt at the internationalization of copyright law.[23] And during the debates of the drafting of the ICESCR, the UNESCO delegation stated its belief that the protection of authors' rights should find a place in the Covenant as a means to enrich 'the cultural heritage of mankind'.[24] The position of the UNESCO delegation was important for the insertion of this provision in the ICESCR, but it was not the only role UNESCO played in this context.

During the debates on the drafting of the ICESCR, a UNESCO-sponsored instrument in the area of IP law, the Universal Copyright Convention, was adopted. And the adoption of this instrument, according to one researcher of the

[18] See for instance Daniel A Farber, 'Conflicting Visions and Contested Baselines: Intellectual Property and Free Speech in the "Digital Millennium"', *Minn L Rev* 89 (2005), 1318 60; P Bernt Hugenholtz, 'Copyright and Freedom of Expression in Europe', in Rochelle Cooper Dreyfuss, Harry First and Diane Leenheer Zimmermann (eds), *Innovation Policy in an Information Age* (Oxford University Press, 2000), 343 64; Laurence R Helfer, 'Toward a Human Rights Framework for Intellectual Property', *UC Davis L Rev* 40 (2007), 970 1020; Maria Green, *Drafting History of the Article 15(1)(c) of the International Covenant on Economic, Social and Cultural Rights*, UN Doc E/C.12/2000/15, of 9 October 2000; Yu, 'International Rights Approaches to Intellectual Property'; and Volker Heins, 'Human Rights, Intellectual Property, and Struggles for Recognition', *Human Rights Rev* 9 (2008), 213 32.

[19] Yu, 'International Rights Approaches to Intellectual Property', 1048.

[20] Green, *Drafting History*, para 5.

[21] Green, *Drafting History*, para 45.

[22] See for instance Helfer, 'Toward a Human Rights Framework'; Green, 'Drafting History'; and Yu, 'International Rights Approaches to Intellectual Property'.

[23] Green, *Drafting History*, para 6.

[24] Green, *Drafting History*, para 21 (citing a statement by the UNESCO representative during a drafting session, at UN Doc E/CN.4/SR.228, para 13).

drafting history of the ICESCR, was decisive in building the consensus around the protection of IP as a human right.[25] This early reference to the connection between IP and cultural heritage by UNESCO is very telling, and it may help explain the resilience of the idea of connecting the two areas even in the early drafting of the 2003 UNESCO Convention, and why the use of IP mechanisms is still so important.

This connection has been asserted even in authoritative interpretations of human rights instruments with provisions on IP. According to the Committee on Economic, Social and Cultural Rights, the connection between human rights and IP serves two functions. One of them is to protect basic economic advantages arising out of this protection, and that enable the livelihood of creators. And the other, more important for our purposes, is to protect the link between authors and their creations on the one hand, and peoples, communities, and other collectivities with their collective heritage on the other.[26]

That said, the core reasons for protecting copyright as a human rights concern are the protection of moral rights, and the protection of the cultural heritage upon which authors rely for their creation. This reading offers a distinct advantage in the present context, since connecting the protection of IP to human rights through the protection of cultural heritage creates an appealing justification for trying to resolve ICH tensions through the normative framework of IP rights. But this connection has other practical effects.

For instance, one can more clearly look at the issue of a monopoly created by human rights as one of balancing of one right (IP protection) against other (freedom of expression of others who want to borrow from the protected work).[27] This angle brings the two competing interests to the same level, and makes it easier to look at the larger picture than it would be in case IP was considered exclusively under the prism of its specialized field of law.

Besides the occasional conflict between IP and freedom of expression, there is still another area into which IP interests can be translated. The right of protection of personal honour and reputation, even though an autonomous right in many human rights instruments, when read from the perspective of IP, becomes part of moral rights in IP. The drawing of this connection is most likely connected to the fact that the protection of moral rights in some Common Law countries still happens through tort causes of action related to personal reputation, rather than

[25] Yu, 'International Rights Approaches to Intellectual Property', 1069.

[26] As analysed by Helfer, 'Toward a Human Rights Framework', 995 6.

[27] See eg Scafidi, *Who Owns Culture?*, 138; Farber, 'Conflicting Visions'; and Hugenholtz, 'Copyright and Freedom of Expression in Europe'. In the constitutional context, see Yochai Benkler, 'Through the Looking Glass: Alice and the Constitutional Foundations of the Public Domain', in James Boyle (ed), *Collected Papers: Duke Conference on the Public Domain* (Center for the Public Domain, 2003), 173 224; William W Van Alstyne, 'Reconciling what the First Amendment Forbids with what the Copyright Clause Permits: A Summary Explanation and Review', in James Boyle (ed), *Collected Papers: Duke Conference on the Public Domain* (2003), 225 38; and Michael Halewood, 'Indigenous and Local Knowledge in International Law: A Preface to Sui Generis Intellectual Property Protection', *McGill LJ* 44 (1999), 953 96 at 992 3.

through specific provisions protecting the reputation of the author as a category distinct from that of any other individual.[28]

This framework of analysis is advantageous from some points of view, but it will not be the focus of this chapter. It will be part of the background against which many of the ideas about IP play out, alongside debates on commodification and cultural flows, but it will not be decisive. Instead, I will focus on IP rights as set forth in specific instruments, that is, on the special regime of private rights created for the protection of IP.

This narrower focus raises the question of lack of uniformity of criteria in municipal IP law. For instance, some national systems require that works, in order to be protected by copyright, be fixated in material means, whereas others do not impose such a requirement. This imposition has consequences for ICH protection through IP, since manifestations of heritage tend not to be documented or fixated in traditional communities; they are rather simply experienced as part of normal social and cultural life, or were documented by others. This inconsistency, and others across national systems, will be resolved in this chapter through looking primarily at the international standards for IP protection, however flawed they might be.[29] When these standards are silent, a compromise will be attempted between common law and civil law criteria, those representing the two most prominent systems of law for IP purposes (which have to a great extent been copied by other countries).

There are two main general objections to the uses of IP. The first one concerns the very nature of intangible heritage. Being intangible means being 'non-specifiable', and therefore any attempt at providing for legal protection would be unfruitful, since it would lack an object of protection. Alternatively, it would result in commodification, as highlighted above. Therefore, only the tangible assets may be protected, not the expression as a whole, these being those specific works which may be catalogued and documented.[30]

Another objection, more important to our analysis, is that IP mechanisms cannot be implemented because many custodial communities have a different conception of 'property', of owning. In this conception, everything around these communities was given by their deity, and intending to be the master of anything would cause severe offence to the deity. For instance, if a member of such a community produces a statue made of clay, such a statue is still thought of as the

[28] One notable exception in the United States is the Visual Artists Rights Act (VARA). For a short commentary on it as it applies to a certain form of 'urban intangible heritage' (mural painting), see Ann Garfinkle, *The Legal and Ethical Consideration of Mural Conservation: Issues and Debates* (The Getty Conservation Institute, 2003).

[29] Critical readings of international intellectual property law highlight how the '[a]ttention to the increased globalisation in knowledge management frameworks of intellectual property and the attempts at harmonisation of standards and procedural rules misunderstands the underlying disparity in social and economic wants of individual countries and stakeholders'. See Jane E Anderson, *Law, Knowledge, Culture: The Production of Indigenous Knowledge in Intellectual Property Law* (Edward Elgar, 2009), 178.

[30] This objection has been raised, among others, by the Brazilian working group on intangible cultural heritage policies, promoted by the Brazilian Association of Folklore.

earth it was made of. The earth can be thought of as belonging to a deity, or it may be a deity itself. There is no added value to this statue by the fact that the artist has put labour into it and transformed the raw materials, because that would imply assuming that the deity can be transformed by the hands of men. Most of the time, the effort of transforming shapeless clay into a statue is simply a religious obligation. In this sense, the capacity of transformation is again a gift, and as such it cannot be appropriated or monetized.

To impose a certain legal understanding of property upon a community implies forcing the community to fundamentally transform itself for the sake of claiming a defence within a legal category that is not necessarily natural to their belief system. In the words of Rosemary J Coombe, '[s]implistic reductions of Native concerns to trademark or copyright considerations and the assertion of IP rights fail to reflect the full dimensions of Native aspirations and impose colonial juridical categories on postcolonial struggles in a fashion that reenacts the cultural violence of colonization'.[31]

Bearing in mind these more general objections, as well as those raised in previous sections, it is important to look at some possibilities for the use of IP for the protection of intangible heritage. IP can be an effective tool in instances where private property is recognized by the community in question, and it is a readily available tool that should be taken into account in some cases.

When it comes to the protection of IP, private means of protection ought not to be relied upon; instead, statutory protections must be available as the only means to validate the assumption that intellectual work should be remunerated and protected.[32] IP has the effect of creating such a barrier as a system of boundaries in the public mind against the abuse of such heritage.[33] The fact that IP mechanisms themselves have checks on creativity and originality (imposing them as requirements for protection via IP rights) also arguably assists in that intangible heritage is not over-propertized, but rather protected in a way that allows for creativity.

Before analysing specific IP tools, there is another general objection that must be raised. It is the fact that, even though IP mechanisms can in some instances be used to the advantage of communities who are the holders of intangible heritage, in practice there are systematic complaints of lack of access to information, legal advice, and financial resources to undertake the necessary steps for successful IP protection.[34] Especially when one cannot specify who the rights holders are for certain manifestations of heritage, this becomes a large obstacle to be overcome.

The following subsections are dedicated to analysing several IP tools that have been mentioned in the literature on the subject. Patents have been excluded from

[31] Rosemary J Coombe, *The Cultural Life of Intellectual Properties* (Duke University Press, 2003), 132.

[32] AL Figueira Barbosa, *Sobre a Propriedade do Trabalho Intelectual Uma Perspectiva Crítica* (UFRJ, 1999), 42 3.

[33] Scafidi, *Who Owns Culture?*, 14 15.

[34] Darrell A Posey and Graham Dutfield, *Beyond Intellectual Property: Toward Traditional Resource Rights for Indigenous Peoples and Local Communities* (International Development Research Center, 1996), 76.

the present analysis because they are more concerned with traditional knowledge (TK) associated with the pharmaceutical industry than to ICH in general. Even though, as argued in Chapter 1, TK is part of ICH, for the purposes of IP protection it is a very specialized part of intangible heritage, calling for an entirely different set of considerations, which fall outside the scope of this chapter.[35]

6.1.2.1 Copyright

Copyright is perhaps the most obvious alternative when one thinks of folklore protection and IP, because both concern mainly artistic expressions. The main copyright solutions adopted concern connected rights, that is, the rights of executing and performing artists. International instruments include the Berne Convention of 1886,[36] the 1961 Rome Convention on the Protection of Performers' Rights,[37] and the Phonograms Convention of 1971.[38]

IP protection, and particularly copyright, draws primarily on one of two justifications for its existence. One justification is that IP protection exists to guarantee the remuneration of copyright owners. This economic incentive-based or utilitarian explanation is found in Common Law countries. The other explanation is known as the 'ethical' justification, and is based on the protection of the creator's personality and integrity. This is more typical of Civil Law countries, and is usually grouped under the French label of '*droit d'auteur*', as opposed to 'copyright'.[39]

The plurality of national interpretations of IP principles mentioned above as a problem to be mediated through the use of international instruments for 'universal' standards is further complicated in the specific field of copyright. There is a rich array of international instruments dealing with copyright, and each has a different

[35] On the uses of intellectual property for the protection of traditional knowledge, see WIPO Intergovernmental Committee on Intellectual Property and Genetic Resources, Traditional Knowledge and Folklore, *Information on National Experiences with the Intellectual Property Protection of Traditional Knowledge*, Doc WIPO/GRTKF/IC/5/INF/2, of 4 April 2003; WIPO Intergovernmental Committee on Intellectual Property and Genetic Resources, Traditional Knowledge and Folklore, *Comparative Summary of Existing National* Sui Generis *Measures and Laws for the Protection of Traditional Knowledge*, Doc WIPO/GRTKF/IC/5/INF/4, of 20 June 2003; and WIPO Intergovernmental Committee on Intellectual Property and Genetic Resources, Traditional Knowledge and Folklore, *Composite Study on the Protection of Traditional Knowledge*, Doc WIPO/GRTKF/IC/5/8, of 28 April 2003.

[36] Berne Convention for the Protection of Literary and Artistic Works, of 9 September 1886, completed at Paris on 4 May 1896, revised at Berlin on 13 November 1908, completed at Berne on 20 March 1914, revised at Rome on 2 June 1928, at Brussels on 26 June 1948, at Stockholm on 14 July 1967, and at Paris on 24 July 1971, and amended on 28 September 1979. Number of contracting parties as of November 2012: 166. On the evolution of the protection of traditional cultural expressions in the Berne Convention, see Michael Blakeney, 'Protecting Traditional Cultural Expressions: The International Dimension', in Fiona Macmillan and Kathy Bowrey (eds), *New Directions in Copyright Law, Vol 3* (Edward Elgar, 2006), 3 14.

[37] International Convention for the Protection of Performers, Producers of Phonograms and Broadcasting Organizations, of 26 October 1961. Number of contracting parties as of November 2012: 91.

[38] Convention for the Protection of Producers of Phonograms Against Unauthorized Duplication of Their Phonograms, of 29 October 1971. Number of contracting parties as of November 2012: 77.

[39] See Scafidi, *Who Owns Culture?*, 17 18.

ideological orientation and attempts to serve a different purpose. The UNESCO-sponsored Universal Copyright Convention, for instance, was drafted as an attempt to mediate between different approaches to the protection of literary creations, those of the French-inspired *droit d'auteur* and Common Law's copyright.[40]

The differences between these two systems are particularly important in the context of the protection of intangible heritage. The French (or European Continental) *droit d'auteur*, as its name suggests, is largely focused on the author as the rights holder (the creative 'spark', or the Romantic genius of the author), whereas copyright focuses on the work (better said, the economic incentives to creators through the selling of copies of the work).[41] This idiosyncrasy of the French system, which is largely based on natural law, clashes with the copyright regime, which favours more of an economic approach, and even more easily accepts a 'total' public domain.[42]

Further, the copyright system requires that creation be fixated in a tangible form for it to be protected, while *droit d'auteur* does not. Common Law countries usually require fixation because this proves the existence of the creation, but the fact is that no treaty regime on copyright imposes an essential form of fixation as a requirement.[43] Manifestations of intangible heritage are often not fixated in any medium, because this type of heritage is largely based on oral transmission. Copyright then imposes an extra burden on the protection of intangible heritage.

Authorship as a concept is deeply connected to originality and uniqueness. One possible reading of originality is connected to the construction of property as the fruit of one's labour (partly inspired by Locke, but also departing from it in some ways), meaning that authorship and ownership are inextricable from one another.[44] In this sense, and with specific regard to traditional music, one scholar has observed that copyright law has two main effects. The first one is that it makes it illegal to create folk songs the way they have been created for centuries (namely, through borrowing and copying of melodic themes). The second one, closely related, is that it 'freezes' the development of melodic themes and their evolution, since they are the exclusive monopoly of their author.[45]

Authorship also imposes a problem in that it is a requirement for the protection of a certain work, and it is not always possible to determine authorship of manifestations of intangible heritage, at least to the extent that they are the product

[40] See for instance Ruth L Okediji, 'An Enduring Legacy For the Knowledge Economy: UNESCO and the International Copyright System', in A Yusuf Abdulqawi (ed), *Standard-Setting in UNESCO Volume I: Normative Action in Education, Science and Culture* (Martinus Nijhoff and UNESCO Publishing, 2007), 113 34 at 115.

[41] Doris Estelle Long, 'The Impact of Foreign Investment on Indigenous Culture: An Intellectual Property Perspective', *NCJ Intl L & Com Reg* 23 (1998), 229 43 at 267 8.

[42] Benjamin Davidson, 'Lost in Translation: Distinguishing Between French and Anglo-American Natural Rights in Literary Property, and How Dastar Proves that the Difference Still Matters', *Cornell Intl LJ* 38 (2005), 583 623 at 588.

[43] WIPO Intergovernmental Committee, *Consolidated Analysis of the Legal Protection of Traditional Cultural Expressions*, Doc WIPO/GRTKF/IC/5/3, of 2 May 2003, Annex, para 127.

[44] McLeod, *Owning Culture*, 15.

[45] McLeod, *Owning Culture*, 42.

of collective creativity (and therefore there is no identified or identifiable individual author).[46] To the extent, however, that all creative work is at least partly the product of a collective pool of creative resources, this objection against finding an identifiable author rests only in the traditional communities' reluctance in pointing to an author (either an individual author or individuals that could claim joint authorship); unless, of course, it is impossible to trace authorship back in time.

This is the second objection: copyright protection is limited in time. Normally, copyright protection will extend to the life of the original copyright holder plus 70 years; when the original copyright holder is a corporation, a single term of 70 years is the rule (which could vary, depending on the type of work being protected). This is inconsistent with intangible heritage, which is by definition a practice passed across generations.

The negotiators of the currently-stalled Free Trade Area of the Americas (FTAA) have looked at the issue of protection of intangible heritage as an IP issue (in many ways mirroring an earlier version of the Draft Inter-American Declaration on the Rights of Indigenous Peoples, analysed in Chapter 3). The proposed provision states the need to protect intangible heritage as an IP concern, and it focuses primarily in its protection via copyright, using moral rights language.[47]

One way to sidestep objections against copyright, and offer a marginal yet potentially strong protection to intangible heritage is through performers' rights. In fact, the WIPO Performances and Phonograms Treaty of 1996 explicitly includes the performers of expressions of intangible heritage in its definition of performer.[48]

By protecting a performance of a manifestation of heritage, as opposed to the actual manifestation, one avoids the temporal limitation (to the extent that every fixation of a performance will have its own term), and one can more easily determine who the performer is, for the purposes of protection. One of the most important features of performers' rights is a derivation of moral rights in copyright, and it is the right of the performer to zeal for the integrity of their performance (which can be used to prevent misuse and de-contextualization by third parties).[49]

[46] Hildebrando Pontes Neto, 'As expressões do folclore e o direito autoral', *Revista da Faculdade de Direito Milton Campos* 9 (2002), 71 96 at 75.

[47] Anthony Carter, 'Protecting the Indigenous Past While Securing the Digital Future: The FTAA and the Protection of Expressions of Folklore', *Loy Intl L Rev* 1 (2004), 203 16 at 212 13.

[48] WIPO Performances and Phonograms Treaty, of 20 December 1996. Number of parties as of November 2012: 90. The relevant provision is the following: 'Article 2. Definitions. For the purposes of this Treaty: (a) "performers" are actors, singers, musicians, dancers, and other persons who act, sing, deliver, declaim, play in, interpret, or otherwise perform literary or artistic works *or expressions of folklore*; [. . .]' (emphasis added).

[49] WIPO Performances and Phonograms Treaty, Article 5. The full text of the provision is the following: '**Article 5. Moral Rights of Performers.**(1) Independently of a performer's economic rights, and even after the transfer of those rights, the performer shall, as regards his live aural performances or performances fixed in phonograms, have the right to claim to be identified as the performer of his performances, except where omission is dictated by the manner of the use of the performance, and to object to any distortion, mutilation or other modification of his performances that would be prejudicial to his reputation. (2) The rights granted to a performer in accordance with paragraph (1) shall, after his death, be maintained, at least until the expiry of the economic rights, and shall be exercisable by the persons or institutions authorized by the legislation of the Contracting Party where protection is

One of the most successful instances of the application of copyright law to the protection of a manifestation of intangible heritage is what has become known as 'the carpets case'.[50] In this case, an Aboriginal artist's paintings displaying symbols sacred to the community of origin of the artist were put on display at the National Australian Gallery, from which a catalogue was produced with permission of the artists. These images were then copied and printed by an Australian company, Indofurn Pty Ltd, to order on carpets by a Vietnamese factory and sold in Australia as Aboriginal art. Such use was problematic, not only because it was done without the consent of the custodial community (or the individual artist, for that matter), but also because it exploited the community's religious beliefs and symbols commercially, arguably profaning the culture of that people. In addition, consumers were deceived. The manufacturers and sellers of the merchandise falsely claimed that the Aboriginal artists received a royalty for the reproductions. The action was brought against the importer of the carpets, who alleged that they had unsuccessfully tried to contact the artists in order to secure the necessary authorization for reproduction of the art on the carpets, which turned out to be untrue.

The artists argued that they were only authorized to paint those artworks in the first place as part of their religious rights within their communities, and that any unauthorized reproduction was a breach by them of their traditional legal obligations. Some of the paintings represented important parts of the mythology of the communities involved, the knowledge of which was very restricted. The fact that the paintings had been reproduced, even without their permission, could expose them to severe penalties under customary laws for the artists, including banishment.

The Australian Court did not acknowledge customary law as a relevant set of rules applicable to the dispute (since the Court's mandate was restricted to applying federal law). Instead, it said that customary law formed part of the 'factual matrix' of the judgment, and would be taken into account in determining the extent of the damages to be paid. And the Court ordered the payment of damages for cultural

claimed. However, those Contracting Parties whose legislation, at the moment of their ratification of or accession to this Treaty, does not provide for protection after the death of the performer of all rights set out in the preceding paragraph may provide that some of these rights will, after his death, cease to be maintained. (3) The means of redress for safeguarding the rights granted under this Article shall be governed by the legislation of the Contracting Party where protection is claimed.' See also Otto W Konrad, 'A Federal Regulation of Performance Art Author Moral Rights', 48 *Wash & Lee L Rev* 1759 (1991), reprinted in Anthony D'Amato and Doris Estelle Long (eds), *International Intellectual Property Anthology* (1996), 157 60 at 159 60. For a case study on the potentials of performers' rights for the protection of traditional dances and rituals, see Terri Janke, *Minding Culture: Case Studies on Intellectual Property and Traditional Cultural Expressions* (WIPO, 2003), 86; and WIPO Intergovernmental Committee, *Consolidated Analysis*, Annex, para 40.

[50] *George Milpurrurru, Banduk Marika, Tim Payunka and the Public Trustee of the Northern Territory v Indofurn Pty Ltd, Brian Alexander Bethune, Raymond King and Robert James Rylands* [1994] 54 FCR 240. More detailed analyses of this case can be found in Anderson, *Law, Knowledge, Culture*; Janke, *Minding Culture*, 8; and Kathy Bowrey, 'Indigenous Culture, Knowledge and Intellectual Property: The Need for a New Category of Rights?', in Kathy Bowrey, Michael Handler, and Dianne Nicoll (eds), *Emerging Challenges in Intellectual Property* (Oxford University Press, 2011), 46 67 at 57 8.

harm, which was then something unheard of in the Australian legal system.[51] The compensation was ordered to be paid to the artists, and they should determine how to distribute the money in accordance with their own customs.

This case is an example of successful application of copyright law to protect a manifestation of heritage. One must take into account, however, that there are several specificities that make the replication of the results difficult in other contexts. For one, the authors were easily identifiable, and they were in a position to accept the attribution of property titles over their work. Further, the works were rather recent and fell therefore within the temporal limitations of protection of artistic works.

The value of this case cannot therefore be overestimated. But one aspect of it has broader implications for the application of copyright to intangible heritage. One of the arguments made by the defendants in the case is that there was no original work involved on the part of the artists, as they were admittedly reproducing parts of their mythology or 'dreaming'. However, the judge concluded that, upon examination of the actual works, their execution involved considerable skill and work, and were therefore susceptible to protection under copyright, even if the themes represented in the works were not original. In other words, works that incorporate intangible heritage are still protectable under copyright law, because, even if they draw inspiration from the intangible heritage of the community, there is still the personal imprint of the individual artist in each work, and that is what can be protected.[52]

Another important aspect of copyright law is the protection of moral rights, which is in many instances what traditional communities are most interested in. There is more of an interest in protecting the integrity and guaranteeing the attribution of a certain manifestation of heritage to the community than in receiving financial benefits from the exploitation of this heritage. The following subsection is dedicated to moral rights.

6.1.2.1.1 Moral rights

The link between moral rights and the protection of authors' rights as a human right has been explored above. It has been stated that much of the literature connecting human rights to IP relies on the idea of moral rights. Some scholars defend the use of 'moral rights' for the protection of folklore, to some extent.[53] Article 15(4) of the Berne Convention for the Protection of Literary and Artistic

[51] A subsequent case in a similar context (this time, involving the printing of a painting of sacred significance on t-shirts sold as souvenirs to tourists) saw compensation being ordered exclusively for cultural harm suffered. The case, also Australian, is *Bulun Bulun v R & T Textiles* [1998] 41 IPR 513. See Janke, *Minding Culture*, 50.

[52] For more on the requirement of originality as applied to manifestations of intangible heritage, see WIPO Intergovernmental Committee, *Consolidated Analysis*, Annex, paras 103 12.

[53] See eg Paul Kuruk, 'Protecting Folklore under Modern Intellectual Property Regimes: A Reappraisal of the Tensions between Individual and Communal Rights in Africa and the United States', *Am U L Rev* 48 (1999), 769 849 at 829 30; Silke von Lewinski, 'The Protection of Folklore' *Cardozo J Intl & Comp L* 11 (2003), 747 68 at 759; and Christine Haight Farley, 'Protecting Folklore of Indigenous Peoples: Is Intellectual Property the Answer?', *Conn L Rev* 30 (1997), 1 57 at 47 8.

Works of 1886, added in the Stockholm revision of 1957 a provision to give the State in which the work is produced the duty to protect it. However, the works go into the public domain, which will be analysed in further detail below. Moral rights, in this sense, are more compatible with intangible heritage because they avoid the commodification of intangible heritage.[54]

A lengthy discussion of the nature of moral rights exceeds the purposes of this chapter. It is important to highlight some of its core features, as well as some of the international standards for their protection.[55] When it comes to the characteristics of moral rights, an important feature is that these rights cannot be transferred,[56] which matches the concerns of intangible heritage. Also, some of these rights are not susceptible to expiration with time,[57] which is also an important feature for ICH protection, which often fails to be protected under other forms of IP precisely for being too old.

The protection of these rights, further, is connected to the protection of cultural values of society in general, and not the interests of a single author. This is the reason why, upon expiration of the economic rights of the author, the protection of moral rights often falls with the State.[58]

The two main features of moral rights are the right to attribution and the right to protect the integrity of one's work.[59] These are the two features protected by the Berne Convention on the Protection of Literary and Artistic Works of 1886. In the Rome revision of 1928, the parties of the Berne Union inserted Article 6*bis* to the Convention, based on an Italian and Polish proposal inspired by the French model of *droit d'auteur*.[60] When the provision came to a vote, however, it was only approved due to a compromise according to which, even though the content of moral rights should be protected by national laws, there was no need for explicit provisions on moral rights in copyright legislation.[61]

[54] David R Downes, 'How Intellectual Property Could Be a Tool to Protect Traditional Knowledge', *Colum J Envtl L* 25 (2000), 253 81 at 259.

[55] A lengthier discussion can be found in Lucas Lixinski, 'O Direito Moral de Autor como Direito de Personalidade e a Universlidade de sua Proteção', *Revista Trimestral de Direito Civil* 27 (2006), 49 79.

[56] Henri Mazeaud, Léon Mazeaud, and Jean Mazeaud, *Leçons de Droit Civil. Tome Premier* (Éditions Montchrestien, 1998), 656.

[57] Gilles Goubeaux, *Traité de Droit Civil. Sous la direction de Jacques Ghestin* (Librairie générale de droit et de jurisprudente, 1977), 310; Miguel Amando and Delia Lipzyc, 'Bienes inmateriales', in Diego Fernández Arroyo (ed) *Derecho Internacional Privado de los Estados del Mercosur* (Zavalia, 2003), 903 36 at 906; and Mazeaud, Mazeaud, and Mazeaud, *Leçons*, 656.

[58] Gobeaux, *Traité*, 311; and Sigfrido Radaelli, 'Direito Moral do Autor', *Revista Forense* 109 (1947), 23 34 at 23 4.

[59] Frederico José da Silva Ramos, 'Direitos de Autor', *Revista dos Tribunais* 274 (1958), 69 85 at 72; and Geri J Yonover, 'Artistic Parody: The Precarious Balance: Moral Rights, Parody, and Fair Use', *Cardozo Arts & Ent LJ* 14 (1996), 79 122, 88 9.

[60] Luiz Gonzaga Silva Adolfo, 'Considerações sobre o Direito Moral do Autor', *Revista da ABPI*, 44 (2000) 3 13 at 5.

[61] David S Glass, 'Moral Rights and the New Copyright Law', 134 *Solicitors Journal* 6 (1990), reprinted in Anthony D'Amato and Doris Estelle Long (eds), *International Intellectual Property Anthology* (1996), 131 3, at 132; and Josselin-Gall, Muriel, *Les contrats d'exploitation du droit de propriété littéraire et artistique Étude de droit comparé et de droit international privé* (GLN Joly Edition, 1995), 309.

Another international treaty to protect moral rights, with a more regional focus, is the Inter-American Convention on Copyright of 1946. This was the first international attempt to conciliate the systems of copyright and *droit d'auteur*, even though it was not ultimately ratified by the United States. The convention avoids using the term 'moral rights', but it does protect the rights to integrity and attribution.[62] The TRIPS agreement, on the other hand, even though it incorporates provisions of the Berne Convention, explicitly excludes the incorporation of Article 6*bis*, as a result of US pressure during the negotiations.[63]

National protection to moral rights exists in most jurisdictions, even if not by mechanisms falling explicitly under the label of 'moral rights'.[64] The United States, for instance, uses the law of publicity, privacy and contract law to protect moral rights, among other tools.[65]

Many of the advantages of moral rights protection, however, clash with the freedom of expression concerns outlined above.[66] There is a concern with the negative effect that a strict enforcement of the right of integrity can have on the development of new works, which can create an overall chilling effect that can be harmful to human creativity.[67]

Also, moral rights only extend to the individualized author, and have not been ordinarily construed as applying to an entire community.[68] It has been argued, however, that moral rights could be applied to a custodial community as a whole, deeming the individualization requirement a formal requirement, and one that does not affect the essence of moral rights. In this sense, moral rights can be collectively translated into the right to attribution, and the communities would be entitled to moral rights similarly to individuals. A suggested exception would be that fair use exceptions would have to be more robust, so as to not stifle creativity and 'to

[62] José de Oliveira Ascensão, *Direito Autoral* (Renovar, 1997), 643 4.

[63] South Centre, *The TRIPs Agreement: A Guide for the South* (South Centre, 1997), 27.

[64] See in general Alain Strowel, *'Droit d'auteur et copyright': Étude de droit comparé* (LGDJ, 1993). See also Thomas Dreier, 'Restoration and Moral Rights of the Artist under Comparative Law', in Quentin Byrne Sutton, Marc-André Renold, and Beatrice Rötheli-Mariotti (eds), *La Restauration des Objets D'Art: Aspects juridiques et éthiques* (Centre du Droit De L'Art, 1994), 105 23 at 107; René David, *Os Grandes Sistemas do Direito Contemporâneo* (Meridiano, 1978), 467; Mike Holderness, 'Moral Rights and Authors' Rights: The Keys to the Information Age'. *J of Information, L and Technology (JILT)* 1998(1), available at <http://www2.warwick.ac.uk/fac/soc/law/elj/jilt/1998 1/holderness/> (accessed 29 November 2012); Harry Hillman Chartrand, 'Towards an American Arts Industry', *Cultural Economics*, available at <http://www.compilerpress.ca/Cultural%20Economics/Works/Towards%202000.htm> (accessed 29 November 2012).

[65] Laura A Pitta, 'Economic and Moral Rights under US Copyright Law: Protecting Authors and Producers in the Motion Picture Industry', 12 *Ent & Sports Lawyer* 3 (1995), reprinted in Anthony D'Amato and Doris Estelle Long (eds), *International Intellectual Property Anthology* (Anderson Publishing Co, 1996), 134 5 at 134. For the situation in the United Kingdom, see William Cornish and David Llewelyn, *Intellectual Property: Patents, Copyright, Trade Marks and Allied Rights* (Sweet & Maxwell, 2003), 454 5.

[66] Michael F Brown, *Who Owns Native Culture?* (Harvard University Press, 2004), 235.

[67] Thomas P Heide, 'The Moral Right of Integrity and the Global Information Infrastructure: Time for a New Approach?', *UC Davis J Intl L & Policy* 2 (1996), 211 66 at 215.

[68] Robert K Paterson and Dennis S Karjala, 'Looking Beyond Intellectual Property in Resolving Protection of the Intangible Cultural Heritage of Indigenous Peoples', *Cardozo J Intl & Comp L* 11 (2003), 633 70 at 644.

promote the civic benefits of limited appropriation'.[69] Of course, the consequence would be to move adjudication of the issue away from the human rights and heritage domains, and closer to the core of IP, which remains primarily a framework about economic rights. In this sense, then, more robust fair use exceptions might defeat the purpose of creating collective moral rights to begin with.

6.1.2.2 Trademarks

Trademarks are an interesting example of how traditional cultures have been historically appropriated and commodified to serve a different purpose from the one they were originally meant to serve. Historically, manufacturers have been advised, when creating their trademarks, to choose marks that were as distant as possible from what they were actually trying to market (looking for 'signs of alterity'), so that their applications would not be rejected on the basis of having chosen an exceedingly obvious word for the area of activity to which the mark was being registered. As a consequence, many manufacturers looked for words within traditional communities,[70] but this sometimes created problems with attempts to register words sacred to certain communities, to the communities' distress. However appealing as a product development tool, the result is that '[w]hether these commodity/signs are commodifications of their heritage or stereotypical signs of their alterity, many peoples find "their own" representations owned by others'.[71]

'The Washington Redskins Case' (*Harjo v Pro-Football Inc*) offers some insight into this situation. In this case, the sports team 'Washington Redskins' had the registration of its trademark challenged by an indigenous community, on the grounds that the trademark was harmful to indigenous peoples in general, for perpetuating racist stereotypes. The case gravitated around procedural issues, but it highlighted the relevance of trademarks (and challenges to trademarks) for the protection of traditional culture,[72] at least to the extent that it protected the identity of a certain traditional community from being essentialized and commodified into a stereotype. I suggest that trademark law should work precisely this way, in avoiding commercial stereotyping of identity that is beyond the control of those being stereotyped.

One of the main advantages of attempting to use trademarks to protect intangible heritage is that the collective registration of a trademark is possible (even if it is subject to special rules in order to ensure the registration does not turn out to be anti-competitive). That is, while one of the objections for the use of copyright is that there can be no collective attribution of a work to an entire community, for

[69] Scafidi, *Who Owns Culture?*, 149.

[70] Coombe, *The Cultural Life*, 175.

[71] Coombe, *The Cultural Life*, 185.

[72] For a full commentary of this case, see Daphne Zografos, 'The Appropriation of American Indian Names and Images in Trade Marks The Washington Redskins Case', in Guido Westkamp (ed), *Emerging Issues in Intellectual Property: Trade Technology and Market Freedom: Essays in Honour of Herchel Smith* (Edward Elgar, 2007), 391 406 at 396 406.

trademarks the entire community can be registered as the owner of the trademark, rights then being granted to a representative of the community.[73]

While the idea of collectively-owned IP rights common to trademarks is appealing in the case of traditional communities, using this tool can potentially exclude the advantageous use of the human rights discourse associated with IP protection. IP rights with a corporate basis do not necessarily qualify for protection as a human right, because the protection granted under human rights (at least in universal instruments) does not extend to corporations.[74] This tension, however, may be renegotiated in the case of traditional communities, especially in light of regional jurisprudence recognizing the trademark rights of a corporation as a human rights issue.[75]

In any event, trademarks are useful also because there is a strong sense of 'authenticity' associated with trademarks. Therefore, if traditional communities are capable of registering a trademark that certifies the authenticity of the traditional character of a certain product, they can use that as a selling point for their products. Naturally, this is a form of mummification of culture, but one that is controlled by the communities themselves, and with an eye to facilitate their cultural development within their own terms. This practice of authenticity labels has the effect of creating obstacles for third parties who offer counterfeit versions of crafts and other products.[76] Another advantage is that trademarks can be renewed for a long period of time, as opposed to copyright, which necessarily expires at some point.[77]

However, trademarks cannot be used as a means to permanently prevent misappropriation by third parties, since trademark registrations can be cancelled if there is no effective commercial use of the mark. Another disadvantage is that there are more technical requirements involved in registering trademarks than with copyright. The problems outlined above with respect to lack of expertise and resources for the use of the IP framework are especially palpable when it comes to trademark law.[78] Further, communities are not always in a position to present an opposition to trademark registration by third parties who have misappropriated their intangible heritage.[79]

6.1.2.3 Appellations of origin

An appellation of origin intends to protect the authenticity of a given product, by creating a designation attached to the product indicating its provenance. It has the

[73] Daniel J Gervais, 'The Internationalization of Intellectual Property: New Challenges from the Very Old and the Very New', *Fordham Intell Prop Media & Ent LJ* 12 (2002), 929 90 at 962.

[74] See Yu, 'International Rights Approaches to Intellectual Property', 1128.

[75] One well-known such instance is the case involving the registration of Budweiser by the American company Anheuser-Busch as a trademark in Portugal, against the opposition of a Czech brewery who had previously registered the same name as its own trademark. See ECtHR, *Case of Anheuser-Busch Inc v Portugal* (Application No 73049/01), judgment of 11 January 2007.

[76] Posey and Dutfield, *Beyond Intellectual Property*, 85.

[77] Janke, *Minding Culture*, 30.

[78] Janke, *Minding Culture*, 34.

[79] Janke, *Minding Culture*, 44.

potential to work well in the context of intangible heritage because it narrows down the number of people who can claim to be putting certain intangible heritage-related products on the market. It has already been applied for a certain time, for example, in Australia[80] by the National Indigenous Arts Advocacy Association (NIAAA).[81] One of the objections to protection via this mechanism, however, is the fact that it only protects one aspect of ICH, designation of its origin.

The main difficulty, however, would be to determine the adequate rights' holder, a problem arising from the lack of recognition of communal laws and practices by IP.[82] More specifically, because IP law does not recognize communal practices in determining who the representative of a certain community is, it is impossible to determine the rights' holder. These problems of agency and representation will be dealt with more closely in Chapter 7, but, to the extent that the customary law of traditional communities is recognized as forming part of the 'factual matrix' for the application of IP law, it is perfectly possible to incorporate these concerns when designing the necessary structure for appellations of origin for traditional communities.

On the other hand, as one commentator put it, appellations of origin are suitable for use by traditional communities precisely because they can be based upon collective decision-making processes and traditions. They reward tradition, while allowing for evolution, but at the same time are not freely transferable (especially to a third party); further, they last for as long as the tradition exists.[83]

This is particularly true when it comes to the protection of wine-making traditions, for instance. A case study on the protection of Chianti wines in Italy under an appellation of origin shows how, even though the Chianti wine-making process has changed because of the use of different grapes (to the point where they no longer resemble the original recipe), Italy still maintains the appellation. That is to say, the appellation of origin has been successful in protecting the intangible heritage associated with the Chianti wine-making by protecting its final product, but at the same time has been able to give space for the practice to evolve and change over time.[84]

Also, an appellation of origin, because it is not freely transferable, cannot be taken away from the traditional community. The traditional community will always be necessarily connected to whatever product that is derived from their intangible heritage.[85]

[80] This initiative was called 'National Aboriginal and Torres Strait Islander Cultural Industry Strategy', and created both an authenticity mark and a collaboration mark, the latter being used in cases where a product was made in cooperation between an Aboriginal and a 'normal' industry. For further information, see Janke, *Minding Culture*, 134.

[81] NIAAA ceased its activities in 2002, due to cessation of its funding. Funding stopped because Aboriginal communities did not support the initiative.

[82] Gervais, 'The Internationalization of Intellectual Property', 968.

[83] Downes, 'How Intellectual Property', 269.

[84] For a full account of the history of Chianti wine and its protection as an appellation of origin, see Tomer Broude, *Taking 'Trade and Culture' Seriously: Geographical Indications and Cultural Protection in WTO Law*, available at <http://papers.ssrn.com/sol3/papers.cfm?abstract id=714981> (accessed 29 November 2012).

[85] Downes, 'How Intellectual Property', 272 3.

6.1.2.4 Industrial designs

Industrial design law is oriented towards protecting the artistic features of a functional object. It focuses on the appearance of an object, and not on its functionality.[86] For protection of an industrial design, this design has to be registered (which creates difficulties for traditional communities, as highlighted above).

Industrial design law is of course very different from copyright law: industrial design law requires registration (copyright is protected automatically upon publication or fixation), and any monopoly is limited to the visual appearance registered (copyright allows for some leeway in the appearance of the final product). But, because industrial design law is aimed at protecting the artistic features of an object, it is to a limited extent similar to copyright law in its characteristics. Therefore, the same objections levelled against copyright (namely, that of lack of identifiable author and the difficulties in tracing the origin of the design for the purposes of beginning of the term of protection), are also applicable in this case. Further, the protection given to industrial designs is very limited in time (with a certain variation across jurisdictions, but it must be at least 10 years, according to the terms of the TRIPS agreement).[87]

In considering these circumstances, an Australian legislative working group concluded that it would be best if the registration of indigenous patterns and designs as industrial designs were prohibited altogether, especially when such reproduction would offend religious feelings of traditional communities.[88]

6.1.2.5 Trade secret law

With regard to trade secret law, it must be said that the recognition of this category by IP law is not uniform across jurisdictions. For one, there is no single universally applicable definition of 'trade secret'. A trade secret can be anything that is used in connection with business for a competitive advantage, as long as the information is secret, identifiable, and not readily ascertainable.[89]

In many jurisdictions a trade secret must be fixated in a tangible medium for it to be protected,[90] which already poses a problem for the use of trade secrets law as a tool to protect intangible heritage. Further, the connection to business is often

86 Janke, *Minding Culture*, 71.

87 Agreement on Trade-Related Aspects of Intellectual Property Rights (TRIPS Agreement), Annex 1C to the Marrakesh Agreement Establishing the World Trade Organization, signed on 15 April 1994. Number of Parties as of November 2012: 155. Article 26.3.

88 Janke, *Minding Culture*, 73.

89 Margaret A Boulware, Jeffrey A Pyle, and Frank C Turner, 'Symposium: Intellectual Property: An Overview of Intellectual Property Rights Abroad', *Hous J Int'l L* 14 (1994), 441, reprinted in Anthony D'Amato and Doris Estelle Long (eds), *International Intellectual Property Anthology* (Anderson Publishing Co, 1996), 20 2, at 20.

90 Boulware, Pyle, and Turner, 'Symposium', 21.

lacking in intangible heritage cases, and can pose a further obstacle to protection through trade secret law.

To the substance of the protection of trade secrets, being the technique behind the production of a given craft or work sacred or otherwise secret, industrial secret law could be applied. It may happen that, for the creation of certain works, such as carpets or basket weaving, for example, the techniques applied are secretive or a certain ritual or religious initiation is required. This is not the case at all times, though, and there is also the fact that an industrial application (or connection to a business practice) is required for protection under this mechanism to be given, which is not necessarily the case concerning intangible heritage.

This mechanism seems particularly appropriate in protecting the 'cultural privacy'[91] of a certain community. It focuses, further, on the methods of production of a certain expression of folklore, going beyond the final products. This can be an effective tool to protect certain techniques related to intangible heritage, when their use by third parties would imply the violation of a sacred or simply otherwise secret aspect of heritage. However, trade secret law is impotent against discovery or reverse engineering of a technique, and thus offers very limited potential to protecting intangible heritage.[92]

6.1.2.6 Unfair competition rules of IP

Use of unfair competition law has been defended because this mechanism may prevent a third party from appropriating intangible heritage in an 'anti-competitive way'. In other words, it may effectively prevent the reproduction of art through cheaper processes whereby 'originals' that have been 'researched and developed' by the custodial communities are taken advantage of. In theory, then, unfair competition law could be used as a means to protect the community as an economic actor, when the commercialization of products of its intangible heritage is commonplace. This type of mechanism cannot be applied to intangible heritage when this heritage refers to '*res extra commercium*', that is, goods out of trade.[93]

In international discussions on the application of unfair competition rules to the protection of intangible heritage, Norway took an interesting position. Norway defended the use of rules on unfair competition to create a general norm on the protection of intangible heritage, one that would protect this type of knowledge without imposing requirements such as prior examination or registration (thus addressing the technical difficulties mentioned above with regard to the use of IP mechanisms to protect ICH). Further, this general norm would be based on blanket concepts such as fairness and equity.[94] A 2003 dispute in Australia over

[91] Brown, *Who Owns Native Culture?*, 27 42.

[92] Posey and Dutfield, *Beyond Intellectual Property*, 87.

[93] Such is the case, for example, in works produced with a religious purpose, or through religious means, containing particular sacred symbols or references. See Agnes Lucas-Schloetter, 'Folklore', in Silke von Lewinski (ed), *Indigenous Heritage and Intellectual Property* (Kluwer Law International, 2003), 259 340 at 312 14.

[94] WIPO Intergovernmental Committee, *Consolidated Analysis*, Annex, para 190.

the selling of hand-carved Aboriginal souvenirs is illustrative of how unfair competition rules, coupled with ideas of fairness and equity, could be applied.[95]

All these IP mechanisms and competition rules offer different advantages and shortcomings when it comes to their potential use for the protection of intangible heritage. They are all based on proprietary regimes, though, and largely fail to address the gravest concern when it comes to misuse of intangible heritage, that is, cultural harm. Even when they do address this harm, it is only after a series of complicated and costly steps have been taken. Perhaps it would be best if there was a tool to directly address cultural harm, avoiding the pitfalls of IP. The next section discusses such a possibility.

6.1.3 IP as a tort and the redressing of cultural harm

Some literature on IP has explored the possibility of treating parts of IP as a torts issue, rather than as a property one. The idea is that intellectual works are protected against deception and confusion, and the focus is more on the remedies than it is on the registration system and the proprietary 'titles' given to IP rights-holders. What is at stake is the integrity of the work of art (or manifestation of heritage), rather than any proprietary or economic claims to it.[96] This option is connected to the idea of moral rights, explored above.

This system creates a presumption against proprietary interests, and it uses more unfair competition concepts. It guarantees that no IP rights (particularly trademarks) will be registered to the detriment of traditional communities.[97] The key interest at stake is confusion rather than misappropriation, at least if one adopts a consumer-oriented logic;[98] from the perspective of manifestations of heritage, what matters is the integrity of the work as an abstract entity, disconnected from the copyright owner inasmuch as economic interests are at stake, while preserving moral rights' claims, including attribution and acknowledgment. Also, in terms of protection from cultural harm, it can be argued that this type of harm amounts to a human rights issue, which can be translated into a torts claim before domestic courts, or at least an affront to native dignity.[99]

One of the advantages of the use of torts (or civil liability) rules for the protection of IP in the ICH context is that it stimulates investment and interest because of the marketing potential of ICH; and it does not create legal barriers to access. This is beneficial to society at large. At the same time, it creates the conditions to redress (and prevent, through punitive damages and other tort mechanisms) inappropriate uses of ICH material in contravention of communities' belief systems.[100] It also

[95] WIPO Intergovernmental Committee, *Consolidated Analysis*, Annex, para 194.

[96] David Lange, 'Reimagining the Public Domain', in James Boyle (ed), *Collected Papers: Duke Conference on the Public Domain* (Center for the Public Domain, 2003), 463 83 at 470.

[97] Chander and Sunder, 'The Romance of the Public Domain', 1369.

[98] Lange, 'Reimagining the Public Domain', 470.

[99] Paterson and Karjala, 'Looking Beyond Intellectual Property', 658.

[100] Ryu Kojima, 'Prior Informed Consent: An Intellectual Property Law Perspective', in Toshiyuki Kono (ed), *Intangible Cultural Heritage and Intellectual Property: Communities, Cultural Diversity and Sustainable Development* (Intersentia, 2009), 309 16 at 314.

creates more direct and efficient mechanisms for the sharing of financial benefits and the payment of compensation.[101] A torts mechanism, as opposed to a property-based registration scheme, results in any monies owed to the community being paid directly to it or its governing body. This is distinct from the system of IP royalties, which are traditionally paid to an agency that administers rights on behalf of authors and would keep a percentage of these values before paying the community.

Within the domain of rights over heritage as private rights, then, the treatment of these interests as torts rather than property offers interesting advantages when it comes to the protection of ICH. Considering the inadequacy of property for dealing with intangible heritage and the overall goal of law in this area being to redress cultural harm, tort rules seem like the best fit.

General torts may also be successfully used in this area. For instance, the torts related to moral rights in copyright countries are not specific torts, but rather general torts on reputation and honour. That said, it is clear that general torts on personality rights or even personal injury[102] can be used to address issues relating to ICH.

Tort rules do not have much of a preventative effect, however; they address cultural harm only once it has occurred, and are not particularly efficient in preventing it. Even the pedagogical function of torts has a limited effect, as the potential for punitive damages, for instance, is unclear in the context of cultural harm. That is to say, someone who is ordered to pay compensation for cultural harm to a community will not necessarily be discouraged from causing harm to another community, as the financial benefits (or some other type of benefit) may outweigh the trouble of paying compensation. Equally, there is no guarantee that a tort action involving community A and unauthorized exploiter of intangible heritage X will prevent exploiter Y from using community B's heritage. In this sense, there is no guarantee that a case-by-case resolution of tort cases will initiate a chain reaction and create a sufficiently known body of law so as to deter parties who have not been previously been involved in a dispute of this sort. In this sense, a set of rules that play out prior to harm to the custodial communities is necessary. The idea of a 'regulated public domain' then becomes appealing, and the following section will analyse it.

6.2 The Public Domain and 'Cultural Commons'

IP instruments in general recognize the existence of a public domain. There seems to be a tendency to think of the public domain as the end of the scope of

[101] Yu, 'International Rights Approaches to Intellectual Property', 1089 90 (quoting Jerome H Reichmann, 'Of Green Tulips and Legal Kudzu: Repackaging Rights in Subpatentable Innovation', *Vand L Rev* 53 (2000), 1743 98).

[102] One common example of this is § 823 of the German Civil Code (BGB), which states: '**Section 823. Liability in damages.** (1) A person who, intentionally or negligently, unlawfully injures the life, body, health, freedom, property or another right of another person is liable to make compensation to the other party for the damage arising from this. (2) The same duty is held by a person who commits a breach of a statute that is intended to protect another person. If, according to the contents of the statute, it may also be breached without fault, then liability to compensation only exists in the case of fault.'

application of the IP instrument. As most IP instruments are concerned primarily with private rights, the topic of the public domain is usually not explored within them. One notable exception is the Universal Copyright Convention, mentioned above. While there are not many provisions on the public domain specifically, the mandate of UNESCO as an organization for the protection and promotion of culture and cultural exchange has led it to draft an instrument that, on top of conciliating different approaches to copyright protection, also had in mind the preservation of a robust public domain.[103]

The public domain is not necessarily the enemy of IP protection. Rather, the public domain is a natural part of the IP cycle, and something that must be carefully considered in the promotion of culture, which is after all one of the main reasons why IP protection exists in the first place.

This section is dedicated to exploring the prospects of using the public domain to safeguard ICH. More specifically, it looks at intangible heritage as 'the common heritage of mankind', which translates in IP terms as thinking of ICH as a 'cultural common'. The first part of the section is dedicated to exploring the public domain and its potential and shortcomings for the protection of intangible heritage. The following subsection differentiates between the public domain and 'cultural commons'. The remainder of the section offers some guidelines for promoting these commons in the best possible way for safeguarding intangible heritage.

6.2.1 Public domain and *domaine public payant*

When IP rights lapse over a certain work, this work passes into the public domain, and may be freely used by all of society. ICH, when treated under the prism of IP law, is usually considered to fall under the public domain, since it is the manifestation of an ancient practice, which, when it can be traced back to a determined point in time, has usually exceeded the timeframe for protection under IP.[104]

Public domain shifts the obligation for protection of manifestations of heritage from the creators to the State. The public domain can be divided in two: public domain, and '*domaine public payant*'. In both of these, a national authority is designated for the defence of interests arising from the exploitation of intangible heritage by whoever intends to use it and does not belong to the custodial community. In the latter scenario, fees are to be paid so authorization is given to the use. These fees, once collected, usually go to a governmental fund oriented to cultural development, not reaching the custodial communities as copyrights or royalties.

The conception of the 'total' public domain mentioned above suggests that when the protection period has lapsed in a particular work or expression, all exclusive rights to it disappear. This is at odds with the *droit d'auteur* system. In this system, certain moral rights, such as those of integrity and attribution, never

[103] Okediji, 'An Enduring Legacy', 120.
[104] Long, 'The Impact of Foreign Investment on Indigenous Culture', 269 70.

cease to exist, the only difference being that the entitlement to uphold these rights passes from the authors and their successors to the State.

A 'total' public domain may seem at first glance to be more protective of creativity, since it gives new creators the chance to freely adapt from pre-existing work. However, the rights of attribution and integrity of the work, which essentially function to prevent plagiarism, in the long run help foster creativity. These rights do not remove works from the public domain; rather, they create a 'bounded' or 'regulated' public domain, which in many ways is what the idea of 'cultural commons' is about.

One of the alternatives to still be able to somehow protect works that have fallen in the public domain is the institution of a 'paying public domain', or '*domaine public payant*', as it is more commonly referred to. This alternative reduces the harm caused by creating property rights over the common cultural pool from which society draws (which, admittedly, could have very harmful effects on cultural diversity), but at the same time it imposes certain conditions for the use of works in the public domain.[105] The most common of these conditions is the payment of fees, which are normally destined to promote ICH practices in the country licensing the manifestation of heritage. This *domaine public payant* is usually administered by the State, as it is normally the case with the protection of moral rights of works that have fallen into the 'normal' public domain.

In this sense, a regulated public domain can perform two functions: it can serve the desire to keep some level of protection to authors' moral rights (more specifically, the rights to attribution and integrity); and it can be useful for the preservation of cultural heritage. While still predicated on the commodification of heritage, it is commodification that happens in terms determined by the custodial communities. The *domaine public payant* is characterized by a stronger emphasis on the protection of cultural heritage, because it provides financial means for safeguarding intangible heritage (which revert to the custodial communities). The main drawback, however, is that there is little international recognition of public domain regulations. There is no international structure through which these mechanisms can be enforced, and, as the *domaine public payant* is more often than not aimed at preventing misuse by *foreign* third parties, it is of limited usefulness.[106]

It is interesting to note that there has been a shift in attitudes towards the public domain in terms of the exploitation of intangible heritage and TK. While traditional communities have often favoured the use of public domain, some authors argue that the awareness of the economic potential of these resources seems to have created a shift: while corporations now try to make sure that these resources fall in the public domain (and can therefore be re-appropriated by corporate actors), traditional communities have largely abandoned the idea of a public domain to

[105] Long, 'The Impact of Foreign Investment on Indigenous Culture', 270.

[106] Cathryn A Berryman, 'Toward More Universal Protection of Intangible Cultural Property', *J Intell Prop L* 1 (1994), 293, reprinted in Anthony D'Amato and Doris Estelle Long (eds), *International Intellectual Property Anthology* (Anderson Publishing Co, 1996), 76 at 77.

favour proprietary rights that can foster their development.[107] They use this argument not to discard the use of the public domain or the idea of commons, but simply to warn that these concepts should be considered carefully, rather than immediately jumped at as the best possible solution.[108] In this sense, while the public domain allows for the 'regeneration and revitalization' of intangible heritage, it does not provide a strong economic incentive for creation and development.[109] It has been pointed out that economic exploitation of these resources is bound to happen asymmetrically. The potential for exploitation by a local community in comparison to that of a multinational corporate partner is unbalanced for a number of reasons.[110] There are limited opportunities for local commercialization of this knowledge, since it is often an integral part of social life, and not something that would be thought of as deserving added commercial value. Further, local communities are often unaware of the tools available to them in regulating the use of their knowledge, in comparison to transnational corporate partners who have the expertise to exploit IP regimes in their favour. Finally, it is more difficult for local communities to raise the capital necessary to launch the commercial exploitation of their manifestations of heritage.[111]

The public domain has also been criticized as insufficient for the protection of intangible heritage on other grounds. First of all, the public domain fails to offer mechanisms to prevent the use of intangible heritage in certain circumstances. Such instances might include: falsely suggesting a connection to the custodial community; offensive, derogatory, or libellous uses; or attempts at using sacred or secret manifestations of intangible heritage. Also, other areas of legislation outside of IP law seem to be more effective than the total lack of regulation, and the conflicts with IP law are not so large that they exclude the application of IP law altogether.[112]

The inequality of access to resources that can create an enabling environment for the exploitation of intangible heritage in favour of the tradition-bearers thus defeats the idea that the public domain is the best way to protect intangible heritage.[113] An alternative must be sought, and perhaps one that is not so far from the idea of non-individual ownership (which is also harmful). The following section is dedicated to differentiating between two similar concepts, 'public domain' and 'commons'.

6.2.2 From 'no one's' to 'everyone's'

One of the early statutes that recognized IP as a legal category is the Statute of Anne of 1709 in England.[114] This Statute has been considered to be a legal landmark of the 'second enclosure movement' (the first one being that which consisted of the

[107] Chander and Sunder, 'The Romance of the Public Domain', 1335.
[108] Chander and Sunder, 'The Romance of the Public Domain', 1336.
[109] WIPO Intergovernmental Committee, *Consolidated Analysis*, para 15.
[110] Chander and Sunder, 'The Romance of the Public Domain', 1351.
[111] Chander and Sunder, 'The Romance of the Public Domain', 1351 2.
[112] WIPO Intergovernmental Committee, *Consolidated Analysis*, para 23.
[113] Chander and Sunder, 'The Romance of the Public Domain', 1354.
[114] For the history of this Statute, see Rose, 'Nine-Tenths of the Law', 77.

enclosure of real property for farming purposes).[115] The first enclosure was highly successful in removing property from public to private ownership, and thus serving to greatly expand productive capabilities.[116]

The second enclosure movement, on the other hand, meant the creation of exclusive rights over intellectual creations and as a means to stimulate productivity. However, the mere transposition of the property model to intellectual creation has seemingly failed to take into account ways in which IP is different from real property. For one, while real property uses are mutually exclusive (that is, if one uses a piece of land, another person cannot use the same land), IP uses are non-rival, as one person using an idea or listening to a song does not prevent another person from doing the exact same thing. Therefore, the threat of overuse of fields and rivers that was one of the justifications for the first enclosure movement cannot be sustained when it comes to 'informational or innovational commons'.[117]

Initial efforts towards the creation of proprietary rights over intellectual creation in the Common Law world were those of publishers,[118] not the creators themselves (which helps explain the sharp difference in focus between the *droit d'auteur* and copyright systems). They advocated for perpetual rights over published works, a view that was forcefully combated by several political thinkers of the period, most notably John Locke, who argued that perpetual monopolies would be harmful to the circulation of knowledge (an Enlightenment ideal). His ideas seeped into the case law in the late 18th century discussing the Statute of Anne (whether knowingly so is unclear), and, even though the Statute opens by saying it is necessary to protect literary property, it also says that the purpose of the legislation is to encourage the production of knowledge. This Statute has even been interpreted by British Courts as placing a higher value on the access to published works than in the protection of an economic monopoly.[119] According to Mark Rose, '[i]n this way, the Statute aligns itself with broad civic purposes as well as with private property'.[120]

The public domain is in many ways different from the idea of commons; while the public domain is seen as 'free' and unregulated, the idea of commons rests on some form of control of distribution. While there are no financial benefits to be accrued from transactions involving the commons, there is still the need for a transaction, some form of authorization, before the commons can be used.[121] And this is very important for intangible heritage, since, as we have seen, communities are less interested in financial benefits from the exploitation of their heritage by third parties than in actually controlling such use, to make sure it is not culturally offensive or harmful in any way.

[115] For the history of the first enclosure movement, see Boyle, 'The Second Enclosure Movement', 33 6.

[116] Boyle, 'The Second Enclosure Movement', 35.

[117] Boyle, 'The Second Enclosure Movement', 41.

[118] Rose, 'Nine-Tenths of the Law', 78.

[119] Davidson, 'Lost in Translation', 584 (citing *Donaldson v Becket*).

[120] Rose, 'Nine-Tenths of the Law', 79.

[121] Boyle, 'The Second Enclosure Movement', 65 6.

The commons, however, require some form of regulation.[122] The next section is aimed at discussing a few ways in which a 'regulated common' can be used to protect intangible heritage.

6.2.3 Regulating the commons

Leaving a resource in the public domain is not enough, at least not unless this public domain is structured.[123] And that is when the idea of commons comes into play. One of the problems with the commons is that any discussion of it seems to be overshadowed by the idea of 'the tragedy of the commons',[124] an idea articulated by Garrett Hardin to say that (environmental) commons were bound to be subject to over-exploitation and therefore be destroyed.[125] This does not hold true when it comes to intellectual or cultural commons, however. The repeated use of informational or cultural commons does not lead to its depletion; on the contrary, it can work to the advantage of certain groups who control these commons.[126] The central question is who should control these resources.

It is also important to consider how the commons (environmental or otherwise) can regulate themselves against overuse. For one, to speak of lack of individualized control over the commons does not mean to speak of no control whatsoever; on the contrary, groups manage the commons. Further, and more importantly for this analysis, the commons are regulated in very nuanced ways, depending on the exact common at stake.[127]

Further, the logic of the tragedy of the commons is based on law and economics, and it fails to take into account social norms that are not necessarily given the status of 'legal norms', but that successfully regulate the commons. It is regrettable that, while academic literature about property in general recognizes interests other than efficiency, the literature on the commons seems to a large extent trapped within this law and economics mindset.[128]

One of the possible theories for offering a regulatory framework for the commons is the Roman Law concept of '*res universitatis*' or communion of assets. This may be translated further as property belonging to a group in its corporate capacity.[129] The regime for the commons is that the resources involved are

[122] The regulation of the public domain fails to deal with the effects of colonialism, which is of course very relevant when it comes to use the public domain as an emancipatory tool for often colonized custodial communities like indigenous peoples. For this critique, see Kathy Bowrey and Jane Anderson, 'The Politics of Global Information Sharing: Whose Cultural Agendas are Being Advanced?', *Social and Legal Studies* 18(4) (2009), 1 26.

[123] Chander and Sunder, 'The Romance of the Public Domain', 1337.

[124] James Boyle, 'Foreword: The Opposite of Property?', in James Boyle (ed), *Collected Papers: Duke Conference on the Public Domain* (Center for the Public Domain, 2003), 1 32 at 7.

[125] For a summary explanation of the idea, see Chander and Sunder, 'The Romance of the Public Domain', 1332.

[126] Chander and Sunder, 'The Romance of the Public Domain', 1337.

[127] Boyle, 'Foreword', 7 8.

[128] Chander and Sunder, 'The Romance of the Public Domain', 1333.

[129] Carol M Rose, 'Romans, Roads, and Romantic Creators: Traditions of Public Property in the Information Age', in James Boyle (ed), *Collected Papers: Duke Conference on the Public Domain* (Center for the Public Domain, 2003), 89 110 at 105 8.

commons on the inside, but they are property vis-à-vis non-members. That is to say, members of a community adopting this regime may freely use the resources within the community, but third parties are excluded from such use.[130] Presumably, third parties can be authorized to certain uses of the commons; the main feature is that such authorization is not presumed, as it would be in the case of the public domain.

In this sense, *res universitatis* is a type of property that, while non-exclusive, is also bounded.[131] Intangible heritage is thus treated not as a freely exploitable resource, but rather as a resource that belongs to the entire (often national) community where it has been nurtured, but that will not be automatically available to third parties who will put interests other than those of the community of origin in their use of the heritage.

The plurality of social norms used to regulate the use of commons makes it very hard to design a model through which cultural commons should be governed. Some elements, however, should always be considered when designing such regimes. This will be the object of detailed analysis in the following chapter, but it is important to outline some of the core ideas.

The sharing of benefits[132] is an important element. It has been stated that the denial of registration of copyright or a patent over intangible heritage that is misappropriated by third parties does not resolve the issue. On the contrary, it has been argued, it prevents the production of knowledge-based products that can benefit a much larger population than that of the traditional community, without necessarily affecting the traditional community's use of its intangible heritage. This argument suggests that if commercial exploitation by a third party is simply forbidden in all instances, society at large is the biggest loser, and the traditional community also loses potential economic benefits. The important thing, then, is to devise a system that ensures that, if appropriation by a third party takes place, it is respectful of cultural sensitivities, and secures benefit-sharing in a way that is also culturally-sensitive (for instance, if the community in question does not use money, then the royalty payments should be directed at the State, for investment in areas that can benefit the community, according to its requests).[133] Naturally, any such scheme for economic or commercial exploitation implies a fair degree of commodification of heritage, but, as discussed in Chapter 1, commodification may in fact benefit the community, if the community is at a position to control the terms of the exploitation. If the community chooses to keep its heritage out of the market, that is their sole prerogative.

There are other factors besides benefit-sharing that must be taken into account. For instance, there is the question of agency (that is, who gets to represent the ICH

[130] Rose, 'Romans, Roads, and Romantic Creators', 106.

[131] Rose, 'Romans, Roads, and Romantic Creators', 108.

[132] On this topic, see Chapter 7. See also Francesco Francioni, 'Equity in International Law', in Rudolf Bernhardt and Rüdiger Wolfrum (eds), *Max Planck Encyclopedia of Public International Law* (2007), available at <http://www.mpepil.com> (accessed 29 November 2012).

[133] Paterson and Karjala, 'Looking Beyond Intellectual Property', 651.

holders in the negotiation of these agreements). There are also pressing issues of prior and informed consent that must be taken into account.

All these elements will be subject to detailed analysis in Chapter 7. But it is important to highlight them here as a counterbalance to use of IP mechanisms that can be exceedingly constraining, at one extreme, and a loose, unregulated use of public domain, which fails to take into account sensitivities invariably at stake when talking about the use of intangible heritage, on the other. The elements for the regulation of the commons present here aim at ensuring that excesses in the attempts to safeguard intangible heritage are still sufficiently protective, but do not freeze this great source of cultural diversity that is ICH.

7

Contractual Approaches

The two previous chapters addressed measures aimed at protecting intangible cultural heritage (ICH) against misappropriation by third parties from a human rights or an intellectual property perspective. These chapters offered tools to remedy what are considered to be undesirable acts in the use of ICH by third parties (that is, parties not belonging to the community where the particular manifestation of heritage originated). This chapter is aimed at offering some elements for what would be possible contractual arrangements between the holders/custodians of intangible heritage and those interested in making use of this heritage. By 'contractual approaches' I mean arrangements directly between custodians of heritage and interested third parties which borrows elements from private law in a broad sense, but are also widely interspersed with more public elements. It relates to what can be referred to as codes of best practice and protocols.

The uses of heritage through contractual approaches include commercial and non-commercial uses alike. Non-commercial uses are understood here as those beyond the industrial processes, focused instead on the intrinsic nature of heritage. Naturally, non-commercial uses (particularly scientific ones) are expected to be subject to a less strict set of rules, because of the greater benefits that presumably arise from this kind of use. They must nevertheless be subject to rules as well.

The main assumption for the purposes of this chapter is that community rules are not particularly rigid, and can be adjusted to the ideas presented here. In other words, it is understandable that the specific social and legal order of each community (particularly traditional and indigenous communities) must be reflected in each specific contractual arrangement, and that the conclusions reached in this chapter must, when incorporated into actual legal arrangements, be adjusted so as to reflect these traditional and customary rules. It is impossible to create a comprehensive codification of customary law across different communities,[1] and I am well aware of that. However, this does not mean one should not try to offer guidelines in what is to a large extent a relationship between traditional and non-traditional legal systems. But one must also be aware of the danger of creating new traditions within a certain group by trying to force upon it a legal system or legal traditions that are foreign to them. This can happen when community norms about access to their

[1] Nicolas Brahy, *The Property Regime of Biodiversity and Traditional Knowledge: Institutions for Conservation and Innovation* (Éditions Larcier, 2008), 296 9.

own resources are not taken into account.[2] However, this is not to say that any effort to provide some degree of generalization in this area would be fruitless. On the contrary, general guidelines are important, as long as they can be adapted to existing customary law and give primacy to it.

One such example of contracting is the Covenant on Intellectual, Cultural and Scientific Resources, a model contract produced by the Global Coalition for Biocultural Diversity, a no longer active NGO that worked on the issue. This Covenant has the potential to protect traditional communities through requirements such as prior and informed consent, benefit sharing and other financial benefits, and general informational duties towards the communities.[3] Cases such as this are the object of this chapter.

In many ways, this chapter brings the work so far full circle. After outlining the main theoretical difficulties relating to the protection of intangible heritage, looking at how different institutional levels address the problem and examining some of the remedies that can exist to misuses of intangible heritage by third parties and the advantages and pitfalls of these remedies, this chapter takes these elements into account and proposes a set of rules that can provide ICH with effective legal protection and prevent harm to communities, attempting to accommodate the theoretical tensions into a set of coherent legal guidelines.

This chapter will proceed as follows: I will first come back to an issue left somewhat open in the previous chapter, namely, that of the regulation of cultural commons. Next, I will move to the issue of agency and representation of collective entities and communities for the purposes of negotiating uses of intangible heritage by third parties. This part will look at the issue of balancing the interests of multiple stakeholders, and means to ensure community participation. I will then look at the delicate issue of free, prior and informed consent, and conclude the analysis with financial issues pertaining to the exploitation of intangible heritage.

7.1 Creating a Structure for Contracting Out the Commons

The protection of intangible heritage through propertization, as seen in Chapter 6, is problematic for many reasons, not the least of which the stifling of creativity that can come out of this type of protection. 'Softer' systems of ICH protection aim at securing the viability of intangible heritage, whereas intellectual property rights aim at protection.[4] Protection, despite the negative fallout, can be necessary in certain

[2] Branislav Hazucha and Toshiyuki Kono, 'Conceptualization of Community as a Holder of Intangible Cultural Heritage', in Kono Toshiyuki (ed), *Intangible Cultural Heritage and Intellectual Property: Communities, Cultural Diversity and Sustainable Development* (Intersentia, 2009), 145 57 at 157.

[3] Darrell A Posey and Graham Dutfield, *Beyond Intellectual Property: Toward Traditional Resource Rights for Indigenous Peoples and Local Communities* (International Development Research Center, 1996), 73 4 and 175 8.

[4] Wend B Wendland, 'Managing Intellectual Property Options when Documenting, Recording and Digitizing Intangible Cultural Heritage', in Toshiyuki Kono (ed), *Intangible Cultural Heritage and Intellectual Property: Communities, Cultural Diversity and Sustainable Development* (Intersentia, 2009),

instances, for example where one deals with perceptions of the sacred of communities that can be misappropriated by others. It protects the cultural process of creativity, as opposed to simply universalizing access to knowledge produced in the context of intangible cultural heritage.[5] However this 'enclosure' is not generally necessary, and for the most part intangible cultural heritage can be considered to be part of a given community's 'cultural commons'. This turn to the commons does not mean the commons should go unprotected against third parties;[6] rather, protection must be secured, and whenever possible to the benefit and empowerment of communities.[7]

It has already been said that many authors draw on a common pool of knowledge; partly this pool comes from the work of folklorists who catalogued oral tradition in the form of books.[8] Perhaps the most prominent of these were the brothers Grimm, who catalogued fairy tales and other stories from a specific region of Germany, originally, later expanding to larger parts of the then forming nation. Many of the tales catalogued by the Grimm brothers were however common to other countries and national oral traditions, and had been catalogued before in those countries by authors such as Perrault (France), Basile (Italy), or Hans Christian Andersen (Denmark).[9]

These authors borrowed from each others' traditions and, even when cataloguing only stories original to their own culture, they still took the liberty of adapting and changing these stories to serve the goal of turning them into moral tales, or simply for the cohesion of their books. None of this was considered misappropriation, and rather was regarded simply as borrowing from and reinvention of the commons.[10]

In other examples, folk singers from minority groups in India had their songs used in Bollywood movies. In two such cases, the performers of the songs in the movies registered the songs as their own original compositions. In one of these

77 99 at 98 9; and Steven Van Uytsel, 'Inventory Making and Fairy Tales: Safeguarding of Intangible Cultural Heritage in Historical Perspective', in Toshiyuki Kono (ed), *Intangible Cultural Heritage and Intellectual Property: Communities, Cultural Diversity and Sustainable Development* (Intersentia, 2009), 113 41 at 136.

[5] Johanna Gibson, *Community Resources: Intellectual Property, International Trade and Protection of Traditional Knowledge* (Ashgate, 2009), 158 9.

[6] Wim van Zanten, 'Prior Informed Consent: Experiences with Ethnomusicology Recordings', in Toshiyuki Kono (ed), *Intangible Cultural Heritage and Intellectual Property: Communities, Cultural Diversity and Sustainable Development* (Intersentia, 2009), 283 308 at 285.

[7] Branislav Hazucha and Toshiyuki Kono, 'Safeguarding of Intangible Cultural Heritage: Benefits and Potential Harms', in Toshiyuki Kono (ed), *Intangible Cultural Heritage and Intellectual Property: Communities, Cultural Diversity and Sustainable Development* (Intersentia, 2009), 319 24 at 320.

[8] See for instance Jaime Ricardo Teixeira Gouveia, *Embate em Debate: História, Administração e Limites do Planalto Ribeirão (Um Estudo de Caso)* (Casa do Povo, 2003); Jaime Ricardo Teixeira Gouveia, *Subsídios para a História de Leomil: 'A-presentação' e 'Re-presentação'* (Casa do Povo, 2004); Antonio Machado y Álvarez, *Bases de el Folk-lore español y reglamento del el Folk-lore andaluz* (Imp y Lit De El Porvernir, 1881); Vânia de Fátima Noronha Alvez, *O Corpo Lúdico Maxakali: Segredos de um 'Programa de Índio'* (C/ Arte, 2003); Júlio Vila Nova, *Panorama de Folião: O Carnaval de Pernambuco na Voz dos Blocos Líricos* (Fundação de Cultura Cidade do Recife, 2007); and Hermilo Borba Filho, *Espetáculos Populares do Nordeste* (Massangana, 2007).

[9] Van Uytsel, 'Inventory Making and Fairy Tales', 119 20.

[10] Van Uytsel, 'Inventory Making and Fairy Tales', 135.

instances, the community author, even though widely recognizing that he drew from traditional music for his composition, had also registered the song as his own. In the other case alluded to above, there was an actual group involved in the song creation at the community of origin level, who had never proceeded with registration.

In the first situation, the author did not mind the fact that his song was used in a movie, even if authorship had been attributed to another person. He was in fact happy with the boost his own career received due to the high profile nature of the movie, and, most importantly, with the wide circulation of his community's traditional music as a result (which amounts to a renunciation of sorts of the moral right of attribution, analysed in Chapter 6, outside the musician's own community). In the second case, the group involved also said it was pleased with the visibility their own traditional music had gained, and lamented only the fact that the new rendition of the song mispronounced some of the words of their own language.[11]

This is by no means a representative sample, but it serves as a reminder that, at least in some instances, people are more than happy to have their own culture be part of a freely accessible pool of knowledge.[12] This means that any broader, more general regulation of the commons must take into account instances in which the commons should not be regulated at all[13] (or at least not seek to assert perceived rights). It is, however, safe to assume that when religious feelings are involved (in both of the cases mentioned above with respect to India, the songs were not religious), communities may be more interested in controlling the uses of their heritage. However, a regulatory framework covering the use of communities' ICH that has to encompass both a commons and highly controlled material, when there is no opposition to use by outsiders from ICH holders to begin with, would be cumbersome to try and construct.

In any case, some sort of attribution right should be guaranteed as a rule. Even if individual or collective artists, or even communities, do not mind having their ICH used by third parties without attribution, they seem to all welcome the visibility their culture gains by the exposure in other cultural circles. And this exposure would be enhanced if attribution were guaranteed, in the fashion of authors' moral rights.[14]

One must consider, however, the possible chilling effect upon third parties who might choose not to use traditional culture simply so that they (1) would not have

[11] Shubha Chaudhuri, 'Who is the "Holder" of Intangible Cultural Heritage? Revisiting the Concept of Community from an Intangible Cultural Heritage Perspective', in Toshiyuki Kono (ed), *Intangible Cultural Heritage and Intellectual Property: Communities, Cultural Diversity and Sustainable Development* (Intersentia, 2009), 189 201 at 196 7.

[12] See also, with regard to traditional communities in Indonesia, van Zanten, 'Prior Informed Consent', 304 6.

[13] Ryu Kojima, 'Prior Informed Consent: An Intellectual Property Law Perspective', in Toshiyuki Kono (ed), *Intangible Cultural Heritage and Intellectual Property: Communities, Cultural Diversity and Sustainable Development* (Intersentia, 2009), 309 16 at 313 (drawing an analogy with computer open-source software).

[14] Gibson, *Community Resources*, 291.

to 'share' authorship by attributing part of it to a community to which they do not belong; and (2) would not have to worry about future royalty requests from a community to whom they attributed. The first objection, I suggest, is minor, and the burden imposed on third parties using intangible heritage would have little impact on actually discouraging the borrowing. But the second claim is more feasible, and presents an actual potential risk. In this sense, one alternative would be to establish, as a ground rule to the 'regulated cultural commons', that no monetary compensation can be sought by those whose work is borrowed from. This mechanism would create more incentives for observing the right to attribution, which is the key right to determine control over the way heritage is presented (because the right of attribution is connected to another moral right, that of integrity of the work).

This suggestion of course creates the problem of who gets to decide that a community shall not have monetary claims, an issue that can be resolved as one of the steps in the inventorying process. Inventories are an essential part of the 'regulated commons', as they will limit the common pool of knowledge that is the object of protection. While public cataloguing arguably makes it easier to facilitate the misuse of intangible heritage by others, because it makes public information that otherwise may be difficult to obtain, it also precludes proprietary claims over heritage by third parties, because it has already been listed as 'prior knowledge' in these catalogues. But cataloguing must be done with an objective of not being seen as exhaustive, and it cannot preclude creation by communities themselves upon what they have deposited in this inventory. That is to say, the inventory serves as a control for use by third parties. However, the communities themselves (from which the manifestation of heritage originated), as well as individuals and groups belonging to it, should be able to freely use their own heritage without having to ask for permission, as limited by their custom.

Inventorying should be conducted by ICH experts and by the community themselves (the latter being the key element, to which experts should defer), much in the fashion suggested by the 2003 UNESCO Convention (with the exception of the prevalence of communities over experts, which lacks from the 2003 UNESCO Convention). Further steps should be added, though. In addition to creating this databank of ICH manifestations, those registering the manifestations should also indicate the limits and extent of availability of their work in the cultural commons. More specifically, those registering the manifestation of heritage should indicate whether the ICH is freely available in the case that the right of attribution is respected, whether the ICH is available upon payment of certain fees to the community of origin, or simply whether any use by a third party is forbidden, thereby laying down the rules of licensing.[15]

The latter scenario is helpful because it puts manifestations of heritage in the public domain, to a certain extent. It also precludes third parties from appropriating it, or claiming that their consulting of an ICH database prior to the registration of

[15] On the use of licensing agreements to protect traditional knowledge, see Posey and Dutfield, *Beyond Intellectual Property*, 69 70.

an intellectual property right makes their request to be in good faith and thus legitimate. At the same time it gives communities the right to prevent third parties from ever using it because they have asserted control over it. This solution can work for manifestations of heritage of sacred or otherwise secret content. It would also reduce the transaction costs of third parties' interest to exploit ICH, as it lowers the necessary amount of evidence to support prior and informed consent, for instance (to be analysed in detail below).[16]

One important question amidst these debates is who gets to register the manifestations of heritage on behalf of the community, and who administers and controls the rights of the community to attribution and even royalties. Issues of agency and representation are the subject of the following section.

7.2 Agency and Representation

Agency here is understood not in the philosophical-anthropological sense (the analysis of reasons why individuals or other entities act the way they do), but rather in the narrower legal sense (a legal relationship of representation within a certain structure).[17] This section will look at how agency and representation can be sought in the identification of the stakeholders of ICH, and also through mechanisms to ensure and widen community participation. These two are pre-requisites to appropriate agency and representation, which then is *conditio sine qua non* of prior and informed consent, the subject of the following section.

Before the analysis of prior and informed consent, though, one must determine who gets to give consent on behalf of a given group. The first step of this assessment lies in analysing the different stakeholders in ICH 'transactional contexts', and the roles they should play.

7.2.1 Negotiating among the different stakeholders

It is obvious that, depending on the types of aims one intends to advance by protecting ICH (identity, property, development, maintenance of ways of life, among others explored in Chapter 1), the choice of means to safeguard intangible heritage will operate on a sliding scale. Property is best protected through intellectual property mechanisms, explored in Chapter 6; development is best obtained through regional mechanisms discussed in Chapters 3 (the OAS being a prime example) and 4 (Laos, Viet Nam, and China in particular); maintenance of ways of life is a goal best served through human rights mechanisms analysed in Chapter 5; and identity, understood as political identity, has been analysed outside the national

[16] Hazucha and Kono, 'Safeguarding of Intangible Cultural Heritage', 321.

[17] Deryck Beyleveld, and Roger Brownsword, *Consent in the Law* (Hart Publishing, 2007), 35. For agency as a philosophical-anthropological concern, see particularly Margaret Archer, *Culture and Agency: The Place of Culture in Social Theory* (Cambridge University Press, 1996); Michael E Bratman, *Structure of Agency* (Oxford University Press, 2007); and J Jeremy Wisnewski, *The Politics of Agency: Towards a Pragmatic Approach to Philosophical Anthropology* (Ashgate, 2008).

context in the discussions about the EU, African Union, and Council of Europe in Chapter 3.

This sliding scale of means, according to one commentator who looked at it from the perspective of the manifestation of heritage alone, will vary from the protection of only the aesthetic values of the manifestation of heritage to the protection of the social context with disregard to the aesthetics. It is up to the stakeholders involved, and more prominently the communities where such ICH originates, to decide how far to go along this spectrum, based on their needs and possibilities. One must always make sure, however, that these decisions are taken to be circumstantial or situational choices, responding to needs and aspirations of a given moment, and not new 'dogmas or orthodoxies'.[18]

Bearing that in mind, the idea of negotiating among the different stakeholders can be thought of as considering the community as a single stakeholder which has to negotiate with the government and third parties interested in exploiting their ICH, for instance (external dimension); or it can be considered from the point of view of the different actors within a community itself (internal dimension).

Relative to the external dimension, there are many issues to be considered. One is that the number of stakeholders must be considered. The community where the ICH originates is on one side of the transaction, and the party/parties intending to exploit this ICH on the other side. This outline makes for a simple, two-party transaction. But where should the State be? Preliminarily, should the State play a role at all? If so, on what grounds?

I suggest the State should in principle be involved in the matter, if anything as a guardian of the interests of the community, and also as a representative of the interests of the broader national polity. This of course seems to reinforce cultural nationalism in heritage issues, and it also seems to enable the State to be in a position to suppress dissent or 'subversive' heritage within its territory. That is one instance in which internationalism (in the form suggested in Chapter 2, that is, moving beyond the still current sovereignty-based models) becomes vital, in creating an alternative to States that abuse their position. But it is best that subsidiarity be respected, especially in the field of heritage, which is very context-driven.

In many legal orders the State is viewed as the keeper of human rights generally, but also particularly it is regarded as a guardian of the rights and interests of traditional and indigenous communities. To the extent intangible heritage has been often articulated in terms of human rights and the protection of cultural identity, it is to be expected that the State be involved as a steward. Also, States can still be legitimately seen as guardians of the indigenous and traditional groups within their territories. The discussion on the constitutional protection of indigeneity, interculturalism, and multiculturalism in Chapter 4 highlighted this function of the State. Both of these ideas echo the Enlightenment canon of freedom 'through' the State, and are not fully compatible with more liberal understandings

[18] Antonio A Arantes, 'Heritage as Culture: Limits, Uses and Implications of Intangible Cultural Heritage Inventories', in Toshiyuki Kono (ed), *Intangible Cultural Heritage and Intellectual Property: Communities, Cultural Diversity and Sustainable Development* (Intersentia, 2009), 51 75 at 70 1.

of rights and the role of the State. This is, however, the model I advocate, for pragmatic reasons, even if I have some reservations about it (to be explored below). Even in more liberal legal regimes the State is still seen as at least a mediator of indigenous and traditional communities' interests before other segments of society, which makes this view more widely acceptable.

In practice, this translates as the State providing resources (legal and informational) to communities to assist them in negotiating with third parties regarding the use of their intangible heritage, either through overseeing contracts or simpler memoranda of understanding and other non-legal instruments, which can be useful to third parties in that they further reduce transactional costs.[19] In this way, the vulnerability of communities can be balanced out against the technical and financial superiority of some of the parties that would otherwise be in a position to offer unfavourable terms for the use of a community's ICH, or to fail to consult them at all.

Another function to be performed by the State in overseeing these transactions is to guarantee that they also take into account the universe outside of that specific transaction. More specifically, negotiations involving intangible heritage, because they involve culture and touch upon the cultural commons and the public domain, must take into account the impact of specific transactions on society at large, so as not to encroach upon the cultural life of the larger community. This is generally likely to occur through the excessive propertization of what should be considered cultural commons. In this sense, the State could act as a control mechanism to prevent transactions over what cannot be the subject of a contract, thus protecting the larger national community.

One obvious critique of this view of the State is that, especially in the developing world that is the repository of a significant amount of the world's intangible heritage, States can be much more concerned with promoting development at the expense of protecting culture and their own traditional communities. In the search for capital, States may be willing to give excessively generous conditions to third parties willing to invest in the exploitation of cultural resources and to look the other way when there are signs of abuse, much in the same fashion of what reportedly happens in cases of exploitation of natural resources. This is thus a serious risk to be taken into account. At the same time it is not one that can warrant excluding the State altogether and leaving communities at the mercy of corporate entities which, if they are sometimes powerful enough to bend a State's machinery to their needs, could also harm a community. International oversight of these contracts can be secured, either through non-governmental organizations assisting the communities alongside the State, or simply through subsequent international action in human rights bodies, for instance, in a similar vein to what has already happened in situations where natural resource exploitation has had a negative impact on traditional communities.[20] The tools outlined in Chapter 5 may also be utilized.

[19] Posey and Dutfield, *Beyond Intellectual Property*, 70.

[20] See for instance the seminal case of the African Commission on Human and Peoples' Rights, *Social and Economic Rights Action Centre (SERAC) and Another v Nigeria* (2001), 2001 AHRLR 60.

Another possible criticism of the role of the State is the potential for abuse. This is highlighted in my critique of the inscription of Tibetan Opera in the UNESCO Representative List (Chapter 2). But to suggest a radical solution in the opposite direction, namely, that the State is not involved at all, may result in States taking no responsibility for the safeguarding of intangible heritage. International remedies should be available to counter possible State abuse, but States should be involved and have a stake in the safeguarding of intangible heritage everywhere. What I propose here is a subsidiary mechanism (or layer of responsibility) rather than a means to bypass international scrutiny.

If the State does play a role, there are at least three stakeholders in each transaction involving ICH. What about when there is more than one community that can be considered the 'owner' of a certain manifestation of heritage? Should this mean such heritage goes immediately into the public domain/cultural commons, and it is therefore no longer possible for it to be involved in financial transactions? If there is more than one community that can be deemed to be the authentic holders of a certain manifestation of heritage (either because both have registered the same form of ICH in the databank of cultural commons outline above, or because there is empirical evidence supporting the claims of all the communities), then the best alternative for all the communities is that they are involved as contracting parties, along with the party interested in the exploitation of the heritage. But this would dramatically increase the negotiating costs, and could potentially discourage the party interested in exploiting ICH from doing so.

Another alternative is to involve only the entity that administers the cultural commons, outlined above. This would have less community involvement, but it might secure the exploitation of the manifestation of heritage (to the subsequent benefit of the communities). This option would reduce negotiation costs, and, because the entity would be well aware of the conditions in which the manifestation of heritage could be exploited (seeing as that is one of the suggested conditions for registration in the databank), there would in principle not be a problem with involving this entity in the negotiations on behalf of the involved communities.

The way communities portray themselves before others connects to another set of concerns, related to the internal dimension of assessing stakeholders in an ICH

This case concerned the harm caused to the Ogoni indigenous community by the actions of an oil company of which Nigeria was the majority shareholder. Although the complaint tried to impute responsibility primarily to the State by its own actions, by alleging that the State was the majority shareholder of the oil consortium, by arguing that the human rights violations had been perpetrated by the military put at the disposal of the oil consortium, or ultimately that the government had a direct participation in the oil development that caused the harm to Ogoniland, the African Commission decided the case based on the State's duty to oversee that the oil exploitation did not affect the rights of people in the area (that is, through the positive duty of the State in the protection of human rights). For an analysis of this case from the perspective of international investment law, see Francesco Francioni, 'Access to Justice, Denial of Justice and International Investment Law', *EJIL* 20 (3) (2009), 729–48. This look through the lenses of investment law can be helpful, at least to the extent traditional communities can be seen as people affected by investments third parties (investors) wish to make, with the blessing of the State. To the extent the development of the right of access to justice in international investment law cuts both ways, according to Francioni, and can be used to protect not only the investor, but also those affected by it, this is a valid perspective to take into account.

transaction. More specifically, the safeguarding process implies an adjustment between the identity sentiments within a community (with all of its tensions, rivalries, and the problems around defining which objects are to be most representative) and its exterior dimension, which is what the community wants to let others see of itself.[21] The community can hardly be considered a single entity with a single will, and assessing this 'will' is all the more problematic when someone is exercising it on behalf of the community. A community's 'amorphous membership' and 'evolving direction' create a central problem in the difficulty of recognizing, monitoring, transferring, and enforcing claims of entitlement. A wide cultural and legal gap is created if enforcement relies on a set of customary rules which are largely unfamiliar to the forum where that enforcement is sought. Transnationally, the scenario creates a major problem of private international law that is beyond the scope of the present work to discuss.[22] It also creates a somewhat less difficult but equally important problem in domestic courts in proving and enforcing customary law.[23] Furthermore, one can argue that the very idea of representation is colonial in framing, and that it is just a means to force indigenous communities to engage with the colonizers, often out of economic necessity.[24]

The Panama Kuna example analysed in Chapter 4 shows that different segments of a same community can feel very differently about the use of the community's heritage. In that instance, on the one hand there was the community's council exercising the role of representative of the community (an all-male body, according to the indigenous people's customary laws), and on the other there were the women of the community, who were in fact the producers of the manifestation of heritage involved in the dispute, and who felt very differently about the ways in which the community's ICH should be exploited.

[21] Sylvie Grenet and Christian Houin, 'Avant-Propos: Un Livre Politique', in Chiara Bortolotto (ed), *Le patrimoine culturel immatériel: Enjeux d'une nouvelle catégorie* (Éditions de la Maison des sciences de l'homme, 2011), 9 19 at 16; and Laurent-Sébastien Fournier, 'Le Tarasque métamorphosée', in Chiara Bortolotto (ed), *Le patrimoine culturel immatériel: Enjeux d'une nouvelle catégorie* (Éditions de la Maison des sciences de l'homme, 2011), 149 66.

[22] The proof of foreign law is already somewhat difficult in Private International Law when the law is of relatively easy access. The problem grows exponentially when the law is unknown and has to be investigated and proven by anthropologists and other experts in customary law, who must first codify the law and then make proof of it for the foreign judge. That, of course, if one is to take into account cultural identity and customary law in the resolution of Private International Law disputes. Advocating such an approach, see generally Erik Jayme, 'Identité culturelle et intégration: le droit international privé postmoderne Cours General de droit international privé', *Collected Courses of the Hague Academy of Intl L* 251 (1995), 9 268. See also Guido Westkamp, 'The Qualification of Traditional Cultural Expressions in Private International Law: A Preliminary Appraisal', in Fiona Macmillan and Kathy Bowrey (eds), *New Directions in Copyright Law, Vol 3* (Edward Elgar, 2006), 198 228.

[23] Branislav Hazucha, 'Community as a Holder of Intangible Cultural Heritage: A Broader Public Policy Perspective', in Toshiyuki Kono (ed), *Intangible Cultural Heritage and Intellectual Property: Communities, Cultural Diversity and Sustainable Development* (Intersentia, 2009), 223 44 at 238; and van Zanten, 'Prior Informed Consent', 302.

[24] Kathy Bowrey, 'Indigenous Culture, Knowledge and Intellectual Property: The Need for a New Category of Rights?', in Kathy Bowrey, Michael Handler, and Dianne Nicoll (eds), *Emerging Challenges in Intellectual Property* (Oxford University Press, 2011), 46 67 at 56 (citing Irene Watson, 'Aboriginal Sovereignties: Past, Present and Future (Im)possibilities', in Suvendrini Perera (ed), *Our Patch: Australian Sovereignties Post-2001* (API Network, 2007), 23 43 at 33).

It is of course impossible to offer a solution to this issue without stepping into the boundaries of the community's self-determination, which is ultimately the best way to resolve issues of control over ICH.[25] But the Panamanian example serves as a reminder that, at least in principle, all segments of a given community should be involved in the decision-making process leading up to the exploitation of their intangible heritage.[26] In other words, not only men and women, but also the elderly, and even children (should it be the case that the specific manifestation of heritage is performed primarily by children), ought to be involved in these decision-making processes. This notion is based on a human rights idea of participation and inclusiveness.

Once the issue of determining who the appropriate stakeholders should be is resolved, it is important to see under which status the community will be able to exercise its rights. Pieces of legislation of many countries (some analysed in Chapter 4) grant traditional communities legal personality, allowing them to appear before courts and generally to transact.[27] Another possibility is for communities to be represented by a State organ, such as the Brazilian example regarding indigenous peoples (even if such a solution is potentially very problematic in that it can strip communities of their agency if not implemented correctly). Yet another alternative is to grant these communities the same status of religious organizations, a solution which is, however, limited to instances in which ICH is of an essentially religious nature.[28]

The determination of roles to be played by each stakeholder (and the identification of the stakeholders) in transactions involving ICH can be aided by the use of guidelines enacted in the context of the Convention on Biological Diversity (CBD) relative to the use of traditional knowledge. The two most prominent of these documents are the Nagoya Protocol on Access to Genetic Resources and the Fair and Equitable Sharing of Benefits Arising from their Utilization (2010)[29] and the Bonn Guidelines on Access to Genetic Resources and Fair and Equitable Sharing of the Benefits Arising out of their Utilization (2002).[30] The European Communities played an active role in the adoption of the Bonn Guidelines.[31] Because the Bonn

[25] Posey and Dutfield, *Beyond Intellectual Property*, 64.

[26] Another example of internal divisions within a community related to the exploitation of ICH is that of the Body Shop and the Kayapó Indians of Brazil. For an analysis of this incident, see Posey and Dutfield, *Beyond Intellectual Property*, 52.

[27] This is the example of Suriname, analysed in detail in the Inter-American Court of Human Rights' judgment in the *Saramaka Community* case. See I/A Court HR, *Case of the Saramaka People v Suriname*. Preliminary Objections, Merits, Reparations, and Costs. Judgment of 28 November 2007, Series C No 172.

[28] Posey and Dutfield, *Beyond Intellectual Property*, 62 3.

[29] Nagoya Protocol on Access to Genetic Resources and the Fair and Equitable Sharing of Benefits Arising from their Utilization. As of November 2012, it had been signed by 91 States and one regional economic organization (the European Union), but only ratified by nine. According to its Art 33, the Protocol requires 50 ratifications to enter into force.

[30] Secretariat of the Convention on Biological Diversity, *Bonn Guidelines on Access to Genetic Resources and Fair and Equitable Sharing of the Benefits Arising out of their Utilization* (2002).

[31] Chidi Oguamanam, 'Documentation and Digitization of Traditional Knowledge and Intangible Cultural Heritage: Challenges and Prospects', in Toshiyuki Kono (ed), *Intangible Cultural Heritage and*

Guidelines are a kind of precursor to the Nagoya Protocol, I will start my analysis with this earlier document.

In the section titled 'key features', the Bonn Guidelines sets out a long list of restrictions to itself, indicating how contentious the process leading to their adoption probably was. These restrictions include deference to national sovereignty over natural resources, and the prevalence of national legislation.[32] The guidelines are voluntary, and prepared with the view that it must be considered they be mutually supportive in relation to other instruments (presumably including the 2003 UNESCO Convention).[33] The relationship with other regimes in a mutually supportive manner is further reinforced, and both national and international regimes, instruments, and legislation must be thought of as mutually supporting the goals of the Bonn Guidelines.[34]

The Bonn Guidelines give an important role to designated national authorities in overseeing the negotiating process leading up to the utilization of resources of traditional communities, including a check on prior and informed consent, the monitoring of compliance with agreements on benefit-sharing, and ensuring the sustainability of practices allowed by these agreements.[35] All the stakeholders in the process are given a series of responsibilities, one set for the countries of origin of the resources, one for the communities, one for the 'users' (those exploiting the resources), and another for the countries of origin of the parties exploiting the resources.[36]

The countries of origin of the resources should, among other things, ensure that the environmental consequences of activities be taken into account; that the decisions taken by the State be made available to all stakeholders, particularly traditional communities; and that measures are taken to increment traditional communities' capacity to represent their interests during negotiations. Communities in which resources originated are under the duty of only making transactions over resources they are entitled to dispose of, and to avoid imposing arbitrary restrictions on access to these resources.

Those interested in exploiting the knowledge of these communities must, among other things, seek free prior informed consent from the communities, respect the customary values and rules of these communities, respond to requests for information, ensure that the uses of their resources are only those expressly provided for in the authorization given by the communities, and guarantee evidence of prior and informed consent. And the States exercising jurisdiction over those exploiting resources must take all necessary measures (legal, administrative, or policy-based) to ensure compliance with prior informed consent, and take measures to encourage

Intellectual Property: Communities, Cultural Diversity and Sustainable Development (Intersentia, 2009), 357 83 at 364.

[32] Secretariat of the Convention on Biological Diversity, *Bonn Guidelines*, Guidelines 2 6.
[33] Secretariat of the Convention on Biological Diversity, *Bonn Guidelines*, Guideline 7.
[34] Secretariat of the Convention on Biological Diversity, *Bonn Guidelines*, Guideline 10.
[35] Secretariat of the Convention on Biological Diversity, *Bonn Guidelines*, Guideline 14.
[36] Secretariat of the Convention on Biological Diversity, *Bonn Guidelines*, Guideline 16.

the disclosure of sources of origin of traditional knowledge in applications for intellectual property rights.

The involvement of stakeholders is highlighted, and some detailed rules are offered regarding informational duties, the need for technical assistance and capacity-building, as well as the use of mediators during negotiations.[37] The Bonn Guidelines also contain detailed rules on prior informed consent and benefit-sharing, and these will be analysed in subsequent sections.

The Nagoya Protocol mirrors several key features of the Bonn Guidelines, starting with the deference to national sovereignty over natural resources and the prevalence of deference to national legislation over indicating specific solutions.[38] Most notably, the Protocol only suggests actual solutions when referring to State-State negotiations over genetic resources. When it comes to actually involving communities (which is where most of the transactions involving traditional knowledge, which is what matters for ICH purposes), there is near-total deference to domestic solutions,[39] even if the Protocol contains several provisions on the make-up and role of national authorities (similarly to the Bonn Guidelines).[40]

But the Protocol tries to establish a stronger position for itself than, for instance, the 2005 UNESCO Convention on the Diversity of Cultural Expressions (analysed in Chapter 2). While the UNESCO instrument's relationship clause essentially empties the Convention, the Nagoya Protocol's relationship clause affirms the principle of mutually supportive interpretation, and expressly says that it does not create a hierarchy with other instruments (therefore suggesting it is equal to other international instruments, unlike the 2005 UNESCO Convention, which seems to suggest it is hierarchically inferior to other instruments).[41]

It is important to note also that the Nagoya Protocol contains specific provisions on private regulation, that is, on directly involving industry stakeholders in the process of exploiting genetic resources and traditional knowledge. Regrettably, these provisions do not accomplish much in the way of requiring that contractual imbalances between communities and industry stakeholders be corrected, which turns a seemingly well-intentioned provision into a means through which to escape governmental oversight.[42] A provision on capacity-building is included in the Protocol as a means to try to correct contractual imbalances, but its effect is yet to be seen.[43]

Another important set of rules enacted under the Convention on Biological Diversity that can be helpful in broader ICH transactions are the *Akwé: Kon Guidelines* on impact assessment of 2004. These guidelines were enacted bearing in mind Article 8(j) of the CBD, which is the core provision relating to traditional knowledge, and they intend to provide a framework that ensures the full involvement of indigenous and local communities in assessing the cultural, environmental, and social impact of proposed developments on the interests and concerns of

[37] Secretariat of the Convention on Biological Diversity, *Bonn Guidelines*, Guidelines 17 21.
[38] Nagoya Protocol, Preamble. [39] Nagoya Protocol, Arts 5 6.
[40] Nagoya Protocol, Arts 13 16. [41] Nagoya Protocol, Art 4.
[42] Nagoya Protocol, Art 20. [43] Nagoya Protocol, Art 22.

traditional communities. They take into account traditional practices and knowledge as part of the impact assessment process.[44]

The guidelines propose a collaborative framework involving governments, indigenous and local communities, decision-makers, and managers of development projects. In this framework, these actors can support full and effective participation of communities, taking into account their cultural, environmental, and social concerns and interests. They take into account traditional knowledge and practices, and should be implemented taking into account other international instruments and obligations (which presumably includes taking ICH-protecting instruments into account).[45]

These rules for the ways in which a community should be involved are empty if one cannot guarantee that the community is in fact involved in the first place. The next section is devoted to the issue of ensuring community participation in ICH transactions.

7.2.2 Ensuring community participation

'Community' is a fairly vague term, but for the purposes of ICH protection it can be loosely defined as a group of people sharing history, customs knowledge, and other cultural and social expressions in sum, a group of people brought together at least partly by commonly shared intangible heritage. ICH helps the community identify its members and exclude others; more specifically, it helps the community identify who the third parties are (if any) in situations involving the use of their heritage.[46]

An important means of ensuring community participation is through cultural impact assessments, one of the objects of the *Akwé: Kon* Guidelines. The idea of promoting cultural impact assessments pre-dates these guidelines (the US case examined in Chapter 4 is one example). But it is nonetheless an important international validation of this type of assessment, which is defined in the guidelines as

> a process of evaluating the likely impacts of a proposed development on the way of life of a particular group or community, with full involvement of this group or community of people and possibly undertaken by this group or community of people; a cultural impact assess ment will generally address the impacts, both beneficial and adverse, of a proposed development that may affect, for example, the *values, belief systems, customary laws, lan guage(s), customs, economy, relationships with the local environment and particular species, social organization and traditions of the affected community*[.][47]

[44] Secretariat of the Convention on Biological Diversity, *Akwé: Kon Voluntary Guidelines for the Conduct of Cultural, Environmental and Social Impact Assessments Regarding Developments Proposed to Take Place on, or which are Likely to Impact on, Sacred Sites, and on Lands and Waters Traditionally Occupied by Indigenous and Local Communities* (2004), 1 2.

[45] Secretariat of the Convention on Biological Diversity, *Akwé: Kon Guidelines*, Guidelines 3 and 4.

[46] Hazucha and Kono, 'Conceptualization of Community', 147.

[47] Secretariat of the Convention on Biological Diversity, *Akwé: Kon Guidelines*, Guideline 6(a) (emphasis added).

The guidelines also offer a definition of a 'cultural heritage impact assessment', understood as 'a process of evaluating the likely impacts, both beneficial and adverse, of a proposed development on the physical manifestations of a community's cultural heritage including *sites, structures and remains of archaeological, architectural, historical, religious, spiritual, cultural, ecological or aesthetical value or significance*[.]'[48] This definition refers primarily to built heritage, but it takes into account the intangible values associated with it.

The guidelines state that a single assessment process should integrate cultural, environmental, and social issues.[49] It also outlines steps that should be taken into account when the developed project takes place in lands or sites that are sacred to or traditionally occupied by indigenous or local communities. These include the identification of all relevant stakeholders likely to be affected by the project, the establishment of effective consulting mechanisms that include all segments of a community, including women, youth, the elderly, and other vulnerable groups, a process of recording the views expressed by members of the community. It also determines that the community should have veto power over a project that can impact the community, and that sufficient human, financial, technical, and legal resources should be given to communities in order to ensure the effectiveness of their participation in all phases of the impact assessment process. Actors should also be identified who would be responsible for liability, redress, insurance, and compensation, and measures must be identified to prevent or mitigate negative impacts.[50]

It is interesting to note that these steps, at least inasmuch as they concern community participation, tend to individualize community members, as opposed to referring to the community as a whole. This individualization implies a disbelief in traditional indigenous agency, in which one single individual or select group of individuals speaks on behalf of the community, and advances a more inclusive model, but one that may come into conflict with perceived notions of group identity and group rights in traditional communities, while at the same time advancing individualism. When it comes to the identification of stakeholders, for instance, the guidelines suggest that a formal process is undertaken to identify all the community members, and that then a committee representative of all the segments of the community be established to advise on the impact assessment process.[51]

Specifically on cultural impact assessments, the guidelines indicate several specific factors to be considered, including impacts on the customary use of biological resources; impact on traditional knowledge; impacts on sacred sites and the associated ceremonial or ritual activities; concerns for cultural privacy (especially regarding the disclosure of sacred or secret knowledge, which then includes protec-

[48] Secretariat of the Convention on Biological Diversity, *Akwé: Kon Guidelines*, Guideline 6(b) (emphasis added).

[49] Secretariat of the Convention on Biological Diversity, *Akwé: Kon Guidelines*, Guideline 7.

[50] Secretariat of the Convention on Biological Diversity, *Akwé: Kon Guidelines*, Guideline 8.

[51] Secretariat of the Convention on Biological Diversity, *Akwé: Kon Guidelines*, Guideline 13.

tion measures and prior informed consent); impacts on customary laws (which may include the need to codify customary law, clarify matters of jurisdiction, and 'negotiate ways to minimize breaches of local laws'); and protocols to be established between the communities and the parties undertaking the developing project to facilitate the conduct of the development project and of the personnel associated with it.[52]

But the cultural dimension extends also to the other areas of impact assessment, such as the requirement for identification of religious sites in environmental assessments,[53] or the inter-generational and gender elements of social impact assessment, which again highlight the group individual tension noted above.[54] And the section of the guidelines on 'general considerations' also highlights some elements more closely related to the cultural dimension of the process, and even to ICH concerns, such as the assessment of impact over ownership, protection, and control of traditional knowledge, and the need for prior and informed consent.[55] Interestingly, legal considerations in the guidelines are always subject to the existence of a mirror requirement in national legislation (consistent with international obligations, but still the international dimension is only secondary).[56] Prior and informed consent is a requirement in the guidelines also only if national legislation in the country where the development is taking place mirrors this requirement.[57] But, as we will see below, prior and informed consent can be argued to be a general requirement of all legal systems and orders.

These guidelines make a substantial effort to include communities in the process of integrated impact assessment. However, they subordinate most of their guidelines to the existence of supporting national legislation. On the positive side, they require that individuals within a community be heard before agency can be exercised, which guarantees that all segments of a community will have a say and problems similar to Panamanian Kuna case examined in Chapter 4 will be avoided.

The connection between a community and its intangible heritage, or the link that makes a certain community feel entitled to certain claims over its heritage, be they property claims or softer aspirations at some form of control, can be justified in two ways. The first way is the idea of inheritance or legacy, meaning that communities feel entitled to their own ICH based on the idea that they simply are the biological and cultural successors of those who have created those practices in the first place. Individuals are then simply deemed as the custodians of manifestations of heritage acting on behalf of past and future generations, and these interests are to be taken into account when making decisions regarding ICH management.[58] This

[52] Secretariat of the Convention on Biological Diversity, *Akwé: Kon Guidelines*, Guidelines 27 34.

[53] Secretariat of the Convention on Biological Diversity, *Akwé: Kon Guidelines*, Guideline 37(f).

[54] Secretariat of the Convention on Biological Diversity, *Akwé: Kon Guidelines*, Guideline 43.

[55] Secretariat of the Convention on Biological Diversity, *Akwé: Kon Guidelines*, Guideline 52.

[56] Secretariat of the Convention on Biological Diversity, *Akwé: Kon Guidelines*, Guidelines 57 and 58.

[57] Secretariat of the Convention on Biological Diversity, *Akwé: Kon Guidelines*, Guideline 53.

[58] Hazucha and Kono, 'Conceptualization of Community', 148.

first justification, because it boils down to an affirmation of temporary custodianship, does not allow for property claims over heritage.

Another justification is the idea that the community is an entity different from its individual members, and that it is this collective creativity that functions in each manifestation of heritage, each social and cultural practice. In this sense, ICH is a product of the moment, less bound to the past and the future, and it is easier to assert property claims. This argument can be read as a collective version of Locke's labour theory, which is by and large the liberal justification for intellectual property rights.[59]

Regardless of the justification for a community asserting control over its heritage, the fact is that the community must always be involved, in some way. As highlighted in Chapter 2, though, community participation in decision-making processes affecting their intangible heritage is a major issue in the system created by the 2003 UNESCO Convention.[60] But this is a problem common to any system aimed at the protection of intangible heritage, at all levels.

One of the problems here is determining who the 'real' or 'qualified' representatives of a certain community or group where a certain manifestation of heritage develops are. Practice under the 2003 UNESCO Convention system shows that, in the case of manifestations of heritage belonging to an entire national group, or to a segment of society that cannot be easily identified and isolated, there are many segments that should be consulted. This type of practice is contained in the documents proving the expression of consent to inscription on the list, attached to the nomination forms.[61]

For instance, when proposing a joint nomination between Buenos Aires and Montevideo (the capitals of Argentina and Uruguay, respectively) for inscription of the Tango in the Representative List of the Intangible Heritage of Mankind, entities consulted included the Argentinean National Secretariat of Culture, the Uruguayan Ministry of Culture, the Legislative City Council of Buenos Aires, a number of citizens through a signed petition, the Uruguayan Association of Musicians, the association *Demilonga* (which calls itself the First Uruguayan Tango Forum), *Joventango*, the Uruguayan Tango Academy, the General Association of Tango Authors, the Montevideo City Legislature, and a list of Uruguayan artists and intellectuals who supported the inscription. In this example, of a manifestation of heritage that is by no means limited to a single community or even to a single nation, UNESCO considered that non-governmental entities, natural persons associated with the manifestation of heritage and the legislature (considered to be the democratic representative of the people par excellence) were the ones whose accordance was sufficient to meet the requirement of community participation and consent for inscription.

[59] Hazucha and Kono, 'Conceptualization of Community', 148 9.

[60] See also Arantes, 'Heritage as Culture', 54.

[61] All the information regarding these nominations is available as downloadable files along with the description of each element inscribed in the list. See UNESCO Intangible Heritage, *The Intangible Heritage Lists*, available at <http://www.unesco.org/culture/ich/index.php?pg=00011> (accessed 29 November 2012).

In the process leading up to the inscription of the Holy Blood Procession of Bruges (therefore, a single city, as opposed to two entire countries), the following parties showed their consent: the Flemish Commission for UNESCO, the Flemish Minister of Culture, the Noble Confraternity of the Holy Blood (who pushed for the nomination at the national level), the Arts and Heritage Agency, the Bishop of Bruges, the Governor of West-Flanders, the Town Clerk and Burgomaster of Bruges, the President of the College of Europe (located in Bruges),[62] natural persons, schools, a traditional musical group involved in the Procession, groups of expats who return to Bruges solely for the Procession (and who see in the Procession a vital part of their identity, and a main reason why they still feel attached to Belgian culture), and the *Confrérie du Saint-Sang* (another group that participates in the organizing of the Procession). For this city-level manifestation of heritage, then, bodies linked to the Executive Branch of government were asked for their assent, along with several segments of the local community and even from abroad, in an attempt to show the international relevance of the festivity.

The nomination process for the Tibetan Opera, already discussed at some length in Chapter 2, reveals a more limited effort in consulting with interested parties. On the nomination form, all there is regarding free, prior and informed consent (the rubric under which community participation is proven in the nomination forms) is the signature of a single individual who is identified as an 'inheritor of Tibetan Opera', and the stamps of two associations of Tibetan Opera. In the nomination for Chinese Sericulture and Silk Craftsmanship, however, many more actors were consulted, including the Chinese Silk Museum, provincial Departments of Culture, municipal governments, local silk museums and institutes, individuals identified as 'inheritors' of the practice, and a silk factory. This latter process, much more extensive than the Tibetan Opera, took into account several segments of society and government, mostly within the Executive Branch.

Finally, one example of a practice that can be geographically restricted is the *Candombe* Cultural Space (Uruguay). For this practice, only actual practitioners and members of the community were consulted, since there was no specific local association that could be consulted, suggesting that the range of actors to be consulted in order to create agency necessary for decision-making relative to ICH will necessarily vary in direct relationship with the geographical expansion of the manifestation of heritage.

I suggest the agency necessary for making transactions with a certain practice is largely the same as it is necessary to inscribe it in one of the lists created by the UNESCO system. That because these are essentially the same segments that are consulted for inscription in the national inventories and, to the extent I believe these inventories or repositories of cultural commons are the starting point for any negotiation regarding the use of ICH by third parties, these are also the same actors

[62] The College of Europe is an international institution (and thus not a Belgian Academic Institution), and in many ways a sister institution to the European University Institute, receiving students from numerous countries across Europe and the world. The letter of support of its President is noteworthy for indicating how the Holy Blood Procession is an important part of the College's efforts to integrate its international studentship into the Bruges local community.

who can make basic decisions regarding the use of their heritage. In this sense, a more 'local' manifestation of heritage can count on its practitioners alone (or a representative when there is one).[63] But when it comes to manifestations of heritage of larger presence, the number of actors multiplies, and representative bodies become the rule, along with 'samples' of individuals involved with the practice and non-governmental organizations and other segments of society.

This option increases transactional costs quite considerably, but at the same time it may reduce the need for transaction in the first place: the more widespread a cultural practice is, the more it belongs to the commonly shared pool of knowledge, and the less subject to appropriation it is.[64] For instance, a Tango school outside Argentina or Uruguay does not need authorization from entities in either one of these countries so it can operate. Concerns for authenticity also diminish, simply because each one of the practitioners across the wide spectrum practise this heritage differently. This makes it very difficult to determine what the authentic form actually is, and who gets to speak on behalf of this authenticity.[65] This is the moment where intangible heritage really moves into general culture. Even though it must still be protected, there is very little reason to justify a 'hard' form of protection.

The powers of agency and representation for each ICH practice vary, in inverse proportion to their reach: the more widespread a practice, the less need (or justification, for that matter) there is for proprietary control. But agency would be nothing if it was not possible to ensure that it was exercised in a free and informed manner. The next section explores this requirement.

7.3 Free, Prior, and Informed Consent

Once the issue of agency and representation has been more or less resolved, one can look at the issues relating to free, prior, and informed consent, an idea that, as one commentator points out, is very difficult to implement in practice, despite seeming natural and easy on paper.[66] Consent as a legal concept, it has been argued, is not

[63] One important factor to be taken into account regarding the existence of representative entities is the example of the PROMAYA incident. In this project, relating to the exploitation of Maya traditional culture by an outsider, an association was created by the developers of the research project themselves in order to represent the Mayan community and give free, prior, and informed consent. This entity failed to genuinely connect with the Mayan people, however, and was discredited, eventually harming the research project. For a detailed account, see Joël-David Dalibard, and Toshiyuki Kono, 'Prior Informed Consent: Empowering the Bearers of Cultural Traditions', in Toshiyuki Kono (ed) *Intangible Cultural Heritage and Intellectual Property: Communities, Cultural Diversity and Sustainable Development* (Intersentia, 2009), 247 59 at 253 8.

[64] Kojima, 'Prior Informed Consent', 314.

[65] See for instance Elazar Barkan, 'Genes and Burkas: Predicaments of Human Rights and Cultural Property', in Helaine Silverman and D Fairchild Ruggles (eds), *Cultural Heritage and Human Rights* (Springer, 2007), 184 200 at 198 (on the Muslim reaction to the Danish cartoons in 2005, and whether there can be anyone to speak on behalf of such a widespread community).

[66] Graham Dutfield, 'Prior Informed Consent and Traditional Knowledge in a Multicultural World', in Toshiyuki Kono (ed), *Intangible Cultural Heritage and Intellectual Property: Communities, Cultural Diversity and Sustainable Development* (Intersentia, 2009), 261 82 at 262.

only part of the law, but also the basis of legal authority and arguably of the legal order itself.[67] Consent can serve three core functions in a legal relationship: it can assist the consenting party to empower the party to whom consent is given; it can be a simple self-limitation of the consenting party; or it can be an act of self-empowerment by the consenting person, shifting a previously disadvantageous legal relationship through the introduction of an 'institutional rule-set'.[68]

In a contract, then, consent also plays one of three functions: it can empower the consenting subject, it can be a function of the rule-set, or it can play a corrective role within the rule-set (compensating a deficiency in the relationship, usually an imbalance in negotiating power between the parties).[69] There are three types of 'improper' consent: where the manifestation is obtained improperly, through duress or misrepresentation; where the consenting subject lacks the capacity to do so; or when the consent given does not correspond to the performance (mistake and frustration, for instance).[70] In the first group are the forms that relate to free and informed consent.

Uninformed consent, in a situation such as those involving ICH, can exist on at least two different grounds: where background positive obligations (specially of the informational type) were not fulfilled; and where there is a supervening material fact that could not reasonably be detected or known (in ICH contexts, one example would be one community contracting the use of ICH by a third party and then subsequently discovering that other communities use the same heritage, but with sacred purposes, and therefore object to the use by a third party, even though not by the first community, as it is a pre-existing, non-commercial use).[71]

The idea of 'free, prior and informed consent' (FPIC) was originally developed in the field of bioethics and medical law.[72] It was later expanded to include informational duties in consumer relations,[73] environmental issues (most notably the Basel Convention on the Control of Transboundary Movement of Hazardous Wastes and their Disposal),[74] and arguably all relationships in which one of the parties is deemed substantially more vulnerable than the other. For this reason (protecting a weaker party) FPIC is an important element of any transaction involving ICH. In fact, one can say that free and informed consent is a requirement of ethical compliance of any legal system for all consent situations.[75]

One of the big questions relating to FPIC is whether misappropriation or misuse of intangible heritage can be avoided by using it.[76] At the same time, though, it is

[67] Beyleveld and Brownsword, *Consent in the Law*, 3.

[68] Beyleveld and Brownsword, *Consent in the Law*, 83.

[69] Beyleveld and Brownsword, *Consent in the Law*, 157.

[70] Beyleveld and Brownsword, *Consent in the Law*, 158.

[71] Beyleveld and Brownsword, *Consent in the Law*, 181 2. The authors actually argue that this type of justification is available in medical and *informal* contexts. Given the specificities of ICH transactions, one may easily consider them to fall under the category of informal contracts.

[72] Dalibard and Kono, 'Prior Informed Consent', 248.

[73] Beyleveld and Brownsword, *Consent in the Law*, 184.

[74] Posey and Dutfield, *Beyond Intellectual Property*, 45; and Dutfield, 'Prior Informed Consent', 267.

[75] Beyleveld and Brownsword, *Consent in the Law*, 131.

[76] Dalibard and Kono, 'Prior Informed Consent', 247.

very difficult to incorporate FPIC in practice because the way ICH is misused is often significantly different from the way it was originally meant to be used.[77]

FPIC was originally meant to emphasize the protection of human dignity.[78] In terms of the issue of consent generally, though, there is some degree of competition among different philosophical grounds for it.[79] One account is that of utilitarianism, which argues that consent is only instrumental to the maximization of utility, but can easily be dispensed with if it fails in this maximization.[80] A second account, and probably the most common one, bases consent on a human rights-based theory according to which consent becomes the basis for human rights and for the limitations to these rights.[81] And a third account, of Kantian inspiration, expands this theory to claim that while rights are the foundation and the purpose of consent, human dignity must also always be observed and consent is necessarily invalidated if as a consequence of consenting a person agrees to a violation of his or her own dignity.[82] This duty-led approach to consent is key to FPIC, and is the one adopted here. In fact, where human dignity is involved, in most instances consent becomes immaterial.[83]

An important element of consent is the idea that a precautionary approach must be adopted to ensure the capacity and competence of the subjects giving the consent.[84] This means, first of all, that the capacity for consent must be a developed one; secondly, that the person consenting fully understands what she or he is consenting to; and thirdly, that the implications of consenting are thoroughly understood by a 'fully developed dispositional capacity'. All of this must be considered alongside a certain communicative competence.[85]

The precautionary approach translates into a careful assessment of whether the person consenting is actually an agent (in the anthropological sense), and whether the consenting subject can exercise will regarding its own rights.[86] Caution must be exercised in relation to those people who seem ostensibly to be consenting subjects, but who for any reason may be reasonably believed not to be.[87] Given the immense difficulties in determining agency (in the legal sense) and representation when it comes to ICH holders, the precautionary approach should be adopted at all times in transactions involving ICH.

In dealing with what has been referred to as 'non-ideal-typical subjects of consent', which is the case in all transactions involving intangible heritage, there are three possible alternatives. The first is substituted judgment by a judicial

[77] Kojima, 'Prior Informed Consent', 310.
[78] Dalibard and Kono, 'Prior Informed Consent', 248.
[79] Beyleveld and Brownsword, *Consent in the Law*, 27.
[80] Beyleveld and Brownsword, *Consent in the Law*, 28.
[81] Beyleveld and Brownsword, *Consent in the Law*, 30.
[82] Beyleveld and Brownsword, *Consent in the Law*, 31 2.
[83] Beyleveld and Brownsword, *Consent in the Law*, 17.
[84] Beyleveld and Brownsword, *Consent in the Law*, 96.
[85] Beyleveld and Brownsword, *Consent in the Law*, 99 100.
[86] Beyleveld and Brownsword, *Consent in the Law*, 101.
[87] Beyleveld and Brownsword, *Consent in the Law*, 104 5.

authority.[88] The second involves interferences in order to protect the consenting subject's 'best interests'[89] (generally adopted in cases of child custody, for instance, and in ICH contexts requiring more of a partnership between the State and the community, along the lines proposed above). The third includes the use of proxies[90] (a strategy adopted towards indigenous peoples in countries such as Brazil, which does not confer legal capacity to its indigenous communities and instead created a legal entity to represent indigenous peoples before the rest of society).

An important regime that has used free, prior, and informed consent in the context of access to knowledge held by traditional groups and communities is the Convention on Biological Diversity (CBD), as highlighted in Chapter 2. Even though the wording of the Convention does not include the term 'free, prior, and informed consent' anywhere, there is a provision suggesting the need to empower the communities holding traditional knowledge, which has been construed as requiring FPIC.[91] The practice of the governing body of the Convention has expanded on this concept since 2000, when it first mentioned the requirement of free, prior, and informed consent.[92] The Conference of the Parties has also determined that a few elements of ensuring compliance with FPIC include the disclosure of origin of traditional knowledge in intellectual property applications, the recognition of customary law and practices of indigenous and tribal communities, and the existence of a code of ethics to ensure FPIC and benefit-sharing.[93]

The World Intellectual Property Organization (WIPO) has also briefly addressed the issue of free, prior, and informed consent in the context of traditional cultural expressions. It has put FPIC in lines similar to authors' moral rights (analysed in Chapter 6), in saying that FPIC is similar to the right of authors not to have their work published.[94]

There are three main requirements to obtaining free, prior, and informed consent: the first one of these is that there be frank and extensive dissemination of information among the stakeholders, particularly between third parties and the community whose knowledge the outsiders want to exploit. The discharge of these informational duties is not a one-time event, and must be done continuously as the exploitation project advances, so as to guarantee that the holders of ICH act in accordance with any subsequent uses of their heritage that were not originally foreseen.[95]

One example of continuous consent is that of the rosy periwinkle.[96] A new use for this plant was discovered subsequent to the original research (and original

[88] Beyleveld and Brownsword, *Consent in the Law*, 114 17.
[89] Beyleveld and Brownsword, *Consent in the Law*, 117 19.
[90] Beyleveld and Brownsword, *Consent in the Law*, 119 21.
[91] Dalibard and Kono, 'Prior Informed Consent', 249.
[92] Dutfield, 'Prior Informed Consent', 267.
[93] Dutfield, 'Prior Informed Consent', 272.
[94] Dutfield, 'Prior Informed Consent', 275.
[95] Dalibard and Kono, 'Prior Informed Consent', 251.
[96] For a longer analysis of this case, see Dutfield, 'Prior Informed Consent', 281 2.

request for FPIC from the community). According to one commentator on this case, FPIC would have been of very little use since the discovery of other uses of the resource was only made after the original use already existed, and as a derivative to this original use.[97] I suggest that, even though it is true that the new use is derivative, it does not mean FPIC can be dispensed with. To the contrary, each use of ICH can have a very different impact on a community. Its authorization must always be sought every step of the way as every use of intangible heritage for a different purpose.[98] Naturally, in the scheme I propose in this chapter, FPIC is not a requirement in all instances, but only in those in which the requirement has been indicated in the registration of the manifestation of heritage (discussed above). Within the context of a manifestation not yet registered, registration must be sought, and it is at that point that the question of whether FPIC is required will be cleared. Naturally, if registration was not agreed to by all parties, and excluded groups only later find out about it, then consent is needed from them anew. The veracity of the register is essential for consent issues, and the question of who needs to give their consent hinges essentially on the fidelity of the registration.

Secondly, consent must be taken in accordance with a procedure that is recognized as valid by the stakeholders. This requirement has already been discussed in the previous section, but it generally means that customary practices must be followed (even though, as highlighted above, the participation of the largest possible number of segments of the community must also be sought).[99] This means not only that consent must be obtained, but that the trust from communities must be obtained,[100] and that requests for confidentiality and cultural privacy are respected.[101] The third requirement is that of benefit-sharing, which will be the subject of the following section.[102]

The Bonn Guidelines on access and benefit-sharing mentioned above offer a very detailed set of rules about obtaining FPIC. They require: '[l]egal certainty and clarity'; '[a]ccess to [traditional] resources should be facilitated at a minimum cost'; '[r]estrictions on access to genetic resources should be transparent, based on legal grounds, and not run counter to the objectives of the [Convention on Biological Diversity]'; and '[c]onsent of the relevant national authority(ies) in the provider country. The consent of relevant stakeholders, such as indigenous and local communities, as appropriate to the circumstances and subject to domestic law, should also be obtained'.[103] Note the prevalence of sovereignty and national authorities as the competent organs to consent to the use of resources. This is reflective of the prevalence of sovereignty over resources, which is a key feature of the Bonn Guidelines, as indicated above.

97 Dutfield, 'Prior Informed Consent', 282 (showing concern that FPIC can have a chilling effect on research and innovation).
98 van Zanten, 'Prior Informed Consent', 298.
99 Dalibard and Kono, 'Prior Informed Consent', 252.
100 Kojima, 'Prior Informed Consent', 311.
101 van Zanten, 'Prior Informed Consent', 287.
102 Dalibard and Kono, 'Prior Informed Consent', 252.
103 Secretariat of the Convention on Biological Diversity, *Bonn Guidelines*, Guideline 26.

The elements of prior informed consent, according to the Bonn Guidelines, include: '[c]ompetent authority(ies) granting or providing for evidence of prior informed consent'; '[t]iming and deadlines'; '[s]pecification of use'; '[p]rocedures for obtaining prior informed consent'; '[m]echanism for consultation of relevant stakeholders'; and process.[104] The competent authority or authorities to grant prior informed consent must be determined in accordance with national legislation, which may require the involvement of different levels of government.[105] Traditional communities and other holders of traditional knowledge must also be consulted and their consent obtained in accordance with their traditional practices and domestic laws.[106]

Several procedures must be observed to obtain prior informed consent, according to the Bonn Guidelines. Some of these steps (a list that, according to the text of the Guidelines, is indicative and must be subject to national legislation) are accurate information regarding the intended use, an explanation on the benefits that could come from the exploitation (commercial or otherwise) of the resource by the interested party, and an indication of benefit-sharing arrangements and of the treatment to be given to confidential information.[107]

The Nagoya Protocol, a more recent set of guidelines, contains only one provision on free, prior, and informed consent, which largely applies only to State-State transactions. It highlights the need to provide for 'legal certainty, clarity and transparency'; 'fair and non-arbitrary rules and procedures'; and a 'clear and transparent written decision'. The one part of this provision concerning communities simply states that communities should be involved and also give free, prior, and informed consent, but 'subject to domestic legislation', a qualification which weakens the provision.[108]

If these requirements, principles, and procedure are observed, free, prior, and informed consent can work in favour of empowering the communities, those giving the consent. But at the same time, the excessive weight given to State sovereignty (who have more authority over the resources than do the communities) is cause for concern. If State interests are restricted to natural resources involved in exploitation and reserve the control over the associated knowledge (which is the intangible heritage in question), then these rules may be more useful in terms of empowering communities. They may also be transplanted to broader ICH contexts (where natural and genetic resources are of secondary importance).

Free, prior, and informed consent is an important element for the use of intangible heritage by parties not belonging to the community of origin of the manifestation of heritage. But it is by no means a fix-all solution, and it must be considered carefully. There are many shortcomings too, especially with regard to

[104] Secretariat of the Convention on Biological Diversity, *Bonn Guidelines*, Guideline 27.
[105] Secretariat of the Convention on Biological Diversity, *Bonn Guidelines*, Guideline 29.
[106] Secretariat of the Convention on Biological Diversity, *Bonn Guidelines*, Guideline 31.
[107] Secretariat of the Convention on Biological Diversity, *Bonn Guidelines*, Guideline 36.
[108] Nagoya Protocol, Art 6(3).

traditional communities.[109] Many of these problems are related to benefit-sharing, which is a financial issue that will be looked at in the next section of this chapter.

7.4 Financial Issues

This section is about the sharing of benefits arising from the commercial exploitation of intangible heritage. One of the issues is the payment of royalties for the use of ICH when such heritage is propertized.

Discussion about financial issues may also refer to benefits that arise from non-commercial uses that develop into commercial ones, such as ethnomusicology recordings that, even though made for the purposes of research, are later sold (a great example being the UNESCO 'Collection of Traditional Music of the World' series),[110] or just non-commercial uses. In the former case, however, one must bear in mind the difference between the expectations of communities, who sometimes believe they will accrue significant royalties for the sale of their music, and the actual market for this type of music, from which royalty payments or profit seldom derive.[111]

In the case of recordings made for scientific purposes only, it has been reported that, at least in the field of ethnomusicology, it is common practice to pay musicians for their work in performing for the recordings, which is often acceptable to most communities and in most contexts (a situation covered by the Performances Treaty, analysed in Chapter 6). The payment also helps reinforce the trust between the researcher and the sources, which ensures the validity of the data obtained.[112] The payment can be given either directly to the musicians, or to the community itself.[113] The latter is often appropriate as musicians may consider themselves to be simply performing their duties towards their community and/or to have no property entitlement of any sort over the ICH.

Another important issue is that of contracting payment for the use of music that is considered sacred and therefore *res extra commercium*. In many cases, payments can still be made to the communities not under the title of royalties, but for other purposes (such as purchase of lands, construction of infrastructure, and so on). This creates a problem of proof of payment, as the receipts for the transfer of values will not contain a reference to payment for intellectual property rights.[114]

One must also consider the financial sustainability of any system for the administration of intangible heritage. A system for the administration of cultural commons, either run by the government or non-governmental institutions, is often not self-sustainable. This is because it does not accrue sufficient resources directly from fees

[109] van Zanten, 'Prior Informed Consent', 306.

[110] UNESCO Intangible Heritage, *UNESCO Collection of Traditional Music of the World*, available at <http://www.unesco.org/culture/ich/index.php?pg=00123> (accessed 29 November 2012).

[111] van Zanten, 'Prior Informed Consent', 289.

[112] van Zanten, 'Prior Informed Consent', 284.

[113] van Zanten, 'Prior Informed Consent', 290.

[114] van Zanten, 'Prior Informed Consent', 297.

related to the exploitation of ICH to even sustain its own administrative operations, let alone to share these benefits with the concerned communities.[115] Even though the priority in the distribution of the benefits should probably be to return them to the communities, rather than use all the money in the administrative maintenance of the system, the system must also be maintained with at least some funds of its own. In the same way as with intellectual property royalties, it is natural that some of these royalty payments go to the institution that administers these payments and makes it possible for those exploiting ICH to be charged for this use in the first place.

However, as with many things related to culture, royalties for ICH should not be thought of as self-sustaining business enterprises. If they happen to evolve into thriving commercial successes, that is most welcome. However, the State (through its own resources or through international assistance), should be willing to step in and cover financial gaps to maintain such systems for the administration of heritage. There are several values associated with ICH (such as the formation and continuation of national political identity, but also cultural diversity as a value to be protected in multicultural and intercultural constitutional frameworks) which justify its protection beyond its financial sustainability.[116]

The Bonn Guidelines discussed above contain a series of provisions relating to benefit-sharing. Benefits may be accrued in favour of traditional knowledge communities of origin, including short-term, medium-term, and long-term benefits.[117] These benefits should be distributed in a fair and equitable manner with all those that have contributed to the management of the resource and its successful commercialization, thus extending the range of beneficiaries also to governmental and non-governmental bodies and academic institutions, aside from the communities of origin.[118] These measures help ensure the continuation of the system, as all actors can share in the benefits and use the resources for the maintenance of their activities.

The Nagoya Protocol, in turn, contains a provision on monetary and non-monetary benefits in an Annex.[119] The monetary benefits include access fees, royalties, milestone payments, licence fees, special fees to trust funds involved in conservation and sustainable use of biodiversity, research funding, and joint ownership of intellectual property rights.

Some of the monetary benefits that may be gained in ICH transactions include access fees, up-front payments, milestone payments (that is, partial payments for each phase of the development of a project), the payment of royalties, licensing fees

[115] Hazucha, 'Community as a Holder', 243.

[116] Hazucha, 'Community as a Holder', 235. He mentions the particular importance of what he calls *non-use* values, including the *bequest value* (the benefit of preserving ICH for future generations), the *option value* (the benefit of members from other communities who have the option to get acquainted with each other's heritages), and the *existence value* (the value of simply having a preserved body of ICH). One must also consider the values mentioned in Chapter 1.

[117] Secretariat of the Convention on Biological Diversity, *Bonn Guidelines*, Guideline 47.

[118] Secretariat of the Convention on Biological Diversity, *Bonn Guidelines*, Guideline 48.

[119] Nagoya Protocol, Annex.

in case of commercialization, special fees to be paid to trust funds for the general conservation of ICH, salaries for those directly involved in the process, and joint ownership of relevant intellectual property rights.[120] But there are also non-monetary benefits that must be considered in balance with financial issues. These include, for traditional communities, the construction of necessary infrastructure as seen above in the ethnomusicology example.

Contractual approaches for the protection of ICH, while promoting the commodification of heritage (since a transaction over ICH is necessarily an assertion of control over it, which implies commodification to a certain extent), are also the ones which empower communities the most, without necessarily creating property interests that may in the long run stifle cultural development, and without necessarily imposing a large legal framework that is foreign to many indigenous and traditional communities. It also allows for the acknowledgment of the important group dimension of ICH, as transactions are done with the community as a whole or with agents on behalf of the community.

There are many requirements to be taken into account. While this chapter has been an attempt at universalizing some of these requirements, they invariably contrast with and so are trumped by the customary law of some communities. But all things considered, it may be that contractual approaches offer the necessary legal tools for safeguarding community interests regarding their intangible heritage.

[120] See, *mutatis mutandis*, Secretariat of the Convention on Biological Diversity, *Bonn Guidelines*, App II.

8
Conclusions

The preceding chapters show that there is a wide array of possibilities that can be employed for the safeguarding of intangible cultural heritage (ICH). Safeguarding is an important verb to indicate the protection of heritage. It means non-encapsulation of heritage, not imposing defined contours that may provide full legal protection but that also ossify heritage and freeze it in time. Rather, safeguarding means constructing a protective cocoon around heritage, allowing it to grow and develop. At the same time it is a kind of permeable capsule, one that allows for cultural exchanges and flows and is important for the development of heritage.

The dichotomy between tangible and intangible heritage is important, but to a great extent this dichotomy is artificial and does not offer an accurate portrayal of cultural heritage and the rationale for its protection in all of its dimensions. While this limitation is true, it is important to note that the discourse of heritage scholars and professionals will be invariably biased (as is probably also my own, in the position of a scholar writing on the legal safeguarding of intangible heritage). Nowadays it tends to converge into a view that acknowledges a symbiotic concept of heritage incorporating tangible and intangible elements.

This symbiosis translates into the different regimes analysed throughout the book. While some regimes have focused exclusively on the protection of intangible heritage, more often than not there has been a greater concern with achieving an integrated approach to heritage protection.

One way to choose the most appropriate tools among those discussed here is to first determine the goal that it is hoped will be advanced through protecting intangible heritage (assuming that there is no inherent value to cultural heritage). If development is prioritized, perhaps trade arrangements and schemes that in substance largely commodify intangible heritage (including intellectual property tools) are the best way to go.

If fostering national identity is the objective, then inventories, lists, and other tools that dispense with the individual dimension of creativity and look at it mostly as part of a collective sense of identity and creativity might be preferred mechanisms. The tools offered by UNESCO and several national schemes provide for this.

If protection of identity at a more intimate level is most important, either group identity of non-majoritarian groups or even individual identity, regimes for protection of minorities and human rights law generally might come in to play. Though not necessarily originally designed to protect cultural distinctiveness, these regimes have all evolved in that direction. The multiplicity of possible goals for protection, and what they may imply in terms of legal tools, is further explained through the flowchart in the Appendix. There, by asking the question of what goal one hopes to achieve through intangible heritage, one can be led into the multiple possible solutions, and ultimately choose the most appropriate for advancing the goal, be it identity, development, regional integration, or simply the advancement of tourism.

That possible justifications (and legal mechanisms) for safeguarding intangible heritage are multiple does not mean that all are equally valuable. In my view, many of these justifications may not amount to anything more than a means to bring a certain regime into play, not in themselves sufficient goals. For instance, trade and development are salutary goals, and have the power of triggering the machineries of economic regional integration processes. At the same time, these goals by themselves can result in the excessive folklorization of intangible heritage, making all practices that lead to its protection product-oriented. ICH may be irretrievably commodified and its very existence threatened. On the other hand, national solutions of the 'fragmented' type, while constituting the majority of countries and sometimes quite effective, should not be thought of as more than temporary arrangements while more tailored solutions are designed. In relying on these arrangements as permanent solutions, implementing actors (generally the State, but also its smaller units cities, provinces and states and also non-governmental entities that operate in such legal environment) tend to lose sight of why safeguarding must be promoted in the first place, by whom, and for whom.

ICH must be protected because it is an essential element of identity. This is perhaps the most relational of values that can be tied to ICH, but at the same time it is the most important of all. Heritage only becomes so when one relates to it, when the experience of a given heritage triggers in a person sentiments of being, of belonging, of completeness. Any other justification behind the protection of heritage is only accessory and, while it can be successfully exploited as a means to trigger legal mechanisms, it must always be borne in mind that heritage is about individual and group identity.

From this assertion it follows that ICH must be safeguarded for the communities where it comes from. To safeguard for any other beneficiary means the beginning of the end of such heritage; if one cannot connect heritage to its source it may disappear or become part of the past. It risks not being the living culture that is what made it so important in the first place.

But to whom does the duty to safeguard ICH fall? To say it is 'everyone's' duty is nearly equivalent to saying it is 'no one's'. At the same time, all that has been said about means of protection so far indicates that, unless a large number of actors are involved, any effort is bound to fail, either by not connecting with the heritage, or by strangling it by cutting it out of its roots. If the 'fragile flowers of difference' that are certain manifestations of heritage are transplanted in some ways, they die. Forcing a shift from their natural growing grounds to a different one, or, more often than not, to a flower pot (that is, to a new and controlled environment) can only have the effect of preventing it from growing, of changing its interaction with the world, of suffocating its roots.

As argued in Chapter 7, it is for the State to be at the forefront of safeguarding intangible cultural heritage. As the protector of its populations, it is for the State to guarantee that the identities of these populations are allowed to flourish. But State action must be necessarily concerned with the communities. The State must move beyond its classic paternalistic role of assuming it knows what is best for its populations through the mechanisms of representative democracy. Rather, because we are talking about manifestations of heritage that are sometimes restricted to small communities, these communities must be directly involved, as representative democracy is not guaranteed to be able to take their interests fully into account. In addition to community involvement, the involvement of other institutions and organizations outside of the State is important. These can offer the expertise to effectively exploit mechanisms within the State to make sure the interests of communities are taken into account.

There are risks associated with this large role of the State, of course, as the example of the Tibetan Opera shows, but the potentially overwhelming and oppressive presence of the State can be counterbalanced with (1) international remedies, such as the human rights mechanisms surveyed in Chapter 5; and, most importantly, (2) ensuring wide community participation in the design of national laws and policies and also in the international fora concerned with intangible heritage, such as the UNESCO system and the OAS negotiations towards a declaration on the rights of indigenous peoples.

When it comes to the articulation of these ideas, there are two main levels of action to be explored: the international/regional (the State as the leading actor around which legal protection issues are articulated), and the national/supranational (beyond the State, with the communities as the main focal point). At the international/regional level, the main mechanism that must be looked at, with a view of safeguarding ICH as a means of protecting identity, is the listing mechanism of the UNESCO Convention (which can be emulated by other organizations).

The UNESCO System is central for the safeguarding of intangible heritage despite its many shortcomings. Its listing mechanism has been much criticized for its lack of teeth, and for simply 'parading' heritage as opposed to offering means for its protection. At the same time, though, it is an important step, even if it falls short of fully-fledged legal protection (which, as noted above, is not always desirable). It is an important step because it brings intangible heritage to the fore, and it fosters debate about the existence of this heritage, giving it an added value internally that would not be achievable if it were not for the international attention.

Struggles over heritage often showcase deeper underlying political issues, especially when it comes to the recognition of cultural minorities, who may or may not have political agendas. It is important that communities have a say in every initiative that involves their heritage so that the necessary control can be asserted by the community. The much-dreaded commodification of heritage can then become a tool in favour of the involved groups, as it can also serve to empower them. On the other hand, the State can also make use of this commodification process to assert control over the meanings to be attributed to such heritage, ultimately making them devoid of any political content.

The experience of UNESCO with the Intangible Heritage Convention can be interpreted through these two different sets of lenses. On the one hand, communities are required to be involved in the preparation of nominations for the UNESCO lists. Ultimately, however, it is the State who determines which manifestations of heritage in its territory are even worth being considered in the first place. The several layers of sovereignty in the UNESCO system for ICH protection seem to be a rather cumbersome obstacle for the international validation of political claims through the assertion of cultural distinctiveness. As the Committee's practice evolves, however, it seems that community participation at the international level will increase and the States can become more deferential to communities and their cultural claims. In its original form the system could not offer communities enough safeguarding. Its first reform has already taken important steps in strengthening the role of communities in heritage management, and ultimately the protection the system gives to intangible heritage. It is still not a sufficiently strong system, but it is moving in the right direction.

Both political and economic regional integration schemes regard the protection of intangible heritage as a desirable goal of integration. Much of this rhetoric, especially at the political level, has been articulated as a human rights concern, particularly in the OAS (with the link between intangible heritage and indigenous rights) and the Council of Europe (with the Faro Convention that creates a non-enforceable collective right to heritage). The African Union has also taken important steps towards acknowledging the importance of intangible heritage for the identity and strengthening of the region, even if their most recent instrument is yet to come into force.

Because the goals of integration are slightly different with respect to economic regionalism, so is the justification for protecting intangible heritage within it. The Andean Community seems to be primarily concerned with the development potential of exploring ICH (seen predominantly as traditional knowledge with biotechnological applications). And the EU, as a matter of policy, deals with cultural heritage in terms of development aid, especially in the EU's external relations. By fostering programmes in its partner countries for the protection of heritage, the EU attempts to build an appropriate environment for responsible and sustainable development, respecting cultural diversity and creating opportunities for cultural tourism in the region. It must be noted that, in doing this, the EU has been criticized for imposing a determined set of values in the selection of heritage 'worth protecting' (that is, in the selection of the programmes it will support, and also interference in the management of the programmes it has selected). It also builds, in a way, upon the creation of a common European heritage, even if only prospectively, considering the beneficiaries of these programmes are more often than not accession States. There are some perils associated with development aid in the field of intangible heritage, mostly because cultural promotion is not a priority area of investment and of the fungibility of aid resources. Tools to counter this shortcoming are being developed, though, and community involvement is critical for ensuring the effectiveness of aid in intangible heritage safeguarding.

On the level of internal policy, however, the EU seems to be more cautious in terms of interfering with each Member State's policy and legal choices. While the provisions on culture of the Treaties preclude the harmonization of laws in the area, the Lisbon Treaty creates the means for protecting ICH through intellectual property.

Cultural heritage is an important international concern and it should not be left in all cases to the States, as it forms part of the 'common heritage of mankind'. However, since the EU Treaties have chosen to leave culture within this reserved domain, it is necessary to find different means and a different justification for the protection of cultural heritage within the EU.

As cultural heritage is part of the subject-matter of intellectual property, especially copyright law, and it can negatively affect the functioning of the internal market, it can be regulated under the EU's new mandate for harmonizing intellectual property laws. While these laws need to observe some specificities of cultural heritage, there are examples of their successful use and the EU legislator can draw inspiration from these. Even though protection can only be built on justifications that are not directly relevant to cultural heritage and subordinate cultural heritage to the mandates of economic freedoms, what is important is that the EU legislator has a tool to protect heritage, even if only indirectly.

The national/supranational dimension of ICH safeguarding means looking beyond the State to where the communities themselves (with or without the assistance of other non-governmental entities) bring forth their own interests related to their intangible heritage. The supranational dimension of ICH is an even more recent topic than that of ICH protection in general. But it is also a very fertile terrain to develop innovative and effective tools for addressing ICH concerns.

In many ways, this supranational dimension of ICH protection should be thought of as 'State +', that is, the involvement of actors other than the State in the international regulation and protection of ICH. The contractual approaches and the solutions explored in Chapter 7 can easily be adapted to a supranational environment. Ideally they should be, as much of the potential harm to intangible heritage is in misappropriation on an international level (for instance, across jurisdictions). Domestic law is generally in a better position to address these issues as a matter of torts or intellectual property (when it comes to remedies), but there is very little that is currently in force internationally to deal with instances of misappropriation.

The international obligations upon the States to safeguard intangible heritage are restricted to the heritage within a State's territory, and from the plain language of some of the provisions of the ICH Convention it does not naturally follow that each State has the obligation to safeguard intangible heritage that is not from its territory. However, if the preamble of the ICH Convention, and the idea that safeguarding ICH is of concern to the whole of humankind are taken into account, the necessary values are in place to make States spring into action to promote the transnational protection of intangible heritage.

This transnational protection must involve other actors as well as States. One of the reasons for this suggestion is that there is no clear obligation upon States to create such a transnational regulatory network. Another is that initiatives for ICH protection must always take into account and actively involve the communities and NGOs that can assist communities in overcoming any informational deficits towards States and third parties interested in exploiting ICH.

I suggest that this transnational network takes into account the principles and rules laid down in Chapter 7, and adopts a system that acts as a facilitator for contact between ICH holders and third parties. This ought to privilege communities as the holders of intangible heritage. This bias is necessary to make sure that ICH is respected at all times and put front and centre in the activities of such a network. In this way communities may ensure the viability and continuity of ICH for the future (and may also assist with the continuity of the network).

This model implies, for instance, dealing with issues of agency/representation, and free, prior, and informed consent. Regarding the former, basic principles of representation and legal agency must be drawn from the customary rules of the communities themselves, as they are the only ones who can actually determine how their members feel best represented. Alongside these customary rules, though, some ideas from human rights practice should be incorporated, in the sense of not excluding any sector of a given community from such representativeness, and trying to ensure the widest possible participation of all members of a community.

And when it comes to free, prior, and informed consent, once issues of representation and agency have been taken care of, it is easy that the representatives of the community be ready to show consent to the exploitation of their heritage. But one must also bear in mind at this stage that there is often a power imbalance between the community and any third parties wishing to exploit their ICH, partly because of sheer economic power. Most importantly this is because the legal universe in which these transactions occur is that of the exploiter, not of the community. The community's legal rules play a smaller part in agency, and generally form part of the 'factual background' of the legal transaction. They are not the main set of applicable rules. This imbalance may be overcome with the assistance of the State and non-governmental entities on the side of the community. This is another reason why the pro-community bias suggested above is so important.

Another instance of this supranational dimension of ICH is when the State is a threat to ICH, and that is resolved internationally through human rights mechanisms. Human rights, incidentally, seem to be the common thread of all attempts at safeguarding ICH. Much is spoken of a 'human rights to heritage'. But how can this right be articulated? Is it a corollary to the human right to identity, which can be individualized, or are we talking about a different, essentially collective, human right?

I suggest that, to the extent heritage has no intrinsic value and is actually instrumental to advancing other goals there is no separate, enforceable human right to the protection of cultural heritage, at least within the existing framework where only individual rights are enforceable internationally. The protection of cultural heritage, particularly of the intangible kind, is a duty of all States towards communities. It cannot be successfully translated into individual entitlements unless one speaks of heritage as a vehicle for identity (and thus turns any heritage claim into a claim for identity protection).

The link to human rights is very present, though, and useful. To a large extent, the rhetoric of rights helps give intangible heritage the necessary international legitimacy for it to seek international protection.

The protection of cultural heritage, from a human rights law perspective, is instrumental for the protection of culture, identity, and ultimately dignity. Therefore, it is only to be expected that this field of law has been influenced by human rights law, an influence that can be seen particularly in the shift from 'cultural property' to 'cultural heritage' as a legal category.

Further, given the proximity of cultural heritage to human rights law, the fact that institutional arrangements for the protection of human rights have developed to the point of finding ways to protect manifestations of culture and ways of life is a compelling reason why resources must be made available for the protection of elements of cultural heritage. Some solutions may provide the necessary tools for implementing this suggestion in practice.

Even though the use of human rights mechanisms imposes a certain narrowing of the goals to be attained by protecting ICH, the protection of cultural identity and human rights is a powerful reason justifying the protection of intangible heritage. And, while the external limitation imposed by the 'individual versus group rights' tension plays a role, this role must not be overestimated.

The use of institutional mechanisms for the international protection of human rights seems to be a good means of protecting ICH internationally. At present this does not exist under regime-specific arrangements (such as the UNESCO framework). The array of rights currently protected by institutional mechanisms at the international level seems sufficient to address most ICH-related concerns, and the fact that there are internal limitations to these rights helps balance conflicting interests that are always at play when talking about ICH.

Another group of scenarios that moves beyond the State is when communities try to articulate their heritage concerns within the realm of each State. This articulation happens, for instance, at the domestic level where a large plethora of solutions exist. This variety of choices of legal tools does not mean that anything goes, and that States can pretend to be meeting their duty to safeguard intangible heritage through just about anything. Countries have generally moved towards the recognition of intangible heritage as a legal good worth protecting. Even in those countries which have failed to adopt regimes, intangible concerns are still taken into account through other mechanisms, or simply because it is an undeniable fact that tangible and intangible heritage are inextricably connected. Thus all legislation protecting cultural heritage will, even if only indirectly, also pay some attention to intangible heritage concerns.

Countries that have so far failed to adopt specific regimes, however, must bear in mind that where other tools can be used to protect intangible heritage, this must be seen as a temporary state of affairs only. Specific regimes are necessary. Regimes must be both preventative, in the sense of creating an environment that allows communities to control their own heritage and prevent cultural harm from occurring in the first place, and also remedy-oriented, creating conditions for the redressing of such harm. This follows also from the legal maxim according to which where there is a right, there is a remedy (*ubi jus, ibi remedium*).

When it comes to offering remedies for the protection of intangible heritage against misappropriation by third parties, there are two main avenues of protection: human rights law (domestically translated) and intellectual property.

In domestic practice, human rights law generally translates into tort actions, which are an important means of redressing harm generally. That there are tort remedies connected to the broader category of personality rights, or just a general tort rule for personal injury, should usually be enough to guarantee that remedies are available also domestically to redress cultural harm caused by the misappropriation of intangible heritage. Legislation on safeguarding intangible heritage should make clear that these remedies are available, and, where they are not, create them. Should domestic legislation fail, international human rights law may again become a useful tool, through the human rights to a remedy, recognized by all human rights adjudicatory and quasi-adjudicatory bodies.

Torts can also be an important part of intellectual property claims (particularly in civil law jurisdictions). But there are other specific features to this type of solution that make it appealing. In relation to intellectual property, the commodification of intangible heritage probably reaches its peak when one speaks of its protection through intellectual property mechanisms. However, to the extent that commodification can be translated into control and empowerment, the use of intellectual property mechanisms can have positive effects in some cases.

The language of human rights is again present in this area of protection of intangible heritage, as is the idea of overlapping regimes. The fact that a public interest-oriented instrument such as the Universal Copyright Convention was the determining factor in the passing of intellectual property protection as a human right in the ICESCR can be read as meaning that the tension between intellectual property as a private right and the public value of cultural exchange has been present since the beginning of these debates.

That is to say, even though intellectual property can serve the protection of intangible heritage in some circumstances, it is a set of tools that must not be abused. The over-use of intellectual property mechanisms in this sense can create an excessive number of access barriers to intangible heritage ultimately forcing creators not to use it which would eventually result in the disappearance of much of this heritage.

The opposite idea, that all intangible heritage belongs to the public domain, also has shortcomings. It fails to take into account the value of the attachment of certain communities to their heritage. In this sense, placing intangible heritage in the public domain does not consider religious and cultural harm that can arise from the use of this heritage by third parties (which they are free to do, according to the rules of the public domain).

The idea of commons seems to be the most appealing option. It does not automatically make intangible heritage freely available to anyone interested but it gives custodial communities the opportunity to exercise some form of control over the uses of their own heritage, and to make sure that cultural sensitivities are respected and that certain elements of their heritage remain out of reach from third parties.

The balancing between private intellectual property and public access to cultural commons would then be as follows. When cultural feelings close to the core of identity of a certain community are involved in a certain manifestation of heritage, then this heritage should be protected by the strongest form of protection available in this spectrum, that is, intellectual property monopolies that enable the copyright holders to exclude third parties. When the manifestations of heritage are still important and unique to a certain community, they should be regulated through the language of commons, which guarantees some oversight and that the communities will be properly acknowledged when their heritage is used by third parties. And finally, when the heritage is not related to religious feelings or for any other reason too important or unique to the community in question, the intangible heritage should simply be in the public domain, and the State will be in charge of protecting basic standards of integrity and attribution.

This proposed scheme disregards the economic aspects of the use of intangible heritage. But these concerns are secondary, and can still be regulated through each of these tools. Licensing fees are available in the case of intellectual property holders, for instance. In this case, though, licensing should not be available, as intellectual property tools are only to be used to completely exclude third parties from accessing intangible heritage that touches upon cultural/religious feelings. The public domain can be converted into a *domaine public payant*, and the regulated commons can institute licensing fees, to be used for the safeguarding and perpetuation of intangible heritage as the source of cultural diversity it is.

And the idea of contractual approaches to ICH protection responds to these concerns. These approaches can be incorporated either as a domestic matter, or as a transnational regulatory issue, as outlined above. Contractual approaches also create the preventive structure that can oversee the uses of intangible heritage by third parties and foster a controlled environment where cultural flows happen while respecting cultural sensitivities (where they exist). While they promote some form of commodification of heritage, this commodification is by no means as totalizing as that promoted through the use of intellectual property mechanisms. But an assertion of power definitely happens here. With the help of some basic tools, including respect for the customary law of communities outside of mainstream society and the observance of important general rules regarding agency and consent, power may be given to communities, to those producing ICH and concerned with its perpetuation.

If applied correctly, contractual approaches can incorporate lessons learned and tools from all other types of experience and avoid the pitfalls of intangible heritage protection. In this sense, even though their promise is still to be fulfilled, and they are still largely subsidiary solutions, contractual approaches (particularly in their transnational version) should be used as a framework for the safeguarding of ICH in international law.

Appendix The Flowchart of Living Heritage

The Flowchart of Living Heritage

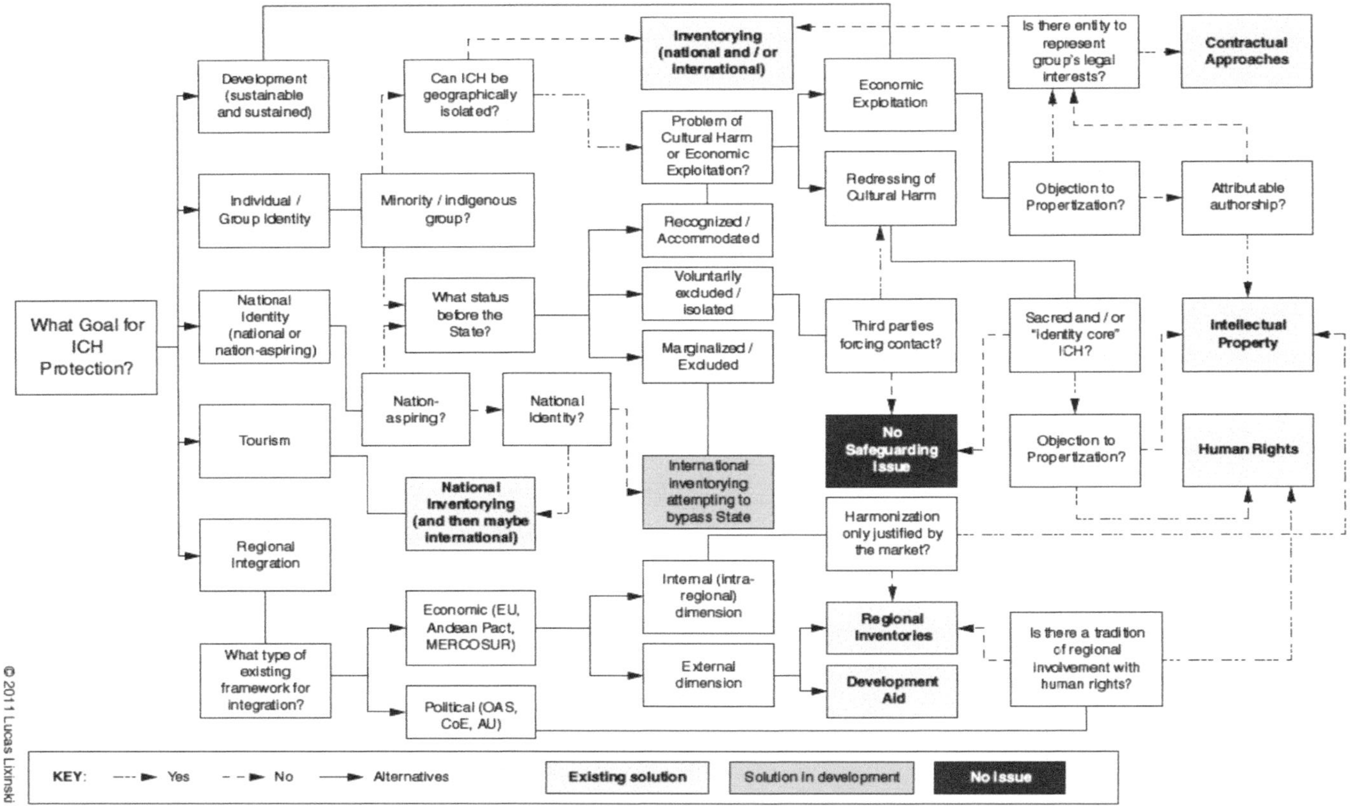

References

Adolfo, Luiz Gonzaga Silva, 'Considerações sobre o Direito Moral do Autor', *Revista da ABPI* 44 (2000), 3 13.

African Union, *Africa, Our Common Destiny Guideline Document prepared by the Commission of the African Commission* (2004).

African Union, *Aide Memoire to the First Pan African Cultural Congress, 13 15 November 2006, Addis Ababa, Ethiopia, General Theme: 'Culture, Integration and African Renaissance'*.

Aguilar, Alonso, *Pan Americanism from Monroe to the Present: A View from the Other Side* (Monthly Review Press, 1968).

Aikawa, Noriko, 'The UNESCO *Recommendation on the Safeguarding of Traditional Culture and Folklore (1989)*: Actions Undertaken by UNESCO for Its Implementation', in Peter Seitel (ed), *Safeguarding Traditional Culture: A Global Assessment* (Smithsonian Institution, 2001), 13 19.

Aikawa Faure, Noriko, 'From the Proclamation of Masterpieces to the *Convention for the Safeguarding of Intangible Cultural Heritage*', in Laurajane Smith and Natsuko Agakawa (eds) *Intangible Heritage* (Routledge, 2009), 1 44.

Albornoz, Orlando (March 2007), 'Relaciones entre Cultura y Desarrollo, informe presentado al Programa Regional Interamericano de Cultura Oficina de Asuntos Culturales', *Workshop on Case Studies in the Protection of Cultural Heritage Central American Region*, available at <http://portal.oas.org/Portal/Topic/SEDI/Educaci%C3%B3nyCultura/Cultura/TemasPrioritarios/Preservaci%C3%B3nyProtecci%C3%B3ndelPatrimonioCultural/Activities/ProtegiendoelPatrimonioCultural/tabid/1447/language/en US/Default.aspx> (accessed 29 November 2012).

Álvarez Molinero, Natalia, *Pueblos indígenas y derecho de autodeterminación. ¿Hacia un derecho internacional multicultural?* (Universidad de Deusto, 2008).

Alvarez, José E., *International Organizations as Law Makers* (Oxford University Press, 2006).

Alvez, Vânia de Fátima Noronha, *O Corpo Lúdico Maxakali: Segredos de um 'Programa de Índio'* (C/ Arte, 2003).

Amando, Migue, and Lipzyc, Delia, 'Bienes inmateriales', in Diego Fernández Arroyo (ed) *Derecho Internacional Privado de los Estados del Mercosur* (Zavalia, 2003), 903 36.

Anderson, Jane E., *Law, Knowledge, Culture: The Production of Indigenous Knowledge in Intellectual Property Law* (Edward Elgar, 2009).

Andrews, Charlotte, Viejo Rose, Dacia, Baillie, Britt, and Morris, Benjamin, 'Conference Report: Tangible Intangible Cultural Heritage: A Sustainable Dichotomy? The 7th Annual Cambridge Heritage Seminar', *Intl J of Intangible Heritage* 2 (2007), 124 9.

Aparo, Nimia, 'Derechos fundamentales de los pueblos indígenas', in *Los Pueblos Indígenas y la Integración Andina Primer Foro de Intelectuales e Investigadores Indígenas* (Comunidad Andina, 2008), 56 8.

Appadurai, Arjun, 'Introduction: Commodities and the Politics of Value', in Arjun Appadurai (ed), *The Social Life of Things: Commodities in Cultural Perspective* (Cambridge University Press, 1986), 3 63.

Arantes, Antonio A., 'Heritage as Culture: Limits, Uses and Implications of Intangible Cultural Heritage Inventories', in Toshiyuki Kono (ed), *Intangible Cultural Heritage and Intellectual Property: Communities, Cultural Diversity and Sustainable Development* (Intersentia, 2009), 51 75.

Archer, Margaret, *Culture and Agency: The Place of Culture in Social Theory* (Cambridge University Press, 1996).

Ascensão, José de Oliveira, *Direito Autoral* (Renovar, 1997).

Ashworth, GJ, Graham, Brian, and Tunbridge, JE, *Pluralising Pasts: Heritage, Identity and Place in Multicultural Societies* (Pluto Press, 2007).

Austin, Regina, 'Kwanzaa and the Commodification of Black Culture', in Martha M Ertman and Joan C Williams (eds), *Rethinking Commodification: Cases and Readings in Law and Culture* (New York University Press, 2005), 178 90.

Bakker, Karel Anthonie, 'Preserving Intangible Heritage Resources: Examples from South Africa', *Proceedings of the ICOMOS 14th General Assembly and Scientific Symposium: Place, Memory, Meaning: Preserving Intangible Values in Monuments and Sites*, available at <http://www.international.icomos.org/victoriafalls2003/papers.htm> (accessed 29 November 2012).

Baltl, Hermann, 'Folklore Research and Legal History in the German Language Area', in Alison Dundes Rentel and Alan Dundes (eds), *Folk Law: Essays on the Theory and Practice of* Lex Non Scripta (University of Wisconsin Press, 1995), 397 407.

Bancroft, Robyne, 'Everything Relates, or a Holistic Approach to Aboriginal Indigenous Cultural Heritage', in Peter Seitel (ed), *Safeguarding Traditional Culture: A Global Assessment* (Smithsonian Institution, 2001), 70 4.

Bannavong, Siho, 'The Lao Front for National Construction and Minority Cultural Heritage', in Yves Goudineau (ed), *Laos and Ethnic Minority Cultures: Promoting Heritage* (UNESCO Publishing, 2003), 255 61.

Barbosa, AL Figueira, *Sobre a Propriedade do Trabalho Intelectual Uma Perspectiva Crítica* (UFRJ, 1999).

Barkan, Elazar, 'Genes and Burkas: Predicaments of Human Rights and Cultural Property', in Helaine Silverman and D Fairchild Ruggles (eds), *Cultural Heritage and Human Rights* (Springer, 2007), 184 200.

Baroness Hooper, *Crafts and Cultural Heritage Conservation Skills, Report to the Committee on Culture, Science and Education of the Council of Europe Parliamentary Assembly*. Doc 11761, 23 October 2008.

Bendix, Regina, 'Héritage et patrimoine: de leurs proximités sémantiques et de leurs implications', in Chiara Bortolotto (ed), *Le patrimoine culturel immaterial: Enjeux d'une nouvelle catégorie* (Éditions de la Maison des sciences de l'homme, 2011), 99 121.

Benkler, Yochai, 'Through the Looking Glass: Alice and the Constitutional Foundations of the Public Domain', in James Boyle (ed), *Collected Papers: Duke Conference on the Public Domain* (Center for the Public Domain, 2003), 173 224.

Benvenisti, Eyal and Downs, George, 'The Empire's New Clothes: Political Economy and the Fragmentation of International Law', *Stanford L Rev* 60 (2007), 595 631.

Berryman, Cathryn A, 'Toward More Universal Protection of Intangible Cultural Property', *J Intell Prop L* 1 (1994), 293, reprinted in Anthony D'Amato and Doris Estelle Long (eds), *International Intellectual Property Anthology* (Anderson Publishing Co, 1996), 76 8.

Beyleveld, Deryck and Brownsword, Roger, *Consent in the Law* (Hart Publishing, 2007).
Biondi, Andrea, 'The Merchant, the Thief and the Citizen: The Circulation of Works of Art within the European Union', *CML Rev* 34 (1997), 1173 95.
Blake, Janet, *Commentary on the UNESCO 2003 Convention on the Safeguarding of the Intangible Cultural Heritage* (Institute for Art and Law, 2006).
Blake, Janet, *Developing a New Standard Setting Instrument for the Safeguarding of Intangible Cultural Heritage: Elements for Consideration* (UNESCO Publishing, 2001).
Blake, Janet, 'On Defining the Cultural Heritage', *ICLQ* 49 (2000), 61 85.
Blake, Janet, 'UNESCO's 2003 Convention on Intangible Cultural Heritage: The Implications of Community Involvement in "Safeguarding"', in Laurajane Smith and Natsuko Akagawa (eds), *Intangible Heritage* (Routledge, 2009), 45 73.
Blakeney, Michael, 'Protecting Traditional Cultural Expressions: The International Dimension', in Fiona Macmillan and Kathy Bowrey (eds), *New Directions in Copyright Law, Vol 3* (Edward Elgar, 2006), 3 14.
Borba Filho, Hermilo, *Espetáculos Populares do Nordeste* (Massangana, 2007).
Bouapao, Lytou, 'Traditional Hmong Weaving and Embroidery', in Yves Goudineau (ed), *Laos and Ethnic Minority Cultures: Promoting Heritage* (UNESCO Publishing, 2003), 119 27.
Bouchenaki, Mounir, 'A Major Advance towards a Holistic Approach to Heritage Conservation: The 2003 Intangible Heritage Convention', *Intl J of Intangible Heritage* 2 (2007), 106 9.
Boulware, Margaret A, Pyle, Jeffrey A, and Turner, Frank C, 'Symposium: Intellectual Property: An Overview of Intellectual Property Rights Abroad', *Hous J Int'l L* 14 (1994), 441, reprinted in Anthony D'Amato and Doris Estelle Long (eds), *International Intellectual Property Anthology* (Anderson Publishing Co, 1996), 20 2.
Bowrey, Kathy, 'Indigenous Culture, Knowledge and Intellectual Property: The Need for a New Category of Rights?', in Kathy Bowrey, Michael Handler, and Dianne Nicoll (eds), *Emerging Challenges in Intellectual Property* (Oxford University Press, 2011), 46 67.
Bowrey, Kathy, 'International Trade in Indigenous Cultural Heritage: An Australian Perspective', in Christoph Beat Graber, Karolina Kuprecht, and Jessica Lai (eds), *International Trade in Indigenous Cultural Heritage: Legal and Policy Issues* (Edward Elgar, 2012), 396 438.
Bowrey, Kathy and Anderson, Jane, 'The Politics of Global Information Sharing: Whose Cultural Agendas are Being Advanced?', *Social and Legal Studies* 18(4) (2009), 1 26.
Boylan, Patrick J, 'The Intangible Heritage: A Challenge and an Opportunity for Museums and Museum Professional Training', *Intl J of Intangible Heritage* 1 (2006), 54 65.
Boyle, James, 'Foreword: The Opposite of Property?', in James Boyle (ed), *Collected Papers: Duke Conference on the Public Domain* (Center for the Public Domain, 2003), 1 32.
Boyle, James, 'The Second Enclosure Movement and the Construction of the Public Domain', in James Boyle (ed), *Collected Papers: Duke Conference on the Public Domain* (Center for the Public Domain, 2003), 33 74.
Brahy, Nicolas, *The Property Regime of Biodiversity and Traditional Knowledge: Institutions for Conservation and Innovation* (Éditions Larcier, 2008).
Bratman, Michael E, *Structure of Agency* (Oxford University Press, 2007).
Brewster, Paul G, 'Traces of Ancient Germanic Law in a German Game Song', in Alison Dundes Rentel and Alan Dundes (eds), *Folk Law: Essays on the Theory and Practice of* Lex Non Scripta (University of Wisconsin Press, 1995), 407 16.

Broude, Tomer, *Taking 'Trade and Culture' Seriously: Geographical Indications and Cultural Protection in WTO Law*, available at <http://papers.ssrn.com/sol3/papers.cfm?abstract id=714981> (accessed 29 November 2012).

Brown, Michael F, 'Heritage Trouble: Recent Work on the Protection of Intangible Cultural Property', *Intl J of Cultural Property* 12 (2005), 40 61.

Brown, Michael F, *Who Owns Native Culture?* (Harvard University Press, 2004).

Bruner, Christopher M, 'Culture, Sovereignty, and Hollywood: UNESCO and the Future of Trade in Cultural Products', *NYU J Intl L & Pol* 40 (2008), 351 436.

Bulfinch, Thomas, *The Golden Age of Myth and Legend* (Wordsworth Editions, 1993).

Burden, Matilda, 'Museums and the Intangible Heritage: The Case Study of the Afrikaans Language Museum', *Intl J of Intangible Heritage* 2 (2007), 82 91.

Calderón Puente and María Cecilia, 'Protección Durable', *ICOMOS 15th General Assembly and Scientific Symposium (2005)*, available at <http://www.international.icomos.org/xian2005/papers.htm> (accessed 29 November 2012).

Cang, Voltaire Garces, 'Defining Intangible Cultural Heritage and its Stakeholders: The Case of Japan', *Intl J of Intangible Heritage* 2 (2007), 46 55.

Carlson, Kirsten Matou, 'Notice: Premature Predictions of Multiculturalism?', *Mich L Rev* 100 (2002), 1470 87.

Carter, Anthony, 'Protecting the Indigenous Past While Securing the Digital Future: The FTAA and the Protection of Expressions of Folklore', *Loy Intl L Rev* 1 (2004), 203 16.

Cavalcanti, Maria Laura Viveiros de Castro and Fonseca, Maria Cecilia Londres, *Patrimônio Imaterial no Brasil: Legislação e Políticas Estaduais* (UNESCO Publishing, 2008).

Chander, Anupam and Sunder, Madhavi, 'The Romance of the Public Domain', *Calif L Rev* 92 (2004), 1331 73.

Chao Ching, Fu, 'Cultural Sensitivity towards Intangible Values in Monuments and Sites A Comparison between Eastern Asian and Western Countries', *ICOMOS 15th General Assembly and Scientific Symposium (2005)*, available at <http://www.international.icomos.org/xian2005/papers.htm> (accessed 29 November 2012).

Chartrand, Harry Hillman, 'Towards an American Arts Industry', *Cultural Economics*, available at <http://www.compilerpress.ca/Cultural%20Economics/Works/Towards%202000.htm> (accessed 29 November 2012).

Chaudhuri, Shubha, 'Who is the "Holder" of Intangible Cultural Heritage? Revisiting the Concept of Community from an Intangible Cultural Heritage Perspective', in Toshiyuki Kono (ed), *Intangible Cultural Heritage and Intellectual Property: Communities, Cultural Diversity and Sustainable Development* (Intersentia, 2009), 189 201.

Clavero, Bartolomé, 'Derechos Indígenas y Constituciones Latinoamericanas', in Mikel Berraondo (ed), *Pueblos Indígenas y Derechos Humanos* (Universidad de Deusto, 2006), 313 38.

Clément, Sophie and Clément, Pierre, 'Architecture as an Expression of Minority Culture', in Yves Goudineau (ed), *Laos and Ethnic Minority Cultures: Promoting Heritage* (UNESCO Publishing, 2003), 137 52.

Commission of the European Communities, *Commission Staff Working Paper on the Review of the EC Legal Framework in the Field of Copyright and Related Rights, 19 July 2004 (SEC (2004) 995).*

'Comunicado sobre la Protección y Recuperación de Bienes del Patrimonio Cultural de los Países Miembros de la Comunidad Andina', in *Los Pueblos Indígenas y la Integración*

Andina Primer Foro de Intelectuales e Investigadores Indígenas (Comunidad Andina, 2008), 96.

Comunidad Andina de Naciones, *Biocomercio en la subregión andina Oportunidades para el desarrollo* (Comunidad Andina, 2005).

Comunidad Andina de Naciones, *Elementos para la protección sui generis de los conocimientos tradicionales colectivos e integrales desde la perspectiva indígena* (Comunidad Andina, 2005).

Comunidad Andina de Naciones, *Negociaciones sobre acceso a recursos genéticos y conocimientos* tradicionales (Comunidad Andina, 2003).

Condominas, Georges, 'Safeguarding and Promoting the Intangible Cultural Heritage of Lao Minority Groups', in Yves Goudineau (ed), *Laos and Ethnic Minority Cultures: Promoting Heritage* (UNESCO Publishing, 2003), 19 26.

Coombe, Rosemary J, *The Cultural Life of Intellectual Properties* (Duke University Press, 2003).

Cornides, Jakob, 'Human Rights and Intellectual Property, Conflict or Convergence?', *The J of World Intellectual Property* 7(2) (2004), 135 67.

Cornish, William and Llewelyn, David, *Intellectual Property: Patents, Copyright, Trade Marks and Allied Rights* (Sweet & Maxwell, 2003).

Costa, Rodrigo Vieira, *A Dimensão Constitucional do Patrimônio Cultural: O Tombamento e o Registro Sob a ötica dos Direitos Culturais* (Lumen Juris, 2011).

Council of Europe, *Explanatory Report to the Council of Europe Framework Convention on the Value of Cultural Heritage to Society* (Council of Europe, 2005).

Council of Europe, *Presentation to the Framework Convention on the Value of Cultural Heritage for Society* (Council of Europe, 2005).

Council of Europe, Steering Committee for Cultural Heritage, *Heritage from Elsewhere, Heritage of Others: Outline of an awareness raising project.* Doc Symbol CDPAT (2004) 30 final, 29 April 2004.

Craig, Paul and de Búrca, Gráinne, *EU Law* (Oxford University Press, 2003).

Cuevas Gayosso and José Luis, 'La autonomía de los derechos de los pueblos indígenas en la constitución mexicana (reforma, 2001). Análisis y propuestas para su ejercicio formal y real', paper presented at the *XIV Congreso Latinoamericano de Derecho Romano, Universidad de Buenos Aires, 15 17 November 2004.*

Cunha, Manuela Carneiro da, 'The Role of UNESCO in the Defense of Traditional Knowledge', in Peter Seitel (ed), *Safeguarding Traditional Culture: A Global Assessment* (Smithsonian Institution, 2001), 143 8.

D'Amato, Anthony and Long, Doris Estelle (eds), *International Intellectual Property Anthology* (Anderson Publishing Co, 1996).

Dalibard, Joël David and Kono, Toshiyuki, 'Prior Informed Consent: Empowering the Bearers of Cultural Traditions', in Toshiyuki Kono (ed) *Intangible Cultural Heritage and Intellectual Property: Communities, Cultural Diversity and Sustainable Development* (Intersentia, 2009), 247 59.

David, René, *Os Grandes Sistemas do Direito Contemporâneo* (Meridiano, 1978).

Davidson, Benjamin, 'Lost in Translation: Distinguishing Between French and Anglo American Natural Rights in Literary Property, and How Dastar Proves that the Difference Still Matters', *Cornell Intl LJ* 38 (2005), 583 623.

Deacon, Harriet, Dondolo, Luvuyo, Mrubata, Mbulelo, and Prosalendis, Sandra, *The Subtle Power of Intangible Heritage: Legal and Financial Instruments for Safeguarding Intangible Heritage* (Human Sciences Research Council, 2004).

Dessaint, William, 'Intangible Cultural Heritage: Tibeto Burmese Peoples and Minority Groups in Viet Nam', in Oscar Salemink (ed), *Viet Nam's Cultural Diversity: Approaches to Preservation* (UNESCO Publishing, 2001), 239 54.

Diegues, Antonio Carlos, *O Mito Moderno da Natureza Intocada* (HUCITEC, 2000).

Dinstein, Yoram, 'Collective Human Rights of Peoples and Minorities', *ICLQ* 25 (1976), 102 20.

Donders, Yvonne, 'The History of the UNESCO Convention on the Protection and Promotion of the Diversity of Cultural Expressions', in H Schneider and P Van den Bossche (eds), *Protection of Cultural Diversity from a European and International Perspective* (Intersentia, 2008), 1 30.

Downes, David R, 'How Intellectual Property Could Be a Tool to Protect Traditional Knowledge', *Colum J Envtl L* 25 (2000), 253 81.

Dreier, Thomas, 'Restoration and Moral Rights of the Artist under Comparative Law', in Quentin Byrne Sutton, Marc André Renold, and Beatrice Rötheli Mariotti (eds), *La Restauration des Objets D'Art: Aspects juridiques et éthiques* (Centre du Droit De L'Art, 1994), 105 23.

Dung, Nguyen Kim, *Intangible Cultural Heritage Safeguarding System in Vietnam*, available at <http://www.unesco.org/culture/ich/doc/src/00174 EN.pdf> (accessed 29 November 2012).

Dutfield, Graham, 'Prior Informed Consent and Traditional Knowledge in a Multicultural World', in Toshiyuki Kono (ed), *Intangible Cultural Heritage and Intellectual Property: Communities, Cultural Diversity and Sustainable Development* (Intersentia, 2009), 261 82.

Easterly, William, *The White Man's Burden: Why the West's Efforts to Aid the Rest Have Done so Much Ill and so Little Good* (Penguin Press, 2006).

Engle, Karen, *The Elusive Promise of Indigenous Development: Rights, Culture, Strategy* (Duke University Press, 2010).

European Communities, *Strategy for the Development of Euro Mediterranean Cultural Heritage: Priorities from Mediterranean Countries (2007 2013)* (European Communities, 2007).

Evans, Grant, 'Tourism and Minorities', in Oscar Salemink (ed), *Viet Nam's Cultural Diversity: Approaches to Preservation* (UNESCO Publishing, 2001), 277 80.

Farber, Daniel A, 'Conflicting Visions and Contested Baselines: Intellectual Property and Free Speech in the "Digital Millennium"', *Minn L Rev* 89 (2005), 1318 60.

Farley, Christine Haight, 'Protecting Folklore of Indigenous Peoples: Is Intellectual Property the Answer?', *Conn L Rev* 30 (1997), 1 57.

Floris Margadant, Guillermo, 'Official Mexican Attitudes toward the Indians: An Historical Essay', *Tul L Rev* 54 (1980), 964 86.

Folsom, Ralph H, *NAFTA* (West Group Publishing, 1999).

Fournier, Laurent Sébastien, 'Le Tarasque métamorphosée', in Chiara Bortolotto (ed), *Le patrimoine culturel immatériel: Enjeux d'une nouvelle catégorie* (Éditions de la Maison des sciences de l'homme, 2011), 149 66.

Francioni, Francesco, 'A Dynamic Evolution of Concept and Scope: From Cultural Property to Cultural Heritage', in Abdulqawi A Yusuf (ed), *Standard Setting in*

UNESCO Vol 1: Normative Action in Education, Science and Culture (Martinus Nijhoff and UNESCO Publishing, 2007), 221 36.

Francioni, Francesco, 'Access to Justice, Denial of Justice and International Investment Law', *EJIL* 20(3) (2009), 729 48.

Francioni, Francesco, 'Culture, Heritage and Human Rights: An Introduction', in Francesco Francioni and Martin Scheinin (eds), *Cultural Human Rights* (Martinus Nijhoff, 2008), 1 15.

Francioni, Francesco, 'Equity in International Law', in Rudolf Bernhardt and Rüdiger Wolfrum (eds), *Max Planck Encyclopedia of Public International Law* (2007), available at <http://www.mpepil.com> (accessed 29 November 2012).

Francioni, Francesco, 'La Protección del patrimonio cultural a la luz de los principios de Derecho Internacional Público', in Carlos R Fernández Liesa and Jesús Prieto de Pedro (eds), *La Protección Jurídico Internacional del Patrimonio Cultural: Especial Referencia a España* (COLEX, 2009), 13 34.

Francioni, Francesco, 'The Human Dimension of International Cultural Heritage Law: An Introduction', *EJIL*, 22(1) (2011), 9 16.

Francioni, Francesco (ed), *The 1972 World Heritage Convention: A Commentary* (Oxford University Press, 2008).

Francioni, Francesco, 'WTO Law in Context: The Integration of International Human Rights and Environmental Law in the Dispute Settlement Process', in Giorgio Sacerdoti, Alan Yanovich, and Jan Bohanes (eds), *The WTO at Ten: The Contribution of the Dispute Settlement System* (Cambridge University Press, 2006), 143 54.

Francioni, Francesco and Lenzerini, Federico, 'The Destruction of the Buddhas of Bamiyan and International Law', *EJIL* 14(4) (2003), 619 51.

Francioni, Francesco and Lenzerini, Federico, 'The Obligation to Prevent and Avoid Destruction of Cultural Heritage: From Bamiyan to Iraq', in Barbara T Hoffman (ed), *Art and Cultural Heritage: Law, Policy and Practice* (Cambridge University Press, 2006), 28 40.

García Canclini, Néstor, 'Las Industrias Culturales y el Desarrollo de los Países Americanos', *Workshop on Case Studies in the Protection of Cultural Heritage Central American Region*, available at <http://portal.oas.org/Portal/Topic/SEDI/Educaci%C3%B3nyCultura/Cultura/TemasPrioritarios/Preservaci%C3%B3nyProtecci%C3%B3ndelPatrimonioCultural/Activities/ProtegiendoelPatrimonioCultural/tabid/1447/language/en US/Default.aspx> (accessed 29 November 2012).

García Ramírez, Sergio, 'La Jurisprudencia de la Corte Interamericana de Derechos Humanos en Materia de Reparaciones', in *La Corte Interamericana de Derechos Humanos: Un Cuarto de Siglo 1979 2004* (Corte Interamericana de Derechos Humanos, 2005), 1 85.

Garfinkle, Ann, *The Legal and Ethical Consideration of Mural Conservation: Issues and Debates* (The Getty Conservation Institute, 2003).

General Assembly of States Parties to the Convention for the Safeguarding of the Intangible Cultural Heritage, *Operational Directives for the Implementation of the Convention for the Safeguarding of the Intangible Cultural Heritage (June 2008).*

Gervais, Daniel J, 'The Internationalization of Intellectual Property: New Challenges from the Very Old and the Very New', *Fordham Intell Prop Media & Ent LJ* 12 (2002), 929 90.

Gibson, Johanna, *Community Resources: Intellectual Property, International Trade and Protection of Traditional Knowledge* (Ashgate, 2009).

Gibson, Johanna, 'Knowledge and Other Values Intellectual Property and the Limitations for Traditional Knowledge', in Guido Westkamp (ed), *Emerging Issues in Intellectual Property: Trade Technology and Market Freedom: Essays in Honour of Herchel Smith* (Edward Elgar, 2007), 309 18.

Gillman, Derek, *The Idea of Cultural Heritage* (Institute for Art and Law, 2006).

Glass, David S, 'Moral Rights and the New Copyright Law', 134 *Solicitors Journal* 6 (1990), reprinted in Anthony D'Amato and Doris Estelle Long (eds), *International Intellectual Property Anthology* (Anderson Publishing Co, 1996), 131 3.

Golding, Viv, '*Inspiration Africa!* Using Tangible and Intangible Heritage to Promote Social Inclusion Amongst Young People with Disabilities', *Intl J of Intangible Heritage* 1 (2006), 84 93.

Gomez, Gail Goodwin, 'Indigenous Rights and the Case of the Yanomami Indians in Brazil', in Cynthia Price Cohen (ed), *The Human Rights of Indigenous Peoples* (Transnational Publishers, 1998), 185 200.

Goubeaux, Gilles, *Traité de Droit Civil. Sous la direction de Jacques Ghestin* (Librairie générale de droit et de jurisprudente, 1977).

Goudineau, Yves, 'Managing the Intangible Cultural Heritage', in Yves Goudineau (ed), *Laos and Ethnic Minority Cultures: Promoting Heritage* (UNESCO Publishing, 2003), 33 7.

Goudineau, Yves (ed), *Laos and Ethnic Minority Cultures: Promoting Heritage* (UNESCO Publishing, 2003).

Gouveia, Jaime Ricardo Teixeira, *Embate em Debate: História, Administração e Limites do Planalto Ribeirão (Um Estudo de Caso)* (Casa do Povo, 2003).

Gouveia, Jaime Ricardo Teixeira, *Subsídios para a História de Leomil: 'A presentação' e 'Re presentação'* (Casa do Povo, 2004).

Graham, Brian, Ashworth, Gregory John, and Tunbridge, John E, 'The Uses and Abuses of Heritage', in Gerard Corsane (ed), *Heritage Museums and Galleries: An Introductory Reader* (Routledge, 2005), 26 37.

Green, Maria, *Drafting History of the Article 15(1)(c) of the International Covenant on Economic, Social and Cultural Rights*, UN Doc E/C.12/2000/15, of 9 October 2000.

Greffe, Xavier, *Arts and Artists from an Economic Perspective* (UNESCO Publishing, 2002).

Grenet, Sylvie and Houin, Christian, 'Avant Propos: Un Livre Politique', in Chiara Bortolotto (ed), *Le patrimoine culturel immatériel: Enjeux d'une nouvelle catégorie* (Éditions de la Maison des sciences de l'homme, 2011), 9 19.

Grijalva, Agustín, 'The Status of Traditional Indian Justice in Ecuador', *Tribal LJ* 2 (2001 2002), 1 20.

Gross, Robin, 'Intellectual Property Rights and the Information Commons', in Rike Frank Jorgensen (ed), *Human Rights in the Global Information Society* (MIT Press, 2006), 107 20.

Gruber, Stefan, 'Protecting China's Cultural Heritage: A Legal and Policy Approach', PhD Thesis (University of Sydney, 2012).

Gruber, Stefan, 'Protecting China's Cultural Heritage Sites in Times of Rapid Change: Current Developments, Practice and Law', *Asia Pacific J of Envl L* 10(3), (4) (2007), 253 301.

Guèvremont, Véronique, 'Industries culturelles et négociations internationals: portrait d'une dynamique multidimensionelle. L'exemple des pays de la zone euro méditerranéenne', *EUI Working Papers RSCAS 2007/33* (2007).

Hafstein, Valdimar Tr, 'Intangible Heritage as a List: From Masterpieces to Representation', in Laurajane Smith and Natsuko Akagawa (eds), *Intangible Heritage* (Routledge, 2009), 93 111.

Halewood, Michael, 'Indigenous and Local Knowledge in International Law: A Preface to Sui Generis Intellectual Property Protection', *McGill LJ* 44 (1999), 953 96.

Hanse, Hugh C, Blakeney, Michael, Lourie, Linda S, Salmon, Paul E, and Visser, Coenraad, 'Symposium: Global Intellectual Property Rights: Boundaries of Access and Enforcement: Panel II: The Law and Policy of Protecting Folklore, Traditional Knowledge, and Genetic Resources', *Fordham Intell Prop Media & Ent LJ* 12 (2002), 753 803.

Harding, Sarah, 'Culture, Commodification and Native American Cultural Patrimony', in Martha M Ertman and Joan C Williams (eds), *Rethinking Commodification: Cases and Readings in Law and Culture* (New York University Press, 2005), 137 55.

Harding, Sarah, 'Value, Obligation and Cultural Heritage', *Ariz St LJ* 31 (1999), 291 354.

Harris, Bryan, *Intellectual Property Law in the European Union* (William S Hein & Co, 2005).

Harris, Stephen, 'Cultural Heritage Protection in Australia Legislation and Some Comments', *Proceedings of the ICOMOS 13th General Assembly Madrid, 2002: Strategies for the World's Cultural Heritage, Preservation in a Globalized World, Principles, Practices, Perspectives*, available at <http://www.international.icomos.org/publications/ga madrid.htm> (accessed 29 November 2012).

Harrison, Rodney, *Heritage: Critical Approaches* (Routledge, 2013).

Hartney, Michael, 'Some Confusions Concerning Collective Rights', 4 *Canadian Journal of Law and Jurisprudence* 293 (1991), reprinted in Will Kymlicka (ed), *The Rights of Minority Cultures* (Oxford University Press, 1995), 202 27.

Hazucha, Branislav, 'Community as a Holder of Intangible Cultural Heritage: A Broader Public Policy Perspective', in Toshiyuki Kono (ed), *Intangible Cultural Heritage and Intellectual Property: Communities, Cultural Diversity and Sustainable Development* (Intersentia, 2009), 223 44.

Hazucha, Branislav and Kono, Toshiyuki, 'Conceptualization of Community as a Holder of Intangible Cultural Heritage', in Toshiyuki Kono (ed), *Intangible Cultural Heritage and Intellectual Property: Communities, Cultural Diversity and Sustainable Development* (Intersentia, 2009), 145 57.

Hazucha, Branislav and Kono, Toshiyuki, 'Safeguarding of Intangible Cultural Heritage: Benefits and Potential Harms', in Toshiyuki Kono (ed), *Intangible Cultural Heritage and Intellectual Property: Communities, Cultural Diversity and Sustainable Development* (Intersentia, 2009), 319 24.

Heide, Thomas P, 'The Moral Right of Integrity and the Global Information Infrastructure: Time for a New Approach?', *UC Davis J Intl L & Policy* 2 (1996), 211 66.

Heins, Volker, 'Human Rights, Intellectual Property, and Struggles for Recognition', *Human Rights Rev* 9 (2008), 213 32.

Helfer, Laurence R, 'Toward a Human Rights Framework for Intellectual Property', *UC Davis L Rev* 40 (2007), 970 1020.

Holderness, Mike, 'Moral Rights and Authors' Rights: The Keys to the Information Age', *J of Information, L and Technology (JILT)*, 1998(1), available at <http://www2.warwick.ac.uk/fac/soc/law/elj/jilt/1998 1/holderness/> (accessed 29 November 2012).

Howard, Peter, *Heritage: Management, Interpretation, Identity* (Continuum, 2003).

Howard, Rhoda, 'Group Versus Individual Identity in the African Debate on Human Rights', in Abdullah An na im and Francis Deng (eds), *Human Rights in Africa, Cross Cultural Perspectives* (The Brookings Institution, 1990), 159 83.

Huanucurú, Fernando, 'Cosmovisión sagrada de la vida', in *Los Pueblos Indígenas y la Integración Andina Primer Foro de Intelectuales e Investigadores Indígenas* (Comunidad Andina, 2008), 66 8.

Hugenholtz, P Bernt, 'Copyright and Freedom of Expression in Europe', in Rochelle Cooper Dreyfuss, Harry First, and Diane Leenheer Zimmermann (eds), *Innovation Policy in an Information Age* (Oxford University Press, 2000), 343 64.

Hyde, Lewis, *The Gift: Creativity and the Artist in the Modern World* (Vintage Books, 2007).

Intergovernmental Committee for the Safeguarding of the Intangible Cultural Heritage, First Extraordinary Session (Chengdu, China, 23 27 May 2007), *Discussion on the Implementation of Article 18 of the Convention for the Safeguarding of the Intangible Cultural Heritage*, Doc ITH/07/1.EXT.COM/CONF.207/11, of 20 April 2007.

Intergovernmental Committee for the Safeguarding of the Intangible Cultural Heritage, Second Session (Tokyo, Japan, 3 7 September 2007), *Preliminary draft directives for implementing Article 18 of the Convention for the Safeguarding of the Intangible Cultural Heritage*, Doc ITH/07/2.COM/CONF.208/12, of 30 July 2007.

Intergovernmental Committee for the Safeguarding of the Intangible Cultural Heritage, *Note by the Office of International Standards and Legal Affairs on the Incorporation of Masterpieces into the Representative List under Article 31 of the Convention for the Safeguarding of the Intangible Cultural Heritage*. Doc ITH/07/2.COM/CONF.208/14, of 23 July 2007, para 14.

Intergovernmental Committee for the Safeguarding of the Intangible Cultural Heritage, *Report of the Rapporteur of the subsidiary body on the modalities for the participation of communities or their representatives, practitioners, experts, centers of expertise and research institutes in the implementation of the Convention*, presented at the Second Extraordinary Session (Sofia, Bulgaria, 18 22 February 2008). Doc ITH/08/2.EXT.COM/CONF.201/INF.4, of 12 February 2008.

Ito, Nobuo, 'Intangible Cultural Heritage Involved in Tangible Cultural Heritage', *ICOMOS 14th General Assembly and Scientific Symposium (2003)*, available at <http://www.international.icomos.org/victoriafalls2003/papers.htm> (accessed 29 November 2012).

Janke, Terri, *Minding Culture: Case Studies on Intellectual Property and Traditional Cultural Expressions* (WIPO, 2003).

Jayme, Erik, 'Identité culturelle et intégration: le droit international privé postmoderne Cours General de droit international privé', *Collected Courses of the Hague Academy of Intl L* 251 (1995), 9 268.

Jett, Allison Carter, 'Domestic, Supranational and International Historic Preservation Legislation: Does it Protect our Cultural Heritage or Restrict Development? Exploring its Impact on Ancient Roman Monuments', *Ga J Intl & Comp L* 31 (2003), 649 80.

Johnston, Darlene M, 'Native Rights as Collective Rights: A Question of Group Self Preservation', 2 *Canadian Journal of Law and Jurisprudence* 19 (1989), reprinted in Will

Kymlicka (ed), *The Rights of Minority Cultures* (Oxford University Press, 1995), 179 201.

Jones, Michael, 'Eldred v. Ashcroft: The Constitutionality of the Copyright Term Extension Act', *Berkeley Technology LJ* 19 (2004), 85 106.

Josselin Gall, Muriel, *Les contrats d'exploitation du droit de propriété littéraire et artistique Étude de droit comparé et de droit international privé* (GLN Joly Edition, 1995).

Jovanović, Miodrag A, 'Recognizing Minority Identities Through Collective Rights', *Human Rights Q* 27 (2005), 625 51.

Karnoouh, Claude, 'Europe: Common Heritage and Differences', in *Forward Planning: The Function of Cultural Heritage in a Changing Europe* (Council of Europe, 2000), 29 52.

Keal, Paul, *European Conquest and the Rights of Indigenous Peoples The Moral Backwardness of International Society* (Cambridge University Press, 2003).

Kearney, Amanda, 'Intangible Cultural Heritage: Global Awareness and Local Interest', in Laurajane Smith and Natsuko Akagawa (eds), *Intangible Heritage* (Routledge, 2009), 209 26.

Kelsey, Jane, 'How Trade Trumps Culture', in *Toward Freedom*, available at <http://www.towardfreedom.com/home/content/view/514/55/> (accessed 29 November 2012).

Kennedy, David, 'Some Caution About Property Rights as a Recipe for Economic Development', *Accounting, Economics and Law* 1 (2011), 1 62.

Kennedy, David, *The Dark Sides of Virtue: Reassessing International Humanitarianism* (Princeton University Press, 2005).

Khê, Trân Van, 'Safeguarding and Promoting the Traditional Musical Heritage of Minority Groups in Viet Nam', in Oscar Salemink (ed), *Viet Nam's Cultural Diversity: Approaches to Preservation* (UNESCO Publishing, 2001), 105 10.

King, Thomas F, *Cultural Resources Laws and Practice* (AltaMira, 2008).

Kingsada, Thongphet, 'Some Vulnerable Languages in the Lao PDR', in Yves Goudineau (ed), *Laos and Ethnic Minority Cultures: Promoting Heritage* (UNESCO Publishing, 2003), 43 4.

Kojima, Ryu, 'Prior Informed Consent: An Intellectual Property Law Perspective', in Toshiyuki Kono (ed), *Intangible Cultural Heritage and Intellectual Property: Communities, Cultural Diversity and Sustainable Development* (Intersentia, 2009), 309 16.

Konigsberg, Stephen R, 'Think Globally, Act Locally: North American Free Trade, Canadian Cultural Industry Exemption, and the Liberalization of the Broadcast Ownership Law', *Cardozo Arts & Ent LJ* 12 (1994), 281 305.

Kono, Toshiyuki, 'UNESCO and Intangible Cultural Heritage from the Viewpoint of Sustainable Development', in Abdulqawi A Yusuf (ed), *Standard Setting in UNESCO Vol 1: Normative Action in Education, Science and Culture* (Martinus Nijhoff and UNESCO Publishing, 2007), 237 65.

Konrad, Otto W, 'A Federal Regulation of Performance Art Author Moral Rights', 48 *Wash & Lee L Rev* 1759 (1991), reprinted in Anthony D'Amato and Doris Estelle Long (eds), *International Intellectual Property Anthology* (Anderson Publishing Co, 1996), 157 60.

Krisch, Nico, 'International Law in Times of Hegemony: Unequal Power and the Shaping of the International Legal Order', *EJIL* 16(3) (2005), 369 408.

Krstić, Durica, 'Symbols in Customary Law', in Alison Dundes Rentel and Alan Dundes (eds), *Folk Law: Essays on the Theory and Practice of* Lex Non Scripta (University of Wisconsin Press,1995), 439 54.

Kukathas, Chandran, 'Are There Any Cultural Rights?', 20 *Political Theory* 105 (1992), reprinted in Will Kymlicka (ed), *The Rights of Minority Cultures* (Oxford University Press, 1995), 228 55.

Kurin, Richard, 'Safeguarding Intangible Cultural Heritage: Key Factors in Implementing the 2003 Convention', *Intl J of Intangible Heritage* 2 (2007), 10 20.

Kurin, Richard, 'The UNESCO Questionnaire on the Application of the 1989 *Recommendation on the Safeguarding of Traditional Culture and Folklore*: Preliminary Results', in Peter Seitel (ed), *Safeguarding Traditional Culture: A Global Assessment* (Smithsonian Institution, 2001), 20 35.

Kuruk, Paul, 'Protecting Folklore under Modern Intellectual Property Regimes: A Reappraisal of the Tensions between Individual and Communal Rights in Africa and the United States', *Am U L Rev* 48 (1999), 769 849.

Kutty, PV Valsala G, *National Experiences with the Protection of Expressions of Folklore/ Traditional Cultural Expressions* (WIPO, 2002).

Kymlicka, Will, *Multicultural Odysseys: Navigating the New International Politics of Diversity* (Oxford University Press, 2007).

Kymlicka, Will, 'Multicultural States and Intercultural Citizens', *Theory and Research in Education* 1(2) (2003), 147 69.

Laborde, Cécile, 'The Culture(s) of the Republic: Nationalism and Multiculturalism in French Republican Thought', *Political Theory* 29 (2001), 716 35.

Lafarge, François, 'Landscapes in International Law and European Law', in Monica Sassatelli (ed), *Landscape as Heritage: Negotiating European Cultural Identity* (EUI Working Papers RSCAS No 2006/03), 37 44.

Lange, David, 'Reimagining the Public Domain', in James Boyle (ed), *Collected Papers: Duke Conference on the Public Domain* (2003), 463 83.

Larrea, Therese Anne, 'Comment: Eliminate the Cultural Industries Exemption from NAFTA', *Santa Clara L Rev* 37 (1997), 1107 50.

Lasoukanh, Phéng, 'Overview of the Ko Ethnic Group', in Yves Goudineau (ed), *Laos and Ethnic Minority Cultures: Promoting Heritage* (UNESCO Publishing, 2003), 181 4.

Lefferts, Jr, H Leedom, 'Textiles for the Preservation of the Lao Intangible Cultural Heritage', in Yves Goudineau (ed), *Laos and Ethnic Minority Cultures: Promoting Heritage* (UNESCO Publishing, 2003), 89 110.

Leitão, Sérgio, *Os Direitos Constitucionais dos Povos Indígenas* (UNAM, 2003).

Lemoine, Jacques, 'Creating an Ethnographical Data Bank in the Lao PDR', in Yves Goudineau (ed), *Laos and Ethnic Minority Cultures: Promoting Heritage* (UNESCO Publishing, 2003), 275 82.

Lenzerini, Federico, 'Articles 15 16: World Heritage Fund', in Francesco Francioni (ed), *The 1972 World Heritage Convention: A Commentary* (Oxford University Press, 2008), 269 88.

Lenzerini, Federico, 'Intangible Cultural Heritage: The Living Culture of Peoples', *EJIL* 22 (1) (2011), 101 20.

Lewinski, Silke von, 'The Protection of Folklore', *Cardozo J Intl & Comp L* 11 (2003), 747 68.

Li, Luo, 'Does Intangible Cultural Heritage Law Resolve Everything in China?', *J of Intl Commercial L and Technology* 7(4) (2012), 355 62.

Lixinski, Lucas, 'Constitutionalism and the Other: Multiculturalism and Indigeneity in Selected Latin American Countries', *Anuario Iberoamericano de Justicia Constitucional* 14 (2010), 235 65.

Lixinski, Lucas, 'Falling Short: The UNESCO Intangible Cultural Heritage Regime, Indigenous Heritage and the UN Declaration on the Rights of Indigenous Peoples', in Sarah Sargent (ed), *A New Millennium for Indigenous Rights: Challenges and Changes* (Buckingham University Press, forthcoming 2013).

Lixinski, Lucas, 'O Direito Moral de Autor como Direito de Personalidade e a Universlidade de sua Proteção', *Revista Trimestral de Direito Civil* 27 (2006), 49 79.

Lixinski, Lucas, 'Selecting Heritage: The Interplay of Art, Politics and Identity', *EJIL* 22(1) (2011), 81 100.

Lixinski, Lucas, 'The Future of the EU Cultural Policy in the Protection of Intangible Cultural Heritage', *The Prague Ybk of Comparative L* 1 (2009), 119 39.

Lixinski, Lucas, 'Treaty Interpretation by the Inter American Court of Human Rights: Expansionism at the Service of the Unity of International Law', *EJIL* 21(3) (2010), 585 604.

Lixinski, Lucas, 'World Heritage and the Heritage of the World Review of: The 1972 World Heritage Convention: A Commentary (Francesco Francioni and Federico Lenzerini eds.) (Oxford, Oxford University Press 2008)', *Eur J of Legal Studies* 2 (2008), 371 86.

Llasag Fernández, Raúl, 'Jurisdicción y competencia en el derecho indígena o consuetudinario', *Anuario de Derecho Constitucional Latinoamericano* (2006), 749 78.

Lohman, Cynthia A, 'Crofting: Securing the Future of the Scottish Highlands Through Legislative Challenge and Cultural Legacy', *Transnational L & Contemporary Problems* 16 (2007), 663 704.

Long, Doris Estelle, 'The Impact of Foreign Investment on Indigenous Culture: An Intellectual Property Perspective', *NCJ Intl L & Com Reg* 23 (1998), 229 43.

Lopes, Cristina Leme, 'La Protection Juridique du Patrimoine Culturel Immatériel: Le Cas Brésilien', Mémoire presented for a Master's Degree at the Universities of Paris I and II (2008).

López Bárcenas, Francisco, 'Autonomías indígenas en América: de la demanda de reconocimiento a su construcción', in Mikel Berraondo (ed), *Pueblos Indígenas y Derechos Humanos* (Universidad de Deusto, 2006), 423 50.

López Bárcenas, Francisco, 'Territorios, Tierras y Recursos Naturales de los Pueblos Indígenas en México', in Jorge Alberto Gonzáles Galván (ed), *Constitución y Derechos Indígenas* (Universidad Nacional Autónoma de México 2002), 121 43.

López y Rivas, Gilberto, 'Las Autonomías Indígenas', in Jorge Alberto Gonzáles Galván (ed), *Constitución y Derechos Indígenas* (Universidad Nacional Autónoma de México, 2002), 113 20.

Lowenthal, David, *The Heritage Crusade and the Spoils of History* (Cambridge University Press, 1998).

Lucas Schloetter, Agnes, 'Folklore', in Silke von Lewinski (ed), *Indigenous Heritage and Intellectual Property* (Kluwer Law International, 2003), 259 340.

Lumley, Robert, 'The Debate on Heritage Reviewed', in Gerard Corsane (ed), *Heritage Museums and Galleries: An Introductory Reader* (Routledge, 2005), 15 25.

Macdonald, Sharon, 'A People's Story: Heritage, Identity and Authenticity', in Gerard Corsane (ed), *Heritage Museums and Galleries: An Introductory Reader* (Routledge, 2005), 272 90.

Machado y Álvarez, Antonio, *Bases de el Folk lore español y reglamento del el Folk lore andaluz* (Imp y Lit De El Porvernir, 1881).

Macklem, Patrick, 'Militant Democracy, Legal Pluralism and the Paradox of Self Determination', *University of Toronto Legal Studies Research Paper No 05 03* (2003).

Macklem, Patrick, 'The Wrong Vocabulary of Right: Minority Rights and the Boundaries of Political Community', *University of Toronto Legal Studies Series Research Paper No XX 05* (2005).

Magannon, Esteban T, 'Philippine Indigenous Cultural Communities: A Historical Perspective', in Oscar Salemink (ed), *Viet Nam's Cultural Diversity: Approaches to Preservation* (UNESCO Publishing, 2001), 133 48.

Marrie, Henrietta, 'The UNESCO *Convention for the Safeguarding of the Intangible Cultural Heritage* and the protection and maintenance of the intangible cultural heritage of indigenous peoples', in Laurajane Smith and Natsuko Akagawa (eds), *Intangible Heritage* (Routledge, 2009), 169 92.

Matthews, Herbert L and Silvert, KH, *Los Estados Unidos y América Latina: De Monroe a Fidel Castro* (Editorial Grijalbo, 1967).

Mauss, Marcel, *The Gift: The Form and Reason for Exchange in Archaic Societies* (Routlege, 1990).

Mazeaud, Henri, Mazeaud, Léon, and Mazeaud, Jean, *Leçons de Droit Civil. Tome Premier* (Éditions Montchrestien, 1998).

McCann, Anthony, et al, 'The 1989 Recommendation Ten Years On: Towards a Critical Analysis', in Peter Seitel (ed), *Safeguarding Traditional Culture: A Global Assessment* (Smithsonian Institution, 2001), 57 64.

McLeod, Kembrew, *Owning Culture: Authorship, Ownership and Intellectual Property Law* (P Lang, 2001).

Merryman, John Henry, 'Cultural Property, International Trade and Human Rights', *Cardozo Arts & Ent LJ* 19 (2001), 51 68.

Merryman, John Henry, 'Thinking about the Elgin Marbles', *Mich L Rev* 83 (1984 85), 1881 923.

Merryman, John Henry, 'Two Ways of Thinking about Cultural Property', *AJIL* 80 (1986), 831 53.

Messenger, Jr, John C, 'The Role of Proverbs in a Nigerian Judicial System', *Southwestern Journal of Anthropology* 15(1) (1959), 64 73.

Mills, Sherylle, 'Indigenous Music and the Law: An Analysis of National and International Legislation', *Ybk for Traditional Music* (1996), 57 86.

Moisés, José Álvaro, 'Cultural Diversity and Development in the Americas', *OAS Unit for Social Development, Education and Cultural, Cultural Studies Series No 9* (2004).

Mowbray, Alastair R, *The Development of Positive Obligations under the European Convention on Human Rights by the European Court of Human Rights* (Hart Publishing, 2004).

Munjeri, Dawson, 'Following the Length and Breadth of the Roots: Some Dimensions of Intangible Heritage', in Laurajane Smith and Natsuko Akagawa (eds), *Intangible Heritage* (Routledge, 2009), 207 42.

Munyaradzi, Manyanga, 'Intangible Cultural Heritage and the Empowerment of Local Communities: Manyanga (Ntaba Zi Ka Mambo) Revisited', *ICOMOS 15th General Assembly and Scientific Symposium (2005)*, available at <http://www.international.icomos.org/xian2005/papers.htm> (accessed 29 November 2012).

Mutua, Makau wa, 'The Ideology of Human Rights', *Va J Intl L* 36 (1996), 589 657.

Nafziger, James AR, 'The Underlying Constitutionalism of the Law Governing Anchaeological and Other Cultural Heritage', *Willamette L Rev* 30 (1994), 581 608.

Negativland, 'Two Relationships to a Cultural Public Domain', in James Boyle (ed), *Collected Papers: Duke Conference on the Public Domain* (Center for the Public Domain, 2003), 239 62.

Nhât, Phang Dang, 'The Timeless Epics of the Ethnic Minorities of Viet Nam', in Oscar Salemink (ed), *Viet Nam's Cultural Diversity: Approaches to Preservation* (UNESCO Publishing, 2001), 85 104.

Nickel, James W, 'Intrinsic Value and Cultural Preservation', *Ariz St LJ* 31 (1999), 355 61.

Nmehielle, Vincent Orlu, *The African Human Rights System: Its Laws, Practice, and Institutions* (Martinus Nijhoff, 2001).

Nordenflycht, José de, 'El Culto Postmoderno a los Monumentos: Patrimonio Local en Contexto Global', *ICOMOS 15th General Assembly and Scientific Symposium (2005)*, available at <http://www.international.icomos.org/xian2005/papers.htm> (accessed 29 November 2012).

Novak, Fabián, 'Biotechnology and Regional Integration Systems: Legislation and Practices in the Andean Community Countries', in Francesco Francioni and Tullio Scovazzi (eds), *Biotechnology and International Law* (Hart Publishing, 2006), 403 38.

Nuti, Giancarlo, 'Cultural Values: Intangible Forms and Places', *ICOMOS 14th General Assembly and Scientific Symposium (2003)*, available at <http://www.international.icomos.org/victoriafalls2003/papers.htm> (accessed 29 November 2012).

O'Keefe, Roger, 'World Cultural Heritage Obligations to the International Community as a Whole?', *ICLQ* 53 (2004), 189 209.

Obaldia, Irma De, 'Western Intellectual Property and Indigenous Cultures: The Case of the Panamanian Indigenous Intellectual Property Law', *BU Intl LJ* 23 (2005), 337 94.

Oguamanam, Chidi, 'Documentation and Digitization of Traditional Knowledge and Intangible Cultural Heritage: Challenges and Prospects', in Toshiyuki Kono (ed), *Intangible Cultural Heritage and Intellectual Property: Communities, Cultural Diversity and Sustainable Development* (Intersentia, 2009), 357 83.

Oguamanam, Chidi, 'Protecting Indigenous Knowledge in International Law: Solidarity Beyond the Nation state', *L Text Culture* 8 (2004), 191 230.

Okediji, Ruth L, 'An Enduring Legacy For the Knowledge Economy: UNESCO and the International Copyright System', in Abdulqawi A Yusuf (ed), *Standard Setting in UNESCO Vol I: Normative Action in Education, Science and Culture* (Martinus Nijhoff and UNESCO Publishing, 2007), 113 34.

Oquendo, Angel R, 'Indigeneity and the State: Comparative Critiques: Indigenous Self Determination in Latin America', *Fla J Intl L* 17 (2005), 625 46.

Ordóñez Cifuentes, José Emilio Rolando, 'Las Demandas Constitucionales en Guatemala y México', *Revista de Derechos Humanos* 1 (2003), 169 88.

Organización de los Estados Americanos, Consejo Interamericano para el Desarrollo Integral, *Documento Conceptual para el Tema Ministerial Cultura y el Rol de los Pueblos*

Indígenas, presentado por la Delegación de Guatemala para la Tercera Reunión Interamericana de Ministros y Máximas Autoridades de Cultura, del 13 al 15 de noviembre de 2006 en Montreal, Canadá. OEA/Sr.K/XXVII.3 CIDI/REMIC III/doc.4/06, 25 October 2006.

Organización de los Estados Americanos, *La Cultura como Finalidad del Desarrollo: Documento para el Seminario de Expertos en Políticas Culturales, Vancouver, Canadá, marzo 18 y 19 de 2002.*

Organization of American States, Inter American Council for Integral Development, *Concept Paper for the Ministerial Theme Culture and the Enhancement of the Dignity and Identity of Our People, presented by the Delegation of Jamaica for the Third Inter American Meeting of Ministers of Culture and Highest Appropriate Authorities, November 13 15, 2006, Montreal, Canada.* OEA/Ser.K/XXVII.3 CIDI/REMIC III/doc.6/06, of 26 October 2006.

Organization of American States, Inter American Council for Integral Development, *Concept Paper for the Ministerial Theme Preservation and Presentation of Cultural Heritage, presented by the Delegation of the United States for the Third Inter American Meeting of Ministers of Culture and Highest Appropriate Authorities, on November 13 15, 2006, in Montreal, Canada.* OEA/Ser.K/XXVII.3 CIDI/REMIC III/doc.5/06, of 26 October 2006.

Paterson, Robert K and Karjala, Dennis S, 'Looking Beyond Intellectual Property in Resolving Protection of the Intangible Cultural Heritage of Indigenous Peoples', *Cardozo J Intl & Comp L* 11 (2003), 633 70.

Pentassuglia, Gaetano, *Minority Groups and Judicial Discourse in International Law: A Comparative Perspective* (Martinus Nijhoff, 2009).

Pettygrove, Joseph C, 'Canyons, Castles & Controversies: A Comparison of Preservation Laws in the United States and Ireland', *Regent J Intl L* 4 (2006), 47 99.

Philp, Janette, 'The Political Appropriation of Burma's Cultural Heritage and its Implications for Human Rights', in Michele Langfield, William Logan, and Máiréad Nic Craith (eds), *Cultural Diversity, Heritage and Human Rights: Intersections in Theory and Practice* (Routledge, 2010), 83 100.

Pitta, Laura A, 'Economic and Moral Rights under US Copyright Law: Protecting Authors and Producers in the Motion Picture Industry', 12 *Ent & Sports Lawyer* 3 (1995), reprinted in Anthony D'Amato and Doris Estelle Long (eds), *International Intellectual Property Anthology* (Anderson Publishing Co, 1996), 134 135.

Pontes Neto, Hildebrando, 'As expressões do folclore e o direito autoral', *Revista da Faculdade de Direito Milton Campos* 9 (2002), 71 96.

Posey, Darrell A and Dutfield, Graham, *Beyond Intellectual Property: Toward Traditional Resource Rights for Indigenous Peoples and Local Communities* (International Development Research Centre, 1996).

Povinelli, Elizabeth A, *The Cunning of Recognition: Indigenous Alterities and the Making of Australian Multiculturalism* (Duke University Press, 2002).

Prott, Lyndel V, 'Some Considerations on the Protection of the Intangible Heritage: Claims and Remedies', in Peter Seitel (ed), *Safeguarding Traditional Culture: A Global Assessment* (Smithsonian Institution, 2001), 104 10.

Prott, Lyndel V and O'Keefe, Patrick J, '"Cultural Heritage" or "Cultural Property"?', *Intl J of Cultural Property* 1 (1992), 307 20.

Psychogiopoulou, Evangelia, 'Euro Mediterranean Cultural Cooperation in the Field of Heritage Conservation and Management', *Eur Foreign Affairs Rev* 10 (2005), 237 55.

Psychogiopoulou, Evangelia, *The Integration of Cultural Considerations in EU Law and Policies* (Martinus Nijhoff Publishers, 2008).

Puri, Kamal, 'Protection of Traditional Culture and Folklore', in Peter Seitel (ed), *Safeguarding Traditional Culture: A Global Assessment* (Smithsonian Institution, 2001), 97 103.

Radaelli, Sigfrido, 'Direito Moral do Autor', *Revista Forense* 109 (1947), 23 34.

Radin, Margareth Jane and Sunder, Madhavi, 'Introduction: The Subject and Object of Commodification', in Martha M Ertman and Joan C Williams (eds), *Rethinking Commodification: Cases and Readings in Law and Culture* (New York University Press, 2005), 8 33.

Ramaga, Philip Vuciri, 'Bases of Minority Identity', *Human Rights Q* 14 (1992), 409 28.

Ramaga, Philip Vuciri, 'Relativity of the Minority Concept', *Human Rights Q* 14 (1992), 104 19.

Ramos, Frederico José da Silva, 'Direitos de Autor', *Revista dos Tribunais* 274 (1958), 69 85.

Rattanavong, Houmphan, 'A Multi Ethnic Culture', in Yves Goudineau (ed), *Laos and Ethnic Minority Cultures: Promoting Heritage* (UNESCO Publishing, 2003), 27 32.

Reap, James K, 'Selected Legislative, Administrative and Management Approaches for Protecting the Setting of Heritage Places in the United States', *Proceedings of the ICOMOS 15th General Assembly and Scientific Symposium: Monuments and Sites in their Setting Conserving Cultural Heritage in Changing Townscapes and Landscapes*, available at <http://www.international.icomos.org/xian2005/papers.htm> (accessed 29 November 2012).

Reichmann, Jerome H, 'Of Green Tulips and Legal Kudzu: Repackaging Rights in Subpatentable Innovation', *Vand L Rev* 53 (2000), 1743 98.

Rentel, Alison Dundes and Dundes, Alan (eds), *Folk Law: Essays on the Theory and Practice of* Lex Non Scripta (University of Wisconsin Press, 1995).

Ringelheim, Julie, 'Minority Protection and Constitutional Recognition of Difference: Reflections on the Diversity of European Approaches', in A Verstichel, A Alen B De Witte, and P Lemmens (eds), *The Framework Convention for the Protection of National Minorities: A Useful Pan European Instrument?* (Intersentia, 2008), 33 50.

Robertson, Margaret Hart, 'The Difficulties of Interpreting Mediterranean Voices: Exhibiting Intangibles Using New Technologies', *Intl J of Intangible Heritage* 1 (2006), 26 34.

Rose, Carol M, 'Romans, Roads, and Romantic Creators: Traditions of Public Property in the Information Age', in James Boyle (ed), *Collected Papers: Duke Conference on the Public Domain* (2003), 89 110.

Rose, Mark, 'Nine Tenths of the Law: The English Copyright Debates and the Rhetoric of the Public Domain', in James Boyle (ed), *Collected Papers: Duke Conference on the Public Domain* (Center for the Public Domain, 2003), 75 88.

Rumrrill, Róger, 'Cosmovisión amazónica', in *Los Pueblos Indígenas y la Integración Andina Primer Foro de Intelectuales e Investigadores Indígenas* (2008), 82 4.

Salemink, Oscar, 'Who Decides Who Preserves What? Cultural Preservation and Cultural Representation', in Oscar Salemink (ed), *Viet Nam's Cultural Diversity: Approaches to Preservation* (UNESCO Publishing, 2001), 205 12.

Sambuc, Henri Philippe, *La Protection Internationale des Savoirs Traditionnels: La Nouvelle Frontière de la Proprieté Intellectuelle* (l'Harmattan, 2003).

Sánchez Botero, Esther, 'Los Derechos Indígenas en las Constituciones de Colombia y Ecuador', in Jorge Alberto Gonzáles Galván (ed), *Constitución y Derechos Indígenas* (Universidad Nacional Autónoma de México, 2002), 69 88.

Sax, Joseph L, *Playing Darts with a Rembrandt: Public and Private Interests in Cultural Treasures* (University of Michigan Press, 1999).

Scafidi, Susan, *Who Owns Culture? Appropriation and Authenticity in American Law* (Rutgers University Press, 2005).

Scheinin, Martin, 'The Right to Enjoy a Distinct Culture: Indigenous and Competing Uses of Land', in Theodore S Orlin, Allan Rosas, and Martin Scheinin (eds), *The Jurisprudence of Human Rights Law: A Comparative Interpretive Approach* (Turku Institute for Human Rights, 2000), 159 222.

Secretariat of the Convention on Biological Diversity, *Akwé: Kon Voluntary Guidelines for the Conduct of Cultural, Environmental and Social Impact Assessments Regarding Developments Proposed to Take Place on, or which are Likely to Impact on, Sacred Sites, and on Lands and Waters Traditionally Occupied by Indigenous and Local Communities* (2004).

Secretariat of the Convention on Biological Diversity, *Bonn Guidelines on Access to Genetic Resources and Fair and Equitable Sharing of the Benefits Arising out of their Utilization* (2002).

Seeger, Anthony, 'Lessons Learned from the ICTM (NGO) Evaluation of Nominations for the UNESCO *Masterpieces of the Oral and Intangible Heritage of Humanity*, 2001 5', in Laurajane Smith and Natsuko Akagawa (eds), *Intangible Heritage* (Routledge, 2009), 112 28.

Seitel, Peter (ed), *Safeguarding Traditional Culture: A Global Assessment* (Smithsonian Institution, 2001).

Sherkin, Samantha, 'A Historical Study on the Preparation of the *1989 Recommendation on the Safeguarding of Traditional Culture and Folklore*', in Peter Seitel (ed), *Safeguarding Traditional Culture: A Global Assessment* (Smithsonian Institution, 2001), 42 56.

Silverman, Helaine and Ruggles, D Fairchild (eds), *Cultural Heritage and Human Rights* (Springer, 2007).

Silverman, Helaine and Ruggles, D Fairchild, 'Cultural Heritage and Human Rights', in Helaine Silverman and D Fairchild Ruggles (eds), *Cultural Heritage and Human Rights* (Springer, 2007), 3 22.

Simana, Suksavang and Preisig, Elisabeth, '"Kmhumu" Music and Musical Instruments', in Yves Goudineau (ed), *Laos and Ethnic Minority Cultures: Promoting Heritage* (UNESCO Publishing, 2003), 123 32.

Simon, Bradford S, 'Global Steps to Local Empowerment in the Next Millennium: An Assessment of UNESCO's 1989 *Recommendation on the Safeguarding of Traditional Culture and Folklore*', in Peter Seitel (ed), *Safeguarding Traditional Culture: A Global Assessment* (Smithsonian Institution, 2001), 111 42.

Sinamai, Ashton, 'Cultural Shifting Sands: Changing Meanings of Zimbabwe Sites in Zimbabwe, South Africa and Botswana', *ICOMOS 15th General Assembly and Scientific Symposium (2005)*, available at <http://www.international.icomos.org/xian2005/papers.htm> (accessed 29 November 2012).

Siphandone, Kamtay, '5th Party Congress Directive on Cultural Activities in the New Era: Ninth meeting of the Administrative Commission of the Party Central Committee', in Yves Goudineau (ed), *Laos and Ethnic Minority Cultures: Promoting Heritage* (UNESCO Publishing, 2003), 289 92.

Skounti, Ahmed, 'The Authentic Illusion: Humanity's Intangible Cultural Heritage, the Moroccan Experience', in Laurajane Smith and Natsuko Akagaway (eds), *Intangible Heritage* (Routledge, 2009), 74 92.

Skrydstrup, Martin, 'Symposium Report: Only in America? Athnographic Archives, Communities of Origin and Intangible Cultural Heritage', *Intl J of Intangible Heritage* 2 (2007), 132 6.

Sljivic, Ana, 'Why Do You Think It's Yours? An Exposition of the Jurisprudence Underlying the Debate between Cultural Nationalism and Cultural Internationalism', *GW J Intl L & Econ* 31 (1997 1998), 393 438.

Smith, Laurajane, *The Uses of Heritage* (Routledge, 2006).

Souksavat, Bouthèng, 'The Tunglung: An Alak Musical Instrument', in Yves Goudineau (ed), *Laos and Ethnic Minority Cultures: Promoting Heritage* (UNESCO Publishing, 2003), 133 6.

South Centre, *The TRIPs Agreement: A Guide for the South* (South Centre, 1997).

Souza Filho, Carlos Frederico Marés de, *Bens Culturais e sua Proteção Jurídica* (Juruá, 2008).

Staneva, Hristina, 'Heritage Legislation Challenges in the Context of European Integration', *ICOMOS 13th General Assembly and International Symposium*, available at <http://www.international.icomos.org/madrid2002/actas/112.pdf> (accessed 29 November 2012).

Stavenhagen, Rodolfo, 'La Diversidad Cultural en el Desarrollo de las Américas: Los pueblos indígenas y los estados nacionales en Hispanoamérica', *OEA, Unidad de Desarrollo Social, Educación y Cultural, Serie de Estudios Culturales No 9* (2004).

Steiner, Henry J and Alston, Philip, *International Human Rights in Context Law, Politics, Morals* (Oxford University Press, 2000).

Strowel, Alain, *'Droit d'auteur et copyright': Étude de droit comparé* (LGDJ, 1993).

Suagee, Dean B, 'The Cultural Heritage of American Indian Tribes and the Preservation of Biological Diversity', *Ariz St LJ* 31 (1999), 483 538.

Sudre, Frédéric, 'Les "obligations positives" dans la jurisprudence européenne des droits de l'homme', *Revue Trimestrielle des Droits de l'homme* 23 (1995), 363 84.

Tariffi, Flavio, Christensen, Peter Holm, and Le Guyader, Hervé, *Third Socio Economic Evaluation of Cultural Heritage Projects under the IST 2001 Work Programme: Report of the Evaluation Panel* (European Communities, 2002).

Thanh, Tô Ngoc, 'Protecting the Intangible Cultural Heritage of Minority Groups in Viet Nam', in Yves Goudineau (ed), *Laos and Ethnic Minority Cultures: Promoting Heritage* (UNESCO Publishing, 2003), 219 22.

Thanh, Tô Ngoc, 'The Intangible Culture of the Vietnamese Minorities: Questions and Answers', in Oscar Salemink (ed), *Viet Nam's Cultural Diversity: Approaches to Preservation* (UNESCO Publishing, 2001), 121 6.

The Press and Communication Department of the European Commission, *Figel' launches landmark process for cultural heritage in the Western Balkans*, available at <http://europa.eu/rapid/pressReleasesAction.do?reference=IP/08/737&format=HTML&aged=0&language=EN> (accessed 29 November 2012).

Thomas, Preston, 'The 1989 UNESCO Recommendation and Aboriginal and Torres Strait Islander Peoples' Intellectual Property Rights', in Peter Seitel (ed), *Safeguarding Traditional Culture: A Global Assessment* (Smithsonian Institution, 2001), 89 96.

Thornberry, Patrick, *International Law and the Rights of Minorities* (Clarendon Press, 1991).

Tokumaru, Yosihiko, 'Transmitting Music: Towards a Re Evaluation of the Human Body', in Oscar Salemink (ed), *Viet Nam's Cultural Diversity: Approaches to Preservation* (UNESCO Publishing, 2001), 233 8.

Tolefo Llancaqueo, Victor, 'El nuevo régimen internacional de derechos de propiedad intelectual y los derechos de los pueblos indígenas', in Mikel Berraondo (ed), *Pueblos Indígenas y Derechos Humanos* (Universidad de Deusto, 2006), 509 36.

Tomaszewski, Andrzej, 'Intellectual Context of Monuments and Sites in their Setting', *ICOMOS 15th General Assembly and Scientific Symposium (2005)*, available at <http://www.international.icomos.org/xian2005/papers.htm> (accessed 29 November 2012).

Trabalhos com Engenho: Escultura de Ídolos Sagrados de Macau (Museu de Macau, 2008).

Tritton, Guy, et al, *Intellectual Property in Europe* (Sweet & Maxwell, 2002).

Tsagourias, Nicholas (ed), *Transnational Constitutionalism: International and European Perspectives* (Cambridge University Press, 2007).

Tzevelekos, Vassilis P, 'The Use of Article 31(3)(c) of the VCLT in the Case Law of the ECtHR: An Effective Anti Fragmentation Tool or a Selective Loophole for the Reinforcement of Human Rights Teleology? Between Evolution and Systemic Integration', *Mich J of Intl L* 31 (2010), 621 90.

UNESCO, *Extracts of States Parties comments on possible modalities for the participation of communities or their representatives, practitioners, experts, centers of expertise and research institutes in the implementation of the Convention for the Safeguarding of the Intangible Cultural Heritage, Working document prepared by the Secretariat of the Intergovernmental Committee for the Safeguarding of the Intangible Cultural Heritage* (January 2008).

UNESCO, *Final Report International Meeting of Experts on Intangible Cultural Heritage: Priority Domains for an International Convention* (Rio de Janeiro, Brazil, 2002).

UNESCO, *International Round Table: 'Intangible Cultural Heritage Working Definitions'*, meeting held in Turin Piedmont (Italy) on 14 17 March 2001.

UNESCO, *Preparation of a preliminary draft International Convention on the Intangible Cultural Heritage, Meeting of the 'Restricted Drafting Group' (RDG) in Paris, 20 22 March 2002 Outline Work Plan.*

UNESCO, *Report on the Expert Meeting on Criteria for Inscription on the Lists Established by the 2003 Convention for the Safeguarding of the Intangible Cultural Heritage* (Paris, 5 6 December 2005).

UNESCO General Conference, *Oral Report of the Chairperson of Commission IV*, Doc 31 C/INF.24, of 12 November 2001.

United Nations Development Programme (UNDP), *Human Development Report 2004 Cultural Liberty in Today's Diverse World.*

Valadés, Diego, 'Los Derechos de los Indígenas y la Renovación Constitucional en México', in Jorge Alberto Gonzáles Galván (ed), *Constitución y Derechos Indígenas* (Universidad Nacional Autónoma de México, 2002), 13 20.

Valenta, Lisa, 'Disconnect: The 1988 Brazilian Constitution, Customary International Law, and Indigenous Land Rights in Northern Brazil', *Tex Intl LJ* 38 (2003), 643 62.

Valladolid, Julio, 'Sabiduría en la crianza de la chacra', in *Los Pueblos Indígenas y la Integración Andina Primer Foro de Intelectuales e Investigadores Indígenas* (2008), 61 5.

Van Alstyne, William W, 'Reconciling what the First Amendment Forbids with what the Copyright Clause Permits: A Summary Explanation and Review', in James Boyle (ed), *Collected Papers: Duke Conference on the Public Domain* (Center for the Public Domain, 2003), 225 38.

Van Cott, Donna Lee, *The Friendly Liquidation of the Past: The Politics of Diversity in Latin America* (University of Pittsburgh Press, 2000).

van de Walle, Dominique and Cratty, Dorothyjean, 'Do Donors Get What They Paid For? Micro Evidence on the Fungibility of Development Project Aid', *World Bank Policy Research Working Paper 3542* (2005).

Van Uytsel, Steven, 'Inventory Making and Fairy Tales: Safeguarding of Intangible Cultural Heritage in Historical Perspective', in Toshiyuki Kono (ed), *Intangible Cultural Heritage and Intellectual Property: Communities, Cultural Diversity and Sustainable Development* (Intersentia, 2009), 113 41.

van Zanten, Wim, 'Prior Informed Consent: Experiences with Ethnomusicology Recordings', in Toshiyuki Kono (ed), *Intangible Cultural Heritage and Intellectual Property: Communities, Cultural Diversity and Sustainable Development* (Intersentia, 2009), 283 308.

Van, Dang Nghiêm, 'Preservation and Development of the Cultural Heritage', in Oscar Salemink (ed), *Viet Nam's Cultural Diversity: Approaches to Preservation* (UNESCO Publishing, 2001), 33 62.

Vargas, Jorge A, 'Mexico's Legal Revolution: An Appraisal of Its Recent Constitutional Changes, 1988 1995', *Ga J Intl & Comp L* 25 (1996), 497 559.

Vargyas, Gábor, 'Intangible Culture of the Bru: Preservation, Promotion and Reassertion of Values', in Oscar Salemink (ed), *Viet Nam's Cultural Diversity: Approaches to Preservation* (UNESCO Publishing, 2001), 199 204.

Vargyas, Gábor, 'The Bru: A Minority Straddling Laos and Viet Nam', in Yves Goudineau (ed), *Laos and Ethnic Minority Cultures: Promoting Heritage* (UNESCO Publishing, 2003), 159 62.

Vila Nova, Júlio, *Panorama de Folião: O Carnaval de Pernambuco na Voz dos Blocos Líricos* (Fundação de Cultura Cidade do Recife, 2007).

Vitrano, Victoria J, 'Protecting Cultural Objects in an Internal Border Free EC: The EC Directive and Regulation for the Protection and Return of Cultural Objects', *Fordham Intl LJ* 17 (1994), 1164 201.

Vlachaki, Maria, 'Crossing Cultures through the Intangible Heritage: An Education Programme about Migration in Greece', *Intl J of Intangible Heritage* 2 (2007), 94 102.

Voon, Tania, 'UNESCO and WTO: A Clash of Cultures?', *ICLQ* 55 (2006), 635 51.

Vorakhoun, Bouabane, 'Survey of Preservation and Promotion of Minority Cultures in the Lao PDR', in Yves Goudineau (ed), *Laos and Ethnic Minority Cultures: Promoting Heritage* (UNESCO Publishing, 2003), 247 50.

Vrdoljak, Ana, *International Law, Museums and the Return of Cultural Objects* (Cambridge University Press, 2006).

Wagner, Peter, 'From Monuments to Human Rights: Redefining "Heritage" in the Work of the Council of Europe', in *Forward Planning: The Function of Cultural Heritage in a Changing Europe* (Council of Europe, 2000), 9 28.

Watson, Irene, 'Aboriginal Sovereignties: Past, Present and Future (Im)possibilities', in Suvendrini Perera (ed), *Our Patch: Australian Sovereignties Post 2001* (API Network, 2007), 23 43.

Weisbrod, Carol, *Emblems of Pluralism: Cultural Differences and the State* (Princeton University Press, 2002).

Wendland, Wend B, 'Managing Intellectual Property Options when Documenting, Recording and Digitizing Intangible Cultural Heritage', in Toshiyuki Kono (ed), *Intangible Cultural Heritage and Intellectual Property: Communities, Cultural Diversity and Sustainable Development* (Intersentia, 2009), 77 99.

Westkamp, Guido, 'The Qualification of Traditional Cultural Expressions in Private International Law: A Preliminary Appraisal', in Fiona Macmillan and Kathy Bowrey (eds), *New Directions in Copyright Law, Vol 3* (Edward Elgar, 2006), 198 228.

Wiessner, Siegfried, 'Rights and Status of Indigenous Peoples: A Global Comparative and International Legal Analysis', *Harv Human Rights J* 12 (1999), 57 128.

WIPO Intergovernmental Committee on Intellectual Property and Genetic Resources, Traditional Knowledge and Folklore, *Comparative Summary of Existing National* Sui Generis *Measures and Laws for the Protection of Traditional Knowledge*, Doc WIPO/GRTKF/IC/5/INF/4, of 20 June 2003.

WIPO Intergovernmental Committee on Intellectual Property and Genetic Resources, Traditional Knowledge and Folklore, *Composite Study on the Protection of Traditional Knowledge*, Doc WIPO/GRTKF/IC/5/8, of 28 April 2003.

WIPO Intergovernmental Committee on Intellectual Property and Genetic Resources, Traditional Culture and Folklore, *Consolidated Analysis of the Legal Protection of Traditional Cultural Expressions*, Doc WIPO/GRTKF/IC/5/3, of 2 May 2003.

WIPO Intergovernmental Committee on Intellectual Property and Genetic Resources, Traditional Knowledge and Folklore, *Information on National Experiences with the Intellectual Property Protection of Traditional Knowledge*, Doc WIPO/GRTKF/IC/5/INF/2, of 4 April 2003.

WIPO Intergovernmental Committee on Intellectual Property, Genetic Resources, Traditional Knowledge and Folklore, *The Protection of Traditional Cultural Expressions/Expressions of Folklore: Draft Objectives and Principles*, WIPO/GRTKF/IC/10/4, of 2 October 2006.

WIPO, *Comparative Summary of Sui Generis Legislation for the Protection of Traditional Cultural Expressions*, WIPO/GRTKF/IC/5/INF/3, Annex.

WIPO, *Consolidated Legal Analysis of the Legal Protection of Traditional Cultural Expressions (2003)*, Doc symbol WIPO/GRTKF/IC/5/3, Annex.

Wisnewski, J Jeremy, *The Politics of Agency: Towards a Pragmatic Approach to Philosophical Anthropology* (Ashgate, 2008).

Witz, Leslie, Rassool, Ciraj, and Minkley, Gary, 'Repackaging the Past for South African Tourism', in Gerard Corsane (ed), *Heritage, Museums and Galleries: An Introductory Reader* (Routledge, 2005), 308 19.

Workshop on Case Studies in the Protection of Cultural Heritage Central American Region, available at <http://portal.oas.org/Portal/Topic/SEDI/Educaci%C3%B3nyCultura/Cultura/TemasPrioritarios/Preservaci%C3%B3nyProtecci%C3%B3ndelPatrimonioCultural/Activities/ProtegiendoelPatrimonioCultural/tabid/1447/language/en US/Default.aspx> (accessed 29 November 2012).

Worthen, Kevin J, 'The Grand Experiment: Evaluating Indian Law in the "New World"', *Tulsa J Comp & Intl L* 5 (1998), 299 334.

Worthen, Kevin J, 'The Role of Indigenous Groups in Constitutional Democracies: A Lesson from Chile and the United States', in Cynthia Price Cohen (ed), *The Human Rights of Indigenous Peoples* (Transnational Publishers, 1998), 235 70.

Wouters, Jan and de Meester, Bart, 'The UNESCO Convention on Cultural Diversity and WTO Law: A Case Study in Fragmentation of International Law', *J of World Trade* 42(1) (2008), 205 40.

Yamaguti, Osamu, 'Harmony in Cultural Projects: Revitalization of the Music and Dance of the Vietnamese Minorities', in Oscar Salemink (ed), *Viet Nam's Cultural Diversity: Approaches to Preservation* (UNESCO Publishing, 2001), 229 32.

Yanagi, Yoshikuni, 'Research on Textile Traditions', in Yves Goudineau (ed), *Laos and Ethnic Minority Cultures: Promoting Heritage* (UNESCO Publishing, 2003), 261 4.

Yerkovich, Sally, 'Linking the Present with the Past through Intangible Heritage in History Museums', *Intl J of Intangible Heritage* 1 (2006), 44 52.

Yonover, Geri J, 'Artistic Parody: The Precarious Balance: Moral Rights, Parody, and Fair Use', *Cardozo Arts & Ent LJ* 14 (1996), 79 122.

Yourow, Howard Charles, *The Margin of Appreciation Doctrine in the Dynamics of European Human Rights Jurisprudence* (Kluwer Law International, 1996).

Yrigoyen Fajardo, Raquel, 'Hitos del reconocimiento del pluralismo jurídico y el derecho indígena en las políticas indigenistas y el constitucionalismo andino', in Mikel Berraondo (ed), *Pueblos Indígenas y Derechos Humanos* (Universidad de Deusto, 2006), 537 67.

Yu, Peter K, 'International Rights Approaches to Intellectual Property: Reconceptualizing Intellectual Property Interests in a Human Rights Framework', *UC Davis L Rev* 40 (2007), 1039 49.

Zhan, Guo, 'Setting Factors and Judging Standards of World Cultural Heritage', *ICOMOS 14th General Assembly and Scientific Symposium (2003)*, available at <http://www.international.icomos.org/victoriafalls2003/papers.htm> (accessed 29 November 2012).

Ziegler, Katja S, 'Cultural Heritage and Human Rights', *Social Sciences Resource Network*, available at <http://ssrn.com/abstract=1002620> (accessed 29 November 2012).

Zografos, Daphne, 'The Appropriation of American Indian Names and Images in Trade Marks The Washington Redskins Case', in Guido Westkamp (ed), *Emerging Issues in Intellectual Property: Trade Technology and Market Freedom: Essays in Honour of Herchel Smith* (Edward Elgar, 2007), 391 406.

Index

Note: Page numbers in bold represent main discussion of the topic.

Afghanistan 13
African Union, *see* regionalism
agency and representation 32, 125 126, 193, 203 204, **210–223**, 238
Andean Community of Nations, *see* regionalism
Argentina 52, 221, 223
Australia **120–122**, 176, 187 188, 193, 194, 195
authenticity **17**, 19 20, 31, 125, 176, 192, 223

Belgium 222
benefit-sharing 179, 197, 213, 226, 227, **229–231**, 241
  and the cultural commons 201, 203, 206, 207
  in the ICH Convention 38
  as a positive consequence of commodification 16, 123
  in relation to Traditional Knowledge 63, 64, 99, 101, 215, 216, 217
biological diversity 99 100
  Convention on Biological Diversity 29, 33, **63–65**, 100, 101, 215, 217, 226, 227
  see also Traditional Knowledge
Bolivia 30, 48, 98, 116 117, **117–120**, 122 123, 141
Brazil 40, 43, 109, 112 116, **134–138**, 140 141, 215, 226
Bulgaria 53

Canada 61, 116, 155, 156, 157
Chile 48
China 46, 53, **128–129**, 210, 222
Colombia 46, 98, 109
colonialism 14, 68, 82, **83–86**, 102 103, 110, 115, 173, 183
commodification **14–18**, 36, 47, 51, 233, 234, 235, 240, 241
  in the definition of heritage 9, 31, 32
  in relation to economic exploitation of heritage 36, 55, 58, 126
  in relation to intellectual property 175, **176–179**, 182, 191, 192, 199, 203
  see also community involvement
community involvement 1, 4, 7, 10, **11–12**, 13, 210, 214 215, **218–223**, 227, 234, 235, 237 238, 240 241
  in relation to commodification and control over heritage 16, 17, 18
  in relation to control over the meaning of tangible artifacts 20
  in relation to development 71, 72 73
  in relation to heritage experts 9, 24
  in relation to human rights 142, 145, 172 173
  in the implementation of the ICH Convention 36, 37, 39, 40, 41, 42 43, 44, 45, 48 49, **53–54**
  in relation to intellectual property 175, 178 179, 183, 187, 196 197, 198, 199, 203, 205, 207 208
  in relation to regional identities 78, 85
  in relation to Traditional Knowledge 64 65, 217
competition law 97
  see also intellectual property
conservationism, *see* preservation
constitutionalism **106–120**, 123, 130, 134, 140
contractual approaches 26, 64, **205–231**, 237, 241
Costa Rica 109, 126
Council of Europe, *see* regionalism
cultural commons 175, **197–204**, 206 210
  see also public domain
cultural diversity 35, 71, 73, 85 86, 107 108, 109, 132, 152, 173, 199, 241
  see also UNESCO, Cultural Diversity Convention
cultural harm 102, 175, 177, 179, 196, 239, 240
  see also intellectual property, tort
cultural heritage
  cultural landscapes 67, 78, 93, 95, 96, 164 165
  definition of Intangible Cultural Heritage 1, **7–10**, 16, 34 35
  heritage as experience 16
  tangible v intangible heritage 2, 8, **18–22**, 233
  versus 'cultural property' 2, **5–7**
cultural identity 4, 7, 15, 25, 33, 73, 99, 123, 145, 146, 173, 191, 210, 211, 233, 234
  see also regionalism, regional identity
cultural impact assessment 217, 218 219
cultural landscapes, *see* cultural heritage
cultural property
  versus 'cultural heritage' 2, 5–7, 239

Denmark 207
development 24, 35 36, 59, 68, 69, **70–73**, 82, 89, 199, 210, 212, 233, 236
  development aid 91 92, 130, 133, 141, 173, 236
  economic development 17, 55, 78, 127, 130
  sustainable development 24, 35, 64, 236

development (*cont.*)
  UNCTAD 64
  see also community involvement
Dominican Republic 72

Ecuador 98, 109, 117
education 5
England, *see* United Kingdom
environmental impact assessments 139, 217, 220
European Union, *see* regionalism

female circumcision, *see* human rights
Finland 97, 156 157
Food and Agriculture Organization (FAO) 64
food as heritage 45, 46
France 126, 155, 160, 163, 164, 166, 167, 184, 185, 189, 207
free, prior, and informed consent 43, 44, 45 46, 75, 140, 204, 206, 210, 220, 222, **223–229**, 238

Germany 97, 207
Greece 46
Guatemala 72, 109

Honduras 109, 162
human rights 1, 9, 15, 25, 36, 68, 99, **145–173**, 180, 188, 191, 192, 196, 205, 211, 212, 225, 233, 235, 236, 238, 239, 240
  African Commission on Human and Peoples' Rights 170
  African Court of Human and Peoples' Rights 170
  collective rights, *see* group rights, below
  cultural privacy 163, 172, 195, 219
  equality and non-discrimination 26, 155, **158–161**, 162, 173
  European Commission of Human Rights 166
  European Court of Human Rights 146, 154, 164 165, 166, 167 168, 170, 192
  fair trial rights 169, 171
  female circumcision 172
  freedom of association 36, 154, 169, 171
  freedom of expression 26, 154, **162–163**, 171, 173, 181
  freedom of religion 26, 36, 154, **166–168**, 171, 173
  group rights 9, 120, 123 125, **154–158**, 165, 166, 171, 173
    versus individual rights 136, **147–152**, 165, 173, 190, 239
  human rights exception to heritage 145
    see also female circumcision
  human rights of indigenous peoples 69, 105, 123, 136 137, 140, 169, 171, 186
  Inter-American Commission on Human Rights 74, 114
  Inter-American Court of Human Rights 148, 154, 158, 159, 161, 162, 163, 169, 170, 171
  limitations to rights **170–172**
  minority rights, *see* group rights, above
  non-discrimination, *see* equality and non-discrimination, above
  personal honour and reputation 181
  right to culture 74, 153, 169 170
  right to heritage **79**, 153, 173
  right to physical integrity 169, 171
  right to private and family life 26, 36, 154, 161, **163–165**, 171
  right to property 169, 171
    see also property
  Roma rights 164 165
  United Nations Human Rights Committee 154 158, 159, 160, 161, 162 163, 164, 170
  women's rights 156, 160, 214 215
    see also female circumcision
  see also community involvement

identity, *see* cultural identity
India 43, 207
indigenous peoples 106 120, 123, 211, 226, 231
  see also human rights of indigenous peoples
  indigenous heritage 8, 23 24, 46 47, 63, 64 65, 67, 69, 71 72, 73, 119, 138, 140
    see also western heritage
  indigenous traditional knowledge, *see* Traditional Knowledge
  OAS Declaration on the Rights of Indigenous Peoples 25, **73–76**, 235
  self-determination / autonomy 13, 72, 101, 215
Indonesia 120, 132 133
Intangible Heritage Convention 3, 8, 9, 17, 19, 22, 29, **34–56**, 63, 80, 82 83, 85, 86, 93, 102, 126, 127, 128, 135, 146, 147, 150, 151, 162, 169, 172, 175, 176, 181, 195, 209, 216, 221, 235, 236
  antecedents 30 33
  basic features 34 37
  catalogue of best practices 43, **47–49**
  complementarity and non-state actors 37 40
  criticism 51 56
  Fund for the Safeguarding of the Intangible Cultural Heritage **49–50**
  List of Intangible Cultural Heritage in Need of Urgent Safeguarding **43–45**, 235
  Representative List of the Intangible Cultural Heritage of Humanity 43, **45–47**, 213, 235
  safeguarding system 40 51
  see also benefit-sharing; community involvement

intellectual property 1, 8, 17, 26, 30, 32, 37, 55, 60, 74 75, 88, 93 98, 99, 100, 120 122, 125, 129, 134, 136, 138, 140, **175–204**, 205, 206, 210, 221, 226, 231, 233, 237, 240, 241
- appellations of origin 125, **192–193**
- competition rules related to intellectual property 191, **195–196**
- copyright 88, 91, 94, 97 98, 175, 176, 177, 178, 179, 180, **184–188**, 191, 194
- industrial design **194**
- moral rights 98, 180, 181, 186, **188–191**, 196, 197, 199, 208, 209, 226
- patents 183 184
- performers' rights 97, 186
- tort, intellectual property as **196–197**, 237, 240
- trade secret **194–195**
- trademarks 127, 179, **191–192**
- TRIPS Agreement, *see* trade
- WIPO 25, 26, 29, 30 31, 35, 37, **56–58**, 176, 186, 226
- *see also* commodification; community involvement

interculturalism, *see* cultural diversity
internationalism
- versus nationalism **10–14**

Iran 177
Ireland 134, 166
Italy 46, 177, 189, 193, 207

Jamaica 73
Japan 128, 132

languages 82 83, 85, 118, 130, 162 163
Laos 128, **129–131**, 141, 210
Latvia 44 45

Mauritius 160
Mexico 72, 111
minorities, *see* cultural diversity; human rights, group rights; indigenous peoples
Morocco 46
multiculturalism, *see* cultural diversity

nationalism
- versus internationalism, *see* internationalism

Netherlands 160
North American Free Trade Area (NAFTA), *see* regionalism
Norway 43, 53 54, 159, 195

Organization of American States (OAS), *see* regionalism
outstanding universal value 33, 50

Panama 122, **123–126**, 141, 214 215, 220
Paraguay 158, 162
Peru 48, 98
Philippines **140–141**
Poland 189
Portugal 110
preservation 12
- conservationism 16

property 6 7, 16, 23, 140, 182 183, 199, 201, 203, 210, 231
- *see also* cultural property; intellectual property; human rights, right to property

public domain 175, **197–204**, 241

regionalism 25, **67–103**
- economic regionalism 5, **86–103**, 105
  - Andean Community of Nations 25, 67, 86, **98–102**, 236
  - European Union 25, 61, 67, 78, 86, **87–98**, 102, 138, 211, 236 237
  - FTAA 186
  - NAFTA 61
- political regionalism **67–86**
  - African Union 25, 34, 67, **81–86**, 102 103, 211, 236
  - Council of Europe 25, 67, **76–81**, 91, 102, 211, 236
  - OAS 25, 67, **68–76**, 100, 102, 210, 236
    - OAS Declaration on the Rights of Indigenous Peoples, *see* indigenous peoples
- regional identity
  - African 82, 85 86
  - European 76, **77–78**, 79 80, 87, 91, 236
  - Inter-American 70
  - *see also* community involvement

representation, *see* agency and representation
representative value 33, 36, 43, 50
ritual slaughter 167 168
Roma rights, *see* human rights
Romania 127 128, 141

social impact assessment 138 139, 217, 220
South Africa 133 134
South Korea 127
sovereignty 40, **52–53**, 65, 211, 216, 217, 227, 228, 236
Spain 36, 46, 110
sui generis solutions 55, 64, 98, **100–102**, 106, **122–126**, 134, 140
Suriname 169
Sweden 156

tangible v intangible heritage, *see* cultural heritage
tax incentives 137
tourism 4, 5, 10, 17, 89, 130, 132, 141
trade 1, **58–63**, 95 97
- GATS 61
- GATT 62, 63
- TRIPS 58, 190, 194
- WTO 25, 29, 35, **60–63**, 105
- *see also* regionalism

Traditional Knowledge (TK) 29, **63–65**, 99 101, 123, 184, 199, 219, 226, 236
see also benefit-sharing; community involvement
Turkey 167

UNESCO 25, **29–33**, 72, 180, 181, 185, 198, 221, 229, 233, 235, 239
Convention on the Return of Cultural Property (1970) 16
Cultural Diversity Convention 29, 58, **59–60**, 61 62, 73, 85, 217
Hague Convention for the Protection of Cultural Property in the Event of Armed Conflict 5, 16
Recommendation on the Safeguarding of Traditional Culture and Folklore **31–32**
Underwater Heritage Convention 16
Universal Copyright Convention 30
World Heritage Convention 29, 34, 35, 36, 37, 40, 42, 55 56
World Heritage Committee 33, 37, 55
World Heritage Fund 50
World Heritage List 16, 23
see also Intangible Heritage Convention
United Kingdom 164 165, 166, 200
United States of America 61, 72, 106, 116, **138–140**, 141, 177 178, 190, 218
Uruguay 46, 110, 221, 222, 223

value of heritage 3 4
Venezuela 46
Viet Nam 128, **131–133**, 141, 187, 210

western heritage 2, 16, **22–25**, 35
World Heritage Convention, *see* UNESCO
World Intellectual Property Organization (WIPO), *see* intellectual property
World Trade Organization (WTO), *see* trade

The manufacturer's authorised representative in the EU for product safety is Oxford University Press España S.A. of El Parque Empresarial San Fernando de Henares, Avenida de Castilla, 2 - 28830 Madrid (www.oup.es/en or product.safety@oup.com). OUP España S.A. also acts as importer into Spain of products made by the manufacturer.
Printed and bound by CPI Group (UK) Ltd, Croydon, CR0 4YY

14/09/2026

02216306-0005

DORA: Interpreting the EU's Digital Operational Resilience Act

DORA: Interpreting the EU's Digital Operational Resilience Act

Dr Paul Lambert

Bloomsbury Professional

LONDON • DUBLIN • EDINBURGH • NEW YORK • NEW DELHI • SYDNEY

BLOOMSBURY PROFESSIONAL

Bloomsbury Publishing Plc
50 Bedford Square, London, WC1B 3DP, UK
1385 Broadway, New York, NY 10018, USA
29 Earlsfort Terrace, Dublin 2, Ireland

British Library Cataloguing-in-Publication Data

A catalogue record for this book is available from the British Library.

ISBN:	PB	978 1 52653 266 4
	ePDF	978 1 52653 268 8
	ePub	978 1 52653 267 1

Typeset by Evolution Design and Digital Ltd (Kent)
Printed and bound by CPI Group (UK) Ltd, Croydon, CR0 4YY

Dedication

My wonderful Mother
and
Fenton and Roswell

Abbreviations

DORA:	Digital Operational Resilience Act
ESAs:	European Supervisory Authorities
EBA:	European Banking Authority
ECB:	European Central Bank
EIOPA:	European Insurance and Occupational Pensions Authority
ESMA:	European Securities and Markets Authority
TLPT:	threat-led penetration testing
ENISA:	European Union Agency on Cybersecurity
CSIRT:	computer security incident response team
JON:	Joint Oversight Network

Contents

Dedication *v*
Abbreviations *vii*
Table of European Legislation *xvii*

Part A: Necessity

Chapter 1 Introduction **3**
Introduction 3
Cyber Threats 4
ICT threats and cost 4
Increased risk 5
Wide universe of ICT risk 5
Temporal risks 6
Payment attacks 6
IT/ICT Threats 7
Imperative Need 7
Threat gaps and vectors 7
Reliance and support 8
Resilience gap 9
Pivotal reliance 9
Payments 9
Trading 9
Funding 10
Insurance 10
Sector reliance 10
Systemic risks 10
International focus and concern 11
Challenge 11
Prior initiatives 12
Lack of harmonisation 12
Need for additional rules 13
Disparities 13
Coverage gaps 13
Outsourcing exposures 14
Group services 15
Cloud 15
Payment services 15
Review of risk and payment services and systems 16
Popularity and reliance on ICT services 16
Threat Solutions 17
Need for digital operational resilience 17
Consolidation 18
Controls and policies 19
Enhanced baseline protections 19

Supervision	19
Enhanced testing	20
Digital operational resilience rules	20
Chapter 2 Sectors and Industries	**23**
Wide Sectoral Remit	23
Wide Financial Sectors	23
ICT Sector	25
Chapter 3 Legal Compliance	**27**
Introduction	27
Requirements on Legal Compliance	28
Policy on Legal Compliance	32
Regulation instrument	33
Prior initiatives	33
New initiative	34
Graduated impact	35
National measures	35
Payment incidents	38
Prime responsibility	38
Emerging risk	38
Requirements on ICT Compliance	41
Simplified risk management framework	55
Identification and classification	57
Reporting incidents	59
Supervisory feedback	64
Payment incidents	65
Testing	65
Chapter 4 Policy on ICT Compliance	**71**
Increased Attention on ICT risk	71
Ineffective Policy	71
Limited Policy Focus	72
Cross-sectoral Influence	72
Testing Gaps, Hidden Concerns	73
Graduated Tests	73
Not one size fits all	75
Sector Testing	76
Management	77
Continuity	77
Reporting and Monitoring	77
International	78
Chapter 5 Law and Governance	**81**
Introduction	81
Requirements on Law and Governance	81
Management responsibility	81
Third-party arrangements	82
Register of information template	85
Arrangements	86
Policy on Law and Governance	94
Policy strategy	94

Limited earlier attention 94
Digital and physical resilience 95
Cloud industry 95
Effective ICT risk strategy 95
Supervisory strategy 96
Complex arrangements 96
Outsourcing rules 97
Varied monitoring 97
Risk multiplied 98
Increased ICT risk complexity 98
Chilling 98
Need for shared intelligence 99
Global ICT risk 99
Disparate resources 100
Board responsibility and input 100
Flexibility 101
Threat evolution 101
Continuity, recovery 101
Market assessment 101
ICT risk sources 102
Responsive monitoring 102
Diligence and ICT partners 103
Competition and concentration 103
Key providers and provisions 104
Additional key provisions 104
Access 105
Exit and transition 105
Standard clauses 105
Consolidated regulatory effects 106
Oversight and criticality 106
Direct services 107
Digital transformation 107
Oversight of critical services 108
Subsidiaries 108
Global service providers 108
Contact designation 109
Additional oversight 109
Regulatory expertise 109
ESA mandate 110
Reporting formats 110
Payment systems 110
Contagion 111

Chapter 6 Regulatory Reports and Reporting 113
Introduction 113
Requirements on Reports 113
Policy on Reports 115
Divergent reporting problems 115
Reporting of incidents 115
Bad actor motivation 116
Timing and sharing 116
Incidents and reports vary 117

Critical incident reporting 117
Register of information 117
Skills 117

Chapter 7 Investigations **119**
Introduction 119
Requirements on Investigations 119
Policy on Investigations 120
Collaboration 120
Communication 120
National efforts 121
European oversight 121
Powers 121
Rights 122
Verifying compliance 122
Oversight principles 122
Risk management obligations remain 123
Shared expertise 123
Oversight costs 123
Further regulation on systemic impacts 124

Chapter 8 Fines, Penalties, Prosecutions **125**
Introduction 125
Requirements on Fines, Penalties, Prosecutions 125
Policy on Fines, Penalties, Prosecutions 130
Engagement 130
New fines and penalties 130

PART B: DORA

Chapter 9 The Digital Operational Resilience Act **133**
Overview 133
Title 133
DORA Chapter Themes 133
DORA Chapter Details 134
DORA Pillars 136
DORA Level 1 137
DORA Level 2 137

Chapter 10 General Provisions **141**
General Provisions 141
Subject Matter 141
Scope 142
Definitions 145
Digital operational resilience 146
Network and information system 146
Legacy ICT system 146
Security of network and information systems 147
ICT risk 147
Information asset 147

ICT asset 147
ICT-related incident 148
Operational or security payment-related incident 148
Major ICT-related incident 148
Major operational or security payment-related incident 149
Cyber threat 149
Significant cyber threat 149
Cyber-attack 150
Threat intelligence 150
Vulnerability 150
Threat-led penetration testing 150
ICT third-party risk 151
ICT third-party service provider 151
ICT intra group service provider 151
ICT services 151
Critical or important function 152
Critical ICT third-party service provider 152
ICT third-party service provider established in third country 152
Subsidiary 152
Group 153
Parent undertaking 153
ICT subcontractor established in a third country 153
ICT concentration risk 153
Management body 153
Credit institution 154
Institution exempted pursuant to Directive 2013/36 154
Investment firm 154
Small and non-interconnected investment firm 154
Payment institution 154
Payment institution exempted 154
Account information service provider 155
Electronic money institution 155
Electronic money institution exempted 155
Central counterparty 155
Trade repository 155
Central securities depository 155
Trading venue 156
Manager of alternative investment funds 156
Management company 156
Data reporting service provider 156
Insurance undertaking 156
Reinsurance undertaking 156
Insurance intermediary 156
Ancillary insurance intermediary 157
Reinsurance intermediary 157
Institution for occupational retirement provision 157
Small institution for occupational retirement provision 157
Credit rating agency 157
Crypto asset service provider 157
Issuer of asset referenced tokens 158
Administrator of critical benchmarks 158
Crowdfunding service provider 158

Securitisation repository 158
Microenterprise 158
Lead Overseer 159
Joint Committee 159
Small enterprise 159
Medium-sized enterprise 159
Public authority 159
Proportionality and Proportionality Principle 160
Governance and Organisation 161
Risk Management and ICT Risk Management Framework 164
ICT Systems, Protocols and Tools 170
Identification 171
Protection and Prevention 174
Detections 177
Response and Recovery 178
Backups and Restoration 181
Learnings 183
Communication 185
Harmonisation of ICT Risk Management Tools, Methods, Processes and Policies 185
Simplified ICT Risk Management Framework 187
Regulation 2024/1774 190
Overall risk profile and complexity 190
General elements of ICT security policies, procedures, protocols, and tools 190
ICT risk management 191
ICT asset management policy 193
ICT asset management procedure 194
Encryption and cryptographic controls 194
Cryptographic key management 195
Policies and procedures for ICT operations 195
Capacity and performance management 197
Vulnerability and patch management 197
Data and system security 199
Logging 201
Network security management 201
Securing information in transit 203
ICT project management 203
ICT systems acquisition, development, and maintenance 204
ICT change management 206
Physical and environmental security 207
Human resources policy 208
Identity management 209
Access control 209
ICT-related incident management policy 211
Anomalous activities detection and criteria for ICT-related incidents detection and response 212
Components of the ICT business continuity policy 213
Testing of the ICT business continuity plans 215
ICT response and recovery plans 217
Format and content of the report on the review of the ICT Risk Management Framework 218

Simplified ICT Risk Management Framework 221
Information security policy and measures 222
Classification of information assets and ICT assets 222
ICT risk management 223
Physical and environmental security 223
Access control 224
ICT operations security 225
Data, system and network security 225
ICT security testing 226
ICT systems acquisition, development, and maintenance 226
ICT project and change management 227
Components of the ICT business continuity plan 227
Testing of business continuity plans 228
Format and content of the report on the review of the Simplified ICT Risk Management Framework 228

Chapter 11 Incident Management, Classification and Reporting **231**
Incident Management, Classification and Reporting 231
ICT Incident Management Process 231
Classification of ICT Incidents and Cyber Threats 232
RTS sub-Regulation 2024/1774 re Article 18(1) and (4) 234
Classification criteria 234
Major incidents and materiality thresholds 237
Significant cyber threats 238
Relevance of major incidents to other competent authorities and reports 239
Regulation 2024/1774 re Article 18(2) 240
Overall risk profile and complexity 240
Incident Reporting 248
Harmonisation of Reporting Content and Templates 251
Centralisation of Reporting of Major ICT Incidents 252
Supervisory Feedback 254
Operational or Security Payment Related Incidents 255

Chapter 12 Digital Operational Resilience Testing **257**
Digital Operational Resilience Testing 257
General Requirements for Digital Operational Resilience Testing 257
Testing of ICT Tools and Systems: DORTP 258
Advanced Testing 260
Requirements for TLPT Testers 264

Chapter 13 Managing ICT Third-party Risk **265**
Managing ICT Third-party Risk 265
General Principles 265
Preliminary Assessment of ICT Concentration Risk 270
Key Contractual Provisions 271
Designation of Critical ICT Third-party Service Providers 275
Structure of the Oversight Framework 278
Tasks of the Lead Overseer 281
Operational Coordination Between Lead Overseers 282
Powers of the Lead Overseer 283
Exercise of Lead Overseer Powers Outside Union 286
Request for Information 288

General Investigations 290
Inspections 291
Ongoing Oversight 293
Harmonisation For Oversight 294
Follow-up by Competent Authorities 295
Oversight Fees 298
International Cooperation 299
ICT Risk Compliance 300

Chapter 14 Information Sharing Arrangements **301**
Information Sharing Arrangements 301
Information Sharing Arrangements on Cyber Threat Information and Intelligence 302

Chapter 15 Competent Authorities **305**
Competent Authorities 305
Cooperation with Structures and Authorities 306
Cooperation Between Authorities 307
Financial Cross Sector Exercises, Communication and Cooperation 307
Administrative Penalties and Remedial Measures 308
Exercise of Administrative Penalties and Remedies 310
Criminal Penalties 311
Publication of Administrative Penalties 311
Professional Secrecy 312
Data Protection 313
Notification Duties 313

Chapter 16 Delegated Acts **315**
Delegated Acts 315
Exercise of the Delegation 315

Chapter 17 Transitional and Final Provisions **319**
Transitional and Final Provisions 319
Entry Into Force and Application of DORA 319
Amendments 320
Review 321

Appendices

Appendix 1 DORA **325**

Appendix 2 DORA Level Two Regulatory Technical Standards and Delegated Regulations **437**
ESA draft Regulatory Technical Standards: Batch 1 437
ESA draft Regulatory Technical Standards: Batch 2 437
ESA/Commission Delegated Regulations Adopted 438
Commission Delegated Regulation (EU) 2024/1774 439

Index **487**

Table of European Legislation

TREATIES AND CONVENTIONS

Treaty on the Functioning of the European Union (Rome, 25 March 1957) ... 9.02
- Art 5 ... 1.37; 3.11
  - 101 ... 5.19
  - 114 ... 9.02
  - 127(2) ... 5.06, 5.37; 13.05
  - 290 ... 4.11; 5.47; 7.14
  - 291 ... 4.11

DIRECTIVES

Directive 2006/43/EC of the European Parliament and of the Council of 17 May 2006 on statutory audits of annual accounts and consolidated accounts, amending Council Directives 78/660/EEC and 83/349/EEC and repealing Council Directive 84/253/EEC ... 17.04

Directive 2009/65/EC of the European Parliament and of the Council of 13 July 2009 on the coordination of laws, regulations and administrative provisions relating to undertakings for collective investment in transferable securities (UCITS) (recast)
- Art 2(1)(b) ... 10.49
  - (5) ... 10.34
  - 97 ... 15.01

Directive 2009/110/EC of the European Parliament and of the Council of 16 September 2009 on the taking up, pursuit and prudential supervision of the business of electronic money institutions amending Directives 2005/60/EC and 2006/48/EC and repealing Directive 2000/46/EC ... 3.13; 10.03, 10.43, 10.82; 15.01
- Art 2(1) ... 10.42
  - 9 ... 3.08
  - (1) ... 10.43

Directive 2009/138/EC of the European Parliament and of the Council of 25 November 2009 on the taking-up and pursuit of the business of Insurance and Reinsurance (Solvency II) (recast)
- Art 4 ... 10.03
  - 13(1) ... 10.51
  - (4) ... 10.52
  - 30 ... 15.01

Directive 2011/61/EU of the European Parliament and of the Council of 8 June 2011 on Alternative Investment Fund Managers and amending Directives 2003/41/EC and 2009/65/EC and Regulations (EC) No 1060/2009 and (EU) No 1095/2010
- Art 3(2) ... 10.03
  - 4(1)(b) ... 10.48
  - 44 ... 15.01

Directive 2013/34/EU of the European Parliament and of the Council of 26 June 2013 on the annual financial statements, consolidated financial statements and related reports of certain types of undertakings, amending Directive 2006/43/EC of the European Parliament and of the Council and repealing Council Directives 78/660/EEC and 83/349/EEC ... 8.04
- Art 2(9) ... 10.31
  - (10) ... 10.29
  - (11) ... 10.30
  - 22 ... 10.29, 10.31

Directive 2013/36/EU of the European Parliament and of the Council of 26 June 2013 on access to the activity of credit institutions and the prudential supervision of credit institutions and investment firms, amending Directive 2002/87/EC and repealing Directives 2006/48/EC and 2006/49/EC 3.08, 3.13; 10.36, 10.82; 15.01
Art 2(4)... 3.13
(5)... 10.03
(3).................................... 10.03
(4)–(23) 3.02, 30.08; 10.03, 10.36
3(1)(7).................................... 10.34
4 .... 3.15; 11.11; 15.01
Directive 2014/59/EU of the European Parliament and of the Council of 15 May 2014 establishing a framework for the recovery and resolution of credit institutions and investment firms and amending Council Directive 82/891/EEC, and Directives 2001/24/EC, 2002/47/EC, 2004/25/EC, 2005/56/EC, 2007/36/EC, 2011/35/EU, 2012/30/EU and 2013/36/EU, and Regulations (EU) No 1093/2010 and (EU) No 648/2012, of the European Parliament and of the Council.. 5.34
Art 2(1)(35)............................ 3.15; 11.11
3 .... 3.15; 11.11; 15.04
Directive 2014/65/EU of the European Parliament and of the Council of 15 May 2014 on markets in financial instruments and amending Directive 2002/92/EC and Directive 2011/61/EU (recast)
Art 2, 3 .... 10.03
4(1)(1).................................... 10.37
(24)................................. 10.47
(36)................................. 10.34
67 .... 15.01
Directive (EU) 2015/2366 of the European Parliament and of the Council of 25 November 2015 on payment services in the internal market, amending Directives 2002/65/EC, 2009/110/EC and 2013/36/EU and Regulation (EU) No 1093/2010, and repealing Directive 2007/64/EC . 1.29; 2.02; 3.09, 3.13; 5.49; 10.03; 10.40, 10.82; 15.01; 17.04
Art 4(4).. 10.39
22 .... 15.01
32(1)................................ 3.08; 10.40
33(1)............................... 10.41; 15.01
108 .... 17.04
Directive (EU) 2016/97 of the European Parliament and of the Council of 20 January 2016 on insurance distribution (recast)
Art 2(1)(3).................................. 10.53
(4).................................. 10.54
(5).................................. 10.55
12 .... 15.01
Directive (EU) 2016/1148 of the European Parliament and of the Council of 6 July 2016 concerning measures for high common level of security of network and information systems across the Union...... 4.03; 5.08
Directive (EU) 2016/2341 of the European Parliament and of the Council of 14 December 2016 on the activities and supervision of institutions for occupational retirement provision (IORPs) 5.11
Art 5 .... 1.35; 3.08; 5.11
6(1).. 10.56
31 .... 1.35; 5.12
47 .... 15.01
Directive (EU) 2019/1937 of the European Parliament and of the Council of 23 October 2019 on the protection of persons who report breaches of Union Law.. 10.102

Directive (EU) 2019/2034 of the European Parliament and of the Council of 27 November 2019 on the prudential supervision of investment firms and amending Directives 2002/87/EC, 2009/65/EC, 2011/61/EU, 2013/36/EU, 2014/59/EU and 2014/65/EU
Art 4 .... 15.01
Directive (EU) 2022/2555 of the European Parliament and of the Council of 14 December 2022 on measures for a high common level of cybersecurity across the Union, amending Regulation (EU) No 910/2014 and Directive (EU) 2018/1972, and repealing Directive (EU) 2016/1148 (NIS 2 Directive) 3.15, 3.16; 4.03, 4.04; 5.06, 5.08, 5.10, 5.46; 6.03, 6.04, 6.06, 6.10; 7.09, 7.10, 7.12; 9.04; 10.02; 11.11, 11.12, 11.14; 13.06, 13.09, 13.16; 15.02, 15.09
Art 3, 4 .... 10.02
6(1) 10.06
(2) 10.08
14 .... 15.02
Directive (EU) 2022/2557 of the European Parliament and of the Council of 14 December 2022 on the resilience of critical entities and repealing Council Directive 2008/114/EC 5.09
Ch III (arts 12–18) 5.09
Ch IV (arts 19, 20) 5.09

REGULATIONS
Regulation (EC) No 1060/2009 of the European Parliament and of the Council of 16 September 2009 on credit rating agencies 3.02; 9.04
Art 3(1)(b) 10.58
21 .... 15.01
Regulation (EU) No 1093/2010 of the European Parliament and of the Council of 24 November 2010 establishing a European Supervisory Authority (European Banking Authority), amending Decision No 716/2009/EC and repealing Commission Decision 2009/78/EC 1.20; 3.05; 5.06; 8.02; 13.05, 13.12, 13.13
Art 10–14 .... 3.12, 3.13, 3.14, 3.15, 3.18; 4.11; 5.04, 5.05, 5.47; 10.81, 10.82; 11.03, 11.12; 12.04; 13.02, 13.04, 13.15
15 .... 4.11; 5.04; 11.12; 13.02
16 .... 3.12; 10.77; 13.06
33 .... 13.18
54 .... 10.66
56(1) 13.06
57(1) 13.06
60, 61 .... 13.11
Regulation (EU) No 1094/2010 of the European Parliament and of the Council of 24 November 2010 establishing a European Supervisory Authority (European Insurance and Occupational Pensions Authority), amending Decision No 716/2009/EC and repealing Commission Decision 2009/79/EC 1.20; 3.05; 5.06; 8.02; 13.05, 13.12, 13.13
Art 10–14 .... 3.12, 3.13, 3.14, 3.15, 3.18; 4.11; 5.04, 5.05, 5.47; 10.81, 10.82; 11.03, 11.12; 12.04; 13.02, 13.04, 13.15
15 .... 4.11; 5.04; 11.12; 13.02
16 .... 3.12; 10.77; 13.06
33 .... 13.18
54 .... 10.66
56(1) 13.06
57(1) 13.06
60, 61 .... 13.11

Regulation (EU) No 1095/2010 of the European Parliament and of the Council of 24 November 2010 establishing a European Supervisory Authority (European Securities and Markets Authority), amending Decision No 716/2009/EC and repealing Commission Decision 2009/77/EC .. 1.20; 3.05; 5.06; 8.02; 13.05, 13.12, 13.13
Art 10–14 .... 3.12, 3.13, 3.14, 3.15, 3.18; 4.11; 5.04, 5.05, 5.47; 10.81, 10.82; 11.03, 11.12; 12.04; 13.02, 13.04, 13.15
15 .... 4.11; 5.04; 11.12; 13.02
16 .... 3.12; 10.77; 13.06
33 .... 13.18
54 .... 10.66
56(1) 13.06
57(1) 13.06
60, 61 .... 13.11
Regulation (EU) No 648/2012 of the European Parliament and of the Council of 4 July 2012 on OTC derivatives, central counterparties and trade repositories 3.02; 9.04; 17.03
Art 2(1) 10.44
(2) 10.45
22 .... 15.01
Regulation (EU) No 1025/2012 of the European Parliament and of the Council of 25 October 2012 on European standardisation, amending Council Directives 89/686/EEC and 93/15/EEC and Directives 94/9/EC, 94/25/EC, 95/16/EC, 97/23/EC, 98/34/EC, 2004/22/EC, 2007/23/EC, 2009/23/EC and 2009/105/EC of the European Parliament and of the Council and repealing Council Decision 87/95/EEC and Decision No 1673/2006/EC of the European Parliament and of the Council
Art 2(1) 10.85, 10.89, 10.94, 10.96
(4), (5) 10.99
Regulation (EU) No 575/2013 of the European Parliament and of the Council of 26 June 2013 on prudential requirements for credit institutions and investment firms and amending Regulation (EU) No 648/2012
Art 4(1)(1) 10.35
Regulation (EU) No 1024/2013 of 15 October 2013 conferring specific tasks on the European Central Bank concerning policies relating to the prudential supervision of credit institutions
Art 6(4) 3.15, 3.18; 6.05; 11.11; 12.04; 15.01
Regulation (EU) No 600/2014 of the European Parliament and of the Council of 15 May 2014 on markets in financial instruments and amending Regulation (EU) No 648/2012 .... 3.02; 6.02; 9.04; 10.50; 17.03
Art 2(1)(18) 15.01
(34)–(36) 6.02; 10.50
Regulation (EU) No 909/2014 of the European Parliament and of the Council of 23 July 2014 on improving securities settlement in the European Union and on central securities depositories and amending Directives 98/26/EC and 2014/65/EU and Regulation (EU) No 236/2012 .... 3.02; 9.04; 17.03
Art 2(1)(1) 10.46
(45) 10.34
11 .... 15.01
Regulation (EU) No 806/2014 of the European Parliament and of the Council of 15 July 2014 establishing uniform rules and a uniform procedure for the resolution of credit institutions and certain investment firms in the framework of a Single Resolution Mechanism and a Single Resolution Fund and amending Regulation (EU) No 1093/2010 .... 15.04
Art 7(2) 3.15; 11.11
(4)(b) 3.15; 11.11
(5) 3.15; 11.11

Regulation (EU) 2016/679 of the European Parliament and of the Council of 27 April 2016 on the protection of natural persons with regard to the processing of personal data and on the free movement of such data, and repealing Directive 95/46/EC (General Data Protection Regulation) 1.02; 3.06; 5.19; 14.02; 15.10
Art 6 .... 5.19
(1)(c), (e), (f)........................ 5.19
Regulation (EU) 2016/1011 of the European Parliament and of the Council of 8 June 2016 on indices used as benchmarks in financial instruments and financial contracts or to measure the performance of investment funds and amending Directives 2008/48/EC and 2014/17/EU and Regulation (EU) No 596/2014...... 3.02; 9.04; 17.03
Art 3(1)(20)................................ 10.34
(25)................................ 10.61
40, 41 .... 15.01
Regulation (EU) 2017/2402 of the European Parliament and of the Council of 12 December 2017 laying down a general framework for securitisation and creating a specific framework for simple, transparent and standardised securitisation, and amending Directives 2009/65/EC, 2009/138/EC and 2011/61 EU and Regulations (EC) No 1060/2009 and (EU) No 648/2012
Art 2(23)..................................... 10.63
10 .... 15.01
14(1)..................................... 15.01
31(1)(b)................................ 10.65
Regulation (EU) 2018/1725 of the European Parliament and of the Council of 23 October 2018 on the protection of natural persons with regard to the processing of personal data by the Union institutions, bodies, offices and agencies and on the free movement of such data, and repealing Regulation (EC) No 45/2001 and Decision No 1247/2002/EC 15.10
Art 42(1)..................................... 3.11
Regulation (EU) 2019/881 of the European Parliament and of the Council of 17 April 2019 on ENISA (the European Union Agency for Cybersecurity) and on information and communications technology cybersecurity certification and repealing Regulation (EU) No 526/2013 (Cybersecurity Act).. 6.03
Art 2(8).. 10.16
Regulation (EU) 2019/2033 of the European Parliament and of the Council of 27 November 2019 on the prudential requirements of investment firms and amending Regulations (EU) No 1093/2010, (EU) No 575/2013, (EU) No 600/2014 and (EU) No 806/2014
Art 12(1)..................................... 10.38
Regulation (EU) 2020/1503 of the European Parliament and of the Council of 7 October 2020 on European crowdfunding service providers for business, and amending Regulation (EU) 2017/1129 and Directive (EU) 2019/1937
Art 2(1)(e).................................. 10.62
29 .... 15.01
Regulation (EU) 2022/2554 of the European Parliament and of the Council of 14 December 2022 on digital operational resilience for the financial sector and amending Regulations (EC) No 1060/2009, (EU) No 648/2021, (EU) No 600/2014, (EU) No 909/2104 and (EU) 2016/1011...... 1.01, 1.04, 1.06, 1.07, 1.08, 1.09, 1.17, 1.24, 1.26, 1.27, 1.29, 1.32, 1.34, 1.37; 2.01, 2.02, 2.03; 3.01, 3.02, 3.03, 3.06, 3.07, 3.08, 3.09, 3.10, 3.11, 3.12, 3.18; 4.02, 4.04, 4.05, 4.06, 4.07, 4.08, 4.11, 4.12; 5.01, 5.09, 5.10, 5.20, 5.21, 5.23, 5.26, 5.27, 5.28, 5.30, 5.31, 5.38, 5.42, 5.44, 5.49; 6.01, 6.04, 6.09; 7.01, 7.02, 7.06, 7.08, 7.10, 7.13; 8.01, 8.02, 8.04; 9.01, 9.02, 9.03, 9.05, 9.06,

Regulation (EU) 2022/2554 of the European Parliament and of the Council of 14 December 2022 on digital operational resilience for the financial sector and amending Regulations (EC) No 1060/2009, (EU) No 648/2021, (EU) No 600/2014, (EU) No 909/2104 and (EU) 2016/1011 – *contd*
9.07; 10.02, 10.03, 10.04, 10.07, 10.09, 10.12, 10.13, 10.14, 10.16, 10.21, 10.22, 10.27, 10.32, 10.33, 10.34, 10.44, 10.50, 10.59, 10.62, 10.64, 10.65, 10.67, 10.68, 10.70, 10.71, 10.72, 10.75, 10.76, 10.77, 10.79, 10.80, 10.81; 11.01, 11.10, 11.14; 12.02, 12.03, 12.04, 12.05; 13.01, 13.02, 13.03, 13.04, 13.05, 13.06, 13.07, 13.09, 13.12, 13.13, 13.19; 14.01; 15.01, 15.03, 15.04, 15.05, 15.07, 15.09, 15.10, 15.11; 17.02, 17.04; App 1
Recital (1) 1.03, 1.09, 1.10
(2) 1.11, 1.12, 1.14, 1.15, 1.16
(3) 1.17
(4) 1.18; 3.05; 4.01
(5) 1.19
(6) 1.31; 10.78
(7) 1.20; 3.05; 4.01; 10.81; 16.02
(8) 1.20, 1.21, 1.22; 10.81; 13.15
(9) 1.23; 10.81; 13.15
(10) 1.24; 10.81; 13.15
(11) 10.81; 13.15
(12) 1.32; 3.06; 4.02; 10.70
(13) 1.32
(14) 5.07; 10.81; 13.15
(15) 4.03; 5.08; 10.81; 13.15
(16) 10.81; 13.15
(18) 4.04
(19) 5.09
(20) 5.10
(21) 1.33, 1.34, 1.35; 5.11, 5.12; 11.12; 13.02

Regulation (EU) 2022/2554 of the European Parliament and of the Council of 14 December 2022 on digital operational resilience for the financial sector and amending Regulations (EC) No 1060/2009, (EU) No 648/2021, (EU) No 600/2014, (EU) No 909/2104 and (EU) 2016/1011 – *contd*
Recital (22) 6.03; 10.70, 10.81; 13.15
(24) 6.04; 10.81; 11.11; 13.15
(25) 1.36
(26) 4.05; 10.81; 12.02; 13.15
(28) 5.13; 13.04
(29) 5.14; 13.04
(30) 1.25; 5.15; 13.04
(31) 1.25, 1.26; 5.16; 13.04
(32) 5.17; 11.11; 14.02
(33) 5.18; 11.11; 14.02
(34) 5.19; 14.02
(35) 1.04; 5.20; 10.25
(36) 3.07; 10.70; 11.12
(38) 3.07; 5.21; 10.70; 11.12
(39) 10.70; 11.12
(40) 3.08; 10.70; 11.12
(42) 3.08; 10.70; 11.12
(43) 3.08; 4.06, 4.07; 10.70, 10.72; 11.12; 12.02
(44) 4.06; 10.70; 11.12; 12.02
(45) 4.09; 5.22
(46) 5.22
(47) 5.23; 10.72
(48) 5.24; 10.72
(49) 4.10; 5.25; 10.72
(50) 5.26; 10.72
(51) 6.05; 11.11
(52) 6.06; 14.02
(53) 6.07; 10.70; 11.12
(54) 3.09
(55) 6.08; 10.81; 11.11; 13.15
(56) 4.06; 12.02
(57) 4.12; 12.02
(59) 4.12; 12.02
(60) 4.08; 12.02
(61) 4.08; 12.02
(63) 1.26, 1.27, 1.28; 5.27; 10.25
(64) 3.10, 3.11; 5.28; 10.70; 11.12

Regulation (EU) 2022/2554 of the European Parliament and of the Council of 14 December 2022 on digital operational resilience for the financial sector and amending Regulations (EC) No 1060/2009, (EU) No 648/2021, (EU) No 600/2014, (EU) No 909/2104 and (EU) 2016/1011 – *contd*
Recital (65) 6.09; 11.11
(66) 5.29; 13.04
(67) 3.11; 5.30; 13.03, 13.04
(69) 5.31; 13.04
(71) 5.31; 13.04
(72) 5.32, 5.33; 13.04
(73) 5.34; 13.04
(74) 5.35; 13.04
(75) 5.36; 13.04
(76) 5.36; 13.06
(77) 5.37; 13.06
(78) 5.38; 13.06
(79) 13.02
(80) 13.06
(81) 1.30; 5.39; 8.04; 13.06
(82) 3.11; 5.40, 5.41; 7.03; 8.03
(83) 3.11; 5.42; 13.06
(84) 5.43; 7.04; 13.06
(85) 5.44; 7.05; 13.06
(87) 7.06; 13.06
(88) 7.07; 13.06
(89) 3.11; 7.08; 13.05, 13.06
(90) 7.09; 13.06
(91) 7.10; 13.06
(92) 7.11; 13.06
(93) 13.06
(94) 3.11; 5.45; 10.81; 13.15
(95) 3.11; 5.46; 6.10; 7.12; 13.06, 13.13
(96) 7.13; 13.17
(97) 15.05
(98) 7.14; 13.05, 13.17
(99) 4.11; 5.47; 10.70, 10.81; 11.12; 13.15
(100) 4.11; 5.48; 10.81
(104) 1.06, 1.29; 5.49; 13.02
(105) 1.37; 3.11; 13.02
(106) 3.11
Ch I (arts 1–4) 9.04; 10.01
Art 1 .... 6.02; 9.04; 10.02, 10.79; 13.16
(1) 10.02

Regulation (EU) 2022/2554 of the European Parliament and of the Council of 14 December 2022 on digital operational resilience for the financial sector and amending Regulations (EC) No 1060/2009, (EU) No 648/2021, (EU) No 600/2014, (EU) No 909/2104 and (EU) 2016/1011 – *contd*
Art 1(1)(a) 11.10
(d) 10.02
(2) 10.02
(3) 10.02
2 .... 2.02; 6.02; 9.04; 10.03
(1) 10.03, 10.70; 11.11
(a), (b) 3.15; 6.02; 10.02, 10.03, 10.13; 11.11
(c) 6.02; 10.02, 10.03, 10.13
(d) 3.15; 6.02; 10.02, 10.03, 10.13; 11.11
(e)–(t) 10.03
(2) 10.03
(3) 10.03
(e) 17.04
(3) 3.02; 10.03
(4) 3.02; 10.03, 10.82
(5) 3.02
3 .... 9.04; 10.04
(1) 10.05
(a) 10.94
(2) 10.06
(3) 10.07
(4) 10.08
(5) 10.09
(6) 10.10
(7) 10.11
(8) 10.12
(9) 10.13
(10) 10.14
(11) 10.15
(12) 10.16
(13) 10.17
(14) 10.18
(15) 10.19
(16) 10.20
(17) 10.21
(18) 10.22
(19) 10.23
(20) 10.24
(21) 10.25
(22) 10.26
(23) 10.27
(24) 10.28
(25) 10.29
(26) 10.30

Regulation (EU) 2022/2554 of the European Parliament and of the Council of 14 December 2022 on digital operational resilience for the financial sector and amending Regulations (EC) No 1060/2009, (EU) No 648/2021, (EU) No 600/2014, (EU) No 909/2104 and (EU) 2016/1011 – *contd*

Art 3(27)........ 10.31
(28)........ 10.32
(29)........ 10.33
(30)........ 10.34
(31)........ 10.35
(32)........ 10.36
(33)........ 10.37
(34)........ 10.38
(35)........ 10.39
(36)........ 10.40
(37)........ 10.41
(38)........ 10.42
(39)........ 10.43
(40)........ 10.44
(41)........ 10.45
(42)........ 10.46
(43)........ 10.47
(44)........ 10.48
(45)........ 10.49, 10.50
(47)........ 10.51
(48)........ 10.52
(49)........ 10.53
(50)........ 10.54
(51)........ 10.55
(52)........ 10.56
(53)........ 10.57
(54)........ 10.58
(55)........ 10.59
(56)........ 10.60
(57)........ 10.61
(58)........ 10.62
(59)........ 10.63
(60)........ 10.64
(61)........ 10.65
(62)........ 10.66
(63)........ 10.67
(64)........ 10.68
(65)........ 10.69
4........ 3.02, 3.12; 9.04; 10.70, 10.73, 10.75
(1)........ 10.70
(2)........ 3.14, 3.18; 5.03; 10.70; 11.03; 12.02, 12.03, 12.04; 13.02
(3)........ 6.02; 10.70
Ch II (arts 5–16)........ 9.04, 10.70, 10.71
Ch II Section I (art 5)........ 10.71
Art 5........ 3.13; 9.04, 9.05; 10.71, 10.82

Regulation (EU) 2022/2554 of the European Parliament and of the Council of 14 December 2022 on digital operational resilience for the financial sector and amending Regulations (EC) No 1060/2009, (EU) No 648/2021, (EU) No 600/2014, (EU) No 909/2104 and (EU) 2016/1011 – *contd*

Art 5(1)–(4)........ 10.71
Ch II Section II (arts 6–16)........ 10.72
Art 6........ 3.02, 3.12, 3.13, 3.18; 9.04, 9.05; 10.72, 10.82; 11.10; 12.02
(1)........ 3.12; 5.02; 10.71, 10.72, 10.74, 10.75, 10.77, 10.79, 10.80; 13.02
(2)........ 3.12; 10.72, 10.96
(d)........ 10.90
(3)........ 3.12; 10.72, 10.89
(4)........ 5.02; 10.71, 10.72, 10.89
(5)........ 3.12; 6.02; 10.70, 10.72, 10.81, 10.85, 10.110
(6)........ 3.12; 10.72, 10.110
(7)........ 3.12; 10.72
(8)........ 3.12; 10.71, 10.72, 10.79, 10.85
(b)........ 10.71, 10.86
(9)........ 3.12; 5.02; 10.72; 13.02
(10)........ 3.12; 10.72
7........ 3.12, 3.13; 9.04, 9.05; 10.73, 10.82
8........ 3.12, 3.13; 9.04, 9.05; 10.74, 10.77, 10.82
(1)........ 3.12; 10.74, 10.87, 10.89, 10.93, 10.94, 10.96, 10.101, 10.104
(2)........ 3.12; 10.74
(3)–(5)........ 3.12; 10.74
(6)........ 3.12
(7)........ 3.12; 10.74, 10.87
9........ 3.12, 3.13; 9.04, 9.05; 10.75, 10.82
(1)........ 3.12; 10.75, 10.92
(2)........ 3.12; 10.75, 10.81, 10.85, 10.87, 10.89, 10.91, 10.92, 10.93, 10.94
(3)........ 3.12; 10.75
(4)........ 3.12; 10.75; 11.10
(c)........ 3.12; 10.81

Regulation (EU) 2022/2554 of the European Parliament and of the Council of 14 December 2022 on digital operational resilience for the financial sector and amending Regulations (EC) No 1060/2009, (EU) No 648/2021, (EU) No 600/2014, (EU) No 909/2104 and (EU) 2016/1011 – *contd*
Art 9(4)(e) ... 10.100
10 ... 3.12, 3.13; 9.04, 9.05; 10.76, 10.82
(1) ... 3.12; 10.76, 10.81, 10.106
(2) ... 3.12; 10.76, 10.81, 10.106
(a) ... 10.89
(3), (4) ... 3.12; 10.76
11 ... 3.12, 3.13; 9.04, 9.05; 10.77, 10.79, 10.82; 11.10
(1) ... 3.12; 10.71, 10.77, 10.81, 10.107
(2) ... 3.12; 10.77
(e) ... 10.107
(3) ... 3.12; 10.71, 10.77, 10.81, 10.109
(4) ... 3.12; 10.77
(5) ... 3.12; 10.77, 10.107
(6) ... 3.12; 10.77, 10.81, 10.108
(7)–(11) ... 3.12; 10.77
12 ... 3.12, 3.13; 9.04, 9.05; 10.77, 10.78, 10.82
(1)–(7) ... 3.12; 10.78
13 ... 3.12, 3.13; 9.04, 9.05; 10.79, 10.82
(1) ... 3.12; 10.79
(a) ... 10.91
(2)–(5) ... 3.12; 10.79
(6) ... 3.12; 5.05; 10.71, 10.79; 13.04
(7) ... 3.12
14 ... 3.12, 3.13, 3.14; 9.04, 9.05; 10.72, 10.77, 10.80, 10.82; 11.02
(1) ... 3.12; 10.80
(2) ... 3.12; 10.80, 10.107
(3) ... 3.12; 10.80
15 ... 3.12, 3.13; 9.04, 9.05; 10.81, 10.82
(1) ... 3.12, 3.13
16 ... 3.02; 9.04, 9.05; 10.82

Regulation (EU) 2022/2554 of the European Parliament and of the Council of 14 December 2022 on digital operational resilience for the financial sector and amending Regulations (EC) No 1060/2009, (EU) No 648/2021, (EU) No 600/2014, (EU) No 909/2104 and (EU) 2016/1011 – *contd*
rt 16(1) ... 3.02, 3.13, 3.18; 5.02; 10.82, 10.111, 10.112, 10.113, 10.114, 10.115, 10.116, 10.117, 10.118, 10.119, 10.120, 10.121, 10.122, 10.123, 10.124; 11.06; 13.02
(a) ... 10.82, 10.113
(f) ... 10.82, 10.111
(2) ... 3.13; 6.02; 10.70, 10.82, 10.124
(3) ... 3.13; 10.82
(6) ... 10.91
Ch III (arts 17–23) ... 3.14; 9.04; 10.70; 11.01, 11.15
Art 17 ... 3.12, 3.14; 9.04, 9.05; 10.76, 10.105; 11.02
(1)–(3) ... 3.14; 11.02
18 ... 3.14; 9.04, 9.05; 11.03
(1) ... 3.14, 3.15; 11.02, 11.03, 11.04, 11.12
(a), (c), (d) ... 11.05
(e) ... 11.05, 11.07
(f) ... 11.05
(2) ... 3.14; 11.03, 11.07, 11.09
(3) ... 3.14; 11.03
(4) ... 3.14, 3.15; 11.03, 11.04
19 ... 3.12, 3.15; 9.04, 9.05; 10.77; 11.10, 11.11; 17.04
(1) ... 3.02, 3.14, 3.15, 3.16; 11.03, 11.06, 11.11, 11.14
(2) ... 3.02, 3.15; 11.11
(3) ... 11.11
(4) ... 3.15, 3.16; 11.08, 11.11, 11.12, 11.14
(5) ... 3.15; 11.11
(6) ... 3.14, 3.15, 3.16; 11.03, 11.08, 11.11, 11.14
(7) ... 3.14, 3.15; 11.03, 11.08, 11.11

Regulation (EU) 2022/2554 of the European Parliament and of the Council of 14 December 2022 on digital operational resilience for the financial sector and amending Regulations (EC) No 1060/2009, (EU) No 648/2021, (EU) No 600/2014, (EU) No 909/2104 and (EU) 2016/1011 – *contd*
Art 19(8).. 11.11
20 .... 3.15; 9.04, 9.05; 11.11, 11.12
(a).. 11.12
(ii) 3.15; 11.12
(b).............................. 11.06, 11.12
21 .... 9.04, 9.05; 11.13
(1)–(3).......................... 3.15; 11.13
22 .... 3.16; 9.04, 9.05; 11.14
(1), (2).......................... 3.16; 11.14
23 .... 3.02, 3.17; 9.04, 9.05; 11.15
Ch IV (arts 24–27) 3.12; 9.04; 10.70, 10.72; 12.01
Art 24 .... 3.18; 9.04, 9.05; 12.02, 12.03
(1)................................ 3.18; 12.02
(2), (3).............................. 3.18
(4)–(6).......................... 3.18; 12.02
25 .... 3.12, 3.18; 9.04, 9.05; 10.76; 12.02, 12.03
(1)–(3).......................... 3.18; 12.03
(6).. 13.09
26 .... 3.02, 3.12, 3.18; 5.05; 9.04, 9.05; 10.79; 12.02, 12.04; 13.04
(1)–(7).......................... 3.18; 12.04
(8)................................ 3.18; 12.04
(9)........................ 3.02, 3.18; 12.04, 12.05
(10).................... 3.18; 12.04, 12.05
(11).............................. 3.18; 12.04
27 .... 3.12, 3.18; 5.05; 9.04, 9.05; 10.79; 12.04, 12.05; 13.04
(1)................................ 3.18; 12.05
(a)–(e)...................... 3.18; 12.04
(2), (3).......................... 3.18; 12.05
Ch V (arts 28–44).......... 5.02; 9.04; 10.70; 13.01
Ch V Section I (arts 28–30) 5.02; 13.02
Art 28 .... 5.02; 6.02; 9.04, 9.05; 13.02, 13.16; 16.02
(1)................................ 5.02; 13.02

Regulation (EU) 2022/2554 of the European Parliament and of the Council of 14 December 2022 on digital operational resilience for the financial sector and amending Regulations (EC) No 1060/2009, (EU) No 648/2021, (EU) No 600/2014, (EU) No 909/2104 and (EU) 2016/1011 – *contd*
Art 28(1)(a)................................ 10.94
(2)........................ 5.02, 5.04; 13.02
(3)........................ 3.02; 5.02, 5.03, 5.04, 5.06; 6.02; 11.10; 13.02, 13.05
(4)................................ 5.03; 13.02
(c) 5.05; 13.03
(5)................................ 5.03; 13.02
(6)........................ 5.03; 7.02; 13.02
(7), (8).......................... 5.03; 13.02
(9)........................ 5.04; 6.02; 13.02
(10).............................. 5.04; 13.02
29 .... 5.03; 9.04, 9.05; 13.02, 13.03
(1), (2).......................... 5.05; 13.03
30 .... 5.05; 9.04, 9.05; 13.04
(1)................................ 5.05; 13.04
(2)...................... 5.05; 11.10; 13.04
(a) 5.05; 13.04
(i) 3.12; 10.79
(3)...................... 5.05; 11.10; 13.04
(e)(i), (ii)....................... 7.02
(f)(i).............................. 7.02
(4), (5).......................... 5.05; 13.04
Ch V Section II (arts 31–44).. 5.06; 11.10; 13.05, 13.17; 15.01
Art 31 .... 5.06; 9.04, 9.05; 10.27; 13.05; 15.02
(1)................................ 5.06; 13.05
(a) 5.06; 13.05, 13.10
(b) 13.06, 13.07, 13.08
(2)...................... 5.06; 13.05; 17.04
(3)–(5).............................. 5.06
(6)...................... 5.06; 13.05; 16.02
(7)–(10)........................ 5.06; 13.05
(11).................... 5.06; 13.05, 13.15
(12).................. 5.06; 13.05, 13.10; 17.04
(13).............................. 5.06; 13.05
32 .... 5.06; 9.04, 9.05; 13.05, 13.06
(1)...................... 5.06; 13.05, 13.06
(2), (3).............................. 13.06
(4).............................. 13.06, 13.17
(a)–(c).......................... 13.16
(e) 13.14
(5)–(9).............................. 13.06

Regulation (EU) 2022/2554 of the European Parliament and of the Council of 14 December 2022 on digital operational resilience for the financial sector and amending Regulations (EC) No 1060/2009, (EU) No 648/2021, (EU) No 600/2014, (EU) No 909/2104 and (EU) 2016/1011 – *contd*

Art 33 ... 9.04, 9.05; 13.07
(1), (2) ... 13.07
(3) ... 13.07, 13.09
(4), (5) ... 13.07
34 ... 5.06; 9.04, 9.05; 13.08
(1) ... 12.02; 13.07, 13.08
(2), (3) ... 12.02; 13.08
(4) ... 13.07
35 ... 5.06; 7.02; 8.02; 9.04, 9.05; 13.09, 13.10, 13.14
(1) ... 13.09, 13.15
(a) ... 8.02; 13.09, 13.10
(b) ... 7.02; 8.02; 13.09, 13.10
(c) ... 8.02; 13.09, 13.16
(d) ... 13.06, 13.09, 13.10, 13.16
(iv) ... 17.04
(2)–(5) ... 13.09
(6) ... 8.01, 8.02; 13.09, 13.11, 13.12, 13.13
(7) ... 8.01, 8.02; 13.09
(8) ... 8.01, 8.02; 13.09
(9), (10) ... 8.02; 13.09
(11) ... 8.01, 8.02; 13.09
36 ... 5.06; 9.04, 9.05; 13.10, 13.18
(1) ... 13.10
(a) ... 13.05
(2) ... 3.02; 13.05, 13.10
(3) ... 13.05, 13.10
(4), (5) ... 13.05
37 ... 3.02; 5.06; 8.02; 9.04, 9.05; 13.09, 13.10, 13.11
(1) ... 3.02; 13.11
(2) ... 13.11
(3) ... 13.11
(d) ... 13.11
(e) ... 8.02
(4), (5) ... 13.11
38 ... 3.02; 5.06; 7.02; 9.04, 9.05; 13.09, 13.12
(1) ... 7.02; 13.12
(2) ... 13.12

Regulation (EU) 2022/2554 of the European Parliament and of the Council of 14 December 2022 on digital operational resilience for the financial sector and amending Regulations (EC) No 1060/2009, (EU) No 648/2021, (EU) No 600/2014, (EU) No 909/2104 and (EU) 2016/1011 – *contd*

Art 38(2)(a), (b), (d) ... 13.10
(3) ... 3.02; 8.02; 13.12
(4) ... 8.02; 13.12
(5) ... 13.12
39 ... 3.02; 5.06; 8.02; 9.04, 9.05; 13.09, 13.13
(1) ... 13.10, 13.13
(2) ... 8.02; 13.13
(a) ... 13.10
(3)–(5) ... 13.13
(6) ... 8.02; 13.13
(7) ... 13.13
40 ... 5.06; 9.04, 9.05; 13.14, 13.17
(1) ... 13.12, 13.13, 13.14
(2), (3) ... 13.14
(4) ... 3.02; 13.14
41 ... 5.06; 9.04, 9.05; 13.15
(1) ... 13.15
(b) ... 13.09
(2) ... 13.15, 13.17
42 ... 5.06; 9.04, 9.05; 13.08, 13.16
(1) ... 13.16
(2) ... 13.16, 13.17
(3) ... 13.15, 13.16
(4)–(9) ... 13.16
43 ... 3.02; 5.06; 9.04, 9.05; 13.17
(1) ... 13.17
(2) ... 13.17; 16.02
44 ... 5.06; 9.04, 9.05; 13.18
(1), (2) ... 13.18
Ch VI (Art 45) ... 9.04; 14.01
Art 45 ... 5.06; 9.04, 9.05; 14.02
(1) ... 14.02
(c) ... 14.02
(2), (3) ... 14.02
Ch VII (arts 46–56) ... 9.04; 15.01, 15.11
Art 46 ... 3.02, 3.15; 5.06; 9.04; 13.06; 15.01
47 ... 5.06; 9.04; 15.02, 15.04
(1)–(4) ... 15.02

Regulation (EU) 2022/2554 of the European Parliament and of the Council of 14 December 2022 on digital operational resilience for the financial sector and amending Regulations (EC) No 1060/2009, (EU) No 648/2021, (EU) No 600/2014, (EU) No 909/2104 and (EU) 2016/1011 – *contd*
Art 48 .... 5.06; 9.04; 15.03, 15.04
(1), (2) 15.03
49 .... 5.06; 9.04; 15.04
(1), (2) 15.04
50 .... 3.02; 5.06; 8.02; 9.04; 15.04, 15.05, 15.06
(1) 15.05
(2) 15.05
(c) 15.05
(3), (4) 3.02; 15.05
(5), (6) 15.05
51 .... 3.02; 5.06; 8.02; 9.04; 15.04, 15.06
(2) 8.02; 15.06
52 .... 3.02; 5.06; 9.04; 15.04, 15.07
(1), (2) 8.02; 15.07
53 .... 5.06; 9.04; 15.04, 15.11
54 .... 5.06; 8.02; 9.04; 15.04, 15.08
(1), (2) 8.02; 15.08
(3) 8.02; 15.08
(b) 15.08
(4)–(6) 8.02; 15.08
55 .... 3.02; 5.06; 9.04; 15.09
(1)–(4) 15.09
56 .... 3.02; 5.06; 9.04; 15.10
(1), (2) 15.10
Ch VIII (Art 57) 9.04; 16.01
Art 57 .... 3.02; 5.06; 9.04; 13.05, 13.17; 16.02
(1)–(6) 16.02
Ch IX (arts 58–64) 9.04; 17.01
Ch IX Section II (arts 59–64) 17.03
Art 58 .... 9.04; 17.04
(1)–(3) 17.04
59–63 .... 3.02; 9.04; 17.03
64 .... 9.04; 17.02
Regulation (EU) 2023/1114 of the European Parliament and of the Council of 31 May 2023 on markets in crypto-assets, and amending Regulations (EU) No 1093/2010 and (EU) No 1095/2010 and Directives 2013/36/EU and (EU) 2019/1937 .... 2.02; 10.03, 10.34, 10.59, 10.60; 15.01
Commission Delegated Regulation (EU) 2024/1502 of 22 February 2024 supplementing Regulation (EU) 2022/2554 of the European Parliament and of the Council by specifying the criteria for the designation of ICT third-party service providers as critical for financial entities .... 9.07; App 2
Commission Delegated Regulation (EU) 2024/1505 of 22 February 2024 supplementing Regulation (EU) 2022/2554 of the European Parliament and of the Council by determining the amount of the oversight fees to be charged by the Land Overseer to critical ICT third-party service providers and the way in which those fees are paid .... 9.07; App 2
Commission Delegated Regulation (EU) 2024/1772 of 13 March 2024 supplementing Regulation (EU) 2022/2554 of the European Parliament and of the Council with regard to regulatory technical standards specifying the criteria for the classification of ICT-related incidents and cyber threats, setting our materiality thresholds and specifying the details of reports of major incidents .... App 2
Art 15 .... 10.105
Commission Delegated Regulation (EU) 2024/1773 of 13 March 2024 supplementing Regulation (EU) 2022/2554 of the European Parliament and of the Council with regard to regulatory technical standards specifying the detailed content of the policy regarding contractual arrangements on the use of ICT services supporting critical or important functions provided by ICT third-party service providers .... App 2

Commission Delegated Regulation (EU) 2024/1774 of 13 March 2024 supplementing Regulation (EU) 2022/2554 of the European Parliament and of the Council with regard to regulatory technical standards specifying ICT risk management tools, methods, processes, and policies and the simplified ICT risk management framework... 10.82, 10.83; 11.03, 11.09; App 2

Ch I (arts 1–18) 11.05

Art 1 .... 10.84; 11.05, 11.10

(3) 11.06

2 .... 10.85; 11.05, 11.10

(a)–(d) 11.06

3 .... 10.86; 11.05, 11.10

(1)(b) 10.108

4 .... 10.87; 11.05, 11.06, 11.10

(1) 10.87

5 .... 10.88; 11.05, 11.06, 11.10

(1) 10.88

6 .... 10.89; 11.05, 11.06, 11.07, 11.10

(1) 10.89

(2)(d) 10.90

(3) 10.89

(a)–(e) 11.10

(4) 10.89

7 .... 10.90; 11.05, 11.10

8 .... 10.91; 11.06, 11.10

(1) 10.91

(2)(b)(v)–(vii) 10.99

(c), (d) 11.10

(4) 11.10

9 .... 10.92; 11.06, 11.10

(1) 11.06, 11.07

(2) 11.06, 11.07, 11.10

(3), (4) 11.06, 11.07

(5) 11.06, 11.07

(b) 11.06

(6) 11.06, 11.07

10 .... 10.93; 11.07, 11.10

(1) 10.93

(3) 10.93

11 .... 10.94; 11.08

(1) 10.94

12 .... 10.95; 11.08

(1) 10.95

13 .... 10.96

(1)(a) 10.91

14 .... 10.97

(1) 10.97

Commission Delegated Regulation (EU) 2024/1774 of 13 March 2024 supplementing Regulation (EU) 2022/2554 of the European Parliament and of the Council with regard to regulatory technical standards specifying ICT risk management tools, methods, processes, and policies and the simplified ICT risk management framework – *contd*

Art 15 .... 10.98

(1) 10.98

(3)(d) 10.98

16 .... 10.83, 10.99

(1)–(8) 10.99

17 .... 10.100

(1) 10.100

18 .... 10.101

(1) 10.101

Ch II (arts 19–21) 11.06

Art 19 .... 10.102

20 .... 10.103

(1) 10.103

21 .... 10.94, 10.95, 10.103, 10.104

(1)(c) 10.103

(g) 10.101

Ch III (arts 22, 23) 11.07

Art 22 .... 10.105

23 .... 10.105, 10.106

(5) 10.106

Ch IV (arts 24–26) 11.08

Art 24 .... 10.95, 10.107

(1) 10.107

25 .... 10.107, 10.108

(1), (2) 10.108

26 .... 10.107, 10.109

(1) 10.109

(2) 10.107, 10.108

27 .... 10.110

(1) 10.110

28 .... 10.111

(5) 10.111

29 .... 10.112

(1) 10.112

30 .... 10.112, 10.113

(1) 10.111, 10.115, 10.116, 10.117, 10.118

31 .... 10.112, 10.114, 10.119

32 .... 10.112, 10.115

(1) 10.115

33 .... 10.112, 10.116, 10.119

Commission Delegated Regulation (EU) 2024/1774 of 13 March 2024 supplementing Regulation (EU) 2022/2554 of the European Parliament and of the Council with regard to regulatory technical standards specifying ICT risk management tools, methods, processes, and policies and the simplified ICT risk management framework – *contd*
Art 34 .... 10.112, 10.117, 10.119
(1)(f).................................. 10.116
35 .... 10.112, 10.118, 10.119
36 .... 10.112, 10.119
37 .... 10.112, 10.119, 10.120

Commission Delegated Regulation (EU) 2024/1774 of 13 March 2024 supplementing Regulation (EU) 2022/2554 of the European Parliament and of the Council with regard to regulatory technical standards specifying ICT risk management tools, methods, processes, and policies and the simplified ICT risk management framework – *contd*
Art 38 .... 10.112, 10.119, 10.121
39 .... 10.122, 10.123
(1)...................................... 10.122
40 .... 10.123
(1)...................................... 10.123
41 .... 10.124
(1), (2)............................... 10.124
46 .... 11.11

PART A:

NECESSITY

CHAPTER 1

Introduction

INTRODUCTION

1.01 Central banks, whether the European Central Bank (ECB), the Bank of England (BOE), or the Federal Reserve in the US, are tasked with protecting the financial stability of the entire financial system. As part of this they need to ensure that financial firms are financially resilient and stable. Part of the rules around financial stability stem from the last great recession.

But today, financial stability is not the only threat to financial entities and the wider financial system. IT, information and communication technology (ICT), and cyber threats must also be reckoned with. An example of an IT vulnerability change, apparently due to lack of testing prior to deployment, which had widespread adverse effects across a range of industries, was the SolarWinds incident. Financial entities often rely on third-party suppliers or even outsource some of their core activities. Firms can be adversely affected when one of these third parties is exposed to a cyber attack. The Bank of America, for example, had to warn its customers after one of its suppliers (IMS) was hacked by bad actors. Financial entities of service providers such as AddComm and Cabot have also encountered problems when these suppliers were involved in cyber attacks. Christine Lagarde (President of the ECB) has stated that 'cyberattacks could trigger a serious financial crisis'. Piero Cipollone (a member of the ECB Executive Board) states that 'cyber risks have become one of the main issues for global security. They have been identified as a systematic risk to the stability of the European financial system.' Unfortunately, it is not limited to just the European financial system.

Now, financial firms must also ensure that they are digitally resilient and prepared for these internal and external tech threats.

Digitisation is increasing and presents many opportunities but also risks.[1] A Foreword to a BOE paper indicates that the financial sector is a complex, interconnected system in which financial services firms and financial market infrastructure firms increasingly rely upon third-party services to support their business operations. Technology services such as cloud computing and data analytics can bring multiple benefits – enabling digital transformation, catalysing innovation, and providing greater resilience (and security) than firms' and

1 Wuermeling, Prof. Joachim, 'Exploring DORA – the Digital Operational Resilience Act and Its Impact on Banks and Their Supervisors', Speech at the European Savings and Retail Banking Group (ESBG) (23 September 2021).

suppliers' own technology infrastructure.[2] However, the BOE also points out that this increasing reliance on third parties also poses growing risks.[3]

The Digital Operational Resilience Act, or DORA as it is known, is an EU regulation[4] that introduces (and in some cases, enhances) the oversight and supervision by relevant financial regulators of financial firms and their cyber security, electronic operations and contracting, and digital operational resilience. A recent paper from the ECB notes that DORA also strengthens cooperative oversight of critical cloud computing service providers by bringing together all relevant supervisory authorities, including prudential supervisors.[5] DORA is described by KPMG as being 'aimed at improving the EU financial system's digital and operational resilience. It creates a holistic regulatory framework, harmonising the current patchwork of financial regulations related to ICT.'[6]

CYBER THREATS

ICT threats and cost

1.02 According to the ECB '[w]ith the use of information technology having become a large part of daily life, and even more so during the coronavirus (COVID-19) pandemic, the potential downsides of an increasing dependence on technology have become even more apparent. Protecting critical services like hospitals, electricity supply and access to the financial system from attacks and outages is crucial.'[7] 'Given the ever-increasing risks of cyber attacks, the EU is strengthening the IT security of financial entities such as banks, insurance companies and investment firms.'[8] DORA will 'make sure the financial sector in Europe is able to stay resilient through a severe operational disruption.'[9]

The cost of the above threats continues to increase. We already see very significant data fines arising under data laws such as personal data rules.[10] Meta (previously Facebook) has been fined €1.2 billion for one set of data breaches concerning data transfers. TikTok has been fined €345 million and €14.5 million for data

2 Foreword, 'DP3/22 – Operational Resilience: Critical Third Parties to the UK Financial Sector', Bank of England (21 July 2022).
3 Ibid.
4 Regulation (EU) 2022/2554 on digital operational resilience for the financial sector and amending Regulations (EC) No 1060/2009, (EU) No 648/2012, (EU) No 600/2014, (EU) No 909/2014 and (EU) 2016/1011. The EU Regulation entered into force on 16 January 2023 and will apply as of 17 January 2025.
5 Papathanassiou, C, 'Digital Innovation and Banking Regulation' (2024).
6 Niedermeier, E, 'Decoding DORA for European Banks', KPMG (May 2024).
7 'IT and Cyber Risk: A Constant Challenge', European Central Bank (18 August 2021).
8 'Digital finance: Council Adopts Digital Operational Resilience Act', European Council (28 November 2022).
9 Ibid.
10 Some examples of these rules include the Data Protection Act 2018, the General Data Protection Regulation 2016/679 (GDPR) and other similar laws.

breaches regarding child data. There have been a number of data fines in the billions across the globe.

Many firms have been fined as a consequence of ineffective security measures leading to them being hacked – demonstration a lack of appropriate and technical security measures and overall digital operational resilience. Already, even before the official go live of DORA, firms have been receiving significant fines and penalties as a result of matters which cross over with digital operational resilience.

Increased risk

1.03 Increased digitalisation – and interconnections – also 'amplify ICT risk', making society as a whole (and the financial sector in particular) more vulnerable to cyber threats and or ICT disruptions[11] and attacks from errant third parties.

The range of cyber threats are increasing. They include, for example, attacks such as bad actor hacking attacks, business email attacks, Phishing, Spear Phishing, Ransomware, viruses, Trojans, Distributed Denial of Service (DDOS), web application attacks, mobile attack, and more.

It can also be wider than direct attacks. There are increasing numbers of indirect attacks, where the bad actors seek to get in via a trusted third-party service provider that the financial company uses. This is supply chain and service provider compromise.

Other risk issues include management risk and system risk, such as failing to patch known vulnerabilities.

The number of attacks is increasing. The level of sophistication and complexity of the attacks are also increasing.

Wide universe of ICT risk

1.04 In order to maintain a high level of digital operational resilience for the whole financial sector, and at the same time to keep pace with technological developments, DORA needs to address risk stemming from 'all types of ICT services'.[12] For that purpose, the definition of ICT services in the context of DORA should be understood in a broad manner, encompassing digital and data services provided through ICT systems to one or more internal or external users on an ongoing basis.[13]

11 Recital 1, DORA.
12 Recital 35, DORA.
13 Recital 35, DORA.

The definition should also include so-called 'over the top' services, which fall within the category of electronic communications services.[14] The ICT service definition should exclude 'only' the limited category of traditional analogue telephone services qualifying as Public Switched Telephone Network (PSTN) services, landline services, Plain Old Telephone Service (POTS), or fixed-line telephone services.[15]

Temporal risks

1.05 Timing is also very important. Some bad actors seek to pressure victims in a deliberate manner by suggesting that a certain action needs to occur quickly. These social engineering tools aim to take away the normal thoughtfulness and caution that individuals have. If an errant attacker is pretending to be the CEO on email and needs something done urgently – even an unusual payment – the normal human defences can be somewhat compromised. As an ECB presentation notes, 'If the institutions affected only detect or learn about such attacks with a delay, the consequences can be immense. We therefore need to monitor all the software and hardware in our IT environments – no matter how small – and not focus solely on our most critical third-party providers. And we need to exchange critical information and tackle this threat.'[16]

Payment attacks

1.06 Numerous large-scale attacks demonstrate how payment systems have become exposed to cyber threats.[17] Placed at the core of the payment services chain and showing strong interconnections with the overall financial system, payment systems and payment processing activities acquired a critical significance for the functioning of the European financial markets.[18] Cyber attacks on such systems can cause severe operational business disruptions with direct repercussions on key economic functions, such as the facilitation of payments, and indirect effects on related economic processes.[19]

However, until a harmonised regime and the supervision of operators of payment systems and processing entities are put in place at European level, Member States may, with a view to applying similar market practices, draw inspiration from the digital operational resilience requirements laid down by DORA, when applying rules to operators of payment systems and processing entities supervised under their own jurisdictions.[20]

14 Recital 35, DORA.
15 Recital 35, DORA.
16 Panetta, F, 'Cyber Risks and the Integrity of Digital Finance', *European Central Bank* (30 September 2021).
17 Recital 104, DORA.
18 Recital 104, DORA.
19 Recital 104, DORA.
20 Recital 104, DORA.

IT/ICT THREATS

1.07 It is very important to also point out that problem issues can arise (as well as fines, penalties and prosecutions) outside of hacking type events instigated by bad actors. The ability to continue delivering financial services to customer and business partners can be disrupted by events which are internal to the financial entity and where no bad actors are attacking the firm.

DORA also seeks to ensure that these types of reliance and preventative measures are developed in financial sector firms.

A perfect example of this is the recent Crowd Strike outage affecting firms around the globe as well as millions of customers including airline passengers and hospital patients. The problem arose with a scheduled update to the Crowd Strike security software. Unfortunately, there was a glitch with the update which knocked out customers' ICT systems. This should not have happened and should have been prevented by robust IT testing processes, procedures, and governance prior to the update being released to customers. In addition to the very significant level of customer disruption, Crowd Strike is reportedly being sued by shareholders, corporate customers and others. Some of the customer firms adversely affected, such as Delta airlines, are also being sued by their own customers. The direct cost to Delta has been $500 million. This may now rise. The direct losses resulting from the outage are estimated to be $5 billion.

While Crowd Strike is a security firm, the effects of the incident were far and wide. These are the types of systemic dangers that the financial regulators and policymakers behind DORA are concerned with. They know that preparing and mandating in advance is a form of preventative safeguard necessary across the financial sector and financial firms.

There are already a number of well publicised ICT outages affecting banking customers where ICT upgrades have not gone as intended, or where online banking has been unavailable due to some internal IT issues (as opposed to third-party attacks). These types of events will now be caught by DORA and fines may be issued after appropriate investigations. It is inevitable that some of these types of events will breach some of the mandated requirements set out in DORA. These early instances will serve to drive greater ICT and operational resilience separate, and in addition to, the requirements of DORA compliance itself.

IMPERATIVE NEED

Threat gaps and vectors

1.08 The policymakers who set the trajectory for the ultimate enactment of the DORA requirements for the wider financial sector were concerned with a number of ICT and resilience issues which posed risks, and even threats to financial entities. Indeed, it is also clear that they were even concerned that potential ICT problems with one or a number of financial entities could create escalating impacts on the wider financial sector – or worse, the wider economy.

DORA 'promotes a common set of rules and standards to mitigate Information and Communications Technology (ICT) risks for financial entities. One of the objectives of DORA is to prevent increased fragmentation of rules applicable to ICT risk management.'[21]

DORA deals with five key areas, namely:

- ICT risk management;
- ICT-related incident management, classification and reporting;
- digital operational resilience testing (DOR testing);
- ICT third-party risk management (TPRM); and
- information-sharing arrangements.[22]

DORA 'addresses today's most important challenges for managing ICT risks at financial institutions and critical ICT third-party service providers. Only if these risks are properly managed can digitalisation truly deliver on the many opportunities it offers for the banking and financial industry. Better analysis and better data management can make banks more resilient. For instance, early warning systems for loan defaults based on automatically evaluated economic news could improve risk management.'[23]

Reliance and support

1.09 Some of these concerns are also outlined in the introductory Recital sections of the final version of DORA. Recital 1, for example, points out that in the new digital era, IT/ICT supports complex systems used for activities in everyday life. It keeps 'economies running in key sectors',[24] including the financial sector. ICT also enhances the functioning of the European internal market.[25]

The use of IT and ICT systems has become ubiquitous. The use of ICT systems and high levels of digitalisation and connectivity are now 'core features' of the activities of European and international financial entities.[26]

21 Boucheta, H, and Joseph, A, 'DORA – Digital Operational Resilience Act – Regulation Memo', BNP Paribas (19 July 2024).
22 Niedermeier, E, KPMG (n 6 above).
23 Wuermeling, Prof. Joachim, 'Exploring DORA – the Digital Operational Resilience Act and Its Impact on Banks and Their Supervisors', Speech at the European Savings and Retail Banking Group (ESBG) (23 September 2021).
24 Recital 1, DORA.
25 Recital 1, DORA.
26 Recital 1, DORA.

Resilience gap

1.10 There is a need, however, to ensure that the digital resilience of such financial entities have are 'better addressed.'[27] There is an acknowledgement that there is a lack of digital resilience in many financial entities. Also acknowledged is the fact that digital and operational resilience are not as 'integrated' into the broader operational frameworks of such entities as they might otherwise be.[28]

Pivotal reliance

1.11 The use of ICT has during recent decades gained a 'pivotal role' in the provision of financial services.[29] This reliance has come to a point where it has 'now acquired a critical importance in the operation' of all of the typical daily activities and functions of 'all' financial entities.[30]

Payments

1.12 Digitalisation now covers essential payment functions. Such payments have increasingly moved from cash and paper-based payment methods to the use of digital payment solutions.[31] Part of the reason for expressly being concerned to protect and ensure resilience regarding payment systems is referred to by Fabio Panetta, a Member of the Executive Board of the ECB. He states that 'digitalisation also brings with it risks to the payment system, to monetary sovereignty and to the financial system as a whole.'[32] He continues that 'there will be no integrity of digital finance and payments without protection against cyber risk.'[33]

Trading

1.13 Electronic and digital solutions are also essential for financial sector activities, as well as securities clearing and settlement. This is also the case with electronic and algorithmic trading. Financial entities even seek to gain commercial advantage by seeking to ensure that they have the fastest ICT and digital communications systems. Even the smallest fraction of difference in digital communications for trading systems can be very significant.

27 See Recital 1, DORA .
28 See Recital 1, DORA .
29 Recital 2, DORA.
30 Recital 2, DORA.
31 Recital 2, DORA.
32 Panetta, F, 'Cyber Risks and the Integrity of Digital Finance', *European Central Bank* (30 September 2021).
33 Ibid.

Funding

1.14 Lending and funding activities, peer-to-peer finance, credit rating, claims management and back-office operations are also almost entirely reliant on digitisation.[34]

Insurance

1.15 The insurance sector has also been fully transformed by the use of ICT. Digitisation and ICT have been central to the 'emergence of insurance intermediaries'.[35] These intermediaries offer their services online operating with InsurTech. There is now an industry supporting digital insurance underwriting.[36]

Sector reliance

1.16 The finance sector has not only become largely digital throughout the whole sector, but digitalisation has also deepened 'interconnections and dependencies' within the financial sector – and with third-party infrastructure and service providers.[37]

Systemic risks

1.17 There are a number of references in DORA pointing to regulators' and policymakers' concern in relation to systemic cyber risks and systemic ICT risks. These concerns centre on the potential for a problem event occurring with one financial entity to affect other firms in the sector and in more significant events can affect the wider financial system.

The European Systemic Risk Board (ESRB) reviewed and researched systemic cyber risk issues.[38] In doing so, it looked at the now high level of interconnectedness across financial entities.[39] It also detailed the nature of financial markets and financial market infrastructures.[40] The ESRB also highlighted the interdependencies of these ICT systems.[41] It assessed that these could constitute 'a systemic vulnerability' because 'localised cyber incidents could quickly spread' from any of the approximately 22,000 European financial entities to the entire financial system, and thus 'unhindered by geographical boundaries'[42].

34 Recital 2, DORA.
35 Recital 2, DORA.
36 Recital 2, DORA.
37 Recital 2, DORA.
38 Recital 3, DORA.
39 Recital 3, DORA.
40 Recital 3, DORA.
41 Recital 3, DORA.
42 Recital 3, DORA.

Serious ICT breaches that arise in the financial sector do not merely affect financial entities in isolation.[43] They also 'smooth the way' for the advent of localised vulnerabilities 'across the financial transmission channels' and potentially can trigger adverse consequences for the stability of the European financial system.[44] One of the examples of such occurrence is the possibility for generating liquidity runs.[45] This can also lead to an 'overall loss of confidence and trust in financial markets'.[46]

International focus and concern

1.18 In recent years, the issue of ICT risk has attracted the attention of national, European, and international policymakers. It has also garnered the attention of others, such as regulators and standards setting bodies. These have all been concerned to enhance digital resilience, and to set appropriate standards and to coordinate regulatory or supervisory activities.[47]

At the international level, there has been repeated interest and focus. Some examples include the Basel Committee on Banking Supervision, the Committee on Payments and Market Infrastructures, the Financial Stability Board, the Financial Stability Institute, as well as the G7 and G20. They seek to provide competent authorities and market operators across various jurisdictions with the 'tools to bolster the resilience of their financial systems'.[48] That work has also been 'driven by the need to duly consider ICT risk in the context of a highly interconnected global financial system' as well as to provide more consistency of appropriate best practices.[49]

Challenge

1.19 However, despite national and European targeted policy and legislative initiatives, ICT risk continues to pose a challenge to the operational resilience, performance and stability of the financial system.[50] Various reforms followed as a result of the 2008 financial crisis. These primarily strengthened the financial resilience of the European financial sector and aimed to safeguard the competitiveness and stability of Europe from economic, prudential and market conduct perspectives.[51]

43 Recital 3, DORA.
44 Recital 3, DORA.
45 Recital 3, DORA.
46 Recital 3, DORA.
47 Recital 4, DORA.
48 Recital 4, DORA.
49 Recital 4, DORA.
50 Recital 5, DORA.
51 Recital 5, DORA.

Even though ICT security and digital resilience are a part of wider operational risk, they have unfortunately been 'less in the focus of the post-financial crisis regulatory agenda'.[52] They have developed in only some areas of Europe's financial services policy and regulatory landscape, or in only a few EU Member States.[53]

Prior initiatives

1.20 There are a number of European level financial bodies or authorities. These are, in particular, the European Banking Authority (EBA),[54] the European Insurance and Occupational Pensions Authority) (EIOPA),[55] and the European Securities and Markets Authority) (ESMA).[56] These are known collectively as 'European Supervisory Authorities' or 'ESAs.' Previously the ESAs jointly issued technical advice[57] calling for a coherent approach to ICT risk in finance and recommending to 'strengthen, in a proportionate way, the digital operational resilience of the financial services industry' through a sector-specific legal and policy initiatives.[58] The European financial sector is also regulated by a Single Rulebook and governed by a European system of financial supervision.[59]

DORA 'aims to establish a much clearer foundation for EU financial regulators and supervisors to be able to expand their focus from ensuring firms remain financially resilient to also making sure they are able to maintain resilient operations through a severe operational disruption.'[60]

Lack of harmonisation

1.21 Nonetheless, it is officially recognised that the above provisions tackling digital operational resilience and ICT security are not yet fully or consistently harmonised. This is despite digital operational resilience being 'vital for ensuring financial stability' and also 'market integrity' in the digital age. It is no less important than, for example, 'common prudential or market conduct standards.'[61]

52 Recital 5, DORA.
53 Recital 5, DORA.
54 Established by Regulation 1093/2010.
55 Established by Regulation 1094/2010.
56 Established by Regulation 1095/2010.
57 In April 2019.
58 Recital 7, DORA.
59 Recital 8, DORA.
60 Mosseray, Q, Martin, S, Brennan, S, Black, S, and Cudworth, R, 'The EU's Digital Operational Resilience Act for Financial Services', Deloitte (2024).
61 Recital 8, DORA.

Need for additional rules

1.22 The Single Rulebook and system of supervision are therefore called upon to be further developed to also include digital operational resilience.[62] This can include strengthening the mandates or powers of competent authorities to permit them to supervise the management of ICT risk in the financial sector.[63] This is also necessary in order to protect the integrity and efficiency of the internal market, and to facilitate its orderly functioning.[64]

Disparities

1.23 Another problem facing a desired appropriate level of resilience in financial entities are a variety of disparities. These include legislative disparities.[65] There was also an uneven national regulatory or supervisory approach with regard to ICT.[66] Hence, this would risk or trigger obstacles to the functioning of the internal market in financial services. As a result, this would impede the smooth exercise of the freedom of establishment and the provision of services for financial entities operating on a cross-border basis.

As an example, competition between the same type of financial entities operating in different European States could also be distorted. This is the case, in particular, for areas where European harmonisation has been very limited (such as digital operational resilience testing) or absent (such as the monitoring of ICT third-party risk).[67] Disparities stemming from developments envisaged at national level could also generate further obstacles to the functioning of the internal market to the detriment of market participants and financial stability.[68]

Coverage gaps

1.24 The background Recitals to DORA also point out that 'due to the ICT risk related provisions being only partially addressed' at European level, there are 'gaps or overlaps' in important areas.[69] For example, this includes ICT-related incident reporting. It also includes digital operational resilience testing. There are also inconsistencies as a result of emerging divergent national rules. Additionally, there is 'cost-ineffective' application of overlapping rules.[70] This is 'particularly detrimental' for an ICT intensive user such as the important

62 Recital 8, DORA.
63 Recital 8, DORA.
64 Recital 8, DORA.
65 Recital 9, DORA.
66 Recital 9, DORA.
67 Recital 9, DORA.
68 Recital 9, DORA.
69 Recital 10, DORA.
70 Recital 10, DORA.

financial sector.[71] One reason given is that technology risks have no borders and the financial sector deploys its services on a wide cross-border basis within Europe and outside Europe.[72] Individual financial entities operating on a cross-border basis or holding several authorisations (eg, one financial entity can have a banking, an investment firm, and a payment institution licence, each issued by a different competent authority in one or several Member States) thus face operational challenges in addressing ICT risk and mitigating adverse impacts of ICT incidents on their own and in a coherent cost-effective way.[73]

Outsourcing exposures

1.25 It is noted that there is a 'lack of homogeneity and convergence' regarding the monitoring of ICT third-party risk and ICT third-party dependencies.[74] There have been some efforts to address outsourcing, such as the 2019 EBA Guidelines on outsourcing and 2021 ESMA Guidelines on outsourcing to cloud service providers of 2021. However, despite these efforts to address outsourcing, the broader issue of counteracting 'systemic risk' which may be triggered by the financial sector's exposure to 'a limited number of critical ICT third party service providers' is not sufficiently addressed.[75]

The lack of rules at European level is compounded by the absence of national rules on mandates that allow the financial supervisors to (1) acquire a good understanding of ICT third-party dependencies; and (2) to monitor adequately risks arising from the concentration of ICT third-party dependencies.[76]

Policymakers must take into account the potential 'systemic risk' entailed by increased outsourcing practices and also by ICT third-party concentration. There is also a need to be mindful of the insufficiency of national mechanisms in providing financial supervisors with adequate 'tools to quantify, qualify and redress the consequences of ICT risk occurring at critical ICT third-party service providers'.[77]

It is necessary to establish an appropriate 'Oversight Framework' allowing for a 'continuous' monitoring of the activities of ICT third-party service providers that are critical ICT third-party service providers to financial entities, while also ensuring that the confidentiality and security of customers other than financial entities is preserved.[78]

71 Recital 10, DORA.
72 Recital 10, DORA.
73 Recital 10, DORA.
74 Recital 30, DORA.
75 Recital 30, DORA.
76 Recital 30, DORA.
77 Recital 31, DORA.
78 Recital 31, DORA.

Group services

1.26 It is also noted that services can sometimes be provided by other group companies. While intra group provision of ICT services entails specific risks and benefits, it should not be automatically considered less risky than the provision of ICT services by providers outside of a financial group and should therefore be subject to the same regulatory framework.[79] However, when ICT services are provided from within the same financial group, financial entities might have an even higher level of control over intra group providers, which ought to be taken into account in the overall risk assessment.[80]

Similarly, since financial entities should effectively and coherently identify and manage all types of risk, including in the context of ICT services procured within a financial group, it should be clarified that undertakings which are part of a financial group and provide ICT services predominantly to their parent undertaking, or to subsidiaries or branches of their parent undertaking, as well as financial entities providing ICT services to other financial entities, should also be considered as ICT third-party service providers under DORA.[81]

Cloud

1.27 There is also a need for enhanced regulation as a result of new dependencies of the wider financial sector. In a recent presentation, Professor Joachim Wuermeling states that '[w]orking in the cloud, having all your data available anytime, anyplace, seems boundless and offers many opportunities. But just like in air traffic, cloud providers and online traffic need rules and oversight in order to be stable and beneficial.'[82]

In order to also address the complexity of the various sources of ICT risk, while taking into account the multitude and diversity of providers of technological solutions which enable a smooth provision of financial services, DORA should cover a wide range of ICT third-party service providers, including providers of cloud computing services, software, data analytics services and providers of data centre services.[83]

Payment services

1.28 There is also increased dependency of the public and industry on new forms of financial services. It is recognised that the payment services market is

79 Recital 31, DORA.

80 Recital 31, DORA.

81 Recital 63, DORA.

82 Wuermeling, Professsor Joachim, 'Exploring DORA – the Digital Operational Resilience Act and Its Impact on Banks and Their Supervisors', speech at the European Savings and Retail Banking Group (ESBG) (23 September 2021).

83 Recital 63, DORA.

evolving rapidly.[84] In addition, there are emerging types of payment services and payment-related solutions.[85] But there is the possibility of it becoming increasingly dependent on complex technical solutions.[86] In light of these changes, participants in the payment services ecosystem (whether providing payment-processing activities, or operating payment infrastructures), should therefore also be considered to be ICT third-party service providers under DORA.[87] This is with the exception of central banks when operating payment or securities settlement systems, and public authorities when providing ICT-related services in the context of fulfilling State functions.[88]

Review of risk and payment services and systems

1.29 ICT infrastructures enable the operation of payment systems and the provision of payment processing activities. The potential systemic cyber risk associated with the use of such systems should be appropriately addressed at European level through harmonised digital resilience rules. To that effect, the EU Commission should swiftly assess the need for reviewing the scope of DORA while aligning such review with the outcome of the comprehensive review envisaged under Directive 2015/2366.[89]

Popularity and reliance on ICT services

1.30 The digital transformation experienced in financial services has brought about an unprecedented level of popular use of, and reliance upon, ICT services. It has become inconceivable to provide financial services without the use of cloud computing services, software solutions and data-related services. The European financial ecosystem has become intrinsically 'co-dependent' on certain ICT services provided by ICT service suppliers.[90] Some of those suppliers, who are innovators in developing and applying ICT-based technologies, 'play a significant role in the delivery of financial services', or have become 'integrated into' the financial services value chain.[91]

They have as a result become critical to the stability and integrity of the European financial system.[92] This widespread reliance on services supplied by critical ICT third-party service providers, combined with the interdependence of the information systems of various market operators, 'create a direct, and potentially severe, risk to' the European financial services system and to the continuity of

84 Recital 63, DORA.
85 Recital 63, DORA.
86 Recital 63, DORA.
87 Recital 63, DORA.
88 Recital 63, DORA.
89 Recital 104, DORA.
90 Recital 81, DORA.
91 Recital 81, DORA.
92 Recital 81, DORA.

delivery of financial services if critical ICT third-party service providers were to be affected by operational disruptions or major cyber incidents.[93]

Cyber incidents and attacks have a distinctive ability to multiply and propagate throughout the financial system at a considerably faster pace than other types of risk monitored in the financial sector.[94] They can also extend across sectors and beyond geographical borders.[95] They have the potential to evolve into a systemic crisis, where trust in the financial system has been eroded due to the disruption of functions supporting the real economy, or to substantial financial losses, reaching a level which the financial system is unable to withstand, or which requires the deployment of 'heavy shock absorption measures'.[96]

To prevent these types of scenarios from taking place and endangering the financial stability and integrity of Europe as a result, it is essential to provide the 'convergence of supervisory practices' relating to ICT third-party risk in finance.[97] This in particular through the means of new rules enabling the European oversight of critical ICT third-party service providers.[98]

THREAT SOLUTIONS

Need for digital operational resilience

1.31 The EU Commission in the 'FinTech Action Plan: For a More Competitive and Innovative European Financial Sector'[99] highlights the 'paramount importance' of ensuring and making the financial sector more resilient, including from an operational perspective lens to ensure 'technological safety', 'good functioning', and 'quick recovery' from ICT breach events and incident events.[100] Ultimately, it must ensure and enable the effective and smooth provision of financial services across the whole EU, including under situations of stress, while also preserving wider consumer and market trust and confidence.[101] Enhanced resilience brings advantages, but is also essential and ultimately cost beneficial. This is stressed by the ECB, for instance, pointing out that 'We need to remain vigilant to the evolving threat landscape and continuously maintain the highest level of resilience. This focus cannot be compromised: although the monetary cost of improving cyber resilience may seem high, the costs of successful attacks – in terms of both financial damage and reputational impact – are far higher.'[102]

93 Recital 81, DORA.
94 Recital 81, DORA.
95 Recital 81, DORA.
96 Recital 81, DORA.
97 Recital 81, DORA.
98 Recital 81, DORA.
99 EU Commission, 'FinTech Action Plan: For a More Competitive and Innovative European Financial Sector', Communication (8 March 2018).
100 Recital 6, DORA.
101 Recital 6, DORA.
102 Panetta, F, 'Cyber Risks and the Integrity of Digital Finance', European Central Bank (30 September 2021).

Consolidation

1.32 The Recitals point out that DORA aims to 'consolidate and upgrade' ICT risk requirements as part of the operational risk requirements that have, up to now, been addressed separately in various legal instruments. While those instruments covered the main categories of financial risk (eg, credit risk, market risk, counterparty credit risk and liquidity risk, market conduct risk), they 'did not comprehensively tackle, at the time of their adoption, all components of operational resilience.'

The operational risk rules, when further developed in those European legal instruments, often favoured a traditional quantitative approach to addressing risk (namely, setting a capital requirement to cover ICT risk).[103] This is as opposed to targeted qualitative rules for the protection, detection, containment, recovery and repair capabilities against ICT-related incidents, or for reporting and digital testing capabilities.[104] Those instruments were primarily meant to cover and update essential rules on prudential supervision, market integrity or conduct. By consolidating and upgrading the different rules on ICT risk, all provisions addressing digital risk in the financial sector should 'for the first time' be brought together in a consistent manner in 'one single legislative act.[105] Therefore, the intention is that DORA fills in the gaps or remedies inconsistencies in some of the prior legal instruments, including in relation to the terminology used therein, and explicitly refers to ICT risk via targeted rules on ICT risk management capabilities, incident reporting, operational resilience testing and ICT third-party risk monitoring.[106] DORA should therefore also raise awareness of ICT risk and acknowledge that ICT incidents and a lack of operational resilience have the possibility to jeopardise the soundness of financial entities.[107]

Financial entities should follow the 'same approach and the same principle-based rules when addressing ICT risk taking into account their size and overall risk profile, and the nature, scale and complexity of their services, activities and operations.'[108] Consistency is indicated to contribute to enhancing confidence in the financial system and preserving its stability especially in times of high reliance on ICT systems, platforms and infrastructures, which entails increased digital risk.[109] Following basic cyber hygiene should also avoid imposing heavy costs on the economy by minimising the impact and costs of ICT disruptions.[110]

103 Recital 12, DORA.
104 Recital 12, DORA.
105 Recital 12, DORA.
106 Recital 12, DORA.
107 Recital 12, DORA.
108 Recital 13, DORA.
109 Recital 13, DORA.
110 Recital 13, DORA.

Controls and policies

1.33 Financial entities should be able to maintain full control over ICT risk. In order to do so, financial entities need to have 'comprehensive capabilities' to enable a 'strong and effective ICT risk management'.[111]

They also require 'specific mechanisms and policies' for handling all ICT-related incidents, events, and for the reporting of major ICT-related incidents. Similarly, financial entities should also have policies in place for the testing of 'ICT systems, controls and processes'.[112]

They also need policies for the management of ICT third-party risk.[113]

Enhanced baseline protections

1.34 The 'digital operational resilience baseline' for financial entities should be increased while also allowing for a proportionate application of requirements for certain financial entities, particularly microenterprises, and financial entities subject to a simplified ICT risk management framework.[114]

Supervision

1.35 To facilitate an efficient supervision of institutions for occupational retirement provision that is proportionate and addresses the need to reduce administrative burdens on the competent authorities, the relevant national supervisory arrangements in respect of such financial entities should take into account their size and overall risk profile, and the nature, scale and complexity of their services, activities and operations.[115] This should be the case even when the relevant thresholds established in Article 5 of Directive 2016/2341[116] are exceeded.[117] In particular, supervisory activities should focus primarily on the need to address 'serious risks' associated with the ICT risk management of a particular entity.[118]

Competent authorities should also maintain a 'vigilant but proportionate approach' in relation to the supervision of institutions for occupational retirement provision which, in accordance with Article 31 of Directive 2016/2341, outsource

111 Recital 21, DORA.
112 Recital 21, DORA.
113 Recital 21, DORA.
114 Recital 21, DORA.
115 Recital 21, DORA.
116 Directive (EU) 2016/2341 on the activities and supervision of institutions for occupational retirement provision (IORPs).
117 Recital 21, DORA.
118 Recital 21, DORA.

a significant part of their core business.[119] Such outsourcing can include asset management, actuarial calculations, accounting and data management, to service providers.[120]

Enhanced testing

1.36 It is emphasised that digital operational resilience testing requirements have been developed in 'certain financial subsectors'.[121] Yet, these testing requirements set out frameworks that are 'not always fully aligned'.[122] This leads to a potential duplication of costs for cross-border financial entities.[123] It also makes the mutual recognition of the results of the digital operational resilience testing 'complex' which, in turn, can also fragment the internal market.[124]

Digital operational resilience rules

1.37 The objective of DORA is to achieve a high level of digital operational resilience for regulated financial entities.[125] This cannot be sufficiently achieved by the Member States because it requires harmonisation of various different rules in European and national law. By reason of its scale and effects, this can be better achieved at European level.[126] The EU may adopt measures in accordance with the principle of subsidiarity as set out in Article 5 of the Treaty on European Union. In accordance with the principle of proportionality as set out in that Article, DORA does not go beyond what is necessary in order to achieve that objective.[127]

DORA represents a shift in focus – a particular attention to wide focus on enhancing standards and diligence against adverse ICT events. According to PWC, DORA 'shifts the focus from guaranteeing firms' financial soundness to also ensuring they can maintain resilient operations through severe operational disruption caused by cyber security and information and communication technology (ICT) issues.'[128]

As a result of the above, concerns for individual financial entities and arguably more particularly for the risk effect for the wider financial sector and even wider economy, it was decided to introduce new more centralised and more comprehensive rules by way of DORA. It is described in the heading as a regulation directed to digital operational resilience for the financial sector.

119 Recital 21, DORA.
120 Recital 21, DORA.
121 Recital 25, DORA.
122 Recital 25, DORA.
123 Recital 25, DORA.
124 Recital 25, DORA.
125 Recital 105, DORA.
126 Recital 105, DORA.
127 Recital 105, DORA.
128 'DORA and Its Impact on UK Financial Entities and ICT Service Providers', PWC, at https://www.pwc.co.uk/industries/financial-services/insights/dora-and-its-impact-on-uk-financial-entities-and-ict-service-providers.html.

DORA introduced five Pillars of rules to enhance digital operational resilience. The five Pillars are:

Pillar 1	ICT Risk Management
Pillar 2	ICT-related Incident Management, Classification and Reporting
Pillar 3	Digital Operational Resilience Testing
Pillar 4	ICT Third-Party Risk Management
Pillar 5	Information Sharing Arrangements

DORA sets out a broad array of new obligations for financial entities, and also outsource companies, and technology companies supporting the financial sector. Some of these new rules mean new or enhanced:

- ICT risk management and governance;
- ICT policies and procedures;
- ICT incident management and reporting;
- change management;
- digital operational resilience;
- digital operational resilience testing;
- ICT third-party risk management;
- business continuity;
- cyber security;
- training; and
- information sharing on threats.

DORA is also a particular example of layered regulatory obligations. In addition to the specific obligations set out directly in DORA itself, there are a variety of rules set out (or that can be set out) in sub regulations. These will in general be approved by the EU Commission, but may in the first instance be drafted and developed by what are referred to as the ESAs or European Supervisory Authorities. These are referred to as *technical standards* but will operate as something which must be adhered to. These sub regulations will also be published in the Official Journal. The ESA are identified below.

EBA	European Banking Authority
EIOPA	European Insurance and Occupational Pensions Authority
ESMA	European Securities and Markets Authority

CHAPTER 2

Sectors and Industries

WIDE SECTORAL REMIT

2.01 DORA at a headline level is described as a regulation directed to digital operational resilience for the financial sector. It would be a misunderstanding to understand this to be limiting, however. The ambit and breadth of DORA is as wide as can be imagined.

WIDE FINANCIAL SECTORS

2.02 The direct impact of DORA is extensive indeed. It captures all of the main financials sectors. One must bear in mind that at most there are many different financial sectors. At a minimum, there are significant numbers of sub sectors within an overarching global financial sector.

Article 2 of DORA sets out the intended scope. DORA applies to entities in the following financial sectors, namely:

- credit institutions;
- payment institutions, including payment institutions exempted pursuant to Directive 2015/2366[1];
- account information service providers;
- electronic money institutions, including electronic money institutions exempted[2];
- investment firms;
- crypto-asset service providers as authorised under Regulation 2023/1114[3] and issuers of asset-referenced tokens;
- central securities depositories;
- central counterparties;
- trading venues;

1 Directive (EU) 2015/2366 on payment services in the internal market, amending Directives 2002/65/EC, 2009/110/EC and 2013/36/EU and Regulation (EU) No 1093/2010, and repealing Directive 2007/64/EC.

2 Electronic money institutions exempted pursuant to Directive 2009/110.

3 Regulation (EU) 2023/1114 on markets in crypto-assets, and amending Regulations (EU) No 1093/2010 and (EU) No 1095/2010 and Directives 2013/36/EU and (EU) 2019/1937.

- trade repositories;
- managers of alternative investment funds;
- management companies;
- data reporting service providers;
- insurance and reinsurance undertakings;
- insurance intermediaries, reinsurance intermediaries and ancillary insurance intermediaries;
- institutions for occupational retirement provision;
- credit rating agencies;
- administrators of critical benchmarks;
- crowdfunding service providers;
- securitisation repositories; and
- information and communication technology (ICT) third-party service providers.

These are collectively referred to as 'financial entities'.

It therefore covers distinct and wide ranging types of financial sectors, including:

- credit sector;
- payment sector;
- account information sector;
- electronic money sector;
- investment sector;
- crypto asset sector;
- central securities sector;
- central counterparties sector;
- trading venues sector;
- trade repositories sector;
- management of alternative investment funds sector;
- management companies sector;
- data reporting sector;
- insurance and reinsurance sectors (each being distinct in themselves);
- insurance intermediaries sectors, reinsurance intermediaries sector and ancillary insurance intermediaries sector;

- occupational retirement sector;
- credit rating sector;
- administration of critical benchmark sector;
- crowdfunding sector; and
- securitisation sector.

ICT SECTOR

2.03 DORA also includes the all-important 'ICT third party service provider sector'.

The ICT sector, or at least the ICT sector that services the financials sectors, should not be considered singular. There are a wide – and growing – number of ICT services and ICT service supplies which support the financial sector. From one perspective, the advent of DORA arises less from the ICT services to the financial sector, but more to the fact that many of these ICT services are now very important support, even essential supports, to the financial sector. Many financial sectors as they exist today may not exist without the underlying ICT capabilities which are required to continue to supply these financial services.

DORA does not supply a definitive list of these ICT services or ICT service suppliers. Indeed, it may be unwise to seek to provide such a list as being definitive, given that such services can adapt quickly or can be supplemented by new types of services which may fall under this umbrella category.

However, it may be of some assistance to at least refer to some of the categories of ICT services that may be encompassed, such as:

- payment services;
- online customer service;
- web services;
- website services;
- hosting services (website);
- hosting services (data);
- data centres;
- Cloud services;
- ICT services for HR;
- ICT services for a firm's customers;
- ICT marketing services;
- financial applications;

- ICT financial services and applications;
- ICT managed services;
- ICT security;
- ICT print services;
- and many more.

CHAPTER 3

Legal Compliance

INTRODUCTION

3.01 Legal compliance in the financial sector is increasingly complex. The increased reliance of the financial sector on complicated information and communication technology (ICT) services adds an immense layer of legal compliance on top of the existing regulations.

It is also important to recognise that ICT legal compliance via DORA cannot be narrow focused and is certainly not a won and done issue. The DORA legal rules cannot be viewed as a simple one-time tick box. No firm will have all DORA measures in place. No firm can take it for granted that even where a particular requirement may be in place already, that all of the tenets of that measure as referred to in DORA are satisfied by a particular pre-existing policy, for example. To take the policy example, DORA may require that the policy needs to be entirely rewritten, or at least expanded in significant and meaningful ways. Simply put, DORA can require substantial additions that need to be made.

While there may be a business continuity policy or a back-up policy in place, for example, merely ticking a box based on the label on the name of a policy, will inevitably lead to such affirm being in breach of the full DORA rules. This will become apparent when an internal audit and/or regulators begin to look into the nature of the DORA compliance programme that the company implemented.

It can also be difficult to separate law from technology, and technology from law. But firms need to be aware of the nexus between these separate disciplines when they consider their legal compliance efforts.

This is also an apt example of *live law*, whereby the legal compliance rules are alive, dynamic, and organic. DORA as an example of modern live law requires not just that the policy is in place (or that the policy is updated if it is a pre-existing policy), but that the legal policy document lives and breathes in the firm and is followed on a day-to-day basis, and that the elements within the policy are actively implemented on a day-to-day basis. Implemented in this context refers to how the elements of the policy are practiced by the firm and its employees. It is a daily activity not a lofty legal tomb taken out off the shelf once a year or if an adverse event was ever to occur. Firms will be familiar with the term business as usual or BAU. DORA's live law requires daily legal compliance as usual.

A firm can only demonstrate DORA compliance effectively if it has implemented DORA legal compliance as usual.

In this context the legal requirements need to be carefully considered of course. But in addition, the nature of the legal compliance documents needs to be considered. These are more extensive than solely having a new 'DORA Policy'. Legal compliance is layered and refers to requirements to have documentation in addition to policies, such as frameworks, systems, reviews, processes, etc.

One of the very important aspects of legal compliance for DORA is that the relevant documented policies and processes are reviewed on a regular basis, and updated accordingly. In addition, they may have to be updated more regularly than annually depending on the circumstances, for instance, if particular events occur in the meantime.

Another important aspect is the requirement for particular types of reports and reviews to be conducted. While some of these may need to occur, others also need to be reported to the appropriate supervisory authority.

REQUIREMENTS ON LEGAL COMPLIANCE

3.02 In order to be legally compliant with DORA firms need to have an extensive strategy. One cannot simply say one looked at DORA and that the firm feels that it satisfies DORA already as a result of its current policies. Invariably, this would not be factually correct.

Even in the best-case scenarios where a firm does have robust mechanisms in place already, these will need to be vetted and cross-checked with DORA. In most instances there will be amendments or enhancements that will need to be made. In addition, it is also most likely that new additional policies or related processes will need to be developed and approved.

The above exercises are significant and time consuming and cannot be underestimated. Legal and risk functions will also then need to be satisfied that the above exercises have occurred and have reached a satisfactory or successful outcome.

There is another important aspect to consider. There is a danger that because the issues in focus with DORA are cast in language such as IT, ICT, operational resilience, digital operational resilience, and event technological terms, that those looking through a legal lens may feel that all of DORA is a non-legal issue. It may be, incorrectly, perceived as only raising issues for the IT technical department or the head of IT. Again, such a presumption is a mistake and will lead to ineffective legal compliance for a variety of reasons.

Legal – and also Risk – need to consider DORA from the perspective of risk identification and risk reduction.

There are also issues to consider quite apart from the initial legal compliance process perspective.

Legal consideration of the nature of DORA and its relationship with other regulatory obligations will also arise.

It will be necessary to consider the ambit and scope of DORA from the perspective of legal applicability to the financial entity in question. Some entities are encompassed – but it may be necessary to see if the given entity is not encompassed or otherwise excluded. Article 2(3), for example, refers to certain entities that are out of scope or to which the Regulation 'does not apply'.

It is sometimes easy to neglect to consider that in a larger group structure, a particular legal regulation may apply to some group entities but not to others. Again, this is an issue that should be considered in terms of DORA legal compliance.

Similar to many other legal measures, DORA is not necessarily coming in a vacuum. While the issues of digital operational resilience have not been comprehensibly addressed before – and particularly for the financial universe – there are relevant and tangentially-related pre-existing laws that may need to be considered. Indeed, DORA has to some extend considered this and the legal policymakers have assessed that some of these prior legal instruments need to be updated.[1] The Legal Function may need to consider and address these amendments as relevant and appropriate.

Without doubt, DORA is a most extensive and complex legal regulation. But, importantly, it is not a one-size-fits-all law. While debate may arise as to how successfully this may have been achieved, there is at least an effort to differentiate between the various types and forms of financial entities within the wider financial sector – and servicing the wider financial sector. Some may argue that the *general* legal policy tools utilised (in particular, using the principle of proportionality;[2] the general ICT risk management framework requirements[3] versus simplified ICT risk management framework requirements[4]) and the *specification* legal policy tools utilised (in particular, identifying and calling out particular financial sector firms for less DORA regulatory legal obligations[5]) are insufficient. (There are also some instances where particular obligations are

1 Article 59, DORA contains amendments to Regulation 1060/2009; Article 60 contains amendments to Regulation 648/2012; Article 61 contains amendments to Regulation 909/2014; Article 62 contains amendments to Regulation 600/2014; and Article 63 contains amendments to Regulation 2016/1011.
2 Article 4 (Proportionality principle), DORA.
3 Article 6 et seq., DORA.
4 Article 16 et seq., DORA.
5 Consider, for example, how institutions for occupational retirement provision, which operate pension schemes which together have less than 100 members in total, institutions for occupational retirement provision which operate pension schemes which together do not have more than 15 members in total, and small institutions for occupational retirement provision are differentiated.

expressly extended to apply to particular sectors and or types of firm.[6]) They may argue that even more firms and more categories of financial firms needed to have DORA legal measures tailored to them. Such arguments may have justified merit. There are many financial sectors which do not have the same high volume of financial transactions as regular high street banks, nor have the same high numbers of customers – yet may be treated identically under DORA. It is fair to say that DORA implicitly if not expressly gives an acknowledgement that the level of risk is not identical for all financial firms.[7] It is indicated more than once that individualised proportionality consideration can (if not should) be applied.

Separate and in addition to the above, other functions within the financial entity (and ICT entity) will need to consider the particular regulations in DORA which are most applicable to them and which require implementing activity on their part. However, in arriving at an understanding of what is meant by particular individual obligations – even some of those of an ICT technical nature – this may not always be a 100 per cent clear. There will be occasions where other functions will need to call upon the Legal Function to assist in clarifying the meaning and interpretation of particular regulatory obligations, and how they may apply in the particular circumstances of the firm.

The various steps in arriving at legal compliance should be documented separate and in addition to the documented demonstration of compliance with the overall DORA requirements. This will involve consideration of the DORA Regulation, the nature of the Regulation, and each of the legal regulatory compliance components.

The Legal Function, as well as other functions, will also need to be keenly aware that while the complex analysis exercises that are required for implementing DORA are of course essential, this is certainly not a one moment in time initiative. Continual ongoing compliance is needed from a legal perspective. The best approach for the firm in doing so needs to be considered. This will inevitably require certain ongoing legal compliance processes.

Legal compliance with DORA also requires consideration of what may happen if things go wrong. As with most legal regulations, there are forms of encouraging compliance (on top of the de facto legal requirements of compliance ab initio). There are provisions providing for regulatory investigation, impositions of costs and penalties, and prosecutions for offences. The following will need to be considered:

- general investigations (Article 38);
- inspections (Article 39);

6 Consider, for example, Article 23 of DORA as it relates to operational or security payment-related incidents concerning credit institutions, payment institutions, account information service providers, and electronic money institutions; and Article 26 of DORA as it relates to advanced testing of ICT tools, systems and processes based on TLPT.

7 Of course, that statement itself needs to be more nuanced and encompass time and change issues.

- oversight fees (Article 43);
- administrative penalties and remedial measures (Article 50);
- exercise of the power to impose administrative penalties and remedial measures (Article 51); and
- criminal penalties (Article 52).

The in-scope firms and Legal Function will also need to consider issues of professional secrecy. This is referred to in Article 55 of DORA. Additionally, data protection and personal data considerations arise. These are referred to in Article 56.

While DORA is prescriptive in terms of the regulations and obligations it sets out, financial entities and legal advisors will also need to be aware that DORA is not the be all and end all. To arrive at legal compliance a firm needs to be aware that the Articles of DORA are less than half of the provisions that need to be considered. This is because there are a wide range of secondary or sub-regulations to be complied with. These are the sub-regulations developed by the European Supervisory Authorities (ESAs) and which are promulgated by the EU Commission (see Appendices).[8]

If this is not complicating enough already, financial entities and Legal Functions need to be aware that there is in addition a range of national DORA legislation. This arises for a number of reasons but it is expressly provided in DORA that national states may develop their own national legislation, which may sometimes compliment and/or help to implement DORA[9] and sometimes provide certain exceptions,[10] or even exclusions from the applicability of DORA,[11] or variations to DORA.[12] National legislation will also provide for or appoint the national regulator or regulators whom will enforce and apply DORA nationally.[13] These nationally appointed regulators will also report and liaise with the ESA and other

8 See, for example, Article 57, DORA, regarding the power to adopt delegated acts is conferred on the EU Commission.

9 See, for example, Article 50(3) which provides, inter alia, that Member States shall lay down rules establishing appropriate administrative penalties and remedial measures for breaches of DORA and shall ensure their effective implementation.

10 See, for example, Article 52, where Member States may decide not to lay down rules for administrative penalties or remedial measures for breaches that are subject to criminal penalties under their national law.

11 Consider Article 2(4) of DORA which provides that Member States may exclude from the scope of DORA entities referred to in Article 2(5), points (4) to (23), of Directive 2013/36 that are located within their respective territories. Also consider Article 16(1) of DORA in this national respect.

12 Consider, for example, Article 19(1), paragraph 5, and Article 19(2), paragraph 3, of DORA.

13 See, for example, Article 50(3) and (4). Also consider, for example, Article 26(9) where Member States may designate a single public authority in the financial sector to be responsible for TLPT-related matters in the financial sector at national level and shall entrust it with all competences and tasks to that effect.

European-level DORA authorities.[14] States may also continue to engage in their own bilateral relations on some of the issues pertaining to DORA.[15] This also applies to national regulators or supervisory authorities.[16]

From a legal perspective, particular attention is required when considering how a firm ensures it complies with regulatory reporting obligations. In this instance there are a variety of reporting issues to be cognisant of, including the:

- register of information;[17]
- report on ICT service providers;[18]
- ICT security audit reports;[19]
- ICT-related incident reports;[20] and
- ICT third-party internal or external audit reports.[21]

Particular legal considerations may also arise if and when an inspection occurs or when particular information is requested from a national or European regulator or supervisory authority.[22] This may involve the fact of the occurrence, the legal basis, the information required, the information available to furnish, and the potential consequences or implications arising from the content of the information. Time requirement issues can also be important.

In addition to requests for particular information, the important issue of inspections may also need to be considered – if not prepared for.[23]

POLICY ON LEGAL COMPLIANCE

3.03 There are a variety of legal and compliance issues raised by DORA. It is obviously a legal requirement to comply. It would be a mistake to assume that the impact of DORA was limited to a small number of entities, or that financial entities per se were of little consequence to wider industry, to the general economy, to society more widely. There are a wide range of impact issues, none least being the legal and compliance issues. These assist in conveying the wider impacts of DORA.

14 Certain national regulators may indeed already be appointed. See also Article 46 of DORA regarding competent authorities.
15 See Article 36(2), DORA.
16 Ibid.
17 See, for example, Article 38(3), DORA.
18 See, for example, Article 28(3), paragraph 3, DORA.
19 See, for example, Article 37(1), DORA.
20 See, for example, Article 37(1), DORA.
21 See, for example, Article 40(4), paragraph 2, DORA.
22 Requests for information are referred to in Article 37, DORA.
23 Inspections are referred to in Article 39, DORA.

Regulation instrument

3.04 By its nature, it is directly applicable as legal Regulations are directly effective. This means that it does not require secondary implementation by way of national legislation in order to be effective and obligatory. (There is a caveat to this, see below at **3.08**.) This is also deliberate. The decision was made that given the importance of ensuring digital operational resilience, the fastest and also most uniform way of doing so, was by way of a legal instrument known as a Regulation – as opposed to a Directive or other legal means.

Prior initiatives

3.05 There is also a recognition that past measures in this space were less effective, or even not effective as otherwise intended.

Clearly, ICT risk has attracted the attention of many policymakers and regulators (and not least international standard setting bodies (SSOs)) in an attempt to enhance digital resilience, set standards and coordinate regulatory or supervisory work.[24] Some examples at international level include the Basel Committee on Banking Supervision, the Committee on Payments and Market Infrastructures, the Financial Stability Board, the Financial Stability Institute, and the G7 and G20. These aim to provide competent authorities and market operators across various jurisdictions with appropriate tools to bolster the resilience of their financial systems.[25]

Such efforts have also been driven by the need to properly consider ICT risk in the context of an increasingly interconnected global financial system.[26] There is also an increasing need to ensure more consistency of relevant best practices.[27]

Europe has also established what are known as 'European Supervisory Authorities' (ESAs). The ESAs comprise:

- the European Supervisory Authority (European Banking Authority) (EBA);[28]
- the European Supervisory Authority (European Insurance and Occupational Pensions Authority) (EIOPA);[29] and
- the European Supervisory Authority (European Securities and Markets Authority) (ESMA).[30]

24 Recital 4, DORA.
25 Recital 4, DORA.
26 Recital 4, DORA.
27 Recital 4, DORA.
28 The European Banking Authority was established by Regulation 1093/2010.
29 The European Supervisory Authority (European Insurance and Occupational Pensions Authority) was established by Regulation 1094/2010.
30 The European Supervisory Authority (European Securities and Markets Authority) was established by Regulation 1095/2010.

These are collectively referred to as the European Supervisory Authorities or 'ESAs'. The ESAs jointly issued technical advice calling for a coherent approach to ICT risk in finance and recommending to strengthen, in a proportionate way, the digital operational resilience of the financial services industry through a sector-specific initiative of Europe.[31]

New initiative

3.06 DORA represents a new legal requirement to move well beyond the past initiatives. The new Regulation aims to 'consolidate and upgrade' ICT risk requirements as part of the operational risk requirements that have previously been addressed separately in different legal initiatives.[32]

The previous legal efforts covered the perceived main categories of financial risk. These included credit risk, market risk, counterparty credit risk, liquidity risk, and also market conduct risk.

The above risk and legal efforts as initiated did not, however, comprehensively tackle all components of operational resilience. The operational risk rules, when further developed in those European legal Acts, often favoured a 'traditional' quantitative approach to addressing risk. What that refers to is setting a capital requirement to cover ICT risk.[33] It does not include or address targeted qualitative rules for the protection, detection, containment, recovery and repair capabilities against ICT-related incidents, nor requiring rules for the reporting of such issues and digital testing capabilities.[34]

The previous legal instruments were primarily meant to cover and update essential rules on prudential supervision, market integrity or conduct. By consolidating and upgrading the different rules on ICT risk, all provisions addressing digital risk in the financial sector should now, as a result of DORA, for the first time be brought together in a consistent manner in one single legislative Act.[35]

Therefore, DORA will fill in the gaps and remedy some of the inconsistencies in some of the previous legal efforts. This effort also includes addressing the terminology and definitions used. DORA explicitly refers to ICT risk via targeted rules on ICT risk management capabilities, incident reporting obligations, operational resilience testing, and ICT third-party risk monitoring.[36]

The new Regulation, not dissimilar to the GDPR, will also raise awareness of ICT risk and the danger of ICT incidents. It will also raise the recognition of the

31 This was issued in April 2019. Recital 7, DORA.
32 Recital 12, DORA.
33 Recital 12, DORA.
34 Recital 12, DORA.
35 Recital 12, DORA.
36 Recital 12, DORA.

fact that a lack of operational resilience can have the possibility of jeopardising the soundness of financial entities.[37]

Graduated impact

3.07 While there is a wide range of financial sectors encompassed, there is also a need to recognise the need for nuanced or graduated impacts. The Recitals point out that '[n]otwithstanding the broad coverage envisaged by this Regulation, the application of the digital operational resilience rules should take into account the significant differences between financial entities in terms of their size and overall risk profile.'[38]

It is indicated that as a 'general principle,' when distributing resources and capabilities for the implementation of the ICT risk management framework, financial entities should duly 'balance their ICT related needs to their size and overall risk profile, and the nature, scale and complexity of their services, activities and operations.'[39] On the other hand, competent authorities should continue to assess and review the approach of such distribution.[40]

Larger financial entities may enjoy wider resources to address the new legal requirements (as well as problem issues as they arise).[41] They can also swiftly deploy funds to develop governance structures and set up various corporate strategies.[42] It is indicated that only financial entities that are not microenterprises in the sense of DORA should be required to establish more complex governance arrangements.[43] Such entities are better equipped in particular to set up dedicated management functions for supervising arrangements with ICT third-party service providers or for dealing with crisis management, to organise their ICT risk management according to the three lines of defence model, or to set up an internal risk management and control model, and to submit their ICT risk management framework to the important internal audits.[44]

National measures

3.08 While DORA is wide in the universe it encompasses, there are certain areas not covered. Sometimes European level laws, even Regulations as referred to above, can include provisions for national policymakers to make exclusions or to implement some of the rues as most appropriately fit the country in question. As a result, it is indicated in DORA that because the entities referred

37 Recital 12, DORA.
38 Recital 36, DORA.
39 Recital 36, DORA.
40 Recital 36, DORA.
41 Recital 38, DORA.
42 Recital 38, DORA.
43 Recital 38, DORA.
44 Recital 38, DORA.

to in Article 2(5), points (4) to (23), of Directive 2013/36 are excluded from the scope of that Directive, Member States should consequently be able to choose to exempt from the application of this Regulation such entities located within their respective territories.[45]

Under sector-specific European law, some financial entities are subject to lighter requirements or exemptions for reasons associated with their size or the services they provide.[46] That category of financial entities includes small and non-interconnected investment firms, small institutions for occupational retirement provision which may be excluded from the scope of Directive 2016/2341 under the conditions laid down in Article 5 of that Directive by the Member State concerned and operate pension schemes which together do not have more than 100 members in total, as well as institutions exempted pursuant to Directive 2013/36.[47] Therefore, in accordance with the principle of proportionality and to preserve the spirit of sector-specific European law, it is also appropriate to subject those financial entities to a simplified ICT risk management framework under DORA.[48]

The proportionate character of the ICT risk management framework covering those financial entities should not be altered by the regulatory technical standards that are to be developed by the ESAs. Moreover, in accordance with the principle of proportionality, it is appropriate to also subject payment institutions[49] and electronic money institutions[50] exempted in accordance with national law transposing those European legal Acts to a simplified ICT risk management framework under DORA, while payment institutions and electronic money institutions which have not been exempted in accordance with their respective national law transposing sectoral European law should comply with the general framework laid down by DORA.[51]

Similarly so, financial entities which qualify as microenterprises, or are subject to the simplified ICT risk management framework under DORA, should not be required to:

- establish a role to monitor their arrangements concluded with ICT third-party service providers on the use of ICT services;
- designate a member of senior management to be responsible for overseeing the related risk exposure and relevant documentation;
- assign the responsibility for managing and overseeing ICT risk to a control function and ensure an appropriate level of independence of such control function in order to avoid conflicts of interest;

45 Recital 40, DORA.
46 Recital 42, DORA.
47 Recital 42, DORA.
48 Recital 42, DORA.
49 Payment institutions referred to in Article 32(1) of Directive 2015/2366.
50 Electronic money institutions referred to in Article 9 of Directive 2009/110.
51 Recital 42, DORA.

- document and review at least once a year the ICT risk management framework;
- subject to internal audit on a regular basis the ICT risk management framework;
- perform in-depth assessments after major changes in their network and information system infrastructures and processes;
- regularly conduct risk analyses on legacy ICT systems;
- subject the implementation of the ICT Response and Recovery plans to independent internal audit reviews;
- have a crisis management function;
- expand the testing of business continuity and response and recovery plans to capture switchover scenarios between primary ICT infrastructure and redundant facilities;
- report to competent authorities, upon their request, an estimation of aggregated annual costs and losses caused by major ICT-related incidents, to maintain redundant ICT capacities;
- communicate to national competent authorities implemented changes following post ICT-related incident reviews; and
- monitor on a continuous basis, relevant technological developments to establish a comprehensive digital operational resilience testing programme as an integral part of the ICT risk management framework provided for in this Regulation, or to adopt and regularly review a strategy on ICT third-party risk.[52]

In addition, it is specified that microenterprises should only be required to assess the need to maintain such redundant ICT capacities based on their risk profile.[53]

Microenterprises should benefit from a more flexible regime as regards digital operational resilience testing programmes. When considering the type and frequency of testing to be performed, they should properly balance the objective of maintaining a high digital operational resilience, the available resources and their overall risk profile.[54]

Microenterprises and financial entities subject to the simplified ICT risk management framework under this Regulation should be exempted from the requirement to perform advanced testing of ICT tools, systems and processes based on threat-led penetration testing (TLPT). This because only financial entities meeting the criteria set out in DORA should be required to carry out such testing. In light of their limited capabilities, microenterprises should be able to agree with the ICT third-party service provider to delegate the financial

52 Recital 43, DORA.
53 Recital 43, DORA.
54 Recital 43, DORA.

entity's rights of access, inspection and audit to an independent third party, to be appointed by the ICT third-party service provider, provided that the financial entity is able to request, at any time, all relevant information and assurance on the ICT third-party service provider's performance from the respective independent third party.[55]

Payment incidents

3.09 DORA requires credit institutions, payment institutions, account information service providers and electronic money institutions to report all operational or security payment-related incidents – previously reported under Directive 2015/2366 – irrespective of the ICT nature of the incident.[56]

Prime responsibility

3.10 A financial entity should at all times remain fully responsible for complying with its obligations set out in DORA.[57] While third-party services providers, particularly ICT providers, will be engaged, the prime responsibility for legal compliance rests with the firm itself. Management and board obligations and responsibilities also need to be borne in mind. In addition, many financial regulations and regulators impose obligations of individual responsibility on certain role holders with the firms – which can be separate and in addition to the firm itself. One consequence of this can be personal sanctions, including up to personal fines.

Emerging risk

3.11 Financial entities should apply a proportionate approach to the monitoring of risks emerging at the level of the ICT third-party service providers. This requires taking into account a number of specified issues. Financial entities should be 'duly considering' the following – namely, nature, scale, complexity and importance of their ICT-related dependencies, the criticality or importance of the services, processes or functions subject to the contractual arrangements and, ultimately, on the basis of a careful assessment of any potential impact on the continuity and quality of financial services at individual and at group level, as appropriate.[58]

To address the systemic impact of ICT third-party concentration risk, DORA promotes a 'balanced solution' by means of taking a 'flexible and gradual approach' to such concentration risk. This is because of the consideration that

55 Recital 43, DORA.
56 Recital 54, DORA.
57 Recital 64, DORA.
58 Recital 64, DORA.

the imposition of any rigid caps or strict limitations might hinder the conduct of business and restrain the contractual freedom.[59]

Financial entities should thoroughly assess their envisaged contractual arrangements to identify the likelihood of such risk emerging. This includes, by means of 'in depth analyses', subcontracting arrangements, in particular when concluded with ICT third-party service providers established in a third country.[60]

However, at this stage, and with a view to striking a fair balance between the imperative of preserving contractual freedom and that of guaranteeing financial stability, it is not considered appropriate to set out rules on strict caps and limits to ICT third-party exposures.[61] In the context of the Oversight Framework, a Lead Overseer appointed pursuant to DORA, should, in respect to critical ICT third-party service providers, pay particular attention to fully grasp the magnitude of interdependences, discover specific instances where a high degree of concentration of critical ICT third-party service providers in the EU is likely to put a strain on a European financial system's stability and integrity and maintain a dialogue with critical ICT third-party service providers where that specific risk is identified.[62]

The requirement to set up a subsidiary in the EU should not prevent the critical ICT third-party service provider from supplying ICT services and related technical support from facilities and infrastructure located outside the EU. DORA does not impose a 'data localisation' obligation as it does not require data storage or processing to be undertaken in the EU.[63]

Critical ICT third-party service providers should be able to provide ICT services from anywhere in the world, not necessarily or not only from premises located in the EU. Oversight activities should be first conducted on premises located in the EU and by interacting with entities located in the EU, including the subsidiaries established by critical ICT third-party service providers pursuant to DORA. However, such actions within the EU might be insufficient to allow the Lead Overseer to fully and effectively perform its duties under this Regulation. The Lead Overseer should, therefore, also be able to 'exercise its relevant oversight powers in third countries.' Exercising those powers in third countries should allow the Lead Overseer to 'examine the facilities' from which the ICT service is or the technical support services are actually provided or managed by the critical ICT third-party service provider, and should give the Lead Overseer a comprehensive and operational understanding of the ICT risk management of the critical ICT third-party service provider. The possibility for the Lead Overseer, as an EU agency, to exercise powers outside the territory of the EU should be duly framed by relevant conditions, in particular the consent of the critical ICT third-party service provider concerned. Similarly, the relevant authorities of the third

59 Recital 67, DORA.
60 Recital 67, DORA.
61 Recital 67, DORA.
62 Recital 67, DORA.
63 Recital 82, DORA.

country should be informed of, and not have objected to, the exercise on their own territory of the activities of the Lead Overseer. However, in order to ensure efficient implementation, and without prejudice to the respective competences of the EU institutions and the Member States, such powers also need to be fully anchored in the conclusion of administrative cooperation arrangements with the relevant authorities of the third country concerned. DORA should, therefore, enable the ESAs to conclude 'administrative cooperation arrangements' with the relevant authorities of third countries, which should not otherwise create legal obligations in respect of the EU and its Member States.[64]

Due to the significant impact of being designated as critical, DORA should ensure that the rights of critical ICT third-party service providers are observed throughout the implementation of the Oversight Framework.[65]

Prior to being designated as critical, such providers should have, for example, the right to submit to the Lead Overseer a 'reasoned statement' containing any relevant information for the purposes of the assessment related to their designation. Since the Lead Overseer should be empowered to submit recommendations on ICT risk matters and suitable remedies thereto, which include the power to oppose certain contractual arrangements ultimately affecting the stability of the financial entity or the financial system, critical ICT third-party service providers should also be given the opportunity to provide, prior to the finalisation of those recommendations, 'explanations' regarding the expected impact of the solutions, envisaged in the recommendations, on customers that are entities falling outside the scope of DORA and to formulate solutions to mitigate risks. Critical ICT third-party service providers disagreeing with the recommendations should submit a 'reasoned explanation' of their intention not to endorse the recommendation. Where such reasoned explanation is not submitted or where it is 'considered' to be insufficient, the Lead Overseer should issue a public notice summarily describing the matter of non-compliance.[66]

To promote convergence at international level as regards the use of best practices in the review and monitoring of ICT third-party service providers' digital risk management, the ESAs should be encouraged to conclude cooperation arrangements with relevant supervisory and regulatory third-country authorities.[67]

To leverage the specific competences, technical skills and expertise of staff specialising in operational and ICT risk within the competent authorities, the three ESAs and, on a voluntary basis, the competent authorities under Directive 2022/2555, the Lead Overseer should draw on national supervisory capabilities and knowledge and set up dedicated 'examination teams' for each critical ICT third-party service provider, pooling 'multidisciplinary teams' in support of the preparation and execution of oversight activities, including general investigations

64 Recital 83, DORA.
65 Recital 89, DORA.
66 Recital 89, DORA.
67 Recital 94, DORA.

and inspections of critical ICT third-party service providers, as well as for any necessary follow up.[68]

Since the objective of DORA, namely to achieve a high level of digital operational resilience for regulated financial entities, cannot be sufficiently achieved (alone) by the Member States because it requires harmonisation of various different rules in Union and national law, but can rather, by reason of its scale and effects, be better achieved at European level, the EU may adopt measures in accordance with the principle of subsidiarity as set out in Article 5 of the Treaty on European Union. In accordance with the principle of proportionality as set out in that Article, DORA does not go beyond what is necessary in order to achieve that objective.[69]

DORA may also raise personal data and data protection considerations. The European Data Protection Supervisor (EDPS) is indicated to have been consulted during the process of developing DORA.[70] The EDPS delivered an opinion on 10 May 2021.[71]

It is inevitable, given that so much of the focus is directed to establishing or improving ICT digital operational resilience, that there is significant reliance and specificity on technical ICT issues. This includes technical tools and systems, to wider governance and policy issues.

REQUIREMENTS ON ICT COMPLIANCE

3.12 A good example of this is Article 6 which specifies requirements in relation to the ICT risk management framework. Financial entities are required to have 'a sound, comprehensive and well-documented ICT risk management framework' – which is to be a part of their overall risk management system to enables them to address ICT risk quickly, efficiently and comprehensively and to ensure a high level of digital operational resilience.[72]

The wide breadth of what ICT issues are encompassed is clear when we see that that the ICT risk management framework must include at least:[73]

- strategies;
- policies,
- procedures;
- ICT protocols; and
- tools,

which must, therefore, be separate.

68 Recital 95, DORA.
69 Recital 105, DORA.
70 In accordance with Article 42(1) of Regulation 2018/1725.
71 Recital 106, DORA.
72 Article 6(1), DORA.
73 Article 6(2), DORA.

It is noted that there is a reference to 'at least'[74] and as such, it is clear that there can also be a wider range of activities to consider, and reference as appropriate.

It is also indicated that the ICT risk management framework shall include at least strategies, policies, procedures, ICT protocols and tools that are necessary to duly and adequately protect all information assets and ICT assets.[75] The information assets and ICT assets include computer software, hardware, and servers.[76] They also include the protection of 'all relevant physical components and infrastructures, such as premises, data centres and sensitive designated areas.'[77] They also include ensuring that 'all information assets and ICT assets are adequately protected from risks including damage and unauthorised access or usage.'[78]

The aim is to reduce ICT risk. In accordance with the ICT risk management framework, financial entities shall 'minimise the impact of ICT risk by deploying appropriate strategies, policies, procedures, ICT protocols and tools.'[79] Firms must provide 'complete and updated information on ICT risk and on their ICT risk management framework to the competent authorities upon their request.'[80]

The ICT risk management framework must be documented.[81] It must also be reviewed at least once a year.[82] (In the case of microenterprises, it must be reviewed periodically[83].) It must also be reviewed upon the occurrence of major ICT-related incidents.[84] Alternatively, it must also be reviewed following supervisory instructions.[85] In addition, it must also be reviewed following conclusions derived from relevant digital operational resilience testing or audit processes.[86] The ICT risk management framework must also be 'continuously improved' on the basis of lessons derived from implementation and monitoring.[87]

There must also be a 'report on the review of the ICT risk management framework.'[88] This report must be submitted to the competent authority upon its request.[89]

74 Article 6(2), DORA.
75 Article 6(2), DORA.
76 Article 6(2), DORA.
77 Article 6(2), DORA.
78 Article 6(2), DORA.
79 Article 6(3), DORA.
80 Article 6(3), DORA.
81 Article 6(5), DORA.
82 Article 6(5), DORA.
83 Article 6(5), DORA.
84 Article 6(5), DORA.
85 Article 6(5), DORA.
86 Article 6(5), DORA.
87 Article 6(5), DORA.
88 Article 6(5), DORA.
89 Article 6(5), DORA.

The ICT risk management framework must be subject to internal audit reviews.[90] (There is an exception for microenterprises) These internal audits will occur a regular basis in line with the financial entities' audit plan.[91] There is a requirement for the auditors to have 'sufficient knowledge, skills and expertise in ICT risk.'[92] The auditors must also have and maintain appropriate independence.[93] It is also provided that the frequency and focus of ICT audits shall be 'commensurate to the ICT risk' of the financial entity.[94]

Financial entities must establish a formal follow-up process based on the conclusions from the internal audit review.[95] This shall include rules for the timely verification and remediation of any critical ICT audit findings.[96]

The ICT risk management framework must include a digital operational resilience strategy which sets out how the framework is to be implemented.[97]

To that end, the digital operational resilience strategy shall include methods to address ICT risk and attain specific ICT objectives, by:

- explaining how the ICT risk management framework supports the financial entity's business strategy and objectives;
- establishing the risk tolerance level for ICT risk, in accordance with the risk appetite of the financial entity, and analysing the impact tolerance for ICT disruptions;
- setting out clear information security objectives, including key performance indicators and key risk metrics;
- explaining the ICT reference architecture and any changes needed to reach specific business objectives;
- outlining the different mechanisms put in place to detect ICT-related incidents, prevent their impact and provide protection from it;
- evidencing the current digital operational resilience situation on the basis of the number of major ICT-related incidents reported and the effectiveness of preventive measures;
- implementing digital operational resilience testing (in accordance with Chapter IV of DORA); and
- outlining a communication strategy in the event of ICT-related incidents the disclosure of which is required (in accordance with Article 14).[98]

90 Article 6(6), DORA.
91 Article 6(6), DORA.
92 Article 6(6), DORA.
93 Article 6(6), DORA.
94 Article 6(6), DORA.
95 Article 6(7), DORA.
96 Article 6(7), DORA.
97 Article 6(8), DORA.
98 Article 6(8), DORA.

Financial entities may in the context of their digital operational resilience strategy, have a holistic ICT multi-vendor strategy (at group or entity level) showing key dependencies on ICT third-party service providers and explaining the 'rationale' behind the procurement mix of ICT third-party service providers.[99]

Financial entities may, in accordance with sectoral law,[100] outsource the tasks of verifying compliance with ICT risk management requirements to intra group or external undertakings. In the case of such outsourcing, the financial entity remains fully responsible for the verification of compliance with the ICT risk management requirements.[101]

There is also further specificity in relation to ICT systems, protocols and tools. Article 7 provides that in order to address and manage ICT risk, financial entities shall use and maintain updated ICT systems, protocols and tools that meet certain requirements.[102] These requirements are:

- appropriate to the magnitude of operations supporting the conduct of their activities, in accordance with the proportionality principle (as referred to in Article 4);
- reliable;
- equipped with sufficient capacity to accurately process the data necessary for the performance of activities and the timely provision of services, and to deal with peak orders, message or transaction volumes, as needed, including where new technology is introduced; and
- technologically resilient in order to adequately deal with additional information processing needs as required under stressed market conditions or other adverse situations.[103]

There is also a requirement, associated with the ICT risk management framework, to undertake an identification exercise. Article 8 provides that '[a]s part of the ICT risk management framework referred to in Article 6(1), financial entities shall identify, classify and adequately document all ICT supported business functions, roles and responsibilities, the information assets and ICT assets supporting those functions, and their roles and dependencies in relation to ICT risk.'[104] Financial entities must also review as needed, and at least yearly, the adequacy of this classification and of any relevant documentation.[105] The exercise must, therefore, identify and classify all:

- ICT-supported business functions;
- roles and responsibilities;

99 Article 6(9), DORA.
100 In accordance with EU and national sectoral law.
101 Article 6(10), DORA.
102 Article 7, DORA.
103 Article 7, DORA.
104 Article 8(1), DORA.
105 Article 8(1), DORA.

- information assets and ICT assets supporting those functions; and
- their roles and dependencies in relation to ICT risk.[106]

In addition, financial entities must on a continuous basis, identify all sources of ICT risk, in particular the risk exposure to and from other financial entities, and assess cyber threats and ICT vulnerabilities relevant to their ICT supported business functions, information assets and ICT assets.[107] Financial entities must review on a regular basis, and at least yearly, the risk scenarios impacting them.[108] Therefore, in addition to the above, firms must identify all sources of ICT risk, in particular risk exposure to and from other financial entities.

Firms must also assess cyber threats and ICT vulnerabilities relevant to their:

- ICT-supported business functions;
- information assets; and
- ICT assets.

Financial entities (other than microenterprises) must perform a risk assessment upon each major change in the network and information system infrastructure, in the processes or procedures affecting their ICT supported business functions, information assets or ICT assets.[109]

Financial entities must identify all information assets and ICT assets, including those on remote sites, network resources and hardware equipment.[110] They must also map those considered critical.[111] Firms must map the configuration of the information assets and ICT assets and the links and interdependencies between the different information assets and ICT assets.[112]

Financial entities must also identify and document all processes that are dependent on ICT third-party service providers.[113] The must identify interconnections with ICT third-party service providers that provide services that support critical or important functions.[114]

For the purposes of the above,[115] financial entities must maintain relevant inventories and update them periodically and every time any major change as referred to above[116] occurs.[117]

106 Article 8(1), DORA.
107 Article 8(2), DORA.
108 Article 8(2), DORA.
109 Article 8(3), DORA.
110 Article 8(4), DORA.
111 Article 8(4), DORA.
112 Article 8(4), DORA.
113 Article 8(5), DORA.
114 Article 8(5), DORA.
115 For paragraphs (1), (4) and (5) of Article 8.
116 Any major change as referred to in paragraph (3).
117 Article 8(6), DORA.

Financial entities (other than microenterprises) must on a regular basis (and at least yearly), conduct a specific ICT risk assessment on all 'legacy ICT systems' and, in any case before and after connecting technologies, applications or systems.[118]

Article 9 refers to issues of protection and prevention. For the purposes of adequately protecting ICT systems and with a view to organising response measures, financial entities must 'continuously monitor and control' the security and functioning of ICT systems and tools.[119] They must also minimise the impact of ICT risk on ICT systems through the deployment of appropriate ICT security tools, policies and procedures.[120]

Financial entities must also design, procure and implement ICT security 'policies, procedures, protocols and tools' that aim to ensure the resilience, continuity and availability of ICT systems.[121] This is in particular for those supporting critical or important functions.[122] This is also to maintain high standards of availability, authenticity, integrity and confidentiality of data, whether at rest, in use or in transit.[123]

In order to achieve the objectives referred to in the above paragraph, financial entities must use ICT solutions and processes that are 'appropriate' (in accordance with Article 4).[124] But what is appropriate, and therefore, not appropriate? Gratefully, it is specified that those ICT solutions and processes shall:

- ensure the security of the means of transfer of data;
- minimise the risk of corruption or loss of data, unauthorised access and technical flaws that may hinder business activity;
- prevent the lack of availability, the impairment of the authenticity and integrity, the breaches of confidentiality and the loss of data; and
- ensure that data is protected from risks arising from data management, including poor administration, processing-related risks and human error.[125]

In addition, as part of the ICT risk management framework, financial entities must:

- develop and document an information security policy defining rules to protect the availability, authenticity, integrity and confidentiality of data, information assets and ICT assets, including those of their customers, where applicable;

118 Article 8(7), DORA.
119 Article 9(1), DORA.
120 Article 9(1), DORA.
121 Article 9(2), DORA.
122 Article 9(2), DORA.
123 Article 9(2), DORA.
124 Article 9(3), DORA.
125 Article 9(3), DORA.

- following a risk-based approach, establish a sound network and infrastructure management structure using appropriate techniques, methods and protocols that may include implementing automated mechanisms to isolate affected information assets in the event of cyber attacks;
- implement policies that limit the physical or logical access to information assets and ICT assets to what is required for legitimate and approved functions and activities only, and establish to that end a set of policies, procedures and controls that address access rights and ensure a sound administration thereof;
- implement policies and protocols for strong authentication mechanisms, based on relevant standards and dedicated control systems, and protection measures of cryptographic keys whereby data is encrypted based on results of approved data classification and ICT risk assessment processes;
- implement documented policies, procedures and controls for ICT change management, including changes to software, hardware, firmware components, systems or security parameters, that are based on a risk assessment approach and are an integral part of the financial entity's overall change management process, in order to ensure that all changes to ICT systems are recorded, tested, assessed, approved, implemented and verified in a controlled manner; and
- have appropriate and comprehensive documented policies for patches and updates.[126]

For the purposes of Article 9(4), first subparagraph, point (b) (bullet point two above), financial entities shall design the network connection infrastructure in a way that allows it to be instantaneously severed or segmented in order to minimise and prevent contagion, especially for interconnected financial processes.[127]

For the purposes of Article 9(4), first subparagraph, point (e) (bullet point five above), the ICT change management process shall be approved by appropriate lines of management and shall have specific protocols in place.[128]

Detection is also an important facet of the ICT risk management framework. Article 10 provides that financial entities must have in place mechanisms to promptly detect anomalous activities (in accordance with Article 17), including ICT network performance issues and ICT-related incidents, and to identify potential material single points of failure.[129]

All detection mechanisms referred to above must be regularly tested in accordance with Article 25.[130]

126 Article 9(4), DORA.
127 Article 9(4), DORA.
128 Article 9(4), DORA.
129 Article 10(1), DORA.
130 Article 10(1), DORA.

The detection mechanisms referred to above shall enable multiple layers of control, define alert thresholds and criteria to trigger and initiate ICT-related incident response processes, including automatic alert mechanisms for relevant staff in charge of ICT-related incident responses.[131]

Financial entities must devote sufficient resources and capabilities to monitor user activity, the occurrence of ICT anomalies and ICT-related incidents, in particular cyber attacks.[132]

Data reporting service providers must, in addition, have in place systems that can effectively check trade reports for completeness, identify omissions and obvious errors, and request re-transmission of those reports.[133]

Response and recovery is another important part of the ICT risk management framework. Article 11 provides that as part of the ICT risk management framework and based on the identification requirements (set out in Article 8), financial entities must put in place a comprehensive ICT business continuity policy, which may be adopted as a dedicated specific policy, forming an integral part of the overall business continuity policy of the financial entity.[134]

The financial entities must implement the ICT business continuity policy through dedicated, appropriate and documented arrangements, plans, procedures and mechanisms aiming to:

- ensure the continuity of the financial entity's critical or important functions;
- quickly, appropriately and effectively respond to, and resolve, all ICT-related incidents in a way that limits damage and prioritises the resumption of activities and recovery actions;
- activate, without delay, dedicated plans that enable containment measures, processes and technologies suited to each type of ICT-related incident and prevent further damage, as well as tailored response and recovery procedures (established in accordance with Article 12);
- estimate preliminary impacts, damages and losses; and
- set out communication and crisis management actions that ensure that updated information is transmitted to all relevant internal staff and external stakeholders (in accordance with Article 14), and report to the competent authorities (in accordance with Article 19).[135]

As part of the ICT risk management framework financial entities must also implement associated ICT response and recovery plans which (in the case of

131 Article 10(2), DORA.
132 Article 10(3), DORA.
133 Article 10(4), DORA.
134 Article 11(1), DORA.
135 Article 11(2), DORA.

financial entities other than microenterprises), must be subject to independent internal audit reviews.[136]

Financial entities must also put in place, maintain and periodically test appropriate ICT business continuity plans.[137] This is notably with regard to critical or important functions outsourced or contracted through arrangements with ICT third-party service providers.[138]

It is further provided that as part of the overall business continuity policy, financial entities must conduct a business impact analysis (BIA) of their exposures to severe business disruptions.[139] Under the BIA, the financial entities must assess the potential impact of severe business disruptions by means of quantitative and qualitative criteria, using internal and external data and scenario analysis, as appropriate.[140] The BIA must consider the criticality of identified and mapped business functions, support processes, third party dependencies and information assets, and their interdependencies.[141] Financial entities must ensure that ICT assets and ICT services are designed and used in full alignment with the BIA, in particular with regard to adequately ensuring the redundancy of all critical components.[142]

As part of their comprehensive ICT risk management, financial entities must:

- test the ICT business continuity plans and the ICT response and recovery plans in relation to ICT systems supporting all functions at least yearly, as well as in the event of any substantive changes to ICT systems supporting critical or important functions; and
- test the crisis communication plans established in accordance with Article 14.[143]

For the purposes of Article 11(6), first subparagraph, point (a), financial entities (other than microenterprises) shall include in the testing plans scenarios of cyber attacks and switchovers between the primary ICT infrastructure and the redundant capacity, backups and redundant facilities necessary to meet the obligations set out in Article 12.[144]

Financial entities must regularly review their ICT business continuity policy and ICT response and recovery plans, taking into account the results of tests carried out in accordance with Article 11(6), first subparagraph and recommendations stemming from audit checks or supervisory reviews.[145]

136 Article 11(3), DORA.
137 Article 11(4), DORA.
138 Article 11(4), DORA.
139 Article 11(5), DORA.
140 Article 11(5), DORA.
141 Article 11(5), DORA.
142 Article 11(5), DORA.
143 Article 11(6), DORA.
144 Article 11(6), DORA.
145 Article 11(6), DORA.

Financial entities (other than microenterprises) must have a crisis management function, which, in the event of activation of their ICT business continuity plans or ICT response and recovery plans, shall, inter alia, set out clear procedures to manage internal and external crisis communications in accordance with Article 14.[146]

Financial entities must keep readily accessible records of activities before and during disruption events when their ICT business continuity plans and ICT response and recovery plans are activated.[147]

Central securities depositories must provide the competent authorities with copies of the results of the ICT business continuity tests, or of similar exercises.[148]

Financial entities (other than microenterprises) must report to the competent authorities, upon their request, an estimation of aggregated annual costs and losses caused by major ICT-related incidents.[149]

The ESAs, through the Joint Committee, shall by 17 July 2024 develop common guidelines on the estimation of aggregated annual costs and losses referred to in Article 11(10).[150]

In any resilience or recovery situation the importance of backups cannot be overstated. Article 12 refers to backup policies and procedures, restoration and recovery procedures and methods.

For the purpose of ensuring the restoration of ICT systems and data with minimum downtime, limited disruption and loss, as part of their ICT risk management framework, financial entities shall develop and document:

- backup policies and procedures specifying the scope of the data that is subject to the backup and the minimum frequency of the backup, based on the criticality of information or the confidentiality level of the data; and
- restoration and recovery procedures and methods.[151]

Financial entities must also set up backup systems that can be activated in accordance with the backup policies and procedures, as well as restoration and recovery procedures and methods. The activation of backup systems must not jeopardise the security of the network and information systems or the availability, authenticity, integrity or confidentiality of data.[152] Testing of the

146 Article 11(7), DORA.
147 Article 11(8), DORA.
148 Article 11(9), DORA.
149 Article 11(10), DORA.
150 In accordance with Article 16 of Regulations 1093/2010, 1094/2010 and 1095/2010. Article 11(11), DORA.
151 Article 12(1), DORA.
152 Article 12(2), DORA.

backup procedures and restoration and recovery procedures and methods must be undertaken periodically.[153]

When restoring backup data using own systems, financial entities must use ICT systems that are physically and logically segregated from the source ICT system.[154] The ICT systems shall be securely protected from any unauthorised access or ICT corruption and allow for the timely restoration of services making use of data and system backups as necessary.[155]

Central counterparties are one of the entities in the wider financial sector. For central counterparties, the recovery plans must enable the recovery of all transactions at the time of disruption to allow the central counterparty to continue to operate with certainty and to complete settlement on the scheduled date.[156]

Data reporting service providers are also referred to. Data reporting service providers must additionally maintain adequate resources and have back up and restoration facilities in place in order to offer and maintain their services at all times.[157]

Financial entities (other than microenterprises) must maintain redundant ICT capacities equipped with resources, capabilities and functions that are adequate to ensure business needs.[158] Microenterprises shall assess the need to maintain such redundant ICT capacities based on their risk profile.[159]

Central securities depositories must maintain at least one secondary processing site endowed with adequate resources, capabilities, functions and staffing arrangements to ensure business needs.[160]

The secondary processing site referred to above must be:

- located at a geographical distance from the primary processing site to ensure that it bears a distinct risk profile and to prevent it from being affected by the event which has affected the primary site;
- capable of ensuring the continuity of critical or important functions identically to the primary site, or providing the level of services necessary to ensure that the financial entity performs its critical operations within the recovery objectives; and
- immediately accessible to the financial entity's staff to ensure continuity of critical or important functions in the event that the primary processing site has become unavailable.[161]

153 Article 12(2), DORA.
154 Article 12(3), DORA.
155 Article 12(3), DORA.
156 Article 12(3), DORA.
157 Article 12(3), DORA.
158 Article 12(4), DORA.
159 Article 12(4), DORA.
160 Article 12(5), DORA.
161 Article 12(5), DORA.

In determining the recovery time and recovery point objectives for each function, financial entities must take into account whether it is a critical or important function and the potential overall impact on market efficiency.[162] Such time objectives shall ensure that, in extreme scenarios, the agreed service levels are met.[163]

When recovering from an ICT-related incident, financial entities shall perform necessary checks, including any multiple checks and reconciliations, in order to ensure that the highest level of data integrity is maintained.[164] These checks shall also be performed when reconstructing data from external stakeholders, in order to ensure that all data is consistent between systems.[165]

Firm must always learn lessons when problem issues or events arise. This is no less so for cyber attacks and other IT resilience issues. Article 13 refers to learning and evolving. Financial entities shall have in place capabilities and staff to gather information on vulnerabilities and cyber threats, ICT-related incidents, in particular cyber attacks, and analyse the impact they are likely to have on their digital operational resilience.[166]

Financial entities must put in place post ICT-related incident reviews after a major ICT-related incident disrupts their core activities, analysing the causes of disruption and identifying required improvements to the ICT operations or within the ICT business continuity policy (as referred to in Article 11).[167]

Financial entities (other than microenterprises) must, upon request, communicate to the competent authorities, the changes that were implemented following post ICT-related incident reviews (as referred to in Article 13(1)).[168]

The post ICT-related incident reviews referred to in Article 13(1) must determine whether the established procedures were followed and the actions taken were effective. This includes in relation to the following:

- the promptness in responding to security alerts and determining the impact of ICT-related incidents and their severity;
- the quality and speed of performing a forensic analysis, where deemed appropriate;
- the effectiveness of incident escalation within the financial entity; and
- the effectiveness of internal and external communication.[169]

162 Article 12(6), DORA.
163 Article 12(6), DORA.
164 Article 12(7), DORA.
165 Article 12(7), DORA.
166 Article 13(1), DORA.
167 Article 13(2), DORA.
168 Article 13(2), DORA.
169 Article 13(2), DORA.

Lessons derived from the digital operational resilience testing (carried out in accordance with Articles 26 and 27) and from real life ICT-related incidents, in particular cyber attacks, along with challenges faced upon the activation of ICT business continuity plans and ICT response and recovery plans, together with relevant information exchanged with counterparts and assessed during supervisory reviews, shall be duly incorporated on a continuous basis into the ICT risk assessment process.[170] Those findings shall form the basis for appropriate reviews of relevant components of the ICT risk management framework.[171]

Financial entities must monitor the effectiveness of the implementation of their digital operational resilience strategy (set out in Article 6(8)).[172] They shall map the evolution of ICT risk over time, analyse the frequency, types, magnitude and evolution of ICT-related incidents, in particular cyber attacks and their patterns, with a view to understanding the level of ICT risk exposure, in particular in relation to critical or important functions, and enhance the cyber maturity and preparedness of the financial entity.[173]

Senior ICT staff shall report at least yearly to the management body on the findings referred to in Article 13(3) and put forward recommendations.[174]

Financial entities must develop ICT security awareness programmes and digital operational resilience training as compulsory modules in their staff training schemes.[175] Those programmes and training shall be applicable to all employees and to senior management staff, and shall have a level of complexity commensurate to the remit of their functions. Where appropriate, financial entities shall also include ICT third-party service providers in their relevant training schemes (in accordance with Article 30(2)(i)).[176]

Financial entities (other than microenterprises) must monitor relevant technological developments on a continuous basis, also with a view to understanding the possible impact of the deployment of such new technologies on ICT security requirements and digital operational resilience.[177] They must also keep up to date with the latest ICT risk management processes, in order to effectively combat current or new forms of cyber attacks.[178]

Communications issues are also critically important. Article 14 refers to these communications aspects. It provides that as part of the ICT risk management framework, financial entities must have in place crisis communication plans

170 Article 13(3), DORA.
171 Article 13(3), DORA.
172 Article 13(4), DORA.
173 Article 13(4), DORA.
174 Article 13(5), DORA.
175 Article 13(6), DORA.
176 Article 13(6), DORA.
177 Article 13(7), DORA.
178 Article 13(7), DORA.

enabling a responsible disclosure of, at least, major ICT-related incidents or vulnerabilities to clients and counterparts as well as to the public, as appropriate.[179]

Also as part of the ICT risk management framework, financial entities shall implement communication policies for internal staff and for external stakeholders.[180] Communication policies for staff shall take into account the need to differentiate between staff involved in ICT risk management, in particular the staff responsible for response and recovery, and staff that needs to be informed.[181]

At least one person in the financial entity shall be tasked with implementing the communication strategy for ICT-related incidents and fulfil the public and media function for that purpose.[182]

The ESAs are also referred to. Article 15 refers to further harmonisation of ICT risk management tools, methods, processes and policies. The ESAs shall, through the Joint Committee, in consultation with the European Union Agency on Cybersecurity (ENISA), develop common draft regulatory technical standards.[183] The purpose of these technical standards is to:

- specify further elements to be included in the ICT security policies, procedures, protocols and tools (referred to in Article 9(2)), with a view to ensuring the security of networks, enable adequate safeguards against intrusions and data misuse, preserve the availability, authenticity, integrity and confidentiality of data, including cryptographic techniques, and guarantee an accurate and prompt data transmission without major disruptions and undue delays;
- develop further components of the controls of access management rights (referred to in Article 9(4)(c)), and associated human resource policy specifying access rights, procedures for granting and revoking rights, monitoring anomalous behaviour in relation to ICT risk through appropriate indicators, including for network use patterns, hours, IT activity and unknown devices;
- develop further the mechanisms (specified in Article 10(1)) enabling a prompt detection of anomalous activities and the criteria (set out in Article 10(2)) triggering ICT-related incident detection and response processes;
- specify further the components of the ICT business continuity policy (referred to in Article 11(1));
- specify further the testing of ICT business continuity plans (referred to in Article 11(6)) to ensure that such testing duly takes into account scenarios in which the quality of the provision of a critical or important function deteriorates to an unacceptable level or fails, and duly considers the

179 Article 14(1), DORA.
180 Article 14(2), DORA.
181 Article 14(2), DORA.
182 Article 14(3), DORA.
183 Article 15(1), DORA.

potential impact of the insolvency, or other failures, of any relevant ICT third-party service provider and, where relevant, the political risks in the respective providers' jurisdictions;

- specify further the components of the ICT response and recovery plans (referred to in Article 11(3)); and
- specify further the content and format of the report on the review of the ICT risk management framework (referred to in Article 6(5)).[184]

When developing those draft regulatory technical standards, the ESAs must take into account the 'size and the overall risk profile' of the financial entity, and the nature, scale and complexity of its services, activities and operations, while duly taking into consideration any specific feature arising from the distinct nature of activities across different financial services sectors.[185]

The ESAs were required to submit those draft regulatory technical standards to the Commission by 17 January 2024. Power is delegated to the Commission to supplement DORA by adopting the regulatory technical standards referred to.[186]

Simplified risk management framework

3.13 As mentioned earlier, there is recognition that not all financial entities are the same, whether in terms of size or activities. Therefore, there is also provided in DORA what is referred to as a simplified risk management framework. Articles 5 to 15 of DORA do not apply to:

- small and non-interconnected investment firms;
- payment institutions exempted pursuant to Directive 2015/2366;
- institutions exempted pursuant to Directive 2013/36 in respect of which Member States have decided not to apply the option referred to in Article 2(4) of this Regulation;
- electronic money institutions exempted pursuant to Directive 2009/110; and
- small institutions for occupational retirement provision.[187]

Without prejudice to Article 16(1), the entities listed in that provision shall:

- put in place and maintain a sound and documented ICT risk management framework that details the mechanisms and measures aimed at a quick,

184 Article 15, DORA.
185 Article 15, DORA.
186 In accordance with Articles 10 to 14 of Regulations 1093/2010, 1094/2010 and 1095/2010, Article 15, DORA.
187 Article 16(1), DORA.

efficient and comprehensive management of ICT risk, including for the protection of relevant physical components and infrastructures;

- continuously monitor the security and functioning of all ICT systems;
- minimise the impact of ICT risk through the use of sound, resilient and updated ICT systems, protocols and tools which are appropriate to support the performance of their activities and the provision of services and adequately protect availability, authenticity, integrity and confidentiality of data in the network and information systems;
- allow sources of ICT risk and anomalies in the network and information systems to be promptly identified and detected and ICT-related incidents to be swiftly handled;
- identify key dependencies on ICT third-party service providers;
- ensure the continuity of critical or important functions, through business continuity plans and response and recovery measures, which include, at least, backup and restoration measures;
- test, on a regular basis, the plans and measures referred to in the bullet point above, as well as the effectiveness of the controls implemented in accordance with bullet points 1 and 3; and
- implement, as appropriate, relevant operational conclusions resulting from the tests referred to in the above bullet point and from post-incident analysis into the ICT risk assessment process and develop, according to needs and ICT risk profile, ICT security awareness programmes and digital operational resilience training for staff and management.[188]

The ICT risk management framework referred to in Article 16(1), second subparagraph, point (a), shall be documented and reviewed periodically and upon the occurrence of major ICT-related incidents in compliance with supervisory instructions.[189] It shall be continuously improved on the basis of lessons derived from implementation and monitoring.[190] A report on the review of the ICT risk management framework shall be submitted to the competent authority upon its request.[191]

The ESAs shall, through the Joint Committee, in consultation with the ENISA, develop common draft regulatory technical standards in order to:

- specify further the elements to be included in the ICT risk management framework referred to in Article 16(1), second subparagraph, point (a);
- specify further the elements in relation to systems, protocols and tools to minimise the impact of ICT risk referred to in Article 16(1), second subparagraph, point (c), with a view to ensuring the security of networks,

188 Article 16(1), DORA.
189 Article 16(2), DORA.
190 Article 16(2), DORA.
191 Article 16(2), DORA.

enabling adequate safeguards against intrusions and data misuse and preserving the availability, authenticity, integrity and confidentiality of data;

- specify further the components of the ICT business continuity plans referred to in Article 16(1), second subparagraph, point (f);
- specify further the rules on the testing of business continuity plans and ensure the effectiveness of the controls referred to in Article 16(1), second subparagraph, point (g) and ensure that such testing duly takes into account scenarios in which the quality of the provision of a critical or important function deteriorates to an unacceptable level or fails; and
- specify further the content and format of the report on the review of the ICT risk management framework referred to in Article 16(2).[192]

When developing those draft regulatory technical standards, the ESAs shall take into account the size and the overall risk profile of the financial entity, and the nature, scale and complexity of its services, activities and operations.[193]

The ESAs were required to submit those draft regulatory technical standards to the Commission by 17 January 2024.[194] Power is delegated to the Commission to supplement this Regulation by adopting the regulatory technical standards referred to in Article 15(1) in accordance with Articles 10 to 14 of Regulations 1093/2010, 1094/2010 and 1095/2010.[195]

Identification and classification

3.14 Chapter III of DORA refers to ICT-related incident management, classification and reporting. Article 17 refers to an ICT-related incident management process. Financial entities must define, establish and implement an ICT-related incident management process to detect, manage and notify ICT-related incidents.[196]

Financial entities must also record all ICT-related incidents and significant cyber threats. Financial entities shall establish appropriate procedures and processes to ensure a consistent and integrated monitoring, handling and follow up of ICT-related incidents, to ensure that root causes are identified, documented and addressed in order to prevent the occurrence of such incidents.[197]

The ICT-related incident management process referred to above shall:

- put in place early warning indicators;

192 Article 16(3), DORA.
193 Article 16(3), DORA.
194 Article 16(3), DORA.
195 Article 16(3), DORA.
196 Article 17(1), DORA.
197 Article 17(2), DORA.

- establish procedures to identify, track, log, categorise and classify ICT-related incidents according to their priority and severity and according to the criticality of the services impacted, in accordance with the criteria set out in Article 18(1);
- assign roles and responsibilities that need to be activated for different ICT-related incident types and scenarios;
- set out plans for communication to staff, external stakeholders and media (in accordance with Article 14) and for notification to clients, for internal escalation procedures, including ICT-related customer complaints, as well as for the provision of information to financial entities that act as counterparts, as appropriate;
- ensure that at least major ICT-related incidents are reported to relevant senior management and inform the management body of at least major ICT-related incidents, explaining the impact, response and additional controls to be established as a result of such ICT-related incidents; and
- establish ICT-related incident response procedures to mitigate impacts and ensure that services become operational and secure in a timely manner.[198]

Article 18 refers to the classification of ICT-related incidents and cyber threats. Financial entities shall classify ICT-related incidents and shall determine their impact based on the following criteria:

- number and/or relevance of clients or financial counterparts affected and, where applicable, the amount or number of transactions affected by the ICT-related incident, and whether the ICT-related incident has caused reputational impact;
- duration of the ICT-related incident, including the service downtime;
- the geographical spread with regard to the areas affected by the ICT-related incident, particularly if it affects more than two Member States;
- data losses that the ICT-related incident entails, in relation to availability, authenticity, integrity or confidentiality of data;
- criticality of the services affected, including the financial entity's transactions and operations; and
- economic impact, in particular direct and indirect costs and losses, of the ICT-related incident in both absolute and relative terms.[199]

Financial entities must classify cyber threats as significant based on the criticality of the services at risk, including the financial entity's transactions and operations, number and/or relevance of clients or financial counterparts targeted and the geographical spread of the areas at risk.[200]

198 Article 17(3), DORA.
199 Article 18(1), DORA.
200 Article 18(3), DORA.

The ESAs shall, through the Joint Committee and in consultation with the European Central Bank (ECB) and ENISA, develop common draft regulatory technical standards further specifying the following:

- the criteria set out in Article 18(1) of DORA, including materiality thresholds for determining major ICT-related incidents or, as applicable, major operational or security payment-related incidents, that are subject to the reporting obligation laid down in Article 19(1);
- the criteria to be applied by competent authorities for the purpose of assessing the relevance of major ICT-related incidents or, as applicable, major operational or security payment-related incidents, to relevant competent authorities in other Member States, and the details of reports of major ICT-related incidents or, as applicable, major operational or security payment-related incidents, to be shared with other competent authorities pursuant to Article 19(6) and (7); and
- the criteria set out in Article 18(2), including high materiality thresholds for determining significant cyber threats.[201]

When developing the common draft regulatory technical standards referred to in Article 18(3), the ESAs shall take into account the criteria set out in Article 4(2), as well as international standards, guidance and specifications developed and published by ENISA, including, where appropriate, specifications for other economic sectors. For the purposes of applying the criteria set out in Article 4(2), the ESAs shall duly consider the need for microenterprises and small and medium-sized enterprises to mobilise sufficient resources and capabilities to ensure that ICT-related incidents are managed swiftly.[202]

The ESAs were required to submit those common draft regulatory technical standards to the Commission by 17 January 2024.[203] Power is delegated to the Commission to supplement this Regulation by adopting the regulatory technical standards referred to in Article 18(3) in accordance with Articles 10 to 14 of Regulations 1093/2010, 1094/2010 and 1095/2010.[204]

Reporting incidents

3.15 Article 19 refers to the reporting of major ICT-related incidents and voluntary notification of significant cyber threats.

Financial entities shall report major ICT-related incidents to the relevant competent authority as referred to in Article 46 in accordance with Article 19(4).[205]

201 Article 18(3), DORA.
202 Article 18(4), DORA.
203 Article 18(4), DORA.
204 Article 18(4), DORA.
205 Article 19(1), DORA.

Where a financial entity is subject to supervision by more than one national competent authority referred to in Article 46, Member States shall designate a single competent authority as the relevant competent authority responsible for carrying out the functions and duties provided for in this Article.[206]

Credit institutions classified as significant, in accordance with Article 6(4) of Regulation 1024/2013, shall report major ICT-related incidents to the relevant national competent authority designated in accordance with Article 4 of Directive 2013/36, which shall immediately transmit that report to the ECB.[207]

For the purpose of Article 19(1), financial entities shall produce, after collecting and analysing all relevant information, the initial notification and reports referred to in Article 19(4) using the templates referred to in Article 20 and submit them to the competent authority. In the event that a technical impossibility prevents the submission of the initial notification using the template, financial entities shall notify the competent authority about it via alternative means.[208]

The initial notification and reports referred to in Article 19(4) shall include all information necessary for the competent authority to determine the significance of the major ICT-related incident and assess possible cross-border impacts.[209]

Without prejudice to the reporting pursuant to Article 19(1) by the financial entity to the relevant competent authority, Member States may additionally determine that some or all financial entities shall also provide the initial notification and each report referred to in Article 19(4) using the templates referred to in Article 20 to the competent authorities or the computer security incident response teams (CSIRTs) designated or established in accordance with Directive 2022/2555.[210]

Financial entities may, on a voluntary basis, notify significant cyber threats to the relevant competent authority when they deem the threat to be of relevance to the financial system, service users or clients. The relevant competent authority may provide such information to other relevant authorities referred to in Article 19(6).[211]

Credit institutions classified as significant, in accordance with Article 6(4) of Regulation 1024/2013, may, on a voluntary basis, notify significant cyber threats to relevant national competent authority, designated in accordance with Article 4 of Directive 2013/36, which shall immediately transmit the notification to the ECB.[212]

206 Article 19(1), DORA.
207 Article 19(1), DORA.
208 Article 19(1), DORA.
209 Article 19(1), DORA.
210 Article 19(1), DORA.
211 Article 19(2), DORA.
212 Article 19(2), DORA.

Member States may determine that those financial entities, who on a voluntary basis notify in accordance with Article 19(1), may also transmit that notification to the CSIRTs designated or established in accordance with Directive 2022/2555.[213]

Where a major ICT-related incident occurs and has an impact on the financial interests of clients, financial entities shall, without undue delay as soon as they become aware of it, inform their clients about the major ICT-related incident and about the measures that have been taken to mitigate the adverse effects of such incident.[214]

In the case of a significant cyber threat, financial entities shall, where applicable, inform their clients that are potentially affected of any appropriate protection measures which the latter may consider taking.[215]

Financial entities shall, within the time limits to be laid down in accordance with Article 20, first paragraph, point (a)(ii), submit the following to the relevant competent authority:

- an initial notification;
- an intermediate report after the initial notification referred to in point (a), as soon as the status of the original incident has changed significantly or the handling of the major ICT-related incident has changed based on new information available, followed, as appropriate, by updated notifications every time a relevant status update is available, as well as upon a specific request of the competent authority; and
- a final report, when the root cause analysis has been completed, regardless of whether mitigation measures have already been implemented, and when the actual impact figures are available to replace estimates.[216]

Financial entities may outsource, in accordance with European and national sectoral law, the reporting obligations under this Article 19 to a third-party service provider. In the case of such outsourcing, the financial entity remains fully responsible for the fulfilment of the incident reporting requirements.[217]

Upon receipt of the initial notification and of each report referred to in Article 19(4), the competent authority shall, in a timely manner, provide details of the major ICT-related incident to the following recipients based, as applicable, on their respective competences:

- EBA, ESMA or EIOPA;
- the ECB, in the case of financial entities referred to in Article 2(1)(a), (b) and (d);

213 Article 19(2), DORA.
214 Article 19(2), DORA.
215 Article 19(2), DORA.
216 Article 19(4), DORA.
217 Article 19(5), DORA.

- the competent authorities, single points of contact or CSIRTs designated or established in accordance with Directive 2022/2555;
- the resolution authorities, as referred to in Article 3 of Directive 2014/59, and the Single Resolution Board (SRB) with respect to entities referred to in Article 7(2) of Regulation 806/2014, and with respect to entities and groups referred to in Article 7(4)(b) and (5) of Regulation 806/2014 if such details concern incidents that pose a risk to ensuring critical functions within the meaning of Article 2(1), point (35), of Directive 2014/59; and
- other relevant public authorities under national law.[218]

Following receipt of information in accordance with Article 19(6), EBA, ESMA or EIOPA and the ECB, in consultation with ENISA and in cooperation with the relevant competent authority, shall assess whether the major ICT-related incident is relevant for competent authorities in other Member States.[219] Following that assessment, EBA, ESMA or EIOPA shall, as soon as possible, notify relevant competent authorities in other Member States accordingly.[220] The ECB shall notify the members of the European System of Central Banks on issues relevant to the payment system.[221] Based on that notification, the competent authorities shall, where appropriate, take all of the necessary measures to protect the immediate stability of the financial system.[222]

The notification to be done by ESMA pursuant to Article 19(7) shall be without prejudice to the responsibility of the competent authority to urgently transmit the details of the major ICT-related incident to the relevant authority in the host Member State, where a central securities depository has significant cross-border activity in the host Member State, the major ICT-related incident is likely to have severe consequences for the financial markets of the host Member State and where there are cooperation arrangements among competent authorities related to the supervision of financial entities.

The ESAs are also tasked in relation to harmonisation of reporting content and templates. The ESAs, through the Joint Committee, and in consultation with ENISA and the ECB, shall develop:

- common draft regulatory technical standards in order to:
  - (i) establish the content of the reports for major ICT-related incidents in order to reflect the criteria laid down in Article 18(1) and incorporate further elements, such as details for establishing the relevance of the reporting for other Member States and whether it constitutes a major operational or security payment-related incident or not;

218 Article 19(6), DORA.
219 Article 19(7), DORA.
220 Article 19(7), DORA.
221 Article 19(7), DORA.
222 Article 19(7), DORA.

(ii) determine the time limits for the initial notification and for each report referred to in Article 19(4); and

(iii) establish the content of the notification for significant cyber threats.

When developing those draft regulatory technical standards, the ESAs shall take into account the size and the overall risk profile of the financial entity, and the nature, scale and complexity of its services, activities and operations, and in particular, with a view to ensuring that, for the purposes of Article 20, point (a), point (ii), different time limits may reflect, as appropriate, specificities of financial sectors, without prejudice to maintaining a consistent approach to ICT-related incident reporting pursuant to this Regulation and to Directive 2022/2555. The ESAs shall, as applicable, provide justification when deviating from the approaches taken in the context of that Directive;

- common draft implementing technical standards in order to establish the standard forms, templates and procedures for financial entities to report a major ICT-related incident and to notify a significant cyber threat.[223]

The ESAs were required to submit the common draft regulatory technical standards referred to in Article 20, first paragraph, point (a), and the common draft implementing technical standards referred to in the first paragraph, point (b), to the Commission by 17 July 2024.[224]

Power is delegated to the Commission to supplement this Regulation by adopting the common regulatory technical standards referred to in Article 20, first paragraph, point (a), in accordance with Articles 10 to 14 of Regulations 1093/2010, 1094/2010 and 1095/2010.[225]

Power is conferred on the Commission to adopt the common implementing technical standards referred to in Article 20, first paragraph, point (b), in accordance with Article 15 of Regulations 1093/2010 1094/2010 and 1095/2010.[226]

The ESAs are also called upon to assist in the centralisation of reporting of major ICT-related incidents. The ESAs, through the Joint Committee, and in consultation with the ECB and ENISA, shall prepare a joint report assessing the feasibility of further centralisation of incident reporting through the establishment of a single EU Hub for major ICT-related incident reporting by financial entities. The joint report shall explore ways to facilitate the flow of ICT-related incident reporting, reduce associated costs and underpin thematic analyses with a view to enhancing supervisory convergence.[227]

223 Article 20, DORA.
224 Article 20, DORA.
225 Article 20, DORA.
226 Article 20, DORA.
227 Article 21(1), DORA.

The joint report referred to in Article 21(1) shall comprise at least the following elements:

- prerequisites for the establishment of a single EU Hub;
- benefits, limitations and risks, including risks associated with the high concentration of sensitive information;
- the necessary capability to ensure interoperability with regard to other relevant reporting schemes;
- elements of operational management;
- conditions of membership;
- technical arrangements for financial entities and national competent authorities to access the single EU Hub; and
- a preliminary assessment of financial costs incurred by setting-up the operational platform supporting the single EU Hub, including the requisite expertise.[228]

The ESAs shall submit the report referred to in Article 21(1) to the European Parliament, to the Council and to the Commission by 17 January 2025.[229]

Supervisory feedback

3.16 Without prejudice to the technical input, advice or remedies and subsequent follow up which may be provided, where applicable, in accordance with national law, by the CSIRTs under Directive 2022/2555, the competent authority shall, upon receipt of the initial notification and of each report as referred to in Article 19(4), acknowledge receipt and may, where feasible, provide in a timely manner relevant and proportionate feedback or high level guidance to the financial entity, in particular by making available any relevant anonymised information and intelligence on similar threats, and may discuss remedies applied at the level of the financial entity and ways to minimise and mitigate adverse impact across the financial sector.[230] Without prejudice to the supervisory feedback received, financial entities shall remain fully responsible for the handling and for consequences of the ICT-related incidents reported pursuant to Article 19(1).[231]

The ESAs shall, through the Joint Committee, on an anonymised and aggregated basis, report yearly on major ICT-related incidents, the details of which shall be provided by competent authorities in accordance with Article 19(6), setting out at least the number of major ICT-related incidents, their nature and their impact

228 Article 21(2), DORA.
229 Article 21(3), DORA.
230 Article 22(1), DORA.
231 Article 22(1), DORA.

on the operations of financial entities or clients, remedial actions taken and costs incurred.[232]

The ESAs shall issue warnings and produce high-level statistics to support ICT threat and vulnerability assessments.[233]

Payment incidents

3.17 There is also a provision in relation to operational or security payment-related incidents concerning credit institutions, payment institutions, account information service providers, and electronic money institutions. The requirements laid down in this chapter shall also apply to operational or security payment related incidents and to major operational or security payment-related incidents, where they concern credit institutions, payment institutions, account information service providers, and electronic money institutions.[234]

Testing

3.18 Article 24 refers to DORA's general requirements for the performance of digital operational resilience testing. For the purpose of assessing preparedness for handling ICT-related incidents, of identifying weaknesses, deficiencies and gaps in digital operational resilience, and of promptly implementing corrective measures, financial entities, other than microenterprises, shall, taking into account the criteria set out in Article 4(2), establish, maintain and review a sound and comprehensive digital operational resilience testing programme as an integral part of the ICT risk-management framework referred to in Article 6.[235]

The digital operational resilience testing programme shall include a range of assessments, tests, methodologies, practices and tools to be applied in accordance with Articles 25 and 26.[236]

When conducting the digital operational resilience testing programme referred to in Article 24(1), financial entities, other than microenterprises, shall follow a risk-based approach taking into account the criteria set out in Article 4(2) duly considering the evolving landscape of ICT risk, any specific risks to which the financial entity concerned is or might be exposed, the criticality of information assets and of services provided, as well as any other factor the financial entity deems appropriate.[237]

232 Article 22(2), DORA.
233 Article 22, DORA.
234 Article 23, DORA.
235 Article 24(1), DORA.
236 Article 24(2), DORA.
237 Article 24(3), DORA.

Financial entities, other than microenterprises, shall ensure that tests are undertaken by independent parties, whether internal or external. Where tests are undertaken by an internal tester, financial entities shall dedicate sufficient resources and ensure that conflicts of interest are avoided throughout the design and execution phases of the test.[238]

Financial entities, other than microenterprises, shall establish procedures and policies to prioritise, classify and remedy all issues revealed throughout the performance of the tests and shall establish internal validation methodologies to ascertain that all identified weaknesses, deficiencies or gaps are fully addressed.[239]

Financial entities, other than microenterprises, shall ensure, at least yearly, that appropriate tests are conducted on all ICT systems and applications supporting critical or important functions.[240]

Article 25 refers to testing of ICT tools and systems. The digital operational resilience testing programme referred to in Article 24 shall provide, in accordance with the criteria set out in Article 4(2), for the execution of appropriate tests, such as vulnerability assessments and scans, open source analyses, network security assessments, gap analyses, physical security reviews, questionnaires and scanning software solutions, source code reviews where feasible, scenario based tests, compatibility testing, performance testing, end to end testing and penetration testing.[241]

Central securities depositories and central counterparties shall perform vulnerability assessments before any deployment or redeployment of new or existing applications and infrastructure components, and ICT services supporting critical or important functions of the financial entity.[242]

Microenterprises shall perform the tests referred to in Article 24(1) by combining a risk-based approach with a strategic planning of ICT testing, by duly considering the need to maintain a balanced approach between the scale of resources and the time to be allocated to the ICT testing provided for in this Article, on the one hand, and the urgency, type of risk, criticality of information assets and of services provided, as well as any other relevant factor, including the financial entity's ability to take calculated risks, on the other hand.[243]

Article 26 refers to advanced testing of ICT tools, systems and processes based on TLPT (threat-led penetration testing). Financial entities, other than entities referred to in Article 16(1), first subparagraph, and other than microenterprises, which are identified in accordance with Article 26(8), third subparagraph, shall carry out at least every three years advanced testing by means of TLPT. Based

238 Article 24(4), DORA.
239 Article 24(5), DORA.
240 Article 24(6), DORA.
241 Article 25(1), DORA.
242 Article 25(2), DORA.
243 Article 25(3), DORA.

on the risk profile of the financial entity and taking into account operational circumstances, the competent authority may, where necessary, request the financial entity to reduce or increase this frequency.[244]

Each TLPT shall cover several or all critical or important functions of a financial entity, and shall be performed on live production systems supporting such functions.[245]

Financial entities shall identify all relevant underlying ICT systems, processes and technologies supporting critical or important functions and ICT services, including those supporting the critical or important functions which have been outsourced or contracted to ICT third-party service providers.[246]

Financial entities shall assess which critical or important functions need to be covered by the TLPT. The result of this assessment shall determine the precise scope of TLPT and shall be validated by the competent authorities.[247]

Where ICT third-party service providers are included in the scope of TLPT, the financial entity shall take the necessary measures and safeguards to ensure the participation of such ICT third-party service providers in the TLPT and shall retain at all times full responsibility for ensuring compliance with DORA.[248]

Without prejudice to Article 26(2), first and second subparagraphs, where the participation of an ICT third-party service provider in the TLPT, referred to in the first subparagraph, is reasonably expected to have an adverse impact on the quality or security of services delivered by the ICT third-party service provider to customers that are entities falling outside the scope of this Regulation, or on the confidentiality of the data related to such services, the financial entity and the ICT third-party service provider may agree in writing that the ICT third-party service provider directly enters into contractual arrangements with an external tester, for the purpose of conducting, under the direction of one designated financial entity, a pooled TLPT involving several financial entities (pooled testing) to which the ICT third-party service provider provides ICT services.[249]

That pooled testing shall cover the relevant range of ICT services supporting critical or important functions contracted to the respective ICT third-party service provider by the financial entities.[250] The pooled testing shall be considered TLPT carried out by the financial entities participating in the pooled testing.[251]

244 Article 26(1), DORA.
245 Article 26(2), DORA.
246 Article 26(2), DORA.
247 Article 26(2), DORA.
248 Article 26(3), DORA.
249 Article 26(4), DORA.
250 Article 26(4), DORA.
251 Article 26(4), DORA.

The number of financial entities participating in the pooled testing shall be duly calibrated taking into account the complexity and types of services involved.[252]

Financial entities shall, with the cooperation of ICT third-party service providers and other parties involved, including the testers but excluding the competent authorities, apply effective risk management controls to mitigate the risks of any potential impact on data, damage to assets, and disruption to critical or important functions, services or operations at the financial entity itself, its counterparts or to the financial sector.[253]

At the end of the testing, after reports and remediation plans have been agreed, the financial entity and, where applicable, the external testers shall provide to the authority, designated in accordance with Article 26(9) or (10), a summary of the relevant findings, the remediation plans and the documentation demonstrating that the TLPT has been conducted in accordance with the requirements.[254]

Authorities shall provide financial entities with an attestation confirming that the test was performed in accordance with the requirements as evidenced in the documentation in order to allow for mutual recognition of TLPTs between competent authorities.[255] The financial entity shall notify the relevant competent authority of the attestation, the summary of the relevant findings and the remediation plans.[256] Without prejudice to such attestation, financial entities shall remain at all times fully responsible for the impact of the tests referred to in Article 26(4).[257]

Financial entities shall contract testers for the purposes of undertaking TLPT in accordance with Article 27. When financial entities use internal testers for the purposes of undertaking TLPT, they shall contract external testers every three tests.[258]

Credit institutions that are classified as significant in accordance with Article 6(4) of Regulation 1024/2013, shall only use external testers in accordance with Article 27(1)(a) to (e).[259]

Competent authorities shall identify financial entities that are required to perform TLPT taking into account the criteria set out in Article 4(2), based on an assessment of the following:

- impact-related factors, in particular the extent to which the services provided and activities undertaken by the financial entity impact the financial sector;

252 Article 26(4), DORA.
253 Article 26(5), DORA.
254 Article 26(6), DORA.
255 Article 26(7), DORA.
256 Article 26(7), DORA.
257 Article 26(7), DORA.
258 Article 26(7), DORA.
259 Article 26(7), DORA.

- possible financial stability concerns, including the systemic character of the financial entity at European or national level, as applicable; and
- specific ICT risk profile, level of ICT maturity of the financial entity or technology features involved.[260]

Member States may designate a single public authority in the financial sector to be responsible for TLPT-related matters in the financial sector at national level and shall entrust it with all competences and tasks to that effect.[261]

In the absence of a designation in accordance with Article 26(9), and without prejudice to the power to identify the financial entities that are required to perform TLPT, a competent authority may delegate the exercise of some or all of the tasks referred to in this Article and Article 27 to another national authority in the financial sector.[262]

The ESAs shall, in agreement with the ECB, develop joint draft regulatory technical standards in accordance with the Threat Intelligence-based Ethical Red Teaming (TIBER)-EU framework in order to specify further:

- the criteria used for the purpose of the application of Article 26(8), second subparagraph;
- the requirements and standards governing the use of internal testers;
- the requirements in relation to:
  - (i) the scope of TLPT referred to in Article 26(2);
  - (ii) the testing methodology and approach to be followed for each specific phase of the testing process; and
  - (iii) the results, closure and remediation stages of the testing; and
- the type of supervisory and other relevant cooperation which are needed for the implementation of TLPT, and for the facilitation of mutual recognition of that testing, in the context of financial entities that operate in more than one Member State, to allow an appropriate level of supervisory involvement and a flexible implementation to cater for specificities of financial sub-sectors or local financial markets.[263]

When developing those draft regulatory technical standards, the ESAs shall give due consideration to any specific feature arising from the distinct nature of activities across different financial services sectors.[264]

260 Article 26(8), DORA.
261 Article 26(9), DORA.
262 Article 26(10), DORA.
263 Article 26(11), DORA.
264 Article 26(11), DORA.

The ESAs were required to submit those draft regulatory technical standards to the Commission by 17 July 2024.[265]

Power is delegated to the Commission to supplement this Regulation by adopting the regulatory technical standards referred to in Article 26(11), first subparagraph in accordance with Articles 10 to 14 of Regulations 1093/2010, 1094/2010 and 1095/2010.[266]

There are also requirements for testers for the carrying out of TLPT. Financial entities shall only use testers for the carrying out of TLPT, that:

- are of the highest suitability and reputability;
- possess technical and organisational capabilities and demonstrate specific expertise in threat intelligence, penetration testing and red team testing;
- are certified by an accreditation body in a Member State or adhere to formal codes of conduct or ethical frameworks;
- provide an independent assurance, or an audit report, in relation to the sound management of risks associated with the carrying out of TLPT, including the due protection of the financial entity's confidential information and redress for the business risks of the financial entity; and
- are duly and fully covered by relevant professional indemnity insurances, including against risks of misconduct and negligence.[267]

When using internal testers, financial entities shall ensure that, in addition to the requirements in Article 27(1), the following conditions are met:

- such use has been approved by the relevant competent authority or by the single public authority designated in accordance with Article 26(9) and (10);
- the relevant competent authority has verified that the financial entity has sufficient dedicated resources and ensured that conflicts of interest are avoided throughout the design and execution phases of the test; and
- the threat intelligence provider is external to the financial entity.[268]

Financial entities shall ensure that contracts concluded with external testers require a sound management of the TLPT results and that any data processing thereof, including any generation, store, aggregation, draft, report, communication or destruction, do not create risks to the financial entity.[269]

265 Article 26(11), DORA.
266 Article 26(11), DORA.
267 Article 27(1), DORA.
268 Article 27(2), DORA.
269 Article 27(3), DORA.

CHAPTER 4

Policy on ICT Compliance

The DORA rules raise a variety of compliance issues. These are included throughout the text of DORA.

INCREASED ATTENTION ON ICT RISK

4.01 Information and communications technology (ICT) risk issues have increasingly attracted the attention of national, European, and international policymakers, as well as of regulatory standard-setting bodies. They have all been concerned to attempt to enhance digital resilience, set standards and coordinate regulatory and or supervisory activities. At international level, the Basel Committee on Banking Supervision, the Committee on Payments and Market Infrastructures, the Financial Stability Board, the Financial Stability Institute, as well as the G7 and G20 have aimed to provide the relevant competent authorities and market operators across various jurisdictions with tools to bolster the resilience of their financial systems. That work has also been driven by the need to duly consider ICT risk in the context of a highly interconnected global financial system and to seek more consistency of relevant best practices.[1]

The European Supervisory Authorities (ESAs) called for a coherent approach to ICT risk in finance.[2] They recommended strengthening the digital operational resilience of the financial services industry.[3]

INEFFECTIVE POLICY

4.02 However, as there was somewhat disparate regulatory attention to the risks associated with errant actors and ICT problem issues, one of the intentions of DORA is to 'consolidate and upgrade ICT risk requirements' as part of the operational risk requirements. It is pointed out that these issues have been addressed separately across a variety of legal measures[4] – that is, if and when addressed. These prior measures left gaps as they only covered the then considered main categories of financial risk. The prior concerns related to what was referred to as

1 Recital 4, DORA.
2 Technical advice document (April 2019). There are three ESAs of relevance, namely the European Banking Authority, the European Insurance and Occupational Pensions Authority, and the European Securities and Markets Authority.
3 Recital 7, DORA.
4 Recital 12, DORA.

credit risk, market risk, counterparty credit risk and liquidity risk, market conduct risk.[5] Perceptions and needs to address new areas, as well as enhanced areas of risk, help to create new priorities. They did not (comprehensively) address 'all components of operational resilience'. The operational risk rules, as referred to in prior legal measures, favoured a 'traditional quantitative approach' to addressing risk by setting a capital requirement to cover ICT risk. They did not involve targeted qualitative rules to protect, detect, contain, recover and repair ICT-related incidents, nor have reporting and digital testing capabilities. Those prior acts were primarily to cover and update essential rules on prudential supervision, market integrity or conduct. One of the aims of DORA is to consolidate (and update) the different rules on ICT risk, and importantly to address digital risk in the financial sector for the 'first time'[6] in a consistent single legislative act. Therefore, DORA fills a number of gaps. It remedies inconsistencies in the prior rules. It also makes the important technical terminology more consistent. It explicitly refers to ICT risk in targeted rules on ICT risk management capabilities, incident reporting, operational resilience testing and ICT third-party risk monitoring. In addition, DORA raises awareness of ICT risk and of the need to plan for sound operational resilience in the financial entities.[7]

LIMITED POLICY FOCUS

4.03 The first horizontal cybersecurity framework, Directive 2016/1148, applies to three types of financial entities, namely, credit institutions, trading venues, and central counterparties. However, that Directive sets out a mechanism of identifying operators of essential services, but only for certain credit institutions, trading venues and central counterparties that were identified by the Member States. Only those so brought into its scope were required to comply with the specified ICT security and incident notification requirements. Directive 2022/2555[8] sets a uniform criterion to determine the entities that fall within the scope of application (via a size cap rule) while referring to the three types of financial entities in its scope.[9]

CROSS-SECTORAL INFLUENCE

4.04 There is an importance attached to learning from other sectors and how adverse issues are identified and addressed. The ESAs and national competent authorities should be able to participate in the strategic policy discussions and

5 Recital 12, DORA.
6 Recital 12, DORA.
7 Recital 12, DORA.
8 Directive (EU) 2022/2555 on measures for a high common level of cybersecurity across the Union, amending Regulation (EU) No 910/2014 and Directive (EU) 2018/1972, and repealing Directive (EU) 2016/1148 (NIS 2 Directive).
9 Recital 15, DORA.

the technical workings of the Cooperation Group under Directive 2022/2555.[10] The ESAs should also be able to exchange information and further cooperate with the single points of contact designated or established in accordance with that Directive. The competent authorities under DORA should also consult and cooperate with the CSIRTs – which are the computer security incident response teams as referred to in Directive 2022/2555. The competent authorities should also be able to request technical advice from the competent authorities designated or established in accordance with the same Directive and to establish cooperation arrangements that aim to ensure effective and fast response coordination mechanisms to adverse events.[11]

TESTING GAPS, HIDDEN CONCERNS

4.05 There is a view expressed that where no ICT testing occurs or is required, vulnerabilities will remain undetected. This can result in exposing a financial entity (or even a wider sector) to ICT risk. It may ultimately create a higher risk to the stability and integrity of the financial sector. Therefore, without legal policymaker intervention, digital operational resilience testing would continue to be inconsistent and could lack a system of mutual recognition of ICT testing results across different jurisdictions.[12]

In addition, it is perceived unlikely that other financial subsectors would adopt testing schemes (or methodologies) on a meaningful scale. They could miss out on the various potential benefits of a testing framework, in terms of revealing ICT vulnerabilities and risks, and importantly testing defences and defence capabilities and business continuity and associated plans. Done properly, this can help to increase the trust of customers, suppliers and business partners. In order to proactively address those respective overlaps, divergences, and gaps, it is 'necessary' to now establish rules for a coordinated testing regime.[13] This also facilitates the mutual recognition of advanced testing for financial entities meeting the criteria of DORA.[14]

GRADUATED TESTS

4.06 Microenterprises should be able to benefit from a more flexible regime as regards digital operational resilience testing programmes.[15] When considering the type and frequency of testing to be performed, microenterprises should 'properly'

10 To enable cross-sector learning and to effectively draw on experiences of other sectors in dealing with cyber threats, the financial entities referred to in Directive 2022/2555 should remain part of the 'ecosystem' of that Directive, for example, Cooperation Group and computer security incident response teams (CSIRTs).
11 Recital 18, DORA.
12 Recital 26, DORA.
13 Recital 26, DORA.
14 Recital 26, DORA.
15 Recital 43, DORA.

'balance the objective of maintaining a high digital operational resilience, the available resources and their overall risk profile.'[16] Microenterprises and financial entities subject to the DORA simplified ICT risk management framework, should be exempted from the requirement to perform advanced testing of ICT tools, systems and processes based on threat-led penetration testing (TLPT), as only financial entities meeting the criteria set out in DORA should be required to carry out such testing.[17] In light of their limited capabilities, microenterprises should be able to agree with the ICT third-party service provider to delegate the financial entity's rights of access, inspection, and audit to an independent third party, to be appointed by the ICT third-party service provider, provided that the financial entity is able to request, at any time, all relevant information and assurance on the ICT third-party service provider's performance from the respective independent third party.[18]

Only financial entities identified for the purposes of the advanced digital resilience testing should be required to conduct TLPT.[19] As a consequence, the administrative processes and financial costs entailed in the performance of such tests should also only be borne by a small percentage of financial entities.[20]

Financial entities should regularly test their ICT systems and staff should have ICT-related responsibilities with regard to the effectiveness of their preventive, detection, response and recovery capabilities, to uncover and address potential ICT vulnerabilities.[21] This is in order to achieve a high level of digital operational resilience, and in line with relevant international standards[22] and EU frameworks.[23] There are differences that exist across, and within, the various financial subsectors as regards financial entities' level of cybersecurity preparedness. Therefore, testing should include a wide variety of tools and actions, ranging from the assessment of basic requirements[24] to more advanced testing by means of TLPT.[25] Such advanced testing should be required 'only' of financial entities that are 'mature' enough from an ICT perspective to reasonably carry it out. The digital operational resilience testing required by DORA should thus be more demanding for 'those' financial entities that meet the criteria set out in DORA – for example, 'large, systemic and ICT mature credit institutions, stock exchanges, central securities depositories and central counterparties.'[26] This is as compared to other financial entities. At the same time, the digital operational resilience testing by

16 Recital 43, DORA.
17 Recital 43, DORA.
18 Recital 43, DORA.
19 Recital 44, DORA.
20 Recital 44, DORA.
21 Recital 56, DORA.
22 For example, the G7 Fundamental Elements for Threat-Led Penetration Testing.
23 Such as the TIBER-EU.
24 For example, vulnerability assessments and scans, open source analyses, network security assessments, gap analyses, physical security reviews, questionnaires and scanning software solutions, source code reviews where feasible, scenario-based tests, compatibility testing, performance testing or end-to-end testing), Recital 56, DORA.
25 Recital 56, DORA.
26 Recital 56, DORA.

means of TLPT should be more relevant for financial entities operating in 'core financial services subsectors' and playing a 'systemic role' and less relevant for other subsectors.[27] The examples given for systemic roles are payments, banking, and clearing and settlement). Examples given for less relevant other subsectors are asset managers and credit rating agencies.[28]

Not one size fits all

4.07 Some financial entities qualify as microenterprises under DORA. Other entities qualify for the DORA simplified ICT risk management framework. Such entities should not be required to:

- establish a 'role' to monitor their arrangements entered into with ICT third-party service providers on the use of ICT services;
- 'designate' a member of senior management to be responsible for overseeing the related risk exposure and relevant documentation;
- assign responsibility for managing and overseeing ICT risk to a control function and ensure an appropriate level of independence of such control function in order to avoid conflicts of interest;
- document and review at least once a year the ICT risk management framework;
- be subject to an internal audit on a regular basis in relation to the ICT risk management framework;
- perform in depth assessments after major changes in their network and information system infrastructures and processes;
- regularly conduct risk analyses on legacy ICT systems;
- subject the implementation of the ICT Response and Recovery plans to independent internal audit reviews;
- have a crisis management function, expand the testing of business continuity and response and recovery plans to capture switchover scenarios between primary ICT infrastructure and redundant facilities;
- report to competent authorities, upon their request, an estimation of aggregated annual costs and losses caused by major ICT-related incidents, to maintain redundant ICT capacities;
- communicate to national competent authorities as regards implementing changes following post ICT-related incident reviews; and
- monitor on a continuous basis, relevant technological developments to establish a comprehensive digital operational resilience testing programme

27 Recital 56, DORA.
28 Recital 56, DORA.

as an integral part of the ICT risk management framework, or to adopt and regularly review a strategy on ICT third-party risk.29

In addition, microenterprises should only be required to assess the need to maintain 'such redundant ICT capacities' based on their 'risk profile'.[30]

SECTOR TESTING

4.08 Pooled testing within the meaning of DORA involves the participation of several financial entities in a TLPT.[31] An ICT third-party service provider can directly enter into contractual arrangements with an external tester.[32] Pooled testing should be allowed only where the quality or security of services delivered by the ICT third-party service provider to customers that are entities falling outside the scope of DORA, or the confidentiality of the data related to such services, are reasonably expected to be adversely impacted.[33] Pooled testing should also be subject to safeguards to ensure a rigorous testing exercise for the financial entities involved which meet the objectives of the TLPT pursuant to DORA.[34] The safeguards are referred to as direction by one designated financial entity, calibration of the number of participating financial entities.[35]

Some financial entities have internal resources available at corporate level. In order to take advantage of the internal resources available at corporate level, DORA should allow the use of resources of internal testers for the purposes of carrying out TLPT.[36] This is provided or conditioned on there being supervisory approval. There must also be no conflicts of interest.[37] There should also be periodical alternation of the use of internal and external testers (every three tests).[38] The threat intelligence in the TLPT required should always be external to the financial entity.[39] The responsibility for conducting TLPT should remain fully with the financial entity.[40] Attestations provided by authorities should be solely for the purpose of mutual recognition and should not preclude any follow-up action needed to address the ICT risk to which the financial entity is exposed.[41] Nor should they be seen as a supervisory endorsement of a financial entity's ICT risk management and mitigation capabilities.[42]

29 Recital 43, DORA.
30 Recital 43, DORA.
31 Recital 60, DORA.
32 Recital 60, DORA.
33 Recital 60, DORA.
34 Recital 60, DORA.
35 Recital 60, DORA.
36 Recital 61, DORA.
37 Recital 61, DORA.
38 Recital 61, DORA.
39 Recital 61, DORA.
40 Recital 61, DORA.
41 Recital 61, DORA.
42 Recital 61, DORA.

MANAGEMENT

4.09 The financial entities' management bodies (often the Board) should be required to maintain a 'pivotal and active role' in steering and adapting the ICT risk management framework and the overall digital operational resilience strategy of the firm.[43] This is to ensure full alignment and overall consistency between financial entities' business strategies, on the one hand, and the conduct of ICT risk management, on the other hand.[44] There is a recommended approach to be adopted.[45] The approach to be taken by management bodies should not only focus on the 'means of ensuring' the resilience of the ICT systems, but should also cover people and processes through a set of policies.[46] These policies should cultivate, at each corporate layer, and for all staff, a strong sense of awareness about cyber risks and a commitment to observe a strict cyber hygiene at all levels.[47] The ultimate responsibility of the management body in managing the financial entity's ICT risk should be 'an overarching principle' of that comprehensive approach.[48] It should further translate into the continuous engagement of the management body in the control of the monitoring of the ICT risk management.[49]

CONTINUITY

4.10 It is indicated that '[e]fficient' business continuity and recovery plans are necessary.[50] This is to ensure that financial entities can promptly and quickly resolve ICT-related incidents. This is especially so for cyber attacks. It will (potentially) limit damage and give priority to the resumption of activities and recovery actions in accordance with the firm's backup policies.[51] However, such resumption should 'in no way jeopardise' the integrity and security of the network and information systems or the availability, authenticity, integrity or confidentiality of data.[52]

REPORTING AND MONITORING

4.11 Reporting of financial entities is required across a range of issues. DORA increases focus on the ability of reports in relation to ICT-related incidents being made in such a manner that they are identical in format across jurisdictions, and hence that comparisons and trends can be identified. There is emphasis on the need to facilitate the comparability of such reports on major ICT-related

43 Recital 45, DORA.
44 Recital 45, DORA.
45 Recital 45, DORA.
46 Recital 45, DORA.
47 Recital 45, DORA.
48 Recital 45, DORA.
49 Recital 45, DORA.
50 Recital 49, DORA.
51 Recital 49, DORA.
52 Recital 49, DORA.

incidents and major operational or security payment-related incidents, as well as to ensure transparency regarding contractual arrangements for the use of ICT services provided by ICT third-party service providers.[53] As a result, the ESAs should develop draft implementing technical standards establishing standardised templates, forms and procedures for financial entities to report a major ICT-related incident and a major operational or security payment-related incident.[54] This also applies to standardised templates for the register of information to be filed by financial entities.[55] When developing those standards, the ESAs should take into account the size and the overall risk profile of the financial entity, and the nature, scale and complexity of its services, activities and operations.[56] The Commission is then empowered to legalise these technical standards.[57]

Regulatory technical standards should be developed in the areas of ICT risk management, major ICT-related incident reporting, testing, as well as in relation to key requirements for a sound monitoring of ICT third-party risk. Regulatory technical standards can assist to ensure the consistent harmonisation of the DORA rules. The ESAs should, therefore, develop draft regulatory technical standards (but which do not involve policy choices) for submission to the Commission to legalise.[58] The Commission and the ESAs will ensure that those standards and requirements can be applied by *all* financial entities in a manner that is 'proportionate to their size' and 'overall risk profile', and the 'nature, scale and complexity of their services, activities and operations.'[59]

INTERNATIONAL

4.12 It is intended that financial entities involved in cross-border activities and exercising the freedoms of establishment, or of provision of services within the EU, should comply with a single set of advanced testing requirements (ie, TLPT) in their home Member State, which should include the ICT infrastructures in all jurisdictions where the cross-border financial group operates within the EU, thus

53 Recital 100, DORA. The Commission should be empowered to adopt those implementing technical standards by means of implementing acts pursuant to Article 291 TFEU and in accordance with Article 15 of Regulations 1093/2010, 1094/2010 and 1095/2010.

54 Recital 100, DORA. The Commission should be empowered to adopt those implementing technical standards by means of implementing acts pursuant to Article 291 TFEU and in accordance with Article 15 of Regulations 1093/2010, 1094/2010 and 1095/2010.

55 Recital 100, DORA. The Commission should be empowered to adopt those implementing technical standards by means of implementing acts pursuant to Article 291 TFEU and in accordance with Article 15 of Regulations 1093/2010, 1094/2010 and 1095/2010.

56 Recital 100, DORA. The Commission should be empowered to adopt those implementing technical standards by means of implementing acts pursuant to Article 291 TFEU and in accordance with Article 15 of Regulations 1093/2010, 1094/2010 and 1095/2010.

57 Recital 100, DORA. The Commission should be empowered to adopt those implementing technical standards by means of implementing acts pursuant to Article 291 TFEU and in accordance with Article 15 of Regulations 1093/2010, 1094/2010 and 1095/2010.

58 The Commission is empowered to adopt those regulatory technical standards by means of delegated acts pursuant to Article 290 TFEU and in accordance with Articles 10 to 14 of Regulations 1093/2010, 1094/2010 and 1095/2010.

59 Recital 99, DORA.

allowing such cross-border financial groups to incur related ICT testing costs in one jurisdiction only.[60]

DORA does not require financial entities to cover all critical or important functions in one single threat-led penetration test.[61] Therefore, financial entities should be free to determine which and how many critical or important functions should be included in the scope of such a test.[62]

60 Recital 57, DORA.
61 Recital 59, DORA.
62 Recital 59, DORA.

CHAPTER 5

Law and Governance

INTRODUCTION

5.01 The importance of governance – and management oversight – of DORA compliance cannot be under-estimated. While it is understandable that some of the main initial corporate efforts regarding DORA will involve immediate compliance (and initial assessments, diligence, gap analysis, etc), and implementation, governance must be of prime importance.

Where governance is missing, lacking, or ineffective, failures will arise. Vulnerabilities which are sought to be identified and mitigation as a purpose of DORA will not be addressed, or will be addressed in a sub optimal manner. The intended level of digital operational resilience for the firm – and potentially the sector – will not be arrived at. From another perspective, the level of maturity sought to be achieved will not be fostered will be undermined.

In order to ensure the appropriate level of governance DORA seeks to imbue appropriate levels of responsibility and layered levels of governance. It is important that initial and ongoing compliance with DORA included multiple levels of governance, oversight, reporting, and action.

REQUIREMENTS ON LAW AND GOVERNANCE

Management responsibility

5.02 Financial entities – other than microenterprises – must assign the responsibility for 'managing and overseeing ICT risk' to a control function.[1] Firms shall also ensure an appropriate level of independence of such control function in order to avoid conflicts of interest. Financial entities must ensure appropriate segregation and independence of information and communication technology (ICT) risk management functions, control functions, and internal audit functions, according to the three lines of defence model – or an internal risk management and control model.[2]

Chapter V of DORA refers to the managing of ICT third-party risk. Section I of the Chapter refers to key principles for a sound management of ICT third-party risk. Article 28 sets out general principles. Financial entities shall manage

1 Article 6(4), DORA.
2 Article 6(4), DORA.

ICT third-party risk as an integral component of ICT risk within their ICT risk management framework as referred to in Article 6(1), and in accordance with the following principles:

- financial entities that have in place contractual arrangements for the use of ICT services to run their business operations shall, at all times, remain fully responsible for compliance with, and the discharge of, all obligations under this Regulation and applicable financial services law;
- financial entities' management of ICT third-party risk shall be implemented in light of the principle of proportionality, taking into account:
  - (i) the nature, scale, complexity and importance of ICT-related dependencies; and
  - (ii) the risks arising from contractual arrangements on the use of ICT services concluded with ICT third-party service providers, taking into account the criticality or importance of the respective service, process or function, and the potential impact on the continuity and availability of financial services and activities, at individual and at group level.[3]

As part of their ICT risk management framework, financial entities, other than entities referred to in Article 16(1), first subparagraph, and other than microenterprises, shall adopt, and regularly review, a strategy on ICT third-party risk, taking into account the multi-vendor strategy referred to in Article 6(9), where applicable. The strategy on ICT third-party risk shall include a policy on the use of ICT services supporting critical or important functions provided by ICT third-party service providers and shall apply on an individual basis and, where relevant, on a sub-consolidated and consolidated basis. The management body shall, on the basis of an assessment of the overall risk profile of the financial entity and the scale and complexity of the business services, regularly review the risks identified in respect to contractual arrangements on the use of ICT services supporting critical or important functions.[4]

As part of their ICT risk management framework, financial entities shall maintain and update at entity level, and at sub-consolidated and consolidated levels, a register of information in relation to all contractual arrangements on the use of ICT services provided by ICT third-party service providers.[5]

Third-party arrangements

5.03 The contractual arrangements referred to in the first subparagraph shall be appropriately documented, distinguishing between those that cover ICT services supporting critical or important functions and those that do not.[6]

3 Article 28(1), DORA.
4 Article 28(2), DORA.
5 Article 28(3), DORA.
6 Article 28(3), DORA.

Financial entities shall report at least yearly to the competent authorities on the number of new arrangements on the use of ICT services, the categories of ICT third-party service providers, the type of contractual arrangements and the ICT services and functions which are being provided.[7]

Financial entities shall make available to the competent authority, upon its request, the full register of information or, as requested, specified sections thereof, along with any information deemed necessary to enable the effective supervision of the financial entity.[8]

Financial entities shall inform the competent authority in a timely manner about any planned contractual arrangement on the use of ICT services supporting critical or important functions as well as when a function has become critical or important.[9]

Before entering into a contractual arrangement on the use of ICT services, financial entities shall:

- assess whether the contractual arrangement covers the use of ICT services supporting a critical or important function;
- assess if supervisory conditions for contracting are met;
- identify and assess all relevant risks in relation to the contractual arrangement, including the possibility that such contractual arrangement may contribute to reinforcing ICT concentration risk as referred to in Article 29;
- undertake all due diligence on prospective ICT third-party service providers and ensure throughout the selection and assessment processes that the ICT third-party service provider is suitable; and
- identify and assess conflicts of interest that the contractual arrangement may cause.[10]

Financial entities may only enter into contractual arrangements with ICT third-party service providers that comply with appropriate information security standards.[11] When those contractual arrangements concern critical or important functions, financial entities shall, prior to concluding the arrangements, take due consideration of the use, by ICT third-party service providers, of the most up-to-date and highest quality information security standards.[12]

In exercising access, inspection and audit rights over the ICT third-party service provider, financial entities shall, on the basis of a risk-based approach, pre-determine the frequency of audits and inspections as well as the areas to be

7 Article 28(3), DORA.
8 Article 28(3), DORA.
9 Article 28(3), DORA.
10 Article 28(4), DORA.
11 Article 28(5), DORA.
12 Article 28(5), DORA.

audited through adhering to commonly accepted audit standards in line with any supervisory instruction on the use and incorporation of such audit standards.[13]

Where contractual arrangements concluded with ICT third-party service providers on the use of ICT services entail high technical complexity, the financial entity shall verify that auditors, whether internal or external, or a pool of auditors, possess appropriate skills and knowledge to effectively perform the relevant audits and assessments.[14]

Financial entities shall ensure that contractual arrangements on the use of ICT services may be terminated in any of the following circumstances:

- significant breach by the ICT third-party service provider of applicable laws, regulations or contractual terms;
- circumstances identified throughout the monitoring of ICT third-party risk that are deemed capable of altering the performance of the functions provided through the contractual arrangement, including material changes that affect the arrangement or the situation of the ICT third-party service provider;
- ICT third-party service provider's evidenced weaknesses pertaining to its overall ICT risk management and in particular in the way it ensures the availability, authenticity, integrity and, confidentiality, of data, whether personal or otherwise sensitive data, or non-personal data; and
- where the competent authority can no longer effectively supervise the financial entity as a result of the conditions of, or circumstances related to, the respective contractual arrangement.[15]

For ICT services supporting critical or important functions, financial entities shall put in place exit strategies.[16] The exit strategies shall take into account risks that may emerge at the level of ICT third-party service providers, in particular a possible failure on their part, a deterioration of the quality of the ICT services provided, any business disruption due to inappropriate or failed provision of ICT services or any material risk arising in relation to the appropriate and continuous deployment of the respective ICT service, or the termination of contractual arrangements with ICT third-party service providers under any of the circumstances listed in Article 28(7).[17]

Financial entities shall ensure that they are able to exit contractual arrangements without:

- disruption to their business activities;

13 Article 28(6), DORA.
14 Article 28(6), DORA.
15 Article 28(7), DORA.
16 Article 28(8), DORA.
17 Article 28(8), DORA.

- limiting compliance with regulatory requirements; and
- detriment to the continuity and quality of services provided to clients.[18]

Exit plans shall be comprehensive, documented and, in accordance with the criteria set out in Article 4(2), shall be sufficiently tested and reviewed periodically.[19]

Financial entities shall identify alternative solutions and develop transition plans enabling them to remove the contracted ICT services and the relevant data from the ICT third-party service provider and to securely and integrally transfer them to alternative providers or reincorporate them in-house.[20]

Financial entities shall have appropriate contingency measures in place to maintain business continuity in the event of the circumstances referred to in the first subparagraph.[21]

Register of information template

5.04 The European Supervisory Authorities (ESAs) shall, through the Joint Committee, develop draft implementing technical standards to establish the standard templates for the purposes of the register of information referred to in Article 28(3), including information that is common to all contractual arrangements on the use of ICT services.[22] The ESAs were required to submit those draft implementing technical standards to the Commission by 17 January 2024.[23] Power is conferred on the Commission to adopt the implementing technical standards referred to above.[24]

The ESAs shall, through the Joint Committee, develop draft regulatory technical standards to further specify the detailed content of the policy referred to above in relation to the contractual arrangements on the use of ICT services supporting critical or important functions provided by ICT third-party service providers.[25]

When developing those draft regulatory technical standards, the ESAs shall take into account the size and the overall risk profile of the financial entity, and the nature, scale and complexity of its services, activities and operations. The ESAs were required to submit those draft regulatory technical standards to the

18 Article 28(8), DORA.
19 Article 28(8), DORA.
20 Article 28(8), DORA.
21 Article 28(8), DORA.
22 Article 28(9), DORA.
23 Article 28(9), DORA.
24 In accordance with Article 15 of Regulations 1093/2010, 1094/2010 and 1095/2010. Article 28(9), DORA.
25 Article 28(10), DORA.

Commission by 17 January 2024.[26] Power is delegated to the Commission to supplement this Regulation by adopting the regulatory technical standards.[27]

Article 29 refers to preliminary assessment of ICT concentration risk at entity level.

Arrangements

5.05 When performing the identification and assessment of risks referred to in Article 28(4)(c), financial entities shall also take into account whether the envisaged conclusion of a contractual arrangement in relation to ICT services supporting critical or important functions would lead to any of the following:

- contracting an ICT third-party service provider that is not easily substitutable; or
- having in place multiple contractual arrangements in relation to the provision of ICT services supporting critical or important functions with the same ICT third-party service provider or with closely connected ICT third-party service providers.[28]

Financial entities shall weigh the benefits and costs of alternative solutions, such as the use of different ICT third-party service providers, taking into account if and how envisaged solutions match the business needs and objectives set out in their digital resilience strategy.[29]

Where the contractual arrangements on the use of ICT services supporting critical or important functions include the possibility that an ICT third-party service provider further subcontracts ICT services supporting a critical or important function to other ICT third-party service providers, financial entities shall weigh benefits and risks that may arise in connection with such subcontracting, in particular in the case of an ICT subcontractor established in a third country.[30]

Where contractual arrangements concern ICT services supporting critical or important functions, financial entities shall duly consider the insolvency law provisions that would apply in the event of the ICT third-party service provider's bankruptcy as well as any constraint that may arise in respect to the urgent recovery of the financial entity's data.[31]

Where contractual arrangements on the use of ICT services supporting critical or important functions are concluded with an ICT third-party service provider

26 Article 28(10), DORA.
27 In accordance with Articles 10 to 14 of Regulations 1093/2010, 1094/2010 and 1095/2010. Article 28(10), DORA.
28 Article 29(1), DORA.
29 Article 29(1), DORA.
30 Article 29(2), DORA.
31 Article 29(2), DORA.

established in a third country, financial entities shall, in addition to the considerations referred to in Article 29(2), second subparagraph, also consider the compliance with European data protection rules and the effective enforcement of the law in that third country.[32]

Where the contractual arrangements on the use of ICT services supporting critical or important functions provide for subcontracting, financial entities shall assess whether and how potentially long or complex chains of subcontracting may impact their ability to fully monitor the contracted functions and the ability of the competent authority to effectively supervise the financial entity in that respect.[33]

Article 30 refers to key contractual provisions. The rights and obligations of the financial entity and of the ICT third-party service provider shall be clearly allocated and set out in writing.[34] The full contract shall include the service level agreements and be documented in one written document which shall be available to the parties on paper, or in a document with another downloadable, durable and accessible format.[35]

The contractual arrangements on the use of ICT services shall include at least the following elements:

- a clear and complete description of all functions and ICT services to be provided by the ICT third-party service provider, indicating whether subcontracting of an ICT service supporting a critical or important function, or material parts thereof, is permitted and, when that is the case, the conditions applying to such subcontracting;
- the locations, namely the regions or countries, where the contracted or subcontracted functions and ICT services are to be provided and where data is to be processed, including the storage location, and the requirement for the ICT third-party service provider to notify the financial entity in advance if it envisages changing such locations;
- provisions on availability, authenticity, integrity and confidentiality in relation to the protection of data, including personal data;
- provisions on ensuring access, recovery and return in an easily accessible format of personal and non-personal data processed by the financial entity in the event of the insolvency, resolution or discontinuation of the business operations of the ICT third-party service provider, or in the event of the termination of the contractual arrangements;
- service level descriptions, including updates and revisions thereof;

32 Article 29(2), DORA.
33 Article 29(2), DORA.
34 Article 30(1), DORA.
35 Article 30(1), DORA.

- the obligation of the ICT third-party service provider to provide assistance to the financial entity at no additional cost, or at a cost that is determined ex-ante, when an ICT incident that is related to the ICT service provided to the financial entity occurs;
- the obligation of the ICT third-party service provider to fully cooperate with the competent authorities and the resolution authorities of the financial entity, including persons appointed by them;
- termination rights and related minimum notice periods for the termination of the contractual arrangements, in accordance with the expectations of competent authorities and resolution authorities; and
- the conditions for the participation of ICT third-party service providers in the financial entities' ICT security awareness programmes and digital operational resilience training in accordance with Article 13(6).[36]

The contractual arrangements on the use of ICT services supporting critical or important functions shall include, in addition to the elements referred to in Article 30(2), at least the following:

- full service level descriptions, including updates and revisions thereof with precise quantitative and qualitative performance targets within the agreed service levels to allow effective monitoring by the financial entity of ICT services and enable appropriate corrective actions to be taken, without undue delay, when agreed service levels are not met;
- notice periods and reporting obligations of the ICT third-party service provider to the financial entity, including notification of any development that might have a material impact on the ICT third-party service provider's ability to effectively provide the ICT services supporting critical or important functions in line with agreed service levels;
- requirements for the ICT third-party service provider to implement and test business contingency plans and to have in place ICT security measures, tools and policies that provide an appropriate level of security for the provision of services by the financial entity in line with its regulatory framework;
- the obligation of the ICT third-party service provider to participate and fully cooperate in the financial entity's TLPT as referred to in Articles 26 and 27;
- the right to monitor, on an ongoing basis, the ICT third-party service provider's performance, which entails the following:
  (i) unrestricted rights of access, inspection and audit by the financial entity, or an appointed third party, and by the competent authority, and the right to take copies of relevant documentation on site if they are critical to the operations of the ICT third-party service provider,

36 Article 30(2), DORA.

the effective exercise of which is not impeded or limited by other contractual arrangements or implementation policies;

(ii) the right to agree on alternative assurance levels if other clients' rights are affected;

(iii) the obligation of the ICT third-party service provider to fully cooperate during the onsite inspections and audits performed by the competent authorities, the Lead Overseer, financial entity or an appointed third party; and

(iv) the obligation to provide details on the scope, procedures to be followed and frequency of such inspections and audits;

- exit strategies, in particular the establishment of a mandatory adequate transition period:

  (i) during which the ICT third-party service provider will continue providing the respective functions, or ICT services, with a view to reducing the risk of disruption at the financial entity or to ensure its effective resolution and restructuring; and

  (ii) allowing the financial entity to migrate to another ICT third-party service provider or change to in house solutions consistent with the complexity of the service provided.[37]

By way of derogation from bullet point five above, the ICT third-party service provider and the financial entity that is a microenterprise may agree that the financial entity's rights of access, inspection and audit can be delegated to an independent third party, appointed by the ICT third-party service provider, and that the financial entity is able to request information and assurance on the ICT third-party service provider's performance from the third party at any time.[38]

When negotiating contractual arrangements, financial entities and ICT third-party service providers shall consider the use of standard contractual clauses developed by public authorities for specific services.[39]

The ESAs shall, through the Joint Committee, develop draft regulatory technical standards to specify further the elements referred to in Article 30(2)(a), which a financial entity needs to determine and assess when subcontracting ICT services supporting critical or important functions.[40]

When developing those draft regulatory technical standards, the ESAs shall take into consideration the size and overall risk profile of the financial entity, and the nature, scale and complexity of its services, activities and operations.[41]

37 Article 30(3), DORA.
38 Article 30(3), DORA.
39 Article 30(4), DORA.
40 Article 30(5), DORA.
41 Article 30(5), DORA.

The ESAs were required submit those draft regulatory technical standards to the Commission by 17 July 2024.[42] Power is delegated to the Commission to supplement this Regulation by adopting the regulatory technical standards referred to above.[43]

Designation as critical

5.06 Section II refers to the Oversight Framework of critical ICT third-party service providers. Article 31 refers to designation of critical ICT third-party service providers. The ESAs, through the Joint Committee and upon recommendation from the Oversight Forum established pursuant to Article 32(1), shall:

- designate the ICT third-party service providers that are critical for financial entities, following an assessment that takes into account the criteria specified in Article 31(2);
- appoint as Lead Overseer for each critical ICT third-party service provider the ESA that is responsible, in accordance with Regulations 1093/2010, 1094/2010 or 1095/2010, for the financial entities having together the largest share of total assets out of the value of total assets of all financial entities using the services of the relevant critical ICT third-party service provider, as evidenced by the sum of the individual balance sheets of those financial entities.[44]

The designation referred to in Article 31(1)(a), shall be based on all of the following criteria in relation to ICT services provided by the ICT third-party service provider:

- the systemic impact on the stability, continuity or quality of the provision of financial services in the event that the relevant ICT third-party service provider would face a large-scale operational failure to provide its services, taking into account the number of financial entities and the total value of assets of financial entities to which the relevant ICT third-party service provider provides services;
- the systemic character or importance of the financial entities that rely on the relevant ICT third-party service provider, assessed in accordance with the following parameters:
  - (i) the number of global systemically important institutions (G-SIIs) or other systemically important institutions (O-SIIs) that rely on the respective ICT third-party service provider;
  - (ii) the interdependence between the G-SIIs or O-SIIs referred to in point (i) and other financial entities, including situations where the G-SIIs

42 Article 30(5), DORA.

43 In accordance with Articles 10 to 14 of Regulations 1093/2010, 1094/2010 and 1095/2010. Article 30(5), DORA.

44 Article 31(1), DORA.

or O-SIIs provide financial infrastructure services to other financial entities;

- the reliance of financial entities on the services provided by the relevant ICT third-party service provider in relation to critical or important functions of financial entities that ultimately involve the same ICT third-party service provider, irrespective of whether financial entities rely on those services directly or indirectly, through subcontracting arrangements;
- the degree of substitutability of the ICT third-party service provider, taking into account the following parameters:
  - (i) the lack of real alternatives, even partial, due to the limited number of ICT third-party service providers active on a specific market, or the market share of the relevant ICT third-party service provider, or the technical complexity or sophistication involved, including in relation to any proprietary technology, or the specific features of the ICT third-party service provider's organisation or activity;
  - (ii) difficulties in relation to partially or fully migrating the relevant data and workloads from the relevant ICT third-party service provider to another ICT third-party service provider, due either to significant financial costs, time or other resources that the migration process may entail, or to increased ICT risk or other operational risks to which the financial entity may be exposed through such migration.[45]

Where the ICT third-party service provider belongs to a group, the criteria referred to in Article 31(2) shall be considered in relation to the ICT services provided by the group as a whole.[46]

Critical ICT third-party service providers which are part of a group shall designate one legal person as a coordination point to ensure adequate representation and communication with the Lead Overseer.[47]

The Lead Overseer shall notify the ICT third-party service provider of the outcome of the assessment leading to the designation referred in Article 31(1)(a).[48] Within six weeks from the date of the notification, the ICT third-party service provider may submit to the Lead Overseer a reasoned statement with any relevant information for the purposes of the assessment.[49] The Lead Overseer shall consider the reasoned statement and may request additional information to be submitted within 30 calendar days of the receipt of such statement.[50]

After designating an ICT third-party service provider as critical, the ESAs, through the Joint Committee, shall notify the ICT third-party service provider

45 Article 31(2), DORA.
46 Article 31(3), DORA.
47 Article 31(4), DORA.
48 Article 31(5), DORA.
49 Article 31(5), DORA.
50 Article 31(5), DORA.

of such designation and the starting date as from which they will effectively be subject to oversight activities.[51] That starting date shall be no later than one month after the notification.[52] The ICT third-party service provider shall notify the financial entities to which they provide services of their designation as critical.[53]

The Commission was empowered to adopt a delegated act in accordance with Article 57 to supplement this Regulation by specifying further the criteria referred to in Article 31(2), by 17 July 2024.[54]

The designation referred to in Article 31(1)(a), shall not be used until the Commission has adopted a delegated act in accordance with Article 31(6).[55]

The designation referred to in Article 31(1)(a), shall not apply to the following:

- financial entities providing ICT services to other financial entities;
- ICT third-party service providers that are subject to oversight frameworks established for the purposes of supporting the tasks referred to in Article 127(2) of the Treaty on the Functioning of the European Union;
- ICT intra group service providers; and
- ICT third-party service providers providing ICT services solely in one Member State to financial entities that are only active in that Member State.[56]

The ESAs, through the Joint Committee, shall establish, publish and update yearly the list of critical ICT third-party service providers at Union level.[57]

For the purposes of Article 31(1)(a), competent authorities shall, on a yearly and aggregated basis, transmit the reports referred to in Article 28(3), third subparagraph, to the Oversight Forum established pursuant to Article 32. The Oversight Forum shall assess the ICT third party dependencies of financial entities based on the information received from the competent authorities.[58]

The ICT third-party service providers that are not included in the list referred to in paragraph 9 may request to be designated as critical in accordance with Article 31(1)(a).[59]

For the purpose of Article 31(1), the ICT third-party service provider shall submit a reasoned application to the European Banking Authority (EBA), the European

51 Article 31(5), DORA.
52 Article 31(5), DORA.
53 Article 31(5), DORA.
54 Article 31(6), DORA.
55 Article 31(7), DORA.
56 Article 31(8), DORA.
57 Article 31(9), DORA.
58 Article 31(10), DORA.
59 Article 31(11), DORA.

Securities and Markets Authority (ESMA) or the European Insurance and Occupational Pensions Authority (EIOPA), which, through the Joint Committee, shall decide whether to designate that ICT third-party service provider as critical in accordance with Article 31(1)(a).[60]

The decision referred to Article 31(11), second subparagraph, shall be adopted and notified to the ICT third-party service provider within six months of receipt of the application.[61]

Financial entities shall only make use of the services of an ICT third-party service provider established in a third country and which has been designated as critical in accordance with Article 31(1)(a), if the latter has established a subsidiary in the EU within the 12 months following the designation.[62]

The critical ICT third-party service provider referred to in Article 31(12) shall notify the Lead Overseer of any changes to the structure of the management of the subsidiary established in Europe.[63]

There are various additional provisions relevant to law and governance consideration, including the following:

- Article 32 refers to the structure of the Oversight Framework;
- Article 34 refers to operational coordination between Lead Overseers;
- Article 35 refers to the powers of the Lead Overseer;
- Article 36 refers to the exercise of the powers of the Lead Overseer outside Europe;
- Article 37 refers to requests for information;
- Article 38 refers to general investigations;
- Article 39 refers to inspections;
- Article 40 refers to ongoing oversight;
- Article 41 refers to the ESAs and harmonisation of conditions enabling the conduct of the oversight activities;
- Article 42 refers to follow up by competent authorities;
- Article 43 refers to oversight fees;
- Article 44 refers to international cooperation;
- Article 45 refers to information-sharing arrangements on cyber threat information and intelligence;

60 Article 31(11), DORA.
61 Article 31(11), DORA.
62 Article 31(12), DORA.
63 Article 31(13), DORA.

- Article 46 refers to competent authorities;
- Article 47 refers to cooperation with structures and authorities established by Directive 2022/2555;
- Article 48 refers to cooperation between authorities;
- Article 49 refers to financial cross sector exercises, communication and cooperation;
- Article 50 refers to administrative penalties and remedial measures;
- Article 51 refers to the exercise of the power to impose administrative penalties and remedial measures;
- Article 52 refers criminal penalties;
- Article 53 refers to notification duties;
- Article 54 refers to publication of administrative penalties;
- Article 55 refers to professional secrecy; and
- Article 56 refers to data protection.

POLICY ON LAW AND GOVERNANCE

Policy strategy

5.07 The format of using a Regulation as a legal instrument helps to reduce regulatory complexity, fosters supervisory convergence and increases legal certainty. It also contributes to limiting compliance costs, especially for financial entities operating across borders. In addition, it contributes to reducing competitive distortions. Therefore, the choice of a Regulation legal instrument for the establishment of a common framework for the digital operational resilience of financial entities is the 'most appropriate way to guarantee a homogenous and coherent application of all components of ICT risk management' by the European financial sector.[64]

Limited earlier attention

5.08 Directive 2016/1148[65] was the first European horizontal cybersecurity framework setting out national cybersecurity rules for the level of operators that could be used for essential services. But the rules only applied to certain credit institutions, trading venues and central counterparties. They needed to be identified at national level, and clearly brought into scope. Only then were they required to comply with the ICT security and incident notification requirements

64 Recital 14, DORA.

65 Directive (EU) 2016/1148 concerning measures for a high common level of security of network and information systems across the Union.

that were set out. Directive 2022/2555[66] sets a uniform criterion[67] to determine the entities that fall within its scope, while also keeping the three types of financial entities within its scope.[68]

Digital and physical resilience

5.09 There are strong links between the digital resilience and the physical resilience of financial entities.[69] A coherent approach with regard to the resilience of critical entities is necessary.[70] This approach is reflected in DORA and Directive 2022/2557.[71] It is suggested that given that the physical resilience of financial entities is addressed in a comprehensive manner by the ICT risk management and reporting obligations covered by DORA, the obligations laid down in Chapters III and IV of Directive 2022/2557 should not apply to financial entities falling within the scope of that Directive.[72]

Cloud industry

5.10 Cloud computing service providers are suggested as being one necessary category of digital infrastructure covered by Directive 2022/2555. The DORA European Oversight Framework (Oversight Framework) applies to all critical ICT third-party service providers, including cloud computing service providers providing ICT services to financial entities. These should be considered complementary to the supervision carried out pursuant to Directive 2022/2555. Moreover, the Oversight Framework established by DORA should cover cloud computing service providers in the absence of a European horizontal framework establishing a digital oversight authority.[73]

Effective ICT risk strategy

5.11 To maintain full control over ICT risk, financial entities need to have comprehensive capabilities to enable a strong and effective ICT risk management. Financial entities must also have specific mechanisms and policies for handling all ICT-related incidents and for reporting major ICT-related incidents. Likewise, financial entities should have policies in place for the testing of ICT systems,

66 Directive (EU) 2022/2555 on measures for a high common level of cybersecurity across the Union, amending Regulation (EU) No 910/2014 and Directive (EU) 2018/1972, and repealing Directive (EU) 2016/1148 (NIS 2 Directive).

67 Based upon a size cap rule.

68 Recital 15, DORA.

69 Recital 19, DORA.

70 Recital 19, DORA.

71 Directive (EU) 2022/2557 on the resilience of critical entities and repealing Council Directive 2008/114/EC.

72 Recital 19, DORA.

73 Recital 20, DORA.

controls and processes, as well as for managing ICT third-party risk. The digital operational resilience *baseline* for financial entities should be increased. However, this is while also allowing for a proportionate application of requirements for certain financial entities, particularly microenterprises, and financial entities subject to a simplified ICT risk management framework. To facilitate an efficient supervision of institutions for occupational retirement provision that is proportionate and addresses the need to reduce administrative burdens on the competent authorities, the relevant national supervisory arrangements in respect of such financial entities should take into account their size and overall risk profile, and the nature, scale and complexity of their services, activities and operations even when the relevant thresholds established in Article 5 of Directive 2016/2341[74] are exceeded. In particular, supervisory activities should focus primarily on the need to address 'serious risks' associated with the ICT risk management of a particular entity.[75]

Supervisory strategy

5.12 Competent authorities should also maintain a vigilant but proportionate approach in relation to the supervision of institutions for occupational retirement provision which[76] outsource a significant part of their core business, such as asset management, actuarial calculations, accounting and data management, to service providers.[77]

Complex arrangements

5.13 The extensive use of ICT services is evidenced by complex contractual arrangements.[78] In such arrangements financial entities often encounter difficulties in negotiating contractual terms that are tailored to the prudential standards or other regulatory requirements to which they are subject, or otherwise in enforcing specific rights, such as access or audit rights, even when the latter are enshrined in their contractual arrangements.[79] Many of those contractual arrangements do not provide for sufficient safeguards allowing for the fully fledged monitoring of subcontracting processes.[80] This deprives the financial entity of its ability to assess the associated risks.[81] In addition, as ICT third-party service providers often provide standardised services to different types of clients, such contractual

74 Directive (EU) 2016/2341 on the activities and supervision of institutions for occupational retirement provision (IORPs) (recast).
75 Recital 21, DORA.
76 In accordance with Article 31 of Directive 2016/2341.
77 Recital 21, DORA.
78 Recital 28, DORA.
79 Recital 28, DORA.
80 Recital 28, DORA.
81 Recital 28, DORA.

arrangements do not always cater adequately for the individual or specific needs of financial industry actors.[82]

Outsourcing rules

5.14 Even though European financial services law contains certain 'general rules' on outsourcing, monitoring of the contractual dimension is not fully anchored into European law.[83] In the absence of clear and bespoke European standards applying to the contractual arrangements concluded with ICT third-party service providers, the external source of ICT risk is not comprehensively addressed.[84] Consequently, it is necessary to set out certain key principles to guide financial entities' management of ICT third-party risk, which are of particular importance when financial entities resort to ICT third-party service providers to support their critical or important functions.[85] Those principles should be accompanied by a set of 'core contractual rights' in relation to several elements in the performance and termination of contractual arrangements with a view to providing certain 'minimum safeguards' in order to strengthen financial entities' ability to effectively monitor all ICT risk emerging at the level of third-party service providers.[86] Those principles are also complementary to the sectoral law applicable to outsourcing.[87]

Varied monitoring

5.15 Lack of 'homogeneity and convergence' regarding the monitoring of ICT third-party risk and ICT third-party dependencies is evident today.[88] Despite efforts to address outsourcing, such as EBA Guidelines on outsourcing of and ESMA Guidelines on outsourcing to cloud service providers of the broader issue of counteracting systemic risk which may be triggered by the financial sector's exposure to a limited number of critical ICT third-party service providers is not sufficiently addressed by European law. The lack of rules at European level is compounded by the absence of national rules on mandates and tools that allow financial supervisors to acquire a good understanding of ICT third-party dependencies and to monitor adequately risks arising from the concentration of ICT third-party dependencies.[89]

82 Recital 28, DORA.
83 Recital 29, DORA.
84 Recital 29, DORA.
85 Recital 29, DORA.
86 Recital 29, DORA.
87 Recital 29, DORA.
88 Recital 30, DORA.
89 Recital 30, DORA.

Risk multiplied

5.16 There can be potential systemic risk entailed by increased outsourcing practices. This can also be the case with ICT third-party concentration. There can also be insufficiency of national mechanisms in providing financial supervisors with adequate tools to quantify, qualify and redress the consequences of ICT risk occurring at critical ICT third-party service providers. Taking the above into account, it is necessary to establish an appropriate Oversight Framework allowing for a continuous monitoring of the activities of ICT third-party service providers that are critical ICT third-party service providers to financial entities, while ensuring that the confidentiality and security of customers other than financial entities is preserved.[90] While intra group provision of ICT services entails specific risks and benefits, it should not be automatically considered less risky than the provision of ICT services by providers outside of a financial group and should therefore be subject to the same regulatory framework.[91] However, when ICT services are provided from within the same financial group, financial entities might have a higher level of control over intra group providers, which ought to be taken into account in the overall risk assessment.[92]

Increased ICT risk complexity

5.17 ICT is risk becoming more and more complex and sophisticated. Good measures for the detection and prevention of ICT risk depend to a great extent on the regular sharing between financial entities of threat and vulnerability intelligence. Information sharing contributes to creating increased awareness of cyber threats.[93] In turn, this enhances the capacity of financial entities to prevent cyber threats from becoming real ICT-related incidents and enables financial entities to more effectively contain the impact of ICT-related incidents and to recover faster. [94] In the absence of guidance at European level, several factors seem to have inhibited such intelligence sharing, in particular uncertainty about its compatibility with data protection, antitrust and liability rules.[95]

Chilling

5.18 In addition, doubts about the type of information that can be shared with other market participants, or with non-supervisory authorities lead to useful information being withheld. Examples include the European Union Agency on Cybersecurity (ENISA) for analytical input, or Europol for law enforcement purposes. Therefore, the extent and quality of information sharing currently

90 Recital 31, DORA.
91 Recital 31, DORA.
92 Recital 31, DORA.
93 Recital 32, DORA.
94 Recital 32, DORA.
95 Recital 32, DORA.

remains limited and fragmented, with relevant exchanges mostly being local (by way of national initiatives) and with no consistent European wide information sharing arrangements tailored to the needs of an integrated financial system.[96] It is therefore important to strengthen those communication channels.[97]

Need for shared intelligence

5.19 Financial entities should be encouraged to exchange among themselves cyber threat information and intelligence. They can collectively leverage their individual knowledge and practical experience at strategic, tactical and operational levels with a view to enhancing their capabilities to adequately assess, monitor, defend against, and respond to cyber threats, by participating in information sharing arrangements. It is, therefore, necessary to enable the emergence at European level of mechanisms for voluntary information sharing arrangements which, when conducted in trusted environments, would help the community of the financial industry to prevent and collectively respond to cyber threats by quickly limiting the spread of ICT risk and impeding potential contagion throughout the financial channels. Those mechanisms should comply with the applicable competition law rules of the European set out in 'Guidelines on the applicability of Article 101 of the Treaty on the Functioning of the European Union to horizontal cooperation agreements',[98] as well as with data protection rules.[99] They should operate based on the use of one or more of the legal bases that are laid down in Article 6 of the General Data Protection Regulation (GDPR), such as in the context of the processing of personal data that is necessary for the purposes of the legitimate interest pursued by the controller or by a third party, as referred to in Article 6(1)(f), of that Regulation, as well as in the context of the processing of personal data necessary for compliance with a legal obligation to which the controller is subject, necessary for the performance of a task carried out in the public interest or in the exercise of official authority vested in the controller, as referred to in Article 6(1)(c) and (e), respectively, of the GDPR.[100]

Global ICT risk

5.20 In order to maintain a high level of digital operational resilience for the whole financial sector, and at the same time to keep pace with technological developments, DORA should address risk stemming from all types of ICT

96 Recital 33, DORA.
97 Recital 33, DORA.
98 The Communication from the Commission of entitled 'Guidelines on the applicability of Article 101 of the Treaty on the Functioning of the European Union to horizontal cooperation agreements' (14 January 2011).
99 In particular Regulation (EU) 2016/679 on the protection of natural persons with regard to the processing of personal data and on the free movement of such data, and repealing Directive 95/46/EC – otherwise known as the GDPR.
100 Recital 34, DORA.

services. To that end, the definition of ICT services in the context of DORA should be understood in a 'broad manner', encompassing 'digital and data' services provided through ICT systems to one or more internal or external users on an ongoing basis. That definition should, for instance, include so-called 'over the top' services, which fall within the category of electronic communications services. It should 'exclude only the limited category' of traditional 'analogue' telephone services qualifying as Public Switched Telephone Network (PSTN) services, landline services, Plain Old Telephone Service (POTS), or fixed-line telephone services.[101]

Disparate resources

5.21 Larger financial entities might enjoy wider resources and can swiftly deploy funds to develop governance structures and set up various corporate strategies. Therefore, only financial entities that are not microenterprises in the sense of DORA should be required to establish more complex governance arrangements. Such entities are better equipped in particular to set up dedicated management functions for supervising arrangements with ICT third-party service providers or for dealing with crisis management, to organise their ICT risk management according to the three lines of defence model, or to set up an internal risk management and control model, and to submit their ICT risk management framework to internal audits.[102]

Board responsibility and input

5.22 To ensure full alignment and overall consistency between financial entities' business strategies, on the one hand, and the conduct of ICT risk management, on the other hand, the financial entities' management bodies (eg, Boards) should be required to maintain a pivotal and active role in steering and adapting the ICT risk management framework and the overall digital operational resilience strategy. The approach to be taken by management bodies should not only focus on the means of ensuring the resilience of the ICT systems, but should also cover people and processes through a set of policies which cultivate, at each corporate layer, and for all staff, a strong sense of awareness about cyber risks and a commitment to observe a strict cyber hygiene at all levels. The ultimate responsibility of the management body in managing a financial entity's ICT risk should be an overarching principle of that 'comprehensive approach', further translated into the continuous engagement of the management body in the control of the monitoring of the ICT risk management.[103]

The principle of the management body's full and ultimate responsibility for the management of the ICT risk of the financial entity goes hand in hand with the

101 Recital 35, DORA.
102 Recital 38, DORA.
103 Recital 45, DORA.

need to secure a level of ICT-related investments and an overall budget for the financial entity that would enable the financial entity to achieve a high level of digital operational resilience.[104]

Flexibility

5.23 DORA is inspired in part by relevant international, national and industry best practices, guidelines, recommendations and approaches to the management of cyber risk. As such, it promotes a set of principles that facilitate the overall structure of ICT risk management. Consequently, as long as the main capabilities which financial entities put in place address the various functions in the ICT risk management (namely, identification, protection and prevention, detection, response and recovery, learning and evolving and communication) set out in DORA, financial entities should 'remain free to use ICT risk management models that are differently framed or categorised.'[105]

Threat evolution

5.24 The pace of the cyber threat landscape is fast evolving. Financial entities should maintain updated ICT systems that are reliable and capable, not only for guaranteeing the processing of data required for their services, but also for ensuring sufficient technological resilience to allow them to deal adequately with additional processing needs due to stressed market conditions or other adverse situations.[106]

Continuity, recovery

5.25 Efficient business continuity and recovery plans are necessary to allow financial entities to promptly and quickly resolve ICT-related incidents, in particular cyber attacks. This includes limiting damage and giving priority to the resumption of activities and recovery actions in accordance with their backup policies. However, such resumption should not jeopardise the integrity and security of the network and information systems or the availability, authenticity, integrity or confidentiality of data.[107]

Market assessment

5.26 While DORA allows financial entities to determine their recovery time and recovery point objectives in a flexible manner and, hence, to set such

104 Recital 46, DORA.
105 Recital 47, DORA.
106 Recital 48, DORA.
107 Recital 49, DORA.

objectives by fully taking into account the nature and the criticality of the relevant functions and any specific business needs, it should nevertheless require them to carry out an assessment of the potential overall impact on market efficiency when determining such objectives.[108]

ICT risk sources

5.27 There are various sources of ICT risk. To address the complexity of the various sources of ICT risk, while taking into account the multitude and diversity of providers of technological solutions which enable a smooth provision of financial services, DORA should cover a wide range of ICT third-party service providers. This includes providers of cloud computing services, software, data analytics services and providers of data centre services. Financial entities should effectively and coherently identify and manage all types of risk, including in the context of ICT services procured within a financial group. It should be clarified that undertakings which are part of a financial group and provide ICT services predominantly to their parent undertaking, or to subsidiaries or branches of their parent undertaking, as well as financial entities providing ICT services to other financial entities. It should also be considered as ICT third-party service providers under DORA. In light of the evolving payment services market becoming increasingly dependent on complex technical solutions, and in view of emerging types of payment services and payment-related solutions, participants in the payment services ecosystem, providing payment processing activities, or operating payment infrastructures, should also be considered to be ICT third-party service providers under DORA, with the exception of central banks when operating payment or securities settlement systems, and public authorities when providing ICT-related services in the context of fulfilling State functions.[109]

Responsive monitoring

5.28 A financial entity should at 'all' times remain fully responsible for complying with its obligations set out in DORA. Financial entities should apply a proportionate approach to the monitoring of risks emerging at the level of the ICT third-party service providers, by duly considering the nature, scale, complexity and importance of their ICT-related dependencies, the criticality or importance of the services, processes or functions subject to the contractual arrangements and, ultimately, on the basis of a careful assessment of any potential impact on the continuity and quality of financial services at individual and at group level, as appropriate.[110]

108 Recital 50, DORA.
109 Recital 63, DORA.
110 Recital 64, DORA.

Diligence and ICT partners

5.29 A thorough pre-contracting analysis should underpin and precede the formal conclusion of contractual arrangements, in particular by focusing on elements such as the criticality or importance of the services supported by the envisaged ICT contract, the necessary supervisory approvals or other conditions, the possible concentration risk entailed, as well as applying due diligence in the process of selection and assessment of ICT third-party service providers and assessing potential conflicts of interest. For contractual arrangements concerning critical or important functions, financial entities should take into consideration the use by ICT third-party service providers of the most up-to-date and highest information security standards. Termination of contractual arrangements could be prompted at least by a series of circumstances showing shortfalls at the ICT third-party service provider level, in particular significant breaches of laws or contractual terms, circumstances revealing a potential alteration of the performance of the functions provided for in the contractual arrangements, evidence of weaknesses of the ICT third-party service provider in its overall ICT risk management, or circumstances indicating the inability of the relevant competent authority to effectively supervise the financial entity.[111]

Competition and concentration

5.30 To address the systemic impact of ICT third-party concentration risk, DORA promotes a balanced solution by means of taking a flexible and gradual approach to such concentration risk since the imposition of any rigid caps or strict limitations might hinder the conduct of business and restrain the contractual freedom. Financial entities should thoroughly assess their envisaged contractual arrangements to identify the likelihood of such risk emerging, including by means of in-depth analyses of subcontracting arrangements, in particular when concluded with ICT third-party service providers established in a third country. At this stage, and with a view to striking a fair balance between the imperative of preserving contractual freedom and that of guaranteeing financial stability, it is not considered appropriate to set out rules on strict caps and limits to ICT third-party exposures. In the context of the Oversight Framework, a Lead Overseer, appointed pursuant to DORA, should, in respect to critical ICT third-party service providers, pay particular attention to fully grasp the magnitude of interdependences, discover specific instances where a high degree of concentration of critical ICT third-party service providers in the Union is likely to put a strain on the European financial system's stability and integrity and maintain a dialogue with critical ICT third-party service providers where that specific risk is identified.[112]

111 Recital 66, DORA.
112 Recital 67, DORA.

Key providers and provisions

5.31 When renegotiating contractual arrangements to seek alignment with the requirements of DORA, financial entities and ICT third-party service providers should ensure the coverage of the key contractual provisions as provided for in DORA.[113]

Irrespective of the criticality or importance of the function supported by the ICT services, contractual arrangements should, in particular, provide for a specification of the complete descriptions of functions and services, of the locations where such functions are provided and where data is to be processed, as well as an indication of service level descriptions. Other essential elements to enable a financial entity's monitoring of ICT third-party risk are: contractual provisions specifying how the accessibility, availability, integrity, security and protection of personal data are ensured by the ICT third-party service provider, provisions laying down the relevant guarantees for enabling the access, recovery and return of data in the case of insolvency, resolution or discontinuation of the business operations of the ICT third-party service provider, as well as provisions requiring the ICT third-party service provider to provide assistance in case of ICT incidents in connection with the services provided, at no additional cost or at a cost determined ex-ante; provisions on the obligation of the ICT third-party service provider to fully cooperate with the competent authorities and resolution authorities of the financial entity; and provisions on termination rights and related minimum notice periods for the termination of the contractual arrangements, in accordance with the expectations of competent authorities and resolution authorities.[114]

Additional key provisions

5.32 In addition to such contractual provisions, and with a view to ensuring that financial entities remain in full control of all developments occurring at third-party level which may impair their ICT security, the contracts for the provision of ICT services supporting critical or important functions should also provide for the following: the specification of the full service level descriptions, with precise quantitative and qualitative performance targets, to enable without undue delay appropriate corrective actions when the agreed service levels are not met; the relevant notice periods and reporting obligations of the ICT third-party service provider in the event of developments with a potential material impact on the ICT third-party service provider's ability to effectively provide their respective ICT services; a requirement upon the ICT third-party service provider to implement and test business contingency plans and have ICT security measures, tools and policies allowing for the secure provision of services, and to participate and fully cooperate in the threat-led penetration testing (TLPT) carried out by the financial entity.[115]

113 Recital 69, DORA.
114 Recital 71, DORA.
115 Recital 72, DORA.

Access

5.33 Contracts for the provision of ICT services supporting critical or important functions should also contain provisions enabling the rights of access, inspection and audit by the financial entity, or an appointed third party, and the right to take copies as crucial instruments in the financial entities' ongoing monitoring of the ICT third-party service provider's performance, coupled with the service provider's full cooperation during inspections. Similarly, the competent authority of the financial entity should have the right, based on notices, to inspect and audit the ICT third-party service provider, subject to the protection of confidential information.[116]

Exit and transition

5.34 Such contractual arrangements should also provide for dedicated exit strategies to enable, in particular, mandatory transition periods during which ICT third-party service providers should continue providing the relevant services with a view to reducing the risk of disruptions at the level of the financial entity, or to allow the latter effectively to switch to the use of other ICT third-party service providers or, alternatively, to change to in-house solutions, consistent with the complexity of the provided ICT service. Moreover, financial entities within the scope of Directive 2014/59[117] should ensure that the relevant contracts for ICT services are robust and fully enforceable in the event of resolution of those financial entities. Therefore, in line with the expectations of the resolution authorities, those financial entities should ensure that the relevant contracts for ICT services are resolution resilient. As long as they continue meeting their payment obligations, those financial entities should ensure, among other requirements, that the relevant contracts for ICT services contain clauses for non-termination, non-suspension and non-modification on grounds of restructuring or resolution.[118]

Standard clauses

5.35 Moreover, the voluntary use of standard contractual clauses developed by public authorities or European institutions, in particular the use of contractual clauses developed by the Commission for cloud computing services could provide further comfort to the financial entities and ICT third-party service providers, by enhancing their level of legal certainty regarding the use of cloud computing services in the financial sector, in full alignment with the requirements and expectations set out by the Union financial services law. The development of standard contractual clauses builds on measures already envisaged in the 2018 Fintech Action Plan that announced the Commission's intention to encourage

116 Recital 72, DORA.
117 Directive 2014/59/EU establishing a framework for the recovery and resolution of credit institutions and investment firms.
118 Recital 73, DORA.

and facilitate the development of standard contractual clauses for the use of cloud computing services outsourcing by financial entities, drawing on cross-sectorial cloud computing services stakeholders' efforts, which the Commission has facilitated with the help of the financial sector's involvement.[119]

Consolidated regulatory effects

5.36 With a view to promoting convergence and efficiency in relation to supervisory approaches when addressing ICT third-party risk in the financial sector, as well as to strengthening the digital operational resilience of financial entities which rely on critical ICT third-party service providers for the provision of ICT services that support the supply of financial services, and thereby to contributing to the preservation of the Union's financial system stability and the integrity of the internal market for financial services, critical ICT third-party service providers should be subject to a Union Oversight Framework. While the setup of the Oversight Framework is justified by the added value of taking action at European level and by virtue of the inherent role and specificities of the use of ICT services in the provision of financial services, it should be recalled, at the same time, that this solution appears suitable only in the context of this Regulation specifically dealing with digital operational resilience in the financial sector.[120] However, such Oversight Framework should not be regarded as a new model for European supervision in other areas of financial services and activities.[121]

Oversight and criticality

5.37 The Oversight Framework should apply only to critical ICT third-party service providers. There should therefore be a designation mechanism to take into account the dimension and nature of the financial sector's reliance on such ICT third-party service providers. That mechanism should involve a set of quantitative and qualitative criteria to set the criticality parameters as a basis for inclusion in the Oversight Framework. In order to ensure the accuracy of that assessment, and regardless of the corporate structure of the ICT third-party service provider, such criteria should, in the case of an ICT third-party service provider that is part of a wider group, take into consideration the entire ICT third-party service provider's group structure. On the one hand, critical ICT third-party service providers, which are not automatically designated by virtue of the application of those criteria, should have the possibility to opt in to the Oversight Framework on a voluntary basis, on the other hand, ICT third-party service providers, that are already subject to oversight mechanism frameworks supporting the fulfilment of the tasks of the European System of Central Banks as referred to in Article 127(2) TFEU, should be exempted.[122]

119 Recital 74, DORA.
120 Recital 75, DORA.
121 Recital 76, DORA.
122 Recital 77, DORA.

Direct services

5.38 Similarly, financial entities providing ICT services to other financial entities, while belonging to the category of ICT third-party service providers under DORA, should also be exempted from the Oversight Framework since they are already subject to supervisory mechanisms established by the relevant Union financial services law. Where applicable, competent authorities should take into account, in the context of their supervisory activities, the ICT risk posed to financial entities by financial entities providing ICT services. Likewise, due to the existing risk monitoring mechanisms at group level, the same exemption should be introduced for ICT third-party service providers delivering services predominantly to the entities of their own group. ICT third-party service providers providing ICT services solely in one Member State to financial entities that are active only in that Member State should also be exempted from the designation mechanism because of their limited activities and lack of cross-border impact.[123]

Digital transformation

5.39 The digital transformation experienced in financial services has brought about an unprecedented level of use of, and reliance upon, ICT services. Since it has become inconceivable to provide financial services without the use of cloud computing services, software solutions and data-related services, the European financial ecosystem has become intrinsically co-dependent on certain ICT services provided by ICT service suppliers. Some of those suppliers, innovators in developing and applying ICT based technologies, play a significant role in the delivery of financial services, or have become integrated into the financial services value chain. They have thus become critical to the stability and integrity of the European financial system. This widespread reliance on services supplied by critical ICT third-party service providers, combined with the interdependence of the information systems of various market operators, create a direct, and potentially severe, risk to the European financial services system and to the continuity of delivery of financial services if critical ICT third-party service providers were to be affected by operational disruptions or major cyber incidents. Cyber incidents have a distinctive ability to multiply and propagate throughout the financial system at a considerably faster pace than other types of risk monitored in the financial sector and can extend across sectors and beyond geographical borders. They have the potential to evolve into a systemic crisis, where trust in the financial system has been eroded due to the disruption of functions supporting the real economy, or to substantial financial losses, reaching a level which the financial system is unable to withstand, or which requires the deployment of heavy shock absorption measures. To prevent these scenarios from taking place and thereby endangering the financial stability and integrity of the EU, it is essential to provide the convergence of supervisory practices relating

123 Recital 78, DORA.

to ICT third-party risk in finance, in particular through new rules enabling the Union oversight of critical ICT third-party service providers.[124]

Oversight of critical services

5.40 The Oversight Framework largely depends on the degree of collaboration between the Lead Overseer and the critical ICT third-party service provider delivering to financial entities services affecting the supply of financial services. Successful oversight is predicated, inter alia, upon the ability of the Lead Overseer to effectively conduct monitoring missions and inspections to assess the rules, controls and processes used by the critical ICT third-party service providers, as well as to assess the potential cumulative impact of their activities on financial stability and the integrity of the financial system. At the same time, it is crucial that critical ICT third-party service providers follow the Lead Overseer's recommendations and address its concerns. Since a lack of cooperation by a critical ICT third-party service provider providing services that affect the supply of financial services, such as the refusal to grant access to its premises or to submit information, would ultimately deprive the Lead Overseer of its essential tools in appraising ICT third-party risk, and could adversely impact the financial stability and the integrity of the financial system, it is necessary to also provide for a commensurate sanctioning regime.[125]

Subsidiaries

5.41 The requirement to set up a subsidiary in the Union should not prevent the critical ICT third-party service provider from supplying ICT services and related technical support from facilities and infrastructure located outside Europe. This Regulation does not impose a data localisation obligation as it does not require data storage or processing to be undertaken in Europe.[126]

Global service providers

5.42 Critical ICT third-party service providers should be able to provide ICT services from anywhere in the world, not necessarily or not only from premises located in the Union. Oversight activities should be first conducted on premises located in the Europe and by interacting with entities located in Europe, including the subsidiaries established by critical ICT third-party service providers pursuant to DORA. However, such actions within Europe might be insufficient to allow the Lead Overseer to fully and effectively perform its duties under DORA. The Lead Overseer should therefore also be able to exercise its relevant oversight powers in third countries. Exercising those powers in third countries should allow

124 Recital 81, DORA.
125 Recital 82, DORA.
126 Recital 82, DORA.

the Lead Overseer to examine the facilities from which the ICT services or the technical support services are actually provided or managed by the critical ICT third-party service provider, and should give the Lead Overseer a comprehensive and operational understanding of the ICT risk management of the critical ICT third-party service provider. The possibility for the Lead Overseer, as a European agency, to exercise powers outside the territory of the EU should be duly framed by relevant conditions, in particular the consent of the critical ICT third-party service provider concerned. Similarly, the relevant authorities of the third country should be informed of, and not have objected to, the exercise on their own territory of the activities of the Lead Overseer. However, in order to ensure efficient implementation, and without prejudice to the respective competences of the European institutions and the Member States, such powers also need to be fully anchored in the conclusion of administrative cooperation arrangements with the relevant authorities of the third country concerned. DORA should, therefore, enable the ESAs to conclude administrative cooperation arrangements with the relevant authorities of third countries, which should not otherwise create legal obligations in respect of the EU and its Member States.[127]

Contact designation

5.43 To facilitate communication with the Lead Overseer and to ensure adequate representation, critical ICT third-party service providers which are part of a group should designate one legal person as their coordination point.[128]

Additional oversight

5.44 The Oversight Framework should be without prejudice to Member States' competence to conduct their own oversight or monitoring missions in respect to ICT third-party service providers which are not designated as critical under DORA, but which are regarded as important at national level.[129]

Regulatory expertise

5.45 To promote convergence at international level as regards the use of best practices in the review and monitoring of ICT third-party service providers' digital risk management, the ESAs should be encouraged to conclude cooperation arrangements with relevant supervisory and regulatory third country authorities.[130]

127 Recital 83, DORA.
128 Recital 84, DORA.
129 Recital 85, DORA.
130 Recital 94, DORA.

ESA mandate

5.46 To leverage the specific competences, technical skills and expertise of staff specialising in operational and ICT risk within the competent authorities, the three ESAs and, on a voluntary basis, the competent authorities under Directive 2022/2555, the Lead Overseer should draw on national supervisory capabilities and knowledge and set up dedicated examination teams for each critical ICT third-party service provider, pooling multidisciplinary teams in support of the preparation and execution of oversight activities, including general investigations and inspections of critical ICT third-party service providers, as well as for any necessary follow up thereto.[131]

Reporting formats

5.47 Regulatory technical standards should ensure the consistent harmonisation of the requirements laid down in this Regulation. In their roles as bodies endowed with highly specialised expertise, the ESAs should develop draft regulatory technical standards which do not involve policy choices, for submission to the Commission. Regulatory technical standards should be developed in the areas of ICT risk management, major ICT-related incident reporting, testing, as well as in relation to key requirements for a sound monitoring of ICT third-party risk. The Commission and the ESAs should ensure that those standards and requirements can be applied by all financial entities in a manner that is proportionate to their size and overall risk profile, and the nature, scale and complexity of their services, activities and operations.[132]

Payment systems

5.48 To facilitate the comparability of reports on major ICT-related incidents and major operational or security payment-related incidents, as well as to ensure transparency regarding contractual arrangements for the use of ICT services provided by ICT third-party service providers, the ESAs should develop draft implementing technical standards establishing standardised templates, forms and procedures for financial entities to report a major ICT-related incident and a major operational or security payment-related incident, as well as standardised templates for the register of information. When developing those standards, the ESAs should take into account the size and the overall risk profile of the financial entity, and the nature, scale and complexity of its services, activities and operations.[133]

131 Recital 95, DORA.

132 Recital 99, DORA. The Commission should be empowered to adopt those regulatory technical standards by means of delegated acts pursuant to Article 290 TFEU and in accordance with Articles 10 to 14 of Regulations 1093/2010, 1094/2010 and 1095/2010.

133 Recital 100, DORA.

Contagion

5.49 The potential systemic cyber risk associated with the use of ICT infrastructures that enable the operation of payment systems and the provision of payment processing activities should be duly addressed at Union level through harmonised digital resilience rules. To that effect, the Commission should swiftly assess the need for reviewing the scope of this Regulation while aligning such review with the outcome of the comprehensive review envisaged under Directive 2015/2366.[134] Numerous large-scale attacks over the past decade demonstrate how payment systems have become exposed to cyber threats. Placed at the core of the payment services chain and showing strong interconnections with the overall financial system, payment systems and payment processing activities acquired a critical significance for the functioning of the Union financial markets. Cyber attacks on such systems can cause severe operational business disruptions with direct repercussions on key economic functions, such as the facilitation of payments, and indirect effects on related economic processes. Until a harmonised regime and the supervision of operators of payment systems and processing entities are put in place at European level, Member States may, with a view to applying similar market practices, draw inspiration from the digital operational resilience requirements laid down by DORA, when applying rules to operators of payment systems and processing entities supervised under their own jurisdictions.[135]

134 Directive (EU) 2015/2366 on payment services in the internal market, amending Directives 2002/65/EC, 2009/110/EC and 2013/36/EU and Regulation (EU) No 1093/2010, and repealing Directive 2007/64/EC.

135 Recital 104, DORA.

CHAPTER 6

Regulatory Reports and Reporting

INTRODUCTION

6.01 Regulatory reporting is important for a number of reasons, such as financial stability, corporate returns, market transparency, outsourcing and other disclosures. While such mandatory reporting is important in and of itself, the nature of such reporting becomes more onerous and detailed as the entities concerned get larger. Certain sectors, such as the financial sector, also have more enhanced regulatory reporting obligations as they are deemed more important enterprises to the wider economy. These financial entities must now also consider DORA from the perspective of identifying the mandatory reports that must be made to regulators or supervisory authorities – on top of all of the pre-existing reporting obligations. It is also important to consider what the required contents of each specific new DORA report will be. Some of these new DORA reports require complicated and exact details to be included.[1] If some pertinent details are missing, this could be viewed as a breach equal to not reporting at all.

In addition to the reporting obligations imposed on the financial entities themselves, there are also reporting obligations imposed on the national regulator or supervisory authorities. A further form of regulatory reporting also arises for the EU Commission.

REQUIREMENTS ON REPORTS

6.02 Article 1 of DORA refers to various focus areas or subject matters. These areas include reporting issues. For example, it states 'this Regulation lays down uniform requirements concerning the security of network and information systems supporting the business processes of financial entities as follows' and refers to:

- 'reporting of major ICT-related incidents and notifying, on a voluntary basis, significant cyber threats to the competent authorities'; and
- 'reporting of major operational or security payment-related incidents to the competent authorities by financial entities referred to in Article 2(1), points (a) to (d)'.

1 Indeed, there has been some criticism levelled at some of the complicated nature of certain of the reporting requirements. Arguably this is at least somewhat justified given that the ESAs and certain national supervisory authorities have engaged in beta testing exercises based on the initial draft version of some of the reporting formats.

Article 2 refers to 'data reporting service providers' being within scope of the Regulation. Data reporting service providers means a data reporting service provider within the meaning of Regulation 600/2014, as referred to in Article 2(1)(34) to (36) thereof.

The competent authorities shall consider the application of the proportionality principle by financial entities when reviewing the consistency of the information and communication technology (ICT) risk management framework on the basis of the reports submitted upon the request of competent authorities pursuant to Articles 6(5) and 16(2).[2]

Article 28 refers to general and key principals in relation to the management of ICT third-party risk. It provides that '[a]s part of their ICT risk management framework, financial entities shall maintain and update at entity level, and at sub-consolidated and consolidated levels, a register of information in relation to all contractual arrangements on the use of ICT services provided by ICT third-party service providers.'[3]

It is also provided that '[f]inancial entities shall make available to the competent authority, upon its request, the full register of information or, as requested, specified sections thereof, along with any information deemed necessary to enable the effective supervision of the financial entity.'[4]

Subsequently it is provided that 'The ESAs shall, through the Joint Committee, develop draft implementing technical standards to establish the standard templates for the purposes of the register of information referred to in paragraph 3, including information that is common to all contractual arrangements on the use of ICT services. The ESAs shall submit those draft implementing technical standards to the Commission by 17 January 2024.'[5]

The ESA's have also developed a very detailed template for what the register of information should look like and also what information categories it should contain. Many financial entities have been concerned at the complexity of the indicative register of information developed by the ESAs. At this stage it is not yet final and there is beta testing being undertaken with certain test firms in various countries. The purpose of the test is to see what problems or difficulty areas arise and to try to iron these out before January 2025. It remains to be seen if these efforts will be successful. It is also important that any lessons learned and amendments are made well in advance of January 2025 to be effective and user friendly for firms.

2 Article 4(3), DORA.
3 Article 28(3), DORA.
4 Article 28(3), DORA.
5 Article 28(9), DORA.

POLICY ON REPORTS

Divergent reporting problems

6.03 ICT-related incident reporting thresholds and taxonomies vary significantly at national level.[6] Some common ground may be achieved through the relevant work undertaken by the European Union Agency for Cybersecurity (ENISA)[7] and the Cooperation Group under Directive 2022/2555.[8] However, divergent approaches on setting the thresholds and use of taxonomies still exist, or can emerge, for the remainder of financial entities.[9] Due to those divergences, there are multiple requirements that financial entities must comply with.[10] This is especially when operating across several territories and when part of a financial group. These divergences have the potential to hinder the creation of further uniform or centralised European mechanisms that speed up the reporting process and support a quick and smooth exchange of information between competent authorities.[11] This type of awareness and reporting can be quite crucial for addressing ICT risk in the event of large-scale attacks with potentially systemic consequences.[12]

Reporting of incidents

6.04 It is important that competent authorities are able to fulfil their supervisory roles by acquiring a complete overview of the nature, frequency, significance and impact of ICT-related incidents. Similarly important is the need to enhance the exchange of information between relevant public authorities, including law enforcement authorities and resolution authorities. In view of these necessities, DORA should lay down a robust ICT-related incident reporting regime whereby the relevant requirements address current gaps in financial services law, and remove existing overlaps and duplications to alleviate costs. It is essential to harmonise the ICT related incident reporting regime by requiring all financial entities to report to their competent authorities through a single streamlined framework as set out in DORA. In addition, the ESAs should be empowered to further specify relevant elements for the ICT-related incident reporting framework, such as taxonomy, timeframes, data sets, templates and applicable thresholds. To ensure full consistency with Directive 2022/2555, financial entities should be allowed, on a voluntary basis, to notify significant

6 Recital 22, DORA.
7 The European Union Agency for Cybersecurity (ENISA) was established by Regulation (EU) 2019/881 of the European Parliament and of the Council.
8 Directive (EU) 2022/2555 on measures for a high common level of cybersecurity across the Union, amending Regulation (EU) No 910/2014 and Directive (EU) 2018/1972, and repealing Directive (EU) 2016/1148 (NIS 2 Directive).
9 Recital 22, DORA.
10 Recital 22, DORA.
11 Recital 22, DORA.
12 Recital 22, DORA.

cyber threats to the relevant competent authority, when they consider that the cyber threat is of relevance to the financial system, service users or clients.[13]

Bad actor motivation

6.05 The bad actors propagating cyber attacks often do so to pursue financial gains directly at the source, thus exposing financial entities to significant consequences. To prevent ICT systems from losing integrity or becoming unavailable, and hence to avoid data breaches and damage to physical ICT infrastructure, the reporting of major ICT-related incidents by financial entities should be significantly improved and streamlined. ICT-related incident reporting should be harmonised through the introduction of a requirement for all financial entities to report directly to their relevant competent authorities. Where a financial entity is subject to supervision by more than one national competent authority, Member States should designate a single competent authority as the addressee of such reporting. Credit institutions classified as significant in accordance with Regulation 1024/2013[14] should submit such reporting to the national competent authorities, which should subsequently transmit the report to the European Central Bank (ECB).[15]

Timing and sharing

6.06 The direct reporting should enable financial supervisors to have immediate access to information about major ICT-related incidents. Financial supervisors should in turn pass on details of major ICT related incidents to public non-financial authorities (such as competent authorities and single points of contact (under Directive 2022/2555), national data protection authorities, and to law enforcement authorities for major ICT-related incidents of a criminal nature), in order to enhance such authorities' awareness of such incidents and, in the case of computer security incident response teams, to facilitate prompt assistance that may be given to financial entities, as appropriate. Member States should, in addition, be able to determine that financial entities themselves should provide such information to public authorities outside the financial services area. Those information flows should allow financial entities to swiftly benefit from any relevant technical input, advice about remedies, and subsequent follow-up from such authorities. The information on major ICT-related incidents should be mutually channelled. Financial supervisors should provide all necessary feedback or guidance to the financial entity, while the European Supervisory Authorities (ESAs) should share anonymised data on cyber threats and vulnerabilities relating to an incident, to aid wider collective defence.[16]

13 Recital 24, DORA.

14 In accordance with Article 6(4) of Regulation (EU) No 1024/2013 of 15 October 2013 conferring specific tasks on the European Central Bank concerning policies relating to the prudential supervision of credit institutions.

15 Recital 51, DORA.

16 Recital 52, DORA.

Incidents and reports vary

6.07 While all financial entities should be required to carry out incident reporting, that requirement is not expected to affect all of them in the same manner. Indeed, relevant materiality thresholds, as well as reporting timelines, should be duly adjusted, in the context of delegated acts based on the regulatory technical standards to be developed by the ESAs, with a view to covering only major ICT-related incidents. In addition, the specificities of financial entities should be taken into account when setting timelines for reporting obligations.[17]

Critical incident reporting

6.08 The ESAs should be tasked with assessing the feasibility and conditions for a possible centralisation of ICT-related incident reports at European level. This centralisation could consist of a single EU Hub for major ICT-related incident reporting either directly receiving relevant reports and automatically notifying national competent authorities, or merely centralising relevant reports forwarded by the national competent authorities and thus fulfilling a coordination role. The ESAs should be tasked with preparing, in consultation with the ECB and ENISA, a joint report exploring the feasibility of setting up a single EU Hub.[18]

Register of information

6.09 The conduct of such monitoring should follow a strategic approach to ICT third-party risk formalised through the adoption by the financial entity's management body (generally the Board) of a dedicated ICT third-party risk strategy, rooted in a continuous screening of all ICT third-party dependencies. To enhance supervisory awareness of ICT third-party dependencies, and with a view to further supporting the work in the context of the Oversight Framework established by DORA, all financial entities should be required to maintain a register of information with all contractual arrangements about the use of ICT services provided by ICT third-party service providers. Financial supervisors should be able to request the full register, or to ask for specific sections of the register of information, and therefore, to obtain essential information for acquiring a broader understanding of the ICT dependencies of financial entities.[19]

Skills

6.10 To leverage the specific competences, technical skills and expertise of staff specialising in operational and ICT risk within the competent authorities, the three ESAs and, on a voluntary basis, the competent authorities under Directive

17 Recital 53, DORA.
18 Recital 55, DORA.
19 Recital 65, DORA.

2022/2555, the Lead Overseer should draw on national supervisory capabilities and knowledge and set up dedicated examination teams for each critical ICT third-party service provider, pooling multidisciplinary teams in support of the preparation and execution of oversight activities, including general investigations and inspections of critical ICT third-party service providers, as well as for any necessary follow ups.[20]

20 Recital 95, DORA.

CHAPTER 7

Investigations

INTRODUCTION

7.01 While inspections and investigations are often perceived as an inconvenience (at best) for companies, their existence is a fact of life. Similar to other regulations, DORA created the power and ability for regulators and or supervisory authorities to carry out inspections and investigations.

While these may indeed arise when a problem issue has arisen, or is suspected, it is more often the case that they arise by way of regular or routine oversight activities without any specific problem issue being suspected.

Regulators and supervisory authorities would also point out that such activities are also an effort to protect and safeguard the sector generally, and hence have indirect but positive impacts for each individual entity in the sector. In addition, and this is reflected in the intentions of a variety of financial and other regulation (but particularly financial regulations), these obligations enhance wider public and consumer trust in the sector.

REQUIREMENTS ON INVESTIGATIONS

7.02 Article 28(6) provides that in exercising access, inspection and audit rights over the information and communication technology (ICT) third-party service provider, financial entities shall, on the basis of a risk-based approach, predetermine the frequency of audits and inspections as well as the areas to be audited through adhering to commonly accepted audit standards in line with any supervisory instruction on the use and incorporation of such audit standards.[1]

Firms must also ensure the right to monitor, on an ongoing basis, the ICT third-party service provider's performance, which entails the following, namely:

- the obligation of the ICT third-party service provider to fully cooperate during the onsite inspections and audits performed by the competent authorities, the Lead Overseer, financial entity or an appointed third party;[2] and

1 Article 28(6), DORA.
2 Article 30(3)(e)(i), DORA.

- the obligation to provide details on the scope, procedures to be followed and frequency of such inspections and audits.[3]

There are also specific provision as regards inspections and microenterprises.[4]

Article 35, referring to the power of the Lead Overseer, provides that there is a power to conduct general investigations and inspections.[5] General investigations are referred to in Article 38. In order to carry out its duties under DORA, the Lead Overseer may, where necessary, conduct investigations of critical ICT third-party service providers.[6]

The national regulators will also have various power of oversight, investigation, and inspection.

POLICY ON INVESTIGATIONS

Collaboration

7.03 The Oversight Framework largely depends on the degree of collaboration between the Lead Overseer and the critical ICT third-party service provider delivering to financial entities services affecting the supply of financial services. Successful oversight is predicated, inter alia, upon the ability of the Lead Overseer to effectively conduct monitoring missions and inspections to assess the rules, controls and processes used by the critical ICT third-party service providers, as well as to assess the potential cumulative impact of their activities on financial stability and the integrity of the financial system. At the same time, it is crucial that critical ICT third-party service providers follow the Lead Overseer's recommendations and address its concerns. Since a lack of cooperation by a critical ICT third-party service provider providing services that affect the supply of financial services, such as the refusal to grant access to its premises or to submit information, would ultimately deprive the Lead Overseer of its essential tools in appraising ICT third-party risk, and could adversely impact the financial stability and the integrity of the financial system, it is necessary to also provide for a commensurate sanctioning regime.[7]

Communication

7.04 To facilitate communication with the Lead Overseer and to ensure adequate representation, critical ICT third-party service providers which are part of a group should designate one legal person as their coordination point.[8]

3 Article 30(3)(e)(ii), DORA.
4 Article 30(3)(f)(i), DORA.
5 Article 35(1)(b), DORA.
6 Article 38(1), DORA.
7 Recital 82, DORA.
8 Recital 84, DORA.

National efforts

7.05 The Oversight Framework should be without prejudice to Member States' competence to conduct their own oversight or monitoring missions in respect to ICT third-party service providers which are not designated as critical under this Regulation, but which are regarded as important at national level.[9]

European oversight

7.06 To ensure that critical ICT third-party service providers are appropriately and effectively overseen on a European level, DORA provides that any of the three European Supervisory Authorities (ESAs) could be designated as a Lead Overseer. The individual assignment of a critical ICT third-party service provider to one of the three ESAs should result from an assessment of the preponderance of financial entities operating in the financial sectors for which that ESA has responsibilities. This approach should lead to a balanced allocation of tasks and responsibilities between the three ESAs, in the context of exercising the oversight functions, and should make the best use of the human resources and technical expertise available in each of the three ESAs.[10]

Powers

7.07 Lead Overseers should be granted the necessary powers to conduct investigations, to carry out onsite and offsite inspections at the premises and locations of critical ICT third-party service providers and to obtain complete and updated information. Those powers should enable the Lead Overseer to acquire real insight into the type, dimension and impact of the ICT third-party risk posed to financial entities and ultimately to the Union's financial system. Entrusting the ESAs with the lead oversight role is a prerequisite for understanding and addressing the systemic dimension of ICT risk in finance. The impact of critical ICT third-party service providers on the European financial sector and the potential issues caused by the ICT concentration risk entailed call for taking a collective approach at Union level. The simultaneous carrying out of multiple audits and access rights, performed separately by numerous competent authorities, with little or no coordination among them, would prevent financial supervisors from obtaining a complete and comprehensive overview of ICT third-party risk in Europe, while also creating redundancy, burden and complexity for critical ICT third-party service providers if they were subject to numerous monitoring and inspection requests.[11]

9 Recital 85, DORA.
10 Recital 87, DORA.
11 Recital 88, DORA.

Rights

7.08 Due to the significant impact of being designated as critical, the Regulation should ensure that the rights of critical ICT third-party service providers are observed throughout the implementation of the Oversight Framework. Prior to being designated as critical, such providers should, for example, have the right to submit to the Lead Overseer a reasoned statement containing any relevant information for the purposes of the assessment related to their designation. Since the Lead Overseer should be empowered to submit recommendations on ICT risk matters and suitable remedies thereto, which include the power to oppose certain contractual arrangements ultimately affecting the stability of the financial entity or the financial system, critical ICT third-party service providers should also be given the opportunity to provide, prior to the finalisation of those recommendations, explanations regarding the expected impact of the solutions, envisaged in the recommendations, on customers that are entities falling outside the scope of DORA and to formulate solutions to mitigate risks. Critical ICT third-party service providers disagreeing with the recommendations should submit a reasoned explanation of their intention not to endorse the recommendation. Where such reasoned explanation is not submitted or where it is considered to be insufficient, the Lead Overseer should issue a public notice summarily describing the matter of non-compliance.[12]

Verifying compliance

7.09 Competent authorities should duly include the task of verifying substantive compliance with recommendations issued by the Lead Overseer in their functions with regard to prudential supervision of financial entities. Competent authorities should be able to require financial entities to take additional measures to address the risks identified in the Lead Overseer's recommendations, and should, in due course, issue notifications to that effect. Where the Lead Overseer addresses recommendations to critical ICT third-party service providers that are supervised under Directive 2022/2555, the competent authorities should be able, on a voluntary basis and before adopting additional measures, to consult the competent authorities under that Directive in order to foster a coordinated approach to dealing with the critical ICT third-party service providers in question.[13]

Oversight principles

7.10 The exercise of the oversight should be guided by three operational principles seeking to ensure:

12 Recital 89, DORA.
13 Recital 90, DORA.

- close coordination among the ESAs in their Lead Overseer roles, through a joint oversight network (JON);
- consistency with the framework established by Directive 2022/2555 (through a voluntary consultation of bodies under that Directive to avoid duplication of measures directed at critical ICT third-party service providers); and
- application of diligence to minimise the potential risk of disruption to services provided by the critical ICT third-party service providers to customers that are entities falling outside the scope of DORA.[14]

Risk management obligations remain

7.11 The Oversight Framework should not replace, or in any way or for any part substitute for, the requirement for financial entities to manage themselves the risks entailed by the use of ICT third-party service providers, including their obligation to maintain an ongoing monitoring of contractual arrangements concluded with critical ICT third-party service providers. Similarly, the Oversight Framework should not affect the full responsibility of financial entities for complying with, and discharging, all the legal obligations laid down in this Regulation and in the relevant financial services law.[15]

Shared expertise

7.12 To leverage the specific competences, technical skills and expertise of staff specialising in operational and ICT risk within the competent authorities, the three ESAs and, on a voluntary basis, the competent authorities under Directive 2022/2555, the Lead Overseer should draw on national supervisory capabilities and knowledge and set up dedicated examination teams for each critical ICT third-party service provider, pooling multidisciplinary teams in support of the preparation and execution of oversight activities, including general investigations and inspections of critical ICT third-party service providers, as well as for any necessary follow up thereto.[16]

Oversight costs

7.13 Whereas costs resulting from oversight tasks would be fully funded from fees levied on critical ICT third-party service providers, the ESAs are. however, likely to incur, before the start of the Oversight Framework, costs for the implementation of dedicated ICT systems supporting the upcoming oversight, since dedicated ICT systems would need to be developed and deployed beforehand. Therefore, DORA provides for a hybrid funding model, whereby the

14 Recital 91, DORA.
15 Recital 92, DORA.
16 Recital 95, DORA.

Oversight Framework would, as such, be fully fee funded, while the development of the ESAs' ICT systems would be funded from Union and national competent authorities' contributions.[17]

Further regulation on systemic impacts

7.14 In order to further quantify and qualify the criteria for the designation of ICT third-party service providers as critical and to harmonise oversight fees, the power to adopt acts in accordance with Article 290 TFEU should be delegated to the Commission to supplement DORA by further specifying the systemic impact that a failure or operational outage of an ICT third-party service provider could have on the financial entities it provides ICT services to, the number of global systemically important institutions (G-SIIs), or other systemically important institutions (O-SIIs), that rely on the ICT third-party service provider in question, the number of ICT third-party service providers active on a given market, the costs of migrating data and ICT workloads to other ICT third-party service providers, as well as the amount of the oversight fees and the way in which they are to be paid. It is of particular importance that the Commission carry out appropriate consultations during its preparatory work, including at expert level, and that those consultations be conducted in accordance with the principles laid down in the Interinstitutional Agreement on Better Law Making[18] In particular, to ensure equal participation in the preparation of delegated acts, the European Parliament and the Council should receive all documents at the same time as Member States' experts, and their experts should systematically have access to meetings of Commission expert groups dealing with the preparation of delegated acts.[19]

17 Recital 96, DORA.

18 The Interinstitutional Agreement of 13 April 2016 on Better Law-Making.

19 Recital 98, DORA.

CHAPTER 8

Fines, Penalties, Prosecutions

INTRODUCTION

8.01 Entities need to be particularly mindful of the potential for fines, penalties and prosecutions which come with the new DORA requirements. This may be especially so for information and communication technology (ICT) service suppliers. There are various policy level reasons for these to arise, but at a headline level it is to assist, encourage, or even require compliance with the DORA rules. If they are not present, official (and possibly legal policymakers) may fear that a lessor level of compliance may arise.

There will also be a complimentary inherent obligation on entities to appropriately assess the exact manner in which the above requirements, powers, and provisions are drafted and formulated. This will also occur with professional legal advisors assisting financial entities as and when required. Such matters are the kinds of issues which will come to be considered in exacting detail in submissions and pleadings when more contentious and court related matters arise. Penalties in the nature of daily fines and turnover thresholds can arise.[1]

There is also an additional aspect of DORA to consider in the context of this chapter, which relates to international issues and large-scale international ICT service providers. Care has been taken to ensure that there is optimum assistance and compliance in these types of circumstances.

REQUIREMENTS ON FINES, PENALTIES, PROSECUTIONS

8.02 Article 35 refers to the powers of the Lead Overseer. It states that '[i] n the event of whole or partial non-compliance with the measures required to be taken pursuant to the exercise of the powers under paragraph 1, points (a), (b) and (c), and after the expiry of a period of at least 30 calendar days from the date on which the critical ICT third-party service provider received notification of the respective measures, the Lead Overseer shall adopt a decision imposing a periodic penalty payment to compel the critical ICT third-party service provider to comply with those measures.'[2]

1 See Article 35(6), (7) and (8), DORA. Also note other subsections therein, including for example subparagraph (11).

2 Article 35(6), DORA.

It continues that '[t]he periodic penalty payment ... shall be imposed on a daily basis until compliance is achieved and for no more than a period of six months following the notification of the decision to impose a periodic penalty payment to the critical ICT third-party service provider.'[3]

In addition, '[t]he amount of the periodic penalty payment, calculated from the date stipulated in the decision imposing the periodic penalty payment, shall be up to 1% of the average daily worldwide turnover of the critical ICT third-party service provider in the preceding business year.'[4]

When determining the amount of the penalty payment, the Lead Overseer shall take into account the following criteria regarding non-compliance with the measures referred to in Article 35(6), namely:

- the gravity and the duration of non-compliance;
- whether non-compliance has been committed intentionally or negligently; and
- the level of cooperation of the ICT third-party service provider with the Lead Overseer.[5]

In order to ensure a consistent approach, the Lead Overseer shall engage in consultation within the Joint Oversight Network (JON).[6]

The form and nature of the penalty payments are also described. The penalty payments shall be 'of an administrative nature and shall be enforceable.'[7] Enforcement is governed by the rules of civil procedure in force in the Member State on the territory of which inspections and access shall be carried out. Courts of the Member State concerned shall have jurisdiction over complaints related to irregular conduct of enforcement. The amounts of the penalty payments shall be allocated to the general budget of the EU.[8]

In terms of transparency, the Lead Overseer will disclose to the public every periodic penalty payment that has been imposed, unless such disclosure would seriously jeopardise the financial markets or cause disproportionate damage to the parties involved.[9]

Prior to a periodic penalty payment, the Lead Overseer will 'give the representatives of the critical ICT third-party service provider subject to the proceedings the opportunity to be heard on the findings and shall base its

3 Article 35(7), DORA.
4 Article 35(8), DORA.
5 Article 35(8), DORA.
6 Article 35(8), DORA.
7 Article 35(9), DORA.
8 Article 35(9), DORA.
9 Article 35(10), DORA.

decisions only on findings on which the critical ICT third-party service provider subject to the proceedings has had an opportunity to comment.'[10]

Article 37 refers to requests for information from supervisory authorities to financial firms. It refers to how when requiring by decision to supply information, the Lead Overseer shall 'indicate the periodic penalty payments provided for in Article 35(6) where the production of the required information is incomplete or when such information is not provided within the time limit referred to in point (d) of this paragraph.'[11]

When investigating, the Lead Overseer shall 'exercise their powers upon production of a written authorisation specifying the subject matter and purpose of the investigation.'[12] 'That authorisation shall also indicate the periodic penalty payments provided for in Article 35(6) where the production of the required records, data, documented procedures or any other material, or the answers to questions asked to representatives of the ICT third-party service provider are not provided or are incomplete.'[13]

Representatives of the critical ICT third-party service providers are required to submit to the investigations on the basis of a decision of the Lead Overseer.[14] The decision must specify 'the subject matter and purpose of the investigation, the periodic penalty payments provided for ..., the legal remedies available' under Regulations 1093/2010, 1094/2010 and 1095/2010, and the right to have the decision reviewed by the Court of Justice.[15]

Article 39 refers to the inspections. It provides that '[t]he officials and other persons authorised by the Lead Overseer shall exercise their powers upon production of a written authorisation specifying the subject matter and the purpose of the inspection, and the periodic penalty payments provided for in Article 35(6) where the representatives of the critical ICT third-party service providers concerned do not submit to the inspection.'[16]

It is further specified that '[t]he critical ICT third-party service provider shall submit to on-site inspections ordered by decision of the Lead Overseer. The decision shall specify the subject matter and purpose of the inspection, fix the date on which the inspection shall begin and shall indicate the periodic penalty payments provided for in Article 35(6), the legal remedies available under Regulations 1093/2010, 1094/2010 and 1095/2010, as well as the right to have the decision reviewed by the Court of Justice.'[17]

10 Article 35(11), DORA.
11 Article 37(3)(e), DORA.
12 Article 38(3), DORA.
13 Article 38(3), DORA.
14 Article 38(4), DORA.
15 Article 38(4), DORA.
16 Article 39(2), DORA.
17 Article 39(6), DORA.

Penalties are also referred to in Article 51. It is provided that '[c]ompetent authorities, when determining the type and level of an administrative penalty or remedial measure to be imposed under Article 50, shall take into account the extent to which the breach is intentional or results from negligence, and all other relevant circumstances, including' a list of specified matters.[18] The matters specified are as follows, namely:

- the materiality, gravity and the duration of the breach;
- the degree of responsibility of the natural or legal person responsible for the breach;
- the financial strength of the responsible natural or legal person;
- the importance of profits gained or losses avoided by the responsible natural or legal person, insofar as they can be determined;
- the losses for third parties caused by the breach, insofar as they can be determined;
- the level of cooperation of the responsible natural or legal person with the competent authority, without prejudice to the need to ensure disgorgement of profits gained or losses avoided by that natural or legal person; and
- previous breaches by the responsible natural or legal person.[19]

DORA also makes provision for criminal penalties. Member States may decide not to lay down rules for administrative penalties or remedial measures for breaches that are subject to criminal penalties under their national law.[20] The same provision also states that '[w]here Member States have chosen to lay down criminal penalties for breaches of this Regulation, they shall ensure that appropriate measures are in place so that competent authorities have all the necessary powers to liaise with judicial, prosecuting, or criminal justice authorities within their jurisdiction to receive specific information related to criminal investigations or proceedings commenced for breaches of this Regulation, and to provide the same information to other competent authorities, as well as the European Banking Authority, the European Securities and Markets Authority or the European Insurance and Occupational Pensions Authority to fulfil their obligations to cooperate for the purposes of the Regulation.'[21]

The administrative penalties may also be published.[22] Competent authorities 'shall publish' on their official websites, without undue delay, 'any decision imposing an administrative penalty' against which there is no appeal after the addressee of the penalty has been notified of that decision.[23]

18 Article 51(2), DORA.
19 Article 51(2), DORA.
20 Article 52(1), DORA.
21 Article 52(2), DORA.
22 Article 54, DORA.
23 Article 54(1), DORA.

The publication shall include information on the type and nature of the breach, the identity of the persons responsible and the penalties imposed.[24]

Where the competent authority, following a case-by-case assessment, considers that the publication of the identity, in the case of legal persons, or of the identity and personal data, in the case of natural persons, would be disproportionate, including risks in relation to the protection of personal data, jeopardise the stability of financial markets or the pursuit of an ongoing criminal investigation, or cause, insofar as these can be determined, disproportionate damages to the person involved, it shall adopt one of a number of specified options.[25] The following solutions are listed in respect of the decision imposing an administrative penalty:

- defer its publication until all reasons for non-publication cease to exist;
- publish it on an anonymous basis, in accordance with national law; or
- refrain from publishing it, where the options set out in bullet points one and two are deemed either insufficient to guarantee a lack of any danger for the stability of financial markets, or where such a publication would not be proportionate to the leniency of the imposed penalty.[26]

In the case of a decision to publish an administrative penalty on an anonymous basis in accordance with bullet point two, the publication of the relevant data may be postponed.[27]

Where a competent authority publishes a decision imposing an administrative penalty against which there is an appeal before the relevant judicial authorities, competent authorities shall immediately add on their official website that information and, at later stages, any subsequent related information on the outcome of such appeal.[28] Any judicial decision annulling a decision imposing an administrative penalty shall also be published.[29]

However, competent authorities must ensure that any such publication shall remain on their official website only for the period which is necessary to bring forth Article 54.[30] There is also a maximum period specified. The period shall not exceed five years after its publication.[31]

24 Article 54(2), DORA.
25 Article 54(3), DORA.
26 Article 54(3), DORA.
27 Article 54(4), DORA.
28 Article 54(5), DORA.
29 Article 54(5), DORA.
30 Article 54(6), DORA.
31 Article 54(6), DORA.

POLICY ON FINES, PENALTIES, PROSECUTIONS

Engagement

8.03 The Oversight Framework largely depends on the degree of collaboration between the Lead Overseer and the critical ICT third-party service provider delivering to financial entities services affecting the supply of financial services. Successful oversight is predicated, inter alia, upon the ability of the Lead Overseer to effectively conduct monitoring missions and inspections to assess the rules, controls and processes used by the critical ICT third-party service providers, as well as to assess the potential cumulative impact of their activities on financial stability and the integrity of the financial system. At the same time, it is crucial that critical ICT third-party service providers follow the Lead Overseer's recommendations and address its concerns. Since a lack of cooperation by a critical ICT third-party service provider providing services that affect the supply of financial services, such as the refusal to grant access to its premises or to submit information, would ultimately deprive the Lead Overseer of its essential tools in appraising ICT third-party risk, and could adversely impact the financial stability and the integrity of the financial system, it is necessary to also provide for a commensurate sanctioning regime.[32]

New fines and penalties

8.04 Against this background, the need of the Lead Overseer to impose penalty payments to compel critical ICT third-party service providers to comply with the transparency and access-related obligations set out in the Regulation should not be jeopardised by difficulties raised by the enforcement of those penalty payments in relation to critical ICT third-party service providers established in third countries. In order to ensure the enforceability of such penalties, and to allow a swift roll out of procedures upholding the critical ICT third-party service providers' rights of defence in the context of the designation mechanism and the issuance of recommendations, those critical ICT third-party service providers, providing services to financial entities that affect the supply of financial services, should be required to maintain an adequate business presence in Europe. Due to the nature of the oversight, and the absence of comparable arrangements in other jurisdictions, there are no suitable alternative mechanisms ensuring this objective by way of effective cooperation with financial supervisors in third countries in relation to the monitoring of the impact of digital operational risks posed by systemic ICT third-party service providers, qualifying as critical ICT third-party service providers established in third countries. Therefore, in order to continue its provision of ICT services to financial entities in the Union, an ICT third-party service provider established in a third country which has been designated as critical in accordance with DORA should undertake, within 12 months of such designation, all necessary arrangements to ensure its incorporation within the Union, by means of establishing a subsidiary, as defined throughout the Union acquis, namely in Directive 2013/34.33

32 Recital 82, DORA.
33 Recital 81, DORA.

PART B:

DORA

CHAPTER 9

The Digital Operational Resilience Act

OVERVIEW

9.01 DORA amounts to 79 pages of technical, legal, and policy text, with 106 detailed Recitals and 64 formal Articles containing mandatory legal rules. The Recitals provide context, background and assistance in understanding each of the formal legal rules contained in the Articles. The rules set out in the Articles are spread across a number of different themes. Financial and technology supplier and service companies must consider each of these broad themes and what is required of them in terms of their business activities.

TITLE

9.02 The formal title of DORA is Regulation (EU) 2022/2554 of the European Parliament and of the Council of 14 December 2022 on digital operational resilience for the financial sector and amending Regulations (EC) No 1060/2009, (EU) No 648/2012, (EU) No 600/2014, (EU) No 909/2014 and (EU) 2016/1011.

The introductory heading also recognises the European Parliament and the Council of the European Union, the Treaty on the Functioning of the European Union, and in particular Article 114 thereof, the proposal from the European Commission, the transmission of the draft legislative act to the national parliaments, the opinion of the European Central Bank, the opinion of the European Economic and Social Committee, and the ordinary legislative procedure.

DORA CHAPTER THEMES

9.03 The nine formal DORA Chapters relate to the following categories of issues:

- general provisions;
- ICT risk management;
- ICT-related incident management, classification and reporting;
- digital operational resilience testing;
- managing of ICT third-party risk;
- information sharing arrangements;

- competent authorities;
- delegated acts; and
- transitional and final provisions.

DORA CHAPTER DETAILS

9.04 Chapter 1 of DORA contains detailed provisions relating to:

- subject matter (Article 1);
- scope (Article 2);
- definitions (Article 3);
- proportionality principle (Article 4); and
- governance and organisation (Article 5).

Chapter 2 of DORA contains detailed provisions relating to:

- ICT risk management framework (Article 6);
- ICT systems, protocols and tools (Article 7);
- identification (Article 8);
- protection and prevention (Article 9);
- detection (Article 10);
- response and recovery (Article 11);
- backup policies and procedures, restoration and recovery procedures and methods (Article 12);
- learning and evolving (Article 13);
- communication (Article 14);
- further harmonisation of ICT risk management tools, methods, processes and policies (Article 15); and
- simplified risk management framework (Article 16).

Chapter 3 of DORA contains detailed provisions relating to:

- ICT-related incident management process (Article 17);
- classification of ICT-related incidents and cyber threats (Article 18);
- reporting of major ICT-related incidents and voluntary notification of significant cyber threats (Article 19);
- harmonisation of reporting content and templates (Article 20);
- centralisation of reporting of major ICT-related incidents (Article 21);

- supervisory feedback (Article 22); and
- operational or security payment-related incidents concerning credit institutions, payment institutions account information service providers, and electronic money institutions (Article 23).

Chapter 4 of DORA contains detailed provisions relating to:

- general requirements for the performance of digital operational resilience testing (Article 24);
- testing of ICT tools and systems (Article 25);
- advanced testing of ICT tools, systems and processes based on threat-led penetration testing (TLPT) (Article 26); and
- requirements for testers for the carrying out of TLPT (Article 27).

Chapter 5 of DORA contains detailed provisions relating to the:

- general principles [re managing of ICT third-party risk] (Article 28);
- preliminary assessment of ICT concentration risk at entity level (Article 29);
- key contractual provisions (Article 30);
- designation of critical ICT third-party services providers (Article 31);
- structure of the Oversight Framework (Article 32);
- tasks of Lead Overseer (Article 33);
- operational coordination between Lead Overseers (Article 34);
- powers of Lead Overseer (Article 35);
- exercise of the powers of the Lead Overseer outside the Union (Article 36);
- request for information (Article 37);
- general investigations (Article 38);
- inspections (Article 39);
- ongoing oversight (Article 40);
- harmonisation of conditions enabling the conduct of the oversight activities (Article 41);
- follow up by competent authority (Article 42);
- oversight fees (Article 43); and
- international cooperation (Article 44).

Chapter 6 of DORA contains provision relating to information sharing arrangements on cyber threat information and intelligence (Article 45).

Chapter 7 of DORA contains detailed provisions relating to:

- competent authorities (Article 46);
- cooperation with structures and authorities established by Directive 2022/2555 (Article 47);
- cooperation between authorities (Article 48);
- financial cross-sector exercises, communication and cooperation (Article 49);
- administrative penalties and remedial measures (Article 50);
- exercise of the power to impose administrative penalties and remedial measures (Article 51);
- criminal penalties (Article 52);
- notification duties (Article 53);
- publication of administrative penalties (Article 54);
- professional secrecy (Article 55); and
- data protection (Article 56).

Chapter 8 of DORA contains provision relating to the exercise of the delegation (Article 57).

Chapter 9 of DORA contains detailed provisions relating to:

- review clause (Article 58);
- amendments to Regulation 1060/2009 (Article 59);
- amendments to Regulation (648/2012 (Article 60);
- amendments to Regulation 909/2014 (Article 61);
- amendments to Regulation 600/2014 (Article 62);
- amendment to Regulation 2016/1011 (Article 63); and
- entry into force and application (Article 64).

DORA PILLARS

9.05 Supervisory authorities and commentators have referred to DORA and the above Chapters as referring to five Pillars. These are referred to as:

- Pillar 1: ICT Risk Management
- Pillar 2: Incident Reporting
- Pillar 3: Testing
- Pillar 4: Third-Party Risk Management
- Pillar 5: Information Sharing

The Articles and Pillars align as follows.

- Pillar 1 (ICT Risk Management) aligns with Articles 5–16.
- Pillar 2 (Incident Reporting) aligns with Articles 17–23.
- Pillar 3 (Testing) aligns with Articles 24–27.
- Pillar 4 (Third-Party Risk Management) aligns with Articles 28–44.
- Pillar 5 (Information Sharing) aligns with Article 45.

DORA LEVEL 1

9.06 Companies must also be aware that they need to be compliant with two levels of DORA. The main DORA rules, or Level 1, are contained in DORA.

DORA LEVEL 2

9.07 In addition to the main DORA rules, companies must also be aware of and comply with a second set of rules sitting below DORA, hence referred to as Level 2.

The Level 2 DORA rules are developed by the three European Supervisory Authorities, namely the European Banking Authority, the European Insurance and Occupational Pensions Authority and the European Securities and Markets Authority (ESAs), and the Commission. Some are developed by the Commission directly and some are initially drafted by the ESAs and then finalised and promulgated by the Commission.

The intention behind the Level 2 rules is to add more detailed technical specification to certain more formal requirements contained at Level 1.

These Level 2 rules are further separated into:

- Regulatory Technical Standards or RTS;
- Implementing Technical Standards or ITS;
- Guidelines; and
- (independent) Commission Delegated Regulations.

The range of these added Level 2 rules has added to the already complicated nature of the technical and regulatory compliance efforts required of firms. An additional difficulty is that the Level 2 rules have come out over different time periods. The ones that are developed by the ESAs generally need to be reviewed, amended and implemented by the Commission. While the ESAs had a specific (split) timetable, the Commission has not had to specify when it would finalise the Level 2 rules at its end. Overall, the rules have come out at different time periods, thus adding added difficulties for firms. Indeed, even as the end of 2024 approaches, not all Level 2 rules are fully clear – event though the go-live date is January 2025.

The RTS are:

- RTS to specify the policy on ICT services supporting critical or important functions provided by ICT third-party services (drafted by ESAs, apparently awaiting a Commission implementing measure);
- RTS on threat led penetrating testing (TLPT) (drafted by ESAs, apparently awaiting a Commission implementing measure);
- RTS and ITS on content timelines and templates on incident reporting (drafted by ESAs, apparently awaiting a Commission implementing measure);
- RTS on oversight harmonization (drafted by ESAs, apparently awaiting a Commission implementing measure); and
- RTS on Joint Examination Teams (JET) (drafted by ESAs, apparently awaiting a Commission implementing measure).

There is also the following ITS:

- ITS on Register of Information (drafted by ESAs, possibly awaiting a Commission implementing measure).

There are two Guidelines as follows:

- Guidelines on aggregated costs and losses from major incidents (adopted by ESAs); and
- Guidelines on oversight cooperation between ESAs and competition authorities (adopted by ESAs).

There are two Commission Delegated Regulations which do not appear to align with the materials developed by the ESAs and which are independent (but apparently required by DORA), as follows:

- Commission Delegated Regulation (EU) 2024/1502 supplementing Regulation (EU) 2022/2554 by specifying the criteria for the designation of ICT third-party service providers as critical for financial entities; and
- Commission Delegated Regulation (EU) 2024/1505s supplementing Regulation (EU) 2022/2554 by determining the amount of the oversight fees to be charged by the Lead Overseer to critical ICT third-party service providers and the way in which those fees are to be paid.

The above appear or are referenced throughout DORA Level 1, and in what one might describe as a non-user-friendly manner. It may have assisted firms more to have, for example, a clear summary table or schedule attached to DORA. It would have also assisted firms if the ESAs and or the Commission also referenced all of the Level 2 measures in some form of summary manner together.

The Level 2 rules referred to above correspond to particular DORA Articles which provide that the respective Level 2 rule is required to be developed.

CHAPTER 10

General Provisions

GENERAL PROVISIONS

10.01 Chapter I of DORA refers to the General Provisions. These are referred to below.

SUBJECT MATTER

10.02 The scope and breath of DORA rules are very wide indeed. This is confirmed in the introductory sections referring to the subject matter and scope of DORA,

Article 1 sets out the subject matter, and hence the specific focus of DORA. In order to achieve a high common level of digital operational resilience, DORA lays down 'uniform requirements concerning the security of network and information systems supporting the business processes of financial entities.'[1] These are as follows:

(a) requirements applicable to financial entities in relation to:

(i) information and communication technology (ICT) risk management;

(ii) reporting of major ICT-related incidents and notifying, on a voluntary basis, significant cyber threats to the competent authorities;

(iii) reporting of major operational or security payment related incidents to the competent authorities by financial entities referred to in Article 2(1)(a) to (d);

(iv) digital operational resilience testing;

(v) information and intelligence sharing in relation to cyber threats and vulnerabilities; and

(vi) measures for the sound management of ICT third-party risk;[2]

(b) requirements in relation to the contractual arrangements concluded between ICT third-party service providers and financial entities;[3]

1 Article 1(1), DORA.
2 Article 1(1)(d), DORA.
3 Article 1(1)(d), DORA.

(c) rules for the establishment and conduct of the Oversight Framework for critical ICT third-party service providers when providing services to financial entities;[4] and

(d) rules on cooperation among competent authorities, and rules on supervision and enforcement by competent authorities in relation to all matters covered by DORA.[5]

In relation to financial entities identified as essential or important entities pursuant to national rules transposing Article 3 of the NIS Directive,[6] DORA shall be considered a sector specific EU legal act for the purposes of Article 4 of that Directive.[7] While it is indeed focused primarily on the financial sector, it can be noted that the financial sector is very wide, and also that the net of effect is wider still in that a wide range of service suppliers to the financial sector are also impacted.

DORA is without prejudice to the responsibility of Member States' regarding essential State functions concerning public security, defence and national security in accordance with EU law.[8] Many legal regulations give deference to issues of national rules regarding public security, defence and national security. However, the nature of DORA is that it stems, in part, from concern form national and international stability of essential financial systems, and with a keen awareness to some of the potential threats to such stability.

SCOPE

10.03 Article 2 sets out the scope of DORA. Without prejudice to paragraphs (3) and (4) of Article 2, DORA applies to the following entities:

- credit institutions;
- payment institutions, including payment institutions exempted pursuant to Directive 2015/2366;
- account information service providers;
- electronic money institutions, including electronic money institutions exempted pursuant to Directive 2009/110;
- investment firms;

4 Article 1(1)(d), DORA.
5 Article 1(1)(d), DORA.
6 Directive (EU) 2022/2555 on measures for a high common level of cybersecurity across the Union, amending Regulation (EU) No 910/2014 and Directive (EU) 2018/1972, and repealing Directive (EU) 2016/1148 (NIS 2 Directive).
7 Article 1(2), DORA.
8 Article 1(3), DORA.

- crypto asset service providers (as authorised under Regulation 2023/1114 on markets in crypto assets[9]) and issuers of asset referenced tokens;
- central securities depositories;
- central counterparties;
- trading venues;
- trade repositories;
- managers of alternative investment funds;
- management companies;
- data reporting service providers;
- insurance and reinsurance undertakings;
- insurance intermediaries, reinsurance intermediaries and ancillary insurance intermediaries;
- institutions for occupational retirement provision;
- credit rating agencies;
- administrators of critical benchmarks;
- crowdfunding service providers;
- securitisation repositories; and
- ICT third-party service providers.[10]

From the get go, we see that the intention is to encompass almost the entire financial services provider industry, regardless of the individual types of activity.

What is also striking is the clear and direct intention to cast the net even wider. In addition to front line financial firms, the indirect service providers to the financial sector are also intended to be within scope. There is an express reference in the scope to 'ICT third-party providers'. While there is clear immediate focus on the broad range of financial entities referred to in Article 2, and their immediate compliance needs, it is arguable the inclusion of the third-party ICT service providers that will be the most interesting to watch in the coming years.

For the purposes of DORA, entities referred to above (in Article 2(1)(a)–(t), are collectively referred to as 'financial entities'.[11] The is significance in that it is expressly extensive and wide in seeking to capture all or almost all types of financial entities. Most of the categories of financial entities are now distinct and identifiable sub sectors of the wider financial sector.

9 Regulation (EU) 2023/1114 on markets in crypto-assets, and amending Regulations (EU) No 1093/2010 and (EU) No 1095/2010 and Directives 2013/36/EU and (EU) 2019/1937.

10 Article 2(1), DORA.

11 Article 2(2), DORA.

Some may argue that they are not actual financial entities per se, such as 'data reporting service providers.' They may argue, for example, that they are suppliers of service to traditional (and non-traditional) financial entities. The counter argument is that they have become so integral to the activities of core financial sector entities that it is difficult to remove them from the financial services ecosystem. Another argument will centre on the point that the very information that these entities collect and deal is financial related data, and often of a sensitive nature, that their very business is financial orientated in nature.

While the last sector mentioned is 'ICT third-party service providers', this should not diminish our consideration of its significance. Some entities in this category may have wished not to be included at all, and would also make the argument that they themselves are not actually core or traditional financial entities. But in today's modern word they have become indispensable to the business models of many financial entities. It is this reliance and dependence which has raised the concern of regulators and the decision to expressly include them. There is a regulatory concern that they need to be included because of their importance to the continued and smooth operation of the wider financial sector. A secondary consideration is that there is a concern that the important services and activities of such supplier/service entities should not fall outside or between regulatory oversight. DORA will provide certain direct oversight and also the capability to directly oversee and investigate these types of entities. It is fair to say that at least some of the impact on this last category of entities will grow more over subsequent years as compared to the more immediate Big Bang effect on the express financial sector entities referred to above.[12]

Respective financial entities will need to assess whether they fall within one of these categories, and then assuming that they do, a complex process of deciding how best to comply will ensue. In particular situations an entity may wish to decide that it does not fall with the inclusivity definition, but in such circumstances, it will need to be properly recorded that such a decision is made, and also backed up by the considerations and factors which enable such a decision. Appropriate third-party advices may also be required. In most instances, however, it may be difficult to fall outside of these descriptions and definitions, in part because they have been widely and deliberately drafted.

However, in spite of the above DORA states that it does not apply to:

- managers of alternative investment funds as referred to in Article 3(2) of Directive 2011/61;

12 That is not to suggest that there will not be immediate and then ongoing (or growing) effects on the core financial entities. There are certainly immediate issues to be addressed from a compliance perspective. But there will also be important issues to learn, develop and comply with as a greater appreciation for a very complex and important piece of legislation such as DORA. Much will also be learned by financial entities once it becomes clearer over time as to what the regulators expect and what information they require of financial entities – and not least, how frequently.

- insurance and reinsurance undertakings as referred to in Article 4 of Directive 2009/138;
- institutions for occupational retirement provision which operate pension schemes which together do not have more than 15 members in total;
- natural or legal persons exempted pursuant to Articles 2 and 3 of Directive 2014/65;
- insurance intermediaries, reinsurance intermediaries and ancillary insurance intermediaries which are microenterprises or small or medium sized enterprises; and
- post office giro institutions as referred to in Article 2(5), point (3) of Directive 2013/36.[13]

Any firm wishing make such an assessment will need to do so carefully. This will also need to be carefully and adequately recorded.

A note of caution will also be required, in addition, where a firm may be involved in more than one technical activity. While one activity may otherwise fall outside of the scope of DORA, the other activity may bring it into scope. This is in part reflective of the highly complex nature of financial sector activities – and which continue to develop and expand over time. This expansion is organic but also reflective of the increasing use of information technologies.

In addition, Member States may exclude from the scope of DORA entities referred to in Article 2(5), points (4)–(23) of Directive 2013/36 that are located within their respective territories. Where a Member State makes use of such option, it must inform the Commission of this decision, as well as informing of any subsequent changes made. The Commission will make that information publicly available.[14] Again, if a firm was seeking to consider this option, it will need to identify the additional regulatory text, and then make an appropriate assessment, and record such assessment. It would be prudent not to proceed with undue haste in such matters.

DEFINITIONS

10.04 The definitions are the important building block of DORA and how its provisions are to be interpreted. The definitions help to set the scope of what is included in scope and what may then be determined as out of scope. As with all regulatory instruments great importance is attached to reviewing, understanding, and interpreting the definitions. In addition, the later sections of DORA can only be properly understood by referring back to the definitions as the defined terms will be discussed in greater detail and rules in relation to what must happen in terms of compliance are built around the definitions.

13 Article 2(3), DORA.
14 Article 2(4), DORA.

Article 3 sets out the all-important definitions of DORA. For the purposes implementing and complying with DORA, the following definitions apply.

Digital operational resilience

10.05 'Digital operational resilience' means the ability of a financial entity to build, assure and review its operational integrity and reliability by ensuring, either directly or indirectly through the use of services provided by ICT third-party service providers, the full range of ICT-related capabilities needed to address the security of the network and information systems which a financial entity uses, and which support the continued provision of financial services and their quality, including throughout disruptions.[15]

Network and information system

10.06 'Network and information system' means a network and information system as defined in Article 6(1) of Directive 2022/2555.[16] The definitions vary between financial sector terms, compliance and regulatory, and also IT technology. This definition is an example of the later.

Legacy ICT system

10.07 'Legacy ICT system' means an ICT system that has reached the end of its lifecycle (end-of-life), that is not suitable for upgrades or fixes, for technological or commercial reasons, or is no longer supported by its supplier or by an ICT third-party service provider, but that is still in use and supports the functions of the financial entity.[17] One of the important issues associated with legacy IT systems and legacy components is that there can sometimes be greater risk associated. If the system is significantly older it may not be as safe, robust, and secure as a more modern system. It may not be supported to the same level, or even at all. It may be more complex or clunky in its architecture and functionality. All of these create operational type risk, but regulators will also be keenly aware that some older legacy systems may present greater opportunities of attack for errant third-party hackers. DORA is making assessment that financial entities need to be aware of these enhanced risks, and also undertake the specific precautions which DORA prescribed for when a financial entity may be utilising such a system. While this is certainly an import aspect of DORA presently, it is predicted that its importance will become even more amplified in future and as our experience with DORA matures. It is also noted that these considerations can also have implications wider than DORA directly.

15 Article 3(1), DORA.
16 Article 3(2), DORA.
17 Article 3(3), DORA.

Security of network and information systems

10.08 'Security of network and information systems' means security of network and information systems as defined in Article 6(2) of Directive 2022/2555.[18] The consideration of this clause and how it is to be interpreted may cause some headaches, notwithstanding its obvious importance. However, greater guidance is provider subsequently. Having said that, issues will remain in terms of determining what is secure, what is not secure, and the range of levels of security in between. Much attention will inevitably focus upon how regulators wish to decide these interpretative issues – and the consequences for determinations as regards failures to comply.

ICT risk

10.09 'ICT risk' means any reasonably identifiable circumstance in relation to the use of network and information systems which, if materialised, may compromise the security of the network and information systems, of any technology dependent tool or process, of operations and processes, or of the provision of services by producing adverse effects in the digital or physical environment.[19] This is an important definition, and in some ways gets to the very rationale at the heart of DORA and why policymakers set about developing DORA in the first instance. This should always be kept in mind even when dealing with the later provisions and associated compliance efforts. ICT risk is also a component of wider risk issues to be addressed by financial entities.

Information asset

10.10 'Information asset' means a collection of information, either tangible or intangible, that is worth protecting.[20] This recognises the importance of information and financial data to the financial sector, customers, and the wider economy. It is also frequently associated with the following definition.

ICT asset

10.11 'ICT asset' means a software or hardware asset in the network and information systems used by the financial entity.[21] This recognises the importance of ICT assets and technology to the daily operation and continued wellbeing of financial sector services. This raises a number of issues. In the first instance, it means that firms need to assess, consider, and provide for their ICT assets. It will also be necessary to consider which of these are more important than others.

18 Article 3(4), DORA.
19 Article 3(5), DORA.
20 Article 3(6), DORA.
21 Article 3(7), DORA.

When considering this issue, and the terms of the definition, some firms may also realise that certain parts of the technology chain and information chain which may have previously been less considered (dare I say under considered) will need to be consider more formally.

ICT-related incident

10.12 'ICT-related incident' means a single event or a series of linked events unplanned by the financial entity that compromises the security of the network and information systems, and have an adverse impact on the availability, authenticity, integrity or confidentiality of data, or on the services provided by the financial entity.[22] This raises a number of issues and consideration in the DORA context. Ideally, a firm will want to prevent such an incident arising – and indeed DORA requires safety and precautionary safeguards. But operational resilience also recognises that incidents can occur and that entities need to also have measures in place to enhance and optimise their processes for dealing with such incidents which occur. One of the background factors to the development of DORA is the impact of such incidents to firms, but also the increasing potential impact for the wider economy. There is also at least implicit recognition that the scale of effect from bad actor attacks is increasing in some instances, and also that the volume of such attacks is also increasing. Recent AI technologies also make it easier for bad actors to develop and propagate such attacks. This later phenomenon is not necessarily at the forefront of the concerns of DORA regulators or the text of DORA, but is certainly encompassed. Over time, the regulators may give more expressed attention to this developing issue.

Operational or security payment-related incident

10.13 'Operational or security payment-related incident' means a single event or a series of linked events unplanned by the financial entities referred to in Article 2(1)(a) to (d), whether ICT related or not, that has an adverse impact on the availability, authenticity, integrity or confidentiality of payment-related data, or on the payment-related services provided by the financial entity.[23] This exemplifies how the details of DORA can get into quite exacting details as regards particular financial sector activities. This definition will apply to some financial entities more than others.

Major ICT-related incident

10.14 'Major ICT-related incident' means an ICT-related incident that has a high adverse impact on the network and information systems that support critical

22 Article 3(8), DORA.
23 Article 3(9), DORA.

or important functions of the financial entity.[24] It is clear that some incident can cause more disruption than others. Some incidents may also be localised to one entity while other may affect more than one entity. The number of customers affected can also vary. In addition, DORA recognises that some of the most severe incidents can affect not just financial entities but the wider financial system across Europe – and wider still.

Major operational or security payment-related incident

10.15 'Major operational or security payment-related incident' means an operational or security payment-related incident that has a high adverse impact on the payment-related services provided.[25] This again refers to the graduated adverse effects of certain incidents. It also points to the need for financial entities to predetermine the most critical assets and systems in advance, and also to assess the gravity of incidents when they occur. This is focused on a particular aspect of activity but again highlights the graduated nature of effects of incidents that may occur.

Cyber threat

10.16 'Cyber threat' means 'cyber threat' as defined in Article 2(8) of Regulation 2019/881.[26] This is one of the particular ICT risks that DORA is concerned with, and which financial entities must consider. However, as the number and nature of such threats are ever increasing (AI being perhaps a good example), financial entities must constantly evolve there understanding, awareness, and preventative and operational resilience measures. Just because a firm is operationally resilient today, does not mean that it will not have gaps in its operational resilience in one or two years from now. Examples are outdated procedures regarding legacy systems, and a failure to have implemented the most up to date software patches.

Significant cyber threat

10.17 'Significant cyber threat' means a cyber threat the technical characteristics of which indicate that it could have the potential to result in a major ICT-related incident or a major operational or security payment-related incident.[27] Some cyber threats are so important because of the damage than can ensure, that greater preventative and resilience measures are required.

24 Article 3(10), DORA.
25 Article 3(11), DORA.
26 Article 3(12), DORA.
27 Article 3(13), DORA.

Cyber-attack

10.18 'Cyber-attack' means a malicious ICT-related incident caused by means of an attempt perpetrated by any threat actor to destroy, expose, alter, disable, steal or gain unauthorised access to, or make unauthorised use of, an asset.[28] It should go without saying that cyber attacks can vary in sophistication, intention, and potential adverse effects. A security and compliance solution to one, may not be fully sufficient for another. A constant level of ongoing awareness and associated processes is required. This leads to the following definition and associated processes.

Threat intelligence

10.19 'Threat intelligence' means information that has been aggregated, transformed, analysed, interpreted or enriched to provide the necessary context for decision making and to enable relevant and sufficient understanding in order to mitigate the impact of an ICT-related incident or of a cyber threat, including the technical details of a cyber attack, those responsible for the attack and their modus operandi and motivations.[29]

Vulnerability

10.20 'Vulnerability' means a weakness, susceptibility or flaw of an asset, system, process or control that can be exploited.[30] This is an important concept and emphasises that firms must not just focus on bad actors but also the vulnerabilities which create potential attack vectors for bad actors. Operational related vulnerabilities can also create risk for potential disruption to operations and services which are unrelated to attack vectors and bad actors.

Threat-led penetration testing

10.21 'Threat-led penetration testing (TLPT)' means a framework that mimics the tactics, techniques and procedures of real-life threat actors perceived as posing a genuine cyber threat, that delivers a controlled, bespoke, intelligence-led (red team) test of the financial entity's critical live production systems.[31] Interestingly, there is no definition of pen testing and TLPT. DORA does, however, introduce the dual concepts of (general) pen testing and advanced pen testing – the latter of which appears to be more complex, stringent, and costly and which must be undertaken in conjunction with regulators. While the importance of pen testing per se is clear, the manner of how these concepts are included and described in

28 Article 3(14), DORA.
29 Article 3(15), DORA.
30 Article 3(16), DORA.
31 Article 3(17), DORA.

DORA has raised some confusion with the financial sector as to how and when they apply. Some feel that it is not fully clear that the more stringent advanced test only applies in a more limited set of situations. There are significant cost and practical considerations arising, and especially for smaller and even mid-size financial entities. Given that financial entities can see different interpretation arising in the context of pen testing, it would assist if greater clarity and guidance was available.

ICT third-party risk

10.22 'ICT third-party risk' means an ICT risk that may arise for a financial entity in relation to its use of ICT services provided by ICT third-party service providers or by subcontractors of the latter, including through outsourcing arrangements.[32] This is one of the core concerns at the heart of DORA, and which involved a number of DORA obligations for financial entities – as well as the third-party service providers. It is predicted that these types of issues will take some time to fully bed down. Indeed, this understanding is reflected in various provisions of DORA, such as enforcement, costs, and penalties.

ICT third-party service provider

10.23 'ICT third-party service provider' means an undertaking providing ICT services.[33] This definition goes wider than some may have initially understood. It refers to ICT services, not ICT financial services.

ICT intra group service provider

10.24 'ICT intra-group service provider' means an undertaking that is part of a financial group and that provides predominantly ICT services to financial entities within the same group or to financial entities belonging to the same institutional protection scheme, including to their parent undertakings, subsidiaries, branches or other entities that are under common ownership or control.[34] This will require to be considered in group settings.

ICT services

10.25 'ICT services' means digital and data services provided through ICT systems to one or more internal or external users on an ongoing basis, including hardware as a service and hardware services which includes the provision of

32 Article 3(18), DORA.
33 Article 3(19), DORA.
34 Article 3(20), DORA.

technical support via software or firmware updates by the hardware provider, excluding traditional analogue telephone services.[35]

Critical or important function

10.26 'Critical or important function' means a function, the disruption of which would materially impair the financial performance of a financial entity, or the soundness or continuity of its services and activities, or the discontinued, defective or failed performance of that function would materially impair the continuing compliance of a financial entity with the conditions and obligations of its authorisation, or with its other obligations under applicable financial services law.[36] This requires careful and formalised exercises on the part of financial entities – and which must be replicated on an ongoing basis.

Critical ICT third-party service provider

10.27 'Critical ICT third-party service provider' means an ICT third-party service provider designated as critical in accordance with Article 31.[37] This also requires careful and formalised exercises on the part of financial entities – and which must be replicated on an ongoing basis. It is also reflective of the more focused regulatory concerns at the heart of DORA.

ICT third-party service provider established in third country

10.28 'ICT third-party service provider established in a third country' means an ICT third-party service provider that is a legal person established in a third-country and that has entered into a contractual arrangement with a financial entity for the provision of ICT services.[38] This recognises that such services can be provided from a variety of locations given modern internet and communications technologies.

Subsidiary

10.29 'Subsidiary' means a subsidiary undertaking within the meaning of Article 2(10) and Article 22 of Directive 2013/34.[39]

35 Article 3(21), DORA. There is a broad definition of ICT services, see Recitals 35 and 63.
36 Article 3(22), DORA.
37 Article 3(23), DORA.
38 Article 3(24), DORA.
39 Article 3(25), DORA.

Group

10.30 'Group' means a group as defined in Article 2(11) of Directive 2013/34.[40]

Parent undertaking

10.31 'Parent undertaking' means a parent undertaking within the meaning of Article 2(9) and Article 22 of Directive 2013/34.[41]

ICT subcontractor established in a third country

10.32 'ICT subcontractor established in a third country' means an ICT subcontractor that is a legal person established in a third country and that has entered into a contractual arrangement either with an ICT third-party service provider, or with an ICT third-party service provider established in a third country.[42] Sub-contracting is a very import concern sought to be addressed both in DORA and other regulations.

ICT concentration risk

10.33 'ICT concentration risk' means an exposure to individual or multiple-related critical ICT third-party service providers creating a degree of dependency on such providers so that the unavailability, failure or other type of shortfall of such provider may potentially endanger the ability of a financial entity to deliver critical or important functions, or cause it to suffer other types of adverse effects, including large losses, or endanger the financial stability of the Union as a whole.[43] This is also one of the concerns behind DORA, namely, that a wide range of financial entities can be reliant on a small number of service providers. It is recognised also that intermediaries and service providers can be a secondary or indirect avenue of attack by bad actor attackers. This is recognised by a number of official statements regarding DORA, and while less expressed in DORA itself, it is at least implicitly recognised.

Management body

10.34 'Management body' means a management body as defined in Article 4(1), point (36) of Directive 2014/65, Article 3(1), point (7) of Directive 2013/36, Article 2(1), point (5) of Directive 2009/65, Article 2(1), point (45) of Regulation 909/2014, Articlc 3(1), point (20) of Regulation 2016/1011, and in the relevant

40 Article 3(26), DORA.
41 Article 3(27), DORA.
42 Article 3(28), DORA.
43 Article 3(29), DORA.

provision of Regulation 2023/1114 on markets in crypto-assets, or the equivalent persons who effectively run the entity or have key functions in accordance with relevant Union or national law.[44] The management body is generally the Board of the firm. It is important for the management body to promote the compliance requirements and message of DORA throughout the firm. DORA also refers in more detail as to how the management body can achieve this.

Credit institution

10.35 'Credit institution' means a credit institution as defined in Article 4(1), point (1) of Regulation 575/2013.[45]

Institution exempted pursuant to Directive 2013/36

10.36 'Institution exempted pursuant to Directive 2013/36/EU' means an entity as referred to in Article 2(5), points (4) to (23) of Directive 2013/36.[46]

Investment firm

10.37 'Investment firm' means an investment firm as defined in Article 4(1), point (1) of Directive 2014/65.[47]

Small and non-interconnected investment firm

10.38 'Small and non-interconnected investment firm' means an investment firm that meets the conditions laid out in Article 12(1) of Regulation 2019/2033.[48]

Payment institution

10.39 'Payment institution' means a payment institution as defined in Article 4(4) of Directive 2015/2366.[49]

Payment institution exempted

10.40 'Payment institution exempted pursuant to Directive 2015/2366' means a payment institution exempted pursuant to Article 32(1) of Directive 2015/2366.[50]

44 Article 3(30), DORA.
45 Article 3(31), DORA.
46 Article 3(32), DORA.
47 Article 3(33), DORA.
48 Article 3(34), DORA.
49 Article 3(35), DORA.
50 Article 3(36), DORA.

As mentioned above, when a firm seeks to fall within a section such as this, it must fully consider the basis for same.

Account information service provider

10.41 'Account information service provider' means an account information service provider as referred to in Article 33(1) of Directive 2015/2366.[51]

Electronic money institution

10.42 'Electronic money institution' means an electronic money institution as defined in Article 2(1) of Directive 2009/110.[52] This is an example of how the internet and technology has expanded the financial sector.

Electronic money institution exempted

10.43 'Electronic money institution exempted pursuant to Directive 2009/110/EC' means an electronic money institution benefitting from a waiver as referred to in Article 9(1) of Directive 2009/110.[53] If a firm seeks to fall within a section such as this, it must fully consider the basis for same.

Central counterparty

10.44 'Central counterparty' means a central counterparty as defined in Article 2(1) of Regulation 648/2012.[54] This is one of the concepts where addition DORA provisions apply.

Trade repository

10.45 'Trade repository' means a trade repository as defined in Article 2(2) of Regulation 648/2012.[55]

Central securities depository

10.46 'Central securities depository' means a central securities depository as defined in Article 2(1), point (1) of Regulation 909/2014.[56]

51 Article 3(37), DORA.
52 Article 3(38), DORA.
53 Article 3(39), DORA.
54 Article 3(40), DORA.
55 Article 3(41), DORA.
56 Article 3(42), DORA.

Trading venue

10.47 'Trading venue' means a trading venue as defined in Article 4(1), point (24) of Directive 2014/65.[57]

Manager of alternative investment funds

10.48 'Manager of alternative investment funds' means a manager of alternative investment funds as defined in Article 4(1)(b) of Directive 2011/61.[58]

Management company

10.49 'Management company' means a management company as defined in Article 2(1)(b) of Directive 2009/65.[59]

Data reporting service provider

10.50 'Data reporting service provider' means a data reporting service provider within the meaning of Regulation 600/2014, as referred to in Article 2(1), points (34) to (36) thereof.[60] This is an example of where the definitional ambit of DORA is wider than mere traditional banks.

Insurance undertaking

10.51 'Insurance undertaking' means an insurance undertaking as defined in Article 13(1) of Directive 2009/138.[61]

Reinsurance undertaking

10.52 'Reinsurance undertaking' means a reinsurance undertaking as defined in Article 13(4) of Directive 2009/138.[62]

Insurance intermediary

10.53 'Insurance intermediary' means an insurance intermediary as defined in Article 2(1), point (3) of Directive 2016/97.[63]

57 Article 3(43), DORA.
58 Article 3(44), DORA.
59 Article 3(45), DORA.
60 Article 3(45), DORA.
61 Article 3(47), DORA.
62 Article 3(48), DORA.
63 Article 3(49), DORA.

Ancillary insurance intermediary

10.54 'Ancillary insurance intermediary' means an ancillary insurance intermediary as defined in Article 2(1), point (4) of Directive 2016/97.[64]

Reinsurance intermediary

10.55 'Reinsurance intermediary' means a reinsurance intermediary as defined in Article 2(1), point (5) of Directive 2016/97.[65]

Institution for occupational retirement provision

10.56 'Institution for occupational retirement provision' means an institution for occupational retirement provision as defined in Article 6(1) of Directive 2016/2341.[66]

Small institution for occupational retirement provision

10.57 'Small institution for occupational retirement provision' means an institution for occupational retirement provision which operates pension schemes which together have less than 100 members in total.[67]

Credit rating agency

10.58 'Credit rating agency' means a credit rating agency as defined in Article 3(1)(b) of Regulation 1060/2009.[68] This another example of how the nature of financial information and financial activities has changed in an expansive manner over time.

Crypto asset service provider

10.59 'Crypto-asset service provider' means a crypto-asset service provider as defined in the relevant provision of Regulation 2023/1114 on markets in crypto-assets.[69] DORA is an example of modern regulations which seek to encompass and address the advent of new form 'crypto' currencies and 'crypto' assets.

64 Article 3(50), DORA.
65 Article 3(51), DORA.
66 Article 3(52), DORA.
67 Article 3(53), DORA.
68 Article 3(54), DORA.
69 Article 3(55), DORA.

Issuer of asset referenced tokens

10.60 'Issuer of asset-referenced tokens' means an issuer of asset referenced tokens as defined in the relevant provision of Regulation 2023/1114 on markets in crypto-assets.[70] This is in some way similar to the comments in the above definition.

Administrator of critical benchmarks

10.61 'Administrator of critical benchmarks' means an administrator of 'critical benchmarks' as defined in Article 3(1), point (25) of Regulation 2016/1011.[71] This is another example of a technical financials sector definition.

Crowdfunding service provider

10.62 'Crowdfunding service provider' means a crowdfunding service provider as defined in Article 2(1)(e) of Regulation 2020/1503.[72] This is another example of how DORA seeks to be widely encompassing of newer forms of financial market activities – and which many may not have initially considered to be addressed under 'traditional' form financial regulations.

Securitisation repository

10.63 'Securitisation repository' means a securitisation repository as defined in Article 2(23) of Regulation 2017/2402.[73] This is another specialised area of the wider financial sector.

Microenterprise

10.64 'Microenterprise' means a financial entity, other than a trading venue, a central counterparty, a trade repository or a central securities depository, which employs fewer than 10 persons and has an annual turnover and/or annual balance sheet total that does not exceed €2 million.[74] This is one of the avenues where firms may have at least initially sought to distance themselves from the full ambit of DORA compliance. However, it may not be as wide as many smaller entities may have wished. The financial threshold is arguably low and excludes very few, and in addition if viewed annually, some firms may hover above and below the threshold and therefore need to adopt a cautious approach of compliance.

70 Article 3(56), DORA.
71 Article 3(57), DORA.
72 Article 3(58), DORA.
73 Article 3(59), DORA.
74 Article 3(60), DORA.

Lead Overseer

10.65 'Lead Overseer' means the European Supervisory Authority (ESA) appointed in accordance with Article 31(1)(b) of this Regulation.[75] This is one of the new forms of regulatory oversight in order to police how DORA is complied with. While initially there are a range of Big Bang issues to address, the Lead Overseer and related provisions will become extremely important in the following years. It is an extremely important area of DORA.

Joint Committee

10.66 'Joint Committee' means the committee referred to in Article 54 of Regulations 1093/2010, 1094/2010 and 1095/2010.[76]

Small enterprise

10.67 'Small enterprise' means a financial entity that employs 10 or more persons, but fewer than 50 persons, and has an annual turnover and/or annual balance sheet total that exceeds €2 million, but does not exceed €10 million.[77] This area will be closely scrutinised in order to alleviate some of the compliance burden created by DORA, but may not apply as frequently as some industry entities may have wished for.

Medium-sized enterprise

10.68 'Medium-sized enterprise' means a financial entity that is not a small enterprise and employs fewer than 250 persons and has an annual turnover that does not exceed €50 million and/or an annual balance sheet that does not exceed €43 million.[78] This area will also be closely scrutinised. Many firms will want to understand if they can potentially alleviate some of the compliance burdens created by DORA. But it may not apply as often as some industry entities may have otherwise wished for.

Public authority

10.69 'Public authority' means any government or other public administration entity, including national central banks.[79]

75 Article 3(61), DORA.
76 Article 3(62), DORA.
77 Article 3(63), DORA.
78 Article 3(64), DORA.
79 Article 3(65), DORA.

PROPORTIONALITY AND PROPORTIONALITY PRINCIPLE

10.70 The financial sector is vast, covering many different types of service provider, as articulated in Article 2(1). However, not every firm is on the same scale. Some are multinational household names, some may be national specific or region specific. Yet others may be much smaller and in a single location and also with a limited number of staff and clients. In that regard, some have been concerned as to whether all of the very detailed provisions – and associated obligations – apply to every firm in the in-scope categories referred to.

For such concerned smaller firms, there are a number of helpful provisions. There are some carveouts referred to above. In addition, there is a provision which provides that the obligation must essentially be considered in context and proportional to each individual entity. This implies consideration of the size, scale, and resources of the entity. Article 4 refers to the proportionality principle.[80] Many smaller firms will, therefore, look to the proportionality principle contained in DORA.

Having said that even certain firms who are not the smallest may also have reason to consider the proportionality principle. While the proportionality principle may not do away with obligations per se for larger entities, it may in particular circumstances be helpful in putting limits on how far an entity needs to go in complying with a specific obligation, the length of effort required, or the quantum of expenditure required in so complying. It may help to put a guardrail on disproportionate efforts and disproportionate expenses. This may be far from an exact science however, and much will depend on the specific circumstances, the obligation in question, as well as official guidance which develops over time. It is encouraging however, that prior to the go-live date in January 2025, regulators have been pointing out the applicability of the proportionality principle to those concerned in industry, and advisors to industry.

It is also necessary to look at the specifics of the DORA proportionality principle. The DORA proportionality principle specifically provides that:

- financial entities shall implement the rules laid down in Chapter II of DORA in accordance with the principle of proportionality, taking into account their size and overall risk profile, and the nature, scale and complexity of their services, activities and operations;[81]
- in addition, the application by financial entities of Chapters III, IV and V of DORA, Section I, shall be proportionate to their size and overall risk profile, and to the nature, scale and complexity of their services, activities and operations, as specifically provided for in the relevant rules of those Chapters of DORA;[82] and

80 Proportionality is also referred to in Recitals 12, 22, 36, 38, 39, 40, 42, 43, 44, 53, 64, and 99.
81 Article 4(1), DORA.
82 Article 4(2), DORA.

- the competent authorities shall consider the application of the proportionality principle by financial entities when reviewing the consistency of the ICT Risk Management Framework on the basis of the reports submitted upon the request of competent authorities (ie, the Article 6(5) reports and Article 16(2) reports).[83]

Article 4(1) therefore provides some guidance on what the DORA proportionality principle encompasses, when it refers to:

- the firm's size and overall risk profile; and
- the nature, scale and complexity of the firm's services, activities and operations.

With some justification, some might also argue that some sectors of the wider financial universe are less risky, so to speak, than others. We might consider many differences between them, for example, traditional deposits, investments, and meme stocks. On that basis, some may argue that there is a justified need for the proportionality principle to apply more to certain sectors or activities – seeking to distinguish stable and safer activities across a specific financial sector versus the proportionality principle being limited to the smallest of firms. Even small firms can specialise in new or less stable activities.

It is also helpful for firms to note that the complex ICT Risk Management Frameworks are also specifically referred to in DORA's proportionality principle. It is perhaps unfortunate, however, that Article 4(3) is drafted as it is. This could be argued to limit or conflict with the DORA proportionality principle established above. For example, Articles 4(1) and 4(2) essentially establish the principle and set out what firms can and should be considering. Yes, Article 4(3) says that while regulators must take into account the proportionality principle, it only refers to this in arguably one single context. If this interpretation as followed this may limit the application and utility of the intended principle.

Other industry focused legislation is also known to contain a proportionality focus. This may be somewhat of assistance while the full scope of the DORA proportionality principle comes to be understood and a shared understanding between regulators and industry develops.

GOVERNANCE AND ORGANISATION

10.71 Chapter II of DORA refers to the important concept of ICT risk management. The first section, Section I of Chapter II refers to and is headed 'Governance and Organisation'. The first specific provision in this section is Article 5 – which refers to governance and organisation. It provides as follows:

83 Article 4(3), DORA. The reports submitted upon the request of competent authorities pursuant to Article 6(5) and Article 16(2) of DORA.

- financial entities shall have in place an internal governance and control framework that ensures an effective and prudent management of ICT risk, in accordance with Article 6(4), in order to achieve a high level of digital operational resilience.[84]

Therefore, in order to achieve the required digital operational resilience, a firm must have a governance and control framework for the management of ICT risk. Article 6(1) mandates that firms have a 'ICT Risk Management Framework'. Article 6(4) requires that firms 'shall assign the responsibility for managing and overseeing ICT risk to a control function and ensure an appropriate level of independence of such control function in order to avoid conflicts of interest.' Article 5, therefore, is requiring appropriate allocation of governance oversight, review and or monitoring of the more operational focused aspects of the ICT Risk Management Framework.

To emphasise this even more, Article 5(2) also provides that:

- the management body of the financial entity shall define, approve, oversee and be responsible for the implementation of all arrangements related to the ICT Risk Management Framework[85] referred to in DORA.[86]

For the purposes of the Article 5(1), the management body (generally the Board) shall:

- bear the ultimate responsibility for managing the financial entity's ICT risk;
- put in place policies that aim to ensure the maintenance of high standards of availability, authenticity, integrity and confidentiality, of data;
- set clear roles and responsibilities for all ICT-related functions and establish appropriate governance arrangements to ensure effective and timely communication, cooperation and coordination among those functions;
- bear the overall responsibility for setting and approving the digital operational resilience strategy (as referred to in Article 6(8)), including the determination of the appropriate risk tolerance level of ICT risk of the financial entity, as referred to in DORA;[87]
- approve, oversee and periodically review the implementation of the financial entity's ICT business continuity policy and ICT response and recovery plans (referred to, respectively, in Article 11(1) and (3)), which may be adopted as a dedicated specific policy forming an integral part of the financial entity's overall business continuity policy and response and recovery plan;
- approve and periodically review the financial entity's ICT internal audit plans, ICT audits and material modifications to them;

84 Article 5(1), DORA.
85 The DORA ICT Risk Management Framework is referred to in Article 6(1).
86 Article 5(2), DORA.
87 As referred to in Article 6(8)(b).

- allocate and periodically review the appropriate budget to fulfil the financial entity's digital operational resilience needs in respect of all types of resources, including relevant ICT security awareness programmes and digital operational resilience training referred to in DORA,[88] and ICT skills for all staff;
- approve and periodically review the financial entity's policy on arrangements regarding the use of ICT services provided by ICT third-party service providers; and
- put in place, at corporate level, reporting channels enabling it to be duly informed of the following:
  - (i) arrangements concluded with ICT third-party service providers on the use of ICT services,
  - (ii) any relevant planned material changes regarding the ICT third-party service providers; and
  - (iii) the potential impact of such changes on the critical or important functions subject to those arrangements, including a risk analysis summary to assess the impact of those changes, and at least major ICT-related incidents and their impact, as well as response, recovery and corrective measures.[89]

There is, therefore, a wide range of issues for firms, and the management body in particular, to consider and ensure.

Article 5(3) provides that:

- financial entities, other than microenterprises, shall establish a role in order to monitor the arrangements concluded with ICT third-party service providers on the use of ICT services, or shall designate a member of senior management as responsible for overseeing the related risk exposure and relevant documentation.[90]

This establishes another important obligation. However, on the one hand, it seems to be suggesting the creation of a new role (which often legislation or regulatory guidance mentions it is not mandating) or that the activity for that role be given to an established role holder. On closer examination, however, we see that the provision before the 'or' and after the 'or' are expressed in quite different language and one could question whether they are the same at all. There is an argument for saying that rather there are two requirements, namely:

- establish a role in order to monitor the arrangements concluded with ICT third-party service providers on the use of ICT services; and

88 Relevant ICT security awareness programmes and digital operational resilience training are referred to in Article 13(6) of DORA.

89 Article 5(2), DORA.

90 Article 5(3), DORA.

- designate a member of senior management as responsible for overseeing the related risk exposure and relevant documentation.

In that case, one may query whether there is a need for the 'or' at all, and whether it meaningfully achieves anything. Alternatively, if the 'or' is to mean anything, it may then suggest that firms need to record somewhere which of the two alternatives they decided to implement. If anything, the manner in which the clause is drafted creates additional and unnecessary complications for firms seeking to understand their compliance obligations.

There is also a form of education and training requirement for the management body. Article 5(4) requires as follows, namely:

- members of the management body of the financial entity shall actively keep up to date with sufficient knowledge and skills to understand and assess ICT risk and its impact on the operations of the financial entity, including by following specific training on a regular basis, commensurate to the ICT risk being managed.[91]

Of course, there is also the issue of individual knowledge, expertise, and training and collective knowledge, expertise, and training. Not every single member of the management body should or is expected to have the exact same skillset. Everyone is not expected to be an accountant, or lawyer, or coder. An important part of the requirement, however, is that a training programme is established, and that training is regular and commensurate as appropriate to the issues mentioned.

RISK MANAGEMENT AND ICT RISK MANAGEMENT FRAMEWORK

10.72 Section II of Chapter II of DORA sets out the requirements and obligations in relation to firms as regards having to establish and maintain an ICT Risk Management Framework. This begins with Article 6 of DORA.[92]

The requirements set out within the mandated ICT Risk Management Framework are most extensive. In addition, it is notable that they are the single biggest set of obligations for firms to comply with. While there are certainly additional obligations, the ICT Risk Management Framework will be a significant core of the gap analysis and development exercises that firms will undertake to ensure DORA compliance.

It can also be noted that while DORA references this set of requirements as an ICT Rick Management Framework, it could in practice also be called an IT Risk Management Framework. There is also scope to align the requirements of the ICT Risk Management Framework to existing policies and processes – or even within some of these existing policies and processes. The ICT Risk Management

91 Article 5(4), DORA.

92 The ICT Risk Management Framework is also referred to in Recitals 43, 47, 48, 49, and 50.

Framework can, for example, be an addition to a Risk Management Framework or other policy-related document already existing within the firm – so long as it covers the respective elements set out within the DORA requirements.

However, regardless of the approach adopted by individual firms, they will need to be ready to identify to supervisory authorities and internal auditors how and where the respective requirements of the ICT Risk Management Framework are set out.

The overarching ICT Risk Management Framework requirement is referred to in Article 6 of DORA. This is certainly one of the more detailed and involved requirements of DORA. Article 6(1) begins by requiring the following, namely:

- Financial entities shall have a sound, comprehensive and well-documented ICT Risk Management Framework as part of their overall risk management system, which enables them to address ICT risk quickly, efficiently and comprehensively and to ensure a high level of digital operational resilience.[93]

It is unequivocal, therefore, that firm must now have, if they had not already, an ICT Risk Management Framework. This needs to be considered as one of the cornerstone obligations of DORA. It is also extremely detailed as we will see below. Significant resources are required of firms in understanding the lengthy specific aspects of this obligation, and even more resources in updating and implementing their ICT processes, procedures, and policies.

The next question, and an important one, is what exactly is meant to be contained within an ICT Risk Management Framework. We must examine Article 6(2) to begin to understand the detail and components. It provides that:

- The ICT Risk Management Framework shall include at least strategies, policies, procedures, ICT protocols and tools that are necessary to duly and adequately protect all information assets and ICT assets, including computer software, hardware, servers, as well as to protect all relevant physical components and infrastructures, such as premises, data centres and sensitive designated areas, to ensure that all information assets and ICT assets are adequately protected from risks including damage and unauthorised access or usage.[94]

Note that there is a requirement much more extensive than merely having policies alone. Firm must have in place (at least):

- strategies;
- policies;
- procedures; and
- ICT protocols and tools.

93 Article 6(1), DORA.
94 Article 6(2), DORA.

The latter may or may not mean ICT protocols *and* ICT tools, which could make sense given that these can be distinguished. An ICT protocol may include a predetermined ICT policy that if A happens, do X. An ICT tool may include, for example, a specific anti-virus software tool. The anti-virus software tool can then be configured according to different settings which are sometimes referred to as ICT protocols or policies, eg, if email A arrives, do X, but if email B arrives, do Y.

Many more technically minded people will be familiar with IT and technical policies. These are separate to more corporate-type compliance policies. These are not expressly differentiated in DORA, but both sets of policies are certainly part of the operation and arsenal of defences that modern firms deploy. Arguably both should be differentiated more expressly in terms of the DORA compliance measures. Perhaps, the reference to 'ICT protocols' is a means of avoiding confusion between tech and non-tech policies, but this is not clear.

As it stands, there may be some scope for confusion and for different firms to refer to their defences and digital operational resilience measures in different ways.

There may also be some initial confusion as to what exactly 'strategies' refers to, and how extensive these must be. Some may also ask whether a set of policies is a strategy in itself.

It is clear, however, that the requirement is for a range of multi layered strategies, policies, procedures, etc, some of which may be policy documented and others which are more ICT technical in nature. Regardless of form, however, there is a need for an awareness of all that is in place, and a need for adequate, documented records of these separate items. This will require a range of different contributions across the firm, not just from one person or one function section but from many.

Article 6 also specifies that:

- in accordance with their ICT Risk Management Framework, financial entities shall minimise the impact of ICT risk by deploying appropriate strategies, policies, procedures, ICT protocols and tools.[95]

There is also a related reporting requirement, which specifies that firms:

- shall provide complete and updated information on ICT risk and on their ICT Risk Management Framework to the competent authorities upon their request.[96]

The issue of roles and responsibilities is again referred to, when Article 6(4) specifies that:

- financial entities, other than microenterprises, shall assign the responsibility for managing and overseeing ICT risk to a control function and ensure an

95 Article 6(3), DORA.
96 Article 6(3), DORA.

appropriate level of independence of such control function in order to avoid conflicts of interest. Financial entities shall ensure appropriate segregation and independence of ICT risk management functions, control functions, and internal audit functions, according to the three lines of defence model, or an internal risk management and control model.[97]

There is an express provision that the ICT Risk Management Framework must be documented and reviewed on a regular basis. It must also be reviewed when a significant event occurs or when so directed by a regulator. It provides as follows, namely:

- The ICT Risk Management Framework shall be documented and reviewed at least once a year, or periodically in the case of microenterprises, as well as upon the occurrence of major ICT-related incidents, and following supervisory instructions or conclusions derived from relevant digital operational resilience testing or audit processes. It shall be continuously improved on the basis of lessons derived from implementation and monitoring. A report on the review of the ICT Risk Management Framework shall be submitted to the competent authority upon its request.[98]

As indicated, there are additional requirements to continually evolve the ICT Risk Management Framework and take on board appropriate lessons that have been learned.

In addition, regulators can request/demand to see a documented review (or summary) of the ICT Risk Management Framework. Firms, therefore, need to consider how to go about regular reviews of the ICT Risk Management Framework; and how they are regularly recording and documenting the review of the ICT Risk Management Framework because, inter alia, these review records can be requested by the regulator. While these review records are internal documents and should be systematised, one should expect that in time regulators will ask to see them. Arguably, these will not be the first type of records or reports that regulators will see immediately following the go-live of DORA, given that there are other reports which will undoubtedly be foremost in the mind of regulators. Firms should commence having these records in place nonetheless, as they can be requested and the fact of having a history of such regular documented records will be important in and of itself.

Separate to the regulatory requests for reports and records, there are important internal audit issues to consider. Article 6(6) requires that:

- the ICT Risk Management Framework of financial entities, other than microenterprises, shall be subject to internal audit by auditors on a regular basis in line with the financial entities' audit plan.[99]

97 Article 6(4), DORA.
98 Article 6(5), DORA.
99 Article 6(6), DORA.

In addition, somewhat similar to the requirement of the management body as referred to above, the internal auditors 'shall possess sufficient knowledge, skills and expertise in ICT risk, as well as appropriate independence.'[100] The frequency and focus of 'ICT audits' (presumably ICT internal audits) 'shall be commensurate to the ICT risk of the financial entity'.[101] This latter provision introduces an element of proportionality. What is less clear is what amounts to being commensurate and or proportional, and whom decides this. Another aspect is whether this is subjective, or whether regulators may seek to interpret or otherwise impose an element of an objective standard. Another issue to consider is when the judgement of being commensurate is made. Something may appear to be commensurate at a given moment in time, but if looked at through a different lens and with the benefit of retrospective hindsight, something that may appear correctly commensurate may come to be subjected to critical reappraisal.

In addition to conducting these types of internal audits, there is a requirement which specifies that '[b]ased on the conclusions from the internal audit review, financial entities shall establish a formal follow-up process, including rules for the timely verification and remediation of critical ICT audit findings.'[102] Arguably, many firms and internal audit processes will already do this, but it may be important to consider this specific requirement to ensure that it is fully met and that no inadvertent gaps or discrepancies arise.

DORA requires that the ICT Risk Management Framework includes a digital operational resilience strategy. Article 6(8) specifies that '[t]he ICT Risk Management Framework shall include a digital operational resilience strategy setting out how the framework shall be implemented.'[103] One wonders if this was intended to mean 'the ICT Risk Management Framework shall include a digital operational resilience strategy setting out how digital operational resilience shall be implemented.' If the 'framework' means the ICT Risk Management Framework, one might query if the reference to 'digital operational resilience' in this provision superfluous and confusing. If the intention was to merely say that the ICT Risk Management Framework must include digital operational resilience, this may have been better achieved in a clear stand-alone provision.

The provision also states that, 'the digital operational resilience strategy shall include methods to address ICT risk and attain specific ICT objectives, by meeting' specified criteria (see below).[104] In the first instance, however, note the reference to ICT risk.[105] The issue arises as to whether and how ICT risk is identified, and then whether this must be pre-recorded and documented in advance. To meet the specified criteria, a firm may first have had to undergo the exercise of documenting its ICT risk in order that the actions are directed to the specific ICT risks of the firm.

100 Article 6(6), DORA.
101 Article 6(6), DORA.
102 Article 6(7), DORA.
103 Article 6(8), DORA.
104 Article 6(8), DORA.
105 Article 6(8), DORA.

In addition, there is a reference to 'specific ICT objectives'.[106] Again, the issue arises for firms to consider whether and how they must undergo an exercise to arrive at its own ICT objectives, and how these may need to be documented. Must the actions to meet the criteria be in light of whatever specific ICT objectives will exist for each individual firm.

It is somewhat clearer that 'the digital operational resilience strategy shall include methods to address ICT risk and attain specific ICT objectives, by':

- explaining how the ICT Risk Management Framework supports the financial entity's business strategy and objectives;
- establishing the risk tolerance level for ICT risk, in accordance with the risk appetite of the financial entity, and analysing the impact tolerance for ICT disruptions;
- setting out clear information security objectives, including key performance indicators and key risk metrics;
- explaining the ICT reference architecture and any changes needed to reach specific business objectives;
- outlining the different mechanisms put in place to detect ICT-related incidents, prevent their impact and provide protection from it;
- evidencing the current digital operational resilience situation on the basis of the number of major ICT-related incidents reported and the effectiveness of preventive measures;
- implementing digital operational resilience testing, in accordance with Chapter IV of DORA; and
- outlining a communication strategy in the event of ICT-related incidents, the disclosure of which is required by DORA (in accordance with Article 14).[107]

Financial entities may, in the context of the 'digital operational resilience strategy' referred to in Article 6(8), 'define' (in the sense of document or establish) 'a holistic ICT multi-vendor strategy, at group or entity level, showing key dependencies on ICT third-party service providers and explaining the rationale behind the procurement mix of ICT third-party service providers.'[108] Some of the keynote issues are showing the 'key dependencies' and documenting an explanation of 'the rationale' for choosing the specific ICT third-party service providers engaged.

It is also provided that '[f]inancial entities may, in accordance with Union and national sectoral law, outsource the tasks of verifying compliance with ICT risk management requirements to intra-group or external undertakings.'[109] It

106 Article 6(8), DORA.
107 Article 6(8), DORA.
108 Article 6(9), DORA.
109 Article 6(10), DORA.

is emphasised that when undertaking such 'outsourcing,' the financial entity 'remains fully responsible for the verification of compliance with the ICT risk management requirements'.[110]

ICT SYSTEMS, PROTOCOLS AND TOOLS

10.73 Article 7 of DORA provides more detail on the obligations regarding ICT systems, protocols and tools. It specifies that in order to address and manage ICT risk, financial entities shall 'use and maintain updated ICT systems, protocols and tools that are':

- appropriate to the magnitude of operations supporting the conduct of their activities, in accordance with the proportionality principle[111] as referred to in DORA;
- reliable;
- equipped with sufficient capacity to accurately process the data necessary for the performance of activities and the timely provision of services, and to deal with peak orders, message or transaction volumes, as needed, including where new technology is introduced; and
- technologically-resilient in order to adequately deal with additional information processing needs as required under stressed market conditions or other adverse situations.[112]

There are many components and requirements contained within this provision. One issue arising will be what is meant by the term 'updated'. For example, one may have to consider when something becomes or potentially becomes outdated and therefore needs to become updated. A further issue will be when such assessments are made, who makes them, upon what criteria and ultimately to what extent such assessments are made based on subjective or objective criteria.

It is also important to note the particular focus of the requirement in the provision. The focus is directed to the specific 'ICT systems, protocols and tools' of the firm.

These ICT systems, protocols and tools of the firm must then satisfy the criteria listed at the four bullets points above. These may seem reasonably intended to raise or establish standards of robust ICT security and resilience. However, when one examines the specific criteria, we can foresee that there is some scope for misunderstanding, if not disagreement, as to what the standard of the specific requirement actually is. What does 'reliable' mean? To what standard? To whom? And at what time? Strategically, firms might consider what is a reasonable set

110 Article 6(10), DORA.
111 The proportionality principle as referred to in Article 4 of DORA.
112 Article 7, DORA.

of recorded documentation and processes to have in place to have available to demonstrate in future that at the appropriate point in time the (updated) ICT systems, protocols and tools.

Another criterion refers to the (updated) ICT systems, protocols and tools being appropriate to the magnitude of operations supporting the conduct of their activities, in accordance with the proportionality principle. One may consider what is appropriate and inappropriate, but when most firms are actually diligently implementing ICT security processes breaches can still occur. It may be easier to identify something that is manifestly outdated or manifestly not appropriate or manifestly no longer appropriate, it may be more difficult to say that software versions which are in date or are generally or often used across the financial sector is not appropriate. Particular circumstances can mean that something is indeed not appropriate (or not appropriate at a point in time), but the nature of the provision means that it may be difficult for a regulator to call something out as being not appropriate or that there is a failure to have something appropriate. There is an associated issue in that the exact parameter rules and expectations should be easily known to firms in advance.

The follow-on text of the above provision also raises the possibility that it may be difficult to enforce this provision against firms. The references to 'appropriate', 'magnitude' and 'proportionality' (in 'appropriate to the magnitude of operations supporting the conduct of their activities, in accordance with the proportionality principle') mean that there is not one but three reasonableness qualifiers which allow a firm ample opportunity to demonstrate that its actions/systems were appropriate *or* magnitude relevant *or* proportionate.

However, while the terms 'sufficient' and 'accurately' may seem to assist firm, this may be discounted by the additional service level referenced, which are capable of being well defined with a level of specificity, downtime, and even KPIs (key performance indicators).

The key point to understand in the fourth bullet above is the capacity criterion 'adequately'. Arguably these will only ever be known after the event and with hindsight. This may not be a reasonable standard, however, for regulators to seek to apply.

IDENTIFICATION

10.74 Article 8 of DORA refers to identification and identification issues. It specifies at Article 8(1) that:

- as part of the ICT Risk Management Framework referred to in Article 6(1), financial entities shall identify, classify and adequately document all ICT supported business functions, roles and responsibilities, the information assets and ICT assets supporting those functions, and their roles and dependencies in relation to ICT risk. Financial entities shall review as needed, and at least yearly, the adequacy of this classification and of any relevant documentation.[113]

Firms must engage in identification and classification exercises, which must then be adequately documented. These identification and classification exercises must occur for:

- all ICT-supported business functions;
- roles and responsibilities;
- the information assets and ICT assets supporting the above functions; and
- roles and dependencies in relation to ICT risk.

These exercises are complex and extensive in nature. The exercises must also be revisited annually.

Article 8(2) provides that:

- financial entities shall, on a continuous basis, identify all sources of ICT risk, in particular the risk exposure to and from other financial entities, and assess cyber threats and ICT vulnerabilities relevant to their ICT supported business functions, information assets and ICT assets. Financial entities shall review on a regular basis, and at least yearly, the risk scenarios impacting them.[114]

Firms must therefore have a system for identifying all ICT risks on a rolling basis. This must include the entity obviously but also other entities.

The requirement also specifies that there needs to a system for assessing cyber threats and ICT vulnerabilities specific to:

- business functions relying on ICT;
- information assets; and
- ICT assets.

In order to make such assessments, a firm needs to be able to identify and list each of these separate areas, namely, business functions relying on ICT; information assets; and ICT assets.

While some of these activities may be undertaken to some extent already, the requirements of this expansive provision need to be studied and assessed in detail as there will likely be addition requirement and or more specificity required.

While the above assessments and reviews are extensive in and of themselves, there are also additional requirements to undertake these at the time of significant

113 Article 8(1), DORA.
114 Article 8(2), DORA.

change events. Financial entities, other than microenterprises, must 'perform a risk assessment upon each major change in the network and information system infrastructure, in the processes or procedures affecting their ICT supported business functions, information assets or ICT assets.'[115]

The need to identify information assets and ICT assets referred to above is reiterated in Article 8(4), which specifies that:

- Financial entities shall identify all information assets and ICT assets, including those on remote sites, network resources and hardware equipment, and shall map those considered critical. They shall map the configuration of the information assets and ICT assets and the links and interdependencies between the different information assets and ICT assets.[116]

These must be identified in all such instances, and where deemed critical they need to be mapped. Therefore, a process of identification is required as well as a process of mapping. Unfortunately, the nature and difference between these exercises is not immediately clear. The difference in focus relates to all such assets, and those considered critical, but the nature of the exercise is less transparent.

The description of the information assets and ICT assets is expanded to include such assets on remote sites, networks and hardware. In addition, those deemed critical must be mapped. The second sentence in the provision seems to refer to some of the detail of the mapping process. However, the second sentence is not limited to specific critical assets. It is unclear if the specificity of critical assets was omitted unintentionally or if there was some kind of error. But making the second sentence non-specific, raises the query as to whether the first and second sentences conflict in direct meaning or effect. In the first sentence mapping is limited, but is not limited in the second sentence.

A cautious interpretation means that firms must assume the widest meaning and widest set of obligations – whether this was originally intended or not.

Financial entities are also required to 'identify and document all processes that are dependent on ICT third-party service providers, and shall identify interconnections with ICT third-party service providers that provide services that support critical or important functions.'[117] In this instance the drafting and intention are clearer than some other instances. Here it is clear that firms must:

- identify and document all firm processes dependent on third-party ICT service providers; and
- identify third-party ICT service providers supporting critical or important functions.

115 Article 8(3), DORA.
116 Article 8(4), DORA.
117 Article 8(5), DORA.

There is no confusion created by referring to *identify* and or *map*.

For the purposes of Article 8(1), (4) and (5), financial entities must 'maintain relevant inventories and update them periodically and every time any major change as referred to in [Article 8(3)] occurs.'[118]

Naturally, entities and the public focus on new fangled gadgets arranged in the latest batch of IT and device product launches. Following behind are the latest batch of apps and software, whether for devices, personal, personnel, or enterprise. But as some data breaches highlight (one example being the British Library ransomware attack), the attack vector used by bad actors involved older legacy systems – not the new up to date systems. Some older systems can be more open to be attacked or exploited in an attack.

This vulnerability of older legacy systems is recognised by DORA. Article 8(7) provides that:

- Financial entities, other than microenterprises, shall on a regular basis, and at least yearly, conduct a specific ICT risk assessment on all legacy ICT systems and, in any case before and after connecting technologies, applications or systems.[119]

This focus is commended. The requirement to at least yearly conduct a specific risk assessment on legacy IT systems is relatively clear. Less clear is the reference to assessments 'before and after connecting'. Presumably, we all have in contemplation existing legacy systems which are still in use by a financial firm. If correct, the second part of the clause is difficult to fully understand. It may make better sense if it referred to before and after 'new additional connections'. It may be difficult for firms to apply this requirement without having to assume that this was the intention, and proceed accordingly (ie, yearly plus when a new connection is proposed) – at least unless and until some specific guidance on this point issues from regulators. This may sit uneasily with some firms, namely, having to re-interpret the second clause. The alternative is equally unattractive, which is to ignore the second clause – unless and until greater clarity arises.

PROTECTION AND PREVENTION

10.75 Article 9 of DORA refers to the concepts of protection and prevention. Article 9(1) requires that for the purposes of adequately protecting ICT systems and with a view to organising response measures, financial entities:

- shall continuously monitor and control the security and functioning of ICT systems and tools and shall minimise the impact of ICT risk on ICT systems through the deployment of appropriate ICT security tools, policies and procedures.[120]

118 Article 8(5), DORA.
119 Article 8(7), DORA.
120 Article 9(1), DORA.

Firms must monitor and control. Specifically, they must monitor and control the security *and* functioning (operation) of ICT systems and tools.

Firms must also minimise the impact of ICT risk on ICT systems. This must be achieved through the deployment of 'appropriate ICT security tools, policies and procedures'. Therefore, firms must consider what their separate tools, policies and processes actually are; and then also consider whether each of these are 'adequate'. This term is also sometimes loaded and sometimes vague. What does it mean, who makes the decision, when is the relevant time to consider, and what is a justified reasonable decision on something being adequate, and importantly when might a regular decide that something was not adequate – and the all-important basis and reasons for making such a finding of inadequacy. One can imagine that firms would prefer to have more assurance on what can reasonably be considered to be adequate. Furthermore, is the consideration of what is adequate encompassed or outside of the principle of proportionality to be applied in DORA. Firms will really have to wait and see, even post January 2025. This will not be an enviable waiting period one imagines.

Note also that the requirement to 'minimise' is a greater obligation than to 'reduce' per se.

These is a further guidance, and requirements, in relation what ICT security policies, procedures, protocols and tools are intended to accomplish. Article 9(2) provides that financial entities shall design, procure and implement ICT security policies, procedures, protocols and tools that:

- aim to ensure the resilience, continuity and availability of ICT systems, in particular for those supporting critical or important functions, and to maintain high standards of availability, authenticity, integrity and confidentiality of data, whether at rest, in use or in transit.[121]

In order to achieve the objectives referred to in Article 9(2), financial entities shall use ICT solutions and processes that are appropriate in accordance DORA.[122] Fortunately, DORA sets out what these will be. It specifies that those ICT solutions and processes must:

- ensure the security of the means of transfer of data;
- minimise the risk of corruption or loss of data, unauthorised access and technical flaws that may hinder business activity;
- prevent the lack of availability, the impairment of the authenticity and integrity, the breaches of confidentiality and the loss of data; and
- ensure that data is protected from risks arising from data management, including poor administration, processing-related risks and human error.[123]

121 Article 9(2), DORA.
122 The ICT solutions and processes that are appropriate are referred to in Article 4 of DORA.
123 Article 9(3), DORA.

The DORA ICT Risk Management Framework is referred to again. Article 9(4) specifies that as part of the ICT Risk Management Framework,[124] financial entities must:

- develop and document an information security policy defining rules to protect the availability, authenticity, integrity and confidentiality of data, information assets and ICT assets, including those of their customers, where applicable;
- follow a risk-based approach, establish a sound network and infrastructure management structure using appropriate techniques, methods and protocols that may include implementing automated mechanisms to isolate affected information assets in the event of cyber attacks;
- implement policies that limit the physical or logical access to information assets and ICT assets to what is required for legitimate and approved functions and activities only, and establish to that end a set of policies, procedures and controls that address access rights and ensure a sound administration thereof;
- implement policies and protocols for strong authentication mechanisms, based on relevant standards and dedicated control systems, and protection measures of cryptographic keys whereby data is encrypted based on results of approved data classification and ICT risk assessment processes;
- implement documented policies, procedures and controls for ICT change management, including changes to software, hardware, firmware components, systems or security parameters, that are based on a risk assessment approach and are an integral part of the financial entity's overall change management process, in order to ensure that all changes to ICT systems are recorded, tested, assessed, approved, implemented and verified in a controlled manner; and
- have appropriate and comprehensive documented policies for patches and updates.

Additionally, for the purposes of bullet point two above, financial entities must design the network connection infrastructure in a way that allows it to be instantaneously severed or segmented in order to minimise and prevent contagion, especially for interconnected financial processes.[125] This means considering active workarounds, segmentation, and alternative network channels. There may be greater applicability to those heavily reliant on ongoing live transactions.

For the purposes of bullet point five above, the ICT change management process must be approved by appropriate lines of management and must have specific protocols in place.[126]

124 The ICT Risk Management Framework is referred to in Article 6(1) of DORA.
125 Article 9(4), DORA.
126 Article 9(4), DORA.

DETECTIONS

10.76 There are also certain activities that DORA requires entities to detect ad to have detection mechanisms in place. Article 10 of DORA refers to these detections.

Financial entities must have in place mechanisms to 'promptly detect anomalous activities' in accordance with DORA,[127] including ICT network performance issues and ICT-related incidents, and to identify potential material single points of failure.[128] Therefore, firms must be able to detect:

- anomalous activities (and to do so promptly);
- network performance issues;
- ICT-related incidents; and
- material single points of failure (in advance).

All such detection mechanisms must also be regularly tested in accordance with Article 25.[129]

The detection mechanisms must 'enable multiple layers of control, define alert thresholds and criteria to trigger and initiate ICT-related incident response processes, including automatic alert mechanisms for relevant staff in charge of ICT-related incident response.'[130] This provision creates multiple layers of compliance requirements. One should not underestimate the complexity of this provision.

There is also an obligation on financial entities to 'devote sufficient resources and capabilities to monitor user activity, the occurrence of ICT anomalies and ICT-related incidents, in particular cyber-attacks.'[131] The scope of the areas to be monitored are wide. In addition, it is not clear what will be deemed by a regulator to be 'sufficient resources and capabilities'. Firms will wish that the mere fact of a disruption or a breach on its own would not amount to sufficient basis for a regulator to deem that there was not 'sufficient resources and capabilities' dedicated by the firm, or arguably worse, at the firm. Issues will surround what was reasonable at the time, what was reasonable for a form to consider, and whether issues of hindsight will be applied to any degree. It is not expressly referred to, but firms would also like to be able to consider the proportionality principle in this regard.

Certain provisions of DORA are specific to particular types of entities in the financial sector, Article 10(4) is one such example. It provides that data reporting

127 The mechanisms to promptly detect anomalous activities are referred to in Article 17 of DORA,
128 Article 10(1), DORA.
129 Article 10(1), DORA.
130 Article 10(2), DORA.
131 Article 10(3), DORA.

service providers shall, in addition to the other requirements of Article 10, have in place systems that can effectively check trade reports for completeness, identify omissions and obvious errors, and request re-transmission of those reports.[132]

RESPONSE AND RECOVERY

10.77 One of the core aspects of operational resilience is and ability to respond and recover in as routine a manner as possible. Article 11 of DORA refers to response and recovery. It provides at Article 11(1) that as part of the DORA ICT Risk Management Framework[133] and based on the identification requirements set out in DORA,[134] financial entities shall put in place a comprehensive ICT business continuity policy, which may be adopted as a dedicated specific policy, forming an integral part of the overall business continuity policy of the financial entity.[135]

Thus, in addition to the ICT Risk Management Framework, firms must also establish an ICT business continuity policy. One might expect that most financial firms (as well as other firms) will have a developed business continuity policy and detailed business continuity plan. In this instance, however, DORA distinguishes the general business continuity policy as a form from the newly referred to ICT business continuity policy. Now as a result of DORA both are required. However, it appears that the separate ICT business continuity policy may be appended or incorporated into the overall business continuity policy. It must be a significant and integral part – as opposed to a mere tick box exercise.

Financial entities are also required to implement the ICT business continuity policy through 'dedicated, appropriate and documented arrangements, plans, procedures and mechanisms aiming to':

- ensure the continuity of the financial entity's critical or important functions;
- quickly, appropriately and effectively respond to, and resolve, all ICT-related incidents in a way that limits damage and prioritises the resumption of activities and recovery actions;
- activate, without delay, dedicated plans that enable containment measures, processes and technologies suited to each type of ICT-related incident and prevent further damage, as well as tailored response and recovery procedures established in accordance with DORA;[136]
- estimate preliminary impacts, damages and losses; and

132 Article 10(4), DORA.
133 The ICT risk management framework is referred to in Article 6(1) of DORA.
134 The identification requirements are set out in Article 8 of DORA.
135 Article 11(1), DORA.
136 The tailored response and recovery procedures are established in accordance with Article 12 of DORA.

- set out communication and crisis management actions that ensure that updated information is transmitted to all relevant internal staff and external stakeholders in accordance with Article 14, and report[137] to the competent authorities in accordance with DORA (the Article 19 report).[138]

As part of the ICT Risk Management Framework[139] financial entities must implement associated ICT response and recovery plans which, in the case of financial entities other than microenterprises, shall be subject to independent internal audit reviews.[140]

Financial entities must also put in place, maintain and periodically test 'appropriate ICT business continuity plans, notably with regard to critical or important functions outsourced or contracted through arrangements with ICT third-party service providers.'[141]

As part of the overall business continuity policy, financial entities must conduct a 'business impact analysis (BIA) of their exposures to severe business disruptions.'[142] Firms may well have BIAs but not as fully expressed here, and so may need to consider expanding their BIAs.

Under the BIA, financial entities must 'assess the potential impact of severe business disruptions by means of quantitative and qualitative criteria, using internal and external data and scenario analysis, as appropriate.'[143]

The BIA must consider the 'criticality of identified and mapped business functions, support processes, third-party dependencies and information assets, and their interdependencies.'[144]

Financial entities must also ensure that ICT assets and ICT services are designed and used in 'full alignment' with the BIA, in particular with regard to 'adequately ensuring' the redundancy of all critical components.[145] Queries may arise as to what is meant by the use of the terms 'full', 'adequately' and 'ensuring' in this instance.

In addition, and as part of their 'comprehensive' ICT risk management, financial entities must:

- test the ICT business continuity plans and the ICT response and recovery plans in relation to ICT systems supporting all functions at least yearly, as

137 The report to the competent authorities in accordance with Article 19 of DORA.
138 Article 11(2), DORA.
139 The ICT Risk Management Framework referred to in Article 6(1) of DORA.
140 Article 11(3), DORA.
141 Article 11(4), DORA.
142 Article 11(5), DORA.
143 Article 11(5), DORA.
144 Article 11(5), DORA.
145 Article 11(5), DORA.

well as in the event of any substantive changes to ICT systems supporting critical or important functions; and

- test the crisis communication plans established in accordance with DORA.[146]

For the purposes of bullet point one above, financial entities, other than microenterprises, must include in their 'testing plans scenarios of cyber-attacks and switchovers between the primary ICT infrastructure and the redundant capacity, backups and redundant facilities necessary to meet the obligations set out in Article 12' of DORA.[147]

Financial entities shall regularly review their ICT business continuity policy and ICT response and recovery plans, taking into account the results of tests carried out in accordance with the first bullet above and recommendations stemming from audit checks or supervisory reviews.[148]

Operational resilience also required preparedness in relation to communications and communications planning. Financial entities, other than microenterprises, must have a crisis management function, which, in the event of activation of their ICT business continuity plans or ICT response and recovery plans, shall, inter alia, set out clear procedures to manage internal and external crisis communications in accordance with DORA.[149]

Operational resilience requires preparedness for the inevitability of business disruptions. Under DORA financial entities must keep readily accessible records of activities before and during disruption events when their ICT business continuity plans and ICT response and recovery plans are activated.[150] This is necessary for compliance but it also assists the learning and improvement of the firm to meet the next challenge.

Firms which are central securities depositories must provide the competent authorities with copies of the results of the ICT business continuity tests, or of similar exercises.[151]

Financial entities, other than microenterprises, must report to the competent authorities, upon their request, an estimation of aggregated annual costs and losses caused by major ICT-related incidents.[152]

146 Article 11(6), DORA. The crisis communication plans are established in accordance with Article 14 of DORA.
147 Article 11(6), DORA.
148 Article 11(6), DORA.
149 Article 11(7), DORA. The internal and external crisis communications in accordance with Article 14 of DORA.
150 Article 11(8), DORA.
151 Article 11(9), DORA.
152 Article 11(10), DORA.

The ESAs (through the Joint Committee) were required by 17 July 2024 develop common guidelines on the estimation of aggregated annual costs and losses referred to in Article 11(10).[153]

The ESAs issued (draft) Guidelines on the estimation of aggregated costs/losses caused by major ICT-related incidents on or about 17 July 2024.

BACKUPS AND RESTORATION

10.78 Operational resilience requires the ability to recover from disruptions.[154] This can involve the need to recover from backup versions of records. Article 12 of DORA refers to backup and restoration issues. The heading expressly refers as follows, namely to 'Backup policies and procedures, restoration and recovery procedures and methods'. Article 12(1) provides that for the purpose of 'ensuring the restoration of ICT systems and data with minimum downtime, limited disruption and loss' as part of their ICT Risk Management Framework, financial entities shall develop and document the following, namely:

- backup policies and procedures specifying the scope of the data that is subject to the backup and the minimum frequency of the backup, based on the criticality of information or the confidentiality level of the data; and
- restoration and recovery procedures and methods.[155]

Article 12(2) requires that financial entities must set up backup systems that can be activated in accordance with the backup policies and procedures, as well as restoration and recovery procedures and methods.[156] The activation of backup systems must not jeopardise the security of the network and information systems or the availability, authenticity, integrity or confidentiality of data.[157] Testing of the backup procedures and restoration and recovery procedures and methods must be undertaken periodically.[158]

In accordance with Article 12(3) '[w]hen restoring backup data using own systems, financial entities shall use ICT systems that are physically and logically segregated from the source ICT system.'[159] In addition, the ICT systems must be 'securely protected from any unauthorised access or ICT corruption and allow for the timely restoration of services making use of data and system backups as necessary.'[160]

153 Article 11(11), DORA. In accordance with Article 16 of Regulations 1093/2010, 1094/2010 and 1095/2010.
154 The need for a quick recovery is referred to in Recital 6.
155 Article 12(1), DORA.
156 Article 12(2), DORA.
157 Article 12(2), DORA.
158 Article 12(2), DORA.
159 Article 12(3), DORA.
160 Article 12(3), DORA.

There is an additional provision for entire which are central counterparties. For central counterparties, the recovery plans must enable the recovery of all transactions at the time of disruption to allow the central counterparty to continue to operate with certainty and to complete settlement on the scheduled date.[161]

Data reporting service providers are also separately referred to. These entities must additionally maintain adequate resources and have backup and restoration facilities in place in order to offer and maintain their services at all times.[162]

Financial entities, other than microenterprises, must maintain redundant ICT capacities equipped with resources, capabilities and functions that are adequate to ensure business needs. Microenterprises shall assess the need to maintain such redundant ICT capacities based on their risk profile.[163]

Central securities depositories must also maintain at least one secondary processing site endowed with adequate resources, capabilities, functions and staffing arrangements to ensure business needs.[164] The secondary processing site must be:

- located at a geographical distance from the primary processing site to ensure that it bears a distinct risk profile and to prevent it from being affected by the event which has affected the primary site;
- capable of ensuring the continuity of critical or important functions identically to the primary site, or providing the level of services necessary to ensure that the financial entity performs its critical operations within the recovery objectives; and
- immediately accessible to the financial entity's staff to ensure continuity of critical or important functions in the event that the primary processing site has become unavailable.[165]

Article 12(6) provides that in determining the recovery time and recovery point objectives for each function, financial entities shall take into account whether it is a critical or important function and the potential overall impact on market efficiency.[166] Such time objectives shall ensure that, in extreme scenarios, the agreed service levels are met.[167]

When recovering from an ICT-related incident, financial entities must perform 'necessary' checks.[168] It is not full clear what necessary means or will be taken to mean. However, it is further specified that it includes 'any multiple checks

161 Article 12(3), DORA.
162 Article 12(3), DORA.
163 Article 12(4), DORA.
164 Article 12(5), DORA.
165 Article 12(5), DORA.
166 Article 12(6), DORA.
167 Article 12(6), DORA.
168 Article 12(7), DORA.

and reconciliations, in order to ensure that the highest level of data integrity is maintained.'[169] These checks must also be performed when reconstructing data from external stakeholders, in order to ensure that all data is consistent between systems.[170]

LEARNINGS

10.79 Operational resilience also requires that firm learn from past disruptions and events. Article 13 of DORA, for example, refers what it terms 'Learning and evolving'. Under Article 13(1) financial entities must have in place capabilities and staff to gather information on 'vulnerabilities and cyber threats, ICT-related incidents, in particular cyber-attacks' and 'analyse the impact they are likely to have' on the firm's digital operational resilience.[171]

Financial entities must also put in place *post* ICT-related incident reviews after a major ICT-related incident disrupts their core activities.[172] The post ICT-related incident reviews will analyse the causes of disruption and identify required improvements to the ICT operations or within the ICT business continuity policy referred to in DORA.[173]

Financial entities, other than microenterprises, must, upon request of competent authorities, furnish details of the changes that were implemented following post ICT-related incident reviews.[174] The post ICT-related incident reviews shall determine whether the established procedures were followed and the actions taken were effective, including in relation to the following:

- the promptness in responding to security alerts and determining the impact of ICT-related incidents and their severity;
- the quality and speed of performing a forensic analysis, where deemed appropriate;
- the effectiveness of incident escalation within the financial entity; and
- the effectiveness of internal and external communication.[175]

Lessons shall be duly incorporated on a continuous basis into the ICT risk assessment process.[176] These lessons or lessons learned are specified in DORA to be those lessons derived from:

169 Article 12(7), DORA.
170 Article 12(7), DORA.
171 Article 13(1), DORA.
172 Article 13(2), DORA. The ICT business continuity policies are referred to in Article 11 of DORA.
173 Article 13(2), DORA. The ICT business continuity policies are referred to in Article 11 of DORA.
174 Article 13(2), DORA.
175 Article 13(2), DORA.
176 Article 13(3), DORA. The ICT Risk Management Framework referred to in Article 6(1) of DORA.

- digital operational resilience testing carried out in accordance with DORA;[177]
- real life ICT-related incidents, in particular cyber attacks;
- challenges faced upon the activation of ICT business continuity plans and ICT response and recovery plans; and
- together with relevant information exchanged with counterparts and assessed during supervisory reviews.[178]

Those findings shall form the basis for appropriate reviews of relevant components of the ICT Risk Management Framework referred to in DORA.[179]

Financial entities are required to monitor the effectiveness of the implementation of their digital operational resilience strategy set out in DORA.[180] They must map the evolution of ICT risk over time, analyse the frequency, types, magnitude and evolution of ICT-related incidents, in particular cyber-attacks and their patterns, with a view to understanding the level of ICT risk exposure, in particular in relation to critical or important functions, and enhance the cyber maturity and preparedness of the financial entity.[181]

Senior ICT staff need to report at least yearly to the management body on the findings referred to above and put forward recommendations.[182]

Financial entities must develop ICT security awareness programmes and digital operational resilience training as compulsory modules for staff training. Those programmes and training shall be applicable to all employees and to senior management staff, and shall have a level of complexity commensurate to the remit of their functions.[183] In addition and where appropriate, financial entities must also include ICT third-party service providers in their relevant training schemes in accordance with DORA.[184]

Financial entities, other than microenterprises, must monitor relevant technological developments on a continuous basis, also with a view to understanding the possible impact of the deployment of such new technologies on ICT security requirements and digital operational resilience.[185] They must also keep up to date

177 The digital operational resilience testing carried out is referred to in Articles 26 and 27.

178 Article 13(3), DORA. The ICT Risk Management Framework referred to in Article 6(1) of DORA.

179 Article 13(3), DORA. The ICT Risk Management Framework referred to in Article 6(1) of DORA.

180 The digital operational resilience strategy set out in Article 6(8) of DORA.

181 Article 13(4), DORA.

182 Article 13(5), DORA.

183 Article 13(6), DORA. The relevant training schemes are in accordance with Article 30(2)(i) of DORA.

184 Article 13(6), DORA. The relevant training schemes are in accordance with Article 30(2)(i) of DORA.

185 Article 1, DORA.

with the latest ICT risk management processes, in order to effectively combat current or new forms of cyber attacks.[186]

COMMUNICATION

10.80 Communication issues are additionally referred to in Article 14 of DORA.

As part of the ICT Risk Management Framework referred to in DORA,[187] financial entities must have in place crisis communication plans enabling a responsible disclosure of, at least, major ICT-related incidents or vulnerabilities to clients and counterparts as well as to the public, as appropriate.[188]

Also as part of the ICT Risk Management Framework, financial entities shall implement communication policies for internal staff and for external stakeholders.[189] Communication policies for staff shall take into account the need to differentiate between staff involved in ICT risk management, in particular the staff responsible for response and recovery, and (other) staff that needs to be informed.[190]

At least one person in the financial entity must be tasked with implementing the communication strategy for ICT-related incidents and fulfil the public and media function for that purpose.[191]

HARMONISATION OF ICT RISK MANAGEMENT TOOLS, METHODS, PROCESSES AND POLICIES

10.81 Article 15 of DORA refers to the need for further harmonisation of ICT risk management tools, methods, processes and policies.[192]

The ESAs,[193] through the Joint Committee, in consultation with the European Union Agency on Cybersecurity (ENISA), are to develop common draft RTS in order to:

- further elements to be included in the ICT security policies, procedures, protocols and tools referred to in DORA,[194] with a view to ensuring the security of networks, enable adequate safeguards against intrusions and data

186 Article 1, DORA.
187 The ICT Risk Management Framework referred to in Article 6(1) of DORA.
188 Article 14(1), DORA.
189 Article 14(2), DORA.
190 Article 14(2), DORA.
191 Article 14(3), DORA.
192 Article 15, DORA. The need to address harmonisation, and gap issues, is also referred to in Recitals 8, 9, 10, 11, 14, 15, 16, 22, 24, 26, 55, 94, and 99.
193 The ESAs are also referred to in Recitals 7, 24, and 100.
194 The ICT security policies, procedures, protocols and tools referred to in Article 9(2) of DORA.

misuse, preserve the availability, authenticity, integrity and confidentiality of data, including cryptographic techniques, and guarantee an accurate and prompt data transmission without major disruptions and undue delays;

- develop further components of the controls of access management rights referred to in DORA,[195] and associated human resource policy specifying access rights, procedures for granting and revoking rights, monitoring anomalous behaviour in relation to ICT risk through appropriate indicators, including for network use patterns, hours, IT activity and unknown devices;
- develop further the mechanisms specified in Article 10(1) enabling a prompt detection of anomalous activities and the criteria set out in Article 10(2) triggering ICT-related incident detection and response processes;
- specify further the components of the ICT business continuity policy referred to in DORA;[196]
- specify further the testing of ICT business continuity plans referred to in DORA[197] to ensure that such testing duly takes into account scenarios in which the quality of the provision of a critical or important function deteriorates to an unacceptable level or fails, and duly considers the potential impact of the insolvency, or other failures, of any relevant ICT third-party service provider and, where relevant, the political risks in the respective providers' jurisdictions;
- specify further the components of the ICT response and recovery plans referred to in DORA;[198] and
- specify further the content and format of the report on the review of the ICT Risk Management Framework referred to in Article 6(5).[199]

When developing these draft RTS, the ESAs must take into account the size and the overall risk profile of the financial entity, and the nature, scale and complexity of its services, activities and operations, while duly taking into consideration any specific feature arising from the distinct nature of activities across different financial services sectors.[200] The ESAs were required to submit these draft RTS to the Commission by 17 January 2024.[201]

Power is delegated to the Commission to supplement DORA by adopting the RTS referred to in the first paragraph in accordance with Articles 10 to 14 of Regulations 1093/2010, 1094/2010, and 1095/2010.[202]

The ESAs published the following draft RTS and Guidelines on 17 January 2024:

195 The controls of access management rights referred to in Article 9(4)(c).
196 The ICT business continuity policy referred to in Article 11(1) of DORA.
197 The ICT business continuity plans referred to in Article 11(6) of DORA.
198 The ICT response and recovery plans referred to in Article 11(3) of DORA.
199 Article 15, DORA.
200 Article 15, DORA.
201 Article 15, DORA.
202 Article 15, DORA.

- RTS on ICT risk management framework and on simplified ICT risk management framework;
- RTS on criteria for the classification of ICT-related incidents;
- RTS to specify the policy on ICT services supporting critical or important functions provided by ICT third-party service providers (TPPs); and
- Implementing Technical Standards (ITS) to establish the templates for the register of information.

The ESAs also published the following draft RTS and Guidelines on 17 July 2024:

- RTS and ITS on the content, format, templates and timelines for reporting major ICT-related incidents and significant cyber threats;
- RTS on the harmonisation of conditions enabling the conduct of the oversight activities;
- RTS specifying the criteria for determining the composition of the joint examination team (JET);
- RTS on threat-led penetration testing (TLPT);
- Guidelines on the estimation of aggregated costs/losses caused by major ICT-related incidents; and
- Guidelines on oversight cooperation.

The above are subject to amendment and adoption by the EU Commission.

SIMPLIFIED ICT RISK MANAGEMENT FRAMEWORK

10.82 We have referred to earlier how there is a recognition of the differing scale on entities within the wide financial sector and the need for the proportionality principal. There is further recognition of this issue by providing for a more reduced or Simplified ICT Risk Management Framework for certain smaller firms. The Simplified ICT Risk Management Framework is provided for in Article 16 of DORA.

The means of deciding which firms are qualified for the Simplified ICT Risk Management Framework is framed in two ways – one by saying that the main ICT Risk Management Framework provisions do not apply to the smaller firms in-scope, and two by providing that they need to comply with the Simplified ICT Risk Management Framework.

Article 16(1) provides that Articles 5 to 15 of DORA shall not apply to small and non-interconnected investment firms, payment institutions exempted pursuant to Directive 2015/2366; institutions exempted pursuant to Directive 2013/36 in respect of which Member States have decided not to apply the option referred to in Article 2(4) of DORA; electronic money institutions exempted pursuant to Directive 2009/110; and small institutions for occupational retirement provision.[203] So these are the firms to which the main ICT Risk Management Framework will not apply.

Next it is provided that without prejudice to Article 16(1), the entities listed above must:

- put in place and maintain a sound and documented ICT Risk Management Framework that details the mechanisms and measures aimed at a quick, efficient and comprehensive management of ICT risk, including for the protection of relevant physical components and infrastructures;
- continuously monitor the security and functioning of all ICT systems;
- minimise the impact of ICT risk through the use of sound, resilient and updated ICT systems, protocols and tools which are appropriate to support the performance of their activities and the provision of services and adequately protect availability, authenticity, integrity and confidentiality of data in the network and information systems;
- allow sources of ICT risk and anomalies in the network and information systems to be promptly identified and detected and ICT-related incidents to be swiftly handled;
- identify key dependencies on ICT third-party service providers;
- ensure the continuity of critical or important functions, through business continuity plans and response and recovery measures, which include, at least, back up and restoration measures;
- test, on a regular basis, the plans and measures referred to in bullet point six above, as well as the effectiveness of the controls implemented in accordance with bullets points one and three; and
- implement, as appropriate, relevant operational conclusions resulting from the tests referred to in bullet point seven above and from post-incident analysis into the ICT risk assessment process and develop, according to needs and ICT risk profile, ICT security awareness programmes and digital operational resilience training for staff and management.[204]

The ICT Risk Management Framework referred to in Article 16(1), second subparagraph, point (a), shall be documented and reviewed periodically and upon the occurrence of major ICT-related incidents in compliance with supervisory instructions. It shall be continuously improved on the basis of lessons derived from implementation and monitoring. A report on the review of the ICT Risk Management Framework shall be submitted to the competent authority upon its request.[205]

203 Article 16(1), DORA.
204 Article 16(1), DORA.
205 Article 16(2), DORA.

The ESAs shall, through the Joint Committee, in consultation with ENISA, develop common draft RTS in order to:

- specify further the elements to be included in the ICT Risk Management Framework referred to in Article 16(1), second subparagraph, point (a);
- specify further the elements in relation to systems, protocols and tools to minimise the impact of ICT risk referred to in Article 16(1), second subparagraph, point (c), with a view to ensuring the security of networks, enabling adequate safeguards against intrusions and data misuse and preserving the availability, authenticity, integrity and confidentiality of data;
- specify further the components of the ICT business continuity plans referred to in Article 16(1), second subparagraph, point (f);
- specify further the rules on the testing of business continuity plans and ensure the effectiveness of the controls referred to in Article 16(1), second subparagraph, point (g) and ensure that such testing duly takes into account scenarios in which the quality of the provision of a critical or important function deteriorates to an unacceptable level or fails; and
- specify further the content and format of the report on the review of the ICT Risk Management Framework referred to in Article 16(1), second subparagraph.[206]

When developing those draft RTS, the ESAs shall take into account the size and the overall risk profile of the financial entity, and the nature, scale and complexity of its services, activities and operations.[207]

The ESAs were required submit those draft RTS to the Commission by 17 January 2024.[208]

Power is delegated to the Commission to supplement DORA by adopting the RTS referred to in the first subparagraph in accordance with Articles 10 to 14 of Regulations 1093/2010, 1094/2010 and 1095/2010.[209]

The ESAs published the draft RTS on ICT risk management framework and on simplified ICT risk management framework on 17 January 2024, subject to amendment and adoption by the EU Commission. The Commission has since adopted a sub-regulation, namely Regulation 2024/1774.

The sub-regulation reflects a differential between the requirement for the general body of financial firms and for those which are designated as being able to use a shorter Simplified ICT Risk Management Framework.

206 Article 16(3), DORA.
207 Article 16(3), DORA.
208 Article 16(3), DORA.
209 Article 16(3), DORA.

Regulation 2024/1774

10.83 The ESA sub-regulation referred to above at **10.82** in relation to Article 16, Regulation 2024/1774,[210] has been approved by and signed on behalf of the Commission.

Overall risk profile and complexity

10.84 Article 1 of Regulation 2024/1774 refers to overall risk profile and complexity. When developing and implementing the ICT security policies, procedures, protocols and tools referred to in Title II and the Simplified ICT Risk Management Framework referred to in Title III, the size and the overall risk profile of the financial entity, and the nature, scale and elements of increased or reduced complexity of its services, activities and operations shall be taken into account, including elements relating to:

- encryption and cryptography;
- ICT operations security;
- network security;
- ICT project and change management; and
- the potential impact of the ICT risk on confidentiality, integrity and availability of data, and of the disruptions on the continuity and availability of the financial entity's activities.

General elements of ICT security policies, procedures, protocols, and tools

10.85 Article 2 of Regulation 2024/1774 refers to general elements of ICT security policies, procedures, protocols, and tools. Financial entities shall ensure that their ICT security policies, information security, and related procedures, protocols, and tools as referred to in Article 9(2) of DORA are embedded in their ICT Risk Management Framework. Financial entities shall establish the ICT security policies, procedures, protocols, and tools that:

- ensure the security of networks;
- contain safeguards against intrusions and data misuse;
- preserve the availability, authenticity, integrity, and confidentiality of data, including via the use of cryptographic techniques; and

210 Commission Delegated Regulation (EU) 2024/1774 of 13 March 2024 supplementing Regulation (EU) 2022/2554 of the European Parliament and of the Council with regard to regulatory technical standards specifying ICT risk management tools, methods, processes, and policies and the simplified ICT risk management framework.

- guarantee an accurate and prompt data transmission without major disruptions and undue delays.

Financial entities shall ensure that the ICT security policies referred to above:

- are aligned to the financial entity's information security objectives included in the digital operational resilience strategy referred to in Article 6(8) of DORA;
- indicate the date of the formal approval of the ICT security policies by the management body;
- contain indicators and measures to:
  (i) monitor the implementation of the ICT security policies, procedures, protocols, and tools;
  (ii) record exceptions from that implementation; and
  (iii) ensure that the digital operational resilience of the financial entity is ensured in case of exceptions as referred to in point (ii);
- specify the responsibilities of staff at all levels to ensure the financial entity's ICT security;
- specify the consequences of non-compliance by staff of the financial entity with the ICT security policies, where provisions to that effect are not laid down in other policies of the financial entity;
- list the documentation to be maintained;
- specify the segregation of duties arrangements in the context of the three lines of defence model or other internal risk management and control model, as applicable, to avoid conflicts of interest;
- consider leading practices and, where applicable, standards as defined in Article 2(1) of Regulation 1025/2012;
- identify the roles and responsibilities for the development, implementation and maintenance of ICT security policies, procedures, protocols, and tools;
- are reviewed in accordance with Article 6(5) of DORA; and
- take into account material changes concerning the financial entity, including material changes to the activities or processes of the financial entity, to the cyber threat landscape, or to applicable legal obligations.

ICT risk management

10.86 Article 3 of Regulation 2024/1774 refers to ICT risk management. Financial entities shall develop, document, and implement ICT risk management policies and procedures that shall contain all of the following:

- an indication of the approval of the risk tolerance level for ICT risk established in accordance with Article 6(8)(b) of DORA;

- a procedure and a methodology to conduct the ICT risk assessment, identifying:
  (i) vulnerabilities and threats that affect or may affect the supported business functions, the ICT systems and ICT assets supporting those functions; and
  (ii) the quantitative or qualitative indicators to measure the impact and likelihood of the vulnerabilities and threats referred to in point (i);
- the procedure to identify, implement, and document ICT risk treatment measures for the ICT risks identified and assessed, including the determination of ICT risk treatment measures necessary to bring ICT risk within the risk tolerance level referred to in bullet point one;
- for the residual ICT risks that are still present following the implementation of the ICT risk treatment measures referred to in bullet point three:
  (i) provisions on the identification of those residual ICT risks;
  (ii) the assignment of roles and responsibilities regarding:
    (1) the acceptance of the residual ICT risks that exceed the financial entity's risk tolerance level referred to in bullet point one; and
    (2) for the review process referred to in point (iv) of this bullet point;
  (iii) the development of an inventory of the accepted residual ICT risks, including a justification for their acceptance; and
  (iv) provisions on the review of the accepted residual ICT risks at least once a year, including:
    (1) the identification of any changes to the residual ICT risks;
    (2) the assessment of available mitigation measures; and
    (3) the assessment of whether the reasons justifying the acceptance of residual ICT risks are still valid and applicable at the date of the review;
- provisions on the monitoring of:
  (i) any changes to the ICT risk and cyber threat landscape;
  (ii) internal and external vulnerabilities and threats; and
  (iii) ICT risk of the financial entity that enables prompt detection of changes that could affect its ICT risk profile;
- provisions on a process to ensure that any changes to the business strategy and the digital operational resilience strategy of the financial entity are taken into account.

For the purposes of Article 3, first paragraph, point (c), the procedure referred to in that point shall ensure:

- the monitoring of the effectiveness of the ICT risk treatment measures implemented;
- the assessment of whether the established risk tolerance levels of the financial entity have been attained; and
- the assessment of whether the financial entity has taken actions to correct or improve those measures where necessary.

ICT asset management policy

10.87 Article 4 of Regulation 2024/1774 refers to the ICT asset management policy. As part of the ICT security policies, procedures, protocols, and tools referred to in Article 9(2) of DORA, financial entities shall develop, document, and implement a policy on management of ICT assets. The policy on management of ICT assets referred to in Article 4(1) shall:

- prescribe the monitoring and management of the lifecycle of ICT assets identified and classified in accordance with Article 8(1) of DORA;
- prescribe that the financial entity keeps records of all of the following:
  - (i) the unique identifier of each ICT asset;
  - (ii) information on the location, either physical or logical, of all ICT assets;
  - (iii) the classification of all ICT assets, as referred to in Article 8(1) of DORA;
  - (iv) the identity of ICT asset owners;
  - (v) the business functions or services supported by the ICT asset;
  - (vi) the ICT business continuity requirements, including recovery time objectives and recovery point objectives;
  - (vii) whether the ICT asset can be or is exposed to external networks, including the internet;
  - (viii) the links and interdependencies among ICT assets and the business functions using each ICT asset; and
  - (ix) where applicable, for all ICT assets, the end dates of the ICT third-party service provider's regular, extended, and custom support services after which those ICT assets are no longer supported by their supplier or by an ICT third-party service provider; and
- for financial entities other than microenterprises, prescribe that those financial entities keep records of the information necessary to perform a specific ICT risk assessment on all legacy ICT systems referred to in Article 8(7) of DORA.

ICT asset management procedure

10.88 Article 5 of Regulation 2024/1774 refers to the ICT asset management procedure. Financial entities shall develop, document, and implement a procedure for the management of ICT assets.

The procedure for management of ICT assets referred to in Article 5(1) shall specify the criteria to perform the criticality assessment of information assets and ICT assets supporting business functions. That assessment shall take into account:

- the ICT risk related to those business functions and their dependencies on the information assets or ICT assets; and
- how the loss of confidentiality, integrity, and availability of such information assets and ICT assets would impact the business processes and activities of the financial entities.

Encryption and cryptographic controls

10.89 Article 6 of Regulation 2024/1774 refers to encryption and cryptographic controls. As part of their ICT security policies, procedures, protocols, and tools referred to in Article 9(2) of DORA, financial entities shall develop, document, and implement a policy on encryption and cryptographic controls.

Financial entities shall design the policy on encryption and cryptographic controls referred to above on the basis of the results of an approved data classification and ICT risk assessment. That policy shall contain rules for all of the following:

- the encryption of data at rest and in transit;
- the encryption of data in use, where necessary;
- the encryption of internal network connections and traffic with external parties; and
- the cryptographic key management referred to in Article 7, laying down rules on the correct use, protection, and lifecycle of cryptographic keys.

For the purposes of bullet point two above, where encryption of data in use is not possible, financial entities shall process data in use in a separated and protected environment, or take equivalent measures to ensure the confidentiality, integrity, authenticity, and availability of data.

Financial entities shall include in the policy on encryption and cryptographic controls, referred to in Article 6(1), criteria for the selection of cryptographic techniques and use practices, taking into account leading practices, and standards as defined in Article 2(1) of Regulation 1025/2012, and the classification of relevant ICT assets established in accordance with Article 8(1) of DORA. Financial entities that are not able to adhere to the leading practices or standards, or to use the most reliable techniques, shall adopt mitigation and monitoring measures that ensure resilience against cyber threats.

Financial entities shall include in the policy on encryption and cryptographic controls, referred to in Article 6(1), provisions for updating or changing, where necessary, the cryptographic technology on the basis of developments in cryptanalysis. Those updates or changes shall ensure that the cryptographic technology remains resilient against cyber threats, as required by Article 10(2)(a). Financial entities that are not able to update or change the cryptographic technology shall adopt mitigation and monitoring measures that ensure resilience against cyber threats.

Financial entities shall include in the policy on encryption and cryptographic controls, referred to in Article 6(1), a requirement to record the adoption of mitigation and monitoring measures adopted in accordance with Article 6(3) and (4) and to provide a reasoned explanation for doing so.

Cryptographic key management

10.90 Article 7 Regulation 2024/1774 refers to cryptographic key management. Financial entities shall include in the cryptographic key management policy referred to in Article 6(2)(d), requirements for managing cryptographic keys through their whole lifecycle, including generating, renewing, storing, backing up, archiving, retrieving, transmitting, retiring, revoking, and destroying those cryptographic keys.

Financial entities shall identify and implement controls to protect cryptographic keys through their whole lifecycle against loss, unauthorised access, disclosure, and modification. Financial entities shall design those controls on the basis of the results of the approved data classification and the ICT risk assessment.

Financial entities shall develop and implement methods to replace the cryptographic keys in the case of loss, or where those keys are compromised or damaged.

Financial entities shall create and maintain a register for all certificates and certificate storing devices for at least ICT assets supporting critical or important functions. Financial entities shall keep that register up to date.

Financial entities shall ensure the prompt renewal of certificates in advance of their expiration.

Policies and procedures for ICT operations

10.91 Article 8 of Regulation 2024/1774 refers to policies and procedures for ICT operations. As part of the ICT security policies, procedures, protocols, and tools referred to in Article 9(2) of DORA, financial entities shall develop, document, and implement policies and procedures to manage the ICT operations. Those policies and procedures shall specify how financial entities operate, monitor, control, and restore their ICT assets, including the documentation of ICT operations.

The policies and procedures for ICT operations, referred to in Article 8(1), shall contain all of the following:

- an ICT assets description, including all of the following:
  - (i) requirements regarding secure installation, maintenance, configuration, and deinstallation of an ICT system;
  - (ii) requirements regarding the management of information assets used by ICT assets, including their processing and handling, both automated and manual; and
  - (iii) requirements regarding the identification and control of legacy ICT systems;
- controls and monitoring of ICT systems, including all of the following:
  - (i) backup and restore requirements of ICT systems;
  - (ii) scheduling requirements, taking into consideration interdependencies among the ICT systems;
  - (iii) protocols for audit trail and system log information;
  - (iv) requirements to ensure that the performance of internal audit and other testing minimises disruptions to business operations;
  - (v) requirements on the separation of ICT production environments from the development, testing, and other non-production environments;
  - (vi) requirements to conduct the development and testing in environments which are separated from the production environment; and
  - (vii) requirements to conduct the development and testing in production environments;
- error handling concerning ICT systems, including all of the following:
  - (i) procedures and protocols for handling errors;
  - (ii) support and escalation contacts, including external support contacts in case of unexpected operational or technical issues; and
  - (iii) ICT system restart, rollback, and recovery procedures for use in the event of ICT system disruption.

For the purposes of bullet point two (v), the separation shall consider all of the components of the environment, including accounts, data or connections, as required by Article 13(1)(a).

For the purposes of bullet point two (vii), the policies and procedures referred to in Article 8(1) shall provide that the instances in which testing is performed in a production environment are clearly identified, reasoned, are for limited periods of time, and are approved by the relevant function in accordance with Article 16(6). Financial entities shall ensure the availability, confidentiality, integrity, and authenticity of ICT systems and production data during development and test activities in the production environment.

Capacity and performance management

10.92 Article 9 Regulation 2024/1774 refers to capacity and performance management. As part of the ICT security policies, procedures, protocols, and tools referred to in Article 9(2) of DORA, financial entities shall develop, document, and implement capacity and performance management procedures for the following:

- the identification of capacity requirements of their ICT systems;
- the application of resource optimisation; and
- the monitoring procedures for maintaining and improving:
  - (i) the availability of data and ICT systems;
  - (ii) the efficiency of ICT systems; and
  - (iii) the prevention of ICT capacity shortages.

The capacity and performance management procedures referred to in Article 9(1) shall ensure that financial entities take measures that are appropriate to cater for the specificities of ICT systems with long or complex procurement or approval processes or ICT systems that are resource-intensive.

Vulnerability and patch management

10.93 Article 10 of Regulation 2024/1774 refers to vulnerability and patch management. As part of the ICT security policies, procedures, protocols, and tools referred to in Article 9(2) of DORA, financial entities shall develop, document, and implement vulnerability management procedures.

The vulnerability management procedures referred to in Article 10(1) shall:

- identify and update relevant and trustworthy information resources to build and maintain awareness about vulnerabilities;
- ensure the performance of automated vulnerability scanning and assessments on ICT assets, whereby the frequency and scope of those activities shall be commensurate to the classification established in accordance with Article 8(1) of DORA and the overall risk profile of the ICT asset;

- verify whether:
  - (i) ICT third-party service providers handle vulnerabilities related to the ICT services provided to the financial entity; and
  - (ii) whether those service providers report to the financial entity at least the critical vulnerabilities and statistics and trends in a timely manner;
- track the usage of:
  - (i) third-party libraries, including open-source libraries, used by ICT services supporting critical or important functions; and
  - (ii) ICT services developed by the financial entity itself or specifically customised or developed for the financial entity by an ICT third-party service provider;
- establish procedures for the responsible disclosure of vulnerabilities to clients, counterparties, and to the public;
- prioritise the deployment of patches and other mitigation measures to address the vulnerabilities identified;
- monitor and verify the remediation of vulnerabilities; and
- require the recording of any detected vulnerabilities affecting ICT systems and the monitoring of their resolution.

For the purposes of bullet point two, financial entities shall perform the automated vulnerability scanning and assessments on ICT assets for the ICT assets supporting critical or important functions on at least a weekly basis.

For the purposes of bullet point three, financial entities shall request that ICT third-party service providers investigate the relevant vulnerabilities, determine the root causes, and implement appropriate mitigating action.

For the purposes of bullet point four, financial entities shall, where appropriate in collaboration with the ICT third-party service provider, monitor the version and possible updates of the third-party libraries. In case of ready to use (off the shelf) ICT assets or components of ICT assets acquired and used in the operation of ICT services not supporting critical or important functions, financial entities shall track the usage to the extent possible of third-party libraries, including open source libraries.

For the purposes of bullet point six, financial entities shall consider the criticality of the vulnerability, the classification established in accordance with Article 8(1) of DORA, and the risk profile of the ICT assets affected by the identified vulnerabilities.

As part of the ICT security policies, procedures, protocols, and tools referred to in Article 9(2) of DORA, financial entities shall develop, document and implement patch management procedures.

The patch management procedures referred to in Article 10(3) shall:

- to the extent possible, identify and evaluate available software and hardware patches and updates using automated tools;
- identify emergency procedures for the patching and updating of ICT assets;
- test and deploy the software and hardware patches and the updates referred to in Article 8(2)(b)(v), (vi) and (vii); and
- set deadlines for the installation of software and hardware patches and updates and escalation procedures in case those deadlines cannot be met.

Data and system security

10.94 Article 11 of Regulation 2024/1774 refers to data and system security. As part of the ICT security policies, procedures, protocols, and tools referred to in Article 9(2) of DORA, financial entities shall develop, document, and implement a data and system security procedure.

The data and system security procedure referred to in Article 11(1) shall contain all of the following elements related to data and ICT system security, in accordance with the classification established in accordance with Article 8(1) of DORA:

- the access restrictions referred to in Article 21 of this Regulation, supporting the protection requirements for each level of classification;
- the identification of a secure configuration baseline for ICT assets that minimise exposure of those ICT assets to cyber threats and measures to verify regularly that those baselines are effectively deployed;
- the identification of security measures to ensure that only authorised software is installed in ICT systems and endpoint devices;
- the identification of security measures against malicious codes;
- the identification of security measures to ensure that only authorised data storage media, systems, and endpoint devices are used to transfer and store data of the financial entity;
- the following requirements to secure the use of portable endpoint devices and private non-portable endpoint devices:
    - (i) the requirement to use a management solution to remotely manage the endpoint devices and remotely wipe the financial entity's data;
    - (ii) the requirement to use security mechanisms that cannot be modified, removed or bypassed by staff members or ICT third-party service providers in an unauthorised manner; and
    - (iii) the requirement to use removable data storage devices only where the residual ICT risk remains within the financial entity's risk tolerance level referred to in Article 3(1)(a);

- the process to securely delete data, present on premises of the financial entity or stored externally, that the financial entity no longer needs to collect or to store;
- the process to securely dispose or decommission of data storage devices present on premises of the financial entity or stored externally containing confidential information;
- the identification and implementation of security measures to prevent data loss and leakage for systems and endpoint devices;
- the implementation of security measures to ensure that teleworking and the use of private endpoint devices does not adversely impact the ICT security of the financial entity; and
- for ICT assets or services operated by an ICT third-party service provider, the identification and implementation of requirements to maintain digital operational resilience, in accordance with the results of the data classification and ICT risk assessment.

For the purposes of bullet point two, the secure configuration baseline referred to in that point shall take into account leading practices and appropriate techniques laid down in the standards defined in Article 2(1) of Regulation 1025/2012.

For the purposes of bullet point 11, financial entities shall consider the following:

- the implementation of vendor recommended settings on the elements operated by the financial entity;
- a clear allocation of information security roles and responsibilities between the financial entity and the ICT third-party service provider, in accordance with the principle of full responsibility of the financial entity over its ICT third-party service provider referred to in Article 28(1)(a) of DORA, and for financial entities referred to in Article 28(2) of that Regulation, and in accordance with the financial entity's policy on the use of ICT services supporting critical or important functions;
- the need to ensure and maintain adequate competences within the financial entity in the management and security of the service used; and
- technical and organisational measures to minimise the risks related to the infrastructure used by the ICT third-party service provider for its ICT services, considering leading practices, and standards, as defined in Article 2(1) of Regulation 1025/2012.

Logging

10.95 Article 12 of Regulation 2024/1774 refers to logging. Financial entities shall, as part of the safeguards against intrusions and data misuse, develop, document, and implement logging procedures, protocols and tools.

The logging procedures, protocols, and tools referred to in Article 12(1) shall contain all of the following:

- the identification of the events to be logged, the retention period of the logs, and the measures to secure and handle the log data, considering the purpose for which the logs are created;
- the alignment of the level of detail of the logs with their purpose and usage to enable the effective detection of anomalous activities as referred to in Article 24;
- the requirement to log events related to all of the following:
  - (i) logical and physical access control, as referred to in Article 21, and identity management;
  - (ii) capacity management;
  - (iii) change management;
  - (iv) ICT operations, including ICT system activities; and
  - (v) network traffic activities, including ICT network performance;
- measures to protect logging systems and log information against tampering, deletion, and unauthorised access at rest, in transit, and, where relevant, in use;
- measures to detect a failure of logging systems; and
- without prejudice to any applicable regulatory requirements under European or national law, the synchronisation of the clocks of each of the financial entity's ICT systems upon a documented reliable reference time source.

For the purposes of bullet point one, financial entities shall establish the retention period, taking into account the business and information security objectives, the reason for recording the event in the logs, and the results of the ICT risk assessment.

Network security management

10.96 Article 13 of Regulation 2024/1774 refers to network security management. Financial entities shall, as part of the safeguards ensuring the security of networks against intrusions and data misuse, develop, document, and implement policies, procedures, protocols, and tools on network security management, including all of the following:

- the segregation and segmentation of ICT systems and networks taking into account:
  - (i) the criticality or importance of the function those ICT systems and networks support;

(ii) the classification established in accordance with Article 8(1) of Regulation 2022/2554; and

(iii) the overall risk profile of ICT assets using those ICT systems and networks;

- the documentation of all of the financial entity's network connections and data flows;
- the use of a separate and dedicated network for the administration of ICT assets;
- the identification and implementation of network access controls to prevent and detect connections to the financial entity's network by any unauthorised device or system, or any endpoint not meeting the financial entity's security requirements;
- the encryption of network connections passing over corporate networks, public networks, domestic networks, third-party networks, and wireless networks, for communication protocols used, taking into account the results of the approved data classification, the results of the ICT risk assessment and the encryption of network connections referred to in Article 6(2);
- the design of networks in line with the ICT security requirements established by the financial entity, taking into account leading practices to ensure the confidentiality, integrity, and availability of the network;
- the securing of network traffic between the internal networks and the internet and other external connections;
- the identification of the roles and responsibilities and steps for the specification, implementation, approval, change, and review of firewall rules and connections filters;
- the performance of reviews of the network architecture and of the network security design once a year, and periodically for microenterprises, to identify potential vulnerabilities;
- the measures to temporarily isolate, where necessary, subnetworks, and network components and devices;
- the implementation of a secure configuration baseline of all network components, and the hardening of the network and of network devices in line with any vendor instructions, where applicable standards, as defined in Article 2(1) of Regulation 1025/2012, and leading practices;
- the procedures to limit, lock, and terminate system and remote sessions after a specified period of inactivity; and
- for network services agreements:

(i) the identification and specification of ICT and information security measures, service levels, and management requirements of all network services; and

(ii) whether those services are provided by an ICT intra group service provider or by ICT third-party service providers.

For the purposes of bullet point eight, financial entities shall perform the review of firewall rules and connections filters on a regular basis in accordance with the classification established in accordance with Article 8(1) of DORA and the overall risk profile of ICT systems involved. For ICT systems that support critical or important functions, financial entities shall verify the adequacy of the existing firewall rules and connection filters at least every six months.

Securing information in transit

10.97 Article 14 of Regulation 2024/1774 refers to securing information in transit. As part of the safeguards to preserve the availability, authenticity, integrity and confidentiality of data, financial entities shall develop, document, and implement the policies, procedures, protocols, and tools to protect information in transit. Financial entities shall in particular ensure all of the following:

- the availability, authenticity, integrity and confidentiality of data during network transmission, and the establishment of procedures to assess compliance with those requirements;
- the prevention and detection of data leakages and the secure transfer of information between the financial entity and external parties; and
- that requirements on confidentiality or non-disclosure arrangements reflecting the financial entity's needs for the protection of information for both the staff of the financial entity and of third parties are implemented, documented, and regularly reviewed.

Financial entities shall design the policies, procedures, protocols, and tools to protect the information in transit referred to in Article 14(1) on the basis of the results of the approved data classification and of the ICT risk assessment

ICT project management

10.98 Article 15 of Regulation 2024/1774 refers to ICT project management. As part of the safeguards to preserve the availability, authenticity, integrity, and confidentiality of data, financial entities shall develop, document, and implement an ICT project management policy.

The ICT project management policy referred to in Article 15(1) shall specify the elements that ensure the effective management of the ICT projects related to the acquisition, maintenance and, where applicable, development of the financial entity's ICT systems.

The ICT project management policy shall contain all of the following:

- ICT project objectives;
- ICT project governance, including roles and responsibilities;
- ICT project planning, timeframe, and steps;
- ICT project risk assessment;
- relevant milestones;
- change management requirements; and
- the testing of all requirements, including security requirements, and the respective approval process when deploying an ICT system in the production environment.

The ICT project management policy shall ensure the secure ICT project implementation through the provision of the necessary information and expertise from the business area or functions impacted by the ICT project.

In accordance with the ICT project risk assessment referred to in Article 15(3)(d), the ICT project management policy shall provide that the establishment and progress of ICT projects impacting critical or important functions of the financial entity and their associated risks are reported to the management body as follows:

- individually or in aggregation, depending on the importance and size of the ICT projects; and
- periodically and, where necessary, on an event driven basis.

ICT systems acquisition, development, and maintenance

10.99 Article 16 of Regulation 2024/1774 refers to ICT systems acquisition, development, and maintenance. As part of the safeguards to preserve the availability, authenticity, integrity, and confidentiality of data, financial entities shall develop, document and implement a policy governing the acquisition, development, and maintenance of ICT systems. That policy shall

- identify security practices and methodologies relating to the acquisition, development, and maintenance of ICT systems;
- require the identification of:

    (i) technical specifications and ICT technical specifications, as defined in Article 2(4) and (5) of Regulation 1025/2012; and

    (ii) requirements relating to the acquisition, development, and maintenance of ICT systems, with a particular focus on ICT security requirements and on their approval by the relevant business function and ICT asset owner in accordance with the financial entity's internal governance arrangements;

- specify measures to mitigate the risk of unintentional alteration or intentional manipulation of the ICT systems during the development, maintenance, and deployment of those ICT systems in the production environment.

Financial entities shall develop, document, and implement an ICT systems' acquisition, development, and maintenance procedure for the testing and approval of all ICT systems prior to their use and after maintenance, in accordance with Article 8(2)(b)(v), (vi) and (vii). The level of testing shall be commensurate to the criticality of the business procedures and ICT assets concerned. The testing shall be designed to verify that new ICT systems are adequate to perform as intended, including the quality of the software developed internally.

Central counterparties shall, in addition to the requirements laid down in Article 16(1), involve, as appropriate, in the design and conduct of the testing:

- clearing members and clients;
- interoperable central counterparties; and
- other interested parties.

Central securities depositories shall, in addition to the requirements laid down Article 16(1), involve, as appropriate, in the design and conduct of the testing:

- users;
- critical utilities and critical service providers;
- other central securities depositories;
- other market infrastructures; and
- any other institutions with which central securities depositories have identified interdependencies in their business continuity policy.

The procedure referred to in Article 16(2) shall contain the performance of source code reviews covering both static and dynamic testing. That testing shall contain security testing for internet-exposed systems and applications in accordance with Article 8(2)(b)(v), (vi) and (vii). Financial entities shall:

- identify and analyse vulnerabilities and anomalies in the source code;
- adopt an action plan to address those vulnerabilities and anomalies; and
- monitor the implementation of that action plan.

The procedure referred to in Article 16(2) shall contain security testing of software packages no later than at the integration phase, in accordance with Article 8(2)(b)(v), (vi) and(vii).

The procedure shall provide that:

- non-production environments only store anonymised, pseudonymised, or randomised production data; and

- financial entities are to protect the integrity and confidentiality of data in non-production environments.

By way of derogation from Article 16(5), the procedure referred to in Article 16(2) may provide that production data are stored only for specific testing occasions, for limited periods of time, and following the approval by the relevant function and the reporting of such occasions to the ICT risk management function.

The procedure shall contain the implementation of controls to protect the integrity of the source code of ICT systems that are developed in house or by an ICT third-party service provider and delivered to the financial entity by an ICT third parties service provider.

The procedure shall provide that proprietary software and, where feasible, the source code provided by ICT third-party service providers or coming from open source projects, are to be analysed and tested in accordance with Article 16(3) prior to their deployment in the production environment.

Paragraphs (1) to (8) of Article 16 shall also apply to ICT systems developed or managed by users outside the ICT function, using a risk-based approach.

ICT change management

10.100 Article 17 of Regulation 2024/1774 refers to ICT change management. As part of the safeguards to preserve the availability, authenticity, integrity, and confidentiality of data, financial entities shall include in the ICT change management procedures referred to in Article 9(4)(e) of DORA, in respect of all changes to software, hardware, firmware components, systems, or security parameters, all of the following elements:

- a verification of whether the ICT security requirements have been met;
- mechanisms to ensure the independence of the functions that approve changes and the functions responsible for requesting and implementing those changes;
- a clear description of the roles and responsibilities to ensure that:
  - (i) changes are specified and planned;
  - (ii) an adequate transition is designed;
  - (iii) the changes are tested and finalised in a controlled manner; and
  - (iv) there is an effective quality assurance;
- the documentation and communication of change details, including:
  - (i) the purpose and scope of the change;
  - (ii) the timeline for the implementation of the change; and
  - (iii) the expected outcomes;

- the identification of fallback procedures and responsibilities, including procedures and responsibilities for aborting changes or recovering from changes not successfully implemented;
- procedures, protocols, and tools to manage emergency changes that provide adequate safeguards;
- procedures to document, re-evaluate, assess, and approve emergency changes after their implementation, including workarounds and patches; and
- the identification of the potential impact of a change on existing ICT security measures and an assessment of whether such change requires the adoption of additional ICT security measures.

After having made significant changes to their ICT systems, central counterparties and central securities depositories shall submit their ICT systems to stringent testing by simulating stressed conditions.

Central counterparties shall involve, as appropriate, in the design and conduct of the testing referred to in Article 17(1):

- clearing members and clients;
- interoperable central counterparties; and
- other interested parties.

Central securities depositories shall, as appropriate, involve in the design and conduct of the testing:

- users;
- critical utilities and critical service providers;
- other central securities depositories;
- other market infrastructures; and
- any other institutions with which central securities depositories have identified interdependencies in their ICT business continuity policy.

Physical and environmental security

10.101 Article 18 of Regulation 2024/1774 refers to physical and environmental security. As part of the safeguards to preserve the availability, authenticity, integrity, and confidentiality of data, financial entities shall specify, document, and implement a physical and environmental security policy. Financial entities shall design that policy in light of the cyber threat landscape, in accordance with the classification established in accordance with Article 8(1) of DORA, and in light of the overall risk profile of ICT assets and accessible information assets.

The physical and environmental security policy referred to in Article 18(1) shall contain all of the following:

- a reference to the section of the policy on control of access management rights referred to in Article 21(1)(g);
- measures to protect from attacks, accidents, and environmental threats and hazards, the premises, data centres of the financial entity, and sensitive designated areas identified by the financial entity, where ICT assets and information assets reside;
- measures to secure ICT assets, both within and outside the premises of the financial entity, taking into account the results of the ICT risk assessment related to the relevant ICT assets; measures to ensure the availability, authenticity, integrity, and confidentiality of ICT assets, information assets, and physical access control devices of the financial entity through the appropriate maintenance; and
- measures to preserve the availability, authenticity, integrity, and confidentiality of the data, including:
  (i) a clear desk policy for papers; and
  (ii) a clear screen policy for information processing facilities.

For the purposes of bullet point two, the measures to protect from environmental threats and hazards shall be commensurate with the importance of the premises, data centres, sensitive designated areas, and the criticality of the operations or ICT systems located therein.

For the purposes of bullet point three, the physical and environmental security policy referred to in Article 18(1) shall contain measures to provide appropriate protection to unattended ICT assets.

Human resources policy

10.102 Article 19 of Regulation 2024/1774 refers to the human resources policy. Financial entities shall include in their human resource policy or other relevant policies all of the following ICT security-related elements:

- the identification and assignment of any specific ICT security responsibilities;
- requirements for staff of the financial entity and of the ICT third-party service providers using or accessing ICT assets of the financial entity to:
  (i) be informed about, and adhere to, the financial entity's ICT security policies, procedures, and protocols;
  (ii) be aware of the reporting channels put in place by the financial entity for the detection of anomalous behaviour, including, where applicable, the reporting channels established in line with Directive 2019/1937; and

(iii) for the staff, to return to the financial entity, upon termination of employment, all ICT assets and tangible information assets in their possession that belong to the financial entity.

Identity management

10.103 Article 20 of Regulation 2024/1774 refers to identity management. As part of their control of access management rights, financial entities shall develop, document, and implement identity management policies and procedures that ensure the unique identification and authentication of natural persons and systems accessing the financial entities' information to enable assignment of user access rights in accordance with Article 21.

The identity management policies and procedures referred to in Article 20(1) shall contain all of the following:

- without prejudice to Article 21(1)(c), a unique identity corresponding to a unique user account shall be assigned to each staff member of the financial entity or staff of the ICT third-party service providers accessing the information assets and ICT assets of the financial entity; and
- a lifecycle management process for identities and accounts managing the creation, change, review and update, temporary deactivation, and termination of all accounts.

For the purposes of bullet point one, financial entities shall maintain records of all identity assignments. Those records shall be kept following a reorganisation of the financial entity or after the end of the contractual relationship without prejudice to the retention requirements laid down in applicable European and national law.

For the purposes of bullet point two, financial entities shall, where feasible and appropriate, deploy automated solutions for the lifecycle identity management process.

Access control

10.104 Article 21 of Regulation 2024/1774 refers to access control. As part of their control of access management rights, financial entities shall develop, document, and implement a policy that contains all of the following:

- the assignment of access rights to ICT assets based on need to know, need to use and least privilege principles, including for remote and emergency access;
- the segregation of duties designed to prevent unjustified access to critical data or to prevent the allocation of combinations of access rights that may be used to circumvent controls;

- a provision on user accountability, by limiting to the extent possible the use of generic and shared user accounts and ensuring that users are identifiable for the actions performed in the ICT systems at all times;
- a provision on restrictions of access to ICT assets, setting out controls and tools to prevent unauthorised access;
- account management procedures to grant, change or revoke access rights for user and generic accounts, including generic administrator accounts, including provision on all of the following:
  - (i) assignment of roles and responsibilities for granting, reviewing, and revoking access rights;
  - (ii) assignment of privileged, emergency, and administrator access on a need to use or an ad hoc basis for all ICT systems;
  - (iii) withdrawal of access rights without undue delay upon termination of the employment or when the access is no longer necessary; and
  - (iv) update of access rights where changes are necessary and at least once a year for all ICT systems, other than ICT systems supporting critical or important functions and at least every six months for ICT systems supporting critical or important functions.
- authentication methods, including all of the following:
  - (i) the use of authentication methods commensurate to the classification established in accordance with Article 8(1) of DORA and to the overall risk profile of ICT assets and considering leading practices; and
  - (ii) the use of strong authentication methods in accordance with leading practices and techniques for remote access to the financial entity's network, for privileged access, for access to ICT assets supporting critical or important functions or ICT assets that are publicly accessible;
- physical access controls measures including:
  - (i) the identification and logging of natural persons that are authorised to access premises, data centres, and sensitive designated areas identified by the financial entity where ICT and information assets reside;
  - (ii) the granting of physical access rights to critical ICT assets to authorised persons only, in accordance with the need to know and least privilege principles, and on an ad hoc basis;
  - (iii) the monitoring of physical access to premises, data centres, and sensitive designated areas identified by the financial entity where ICT and information assets or both reside; and
  - (iv) the review of physical access rights to ensure that unnecessary access rights are promptly revoked.

For the purposes of bullet point five (i), financial entities shall establish the retention period taking into account the business and information security objectives, the reasons for recording the event in the logs, and the results of the ICT risk assessment.

For the purposes of bullet point five (ii), financial entities shall, where possible, use dedicated accounts for the performance of administrative tasks on ICT systems. Where feasible and appropriate, financial entities shall deploy automated solutions for the privilege access management.

For the purposes of bullet point seven (i), the identification and logging shall be commensurate with the importance of the premises, data centres, sensitive designated areas, and the criticality of the operations or ICT systems located therein.

For the purposes of bullet point seven (iii), the monitoring shall be commensurate to the classification established in accordance with Article 8(1) of DORA and the criticality of the area accessed.

ICT-related incident management policy

10.105 Article 22 of Regulation 2024/1774 refers to the ICT-related incident management policy. As part of the mechanisms to detect anomalous activities, including ICT network performance issues and ICT-related incidents, financial entities shall develop, document, and implement an ICT-related incident policy through which they shall:

- document the ICT-related incident management process referred to in Article 17 of DORA;
- establish a list of relevant contacts with internal functions and external stakeholders that are directly involved in ICT operations security, including on:
  - (i) the detection and monitoring of cyber threats;
  - (ii) the detection of anomalous activities; and
  - (iii) vulnerability management;
- establish, implement, and operate technical, organisational, and operational mechanisms to support the ICT-related incident management process, including mechanisms to enable a prompt detection of anomalous activities and behaviours in accordance with Article 23 of this Regulation;
- retain all evidence relating to ICT-related incidents for a period that shall be no longer than necessary for the purposes for which the data are collected, commensurate with the criticality of the affected business functions, supporting processes, and ICT and information assets, in accordance with Article 15 of Regulation 2024/1772 on classification of ICT-related incidents and with any applicable retention requirement pursuant to Union law; and

- establish and implement mechanisms to analyse significant or recurring ICT-related incidents and patterns in the number and the occurrence of ICT-related incidents.

For the purposes of bullet point four, financial entities shall retain the evidence referred to in that point in a secure manner.

Anomalous activities detection and criteria for ICT-related incidents detection and response

10.106 Article 23 of Regulation 2024/1774 refers to anomalous activities detection and criteria for ICT-related incidents detection and response.

Financial entities shall set clear roles and responsibilities to effectively detect and respond to ICT-related incidents and anomalous activities.

The mechanism to promptly detect anomalous activities, including ICT network performance issues and ICT-related incidents, as referred to in Article 10(1) of DORA, shall enable financial entities to:

- collect, monitor, and analyse all of the following:
  - (i) internal and external factors, including at least the logs collected in accordance with Article 12 of this Regulation, information from business and ICT functions, and any problem reported by users of the financial entity;
  - (ii) potential internal and external cyber threats, considering scenarios commonly used by threat actors and scenarios based on threat intelligence activity; and
  - (iii) ICT-related incident notification from an ICT third-party service provider of the financial entity detected in the ICT systems and networks of the ICT third-party service provider and that may affect the financial entity;
- identify anomalous activities and behaviour, and implement tools generating alerts for anomalous activities and behaviour, at least for ICT assets and information assets supporting critical or important functions;
- prioritise the alerts referred to in bullet point two to allow for the management of the detected ICT-related incidents within the expected resolution time, as specified by financial entities, both during and outside working hours; and
- record, analyse, and evaluate any relevant information on all anomalous activities and behaviours automatically or manually.

For the purposes of bullet point two, the tools referred to in that point shall contain the tools that provide automated alerts based on pre-defined rules to identify anomalies affecting the completeness and integrity of the data sources or log collection.

Financial entities shall protect any recording of the anomalous activities against tampering and unauthorised access at rest, in transit and, where relevant, in use.

Financial entities shall log all relevant information for each detected anomalous activity enabling:

- the identification of the date and time of occurrence of the anomalous activity;
- the identification of the date and time of detection of the anomalous activity; and
- the identification of the type of the anomalous activity.

Financial entities shall consider all of the following criteria to trigger the ICT-related incident detection and response processes referred to in Article 10(2) of DORA:

- indications that malicious activity may have been carried out in an ICT system or network, or that such ICT system or network may have been compromised;
- data losses detected in relation to the availability, authenticity, integrity, and confidentiality of data;
- adverse impact detected on financial entity's transactions and operations; and
- ICT systems' and network unavailability.

For the purposes of Article 23(5), financial entities shall also consider the criticality of the services affected.

Components of the ICT business continuity policy

10.107 Article 24 of Regulation 2024/1774 refers to components of the ICT business continuity policy. Financial entities shall include in their ICT business continuity policy, referred to in Article 11(1) of DORA, all of the following:

- a description of:

  (i) the objectives of the ICT business continuity policy, including the interrelation of ICT and overall business continuity, and considering the results of the business impact analysis (BIA) referred to in Article 11(5) of DORA;

  (ii) the scope of the ICT business continuity arrangements, plans, procedures, and mechanisms, including limitations and exclusions;

  (iii) the timeframe to be covered by the ICT business continuity arrangements, plans, procedures, and mechanisms; and

(iv) the criteria to activate and deactivate ICT business continuity plans, ICT response and recovery plans, and crisis communications plans; and

- provisions on:

(i) the governance and organisation to implement the ICT business continuity policy, including roles, responsibilities and escalation procedures ensuring that sufficient resources are available;

(ii) the alignment between the ICT business continuity plans and the overall business continuity plans, concerning at least all of the following:

(1) potential failure scenarios, including the scenarios referred to in Article 26(2) of this Regulation; and

(2) recovery objectives, specifying that the financial entity shall be able to recover the operations of its critical or important functions after disruptions within a recovery time objective and a recovery point objective;

(iii) the development of ICT business continuity plans for severe business disruptions as part of those plans, and the prioritisation of ICT business continuity actions using a risk-based approach;

(iv) the development, testing and review of ICT response and recovery plans, in accordance with Articles 25 and 26 of this Regulation;

(v) the review of the effectiveness of the implemented ICT business continuity arrangements, plans, procedures and mechanisms, in accordance with Article 26 of this Regulation; and

(vi) the alignment of the ICT business continuity policy to:

(1) the communication policy referred to in Article 14(2) of DORA; and

(2) the communication and crisis communication actions referred to in Article 11(2)(e), of DORA.

In addition to the requirements referred to in Article 24(1), central counterparties shall ensure that their ICT business continuity policy:

- contains a maximum recovery time for their critical functions that is not longer than two hours; takes into account external links and interdependencies within the financial infrastructures, including trading venues cleared by the central counterparty, securities settlement and payment systems, and credit institutions used by the central counterparty or a linked central counterparty; and
- requires that arrangements are in place to:

(i) ensure the continuity of critical or important functions of the central counterparty based on disaster scenarios;

(ii) maintain a secondary processing site capable of ensuring continuity of critical or important functions of the central counterparty identical to the primary site;

(iii) maintain or have immediate access to a secondary business site, to allow staff to ensure continuity of the service if the primary location of business is not available; and

(iv) consider the need for additional processing sites, in particular where the diversity of the risk profiles of the primary and secondary sites does not provide sufficient confidence that the central counterparty's business continuity objectives will be met in all scenarios.

For the purposes of bullet point one, central counterparties shall complete end of day procedures and payments on the required time and day in all circumstances.

For the purposes of bullet point three (i), arrangements referred to in that point shall address the availability of adequate human resources, the maximum downtime of critical functions, and fail over and recovery to a secondary site.

For the purposes of bullet point three (ii), the secondary processing site referred to in that point shall have a geographical risk profile which is distinct from that of the primary site.

In addition to the requirements referred to in paragraph 1, central securities depositories shall ensure that their ICT business continuity policy:

- takes into account any links and interdependencies to users, critical utilities and critical service providers, other central securities depositories and other market infrastructures; and
- requires its ICT business continuity arrangements to ensure that the recovery time objective for their critical or important functions shall not be longer than 2 hours.

In addition to the requirements referred to in Article 24(1), trading venues shall ensure that their ICT business continuity policy ensures that:

- trading can be resumed within or close to two hours of a disruptive incident; and
- the maximum amount of data that may be lost from any IT service of the trading venue after a disruptive incident is close to zero.

Testing of the ICT business continuity plans

10.108 Article 25 of Regulation 2024/1774 refers to testing of the ICT business continuity plans. When testing the ICT business continuity plans in accordance with Article 11(6) of DORA, financial entities shall take into account the financial entity's BIA and the ICT risk assessment referred to in Article 3(1)(b), of this Regulation.

Financial entities shall assess through the testing of their ICT business continuity plans referred to in Article 25(1) whether they are able to ensure the continuity of the financial entity's critical or important functions. That testing shall:

- be performed on the basis of test scenarios that simulate potential disruptions, including an adequate set of severe but plausible scenarios;
- contain the testing of ICT services provided by ICT third-party service providers, where applicable;
- for financial entities, other than microenterprises, as referred to in Article 11(6), second subparagraph of DORA, contain scenarios of switchover from primary ICT infrastructure to the redundant capacity, backups and redundant facilities;
- be designed to challenge the assumptions on which the business continuity plans are based, including governance arrangements and crisis communication plans; and
- contain procedures to verify the ability of the financial entities' staff, of ICT third-party service providers, of ICT systems, and ICT services to respond adequately to the scenarios duly taken into account in accordance with Article 26(2).

For the purposes of bullet point one, financial entities shall always include in the testing the scenarios considered for the development of the business continuity plans.

For the purposes of bullet point two, financial entities shall duly consider scenarios linked to insolvency or failures of the ICT third-party service providers or linked to political risks in the ICT third-party service providers' jurisdictions, where relevant.

For the purposes of bullet point three, the testing shall verify whether at least critical or important functions can be operated appropriately for a sufficient period of time, and whether the normal functioning may be restored.

In addition to the requirements referred to in Article 25(2), central counterparties shall involve in the testing of their ICT business continuity plans referred to in Article 25(1):

- clearing members;
- external providers; and
- relevant institutions in the financial infrastructure with which central counterparties have identified interdependencies in their business continuity policies.

In addition to the requirements referred to in Article 25(2), central securities depositories shall involve in the testing of their ICT business continuity plans referred to in Article 25(1), as appropriate:

- users of the central securities depositories;
- critical utilities and critical service providers;
- other central securities depositories;
- other market infrastructures;
- any other institutions with which central securities depositories have identified; and
- interdependencies in their business continuity policy.

Financial entities shall document the results of the testing referred to in Article 25(1).

Any identified deficiencies resulting from that testing shall be analysed, addressed, and reported to the management body.

ICT response and recovery plans

10.109 Article 26 of Regulation 2024/1774 refers to ICT response and recovery plans. When developing the ICT response and recovery plans referred to in Article 11(3) of DORA, financial entities shall take into account the results of the financial entity's BIA. Those ICT response and recovery plans shall:

- specify the conditions prompting their activation or deactivation, and any exceptions for such activation or deactivation;
- describe what actions are to be taken to ensure the availability, integrity, continuity, and recovery of at least ICT systems and services supporting critical or important functions of the financial entity;
- be designed to meet the recovery objectives of the operations of the financial entities;
- be documented and made available to the staff involved in the execution of ICT response and recovery plans and be readily accessible in case of emergency;
- provide for both short-term and long-term recovery options, including partial systems recovery; and
- lay down the objectives of ICT response and recovery plans and the conditions to declare a successful execution of those plans.

For the purposes of bullet point four, financial entities shall clearly specify roles and responsibilities.

The ICT response and recovery plans referred to in Article 26(1) shall identify relevant scenarios, including scenarios of severe business disruptions and increased likelihood of occurrence of disruption. Those plans shall develop scenarios based on current information on threats and on lessons learned from previous occurrences of business disruptions. Financial entities shall duly take into account all of the following scenarios:

- cyber-attacks and switchovers between the primary ICT infrastructure and the redundant capacity, backups, and redundant facilities;
- scenarios in which the quality of the provision of a critical or important function deteriorates to an unacceptable level or fails, and duly consider the potential impact of the insolvency, or other failures, of any relevant ICT third-party service provider;
- partial or total failure of premises, including office and business premises, and data centres;
- substantial failure of ICT assets or of the communication infrastructure;
- the non-availability of a critical number of staff or staff members in charge of guaranteeing the continuity of operations;
- impact of climate change and environment degradation related events, natural disasters, pandemics, and physical attacks, including intrusions and terrorist attacks;
- insider attacks;
- political and social instability, including, where relevant, in the ICT third-party service provider's jurisdiction and the location where the data are stored and processed; and
- widespread power outages.

Where the primary recovery measures may not be feasible in the short term because of costs, risks, logistics, or unforeseen circumstances, the ICT response and recovery plans referred to in paragraph 1 shall consider alternative options.

As part of the ICT response and recovery plans referred to in Article 26(1), financial entities shall consider and implement continuity measures to mitigate failures of ICT third-party service providers of ICT services supporting critical or important functions of the financial entity.

Format and content of the report on the review of the ICT Risk Management Framework

10.110 Article 27 of Regulation 2024/1774 refers to the format and content of the report on the review of the ICT Risk Management Framework. Financial entities shall submit the report on the review of the ICT Risk Management Framework referred to in Article 6(5) of DORA in a searchable electronic format.

Financial entities shall include all of the following information in the report referred to in Article 27(1):

- an introductory section that:
  - (i) clearly identifies the financial entity that is the subject of the report, and describes its group structure, where relevant;
  - (ii) describes the context of the report in terms of the nature, scale, and complexity of the financial entity's services, activities, and operations, its organisation, identified critical functions, strategy, major ongoing projects or activities, relationships and its dependence on in-house and contracted ICT services and systems or the implications that a total loss or severe degradation of such systems would have in terms of critical or important functions and market efficiency;
  - (iii) summarises the major changes in the ICT Risk Management Framework since the previous report submitted; and
  - (iv) provides an executive level summary of the current and near term ICT risk profile, threat landscape, the assessed effectiveness of its controls, and the security posture of the financial entity;
- the date of the approval of the report by the management body of the financial entity;
- a description of the reason for the review of the ICT Risk Management Framework in accordance with Article 6(5) of DORA;
- the start and end dates of the review period;
- an indication of the function responsible for the review;
- a description of the major changes and improvements to the ICT Risk Management Framework since the previous review;
- a summary of the findings of the review and detailed analysis and assessment of the severity of the weaknesses, deficiencies, and gaps in the ICT Risk Management Framework during the review period;
- a description of the measures to address identified weaknesses, deficiencies, and gaps, including all of the following:
  - (i) a summary of measures taken to remediate to identified weaknesses, deficiencies and gaps;
  - (ii) an expected date for implementing the measures and dates related to the internal control of the implementation, including information on the state of progress of the implementation of those measures as at the date of drafting of the report, explaining, where applicable, if there is a risk that deadlines may not be respected;
  - (iii) tools to be used, and the identification of the function responsible for carrying out the measures, detailing whether the tools and functions are internal or external;

(iv) a description of the impact of the changes envisaged in the measures on the financial entity's budgetary, human, and material resources, including resources dedicated to the implementation of any corrective measures;

(v) information on the process for informing the competent authority, where appropriate; and

(vi) where the weaknesses, deficiencies, or gaps identified are not subject to corrective measures, a detailed explanation of the criteria used to analyse the impact of those weaknesses, deficiencies, or gaps, to evaluate the related residual ICT risk, and of the criteria used to accept the related residual risk;

- information on planned further developments of the ICT Risk Management Framework;
- conclusions resulting from the review of the ICT Risk Management Framework;
- information on past reviews, including:

  (i) a list of past reviews to date;

  (ii) where applicable, a state of implementation of the corrective measures identified by the last report; and

  (iii) where the proposed corrective measures in past reviews have proven ineffective or have created unexpected challenges, a description of how those corrective measures could be improved or of those unexpected challenges; and
- sources of information used in the preparation of the report, including all of the following:

  (i) for financial entities other than microenterprises as referred to in Article 6(6) of DORA, the results of internal audits;

  (ii) the results of compliance assessments;

  (iii) results of digital operational resilience testing, and where applicable the results of advanced testing, based on threat-led penetration testing (TLPT), of ICT tools, systems, and processes; and

  (iv) external sources.

For the purposes of bullet point three, where the review was initiated following supervisory instructions, or conclusions derived from relevant digital operational resilience testing or audit processes, the report shall contain explicit references to such instructions or conclusions, allowing for the identification of the reason for initiating the review. Where the review was initiated following ICT-related incidents, the report shall contain the list of all ICT-related incidents with incident root cause analysis.

For the purposes of bullet point six, the description shall contain an analysis of the impact of the changes on the financial entity's digital operational resilience strategy, on the governance.

Simplified ICT Risk Management Framework

10.111 Article 28 of the sub-regulation, Regulation 2024/1774, refers to governance and organisation. The financial entities referred to in Article 16(1) of DORA shall have in place an internal governance and control framework that ensures an effective and prudent management of ICT risk to achieve a high level of digital operational resilience.

The financial entities referred to in Article 16(1) of DORA shall, as part of their Simplified ICT Risk Management Framework, ensure that their management body:

- bears the overall responsibility for ensuring that the Simplified ICT Risk Management Framework allows for the achievement of the financial entity's business strategy in accordance with the risk appetite of that financial entity, and ensures that ICT risk is considered in that context;
- sets clear roles and responsibilities for all ICT-related tasks;
- sets out information security objectives and ICT requirements;
- approves, oversees, and periodically reviews:
  - (i) the classification of information assets of the financial entity as referred to in Article 30(1) of this Regulation, the list of main risks identified, and the business impact analysis and related policies; and
  - (ii) the business continuity plans of the financial entity, and the response and recovery measures referred to in Article 16(1)(f), of DORA;
- allocates and reviews at least once a year the budget necessary to fulfil the financial entity's digital operational resilience needs in respect of all types of resources, including relevant ICT security awareness programmes and digital operational resilience training and ICT skills for all staff;
- specifies and implements the policies and measures included in Chapters I, II and III of Title III (of the sub-regulation) to identify, assess and manage the ICT risk the financial entity is exposed to;
- identifies and implements procedures, ICT protocols, and tools that are necessary to protect all information assets and ICT assets;
- ensures that the staff of the financial entity is kept up to date with sufficient knowledge and skills to understand and assess ICT risk and its impact on the operations of the financial entity, commensurate to the ICT risk being managed; and
- establishes reporting arrangements, including the frequency, form, and content of reporting to the management body on the information security and digital operational resilience.

The financial entities referred to in Article 16(1) may, in accordance with Union and national sectoral law, outsource the tasks of verifying compliance with ICT risk management requirements to ICT intra group or ICT third-party service providers. In the case of such outsourcing, financial entities shall remain fully responsible for the verification of compliance with the ICT risk management requirements.

The financial entities referred to in Article 16(1) shall ensure an appropriate segregation and the independence of control functions and internal audit functions.

The financial entities referred to in Article 16(1) shall ensure that their Simplified ICT Risk Management Framework is subject to an internal audit by auditors, in line with the financial entities' audit plan. The auditors shall have sufficient knowledge, skills, and expertise in ICT risk, and shall be independent. The frequency and focus of ICT audits shall be commensurate to the ICT risk of the financial entity.

Based on the outcome of the audit referred to in Article 28(5), the financial entities referred to in Article 16(1) shall ensure the timely verification and remediation of critical ICT audit findings.

Information security policy and measures

10.112 Article 29 of Regulation 2024/1774 refers to information security policy and measures. The financial entities referred to in Article 16(1) of DORA shall develop, document, and implement an information security policy in the context of the Simplified ICT Risk Management Framework. That information security policy shall specify the high-level principles and rules to protect the confidentiality, integrity, availability, and authenticity of data and of the services those financial entities provide.

Based on their information security policy referred to in Article 29(1), the financial entities referred to in Article 16(1) of DORA shall establish and implement ICT security measures to mitigate their exposure to ICT risk, including mitigating measures implemented by ICT third-party service providers.

The ICT security measures shall include all of the measures referred to in Articles 30 to 38.

Classification of information assets and ICT assets

10.113 Article 30 of Regulation 2024/1774 refers to classification of information assets and ICT assets. As part of the Simplified ICT Risk Management Framework referred to in Article 16(1)(a) of DORA, the financial entities referred to in paragraph (1) of that Article shall identify, classify, and document all critical or important functions, the information assets and ICT assets supporting them and their interdependencies. Financial entities shall review that identification and classification as needed.

The financial entities referred to in Article 16(1) shall identify all critical or important functions supported by ICT third-party service providers.

ICT risk management

10.114 Article 31 of Regulation 2024/1774 refers to ICT risk management. The financial entities referred to in Article 16(1) of DORA shall include in their Simplified ICT Risk Management Framework all of the following:

- a determination of the risk tolerance levels for ICT risk, in accordance with the risk appetite of the financial entity;
- the identification and assessment of the ICT risks to which the financial entity is exposed;
- the specification of mitigation strategies at least for the ICT risks that are not within the risk tolerance levels of the financial entity;
- the monitoring of the effectiveness of the mitigation strategies referred to in bullet point three; and
- the identification and assessment of any ICT and information security risks resulting from any major change in ICT system or ICT services, processes, or procedures, and from ICT security testing results and after any major ICT-related incident.

The financial entities referred to in paragraph 1 shall carry out and document the ICT risk assessment periodically commensurate to the financial entities' ICT risk profile.

The financial entities referred to in Article 16(1) of DORA shall continuously monitor threats and vulnerabilities that are relevant to their critical or important functions, and information assets and ICT assets, and shall regularly review the risk scenarios impacting those critical or important functions.

The financial entities referred to in Article 16(1) shall set out alert thresholds and criteria to trigger and initiate ICT-related incident response processes.

Physical and environmental security

10.115 Article 32 of Regulation 2024/1774 refers to physical and environmental security. The financial entities referred to in Article 16(1) of DORA shall identify and implement physical security measures designed on the basis of the threat landscape and in accordance with the classification referred to in Article 30(1) of this Regulation, the overall risk profile of ICT assets, and accessible information assets.

The measures referred to in Article 32(1) shall protect the premises of financial entities and, where applicable, data centres of financial entities where ICT assets and information assets reside from unauthorised access, attacks, and accidents, and from environmental threats and hazards.

The protection from environmental threats and hazards shall be commensurate with the importance of the premises concerned and, where applicable, the data centres and the criticality of the operations or ICT systems located therein.

Access control

10.116 Article 33 of Regulation 2024/1774 refers to access control. The financial entities referred to in Article 16(1) of DORA shall develop, document, and implement procedures for the control of logical and physical access and shall enforce, monitor, and periodically review those procedures. Those procedures shall contain the following elements of control of logical and physical access:

- access rights to information assets, ICT assets, and their supported functions, and to critical locations of operation of the financial entity, are managed on a need to know, need-to-use and least privileges basis, including for remote and emergency access;
- user accountability, which ensures that users can be identified for the actions performed in the ICT systems;
- account management procedures to grant, change, or revoke access rights for user and generic accounts, including generic administrator accounts;
- authentication methods that are commensurate to the classification referred to in Article 30(1) and to the overall risk profile of ICT assets, and which are based on leading practices; and
- access rights that are periodically reviewed and are withdrawn when no longer required.

For the purposes of bullet point three, the financial entity shall assign privileged, emergency, and administrator access on a need to use or an ad hoc basis for all ICT systems, and shall be logged in accordance with Article 34(1)(f).

For the purposes of bullet point four, financial entities shall use strong authentication methods that are based on leading practices for remote access to the financial entities' network, for privileged access, and for access to ICT assets supporting critical or important functions that are publicly available.

ICT operations security

10.117 Article 34 of Regulation 2024/1774 refers to ICT operations security. The financial entities referred to in Article 16(1) of DORA shall, as part of their systems, protocols, and tools, and for all ICT assets:

- monitor and manage the lifecycle of all ICT assets;
- monitor whether the ICT assets are supported by ICT third-party service providers of financial entities, where applicable;
- identify capacity requirements of their ICT assets and measures to maintain and improve the availability and efficiency of ICT systems and prevent ICT capacity shortages before they materialise;
- perform automated vulnerability scanning and assessments of ICT assets commensurate to their classification as referred to in Article 30(1) and to the overall risk profile of the ICT asset, and deploy patches to address identified vulnerabilities;
- manage the risks related to outdated, unsupported, or legacy ICT assets;
- log events related to logical and physical access control, ICT operations, including system and network traffic activities, and ICT change management identify and implement measures to monitor and analyse information on anomalous activities and behaviour for critical or important ICT operations;
- implement measures to monitor relevant and up-to-date information about cyber threats; and
- other security threats, and publicly known vulnerabilities in software and hardware, and check for corresponding new security updates.

For the purposes of bullet point six, financial entities shall align the level of detail of the logs with their purpose and usage of the ICT asset producing those logs.

Data, system and network security

10.118 Article 35 of Regulation 2024/1774 refers to data, system and network security. The financial entities referred to in Article 16(1) of DORA shall, as part of their systems, protocols, and tools, develop and implement safeguards that ensure the security of networks against intrusions and data misuse and that preserve the availability, authenticity, integrity, and confidentiality of data. In particular, financial entities shall, taking into account the classification referred to in Article 30(1) of this Regulation, establish all of the following:

- the identification and implementation of measures to protect data in use, in transit, and at rest;
- the identification and implementation of security measures regarding the use of software, data storage media, systems and endpoint devices that transfer and store data of the financial entity;

- the identification and implementation of measures to prevent and detect unauthorised connections to the financial entity's network, and to secure the network traffic between the financial entity's internal networks and the internet and other external connections;
- the identification and implementation of measures that ensure the availability, authenticity, integrity, and confidentiality of data during network transmissions;
- a process to securely delete data on premises, or that are stored externally, that the financial entity no longer needs to collect or store;
- a process to securely dispose of, or decommission, data storage devices on premises, or data storage devices that are stored externally, that contain confidential information; and
- the identification and implementation of measures to ensure that teleworking and the use of private endpoint devices does not adversely impact the financial entity's ability to carry out its critical activities in an adequate, timely, and secure manner.

ICT security testing

10.119 Article 36 of Regulation 2024/1774 refers to ICT security testing. The financial entities referred to in Article 16(1) of DORA shall establish and implement an ICT security testing plan to validate the effectiveness of their ICT security measures developed in accordance with Articles 33, 34 and 35 and Articles 37 and 38 of this Regulation. Financial entities shall ensure that that plan considers threats and vulnerabilities identified as part of the Simplified ICT Risk Management Framework referred to in Article 31 of this Regulation.

The financial entities referred to in Article 16(1) of DORA shall review, asses and test ICT security measures, taking into consideration the overall risk profile of the ICT assets of the financial entity.

The financial entities referred to in Article 16(1) shall monitor and evaluate the results of the security tests and update their security measures accordingly without undue delay in the case of ICT systems supporting critical or important functions.

ICT systems acquisition, development, and maintenance

10.120 Article 37 of Regulation 2024/1774 refers to ICT systems acquisition, development, and maintenance. The financial entities referred to in Article 16(1) of DORA shall design and implement, where appropriate, a procedure governing the acquisition, development, and maintenance of ICT systems following a risk-based approach. That procedure shall:

- ensure that, before any acquisition or development of ICT systems takes place, the functional and non-functional requirements, including information security requirements, are clearly specified and approved by the business function concerned;
- ensure the testing and approval of ICT systems prior to their first use and before introducing changes to the production environment; and
- identify measures to mitigate the risk of unintentional alteration or intentional manipulation of the ICT systems during development and implementation in the production environment.

ICT project and change management

10.121 Article 38 of the Regulation 2024/1774 refers to ICT project and change management. The financial entities referred to in Article 16(1) of DORA shall develop, document, and implement an ICT project management procedure and shall specify the roles and responsibilities for its implementation. That procedure shall cover all stages of the ICT projects from their initiation to their closure.

The financial entities referred to in Article 16(1) of DORA shall develop, document, and implement an ICT change management procedure to ensure that all changes to ICT systems are recorded, tested, assessed, approved, implemented, and verified in a controlled manner and with the adequate safeguards to preserve the financial entity's digital operational resilience.

Components of the ICT business continuity plan

10.122 Article 39 of Regulation 2024/1774 refers to components of the ICT business continuity plan. The financial entities referred to in Article 16(1) of DORA shall develop their ICT business continuity plans considering the results of the analysis of their exposures to and potential impact of severe business disruptions and scenarios to which their ICT assets supporting critical or important functions might be exposed, including a cyber attack scenario.

The ICT business continuity plans referred to in Article 39(1) shall:

- be approved by the management body of the financial entity;
- be documented and readily accessible in the event of an emergency or crisis;
- allocate sufficient resources for their execution;
- establish planned recovery levels and timeframes for the recovery and resumption of functions and key internal and external dependencies, including ICT third-party service providers;
- identify the conditions that may prompt the activation of the ICT business continuity plans and what actions are to be taken to ensure the availability,

continuity, and recovery of the financial entities' ICT assets supporting critical or important functions;

- identify the restoration and recovery measures for critical or important business functions, supporting processes, information assets, and their interdependencies to avoid adverse effects on the functioning of the financial entities;
- identify backup procedures and measures that specify the scope of the data that are subject to the backup, and the minimum frequency of the backup, based on the criticality of the function using those data;
- consider alternative options where recovery may not be feasible in the short term because of costs, risks, logistics, or unforeseen circumstances;
- specify the internal and external communication arrangements, including escalation plans; and
- be updated in line with lessons learned from incidents, tests, new risks, and threats identified, changed recovery objectives, major changes to the financial entity's organisation, and to the ICT assets supporting critical or business functions.

For the purposes of bullet point six, the measures referred to in that point shall provide for the mitigation of failures of critical third-party providers

Testing of business continuity plans

10.123 Article 40 of Regulation 2024/1774 refers to the testing of business continuity plans. The financial entities referred to in Article 16(1) of DORA shall test their business continuity plans referred to in Article 39 of this Regulation, including the scenarios referred to in that Article, at least once every year for the backup and restore procedures, or upon every major change of the business continuity plan.

The testing of business continuity plans referred to in Article 40(1) shall demonstrate that the financial entities referred to in Article 16(1) of DORA are able to sustain the viability of their businesses until critical operations are re-established and identify any deficiencies in those plans.

The financial entities referred to in Article 16(1) of DORA shall document the results of the testing of business continuity plans and any identified deficiencies resulting from that testing shall be analysed, addressed, and reported to the management body.

Format and content of the report on the review of the Simplified ICT Risk Management Framework

10.124 Article 41 of Regulation 2024/1774 refers to format and content of the report on the review of the Simplified ICT Risk Management Framework. The financial entities referred to in Article 16(1) of DORA shall submit the report on the review of the ICT Risk Management Framework referred to in paragraph (2) of that Article in a searchable electronic format.

The report referred to in Article 41(1) shall contain all of the following information:

- an introductory section providing:
  - (i) a description of the context of the report in terms of the nature, scale, and complexity of the financial entity's services, activities, and operations, the financial entity's organisation, identified critical functions, strategy, major ongoing projects or activities, and relationships, and the financial entity's dependence on in-house and outsourced ICT services and systems, or the implications that a total loss or severe degradation of such systems would have on critical or important functions and market efficiency;
  - (ii) an executive level summary of the current and near term ICT risk identified, threat landscape, the assessed effectiveness of its controls, and the security posture of the financial entity;
  - (iii) information about the reported area;
  - (iv) a summary of the major changes in the ICT Risk Management Framework since the previous report; and
  - (v) a summary and a description of the impact of major changes to the Simplified ICT Risk Management Framework since the previous report;
- where applicable, the date of the approval of the report by the management body of the financial entity;
- a description of the reasons for the review, including:
  - (i) where the review has been initiated following supervisory instructions, evidence of such instructions; and
  - (ii) where the review has been initiated following the occurrence of ICT-related incidents, the list of all those ICT-related incidents with related incident root cause analysis;
- the start and end date of the review period;
- the person responsible for the review;
- a summary of findings, and a self assessment of the severity of the weaknesses, deficiencies, and gaps identified in ICT Risk Management Framework for the review period, including a detailed analysis thereof;
- remedying measures identified to address weaknesses, deficiencies, and gaps in the Simplified ICT Risk Management Framework, and the expected date for implementing those measures, including the follow up

on weaknesses, deficiencies, and gaps identified in previous reports, where those weaknesses, deficiencies, and gaps have not yet been remedied; and

- overall conclusions on the review of the Simplified ICT Risk Management Framework, including any further planned developments.

It will likely be that most queries from an internal audit will initially refer to the policies required by DORA and the ICT Risk Management Framework.

The likely initial queries from data supervisors may relate to the Register of Information and other reporting requirements. Subsequently, the supervisory authorities will expand their queries into the policies and ICT Risk Management Framework.

CHAPTER 11

Incident Management, Classification and Reporting

INCIDENT MANAGEMENT, CLASSIFICATION, AND REPORTING

11.01 It is clear that regulators and supervisory authorities are concerned with the potential threats facing firms as a result of their use of information and communication technologies (ICT), which include internal vulnerabilities, third-party bad actor threats, as well as third-party service providers. While it would be nice to think that all of these different risks and threats can be prevented, this is sadly not likely to be the case. Instead, it is recognised that firms while deploying protective measures, also need to establish processes to ensure that they are prepared and resilient in order to deal with these adverse ICT events once they occur. The more mature and developed these digital operational resilience measures are, the better firms will be able to react and resolve problem issues that do arise. DORA establishes significant obligations and requirements for digital operational resilience activities.

It is also the case that in order for these new digital operational resilience processes to be prioritised and effective, there needs to be a method for firms to be able to identify and assess their most vulnerable services and dependencies. They also need to be able to identify, and protect, their most critical areas of activity. While incidents will occur, these need to be assessed and categorised. Some will cause more potential disruption and may need to be prioritised over other potential issues.

The supervisory authorities will also require to be alerted in relation what are assessed as the most important and critical types of ICT incidents.

It is for this reason that DORA, as well as the Level 2 sub-regulations, seek to directly provide a framework for firms in classifying and assessing incidents and digital operational resilience. This common framework is to ensure that all firms understand a common framework, and also that the same levels of incidents get reported to the supervisory authorities. Chapter III of DORA refers to ICT-related incident management, classification and reporting. These are referred to below.

ICT INCIDENT MANAGEMENT PROCESS

11.02 Article 17 of DORA refers to 'ICT-related incident management process'. Financial entities must define, establish and implement an ICT related incident management process to detect, manage and notify ICT related incidents.[1]

1 Article 17(1), DORA.

Financial entities must record all ICT related incidents and significant cyber threats.[2] There must be a recording and logging recording process in place.

Financial entities are required to establish appropriate procedures and processes to ensure a consistent and integrated monitoring, handling and follow up of ICT related incidents, to ensure that root causes are identified, documented and addressed in order to prevent the occurrence of such incidents.[3]

The ICT related incident management process referred to above must:

- put in place early warning indicators;
- establish procedures to identify, track, log, categorise and classify ICT related incidents according to their priority and severity and according to the criticality of the services impacted, in accordance with the criteria set out in Article 18(1);
- assign roles and responsibilities that need to be activated for different ICT related incident types and scenarios;
- set out plans for communication to staff, external stakeholders and media in accordance with Article 14 and for notification to clients, for internal escalation procedures, including ICT related customer complaints, as well as for the provision of information to financial entities that act as counterparts, as appropriate;
- ensure that at least major ICT related incidents are reported to relevant senior management and inform the management body of at least major ICT related incidents, explaining the impact, response and additional controls to be established as a result of such ICT related incidents; and
- establish ICT-related incident response procedures to mitigate impacts and ensure that services become operational and secure in a timely manner.[4]

It can be seen, therefore, that these are significant and detailed requirements.

CLASSIFICATION OF ICT INCIDENTS AND CYBER THREATS

11.03 The importance of classification of threats and incidents is a core part of the new DORA rules. Article 18 of DORA refers to 'Classification of ICT-related incidents and cyber threats'. Financial entities must classify ICT related incidents and shall determine their impact based on the following criteria:

- the number and/or relevance of clients or financial counterparts affected and, where applicable, the amount or number of transactions affected by the ICT related incident, and whether the ICT related incident has caused reputational impact;

2 Article 17(2), DORA.
3 Article 17(2), DORA.
4 Article 17(3), DORA.

- the duration of the ICT related incident, including the service downtime;
- the geographical spread with regard to the areas affected by the ICT related incident, particularly if it affects more than two Member States;
- the data losses that the ICT-related incident entails, in relation to availability, authenticity, integrity or confidentiality of data;
- the criticality of the services affected, including the financial entity's transactions and operations; and
- the economic impact, in particular direct and indirect costs and losses, of the ICT related incident in both absolute and relative terms.[5]

Financial entities must also classify cyber threats as significant based on the criticality of the services at risk, including the financial entity's transactions and operations, number and/or relevance of clients or financial counterparts targeted and the geographical spread of the areas at risk.[6]

The European Supervisory Authorities (ESAs) must, through the Joint Committee and in consultation with the European Central Bank (ECB) and the European Union Agency on Cybersecurity (ENISA), develop common draft Regulatory Technical Standards (RTS) sub-regulation further specifying the following:

- the criteria set out in Article 18(1) above, including materiality thresholds for determining major ICT related incidents or, as applicable, major operational or security payment related incidents, that are subject to the Article 19(1) reporting obligation;[7]
- the criteria to be applied by competent authorities for the purpose of assessing the relevance of major ICT-related incidents or, as applicable, major operational or security payment related incidents, to relevant competent authorities in other Member States', and the details of reports of major ICT-related incidents or, as applicable, major operational or security payment-related incidents, to be shared with other competent authorities pursuant to DORA;[8] and
- the criteria set out in Article 18(2) above, including high materiality thresholds for determining significant cyber threats.[9]

When developing the common draft RTS referred to in Article 18(3) above, the ESAs must take into account the criteria set out in Article 4(2), as well as international standards, guidance and specifications developed and published by ENISA, including, where appropriate, specifications for other economic sectors. For the purposes of applying the criteria set out in Article 4(2), the ESAs shall duly consider the need for microenterprises and small and medium-sized

5 Article 18(1), DORA.
6 Article 18(2), DORA.
7 The reporting obligation laid down in Article 19(1) of DORA.
8 To be shared with other competent authorities pursuant to Article 19(6) and (7) of DORA.
9 Article 18(3), DORA.

enterprises to mobilise sufficient resources and capabilities to ensure that ICT related incidents are managed swiftly.[10]

The ESAs were required to submit these common draft RTS to the Commission by 17 January 2024.[11] Power is delegated to the Commission to supplement DORA by adopting the RTS referred to in Article 18(3) in accordance with Articles 10 to 14 of Regulations 1093/2010, 1094/2010 and 1095/2010.[12]

The ESAs published the following draft RTS and on 17 January 2024:

- RTS on criteria for the classification of ICT related incidents; and
- RTS to specify the policy on ICT services supporting critical or important functions provided by ICT third-party service providers (TPPs).

The ESAs also published the following draft RTS and Guidelines on 17 July 2024:

- RTS and Implementing Technical Standard on the content, format, templates and timelines for reporting major ICT related incidents and significant cyber threats; and
- Guidelines on the estimation of aggregated costs/losses caused by major ICT-related incidents.

The above are subject to amendment and adoption by the EU Commission. The Commission has since adopted a sub-regulation, namely Regulation 2024/1774.

RTS sub-Regulation 2024/1774 re Article 18(1) and (4)

11.04 The ESA RTS sub-regulation on classification criteria referred to at **11.03** above in relation to Article 18(1), Regulation 2024/1774, has been approved by and signed on behalf of the Commission.[13]

Classification criteria

11.05 Chapter I of Regulation 2024/1774 refers to the specified classification criteria.

Article 1 sets out the technical criteria in relation to clients, financial counterparts and transactions.

10 Article 18(4), DORA.
11 Article 18(4), DORA.
12 Article 18(4), DORA.
13 Commission Delegated Regulation (EU) 2024/1774 of 13 March 2024 supplementing Regulation (EU) 2022/2554 of the European Parliament and of the Council with regard to regulatory technical standards specifying ICT risk management tools, methods, processes, and policies and the simplified ICT risk management framework.

Article 2 refers to reputational impact. For the purposes of determining the reputational impact of the incident (as referred to in Article 18(1)(a) of DORA), financial entities shall consider that a reputational impact has occurred where at least one of the following criteria is met:

- the incident has been reflected in the media;
- the incident has resulted in repetitive complaints from different clients or financial counterparts on client facing services or critical business relationships;
- the financial entity will not be able to or is likely not to be able to meet regulatory requirements as a result of the incident; and
- the financial entity will or is likely to lose clients or financial counterparts with a material impact on its business as a result of the incident.

When assessing the reputational impact of the incident, financial entities shall take into account the level of visibility that the incident has gained or is likely to gain in relation to each criterion listed above. It is not clear how 'level of visibility' may be interpreted.

Article 3 refers to the duration and service downtime. It is specified how this is to be applied.

Article 4 refers to geographical spread. It is provided that for the purpose of determining the geographical spread with regard to the areas affected by the incident as referred to in Article 18(1)(c) of DORA, financial entities shall assess whether the incident has or had an impact in other Member States, and in particular the significance of the impact in relation to any of the following:

- clients and financial counterparts in other Member States;
- branches or other financial entities within the group carrying out activities in other Member States; and
- financial market infrastructures or third-party providers, which may affect financial entities in other Member States to which they provide services, to the extent such information is available.

Article 5 refers to data losses. For the purpose of determining the data losses that the incident entails as referred to in Article 18(1)(d) of DORA, financial entities shall take into account the following:

- in relation to the availability of data, whether the incident has rendered the data on demand by the financial entity, its clients or its counterparts temporarily or permanently inaccessible or unusable;
- in relation to the authenticity of data, whether the incident has compromised the trustworthiness of the source of data;
- in relation to the integrity of data, whether the incident has resulted in non-authorised modification of data that has rendered it inaccurate or incomplete; and

- in relation to the confidentiality of data, whether the incident has resulted in data having been accessed by or disclosed to an unauthorised party or system.

Article 6 refers to the criticality of services affected. For the purpose of determining the criticality of the services affected as referred to in Article 18(1)(e) of DORA, financial entities shall assess whether the incident:

- affects or has affected ICT services or network and information systems that support critical or important functions of the financial entity;
- affects or has affected financial services provided by the financial entity that require authorisation, registration or that are supervised by competent authorities; and
- constitutes or has constituted a successful, malicious and unauthorised access to the network and information systems of the financial entity.

Article 7 refers to the economic impact. For the purpose of determining the economic impact of the incident as referred to in Article 18(1)(f) of DORA, financial entities shall, without accounting for financial recoveries, take into account the following types of direct and indirect costs and losses which they have incurred as a result of the incident:

- expropriated funds or financial assets for which they are liable, including assets lost to theft;
- costs for replacement or relocation of software, hardware or infrastructure;
- staff costs, including costs associated with replacement or relocation of staff, recruitment of extra staff, remuneration of overtime and recovery of lost or impaired skills;
- fees due to non-compliance with contractual obligations;
- costs for redress and compensation to customers;
- losses due to forgone revenues;
- costs associated with internal and external communication; and
- advisory costs, including costs associated with legal counselling, forensic services and remediation services.

Costs and losses referred to above shall not include costs that are necessary for the day-to-day operation of the business, in particular the following:

- costs for general maintenance of infrastructure, equipment, hardware and software, and costs for keeping skills of staff up to date;
- internal or external costs to enhance the business after the incident, including upgrades, improvements and risk assessment initiatives; and
- insurance premiums.

Perhaps importantly, firms shall calculate the amount of costs and losses based on data available at the time of reporting. If the actual amount of costs and losses cannot be determined, firms shall estimate.

When assessing the economic impact of the incident, financial entities shall sum up the costs and losses.

Major incidents and materiality thresholds

11.06 Chapter II of Regulation 2024/1774 refers to major incidents and materiality thresholds.

Article 8 refers to major incidents. An incident shall be considered a major incident for the purposes of Article 19(1) of DORA where it has affected critical services as referred to in Article 6 and where either of the following conditions is fulfilled:

- the materiality threshold referred to in Article 9(5)(b) is met; or
- two or more of the other materiality thresholds referred to in Articles 9(1) to (6) are met.

Recurring incidents that individually are not considered a major incident shall be considered as one major incident where they meet all of the following conditions:

- they have occurred at least twice within six months;
- they have the same apparent root cause as referred to in Article 20(b) of DORA; and
- they collectively fulfil the criteria for being considered a major incident.

Financial entities shall assess the existence of recurring incidents on a *monthly* basis.

However, this Article does not apply to microenterprises and to financial entities listed in Article 16(1) of DORA.

Article 9 refers to materiality thresholds for determining major incidents. The materiality threshold for the criterion 'clients, financial counterparts and transactions' is met where any of the following conditions are fulfilled:

- the number of affected clients is higher than 10 per cent of all clients using the affected service;
- the number of affected clients using the affected service is higher than 100,000;
- the number of affected financial counterparts is higher than 30 per cent of all financial counterparts carrying out activities related to the provision of the affected service;

- the number of affected transactions is higher than 10 per cent of the daily average number of transactions carried out by the financial entity related to the affected service;
- the amount of affected transactions is higher than 10 per cent of the daily average value of transactions carried out by the financial entity related to the affected service; and
- clients or financial counterparts which have been identified as relevant in accordance with Article 1(3) have been affected.

If the actual number of clients or financial counterparts affected or the actual number or amount of transactions affected cannot be determined, the financial entity shall estimate those numbers or amounts based on available data from comparable reference periods.

The materiality threshold for the criterion 'reputational impact' is met where *any* of the conditions set out in Article 2(a) to (d) are fulfilled.

The materiality threshold for the criterion 'duration and service downtime' is met where any of the following conditions are fulfilled:

- the duration of the incident is longer than 24 hours; and
- the service downtime is longer than two hours for ICT services that support critical or important functions.

The materiality threshold for the criterion 'geographical spread' is met where the incident has an impact in two or more Member States in accordance with Article 4.

The materiality threshold for the criterion 'data losses' is met where any of the following conditions are fulfilled:

- any impact as referred to in Article 5 on the availability, authenticity, integrity or confidentiality of data has or will have an adverse impact on the implementation of the business objectives of the financial entity or on its ability to meet regulatory requirements; or
- any successful, malicious and unauthorised access not covered by the above bullet point occurs to network and information systems, where such access may result in data losses.

The materiality threshold for the criterion 'economic impact' is met where the costs and losses incurred by the financial entity due to the incident have exceeded or are likely to exceed €100,000.

Significant cyber threats

11.07 Chapter III of Regulation 2024/1774 refers to significant cyber threats.

Article 10 refers to high materiality thresholds for determining significant cyber threats.

For the purposes of Article 18(2) of DORA, a cyber threat shall be considered significant where all of the following conditions are fulfilled:

- the cyber threat, if materialised, could affect or could have affected critical or important functions of the financial entity, or could affect other financial entities, third-party providers, clients or financial counterparts, based on information available to the financial entity;
- the cyber threat has a high probability of materialisation at the financial entity or at other financial entities, taking into account at least the following elements:
  (i) applicable risks related to the cyber threat referred to in bullet point one, including potential vulnerabilities of the systems of the financial entity that can be exploited;
  (ii) the capabilities and intent of threat actors to the extent known by the financial entity; and
  (iii) the persistence of the threat and any accrued knowledge about incidents that have impacted the financial entity or its third-party provider, clients or financial counterparts;
- the cyber threat could, if materialised, meet any of the following:
  (i) the criterion regarding criticality of services set out in Article 18(1)(e) of DORA, as specified in Article 6 of this Regulation;
  (ii) the materiality threshold set out in Article 9(1); and
  (iii) the materiality threshold set out in Article 9(4).

Where, depending on the type of cyber threat and available information, the financial entity concludes that the materiality thresholds set out in Article 9(2), (3), (5) and (6) could be met, those thresholds may also be considered

Relevance of major incidents to other competent authorities and reports

11.08 Chapter IV of Regulation 2024/1774 refers to the relevance of major incidents to competent authorities in other Member States and details of reports to be shared with other competent authorities.

Article 11 refers to relevance of major incidents to competent authorities in other Member States.

The assessment of whether the major incident is relevant for competent authorities in other Member States as referred to in Article 19(7) of DORA shall be based on whether the incident has a root cause originating from another Member State or whether the incident has or has had a significant impact in another Member State in relation to any of the following:

- clients or financial counterparts;
- a branch of the financial entity or another financial entity within the group; and
- a financial market infrastructure or a third-party provider which may affect financial entities to which they provide services.

Article 12 refers to the details of major incidents to be shared with other competent authorities. The details of major incidents to be submitted by competent authorities to other competent authorities in accordance with Article 19(6) of DORA and the notifications to be submitted by the European Banking Authority, the European Securities and Markets Authority or the European Insurance and Occupational Pensions Authority and the ECB to the relevant competent authorities in other Member States in accordance with Article 19(7) of DORA, shall contain the same level of information, without any anonymisation, as the notifications and reports of major incidents received from financial entities in accordance with Article 19(4) of DORA.

Regulation 2024/1774 re Article 18(2)

11.09 The ESA RTS sub-regulation referred to above in relation to Article 18(2), Regulation 2024/1174, has been approved by and signed on behalf of the Commission.

Overall risk profile and complexity

11.10 Article 1 of Regulation 2024/1774 refers to overall risk profile and complexity. The policy on the use of ICT services supporting critical or important functions provided by ICT third-party service providers (the 'policy') shall take into account the size and the overall risk profile of the financial entity, and the nature, scale and elements of increased or reduced complexity of its services, activities and operations, including elements relating to:

- the type of ICT services included in the contractual arrangement on the use of ICT services supporting critical or important functions provided by ICT third-party service providers (the 'contractual arrangement') between the financial entity and the ICT third-party service provider;
- the location of the ICT third-party service provider or the location of its parent company;
- whether the ICT services supporting critical or important functions are provided by an ICT third-party service provider located within a Member State or in a third country, also considering the location from where the

ICT services are provided and the location where the data is processed and stored;

- the nature of the data shared with the ICT third-party service provider;
- whether the ICT third-party service provider is part of the same group as the financial entity to which the services are provided;
- the use of ICT third-party service providers that are authorised, registered or subject to supervision or oversight by a competent authority in a Member State or subject to the oversight framework under Chapter V, Section II of DORA, and the use of ICT third-party service providers that are not;
- the use of ICT third-party service providers that are authorised, registered or subject to supervision or oversight by a supervisory authority in a third country, and the use of ICT third-party service providers that are not;
- whether the provision of ICT services supporting critical or important functions are concentrated to a single ICT third-party service provider or a small number of such service providers;
- the transferability of the ICT services supporting critical or important functions to another ICT third-party service provider, including as a result of technology specificities; and
- the potential impact of disruptions in the provision of the ICT services supporting critical or important functions on the continuity of the financial entity's activities and on the availability of its services.

Article 2 refers to group application. Where this Regulation applies on a sub consolidated or consolidated basis, the parent undertaking that is responsible for providing the consolidated or sub-consolidated financial statements for the group shall ensure that the policy is implemented consistently in all financial entities that are part of the group and is adequate for the effective application of this Regulation at all relevant levels of the group.

Article 3 refers to governance arrangements. The management body shall review the policy at least once a year and update it where necessary. Changes made to the policy shall be implemented in a timely manner and as soon as it is possible within the relevant contractual arrangements. The financial entity shall document the planned timeline for the implementation.

The policy shall establish or refer to a methodology for determining which ICT services support critical or important functions. The policy shall also specify when this assessment is to be conducted and reviewed.

The policy shall clearly assign the internal responsibilities for the approval, management, control, and documentation of relevant contractual arrangements and shall ensure that appropriate skills, experience and knowledge are maintained within the financial entity to effectively oversee the relevant contractual arrangements, including the ICT services provided under those arrangements.

Without prejudice to the final responsibility of the financial entity to effectively oversee relevant contractual arrangements, the policy shall require that the ICT third-party service provider is assessed to have sufficient resources to ensure that the financial entity complies with all its legal and regulatory requirements regarding the ICT services supporting critical or important functions that are provided.

The policy shall clearly identify the role or member of senior management responsible for monitoring the relevant contractual arrangements. The policy shall specify how that role or member of senior management shall cooperate with the control functions, unless it is part of it, and shall set out the reporting lines to the management body, including the nature of the information to report and the documents to provide. It shall also set out the frequency of such reporting,

The policy shall ensure that the contractual arrangements are consistent with the following:

- the ICT risk management framework;[14]
- the information security policy;[15]
- the ICT business continuity policy;[16] and
- the requirements on incident reporting.[17]

The policy shall require that ICT services supporting critical or important functions provided by ICT third-party service providers are subject to independent review and are included in the audit plan.

The policy shall explicitly specify that the contractual arrangements:

- do not relieve the financial entity and its management body of its regulatory obligations and its responsibilities to its clients;
- are not to prevent effective supervision of a financial entity and are not to contravene any supervisory restrictions on services and activities;
- are to require that the ICT third-party service providers cooperate with the competent authorities; and
- are to require that the financial entity, its auditors, and competent authorities have effective access to data and premises relating to the use of ICT services supporting critical or important functions.

Article 4 refers to the main phases of the life cycle for the adoption and use of contractual arrangements. The policy shall specify the requirements, including

14 Referred to in Article 6, DORA.
15 Referred to in Article 9(4), DORA.
16 Referred to in Article 11, DORA.
17 Set out in Article 19, DORA.

the rules, the responsibilities and the processes, for each main phase of the lifecycle of the contractual arrangement, covering at least the following:

- the responsibilities of the management body, including its involvement, as appropriate, in the decision-making process on the use of ICT services supporting critical or important functions provided by ICT third-party service providers;
- the planning of contractual arrangements, including the risk assessment, the due diligence as set out in Articles 5 and 6 and the approval process regarding new or material changes to contractual arrangements as set out in Article 8(4);
- the involvement of business units, internal controls and other relevant units in respect of contractual arrangements;
- the implementation, monitoring and management of contractual arrangements as referred to in Articles 7, 8 and 9, including at consolidated and sub consolidated level, where applicable;
- the documentation and record keeping, taking into account the requirements with regard to the register of information laid down in Article 28(3) of DORA; and
- the exit strategies and termination processes as set out in Article 10.

Article 5 refers to an ex-ante risk assessment. The policy shall require that the business needs of the financial entity are defined before a contractual arrangement is concluded.

The policy shall require that a risk assessment is conducted at financial entity level and, where applicable, at consolidated and sub-consolidated level before a contractual arrangement is concluded.

The risk assessment shall take into account all the relevant requirements laid down in DORA and applicable sectoral Union legislation. It shall consider, in particular, the impact of the provision of ICT services supporting critical or important functions by ICT third-party service providers on the financial entity and all the risks posed by the provision of those ICT services supporting critical or important functions by ICT third-party service providers, including the following:

- operational risks;
- legal risks;
- ICT risks;
- reputational risks;
- risks linked to the protection of confidential or personal data;
- risks linked to the availability of data;

- risks linked to the location where the data is processed and stored;
- risks linked to the location of the ICT third-party service provider; and
- ICT concentration risks at entity level.

Article 6 refers to due diligence. The policy shall set out an appropriate and proportionate process for selecting and assessing the prospective ICT third-party service providers taking into account whether or not the ICT third-party service provider is an intragroup ICT service provider, and shall require that the financial entity assesses, before entering into a contractual arrangement, whether the ICT third-party service provider:

- has the business reputation, sufficient abilities, expertise and adequate financial, human and technical resources, information security standards, appropriate organisational structure, risk management and internal controls and, if applicable, the required authorisations or registrations to provide the ICT services supporting the critical or important function in a reliable and professional manner;
- has the ability to monitor relevant technological developments and identify ICT security leading practices and implement them where appropriate to have an effective and sound digital operational resilience framework;
- uses or intends to use ICT subcontractors to perform the ICT services supporting critical or important functions or material parts thereof;
- is located, or processes or stores the data in a third country and, if this is the case, whether this practice affects the level of operational or reputational risks or the risk of being affected by restrictive measures, including embargos and sanctions, that may impact the ability of the ICT third-party service provider to provide the ICT services or the financial entity to receive those ICT services;
- consents to contractual arrangements that ensure that it is effectively possible to conduct audits at the ICT third-party service provider, including onsite, by the financial entity itself, appointed third parties, and competent authorities; and
- acts in an ethical and socially responsible manner, respects human rights and children's rights, including the prohibition of child labour, respects applicable principles on environmental protection, and ensures appropriate working conditions.

The policy shall specify the required level of assurance concerning the effectiveness of ICT third-party service providers' risk management framework for the ICT services supporting critical or important functions to be provided by an ICT third-party service provider. The policy shall require that the due diligence process includes an assessment of the existence of risk mitigation and business continuity measures and of how their functioning within the ICT third-party service provider is ensured.

The policy shall determine the due diligence process for selecting and assessing the prospective ICT third-party service providers and shall indicate which of the following elements are to be used for the required level of assurance on the ICT third-party service provider's performance:

- audits or independent assessments performed by the financial entity itself or on its behalf;
- the use of independent audit reports made on request by the ICT third-party service provider;
- the use of audit reports made by the internal audit function of the ICT third-party service provider;
- the use of appropriate third-party certifications; and
- the use of other relevant information available to the financial entity or other information provided by the ICT third-party service provider.

Financial entities shall ensure an appropriate level of assurance on the ICT third-party service provider's performance, taking into account the elements listed in Article 6(3)(a) to (e). Where appropriate, more than one element listed in those points shall be used.

Article 7 refers to conflicts of interest. The policy shall specify the appropriate measures to identify, prevent and manage actual or potential conflicts of interest arising from the use of ICT third-party service providers that are to be taken before entering relevant contractual arrangements and shall provide for an ongoing monitoring of such conflicts of interest. Where ICT services supporting critical or important functions are provided by ICT intra group service providers, the policy shall specify that decisions on the conditions, including the financial conditions, for the ICT services are to be taken objectively.

Article 8 refers to contractual clauses. The policy shall specify that the relevant contractual arrangement is to be in written form and are to include all the elements referred to in Article 30(2) and (3) of DORA. The policy shall also include elements regarding requirements referred to in Article 1(1)(a) of DORA, as well as other relevant Union and national law as appropriate.

The policy shall specify that the relevant contractual arrangements are to include the right for the financial entity to access information, to carry out inspections and audits, and to perform tests on ICT. For that purpose, the policy shall require that the financial entity uses the following methods, without prejudice to the ultimate responsibility of the financial entity:

- its own internal audit or an audit by an appointed third party;
- where appropriate, pooled audits and pooled ICT testing, including threat led penetration testing, that are organised jointly with other contracting financial entities or firms that use ICT services of the same ICT third-party service provider and that are performed by those contracting financial entities or firms or by a third party appointed by them;

- where appropriate, third-party certifications; and
- where appropriate, internal or third-party audit reports made available by the ICT third-party service provider.

The financial entity shall not over time rely solely on certifications referred to in Article 8(2)(c), or audit reports referred to in Article 8(2)(d). The policy shall only permit the use of the methods referred to in Article 8(2)(c) and (d) where the financial entity:

- is satisfied with the audit plan of the ICT third-party service provider for the relevant contractual arrangements;
- ensures that the scope of the certifications or audit reports cover the systems and key controls identified by it and ensures compliance with relevant regulatory requirements;
- thoroughly assesses the content of the certifications or audit reports on an ongoing basis and verifies that the reports or certifications are not obsolete;
- ensures that key systems and controls are covered in future versions of the certification or audit report;
- is satisfied with the aptitude of the certifying or auditing party;
- is satisfied that the certifications are issued, and the audits are performed against widely recognised relevant professional standards and include a test of the operational effectiveness of the key controls in place;
- has the contractual right to request, with a frequency that is reasonable and legitimate from a risk management perspective, modifications of the scope of the certifications or audit reports to other relevant systems and controls; and
- has the contractual right to perform individual and pooled audits at its discretion with regard to the contractual arrangements and execute those rights in line with the agreed frequency.

The policy shall ensure that material changes to the contractual agreement are to be formalised in a written document which is dated and signed by all parties and shall specify the renewal process for the contractual arrangements.

Article 9 refers to monitoring of the contractual arrangements. The policy shall require that the contractual arrangements specify the measures and key indicators to monitor, on an ongoing basis, the performance of ICT third-party service providers, including measures to monitor compliance with requirements regarding the confidentiality, availability, integrity and authenticity of data and information, and the compliance of the ICT third-party service providers with the financial entity's relevant policies and procedures. The policy shall also specify measures that apply when service level agreements are not met, including contractual penalties where appropriate.

The policy shall specify how the financial entity is to assess whether the ICT third-party service providers used for the ICT services supporting critical or important functions meet appropriate performance and quality standards in line with the contractual arrangement and the financial entity's own policies. The policy shall, in particular, ensure the following:

- that the ICT third-party service providers provide appropriate reports on their activities and services to the financial entity, including periodic reports, incidents reports, service delivery reports, reports on ICT security and reports on business continuity measures and testing;
- that the performance of ICT third-party service providers is assessed with key performance indicators, key control indicators, audits, self-certifications and independent reviews in line with the financial entity's ICT risk management framework;
- that the financial entity receives other relevant information from the ICT third-party service provider;
- that the financial entity is notified, where appropriate, of ICT-related incidents and operational or security payment related incidents; and
- that an independent review and audits verifying compliance with legal and regulatory requirements and policies are performed.

The policy shall specify that the assessment referred to in Article 9(2) is to be documented and its results to be used to update the financial entity's risk assessment referred to in Article 6.

The policy shall establish the appropriate measures that the financial entity is to adopt if it identifies shortcomings of the ICT third-party service providers, including ICT-related incidents and operational or security payment related incidents, in the provision of the ICT services supporting critical or important functions or in the compliance with contractual arrangements or legal requirements. It shall also specify how the implementation of such measures is to be monitored in order to ensure that they are effectively complied with within a defined timeframe, taking into account the materiality of the shortcomings.

Article 10 refers to the exit from and termination of the contractual arrangements. The policy shall contain requirements for a documented exit plan for each contractual arrangement and for the periodic review and testing of the documented exit plan. When establishing the exit plan, the following shall be taken into account:

- unforeseen and persistent service interruptions;
- inappropriate or failed service delivery; and
- the unexpected termination of the contractual arrangement.

The exit plan shall be realistic, feasible, based on plausible scenarios and reasonable assumptions and shall have a planned implementation schedule compatible with the exit and termination terms established in the contractual arrangements.

INCIDENT REPORTING

11.11 There is an important requirement for supervisory authorities to be informed of the more important incidents that arise. (In turn, the national supervisory authorities will report to the European level regulators.)

Article 19 of DORA refers to 'Reporting of major ICT-related incidents and voluntary notification of significant cyber threats'.[18]

Financial entities must report major ICT-related incidents to the relevant competent authority as referred to in Article 46 in accordance with Article 19(4).[19]

Where a financial entity is subject to supervision by more than one national competent authority referred to in Article 46, Member States shall designate a single competent authority as the relevant competent authority responsible for carrying out the functions and duties provided for in this Article.[20]

Credit institutions classified as significant, in accordance with Article 6(4) of Regulation 1024/2013, shall report major ICT-related incidents to the relevant national competent authority designated in accordance with Article 4 of Directive 2013/36, which shall immediately transmit that report to the ECB.[21]

For the purpose of the Article 19(1) of DORA, financial entities shall produce, after collecting and analysing all relevant information, the initial notification and reports referred to in Article 19(4) using the templates referred to in Article 20 and submit them to the competent authority. In the event that a technical impossibility prevents the submission of the initial notification using the template, financial entities shall notify the competent authority about it via alternative means.[22]

The initial notification and reports referred to in Article 19(4) shall include all information necessary for the competent authority to determine the significance of the major ICT-related incident and assess possible cross-border impacts.[23]

Without prejudice to the reporting pursuant to Article 19(1) by the financial entity to the relevant competent authority, Member States may additionally determine that some or all financial entities shall also provide the initial notification and each report referred to in Article 19(4) using the templates referred to in Article 20

18 The issue of reporting is also referred to in Recitals 24, 32, 33, 51, 55, and 65.
19 Article 19(1), DORA.
20 Article 19(1), DORA.
21 Article 19(1), DORA.
22 Article 19(1), DORA.
23 Article 19(1), DORA.

to the competent authorities or the computer security incident response teams (CSIRTs) designated or established in accordance with Directive 2022/2555.[24]

Financial entities may, on a voluntary basis, notify significant cyber threats to the relevant competent authority when they deem the threat to be of relevance to the financial system, service users or clients. The relevant competent authority may provide such information to other relevant authorities referred to in Article 19(6).[25]

Credit institutions classified as significant, in accordance with Article 6(4) of Regulation 1024/2013, may, on a voluntary basis, notify significant cyber threats to relevant national competent authority, designated in accordance with Article 4 of Directive 2013/36, which shall immediately transmit the notification to the ECB.[26]

Member States may determine that those financial entities that on a voluntary basis notify in accordance with Article 19(1) may also transmit that notification to the CSIRTs designated or established in accordance with Directive 2022/2555.[27]

Where a major ICT-related incident occurs and has an impact on the financial interests of clients, financial entities shall, without undue delay as soon as they become aware of it, inform their clients about the major ICT-related incident and about the measures that have been taken to mitigate the adverse effects of such incident.[28]

In the case of a significant cyber threat, financial entities shall, where applicable, inform their clients that are potentially affected of any appropriate protection measures which the latter may consider taking.[29]

Financial entities must, within the time limits to be laid down in accordance with DORA,[30] submit the following to the relevant competent authority:

- an initial notification;
- an intermediate report after the initial notification referred to in bullet point one, as soon as the status of the original incident has changed significantly or the handling of the major ICT-related incident has changed based on new information available, followed, as appropriate, by updated notifications every time a relevant status update is available, as well as upon a specific request of the competent authority; and

24 Article 19(1), DORA.
25 Article 19(2), DORA.
26 Article 19(2), DORA.
27 Article 19(2), DORA.
28 Article 19(3), DORA.
29 Article 19(3), DORA.
30 Within the time limits to be laid down in accordance with Article 20(a)(ii) of DORA.

- a final report, when the root cause analysis has been completed, regardless of whether mitigation measures have already been implemented, and when the actual impact figures are available to replace estimates.[31]

Financial entities may outsource, in accordance with Union and national sectoral law, the reporting obligations under this Article to a third-party service provider. In case of such outsourcing, the financial entity remains fully responsible for the fulfilment of the incident reporting requirements.[32]

Upon receipt of the initial notification and of each report referred to above, the competent authority shall, in a timely manner, provide details of the major ICT-related incident to the following recipients based, as applicable, on their respective competences:

- the European Banking Authority (EBA), ESMA or EIOPA;
- the ECB, in the case of financial entities referred to in Article 2(1) of DORA;[33]
- the competent authorities, single points of contact or CSIRTs designated or established in accordance with Directive 2022/2555;
- the resolution authorities, as referred to in Article 3 of Directive 2014/59/EU, and the Single Resolution Board (SRB) with respect to entities referred to in Article 7(2) of Regulation 806/2014, and with respect to entities and groups referred to in Article 7(4)(b) and (5) of Regulation 806/2014 if such details concern incidents that pose a risk to ensuring critical functions within the meaning of Article 2(1), point (35) of Directive 2014/59/EU; and
- other relevant public authorities under national law.[34]

Following the receipt of information in accordance with Article 19(6), the EBA, ESMA or EIOPA and the ECB, in consultation with ENISA and in cooperation with the relevant competent authority, shall assess whether the major ICT-related incident is relevant for competent authorities in other Member States.[35] Following that assessment, the EBA, ESMA or EIOPA shall, as soon as possible, notify relevant competent authorities in other Member States accordingly.[36] The ECB shall notify the members of the European System of Central Banks on issues relevant to the payment system. Based on that notification, the competent authorities shall, where appropriate, take all of the necessary measures to protect the immediate stability of the financial system.[37]

31 Article 19(4), DORA.
32 Article 19(5), DORA.
33 The financial entities referred to in Article 2(1)(a), (b) and (d) of DORA.
34 Article 19(6), DORA.
35 Article 19(7), DORA.
36 Article 19(7), DORA.
37 Article 19(7), DORA.

The notification to be done by ESMA pursuant to Article 19(7) shall be without prejudice to the responsibility of the competent authority to urgently transmit the details of the major ICT-related incident to the relevant authority in the host Member State, where a central securities depository has significant cross-border activity in the host Member State, the major ICT-related incident is likely to have severe consequences for the financial markets of the host Member State and where there are cooperation arrangements among competent authorities related to the supervision of financial entities.[38]

HARMONISATION OF REPORTING CONTENT AND TEMPLATES

11.12 Article 20 of DORA refers to harmonisation of reporting content and templates.[39]

The ESAs, through the Joint Committee, and in consultation with ENISA and the ECB, shall develop common draft RTS in order to:

- establish the content of the reports for major ICT-related incidents in order to reflect the criteria laid down in DORA[40] and incorporate further elements, such as details for establishing the relevance of the reporting for other Member States and whether it constitutes a major operational or security payment-related incident or not;
- determine the time limits for the initial notification and for each report referred to in Article 19(4); and
- establish the content of the notification for significant cyber threats.[41]

When developing those draft RTS, the ESAs shall take into account the size and the overall risk profile of the financial entity, and the nature, scale and complexity of its services, activities and operations, and in particular, with a view to ensuring that, for the purposes of Article 20(a)(ii), different time limits may reflect, as appropriate, specificities of financial sectors, without prejudice to maintaining a consistent approach to ICT-related incident reporting pursuant to DORA and to Directive 2022/2555. The ESAs shall, as applicable, provide justification when deviating from the approaches taken in the context of that Directive.

The ESAs shall also develop common draft Implementing Technical Standards (ITS) in order to establish the standard forms, templates and procedures for financial entities to report a major ICT-related incident and to notify a significant cyber threat.[42]

38 Article 19(8), DORA.

39 Harmonisation issues generally are referred to in Recitals 21, 36, 38, 39, 40, 42, 43, 44, 53, 64, and 99.

40 The criteria laid down in Article 18(1) of DORA.

41 Article 20, DORA.

42 Article 20, DORA.

The ESAs were required to submit the common draft RTS referred to in Article 20(a), and the common draft ITS referred to in Article 20(b), to the Commission by 17 July 2024.[43]

Power is delegated to the Commission to supplement DORA by adopting the common RTS referred to in the Article 20(1)(a), in accordance with Articles 10 to 14 of Regulations 1093/2010, 1094/2010 and 1095/2010.[44]

Power is conferred on the Commission to adopt the common ITS referred to in Article 20(b), in accordance with Article 15 of Regulations 1093/2010, 1094/2010 and 1095/2010.[45]

The ESAs published the following draft RTS and Guidelines on 17 July 2024:

- RTS and ITS on the content, format, templates and timelines for reporting major ICT related incidents and significant cyber threats;
- RTS on the harmonisation of conditions enabling the conduct of the oversight activities;
- Guidelines on the estimation of aggregated costs/losses caused by major ICT related incidents; and
- Guidelines on oversight cooperation.

The above are subject to amendment and adoption by the EU Commission.

CENTRALISATION OF REPORTING OF MAJOR ICT INCIDENTS

11.13 Article 21 of DORA refers to 'Centralisation of reporting of major ICT-related incidents'. The ESAs, through the Joint Committee, and in consultation with the ECB and ENISA, shall prepare a joint report assessing the feasibility of further centralisation of incident reporting through the establishment of a single EU Hub for major ICT-related incident reporting by financial entities. The joint report shall explore ways to facilitate the flow of ICT-related incident reporting, reduce associated costs and underpin thematic analyses with a view to enhancing supervisory convergence.[46]

The joint report referred to in Article 21(1) shall comprise at least the following elements:

- prerequisites for the establishment of a single EU Hub;
- benefits, limitations and risks, including risks associated with the high concentration of sensitive information;

43 Article 20, DORA.
44 Article 20, DORA.
45 Article 20, DORA.
46 Article 21(1), DORA.

- the necessary capability to ensure interoperability with regard to other relevant reporting schemes;
- elements of operational management;
- conditions of membership;
- technical arrangements for financial entities and national competent authorities to access the single EU Hub; and
- a preliminary assessment of financial costs incurred by setting up the operational platform supporting the single EU Hub, including the requisite expertise.[47]

The ESAs shall submit the report referred to in Article 21(1) to the European Parliament, to the Council and to the Commission by 17 January 2025.[48]

The ESAs published the following draft RTS and Guidelines on 17 January 2024:

- RTS on criteria for the classification of ICT-related incidents;
- RTS to specify the policy on ICT services supporting critical or important functions provided by ICT third-party service providers (TPPs); and
- ITS to establish the templates for the register of information.

The ESAs also published the following draft RTS and Guidelines on 17 July 2024:

- RTS and ITS on the content, format, templates and timelines for reporting major ICT related incidents and significant cyber threats;
- RTS on the harmonisation of conditions enabling the conduct of the oversight activities;
- RTS specifying the criteria for determining the composition of the joint examination team (JET);
- Guidelines on the estimation of aggregated costs/losses caused by major ICT related incidents; and
- Guidelines on oversight cooperation.

The above are subject to amendment and adoption by the EU Commission.

Reports such as this as well as how the Lead Overseer mechanisms are seen to operate, particularly as regard third parties, will determine how successful the intentions behind DORA are, and ultimately whether additional enhancements may be required. This will become more apparent in the following years.

47 Article 21(2), DORA.
48 Article 21(3), DORA.

SUPERVISORY FEEDBACK

11.14 Article 22 of DORA refers to supervisory feedback.

Without prejudice to the technical input, advice or remedies and subsequent follow-up which may be provided, where applicable, in accordance with national law, by the CSIRTs under Directive 2022/2555, the competent authority shall, upon receipt of the initial notification and of each report as referred to in Article 19(4), acknowledge receipt and may, where feasible, provide in a timely manner relevant and proportionate feedback or high-level guidance to the financial entity, in particular by making available any relevant anonymised information and intelligence on similar threats, and may discuss remedies applied at the level of the financial entity and ways to minimise and mitigate adverse impact across the financial sector. Without prejudice to the supervisory feedback received, financial entities shall remain fully responsible for the handling and for consequences of the ICT-related incidents reported pursuant to DORA.[49]

The ESAs shall, through the Joint Committee, on an anonymised and aggregated basis, report yearly on major ICT related incidents, the details of which shall be provided by competent authorities in accordance with DORA,[50] setting out at least the number of major ICT related incidents, their nature and their impact on the operations of financial entities or clients, remedial actions taken and costs incurred.[51]

The ESAs shall issue warnings and produce high level statistics to support ICT threat and vulnerability assessments.[52]

The ESAs published the draft RTS on criteria for the classification of ICT-related incidents on 17 January 2024:

The ESAs also published the following draft RTS and Guidelines on 17 July 2024:

- RTS and ITS on the content, format, templates and timelines for reporting major ICT related incidents and significant cyber threats;
- RTS on the harmonisation of conditions enabling the conduct of the oversight activities;
- Guidelines on the estimation of aggregated costs/losses caused by major ICT related incidents; and
- Guidelines on oversight cooperation.

The above are subject to amendment and adoption by the EU Commission.

49 Article 22(1), DORA. The ICT-related incidents reported pursuant to Article 19(1) of DORA.
50 In accordance with Article 19(6) of DORA.
51 Article 22(2), DORA.
52 Article 22(2), DORA.

OPERATIONAL OR SECURITY PAYMENT RELATED INCIDENTS

11.15 While there are general framework requirements for classification and reporting of ICT-related incidents, there are also some variations for particular types of firms. Article 23 of DORA refers to what is referred to as 'Operational or security payment-related incidents concerning credit institutions, payment institutions, account information service providers, and electronic money institutions.' The requirements laid down in Chapter III of DORA shall also apply to operational or security payment-related incidents and to major operational or security payment related incidents, where they concern credit institutions, payment institutions, account information service providers, and electronic money institutions.[53]

53 Article 23, DORA.

CHAPTER 12

Digital Operational Resilience Testing

DIGITAL OPERATIONAL RESILIENCE TESTING

12.01 Chapter IV of DORA refers to digital operational resilience testing. This should not be confused with pen testing or penetration testing which many firms will already be undertaking from a security and preparedness perspective, but also because supervisory authorities wish to ensure that firms are attuned to the benefits, if not requirements, of testing their systems to identify gaps or vulnerabilities that may be exploited by bad actors if they remain unaddressed. It would be a grave mistake for firms to assume that their existing pen testing activities (which should regular and ongoing) satisfy DORA's digital operational resilience testing rules. These issues are referred to below.

General Requirements for Digital Operational Resilience Testing

12.02 Article 24 of DORA refers to 'General requirements for the performance of digital operational resilience testing.'[1] For the purpose of assessing preparedness for handling information and communication technology (ICT)-related incidents, of identifying weaknesses, deficiencies and gaps in digital operational resilience, and of promptly implementing corrective measures, financial entities, other than microenterprises, shall, taking into account the criteria set out in DORA,[2] establish, maintain and review a sound and comprehensive digital operational resilience testing programme as an integral part of the ICT risk management framework referred to in DORA.[3]

The digital operational resilience testing programme shall include a range of assessments, tests, methodologies, practices and tools to be applied in accordance with DORA.[4]

When conducting the digital operational resilience testing programme referred to in Article 24(1), financial entities, other than microenterprises, shall follow a risk-based approach taking into account the criteria set out in DORA[5] duly considering the evolving landscape of ICT risk, any specific risks to which the financial entity concerned is or might be exposed, the criticality of information

1 Testing issues are also referred to in Recitals 26, 43, 44, 56, 57, 59, 60, and 61.
2 The criteria set out in Article 4(2) of DORA.
3 Article 34(1), DORA. The ICT Risk Management Framework referred to in Article 6 of DORA.
4 Article 34(2), DORA. A range of assessments, tests, methodologies, practices and tools to be applied in accordance with Articles 25 and 26 of DORA.
5 The criteria set out in Article 4(2) of DORA.

assets and of services provided, as well as any other factor the financial entity deems appropriate.[6]

Financial entities, other than microenterprises, must ensure that tests are undertaken by independent parties, whether internal or external. Where tests are undertaken by an internal tester, financial entities shall dedicate sufficient resources and ensure that conflicts of interest are avoided throughout the design and execution phases of the test.[7]

Financial entities, other than microenterprises, must establish procedures and policies to prioritise, classify and remedy all issues revealed throughout the performance of the tests and shall establish internal validation methodologies to ascertain that all identified weaknesses, deficiencies or gaps are fully addressed.[8]

Financial entities, other than microenterprises, must also ensure, at least yearly, that appropriate tests are conducted on all ICT systems and applications supporting critical or important functions.[9]

TESTING OF ICT TOOLS AND SYSTEMS: DORTP

12.03 Article 25 of DORA refers to Testing of ICT tools and systems.

Under Article 25(1) the digital operational resilience testing programme referred to in DORA[10] shall provide, in accordance with the criteria set out in Article 4(2), for the execution of appropriate tests, such as vulnerability assessments and scans, open source analyses, network security assessments, gap analyses, physical security reviews, questionnaires and scanning software solutions, source code reviews where feasible, scenario-based tests, compatibility testing, performance testing, end-to-end testing and penetration testing.[11]

There is, therefore, an express requirement for a Digital Operational Resilience Testing Programme ('DORTP' or 'DORT-P'). There are a number of requirements for a firm's DORTP. This includes considering the Article 4(2) proportionality provisions and also the range of appropriate tests.

There are a number of points to be made. These tests are deemed at a headline level to be appropriate to satisfy the requirements of DORA to have a DORTP. Firms who undertake these types of tests will have some assurance that they are satisfying these particular DORA requirements.

The tests to be included in a Digital Operational Resilience Testing Programme are:

6 Article 34(3), DORA.
7 Article 24(4), DORA.
8 Article 24(5), DORA.
9 Article 24(6), DORA.
10 The digital operational resilience testing programme referred to in Article 24 of DORA.
11 Article 25(1), DORA.

- vulnerability assessments and scans;
- open source analyses;
- network security assessments;
- gap analyses;
- physical security reviews;
- questionnaires and scanning software solutions;
- source code reviews where feasible;
- scenario-based tests;
- compatibility testing;
- performance testing;
- end-to-end testing; and
- penetration testing.

As is clear from the above DORA list, pen tests of penetration tests alone are not sufficient to satisfy this part of DORA and the Digital Operational Resilience Testing Programme requirement.

It is important to say that these tests are not a closed list of required tests. They are referred to as examples only – given the use of the term 'such as'.

A further point to note is that it not expressly required that each and every one of these tests must be carried out at the same time. Nor is expressly required that all of these tests are required to be carried out within each testing cycle. However, it will be necessary to consider final sub-regulations and also what individual supervisory authorities say in terms of their expectations for testing.

There are some carveouts to be aware of, namely, for central securities depositories and for microenterprises. These are specific to the categories mentioned, and are not generally applicable.

Central securities depositories and central counterparties shall perform vulnerability assessments before any deployment or redeployment of new or existing applications and infrastructure components, and ICT services supporting critical or important functions of the financial entity.[12]

Microenterprises shall perform the tests referred to in Article 25(1) by combining a risk-based approach with a strategic planning of ICT testing, by duly considering the need to maintain a balanced approach between the scale of resources and the time to be allocated to the ICT testing provided for in this Article, on the one hand, and the urgency, type of risk, criticality of information assets and of

12 Article 25(2), DORA.

services provided, as well as any other relevant factor, including the financial entity's ability to take calculated risks, on the other hand.[13]

ADVANCED TESTING

12.04 Article 26 of DORA refers to advanced testing of ICT tools, systems and processes based on threat-led penetration testing (TLPT). Article 26(1) provides that financial entities, other than entities referred to in Article 16(1), first subparagraph, and other than microenterprises, which are identified in accordance with Article 26(8), third subparagraph, shall carry out at least every three years advanced testing by means of TLPT.[14] Based on the risk profile of the financial entity and taking into account operational circumstances, the competent authority may, where necessary, request the financial entity to reduce or increase this frequency.[15]

Each TLPT shall cover several or all critical or important functions of a financial entity, and shall be performed on live production systems supporting such functions.[16]

Financial entities shall identify all relevant underlying ICT systems, processes and technologies supporting critical or important functions and ICT services, including those supporting the critical or important functions which have been outsourced or contracted to ICT third-party service providers.[17]

Financial entities shall assess which critical or important functions need to be covered by the TLPT. The result of this assessment shall determine the precise scope of TLPT and shall be validated by the competent authorities.[18]

Where ICT third-party service providers are included in the scope of TLPT, the financial entity shall take the necessary measures and safeguards to ensure the participation of such ICT third-party service providers in the TLPT and shall retain at all times full responsibility for ensuring compliance with DORA.[19]

Without prejudice to Article 26(2), first and second subparagraphs, where the participation of an ICT third-party service provider in the TLPT, referred to in Article 26(3), is reasonably expected to have an adverse impact on the quality or security of services delivered by the ICT third-party service provider to customers that are entities falling outside the scope of DORA, or on the confidentiality of the data related to such services, the financial entity and the ICT third-party service provider may agree in writing that the ICT third-party service provider directly enters into contractual arrangements with an external tester, for the purpose of

13 Article 25(3), DORA.
14 Article 26(1), DORA.
15 Article 26(1), DORA.
16 Article 26(2), DORA.
17 Article 26(2), DORA.
18 Article 26(2), DORA.
19 Article 26(3), DORA.

conducting, under the direction of one designated financial entity, a pooled TLPT involving several financial entities (pooled testing) to which the ICT third-party service provider provides ICT services.[20]

That pooled testing shall cover the relevant range of ICT services supporting critical or important functions contracted to the respective ICT third-party service provider by the financial entities. The pooled testing shall be considered TLPT carried out by the financial entities participating in the pooled testing.[21]

The number of financial entities participating in the pooled testing shall be duly calibrated taking into account the complexity and types of services involved.[22]

Financial entities shall, with the cooperation of ICT third-party service providers and other parties involved, including the testers but excluding the competent authorities, apply effective risk management controls to mitigate the risks of any potential impact on data, damage to assets, and disruption to critical or important functions, services or operations at the financial entity itself, its counterparts or to the financial sector.[23]

At the end of the testing, after reports and remediation plans have been agreed, the financial entity and, where applicable, the external testers shall provide to the designated authority,[24] a summary of the relevant findings, the remediation plans and the documentation demonstrating that the TLPT has been conducted in accordance with the requirements.[25]

Authorities shall provide financial entities with an attestation confirming that the test was performed in accordance with the requirements as evidenced in the documentation in order to allow for mutual recognition of threat led penetration tests between competent authorities. The financial entity shall notify the relevant competent authority of the attestation, the summary of the relevant findings and the remediation plans.[26]

Without prejudice to such attestation, financial entities shall remain at all times fully responsible for the impact of the tests referred to above.[27]

Financial entities shall contract testers for the purposes of undertaking TLPT.[28] When financial entities use internal testers for the purposes of undertaking TLPT, they shall contract external testers every three tests.[29]

20 Article 26(4), DORA.
21 Article 26(4), DORA.
22 Article 26(4), DORA.
23 Article 26(5), DORA.
24 Designated in accordance with Article 26(9) or (10).
25 Article 26(6), DORA.
26 Article 26(7), DORA.
27 Article 26(7), DORA. The tests referred to in Article 26(4).
28 Undertaking TLPT in accordance with Article 27 of DORA.
29 Article 26(8), DORA.

Credit institutions that are classified as significant in accordance with Article 6(4) of Regulation 1024/2013, shall only use external testers in accordance with DORA.[30]

Competent authorities shall identify financial entities that are required to perform TLPT taking into account the criteria set out in DORA,[31] based on an assessment of the following:

- impact-related factors, in particular the extent to which the services provided and activities undertaken by the financial entity impact the financial sector;
- possible financial stability concerns, including the systemic character of the financial entity at Union or national level, as applicable; and
- specific ICT risk profile, level of ICT maturity of the financial entity or technology features involved.[32]

Member States may designate a single public authority in the financial sector to be responsible for TLPT-related matters in the financial sector at national level and shall entrust it with all competences and tasks to that effect.[33]

In the absence of a designation in accordance with Article 26(9), and without prejudice to the power to identify the financial entities that are required to perform TLPT, a competent authority may delegate the exercise of some or all of the tasks referred to in Article 26 and Article 27 to another national authority in the financial sector.[34]

The European Supervisory Authorities (ESAs) shall, in agreement with the European Central Bank, develop joint draft RTS in accordance with the TIBER-EU framework in order to specify further:

- the criteria used for the purpose of the application of Article 26(8), second subparagraph;
- the requirements and standards governing the use of internal testers;
- the requirements in relation to:
  (i) the scope of TLPT referred to in Article 26(2);
  (ii) the testing methodology and approach to be followed for each specific phase of the testing process; and
  (iii) the results, closure and remediation stages of the testing; and
- the type of supervisory and other relevant cooperation which are needed for the implementation of TLPT, and for the facilitation of mutual recognition

30 Article 26(8), DORA. In accordance with Article 27(1)(a)–(e) of DORA.
31 The criteria set out in Article 4(2) of DORA.
32 Article 26(8), DORA.
33 Article 26(9), DORA.
34 Article 26(10), DORA.

of that testing, in the context of financial entities that operate in more than one Member State, to allow an appropriate level of supervisory involvement and a flexible implementation to cater for specificities of financial sub-sectors or local financial markets.[35]

When developing those draft RTS, the ESAs shall give due consideration to any specific feature arising from the distinct nature of activities across different financial services sectors.[36]

The ESAs were required to submit those draft RTS to the Commission by 17 July 2024.[37] Power is delegated to the Commission to supplement DORA by adopting the RTS referred to in Article 26, first subparagraph, in accordance with Articles 10 to 14 of Regulations 1093/2010, 1094/2010 and 1095/2010.[38]

The ESAs published the following draft Regulatory Technical Standards (RTS) and Guidelines on 17 January 2024:

- RTS on ICT risk management framework and on simplified ICT risk management framework;
- RTS on criteria for the classification of ICT-related incidents;
- RTS to specify the policy on ICT services supporting critical or important functions provided by ICT third-party service providers (TPPs); and
- Implementing Technical Standards (ITS) to establish the templates for the register of information.

The ESAs also published the following draft RTS and Guidelines on 17 July 2024:

- RTS and ITS on the content, format, templates and timelines for reporting major ICT-related incidents and significant cyber threats;
- RTS on the harmonisation of conditions enabling the conduct of the oversight activities;
- RTS specifying the criteria for determining the composition of the joint examination team (JET);
- RTS on threat-led penetration testing (TLPT);
- Guidelines on the estimation of aggregated costs/losses caused by major ICT-related incidents; and
- Guidelines on oversight cooperation.

The above are subject to amendment and adoption by the EU Commission.

35 Article 26(11), DORA.
36 Article 26(11), DORA.
37 Article 26(11), DORA.
38 Article 26(11), DORA.

REQUIREMENTS FOR TLPT TESTERS

12.05 Article 27 of DORA refers to the necessary requirements for testers for the carrying out of TLPT. Financial entities shall only use testers for the carrying out of TLPT, that:

- are of the highest suitability and reputability;
- possess technical and organisational capabilities and demonstrate specific expertise in threat intelligence, penetration testing and red team testing;
- are certified by an accreditation body in a Member State or adhere to formal codes of conduct or ethical frameworks;
- provide an independent assurance, or an audit report, in relation to the sound management of risks associated with the carrying out of TLPT, including the due protection of the financial entity's confidential information and redress for the business risks of the financial entity; and
- are duly and fully covered by relevant professional indemnity insurances, including against risks of misconduct and negligence.[39]

When using internal testers, financial entities shall ensure that, in addition to the requirements in Article 27(1), the following conditions are met:

- such use has been approved by the relevant competent authority or by the single public authority designated in accordance with DORA;[40]
- the relevant competent authority has verified that the financial entity has sufficient dedicated resources and ensured that conflicts of interest are avoided throughout the design and execution phases of the test; and
- the threat intelligence provider is external to the financial entity.[41]

Financial entities must ensure that contracts concluded with external testers require a sound management of the TLPT results and that any data processing thereof, including any generation, store, aggregation, draft, report, communication or destruction, do not create risks to the financial entity.[42]

Supervisory authorities and internal auditors will be asking firms to demonstrate that they have a Digital Operational Resilience Testing Programme in place, and that it is active and effective.

Depending on the type and size of firm, additional and more detailed forms of testing may also be required, in particular advanced testing. This will no doubt be more expensive and time consuming for the firms concerned.

39 Article 27(1), DORA.

40 The single public authority designated in accordance with Article 26(9) and (10) of DORA.

41 Article 27(2), DORA.

42 Article 27(3), DORA.

CHAPTER 13

Managing ICT Third-party Risk

MANAGING ICT THIRD-PARTY RISK

13.01 It is increasingly recognised that focusing on the company itself, and its own defences, is too limiting an approach for considering information and communication technology (ICT) risk (and indeed risk more widely).

The reason for this is that in the modern services world – and the modern ICT connected telecoms and internet world – attacks and vulnerabilities arise beyond the walls of the enterprise itself.

There are very few companies who do not, to a small or large extent, rely on third-party service providers – or indeed whom outsource some of their prior core functions to a third-party company.

It is for these reasons that financial regulation policymakers and supervisory authorities concerned with increasing the defences and digital operational resilience of firms are beginning to require higher standards. This arises in a twofold manner. The standards of compliance are being raised as well as the types and amount of information that firms are being required to produce to the supervisory authorities.

DORA is at the cutting edge of this in terms of IT and ICT risks for firms, even though there are some earlier examples of this general concept such as firms being asked to provide details on their outsourcing arrangements to supervisory authorities. DORA is a significant advancement on this area of risk.

Chapter V of DORA refers to the managing of ICT third-party risk. This is referred to in detail below.

GENERAL PRINCIPLES

13.02 Section I of Chapter V of DORA refers to key principles for the sound management of ICT third-party risk.[1]

Article 28 of DORA refers to 'General principles'. Under Article 28(1) financial entities must manage ICT third-party risk as an integral component of ICT risk

1 The need to control ICT risk is also referred to in Recitals 21, 79, 104, and 105.

within their ICT risk management framework as referred to in DORA,[2] and in accordance with the following principles:

- financial entities that have in place contractual arrangements for the use of ICT services to run their business operations shall, at all times, remain fully responsible for compliance with, and the discharge of, all obligations under DORA and applicable financial services law; and
- financial entities' management of ICT third-party risk shall be implemented in light of the principle of proportionality, taking into account:
  - (i) the nature, scale, complexity and importance of ICT-related dependencies; and
  - (ii) the risks arising from contractual arrangements on the use of ICT services concluded with ICT third-party service providers, taking into account the criticality or importance of the respective service, process or function, and the potential impact on the continuity and availability of financial services and activities, at individual and at group level.[3]

As part of their ICT Risk Management Framework, financial entities, other than entities referred to in Article 16(1), first subparagraph, and other than microenterprises, shall adopt, and regularly review, a strategy on ICT third-party risk, taking into account the multi-vendor strategy referred to in Article 6(9), where applicable. The strategy on ICT third-party risk shall include a policy on the use of ICT services supporting critical or important functions provided by ICT third-party service providers and shall apply on an individual basis and, where relevant, on a sub-consolidated and consolidated basis. The management body shall, on the basis of an assessment of the overall risk profile of the financial entity and the scale and complexity of the business services, regularly review the risks identified in respect to contractual arrangements on the use of ICT services supporting critical or important functions.[4]

As part of their ICT risk management framework, financial entities shall maintain and update at entity level, and at sub-consolidated and consolidated levels, a register of information in relation to all contractual arrangements on the use of ICT services provided by ICT third-party service providers.[5]

The contractual arrangements referred to in Article 16(1), first subparagraph shall be appropriately documented, distinguishing between those that cover ICT services supporting critical or important functions and those that do not.[6]

Financial entities shall report at least yearly to the competent authorities on the number of new arrangements on the use of ICT services, the categories of ICT

2 The ICT Risk Management Framework as referred to in Article 6(1) of DORA.
3 Article 28(1), DORA.
4 Article 28(2), DORA.
5 Article 28(3), DORA.
6 Article 28(3), DORA.

third-party service providers, the type of contractual arrangements and the ICT services and functions which are being provided.[7]

Financial entities shall make available to the competent authority, upon its request, the full register of information or, as requested, specified sections thereof, along with any information deemed necessary to enable the effective supervision of the financial entity.[8]

Financial entities shall inform the competent authority in a timely manner about any planned contractual arrangement on the use of ICT services supporting critical or important functions as well as when a function has become critical or important.[9]

Before entering into a contractual arrangement on the use of ICT services, financial entities must:

- assess whether the contractual arrangement covers the use of ICT services supporting a critical or important function;
- assess if supervisory conditions for contracting are met;
- identify and assess all relevant risks in relation to the contractual arrangement, including the possibility that such contractual arrangement may contribute to reinforcing ICT concentration risk as referred to in DORA;[10]
- undertake all due diligence on prospective ICT third-party service providers and ensure throughout the selection and assessment processes that the ICT third-party service provider is suitable; and
- identify and assess conflicts of interest that the contractual arrangement may cause.[11]

Financial entities may only enter into contractual arrangements with ICT third-party service providers that comply with appropriate information security standards. When those contractual arrangements concern critical or important functions, financial entities shall, prior to concluding the arrangements, take due consideration of the use, by ICT third-party service providers, of the most up-to-date and highest quality information security standards.[12]

In exercising access, inspection and audit rights over the ICT third-party service provider, financial entities shall, on the basis of a risk-based approach, pre-determine the frequency of audits and inspections as well as the areas to be

7 Article 28(3), DORA.
8 Article 28(3), DORA.
9 Article 28(3), DORA.
10 Reinforcing ICT concentration risk as referred to in Article 29 of DORA.
11 Article 28(4), DORA.
12 Article 28(5), DORA.

audited through adhering to commonly accepted audit standards in line with any supervisory instruction on the use and incorporation of such audit standards.[13]

Where contractual arrangements concluded with ICT third-party service providers on the use of ICT services entail high technical complexity, the financial entity shall verify that auditors, whether internal or external, or a pool of auditors, possess appropriate skills and knowledge to effectively perform the relevant audits and assessments.[14]

Financial entities shall ensure that contractual arrangements on the use of ICT services may be terminated in any of the following circumstances:

- significant breach by the ICT third-party service provider of applicable laws, regulations or contractual terms;
- circumstances identified throughout the monitoring of ICT third-party risk that are deemed capable of altering the performance of the functions provided through the contractual arrangement, including material changes that affect the arrangement or the situation of the ICT third-party service provider;
- ICT third-party service provider's evidenced weaknesses pertaining to its overall ICT risk management and in particular in the way it ensures the availability, authenticity, integrity and, confidentiality, of data, whether personal or otherwise sensitive data, or non-personal data; and
- where the competent authority can no longer effectively supervise the financial entity as a result of the conditions of, or circumstances related to, the respective contractual arrangement.[15]

For ICT services supporting critical or important functions, financial entities shall put in place exit strategies. The exit strategies shall take into account risks that may emerge at the level of ICT third-party service providers, in particular a possible failure on their part, a deterioration of the quality of the ICT services provided, any business disruption due to inappropriate or failed provision of ICT services or any material risk arising in relation to the appropriate and continuous deployment of the respective ICT service, or the termination of contractual arrangements with ICT third-party service providers under any of the circumstances listed in Article 28(7).[16]

Financial entities must ensure that they are able to exit contractual arrangements without:

- disruption to their business activities;
- limiting compliance with regulatory requirements; and

13 Article 28(6), DORA.
14 Article 28(6), DORA.
15 Article 28(7), DORA.
16 Article 28(8), DORA.

- detriment to the continuity and quality of services provided to clients.[17]

Exit plans shall be comprehensive, documented and, in accordance with the criteria set out in Article 4(2), shall be sufficiently tested and reviewed periodically.[18]

Financial entities shall identify alternative solutions and develop transition plans enabling them to remove the contracted ICT services and the relevant data from the ICT third-party service provider and to securely and integrally transfer them to alternative providers or reincorporate them inhouse.[19]

Financial entities shall have appropriate contingency measures in place to maintain business continuity in the event of the circumstances referred to in the first subparagraph.[20]

The European Supervisory Authorities (ESAs) shall, through the Joint Committee, develop draft Implementing Technical Standards (ITS) to establish the standard templates for the purposes of the register of information referred to above,[21] including information that is common to all contractual arrangements on the use of ICT services. The ESAs were required to submit those draft ITS to the Commission by 17 January 2024.[22] Power is conferred on the Commission to adopt the ITS in accordance with Article 15 of Regulations 1093/2010, 1094/2010 and 1095/2010.[23]

The ESAs shall develop draft Regulatory Technical Standards (RTS) to further specify the detailed content of the policy referred to above[24] in relation to the contractual arrangements on the use of ICT services supporting critical or important functions provided by ICT third-party service providers.[25]

When developing those draft RTS, the ESAs shall take into account the size and the overall risk profile of the financial entity, and the nature, scale and complexity of its services, activities and operations. The ESAs were required to submit those draft RTS to the Commission by 17 January 2024.[26]

Power is delegated to the Commission to supplement DORA by adopting the RTS in accordance with Articles 10 to 14 of Regulations 1093/2010, 1094/2010 and 1095/2010.[27]

17 Article 28(8), DORA.
18 Article 28(8), DORA.
19 Article 28(8), DORA.
20 Article 28(8), DORA.
21 The register of information referred to in Article 28(3).
22 Article 28(9), DORA.
23 Article 28(9), DORA.
24 Referred to in Article 28(2).
25 Article 28(10), DORA.
26 Article 28(10), DORA.
27 Article 28(10), DORA.

The ESAs published the following draft RTS and Guidelines on 17 January 2024:

- RTS on ICT risk management framework and on simplified ICT risk management framework;
- RTS on criteria for the classification of ICT-related incidents;
- RTS to specify the policy on ICT services supporting critical or important functions provided by ICT third-party service providers (TPPs); and
- ITS to establish the templates for the register of information.

The ESAs also published the following draft RTS and Guidelines on 17 July 2024:

- RTS and ITS on the content, format, templates and timelines for reporting major ICT-related incidents and significant cyber threats;
- RTS on the harmonisation of conditions enabling the conduct of the oversight activities;
- RTS specifying the criteria for determining the composition of the joint examination team (JET);
- RTS on threat-led penetration testing (TLPT);
- Guidelines on the estimation of aggregated costs/losses caused by major ICT-related incidents; and
- Guidelines on oversight cooperation.

The above are subject to amendment and adoption by the EU Commission.

PRELIMINARY ASSESSMENT OF ICT CONCENTRATION RISK

13.03 Article 29 of DORA refers to 'Preliminary assessment of ICT concentration risk at entity level'.[28] Article 29(1) provides that when performing the identification and assessment of risks referred to in DORA,[29] financial entities shall also take into account whether the envisaged conclusion of a contractual arrangement in relation to ICT services supporting critical or important functions would lead to any of the following:

- contracting an ICT third-party service provider that is not easily substitutable; or
- having in place multiple contractual arrangements in relation to the provision of ICT services supporting critical or important functions with the same ICT third-party service provider or with closely connected ICT third-party service providers.[30]

28 Concentration is also referred to in Recital 67.

29 Referred to in Article 28(4)(c) of DORA.

30 Article 29(1), DORA.

Financial entities shall weigh the benefits and costs of alternative solutions, such as the use of different ICT third-party service providers, taking into account if and how envisaged solutions match the business needs and objectives set out in their digital resilience strategy.[31]

Where the contractual arrangements on the use of ICT services supporting critical or important functions include the possibility that an ICT third-party service provider further subcontracts ICT services supporting a critical or important function to other ICT third-party service providers, financial entities shall weigh benefits and risks that may arise in connection with such subcontracting, in particular in the case of an ICT subcontractor established in a third-country.[32]

Where contractual arrangements concern ICT services supporting critical or important functions, financial entities shall duly consider the insolvency law provisions that would apply in the event of the ICT third-party service provider's bankruptcy as well as any constraint that may arise in respect to the urgent recovery of the financial entity's data.[33]

Where contractual arrangements on the use of ICT services supporting critical or important functions are concluded with an ICT third-party service provider established in a third country, financial entities shall, in addition to the considerations referred to in Article 29(2), second subparagraph, also consider the compliance with Union data protection rules and the effective enforcement of the law in that third country.[34]

Where the contractual arrangements on the use of ICT services supporting critical or important functions provide for subcontracting, financial entities shall assess whether and how potentially long or complex chains of subcontracting may impact their ability to fully monitor the contracted functions and the ability of the competent authority to effectively supervise the financial entity in that respect.[35]

KEY CONTRACTUAL PROVISIONS

13.04 Article 30 of DORA refers to key contractual provisions.[36] Under Article 30(1) the rights and obligations of the financial entity and of the ICT third-party service provider shall be clearly allocated and set out in writing. The full contract shall include the service level agreements and be documented in one written document which shall be available to the parties on paper, or in a document with another downloadable, durable and accessible format.[37]

31 Article 29(1), DORA.
32 Article 29(2), DORA.
33 Article 29(2), DORA.
34 Article 29(2), DORA.
35 Article 29(2), DORA.
36 Contract issues are also referred to in Recitals 28, 29, 30, 31, 66, 67, 69, 71, 72, 73, 74, and 75.
37 Article 30(1), DORA.

The contractual arrangements on the use of ICT services shall include at least the following elements:

- a clear and complete description of all functions and ICT services to be provided by the ICT third-party service provider, indicating whether subcontracting of an ICT service supporting a critical or important function, or material parts thereof, is permitted and, when that is the case, the conditions applying to such subcontracting;
- the locations, namely the regions or countries, where the contracted or subcontracted functions and ICT services are to be provided and where data is to be processed, including the storage location, and the requirement for the ICT third-party service provider to notify the financial entity in advance if it envisages changing such locations;
- provisions on availability, authenticity, integrity and confidentiality in relation to the protection of data, including personal data;
- provisions on ensuring access, recovery and return in an easily accessible format of personal and non-personal data processed by the financial entity in the event of the insolvency, resolution or discontinuation of the business operations of the ICT third-party service provider, or in the event of the termination of the contractual arrangements;
- service level descriptions, including updates and revisions thereof;
- the obligation of the ICT third-party service provider to provide assistance to the financial entity at no additional cost, or at a cost that is determined ex-ante, when an ICT incident that is related to the ICT service provided to the financial entity occurs;
- the obligation of the ICT third-party service provider to fully cooperate with the competent authorities and the resolution authorities of the financial entity, including persons appointed by them;
- termination rights and related minimum notice periods for the termination of the contractual arrangements, in accordance with the expectations of competent authorities and resolution authorities; and
- the conditions for the participation of ICT third-party service providers in the financial entities' ICT security awareness programmes and digital operational resilience training in accordance with DORA.[38]

The contractual arrangements on the use of ICT services supporting critical or important functions shall include, in addition to the elements referred to above,[39] at least the following:

- full service level descriptions, including updates and revisions thereof with precise quantitative and qualitative performance targets within the agreed service levels to allow effective monitoring by the financial entity of ICT

38 Article 30(2), DORA. In accordance with Article 13(6) of DORA.
39 Referred to in Article 30(2).

services and enable appropriate corrective actions to be taken, without undue delay, when agreed service levels are not met;

- notice periods and reporting obligations of the ICT third-party service provider to the financial entity, including notification of any development that might have a material impact on the ICT third-party service provider's ability to effectively provide the ICT services supporting critical or important functions in line with agreed service levels;
- requirements for the ICT third-party service provider to implement and test business contingency plans and to have in place ICT security measures, tools and policies that provide an appropriate level of security for the provision of services by the financial entity in line with its regulatory framework;
- the obligation of the ICT third-party service provider to participate and fully cooperate in the financial entity's TLPT as referred to in DORA;[40]
- the right to monitor, on an ongoing basis, the ICT third-party service provider's performance, which entails the following:
  (i) unrestricted rights of access, inspection and audit by the financial entity, or an appointed third party, and by the competent authority, and the right to take copies of relevant documentation on-site if they are critical to the operations of the ICT third-party service provider, the effective exercise of which is not impeded or limited by other contractual arrangements or implementation policies;
  (ii) the right to agree on alternative assurance levels if other clients' rights are affected;
  (iii) the obligation of the ICT third-party service provider to fully cooperate during the onsite inspections and audits performed by the competent authorities, the Lead Overseer, financial entity or an appointed third party; and
  (iv) the obligation to provide details on the scope, procedures to be followed and frequency of such inspections and audits; and
- exit strategies, in particular the establishment of a mandatory adequate transition period:
  (i) during which the ICT third-party service provider will continue providing the respective functions, or ICT services, with a view to reducing the risk of disruption at the financial entity or to ensure its effective resolution and restructuring; and
  (ii) allowing the financial entity to migrate to another ICT third-party service provider or change to in-house solutions consistent with the complexity of the service provided.[41]

40 As referred to in Articles 26 and 27 of DORA.
41 Article 30(3), DORA.

By way of derogation from bullet point five above, the ICT third-party service provider and the financial entity that is a microenterprise may agree that the financial entity's rights of access, inspection and audit can be delegated to an independent third-party, appointed by the ICT third-party service provider, and that the financial entity is able to request information and assurance on the ICT third-party service provider's performance from the third party at any time.[42]

When negotiating contractual arrangements, financial entities and ICT third-party service providers shall consider the use of standard contractual clauses developed by public authorities for specific services.[43]

The ESAs shall, via the Joint Committee, develop draft RTS to specify further the elements referred to above,[44] which a financial entity needs to determine and assess when subcontracting ICT services supporting critical or important functions.[45]

When developing those draft RTS, the ESAs shall take into consideration the size and overall risk profile of the financial entity, and the nature, scale and complexity of its services, activities and operations.[46]

The ESAs were required to submit those draft RTS to the Commission by 17 July 2024.[47] Power is delegated to the Commission to supplement DORA by adopting the RTS in accordance with Articles 10 to 14 of Regulations 1093/2010, 1094/2010 and 1095/2010.[48]

The ESAs draft RTS and Guidelines with relevance to third parties and contracting with third parties are:

- RTS to specify the policy on ICT services supporting critical or important functions provided by ICT third-party service providers (TPPs);
- RTS on ICT risk management framework and on simplified ICT risk management framework;
- RTS on criteria for the classification of ICT-related incidents;
- ITS to establish the templates for the register of information;
- RTS on threat led penetration testing (TLPT); and
- Guidelines on the estimation of aggregated costs/losses caused by major ICT-related incidents.

42 Article 30(3), DORA.
43 Article 30(4), DORA.
44 The elements referred to in Article 30(2)(a), of this Article.
45 Article 30(5), DORA.
46 Article 30(5), DORA.
47 Article 30(5), DORA.
48 Article 30(5), DORA.

DESIGNATION OF CRITICAL ICT THIRD-PARTY SERVICE PROVIDERS

13.05 Section II of Chapter V of DORA refers to Oversight Framework of critical ICT third-party service providers.

Article 31 of DORA refers to the designation of critical ICT third-party service providers.[49]

The ESAs, through the Joint Committee and upon recommendation from the Oversight Forum established pursuant to DORA,[50] shall:

- designate the ICT third-party service providers that are critical for financial entities, following an assessment that takes into account the criteria specified below;[51] and
- appoint as Lead Overseer for each critical ICT third-party service provider the ESA that is responsible, in accordance with Regulations 1093/2010, 1094/2010 or 1095/2010, for the financial entities having together the largest share of total assets out of the value of total assets of all financial entities using the services of the relevant critical ICT third-party service provider, as evidenced by the sum of the individual balance sheets of those financial entities.[52]

The designation referred to in Article 31(1)(a), shall be based on all of the following criteria in relation to ICT services provided by the ICT third-party service provider:

- the systemic impact on the stability, continuity or quality of the provision of financial services in the event that the relevant ICT third-party service provider would face a large scale operational failure to provide its services, taking into account the number of financial entities and the total value of assets of financial entities to which the relevant ICT third-party service provider provides services;
- the systemic character or importance of the financial entities that rely on the relevant ICT third-party service provider, assessed in accordance with the following parameters:
  - (i) the number of global systemically important institutions (G-SIIs) or other systemically important institutions (O-SIIs) that rely on the respective ICT third-party service provider; and
  - (ii) the interdependence between the G-SIIs or O-SIIs referred to in point (i) and other financial entities, including situations where the G-SIIs or O-SIIs provide financial infrastructure services to other financial entities;

49 Also see Recitals 89 and 98.
50 The Oversight Forum established pursuant to Article 32(1) of DORA.
51 The criteria specified in Article 31(2).
52 Article 31(1), DORA.

- the reliance of financial entities on the services provided by the relevant ICT third-party service provider in relation to critical or important functions of financial entities that ultimately involve the same ICT third-party service provider, irrespective of whether financial entities rely on those services directly or indirectly, through subcontracting arrangements; and
- the degree of substitutability of the ICT third-party service provider, taking into account the following parameters:
  (i) the lack of real alternatives, even partial, due to the limited number of ICT third-party service providers active on a specific market, or the market share of the relevant ICT third-party service provider, or the technical complexity or sophistication involved, including in relation to any proprietary technology, or the specific features of the ICT third-party service provider's organisation or activity; and
  (ii) difficulties in relation to partially or fully migrating the relevant data and workloads from the relevant ICT third-party service provider to another ICT third-party service provider, due either to significant financial costs, time or other resources that the migration process may entail, or to increased ICT risk or other operational risks to which the financial entity may be exposed through such migration.[53]

Where the ICT third-party service provider belongs to a group, the criteria referred to above[54] shall be considered in relation to the ICT services provided by the group as a whole.[55]

Critical ICT third-party service providers which are part of a group shall designate one legal person as a coordination point to ensure adequate representation and communication with the Lead Overseer.[56]

The Lead Overseer shall notify the ICT third-party service provider of the outcome of the assessment leading to the designation referred to above.[57] Within six weeks from the date of the notification, the ICT third-party service provider may submit to the Lead Overseer a reasoned statement with any relevant information for the purposes of the assessment. The Lead Overseer shall consider the reasoned statement and may request additional information to be submitted within 30 calendar days of the receipt of such statement.[58]

After designating an ICT third-party service provider as critical, the ESAs, through the Joint Committee, shall notify the ICT third-party service provider of such designation and the starting date as from which they will effectively be subject to oversight activities. That starting date shall be no later than one

53 Article 36(2), DORA.
54 The criteria referred to in Article 31(2).
55 Article 36(3), DORA.
56 Article 36(4), DORA.
57 Referred in Article 36(1)(a).
58 Article 36(5), DORA.

month after the notification. The ICT third-party service provider shall notify the financial entities to which they provide services of their designation as critical.[59]

The Commission was empowered to adopt a delegated act in accordance with Article 57 to supplement DORA by specifying further the criteria referred to above,[60] by 17 July 2024.[61]

The designation referred to above,[62] shall not be used until the Commission has adopted a delegated act.[63]

The designation[64] shall not apply to the following:

- financial entities providing ICT services to other financial entities;
- ICT third-party service providers that are subject to oversight frameworks established for the purposes of supporting the tasks referred to in the Treaty on the Functioning of the European Union (TFEU);[65]
- ICT intra-group service providers; and
- ICT third-party service providers providing ICT services solely in one Member State to financial entities that are only active in that Member State.[66]

The ESAs, through the Joint Committee, shall establish, publish and update yearly the list of critical ICT third-party service providers at Union level.[67]

For the purposes of Article 31(1)(a), competent authorities shall, on a yearly and aggregated basis, transmit the reports,[68] to the Oversight Forum.[69] The Oversight Forum shall assess the ICT third-party dependencies of financial entities based on the information received from the competent authorities.[70]

Consequently, the ESAs published various draft RTS and Guidelines on 17 January 2024 and 17 July 2024 (see above at **13.02** for more detail). These are subject to amendment and subsequent adoption by the EU Commission.

59 Article 36(5), DORA.
60 Referred to Article 31(2).
61 Article 31(6), DORA.
62 Referred to in paragraph 1, point (a), of this Article.
63 Article 31(7), DORA. A delegated act in accordance with Article 31(6).
64 The designation referred to in Article 31(1)(a).
65 The tasks referred to in Article 127(2) of the Treaty on the Functioning of the European Union (TFEU).
66 Article 31(8), DORA.
67 Article 31(9), DORA.
68 The reports referred to in Article 28(3), third subparagraph.
69 The Oversight Forum established pursuant to Article 32 of DORA.
70 Article 31(10), DORA.

The ICT third-party service providers that are not included in the list referred to in Article 31(9) may request to be designated as critical in accordance with Article 31(1)(a).[71]

For the purpose of Article 31(11), first subparagraph, the ICT third-party service provider shall submit a reasoned application to European Banking Authority (EBA), the European Securities and Markets Authority (ESMA) or the European Insurance and Occupational Pensions Authority (EIOPA), which, through the Joint Committee, shall decide whether to designate that ICT third-party service provider as critical.[72]

The decision referred to in Article 31(11), second subparagraph shall be adopted and notified to the ICT third-party service provider within 6 months of receipt of the application.[73]

Financial entities shall only make use of the services of an ICT third-party service provider established in a third country and which has been designated as critical,[74] if the latter has established a subsidiary in the Union within the 12 months following the designation.[75]

The critical ICT third-party service provider referred to in Article 31(12) shall notify the Lead Overseer of any changes to the structure of the management of the subsidiary established in the Union.[76]

STRUCTURE OF THE OVERSIGHT FRAMEWORK

13.06 Article 32 of DORA refers to the structure of the Oversight Framework.[77]

The Joint Committee, in accordance with Article 57(1) of Regulations 1093/2010, 1094/2010 and 1095/2010, shall establish the Oversight Forum as a sub-committee for the purposes of supporting the work of the Joint Committee and of the Lead Overseer referred to in Article 31(1)(b),[78] in the area of ICT third-party risk across financial sectors. The Oversight Forum shall prepare the draft joint positions and the draft common acts of the Joint Committee in that area.[79]

71 Article 31(11), DORA.
72 Article 31(11), DORA. In accordance with Article 31(1)(a).
73 Article 31(11), DORA.
74 Designated as critical in accordance with Article 31(1)(a).
75 Article 31(12), DORA.
76 Article 31(13), DORA.
77 The Oversight Framework is also referred to in Recitals 76, 77, 78, 80, 81, 83, 84, 85, 87, 88, 89, 90, 91, 92, 93, and 95.
78 The Joint Committee and of the Lead Overseer referred to in Article 31(1)(b) of DORA.
79 Article 32(1), DORA.

The Oversight Forum shall regularly discuss relevant developments on ICT risk and vulnerabilities and promote a consistent approach in the monitoring of ICT third-party risk at Union level.[80]

The Oversight Forum shall, on a yearly basis, undertake a collective assessment of the results and findings of the oversight activities conducted for all critical ICT third-party service providers and promote coordination measures to increase the digital operational resilience of financial entities, foster best practices on addressing ICT concentration risk and explore mitigants for cross-sector risk transfers.[81]

The Oversight Forum shall submit comprehensive benchmarks for critical ICT third-party service providers to be adopted by the Joint Committee as joint positions of the ESAs in accordance with Article 56(1) of Regulations 1093/2010, 1094/2010 and 1095/2010.[82]

The Oversight Forum shall be composed of:

- the Chairpersons of the ESAs;
- one high-level representative from the current staff of the relevant competent authority referred to in Article 46 from each Member State;
- the Executive Directors of each ESA and one representative from the Commission, from the European Systemic Risk Board (ESRB), from the ECB and from the European Union Agency on Cybersecurity (ENISA) as observers;
- where appropriate, one additional representative of a competent authority referred to in Article 46 from each Member State as observer; and
- where applicable, one representative of the competent authorities designated or established in accordance with Directive 2022/2555 responsible for the supervision of an essential or important entity subject to that Directive, which has been designated as a critical ICT third-party service provider, as observer.[83]

The Oversight Forum may, where appropriate, seek the advice of independent experts appointed in accordance with DORA.[84]

Each Member State shall designate the relevant competent authority whose staff member shall be the high-level representative referred to above,[85] and shall inform the Lead Overseer thereof.[86]

80 Article 32(1), DORA.
81 Article 32(2), DORA.
82 Article 32(3), DORA.
83 Article 32(4), DORA.
84 Article 32(4), DORA. Appointed in accordance with Article 32(6).
85 The high-level representative referred in Article 32(4), first subparagraph, point (b).
86 Article 32(5), DORA.

The ESAs shall publish on their website the list of high-level representatives from the current staff of the relevant competent authority designated by Member States.[87]

The independent experts referred to above,[88] shall be appointed by the Oversight Forum from a pool of experts selected following a public and transparent application process.[89]

The independent experts shall be appointed on the basis of their expertise in financial stability, digital operational resilience and ICT security matters. They shall act independently and objectively in the sole interest of the Union as a whole and shall neither seek nor take instructions from Union institutions or bodies, from any government of a Member State or from any other public or private body.[90]

In accordance with Article 16 of Regulations 1093/2010, 1094/2010 and 1095/2010, the ESAs were required by 17 July 2024 to issue, for the purposes of Section II, guidelines on the cooperation between the ESAs and the competent authorities covering the detailed procedures and conditions for the allocation and execution of tasks between competent authorities and the ESAs and the details on the exchanges of information which are necessary for competent authorities to ensure the follow-up of recommendations pursuant to Article 35(1)(d), addressed to critical ICT third-party service providers.[91]

The requirements set out in Section II shall be without prejudice to the application of Directive 2022/2555 and of other Union rules on oversight applicable to providers of cloud computing services.[92]

The ESAs, through the Joint Committee and based on preparatory work conducted by the Oversight Forum, shall, on yearly basis, submit a report on the application of this Section to the European Parliament, the Council and the Commission.[93]

Consequently, the ESAs published various draft RTS and Guidelines on 17 January 2024 and 17 July 2024 (see above at **13.02** for more detail). These are subject to amendment and subsequent adoption by the EU Commission.

87 Article 32(5), DORA.
88 The independent experts referred to in Article 32(4), second subparagraph.
89 Article 32(6), DORA.
90 Article 32(6), DORA.
91 Article 32(7), DORA.
92 Article 32(8), DORA.
93 Article 32(9), DORA.

TASKS OF THE LEAD OVERSEER

13.07 Article 33 of DORA refers to the tasks of the Lead Overseer. The Lead Overseer, appointed in accordance with DORA,[94] shall conduct the oversight of the assigned critical ICT third-party service providers and shall be, for the purposes of all matters related to the oversight, the primary point of contact for those critical ICT third-party service providers.[95]

For the purposes of Article 33(1), the Lead Overseer shall assess whether each critical ICT third-party service provider has in place comprehensive, sound and effective rules, procedures, mechanisms and arrangements to manage the ICT risk which it may pose to financial entities.[96]

The assessment shall focus mainly on ICT services provided by the critical ICT third-party service provider supporting the critical or important functions of financial entities. Where necessary to address all relevant risks, that assessment shall extend to ICT services supporting functions other than those that are critical or important.[97]

The assessment shall cover:

- ICT requirements to ensure, in particular, the security, availability, continuity, scalability and quality of services which the critical ICT third-party service provider provides to financial entities, as well as the ability to maintain at all times high standards of availability, authenticity, integrity or confidentiality of data;
- the physical security contributing to ensuring the ICT security, including the security of premises, facilities, data centres;
- the risk management processes, including ICT risk management policies, ICT business continuity policy and ICT response and recovery plans;
- the governance arrangements, including an organisational structure with clear, transparent and consistent lines of responsibility and accountability rules enabling effective ICT risk management;
- the identification, monitoring and prompt reporting of material ICT-related incidents to financial entities, the management and resolution of those incidents, in particular cyber attacks;
- the mechanisms for data portability, application portability and interoperability, which ensure an effective exercise of termination rights by the financial entities;
- the testing of ICT systems, infrastructure and controls;

94 Appointed in accordance with Article 31(1)(b).
95 Article 33(1), DORA.
96 Article 33(2), DORA.
97 Article 33(2), DORA.

- the ICT audits; and
- the use of relevant national and international standards applicable to the provision of its ICT services to the financial entities.[98]

Based on the assessment referred to above,[99] and in coordination with the Joint Oversight Network (JON) referred to in Article 34(1), the Lead Overseer shall adopt a clear, detailed and reasoned individual oversight plan describing the annual oversight objectives and the main oversight actions planned for each critical ICT third-party service provider. That plan shall be communicated yearly to the critical ICT third-party service provider.[100]

Prior to the adoption of the oversight plan, the Lead Overseer shall communicate the draft oversight plan to the critical ICT third-party service provider.[101]

Upon receipt of the draft oversight plan, the critical ICT third-party service provider may submit a reasoned statement within 15 calendar days evidencing the expected impact on customers which are entities falling outside of the scope of DORA and where appropriate, formulating solutions to mitigate risks.[102]

Once the annual oversight plans referred to in Article 34(4) have been adopted and notified to the critical ICT third-party service providers, competent authorities may take measures concerning such critical ICT third-party service providers only in agreement with the Lead Overseer.[103]

OPERATIONAL COORDINATION BETWEEN LEAD OVERSEERS

13.08 Article 34 of DORA refers to the operational coordination between Lead Overseers.

To ensure a consistent approach to oversight activities and with a view to enabling coordinated general oversight strategies and cohesive operational approaches and work methodologies, the three Lead Overseers appointed in accordance with DORA,[104] shall set up a JON to coordinate among themselves in the preparatory stages and to coordinate the conduct of oversight activities over their respective overseen critical ICT third-party service providers, as well as in the course of any action that may be needed pursuant to Article 42.[105]

98 Article 33(3), DORA.
99 The assessment referred to in Article 33(2).
100 Article 33(4), DORA.
101 Article 33(4), DORA.
102 Article 33(4), DORA.
103 Article 33(5), DORA.
104 The three Lead Overseers appointed in accordance with Article 31(1)(b).
105 Article 34(1), DORA.

For the purposes of Article 34(1), the Lead Overseers shall draw up a common oversight protocol specifying the detailed procedures to be followed for carrying out the day-to-day coordination and for ensuring swift exchanges and reactions. The protocol shall be periodically revised to reflect operational needs, in particular the evolution of practical oversight arrangements.[106]

The Lead Overseers may, on an ad-hoc basis, call on the ECB and ENISA to provide technical advice, share hands on experience or join specific coordination meetings of the JON.[107]

POWERS OF THE LEAD OVERSEER

13.09 Article 35 of DORA refers to the powers of the Lead Overseer. For the purposes of carrying out the duties laid down in Section II, the Lead Overseer shall have the following powers in respect of the critical ICT third-party service providers:

- to request all relevant information and documentation in accordance with DORA;[108]
- to conduct general investigations and inspections in accordance with DORA, respectively;[109]
- to request, after the completion of the oversight activities, reports specifying the actions that have been taken or the remedies that have been implemented by the critical ICT third-party service providers in relation to the recommendations referred in the bullet point below;[110] and
- to issue recommendations on the areas referred to in Article 33(3), in particular concerning the following:
  - (i) the use of specific ICT security and quality requirements or processes, in particular in relation to the roll out of patches, updates, encryption and other security measures which the Lead Overseer deems relevant for ensuring the ICT security of services provided to financial entities;
  - (ii) the use of conditions and terms, including their technical implementation, under which the critical ICT third-party service providers provide ICT services to financial entities, which the Lead Overseer deems relevant for preventing the generation of single points of failure, the amplification thereof, or for minimising the possible systemic impact across the Union's financial sector in the event of ICT concentration risk; and

106 Article 34(2), DORA.
107 Article 34(3), DORA.
108 All relevant information and documentation in accordance with Article 37 of DORA.
109 General investigations and inspections in accordance with Articles 38 and 39 of DORA.
110 Recommendations referred to in Article 35(1)(d).

(iii) any planned subcontracting, where the Lead Overseer deems that further subcontracting, including subcontracting arrangements which the critical ICT third-party service providers plan to enter into with ICT third-party service providers or with ICT subcontractors established in a third country, may trigger risks for the provision of services by the financial entity, or risks to the financial stability, based on the examination of the information gathered in accordance with Articles 37 and 38;

(iv) refraining from entering into a further subcontracting arrangement, where the following cumulative conditions are met:

- the envisaged subcontractor is an ICT third-party service provider or an ICT subcontractor established in a third country;
- the subcontracting concerns critical or important functions of the financial entity; and
- the Lead Overseer deems that the use of such subcontracting poses a clear and serious risk to the financial stability of the Union or to financial entities, including to the ability of financial entities to comply with supervisory requirements.[111]

For the purpose of point (iv), ICT third-party service providers shall, using the template referred to in DORA,[112] transmit the information regarding subcontracting to the Lead Overseer.[113]

When exercising the powers referred to in this Article, the Lead Overseer shall:

- ensure regular coordination within the JON, and in particular shall seek consistent approaches, as appropriate, with regard to the oversight of critical ICT third-party service providers;
- take due account of the framework established by Directive 2022/2555 and, where necessary, consult the relevant competent authorities designated or established in accordance with that Directive, in order to avoid duplication of technical and organisational measures that might apply to critical ICT third-party service providers pursuant to that Directive; and
- seek to minimise, to the extent possible, the risk of disruption to services provided by critical ICT third-party service providers to customers that are entities falling outside the scope of DORA.[114]

The Lead Overseer shall consult the Oversight Forum before exercising the powers referred to above.[115]

111 Article 35(1), DORA.
112 The template referred to in Article 41(1)(b) of DORA.
113 Article 35(1), DORA.
114 Article 35(2), DORA.
115 Article 35(3), DORA. The powers referred to in Article 35(1).

Before issuing recommendations in accordance with the above,[116] the Lead Overseer shall give the opportunity to the ICT third-party service provider to provide, within 30 calendar days, relevant information evidencing the expected impact on customers that are entities falling outside the scope of DORA and, where appropriate, formulating solutions to mitigate risks.[117]

The Lead Overseer shall inform the JON of the outcome of the exercise of the powers referred to above.[118] The Lead Overseer shall, without undue delay, transmit the reports referred to above,[119] to the JON and to the competent authorities of the financial entities using the ICT services of that critical ICT third-party service provider.[120]

Critical ICT third-party service providers shall cooperate in good faith with the Lead Overseer, and assist it in the fulfilment of its tasks.[121]

In the event of whole or partial non-compliance with the measures required to be taken pursuant to the exercise of the powers above,[122] and after the expiry of a period of at least 30 calendar days from the date on which the critical ICT third-party service provider received notification of the respective measures, the Lead Overseer shall adopt a decision imposing a periodic penalty payment to compel the critical ICT third-party service provider to comply with those measures.[123]

The periodic penalty payment referred to in Article 35(6) shall be imposed on a daily basis until compliance is achieved and for no more than a period of six months following the notification of the decision to impose a periodic penalty payment to the critical ICT third-party service provider.[124]

The amount of the periodic penalty payment, calculated from the date stipulated in the decision imposing the periodic penalty payment, shall be up to 1% of the average daily worldwide turnover of the critical ICT third-party service provider in the preceding business year. When determining the amount of the penalty payment, the Lead Overseer shall take into account the following criteria regarding non-compliance with the measures referred to in Article 25(6):

- the gravity and the duration of non-compliance;
- whether non-compliance has been committed intentionally or negligently; and

116 In accordance with Article 35(1)(d).
117 Article 35(3), DORA.
118 The powers referred to in Article 35(1)(a) and (b).
119 The reports referred to in Article 35(1)(c).
120 Article 35(4), DORA.
121 Article 35(5), DORA.
122 The powers under Article 35(1)(a), (b) and (c).
123 Article 35(6), DORA.
124 Article 35(7), DORA.

- the level of cooperation of the ICT third-party service provider with the Lead Overseer.[125]

For the purposes of Article 35(8), first subparagraph, in order to ensure a consistent approach, the Lead Overseer shall engage in consultation within the JON.[126]

Penalty payments shall be of an administrative nature and shall be enforceable. Enforcement shall be governed by the rules of civil procedure in force in the Member State on the territory of which inspections and access shall be carried out. Courts of the Member State concerned shall have jurisdiction over complaints related to irregular conduct of enforcement. The amounts of the penalty payments shall be allocated to the general budget of the European Union.[127]

The Lead Overseer shall disclose to the public every periodic penalty payment that has been imposed, unless such disclosure would seriously jeopardise the financial markets or cause disproportionate damage to the parties involved.[128]

Before imposing a periodic penalty payment under Article 35(6), the Lead Overseer shall give the representatives of the critical ICT third-party service provider subject to the proceedings the opportunity to be heard on the findings and shall base its decisions only on findings on which the critical ICT third-party service provider subject to the proceedings has had an opportunity to comment.[129]

The rights of the defence of the persons subject to the proceedings shall be fully respected in the proceedings. The critical ICT third-party service provider subject to the proceedings shall be entitled to have access to the file, subject to the legitimate interest of other persons in the protection of their business secrets. The right of access to the file shall not extend to confidential information or to the Lead Overseer's internal preparatory documents.[130]

EXERCISE OF LEAD OVERSEER POWERS OUTSIDE UNION

13.10 Article 36 of DORA refers to the exercise of the powers of the Lead Overseer outside the Union.

When oversight objectives cannot be attained by means of interacting with the subsidiary set up for the purpose of Article 31(12), or by exercising oversight activities on premises located in the Union, the Lead Overseer may exercise the powers, referred to in the following provisions, on any premises located in a third country which is owned, or used in any way, for the purposes of providing

125 Article 35(8), DORA.
126 Article 35(8), DORA.
127 Article 35(9), DORA.
128 Article 35(10), DORA.
129 Article 35(11), DORA.
130 Article 35(11), DORA.

services to Union financial entities, by a critical ICT third-party service provider, in connection with its business operations, functions or services, including any administrative, business or operational offices, premises, lands, buildings or other properties:

- in Article 35(1)(a); and
- in Article 35(1)(b), in accordance with Article 38(2)(a), (b) and (d), and in Article 39(1) and (2)(a).[131]

The powers referred to in Article 36(1), first subparagraph, may be exercised subject to all of the following conditions:

- the conduct of an inspection in a third country is deemed necessary by the Lead Overseer to allow it to fully and effectively perform its duties under DORA;
- the inspection in a third country is directly related to the provision of ICT services to financial entities in the Union;
- the critical ICT third-party service provider concerned consents to the conduct of an inspection in a third country; and
- the relevant authority of the third country concerned has been officially notified by the Lead Overseer and raised no objection thereto.[132]

Without prejudice to the respective competences of the Union institutions and of Member States, for the purposes of Article 36(1), the EBA, ESMA or EIOPA shall conclude administrative cooperation arrangements with the relevant authority of the third country in order to enable the smooth conduct of inspections in the third country concerned by the Lead Overseer and its designated team for its mission in that third country. Those cooperation arrangements shall not create legal obligations in respect of the Union and its Member States nor shall they prevent Member States and their competent authorities from concluding bilateral or multilateral arrangements with those third countries and their relevant authorities.[133]

Those cooperation arrangements shall specify at least the following elements:

- the procedures for the coordination of oversight activities carried out under DORA and any analogous monitoring of ICT third-party risk in the financial sector exercised by the relevant authority of the third country concerned, including details for transmitting the agreement of the latter to allow the conduct, by the Lead Overseer and its designated team, of general investigations and on-site inspections as referred to above,[134] on the territory under its jurisdiction;

131 Article 36(1), DORA.
132 Article 36(1), DORA.
133 Article 36(2), DORA.
134 The general investigations and on-site inspections as referred to in Article 36(1), first subparagraph.

- the mechanism for the transmission of any relevant information between the EBA, ESMA or EIOPA and the relevant authority of the third country concerned, in particular in connection with information that may be requested by the Lead Overseer pursuant to DORA;[135]
- the mechanisms for the prompt notification by the relevant authority of the third country concerned to the EBA, ESMA or EIOPA of cases where an ICT third-party service provider established in a third country and designated as critical in accordance with DORA,[136] is deemed to have infringed the requirements to which it is obliged to adhere pursuant to the applicable law of the third country concerned when providing services to financial institutions in that third country, as well as the remedies and penalties applied;
- the regular transmission of updates on regulatory or supervisory developments on the monitoring of ICT third-party risk of financial institutions in the third country concerned; and
- the details for allowing, if needed, the participation of one representative of the relevant third-country authority in the inspections conducted by the Lead Overseer and the designated team.[137]

When the Lead Overseer is not able to conduct oversight activities outside the Union, referred to in Article 36(1) and (2), the Lead Overseer shall:

- exercise its powers under Article 35 on the basis of all facts and documents available to it; and
- document and explain any consequence of its inability to conduct the envisaged oversight activities as referred to in this Article.[138]

The potential consequences shall be taken into consideration in the Lead Overseer's recommendations issued pursuant to DORA.[139]

REQUEST FOR INFORMATION

13.11 Article 37 of DORA refers to requests for information.

The Lead Overseer may, by simple request or by decision, require critical ICT third-party service providers to provide all information that is necessary for the Lead Overseer to carry out its duties under DORA, including all relevant business or operational documents, contracts, policies, documentation, ICT security audit reports, ICT-related incident reports, as well as any information relating to parties

135 Pursuant to Article 37 of DORA.
136 Designated as critical in accordance with Article 31(1)(a) of DORA.
137 Article 36(2), DORA.
138 Article 36(3), DORA.
139 Article 36(3), DORA. The Lead Overseer's recommendations issued pursuant to Article 35(1)(d) of DORA.

to whom the critical ICT third-party service provider has outsourced operational functions or activities.[140]

When sending a simple request for information,[141] the Lead Overseer shall:

- refer to this Article as the legal basis of the request;
- state the purpose of the request;
- specify what information is required;
- set a time limit within which the information is to be provided; and
- inform the representative of the critical ICT third-party service provider from whom the information is requested that he or she is not obliged to provide the information, but in the event of a voluntary reply to the request the information provided must not be incorrect or misleading.[142]

When requiring by decision to supply information,[143] the Lead Overseer shall:

- refer to this Article as the legal basis of the request;
- state the purpose of the request;
- specify what information is required;
- set a time limit within which the information is to be provided;
- indicate the periodic penalty payments[144] where the production of the required information is incomplete or when such information is not provided within the time limit referred to in the bullet point above;[145] and
- indicate the right to appeal the decision to ESA's Board of Appeal and to have the decision reviewed by the Court of Justice of the European Union (Court of Justice).[146]

The representatives of the critical ICT third-party service providers shall supply the information requested. Lawyers duly authorised to act may supply the information on behalf of their clients. The critical ICT third-party service provider shall remain fully responsible if the information supplied is incomplete, incorrect or misleading.[147]

140 Article 37(1), DORA.
141 A simple request for information under Article 37(1).
142 Article 37(2), DORA.
143 A decision to supply information under Article 37(1).
144 The periodic penalty payments provided for in Article 35(6) of DORA.
145 Referred to in Article 37(3)(d).
146 Article 37(3), DORA. Reviewed by the Court of Justice of the European Union (Court of Justice) in accordance with Articles 60 and 61 of Regulations 1093/2010, 1094/2010 and 1095/2010.
147 Article 37(4), DORA.

The Lead Overseer shall, without delay, transmit a copy of the decision to supply information to the competent authorities of the financial entities using the services of the relevant critical ICT third-party service providers and to the JON.[148]

The disputes and appeals that occur will ultimately be important in assessing how well the policy intentions behind DORA are achieved. This is particularly so given the importance of third-party suppliers to the wider financial sector.

GENERAL INVESTIGATIONS

13.12 There are a variety of important obligations created with DORA. While these arise by way of the legislation there are also regulatory enforcement mechanisms. For instance, Article 38 of DORA refers to general investigations. Under Article 38(1), in order to carry out its duties under DORA, the Lead Overseer, assisted by the joint examination team referred to in Article 40(1), may, where necessary, conduct investigations of critical ICT third-party service providers.[149]

Powers of investigators are important. Article 38(2) sets out the following powers of the Lead Overseer, namely to:

- examine records, data, procedures and any other material relevant to the execution of its tasks, irrespective of the medium on which they are stored;
- take or obtain certified copies of, or extracts from, such records, data, documented procedures and any other material;
- summon representatives of the critical ICT third-party service provider for oral or written explanations on facts or documents relating to the subject matter and purpose of the investigation and to record the answers;
- interview any other natural or legal person who consents to be interviewed for the purpose of collecting information relating to the subject matter of an investigation; and
- request records of telephone and data traffic.[150]

The officials and other persons authorised by the Lead Overseer for the purposes of the investigation referred to in Article 38(1) above shall exercise their powers upon production of a written authorisation specifying the subject matter and purpose of the investigation.[151]

That authorisation shall also indicate the periodic penalty payments[152] where the production of the required records, data, documented procedures or any other

148 Article 37(5), DORA.
149 Article 38(1), DORA.
150 Article 38(2), DORA.
151 Article 38(3), DORA.
152 The periodic penalty payments provided for in Article 35(6) of DORA.

material, or the answers to questions asked to representatives of the ICT third-party service provider are not provided or are incomplete.[153]

The representatives of the critical ICT third-party service providers are 'required to submit to the investigations on the basis of a decision of the Lead Overseer.' The decision shall specify the subject matter and purpose of the investigation, the periodic penalty payments,[154] the legal remedies available under Regulations 1093/2010, 1094/2010 and 1095/2010, and the 'right to have the decision reviewed by the Court of Justice'.[155]

In 'good time' before the start of the investigation, the Lead Overseer shall inform competent authorities of the financial entities using the ICT services of that critical ICT third-party service provider of the envisaged investigation and of the identity of the authorised persons.[156] This creates an interesting issue as to whether any prior or pre investigative steps whatsoever can be conducted, which one might expect from regulators. Arguably, these seem to be excluded in this instance, unless some other activities can be sufficiently distinguished from being an 'investigation'. This may result on some objections or even litigation until this aspect if more fully clarified.

The Lead Overseer shall also communicate to the JON all information transmitted pursuant to the first subparagraph above.[157]

INSPECTIONS

13.13 Article 39 of DORA refers to inspections, as opposed to investigations. In light of the comments above, however, some might argue that an inspection is part of an investigation, at least in some instances.[158] This will of course not always be the case.

Article 39(1) provides that in order to carry out its duties under DORA, the Lead Overseer, assisted by the joint examination teams,[159] may enter in, and conduct all necessary onsite inspections on, any business premises, land or property of the ICT third-party service providers, such as head offices, operation centres, secondary premises, as well as to conduct off-site inspections.[160] Presumably off-site inspections will still be at locations that are still the premises of, or under the control of, the target of the inspection.

153 Article 38(3), DORA.
154 The periodic penalty payments provided for in Article 35(6) of DORA.
155 Article 38(4), DORA.
156 Article 38(5), DORA.
157 Article 38(5), DORA.
158 Inspections is also referred to in Recital 95 for example.
159 The joint examination teams referred to in Article 40(1) of DORA.
160 Article 39(1), DORA.

For the purposes of exercising the powers referred to in the Article 39(1), the Lead Overseer shall consult the JON.[161]

The officials and other persons authorised by the Lead Overseer to conduct an on-site inspection have the power to:

- enter any such business premises, land or property; and
- seal any such business premises, books or records, for the period of, and to the extent necessary for, the inspection.[162]

It is not clear in this reference as to what may happen to electronic records. Not does this reference refer to the collection or taking of records.

The officials and other persons authorised by the Lead Overseer shall exercise their powers upon production of a written authorisation specifying the subject matter and the purpose of the inspection, and the periodic penalty payments provided for in Article 35(6) where the representatives of the critical ICT third-party service providers concerned do not submit to the inspection.[163]

In 'good time' before the start of the inspection, the Lead Overseer must inform the competent authorities of the financial entities using that ICT third-party service provider.[164]

Inspections shall 'cover' the 'full range of relevant ICT systems, networks, devices, information and data either used for, or contributing to, the provision of ICT services to financial entities.'[165] This would seem to cover both direct and indirect supply of such services.

Importantly, the Lead Overseer shall give 'reasonable notice' to the critical ICT third-party service providers '[b]efore any planned on-site inspection' 'unless' such notice is not 'possible' 'due to an emergency or crisis situation,' 'or' if it would lead to a situation where the inspection or audit 'would no longer be effective.'[166] While the intention of the last clause may seem somewhat clear, by including 'would' and 'effective' may create an unintended very high standard. It is a higher standard than, for example, 'may no longer be effective' or 'may not be effective'. It is a standard where arguably the only possible outcome *would be* what is stated, and with no other possibilities. It is also a high standard that it would not be effective – suggesting that there needs to be evidence that the target of the inspection would or has definite plane to hinder the investigation, destroy evidence, or such like. This is well beyond some general fear and into the realm of direct knowledge of definitive plans or action by the target. It is not clear if this an intentional high bar, or whether it is unintended. Overall, there is a risk that

161 Article 39(1), DORA.
162 Article 39(2), DORA.
163 Article 39(2), DORA.
164 Article 39(3), DORA.
165 Article 39(4), DORA.
166 Article 39(5), DORA.

officials may be somewhat hampered as compared to officials under alternative legislation such as in the competition sector or anti-counterfeiting sector.

Article 39(6) provides that the critical ICT third-party service provider shall submit to on-site inspections ordered by decision of the Lead Overseer. The decision shall specify the subject matter and purpose of the inspection, fix the date on which the inspection shall begin and shall indicate the periodic penalty payments provided for in Article 35(6), the legal remedies available under Regulations 1093/2010, 1094/2010 and (1095/2010, as well as the right to have the decision 'reviewed' by the Court of Justice.[167]

Where the officials and other persons authorised by the Lead Overseer find that a critical ICT third-party service provider 'opposes' an inspection ordered pursuant to this Article, the Lead Overseer shall inform the critical ICT third-party service provider of the consequences of such opposition, including the possibility for competent authorities of the relevant financial entities to 'require financial entities to terminate the contractual arrangements concluded with that critical ICT third-party service provider.'[168]

ONGOING OVERSIGHT

13.14 Article 40 of DORA refers to ongoing oversight. When conducting oversight activities, in particular general investigations or inspections, the Lead Overseer shall be assisted by a joint examination team established for each critical ICT third-party service provider.[169]

The joint examination team is composed of staff members from:

- the ESAs;
- the relevant competent authorities supervising the financial entities to which the critical ICT third-party service provider provides ICT services;
- the national competent authority[170] on a voluntary basis; and
- one national competent authority from the Member State where the critical ICT third-party service provider is established, on a voluntary basis.[171]

The reference to a voluntary basis suggests that their presence is not required in order to proceed.

Members of the joint examination team shall have expertise in ICT matters and in operational risk.[172] It might be reasonable that some member have a detailed

167 Article 39(6), DORA.
168 Article 39(7), DORA.
169 Article 40(1), DORA.
170 The national competent authority referred to in Article 32(4)(e) of DORA.
171 Article 40(2), DORA.
172 Article 40(2), DORA.

expertise of ICT matter, but the issue arises as to whether all members need such detailed expertise. Another issue is the level of expertise, such as a high general knowledge or detailed technical knowledge.

The joint examination team shall work under the coordination of a designated Lead Overseer staff member (the 'Lead Overseer coordinator').[173]

Then within three months of the completion of an investigation or inspection, the Lead Overseer, after consulting the Oversight Forum, shall adopt recommendations to be addressed to the critical ICT third-party service provider pursuant to the powers referred to in Article 35.[174] This appears to be a fixed-time period.

The recommendations referred to in Article 40(3) shall be immediately communicated to the critical ICT third-party service provider and to the competent authorities of the financial entities to which it provides ICT services.[175]

For the purposes of fulfilling the oversight activities, the Lead Overseer may take into consideration any relevant third-party certifications and ICT third-party internal or external audit reports made available by the critical ICT third-party service provider.[176] This highlights the benefit or importance of firms and/or their suppliers have certifications and or audits.

HARMONISATION FOR OVERSIGHT

13.15 Article 41 of DORA refers to the harmonisation of conditions enabling the conduct of the oversight activities.[177]

The ESAs shall, through the Joint Committee, develop draft RTS to specify:

- the information to be provided by an ICT third-party service provider in the application for a voluntary request to be designated as critical;[178]
- the content, structure and format of the information to be submitted, disclosed or reported by the ICT third-party service providers pursuant to Article 35(1), including the template for providing information on subcontracting arrangements;
- the criteria for determining the composition of the joint examination team ensuring a balanced participation of staff members from the ESAs and from

173 Article 40(2), DORA.
174 Article 40(3), DORA.
175 Article 40(4), DORA.
176 Article 40(4), DORA.
177 Harmonisation aspects are also referred to in Recitals 8, 9, 10, 11, 14, 15, 16, 22, 24, 26, 55, 94, and 99.
178 Provided by an ICT third-party service provider in the application for a voluntary request to be designated as critical under Article 31(11) of DORA.

the relevant competent authorities, their designation, tasks, and working arrangements; and

- the details of the competent authorities' assessment of the measures taken by critical ICT third-party service providers based on the recommendations of the Lead Overseer pursuant to Article 42(3).[179]

The ESAs were required submit those draft RTS to the Commission by 17 July 2024.[180]

Power is delegated to the Commission to supplement DORA by adopting the RTS referred to in paragraph 1 in accordance with the procedure laid down in Articles 10 to 14 of Regulations 1093/2010, 1094/2010 and 1095/2010.[181]

The ESAs published draft RTS and Guidelines on 17 January 2024 and 17 July 2024 (see above at **13.02**).

FOLLOW-UP BY COMPETENT AUTHORITIES

13.16 Article 42 of DORA refers to follow-up by competent authorities.

Article 42(1) provides that within 60 calendar days of the receipt of the recommendations issued by the Lead Overseer[182] critical ICT third-party service providers shall either notify the Lead Overseer of their intention to follow the recommendations or provide a reasoned explanation for not following such recommendations. The Lead Overseer shall immediately transmit this information to the competent authorities of the financial entities concerned.[183]

The Lead Overseer shall 'publicly disclose' where a critical ICT third-party service provider 'fails to notify' the Lead Overseer in accordance with Article 42(1) or where the explanation provided by the critical ICT third-party service provider is 'not deemed sufficient.' The information published shall disclose the identity of the critical ICT third-party service provider as well as information on the type and nature of the non-compliance. Such information shall be limited to what is 'relevant and proportionate' for the purpose of ensuring public awareness, unless such publication would cause disproportionate damage to the parties involved or could seriously jeopardise the orderly functioning and integrity of financial markets or the stability of the whole or part of the financial system of the Union.[184]

179 Article 41(1), DORA.
180 Article 41(2), DORA.
181 Article 41(2), DORA.
182 The recommendations issued by the Lead Overseer pursuant to Article 35(1)(d) of DORA.
183 Article 42(1), DORA.
184 Article 42(2), DORA.

The Lead Overseer shall notify the ICT third-party service provider of that public disclosure.[185]

This will therefore amount to a soft power mechanism to encourage service providers to enhance their digital operational resilience and or to cooperate. While regulators can mandate firms to cease using a particular service provider, the above public mechanism will also encourage or put pressure on firms to discontinue using service providers who have been the subject of certain of the above public notifications.

In addition, competent authorities shall inform the relevant financial entities of the 'risks identified' in the recommendations addressed to critical ICT third-party service providers in accordance with Article 35(1)(d).[186]

When managing ICT third-party risk, financial entities 'shall take into account the risks referred to' in Article 42(1).[187]

Where a competent authority deems that a financial entity 'fails to take into account or to sufficiently address within its management of ICT third-party risk the specific risks identified in the recommendations', it shall notify the financial entity of the possibility of a decision being taken, within 60 calendar days of the receipt of such notification, pursuant to Article 42(6), in the absence of appropriate contractual arrangements aiming to address such risks.[188] One must assume that most service suppliers will of course make some effort and indeed some diligent effort to act on the recommendations. In that regard it may be that there will be few actual instances where a service provider fully fails to take into account the recommendations. It is expected, therefore, that the second part of the clause will be more operable in practice, namely, 'fails to … sufficiently address within its management of ICT third-party risk the specific risks identified in the recommendations.' In this case the issue becomes what is meant by 'sufficiently' and 'sufficiently address' – and importantly who gets to decide and on what basis and upon what justification. One imagines, if not expects, that in the years after the go-live of DORA that these sorts of issues will be the subject of ample disagreement, correspondence, and perhaps even litigation.

It is further provided that '[u]pon receiving' the reports,[189] and prior to taking a decision as referred to in Article 42(6), competent authorities may, on a voluntary basis, consult the competent authorities designated or established in accordance with Directive 2022/2555 responsible for the supervision of an essential or important entity subject to that Directive, which has been designated as a critical ICT third-party service provider.[190]

185 Article 42(2), DORA.
186 Article 42(3), DORA.
187 Article 42(3), DORA.
188 Article 42(4), DORA.
189 The reports referred to in Article 35(1)(c) of DORA.
190 Article 42(5), DORA.

The competent authorities may, as a measure of last resort, following the notification and, if appropriate, the consultation as set out in Article 42(4) and (5), in accordance with Article 50, take a decision requiring financial entities to temporarily suspend, either in part or completely, the use or deployment of a service provided by the critical ICT third-party service provider until the risks identified in the recommendations addressed to critical ICT third-party service providers have been 'addressed'. Where 'necessary', they may require financial entities to terminate, in part or completely, the relevant contractual arrangements concluded with the critical ICT third-party service providers.[191] There is no reference to suspension.

Where a critical ICT third-party service provider refuses to 'endorse' recommendations, based on a divergent approach from the one advised by the Lead Overseer, and such a divergent approach may 'adversely impact' a 'large number' of financial entities, or a 'significant' part of the financial sector, and individual warnings issued by competent authorities have not resulted in consistent approaches 'mitigating' the potential risk to financial stability, the Lead Overseer may, after consulting the Oversight Forum, issue non-binding and non-public opinions to competent authorities, in order to promote consistent and convergent supervisory follow-up measures, as appropriate.[192]

Upon receiving the reports,[193] competent authorities, when taking a decision as referred to in Article 42(6), shall take into account the type and 'magnitude of risk' that is not addressed by the critical ICT third-party service provider, as well as the 'seriousness' of the non-compliance, having regard to the following criteria, namely:

- the gravity and the duration of the non-compliance;
- whether the non-compliance has revealed serious weaknesses in the critical ICT third-party service provider's procedures, management systems, risk management and internal controls;
- whether a financial crime was facilitated, occasioned or is otherwise attributable to the non-compliance;
- whether the non-compliance has been intentional or negligent;
- whether the suspension or termination of the contractual arrangements introduces a risk for continuity of the financial entity's business operations notwithstanding the financial entity's efforts to avoid disruption in the provision of its services; and
- where applicable, the opinion of the competent authorities designated or established in accordance with Directive 2022/2555 responsible for the supervision of an essential or important entity subject to that Directive,

191 Article 42(6), DORA.
192 Article 42(7), DORA.
193 The reports referred to in Article 35(1)(c) of DORA.

which has been designated as a critical ICT third-party service provider, requested on a voluntary basis in accordance with Article 42(5).[194]

Competent authorities shall grant financial entities the necessary period of time to enable them to adjust the contractual arrangements with critical ICT third-party service providers in order to avoid detrimental effects on their digital operational resilience and to allow them to deploy exit strategies and transition plans.[195]

The decision referred to in Article 42(6) shall be notified to the members of the Oversight Forum,[196] and to the JON.[197]

The critical ICT third-party service providers affected by the decisions provided for in Article 42(6) shall fully cooperate with the financial entities impacted, in particular in the context of the process of 'suspension or termination' of their contractual arrangements.[198]

The competent authorities shall regularly inform the Lead Overseer on the approaches and measures taken in their supervisory tasks in relation to financial entities as well as on the contractual arrangements concluded by financial entities where critical ICT third-party service providers have not endorsed in part or entirely recommendations addressed to them by the Lead Overseer.[199]

The Lead Overseer may also, upon request, provide further clarifications on the recommendations issued to guide the competent authorities on the follow-up measures.[200] This suggests that only the competent authorities can ask for clarification.

OVERSIGHT FEES

13.17 Article 43 of DORA refers to oversight fees.[201] This is to cater for some or all of the costs that will be associated to the particular oversight. According to Article 43(1), the Lead Overseer shall, in accordance with the delegated act referred to in Article 42(2), charge critical ICT third-party service providers 'fees that fully cover' the Lead Overseer's 'necessary expenditure' in relation to the conduct of oversight tasks pursuant to DORA, including the reimbursement of any costs which may be incurred as a result of work carried out by the joint examination team,[202] as well as the costs of advice provided by the independent

194 Article 42(8), DORA.
195 Article 42(8), DORA. Deploy exit strategies and transition plans as referred to in Article 28 of DORA.
196 The Oversight Forum referred to in Article 32(4)(a), (b) and (c) of DORA.
197 Article 42(9), DORA.
198 Article 1, DORA.
199 Article 1, DORA.
200 Article 1, DORA.
201 The issue of fees is also referred to in Recitals 96 and 98.
202 The joint examination team referred to in Article 40 of DORA.

experts,[203] in relation to matters falling under the remit of direct oversight activities.[204]

The amount of a fee charged to a critical ICT third-party service provider shall cover 'all costs derived from the execution of the duties' set out in Section II of DORA and shall be 'proportionate to its turnover'.[205] This introduces two potentially divergent concepts. The fees will be whatever they amount to under the provision. However, the separate reference to a process to calculate in some way fees linked to or capped by way of turnover (whether national, EU, or global) is a little vaguer, at least in the provision itself. This may be more specified by way of delegated legislation. In that regard, the Commission was empowered to adopt a delegated act[206] to supplement DORA by determining the amount of the fees and the way in which they are to be paid by 17 July 2024.[207]

INTERNATIONAL COOPERATION

13.18 The whole world is connected by the internet, and not least financial services. This leads itself to a situation where the range of ICT suppliers to the financial sector can be located in many counties, and sometimes many countries at once. Article 44 of DORA refers to the need for international cooperation.

Article 44(1) provides that without prejudice to Article 36, the EBA, ESMA and EIOPA may, in accordance with Article 33 of Regulations 1093/2010, 1095/2010 and 1094/2010, respectively, conclude administrative arrangements with third-country regulatory and supervisory authorities to foster international cooperation on ICT third-party risk across different financial sectors, in particular by developing best practices for the review of ICT risk management practices and controls, mitigation measures and incident responses.[208]

The ESAs, through the Joint Committee, submit every five years a joint confidential report to the European Parliament, to the Council and to the Commission, summarising the findings of relevant discussions held with the third countries' authorities referred to Article 44(1), focusing on the evolution of ICT third-party risk and the implications for financial stability, market integrity, investor protection and the functioning of the internal market.[209]

203 The independent experts as referred to in Article 32(4), second subparagraph, of DORA.
204 Article 43(1), DORA.
205 Article 43(1), DORA.
206 A delegated act in accordance with Article 57 of DORA.
207 Article 43(2), DORA.
208 Article 44(1), DORA.
209 Article 44(2), DORA.

ICT RISK COMPLIANCE

13.19 The new DORA requirements as they relate to ICT risk posed to firms as a result of their engagement of third parties are a clear marker of where supervisory authorities and regulators see an exposure – both to firms individually and to wider financial markets and the economy. The above requirements are detailed and significant.

While there may be more immediate focus on some of the internally focused obligations of DORA, it is predicted that over time supervisory authorities will focus more and more attention on these external-focused risk issues, and elevate their interpretation of what is required of firms in order to comply with these obligations. This view is further enhanced by the fact that supervisory authorities and the newly created Lead Overseer, Joint Committee, joint examination teams (JETs), ESAs, and Commission have significant influence in terms of how these risk-focused areas of DORA will be interpreted, applied, and even expanded in future. In addition, there is clear scope and even an intention to draw more firms, particularly non-financial third-party service supplier firms into the umbrella and scope of DORA and its rules. It may take a year or so to develop post the go-live date of January 2025, but the direction seems to be clear. This will be how the teeth of DORA will grow.

CHAPTER 14

Information Sharing Arrangements

INFORMATION SHARING ARRANGEMENTS

14.01 Digital operational resilience refers, in part, to processes that firms should implement to be prepared to protect against and for dealing with cyber attacks and other adverse digital events. While the world of big business and finance is extremely wide as well as international, the bad actors who target individual consumers and financial firms frequently target more than one firm at the same time.[1] Even where the bad actors target different firms at different times, they will often use similar attack techniques.[2]

While individual firms will seek to deploy a variety of defences, and layered defences, against bad actors (such as anti-virus, perimeter security, access controls, platform security, etc), these are not the only safeguards.

It is often indicated in the cyber security world that the biggest threat is human, which refers to the propensity for employees to do or not do something which will assist a bad actor attack. Unfortunately, many attacks have been successful when an employee clicks a link on an errant email which in a manner of speaking 'opens the door' to the attacker. One of the best methods to prevent attacks in these examples, and indeed one of the most effective defences overall, is to implement effective cyber security training.[3]

However, DORA now recognises that there need to be additional methods to combat cyber criminals. In this regard, DORA recognises the fact that many attacks occur at the same time and/or utilise the same methods of attack.

That being the case, it can be effective for firms who are potential victims of cyber criminals to share information and intelligence on such attacks. If one firm discovers that it is being attacked, it can be of assistance to share some of this information with other firms in the same sector or an industry body. In many instances not every firm will be immediately aware that it is being attacked,

1 On some occasions, they can also be very specific and target an individual firm or a specific individual in a particular firm. An example is spear phishing attacks.

2 While this is generally and predominantly the case, over time there can be new forms of attack discovered or developed. When these new forms of attack involve a new attack tool or new code to enable an attack, or a new attack vector, this is sometimes referred to as a zero-day attack. This means that this is an attack which has not occurred previously.

3 Indeed, this is referenced as one of the DORA requirements. However, this will hopefully not be the first time that an in-scope firm will have commenced cyber security training for its staff. Arguably, it would be remiss if this was the case.

and if a sector-type alert goes out, such firms can take precautionary measures which may thwart the attack. Alternatively, it can shorten the time that it takes to respond and recover.

This is a developing space and many of the parameters are not yet fully developed – but the concept is clear, as is the benefit.

Chapter VI of DORA refers to these information sharing arrangements. These are referred to below.

INFORMATION SHARING ARRANGEMENTS ON CYBER THREAT INFORMATION AND INTELLIGENCE

14.02 Article 45 of DORA refers to information sharing arrangements on cyber threat information and intelligence.[4]

Financial entities 'may' exchange amongst themselves cyber threat information and intelligence, including indicators of compromise, tactics, techniques, and procedures, cyber security alerts and configuration tools, to the extent that such information and intelligence sharing:

- aims to enhance the digital operational resilience of financial entities, in particular through raising awareness in relation to cyber threats, limiting or impeding the cyber threats' ability to spread, supporting defence capabilities, threat detection techniques, mitigation strategies or response and recovery stages;
- takes places within trusted communities of financial entities; and
- is implemented 'through information-sharing arrangements that protect the potentially sensitive nature of the information shared', and that are 'governed by rules of conduct' in full respect of business confidentiality, protection of personal data in accordance with Regulation 2016/679 and guidelines on competition policy.[5]

For the purpose of Article 45(1)(c) (bullet point three above), the information sharing arrangements shall define the conditions for participation and, where appropriate, shall set out the details on the involvement of public authorities and the capacity in which they may be associated to the information-sharing arrangements, on the involvement of ICT third-party service providers, and on operational elements, including the use of dedicated IT platforms.[6]

4 Information sharing issues are referred to in Recitals 32, 33, 34, and 52.
5 Article 45(1), DORA.
6 Article 45(2), DORA.

Financial entities shall notify competent authorities of their participation in the information sharing arrangements, upon validation of their membership, or, as applicable, of the cessation of their membership, once it takes effect.[7]

While this is a developing area, as indicated above, it is predicted that over time those who do not embrace this concept will increase their own risks, and furthermore create circumstances where the respective supervisory authorities will potentially seek to use this as a factor in reprimanding or even sanctioning such firms.

7 Article 45(3), DORA.

CHAPTER 15

Competent Authorities

COMPETENT AUTHORITIES

15.01 The authorities who oversee the many in-scope firms under DORA will have a significant impact – in terms of requiring compliance, monitoring compliance, carrying out investigations, and also imposing sanctions for breaches. Article 46 in Chapter VII of DORA refers to competent authorities, that is, the supervisory regulators involved.

Without prejudice to the provisions on the Oversight Framework for critical information and communication technology (ICT) third-party service providers referred to in Chapter V, Section II of DORA, compliance with DORA shall be ensured by the following competent authorities in accordance with the powers granted by the respective legal acts:

- for credit institutions and for institutions exempted pursuant to Directive 2013/36, the competent authority designated in accordance with Article 4 of that Directive, and for credit institutions classified as significant in accordance with Article 6(4) of Regulation 1024/2013, the European Central Bank (ECB) in accordance with the powers and tasks conferred by that Regulation;
- for payment institutions, including payment institutions exempted pursuant to Directive 2015/2366, electronic money institutions, including those exempted pursuant to Directive 2009/110, and account information service providers as referred to in Article 33(1) of Directive 2015/2366, the competent authority designated in accordance with Article 22 of Directive 2015/2366;
- for investment firms, the competent authority designated in accordance with Article 4 of Directive 2019/2034;
- for crypto asset service providers as authorised under Regulation 2023/1114 on markets in crypto assets and issuers of asset-referenced tokens, the competent authority designated in accordance with the relevant provision of that Regulation;
- for central securities depositories, the competent authority designated in accordance with Article 11 of Regulation 909/2014;
- for central counterparties, the competent authority designated in accordance with Article 22 of Regulation 648/2012;
- for trading venues and data reporting service providers, the competent authority designated in accordance with Article 67 of Directive 2014/65/

EU, and the competent authority as defined in Article 2(1), point (18) of Regulation 600/2014;

- for trade repositories, the competent authority designated in accordance with Article 22 of Regulation 648/2012;
- for managers of alternative investment funds, the competent authority designated in accordance with Article 44 of Directive 2011/61;
- for management companies, the competent authority designated in accordance with Article 97 of Directive 2009/65;
- for insurance and reinsurance undertakings, the competent authority designated in accordance with Article 30 of Directive 2009/138;
- for insurance intermediaries, reinsurance intermediaries and ancillary insurance intermediaries, the competent authority designated in accordance with Article 12 of Directive 2016/97;
- for institutions for occupational retirement provision, the competent authority designated in accordance with Article 47 of Directive 2016/2341;
- for credit rating agencies, the competent authority designated in accordance with Article 21 of Regulation 1060/2009;
- for administrators of critical benchmarks, the competent authority designated in accordance with Articles 40 and 41 of Regulation 2016/1011;
- for crowdfunding service providers, the competent authority designated in accordance with Article 29 of Regulation 2020/1503; and
- for securitisation repositories, the competent authority designated in accordance with Articles 10 and 14(1) of Regulation 2017/2402.[1]

COOPERATION WITH STRUCTURES AND AUTHORITIES

15.02 Article 47 of DORA refers to cooperation with structures and authorities established by Directive 2022/2555.

In order to foster cooperation and enable supervisory exchanges between the competent authorities designated under DORA and the Cooperation Group established by Article 14 of Directive 2022/2555, the European Supervisory Authorities (ESAs) and the competent authorities may participate in the activities of the Cooperation Group for matters that concern their supervisory activities in relation to financial entities.[2] The ESAs and the competent authorities may request to be invited to participate in the activities of the Cooperation Group for matters in relation to essential or important entities subject to Directive 2022/2555 that

1 Article 46, DORA.
2 Article 47(1), DORA.

have also been designated as critical ICT third-party service providers pursuant to Article 31 of DORA.[3]

Where appropriate, competent authorities may consult and share information with the single points of contact and the computer security incident response teams designated or established in accordance with Directive 2022/2555.[4]

Where appropriate, competent authorities may request any relevant technical advice and assistance from the competent authorities designated or established in accordance with Directive 2022/2555 and establish cooperation arrangements to allow effective and fast-response coordination mechanisms to be set up.[5]

The arrangements referred to Article 47(3) may, inter alia, specify the procedures for the coordination of supervisory and oversight activities in relation to essential or important entities subject to Directive 2022/2555 that have been designated as critical ICT third-party service providers pursuant to Article 31 of DORA, including for the conduct, in accordance with national law, of investigations and on-site inspections, as well as for mechanisms for the exchange of information between the competent authorities under DORA and the competent authorities designated or established in accordance with that Directive which includes access to information requested by the latter authorities.[6]

COOPERATION BETWEEN AUTHORITIES

15.03 Article 48 of DORA refers to cooperation between authorities. The competent authorities shall cooperate closely among themselves and, where applicable, with the Lead Overseer.[7] The competent authorities and the Lead Overseer shall, in a timely manner, mutually exchange all relevant information concerning critical ICT third-party service providers which is necessary for them to carry out their respective duties under DORA, in particular in relation to identified risks, approaches and measures taken as part of the Lead Overseer's oversight tasks.[8]

FINANCIAL CROSS SECTOR EXERCISES, COMMUNICATION AND COOPERATION

15.04 Article 49 refers to financial cross-sector exercises, communication and cooperation. The ESAs, through the Joint Committee and in collaboration with competent authorities, resolution authorities as referred to in Article 3 of Directive 2014/59, the ECB, and the Single Resolution Board as regards

3 Article 47(1), DORA.
4 Article 47(2), DORA.
5 Article 47(3), DORA.
6 Article 47(4), DORA.
7 Article 48(1), DORA.
8 Article 48(2), DORA.

information relating to entities falling under the scope of Regulation 806/2014, the European Systemic Risk Board (ESRB) and the European Union Agency on Cybersecurity, as appropriate, may establish mechanisms to enable the sharing of effective practices across financial sectors to enhance situational awareness and identify common cyber vulnerabilities and risks across sectors.[9]

They may develop crisis management and contingency exercises involving cyber attack scenarios with a view to developing communication channels and gradually enabling an effective coordinated response at Union level in the event of a major cross-border ICT-related incident or related threat having a systemic impact on the Union's financial sector as a whole.[10]

Those exercises may, as appropriate, also test the financial sector's dependencies on other economic sectors.[11]

The competent authorities, ESAs and the ECB shall cooperate closely with each other and exchange information to carry out their duties.[12] They shall closely coordinate their supervision in order to identify and remedy breaches of DORA, develop and promote best practices, facilitate collaboration, foster consistency of interpretation and provide cross-jurisdictional assessments in the event of any disagreements.[13]

ADMINISTRATIVE PENALTIES AND REMEDIAL MEASURES

15.05 Article 50 of DORA refers to administrative penalties and remedial measures.[14] The competent authorities shall have all supervisory, investigatory and sanctioning powers necessary to fulfil their duties under DORA.[15]

These powers shall 'include' at least the following powers to:

- have access to any document or data held in any form that the competent authority considers relevant for the performance of its duties and receive or take a copy of it;
- carry out on-site inspections or investigations, which shall include but shall not be limited to;
  - (i) summoning representatives of the financial entities for oral or written explanations on facts or documents relating to the subject matter and purpose of the investigation and to record the answers; and

9 Article 49(1), DORA.
10 Article 49(1), DORA.
11 Article 49(1), DORA.
12 Their duties pursuant to Articles 47 to 54 of DORA.
13 Article 49(2), DORA.
14 Recital 97 also refers to penalties.
15 Article 50(1), DORA.

(ii) interviewing any other natural or legal person who consents to be interviewed for the purpose of collecting information relating to the subject matter of an investigation; and

- require corrective and remedial measures for breaches of the requirements of DORA.[16]

Without prejudice to the right of Member States to impose criminal penalties,[17] Member States shall lay down rules establishing appropriate administrative penalties and remedial measures for breaches of DORA and shall ensure their effective implementation.[18]

Those penalties and measures shall be effective, proportionate and dissuasive.[19] This is similar language to other legislation of this nature,

Member States shall confer on competent authorities the power to apply at least the following administrative penalties or remedial measures for breaches of DORA:

- issue an order requiring the natural or legal person to cease conduct that is in breach of DORA and to desist from a repetition of that conduct;
- require the temporary or permanent cessation of any practice or conduct that the competent authority considers to be contrary to the provisions of DORA and prevent repetition of that practice or conduct;
- adopt any type of measure, including of pecuniary nature, to ensure that financial entities continue to comply with legal requirements;
- require, insofar as permitted by national law, existing data traffic records held by a telecommunication operator, where there is a reasonable suspicion of a breach of DORA and where such records may be relevant to an investigation into breaches of DORA; and
- issue public notices, including public statements indicating the identity of the natural or legal person and the nature of the breach.[20]

Where Article 50(2)(c), and (4) apply to legal persons, Member States shall confer on competent authorities the power to apply the administrative penalties and remedial measures, subject to the conditions provided for in national law, to members of the management body, and to other individuals who under national law are responsible for the breach.[21]

16 Article 50(2), DORA.
17 In accordance with Article 52 of DORA.
18 Article 50(3), DORA.
19 Article 50(3), DORA.
20 Article 50(4), DORA.
21 Article 50(5), DORA.

Member States shall ensure that any decision imposing administrative penalties or remedial measures set out in Article 50(2)(c), is properly reasoned and is subject to a right of appeal.[22]

EXERCISE OF ADMINISTRATIVE PENALTIES AND REMEDIES

15.06 Article 51 of DORA refers to the exercise of the power to impose administrative penalties and remedial measures.

The competent authorities shall exercise the powers to impose administrative penalties and remedial measures referred to in Article 50 in accordance with their national legal frameworks, where appropriate, as follows:

- directly;
- in collaboration with other authorities;
- under their responsibility by delegation to other authorities; or
- by application to the competent judicial authorities.[23]

The competent authorities, when determining the type and level of an administrative penalty or remedial measure to be imposed under Article 50, shall take into account the extent to which the breach is intentional or results from negligence, and all other relevant circumstances, including the following, where appropriate:

- the materiality, gravity and the duration of the breach;
- the degree of responsibility of the natural or legal person responsible for the breach;
- the financial strength of the responsible natural or legal person;
- the importance of profits gained or losses avoided by the responsible natural or legal person, insofar as they can be determined;
- the losses for third parties caused by the breach, insofar as they can be determined;
- the level of cooperation of the responsible natural or legal person with the competent authority, without prejudice to the need to ensure disgorgement of profits gained or losses avoided by that natural or legal person; and
- previous breaches by the responsible natural or legal person.[24]

22 Article 50(6), DORA.
23 Article 51(1), DORA.
24 Article 51(2), DORA.

CRIMINAL PENALTIES

15.07 Article 52 of DORA refers to criminal penalties. Member States may decide not to lay down rules for administrative penalties or remedial measures for breaches that are subject to criminal penalties under their national law.[25]

Where Member States have chosen to lay down criminal penalties for breaches of DORA, they shall ensure that appropriate measures are in place so that competent authorities have all the necessary powers to liaise with judicial, prosecuting, or criminal justice authorities within their jurisdiction to receive specific information related to criminal investigations or proceedings commenced for breaches of DORA, and to provide the same information to other competent authorities, as well as the European Banking Authority (EBA), the European Securities and Markets Authority (ESMA) or the European Insurance and Occupational Pensions Authority (EIOPA) to fulfil their obligations to cooperate for the purposes of DORA.[26]

PUBLICATION OF ADMINISTRATIVE PENALTIES

15.08 Article 54 of DORA refers to the publication of administrative penalties. The competent authorities shall publish on their official websites, without undue delay, any decision imposing an administrative penalty against which there is no appeal after the addressee of the penalty has been notified of that decision.[27]

The publication referred to in Article 54(1) above shall include information on the type and nature of the breach, the identity of the persons responsible and the penalties imposed.[28]

Where the competent authority, following a case-by-case assessment, considers that the publication of the identity, in the case of legal persons, or of the identity and personal data, in the case of natural persons, would be disproportionate, including risks in relation to the protection of personal data, jeopardise the stability of financial markets or the pursuit of an ongoing criminal investigation, or cause, insofar as these can be determined, disproportionate damages to the person involved, it shall adopt one of the following solutions in respect of the decision imposing an administrative penalty:

- defer its publication until all reasons for non-publication cease to exist;
- publish it on an anonymous basis, in accordance with national law; or
- refrain from publishing it, where the options set out in bullet points one and two are deemed either insufficient to guarantee a lack of any danger for

25 Article 52(1), DORA.
26 Article 52(2), DORA.
27 Article 54(1), DORA.
28 Article 54(2), DORA.

the stability of financial markets, or where such a publication would not be proportionate to the leniency of the imposed penalty.[29]

In the case of a decision to publish an administrative penalty on an anonymous basis in accordance with Article 54(3)(b), the publication of the relevant data may be postponed.[30]

Where a competent authority publishes a decision imposing an administrative penalty against which there is an appeal before the relevant judicial authorities, competent authorities shall immediately add on their official website that information and, at later stages, any subsequent related information on the outcome of such appeal. Any judicial decision annulling a decision imposing an administrative penalty shall also be published.[31]

The competent authorities shall ensure that any publication referred to in Article 54(1) to (4) shall remain on their official website only for the period which is necessary to bring forth this Article. This period shall not exceed five years after its publication.[32]

PROFESSIONAL SECRECY

15.09 Article 55 of DORA refers to the issue of professional secrecy. Importantly, any confidential information received, exchanged or transmitted pursuant to DORA shall be subject to the conditions of professional secrecy laid down in Article 55(2) below.[33]

The obligation of professional secrecy applies to all persons who work, or who have worked, for the competent authorities pursuant to DORA, or for any authority or market undertaking or natural or legal person to whom those competent authorities have delegated their powers, including auditors and experts contracted by them.[34]

In addition, information covered by professional secrecy, including the exchange of information among competent authorities under DORA and competent authorities designated or established in accordance with Directive 2022/2555, shall not be disclosed to any other person or authority except by virtue of provisions laid down by Union or national law.[35]

All information exchanged between the competent authorities pursuant to DORA that concerns business or operational conditions and other economic or personal

29 Article 54(3), DORA.
30 Article 54(4), DORA.
31 Article 54(5), DORA.
32 Article 54(6), DORA.
33 Article 55(1), DORA.
34 Article 55(2), DORA.
35 Article 55(3), DORA.

affairs shall be considered confidential and shall be subject to the requirements of professional secrecy, except where the competent authority states, at the time of communication, that such information may be disclosed or where such disclosure is necessary for legal proceedings.[36]

DATA PROTECTION

15.10 Article 56 of DORA refers to data protection and personal data. The ESAs and the competent authorities shall be allowed to process personal data only where necessary for the purpose of carrying out their respective obligations and duties pursuant to DORA, in particular for investigation, inspection, request for information, communication, publication, evaluation, verification, assessment and drafting of oversight plans. The personal data shall be processed in accordance with Regulation 2016/679 or Regulation 2018/1725, whichever is applicable.[37]

Except where otherwise provided in other sectoral acts, the personal data referred to in Article 56(1) above shall be retained until the discharge of the applicable supervisory duties and in any case for a maximum period of 15 years, except in the event of pending court proceedings requiring further retention of such data.[38]

NOTIFICATION DUTIES

15.11 In addition to DORA being directly effective, respective states may also introduce supplementary national legislation. Article 53 of DORA refers to notification duties. Member States shall notify the laws, regulations and administrative provisions implementing Chapter VII, including any relevant criminal law provisions, to the Commission, ESMA, the EBA and EIOPA by 17 January 2025. Member States shall notify the Commission, ESMA, the EBA and EIOPA without undue delay of any subsequent amendments thereto.39

36 Article 55(4), DORA.
37 Article 56(1), DORA.
38 Article 56(2), DORA.
39 Article 53, DORA.

CHAPTER 16

Delegated Acts

DELEGATED ACTS

16.01 Chapter VIII of DORA refers to delegated acts. These are referred to below.

EXERCISE OF THE DELEGATION

16.02 Article 57 of DORA refers to the exercise of the delegation. The power to adopt delegated acts is conferred on the Commission subject to the conditions laid down in this Article.[1] The power to adopt delegated acts[2] is conferred on the Commission for a period of five years from 17 January 2024. The Commission shall draw up a report in respect of the delegation of power not later than nine months before the end of the five-year period. The delegation of power shall be tacitly extended for periods of an identical duration, unless the European Parliament or the Council opposes such extension not later than three months before the end of each period.[3]

The delegation of power[4] may be revoked at any time by the European Parliament or by the Council. A decision to revoke shall put an end to the delegation of the power specified in that decision. It shall take effect the day following the publication of the decision in the Official Journal of the European Union or at a later date specified therein. It shall not affect the validity of any delegated acts already in force.[5]

Before adopting a delegated act, the Commission shall consult experts designated by each Member State in accordance with the principles laid down in the Interinstitutional Agreement on Better Law Making.[6]

As soon as it adopts a delegated act, the Commission shall notify it simultaneously to the European Parliament and to the Council.[7]

1 Article 57(1), DORA.
2 Referred to in Articles 31(6) and 43(2) of DORA.
3 Article 57(2), DORA.
4 Referred to in Articles 31(6) and 43(2) of DORA.
5 Article 57(3), DORA.
6 Article 57(4), DORA. The Interinstitutional Agreement of 13 April 2016 on Better Law-Making.
7 Article 57(5), DORA.

A delegated act[8] shall enter into force only if no objection has been expressed either by the European Parliament or by the Council within a period of three months of notification of that act to the European Parliament and the Council or if, before the expiry of that period, the European Parliament and the Council have both informed the Commission that they will not object. That period shall be extended by three months at the initiative of the European Parliament or of the Council.[9]

In some instances, the Commission may act and make its own Commission-initiated DORA sub-regulations. The majority of sub-regulations, however, are initiated and drafted by the European Supervisory Authorities (ESAs). The ESAs then submit them to the Commission for review and approval. If the Commission is satisfied, it will issue the respective sub-regulation as a legal measure which will become effective as specified after publication in the Official Journal. In most instances so far, the Commission has only made small amendments to the draft sub-regulations.

In one notable example, however, the Commission has rejected one of the measures furnished by the ESAs. The ESAs submitted a draft implementing technical standards (ITS) to the Commission on 17 January 2024 in relation to the register of information required under DORA, Article 28.[10] The Commission rejected the draft ITS on 3 September 2024. The reason for the rejection was the envisaged mandatory use of the Legal Entity Identifier (LEI) number to identify ICT third-party service providers in the registers of information reports. The Commission wished for an alternative to the LEI to be included in the proposed template, namely, the European Unique Identifier.

In response to the rejection, the ESAs wrote that the suggestion to require the inclusion of the European Unique Identifier would add extra costs and effort to firms – the implication being that this may be in some way contrary to one of the policies incorporated into DORA.

While the ESAs have responded with an updated proposed ITS and provisions regarding the register of information, the matter is not yet resolved.[11] This adds extra confusion and complications to the many firms who are developing their compliance initiatives.

8 A delegated act adopted pursuant to Articles 31(6) and 43(2) of DORA.

9 Article 57(6), DORA.

10 Consultation Paper on ITS to Establish the Templates for the Register of Information (Art.28.9) (19 June 2023); Implementing Technical Standards (ITS) to Establish the Templates for the Register of Information (17 January 2024), contained in the first batch of draft rules developed by the ESAs and presented to the Commission.

11 See, for example, JC 2024 75 – Opinion on the Rejection of the ITS on RoI Under DORA (15 October 2024); JC 2024 78 – ESAs Proposals for Further Changes to the ITS on RoI (15 October 2024); JC 2024 79 – ESAs Proposals for Further Changes to the Annex of the ITS on RoI (15 October 2024).

It is noted that while the ESAs have made updated proposals in relation to the LEI number and the European Unique Identifier, it has also made additional amendments, so as to:

- ensure as much consistency as possible in data modelling and reporting already in place for some of the types of financial entities under DORA, which also fall under the sectoral prudential regulation (prudential reporting). These changes would allow for greater consistency among the different types of existing sectoral reporting frameworks and thus would reduce the implementation efforts for the respective types of financial entities;
- reflect the practical feedback received from financial entities participating in the voluntary dry run exercise on reporting of registers of information the ESAs have carried out. These changes are mostly focused on the reporting instructions, with the view to improving their understanding by the financial entities through additional clarifications or simplifications; and
- reinstating important provisions clarifying some requirements. In particular, Recital 7 has been amended with a new drafting to avoid misinterpretation of the initial meaning.[12]

As indicated above, this remains an unresolved issue at the time of publication, which is certainly not ideal in October 2024 as the go-live date of January 2025 approaches.

12 See Opinion of the European Supervisory Authorities, JC 2024 75 (15 October 2024) at para 15. (This is the same as documented JC 2024 75 – Opinion on the Rejection of the ITS on RoI Under DORA, referred to in note 11 above.)

CHAPTER 17

Transitional and Final Provisions

TRANSITIONAL AND FINAL PROVISIONS

17.01 Chapter IX of DORA refers to the transitional and final provisions. These are referred to below.

ENTRY INTO FORCE AND APPLICATION OF DORA

17.02 DORA enters into force on the twentieth day following that of its publication in the Official Journal of the European Union.[1] In terms of day-to-day application, however, DORA applies in effect from the so-called go-live date of 17 January 2025.[2] It is from 17 January 2025 that firms have to be compliant. Of course, they should have many compliance mechanisms already in place, and should in addition also have had ongoing programmes and processes in place in direct preparation for DORA's go live.

It is from this go-live date that compliance or non-compliance will be benchmarked by respective regulators and supervisory authorities – and in addition the European Supervisory Authorities (ESAs). From the go-live date onwards, the supervisory authorities will be progressively calling on firms to demonstrate to them that they are compliant.

In addition, from or soon after the go live date, firms will be expected to start making the mandatory reports to the supervisory authorities on specific DORA compliance matters. In some instances, these reports may be immediately required to be submitted, and in certain instances, only after receiving a specific request from a supervisory authority. However, it may transpire that some of the supervisory authorities may decide to require all in-scope firms to have to make specific reports on an annual basis, as opposed to making individual requests to only a small number of firms.

DORA is binding in its entirety and directly applicable in all Member States,[3] which therefore does not necessitate further local implanting laws to be implemented in individual Member States. It is unlike a Directive which does generally require local implantation. In effect, therefore, DORA arrives with a Big Bang in January 2025 without the lag or delays that awaiting later local

1 Article 64, DORA.
2 Article 64, DORA.
3 Article 64, DORA. DORA was agreed in Strasbourg on 14 December 2022, ibid.

implementing measures sometimes brings. A series of local implementing laws can also bring the disadvantage of staggered implementations. This does not occur with DORA, which may well have something to do with sensitivities and stability of the European financial system as a whole.

It is also appropriate to point out that separate to reports and information to be supplied to supervisory authorities, firm also have internal audit functions. Even where a specific request (or direction as the case may be) arises in relation to a supervisory authority, the internal audit function will sooner or later be making audit requests for information on how the firm is complying with DORA.

A word of caution is advised in terms of reporting. A firm should not take a narrow view in terms of interpreting certain provisions as only requiring particular information or reports to be gathered at the time that an official request is received from a regulator or supervisory authority.

The more correct expectation of DORA, and likely of supervisory authorities, is that information and reporting should become an ongoing business task. These ongoing records of these rolling sets of information and reports should be available to the supervisory authorities on demand. This means that a supervisory authority may ask for past information and past internal reports – not just for the current period.

Therefore, the scope of materials that may need to be supplied has expanded under DORA, but will also expand exponentially over the coming years. One saver may be that some (but not all) of these may in practical terms only be demanded from 2026 onwards as the go-live date is 2025. But this is only a temporary relief. Overall, firms have a lot of ramp-up work to do, as well as a lot of permanent ongoing work to do to be DORA compliant.

AMENDMENTS

17.03 Section II of Chapter IX of DORA refers to amendments. Article 59 of DORA contains amendments to Regulation 1060/2009, but for full details of the specific amendments, see the full text of Article 59 contained in Appendix 1 in this book.

Article 60 of DORA contains amendments to Regulation 648/2012, but for full details of the specific amendments, see the full text of Article 60 contained in Appendix 1 in this book.

Article 61 of DORA contains amendments to Regulation 909/2014, but for full details of the specific amendments, see the full text of Article 61 contained in Appendix 1 in this book.

Article 62 of DORA contains amendments to Regulation 600/2014, but for full details of the specific amendments, see the full text of Article 62 contained in Appendix 1 in this book.

Article 63 of DORA contains amendments to Regulation 2016/1011, but for full details of the specific amendments, see the full text of Article 63 contained in Appendix 1 in this book.

REVIEW

17.04 Article 58 of DORA refers to a review clause. By 17 January 2028, the Commission shall, after consulting the ESAs and the European Systemic Risk Board (ESRB), as appropriate, carry out a review and submit a report to the European Parliament and the Council, accompanied, where appropriate, by a legislative proposal. The review shall include at least the following:

- the criteria for the designation of critical ICT third-party service providers;[4]
- the voluntary nature of the notification of significant cyber threats;[5]
- the regime referred to in Article 31(12) and the powers of the Lead Overseer,[6] with a view to evaluating the effectiveness of those provisions with regard to ensuring effective oversight of critical ICT third-party service providers established in a third country, and the necessity to establish a subsidiary in the Union.[7]

  The review shall include an analysis of the regime referred to in Article 31(12), including in terms of access for Union financial entities to services from third countries and availability of such services on the Union market and it shall take into account further developments in the markets for the services covered by DORA, the practical experience of financial entities and financial supervisors with regard to the application and, respectively, supervision of that regime, and any relevant regulatory and supervisory developments taking place at international level;[8]
- the appropriateness of including in the scope of DORA financial entities referred to in Article 2(3)(e), making use of automated sales systems, in light of future market developments on the use of such systems; and
- the functioning and effectiveness of the joint oversight network in supporting the consistency of the oversight and the efficiency of the exchange of information within the Oversight Framework.[9]

In the context of the review of Directive 2015/2366, the Commission shall assess the need for increased cyber resilience of payment systems and payment processing activities and the appropriateness of extending the scope of DORA to operators of payment systems and entities involved in payment processing activities. In light of this assessment, the Commission was required to submit, as

4 In accordance with Article 31(2) of DORA.
5 Referred to in Article 19 of DORA.
6 Provided for in Article 35(1)(d)(iv), first indent of DORA.
7 Article 58(1), DORA.
8 Article 58(1), DORA.
9 Article 58(1), DORA.

part of the review of Directive 2015/2366, a report to the European Parliament and the Council no later than 17 July 2023.[10]

Based on that review report, and after consulting ESAs, the European Central Bank and the ESRB, the Commission may submit, where appropriate and as part of the legislative proposal that it may adopt pursuant to Article 108, second paragraph of Directive 2015/2366, a proposal to ensure that all operators of payment systems and entities involved in payment processing activities are subject to an appropriate oversight, while taking into account existing oversight by the central bank.[11]

By 17 January 2026, the Commission shall, after consulting the ESAs and the Committee of European Auditing Oversight Bodies, carry out a review and submit a report to the European Parliament and the Council, accompanied, where appropriate, by a legislative proposal, on the appropriateness of strengthened requirements for statutory auditors and audit firms as regards digital operational resilience, by means of the inclusion of statutory auditors and audit firms into the scope of this Regulation or by means of amendments to Directive 2006/43.[12]

10 Article 58(2), DORA.
11 Article 58(2), DORA.
12 Article 58(3), DORA.

Appendices

APPENDIX 1

DORA

REGULATION (EU) 2022/2554 OF THE EUROPEAN PARLIAMENT AND OF THE COUNCIL

of 14 December 2022

on digital operational resilience for the financial sector and amending Regulations (EC) No 1060/2009, (EU) No 648/2012, (EU) No 600/2014, (EU) No 909/2014 and (EU) 2016/1011

(Text with EEA relevance)

THE EUROPEAN PARLIAMENT AND THE COUNCIL OF THE EUROPEAN UNION,

Having regard to the Treaty on the Functioning of the European Union, and in particular Article 114 thereof,

Having regard to the proposal from the European Commission,

After transmission of the draft legislative act to the national parliaments,

Having regard to the opinion of the European Central Bank([1]),

Having regard to the opinion of the European Economic and Social Committee([2]),

Acting in accordance with the ordinary legislative procedure([3]),

Whereas:

(1) In the digital age, information and communication technology (ICT) supports complex systems used for everyday activities. It keeps our economies running in key sectors, including the financial sector, and enhances the functioning of the internal market. Increased digitalisation and interconnectedness also amplify ICT risk, making society as a whole, and the financial system in particular, more vulnerable to cyber threats or ICT disruptions. While the ubiquitous use of ICT systems and high digitalisation and connectivity are today core features of the activities of Union financial entities, their digital resilience has yet to be better addressed and integrated into their broader operational frameworks.

1 OJ C 343, 26.8.2021, p. 1.

2 OJ C 155, 30.4.2021, p. 38.

3 Position of the European Parliament of 10 November 2022 (not yet published in the Official Journal) and decision of the Council of 28 November 2022.

(2) The use of ICT has in the past decades gained a pivotal role in the provision of financial services, to the point where it has now acquired a critical importance in the operation of typical daily functions of all financial entities. Digitalisation now covers, for instance, payments, which have increasingly moved from cash and paper-based methods to the use of digital solutions, as well as securities clearing and settlement, electronic and algorithmic trading, lending and funding operations, peer-to-peer finance, credit rating, claim management and back-office operations. The insurance sector has also been transformed by the use of ICT, from the emergence of insurance intermediaries offering their services online operating with InsurTech, to digital insurance underwriting. Finance has not only become largely digital throughout the whole sector, but digitalisation has also deepened interconnections and dependencies within the financial sector and with third-party infrastructure and service providers.

(3) The European Systemic Risk Board (ESRB) reaffirmed in a 2020 report addressing systemic cyber risk how the existing high level of interconnectedness across financial entities, financial markets and financial market infrastructures, and particularly the interdependencies of their ICT systems, could constitute a systemic vulnerability because localised cyber incidents could quickly spread from any of the approximately 22 000 Union financial entities to the entire financial system, unhindered by geographical boundaries. Serious ICT breaches that occur in the financial sector do not merely affect financial entities taken in isolation. They also smooth the way for the propagation of localised vulnerabilities across the financial transmission channels and potentially trigger adverse consequences for the stability of the Union's financial system, such as generating liquidity runs and an overall loss of confidence and trust in financial markets.

(4) In recent years, ICT risk has attracted the attention of international, Union and national policy makers, regulators and standard-setting bodies in an attempt to enhance digital resilience, set standards and coordinate regulatory or supervisory work. At international level, the Basel Committee on Banking Supervision, the Committee on Payments and Market Infrastructures, the Financial Stability Board, the Financial Stability Institute, as well as the G7 and G20 aim to provide competent authorities and market operators across various jurisdictions with tools to bolster the resilience of their financial systems. That work has also been driven by the need to duly consider ICT risk in the context of a highly interconnected global financial system and to seek more consistency of relevant best practices.

(5) Despite Union and national targeted policy and legislative initiatives, ICT risk continues to pose a challenge to the operational resilience, performance and stability of the Union financial system. The reforms that followed the 2008 financial crisis primarily strengthened the financial resilience of the Union financial sector and aimed to safeguard the competitiveness and stability of the Union from economic, prudential and market conduct perspectives. Although ICT security and digital resilience are part of

operational risk, they have been less in the focus of the post-financial crisis regulatory agenda and have developed in only some areas of the Union's financial services policy and regulatory landscape, or in only a few Member States.

(6) In its Communication of 8 March 2018 entitled 'FinTech Action plan: For a more competitive and innovative European financial sector', the Commission highlighted the paramount importance of making the Union financial sector more resilient, including from an operational perspective to ensure its technological safety and good functioning, its quick recovery from ICT breaches and incidents, ultimately enabling the effective and smooth provision of financial services across the whole Union, including under situations of stress, while also preserving consumer and market trust and confidence.

(7) In April 2019, the European Supervisory Authority (European Banking Authority), (EBA) established by Regulation (EU) No 1093/2010 of the European Parliament and of the Council([4]), the European Supervisory Authority (European Insurance and Occupational Pensions Authority), ('EIOPA') established by Regulation (EU) No 1094/2010 of the European Parliament and of the Council([5]) and the European Supervisory Authority (European Securities and Markets Authority), ('ESMA') established by Regulation (EU) No 1095/2010 of the European Parliament and of the Council([6]) (known collectively as 'European Supervisory Authorities' or 'ESAs') jointly issued technical advice calling for a coherent approach to ICT risk in finance and recommending to strengthen, in a proportionate way, the digital operational resilience of the financial services industry through a sector-specific initiative of the Union.

(8) The Union financial sector is regulated by a Single Rulebook and governed by a European system of financial supervision. Nonetheless, provisions tackling digital operational resilience and ICT security are not yet fully or consistently harmonised, despite digital operational resilience being vital for ensuring financial stability and market integrity in the digital age, and no less important than, for example, common prudential or market conduct standards. The Single Rulebook and system of supervision should therefore be developed to also cover digital operational resilience, by strengthening the mandates of competent authorities to enable them to

4 Regulation (EU) No 1093/2010 of the European Parliament and of the Council of 24 November 2010 establishing a European Supervisory Authority (European Banking Authority), amending Decision No 716/2009/EC and repealing Commission Decision 2009/78/EC (OJ L 331, 15.12.2010, p. 12).

5 Regulation (EU) No 1094/2010 of the European Parliament and of the Council of 24 November 2010 establishing a European Supervisory Authority (European Insurance and Occupational Pensions Authority), amending Decision No 716/2009/EC and repealing Commission Decision 2009/79/EC (OJ L 331, 15.12.2010, p. 48).

6 Regulation (EU) No 1095/2010 of the European Parliament and of the Council of 24 November 2010 establishing a European Supervisory Authority (European Securities and Markets Authority), amending Decision No 716/2009/EC and repealing Commission Decision 2009/77/EC (OJ L 331, 15.12.2010, p. 84).

supervise the management of ICT risk in the financial sector in order to protect the integrity and efficiency of the internal market, and to facilitate its orderly functioning.

(9) Legislative disparities and uneven national regulatory or supervisory approaches with regard to ICT risk trigger obstacles to the functioning of the internal market in financial services, impeding the smooth exercise of the freedom of establishment and the provision of services for financial entities operating on a cross-border basis. Competition between the same type of financial entities operating in different Member States could also be distorted. This is the case, in particular, for areas where Union harmonisation has been very limited, such as digital operational resilience testing, or absent, such as the monitoring of ICT third-party risk. Disparities stemming from developments envisaged at national level could generate further obstacles to the functioning of the internal market to the detriment of market participants and financial stability.

(10) To date, due to the ICT risk related provisions being only partially addressed at Union level, there are gaps or overlaps in important areas, such as ICT-related incident reporting and digital operational resilience testing, and inconsistencies as a result of emerging divergent national rules or cost-ineffective application of overlapping rules. This is particularly detrimental for an ICT-intensive user such as the financial sector since technology risks have no borders and the financial sector deploys its services on a wide cross-border basis within and outside the Union. Individual financial entities operating on a cross-border basis or holding several authorisations (e.g. one financial entity can have a banking, an investment firm, and a payment institution licence, each issued by a different competent authority in one or several Member States) face operational challenges in addressing ICT risk and mitigating adverse impacts of ICT incidents on their own and in a coherent cost-effective way.

(11) As the Single Rulebook has not been accompanied by a comprehensive ICT or operational risk framework, further harmonisation of key digital operational resilience requirements for all financial entities is required. The development of ICT capabilities and overall resilience by financial entities, based on those key requirements, with a view to withstanding operational outages, would help preserve the stability and integrity of the Union financial markets and thus contribute to ensuring a high level of protection of investors and consumers in the Union. Since this Regulation aims to contribute to the smooth functioning of the internal market, it should be based on the provisions of Article 114 of the Treaty on the Functioning of the European Union (TFEU) as interpreted in accordance with the consistent case law of the Court of Justice of the European Union (Court of Justice).

(12) This Regulation aims to consolidate and upgrade ICT risk requirements as part of the operational risk requirements that have, up to this point, been addressed separately in various Union legal acts. While those acts covered the main categories of financial risk (e.g. credit risk, market

risk, counterparty credit risk and liquidity risk, market conduct risk), they did not comprehensively tackle, at the time of their adoption, all components of operational resilience. The operational risk rules, when further developed in those Union legal acts, often favoured a traditional quantitative approach to addressing risk (namely setting a capital requirement to cover ICT risk) rather than targeted qualitative rules for the protection, detection, containment, recovery and repair capabilities against ICT-related incidents, or for reporting and digital testing capabilities. Those acts were primarily meant to cover and update essential rules on prudential supervision, market integrity or conduct. By consolidating and upgrading the different rules on ICT risk, all provisions addressing digital risk in the financial sector should for the first time be brought together in a consistent manner in one single legislative act. Therefore, this Regulation fills in the gaps or remedies inconsistencies in some of the prior legal acts, including in relation to the terminology used therein, and explicitly refers to ICT risk via targeted rules on ICT risk-management capabilities, incident reporting, operational resilience testing and ICT third-party risk monitoring. This Regulation should thus also raise awareness of ICT risk and acknowledge that ICT incidents and a lack of operational resilience have the possibility to jeopardise the soundness of financial entities.

(13) Financial entities should follow the same approach and the same principle-based rules when addressing ICT risk taking into account their size and overall risk profile, and the nature, scale and complexity of their services, activities and operations. Consistency contributes to enhancing confidence in the financial system and preserving its stability especially in times of high reliance on ICT systems, platforms and infrastructures, which entails increased digital risk. Observing basic cyber hygiene should also avoid imposing heavy costs on the economy by minimising the impact and costs of ICT disruptions.

(14) A Regulation helps reduce regulatory complexity, fosters supervisory convergence and increases legal certainty, and also contributes to limiting compliance costs, especially for financial entities operating across borders, and to reducing competitive distortions. Therefore, the choice of a Regulation for the establishment of a common framework for the digital operational resilience of financial entities is the most appropriate way to guarantee a homogenous and coherent application of all components of ICT risk management by the Union financial sector.

(15) Directive (EU) 2016/1148 of the European Parliament and of the Council([7]) was the first horizontal cybersecurity framework enacted at Union level, applying also to three types of financial entities, namely credit institutions, trading venues and central counterparties. However, since Directive (EU) 2016/1148 set out a mechanism of identification at national level of operators of essential services, only certain credit institutions, trading

7 Directive (EU) 2016/1148 of the European Parliament and of the Council of 6 July 2016 concerning measures for a high common level of security of network and information systems across the Union (OJ L 194, 19.7.2016, p. 1).

venues and central counterparties that were identified by the Member States, have been brought into its scope in practice, and hence required to comply with the ICT security and incident notification requirements laid down in it. Directive (EU) 2022/2555 of the European Parliament and of the Council([8]) sets a uniform criterion to determine the entities falling within its scope of application (size-cap rule) while also keeping the three types of financial entities in its scope.

(16) However, as this Regulation increases the level of harmonisation of the various digital resilience components, by introducing requirements on ICT risk management and ICT-related incident reporting that are more stringent in comparison to those laid down in the current Union financial services law, this higher level constitutes an increased harmonisation also in comparison with the requirements laid down in Directive (EU) 2022/2555. Consequently, this Regulation constitutes lex specialis with regard to Directive (EU) 2022/2555. At the same time, it is crucial to maintain a strong relationship between the financial sector and the Union horizontal cybersecurity framework as currently laid out in Directive (EU) 2022/2555 to ensure consistency with the cyber security strategies adopted by Member States and to allow financial supervisors to be made aware of cyber incidents affecting other sectors covered by that Directive.

(17) In accordance with Article 4(2) of the Treaty on European Union and without prejudice to the judicial review by the Court of Justice, this Regulation should not affect the responsibility of Member States with regard to essential State functions concerning public security, defence and the safeguarding of national security, for example concerning the supply of information which would be contrary to the safeguarding of national security.

(18) To enable cross-sector learning and to effectively draw on experiences of other sectors in dealing with cyber threats, the financial entities referred to in Directive (EU) 2022/2555 should remain part of the 'ecosystem' of that Directive (for example, Cooperation Group and computer security incident response teams (CSIRTs)). The ESAs and national competent authorities should be able to participate in the strategic policy discussions and the technical workings of the Cooperation Group under that Directive, and to exchange information and further cooperate with the single points of contact designated or established in accordance with that Directive. The competent authorities under this Regulation should also consult and cooperate with the CSIRTs. The competent authorities should also be able to request technical advice from the competent authorities designated or established in accordance with Directive (EU) 2022/2555 and establish cooperation arrangements that aim to ensure effective and fast-response coordination mechanisms.

8 Directive (EU) 2022/2555 of the European Parliament and of the Council of 14 December 2022 on measures for a high common level of cybersecurity across the Union, amending Regulation (EU) No 910/2014 and Directive (EU) 2018/1972, and repealing Directive (EU) 2016/1148 (NIS 2 Directive) (see page 80 of this Official Journal).

(19) Given the strong interlinkages between the digital resilience and the physical resilience of financial entities, a coherent approach with regard to the resilience of critical entities is necessary in this Regulation and Directive (EU) 2022/2557 of the European Parliament and the Council([9]). Given that the physical resilience of financial entities is addressed in a comprehensive manner by the ICT risk management and reporting obligations covered by this Regulation, the obligations laid down in Chapters III and IV of Directive (EU) 2022/2557 should not apply to financial entities falling within the scope of that Directive.

(20) Cloud computing service providers are one category of digital infrastructure covered by Directive (EU) 2022/2555. The Union Oversight Framework ('Oversight Framework') established by this Regulation applies to all critical ICT third-party service providers, including cloud computing service providers providing ICT services to financial entities, and should be considered complementary to the supervision carried out pursuant to Directive (EU) 2022/2555. Moreover, the Oversight Framework established by this Regulation should cover cloud computing service providers in the absence of a Union horizontal framework establishing a digital oversight authority.

(21) In order to maintain full control over ICT risk, financial entities need to have comprehensive capabilities to enable a strong and effective ICT risk management, as well as specific mechanisms and policies for handling all ICT-related incidents and for reporting major ICT-related incidents. Likewise, financial entities should have policies in place for the testing of ICT systems, controls and processes, as well as for managing ICT third-party risk. The digital operational resilience baseline for financial entities should be increased while also allowing for a proportionate application of requirements for certain financial entities, particularly microenterprises, as well as financial entities subject to a simplified ICT risk management framework. To facilitate an efficient supervision of institutions for occupational retirement provision that is proportionate and addresses the need to reduce administrative burdens on the competent authorities, the relevant national supervisory arrangements in respect of such financial entities should take into account their size and overall risk profile, and the nature, scale and complexity of their services, activities and operations even when the relevant thresholds established in Article 5 of Directive (EU) 2016/2341 of the European Parliament and of the Council([10]) are exceeded. In particular, supervisory activities should focus primarily on the need to address serious risks associated with the ICT risk management of a particular entity.

9 Directive (EU) 2022/2557 of the European Parliament and of the Council of 14 December 2022 on the resilience of critical entities and repealing Council Directive 2008/114/EC (see page 164 of this Official Journal).

10 Directive (EU) 2016/2341 of the European Parliament and of the Council of 14 December 2016 on the activities and supervision of institutions for occupational retirement provision (IORPs) (OJ L 354, 23.12.2016, p. 37).

Competent authorities should also maintain a vigilant but proportionate approach in relation to the supervision of institutions for occupational retirement provision which, in accordance with Article 31 of Directive (EU) 2016/2341, outsource a significant part of their core business, such as asset management, actuarial calculations, accounting and data management, to service providers.

(22) ICT-related incident reporting thresholds and taxonomies vary significantly at national level. While common ground may be achieved through the relevant work undertaken by the European Union Agency for Cybersecurity (ENISA) established by Regulation (EU) 2019/881 of the European Parliament and of the Council([11]) and the Cooperation Group under Directive (EU) 2022/2555, divergent approaches on setting the thresholds and use of taxonomies still exist, or can emerge, for the remainder of financial entities. Due to those divergences, there are multiple requirements that financial entities must comply with, especially when operating across several Member States and when part of a financial group. Moreover, such divergences have the potential to hinder the creation of further uniform or centralised Union mechanisms that speed up the reporting process and support a quick and smooth exchange of information between competent authorities, which is crucial for addressing ICT risk in the event of large-scale attacks with potentially systemic consequences.

(23) To reduce the administrative burden and potentially duplicative reporting obligations for certain financial entities, the requirement for the incident reporting pursuant to Directive (EU) 2015/2366 of the European Parliament and of the Council([12]) should cease to apply to payment service providers that fall within the scope of this Regulation. Consequently, credit institutions, e-money institutions, payment institutions and account information service providers, as referred to in Article 33(1) of that Directive, should, from the date of application of this Regulation, report pursuant to this Regulation, all operational or security payment-related incidents which have been previously reported pursuant to that Directive, irrespective of whether such incidents are ICT-related.

(24) To enable competent authorities to fulfil supervisory roles by acquiring a complete overview of the nature, frequency, significance and impact of ICT-related incidents and to enhance the exchange of information between relevant public authorities, including law enforcement authorities and resolution authorities, this Regulation should lay down a robust ICT-related incident reporting regime whereby the relevant requirements address

11 Regulation (EU) 2019/881 of the European Parliament and of the Council of 17 April 2019 on ENISA (the European Union Agency for Cybersecurity) and on information and communications technology cybersecurity certification and repealing Regulation (EU) No 526/2013 (Cybersecurity Act) (OJ L 151, 7.6.2019, p. 15).

12 Directive (EU) 2015/2366 of the European Parliament and of the Council of 25 November 2015 on payment services in the internal market, amending Directives 2002/65/EC, 2009/110/EC and 2013/36/EU and Regulation (EU) No 1093/2010, and repealing Directive 2007/64/EC (OJ L 337, 23.12.2015, p. 35).

current gaps in financial services law, and remove existing overlaps and duplications to alleviate costs. It is essential to harmonise the ICT-related incident reporting regime by requiring all financial entities to report to their competent authorities through a single streamlined framework as set out in this Regulation. In addition, the ESAs should be empowered to further specify relevant elements for the ICT-related incident reporting framework, such as taxonomy, timeframes, data sets, templates and applicable thresholds. To ensure full consistency with Directive (EU) 2022/2555, financial entities should be allowed, on a voluntary basis, to notify significant cyber threats to the relevant competent authority, when they consider that the cyber threat is of relevance to the financial system, service users or clients.

(25) Digital operational resilience testing requirements have been developed in certain financial subsectors setting out frameworks that are not always fully aligned. This leads to a potential duplication of costs for cross-border financial entities and makes the mutual recognition of the results of digital operational resilience testing complex which, in turn, can fragment the internal market.

(26) In addition, where no ICT testing is required, vulnerabilities remain undetected and result in exposing a financial entity to ICT risk and ultimately create a higher risk to the stability and integrity of the financial sector. Without Union intervention, digital operational resilience testing would continue to be inconsistent and would lack a system of mutual recognition of ICT testing results across different jurisdictions. In addition, as it is unlikely that other financial subsectors would adopt testing schemes on a meaningful scale, they would miss out on the potential benefits of a testing framework, in terms of revealing ICT vulnerabilities and risks, and testing defence capabilities and business continuity, which contributes to increasing the trust of customers, suppliers and business partners. To remedy those overlaps, divergences and gaps, it is necessary to lay down rules for a coordinated testing regime and thereby facilitate the mutual recognition of advanced testing for financial entities meeting the criteria set out in this Regulation.

(27) Financial entities' reliance on the use of ICT services is partly driven by their need to adapt to an emerging competitive digital global economy, to boost their business efficiency and to meet consumer demand. The nature and extent of such reliance has been continuously evolving in recent years, driving cost reduction in financial intermediation, enabling business expansion and scalability in the deployment of financial activities while offering a wide range of ICT tools to manage complex internal processes.

(28) The extensive use of ICT services is evidenced by complex contractual arrangements, whereby financial entities often encounter difficulties in negotiating contractual terms that are tailored to the prudential standards or other regulatory requirements to which they are subject, or otherwise in enforcing specific rights, such as access or audit rights, even when the latter are enshrined in their contractual arrangements. Moreover, many of

those contractual arrangements do not provide for sufficient safeguards allowing for the fully-fledged monitoring of subcontracting processes, thus depriving the financial entity of its ability to assess the associated risks. In addition, as ICT third-party service providers often provide standardised services to different types of clients, such contractual arrangements do not always cater adequately for the individual or specific needs of financial industry actors.

(29) Even though Union financial services law contains certain general rules on outsourcing, monitoring of the contractual dimension is not fully anchored into Union law. In the absence of clear and bespoke Union standards applying to the contractual arrangements concluded with ICT third-party service providers, the external source of ICT risk is not comprehensively addressed. Consequently, it is necessary to set out certain key principles to guide financial entities' management of ICT third-party risk, which are of particular importance when financial entities resort to ICT third-party service providers to support their critical or important functions. Those principles should be accompanied by a set of core contractual rights in relation to several elements in the performance and termination of contractual arrangements with a view to providing certain minimum safeguards in order to strengthen financial entities' ability to effectively monitor all ICT risk emerging at the level of third-party service providers. Those principles are complementary to the sectoral law applicable to outsourcing.

(30) A certain lack of homogeneity and convergence regarding the monitoring of ICT third-party risk and ICT third-party dependencies is evident today. Despite efforts to address outsourcing, such as EBA Guidelines on outsourcing of 2019 and ESMA Guidelines on outsourcing to cloud service providers of 2021 the broader issue of counteracting systemic risk which may be triggered by the financial sector's exposure to a limited number of critical ICT third-party service providers is not sufficiently addressed by Union law. The lack of rules at Union level is compounded by the absence of national rules on mandates and tools that allow financial supervisors to acquire a good understanding of ICT third-party dependencies and to monitor adequately risks arising from the concentration of ICT third-party dependencies.

(31) Taking into account the potential systemic risk entailed by increased outsourcing practices and by the ICT third-party concentration, and mindful of the insufficiency of national mechanisms in providing financial supervisors with adequate tools to quantify, qualify and redress the consequences of ICT risk occurring at critical ICT third-party service providers, it is necessary to establish an appropriate Oversight Framework allowing for a continuous monitoring of the activities of ICT third-party service providers that are critical ICT third-party service providers to financial entities, while ensuring that the confidentiality and security of customers other than financial entities is preserved. While intra-group provision of ICT services entails specific risks and benefits, it should not be automatically considered less risky than the provision of ICT services by providers outside of a financial group and should therefore be subject to

the same regulatory framework. However, when ICT services are provided from within the same financial group, financial entities might have a higher level of control over intra-group providers, which ought to be taken into account in the overall risk assessment.

(32) With ICT risk becoming more and more complex and sophisticated, good measures for the detection and prevention of ICT risk depend to a great extent on the regular sharing between financial entities of threat and vulnerability intelligence. Information sharing contributes to creating increased awareness of cyber threats. In turn, this enhances the capacity of financial entities to prevent cyber threats from becoming real ICT-related incidents and enables financial entities to more effectively contain the impact of ICT-related incidents and to recover faster. In the absence of guidance at Union level, several factors seem to have inhibited such intelligence sharing, in particular uncertainty about its compatibility with data protection, anti-trust and liability rules.

(33) In addition, doubts about the type of information that can be shared with other market participants, or with non-supervisory authorities (such as ENISA, for analytical input, or Europol, for law enforcement purposes) lead to useful information being withheld. Therefore, the extent and quality of information sharing currently remains limited and fragmented, with relevant exchanges mostly being local (by way of national initiatives) and with no consistent Union-wide information-sharing arrangements tailored to the needs of an integrated financial system. It is therefore important to strengthen those communication channels.

(34) Financial entities should be encouraged to exchange among themselves cyber threat information and intelligence, and to collectively leverage their individual knowledge and practical experience at strategic, tactical and operational levels with a view to enhancing their capabilities to adequately assess, monitor, defend against, and respond to cyber threats, by participating in information sharing arrangements. It is therefore necessary to enable the emergence at Union level of mechanisms for voluntary information-sharing arrangements which, when conducted in trusted environments, would help the community of the financial industry to prevent and collectively respond to cyber threats by quickly limiting the spread of ICT risk and impeding potential contagion throughout the financial channels. Those mechanisms should comply with the applicable competition law rules of the Union set out in the Communication from the Commission of 14 January 2011 entitled 'Guidelines on the applicability of Article 101 of the Treaty on the Functioning of the European Union to horizontal cooperation agreements', as well as with Union data protection rules, in particular Regulation (EU) 2016/679 of the European Parliament and of the Council([13]). They should operate based on the use of one or more

13 Regulation (EU) 2016/679 of the European Parliament and of the Council of 27 April 2016 on the protection of natural persons with regard to the processing of personal data and on the free movement of such data, and repealing Directive 95/46/EC (General Data Protection Regulation) (OJ L 119, 4.5.2016, p. 1).

of the legal bases that are laid down in Article 6 of that Regulation, such as in the context of the processing of personal data that is necessary for the purposes of the legitimate interest pursued by the controller or by a third party, as referred to in Article 6(1), point (f), of that Regulation, as well as in the context of the processing of personal data necessary for compliance with a legal obligation to which the controller is subject, necessary for the performance of a task carried out in the public interest or in the exercise of official authority vested in the controller, as referred to in Article 6(1), points (c) and (e), respectively, of that Regulation.

(35) In order to maintain a high level of digital operational resilience for the whole financial sector, and at the same time to keep pace with technological developments, this Regulation should address risk stemming from all types of ICT services. To that end, the definition of ICT services in the context of this Regulation should be understood in a broad manner, encompassing digital and data services provided through ICT systems to one or more internal or external users on an ongoing basis. That definition should, for instance, include so called 'over the top' services, which fall within the category of electronic communications services. It should exclude only the limited category of traditional analogue telephone services qualifying as Public Switched Telephone Network (PSTN) services, landline services, Plain Old Telephone Service (POTS), or fixed-line telephone services.

(36) Notwithstanding the broad coverage envisaged by this Regulation, the application of the digital operational resilience rules should take into account the significant differences between financial entities in terms of their size and overall risk profile. As a general principle, when distributing resources and capabilities for the implementation of the ICT risk management framework, financial entities should duly balance their ICT-related needs to their size and overall risk profile, and the nature, scale and complexity of their services, activities and operations, while competent authorities should continue to assess and review the approach of such distribution.

(37) Account information service providers, referred to in Article 33(1) of Directive (EU) 2015/2366, are explicitly included in the scope of this Regulation, taking into account the specific nature of their activities and the risks arising therefrom. In addition, electronic money institutions and payment institutions exempted pursuant to Article 9(1) of Directive 2009/110/EC of the European Parliament and of the Council([14]) and Article 32(1) of Directive (EU) 2015/2366 are included in the scope of this Regulation even if they have not been granted authorisation in accordance Directive 2009/110/EC to issue electronic money, or if they have not been granted authorisation in accordance with Directive (EU) 2015/2366 to provide and execute payment services. However, post office

14 Directive 2009/110/EC of the European Parliament and of the Council of 16 September 2009 on the taking up, pursuit and prudential supervision of the business of electronic money institutions amending Directives 2005/60/EC and 2006/48/EC and repealing Directive 2000/46/EC (OJ L 267, 10.10.2009, p. 7).

giro institutions, referred to in Article 2(5), point (3), of Directive 2013/36/EU of the European Parliament and of the Council([15]), are excluded from the scope of this Regulation. The competent authority for payment institutions exempted pursuant to Directive (EU) 2015/2366, electronic money institutions exempted pursuant to Directive 2009/110/EC and account information service providers as referred to in Article 33(1) of Directive (EU) 2015/2366, should be the competent authority designated in accordance with Article 22 of Directive (EU) 2015/2366.

(38) As larger financial entities might enjoy wider resources and can swiftly deploy funds to develop governance structures and set up various corporate strategies, only financial entities that are not microenterprises in the sense of this Regulation should be required to establish more complex governance arrangements. Such entities are better equipped in particular to set up dedicated management functions for supervising arrangements with ICT third-party service providers or for dealing with crisis management, to organise their ICT risk management according to the three lines of defence model, or to set up an internal risk management and control model, and to submit their ICT risk management framework to internal audits.

(39) Some financial entities benefit from exemptions or are subject to a very light regulatory framework under the relevant sector-specific Union law. Such financial entities include managers of alternative investment funds referred to in Article 3(2) of Directive 2011/61/EU of the European Parliament and of the Council([16]), insurance and reinsurance undertakings referred to in Article 4 of Directive 2009/138/EC of the European Parliament and of the Council([17]), and institutions for occupational retirement provision which operate pension schemes which together do not have more than 15 members in total. In light of those exemptions it would not be proportionate to include such financial entities in the scope of this Regulation. In addition, this Regulation acknowledges the specificities of the insurance intermediation market structure, with the result that insurance intermediaries, reinsurance intermediaries and ancillary insurance intermediaries qualifying as microenterprises or as small or medium-sized enterprises should not be subject to this Regulation.

(40) Since the entities referred to in Article 2(5), points (4) to (23), of Directive 2013/36/EU are excluded from the scope of that Directive, Member States should consequently be able to choose to exempt from the application of this Regulation such entities located within their respective territories.

15 Directive 2013/36/EU of the European Parliament and of the Council of 26 June 2013 on access to the activity of credit institutions and the prudential supervision of credit institutions, amending Directive 2002/87/EC and repealing Directives 2006/48/EC and 2006/49/EC (OJ L 176, 27.6.2013, p. 338).

16 Directive 2011/61/EU of the European Parliament and of the Council of 8 June 2011 on Alternative Investment Fund Managers and amending Directives 2003/41/EC and 2009/65/EC and Regulations (EC) No 1060/2009 and (EU) No 1095/2010 (OJ L 174, 1.7.2011, p. 1).

17 Directive 2009/138/EC of the European Parliament and of the Council of 25 November 2009 on the taking-up and pursuit of the business of Insurance and Reinsurance (Solvency II) (OJ L 335, 17.12.2009, p. 1).

(41) Similarly, in order to align this Regulation to the scope of Directive 2014/65/EU of the European Parliament and of the Council([18]), it is also appropriate to exclude from the scope of this Regulation natural and legal persons referred in Articles 2 and 3 of that Directive which are allowed to provide investment services without having to obtain an authorisation under Directive 2014/65/EU. However, Article 2 of Directive 2014/65/EU also excludes from the scope of that Directive entities which qualify as financial entities for the purposes of this Regulation such as, central securities depositories, collective investment undertakings or insurance and reinsurance undertakings. The exclusion from the scope of this Regulation of the persons and entities referred to in Articles 2 and 3 of that Directive should not encompass those central securities depositories, collective investment undertakings or insurance and reinsurance undertakings.

(42) Under sector-specific Union law, some financial entities are subject to lighter requirements or exemptions for reasons associated with their size or the services they provide. That category of financial entities includes small and non-interconnected investment firms, small institutions for occupational retirement provision which may be excluded from the scope of Directive (EU) 2016/2341 under the conditions laid down in Article 5 of that Directive by the Member State concerned and operate pension schemes which together do not have more than 100 members in total, as well as institutions exempted pursuant to Directive 2013/36/EU. Therefore, in accordance with the principle of proportionality and to preserve the spirit of sector-specific Union law, it is also appropriate to subject those financial entities to a simplified ICT risk management framework under this Regulation. The proportionate character of the ICT risk management framework covering those financial entities should not be altered by the regulatory technical standards that are to be developed by the ESAs. Moreover, in accordance with the principle of proportionality, it is appropriate to also subject payment institutions referred to in Article 32(1) of Directive (EU) 2015/2366 and electronic money institutions referred to in Article 9 of Directive 2009/110/EC exempted in accordance with national law transposing those Union legal acts to a simplified ICT risk management framework under this Regulation, while payment institutions and electronic money institutions which have not been exempted in accordance with their respective national law transposing sectoral Union law should comply with the general framework laid down by this Regulation.

(43) Similarly, financial entities which qualify as microenterprises or are subject to the simplified ICT risk management framework under this Regulation should not be required to establish a role to monitor their arrangements concluded with ICT third-party service providers on the use of ICT services; or to designate a member of senior management to be responsible

18 Directive 2014/65/EU of the European Parliament and of the Council of 15 May 2014 on markets in financial instruments and amending Directive 2002/92/EC and Directive 2011/61/EU (OJ L 173, 12.6.2014, p. 349).

for overseeing the related risk exposure and relevant documentation; to assign the responsibility for managing and overseeing ICT risk to a control function and ensure an appropriate level of independence of such control function in order to avoid conflicts of interest; to document and review at least once a year the ICT risk management framework; to subject to internal audit on a regular basis the ICT risk management framework; to perform in-depth assessments after major changes in their network and information system infrastructures and processes; to regularly conduct risk analyses on legacy ICT systems; to subject the implementation of the ICT Response and Recovery plans to independent internal audit reviews; to have a crisis management function, to expand the testing of business continuity and response and recovery plans to capture switchover scenarios between primary ICT infrastructure and redundant facilities; to report to competent authorities, upon their request, an estimation of aggregated annual costs and losses caused by major ICT-related incidents, to maintain redundant ICT capacities; to communicate to national competent authorities implemented changes following post ICT-related incident reviews; to monitor on a continuous basis relevant technological developments, to establish a comprehensive digital operational resilience testing programme as an integral part of the ICT risk management framework provided for in this Regulation, or to adopt and regularly review a strategy on ICT third-party risk. In addition, microenterprises should only be required to assess the need to maintain such redundant ICT capacities based on their risk profile. Microenterprises should benefit from a more flexible regime as regards digital operational resilience testing programmes. When considering the type and frequency of testing to be performed, they should properly balance the objective of maintaining a high digital operational resilience, the available resources and their overall risk profile. Microenterprises and financial entities subject to the simplified ICT risk management framework under this Regulation should be exempted from the requirement to perform advanced testing of ICT tools, systems and processes based on threat-led penetration testing (TLPT), as only financial entities meeting the criteria set out in this Regulation should be required to carry out such testing. In light of their limited capabilities, microenterprises should be able to agree with the ICT third-party service provider to delegate the financial entity's rights of access, inspection and audit to an independent third-party, to be appointed by the ICT third-party service provider, provided that the financial entity is able to request, at any time, all relevant information and assurance on the ICT third-party service provider's performance from the respective independent third-party.

(44) As only those financial entities identified for the purposes of the advanced digital resilience testing should be required to conduct threat-led penetration tests, the administrative processes and financial costs entailed in the performance of such tests should be borne by a small percentage of financial entities.

(45) To ensure full alignment and overall consistency between financial entities' business strategies, on the one hand, and the conduct of ICT

risk management, on the other hand, the financial entities' management bodies should be required to maintain a pivotal and active role in steering and adapting the ICT risk management framework and the overall digital operational resilience strategy. The approach to be taken by management bodies should not only focus on the means of ensuring the resilience of the ICT systems, but should also cover people and processes through a set of policies which cultivate, at each corporate layer, and for all staff, a strong sense of awareness about cyber risks and a commitment to observe a strict cyber hygiene at all levels. The ultimate responsibility of the management body in managing a financial entity's ICT risk should be an overarching principle of that comprehensive approach, further translated into the continuous engagement of the management body in the control of the monitoring of the ICT risk management.

(46) Moreover, the principle of the management body's full and ultimate responsibility for the management of the ICT risk of the financial entity goes hand in hand with the need to secure a level of ICT-related investments and an overall budget for the financial entity that would enable the financial entity to achieve a high level of digital operational resilience.

(47) Inspired by relevant international, national and industry best practices, guidelines, recommendations and approaches to the management of cyber risk, this Regulation promotes a set of principles that facilitate the overall structure of ICT risk management. Consequently, as long as the main capabilities which financial entities put in place address the various functions in the ICT risk management (identification, protection and prevention, detection, response and recovery, learning and evolving and communication) set out in this Regulation, financial entities should remain free to use ICT risk management models that are differently framed or categorised.

(48) To keep pace with an evolving cyber threat landscape, financial entities should maintain updated ICT systems that are reliable and capable, not only for guaranteeing the processing of data required for their services, but also for ensuring sufficient technological resilience to allow them to deal adequately with additional processing needs due to stressed market conditions or other adverse situations.

(49) Efficient business continuity and recovery plans are necessary to allow financial entities to promptly and quickly resolve ICT-related incidents, in particular cyber-attacks, by limiting damage and giving priority to the resumption of activities and recovery actions in accordance with their back-up policies. However, such resumption should in no way jeopardise the integrity and security of the network and information systems or the availability, authenticity, integrity or confidentiality of data.

(50) While this Regulation allows financial entities to determine their recovery time and recovery point objectives in a flexible manner and hence to set such objectives by fully taking into account the nature and the criticality of the relevant functions and any specific business needs, it should nevertheless

require them to carry out an assessment of the potential overall impact on market efficiency when determining such objectives.

(51) The propagators of cyber-attacks tend to pursue financial gains directly at the source, thus exposing financial entities to significant consequences. To prevent ICT systems from losing integrity or becoming unavailable, and hence to avoid data breaches and damage to physical ICT infrastructure, the reporting of major ICT-related incidents by financial entities should be significantly improved and streamlined. ICT-related incident reporting should be harmonised through the introduction of a requirement for all financial entities to report directly to their relevant competent authorities. Where a financial entity is subject to supervision by more than one national competent authority, Member States should designate a single competent authority as the addressee of such reporting. Credit institutions classified as significant in accordance with Article 6(4) of Council Regulation (EU) No 1024/2013([19]) should submit such reporting to the national competent authorities, which should subsequently transmit the report to the European Central Bank (ECB).

(52) The direct reporting should enable financial supervisors to have immediate access to information about major ICT-related incidents. Financial supervisors should in turn pass on details of major ICT-related incidents to public non-financial authorities (such as competent authorities and single points of contact under Directive (EU) 2022/2555, national data protection authorities, and to law enforcement authorities for major ICT-related incidents of a criminal nature) in order to enhance such authorities awareness of such incidents and, in the case of CSIRTs, to facilitate prompt assistance that may be given to financial entities, as appropriate. Member States should, in addition, be able to determine that financial entities themselves should provide such information to public authorities outside the financial services area. Those information flows should allow financial entities to swiftly benefit from any relevant technical input, advice about remedies, and subsequent follow-up from such authorities. The information on major ICT-related incidents should be mutually channelled: financial supervisors should provide all necessary feedback or guidance to the financial entity, while the ESAs should share anonymised data on cyber threats and vulnerabilities relating to an incident, to aid wider collective defence.

(53) While all financial entities should be required to carry out incident reporting, that requirement is not expected to affect all of them in the same manner. Indeed, relevant materiality thresholds, as well as reporting timelines, should be duly adjusted, in the context of delegated acts based on the regulatory technical standards to be developed by the ESAs, with a view to covering only major ICT-related incidents. In addition, the

19 Council Regulation (EU) No 1024/2013 of 15 October 2013 conferring specific tasks on the European Central Bank concerning policies relating to the prudential supervision of credit institutions (OJ L 287, 29.10.2013, p. 63).

specificities of financial entities should be taken into account when setting timelines for reporting obligations.

(54) This Regulation should require credit institutions, payment institutions, account information service providers and electronic money institutions to report all operational or security payment-related incidents – previously reported under Directive (EU) 2015/2366 – irrespective of the ICT nature of the incident.

(55) The ESAs should be tasked with assessing the feasibility and conditions for a possible centralisation of ICT-related incident reports at Union level. Such centralisation could consist of a single EU Hub for major ICT-related incident reporting either directly receiving relevant reports and automatically notifying national competent authorities, or merely centralising relevant reports forwarded by the national competent authorities and thus fulfilling a coordination role. The ESAs should be tasked with preparing, in consultation with the ECB and ENISA, a joint report exploring the feasibility of setting up a single EU Hub.

(56) In order to achieve a high level of digital operational resilience, and in line with both the relevant international standards (e.g. the G7 Fundamental Elements for Threat-Led Penetration Testing) and with the frameworks applied in the Union, such as the TIBER-EU, financial entities should regularly test their ICT systems and staff having ICT-related responsibilities with regard to the effectiveness of their preventive, detection, response and recovery capabilities, to uncover and address potential ICT vulnerabilities. To reflect differences that exist across, and within, the various financial subsectors as regards financial entities' level of cybersecurity preparedness, testing should include a wide variety of tools and actions, ranging from the assessment of basic requirements (e.g. vulnerability assessments and scans, open source analyses, network security assessments, gap analyses, physical security reviews, questionnaires and scanning software solutions, source code reviews where feasible, scenario-based tests, compatibility testing, performance testing or end-to-end testing) to more advanced testing by means of TLPT. Such advanced testing should be required only of financial entities that are mature enough from an ICT perspective to reasonably carry it out. The digital operational resilience testing required by this Regulation should thus be more demanding for those financial entities meeting the criteria set out in this Regulation (for example, large, systemic and ICT-mature credit institutions, stock exchanges, central securities depositories and central counterparties) than for other financial entities. At the same time, the digital operational resilience testing by means of TLPT should be more relevant for financial entities operating in core financial services subsectors and playing a systemic role (for example, payments, banking, and clearing and settlement), and less relevant for other subsectors (for example, asset managers and credit rating agencies).

(57) Financial entities involved in cross-border activities and exercising the freedoms of establishment, or of provision of services within the Union, should comply with a single set of advanced testing requirements (i.e.

TLPT) in their home Member State, which should include the ICT infrastructures in all jurisdictions where the cross-border financial group operates within the Union, thus allowing such cross-border financial groups to incur related ICT testing costs in one jurisdiction only.

(58) To draw on the expertise already acquired by certain competent authorities, in particular with regard to implementing the TIBER-EU framework, this Regulation should allow Member States to designate a single public authority as responsible in the financial sector, at national level, for all TLPT matters, or competent authorities, to delegate, in the absence of such designation, the exercise of TLPT related tasks to another national financial competent authority.

(59) Since this Regulation does not require financial entities to cover all critical or important functions in one single threat-led penetration test, financial entities should be free to determine which and how many critical or important functions should be included in the scope of such a test.

(60) Pooled testing within the meaning of this Regulation – involving the participation of several financial entities in a TLPT and for which an ICT third-party service provider can directly enter into contractual arrangements with an external tester – should be allowed only where the quality or security of services delivered by the ICT third-party service provider to customers that are entities falling outside the scope of this Regulation, or the confidentiality of the data related to such services, are reasonably expected to be adversely impacted. Pooled testing should also be subject to safeguards (direction by one designated financial entity, calibration of the number of participating financial entities) to ensure a rigorous testing exercise for the financial entities involved which meet the objectives of the TLPT pursuant to this Regulation.

(61) In order to take advantage of internal resources available at corporate level, this Regulation should allow the use of internal testers for the purposes of carrying out TLPT, provided there is supervisory approval, no conflicts of interest, and periodical alternation of the use of internal and external testers (every three tests), while also requiring the provider of the threat intelligence in the TLPT to always be external to the financial entity. The responsibility for conducting TLPT should remain fully with the financial entity. Attestations provided by authorities should be solely for the purpose of mutual recognition and should not preclude any follow-up action needed to address the ICT risk to which the financial entity is exposed, nor should they be seen as a supervisory endorsement of a financial entity's ICT risk management and mitigation capabilities.

(62) To ensure a sound monitoring of ICT third-party risk in the financial sector, it is necessary to lay down a set of principle-based rules to guide financial entities' when monitoring risk arising in the context of functions outsourced to ICT third-party service providers, particularly for ICT services supporting critical or important functions, as well as more generally in the context of all ICT third-party dependencies.

(63) To address the complexity of the various sources of ICT risk, while taking into account the multitude and diversity of providers of technological solutions which enable a smooth provision of financial services, this Regulation should cover a wide range of ICT third-party service providers, including providers of cloud computing services, software, data analytics services and providers of data centre services. Similarly, since financial entities should effectively and coherently identify and manage all types of risk, including in the context of ICT services procured within a financial group, it should be clarified that undertakings which are part of a financial group and provide ICT services predominantly to their parent undertaking, or to subsidiaries or branches of their parent undertaking, as well as financial entities providing ICT services to other financial entities, should also be considered as ICT third-party service providers under this Regulation. Lastly, in light of the evolving payment services market becoming increasingly dependent on complex technical solutions, and in view of emerging types of payment services and payment-related solutions, participants in the payment services ecosystem, providing payment-processing activities, or operating payment infrastructures, should also be considered to be ICT third-party service providers under this Regulation, with the exception of central banks when operating payment or securities settlement systems, and public authorities when providing ICT related services in the context of fulfilling State functions.

(64) A financial entity should at all times remain fully responsible for complying with its obligations set out in this Regulation. Financial entities should apply a proportionate approach to the monitoring of risks emerging at the level of the ICT third-party service providers, by duly considering the nature, scale, complexity and importance of their ICT-related dependencies, the criticality or importance of the services, processes or functions subject to the contractual arrangements and, ultimately, on the basis of a careful assessment of any potential impact on the continuity and quality of financial services at individual and at group level, as appropriate.

(65) The conduct of such monitoring should follow a strategic approach to ICT third-party risk formalised through the adoption by the financial entity's management body of a dedicated ICT third-party risk strategy, rooted in a continuous screening of all ICT third-party dependencies. To enhance supervisory awareness of ICT third-party dependencies, and with a view to further supporting the work in the context of the Oversight Framework established by this Regulation, all financial entities should be required to maintain a register of information with all contractual arrangements about the use of ICT services provided by ICT third-party service providers. Financial supervisors should be able to request the full register, or to ask for specific sections thereof, and thus to obtain essential information for acquiring a broader understanding of the ICT dependencies of financial entities.

(66) A thorough pre-contracting analysis should underpin and precede the formal conclusion of contractual arrangements, in particular by focusing

on elements such as the criticality or importance of the services supported by the envisaged ICT contract, the necessary supervisory approvals or other conditions, the possible concentration risk entailed, as well as applying due diligence in the process of selection and assessment of ICT third-party service providers and assessing potential conflicts of interest. For contractual arrangements concerning critical or important functions, financial entities should take into consideration the use by ICT third-party service providers of the most up-to-date and highest information security standards. Termination of contractual arrangements could be prompted at least by a series of circumstances showing shortfalls at the ICT third-party service provider level, in particular significant breaches of laws or contractual terms, circumstances revealing a potential alteration of the performance of the functions provided for in the contractual arrangements, evidence of weaknesses of the ICT third-party service provider in its overall ICT risk management, or circumstances indicating the inability of the relevant competent authority to effectively supervise the financial entity.

(67) To address the systemic impact of ICT third-party concentration risk, this Regulation promotes a balanced solution by means of taking a flexible and gradual approach to such concentration risk since the imposition of any rigid caps or strict limitations might hinder the conduct of business and restrain the contractual freedom. Financial entities should thoroughly assess their envisaged contractual arrangements to identify the likelihood of such risk emerging, including by means of in-depth analyses of subcontracting arrangements, in particular when concluded with ICT third-party service providers established in a third country. At this stage, and with a view to striking a fair balance between the imperative of preserving contractual freedom and that of guaranteeing financial stability, it is not considered appropriate to set out rules on strict caps and limits to ICT third-party exposures. In the context of the Oversight Framework, a Lead Overseer, appointed pursuant to this Regulation, should, in respect to critical ICT third-party service providers, pay particular attention to fully grasp the magnitude of interdependences, discover specific instances where a high degree of concentration of critical ICT third-party service providers in the Union is likely to put a strain on the Union financial system's stability and integrity and maintain a dialogue with critical ICT third-party service providers where that specific risk is identified.

(68) To evaluate and monitor on a regular basis the ability of an ICT third party service provider to securely provide services to a financial entity without adverse effects on a financial entity's digital operational resilience, several key contractual elements with ICT third-party service providers should be harmonised. Such harmonisation should cover minimum areas which are crucial for enabling a full monitoring by the financial entity of the risks that could emerge from the ICT third-party service provider, from the perspective of a financial entity's need to secure its digital resilience because it is deeply dependent on the stability, functionality, availability and security of the ICT services received.

(69) When renegotiating contractual arrangements to seek alignment with the requirements of this Regulation, financial entities and ICT third-party service providers should ensure the coverage of the key contractual provisions as provided for in this Regulation.

(70) The definition of 'critical or important function' provided for in this Regulation encompasses the 'critical functions' as defined in Article 2(1), point (35), of Directive 2014/59/EU of the European Parliament and of the Council([20]). Accordingly, functions deemed to be critical pursuant to Directive 2014/59/EU are included in the definition of critical functions within the meaning of this Regulation.

(71) Irrespective of the criticality or importance of the function supported by the ICT services, contractual arrangements should, in particular, provide for a specification of the complete descriptions of functions and services, of the locations where such functions are provided and where data is to be processed, as well as an indication of service level descriptions. Other essential elements to enable a financial entity's monitoring of ICT third party risk are: contractual provisions specifying how the accessibility, availability, integrity, security and protection of personal data are ensured by the ICT third-party service provider, provisions laying down the relevant guarantees for enabling the access, recovery and return of data in the case of insolvency, resolution or discontinuation of the business operations of the ICT third-party service provider, as well as provisions requiring the ICT third-party service provider to provide assistance in case of ICT incidents in connection with the services provided, at no additional cost or at a cost determined ex-ante; provisions on the obligation of the ICT third-party service provider to fully cooperate with the competent authorities and resolution authorities of the financial entity; and provisions on termination rights and related minimum notice periods for the termination of the contractual arrangements, in accordance with the expectations of competent authorities and resolution authorities.

(72) In addition to such contractual provisions, and with a view to ensuring that financial entities remain in full control of all developments occurring at third-party level which may impair their ICT security, the contracts for the provision of ICT services supporting critical or important functions should also provide for the following: the specification of the full service level descriptions, with precise quantitative and qualitative performance targets, to enable without undue delay appropriate corrective actions when the agreed service levels are not met; the relevant notice periods and reporting obligations of the ICT third-party service provider in the event of developments with a potential material impact on the ICT third-

20 Directive 2014/59/EU of the European Parliament and of the Council of 15 May 2014 establishing a framework for the recovery and resolution of credit institutions and investment firms and amending Council Directive 82/891/EEC, and Directives 2001/24/EC, 2002/47/EC, 2004/25/EC, 2005/56/EC, 2007/36/EC, 2011/35/EU, 2012/30/EU and 2013/36/EU, and Regulations (EU) No 1093/2010 and (EU) No 648/2012, of the European Parliament and of the Council (OJ L 173, 12.6.2014, p. 190).

party service provider's ability to effectively provide their respective ICT services; a requirement upon the ICT third-party service provider to implement and test business contingency plans and have ICT security measures, tools and policies allowing for the secure provision of services, and to participate and fully cooperate in the TLPT carried out by the financial entity.

(73) Contracts for the provision of ICT services supporting critical or important functions should also contain provisions enabling the rights of access, inspection and audit by the financial entity, or an appointed third party, and the right to take copies as crucial instruments in the financial entities' ongoing monitoring of the ICT third-party service provider's performance, coupled with the service provider's full cooperation during inspections. Similarly, the competent authority of the financial entity should have the right, based on notices, to inspect and audit the ICT third-party service provider, subject to the protection of confidential information.

(74) Such contractual arrangements should also provide for dedicated exit strategies to enable, in particular, mandatory transition periods during which ICT third-party service providers should continue providing the relevant services with a view to reducing the risk of disruptions at the level of the financial entity, or to allow the latter effectively to switch to the use of other ICT third-party service providers or, alternatively, to change to in-house solutions, consistent with the complexity of the provided ICT service. Moreover, financial entities within the scope of Directive 2014/59/EU should ensure that the relevant contracts for ICT services are robust and fully enforceable in the event of resolution of those financial entities. Therefore, in line with the expectations of the resolution authorities, those financial entities should ensure that the relevant contracts for ICT services are resolution resilient. As long as they continue meeting their payment obligations, those financial entities should ensure, among other requirements, that the relevant contracts for ICT services contain clauses for non-termination, non-suspension and non-modification on grounds of restructuring or resolution.

(75) Moreover, the voluntary use of standard contractual clauses developed by public authorities or Union institutions, in particular the use of contractual clauses developed by the Commission for cloud computing services could provide further comfort to the financial entities and ICT third-party service providers, by enhancing their level of legal certainty regarding the use of cloud computing services in the financial sector, in full alignment with the requirements and expectations set out by the Union financial services law. The development of standard contractual clauses builds on measures already envisaged in the 2018 Fintech Action Plan that announced the Commission's intention to encourage and facilitate the development of standard contractual clauses for the use of cloud computing services outsourcing by financial entities, drawing on cross-sectorial cloud computing services stakeholders' efforts, which the Commission has facilitated with the help of the financial sector's involvement.

(76) With a view to promoting convergence and efficiency in relation to supervisory approaches when addressing ICT third-party risk in the financial sector, as well as to strengthening the digital operational resilience of financial entities which rely on critical ICT third-party service providers for the provision of ICT services that support the supply of financial services, and thereby to contributing to the preservation of the Union's financial system stability and the integrity of the internal market for financial services, critical ICT third-party service providers should be subject to a Union Oversight Framework. While the set-up of the Oversight Framework is justified by the added value of taking action at Union level and by virtue of the inherent role and specificities of the use of ICT services in the provision of financial services, it should be recalled, at the same time, that this solution appears suitable only in the context of this Regulation specifically dealing with digital operational resilience in the financial sector. However, such Oversight Framework should not be regarded as a new model for Union supervision in other areas of financial services and activities.

(77) The Oversight Framework should apply only to critical ICT third-party service providers. There should therefore be a designation mechanism to take into account the dimension and nature of the financial sector's reliance on such ICT third-party service providers. That mechanism should involve a set of quantitative and qualitative criteria to set the criticality parameters as a basis for inclusion in the Oversight Framework. In order to ensure the accuracy of that assessment, and regardless of the corporate structure of the ICT third-party service provider, such criteria should, in the case of a ICT third-party service provider that is part of a wider group, take into consideration the entire ICT third-party service provider's group structure. On the one hand, critical ICT third-party service providers, which are not automatically designated by virtue of the application of those criteria, should have the possibility to opt in to the Oversight Framework on a voluntary basis, on the other hand, ICT third-party service providers, that are already subject to oversight mechanism frameworks supporting the fulfilment of the tasks of the European System of Central Banks as referred to in Article 127(2) TFEU, should be exempted.

(78) Similarly, financial entities providing ICT services to other financial entities, while belonging to the category of ICT third-party service providers under this Regulation, should also be exempted from the Oversight Framework since they are already subject to supervisory mechanisms established by the relevant Union financial services law. Where applicable, competent authorities should take into account, in the context of their supervisory activities, the ICT risk posed to financial entities by financial entities providing ICT services. Likewise, due to the existing risk monitoring mechanisms at group level, the same exemption should be introduced for ICT third-party service providers delivering services predominantly to the entities of their own group. ICT third-party service providers providing ICT services solely in one Member State to financial entities that are active only in that Member State should also be exempted from the designation

mechanism because of their limited activities and lack of cross-border impact.

(79) The digital transformation experienced in financial services has brought about an unprecedented level of use of, and reliance upon, ICT services. Since it has become inconceivable to provide financial services without the use of cloud computing services, software solutions and data-related services, the Union financial ecosystem has become intrinsically co-dependent on certain ICT services provided by ICT service suppliers. Some of those suppliers, innovators in developing and applying ICT-based technologies, play a significant role in the delivery of financial services, or have become integrated into the financial services value chain. They have thus become critical to the stability and integrity of the Union financial system. This widespread reliance on services supplied by critical ICT third-party service providers, combined with the interdependence of the information systems of various market operators, create a direct, and potentially severe, risk to the Union financial services system and to the continuity of delivery of financial services if critical ICT third-party service providers were to be affected by operational disruptions or major cyber incidents. Cyber incidents have a distinctive ability to multiply and propagate throughout the financial system at a considerably faster pace than other types of risk monitored in the financial sector and can extend across sectors and beyond geographical borders. They have the potential to evolve into a systemic crisis, where trust in the financial system has been eroded due to the disruption of functions supporting the real economy, or to substantial financial losses, reaching a level which the financial system is unable to withstand, or which requires the deployment of heavy shock absorption measures. To prevent these scenarios from taking place and thereby endangering the financial stability and integrity of the Union, it is essential to provide the convergence of supervisory practices relating to ICT third-party risk in finance, in particular through new rules enabling the Union oversight of critical ICT third-party service providers.

(80) The Oversight Framework largely depends on the degree of collaboration between the Lead Overseer and the critical ICT third-party service provider delivering to financial entities services affecting the supply of financial services. Successful oversight is predicated, inter alia, upon the ability of the Lead Overseer to effectively conduct monitoring missions and inspections to assess the rules, controls and processes used by the critical ICT third-party service providers, as well as to assess the potential cumulative impact of their activities on financial stability and the integrity of the financial system. At the same time, it is crucial that critical ICT third-party service providers follow the Lead Overseer's recommendations and address its concerns. Since a lack of cooperation by a critical ICT third-party service provider providing services that affect the supply of financial services, such as the refusal to grant access to its premises or to submit information, would ultimately deprive the Lead Overseer of its essential tools in appraising ICT third-party risk, and could adversely impact the

financial stability and the integrity of the financial system, it is necessary to also provide for a commensurate sanctioning regime.

(81) Against this background, the need of the Lead Overseer to impose penalty payments to compel critical ICT third-party service providers to comply with the transparency and access-related obligations set out in this Regulation should not be jeopardised by difficulties raised by the enforcement of those penalty payments in relation to critical ICT third-party service providers established in third countries. In order to ensure the enforceability of such penalties, and to allow a swift roll out of procedures upholding the critical ICT third-party service providers' rights of defence in the context of the designation mechanism and the issuance of recommendations, those critical ICT third-party service providers, providing services to financial entities that affect the supply of financial services, should be required to maintain an adequate business presence in the Union. Due to the nature of the oversight, and the absence of comparable arrangements in other jurisdictions, there are no suitable alternative mechanisms ensuring this objective by way of effective cooperation with financial supervisors in third countries in relation to the monitoring of the impact of digital operational risks posed by systemic ICT third-party service providers, qualifying as critical ICT third-party service providers established in third countries. Therefore, in order to continue its provision of ICT services to financial entities in the Union, an ICT third-party service provider established in a third country which has been designated as critical in accordance with this Regulation should undertake, within 12 months of such designation, all necessary arrangements to ensure its incorporation within the Union, by means of establishing a subsidiary, as defined throughout the Union acquis, namely in Directive 2013/34/EU of the European Parliament and of the Council([21]).

(82) The requirement to set up a subsidiary in the Union should not prevent the critical ICT third-party service provider from supplying ICT services and related technical support from facilities and infrastructure located outside the Union. This Regulation does not impose a data localisation obligation as it does not require data storage or processing to be undertaken in the Union.

(83) Critical ICT third-party service providers should be able to provide ICT services from anywhere in the world, not necessarily or not only from premises located in the Union. Oversight activities should be first conducted on premises located in the Union and by interacting with entities located in the Union, including the subsidiaries established by critical ICT third-party service providers pursuant to this Regulation. However, such actions within the Union might be insufficient to allow the Lead Overseer

21 Directive 2013/34/EU of the European Parliament and of the Council of 26 June 2013 on the annual financial statements, consolidated financial statements and related reports of certain types of undertakings, amending Directive 2006/43/EC of the European Parliament and of the Council and repealing Council Directives 78/660/EEC and 83/349/EEC (OJ L 182, 29.6.2013, p. 19).

to fully and effectively perform its duties under this Regulation. The Lead Overseer should therefore also be able to exercise its relevant oversight powers in third countries. Exercising those powers in third countries should allow the Lead Overseer to examine the facilities from which the ICT services or the technical support services are actually provided or managed by the critical ICT third-party service provider, and should give the Lead Overseer a comprehensive and operational understanding of the ICT risk management of the critical ICT third-party service provider. The possibility for the Lead Overseer, as a Union agency, to exercise powers outside the territory of the Union should be duly framed by relevant conditions, in particular the consent of the critical ICT third-party service provider concerned. Similarly, the relevant authorities of the third country should be informed of, and not have objected to, the exercise on their own territory of the activities of the Lead Overseer. However, in order to ensure efficient implementation, and without prejudice to the respective competences of the Union institutions and the Member States, such powers also need to be fully anchored in the conclusion of administrative cooperation arrangements with the relevant authorities of the third country concerned. This Regulation should therefore enable the ESAs to conclude administrative cooperation arrangements with the relevant authorities of third countries, which should not otherwise create legal obligations in respect of the Union and its Member States.

(84) To facilitate communication with the Lead Overseer and to ensure adequate representation, critical ICT third-party service providers which are part of a group should designate one legal person as their coordination point.

(85) The Oversight Framework should be without prejudice to Member States' competence to conduct their own oversight or monitoring missions in respect to ICT third-party service providers which are not designated as critical under this Regulation, but which are regarded as important at national level.

(86) To leverage the multi-layered institutional architecture in the financial services area, the Joint Committee of the ESAs should continue to ensure overall cross-sectoral coordination in relation to all matters pertaining to ICT risk, in accordance with its tasks on cybersecurity. It should be supported by a new Subcommittee (the 'Oversight Forum') carrying out preparatory work both for the individual decisions addressed to critical ICT third-party service providers, and for the issuing of collective recommendations, in particular in relation to benchmarking the oversight programmes for critical ICT third-party service providers, and identifying best practices for addressing ICT concentration risk issues.

(87) To ensure that critical ICT third-party service providers are appropriately and effectively overseen on a Union level, this Regulation provides that any of the three ESAs could be designated as a Lead Overseer. The individual assignment of a critical ICT third-party service provider to one of the three ESAs should result from an assessment of the preponderance of financial entities operating in the financial sectors for which that ESA

has responsibilities. This approach should lead to a balanced allocation of tasks and responsibilities between the three ESAs, in the context of exercising the oversight functions, and should make the best use of the human resources and technical expertise available in each of the three ESAs.

(88) Lead Overseers should be granted the necessary powers to conduct investigations, to carry out onsite and offsite inspections at the premises and locations of critical ICT third-party service providers and to obtain complete and updated information. Those powers should enable the Lead Overseer to acquire real insight into the type, dimension and impact of the ICT third-party risk posed to financial entities and ultimately to the Union's financial system. Entrusting the ESAs with the lead oversight role is a prerequisite for understanding and addressing the systemic dimension of ICT risk in finance. The impact of critical ICT third-party service providers on the Union financial sector and the potential issues caused by the ICT concentration risk entailed call for taking a collective approach at Union level. The simultaneous carrying out of multiple audits and access rights, performed separately by numerous competent authorities, with little or no coordination among them, would prevent financial supervisors from obtaining a complete and comprehensive overview of ICT third-party risk in the Union, while also creating redundancy, burden and complexity for critical ICT third-party service providers if they were subject to numerous monitoring and inspection requests.

(89) Due to the significant impact of being designated as critical, this Regulation should ensure that the rights of critical ICT third-party service providers are observed throughout the implementation of the Oversight Framework. Prior to being designated as critical, such providers should, for example, have the right to submit to the Lead Overseer a reasoned statement containing any relevant information for the purposes of the assessment related to their designation. Since the Lead Overseer should be empowered to submit recommendations on ICT risk matters and suitable remedies thereto, which include the power to oppose certain contractual arrangements ultimately affecting the stability of the financial entity or the financial system, critical ICT third-party service providers should also be given the opportunity to provide, prior to the finalisation of those recommendations, explanations regarding the expected impact of the solutions, envisaged in the recommendations, on customers that are entities falling outside the scope of this Regulation and to formulate solutions to mitigate risks. Critical ICT third-party service providers disagreeing with the recommendations should submit a reasoned explanation of their intention not to endorse the recommendation. Where such reasoned explanation is not submitted or where it is considered to be insufficient, the Lead Overseer should issue a public notice summarily describing the matter of non-compliance.

(90) Competent authorities should duly include the task of verifying substantive compliance with recommendations issued by the Lead Overseer in their

functions with regard to prudential supervision of financial entities. Competent authorities should be able to require financial entities to take additional measures to address the risks identified in the Lead Overseer's recommendations, and should, in due course, issue notifications to that effect. Where the Lead Overseer addresses recommendations to critical ICT third-party service providers that are supervised under Directive (EU) 2022/2555, the competent authorities should be able, on a voluntary basis and before adopting additional measures, to consult the competent authorities under that Directive in order to foster a coordinated approach to dealing with the critical ICT third-party service providers in question.

(91) The exercise of the oversight should be guided by three operational principles seeking to ensure: (a) close coordination among the ESAs in their Lead Overseer roles, through a joint oversight network (JON), (b) consistency with the framework established by Directive (EU) 2022/2555 (through a voluntary consultation of bodies under that Directive to avoid duplication of measures directed at critical ICT third-party service providers), and (c) applying diligence to minimise the potential risk of disruption to services provided by the critical ICT third-party service providers to customers that are entities falling outside the scope of this Regulation.

(92) The Oversight Framework should not replace, or in any way or for any part substitute for, the requirement for financial entities to manage themselves the risks entailed by the use of ICT third-party service providers, including their obligation to maintain an ongoing monitoring of contractual arrangements concluded with critical ICT third-party service providers. Similarly, the Oversight Framework should not affect the full responsibility of financial entities for complying with, and discharging, all the legal obligations laid down in this Regulation and in the relevant financial services law.

(93) To avoid duplications and overlaps, competent authorities should refrain from taking individually any measures aiming to monitor the critical ICT third-party service provider's risks and should, in that respect, rely on the relevant Lead Overseer's assessment. Any measures should in any case be coordinated and agreed in advance with the Lead Overseer in the context of the exercise of tasks in the Oversight Framework.

(94) To promote convergence at international level as regards the use of best practices in the review and monitoring of ICT third-party service providers' digital risk-management, the ESAs should be encouraged to conclude cooperation arrangements with relevant supervisory and regulatory third-country authorities.

(95) To leverage the specific competences, technical skills and expertise of staff specialising in operational and ICT risk within the competent authorities, the three ESAs and, on a voluntary basis, the competent authorities under Directive (EU) 2022/2555, the Lead Overseer should draw on national supervisory capabilities and knowledge and set up dedicated examination

teams for each critical ICT third-party service provider, pooling multidisciplinary teams in support of the preparation and execution of oversight activities, including general investigations and inspections of critical ICT third-party service providers, as well as for any necessary follow-up thereto.

(96) Whereas costs resulting from oversight tasks would be fully funded from fees levied on critical ICT third-party service providers, the ESAs are. however, likely to incur, before the start of the Oversight Framework, costs for the implementation of dedicated ICT systems supporting the upcoming oversight, since dedicated ICT systems would need to be developed and deployed beforehand. This Regulation therefore provides for a hybrid funding model, whereby the Oversight Framework would, as such, be fully fee-funded, while the development of the ESAs' ICT systems would be funded from Union and national competent authorities' contributions.

(97) Competent authorities should have all required supervisory, investigative and sanctioning powers to ensure the proper exercise of their duties under this Regulation. They should, in principle, publish notices of the administrative penalties they impose. Since financial entities and ICT third-party service providers can be established in different Member States and supervised by different competent authorities, the application of this Regulation should be facilitated by, on the one hand, close cooperation among relevant competent authorities, including the ECB with regard to specific tasks conferred on it by Council Regulation (EU) No 1024/2013, and, on the other hand, by consultation with the ESAs through the mutual exchange of information and the provision of assistance in the context of relevant supervisory activities.

(98) In order to further quantify and qualify the criteria for the designation of ICT third-party service providers as critical and to harmonise oversight fees, the power to adopt acts in accordance with Article 290 TFEU should be delegated to the Commission to supplement this Regulation by further specifying the systemic impact that a failure or operational outage of an ICT third-party service provider could have on the financial entities it provides ICT services to, the number of global systemically important institutions (G-SIIs), or other systemically important institutions (O-SIIs), that rely on the ICT third-party service provider in question, the number of ICT third-party service providers active on a given market, the costs of migrating data and ICT workloads to other ICT third-party service providers, as well as the amount of the oversight fees and the way in which they are to be paid. It is of particular importance that the Commission carry out appropriate consultations during its preparatory work, including at expert level, and that those consultations be conducted in accordance with the principles laid down in the Interinstitutional Agreement of 13 April 2016 on Better Law-Making([22]). In particular,

22 OJ L 123, 12.5.2016, p. 1.

to ensure equal participation in the preparation of delegated acts, the European Parliament and the Council should receive all documents at the same time as Member States' experts, and their experts should systematically have access to meetings of Commission expert groups dealing with the preparation of delegated acts.

(99) Regulatory technical standards should ensure the consistent harmonisation of the requirements laid down in this Regulation. In their roles as bodies endowed with highly specialised expertise, the ESAs should develop draft regulatory technical standards which do not involve policy choices, for submission to the Commission. Regulatory technical standards should be developed in the areas of ICT risk management, major ICT-related incident reporting, testing, as well as in relation to key requirements for a sound monitoring of ICT third-party risk. The Commission and the ESAs should ensure that those standards and requirements can be applied by all financial entities in a manner that is proportionate to their size and overall risk profile, and the nature, scale and complexity of their services, activities and operations. The Commission should be empowered to adopt those regulatory technical standards by means of delegated acts pursuant to Article 290 TFEU and in accordance with Articles 10 to 14 of Regulations (EU) No 1093/2010, (EU) No 1094/2010 and (EU) No 1095/2010.

(100) To facilitate the comparability of reports on major ICT-related incidents and major operational or security payment-related incidents, as well as to ensure transparency regarding contractual arrangements for the use of ICT services provided by ICT third-party service providers, the ESAs should develop draft implementing technical standards establishing standardised templates, forms and procedures for financial entities to report a major ICT-related incident and a major operational or security payment-related incident, as well as standardised templates for the register of information. When developing those standards, the ESAs should take into account the size and the overall risk profile of the financial entity, and the nature, scale and complexity of its services, activities and operations. The Commission should be empowered to adopt those implementing technical standards by means of implementing acts pursuant to Article 291 TFEU and in accordance with Article 15 of Regulations (EU) No 1093/2010, (EU) No 1094/2010 and (EU) No 1095/2010.

(101) Since further requirements have already been specified through delegated and implementing acts based on technical regulatory and implementing technical standards in Regulations (EC) No 1060/2009([23]), (EU) No 648/2012([24]), (EU)

23 Regulation (EC) No 1060/2009 of the European Parliament and of the Council of 16 September 2009 on credit rating agencies (OJ L 302, 17.11.2009, p. 1).

24 Regulation (EU) No 648/2012 of the European Parliament and of the Council of 4 July 2012 on OTC derivatives, central counterparties and trade repositories (OJ L 201, 27.7.2012, p. 1).

No 600/2014([25]) and (EU) No 909/2014([26]) of the European Parliament and of the Council, it is appropriate to mandate the ESAs, either individually or jointly through the Joint Committee, to submit regulatory and implementing technical standards to the Commission for adoption of delegated and implementing acts carrying over and updating existing ICT risk management rules.

(102) Since this Regulation, together with Directive (EU) 2022/2556 of the European Parliament and of the Council([27]), entails a consolidation of the ICT risk management provisions across multiple regulations and directives of the Union's financial services acquis, including Regulations (EC) No 1060/2009, (EU) No 648/2012, (EU) No 600/2014 and (EU) No 909/2014, and Regulation (EU) 2016/1011 of the European Parliament and of the Council([28]), in order to ensure full consistency, those Regulations should be amended to clarify that the applicable ICT risk-related provisions are laid down in this Regulation.

(103) Consequently, the scope of the relevant articles related to operational risk, upon which empowerments laid down in Regulations (EC) No 1060/2009, (EU) No 648/2012, (EU) No 600/2014, (EU) No 909/2014, and (EU) 2016/1011 had mandated the adoption of delegated and implementing acts, should be narrowed down with a view to carry over into this Regulation all provisions covering the digital operational resilience aspects which today are part of those Regulations.

(104) The potential systemic cyber risk associated with the use of ICT infrastructures that enable the operation of payment systems and the provision of payment processing activities should be duly addressed at Union level through harmonised digital resilience rules. To that effect, the Commission should swiftly assess the need for reviewing the scope of this Regulation while aligning such review with the outcome of the comprehensive review envisaged under Directive (EU) 2015/2366. Numerous large-scale attacks over the past decade demonstrate how payment systems have become exposed to cyber threats. Placed at the core of the payment services chain and showing strong interconnections with the overall financial system, payment systems and payment processing activities acquired a critical significance for the functioning

25 Regulation (EU) No 600/2014 of the European Parliament and of the Council of 15 May 2014 on markets in financial instruments and amending Regulation (EU) No 648/2012 (OJ L 173, 12.6.2014, p. 84).

26 Regulation (EU) No 909/2014 of the European Parliament and of the Council of 23 July 2014 on improving securities settlement in the European Union and on central securities depositories and amending Directives 98/26/EC and 2014/65/EU and Regulation (EU) No 236/2012 (OJ L 257, 28.8.2014, p. 1).

27 Directive (EU) 2022/2556 of the European Parliament and of the Council of 14 December 2022 amending Directives 2009/65/EC, 2009/138/EC, 2011/61/EU, 2013/36/EU, 2014/59/EU, 2014/65/EU, (EU) 2015/2366 and (EU) 2016/2341 as regards digital operational resilience for the financial sector (see page 153 of this Official Journal).

28 Regulation (EU) 2016/1011 of the European Parliament and of the Council of 8 June 2016 on indices used as benchmarks in financial instruments and financial contracts or to measure the performance of investment funds and amending Directives 2008/48/EC and 2014/17/EU and Regulation (EU) No 596/2014 (OJ L 171, 29.6.2016, p. 1).

of the Union financial markets. Cyber-attacks on such systems can cause severe operational business disruptions with direct repercussions on key economic functions, such as the facilitation of payments, and indirect effects on related economic processes. Until a harmonised regime and the supervision of operators of payment systems and processing entities are put in place at Union level, Member States may, with a view to applying similar market practices, draw inspiration from the digital operational resilience requirements laid down by this Regulation, when applying rules to operators of payment systems and processing entities supervised under their own jurisdictions.

(105) Since the objective of this Regulation, namely to achieve a high level of digital operational resilience for regulated financial entities, cannot be sufficiently achieved by the Member States because it requires harmonisation of various different rules in Union and national law, but can rather, by reason of its scale and effects, be better achieved at Union level, the Union may adopt measures in accordance with the principle of subsidiarity as set out in Article 5 of the Treaty on European Union. In accordance with the principle of proportionality as set out in that Article, this Regulation does not go beyond what is necessary in order to achieve that objective.

(106) The European Data Protection Supervisor was consulted in accordance with Article 42(1) of Regulation (EU) 2018/1725 of the European Parliament and of the Council([29]) and delivered an opinion on 10 May 2021([30]),

HAVE ADOPTED THIS REGULATION:

CHAPTER I
General provisions
Article 1
Subject matter

1. In order to achieve a high common level of digital operational resilience, this Regulation lays down uniform requirements concerning the security of network and information systems supporting the business processes of financial entities as follows:

   (a) requirements applicable to financial entities in relation to:

      (i) information and communication technology (ICT) risk management;

29 Regulation (EU) 2018/1725 of the European Parliament and of the Council of 23 October 2018 on the protection of natural persons with regard to the processing of personal data by the Union institutions, bodies, offices and agencies and on the free movement of such data, and repealing Regulation (EC) No 45/2001 and Decision No 1247/2002/EC (OJ L 295, 21.11.2018, p. 39).

30 OJ C 229, 15.6.2021, p. 16.

(ii) reporting of major ICT-related incidents and notifying, on a voluntary basis, significant cyber threats to the competent authorities;

(iii) reporting of major operational or security payment-related incidents to the competent authorities by financial entities referred to in Article 2(1), points (a) to (d);

(iv) digital operational resilience testing;

(v) information and intelligence sharing in relation to cyber threats and vulnerabilities;

(vi) measures for the sound management of ICT third-party risk;

(b) requirements in relation to the contractual arrangements concluded between ICT third-party service providers and financial entities;

(c) rules for the establishment and conduct of the Oversight Framework for critical ICT third-party service providers when providing services to financial entities;

(d) rules on cooperation among competent authorities, and rules on supervision and enforcement by competent authorities in relation to all matters covered by this Regulation.

2. In relation to financial entities identified as essential or important entities pursuant to national rules transposing Article 3 of Directive (EU) 2022/2555, this Regulation shall be considered a sector-specific Union legal act for the purposes of Article 4 of that Directive.

3. This Regulation is without prejudice to the responsibility of Member States' regarding essential State functions concerning public security, defence and national security in accordance with Union law.

Article 2
Scope

1. Without prejudice to paragraphs 3 and 4, this Regulation applies to the following entities:

(a) credit institutions;

(b) payment institutions, including payment institutions exempted pursuant to Directive (EU) 2015/2366;

(c) account information service providers;

(d) electronic money institutions, including electronic money institutions exempted pursuant to Directive 2009/110/EC;

(e) investment firms;

(f) crypto-asset service providers as authorised under a Regulation of the European Parliament and of the Council on markets in crypto-assets, and amending Regulations (EU) No 1093/2010 and (EU)

No 1095/2010 and Directives 2013/36/EU and (EU) 2019/1937 ('the Regulation on markets in crypto-assets') and issuers of asset-referenced tokens;

(g) central securities depositories;

(h) central counterparties;

(i) trading venues;

(j) trade repositories;

(k) managers of alternative investment funds;

(l) management companies;

(m) data reporting service providers;

(n) insurance and reinsurance undertakings;

(o) insurance intermediaries, reinsurance intermediaries and ancillary insurance intermediaries;

(p) institutions for occupational retirement provision;

(q) credit rating agencies;

(r) administrators of critical benchmarks;

(s) crowdfunding service providers;

(t) securitisation repositories;

(u) ICT third-party service providers.

2. For the purposes of this Regulation, entities referred to in paragraph 1, points (a) to (t), shall collectively be referred to as 'financial entities'.

3. This Regulation does not apply to:

(a) managers of alternative investment funds as referred to in Article 3(2) of Directive 2011/61/EU;

(b) insurance and reinsurance undertakings as referred to in Article 4 of Directive 2009/138/EC;

(c) institutions for occupational retirement provision which operate pension schemes which together do not have more than 15 members in total;

(d) natural or legal persons exempted pursuant to Articles 2 and 3 of Directive 2014/65/EU;

(e) insurance intermediaries, reinsurance intermediaries and ancillary insurance intermediaries which are microenterprises or small or medium-sized enterprises;

(f) post office giro institutions as referred to in Article 2(5), point (3), of Directive 2013/36/EU.

4. Member States may exclude from the scope of this Regulation entities referred to in Article 2(5), points (4) to (23), of Directive 2013/36/EU that are located within their respective territories. Where a Member State makes use of such option, it shall inform the Commission thereof as well as of any subsequent changes thereto. The Commission shall make that information publicly available on its website or other easily accessible means.

Article 3
Definitions

For the purposes of this Regulation, the following definitions shall apply:

(1) 'digital operational resilience' means the ability of a financial entity to build, assure and review its operational integrity and reliability by ensuring, either directly or indirectly through the use of services provided by ICT third-party service providers, the full range of ICT-related capabilities needed to address the security of the network and information systems which a financial entity uses, and which support the continued provision of financial services and their quality, including throughout disruptions;

(2) 'network and information system' means a network and information system as defined in Article 6, point 1, of Directive (EU) 2022/2555;

(3) 'legacy ICT system' means an ICT system that has reached the end of its lifecycle (end-of-life), that is not suitable for upgrades or fixes, for technological or commercial reasons, or is no longer supported by its supplier or by an ICT third-party service provider, but that is still in use and supports the functions of the financial entity;

(4) 'security of network and information systems' means security of network and information systems as defined in Article 6, point 2, of Directive (EU) 2022/2555;

(5) 'ICT risk' means any reasonably identifiable circumstance in relation to the use of network and information systems which, if materialised, may compromise the security of the network and information systems, of any technology dependent tool or process, of operations and processes, or of the provision of services by producing adverse effects in the digital or physical environment;

(6) 'information asset' means a collection of information, either tangible or intangible, that is worth protecting;

(7) 'ICT asset' means a software or hardware asset in the network and information systems used by the financial entity;

(8) 'ICT-related incident' means a single event or a series of linked events unplanned by the financial entity that compromises the security of the network and information systems, and have an adverse impact on the availability, authenticity, integrity or confidentiality of data, or on the services provided by the financial entity;

(9) 'operational or security payment-related incident' means a single event or a series of linked events unplanned by the financial entities referred to in Article 2(1), points (a) to (d), whether ICT-related or not, that has an adverse impact on the availability, authenticity, integrity or confidentiality of payment-related data, or on the payment-related services provided by the financial entity;

(10) 'major ICT-related incident' means an ICT-related incident that has a high adverse impact on the network and information systems that support critical or important functions of the financial entity;

(11) 'major operational or security payment-related incident' means an operational or security payment-related incident that has a high adverse impact on the payment-related services provided;

(12) 'cyber threat' means 'cyber threat' as defined in Article 2, point (8), of Regulation (EU) 2019/881;

(13) 'significant cyber threat' means a cyber threat the technical characteristics of which indicate that it could have the potential to result in a major ICT-related incident or a major operational or security payment-related incident;

(14) 'cyber-attack' means a malicious ICT-related incident caused by means of an attempt perpetrated by any threat actor to destroy, expose, alter, disable, steal or gain unauthorised access to, or make unauthorised use of, an asset;

(15) 'threat intelligence' means information that has been aggregated, transformed, analysed, interpreted or enriched to provide the necessary context for decision-making and to enable relevant and sufficient understanding in order to mitigate the impact of an ICT-related incident or of a cyber threat, including the technical details of a cyber-attack, those responsible for the attack and their modus operandi and motivations;

(16) 'vulnerability' means a weakness, susceptibility or flaw of an asset, system, process or control that can be exploited;

(17) 'threat-led penetration testing (TLPT)' means a framework that mimics the tactics, techniques and procedures of real-life threat actors perceived as posing a genuine cyber threat, that delivers a controlled, bespoke, intelligence-led (red team) test of the financial entity's critical live production systems;

(18) 'ICT third-party risk' means an ICT risk that may arise for a financial entity in relation to its use of ICT services provided by ICT third-party service providers or by subcontractors of the latter, including through outsourcing arrangements;

(19) 'ICT third-party service provider' means an undertaking providing ICT services;

(20) 'ICT intra-group service provider' means an undertaking that is part of a financial group and that provides predominantly ICT services to financial

entities within the same group or to financial entities belonging to the same institutional protection scheme, including to their parent undertakings, subsidiaries, branches or other entities that are under common ownership or control;

(21) 'ICT services' means digital and data services provided through ICT systems to one or more internal or external users on an ongoing basis, including hardware as a service and hardware services which includes the provision of technical support via software or firmware updates by the hardware provider, excluding traditional analogue telephone services;

(22) 'critical or important function' means a function, the disruption of which would materially impair the financial performance of a financial entity, or the soundness or continuity of its services and activities, or the discontinued, defective or failed performance of that function would materially impair the continuing compliance of a financial entity with the conditions and obligations of its authorisation, or with its other obligations under applicable financial services law;

(23) 'critical ICT third-party service provider' means an ICT third-party service provider designated as critical in accordance with Article 31;

(24) 'ICT third-party service provider established in a third country' means an ICT third-party service provider that is a legal person established in a third-country and that has entered into a contractual arrangement with a financial entity for the provision of ICT services;

(25) 'subsidiary' means a subsidiary undertaking within the meaning of Article 2, point (10), and Article 22 of Directive 2013/34/EU;

(26) 'group' means a group as defined in Article 2, point (11), of Directive 2013/34/EU;

(27) 'parent undertaking' means a parent undertaking within the meaning of Article 2, point (9), and Article 22 of Directive 2013/34/EU;

(28) 'ICT subcontractor established in a third country' means an ICT subcontractor that is a legal person established in a third-country and that has entered into a contractual arrangement either with an ICT third-party service provider, or with an ICT third-party service provider established in a third country;

(29) 'ICT concentration risk' means an exposure to individual or multiple related critical ICT third-party service providers creating a degree of dependency on such providers so that the unavailability, failure or other type of shortfall of such provider may potentially endanger the ability of a financial entity to deliver critical or important functions, or cause it to suffer other types of adverse effects, including large losses, or endanger the financial stability of the Union as a whole;

(30) 'management body' means a management body as defined in Article 4(1), point (36), of Directive 2014/65/EU, Article 3(1), point (7), of Directive 2013/36/EU, Article 2(1), point (s), of Directive 2009/65/EC of the

European Parliament and of the Council([31]), Article 2(1), point (45), of Regulation (EU) No 909/2014, Article 3(1), point (20), of Regulation (EU) 2016/1011, and in the relevant provision of the Regulation on markets in crypto-assets, or the equivalent persons who effectively run the entity or have key functions in accordance with relevant Union or national law;

(31) 'credit institution' means a credit institution as defined in Article 4(1), point (1), of Regulation (EU) No 575/2013 of the European Parliament and of the Council([32]);

(32) 'institution exempted pursuant to Directive 2013/36/EU' means an entity as referred to in Article 2(5), points (4) to (23), of Directive 2013/36/EU;

(33) 'investment firm' means an investment firm as defined in Article 4(1), point (1), of Directive 2014/65/EU;

(34) 'small and non-interconnected investment firm' means an investment firm that meets the conditions laid out in Article 12(1) of Regulation (EU) 2019/2033 of the European Parliament and of the Council([33]);

(35) 'payment institution' means a payment institution as defined in Article 4, point (4), of Directive (EU) 2015/2366;

(36) 'payment institution exempted pursuant to Directive (EU) 2015/2366' means a payment institution exempted pursuant to Article 32(1) of Directive (EU) 2015/2366;

(37) 'account information service provider' means an account information service provider as referred to in Article 33(1) of Directive (EU) 2015/2366;

(38) 'electronic money institution' means an electronic money institution as defined in Article 2, point (1), of Directive 2009/110/EC of the European Parliament and of the Council;

(39) 'electronic money institution exempted pursuant to Directive 2009/110/EC' means an electronic money institution benefitting from a waiver as referred to in Article 9(1) of Directive 2009/110/EC;

(40) 'central counterparty' means a central counterparty as defined in Article 2, point (1), of Regulation (EU) No 648/2012;

(41) 'trade repository' means a trade repository as defined in Article 2, point (2), of Regulation (EU) No 648/2012;

31 Directive 2009/65/EC of the European Parliament and of the Council of 13 July 2009 on the coordination of laws, regulations and administrative provisions relating to undertakings for collective investment in transferable securities (UCITS) (OJ L 302, 17.11.2009, p. 32).

32 Regulation (EU) No 575/2013 of the European Parliament and of the Council of 26 June 2013 on prudential requirements for credit institutions and amending Regulation (EU) No 648/2012 (OJ L 176, 27.6.2013, p. 1).

33 Regulation (EU) 2019/2033 of the European Parliament and of the Council of 27 November 2019 on the prudential requirements of investment firms and amending Regulations (EU) No 1093/2010, (EU) No 575/2013, (EU) No 600/2014 and (EU) No 806/2014 (OJ L 314, 5.12.2019, p. 1).

(42) 'central securities depository' means a central securities depository as defined in Article 2(1), point (1), of Regulation (EU) No 909/2014;

(43) 'trading venue' means a trading venue as defined in Article 4(1), point (24), of Directive 2014/65/EU;

(44) 'manager of alternative investment funds' means a manager of alternative investment funds as defined in Article 4(1), point (b), of Directive 2011/61/EU;

(45) 'management company' means a management company as defined in Article 2(1), point (b), of Directive 2009/65/EC;

(46) 'data reporting service provider' means a data reporting service provider within the meaning of Regulation (EU) No 600/2014, as referred to in Article 2(1), points (34) to (36) thereof;

(47) 'insurance undertaking' means an insurance undertaking as defined in Article 13, point (1), of Directive 2009/138/EC;

(48) 'reinsurance undertaking' means a reinsurance undertaking as defined in Article 13, point (4), of Directive 2009/138/EC;

(49) 'insurance intermediary' means an insurance intermediary as defined in Article 2(1), point (3), of Directive (EU) 2016/97 of the European Parliament and of the Council([34]);

(50) 'ancillary insurance intermediary' means an ancillary insurance intermediary as defined in Article 2(1), point (4), of Directive (EU) 2016/97;

(51) 'reinsurance intermediary' means a reinsurance intermediary as defined in Article 2(1), point (5), of Directive (EU) 2016/97;

(52) 'institution for occupational retirement provision' means an institution for occupational retirement provision as defined in Article 6, point (1), of Directive (EU) 2016/2341;

(53) 'small institution for occupational retirement provision' means an institution for occupational retirement provision which operates pension schemes which together have less than 100 members in total;

(54) 'credit rating agency' means a credit rating agency as defined in Article 3(1), point (b), of Regulation (EC) No 1060/2009;

(55) 'crypto-asset service provider' means a crypto-asset service provider as defined in the relevant provision of the Regulation on markets in crypto-assets;

(56) 'issuer of asset-referenced tokens' means an issuer of asset-referenced tokens as defined in the relevant provision of the Regulation on markets in crypto-assets;

34 Directive (EU) 2016/97 of the European Parliament and of the Council of 20 January 2016 on insurance distribution (OJ L 26, 2.2.2016, p. 19).

(57) 'administrator of critical benchmarks' means an administrator of 'critical benchmarks' as defined in Article 3(1), point (25), of Regulation (EU) 2016/1011;

(58) 'crowdfunding service provider' means a crowdfunding service provider as defined in Article 2(1), point (e), of Regulation (EU) 2020/1503 of the European Parliament and of the Council([35]);

(59) 'securitisation repository' means a securitisation repository as defined in Article 2, point (23), of Regulation (EU) 2017/2402 of the European Parliament and of the Council([36]);

(60) 'microenterprise' means a financial entity, other than a trading venue, a central counterparty, a trade repository or a central securities depository, which employs fewer than 10 persons and has an annual turnover and/or annual balance sheet total that does not exceed EUR 2 million;

(61) 'Lead Overseer' means the European Supervisory Authority appointed in accordance with Article 31(1), point (b) of this Regulation;

(62) 'Joint Committee' means the committee referred to in Article 54 of Regulations (EU) No 1093/2010, (EU) No 1094/2010 and (EU) No 1095/2010;

(63) 'small enterprise' means a financial entity that employs 10 or more persons, but fewer than 50 persons, and has an annual turnover and/or annual balance sheet total that exceeds EUR 2 million, but does not exceed EUR 10 million;

(64) 'medium-sized enterprise' means a financial entity that is not a small enterprise and employs fewer than 250 persons and has an annual turnover that does not exceed EUR 50 million and/or an annual balance sheet that does not exceed EUR 43 million;

(65) 'public authority' means any government or other public administration entity, including national central banks.

Article 4
Proportionality principle

1. Financial entities shall implement the rules laid down in Chapter II in accordance with the principle of proportionality, taking into account their size and overall risk profile, and the nature, scale and complexity of their services, activities and operations.

35 Regulation (EU) 2020/1503 of the European Parliament and of the Council of 7 October 2020 on European crowdfunding service providers for business, and amending Regulation (EU) 2017/1129 and Directive (EU) 2019/1937 (OJ L 347, 20.10.2020, p. 1).

36 Regulation (EU) 2017/2402 of the European Parliament and of the Council of 12 December 2017 laying down a general framework for securitisation and creating a specific framework for simple, transparent and standardised securitisation, and amending Directives 2009/65/EC, 2009/138/EC and 2011/61/EU and Regulations (EC) No 1060/2009 and (EU) No 648/2012 (OJ L 347, 28.12.2017, p. 35).

2. In addition, the application by financial entities of Chapters III, IV and V, Section I, shall be proportionate to their size and overall risk profile, and to the nature, scale and complexity of their services, activities and operations, as specifically provided for in the relevant rules of those Chapters.

3. The competent authorities shall consider the application of the proportionality principle by financial entities when reviewing the consistency of the ICT risk management framework on the basis of the reports submitted upon the request of competent authorities pursuant to Article 6(5) and Article 16(2).

CHAPTER II
ICT risk management

Section I
Article 5
Governance and organisation

1. Financial entities shall have in place an internal governance and control framework that ensures an effective and prudent management of ICT risk, in accordance with Article 6(4), in order to achieve a high level of digital operational resilience.

2. The management body of the financial entity shall define, approve, oversee and be responsible for the implementation of all arrangements related to the ICT risk management framework referred to in Article 6(1).

For the purposes of the first subparagraph, the management body shall:

(a) bear the ultimate responsibility for managing the financial entity's ICT risk;

(b) put in place policies that aim to ensure the maintenance of high standards of availability, authenticity, integrity and confidentiality, of data;

(c) set clear roles and responsibilities for all ICT-related functions and establish appropriate governance arrangements to ensure effective and timely communication, cooperation and coordination among those functions;

(d) bear the overall responsibility for setting and approving the digital operational resilience strategy as referred to in Article 6(8), including the determination of the appropriate risk tolerance level of ICT risk of the financial entity, as referred to in Article 6(8), point (b);

(e) approve, oversee and periodically review the implementation of the financial entity's ICT business continuity policy and ICT response and recovery plans, referred to, respectively, in Article 11(1) and (3), which may be adopted as a dedicated specific policy forming an integral part of the financial entity's overall business continuity policy and response and recovery plan;

(f) approve and periodically review the financial entity's ICT internal audit plans, ICT audits and material modifications to them;

(g) allocate and periodically review the appropriate budget to fulfil the financial entity's digital operational resilience needs in respect of all types of resources, including relevant ICT security awareness programmes and digital operational resilience training referred to in Article 13(6), and ICT skills for all staff;

(h) approve and periodically review the financial entity's policy on arrangements regarding the use of ICT services provided by ICT third-party service providers;

(i) put in place, at corporate level, reporting channels enabling it to be duly informed of the following:

(i) arrangements concluded with ICT third-party service providers on the use of ICT services,

(ii) any relevant planned material changes regarding the ICT third-party service providers,

(iii) the potential impact of such changes on the critical or important functions subject to those arrangements, including a risk analysis summary to assess the impact of those changes, and at least major ICT-related incidents and their impact, as well as response, recovery and corrective measures.

3. Financial entities, other than microenterprises, shall establish a role in order to monitor the arrangements concluded with ICT third-party service providers on the use of ICT services, or shall designate a member of senior management as responsible for overseeing the related risk exposure and relevant documentation.

4. Members of the management body of the financial entity shall actively keep up to date with sufficient knowledge and skills to understand and assess ICT risk and its impact on the operations of the financial entity, including by following specific training on a regular basis, commensurate to the ICT risk being managed.

Section II
Article 6
ICT risk management framework

1. Financial entities shall have a sound, comprehensive and well-documented ICT risk management framework as part of their overall risk management system, which enables them to address ICT risk quickly, efficiently and comprehensively and to ensure a high level of digital operational resilience.

2. The ICT risk management framework shall include at least strategies, policies, procedures, ICT protocols and tools that are necessary to duly and adequately protect all information assets and ICT assets, including computer software, hardware, servers, as well as to protect all relevant

physical components and infrastructures, such as premises, data centres and sensitive designated areas, to ensure that all information assets and ICT assets are adequately protected from risks including damage and unauthorised access or usage.

3. In accordance with their ICT risk management framework, financial entities shall minimise the impact of ICT risk by deploying appropriate strategies, policies, procedures, ICT protocols and tools. They shall provide complete and updated information on ICT risk and on their ICT risk management framework to the competent authorities upon their request.

4. Financial entities, other than microenterprises, shall assign the responsibility for managing and overseeing ICT risk to a control function and ensure an appropriate level of independence of such control function in order to avoid conflicts of interest. Financial entities shall ensure appropriate segregation and independence of ICT risk management functions, control functions, and internal audit functions, according to the three lines of defence model, or an internal risk management and control model.

5. The ICT risk management framework shall be documented and reviewed at least once a year, or periodically in the case of microenterprises, as well as upon the occurrence of major ICT-related incidents, and following supervisory instructions or conclusions derived from relevant digital operational resilience testing or audit processes. It shall be continuously improved on the basis of lessons derived from implementation and monitoring. A report on the review of the ICT risk management framework shall be submitted to the competent authority upon its request.

6. The ICT risk management framework of financial entities, other than microenterprises, shall be subject to internal audit by auditors on a regular basis in line with the financial entities' audit plan. Those auditors shall possess sufficient knowledge, skills and expertise in ICT risk, as well as appropriate independence. The frequency and focus of ICT audits shall be commensurate to the ICT risk of the financial entity.

7. Based on the conclusions from the internal audit review, financial entities shall establish a formal follow-up process, including rules for the timely verification and remediation of critical ICT audit findings.

8. The ICT risk management framework shall include a digital operational resilience strategy setting out how the framework shall be implemented. To that end, the digital operational resilience strategy shall include methods to address ICT risk and attain specific ICT objectives, by:

   (a) explaining how the ICT risk management framework supports the financial entity's business strategy and objectives;

   (b) establishing the risk tolerance level for ICT risk, in accordance with the risk appetite of the financial entity, and analysing the impact tolerance for ICT disruptions;

   (c) setting out clear information security objectives, including key performance indicators and key risk metrics;

(d) explaining the ICT reference architecture and any changes needed to reach specific business objectives;

(e) outlining the different mechanisms put in place to detect ICT-related incidents, prevent their impact and provide protection from it;

(f) evidencing the current digital operational resilience situation on the basis of the number of major ICT-related incidents reported and the effectiveness of preventive measures;

(g) implementing digital operational resilience testing, in accordance with Chapter IV of this Regulation;

(h) outlining a communication strategy in the event of ICT-related incidents the disclosure of which is required in accordance with Article 14.

9. Financial entities may, in the context of the digital operational resilience strategy referred to in paragraph 8, define a holistic ICT multi-vendor strategy, at group or entity level, showing key dependencies on ICT third-party service providers and explaining the rationale behind the procurement mix of ICT third-party service providers.

10. Financial entities may, in accordance with Union and national sectoral law, outsource the tasks of verifying compliance with ICT risk management requirements to intra-group or external undertakings. In case of such outsourcing, the financial entity remains fully responsible for the verification of compliance with the ICT risk management requirements.

Article 7
ICT systems, protocols and tools

In order to address and manage ICT risk, financial entities shall use and maintain updated ICT systems, protocols and tools that are:

(a) appropriate to the magnitude of operations supporting the conduct of their activities, in accordance with the proportionality principle as referred to in Article 4;

(b) reliable;

(c) equipped with sufficient capacity to accurately process the data necessary for the performance of activities and the timely provision of services, and to deal with peak orders, message or transaction volumes, as needed, including where new technology is introduced;

(d) technologically resilient in order to adequately deal with additional information processing needs as required under stressed market conditions or other adverse situations.

Article 8
Identification

1. As part of the ICT risk management framework referred to in Article 6(1), financial entities shall identify, classify and adequately document all ICT supported business functions, roles and responsibilities, the information

assets and ICT assets supporting those functions, and their roles and dependencies in relation to ICT risk. Financial entities shall review as needed, and at least yearly, the adequacy of this classification and of any relevant documentation.

2. Financial entities shall, on a continuous basis, identify all sources of ICT risk, in particular the risk exposure to and from other financial entities, and assess cyber threats and ICT vulnerabilities relevant to their ICT supported business functions, information assets and ICT assets. Financial entities shall review on a regular basis, and at least yearly, the risk scenarios impacting them.

3. Financial entities, other than microenterprises, shall perform a risk assessment upon each major change in the network and information system infrastructure, in the processes or procedures affecting their ICT supported business functions, information assets or ICT assets.

4. Financial entities shall identify all information assets and ICT assets, including those on remote sites, network resources and hardware equipment, and shall map those considered critical. They shall map the configuration of the information assets and ICT assets and the links and interdependencies between the different information assets and ICT assets.

5. Financial entities shall identify and document all processes that are dependent on ICT third-party service providers, and shall identify interconnections with ICT third-party service providers that provide services that support critical or important functions.

6. For the purposes of paragraphs 1, 4 and 5, financial entities shall maintain relevant inventories and update them periodically and every time any major change as referred to in paragraph 3 occurs.

7. Financial entities, other than microenterprises, shall on a regular basis, and at least yearly, conduct a specific ICT risk assessment on all legacy ICT systems and, in any case before and after connecting technologies, applications or systems.

Article 9
Protection and prevention

1. For the purposes of adequately protecting ICT systems and with a view to organising response measures, financial entities shall continuously monitor and control the security and functioning of ICT systems and tools and shall minimise the impact of ICT risk on ICT systems through the deployment of appropriate ICT security tools, policies and procedures.

2. Financial entities shall design, procure and implement ICT security policies, procedures, protocols and tools that aim to ensure the resilience, continuity and availability of ICT systems, in particular for those supporting critical or important functions, and to maintain high standards of availability, authenticity, integrity and confidentiality of data, whether at rest, in use or in transit.

3. In order to achieve the objectives referred to in paragraph 2, financial entities shall use ICT solutions and processes that are appropriate in accordance with Article 4. Those ICT solutions and processes shall:

   (a) ensure the security of the means of transfer of data;

   (b) minimise the risk of corruption or loss of data, unauthorised access and technical flaws that may hinder business activity;

   (c) prevent the lack of availability, the impairment of the authenticity and integrity, the breaches of confidentiality and the loss of data;

   (d) ensure that data is protected from risks arising from data management, including poor administration, processing-related risks and human error.

4. As part of the ICT risk management framework referred to in Article 6(1), financial entities shall:

   (a) develop and document an information security policy defining rules to protect the availability, authenticity, integrity and confidentiality of data, information assets and ICT assets, including those of their customers, where applicable;

   (b) following a risk-based approach, establish a sound network and infrastructure management structure using appropriate techniques, methods and protocols that may include implementing automated mechanisms to isolate affected information assets in the event of cyber-attacks;

   (c) implement policies that limit the physical or logical access to information assets and ICT assets to what is required for legitimate and approved functions and activities only, and establish to that end a set of policies, procedures and controls that address access rights and ensure a sound administration thereof;

   (d) implement policies and protocols for strong authentication mechanisms, based on relevant standards and dedicated control systems, and protection measures of cryptographic keys whereby data is encrypted based on results of approved data classification and ICT risk assessment processes;

   (e) implement documented policies, procedures and controls for ICT change management, including changes to software, hardware, firmware components, systems or security parameters, that are based on a risk assessment approach and are an integral part of the financial entity's overall change management process, in order to ensure that all changes to ICT systems are recorded, tested, assessed, approved, implemented and verified in a controlled manner;

   (f) have appropriate and comprehensive documented policies for patches and updates.

For the purposes of the first subparagraph, point (b), financial entities shall design the network connection infrastructure in a way that allows it to be instantaneously severed or segmented in order to minimise and prevent contagion, especially for interconnected financial processes.

For the purposes of the first subparagraph, point (e), the ICT change management process shall be approved by appropriate lines of management and shall have specific protocols in place.

Article 10
Detection

1. Financial entities shall have in place mechanisms to promptly detect anomalous activities, in accordance with Article 17, including ICT network performance issues and ICT-related incidents, and to identify potential material single points of failure.

   All detection mechanisms referred to in the first subparagraph shall be regularly tested in accordance with Article 25.

2. The detection mechanisms referred to in paragraph 1 shall enable multiple layers of control, define alert thresholds and criteria to trigger and initiate ICT-related incident response processes, including automatic alert mechanisms for relevant staff in charge of ICT-related incident response.

3. Financial entities shall devote sufficient resources and capabilities to monitor user activity, the occurrence of ICT anomalies and ICT-related incidents, in particular cyber-attacks.

4. Data reporting service providers shall, in addition, have in place systems that can effectively check trade reports for completeness, identify omissions and obvious errors, and request re-transmission of those reports.

Article 11
Response and recovery

1. As part of the ICT risk management framework referred to in Article 6(1) and based on the identification requirements set out in Article 8, financial entities shall put in place a comprehensive ICT business continuity policy, which may be adopted as a dedicated specific policy, forming an integral part of the overall business continuity policy of the financial entity.

2. Financial entities shall implement the ICT business continuity policy through dedicated, appropriate and documented arrangements, plans, procedures and mechanisms aiming to:

   (a) ensure the continuity of the financial entity's critical or important functions;

   (b) quickly, appropriately and effectively respond to, and resolve, all ICT-related incidents in a way that limits damage and prioritises the resumption of activities and recovery actions;

(c) activate, without delay, dedicated plans that enable containment measures, processes and technologies suited to each type of ICT-related incident and prevent further damage, as well as tailored response and recovery procedures established in accordance with Article 12;

(d) estimate preliminary impacts, damages and losses;

(e) set out communication and crisis management actions that ensure that updated information is transmitted to all relevant internal staff and external stakeholders in accordance with Article 14, and report to the competent authorities in accordance with Article 19.

3. As part of the ICT risk management framework referred to in Article 6(1), financial entities shall implement associated ICT response and recovery plans which, in the case of financial entities other than microenterprises, shall be subject to independent internal audit reviews.

4. Financial entities shall put in place, maintain and periodically test appropriate ICT business continuity plans, notably with regard to critical or important functions outsourced or contracted through arrangements with ICT third-party service providers.

5. As part of the overall business continuity policy, financial entities shall conduct a business impact analysis (BIA) of their exposures to severe business disruptions. Under the BIA, financial entities shall assess the potential impact of severe business disruptions by means of quantitative and qualitative criteria, using internal and external data and scenario analysis, as appropriate. The BIA shall consider the criticality of identified and mapped business functions, support processes, third-party dependencies and information assets, and their interdependencies. Financial entities shall ensure that ICT assets and ICT services are designed and used in full alignment with the BIA, in particular with regard to adequately ensuring the redundancy of all critical components.

6. As part of their comprehensive ICT risk management, financial entities shall:

(a) test the ICT business continuity plans and the ICT response and recovery plans in relation to ICT systems supporting all functions at least yearly, as well as in the event of any substantive changes to ICT systems supporting critical or important functions;

(b) test the crisis communication plans established in accordance with Article 14.

For the purposes of the first subparagraph, point (a), financial entities, other than microenterprises, shall include in the testing plans scenarios of cyber-attacks and switchovers between the primary ICT infrastructure and the redundant capacity, backups and redundant facilities necessary to meet the obligations set out in Article 12.

Financial entities shall regularly review their ICT business continuity policy and ICT response and recovery plans, taking into account the results of tests carried out in accordance with the first subparagraph and recommendations stemming from audit checks or supervisory reviews.

7. Financial entities, other than microenterprises, shall have a crisis management function, which, in the event of activation of their ICT business continuity plans or ICT response and recovery plans, shall, inter alia, set out clear procedures to manage internal and external crisis communications in accordance with Article 14.

8. Financial entities shall keep readily accessible records of activities before and during disruption events when their ICT business continuity plans and ICT response and recovery plans are activated.

9. Central securities depositories shall provide the competent authorities with copies of the results of the ICT business continuity tests, or of similar exercises.

10. Financial entities, other than microenterprises, shall report to the competent authorities, upon their request, an estimation of aggregated annual costs and losses caused by major ICT-related incidents.

11. In accordance with Article 16 of Regulations (EU) No 1093/2010, (EU) No 1094/2010 and (EU) No 1095/2010, the ESAs, through the Joint Committee, shall by 17 July 2024 develop common guidelines on the estimation of aggregated annual costs and losses referred to in paragraph 10.

Article 12

Backup policies and procedures, restoration and recovery procedures and methods

1. For the purpose of ensuring the restoration of ICT systems and data with minimum downtime, limited disruption and loss, as part of their ICT risk management framework, financial entities shall develop and document:

   (a) backup policies and procedures specifying the scope of the data that is subject to the backup and the minimum frequency of the backup, based on the criticality of information or the confidentiality level of the data;

   (b) restoration and recovery procedures and methods.

2. Financial entities shall set up backup systems that can be activated in accordance with the backup policies and procedures, as well as restoration and recovery procedures and methods. The activation of backup systems shall not jeopardise the security of the network and information systems or the availability, authenticity, integrity or confidentiality of data. Testing of the backup procedures and restoration and recovery procedures and methods shall be undertaken periodically.

3. When restoring backup data using own systems, financial entities shall use ICT systems that are physically and logically segregated from the source ICT system. The ICT systems shall be securely protected from any unauthorised access or ICT corruption and allow for the timely restoration of services making use of data and system backups as necessary.

For central counterparties, the recovery plans shall enable the recovery of all transactions at the time of disruption to allow the central counterparty to continue to operate with certainty and to complete settlement on the scheduled date.

Data reporting service providers shall additionally maintain adequate resources and have back-up and restoration facilities in place in order to offer and maintain their services at all times.

4. Financial entities, other than microenterprises, shall maintain redundant ICT capacities equipped with resources, capabilities and functions that are adequate to ensure business needs. Microenterprises shall assess the need to maintain such redundant ICT capacities based on their risk profile.

5. Central securities depositories shall maintain at least one secondary processing site endowed with adequate resources, capabilities, functions and staffing arrangements to ensure business needs.

   The secondary processing site shall be:

   (a) located at a geographical distance from the primary processing site to ensure that it bears a distinct risk profile and to prevent it from being affected by the event which has affected the primary site;

   (b) capable of ensuring the continuity of critical or important functions identically to the primary site, or providing the level of services necessary to ensure that the financial entity performs its critical operations within the recovery objectives;

   (c) immediately accessible to the financial entity's staff to ensure continuity of critical or important functions in the event that the primary processing site has become unavailable.

6. In determining the recovery time and recovery point objectives for each function, financial entities shall take into account whether it is a critical or important function and the potential overall impact on market efficiency. Such time objectives shall ensure that, in extreme scenarios, the agreed service levels are met.

7. When recovering from an ICT-related incident, financial entities shall perform necessary checks, including any multiple checks and reconciliations, in order to ensure that the highest level of data integrity is maintained. These checks shall also be performed when reconstructing data from external stakeholders, in order to ensure that all data is consistent between systems.

Article 13
Learning and evolving

1. Financial entities shall have in place capabilities and staff to gather information on vulnerabilities and cyber threats, ICT-related incidents, in particular cyber-attacks, and analyse the impact they are likely to have on their digital operational resilience.

2. Financial entities shall put in place post ICT-related incident reviews after a major ICT-related incident disrupts their core activities, analysing the causes of disruption and identifying required improvements to the ICT operations or within the ICT business continuity policy referred to in Article 11.

   Financial entities, other than microenterprises, shall, upon request, communicate to the competent authorities, the changes that were implemented following post ICT-related incident reviews as referred to in the first subparagraph.

   The post ICT-related incident reviews referred to in the first subparagraph shall determine whether the established procedures were followed and the actions taken were effective, including in relation to the following:

   (a) the promptness in responding to security alerts and determining the impact of ICT-related incidents and their severity;

   (b) the quality and speed of performing a forensic analysis, where deemed appropriate;

   (c) the effectiveness of incident escalation within the financial entity;

   (d) the effectiveness of internal and external communication.

3. Lessons derived from the digital operational resilience testing carried out in accordance with Articles 26 and 27 and from real life ICT-related incidents, in particular cyber-attacks, along with challenges faced upon the activation of ICT business continuity plans and ICT response and recovery plans, together with relevant information exchanged with counterparts and assessed during supervisory reviews, shall be duly incorporated on a continuous basis into the ICT risk assessment process. Those findings shall form the basis for appropriate reviews of relevant components of the ICT risk management framework referred to in Article 6(1).

4. Financial entities shall monitor the effectiveness of the implementation of their digital operational resilience strategy set out in Article 6(8). They shall map the evolution of ICT risk over time, analyse the frequency, types, magnitude and evolution of ICT-related incidents, in particular cyber-attacks and their patterns, with a view to understanding the level of ICT risk exposure, in particular in relation to critical or important functions, and enhance the cyber maturity and preparedness of the financial entity.

5. Senior ICT staff shall report at least yearly to the management body on the findings referred to in paragraph 3 and put forward recommendations.

6. Financial entities shall develop ICT security awareness programmes and digital operational resilience training as compulsory modules in their staff training schemes. Those programmes and training shall be applicable to all employees and to senior management staff, and shall have a level of complexity commensurate to the remit of their functions. Where appropriate, financial entities shall also include ICT third-party service providers in their relevant training schemes in accordance with Article 30(2), point (i).

7. Financial entities, other than microenterprises, shall monitor relevant technological developments on a continuous basis, also with a view to understanding the possible impact of the deployment of such new technologies on ICT security requirements and digital operational resilience. They shall keep up-to-date with the latest ICT risk management processes, in order to effectively combat current or new forms of cyber-attacks.

Article 14
Communication

1. As part of the ICT risk management framework referred to in Article 6(1), financial entities shall have in place crisis communication plans enabling a responsible disclosure of, at least, major ICT-related incidents or vulnerabilities to clients and counterparts as well as to the public, as appropriate.

2. As part of the ICT risk management framework, financial entities shall implement communication policies for internal staff and for external stakeholders. Communication policies for staff shall take into account the need to differentiate between staff involved in ICT risk management, in particular the staff responsible for response and recovery, and staff that needs to be informed.

3. At least one person in the financial entity shall be tasked with implementing the communication strategy for ICT-related incidents and fulfil the public and media function for that purpose.

Article 15
Further harmonisation of ICT risk management tools, methods, processes and policies

The ESAs shall, through the Joint Committee, in consultation with the European Union Agency on Cybersecurity (ENISA), develop common draft regulatory technical standards in order to:

(a) further elements to be included in the ICT security policies, procedures, protocols and tools referred to in Article 9(2), with a view to ensuring the security of networks, enable adequate safeguards against intrusions and data misuse, preserve the availability, authenticity, integrity and confidentiality of data, including cryptographic techniques, and guarantee an accurate and prompt data transmission without major disruptions and undue delays;

(b) develop further components of the controls of access management rights referred to in Article 9(4), point (c), and associated human resource policy specifying access rights, procedures for granting and revoking rights, monitoring anomalous behaviour in relation to ICT risk through appropriate indicators, including for network use patterns, hours, IT activity and unknown devices;

(c) develop further the mechanisms specified in Article 10(1) enabling a prompt detection of anomalous activities and the criteria set out in Article 10(2) triggering ICT-related incident detection and response processes;

(d) specify further the components of the ICT business continuity policy referred to in Article 11(1);

(e) specify further the testing of ICT business continuity plans referred to in Article 11(6) to ensure that such testing duly takes into account scenarios in which the quality of the provision of a critical or important function deteriorates to an unacceptable level or fails, and duly considers the potential impact of the insolvency, or other failures, of any relevant ICT third-party service provider and, where relevant, the political risks in the respective providers' jurisdictions;

(f) specify further the components of the ICT response and recovery plans referred to in Article 11(3);

(g) specifying further the content and format of the report on the review of the ICT risk management framework referred to in Article 6(5);

When developing those draft regulatory technical standards, the ESAs shall take into account the size and the overall risk profile of the financial entity, and the nature, scale and complexity of its services, activities and operations, while duly taking into consideration any specific feature arising from the distinct nature of activities across different financial services sectors.

The ESAs shall submit those draft regulatory technical standards to the Commission by 17 January 2024.

Power is delegated to the Commission to supplement this Regulation by adopting the regulatory technical standards referred to in the first paragraph in accordance with Articles 10 to 14 of Regulations (EU) No 1093/2010, (EU) No 1094/2010 and (EU) No 1095/2010.

Article 16
Simplified ICT risk management framework

1. Articles 5 to 15 of this Regulation shall not apply to small and non-interconnected investment firms, payment institutions exempted pursuant to Directive (EU) 2015/2366; institutions exempted pursuant to Directive 2013/36/EU in respect of which Member States have decided not to apply the option referred to in Article 2(4) of this Regulation; electronic money institutions exempted pursuant to Directive 2009/110/EC; and small institutions for occupational retirement provision.

   Without prejudice to the first subparagraph, the entities listed in the first subparagraph shall:

   (a) put in place and maintain a sound and documented ICT risk management framework that details the mechanisms and measures aimed at a quick, efficient and comprehensive management of ICT risk, including for the protection of relevant physical components and infrastructures;

(b) continuously monitor the security and functioning of all ICT systems;

(c) minimise the impact of ICT risk through the use of sound, resilient and updated ICT systems, protocols and tools which are appropriate to support the performance of their activities and the provision of services and adequately protect availability, authenticity, integrity and confidentiality of data in the network and information systems;

(d) allow sources of ICT risk and anomalies in the network and information systems to be promptly identified and detected and ICT-related incidents to be swiftly handled;

(e) identify key dependencies on ICT third-party service providers;

(f) ensure the continuity of critical or important functions, through business continuity plans and response and recovery measures, which include, at least, back-up and restoration measures;

(g) test, on a regular basis, the plans and measures referred to in point (f), as well as the effectiveness of the controls implemented in accordance with points (a) and (c);

(h) implement, as appropriate, relevant operational conclusions resulting from the tests referred to in point (g) and from post-incident analysis into the ICT risk assessment process and develop, according to needs and ICT risk profile, ICT security awareness programmes and digital operational resilience training for staff and management.

2. The ICT risk management framework referred to in paragraph 1, second subparagraph, point (a), shall be documented and reviewed periodically and upon the occurrence of major ICT-related incidents in compliance with supervisory instructions. It shall be continuously improved on the basis of lessons derived from implementation and monitoring. A report on the review of the ICT risk management framework shall be submitted to the competent authority upon its request.

3. The ESAs shall, through the Joint Committee, in consultation with the ENISA, develop common draft regulatory technical standards in order to:

(a) specify further the elements to be included in the ICT risk management framework referred to in paragraph 1, second subparagraph, point (a);

(b) specify further the elements in relation to systems, protocols and tools to minimise the impact of ICT risk referred to in paragraph 1, second subparagraph, point (c), with a view to ensuring the security of networks, enabling adequate safeguards against intrusions and data misuse and preserving the availability, authenticity, integrity and confidentiality of data;

(c) specify further the components of the ICT business continuity plans referred to in paragraph 1, second subparagraph, point (f);

(d) specify further the rules on the testing of business continuity plans and ensure the effectiveness of the controls referred to in paragraph 1, second subparagraph, point (g) and ensure that such testing duly takes into account scenarios in which the quality of the provision of a critical or important function deteriorates to an unacceptable level or fails;

(e) specify further the content and format of the report on the review of the ICT risk management framework referred to in paragraph 2.

When developing those draft regulatory technical standards, the ESAs shall take into account the size and the overall risk profile of the financial entity, and the nature, scale and complexity of its services, activities and operations.

The ESAs shall submit those draft regulatory technical standards to the Commission by 17 January 2024.

Power is delegated to the Commission to supplement this Regulation by adopting the regulatory technical standards referred to in the first subparagraph in accordance with Articles 10 to 14 of Regulations (EU) No 1093/2010, (EU) No 1094/2010 and (EU) No 1095/2010.

CHAPTER III
ICT-related incident management, classification and reporting

Article 17
ICT-related incident management process

1. Financial entities shall define, establish and implement an ICT-related incident management process to detect, manage and notify ICT-related incidents.

2. Financial entities shall record all ICT-related incidents and significant cyber threats. Financial entities shall establish appropriate procedures and processes to ensure a consistent and integrated monitoring, handling and follow-up of ICT-related incidents, to ensure that root causes are identified, documented and addressed in order to prevent the occurrence of such incidents.

3. The ICT-related incident management process referred to in paragraph 1 shall:

(a) put in place early warning indicators;

(b) establish procedures to identify, track, log, categorise and classify ICT-related incidents according to their priority and severity and according to the criticality of the services impacted, in accordance with the criteria set out in Article 18(1);

(c) assign roles and responsibilities that need to be activated for different ICT-related incident types and scenarios;

(d) set out plans for communication to staff, external stakeholders and media in accordance with Article 14 and for notification to clients, for internal escalation procedures, including ICT-related customer complaints, as well as for the provision of information to financial entities that act as counterparts, as appropriate;

(e) ensure that at least major ICT-related incidents are reported to relevant senior management and inform the management body of at least major ICT-related incidents, explaining the impact, response and additional controls to be established as a result of such ICT-related incidents;

(f) establish ICT-related incident response procedures to mitigate impacts and ensure that services become operational and secure in a timely manner.

Article 18

Classification of ICT-related incidents and cyber threats

1. Financial entities shall classify ICT-related incidents and shall determine their impact based on the following criteria:

(a) the number and/or relevance of clients or financial counterparts affected and, where applicable, the amount or number of transactions affected by the ICT-related incident, and whether the ICT-related incident has caused reputational impact;

(b) the duration of the ICT-related incident, including the service downtime;

(c) the geographical spread with regard to the areas affected by the ICT-related incident, particularly if it affects more than two Member States;

(d) the data losses that the ICT-related incident entails, in relation to availability, authenticity, integrity or confidentiality of data;

(e) the criticality of the services affected, including the financial entity's transactions and operations;

(f) the economic impact, in particular direct and indirect costs and losses, of the ICT-related incident in both absolute and relative terms.

2. Financial entities shall classify cyber threats as significant based on the criticality of the services at risk, including the financial entity's transactions and operations, number and/or relevance of clients or financial counterparts targeted and the geographical spread of the areas at risk.

3. The ESAs shall, through the Joint Committee and in consultation with the ECB and ENISA, develop common draft regulatory technical standards further specifying the following:

(a) the criteria set out in paragraph 1, including materiality thresholds for determining major ICT-related incidents or, as applicable, major operational or security payment-related incidents, that are subject to the reporting obligation laid down in Article 19(1);

(b) the criteria to be applied by competent authorities for the purpose of assessing the relevance of major ICT-related incidents or, as applicable, major operational or security payment-related incidents, to relevant competent authorities in other Member States', and the details of reports of major ICT-related incidents or, as applicable, major operational or security payment-related incidents, to be shared with other competent authorities pursuant to Article 19(6) and (7);

(c) the criteria set out in paragraph 2 of this Article, including high materiality thresholds for determining significant cyber threats.

4. When developing the common draft regulatory technical standards referred to in paragraph 3 of this Article, the ESAs shall take into account the criteria set out in Article 4(2), as well as international standards, guidance and specifications developed and published by ENISA, including, where appropriate, specifications for other economic sectors. For the purposes of applying the criteria set out in Article 4(2), the ESAs shall duly consider the need for microenterprises and small and medium-sized enterprises to mobilise sufficient resources and capabilities to ensure that ICT-related incidents are managed swiftly.

The ESAs shall submit those common draft regulatory technical standards to the Commission by 17 January 2024.

Power is delegated to the Commission to supplement this Regulation by adopting the regulatory technical standards referred to in paragraph 3 in accordance with Articles 10 to 14 of Regulations (EU) No 1093/2010, (EU) No 1094/2010 and (EU) No 1095/2010.

Article 19
Reporting of major ICT-related incidents and voluntary notification of significant cyber threats

1. Financial entities shall report major ICT-related incidents to the relevant competent authority as referred to in Article 46 in accordance with paragraph 4 of this Article.

Where a financial entity is subject to supervision by more than one national competent authority referred to in Article 46, Member States shall designate a single competent authority as the relevant competent authority responsible for carrying out the functions and duties provided for in this Article.

Credit institutions classified as significant, in accordance with Article 6(4) of Regulation (EU) No 1024/2013, shall report major ICT-related incidents to the relevant national competent authority designated in accordance with Article 4 of Directive 2013/36/EU, which shall immediately transmit that report to the ECB.

For the purpose of the first subparagraph, financial entities shall produce, after collecting and analysing all relevant information, the initial notification and reports referred to in paragraph 4 of this Article using the templates referred to in Article 20 and submit them to the competent authority. In the event that a technical impossibility prevents the submission of the initial notification using the template, financial entities shall notify the competent authority about it via alternative means.

The initial notification and reports referred to in paragraph 4 shall include all information necessary for the competent authority to determine the significance of the major ICT-related incident and assess possible cross-border impacts.

Without prejudice to the reporting pursuant to the first subparagraph by the financial entity to the relevant competent authority, Member States may additionally determine that some or all financial entities shall also provide the initial notification and each report referred to in paragraph 4 of this Article using the templates referred to in Article 20 to the competent authorities or the computer security incident response teams (CSIRTs) designated or established in accordance with Directive (EU) 2022/2555.

2. Financial entities may, on a voluntary basis, notify significant cyber threats to the relevant competent authority when they deem the threat to be of relevance to the financial system, service users or clients. The relevant competent authority may provide such information to other relevant authorities referred to in paragraph 6.

Credit institutions classified as significant, in accordance with Article 6(4) of Regulation (EU) No 1024/2013, may, on a voluntary basis, notify significant cyber threats to relevant national competent authority, designated in accordance with Article 4 of Directive 2013/36/EU, which shall immediately transmit the notification to the ECB.

Member States may determine that those financial entities that on a voluntary basis notify in accordance with the first subparagraph may also transmit that notification to the CSIRTs designated or established in accordance with Directive (EU) 2022/2555.

3. Where a major ICT-related incident occurs and has an impact on the financial interests of clients, financial entities shall, without undue delay as soon as they become aware of it, inform their clients about the major ICT-related incident and about the measures that have been taken to mitigate the adverse effects of such incident.

In the case of a significant cyber threat, financial entities shall, where applicable, inform their clients that are potentially affected of any appropriate protection measures which the latter may consider taking.

4. Financial entities shall, within the time limits to be laid down in accordance with Article 20, first paragraph, point (a), point (ii), submit the following to the relevant competent authority:

   (a) an initial notification;

   (b) an intermediate report after the initial notification referred to in point (a), as soon as the status of the original incident has changed significantly or the handling of the major ICT-related incident has changed based on new information available, followed, as appropriate, by updated notifications every time a relevant status update is available, as well as upon a specific request of the competent authority;

   (c) a final report, when the root cause analysis has been completed, regardless of whether mitigation measures have already been implemented, and when the actual impact figures are available to replace estimates.

5. Financial entities may outsource, in accordance with Union and national sectoral law, the reporting obligations under this Article to a third-party service provider. In case of such outsourcing, the financial entity remains fully responsible for the fulfilment of the incident reporting requirements.

6. Upon receipt of the initial notification and of each report referred to in paragraph 4, the competent authority shall, in a timely manner, provide details of the major ICT-related incident to the following recipients based, as applicable, on their respective competences:

   (a) EBA, ESMA or EIOPA;

   (b) the ECB, in the case of financial entities referred to in Article 2(1), points (a), (b) and (d);

   (c) the competent authorities, single points of contact or CSIRTs designated or established in accordance with Directive (EU) 2022/2555;

   (d) the resolution authorities, as referred to in Article 3 of Directive 2014/59/EU, and the Single Resolution Board (SRB) with respect to entities referred to in Article 7(2) of Regulation (EU) No 806/2014 of the European Parliament and of the Council([37]), and with respect to entities and groups referred to in Article 7(4)(b) and (5) of Regulation (EU) No 806/2014 if such details concern incidents that pose a risk to ensuring critical functions within the meaning of Article 2(1), point (35), of Directive 2014/59/EU; and

   (e) other relevant public authorities under national law.

37 Regulation (EU) No 806/2014 of the European Parliament and of the Council of 15 July 2014 establishing uniform rules and a uniform procedure for the resolution of credit institutions and certain investment firms in the framework of a Single Resolution Mechanism and a Single Resolution Fund and amending Regulation (EU) No 1093/2010 (OJ L 225, 30.7.2014, p. 1).

7. Following receipt of information in accordance with paragraph 6, EBA, ESMA or EIOPA and the ECB, in consultation with ENISA and in cooperation with the relevant competent authority, shall assess whether the major ICT-related incident is relevant for competent authorities in other Member States. Following that assessment, EBA, ESMA or EIOPA shall, as soon as possible, notify relevant competent authorities in other Member States accordingly. The ECB shall notify the members of the European System of Central Banks on issues relevant to the payment system. Based on that notification, the competent authorities shall, where appropriate, take all of the necessary measures to protect the immediate stability of the financial system.

8. The notification to be done by ESMA pursuant to paragraph 7 of this Article shall be without prejudice to the responsibility of the competent authority to urgently transmit the details of the major ICT-related incident to the relevant authority in the host Member State, where a central securities depository has significant cross-border activity in the host Member State, the major ICT-related incident is likely to have severe consequences for the financial markets of the host Member State and where there are cooperation arrangements among competent authorities related to the supervision of financial entities.

Article 20
Harmonisation of reporting content and templates

The ESAs, through the Joint Committee, and in consultation with ENISA and the ECB, shall develop:

(a) common draft regulatory technical standards in order to:

(i) establish the content of the reports for major ICT-related incidents in order to reflect the criteria laid down in Article 18(1) and incorporate further elements, such as details for establishing the relevance of the reporting for other Member States and whether it constitutes a major operational or security payment-related incident or not;

(ii) determine the time limits for the initial notification and for each report referred to in Article 19(4);

(iii) establish the content of the notification for significant cyber threats.

When developing those draft regulatory technical standards, the ESAs shall take into account the size and the overall risk profile of the financial entity, and the nature, scale and complexity of its services, activities and operations, and in particular, with a view to ensuring that, for the purposes of this paragraph, point (a), point (ii), different time limits may reflect, as appropriate, specificities of financial sectors, without prejudice to maintaining a consistent approach to ICT-related incident reporting pursuant to this Regulation and to Directive (EU) 2022/2555. The ESAs shall, as applicable, provide justification when deviating from the approaches taken in the context of that Directive;

(b) common draft implementing technical standards in order to establish the standard forms, templates and procedures for financial entities to report a major ICT-related incident and to notify a significant cyber threat.

The ESAs shall submit the common draft regulatory technical standards referred to in the first paragraph, point (a), and the common draft implementing technical standards referred to in the first paragraph, point (b), to the Commission by 17 July 2024.

Power is delegated to the Commission to supplement this Regulation by adopting the common regulatory technical standards referred to in the first paragraph, point (a), in accordance with Articles 10 to 14 of Regulations (EU) No 1093/2010, (EU) No 1094/2010 and (EU) No 1095/2010.

Power is conferred on the Commission to adopt the common implementing technical standards referred to in the first paragraph, point (b), in accordance with Article 15 of Regulations (EU) No 1093/2010, (EU) No 1094/2010 and (EU) No 1095/2010.

Article 21
Centralisation of reporting of major ICT-related incidents

1. The ESAs, through the Joint Committee, and in consultation with the ECB and ENISA, shall prepare a joint report assessing the feasibility of further centralisation of incident reporting through the establishment of a single EU Hub for major ICT-related incident reporting by financial entities. The joint report shall explore ways to facilitate the flow of ICT-related incident reporting, reduce associated costs and underpin thematic analyses with a view to enhancing supervisory convergence.

2. The joint report referred to in paragraph 1 shall comprise at least the following elements:

    (a) prerequisites for the establishment of a single EU Hub;

    (b) benefits, limitations and risks, including risks associated with the high concentration of sensitive information;

    (c) the necessary capability to ensure interoperability with regard to other relevant reporting schemes;

    (d) elements of operational management;

    (e) conditions of membership;

    (f) technical arrangements for financial entities and national competent authorities to access the single EU Hub;

    (g) a preliminary assessment of financial costs incurred by setting-up the operational platform supporting the single EU Hub, including the requisite expertise.

3. The ESAs shall submit the report referred to in paragraph 1 to the European Parliament, to the Council and to the Commission by 17 January 2025.

Article 22
Supervisory feedback

1. Without prejudice to the technical input, advice or remedies and subsequent follow-up which may be provided, where applicable, in accordance with national law, by the CSIRTs under Directive (EU) 2022/2555, the competent authority shall, upon receipt of the initial notification and of each report as referred to in Article 19(4), acknowledge receipt and may, where feasible, provide in a timely manner relevant and proportionate feedback or high-level guidance to the financial entity, in particular by making available any relevant anonymised information and intelligence on similar threats, and may discuss remedies applied at the level of the financial entity and ways to minimise and mitigate adverse impact across the financial sector. Without prejudice to the supervisory feedback received, financial entities shall remain fully responsible for the handling and for consequences of the ICT-related incidents reported pursuant to Article 19(1).

2. The ESAs shall, through the Joint Committee, on an anonymised and aggregated basis, report yearly on major ICT-related incidents, the details of which shall be provided by competent authorities in accordance with Article 19(6), setting out at least the number of major ICT-related incidents, their nature and their impact on the operations of financial entities or clients, remedial actions taken and costs incurred.

   The ESAs shall issue warnings and produce high-level statistics to support ICT threat and vulnerability assessments.

Article 23
Operational or security payment-related incidents concerning credit institutions, payment institutions, account information service providers, and electronic money institutions

The requirements laid down in this Chapter shall also apply to operational or security payment-related incidents and to major operational or security payment-related incidents, where they concern credit institutions, payment institutions, account information service providers, and electronic money institutions.

CHAPTER IV
Digital operational resilience testing

Article 24
General requirements for the performance of digital operational resilience testing

1. For the purpose of assessing preparedness for handling ICT-related incidents, of identifying weaknesses, deficiencies and gaps in digital operational resilience, and of promptly implementing corrective measures, financial entities, other than microenterprises, shall, taking into account the criteria set out in Article 4(2), establish, maintain and review a sound and comprehensive digital operational resilience testing programme as

an integral part of the ICT risk-management framework referred to in Article 6.

2. The digital operational resilience testing programme shall include a range of assessments, tests, methodologies, practices and tools to be applied in accordance with Articles 25 and 26.

3. When conducting the digital operational resilience testing programme referred to in paragraph 1 of this Article, financial entities, other than microenterprises, shall follow a risk-based approach taking into account the criteria set out in Article 4(2) duly considering the evolving landscape of ICT risk, any specific risks to which the financial entity concerned is or might be exposed, the criticality of information assets and of services provided, as well as any other factor the financial entity deems appropriate.

4. Financial entities, other than microenterprises, shall ensure that tests are undertaken by independent parties, whether internal or external. Where tests are undertaken by an internal tester, financial entities shall dedicate sufficient resources and ensure that conflicts of interest are avoided throughout the design and execution phases of the test.

5. Financial entities, other than microenterprises, shall establish procedures and policies to prioritise, classify and remedy all issues revealed throughout the performance of the tests and shall establish internal validation methodologies to ascertain that all identified weaknesses, deficiencies or gaps are fully addressed.

6. Financial entities, other than microenterprises, shall ensure, at least yearly, that appropriate tests are conducted on all ICT systems and applications supporting critical or important functions.

Article 25
Testing of ICT tools and systems

1. The digital operational resilience testing programme referred to in Article 24 shall provide, in accordance with the criteria set out in Article 4(2), for the execution of appropriate tests, such as vulnerability assessments and scans, open source analyses, network security assessments, gap analyses, physical security reviews, questionnaires and scanning software solutions, source code reviews where feasible, scenario-based tests, compatibility testing, performance testing, end-to-end testing and penetration testing.

2. Central securities depositories and central counterparties shall perform vulnerability assessments before any deployment or redeployment of new or existing applications and infrastructure components, and ICT services supporting critical or important functions of the financial entity.

3. Microenterprises shall perform the tests referred to in paragraph 1 by combining a risk-based approach with a strategic planning of ICT testing, by duly considering the need to maintain a balanced approach between the scale of resources and the time to be allocated to the ICT testing provided for in this Article, on the one hand, and the urgency, type of risk, criticality

of information assets and of services provided, as well as any other relevant factor, including the financial entity's ability to take calculated risks, on the other hand.

Article 26

Advanced testing of ICT tools, systems and processes based on TLPT

1. Financial entities, other than entities referred to in Article 16(1), first subparagraph, and other than microenterprises, which are identified in accordance with paragraph 8, third subparagraph, of this Article, shall carry out at least every 3 years advanced testing by means of TLPT. Based on the risk profile of the financial entity and taking into account operational circumstances, the competent authority may, where necessary, request the financial entity to reduce or increase this frequency.

2. Each threat-led penetration test shall cover several or all critical or important functions of a financial entity, and shall be performed on live production systems supporting such functions.

Financial entities shall identify all relevant underlying ICT systems, processes and technologies supporting critical or important functions and ICT services, including those supporting the critical or important functions which have been outsourced or contracted to ICT third-party service providers.

Financial entities shall assess which critical or important functions need to be covered by the TLPT. The result of this assessment shall determine the precise scope of TLPT and shall be validated by the competent authorities.

3. Where ICT third-party service providers are included in the scope of TLPT, the financial entity shall take the necessary measures and safeguards to ensure the participation of such ICT third-party service providers in the TLPT and shall retain at all times full responsibility for ensuring compliance with this Regulation.

4. Without prejudice to paragraph 2, first and second subparagraphs, where the participation of an ICT third-party service provider in the TLPT, referred to in paragraph 3, is reasonably expected to have an adverse impact on the quality or security of services delivered by the ICT third-party service provider to customers that are entities falling outside the scope of this Regulation, or on the confidentiality of the data related to such services, the financial entity and the ICT third-party service provider may agree in writing that the ICT third-party service provider directly enters into contractual arrangements with an external tester, for the purpose of conducting, under the direction of one designated financial entity, a pooled TLPT involving several financial entities (pooled testing) to which the ICT third-party service provider provides ICT services.

That pooled testing shall cover the relevant range of ICT services supporting critical or important functions contracted to the respective ICT third-party service provider by the financial entities. The pooled testing shall be considered TLPT carried out by the financial entities participating in the pooled testing.

The number of financial entities participating in the pooled testing shall be duly calibrated taking into account the complexity and types of services involved.

5. Financial entities shall, with the cooperation of ICT third-party service providers and other parties involved, including the testers but excluding the competent authorities, apply effective risk management controls to mitigate the risks of any potential impact on data, damage to assets, and disruption to critical or important functions, services or operations at the financial entity itself, its counterparts or to the financial sector.

6. At the end of the testing, after reports and remediation plans have been agreed, the financial entity and, where applicable, the external testers shall provide to the authority, designated in accordance with paragraph 9 or 10, a summary of the relevant findings, the remediation plans and the documentation demonstrating that the TLPT has been conducted in accordance with the requirements.

7. Authorities shall provide financial entities with an attestation confirming that the test was performed in accordance with the requirements as evidenced in the documentation in order to allow for mutual recognition of threat led penetration tests between competent authorities. The financial entity shall notify the relevant competent authority of the attestation, the summary of the relevant findings and the remediation plans.

Without prejudice to such attestation, financial entities shall remain at all times fully responsible for the impact of the tests referred to in paragraph 4.

8. Financial entities shall contract testers for the purposes of undertaking TLPT in accordance with Article 27. When financial entities use internal testers for the purposes of undertaking TLPT, they shall contract external testers every three tests.

Credit institutions that are classified as significant in accordance with Article 6(4) of Regulation (EU) No 1024/2013, shall only use external testers in accordance with Article 27(1), points (a) to (e).

Competent authorities shall identify financial entities that are required to perform TLPT taking into account the criteria set out in Article 4(2), based on an assessment of the following:

(a) impact-related factors, in particular the extent to which the services provided and activities undertaken by the financial entity impact the financial sector;

(b) possible financial stability concerns, including the systemic character of the financial entity at Union or national level, as applicable;

(c) specific ICT risk profile, level of ICT maturity of the financial entity or technology features involved.

9. Member States may designate a single public authority in the financial sector to be responsible for TLPT-related matters in the financial sector at national level and shall entrust it with all competences and tasks to that effect.

10. In the absence of a designation in accordance with paragraph 9 of this Article, and without prejudice to the power to identify the financial entities that are required to perform TLPT, a competent authority may delegate the exercise of some or all of the tasks referred to in this Article and Article 27 to another national authority in the financial sector.

11. The ESAs shall, in agreement with the ECB, develop joint draft regulatory technical standards in accordance with the TIBER-EU framework in order to specify further:

(a) the criteria used for the purpose of the application of paragraph 8, second subparagraph;

(b) the requirements and standards governing the use of internal testers;

(c) the requirements in relation to:

(i) the scope of TLPT referred to in paragraph 2;

(ii) the testing methodology and approach to be followed for each specific phase of the testing process;

(iii) the results, closure and remediation stages of the testing;

(d) the type of supervisory and other relevant cooperation which are needed for the implementation of TLPT, and for the facilitation of mutual recognition of that testing, in the context of financial entities that operate in more than one Member State, to allow an appropriate level of supervisory involvement and a flexible implementation to cater for specificities of financial sub-sectors or local financial markets.

When developing those draft regulatory technical standards, the ESAs shall give due consideration to any specific feature arising from the distinct nature of activities across different financial services sectors.

The ESAs shall submit those draft regulatory technical standards to the Commission by 17 July 2024.

Power is delegated to the Commission to supplement this Regulation by adopting the regulatory technical standards referred to in the first subparagraph in accordance with Articles 10 to 14 of Regulations (EU) No 1093/2010, (EU) No 1094/2010 and (EU) No 1095/2010.

Article 27
Requirements for testers for the carrying out of TLPT

1. Financial entities shall only use testers for the carrying out of TLPT, that:

(a) are of the highest suitability and reputability;

(b) possess technical and organisational capabilities and demonstrate specific expertise in threat intelligence, penetration testing and red team testing;

(c) are certified by an accreditation body in a Member State or adhere to formal codes of conduct or ethical frameworks;

(d) provide an independent assurance, or an audit report, in relation to the sound management of risks associated with the carrying out of TLPT, including the due protection of the financial entity's confidential information and redress for the business risks of the financial entity;

(e) are duly and fully covered by relevant professional indemnity insurances, including against risks of misconduct and negligence.

2. When using internal testers, financial entities shall ensure that, in addition to the requirements in paragraph 1, the following conditions are met:

(a) such use has been approved by the relevant competent authority or by the single public authority designated in accordance with Article 26(9) and (10);

(b) the relevant competent authority has verified that the financial entity has sufficient dedicated resources and ensured that conflicts of interest are avoided throughout the design and execution phases of the test; and

(c) the threat intelligence provider is external to the financial entity.

3. Financial entities shall ensure that contracts concluded with external testers require a sound management of the TLPT results and that any data processing thereof, including any generation, store, aggregation, draft, report, communication or destruction, do not create risks to the financial entity.

CHAPTER V
Managing of ICT third-party risk

Section I
Key principles for a sound management of ICT third-party risk

Article 28
General principles

1. Financial entities shall manage ICT third-party risk as an integral component of ICT risk within their ICT risk management framework as referred to in Article 6(1), and in accordance with the following principles:

(a) financial entities that have in place contractual arrangements for the use of ICT services to run their business operations shall, at all times, remain fully responsible for compliance with, and the discharge of, all obligations under this Regulation and applicable financial services law;

(b) financial entities' management of ICT third-party risk shall be implemented in light of the principle of proportionality, taking into account:

(i) the nature, scale, complexity and importance of ICT-related dependencies,

(ii) the risks arising from contractual arrangements on the use of ICT services concluded with ICT third-party service providers, taking into account the criticality or importance of the respective service, process or function, and the potential impact on the continuity and availability of financial services and activities, at individual and at group level.

2. As part of their ICT risk management framework, financial entities, other than entities referred to in Article 16(1), first subparagraph, and other than microenterprises, shall adopt, and regularly review, a strategy on ICT third-party risk, taking into account the multi-vendor strategy referred to in Article 6(9), where applicable. The strategy on ICT third-party risk shall include a policy on the use of ICT services supporting critical or important functions provided by ICT third-party service providers and shall apply on an individual basis and, where relevant, on a sub-consolidated and consolidated basis. The management body shall, on the basis of an assessment of the overall risk profile of the financial entity and the scale and complexity of the business services, regularly review the risks identified in respect to contractual arrangements on the use of ICT services supporting critical or important functions.

3. As part of their ICT risk management framework, financial entities shall maintain and update at entity level, and at sub-consolidated and consolidated levels, a register of information in relation to all contractual arrangements on the use of ICT services provided by ICT third-party service providers.

The contractual arrangements referred to in the first subparagraph shall be appropriately documented, distinguishing between those that cover ICT services supporting critical or important functions and those that do not.

Financial entities shall report at least yearly to the competent authorities on the number of new arrangements on the use of ICT services, the categories of ICT third-party service providers, the type of contractual arrangements and the ICT services and functions which are being provided.

Financial entities shall make available to the competent authority, upon its request, the full register of information or, as requested, specified sections thereof, along with any information deemed necessary to enable the effective supervision of the financial entity.

Financial entities shall inform the competent authority in a timely manner about any planned contractual arrangement on the use of ICT services supporting critical or important functions as well as when a function has become critical or important.

4. Before entering into a contractual arrangement on the use of ICT services, financial entities shall:

   (a) assess whether the contractual arrangement covers the use of ICT services supporting a critical or important function;

   (b) assess if supervisory conditions for contracting are met;

   (c) identify and assess all relevant risks in relation to the contractual arrangement, including the possibility that such contractual arrangement may contribute to reinforcing ICT concentration risk as referred to in Article 29;

   (d) undertake all due diligence on prospective ICT third-party service providers and ensure throughout the selection and assessment processes that the ICT third-party service provider is suitable;

   (e) identify and assess conflicts of interest that the contractual arrangement may cause.

5. Financial entities may only enter into contractual arrangements with ICT third-party service providers that comply with appropriate information security standards. When those contractual arrangements concern critical or important functions, financial entities shall, prior to concluding the arrangements, take due consideration of the use, by ICT third-party service providers, of the most up-to-date and highest quality information security standards.

6. In exercising access, inspection and audit rights over the ICT third-party service provider, financial entities shall, on the basis of a risk-based approach, pre-determine the frequency of audits and inspections as well as the areas to be audited through adhering to commonly accepted audit standards in line with any supervisory instruction on the use and incorporation of such audit standards.

   Where contractual arrangements concluded with ICT third-party service providers on the use of ICT services entail high technical complexity, the financial entity shall verify that auditors, whether internal or external, or a pool of auditors, possess appropriate skills and knowledge to effectively perform the relevant audits and assessments.

7. Financial entities shall ensure that contractual arrangements on the use of ICT services may be terminated in any of the following circumstances:

   (a) significant breach by the ICT third-party service provider of applicable laws, regulations or contractual terms;

   (b) circumstances identified throughout the monitoring of ICT third-party risk that are deemed capable of altering the performance of the functions provided through the contractual arrangement, including material changes that affect the arrangement or the situation of the ICT third-party service provider;

(c) ICT third-party service provider's evidenced weaknesses pertaining to its overall ICT risk management and in particular in the way it ensures the availability, authenticity, integrity and, confidentiality, of data, whether personal or otherwise sensitive data, or non-personal data;

(d) where the competent authority can no longer effectively supervise the financial entity as a result of the conditions of, or circumstances related to, the respective contractual arrangement.

8. For ICT services supporting critical or important functions, financial entities shall put in place exit strategies. The exit strategies shall take into account risks that may emerge at the level of ICT third-party service providers, in particular a possible failure on their part, a deterioration of the quality of the ICT services provided, any business disruption due to inappropriate or failed provision of ICT services or any material risk arising in relation to the appropriate and continuous deployment of the respective ICT service, or the termination of contractual arrangements with ICT third-party service providers under any of the circumstances listed in paragraph 7.

Financial entities shall ensure that they are able to exit contractual arrangements without:

(a) disruption to their business activities,

(b) limiting compliance with regulatory requirements,

(c) detriment to the continuity and quality of services provided to clients.

Exit plans shall be comprehensive, documented and, in accordance with the criteria set out in Article 4(2), shall be sufficiently tested and reviewed periodically.

Financial entities shall identify alternative solutions and develop transition plans enabling them to remove the contracted ICT services and the relevant data from the ICT third-party service provider and to securely and integrally transfer them to alternative providers or reincorporate them in-house.

Financial entities shall have appropriate contingency measures in place to maintain business continuity in the event of the circumstances referred to in the first subparagraph.

9. The ESAs shall, through the Joint Committee, develop draft implementing technical standards to establish the standard templates for the purposes of the register of information referred to in paragraph 3, including information that is common to all contractual arrangements on the use of ICT services. The ESAs shall submit those draft implementing technical standards to the Commission by 17 January 2024.

Power is conferred on the Commission to adopt the implementing technical standards referred to in the first subparagraph in accordance with Article 15 of Regulations (EU) No 1093/2010, (EU) No 1094/2010 and (EU) No 1095/2010.

10. The ESAs shall, through the Joint Committee, develop draft regulatory technical standards to further specify the detailed content of the policy referred to in paragraph 2 in relation to the contractual arrangements on the use of ICT services supporting critical or important functions provided by ICT third-party service providers.

When developing those draft regulatory technical standards, the ESAs shall take into account the size and the overall risk profile of the financial entity, and the nature, scale and complexity of its services, activities and operations. The ESAs shall submit those draft regulatory technical standards to the Commission by 17 January 2024.

Power is delegated to the Commission to supplement this Regulation by adopting the regulatory technical standards referred to in the first subparagraph in accordance with Articles 10 to 14 of Regulations (EU) No 1093/2010, (EU) No 1094/2010 and (EU) No 1095/2010.

Article 29
Preliminary assessment of ICT concentration risk at entity level

1. When performing the identification and assessment of risks referred to in Article 28(4), point (c), financial entities shall also take into account whether the envisaged conclusion of a contractual arrangement in relation to ICT services supporting critical or important functions would lead to any of the following:

   (a) contracting an ICT third-party service provider that is not easily substitutable; or

   (b) having in place multiple contractual arrangements in relation to the provision of ICT services supporting critical or important functions with the same ICT third-party service provider or with closely connected ICT third-party service providers.

   Financial entities shall weigh the benefits and costs of alternative solutions, such as the use of different ICT third-party service providers, taking into account if and how envisaged solutions match the business needs and objectives set out in their digital resilience strategy.

2. Where the contractual arrangements on the use of ICT services supporting critical or important functions include the possibility that an ICT third-party service provider further subcontracts ICT services supporting a critical or important function to other ICT third-party service providers, financial entities shall weigh benefits and risks that may arise in connection with such subcontracting, in particular in the case of an ICT subcontractor established in a third-country.

Where contractual arrangements concern ICT services supporting critical or important functions, financial entities shall duly consider the insolvency law provisions that would apply in the event of the ICT third-party service provider's bankruptcy as well as any constraint that may arise in respect to the urgent recovery of the financial entity's data.

Where contractual arrangements on the use of ICT services supporting critical or important functions are concluded with an ICT third-party service provider established in a third country, financial entities shall, in addition to the considerations referred to in the second subparagraph, also consider the compliance with Union data protection rules and the effective enforcement of the law in that third country.

Where the contractual arrangements on the use of ICT services supporting critical or important functions provide for subcontracting, financial entities shall assess whether and how potentially long or complex chains of subcontracting may impact their ability to fully monitor the contracted functions and the ability of the competent authority to effectively supervise the financial entity in that respect.

Article 30
Key contractual provisions

1. The rights and obligations of the financial entity and of the ICT third-party service provider shall be clearly allocated and set out in writing. The full contract shall include the service level agreements and be documented in one written document which shall be available to the parties on paper, or in a document with another downloadable, durable and accessible format.

2. The contractual arrangements on the use of ICT services shall include at least the following elements:

(a) a clear and complete description of all functions and ICT services to be provided by the ICT third-party service provider, indicating whether subcontracting of an ICT service supporting a critical or important function, or material parts thereof, is permitted and, when that is the case, the conditions applying to such subcontracting;

(b) the locations, namely the regions or countries, where the contracted or subcontracted functions and ICT services are to be provided and where data is to be processed, including the storage location, and the requirement for the ICT third-party service provider to notify the financial entity in advance if it envisages changing such locations;

(c) provisions on availability, authenticity, integrity and confidentiality in relation to the protection of data, including personal data;

(d) provisions on ensuring access, recovery and return in an easily accessible format of personal and non-personal data processed by the financial entity in the event of the insolvency, resolution or discontinuation of the business operations of the ICT third-party service provider, or in the event of the termination of the contractual arrangements;

(e) service level descriptions, including updates and revisions thereof;

(f) the obligation of the ICT third-party service provider to provide assistance to the financial entity at no additional cost, or at a cost that is determined ex-ante, when an ICT incident that is related to the ICT service provided to the financial entity occurs;

(g) the obligation of the ICT third-party service provider to fully cooperate with the competent authorities and the resolution authorities of the financial entity, including persons appointed by them;

(h) termination rights and related minimum notice periods for the termination of the contractual arrangements, in accordance with the expectations of competent authorities and resolution authorities;

(i) the conditions for the participation of ICT third-party service providers in the financial entities' ICT security awareness programmes and digital operational resilience training in accordance with Article 13(6).

3. The contractual arrangements on the use of ICT services supporting critical or important functions shall include, in addition to the elements referred to in paragraph 2, at least the following:

(a) full service level descriptions, including updates and revisions thereof with precise quantitative and qualitative performance targets within the agreed service levels to allow effective monitoring by the financial entity of ICT services and enable appropriate corrective actions to be taken, without undue delay, when agreed service levels are not met;

(b) notice periods and reporting obligations of the ICT third-party service provider to the financial entity, including notification of any development that might have a material impact on the ICT third-party service provider's ability to effectively provide the ICT services supporting critical or important functions in line with agreed service levels;

(c) requirements for the ICT third-party service provider to implement and test business contingency plans and to have in place ICT security measures, tools and policies that provide an appropriate level of security for the provision of services by the financial entity in line with its regulatory framework;

(d) the obligation of the ICT third-party service provider to participate and fully cooperate in the financial entity's TLPT as referred to in Articles 26 and 27;

(e) the right to monitor, on an ongoing basis, the ICT third-party service provider's performance, which entails the following:

(i) unrestricted rights of access, inspection and audit by the financial entity, or an appointed third party, and by the competent authority, and the right to take copies of relevant documentation on-site if they are critical to the operations of the ICT third-party service provider, the effective exercise of which is not impeded or limited by other contractual arrangements or implementation policies;

(ii) the right to agree on alternative assurance levels if other clients' rights are affected;

(iii) the obligation of the ICT third-party service provider to fully cooperate during the onsite inspections and audits performed by the competent authorities, the Lead Overseer, financial entity or an appointed third party; and

(iv) the obligation to provide details on the scope, procedures to be followed and frequency of such inspections and audits;

(f) exit strategies, in particular the establishment of a mandatory adequate transition period:

(i) during which the ICT third-party service provider will continue providing the respective functions, or ICT services, with a view to reducing the risk of disruption at the financial entity or to ensure its effective resolution and restructuring;

(ii) allowing the financial entity to migrate to another ICT third-party service provider or change to in-house solutions consistent with the complexity of the service provided.

By way of derogation from point (e), the ICT third-party service provider and the financial entity that is a microenterprise may agree that the financial entity's rights of access, inspection and audit can be delegated to an independent third party, appointed by the ICT third-party service provider, and that the financial entity is able to request information and assurance on the ICT third-party service provider's performance from the third party at any time.

4. When negotiating contractual arrangements, financial entities and ICT third-party service providers shall consider the use of standard contractual clauses developed by public authorities for specific services.

5. The ESAs shall, through the Joint Committee, develop draft regulatory technical standards to specify further the elements referred to in paragraph 2, point (a), which a financial entity needs to determine and assess when subcontracting ICT services supporting critical or important functions.

When developing those draft regulatory technical standards, the ESAs shall take into consideration the size and overall risk profile of the financial entity, and the nature, scale and complexity of its services, activities and operations.

The ESAs shall submit those draft regulatory technical standards to the Commission by 17 July 2024.

Power is delegated to the Commission to supplement this Regulation by adopting the regulatory technical standards referred to in the first subparagraph in accordance with Articles 10 to 14 of Regulations (EU) No 1093/2010, (EU) No 1094/2010 and (EU) No 1095/2010.

Section II
Oversight Framework of critical ICT third-party service providers

Article 31
Designation of critical ICT third-party service providers

1. The ESAs, through the Joint Committee and upon recommendation from the Oversight Forum established pursuant to Article 32(1), shall:

    (a) designate the ICT third-party service providers that are critical for financial entities, following an assessment that takes into account the criteria specified in paragraph 2;

    (b) appoint as Lead Overseer for each critical ICT third-party service provider the ESA that is responsible, in accordance with Regulations (EU) No 1093/2010, (EU) No 1094/2010 or (EU) No 1095/2010, for the financial entities having together the largest share of total assets out of the value of total assets of all financial entities using the services of the relevant critical ICT third-party service provider, as evidenced by the sum of the individual balance sheets of those financial entities.

2. The designation referred to in paragraph 1, point (a), shall be based on all of the following criteria in relation to ICT services provided by the ICT third-party service provider:

    (a) the systemic impact on the stability, continuity or quality of the provision of financial services in the event that the relevant ICT third-party service provider would face a large scale operational failure to provide its services, taking into account the number of financial entities and the total value of assets of financial entities to which the relevant ICT third-party service provider provides services;

    (b) the systemic character or importance of the financial entities that rely on the relevant ICT third-party service provider, assessed in accordance with the following parameters:

        (i) the number of global systemically important institutions (G-SIIs) or other systemically important institutions (O-SIIs) that rely on the respective ICT third-party service provider;

(ii) the interdependence between the G-SIIs or O-SIIs referred to in point (i) and other financial entities, including situations where the G-SIIs or O-SIIs provide financial infrastructure services to other financial entities;

(c) the reliance of financial entities on the services provided by the relevant ICT third-party service provider in relation to critical or important functions of financial entities that ultimately involve the same ICT third-party service provider, irrespective of whether financial entities rely on those services directly or indirectly, through subcontracting arrangements;

(d) the degree of substitutability of the ICT third-party service provider, taking into account the following parameters:

(i) the lack of real alternatives, even partial, due to the limited number of ICT third-party service providers active on a specific market, or the market share of the relevant ICT third-party service provider, or the technical complexity or sophistication involved, including in relation to any proprietary technology, or the specific features of the ICT third-party service provider's organisation or activity;

(ii) difficulties in relation to partially or fully migrating the relevant data and workloads from the relevant ICT third-party service provider to another ICT third-party service provider, due either to significant financial costs, time or other resources that the migration process may entail, or to increased ICT risk or other operational risks to which the financial entity may be exposed through such migration.

3. Where the ICT third-party service provider belongs to a group, the criteria referred to in paragraph 2 shall be considered in relation to the ICT services provided by the group as a whole.

4. Critical ICT third-party service providers which are part of a group shall designate one legal person as a coordination point to ensure adequate representation and communication with the Lead Overseer.

5. The Lead Overseer shall notify the ICT third-party service provider of the outcome of the assessment leading to the designation referred in paragraph 1, point (a). Within 6 weeks from the date of the notification, the ICT third-party service provider may submit to the Lead Overseer a reasoned statement with any relevant information for the purposes of the assessment. The Lead Overseer shall consider the reasoned statement and may request additional information to be submitted within 30 calendar days of the receipt of such statement.

After designating an ICT third-party service provider as critical, the ESAs, through the Joint Committee, shall notify the ICT third-party service provider of such designation and the starting date as from which they will effectively be subject to oversight activities. That starting date shall be no later than one month after the notification. The ICT third-party service provider shall notify the financial entities to which they provide services of their designation as critical.

6. The Commission is empowered to adopt a delegated act in accordance with Article 57 to supplement this Regulation by specifying further the criteria referred to in paragraph 2 of this Article, by 17 July 2024.

7. The designation referred to in paragraph 1, point (a), shall not be used until the Commission has adopted a delegated act in accordance with paragraph 6.

8. The designation referred to in paragraph 1, point (a), shall not apply to the following:

   (i) financial entities providing ICT services to other financial entities;

   (ii) ICT third-party service providers that are subject to oversight frameworks established for the purposes of supporting the tasks referred to in Article 127(2) of the Treaty on the Functioning of the European Union;

   (iii) ICT intra-group service providers;

   (iv) ICT third-party service providers providing ICT services solely in one Member State to financial entities that are only active in that Member State.

9. The ESAs, through the Joint Committee, shall establish, publish and update yearly the list of critical ICT third-party service providers at Union level.

10. For the purposes of paragraph 1, point (a), competent authorities shall, on a yearly and aggregated basis, transmit the reports referred to in Article 28(3), third subparagraph, to the Oversight Forum established pursuant to Article 32. The Oversight Forum shall assess the ICT third-party dependencies of financial entities based on the information received from the competent authorities.

11. The ICT third-party service providers that are not included in the list referred to in paragraph 9 may request to be designated as critical in accordance with paragraph 1, point (a).

    For the purpose of the first subparagraph, the ICT third-party service provider shall submit a reasoned application to EBA, ESMA or EIOPA, which, through the Joint Committee, shall decide whether to designate that ICT third-party service provider as critical in accordance with paragraph 1, point (a).

    The decision referred to in the second subparagraph shall be adopted and notified to the ICT third-party service provider within 6 months of receipt of the application.

12. Financial entities shall only make use of the services of an ICT third-party service provider established in a third country and which has been

designated as critical in accordance with paragraph 1, point (a), if the latter has established a subsidiary in the Union within the 12 months following the designation.

13. The critical ICT third-party service provider referred to in paragraph 12 shall notify the Lead Overseer of any changes to the structure of the management of the subsidiary established in the Union.

Article 32
Structure of the Oversight Framework

1. The Joint Committee, in accordance with Article 57(1) of Regulations (EU) No 1093/2010, (EU) No 1094/2010 and (EU) No 1095/2010, shall establish the Oversight Forum as a sub-committee for the purposes of supporting the work of the Joint Committee and of the Lead Overseer referred to in Article 31(1), point (b), in the area of ICT third-party risk across financial sectors. The Oversight Forum shall prepare the draft joint positions and the draft common acts of the Joint Committee in that area.

   The Oversight Forum shall regularly discuss relevant developments on ICT risk and vulnerabilities and promote a consistent approach in the monitoring of ICT third-party risk at Union level.

2. The Oversight Forum shall, on a yearly basis, undertake a collective assessment of the results and findings of the oversight activities conducted for all critical ICT third-party service providers and promote coordination measures to increase the digital operational resilience of financial entities, foster best practices on addressing ICT concentration risk and explore mitigants for cross-sector risk transfers.

3. The Oversight Forum shall submit comprehensive benchmarks for critical ICT third-party service providers to be adopted by the Joint Committee as joint positions of the ESAs in accordance with Article 56(1) of Regulations (EU) No 1093/2010, (EU) No 1094/2010 and (EU) No 1095/2010.

4. The Oversight Forum shall be composed of:

   (a) the Chairpersons of the ESAs;

   (b) one high-level representative from the current staff of the relevant competent authority referred to in Article 46 from each Member State;

   (c) the Executive Directors of each ESA and one representative from the Commission, from the ESRB, from ECB and from ENISA as observers;

   (d) where appropriate, one additional representative of a competent authority referred to in Article 46 from each Member State as observer;

   (e) where applicable, one representative of the competent authorities designated or established in accordance with Directive (EU)

2022/2555 responsible for the supervision of an essential or important entity subject to that Directive, which has been designated as a critical ICT third-party service provider, as observer.

The Oversight Forum may, where appropriate, seek the advice of independent experts appointed in accordance with paragraph 6.

5. Each Member State shall designate the relevant competent authority whose staff member shall be the high-level representative referred in paragraph 4, first subparagraph, point (b), and shall inform the Lead Overseer thereof.

The ESAs shall publish on their website the list of high-level representatives from the current staff of the relevant competent authority designated by Member States.

6. The independent experts referred to in paragraph 4, second subparagraph, shall be appointed by the Oversight Forum from a pool of experts selected following a public and transparent application process.

The independent experts shall be appointed on the basis of their expertise in financial stability, digital operational resilience and ICT security matters. They shall act independently and objectively in the sole interest of the Union as a whole and shall neither seek nor take instructions from Union institutions or bodies, from any government of a Member State or from any other public or private body.

7. In accordance with Article 16 of Regulations (EU) No 1093/2010, (EU) No 1094/2010 and (EU) No 1095/2010, the ESAs shall by 17 July 2024 issue, for the purposes of this Section, guidelines on the cooperation between the ESAs and the competent authorities covering the detailed procedures and conditions for the allocation and execution of tasks between competent authorities and the ESAs and the details on the exchanges of information which are necessary for competent authorities to ensure the follow-up of recommendations pursuant to Article 35(1), point (d), addressed to critical ICT third-party service providers.

8. The requirements set out in this Section shall be without prejudice to the application of Directive (EU) 2022/2555 and of other Union rules on oversight applicable to providers of cloud computing services.

9. The ESAs, through the Joint Committee and based on preparatory work conducted by the Oversight Forum, shall, on yearly basis, submit a report on the application of this Section to the European Parliament, the Council and the Commission.

Article 33
Tasks of the Lead Overseer

1. The Lead Overseer, appointed in accordance with Article 31(1), point (b), shall conduct the oversight of the assigned critical ICT third-party service providers and shall be, for the purposes of all matters related to the oversight, the primary point of contact for those critical ICT third-party service providers.

2. For the purposes of paragraph 1, the Lead Overseer shall assess whether each critical ICT third-party service provider has in place comprehensive, sound and effective rules, procedures, mechanisms and arrangements to manage the ICT risk which it may pose to financial entities.

The assessment referred to in the first subparagraph shall focus mainly on ICT services provided by the critical ICT third-party service provider supporting the critical or important functions of financial entities. Where necessary to address all relevant risks, that assessment shall extend to ICT services supporting functions other than those that are critical or important

3. The assessment referred to in paragraph 2 shall cover:

(a) ICT requirements to ensure, in particular, the security, availability, continuity, scalability and quality of services which the critical ICT third-party service provider provides to financial entities, as well as the ability to maintain at all times high standards of availability, authenticity, integrity or confidentiality of data;

(b) the physical security contributing to ensuring the ICT security, including the security of premises, facilities, data centres;

(c) the risk management processes, including ICT risk management policies, ICT business continuity policy and ICT response and recovery plans;

(d) the governance arrangements, including an organisational structure with clear, transparent and consistent lines of responsibility and accountability rules enabling effective ICT risk management;

(e) the identification, monitoring and prompt reporting of material ICT-related incidents to financial entities, the management and resolution of those incidents, in particular cyber-attacks;

(f) the mechanisms for data portability, application portability and interoperability, which ensure an effective exercise of termination rights by the financial entities;

(g) the testing of ICT systems, infrastructure and controls;

(h) the ICT audits;

(i) the use of relevant national and international standards applicable to the provision of its ICT services to the financial entities.

4. Based on the assessment referred to in paragraph 2, and in coordination with the Joint Oversight Network (JON) referred to in Article 34(1), the Lead Overseer shall adopt a clear, detailed and reasoned individual oversight plan describing the annual oversight objectives and the main oversight actions planned for each critical ICT third-party service provider. That plan shall be communicated yearly to the critical ICT third-party service provider.

Prior to the adoption of the oversight plan, the Lead Overseer shall communicate the draft oversight plan to the critical ICT third-party service provider.

Upon receipt of the draft oversight plan, the critical ICT third-party service provider may submit a reasoned statement within 15 calendar days evidencing the expected impact on customers which are entities falling outside of the scope of this Regulation and where appropriate, formulating solutions to mitigate risks.

5. Once the annual oversight plans referred to in paragraph 4 have been adopted and notified to the critical ICT third-party service providers, competent authorities may take measures concerning such critical ICT third-party service providers only in agreement with the Lead Overseer.

Article 34
Operational coordination between Lead Overseers

1. To ensure a consistent approach to oversight activities and with a view to enabling coordinated general oversight strategies and cohesive operational approaches and work methodologies, the three Lead Overseers appointed in accordance with Article 31(1), point (b), shall set up a JON to coordinate among themselves in the preparatory stages and to coordinate the conduct of oversight activities over their respective overseen critical ICT third-party service providers, as well as in the course of any action that may be needed pursuant to Article 42.

2. For the purposes of paragraph 1, the Lead Overseers shall draw up a common oversight protocol specifying the detailed procedures to be followed for carrying out the day-to-day coordination and for ensuring swift exchanges and reactions. The protocol shall be periodically revised to reflect operational needs, in particular the evolution of practical oversight arrangements.

3. The Lead Overseers may, on an ad-hoc basis, call on the ECB and ENISA to provide technical advice, share hands-on experience or join specific coordination meetings of the JON.

Article 35
Powers of the Lead Overseer

1. For the purposes of carrying out the duties laid down in this Section, the Lead Overseer shall have the following powers in respect of the critical ICT third-party service providers:

   (a) to request all relevant information and documentation in accordance with Article 37;

   (b) to conduct general investigations and inspections in accordance with Articles 38 and 39, respectively;

   (c) to request, after the completion of the oversight activities, reports specifying the actions that have been taken or the remedies that have been implemented by the critical ICT third-party service providers in relation to the recommendations referred to in point (d) of this paragraph;

(d) to issue recommendations on the areas referred to in Article 33(3), in particular concerning the following:

(i) the use of specific ICT security and quality requirements or processes, in particular in relation to the roll-out of patches, updates, encryption and other security measures which the Lead Overseer deems relevant for ensuring the ICT security of services provided to financial entities;

(ii) the use of conditions and terms, including their technical implementation, under which the critical ICT third-party service providers provide ICT services to financial entities, which the Lead Overseer deems relevant for preventing the generation of single points of failure, the amplification thereof, or for minimising the possible systemic impact across the Union's financial sector in the event of ICT concentration risk;

(iii) any planned subcontracting, where the Lead Overseer deems that further subcontracting, including subcontracting arrangements which the critical ICT third-party service providers plan to enter into with ICT third-party service providers or with ICT subcontractors established in a third country, may trigger risks for the provision of services by the financial entity, or risks to the financial stability, based on the examination of the information gathered in accordance with Articles 37 and 38;

(iv) refraining from entering into a further subcontracting arrangement, where the following cumulative conditions are met:

— the envisaged subcontractor is an ICT third-party service provider or an ICT subcontractor established in a third country;

— the subcontracting concerns critical or important functions of the financial entity; and

— the Lead Overseer deems that the use of such subcontracting poses a clear and serious risk to the financial stability of the Union or to financial entities, including to the ability of financial entities to comply with supervisory requirements.

For the purpose of point (iv) of this point, ICT third-party service providers shall, using the template referred to in Article 41(1), point (b), transmit the information regarding subcontracting to the Lead Overseer.

2. When exercising the powers referred to in this Article, the Lead Overseer shall:

(a) ensure regular coordination within the JON, and in particular shall seek consistent approaches, as appropriate, with regard to the oversight of critical ICT third-party service providers;

(b) take due account of the framework established by Directive (EU) 2022/2555 and, where necessary, consult the relevant competent authorities designated or established in accordance with that Directive, in order to avoid duplication of technical and organisational measures that might apply to critical ICT third-party service providers pursuant to that Directive;

(c) seek to minimise, to the extent possible, the risk of disruption to services provided by critical ICT third-party service providers to customers that are entities falling outside the scope of this Regulation.

3. The Lead Overseer shall consult the Oversight Forum before exercising the powers referred to in paragraph 1.

Before issuing recommendations in accordance with paragraph 1, point (d), the Lead Overseer shall give the opportunity to the ICT third-party service provider to provide, within 30 calendar days, relevant information evidencing the expected impact on customers that are entities falling outside the scope of this Regulation and, where appropriate, formulating solutions to mitigate risks.

4. The Lead Overseer shall inform the JON of the outcome of the exercise of the powers referred to in paragraph 1, points (a) and (b). The Lead Overseer shall, without undue delay, transmit the reports referred to in paragraph 1, point (c), to the JON and to the competent authorities of the financial entities using the ICT services of that critical ICT third-party service provider.

5. Critical ICT third-party service providers shall cooperate in good faith with the Lead Overseer, and assist it in the fulfilment of its tasks.

6. In the event of whole or partial non-compliance with the measures required to be taken pursuant to the exercise of the powers under paragraph 1, points (a), (b) and (c), and after the expiry of a period of at least 30 calendar days from the date on which the critical ICT third-party service provider received notification of the respective measures, the Lead Overseer shall adopt a decision imposing a periodic penalty payment to compel the critical ICT third-party service provider to comply with those measures.

7. The periodic penalty payment referred to in paragraph 6 shall be imposed on a daily basis until compliance is achieved and for no more than a period of six months following the notification of the decision to impose a periodic penalty payment to the critical ICT third-party service provider.

8. The amount of the periodic penalty payment, calculated from the date stipulated in the decision imposing the periodic penalty payment, shall be up to 1 % of the average daily worldwide turnover of the critical

ICT third-party service provider in the preceding business year. When determining the amount of the penalty payment, the Lead Overseer shall take into account the following criteria regarding non-compliance with the measures referred to in paragraph 6:

(a) the gravity and the duration of non-compliance;

(b) whether non-compliance has been committed intentionally or negligently;

(c) the level of cooperation of the ICT third-party service provider with the Lead Overseer.

For the purposes of the first subparagraph, in order to ensure a consistent approach, the Lead Overseer shall engage in consultation within the JON.

9. Penalty payments shall be of an administrative nature and shall be enforceable. Enforcement shall be governed by the rules of civil procedure in force in the Member State on the territory of which inspections and access shall be carried out. Courts of the Member State concerned shall have jurisdiction over complaints related to irregular conduct of enforcement. The amounts of the penalty payments shall be allocated to the general budget of the European Union.

10. The Lead Overseer shall disclose to the public every periodic penalty payment that has been imposed, unless such disclosure would seriously jeopardise the financial markets or cause disproportionate damage to the parties involved.

11. Before imposing a periodic penalty payment under paragraph 6, the Lead Overseer shall give the representatives of the critical ICT third-party service provider subject to the proceedings the opportunity to be heard on the findings and shall base its decisions only on findings on which the critical ICT third-party service provider subject to the proceedings has had an opportunity to comment.

The rights of the defence of the persons subject to the proceedings shall be fully respected in the proceedings. The critical ICT third-party service provider subject to the proceedings shall be entitled to have access to the file, subject to the legitimate interest of other persons in the protection of their business secrets. The right of access to the file shall not extend to confidential information or to the Lead Overseer's internal preparatory documents.

Article 36
Exercise of the powers of the Lead Overseer outside the Union

1. When oversight objectives cannot be attained by means of interacting with the subsidiary set up for the purpose of Article 31(12), or by exercising oversight activities on premises located in the Union, the Lead Overseer may exercise the powers, referred to in the following provisions, on any premises located in a third-country which is owned, or used in any way,

for the purposes of providing services to Union financial entities, by a critical ICT third-party service provider, in connection with its business operations, functions or services, including any administrative, business or operational offices, premises, lands, buildings or other properties:

(a) in Article 35(1), point (a); and

(b) in Article 35(1), point (b), in accordance with Article 38(2), points (a), (b) and (d), and in Article 39(1) and (2), point (a).

The powers referred to in the first subparagraph may be exercised subject to all of the following conditions:

(i) the conduct of an inspection in a third-country is deemed necessary by the Lead Overseer to allow it to fully and effectively perform its duties under this Regulation;

(ii) the inspection in a third-country is directly related to the provision of ICT services to financial entities in the Union;

(iii) the critical ICT third-party service provider concerned consents to the conduct of an inspection in a third-country; and

(iv) the relevant authority of the third-country concerned has been officially notified by the Lead Overseer and raised no objection thereto.

2. Without prejudice to the respective competences of the Union institutions and of Member States, for the purposes of paragraph 1, EBA, ESMA or EIOPA shall conclude administrative cooperation arrangements with the relevant authority of the third country in order to enable the smooth conduct of inspections in the third country concerned by the Lead Overseer and its designated team for its mission in that third country. Those cooperation arrangements shall not create legal obligations in respect of the Union and its Member States nor shall they prevent Member States and their competent authorities from concluding bilateral or multilateral arrangements with those third countries and their relevant authorities.

Those cooperation arrangements shall specify at least the following elements:

(a) the procedures for the coordination of oversight activities carried out under this Regulation and any analogous monitoring of ICT third-party risk in the financial sector exercised by the relevant authority of the third country concerned, including details for transmitting the agreement of the latter to allow the conduct, by the Lead Overseer and its designated team, of general investigations and on-site inspections as referred to in paragraph 1, first subparagraph, on the territory under its jurisdiction;

(b) the mechanism for the transmission of any relevant information between EBA, ESMA or EIOPA and the relevant authority of the third country concerned, in particular in connection with information that may be requested by the Lead Overseer pursuant to Article 37;

(c) the mechanisms for the prompt notification by the relevant authority of the third-country concerned to EBA, ESMA or EIOPA of cases where an ICT third-party service provider established in a third country and designated as critical in accordance with Article 31(1), point (a), is deemed to have infringed the requirements to which it is obliged to adhere pursuant to the applicable law of the third country concerned when providing services to financial institutions in that third country, as well as the remedies and penalties applied;

(d) the regular transmission of updates on regulatory or supervisory developments on the monitoring of ICT third-party risk of financial institutions in the third country concerned;

(e) the details for allowing, if needed, the participation of one representative of the relevant third-country authority in the inspections conducted by the Lead Overseer and the designated team.

3. When the Lead Overseer is not able to conduct oversight activities outside the Union, referred to in paragraphs 1 and 2, the Lead Overseer shall:

(a) exercise its powers under Article 35 on the basis of all facts and documents available to it;

(b) document and explain any consequence of its inability to conduct the envisaged oversight activities as referred to in this Article.

The potential consequences referred to in point (b) of this paragraph shall be taken into consideration in the Lead Overseer's recommendations issued pursuant to Article 35(1), point (d).

Article 37
Request for information

1. The Lead Overseer may, by simple request or by decision, require critical ICT third-party service providers to provide all information that is necessary for the Lead Overseer to carry out its duties under this Regulation, including all relevant business or operational documents, contracts, policies, documentation, ICT security audit reports, ICT-related incident reports, as well as any information relating to parties to whom the critical ICT third-party service provider has outsourced operational functions or activities.

2. When sending a simple request for information under paragraph 1, the Lead Overseer shall:

(a) refer to this Article as the legal basis of the request;

(b) state the purpose of the request;

(c) specify what information is required;

(d) set a time limit within which the information is to be provided;

(e) inform the representative of the critical ICT third-party service provider from whom the information is requested that he or she is not obliged to provide the information, but in the event of a voluntary reply to the request the information provided must not be incorrect or misleading.

3. When requiring by decision to supply information under paragraph 1, the Lead Overseer shall:

   (a) refer to this Article as the legal basis of the request;

   (b) state the purpose of the request;

   (c) specify what information is required;

   (d) set a time limit within which the information is to be provided;

   (e) indicate the periodic penalty payments provided for in Article 35(6) where the production of the required information is incomplete or when such information is not provided within the time limit referred to in point (d) of this paragraph;

   (f) indicate the right to appeal the decision to ESA's Board of Appeal and to have the decision reviewed by the Court of Justice of the European Union (Court of Justice) in accordance with Articles 60 and 61 of Regulations (EU) No 1093/2010, (EU) No 1094/2010 and (EU) No 1095/2010.

4. The representatives of the critical ICT third-party service providers shall supply the information requested. Lawyers duly authorised to act may supply the information on behalf of their clients. The critical ICT third-party service provider shall remain fully responsible if the information supplied is incomplete, incorrect or misleading.

5. The Lead Overseer shall, without delay, transmit a copy of the decision to supply information to the competent authorities of the financial entities using the services of the relevant critical ICT third-party service providers and to the JON.

Article 38
General investigations

1. In order to carry out its duties under this Regulation, the Lead Overseer, assisted by the joint examination team referred to in Article 40(1), may, where necessary, conduct investigations of critical ICT third-party service providers.

2. The Lead Overseer shall have the power to:

   (a) examine records, data, procedures and any other material relevant to the execution of its tasks, irrespective of the medium on which they are stored;

   (b) take or obtain certified copies of, or extracts from, such records, data, documented procedures and any other material;

(c) summon representatives of the critical ICT third-party service provider for oral or written explanations on facts or documents relating to the subject matter and purpose of the investigation and to record the answers;

(d) interview any other natural or legal person who consents to be interviewed for the purpose of collecting information relating to the subject matter of an investigation;

(e) request records of telephone and data traffic.

3. The officials and other persons authorised by the Lead Overseer for the purposes of the investigation referred to in paragraph 1 shall exercise their powers upon production of a written authorisation specifying the subject matter and purpose of the investigation.

That authorisation shall also indicate the periodic penalty payments provided for in Article 35(6) where the production of the required records, data, documented procedures or any other material, or the answers to questions asked to representatives of the ICT third-party service provider are not provided or are incomplete.

4. The representatives of the critical ICT third-party service providers are required to submit to the investigations on the basis of a decision of the Lead Overseer. The decision shall specify the subject matter and purpose of the investigation, the periodic penalty payments provided for in Article 35(6), the legal remedies available under Regulations (EU) No 1093/2010, (EU) No 1094/2010 and (EU) No 1095/2010, and the right to have the decision reviewed by the Court of Justice.

5. In good time before the start of the investigation, the Lead Overseer shall inform competent authorities of the financial entities using the ICT services of that critical ICT third-party service provider of the envisaged investigation and of the identity of the authorised persons.

The Lead Overseer shall communicate to the JON all information transmitted pursuant to the first subparagraph.

Article 39
Inspections

1. In order to carry out its duties under this Regulation, the Lead Overseer, assisted by the joint examination teams referred to in Article 40(1), may enter in, and conduct all necessary onsite inspections on, any business premises, land or property of the ICT third-party service providers, such as head offices, operation centres, secondary premises, as well as to conduct off-site inspections.

For the purposes of exercising the powers referred to in the first subparagraph, the Lead Overseer shall consult the JON.

2. The officials and other persons authorised by the Lead Overseer to conduct an on-site inspection shall have the power to:

(a) enter any such business premises, land or property; and

(b) seal any such business premises, books or records, for the period of, and to the extent necessary for, the inspection.

The officials and other persons authorised by the Lead Overseer shall exercise their powers upon production of a written authorisation specifying the subject matter and the purpose of the inspection, and the periodic penalty payments provided for in Article 35(6) where the representatives of the critical ICT third-party service providers concerned do not submit to the inspection.

3. In good time before the start of the inspection, the Lead Overseer shall inform the competent authorities of the financial entities using that ICT third-party service provider.

4. Inspections shall cover the full range of relevant ICT systems, networks, devices, information and data either used for, or contributing to, the provision of ICT services to financial entities.

5. Before any planned on-site inspection, the Lead Overseer shall give reasonable notice to the critical ICT third-party service providers, unless such notice is not possible due to an emergency or crisis situation, or if it would lead to a situation where the inspection or audit would no longer be effective.

6. The critical ICT third-party service provider shall submit to on-site inspections ordered by decision of the Lead Overseer. The decision shall specify the subject matter and purpose of the inspection, fix the date on which the inspection shall begin and shall indicate the periodic penalty payments provided for in Article 35(6), the legal remedies available under Regulations (EU) No 1093/2010, (EU) No 1094/2010 and (EU) No 1095/2010, as well as the right to have the decision reviewed by the Court of Justice.

7. Where the officials and other persons authorised by the Lead Overseer find that a critical ICT third-party service provider opposes an inspection ordered pursuant to this Article, the Lead Overseer shall inform the critical ICT third-party service provider of the consequences of such opposition, including the possibility for competent authorities of the relevant financial entities to require financial entities to terminate the contractual arrangements concluded with that critical ICT third-party service provider.

Article 40
Ongoing oversight

1. When conducting oversight activities, in particular general investigations or inspections, the Lead Overseer shall be assisted by a joint examination team established for each critical ICT third-party service provider.

2. The joint examination team referred to in paragraph 1 shall be composed of staff members from:

(a) the ESAs;

(b) the relevant competent authorities supervising the financial entities to which the critical ICT third-party service provider provides ICT services;

(c) the national competent authority referred to in Article 32(4), point (e), on a voluntary basis;

(d) one national competent authority from the Member State where the critical ICT third-party service provider is established, on a voluntary basis.

Members of the joint examination team shall have expertise in ICT matters and in operational risk. The joint examination team shall work under the coordination of a designated Lead Overseer staff member (the 'Lead Overseer coordinator').

3. Within 3 months of the completion of an investigation or inspection, the Lead Overseer, after consulting the Oversight Forum, shall adopt recommendations to be addressed to the critical ICT third-party service provider pursuant to the powers referred to in Article 35.

4. The recommendations referred to in paragraph 3 shall be immediately communicated to the critical ICT third-party service provider and to the competent authorities of the financial entities to which it provides ICT services.

For the purposes of fulfilling the oversight activities, the Lead Overseer may take into consideration any relevant third-party certifications and ICT third-party internal or external audit reports made available by the critical ICT third-party service provider.

Article 41
Harmonisation of conditions enabling the conduct of the oversight activities

1. The ESAs shall, through the Joint Committee, develop draft regulatory technical standards to specify:

(a) the information to be provided by an ICT third-party service provider in the application for a voluntary request to be designated as critical under Article 31(11);

(b) the content, structure and format ofthe information to be submitted, disclosed or reported by the ICT third-party service providers pursuant to Article 35(1), including the template for providing information on subcontracting arrangements;

(c) the criteria for determining the composition of the joint examination team ensuring a balanced participation of staff members from the ESAs and from the relevant competent authorities, their designation, tasks, and working arrangements.

(d) the details of the competent authorities' assessment of the measures taken by critical ICT third-party service providers based on the recommendations of the Lead Overseer pursuant to Article 42(3).

2. The ESAs shall submit those draft regulatory technical standards to the Commission by 17 July 2024.

Power is delegated to the Commission to supplement this Regulation by adopting the regulatory technical standards referred to in paragraph 1 in accordance with the procedure laid down in Articles 10 to 14 of Regulations (EU) No 1093/2010, (EU) No 1094/2010 and (EU) No 1095/2010.

Article 42
Follow-up by competent authorities

1. Within 60 calendar days of the receipt of the recommendations issued by the Lead Overseer pursuant to Article 35(1), point (d), critical ICT third-party service providers shall either notify the Lead Overseer of their intention to follow the recommendations or provide a reasoned explanation for not following such recommendations. The Lead Overseer shall immediately transmit this information to the competent authorities of the financial entities concerned.

2. The Lead Overseer shall publicly disclose where a critical ICT third-party service provider fails to notify the Lead Overseer in accordance with paragraph 1 or where the explanation provided by the critical ICT third-party service provider is not deemed sufficient. The information published shall disclose the identity of the critical ICT third-party service provider as well as information on the type and nature of the non-compliance. Such information shall be limited to what is relevant and proportionate for the purpose of ensuring public awareness, unless such publication would cause disproportionate damage to the parties involved or could seriously jeopardise the orderly functioning and integrity of financial markets or the stability of the whole or part of the financial system of the Union.

The Lead Overseer shall notify the ICT third-party service provider of that public disclosure.

3. Competent authorities shall inform the relevant financial entities of the risks identified in the recommendations addressed to critical ICT third-party service providers in accordance with Article 35(1), point (d).

When managing ICT third-party risk, financial entities shall take into account the risks referred to in the first subparagraph.

4. Where a competent authority deems that a financial entity fails to take into account or to sufficiently address within its management of ICT third-party risk the specific risks identified in the recommendations, it shall notify the financial entity of the possibility of a decision being taken, within 60 calendar days of the receipt of such notification, pursuant to paragraph 6, in the absence of appropriate contractual arrangements aiming to address such risks.

5. Upon receiving the reports referred to in Article 35(1), point (c), and prior to taking a decision as referred to in paragraph 6 of this Article, competent authorities may, on a voluntary basis, consult the competent authorities designated or established in accordance with Directive (EU) 2022/2555 responsible for the supervision of an essential or important entity subject to that Directive, which has been designated as a critical ICT third-party service provider.

6. Competent authorities may, as a measure of last resort, following the notification and, if appropriate, the consultation as set out in paragraph 4 and 5 of this Article, in accordance with Article 50, take a decision requiring financial entities to temporarily suspend, either in part or completely, the use or deployment of a service provided by the critical ICT third-party service provider until the risks identified in the recommendations addressed to critical ICT third-party service providers have been addressed. Where necessary, they may require financial entities to terminate, in part or completely, the relevant contractual arrangements concluded with the critical ICT third-party service providers.

7. Where a critical ICT third-party service provider refuses to endorse recommendations, based on a divergent approach from the one advised by the Lead Overseer, and such a divergent approach may adversely impact a large number of financial entities, or a significant part of the financial sector, and individual warnings issued by competent authorities have not resulted in consistent approaches mitigating the potential risk to financial stability, the Lead Overseer may, after consulting the Oversight Forum, issue non-binding and non-public opinions to competent authorities, in order to promote consistent and convergent supervisory follow-up measures, as appropriate.

8. Upon receiving the reports referred to in Article 35(1), point (c), competent authorities, when taking a decision as referred to in paragraph 6 of this Article, shall take into account the type and magnitude of risk that is not addressed by the critical ICT third-party service provider, as well as the seriousness of the non-compliance, having regard to the following criteria:

(a) the gravity and the duration of the non-compliance;

(b) whether the non-compliance has revealed serious weaknesses in the critical ICT third-party service provider's procedures, management systems, risk management and internal controls;

(c) whether a financial crime was facilitated, occasioned or is otherwise attributable to the non-compliance;

(d) whether the non-compliance has been intentional or negligent;

(e) whether the suspension or termination of the contractual arrangements introduces a risk for continuity of the financial entity's business operations notwithstanding the financial entity's efforts to avoid disruption in the provision of its services;

(f) where applicable, the opinion of the competent authorities designated or established in accordance with Directive (EU) 2022/2555 responsible for the supervision of an essential or important entity subject to that Directive, which has been designated as a critical ICT third-party service provider, requested on a voluntary basis in accordance with paragraph 5 of this Article.

Competent authorities shall grant financial entities the necessary period of time to enable them to adjust the contractual arrangements with critical ICT third-party service providers in order to avoid detrimental effects on their digital operational resilience and to allow them to deploy exit strategies and transition plans as referred to in Article 28.

9. The decision referred to in paragraph 6 of this Article shall be notified to the members of the Oversight Forum referred to in Article 32(4), points (a), (b) and (c), and to the JON.

The critical ICT third-party service providers affected by the decisions provided for in paragraph 6 shall fully cooperate with the financial entities impacted, in particular in the context of the process of suspension or termination of their contractual arrangements.

10. Competent authorities shall regularly inform the Lead Overseer on the approaches and measures taken in their supervisory tasks in relation to financial entities as well as on the contractual arrangements concluded by financial entities where critical ICT third-party service providers have not endorsed in part or entirely recommendations addressed to them by the Lead Overseer.

11. The Lead Overseer may, upon request, provide further clarifications on the recommendations issued to guide the competent authorities on the follow-up measures.

Article 43
Oversight fees

1. The Lead Overseer shall, in accordance with the delegated act referred to in paragraph 2 of this Article, charge critical ICT third-party service providers fees that fully cover the Lead Overseer's necessary expenditure in relation to the conduct of oversight tasks pursuant to this Regulation, including the reimbursement of any costs which may be incurred as a result of work carried out by the joint examination team referred to in Article 40, as well as the costs of advice provided by the independent experts as referred to in Article 32(4), second subparagraph, in relation to matters falling under the remit of direct oversight activities.

The amount of a fee charged to a critical ICT third-party service provider shall cover all costs derived from the execution of the duties set out in this Section and shall be proportionate to its turnover.

2. The Commission is empowered to adopt a delegated act in accordance with Article 57 to supplement this Regulation by determining the amount of the fees and the way in which they are to be paid by 17 July 2024.

Article 44
International cooperation

1. Without prejudice to Article 36, EBA, ESMA and EIOPA may, in accordance with Article 33 of Regulations (EU) No 1093/2010, (EU) No 1095/2010 and (EU) No 1094/2010, respectively, conclude administrative arrangements with third-country regulatory and supervisory authorities to foster international cooperation on ICT third-party risk across different financial sectors, in particular by developing best practices for the review of ICT risk management practices and controls, mitigation measures and incident responses.

2. The ESAs shall, through the Joint Committee, submit every five years a joint confidential report to the European Parliament, to the Council and to the Commission, summarising the findings of relevant discussions held with the third countries' authorities referred to in paragraph 1, focusing on the evolution of ICT third-party risk and the implications for financial stability, market integrity, investor protection and the functioning of the internal market.

CHAPTER VI
Information-sharing arrangements

Article 45
Information-sharing arrangements on cyber threat information and intelligence

1. Financial entities may exchange amongst themselves cyber threat information and intelligence, including indicators of compromise, tactics, techniques, and procedures, cyber security alerts and configuration tools, to the extent that such information and intelligence sharing:

    (a) aims to enhance the digital operational resilience of financial entities, in particular through raising awareness in relation to cyber threats, limiting or impeding the cyber threats' ability to spread, supporting defence capabilities, threat detection techniques, mitigation strategies or response and recovery stages;

    (b) takes places within trusted communities of financial entities;

    (c) is implemented through information-sharing arrangements that protect the potentially sensitive nature of the information shared, and that are governed by rules of conduct in full respect of business confidentiality, protection of personal data in accordance with Regulation (EU) 2016/679 and guidelines on competition policy.

2. For the purpose of paragraph 1, point (c), the information-sharing arrangements shall define the conditions for participation and, where appropriate, shall set out the details on the involvement of public authorities and the capacity in which they may be associated to the information-sharing arrangements, on the involvement of ICT third-party service providers, and on operational elements, including the use of dedicated IT platforms.

3. Financial entities shall notify competent authorities of their participation in the information-sharing arrangements referred to in paragraph 1, upon validation of their membership, or, as applicable, of the cessation of their membership, once it takes effect.

CHAPTER VII
Competent authorities

Article 46
Competent authorities

Without prejudice to the provisions on the Oversight Framework for critical ICT third-party service providers referred to in Chapter V, Section II, of this Regulation, compliance with this Regulation shall be ensured by the following competent authorities in accordance with the powers granted by the respective legal acts:

(a) for credit institutions and for institutions exempted pursuant to Directive 2013/36/EU, the competent authority designated in accordance with Article 4 of that Directive, and for credit institutions classified as significant in accordance with Article 6(4) of Regulation (EU) No 1024/2013, the ECB in accordance with the powers and tasks conferred by that Regulation;

(b) for payment institutions, including payment institutions exempted pursuant to Directive (EU) 2015/2366, electronic money institutions, including those exempted pursuant to Directive 2009/110/EC, and account information service providers as referred to in Article 33(1) of Directive (EU) 2015/2366, the competent authority designated in accordance with Article 22 of Directive (EU) 2015/2366;

(c) for investment firms, the competent authority designated in accordance with Article 4 of Directive (EU) 2019/2034 of the European Parliament and of the Council([38]);

(d) for crypto-asset service providers as authorised under the Regulation on markets in crypto-assets and issuers of asset-referenced tokens, the competent authority designated in accordance with the relevant provision of that Regulation;

(e) for central securities depositories, the competent authority designated in accordance with Article 11 of Regulation (EU) No 909/2014;

(f) for central counterparties, the competent authority designated in accordance with Article 22 of Regulation (EU) No 648/2012;

(g) for trading venues and data reporting service providers, the competent authority designated in accordance with Article 67 of Directive 2014/65/

38 Directive (EU) 2019/2034 of the European Parliament and of the Council of 27 November 2019 on the prudential supervision of investment firms and amending Directives 2002/87/EC, 2009/65/EC, 2011/61/EU, 2013/36/EU, 2014/59/EU and 2014/65/EU (OJ L 314, 5.12.2019, p. 64).

EU, and the competent authority as defined in Article 2(1), point (18), of Regulation (EU) No 600/2014;

(h) for trade repositories, the competent authority designated in accordance with Article 22 of Regulation (EU) No 648/2012;

(i) for managers of alternative investment funds, the competent authority designated in accordance with Article 44 of Directive 2011/61/EU;

(j) for management companies, the competent authority designated in accordance with Article 97 of Directive 2009/65/EC;

(k) for insurance and reinsurance undertakings, the competent authority designated in accordance with Article 30 of Directive 2009/138/EC;

(l) for insurance intermediaries, reinsurance intermediaries and ancillary insurance intermediaries, the competent authority designated in accordance with Article 12 of Directive (EU) 2016/97;

(m) for institutions for occupational retirement provision, the competent authority designated in accordance with Article 47 of Directive (EU) 2016/2341;

(n) for credit rating agencies, the competent authority designated in accordance with Article 21 of Regulation (EC) No 1060/2009;

(o) for administrators of critical benchmarks, the competent authority designated in accordance with Articles 40 and 41 of Regulation (EU) 2016/1011;

(p) for crowdfunding service providers, the competent authority designated in accordance with Article 29 of Regulation (EU) 2020/1503;

(q) for securitisation repositories, the competent authority designated in accordance with Articles 10 and 14(1) of Regulation (EU) 2017/2402.

Article 47
Cooperation with structures and authorities established by Directive (EU) 2022/2555

1. To foster cooperation and enable supervisory exchanges between the competent authorities designated under this Regulation and the Cooperation Group established by Article 14 of Directive (EU) 2022/2555, the ESAs and the competent authorities may participate in the activities of the Cooperation Group for matters that concern their supervisory activities in relation to financial entities. The ESAs and the competent authorities may request to be invited to participate in the activities of the Cooperation Group for matters in relation to essential or important entities subject to Directive (EU) 2022/2555 that have also been designated as critical ICT third-party service providers pursuant to Article 31 of this Regulation.

2. Where appropriate, competent authorities may consult and share information with the single points of contact and the CSIRTs designated or established in accordance with Directive (EU) 2022/2555.

3. Where appropriate, competent authorities may request any relevant technical advice and assistance from the competent authorities designated or established in accordance with Directive (EU) 2022/2555 and establish cooperation arrangements to allow effective and fast-response coordination mechanisms to be set up.

4. The arrangements referred to in paragraph 3 of this Article may, inter alia, specify the procedures for the coordination of supervisory and oversight activities in relation to essential or important entities subject to Directive (EU) 2022/2555 that have been designated as critical ICT third-party service providers pursuant to Article 31 of this Regulation, including for the conduct, in accordance with national law, of investigations and on-site inspections, as well as for mechanisms for the exchange of information between the competent authorities under this Regulation and the competent authorities designated or established in accordance with that Directive which includes access to information requested by the latter authorities.

Article 48
Cooperation between authorities

1. Competent authorities shall cooperate closely among themselves and, where applicable, with the Lead Overseer.

2. Competent authorities and the Lead Overseer shall, in a timely manner, mutually exchange all relevant information concerning critical ICT third-party service providers which is necessary for them to carry out their respective duties under this Regulation, in particular in relation to identified risks, approaches and measures taken as part of the Lead Overseer's oversight tasks.

Article 49
Financial cross-sector exercises, communication and cooperation

1. The ESAs, through the Joint Committee and in collaboration with competent authorities, resolution authorities as referred to in Article 3 of Directive 2014/59/EU, the ECB, the Single Resolution Board as regards information relating to entities falling under the scope of Regulation (EU) No 806/2014, the ESRB and ENISA, as appropriate, may establish mechanisms to enable the sharing of effective practices across financial sectors to enhance situational awareness and identify common cyber vulnerabilities and risks across sectors.

   They may develop crisis management and contingency exercises involving cyber-attack scenarios with a view to developing communication channels and gradually enabling an effective coordinated response at Union level in the event of a major cross-border ICT-related incident or related threat having a systemic impact on the Union's financial sector as a whole.

   Those exercises may, as appropriate, also test the financial sector's dependencies on other economic sectors.

2. Competent authorities, ESAs and the ECB shall cooperate closely with each other and exchange information to carry out their duties pursuant to Articles 47 to 54. They shall closely coordinate their supervision in order to identify and remedy breaches of this Regulation, develop and promote best practices, facilitate collaboration, foster consistency of interpretation and provide cross-jurisdictional assessments in the event of any disagreements.

Article 50
Administrative penalties and remedial measures

1. Competent authorities shall have all supervisory, investigatory and sanctioning powers necessary to fulfil their duties under this Regulation.

2. The powers referred to in paragraph 1 shall include at least the following powers to:

   (a) have access to any document or data held in any form that the competent authority considers relevant for the performance of its duties and receive or take a copy of it;

   (b) carry out on-site inspections or investigations, which shall include but shall not be limited to;

      (i) summoning representatives of the financial entities for oral or written explanations on facts or documents relating to the subject matter and purpose of the investigation and to record the answers;

      (ii) Interviewing any other natural or legal person who consents to be interviewed for the purpose of collecting information relating to the subject matter of an investigation;

   (c) require corrective and remedial measures for breaches of the requirements of this Regulation.

3. Without prejudice to the right of Member States to impose criminal penalties in accordance with Article 52, Member States shall lay down rules establishing appropriate administrative penalties and remedial measures for breaches of this Regulation and shall ensure their effective implementation.

   Those penalties and measures shall be effective, proportionate and dissuasive.

4. Member States shall confer on competent authorities the power to apply at least the following administrative penalties or remedial measures for breaches of this Regulation:

   (a) issue an order requiring the natural or legal person to cease conduct that is in breach of this Regulation and to desist from a repetition of that conduct;

(b) require the temporary or permanent cessation of any practice or conduct that the competent authority considers to be contrary to the provisions of this Regulation and prevent repetition of that practice or conduct;

(c) adopt any type of measure, including of pecuniary nature, to ensure that financial entities continue to comply with legal requirements;

(d) require, insofar as permitted by national law, existing data traffic records held by a telecommunication operator, where there is a reasonable suspicion of a breach of this Regulation and where such records may be relevant to an investigation into breaches of this Regulation; and

(e) issue public notices, including public statements indicating the identity of the natural or legal person and the nature of the breach.

5. Where paragraph 2, point (c), and paragraph 4 apply to legal persons, Member States shall confer on competent authorities the power to apply the administrative penalties and remedial measures, subject to the conditions provided for in national law, to members of the management body, and to other individuals who under national law are responsible for the breach.

6. Member States shall ensure that any decision imposing administrative penalties or remedial measures set out in paragraph 2, point (c), is properly reasoned and is subject to a right of appeal.

Article 51
Exercise of the power to impose administrative penalties and remedial measures

1. Competent authorities shall exercise the powers to impose administrative penalties and remedial measures referred to in Article 50 in accordance with their national legal frameworks, where appropriate, as follows:

(a) directly;

(b) in collaboration with other authorities;

(c) under their responsibility by delegation to other authorities; or

(d) by application to the competent judicial authorities.

2. Competent authorities, when determining the type and level of an administrative penalty or remedial measure to be imposed under Article 50, shall take into account the extent to which the breach is intentional or results from negligence, and all other relevant circumstances, including the following, where appropriate:

(a) the materiality, gravity and the duration of the breach;

(b) the degree of responsibility of the natural or legal person responsible for the breach;

(c) the financial strength of the responsible natural or legal person;

(d) the importance of profits gained or losses avoided by the responsible natural or legal person, insofar as they can be determined;

(e) the losses for third parties caused by the breach, insofar as they can be determined;

(f) the level of cooperation of the responsible natural or legal person with the competent authority, without prejudice to the need to ensure disgorgement of profits gained or losses avoided by that natural or legal person;

(g) previous breaches by the responsible natural or legal person.

Article 52
Criminal penalties

1. Member States may decide not to lay down rules for administrative penalties or remedial measures for breaches that are subject to criminal penalties under their national law.

2. Where Member States have chosen to lay down criminal penalties for breaches of this Regulation, they shall ensure that appropriate measures are in place so that competent authorities have all the necessary powers to liaise with judicial, prosecuting, or criminal justice authorities within their jurisdiction to receive specific information related to criminal investigations or proceedings commenced for breaches of this Regulation, and to provide the same information to other competent authorities, as well as EBA, ESMA or EIOPA to fulfil their obligations to cooperate for the purposes of this Regulation.

Article 53
Notification duties

Member States shall notify the laws, regulations and administrative provisions implementing this Chapter, including any relevant criminal law provisions, to the Commission, ESMA, the EBA and EIOPA by 17 January 2025. Member States shall notify the Commission, ESMA, the EBA and EIOPA without undue delay of any subsequent amendments thereto.

Article 54
Publication of administrative penalties

1. Competent authorities shall publish on their official websites, without undue delay, any decision imposing an administrative penalty against which there is no appeal after the addressee of the penalty has been notified of that decision.

2. The publication referred to in paragraph 1 shall include information on the type and nature of the breach, the identity of the persons responsible and the penalties imposed.

3. Where the competent authority, following a case-by-case assessment, considers that the publication of the identity, in the case of legal persons, or of the identity and personal data, in the case of natural persons, would be disproportionate, including risks in relation to the protection of personal data, jeopardise the stability of financial markets or the pursuit of an ongoing criminal investigation, or cause, insofar as these can be determined, disproportionate damages to the person involved, it shall adopt one of the following solutions in respect of the decision imposing an administrative penalty:

   (a) defer its publication until all reasons for non-publication cease to exist;

   (b) publish it on an anonymous basis, in accordance with national law; or

   (c) refrain from publishing it, where the options set out in points (a) and (b) are deemed either insufficient to guarantee a lack of any danger for the stability of financial markets, or where such a publication would not be proportionate to the leniency of the imposed penalty.

4. In the case of a decision to publish an administrative penalty on an anonymous basis in accordance with paragraph 3, point (b), the publication of the relevant data may be postponed.

5. Where a competent authority publishes a decision imposing an administrative penalty against which there is an appeal before the relevant judicial authorities, competent authorities shall immediately add on their official website that information and, at later stages, any subsequent related information on the outcome of such appeal. Any judicial decision annulling a decision imposing an administrative penalty shall also be published.

6. Competent authorities shall ensure that any publication referred to in paragraphs 1 to 4 shall remain on their official website only for the period which is necessary to bring forth this Article. This period shall not exceed five years after its publication.

Article 55
Professional secrecy

1. Any confidential information received, exchanged or transmitted pursuant to this Regulation shall be subject to the conditions of professional secrecy laid down in paragraph 2.

2. The obligation of professional secrecy applies to all persons who work, or who have worked, for the competent authorities pursuant to this Regulation, or for any authority or market undertaking or natural or legal person to whom those competent authorities have delegated their powers, including auditors and experts contracted by them.

3. Information covered by professional secrecy, including the exchange of information among competent authorities under this Regulation and

competent authorities designated or established in accordance with Directive (EU) 2022/2555, shall not be disclosed to any other person or authority except by virtue of provisions laid down by Union or national law;

4. All information exchanged between the competent authorities pursuant to this Regulation that concerns business or operational conditions and other economic or personal affairs shall be considered confidential and shall be subject to the requirements of professional secrecy, except where the competent authority states, at the time of communication, that such information may be disclosed or where such disclosure is necessary for legal proceedings.

Article 56
Data Protection

1. The ESAs and the competent authorities shall be allowed to process personal data only where necessary for the purpose of carrying out their respective obligations and duties pursuant to this Regulation, in particular for investigation, inspection, request for information, communication, publication, evaluation, verification, assessment and drafting of oversight plans. The personal data shall be processed in accordance with Regulation (EU) 2016/679 or Regulation (EU) 2018/1725, whichever is applicable.

2. Except where otherwise provided in other sectoral acts, the personal data referred to in paragraph 1 shall be retained until the discharge of the applicable supervisory duties and in any case for a maximum period of 15 years, except in the event of pending court proceedings requiring further retention of such data.

CHAPTER VIII
Delegated acts

Article 57
Exercise of the delegation

1. The power to adopt delegated acts is conferred on the Commission subject to the conditions laid down in this Article.

2. The power to adopt delegated acts referred to in Articles 31(6) and 43(2) shall be conferred on the Commission for a period of five years from 17 January 2024. The Commission shall draw up a report in respect of the delegation of power not later than nine months before the end of the five-year period. The delegation of power shall be tacitly extended for periods of an identical duration, unless the European Parliament or the Council opposes such extension not later than three months before the end of each period.

3. The delegation of power referred to in Articles 31(6) and 43(2) may be revoked at any time by the European Parliament or by the Council. A decision to revoke shall put an end to the delegation of the power specified in that decision. It shall take effect the day following the publication of

the decision in the Official Journal of the European Union or at a later date specified therein. It shall not affect the validity of any delegated acts already in force.

4. Before adopting a delegated act, the Commission shall consult experts designated by each Member State in accordance with the principles laid down in the Interinstitutional Agreement of 13 April 2016 on Better Law-Making.

5. As soon as it adopts a delegated act, the Commission shall notify it simultaneously to the European Parliament and to the Council.

6. A delegated act adopted pursuant to Articles 31(6) and 43(2) shall enter into force only if no objection has been expressed either by the European Parliament or by the Council within a period of three months of notification of that act to the European Parliament and the Council or if, before the expiry of that period, the European Parliament and the Council have both informed the Commission that they will not object. That period shall be extended by three months at the initiative of the European Parliament or of the Council.

CHAPTER IX
Transitional and final provisions

Section I
Article 58
Review clause

1. By 17 January 2028, the Commission shall, after consulting the ESAs and the ESRB, as appropriate, carry out a review and submit a report to the European Parliament and the Council, accompanied, where appropriate, by a legislative proposal. The review shall include at least the following:

   (a) the criteria for the designation of critical ICT third-party service providers in accordance with Article 31(2);

   (b) the voluntary nature of the notification of significant cyber threats referred to in Article 19;

   (c) the regime referred to in Article 31(12) and the powers of the Lead Overseer provided for in Article 35(1), point (d), point (iv), first indent, with a view to evaluating the effectiveness of those provisions with regard to ensuring effective oversight of critical ICT third-party service providers established in a third country, and the necessity to establish a subsidiary in the Union.

   For the purposes of the first subparagraph of this point, the review shall include an analysis of the regime referred to in Article 31(12), including in terms of access for Union financial entities to services from third countries and availability of such services on the Union market and it shall take into account further developments in the markets for the services covered by this Regulation, the practical experience of financial entities and financial supervisors with regard to the application and, respectively, supervision of that regime, and any relevant regulatory and supervisory developments taking place at international level.

(d) the appropriateness of including in the scope of this Regulation financial entities referred to in Article 2(3), point (e), making use of automated sales systems, in light of future market developments on the use of such systems;

(e) the functioning and effectiveness of the JON in supporting the consistency of the oversight and the efficiency of the exchange of information within the Oversight Framework.

2. In the context of the review of Directive (EU) 2015/2366, the Commission shall assess the need for increased cyber resilience of payment systems and payment-processing activities and the appropriateness of extending the scope of this Regulation to operators of payment systems and entities involved in payment-processing activities. In light of this assessment, the Commission shall submit, as part of the review of Directive (EU) 2015/2366, a report to the European Parliament and the Council no later than 17 July 2023.

Based on that review report, and after consulting ESAs, ECB and the ESRB, the Commission may submit, where appropriate and as part of the legislative proposal that it may adopt pursuant to Article 108, second paragraph, of Directive (EU) 2015/2366, a proposal to ensure that all operators of payment systems and entities involved in payment-processing activities are subject to an appropriate oversight, while taking into account existing oversight by the central bank.

3. By 17 January 2026, the Commission shall, after consulting the ESAs and the Committee of European Auditing Oversight Bodies, carry out a review and submit a report to the European Parliament and the Council, accompanied, where appropriate, by a legislative proposal, on the appropriateness of strengthened requirements for statutory auditors and audit firms as regards digital operational resilience, by means of the inclusion of statutory auditors and audit firms into the scope of this Regulation or by means of amendments to Directive 2006/43/EC of the European Parliament and of the Council([39]).

Section II
Amendments

Article 59
Amendments to Regulation (EC) No 1060/2009

Regulation (EC) No 1060/2009 is amended as follows:

39 Directive 2006/43/EC of the European Parliament and of the Council of 17 May 2006 on statutory audits of annual accounts and consolidated accounts, amending Council Directives 78/660/EEC and 83/349/EEC and repealing Council Directive 84/253/EEC (OJ L 157, 9.6.2006, p. 87).

(1) in Annex I, Section A, point 4, the first subparagraph is replaced by the following:

'A credit rating agency shall have sound administrative and accounting procedures, internal control mechanisms, effective procedures for risk assessment, and effective control and safeguard arrangements for managing ICT systems in accordance with Regulation (EU) 2022/2554 of the European Parliament and of the Council([40]*)

(2) in Annex III, point 12 is replaced by the following:

'12. The credit rating agency infringes Article 6(2), in conjunction with point 4 of Section A of Annex I, by not having sound administrative or accounting procedures, internal control mechanisms, effective procedures for risk assessment, or effective control or safeguard arrangements for managing ICT systems in accordance with Regulation (EU) 2022/2554; or by not implementing or maintaining decision-making procedures or organisational structures as required by that point.'.

Article 60
Amendments to Regulation (EU) No 648/2012

Regulation (EU) No 648/2012 is amended as follows:

(1) Article 26 is amended as follows:

(a) paragraph 3 is replaced by the following:

'3. A CCP shall maintain and operate an organisational structure that ensures continuity and orderly functioning in the performance of its services and activities. It shall employ appropriate and proportionate systems, resources and procedures, including ICT systems managed in accordance with Regulation (EU) 2022/2554 of the European Parliament and of the Council([41]*).

(b) paragraph 6 is deleted;

(2) Article 34 is amended as follows:

(a) paragraph 1 is replaced by the following:

'1. A CCP shall establish, implement and maintain an adequate business continuity policy and disaster recovery plan, which shall include ICT business continuity policy and ICT response and recovery

40 *Regulation (EU) 2022/2554 of the European Parliament and of the Council of 14 December 2022 on digital operational resilience for the financial sector and amending Regulations (EC) No 1060/2009, (EU) No 648/2012, (EU) No 600/2014, (EU) No 909/2014 and (EU) 2016/1011 (OJ L 333, 27.12.2022, p. 1).';"

41 *Regulation (EU) 2022/2554 of the European Parliament and of the Council of 14 December 2022 on digital operational resilience for the financial sector and amending Regulations (EC) No 1060/2009, (EU) No 648/2012, (EU) No 600/2014, (EU) No 909/2014 and (EU) 2016/1011 (OJ L 333, 27.12.2022, p. 1).';"

plans put in place and implemented in accordance with Regulation (EU) 2022/2554, aiming to ensure the preservation of its functions, the timely recovery of operations and the fulfilment of the CCP's obligations.';

(b) in paragraph 3, the first subparagraph is replaced by the following:

'3. In order to ensure consistent application of this Article, ESMA shall, after consulting the members of the ESCB, develop draft regulatory technical standards specifying the minimum content and requirements of the business continuity policy and of the disaster recovery plan, excluding ICT business continuity policy and disaster recovery plans.';

(2) in Article 56(3), the first subparagraph is replaced by the following:

'3. In order to ensure consistent application of this Article, ESMA shall develop draft regulatory technical standards specifying the details, other than for requirements related to ICT risk management, of the application for registration referred to in paragraph 1.';

(3) in Article 79, paragraphs 1 and 2 are replaced by the following:

'1. A trade repository shall identify sources of operational risk and minimise them also through the development of appropriate systems, controls and procedures, including ICT systems managed in accordance with Regulation (EU) 2022/2554.

2. A trade repository shall establish, implement and maintain an adequate business continuity policy and disaster recovery plan including ICT business continuity policy and ICT response and recovery plans established in accordance with Regulation (EU) 2022/2554, aiming to ensure the maintenance of its functions, the timely recovery of operations and the fulfilment of the trade repository's obligations.';

(5) in Article 80, paragraph 1 is deleted.

(6) in Annex I, Section II is amended as follows:

(a) points (a) and (b) are replaced by the following:

'(a) a trade repository infringes Article 79(1) by not identifying sources of operational risk or by not minimising those risks through the development of appropriate systems, controls and procedures including ICT systems managed in accordance with Regulation (EU) 2022/2554;

(b) a trade repository infringes Article 79(2) by not establishing, implementing or maintaining an adequate business continuity policy and disaster recovery plan established in accordance with Regulation (EU) 2022/2554, aiming to ensure the maintenance of its functions, the timely recovery of operations and the fulfilment of the trade repository's obligations;';

(b) point (c) is deleted.

(7) Annex III is amended as follows:

(a) Section II is amended as follows:

(i) point (c) is replaced by the following:

'(c) a Tier 2 CCP infringes Article 26(3) by not maintaining or operating an organisational structure that ensures continuity and orderly functioning in the performance of its services and activities or by not employing appropriate and proportionate systems, resources or procedures including ICT systems managed in accordance with Regulation (EU) 2022/2554;';

(ii) point (f) is deleted.

(b) in Section III, point (a) is replaced by the following:

'(a) a Tier 2 CCP infringes Article 34(1) by not establishing, implementing or maintaining an adequate business continuity policy and response and recovery plan set up in accordance with Regulation (EU) 2022/2554, aiming to ensure the preservation of its functions, the timely recovery of operations and the fulfilment of the CCP's obligations, which at least allows for the recovery of all transactions at the time of disruption to allow the CCP to continue to operate with certainty and to complete settlement on the scheduled date;'.

Article 61
Amendments to Regulation (EU) No 909/2014

Article 45 of Regulation (EU) No 909/2014 is amended as follows:

(1) paragraph 1 is replaced by the following:

'1. A CSD shall identify sources of operational risk, both internal and external, and minimise their impact also through the deployment of appropriate ICT tools, processes and policies set up and managed in accordance with Regulation (EU) 2022/2554 of the European Parliament and of the Council([42]*), as well as through any other relevant appropriate tools, controls and procedures for other types of operational risk, including for all the securities settlement systems it operates.

(2) paragraph 2 is deleted;

(3) paragraphs 3 and 4 are replaced by the following:

'3. For services that it provides as well as for each securities settlement system that it operates, a CSD shall establish, implement and maintain an adequate business continuity policy and disaster

42 *Regulation (EU) 2022/2554 of the European Parliament and of the Council of 14 December 2022 on digital operational resilience for the financial sector and amending Regulations (EC) No 1060/2009, (EU) No 648/2012, (EU) No 600/2014, (EU) No 909/2014 and (EU) 2016/1011 (OJ L 333, 27.12.2022, p. 1).';"

recovery plan, including ICT business continuity policy and ICT response and recovery plans established in accordance with Regulation (EU) 2022/2554, to ensure the preservation of its services, the timely recovery of operations and the fulfilment of the CSD's obligations in the case of events that pose a significant risk to disrupting operations.

4. The plan referred to in paragraph 3 shall provide for the recovery of all transactions and participants' positions at the time of disruption to allow the participants of a CSD to continue to operate with certainty and to complete settlement on the scheduled date, including by ensuring that critical IT systems can resume operations from the time of disruption as provided for in Article 12(5) and (7) of Regulation (EU) 2022/2554.';

(4) paragraph 6 is replaced by the following:

'6. A CSD shall identify, monitor and manage the risks that key participants in the securities settlement systems it operates, as well as service and utility providers, and other CSDs or other market infrastructures might pose to its operations. It shall, upon request, provide competent and relevant authorities with information on any such risk identified. It shall also inform the competent authority and relevant authorities without delay of any operational incidents, other than in relation to ICT risk, resulting from such risks.';

(4) in paragraph 7, the first subparagraph is replaced by the following:

'7. ESMA shall, in close cooperation with the members of the ESCB, develop draft regulatory technical standards to specify the operational risks referred to in paragraphs 1 and 6, other than ICT risk, and the methods to test, to address or to minimise those risks, including the business continuity policies and disaster recovery plans referred to in paragraphs 3 and 4 and the methods of assessment thereof.'.

Article 62
Amendments to Regulation (EU) No 600/2014

Regulation (EU) No 600/2014 is amended as follows:

(1) Article 27g is amended as follows:

(a) paragraph 4 is replaced by the following:

'4. An APA shall comply with the requirements concerning the security of network and information systems set out in Regulation (EU) 2022/2554 of the European Parliament and of the Council([43*]).

43 *Regulation (EU) 2022/2554 of the European Parliament and of the Council of 14 December 2022 on digital operational resilience for the financial sector and amending Regulations (EC) No 1060/2009, (EU) No 648/2012, (EU) No 600/2014, (EU) No 909/2014 and (EU) 2016/1011 (OJ L 333, 27.12.2022, p. 1).';"

(b) in paragraph 8, point (c) is replaced by the following:

'(c) the concrete organisational requirements laid down in paragraphs 3 and 5.';

(2) Article 27h is amended as follows:

(a) paragraph 5 is replaced by the following:

'5. A CTP shall comply with the requirements concerning the security of network and information systems set out in Regulation (EU) 2022/2554.'.

(b) in paragraph 8, point (e) is replaced by the following:

'(e) the concrete organisational requirements laid down in paragraph 4.';

(3) Article 27i is amended as follows:

(a) paragraph 3 is replaced by the following:

'3. An ARM shall comply with the requirements concerning the security of network and information systems set out in Regulation (EU) 2022/2554.';

(b) in paragraph 5, point (b) is replaced by the following:

'(b) the concrete organisational requirements laid down in paragraphs 2 and 4.'.

Article 63
Amendment to Regulation (EU) 2016/1011

In Article 6 of Regulation (EU) 2016/1011, the following paragraph is added:

'6. For critical benchmarks, an administrator shall have sound administrative and accounting procedures, internal control mechanisms, effective procedures for risk assessment, and effective control and safeguard arrangements for managing ICT systems in accordance with Regulation (EU) 2022/2554 of the European Parliament and of the Council([44]*).

Article 64
Entry into force and application

This Regulation shall enter into force on the twentieth day following that of its publication in the Official Journal of the European Union.

It shall apply from 17 January 2025.

44 *Regulation (EU) 2022/2554 of the European Parliament and of the Council of 14 December 2022 on digital operational resilience for the financial sector and amending Regulations (EC) No 1060/2009, (EU) No 648/2012, (EU) No 600/2014, (EU) No 909/2014 and (EU) 2016/1011 (OJ L 333, 27.12.2022, p. 1).'.

This Regulation shall be binding in its entirety and directly applicable in all Member States.

Done at Strasbourg, 14 December 2022.

For the European Parliament

The President

R. METSOLA

For the Council

The President

M. BEK

APPENDIX 2

DORA Level Two Regulatory Technical Standards and Delegated Regulations

ESA DRAFT REGULATORY TECHNICAL STANDARDS: BATCH 1

The following lists the first batch of draft Regulatory Technical Standards (RTS) developed by the European Supervisory Authorities (ESAs):

- RTS on ICT risk management framework and on simplified ICT risk management framework;
- RTS on criteria for the classification of ICT-related incidents;
- RTS to specify the policy on ICT services supporting critical or important functions provided by ICT third-party service providers (TPPs); and
- Implementing Technical Standards (ITS) to establish the templates for the register of information.

ESA DRAFT REGULATORY TECHNICAL STANDARDS: BATCH 2

The following lists the second batch of draft RTS and Guidelines developed by the ESAs:

- RTS and ITS on the content, format, templates and timelines for reporting major ICT-related incidents and significant cyber threats;
- RTS on the harmonisation of conditions enabling the conduct of the oversight activities;
- RTS specifying the criteria for determining the composition of the joint examination team (JET);
- RTS on threat-led penetration testing (TLPT);
- Guidelines on the estimation of aggregated costs/losses caused by major ICT-related incidents; and
- Guidelines on oversight cooperation.

ESA/COMMISSION DELEGATED REGULATIONS ADOPTED

The following lists DORA sub-regulations on RTS which have so far been adopted by the EU Commission after initial recommendation by the ESA's including amendments by the Commission:

- Commission Delegated Regulation (EU) 2024/1772 supplementing Regulation (EU) 2022/2554 with regard to regulatory technical standards specifying the criteria for the classification of ICT-related incidents and cyber threats, setting out materiality thresholds and specifying the details of reports of major incidents. This was adopted by the EU Commission on 13 March 2024 and was published in the Official Journal on 25 June 2024;
- Commission Delegated Regulation (EU) 2024/1773 supplementing Regulation (EU) 2022/2554 with regard to regulatory technical standards specifying the detailed content of the policy regarding contractual arrangements on the use of ICT services supporting critical or important functions provided by ICT third-party service providers. This was adopted by the EU Commission on 13 March 2024 and was published in the Official Journal on 25 June 2024;
- Commission Delegated Regulation (EU) 2024/1774 supplementing Regulation (EU) 2022/2554 with regard to regulatory technical standards specifying ICT risk management tools, methods, processes, and policies and the simplified ICT risk management framework [as set out below]. This was adopted by the EU Commission on 13 March 2024 and was published in the Official Journal on 25 June 2024;
- Commission Delegated Regulation (EU) 2024/1505 supplementing Regulation (EU) 2022/2554 by determining the amount of the oversight fees to be charged by the Lead Overseer to critical ICT third-party service providers and the way in which those fees are to be paid. This was adopted by the EU Commission on 22 February 2024 and was published in the Official Journal on 30 May 2024; and
- Commission Delegated Regulation (EU) 2024/1502 supplementing Regulation (EU) 2022/2554 by specifying the criteria for the designation of ICT third-party service providers as critical for financial entities. This was adopted by the EU Commission on 22 February 2024 and was published in the Official Journal on 30 May 2024.

Commission Delegated Regulation (EU) 2024/1774

COMMISSION DELEGATED REGULATION (EU) 2024/1774

of 13 March 2024

supplementing Regulation (EU) 2022/2554 of the European Parliament and of the Council with regard to regulatory technical standards specifying ICT risk management tools, methods, processes, and policies and the simplified ICT risk management framework

(Text with EEA relevance)

THE EUROPEAN COMMISSION,

Having regard to the Treaty on the Functioning of the European Union,

Having regard to Regulation (EU) 2022/2554 of the European Parliament and of the Council of 14 December 2022 on digital operational resilience for the financial sector and amending Regulations (EC) No 1060/2009, (EU) No 648/2012, (EU) No 600/2014, (EU) No 909/2014 and (EU) 2016/10112, and in particular Article 15, fourth subparagraph, and Article 16(3), fourth subparagraph, thereof,

Whereas:

(1) Regulation (EU) 2022/2554 covers a wide variety of financial entities that differ in size, structure, internal organisation, and in the nature and complexity of their activities, and thus have increased or reduced elements of complexity or risks. To ensure that that variety is duly taken into account, any requirements as regards ICT security policies, procedures, protocols and tools, and as regards a simplified ICT risk management framework, should be proportionate to that size, structure, internal organisation, nature and complexity of those financial entities, and to the corresponding risks.

(2) For the same reason, financial entities subject to Regulation (EU) 2022/2554 should have a certain flexibility in the way they comply with any requirements as regards ICT security policies, procedures, protocols and tools, and as regards any simplified ICT risk management framework. For that reason, financial entities should be allowed to use any documentation they have already to comply with any documentation requirements that flow from those requirements. It follows that the development, documentation, and implementation of specific ICT security policies should be required only for certain essential elements, taking into account, inter alia, leading industry practices and standards. Furthermore, to cover specific technical implementation aspects, it is necessary to develop, document and implement ICT security procedures to cover specific technical implementation aspects, including capacity and performance management, vulnerability and patch management, data and system security, and logging.

(3) To ensure the correct implementation over time of ICT security policies, procedures, protocols, and tools referred to in Title II, Chapter I of this

Regulation, it is important that financial entities correctly assign and maintain any roles and responsibilities relating to ICT security, and that they lay down the consequences of non-compliance with ICT security policies or procedures.

(4) To limit the risk of conflicts of interests, financial entities should ensure the segregation of duties when assigning ICT roles and responsibilities.

(5) To ensure flexibility and to simplify the financial entities' control framework, financial entities should not be required to develop specific provisions on the consequences of non-compliance with ICT security policies, procedures and protocols referred to in Title II, Chapter I of this Regulation where such provisions are already set out in another policy or procedure.

(6) In a dynamic environment where ICT risks constantly evolve, it is important that financial entities develop their set of ICT security policies on the basis of leading practices, and where applicable, of standards as defined in Article 2, point (1), of Regulation (EU) No 1025/2012 of the European Parliament and of the Council. This should enable financial entities referred to in Title II of this Regulation to remain informed and prepared in a changing landscape.

(7) To ensure their digital operational resilience, financial entities referred to in Title II of this Regulation should, as part of their ICT security policies, procedures, protocols, and tools, develop and implement an ICT asset management policy, capacity and performance management procedures, and policies and procedures for ICT operations.

Those policies and procedures are necessary to ensure the monitoring of the status of ICT assets throughout their lifecycles, so that those assets are used and maintained effectively (ICT asset management). Those policies and procedures should also ensure the optimisation of ICT systems' operation and that the ICT systems' and capacity's performance meets the established business and information security objectives (capacity and performance management). Lastly, those policies and procedures should ensure the effective and smooth day-to-day management and operation of ICT systems (ICT operations), thereby minimising the risk of loss of confidentiality, integrity, and availability of data. Those policies and procedures are thus necessary to ensure the security of networks, to provide for adequate safeguards against intrusions and data misuse, and to preserve the availability, authenticity, integrity, and confidentiality of data.

(8) To ensure a proper management of the legacy ICT systems risk, financial entities should record and monitor end-dates of ICT third party support services. Because of the potential impact that a loss of confidentiality, integrity and availability of data may have, financial entities should focus on those ICT assets or systems that are critical for business operation when recording and monitoring those end-dates.

(9) Cryptographic controls can ensure the availability, authenticity, integrity, and confidentiality of data. Financial entities referred to in Title II of

this Regulation should therefore identify and implement such controls on the basis of a risk-based approach. To that end, financial entities should encrypt the data concerned at rest, in transit or, where necessary, in use, on the basis of the results of a two-pronged process, namely data classification and a comprehensive ICT risk assessment. Given the complexity of encrypting data in use, financial entities referred to in Title II of this Regulation should encrypt date in use only where that would be appropriate in light of the results of the ICT risk assessment. Financial entities referred to in Title II of this Regulation should, however, be able, where encryption of data in use is not feasible or is too complex, to protect the confidentiality, integrity, and availability of the data concerned through other ICT security measures. Given the rapid technological developments in the field of cryptographic techniques, financial entities referred to in Title II of this Regulation should remain abreast of relevant developments in cryptanalysis and consider leading practices and standards. Financial entities referred to in Title II of this Regulation should hence follow a flexible approach, based on risk mitigation and monitoring, to deal with the dynamic landscape of cryptographic threats, including threats from quantum advancements.

(10) ICT operations security and operational policies, procedures, protocols, and tools are essential to ensure the confidentiality, integrity, and availability of data. One pivotal aspect is the strict separation of ICT production environments from the environments where ICT systems are developed and tested or from other non-production environments. That separation should serve as an important ICT security measure against unintended and unauthorised access to, modifications of, and deletions of data in the production environment, which could result in major disruptions in the business operations of financial entities referred to in Title II of this Regulation. However, considering current ICT system development practices, in exceptional circumstances, financial entities should be allowed to test in production environments, provided that they justify such testing and obtain the required approval.

(11) The fast-evolving nature of ICT landscapes, ICT vulnerabilities and cyber threats necessitates a proactive and comprehensive approach to identifying, evaluating, and addressing ICT vulnerabilities. Without such an approach, financial entities, their customers, users, or counterparties may be severely exposed to risks, which would put at risk their digital operational resilience, the security of their networks, and the availability, authenticity, integrity, and confidentiality of data that ICT security policies and procedures should protect. Financial entities referred to in Title II of this Regulation should therefore identify and remedy vulnerabilities in their ICT environment, and both the financial entities and their ICT third-party service providers should adhere to a coherent, transparent, and responsible vulnerability management framework. For the same reason, financial entities should monitor ICT vulnerabilities using reliable resources and automated tools, verifying that ICT third-party service providers ensure prompt action on vulnerabilities in provided ICT services.

(12) Patch management should be a crucial part of those ICT security policies and procedures that, through testing and deployment in a controlled environment, are to resolve identified vulnerabilities and to prevent disruptions from the installation of patches.

(13) To ensure timely and transparent communication of potential security threats that could impact the financial entity and its stakeholders, financial entities should establish procedures for the responsible disclosure of ICT vulnerabilities to clients, counterparts, and the public. When establishing those procedures, financial entities should consider factors, including the severity of the vulnerability, the potential impact of such vulnerability on stakeholders, and the readiness of a fix or mitigation measures.

(14) To allow for the assignment of user access rights, financial entities referred to in Title II of this Regulation should establish strong measures to ascertain the unique identification of individuals and systems that will access the financial entity's information. A failure to do so would expose financial entities to potential unauthorised access, data breaches, and fraudulent activities, thus compromising the confidentiality, integrity, and availability of sensitive financial data. While the use of generic or shared accounts should exceptionally be permitted under circumstances specified by financial entities, financial entities should ensure that the accountability for actions taken through those accounts is maintained. Without that safeguard, potential malicious users would be able to hinder investigative and corrective measures, leaving financial entities vulnerable to undetected malicious activities or non-compliance penalties.

(15) To manage the rapid advancement in ICT environments, financial entities referred to in Title II of this Regulation should implement robust ICT project management policies and procedures to maintain data availability, authenticity, integrity, and confidentiality. Those ICT project management policies and procedures should identify the elements that are necessary to successfully manage ICT projects, including changes to, acquisitions of, the maintenance of, and developments of the financial entity's ICT systems, regardless of the ICT project management methodology chosen by the financial entity. In the context of those policies and procedures, financial entities should adopt testing practices and methods that suit their needs, while adhering to a risk-based approach and ensuring that a secure, reliable, and resilient ICT environment is maintained. To guarantee the secure implementation of an ICT project, financial entities should ensure that staff from specific business sectors or roles influenced or impacted by that ICT project can provide the necessary information and expertise. To ensure effective oversight, reports on ICT projects, in particular about projects that affect critical or important functions and about their associated risks, should be submitted to the management body. Financial entities should tailor the frequency and details of the systematic and ongoing reviews and reports to the importance and the size of the ICT projects concerned.

(16) It is necessary to ensure that software packages that financial entities referred to in Title II of this Regulation acquire and develop are effectively and

securely integrated into the existing ICT environment, in accordance with established business and information security objectives. Financial entities should therefore thoroughly evaluate such software packages. For that purpose, and to identify vulnerabilities and potential security gaps within both software packages and the broader ICT systems, financial entities should carry out ICT security testing. To assess the integrity of the software and to ensure that the use of that software does not pose ICT security risks, financial entities should also review source codes of software acquired, including, where feasible, of proprietary software provided by ICT third-party service providers, using both static and dynamic testing methods.

(17) Changes, regardless of their scale, carry inherent risks and may pose significant risks of loss of confidentiality, integrity, and availability of data, and could thus lead to severe business disruptions. To safeguard financial entities from potential ICT vulnerabilities and weaknesses that could expose them to significant risks, a rigorous verification process is necessary to confirm that all changes meet the necessary ICT security requirements. Financial entities referred to in Title II of this Regulation should therefore, as an essential element of their ICT security policies and procedures, have in place sound ICT change management policies and procedures. To uphold the objectivity and effectiveness of the ICT change management process, to prevent conflicts of interest, and to ensure that ICT changes are evaluated objectively, it is necessary to separate the functions responsible for approving those changes from the functions that request and implement those changes. To achieve effective transitions, controlled ICT change implementation, and minimal disruptions to the operation of the ICT systems, financial entities should assign clear roles and responsibilities that ensure that ICT changes are planned, adequately tested, and that quality is ensured. To ensure that ICT systems continue to operate effectively, and to provide a safety net for financial entities, financial entities should also develop and implement fall-back procedures. Financial entities should clearly identify those fall-back procedures and assign responsibilities to ensure a swift and effective response in the event of unsuccessful ICT changes.

(18) To detect, manage, and report ICT-related incidents, financial entities referred to in Title II of this Regulation should establish an ICT-related incident policy encompassing the components of an ICT-related incident management process. For that purpose, financial entities should identify all relevant contacts inside and outside the organisation that can facilitate the correct coordination and implementation of the different phases within that process. To optimise the detection of, and response to, ICT-related incidents, and to identify trends among those incidents, which are a valuable source of information enabling financial entities to identify and address root causes and problems in an effective manner, financial entities should in particular analyse in detail the ICT-related incidents that they consider to be most significant, inter alia because of their regular reoccurrence.

(19) To guarantee an early and effective detection of anomalous activities, financial entities referred to in Title II of this Regulation should collect,

monitor, and analyse the different sources of information and should allocate related roles and responsibilities.

As regards internal sources of information, logs are an extremely relevant source, but financial entities should not rely on logs alone. Instead, financial entities should consider broader information to include what is reported by other internal functions, as those functions are often a valuable source of relevant information. For the same reason, financial entities should analyse and monitor information gathered from external sources, including information provided by ICT third-party providers on incidents affecting their systems and networks, and other sources of information that financial entities consider relevant. In so far as such information constitutes personal data, the Union data protection law applies. The personal data should be limited to what is necessary for the incident detection.

(20) To facilitate ICT-related incidents detection, financial entities should retain evidence of those incidents. To ensure, on the one hand, that such evidence is retained sufficiently long and to avoid, on the other hand, an excessive regulatory burden, financial entities should determine the retention period considering, among other things, the criticality of the data and retention requirements stemming from Union law.

(21) To ensure that ICT-related incidents are detected in time, financial entities referred to in Title II of this Regulation should consider the criteria identified for triggering the detection of and responses to ICT-related incidents as not exhaustive. Moreover, while financial entities should consider each of those criteria, the circumstances described in the criteria should not need to occur simultaneously and the importance of the affected ICT services should be appropriately considered to trigger ICT-related incident detection and response processes.

(22) When developing an ICT business continuity policy, financial entities referred to in Title II of this Regulation should take into account the essential components of ICT risk management, including ICT-related incident management and communication strategies, the ICT change management process, and risks associated with ICT third party service providers.

(23) It is necessary to set out the set of scenarios that financial entities referred to in Title II of this Regulation should take into account both for the implementation of ICT response and recovery plans and for the testing of ICT business continuity plans.

Those scenarios should serve as a starting point for financial entities to analyse both the relevance and plausibility of each scenario and the need to develop alternative scenarios. Financial entities should focus on those scenarios in which investment in resilience measures could be more efficient and effective. By testing switchovers between the primary ICT infrastructure and any redundant capacity, backups and redundant facilities, financial institutions should assess whether that capacity, backup, and those facilities operate effectively for a sufficient period of time and ensure that the normal functioning of the primary ICT infrastructure is restored in accordance with the recovery objectives.

(24) It is necessary to lay down requirements for operational risk, and more particularly requirements for ICT project and change management and ICT business continuity management building on those that apply already to central counterparties, central securities depositories and trading venues under, respectively, Regulations (EU) No 648/20124, (EU) No 600/20145 and (EU) No 909/20146 of the European Parliament and of the Council.

(25) Article 6(5) of Regulation (EU) 2022/2554 requires financial entities to review their ICT risk management framework and to provide their competent authority with a report on that review. To enable competent authorities to easily process the information in those reports, and to guarantee an adequate transmission of that information, financial entities should submit those reports in a searchable electronic format.

(26) The requirements for financial entities that are subject to the simplified ICT risk management framework referred to in Article 16 of Regulation (EU) 2022/2554 should be focused on those essential areas and elements that, in light of the scale, risk, size, and complexity of those financial entities, are as a minimum necessary to ensure the confidentiality, integrity, availability, and authenticity of the data and services of those financial entities. In that context, those financial entities should have in place an internal governance and control framework with clear responsibilities to enable an effective and sound risk management framework. Furthermore, to reduce the administrative and operational burden, those financial entities should develop and document only one policy, that is an information security policy, that specifies the high-level principles and rules necessary to protect the confidentiality, integrity, availability, and authenticity of data and of the services of those financial entities.

(27) The provisions of this Regulation relate to the area of the ICT risk management framework, by detailing specific elements applicable to the financial entities in accordance with Article 15 of Regulation (EU) 2022/2554 and by designing the simplified ICT risk management framework for the financial entities set out in Article 16(1) of that Regulation. To ensure coherence between the ordinary and the simplified ICT risk management framework, and considering that those provisions should become applicable at the same time, it is appropriate to include those provisions in a single legislative act.

(28) This Regulation is based on the draft regulatory technical standards submitted to the Commission by the European Banking Authority, the European Insurance and Occupational Pensions Authority and the European Securities and Markets Authority (European Supervisory Authorities), in consultation with the European Union Agency for Cyber security (ENISA).

(29) The Joint Committee of the European Supervisory Authorities referred to in Article 54 of Regulation (EU) No 1093/2010 of the European Parliament and of the Council7, in Article 54 of Regulation (EU) No 1094/2010 of the European Parliament and of the Council and in Article 54 of Regulation

(EU) No 1095/2010 of the European Parliament and of the Council has conducted open public consultations on the draft regulatory technical standards on which this Regulation is based, analysed the potential costs and benefits of the proposed standards and requested advice of the Banking Stakeholder Group established in accordance with Article 37 of Regulation (EU) No 1093/2010, the Insurance and Reinsurance Stakeholder Group and the Occupational Pensions Stakeholder Group established in accordance with Article 37 of Regulation (EU) No 1094/2010, and the Securities and Markets Stakeholder Group established in accordance with Article 37 of Regulation (EU) No 1095/2010.

(30) To the extent to which processing of personal data is required to comply with the obligations set out in this Act, Regulation (EU) 2016/679 of the European Parliament and of the Council of 27 April 2016 and Regulation (EU) 2018/1725 of the European Parliament and of the Council of 23 October 2018 should fully apply. For instance, the data minimisation principle should be complied with where personal data are controlled to ensure an appropriate incident detection. The European Data Protection Supervisor has also been consulted on the draft text of this Act,

HAS ADOPTED THIS REGULATION:

TITLE I
GENERAL PRINCIPLE

Article 1
Overall risk profile and complexity

When developing and implementing the ICT security policies, procedures, protocols and tools referred to in Title II and the simplified ICT risk management framework referred to in Title III, the size and the overall risk profile of the financial entity, and the nature, scale and elements of increased or reduced complexity of its services, activities and operations shall be taken into account, including elements relating to:

(a) encryption and cryptography;

(b) ICT operations security;

(c) network security;

(d) ICT project and change management;

(e) the potential impact of the ICT risk on confidentiality, integrity and availability of data, and of the disruptions on the continuity and availability of the financial entity's activities.

TITLE II
FURTHER HARMONISATION OF ICT RISK MANAGEMENT TOOLS, METHODS, PROCESSES, AND POLICIES IN ACCORDANCE WITH ARTICLE 15 OF REGULATION (EU) 2022/2554

CHAPTER I
ICT SECURITY POLICIES, PROCEDURES, PROTOCOLS, AND TOOLS

SECTION 1

Article 2
General elements of ICT security policies, procedures, protocols, and tools

1. Financial entities shall ensure that their ICT security policies, information security, and related procedures, protocols, and tools as referred to in Article 9(2) of Regulation (EU) 2022/2554 are embedded in their ICT risk management framework.

   Financial entities shall establish the ICT security policies, procedures, protocols, and tools laid down in this Chapter that:

   (a) ensure the security of networks;

   (b) contain safeguards against intrusions and data misuse;

   (c) preserve the availability, authenticity, integrity, and confidentiality of data, including via the use of cryptographic techniques;

   (d) guarantee an accurate and prompt data transmission without major disruptions and undue delays.

2. Financial entities shall ensure that the ICT security policies referred to in paragraph 1:

   (a) are aligned to the financial entity's information security objectives included in the digital operational resilience strategy referred to in Article 6(8) of Regulation (EU) 2022/2554;

   (b) indicate the date of the formal approval of the ICT security policies by the management body;

   (c) contain indicators and measures to:

      (i) monitor the implementation of the ICT security policies, procedures, protocols, and tools;

      (ii) record exceptions from that implementation

      (iii) ensure that the digital operational resilience of the financial entity is ensured in case of exceptions as referred to in point (ii);

   (d) specify the responsibilities of staff at all levels to ensure the financial entity's ICT security;

   (e) specify the consequences of non-compliance by staff of the financial entity with the ICT security policies, where provisions to that effect are not laid down in other policies of the financial entity;

(f) list the documentation to be maintained;

(g) specify the segregation of duties arrangements in the context of the three lines of defence model or other internal risk management and control model, as applicable, to avoid conflicts of interest;

(h) consider leading practices and, where applicable, standards as defined in Article 2, point (1), of Regulation (EU) No 1025/2012;

(i) identify the roles and responsibilities for the development, implementation and maintenance of ICT security policies, procedures, protocols, and tools;

(j) are reviewed in accordance with Article 6(5) of Regulation (EU) 2022/2554;

(k) take into account material changes concerning the financial entity, including material changes to the activities or processes of the financial entity, to the cyber threat landscape, or to applicable legal obligations.

SECTION 2

Article 3
ICT risk management

Financial entities shall develop, document, and implement ICT risk management policies and procedures that shall contain all of the following:

(a) an indication of the approval of the risk tolerance level for ICT risk established in accordance with Article 6(8), point (b), of Regulation (EU) 2022/2554;

(b) a procedure and a methodology to conduct the ICT risk assessment, identifying:

 (i) vulnerabilities and threats that affect or may affect the supported business functions, the ICT systems and ICT assets supporting those functions;

 (ii) the quantitative or qualitative indicators to measure the impact and likelihood of the vulnerabilities and threats referred to in point (i);

(c) the procedure to identify, implement, and document ICT risk treatment measures for the ICT risks identified and assessed, including the determination of ICT risk treatment measures necessary to bring ICT risk within the risk tolerance level referred to in point (a);

(d) for the residual ICT risks that are still present following the implementation of the ICT risk treatment measures referred to in point (c):

 (i) provisions on the identification of those residual ICT risks;

 (ii) the assignment of roles and responsibilities regarding:

(1) the acceptance of the residual ICT risks that exceed the financial entity's risk tolerance level referred to in point (a);

(1) for the review process referred to in point (iv) of this point (d);

(iii) the development of an inventory of the accepted residual ICT risks, including a

(2) justification for their acceptance;

(iv) provisions on the review of the accepted residual ICT risks at least once a year, including:

(1) the identification of any changes to the residual ICT risks;

(2) the assessment of available mitigation measures;

(3) the assessment of whether the reasons justifying the acceptance of residual ICT risks are still valid and applicable at the date of the review;

(e) provisions on the monitoring of:

(i) any changes to the ICT risk and cyber threat landscape;

(ii) internal and external vulnerabilities and threats:

(iii) ICT risk of the financial entity that enables promp detection of changes that could affect its ICT risk profile;

(f) provisions on a process to ensure that any changes to the business strategy and the digital operational resilience strategy of the financial entity are taken into account.

For the purposes of the first paragraph, point (c), the procedure referred to in that point shall ensure:

(a) the monitoring of the effectiveness of the ICT risk treatment measures implemented;

(b) the assessment of whether the established risk tolerance levels of the financial entity have been attained;

(c) the assessment of whether the financial entity has taken actions to correct or improve those measures where necessary.

SECTION 3
ICT ASSET MANAGEMENT

Article 4
ICT asset management policy

1. As part of the ICT security policies, procedures, protocols, and tools referred to in Article 9(2) of Regulation (EU) 2022/2554, financial entities shall develop, document, and implement a policy on management of ICT assets.

2. The policy on management of ICT assets referred to in paragraph 1 shall:

   (a) prescribe the monitoring and management of the lifecycle of ICT assets identified and classified in accordance with Article 8(1) of Regulation (EU) 2022/2554;

   (b) prescribe that the financial entity keeps records of all of the following:

      (i) the unique identifier of each ICT asset;

      (ii) information on the location, either physical or logical, of all ICT assets;

      (iii) the classification of all ICT assets, as referred to in Article 8(1) of Regulation (EU) 2022/2254;

      (iv) the identity of ICT asset owners;

      (v) the business functions or services supported by the ICT asset;

      (vi) the ICT business continuity requirements, including recovery time objectives and recovery point objectives;

      (vii) whether the ICT asset can be or is exposed to external networks, including the internet;

      (viii) the links and interdependencies among ICT assets and the business functions using each ICT asset;

      (ix) where applicable, for all ICT assets, the end dates of the ICT third-party service provider's regular, extended, and custom support services after which those ICT assets are no longer supported by their supplier or by an ICT third-party service provider;

   (c) for financial entities other than microenterprises, prescribe that those financial entities keep records of the information necessary to perform a specific ICT risk assessment on all legacy ICT systems referred to in Article 8(7) of Regulation (EU) 2022/2554.

Article 5
ICT asset management procedure

1. Financial entities shall develop, document, and implement a procedure for the management of ICT assets.

2. The procedure for management of ICT assets referred to in paragraph 1 shall specify the criteria to perform the criticality assessment of information assets and ICT assets supporting business functions. That assessment shall take into account:

   (a) the ICT risk related to those business functions and their dependencies on the information assets or ICT assets;

   (b) how the loss of confidentiality, integrity, and availability of such information assets and ICT assets would impact the business processes and activities of the financial entities.

SECTION 4
ENCRYPTION AND CRYPTOGRAPHY

Article 6
Encryption and cryptographic controls

1. As part of their ICT security policies, procedures, protocols, and tools referred to in Article 9(2) of Regulation (EU) 2022/2554, financial entities shall develop, document, and implement a policy on encryption and cryptographic controls.

2. Financial entities shall design the policy on encryption and cryptographic controls referred to in paragraph 1 on the basis of the results of an approved data classification and ICT risk assessment. That policy shall contain rules for all of the following:

   (a) the encryption of data at rest and in transit;

   (b) the encryption of data in use, where necessary;

   (c) the encryption of internal network connections and traffic with external parties.

   (d) the cryptographic key management referred to in Article 7, laying down rules on the correct use, protection, and lifecycle of cryptographic keys.

   For the purposes of point (b), where encryption of data in use is not possible, financial entities shall process data in use in a separated and protected environment, or take equivalent measures to ensure the confidentiality, integrity, authenticity, and availability of data.

3. Financial entities shall include in the policy on encryption and cryptographic controls referred to in paragraph 1 criteria for the selection of cryptographic techniques and use practices, taking into account leading practices, and standards as defined in Article 2, point (1), of Regulation (EU) No 1025/2012, and the classification of relevant ICT assets established in accordance with Article 8(1) of Regulation (EU) 2022/2554. Financial entities that are not able to adhere to the leading practices or standards, or to use the most reliable techniques, shall adopt mitigation and monitoring measures that ensure resilience against cyber threats.

4. Financial entities shall include in the policy on encryption and cryptographic controls referred to in paragraph 1 provisions for updating or changing, where necessary, the cryptographic technology on the basis of developments in cryptanalysis. Those updates or changes shall ensure that the cryptographic technology remains resilient against cyber threats, as required by Article 10(2), point (a). Financial entities that are not able to update or change the cryptographic technology shall adopt mitigation and monitoring measures that ensure resilience against cyber threats.

5. Financial entities shall include in the policy on encryption and cryptographic controls referred to in paragraph 1 a requirement to record the adoption of mitigation and monitoring measures adopted in accordance with paragraphs 3 and 4 and to provide a reasoned explanation for doing so.

Article 7
Cryptographic key management

1. Financial entities shall include in the cryptographic key management policy referred to in Article 6(2), point (d), requirements for managing cryptographic keys through their whole lifecycle, including generating, renewing, storing, backing up, archiving, retrieving, transmitting, retiring, revoking, and destroying those cryptographic keys.
2. Financial entities shall identify and implement controls to protect cryptographic keys through their whole lifecycle against loss, unauthorised access, disclosure, and modification. Financial entities shall design those controls on the basis of the results of the approved data classification and the ICT risk assessment.
3. Financial entities shall develop and implement methods to replace the cryptographic keys in the case of loss, or where those keys are compromised or damaged.
4. Financial entities shall create and maintain a register for all certificates and certificate-storing devices for at least ICT assets supporting critical or important functions. Financial entities shall keep that register up to date.
5. Financial entities shall ensure the prompt renewal of certificates in advance of their expiration.

SECTION 5
ICT OPERATIONS SECURITY

Article 8
Policies and procedures for ICT operations

1. As part of the ICT security policies, procedures, protocols, and tools referred to in Article 9(2) of Regulation (EU) 2022/2554, financial entities shall develop, document, and implement policies and procedures to manage the ICT operations.

   Those policies and procedures shall specify how financial entities operate, monitor, control, and restore their ICT assets, including the documentation of ICT operations.

2. The policies and procedures for ICT operations referred to in paragraph 1 shall contain all of the following:

   (a) an ICT assets description, including all of the following:

      (i) requirements regarding secure installation, maintenance, configuration, and deinstallation of an ICT system;

      (ii) requirements regarding the management of information assets used by ICT assets, including their processing and handling, both automated and manual;

      (iii) requirements regarding the identification and control of legacy ICT systems;

(b) controls and monitoring of ICT systems, including all of the following:

(i) backup and restore requirements of ICT systems;

(ii) scheduling requirements, taking into consideration interdependencies among the ICT systems;

(iii) protocols for audit-trail and system log information;

(iv) requirements to ensure that the performance of internal audit and other testing minimises disruptions to business operations;

(v) requirements on the separation of ICT production environments from the development, testing, and other non-production environments;

(vi) requirements to conduct the development and testing in environments which are separated from the production environment;

(vii) requirements to conduct the development and testing in production environments;

(c) error handling concerning ICT systems, including all of the following:

(i) procedures and protocols for handling errors;

(ii) support and escalation contacts, including external support contacts in case of unexpected operational or technical issues;

(iii) ICT system restart, rollback, and recovery procedures for use in the event of ICT system disruption.

For the purposes of point (b)(v), the separation shall consider all of the components of the environment, including accounts, data or connections, as required by Article 13(1), point (a).

For the purposes of point (b)(vii), the policies and procedures referred to in paragraph 1 shall provide that the instances in which testing is performed in a production environment are clearly identified, reasoned, are for limited periods of time, and are approved by the relevant function in accordance with Article 16(6).

Financial entities shall ensure the availability, confidentiality, integrity, and authenticity of ICT systems and production data during development and test activities in the production environment.

Article 9
Capacity and performance management

1. As part of the ICT security policies, procedures, protocols, and tools referred to in Article 9(2) of Regulation (EU) 2022/2554, financial entities shall develop, document, and implement capacity and performance management procedures for the following:

(a) the identification of capacity requirements of their ICT systems;

(b) the application of resource optimisation;

(c) the monitoring procedures for maintaining and improving:

(i) the availability of data and ICT systems;

(ii) the efficiency of ICT systems;

(iii) the prevention of ICT capacity shortages.

2. The capacity and performance management procedures referred to in paragraph 1 shall ensure that financial entities take measures that are appropriate to cater for the specificities of ICT systems with long or complex procurement or approval processes or ICT systems that are resource-intensive.

Article 10
Vulnerability and patch management

1. As part of the ICT security policies, procedures, protocols, and tools referred to in Article 9(2) of Regulation (EU) 2022/2554, financial entities shall develop, document, and implement vulnerability management procedures.

2. The vulnerability management procedures referred to in paragraph 1 shall:

(a) identify and update relevant and trustworthy information resources to build and maintain awareness about vulnerabilities;

(b) ensure the performance of automated vulnerability scanning and assessments on ICT assets, whereby the frequency and scope of those activities shall be commensurate to the classification established in accordance with Article 8(1) of Regulation (EU) 2022/2554 and the overall risk profile of the ICT asset;

(c) verify whether:

(i) ICT third-party service providers handle vulnerabilities related to the ICT services provided to the financial entity;

(ii) whether those service providers report to the financial entity at least the critical vulnerabilities and statistics and trends in a timely manner;

(d) track the usage of:

(i) third-party libraries, including open-source libraries, used by ICT services supporting critical or important functions;

(ii) ICT services developed by the financial entity itself or specifically customised or developed for the financial entity by an ICT third-party service provider;

(e) establish procedures for the responsible disclosure of vulnerabilities to clients, counterparties, and to the public;

(f) prioritise the deployment of patches and other mitigation measures to address the vulnerabilities identified;

(g) monitor and verify the remediation of vulnerabilities;

(h) require the recording of any detected vulnerabilities affecting ICT systems and the monitoring of their resolution.

For the purposes of point (b), financial entities shall perform the automated vulnerability scanning and assessments on ICT assets for the ICT assets supporting critical or important functions on at least a weekly basis.

For the purposes of point (c), financial entities shall request that ICT third-party service providers investigate the relevant vulnerabilities, determine the root causes, and implement appropriate mitigating action.

For the purposes of point (d), financial entities shall, where appropriate in collaboration with the ICT third-party service provider, monitor the version and possible updates of the third-party libraries. In case of ready to use (off-the-shelf) ICT assets or components of ICT assets acquired and used in the operation of ICT services not supporting critical or important functions, financial entities shall track the usage to the extent possible of third-party libraries, including open-source libraries.

For the purposes of point (f), financial entities shall consider the criticality of the vulnerability, the classification established in accordance with Article 8(1) of Regulation (EU) 2022/2554, and the risk profile of the ICT assets affected by the identified vulnerabilities.

3. As part of the ICT security policies, procedures, protocols, and tools referred to in Article 9(2) of Regulation (EU) 2022/2554, financial entities shall develop, document and implement patch management procedures.

4. The patch management procedures referred to in paragraph 3 shall:

(a) to the extent possible identify and evaluate available software and hardware patches and updates using automated tools;

(b) identify emergency procedures for the patching and updating of ICT assets;

(c) test and deploy the software and hardware patches and the updates referred to in Article 8(2), points (b)(v), (vi) and (vii);

(d) set deadlines for the installation of software and hardware patches and updates and escalation procedures in case those deadlines cannot be met.

Article 11
Data and system security

1. As part of the ICT security policies, procedures, protocols, and tools referred to in Article 9(2) of Regulation (EU) 2022/2554, financial entities shall develop, document, and implement a data and system security procedure.

2. The data and system security procedure referred to in paragraph 1 shall contain all of the following elements related to data and ICT system

security, in accordance with the classification established in accordance with Article 8(1) of Regulation (EU) 2022/2554:

(a) the access restrictions referred to in Article 21 of this Regulation, supporting the protection requirements for each level of classification;

(b) the identification of a secure configuration baseline for ICT assets that minimise exposure of those ICT assets to cyber threats and measures to verify regularly that those baselines are effectively deployed;

(c) the identification of security measures to ensure that only authorised software is installed in ICT systems and endpoint devices;

(d) the identification of security measures against malicious codes;

(e) the identification of security measures to ensure that only authorised data storage media, systems, and endpoint devices are used to transfer and store data of the financial entity;

(f) the following requirements to secure the use of portable endpoint devices and private non-portable endpoint devices:

  (i) the requirement to use a management solution to remotely manage the endpoint devices and remotely wipe the financial entity's data;

  (ii) the requirement to use security mechanisms that cannot be modified, removed or bypassed by staff members or ICT third-party service providers in an unauthorised manner;

  (iii) the requirement to use removable data storage devices only where the residual ICT risk remains within the financial entity's risk tolerance level referred to in Article 3(1), point (a);

(g) the process to securely delete data, present on premises of the financial entity or stored externally, that the financial entity no longer needs to collect or to store;

(h) the process to securely dispose or decommission of data storage devices present on premises of the financial entity or stored externally containing confidential information;

(i) the identification and implementation of security measures to prevent data loss and leakage for systems and endpoint devices;

(j) the implementation of security measures to ensure that teleworking and the use of private endpoint devices does not adversely impact the ICT security of the financial entity;

(k) for ICT assets or services operated by an ICT third-party service provider, the identification and implementation of requirements to maintain digital operational resilience, in accordance with the results of the data classification and ICT risk assessment.

For the purposes of point (b), the secure configuration baseline referred to in that point shall take into account leading practices and appropriate techniques laid down in the standards defined in Article 2, point (1), of Regulation (EU) No 1025/2012.

For the purposes of point (k), financial entities shall consider the following:

(a) the implementation of vendor recommended settings on the elements operated by the financial entity;

(b) a clear allocation of information security roles and responsibilities between the financial entity and the ICT third-party service provider, in accordance with the principle of full responsibility of the financial entity over its ICT third-party service provider referred to in Article 28(1), point (a), of Regulation (EU) 2022/2554, and for financial entities referred to in Article 28(2) of that Regulation, and in accordance with the financial entity's policy on the use of ICT services supporting critical or important functions;

(c) the need to ensure and maintain adequate competences within the financial entity in the management and security of the service used;

(d) technical and organisational measures to minimise the risks related to the infrastructure used by the ICT third-party service provider for its ICT services, considering leading practices, and standards as defined in Article 2, point (1), of Regulation (EU) No 1025/2012.

Article 12
Logging

1. Financial entities shall, as part of the safeguards against intrusions and data misuse, develop, document, and implement logging procedures, protocols and tools.

2. The logging procedures, protocols, and tools referred to in paragraph 1 shall contain all of the following:

(a) the identification of the events to be logged, the retention period of the logs, and the measures to secure and handle the log data, considering the purpose for which the logs are created;

(b) the alignment of the level of detail of the logs with their purpose and usage to enable the effective detection of anomalous activities as referred to in Article 24;

(c) the requirement to log events related to all of the following:

(i) logical and physical access control, as referred to in Article 21, and identity management;

(ii) capacity management;

(iii) change management;

(iv) ICT operations, including ICT system activities;

(v) network traffic activities, including ICT network performance;

(d) measures to protect logging systems and log information against tampering, deletion, and unauthorised access at rest, in transit, and, where relevant, in use;

(e) measures to detect a failure of logging systems;

(f) without prejudice to any applicable regulatory requirements under Union or national law, the synchronisation of the clocks of each of the financial entity's ICT systems upon a documented reliable reference time source.

For the purposes of point (a), financial entities shall establish the retention period, taking into account the business and information security objectives, the reason for recording the event in the logs, and the results of the ICT risk assessment.

SECTION 6
NETWORK SECURITY

Article 13
Network security management

1. Financial entities shall, as part of the safeguards ensuring the security of networks against intrusions and data misuse, develop, document, and implement policies, procedures, protocols, and tools on network security management, including all of the following:

   (a) the segregation and segmentation of ICT systems and networks taking into account:

      (i) the criticality or importance of the function those ICT systems and networks support;

      (ii) the classification established in accordance with Article 8(1) of Regulation (EU) 2022/2554;

      (iii) the overall risk profile of ICT assets using those ICT systems and networks;

   (b) the documentation of all of the financial entity's network connections and data flows;

   (c) the use of a separate and dedicated network for the administration of ICT assets;

   (d) the identification and implementation of network access controls to prevent and detect connections to the financial entity's network by any unauthorised device or system, or any endpoint not meeting the financial entity's security requirements;

   (e) the encryption of network connections passing over corporate networks, public networks, domestic networks, third-party networks, and wireless networks, for communication protocols used, taking into account the results of the approved data classification, the results of the ICT risk assessment and the encryption of network connections referred to in Article 6(2);

(f) the design of networks in line with the ICT security requirements established by the financial entity, taking into account leading practices to ensure the confidentiality, integrity, and availability of the network;

(g) the securing of network traffic between the internal networks and the internet and other external connections;

(h) the identification of the roles and responsibilities and steps for the specification, implementation, approval, change, and review of firewall rules and connections filters;

(i) the performance of reviews of the network architecture and of the network security design once a year, and periodically for microenterprises, to identify potential vulnerabilities;

(j) the measures to temporarily isolate, where necessary, subnetworks, and network components and devices;

(k) the implementation of a secure configuration baseline of all network components, and the hardening of the network and of network devices in line with any vendor instructions, where applicable standards, as defined in Article 2, point (1), of Regulation (EU) No 1025/2012, and leading practices;

(l) the procedures to limit, lock, and terminate system and remote sessions after a specified period of inactivity;

(m) for network services agreements:

  (i) the identification and specification of ICT and information security measures, service levels, and management requirements of all network services;

  (ii) whether those services are provided by an ICT intra-group service provider or by ICT third-party service providers.

For the purposes of point (h), financial entities shall perform the review of firewall rules and connections filters on a regular basis in accordance with the classification established in accordance with Article 8(1) of Regulation (EU) 2022/2554 and the overall risk profile of ICT systems involved. For ICT systems that support critical or important functions, financial entities shall verify the adequacy of the existing firewall rules and connection filters at least every 6 months.

Article 14
Securing information in transit

1. As part of the safeguards to preserve the availability, authenticity, integrity and confidentiality of data, financial entities shall develop, document, and implement the policies, procedures, protocols, and tools to protect

information in transit. Financial entities shall in particular ensure all of the following:

(a) the availability, authenticity, integrity and confidentiality of data during network transmission, and the establishment of procedures to assess compliance with those requirements;

(b) the prevention and detection of data leakages and the secure transfer of information between the financial entity and external parties;

(c) that requirements on confidentiality or non-disclosure arrangements reflecting the financial entity's needs for the protection of information for both the staff of the financial entity and of third parties are implemented, documented, and regularly reviewed.

2. Financial entities shall design the policies, procedures, protocols, and tools to protect the information in transit referred to in paragraph 1 on the basis of the results of the approved data classification and of the ICT risk assessment.

SECTION 7
ICT PROJECT AND CHANGE MANAGEMENT
Article 15
ICT project management

1. As part of the safeguards to preserve the availability, authenticity, integrity, and confidentiality of data, financial entities shall develop, document, and implement an ICT project management policy.

2. The ICT project management policy referred to in paragraph 1 shall specify the elements that ensure the effective management of the ICT projects related to the acquisition, maintenance and, where applicable, development of the financial entity's ICT systems.

3. The ICT project management policy referred to in paragraph 1 shall contain all of the following:

(a) ICT project objectives;

(b) ICT project governance, including roles and responsibilities;

(c) ICT project planning, timeframe, and steps;

(d) ICT project risk assessment;

(e) relevant milestones;

(f) change management requirements;

(g) the testing of all requirements, including security requirements, and the respective approval process when deploying an ICT system in the production environment.

4. The ICT project management policy referred to in paragraph 1 shall ensure the secure ICT project implementation through the provision of the

necessary information and expertise from the business area or functions impacted by the ICT project.

5. In accordance with the ICT project risk assessment referred to in paragraph 3, point (d), the ICT project management policy referred to in paragraph 1 shall provide that the establishment and progress of ICT projects impacting critical or important functions of the financial entity and their associated risks are reported to the management body as follows:

   (a) individually or in aggregation, depending on the importance and size of the ICT projects;

   (b) periodically and, where necessary, on an event-driven basis.

Article 16
ICT systems acquisition, development, and maintenance

1. As part of the safeguards to preserve the availability, authenticity, integrity, and confidentiality of data, financial entities shall develop, document and implement a policy governing the acquisition, development, and maintenance of ICT systems.

   That policy shall:

   (a) identify security practices and methodologies relating to the acquisition, development, and maintenance of ICT systems;

   (b) require the identification of:

      (i) technical specifications and ICT technical specifications, as defined in Article 2, points (4) and (5), of Regulation (EU) No 1025/2012;

      (ii) requirements relating to the acquisition, development, and maintenance of ICT systems, with a particular focus on ICT security requirements and on their approval by the relevant business function and ICT asset owner in accordance with the financial entity's internal governance arrangements;

   (c) specify measures to mitigate the risk of unintentional alteration or intentional manipulation of the ICT systems during the development, maintenance, and deployment of those ICT systems in the production environment.

2. Financial entities shall develop, document, and implement an ICT systems' acquisition, development, and maintenance procedure for the testing and approval of all ICT systems prior to their use and after maintenance, in accordance with Article 8(2), point (b), points (v), (vi) and (vii). The level of testing shall be commensurate to the criticality of the business procedures and ICT assets concerned. The testing shall be designed to verify that new ICT systems are adequate to perform as intended, including the quality of the software developed internally.

Central counterparties shall, in addition to the requirements laid down in the first subparagraph, involve, as appropriate, in the design and conduct of the testing referred to in the first subparagraph:

(a) clearing members and clients;

(b) interoperable central counterparties;

(c) other interested parties.

Central securities depositories shall, in addition to the requirements laid down in the first subparagraph, involve, as appropriate, in the design and conduct of the testing referred to in the first subparagraph:

(a) users;

(b) critical utilities and critical service providers;

(c) other central securities depositories;

(d) other market infrastructures;

(e) any other institutions with which central securities depositories have identified interdependencies in their business continuity policy.

3. The procedure referred to in paragraph 2 shall contain the performance of source code reviews covering both static and dynamic testing. That testing shall contain security testing for internet-exposed systems and applications in accordance with Article 8(2), point (b), points (v), (vi) and (vii).

Financial entities shall:

(a) identify and analyse vulnerabilities and anomalies in the source code;

(b) adopt an action plan to address those vulnerabilities and anomalies;

(c) monitor the implementation of that action plan.

4. The procedure referred to in paragraph 2 shall contain security testing of software packages no later than at the integration phase, in accordance with Article 8(2), points (b)(v), (vi) and(vii).

5. The procedure referred to in paragraph 2 shall provide that:

(a) non-production environments only store anonymised, pseudonymised, or randomised production data;

(b) financial entities are to protect the integrity and confidentiality of data in nonproduction environments.

6. By way of derogation from paragraph 5, the procedure referred to in paragraph 2 may provide that production data are stored only for specific testing occasions, for limited periods of time, and following the approval by the relevant function and the reporting of such occasions to the ICT risk management function.

7. The procedurereferred to in paragraph 2 shall contain the implementation of controls to protect the integrity of the source code of ICT systems that are

developed in-house or by an ICT third-party service provider and delivered to the financial entity by an ICT third-parties service provider.

8. The procedure referred to in paragraph 2 shall provide that proprietary software and, where feasible, the source code provided by ICT third-party service providers or coming from open-source projects, are to be analysed and tested in accordance with paragraph 3 prior to their deployment in the production environment.

9. Paragraph 1 to 8 of this Article shall also apply to ICT systems developed or managed by users outside the ICT function, using a risk-based approach.

Article 17
ICT change management

1. As part of the safeguards to preserve the availability, authenticity, integrity, and confidentiality of data, financial entities shall include in the ICT change management procedures referred to in Article 9(4), point (e), of Regulation (EU) 2022/2554, in respect of all changes to software, hardware, firmware components, systems, or security parameters, all of the following elements:
   - (a) a verification of whether the ICT security requirements have been met;
   - (b) mechanisms to ensure the independence of the functions that approve changes and the functions responsible for requesting and implementing those changes;
   - (c) a clear description of the roles and responsibilities to ensure that:
     - (i) changes are specified and planned;
     - (ii) an adequate transition is designed;
     - (iii) the changes are tested and finalised in a controlled manner;
     - (iv) there is an effective quality assurance;
   - (d) the documentation and communication of change details, including:
     - (i) the purpose and scope of the change;
     - (ii) the timeline for the implementation of the change;
     - (iii) the expected outcomes;
   - (e) the identification of fall-back procedures and responsibilities, including procedures and responsibilities for aborting changes or recovering from changes not successfully implemented;
   - (f) procedures, protocols, and tools to manage emergency changes that provide adequate safeguards;
   - (g) procedures to document, re-evaluate, assess, and approve emergency changes after their implementation, including workarounds and patches;
   - (h) the identification of the potential impact of a change on existing ICT security measures and an assessment of whether such change requires the adoption of additional ICT security measures.

2. After having made significant changes to their ICT systems, central counterparties and central securities depositories shall submit their ICT systems to stringent testing by simulating stressed conditions.

   Central counterparties shall involve, as appropriate, in the design and conduct of the testing referred to in the first subparagraph:

   (a) clearing members and clients;

   (b) interoperable central counterparties;

   (c) other interested parties;

   Central securities depositories shall, as appropriate, involve in the design and conduct of the testing referred to in the first subparagraph:

   (a) users;

   (b) critical utilities and critical service providers;

   (c) other central securities depositories;

   (d) other market infrastructures;

   (e) any other institutions with which central securities depositories have identified interdependencies in their ICT business continuity policy.

SECTION 8

Article 18
Physical and environmental security

1. As part of the safeguards to preserve the availability, authenticity, integrity, and confidentiality of data, financial entities shall specify, document, and implement a physical and environmental security policy. Financial entities shall design that policy in light of the cyber threat landscape, in accordance with the classification established in accordance with Article 8(1) of Regulation (EU) 2022/2554, and in light of the overall risk profile of ICT assets and accessible information assets.

2. The physical and environmental security policy referred to in paragraph 1 shall contain all of the following:

   (a) a reference to the section of the policy on control of access management rights referred to in Article 21(1) point (g);

   (b) measures to protect from attacks, accidents, and environmental threats and hazards, the premises, data centres of the financial entity, and sensitive designated areas identified by the financial entity, where ICT assets and information assets reside;

   (c) measures to secure ICT assets, both within and outside the premises of the financial entity, taking into account the results of the ICT risk assessment related to the relevant ICT assets;

   (d) measures to ensure the availability, authenticity, integrity, and confidentiality of ICT assets, information assets, and physical access control devices of the financial entity through the appropriate maintenance;

(e) measures to preserve the availability, authenticity, integrity, and confidentiality of the data, including:

   (i) a clear desk policy for papers;

   (ii) a clear screen policy for information processing facilities.

For the purposes of point (b), the measures to protect from environmental threats and hazards shall be commensurate with the importance of the premises, data centres, sensitive designated areas, and the criticality of the operations or ICT systems located therein.

For the purposes of point (c), the physical and environmental security policy referred to in paragraph 1 shall contain measures to provide appropriate protection to unattended ICT assets.

Chapter II
HUMAN RESOURCES POLICY AND ACCESS CONTROL

Article 19
Human resources policy

Financial entities shall include in their human resource policy or other relevant policies all of the following ICT security related elements:

(a) the identification and assignment of any specific ICT security responsibilities;

(b) requirements for staff of the financial entity and of the ICT third-party service providers using or accessing ICT assets of the financial entity to:

   (i) be informed about, and adhere to, the financial entity's ICT security policies, procedures, and protocols;

   (ii) be aware of the reporting channels put in place by the financial entity for the detection of anomalous behaviour, including, where applicable, the reporting channels established in line with Directive (EU) 2019/1937 of the European Parliament and of the Council10;

   (iii) for the staff, to return to the financial entity, upon termination of employment, all ICT assets and tangible information assets in their possession that belong to the financial entity.

Article 20
Identity management

1. As part of their control of access management rights, financial entities shall develop, document, and implement identity management policies and procedures that ensure the unique identification and authentication of natural persons and systems accessing the financial entities' information to enable assignment of user access rights in accordance with Article 21.

2. The identity management policies and procedures referred to in paragraph 1 shall contain all of the following:

   (a) without prejudice to Article 21(1), point (c), a unique identity corresponding to a unique user account shall be assigned to each staff member of the financial entity or staff of the ICT third-party service providers accessing the information assets and ICT assets of the financial entity;

   (b) a lifecycle management process for identities and accounts managing the creation, change, review and update, temporary deactivation, and termination of all accounts.

   For the purposes of point (a), financial entities shall maintain records of all identity assignments. Those records shall be kept following a reorganisation of the financial entity or after the end of the contractual relationship without prejudice to the retention requirements laid down in applicable Union and national law.

   For the purposes of point (b), financial entities shall, where feasible and appropriate, deploy automated solutions for the lifecycle identity management process.

Article 21
Access control

As part of their control of access management rights, financial entities shall develop, document, and implement a policy that contains all of the following:

(a) the assignment of access rights to ICT assets based on need-to-know, need-to-use and least privilege principles, including for remote and emergency access;

(b) the segregation of duties designed to prevent unjustified access to critical data or to prevent the allocation of combinations of access rights that may be used to circumvent controls;

(c) a provision on user accountability, by limiting to the extent possible the use of generic and shared user accounts and ensuring that users are identifiable for the actions performed in the ICT systems at all times;

(d) a provision on restrictions of access to ICT assets, setting out controls and tools to prevent unauthorised access;

(e) account management procedures to grant, change or revoke access rights for user and generic accounts, including generic administrator accounts, including provision on all of the following:

   (i) assignment of roles and responsibilities for granting, reviewing, and revoking access rights;

   (ii) assignment of privileged, emergency, and administrator access on a need-touse or an ad-hoc basis for all ICT systems;

(iii) withdrawal of access rights without undue delay upon termination of the employment or when the access is no longer necessary;

(iv) update of access rights where changes are necessary and at least once a year for all ICT systems, other than ICT systems supporting critical or important functions and at least every 6 months for ICT systems supporting critical or important functions.

(f) authentication methods, including all of the following:

(i) the use of authentication methods commensurate to the classification established in accordance with Article 8(1) of Regulation (EU) 2022/2554 and to the overall risk profile of ICT assets and considering leading practices;

(ii) the use of strong authentication methods in accordance with leading practices and techniques for remote access to the financial entity's network, for privileged access, for access to ICT assets supporting critical or important functions or ICT assets that are publicly accessible;

(g) physical access controls measures including:

(i) the identification and logging of natural persons that are authorised to access premises, data centres, and sensitive designated areas identified by the financial entity where ICT and information assets reside;

(ii) the granting of physical access rights to critical ICT assets to authorised persons only, in accordance with the need-to-know and least privilege principles, and on an ad-hoc basis;

(iii) the monitoring of physical access to premises, data centres, and sensitive designated areas identified by the financial entity where ICT and information assets or both reside;

(iv) the review of physical access rights to ensure that unnecessary access rights are promptly revoked.

For the purposes of point (e)(i), financial entities shall establish the retention period taking into account the business and information security objectives, the reasons for recording the event in the logs, and the results of the ICT risk assessment.

For the purposes of point (e)(ii), financial entities shall, where possible, use dedicated accounts for the performance of administrative tasks on ICT systems. Where feasible and appropriate, financial entities shall deploy automated solutions for the privilege access management.

For the purposes of point (g)(i), the identification and logging shall be commensurate with the importance of the premises, data centres, sensitive designated areas, and the criticality of the operations or ICT systems located therein.

For the purposes of point (g)(iii), the monitoring shall be commensurate to the classification established in accordance with Article 8(1) of Regulation (EU) 2022/2554 and the criticality of the area accessed.

CHAPTER III
ICT-RELATED INCIDENT DETECTION AND RESPONSE

Article 22
ICT-related incident management policy

As part of the mechanisms to detect anomalous activities, including ICT network performance issues and ICT-related incidents, financial entities shall develop, document, and implement an ICT-related incident policy through which they shall:

(a) document the ICT-related incident management process referred to in Article 17 of Regulation (EU) 2022/2554;

(b) establish a list of relevant contacts with internal functions and external stakeholders that are directly involved in ICT operations security, including on:

 (i) the detection and monitoring of cyber threats;

 (ii) the detection of anomalous activities;

 (iii) vulnerability management;

(c) establish, implement, and operate technical, organisational, and operational mechanisms to support the ICT-related incident management process, including mechanisms to enable a prompt detection of anomalous activities and behaviours in accordance with Article 23 of this Regulation;

(d) retain all evidence relating to ICT-related incidents for a period that shall be no longer than necessary for the purposes for which the data are collected, commensurate with the criticality of the affected business functions, supporting processes, and ICT and information assets, in accordance with [Article [15] of Commission Delegated Regulation (EU) […]/[…] [Commission Delegated Regulation on classification of ICT related incidents]11 and with any applicable retention requirement pursuant to Union law;

(e) establish and implement mechanisms to analyse significant or recurring ICT-related incidents and patterns in the number and the occurrence of ICT-related incidents.

For the purposes of point (d), financial entities shall retain the evidence referred to in that point in a secure manner.

Article 23
Anomalous activities detection and criteria for ICT-related incidents detection and response

1. Financial entities shall set clear roles and responsibilities to effectively detect and respond to ICT-related incidents and anomalous activities.

2. The mechanism to promptly detect anomalous activities, including ICT network performance issues and ICT-related incidents, as referred to

in Article 10(1) of Regulation (EU) 2022/2554, shall enable financial entities to:

(a) collect, monitor, and analyse all of the following:

  (i) internal and external factors, including at least the logs collected in accordance with Article 12 of this Regulation, information from business and ICT functions, and any problem reported by users of the financial entity;

  (ii) potential internal and external cyber threats, considering scenarios commonly used by threat actors and scenarios based on threat intelligence activity;

  (iii) ICT-related incident notification from an ICT third-party service provider of the financial entity detected in the ICT systems and networks of the ICT third-party service provider and that may affect the financial entity;

(b) identify anomalous activities and behaviour, and implement tools generating alerts for anomalous activities and behaviour, at least for ICT assets and information assets supporting critical or important functions;

(c) prioritise the alerts referred to in point (b) to allow for the management of the detected ICT-related incidents within the expected resolution time, as specified by financial entities, both during and outside working hours;

(d) record, analyse, and evaluate any relevant information on all anomalous activities and behaviours automatically or manually.

For the purposes of point (b), the tools referred to in that point shall contain the tools that provide automated alerts based on pre-defined rules to identify anomalies affecting the completeness and integrity of the data sources or log collection.

3. Financial entities shall protect any recording of the anomalous activities against tampering and unauthorised access at rest, in transit and, where relevant, in use.

4. Financial entities shall log all relevant information for each detected anomalous activity enabling:

(a) the identification of the date and time of occurrence of the anomalous activity;

(b) the identification of the date and time of detection of the anomalous activity;

(c) the identification of the type of the anomalous activity.

5. Financial entities shall consider all of the following criteria to trigger the ICT-related incident detection and response processes referred to in Article 10(2) of Regulation (EU) 2022/2554:

(a) indications that malicious activity may have been carried out in an ICT system or network, or that such ICT system or network may have been compromised;

(b) data losses detected in relation to the availability, authenticity, integrity, and confidentiality of data;

(c) adverse impact detected on financial entity's transactions and operations;

(d) ICT systems' and network unavailability;

6. For the purposes of paragraph 5, financial entities shall also consider the criticality of the services affected.

CHAPTER IV
ICT BUSINESS CONTINUITY MANAGEMENT

Article 24
Components of the ICT business continuity policy

1. Financial entities shall include in their ICT business continuity policy referred to in Article 11(1) of Regulation (EU) 2022/2554 all of the following:

(a) a description of:

(i) the objectives of the ICT business continuity policy, including the interrelation of ICT and overall business continuity, and considering the results of the business impact analysis (BIA) referred to in Article 11(5) of Regulation (EU) 2022/2554;

(ii) the scope of the ICT business continuity arrangements, plans, procedures, and mechanisms, including limitations and exclusions;

(iii) the timeframe to be covered by the ICT business continuity arrangements, plans, procedures, and mechanisms;

(iv) the criteria to activate and deactivate ICT business continuity plans, ICT response and recovery plans, and crisis communications plans;

(b) provisions on:

(i) the governance and organisation to implement the ICT business continuity policy, including roles, responsibilities and escalation procedures ensuring that sufficient resources are available;

(ii) the alignment between the ICT business continuity plans and the overall business continuity plans, concerning at least all of the following:

(1) potential failure scenarios, including the scenarios referred to in Article 26(2) of this Regulation;

(2) recovery objectives, specifying that the financial entity shall be able to recover the operations of its critical or important functions after disruptions within a recovery time objective and a recovery point objective;

(iii) the development of ICT business continuity plans for severe business disruptions as part of those plans, and the prioritisation of ICT business continuity actions using a risk-based approach;

(iv) the development, testing and review of ICT response and recovery plans, in accordance with Articles 25 and 26 of this Regulation;

(v) the review of the effectiveness of the implemented ICT business continuity arrangements, plans, procedures and mechanisms, in accordance with Article 26 of this Regulation;

(vi) the alignment of the ICT business continuity policy to:

(1) the communication policy referred to in Article 14(2) of Regulation (EU) 2022/2554;

(2) the communication and crisis communication actions referred to in Article 11(2), point (e), of Regulation (EU) 2022/2554.

2. In addition to the requirements referred to in paragraph 1, central counterparties shall ensure that their ICT business continuity policy:

(a) contains a maximum recovery time for their critical functions that is not longer than 2 hours;

(b) takes into account external links and interdependencies within the financial infrastructures, including trading venues cleared by the central counterparty, securities settlement and payment systems, and credit institutions used by the central counterparty or a linked central counterparty;

(c) requires that arrangements are in place to:

(i) ensure the continuity of critical or important functions of the central counterparty based on disaster scenarios;

(ii) maintain a secondary processing site capable of ensuring continuity of critical or important functions of the central counterparty identical to the primary site;

(iii) maintain or have immediate access to a secondary business site, to allow staff to ensure continuity of the service if the primary location of business is not available;

(iv) consider the need for additional processing sites, in particular where the diversity of the risk profiles of the primary and secondary sites does not provide sufficient confidence that the central counterparty's business continuity objectives will be met in all scenarios.

For the purposes of point (a), central counterparties shall complete end of day procedures and payments on the required time and day in all circumstances.

For the purposes of point (c)(i), arrangements referred to in that point shall address the availability of adequate human resources, the maximum downtime of critical functions, and fail over and recovery to a secondary site.

For the purposes of point (c)(ii), the secondary processing site referred to in that point shall have a geographical risk profile which is distinct from that of the primary site.

3. In addition to the requirements referred to in paragraph 1, central securities depositories shall ensure that their ICT business continuity policy:

   (a) takes into account any links and interdependencies to users, critical utilities and critical service providers, other central securities depositories and other market infrastructures;

   (b) requires its ICT business continuity arrangements to ensure that the recovery time objective for their critical or important functions shall not be longer than 2 hours.

4. In addition to the requirements referred to in paragraph 1, trading venues shall ensure that their ICT business continuity policy ensures that:

   (a) trading can be resumed within or close to 2 hours of a disruptive incident;

   (b) the maximum amount of data that may be lost from any IT service of the trading venue after a disruptive incident is close to zero.

Article 25
Testing of the ICT business continuity plans

1. When testing the ICT business continuity plans in accordance with Article 11(6), of Regulation (EU) 2022/2554, financial entities shall take into account the financial entity's business impact analysis (BIA) and the ICT risk assessment referred to in Article 3(1), point (b), of this Regulation.

2. Financial entities shall assess through the testing of their ICT business continuity plans referred to in paragraph 1 whether they are able to ensure the continuity of the financial entity's critical or important functions. That testing shall:

   (a) be performed on the basis of test scenarios that simulate potential disruptions, including an adequate set of severe but plausible scenarios;

   (b) contain the testing of ICT services provided by ICT third-party service providers, where applicable;

   (c) for financial entities, other than microenterprises, as referred to in Article 11(6), second subparagraph, of Regulation (EU) 2022/2554, contain scenarios of switchover from primary ICT infrastructure to the redundant capacity, backups and redundant facilities;

(d) be designed to challenge the assumptions on which the business continuity plans are based, including governance arrangements and crisis communication plans;

(e) contain procedures to verify the ability of the financial entities' staff, of ICT third-party service providers, of ICT systems, and ICT services to respond adequately to the scenarios duly taken into account in accordance with Article 26(2).

For the purposes of point (a), financial entities shall always include in the testing the scenarios considered for the development of the business continuity plans.

For the purposes of point (b), financial entities shall duly consider scenarios linked to insolvency or failures of the ICT third-party service providers or linked to political risks in the ICT third-party service providers' jurisdictions, where relevant.

For the purposes of point (c), the testing shall verify whether at least critical or important functions can be operated appropriately for a sufficient period of time, and whether the normal functioning may be restored.

3. In addition to the requirements referred to in paragraph 2, central counterparties shall involve in the testing of their ICT business continuity plans referred to in paragraph 1:

(a) clearing members;

(b) external providers;

(c) relevant institutions in the financial infrastructure with which central counterparties have identified interdependencies in their business continuity policies.

4. In addition to the requirements referred to in paragraph 2, central securities depositories shall involve in the testing of their ICT business continuity plans referred to in paragraph 1, as appropriate:

(a) users of the central securities depositories;

(b) critical utilities and critical service providers;

(c) other central securities depositories;

(d) other market infrastructures;

(e) any other institutions with which central securities depositories have identified interdependencies in their business continuity policy.

5. Financial entities shall document the results of the testing referred to in paragraph 1.

Any identified deficiencies resulting from that testing shall be analysed, addressed, and reported to the management body.

Article 26
ICT response and recovery plans

1. When developing the ICT response and recovery plans referred to in Article 11(3) of Regulation (EU) 2022/2554, financial entities shall take into account the results of the financial entity's business impact analysis (BIA). Those ICT response and recovery plans shall:

   (a) specify the conditions prompting their activation or deactivation, and any exceptions for such activation or deactivation;

   (b) describe what actions are to be taken to ensure the availability, integrity, continuity, and recovery of at least ICT systems and services supporting critical or important functions of the financial entity;

   (c) be designed to meet the recovery objectives of the operations of the financial entities;

   (d) be documented and made available to the staff involved in the execution of ICT response and recovery plans and be readily accessible in case of emergency;

   (e) provide for both short-term and long-term recovery options, including partial systems recovery;

   (f) lay down the objectives of ICT response and recovery plans and the conditions to declare a successful execution of those plans.

   For the purposes of point (d), financial entities shall clearly specify roles and responsibilities.

2. The ICT response and recovery plans referred to in paragraph 1 shall identify relevant scenarios, including scenarios of severe business disruptions and increased likelihood of occurrence of disruption. Those plans shall develop scenarios based on current information on threats and on lessons learned from previous occurrences of business disruptions. Financial entities shall duly take into account all of the following scenarios:

   (a) cyber-attacks and switchovers between the primary ICT infrastructure and the redundant capacity, backups, and redundant facilities;

   (b) scenarios in which the quality of the provision of a critical or important function deteriorates to an unacceptable level or fails, and duly consider the potential impact of the insolvency, or other failures, of any relevant ICT third party service provider;

   (c) partial or total failure of premises, including office and business premises, and data centres;

   (d) substantial failure of ICT assets or of the communication infrastructure;

   (e) the non-availability of a critical number of staff or staff members in charge of guaranteeing the continuity of operations;

   (f) impact of climate change and environment degradation related events, natural disasters, pandemics, and physical attacks, including intrusions and terrorist attacks;

(g) insider attacks;

(h) political and social instability, including, where relevant, in the ICT third-party service provider's jurisdiction and the location where the data are stored and processed;

(i) widespread power outages.

3. Where the primary recovery measures may not be feasible in the short term because of costs, risks, logistics, or unforeseen circumstances, the ICT response and recovery plans referred to in paragraph 1 shall consider alternative options.

4. As part of the ICT response and recovery plans referred to in paragraph 1, financial entities shall consider and implement continuity measures to mitigate failures of ICT third-party service providers of ICT services supporting critical or important functions of the financial entity.

CHAPTER V
REPORT ON THE ICT RISK MANAGEMENT FRAMEWORK REVIEW

Article 27
Format and content of the report on the review of the ICT risk management framework

1. Financial entities shall submit the report on the review of the ICT risk management framework referred to in Article 6(5) of Regulation (EU) 2022/2554 in a searchable electronic format.

2. Financial entities shall include all of the following information in the report referred to in paragraph 1:

   (a) an introductory section that:

      (i) clearly identifies the financial entity that is the subject of the report, and describes its group structure, where relevant;

      (ii) describes the context of the report in terms of the nature, scale, and complexity of the financial entity's services, activities, and operations, its organisation, identified critical functions, strategy, major ongoing projects or activities, relationships and its dependence on in-house and contracted ICT services and systems or the implications that a total loss or severe degradation of such systems would have in terms of critical or important functions and market efficiency;

      (iii) summarises the major changes in the ICT risk management framework since the previous report submitted;

      (iv) provides an executive level summary of the current and near-term ICT risk profile, threat landscape, the assessed effectiveness of its controls, and the security posture of the financial entity;

   (b) the date of the approval of the report by the management body of the financial entity;

(c) a description of the reason for the review of the ICT risk management framework in accordance with Article 6(5) of Regulation (EU) 2022/2554.;

(d) the start and end dates of the review period;

(e) an indication of the function responsible for the review;

(f) a description of the major changes and improvements to the ICT risk management framework since the previous review;

(g) a summary of the findings of the review and detailed analysis and assessment of the severity of the weaknesses, deficiencies, and gaps in the ICT risk management framework during the review period;

(h) a description of the measures to address identified weaknesses, deficiencies, and gaps, including all of the following:

  (i) a summary of measures taken to remediate to identified weaknesses, deficiencies and gaps;

  (ii) an expected date for implementing the measures and dates related to the internal control of the implementation, including information on the state of progress of the implementation of those measures as at the date of drafting of the report, explaining, where applicable, if there is a risk that deadlines may not be respected;

  (iii) tools to be used, and the identification of the function responsible for carrying out the measures, detailing whether the tools and functions are internal or external;

  (iv) a description of the impact of the changes envisaged in the measures on the financial entity's budgetary, human, and material resources, including resources dedicated to the implementation of any corrective measures;

  (v) information on the process for informing the competent authority, where appropriate;

  (vi) where the weaknesses, deficiencies, or gaps identified are not subject to corrective measures, a detailed explanation of the criteria used to analyse the impact of those weaknesses, deficiencies, or gaps, to evaluate the related residual ICT risk, and of the criteria used to accept the related residual risk;

(i) information on planned further developments of the ICT risk management framework;

(j) conclusions resulting from the review of the ICT risk management framework;

(k) information on past reviews, including:

  (i) a list of past reviews to date;

(ii) where applicable, a state of implementation of the corrective measures identified by the last report;

(iii) where the proposed corrective measures in past reviews have proven ineffective or have created unexpected challenges, a description of how those corrective measures could be improved or of those unexpected challenges;

(l) sources of information used in the preparation of the report, including all of the following:

(i) for financial entities other than microenterprises as referred to in Article 6(6) of Regulation (EU) 2022/2554, the results of internal audits;

(ii) the results of compliance assessments;

(iii) results of digital operational resilience testing, and where applicable the results of advanced testing, based on threat-led penetration testing (TLPT), of ICT tools, systems, and processes;

(iv) external sources.

For the purposes of point (c), where the review was initiated following supervisory instructions, or conclusions derived from relevant digital operational resilience testing or audit processes, the report shall contain explicit references to such instructions or conclusions, allowing for the identification of the reason for initiating the review. Where the review was initiated following ICT-related incidents, the report shall contain the list of all ICT-related incidents with incident root-cause analysis.

For the purposes of point (f), the description shall contain an analysis of the impact of the changes on the financial entity's digital operational resilience strategy, on the financial entity's ICT internal control framework, and on the financial entity's ICT risk management governance.

TITLE III – SIMPLIFIED ICT RISK MANAGEMENT

FRAMEWORK FOR FINANCIAL ENTITIES REFERRED TO IN ARTICLE 16(1) OF REGULATION (EU) 2022/2554

CHAPTER I
SIMPLIFIED ICT RISK MANAGEMENT FRAMEWORK

Article 28
Governance and organisation

1. The financial entities referred to in Article 16(1) of Regulation (EU) 2022/2554 shall have in place an internal governance and control framework that ensures an effective and prudent management of ICT risk to achieve a high level of digital operational resilience.

2. The financial entities referred to in paragraph 1 shall, as part of their simplified ICT risk management framework, ensure that their management body:

(a) bears the overall responsibility for ensuring that the simplified ICT risk management framework allows for the achievement of the financial entity's business strategy in accordance with the risk appetite of that financial entity, and ensures that ICT risk is considered in that context;

(b) sets clear roles and responsibilities for all ICT-related tasks;

(c) sets out information security objectives and ICT requirements;

(d) approves, oversees, and periodically reviews:

 (i) the classification of information assets of the financial entity as referred to in Article 30(1) of this Regulation, the list of main risks identified, and the business impact analysis and related policies;

 (ii) the business continuity plans of the financial entity, and the response and recovery measures referred to in Article 16(1), point (f), of Regulation (EU) 2022/2554;

(e) allocates and reviews at least once a year the budget necessary to fulfil the financial entity's digital operational resilience needs in respect of all types of resources, including relevant ICT security awareness programmes and digital operational resilience training and ICT skills for all staff;

(f) specifies and implements the policies and measures included in Chapters I, II and III of this Title to identify, assess and manage the ICT risk the financial entity is exposed to;

(g) identifies and implements procedures, ICT protocols, and tools that are necessary to protect all information assets and ICT assets;

(h) ensures that the staff of the financial entity is kept up to date with sufficient knowledge and skills to understand and assess ICT risk and its impact on the operations of the financial entity, commensurate to the ICT risk being managed;

(i) establishes reporting arrangements, including the frequency, form, and content of reporting to the management body on the information security and digital operational resilience.

3. The financial entities referred to in paragraph 1 may, in accordance with Union and national sectoral law, outsource the tasks of verifying compliance with ICT risk management requirements to ICT intra-group or ICT third-party service providers. In case of such outsourcing, financial entities shall remain fully responsible for the verification of compliance with the ICT risk management requirements.

4. The financial entities referred to in paragraph 1 shall ensure an appropriate segregation and the independence of control functions and internal audit functions.

5. The financial entities referred to in paragraph 1 shall ensure that their simplified ICT risk management framework is subject to an internal audit

by auditors, in line with the financial entities' audit plan. The auditors shall have sufficient knowledge, skills, and expertise in ICT risk, and shall be independent. The frequency and focus of ICT audits shall be commensurate to the ICT risk of the financial entity.

6. Based on the outcome of the audit referred to in paragraph 5, the financial entities referred to in paragraph 1 shall ensure the timely verification and remediation of critical ICT audit findings.

Article 29
Information security policy and measures

1. The financial entities referred to in Article 16(1) of Regulation (EU) 2022/2554 shall develop, document, and implement an information security policy in the context of the simplified ICT risk management framework. That information security policy shall specify the high-level principles and rules to protect the confidentiality, integrity, availability, and authenticity of data and of the services those financial entities provide.

2. Based on their information security policy referred to in paragraph 1, the financial entities referred to in paragraph 1 shall establish and implement ICT security measures to mitigate their exposure to ICT risk, including mitigating measures implemented by ICT third-party service providers.

   The ICT security measures shall include all of the measures referred to in Articles 30 to 38.

Article 30
Classification of information assets and ICT assets

1. As part of the simplified ICT risk management framework referred to in Article 16(1), point (a), of Regulation (EU) 2022/2554, the financial entities referred to in paragraph 1 of that Article shall identify, classify, and document all critical or important functions, the information assets and ICT assets supporting them and their interdependencies. Financial entities shall review that identification and classification as needed.

2. The financial entities referred to in paragraph 1 shall identify all critical or important functions supported by ICT third-party service providers.

Article 31
ICT risk management

1. The financial entities referred to in Article 16(1) of Regulation (EU) 2022/2554 shall include in their simplified ICT risk management framework all of the following:

   (a) a determination of the risk tolerance levels for ICT risk, in accordance with the risk appetite of the financial entity;

   (b) the identification and assessment of the ICT risks to which the financial entity is exposed;

(c) the specification of mitigation strategies at least for the ICT risks that are not within the risk tolerance levels of the financial entity;

(d) the monitoring of the effectiveness of the mitigation strategies referred to in point (c);

(e) the identification and assessment of any ICT and information security risks resulting from any major change in ICT system or ICT services, processes, or procedures, and from ICT security testing results and after any major ICT related incident.

2. The financial entities referred to in paragraph 1 shall carry out and document the ICT risk assessment periodically commensurate to the financial entities' ICT risk profile.

3. The financial entities referred to in paragraph 1 shall continuously monitor threats and vulnerabilities that are relevant to their critical or important functions, and information assets and ICT assets, and shall regularly review the risk scenarios impacting those critical or important functions.

4. The financial entities referred to in paragraph 1 shall set out alert thresholds and criteria to trigger and initiate ICT-related incident response processes.

Article 32
Physical and environmental security

1. The financial entities referred to in Article 16(1) of Regulation (EU) 2022/2554 shall identify and implement physical security measures designed on the basis of the threat landscape and in accordance with the classification referred to in Article 30(1) of this Regulation, the overall risk profile of ICT assets, and accessible information assets.

2. The measures referred to in paragraph 1 shall protect the premises of financial entities and, where applicable, data centres of financial entities where ICT assets and information assets reside from unauthorised access, attacks, and accidents, and from environmental threats and hazards.

3. The protection from environmental threats and hazards shall be commensurate with the importance of the premises concerned and, where applicable, the data centres and the criticality of the operations or ICT systems located therein.

CHAPTER II
FURTHER ELEMENTS OF SYSTEMS, PROTOCOLS, AND TOOLS TO MINIMISE THE IMPACT OF ICT RISK

Article 33
Access Control

1. The financial entities referred to in Article 16(1) of Regulation (EU) 2022/2554 shall develop, document, and implement procedures for the control of logical and physical access and shall enforce, monitor, and

periodically review those procedures. Those procedures shall contain the following elements of control of logical and physical access:

(a) access rights to information assets, ICT assets, and their supported functions, and to critical locations of operation of the financial entity, are managed on a need-to-know, need-to-use and least privileges basis, including for remote and emergency access;

(b) user accountability, which ensures that users can be identified for the actions performed in the ICT systems;

(c) account management procedures to grant, change, or revoke access rights for user and generic accounts, including generic administrator accounts;

(d) authentication methods that are commensurate to the classification referred to in Article 30(1) and to the overall risk profile of ICT assets, and which are based on leading practices;

(e) access rights are periodically reviewed and are withdrawn when no longer required.

For the purposes of point (c), the financial entity shall assign privileged, emergency, and administrator access on a need-to-use or an ad-hoc basis for all ICT systems, and shall be logged in accordance with Article 34(1), point (f).

For the purposes of point (d), financial entities shall use strong authentication methods that are based on leading practices for remote access to the financial entities' network, for privileged access, and for access to ICT assets supporting critical or important functions that are publicly available.

Article 34
ICT operations security

The financial entities referred to in Article 16(1) of Regulation (EU) 2022/2554 shall, as part of their systems, protocols, and tools, and for all ICT assets:

(a) monitor and manage the lifecycle of all ICT assets;

(b) monitor whether the ICT assets are supported by ICT third-party service providers of financial entities, where applicable;

(c) identify capacity requirements of their ICT assets and measures to maintain and improve the availability and efficiency of ICT systems and prevent ICT capacity shortages before they materialise;

(d) perform automated vulnerability scanning and assessments of ICT assets commensurate to their classification as referred to in Article 30(1) and to the overall risk profile of the ICT asset, and deploy patches to address identified vulnerabilities;

(e) manage the risks related to outdated, unsupported, or legacy ICT assets;

(f) log events related to logical and physical access control, ICT operations, including system and network traffic activities, and ICT change management;

(g) identify and implement measures to monitor and analyse information on anomalous activities and behaviour for critical or important ICT operations;

(h) implement measures to monitor relevant and up-to-date information about cyber threats;

(i) implement measures to identify possible information leakages, malicious code and other security threats, and publicly known vulnerabilities in software and hardware, and check for corresponding new security updates.

For the purposes of point (f), financial entities shall align the level of detail of the logs with their purpose and usage of the ICT asset producing those logs.

Article 35
Data, system and network security

The financial entities referred to in Article 16(1) of Regulation (EU) 2022/2554 shall, as part of their systems, protocols, and tools, develop and implement safeguards that ensure the security of networks against intrusions and data misuse and that preserve the availability, authenticity, integrity, and confidentiality of data. In particular, financial entities shall, taking into account the classification referred to in Article 30(1) of this Regulation, establish all of the following:

(a) the identification and implementation of measures to protect data in use, in transit, and at rest;

(b) the identification and implementation of security measures regarding the use of software, data storage media, systems and endpoint devices that transfer and store data of the financial entity;

(c) the identification and implementation of measures to prevent and detect unauthorised connections to the financial entity's network, and to secure the network traffic between the financial entity's internal networks and the internet and other external connections;

(d) the identification and implementation of measures that ensure the availability, authenticity, integrity, and confidentiality of data during network transmissions;

(e) a process to securely delete data on premises, or that are stored externally, that the financial entity no longer needs to collect or store;

(f) a process to securely dispose of, or decommission, data storage devices on premises, or data storage devices that are stored externally, that contain confidential information;

(g) the identification and implementation of measures to ensure that teleworking and the use of private endpoint devices does not adversely impact the financial entity's ability to carry out its critical activities in an adequate, timely, and secure manner.

Article 36
ICT security testing

1. The financial entities referred to in Article 16(1) of Regulation (EU) 2022/2554 shall establish and implement an ICT security testing plan to validate the effectiveness of their ICT security measures developed in accordance with Articles 33, 34 and 35 and Articles 37 and 38 of this Regulation. Financial entities shall ensure that that plan considers threats and vulnerabilities identified as part of the simplified ICT risk management framework referred to in Article 31 of this Regulation.
2. The financial entities referred to in paragraph 1 shall review, asses and test ICT security measures, taking into consideration the overall risk profile of the ICT assets of the financial entity.
3. The financial entities referred to in paragraph 1 shall monitor and evaluate the results of the security tests and update their security measures accordingly without undue delay in the case of ICT systems supporting critical or important functions.

Article 37
ICT systems acquisition, development, and maintenance

The financial entities referred to in Article 16(1) of Regulation (EU) 2022/2554 shall design and implement, where appropriate, a procedure governing the acquisition, development, and maintenance of ICT systems following a risk-based approach. That procedure shall:

(a) ensure that, before any acquisition or development of ICT systems takes place, the functional and non-functional requirements, including information security requirements, are clearly specified and approved by the business function concerned;

(b) ensure the testing and approval of ICT systems prior to their first use and before introducing changes to the production environment;

(c) identify measures to mitigate the risk of unintentional alteration or intentional manipulation of the ICT systems during development and implementation in the production environment.

Article 38
ICT project and change management

1. The financial entities referred to in Article 16(1) of Regulation (EU) 2022/2554 shall develop, document, and implement an ICT project management procedure and shall specify the roles and responsibilities for its implementation. That procedure shall cover all stages of the ICT projects from their initiation to their closure.
2. The financial entities referred to in paragraph 1 shall develop, document, and implement an ICT change management procedure to ensure that all changes to ICT systems are recorded, tested, assessed, approved, implemented, and

verified in a controlled manner and with the adequate safeguards to preserve the financial entity's digital operational resilience.

Chapter III
ICT BUSINESS CONTINUITY MANAGEMENT

Article 39
Components of the ICT business continuity plan

1. The financial entities referred to in Article 16(1) of Regulation (EU) 2022/2554 shall develop their ICT business continuity plans considering the results of the analysis of their exposures to and potential impact of severe business disruptions and scenarios to which their ICT assets supporting critical or important functions might be exposed, including a cyber-attack scenario.

2. The ICT business continuity plans referred to in paragraph 1 shall:

   (a) be approved by the management body of the financial entity;

   (b) be documented and readily accessible in the event of an emergency or crisis;

   (c) allocate sufficient resources for their execution;

   (d) establish planned recovery levels and timeframes for the recovery and resumption of functions and key internal and external dependencies, including ICT third-party service providers;

   (e) identify the conditions that may prompt the activation of the ICT business continuity plans and what actions are to be taken to ensure the availability, continuity, and recovery of the financial entities' ICT assets supporting critical or important functions;

   (f) identify the restoration and recovery measures for critical or important business functions, supporting processes, information assets, and their interdependencies to avoid adverse effects on the functioning of the financial entities;

   (g) identify backup procedures and measures that specify the scope of the data that are subject to the backup, and the minimum frequency of the backup, based on the criticality of the function using those data;

   (h) consider alternative options where recovery may not be feasible in the short term because of costs, risks, logistics, or unforeseen circumstances;

   (i) specify the internal and external communication arrangements, including escalation plans;

   (j) be updated in line with lessons learned from incidents, tests, new risks, and threats identified, changed recovery objectives, major changes to the financial entity's organisation, and to the ICT assets supporting critical or business functions.

For the purposes of point (f), the measures referred to in that point shall provide for the mitigation of failures of critical third-party providers.

Article 40
Testing of business continuity plans

1. The financial entities referred to in Article 16(1) of Regulation (EU) 2022/2554 shall test their business continuity plans referred to in Article 39 of this Regulation, including the scenarios referred to in that Article, at least once every year for the back-up and restore procedures, or upon every major change of the business continuity plan.
2. The testing of business continuity plans referred to in paragraph 1 shall demonstrate that the financial entities referred to in that paragraph are able to sustain the viability of their businesses until critical operations are re-established and identify any deficiencies in those plans.
3. The financial entities referred to in paragraph 1 shall document the results of the testing of business continuity plans and any identified deficiencies resulting from that testing shall be analysed, addressed, and reported to the management body.

CHAPTER IV
REPORT ON THE REVIEW OF THE SIMPLIFIED ICT RISK MANAGEMENT FRAMEWORK

Article 41
Format and content of the report on the review of the simplified ICT risk management framework

1. The financial entities referred to in Article 16(1) of Regulation (EU) 2022/2554 shall submit the report on the review of the ICT risk management framework referred to in paragraph 2 of that Article in a searchable electronic format.
2. The report referred to in paragraph 1 shall contain all of the following information:
   (a) an introductory section providing:
      (i) a description of the context of the report in terms of the nature, scale, and complexity of the financial entity's services, activities, and operations, the financial entity's organisation, identified critical functions, strategy, major ongoing projects or activities, and relationships, and the financial entity's dependence on in-house and outsourced ICT services and systems, or the implications that a total loss or severe degradation of such systems would have on critical or important functions and market efficiency;
      (ii) an executive level summary of the current and near-term ICT risk identified, threat landscape, the assessed effectiveness of its controls, and the security posture of the financial entity;

(iii) information about the reported area;

(iv) a summary of the major changes in the ICT risk management framework since the previous report;

(v) a summary and a description of the impact of major changes to the simplified ICT risk management framework since the previous report;

(b) where applicable, the date of the approval of the report by the management body of the financial entity;

(c) a description of the reasons for the review, including:

(i) where the review has been initiated following supervisory instructions, evidence of such instructions;

(ii) where the review has been initiated following the occurrence of ICT related incidents, the list of all those ICT-related incidents with related incident root-cause analysis;

(d) the start and end date of the review period;

(e) the person responsible for the review;

(f) a summary of findings, and a self-assessment of the severity of the weaknesses, deficiencies, and gaps identified in ICT risk management framework for the review period, including a detailed analysis thereof;

(g) remedying measures identified to address weaknesses, deficiencies, and gaps in the simplified ICT risk management framework, and the expected date for implementing those measures, including the follow-up on weaknesses, deficiencies, and gaps identified in previous reports, where those weaknesses, deficiencies, and gaps have not yet been remedied;

(h) overall conclusions on the review of the simplified ICT risk management framework, including any further planned developments.

TITLE IV – FINAL PROVISIONS

Article 42
Entry into force

This Regulation shall enter into force on the twentieth day following that of its publication in the Official Journal of the European Union.

This Regulation shall be binding in its entirety and directly applicable in all Member States.

Done at Brussels, 13.3.2024

For the Commission
The President
Ursula VON DER LEYEN

Index

[all references are to paragraph number]

Access control
ICT risk management framework, 10.104
Simplified ICT risk management framework, 10.116
Account information service provider
definition, 10.41
scope of DORA, 2.02
Acquisition of systems
ICT risk management framework, 10.99
Simplified ICT risk management framework, 10.120
Administrative penalties
exercise, 15.06
generally, 15.05
publication, 15.08
Administrator of critical benchmarks
definition, 10.61
Alternative investment fund managers
definition, 10.48
scope of DORA, 2.02
Alternative investment intermediaries
scope of DORA, 2.02
Ancillary insurance intermediary
definition, 10.54
Anomalous activities detection
ICT risk management framework, 10.106
Asset management policy
ICT risk management framework, 10.87
Asset management procedure
ICT risk management framework, 10.88
Asset-referenced token issuers
scope of DORA, 2.02

Backup of records
ICT risk management framework, 10.78
Bad actor hacking
cyber threats, 1.03
regulatory reports, 6.05
Baseline protections
imperative need, and, 1.34
Board responsibility
governance, 5.22
Business continuity policy
ICT risk management framework
components, 10.107
generally, 10.77
testing, 10.108
Simplified ICT risk management framework
components, 10.122
testing, 10.123
Business email attacks
cyber threats, and, 1.03
Business impact analysis (BIA)
ICT risk management framework, 10.77

Capacity management
ICT risk management framework, 10.92
Central counterparty
definition, 10.44
scope of DORA, 2.02
Central securities depository
definition, 10.46
scope of DORA, 2.02
Centralisation of reporting
incident management, 11.13
Change management
ICT risk management framework, 10.100
Simplified ICT risk management framework, 10.121
Classification of functions, roles and responsibilities
ICT risk management framework, 10.74
Classification of information assets and ICT assets
Simplified ICT risk management framework, 10.113
Cloud services
governance, 5.10
imperative need, and, 1.27
scope of DORA, 2.03
Co-dependency
imperative need, and, 1.30

Communication policies
ICT risk management framework, 10.80
Competent authorities
administrative penalties
exercise, 15.06
generally, 15.05
publication, 15.08
co-operation
between authorities, 15.03
financial cross sector exercises, 15.04
generally, 15.02
criminal penalties, 15.07
data protection, 15.10
generally, 15.01
investigations, 15.05
notification duties, 15.11
penalties
administrative, 15.05—15.08
criminal, 15.07
powers
generally, 15.01
sanctions, 15.05
secrecy, 15.09
Compliance
emerging risk, 3.11
European Supervisory Bodies, and, 3.05
graduated impact, 3.07
ICT, for
classification, 3.14
generally, 3.12
identification, 3.14
payment incidents, 3.17
policy, 4.01—4.12
reporting incidents, 3.15
risk management, 3.13
supervisory feedback, 3.16
initiatives
new, 3.06
prior, 3.05
introduction, 3.01
management of third-party risk, 13.19
national measures, 3.08
new initiatives, 3.06
payment incidents
ICT, for, 3.17
policy, 3.09
policy
emerging risk, 3.11
graduated impact, 3.07
ICT compliance, on, 4.01—4.12
introduction, 3.03
national measures, 3.08
Compliance – *contd*
policy – *contd*
new initiatives, 3.06
payment incidents, 3.09
prior initiatives, 3.05
regulatory framework, 3.04
responsibility, 3.10
policy on ICT compliance
continuity, 4.10
cross-border activities, 4.12
cross-sectoral influence, 4.04
graduated tests, 4.06—4.07
increased attention on risk, 4.01
international requirements, 4.12
lack of effectiveness, 4.02
limited focus, 4.03
management, 4.09
monitoring, 4.11
reporting, 4.11
sector testing, 4.08
vulnerability testing, 4.05
prior initiatives, 3.05
regulatory framework, 3.04
reporting incidents
generally, 3.15
ICT compliance, of, 4.11
requirements
generally, 3.02
ICT compliance, for, 3.12—3.14
responsibility, 3.10
risk identification, 3.02
risk management framework, 3.13
strategy, 3.02
supervisory feedback, 3.16
third-party risk, 13.19
Contractual arrangements
governance, 5.35
managing third-party risk, 13.04
Co-operation
competent authorities
between authorities, 15.03
financial cross sector exercises, 15.04
generally, 15.02
management of third-party risk, 13.18
Cost
threats, and, 1.02
Credit institution
definition, 10.35
scope of DORA, 2.02
Credit rating agency
definition, 10.58
scope of DORA, 2.02

Criminal penalties
generally, 15.07
Critical ICT third-party service provider
definition, 10.27
designation, 13.05
Critical incidents
regulatory reports, 6.08
Critical or important function
definition, 10.26
Critical services
governance, 5.40
Crowdfunding service provider
definition, 10.62
scope of DORA, 2.02
Crypto-asset service provider
definition, 10.59
scope of DORA, 2.02
Cryptographic controls
ICT risk management framework, 10.89
Cryptographic key management
ICT risk management framework, 10.90
Customer services
scope of DORA, 2.03
Cyber-attack
definition, 10.18
Cyber threats
cost, 1.02
definition, 10.16
incident management, 11.03
payment systems, 1.06
risk, 1.03—1.05
temporal risks, 1.05

Data and system security
ICT risk management framework, 10.94
Data centres
scope of DORA, 2.03
Data protection
competent authorities, 15.10
Data reporting service provider
definition, 10.50
scope of DORA, 2.02
Data security
Simplified ICT risk management framework, 10.118
Definitions
account information service provider, 10.41
administrator of critical benchmarks, 10.61
ancillary insurance intermediary, 10.54
central counterparty, 10.44

Definitions – *contd*
central securities depository, 10.46
credit institution, 10.35
credit rating agency, 10.58
critical ICT third-party service provider, 10.27
critical or important function, 10.26
crowdfunding service provider, 10.62
crypto asset service provider, 10.59
cyber-attack, 10.18
cyber threat, 10.16
data reporting service provider, 10.50
digital operational resilience, 10.05
electronic money institution, 10.42
electronic money institution exempted, 10.43
group, 10.30
ICT asset, 10.11
ICT concentration risk, 10.33
ICT intra-group service provider, 10.24
ICT-related incident, 10.12
ICT risk, 10.09
ICT services, 10.25
ICT subcontractor established in third country, 10.28
ICT third-party risk, 10.22
ICT third-party service provider, 10.23
ICT third-party service provider established in third country, 10.28
information asset, 10.10
institution exempted pursuant to Directive 2013/36, 10.36
institution for occupational retirement provision, 10.56
insurance intermediary, 10.53
insurance undertaking, 10.51
introduction, 10.04
investment firm, 10.37
issuer of asset referenced tokens, 10.60
Joint Committee, 10.66
Lead Overseer, 10.65
legacy ICT system, 10.07
major ICT-related incident, 10.14
major operational or security payment-related incident, 10.13
management body, 10.34
management company, 10.49
manager of alternative investment funds, 10.48
medium-sized enterprise, 10.68
microenterprise, 10.64
network and information system, 10.06

Definitions – *contd*
operational or security payment-related incident, 10.13
parent undertaking, 10.31
payment institution, 10.39
payment institution exempted, 10.40
public authority, 10.69
reinsurance intermediary, 10.55
reinsurance undertaking, 10.52
securitisation repository, 10.63
security of network and information systems, 10.08
significant cyber threat, 10.17
small and non-interconnected investment firm, 10.38
small enterprise, 10.67
small institution for occupational retirement provision, 10.57
subsidiary, 10.29
threat intelligence, 10.19
threat-led penetration testing, 10.21
trade repository, 10.45
trading venue, 10.47
vulnerability, 10.20
Delegated acts
generally, 16.01—16.02
Regulations, Appendix 2
Depositaries
central securities, 10.46
Designation
critical ICT third-party service providers, 13.05
Detection
ICT risk management framework, 10.76
Development of systems
ICT risk management framework, 10.99
Simplified ICT risk management framework, 10.120
Digital Operational Resilience Act (EU 2022/2554)
amendments, 17.03
application, 17.02
chapter details, 9.04
chapter themes, 9.03
citation, 9.02
commencement, 17.02
competent authorities
See also **Competent authorities**
co-operation, 15.02—15.04
data protection, 15.10
generally, 15.01
notification duties, 15.11
Digital Operational Resilience Act (EU 2022/2554) – *contd*
competent authorities – *contd*
penalties, 15.05—15.08
secrecy, 15.09
cyber threats, 1.06
definitions
See also **Definitions**
introduction, 10.04
list, 10.05—10.69
delegated acts, 16.01—16.02
entry into force, 17.02
final provisions, 17.01—17.04
fines and penalties, 8.01
formal title, 9.02
general provisions
definitions, 10.04—10.69
governance, 10.71
introduction, 10.01
organisation, 10.71
proportionality, 10.70
scope, 10.03
subject-matter, 10.02
governance
generally, 5.01
risk management, 10.71
ICT threats, 1.07
incident management
See also **Incident management**
centralisation of reporting of incidents, 11.13
classification of incidents, 11.03—11.10
generally, 11.02
harmonisation of reporting content, 11.12
introduction, 11.01
operational or security payment related incidents, 11.15
process, 11.02
reporting incidents, 11.11
supervisory feedback, 11.14
information sharing arrangements, 14.01—14.02
introduction, 1.01
investigations, 7.01
legal compliance, 3.01
levels, 9.06—9.07
need, and, 1.08—1.09
overview, 9.01
pillars, 9.05
proportionality, 10.70

Digital Operational Resilience Act (EU 2022/2554) – *contd*
regulatory reports, 6.01
remedies, 8.01
resilience testing
See also **Digital operational resilience testing**
advanced testing, 12.04
general requirements, 12.02
ICT tools and systems, 12.03
introduction, 12.01
requirements for TLPT testers, 12.05
review clause, 17.04
risk management
See also **Risk management**
backups, 10.78
communication, 10.80
detection, 10.76
generally, 10.72
governance, and, 10.71
harmonisation of tools, methods, processes and policies, 10.81
identification, 10.74
learning, 10.79
protection and prevention, 10.75
response and recovery, 10.77
restoration, 10.78
simplified framework, 10.82—10.141
systems, protocols and tools, 10.73
third-party risk, 13.01—13.19
scope, 10.03
sectoral remit, 2.01—2.03
structure, 9.03
subject-matter, 10.02
text, Appendix 1
themes, 9.03
third-party risk
See also **Third-party risk**
compliance, 13.19
continuing oversight, 13.14
contractual provisions, 13.04
designation of critical service providers, 13.05
fees for oversight, 13.17
follow-up by competent authorities, 13.16
general principles, 13.02
harmonisation of oversight, 13.15
inspections, 13.13
international cooperation, 13.18
introduction, 13.01
investigations, 13.12

Digital Operational Resilience Act (EU 2022/2554) – *contd*
third-party risk – *contd*
Lead Overseer, 13.07—13.10
operational coordination, 13.08
oversight, 13.06—13.17
powers of Lead Overseer, 13.09—13.10
preliminary assessment of concentration risk, 13.03
request for information, 13.11
role of Lead Overseer, 13.07
title, 9.02

Digital operational resilience testing
advanced testing, 12.04
DORT-P, 12.03
general performance requirements, 12.02
ICT tools and systems, 12.03
introduction, 12.01
requirements for TLPT testers, 12.05
threat-led penetration testing (TLPT), 12.04

Digital transformation
governance, 5.39

Distributed denial of service (DDOS)
cyber threats, and, 1.03

Documentation of functions, roles and responsibilities
ICT risk management framework, 10.74

Documentation of policies and procedures
ICT risk management framework, 10.86

Electric money institution
definition, 10.42
scope of DORA, 2.02

Electronic money institution exempted
definition, 10.43

Encryption controls
ICT risk management framework, 10.89

Environmental security
ICT risk management framework, 10.101
Simplified ICT risk management framework, 10.115

European Supervisory Authorities (ESA)
administrative cooperation arrangements, 5.42
competent authorities
cooperation, 15.02
cross sector exercises, 15.04
data protection, 15.10
delegated regulations, Appendix 2
designation of critical service providers, 5.06

European Supervisory Authorities (ESA)
– *contd*
digital operational resilience testing
advanced testing, 12.04
establishment, 3.05
governance mandate, 5.46
harmonisation of tools, methods, processes and policies, 10.81
incident management
classification of incidents, 11.03
investigation oversight
costs, 7.13
generally, 7.06
powers of Lead Overseer, 7.07
principles, 7.10
legal compliance
emerging risk, 3.11
identification and classification, 3.14
introduction, 3.02
national measures, 3.08
prior initiatives, 3.05
requirements, 3.12
reporting incidents, 3.15
risk management framework, 3.13
supervisory feedback, 3.16
testing, 3.18
management of third party risk
continuing oversight, 13.14
contractual arrangements, 13.04
designation of critical service providers, 13.05
general principles, 13.02
harmonisation of oversight, 13.15
international cooperation, 13.16
oversight framework, 13.06
requests for information, 13.11
payment systems, 5.48
policy on ICT compliance, 4.01
register of information, 5.04
regulatory cooperation, 5.45
regulatory reporting
policy, 6.04
requirements, 6.02
reporting formats, 5.47
subcontracting services, 5.05
third party risk, 13.02

Fees
managing third-party risk, 13.17
FinTech Action Plan
imperative need, and, 1.31
Finance activities
imperative need, and, 1.14—1.16
scope of DORA, 2.03
Financial entities
scope of DORA, 2.02
Financial services
imperative need, 1.14—1.16
scope of DORA, 2.03
Fines
See also **Penalties**
engagement, 8.03
introduction, 8.01
policy, 8.03—8.04
requirements, 8.02

Global service providers
governance, 5.42
Governance
access, 5.33
additional oversight, 5.44
arrangement
designation, 5.06
generally, 5.05
board responsibility, 5.22
cloud services, 5.10
competition, 5.30
consolidated regulatory effects, 5.36
contact designation, 5.43
contagion, 5.49
continuity, 5.25
critical services oversight, 5.40
criticality, 5.37
designation, 5.06
digital resilience, 5.09
digital transformation, 5.39
diligence, 5.29
direct services, 5.38
effectiveness of risk strategy, 5.11
ESA mandate, 5.46
exit, 5.34
flexibility of approach, 5.23
global risk, 5.20
global service providers, 5.42
ICT risk management framework, 10.71
information sharing, 5.18
introduction, 5.01
key providers and provision
additional provision, 5.32
generally, 5.31
limited earlier attention, 5.08
management responsibility, 5.02
market assessment, 5.26

Governance – *contd*
monitoring, 5.15, 5.28
outsourcing rules, 5.14
oversight
additional, 5.44
critical services, 5.40
digital transformation, 5.39
direct services, 5.38
generally, 5.37
global service providers, 5.42
introduction, 5.36
payment systems, 5.48
physical resilience, 5.09
policy, 5.07—5.49
recovery from attacks, 5.25
register of information, 5.04
regulatory expertise, 5.45
reporting formats, 5.47
requirements, 5.02—5.06
resources, 5.21
responsive monitoring, 5.28
risk complexity, 5.17
risk management
generally, 10.71
responsibility, 5.02
risk multiplication, 5.16
shared intelligence, 5.19
Simplified ICT risk management framework, 10.111
sources of risk, 5.27
standard contractual clauses, 5.35
strategy, 5.07
subsidiaries, 5.41
supervisory strategy, 5.13
third-party arrangements, 5.03
threat evolution, 5.24
transition, 5.34
Group
definition, 10.30
Group services
imperative need, 1.26

Harmonisation
ICT risk management framework, 10.81
imperative need, 1.21
incident management reporting, 11.12
tools, methods, processes and policies, 10.81
Hosting services
scope of DORA, 2.03
Human resources
ICT risk management framework, 10.102
scope of DORA, 2.03

ICT asset
definition, 10.11
ICT concentration risk
definition, 10.33
ICT intra-group service provider
definition, 10.24
ICT-related incident
definition, 10.12
ICT-related incident detection and response
ICT risk management framework, 10.106
ICT-related incident management policy
ICT risk management framework, 10.105
ICT risk
definition, 10.09
ICT risk management framework
See also **Simplified ICT risk management framework**
access control, 10.104
acquisition of systems, 10.99
anomalous activities detection, 10.106
asset management policy, 10.87
asset management procedure, 10.88
backup of records, 10.78
business continuity policy
components, 10.107
generally, 10.77
testing, 10.108
business impact analysis (BIA), 10.77
capacity management, 10.92
change management, 10.100
classification of functions, roles and responsibilities, 10.74
communication policies, 10.80
cryptographic controls, 10.89
cryptographic key management, 10.90
data and system security, 10.94
detection, 10.76
development of systems, 10.99
documentation of functions, roles and responsibilities, 10.74
documentation of policies and procedures, 10.86
elements of policies, procedures, protocols and tools,10.85
encryption controls, 10.89
environmental security, 10.101
generally, 10.72
governance, 10.71
harmonisation of tools, methods, processes and policies, 10.81
human resources policy, 10.102

ICT risk management framework – *contd*
ICT-related incident detection and response, 10.106
ICT-related incident management policy, 10.105
identification of functions, roles and responsibilities, 10.74
identity management, 10.103
implementation of policies and procedures, 10.86
incident management policy, 10.105
in-transit information, 10.97
learning from past disruption and events, 10.79
logging, 10.95
maintenance of systems, 10.99
network security, 10.96
operational policies and procedures, 10.91
overall risk profile and complexity, 10.84
patch management, 10.93
performance management, 10.92
physical security, 10.101
policies, procedures, protocols and tools,10.85
prevention of risk, 10.75
project management, 10.98
protection of systems, 10.75
recovery procedures
generally, 10.77—10.78
Regulation, 10.109
Regulation 2024/1774
generally, 10.83—10.110
text, Appendix 2
report on review, 10.110
resilience strategy, 10.72
response procedures
generally, 10.77
Regulation, 10.109
restoration of records, 10.78
review of disruption and events, 10.79
securing information in transit, 10.97
strategy, 10.72
system security, 10.94
systems acquisition, development and maintenance, 10.99
systems, protocols and tools, 10.73
third-party risk
See also **Third-party risk**
compliance, 13.19
continuing oversight, 13.14
contractual arrangements, 13.04

ICT risk management framework – *contd*
third-party risk – *contd*
designation of critical service providers, 13.05
fees for oversight, 13.17
follow-up by competent authorities, 13.16
general principles, 13.02
harmonisation of oversight, 13.15
inspections, 13.13
international cooperation, 13.18
introduction, 13.01
investigations, 13.12
Lead Overseer, 13.07—13.10
operational coordination, 13.08
oversight, 13.06—13.17
powers of Lead Overseer, 13.09—13.10
preliminary assessment of concentration risk, 13.03
request for information, 13.11
role of Lead Overseer, 13.07
tools, methods, processes and policies, 10.81
user activity monitoring, 10.75
vulnerability and patch management, 10.93

ICT services
definition, 10.25
introduction, 1.04

ICT subcontractor established in third country
definition, 10.28

ICT third-party risk
definition, 10.22

ICT third-party service provider
definition, 10.23

ICT third-party service provider established in third country
definition, 10.28

Identification and classification
ICT risk management framework, 10.74
legal compliance, 3.14

Identity management
ICT risk management framework, 10.103

Implementation of policies and procedures
ICT risk management framework, 10.86

Incident management
centralisation of reporting of incidents, 11.13

Incident management – *contd*
classification of incidents
criteria, 11.05
generally, 11.03
major incidents, 11.06
materiality thresholds, 11.06
Regulation 2024/1774, 11.04—11.10
relevance of incidents to other authorities, 11.08
risk profile and complexity, 11.10
significant cyber threats, 11.07
cyber threats, 11.03
generally, 11.02
harmonisation of reporting content, 11.12
ICT risk management framework, 10.105
introduction, 11.01
operational or security payment related incidents, 11.15
process, 11.02
reporting incidents
centralisation, 11.13
generally, 11.11
harmonisation, 11.12
requirements, 11.02
supervisory feedback, 11.14
Incident management policy
ICT risk management framework, 10.105
Incidents
regulatory reports
bad actor motivation, 6.05
critical incidents, 6.08
generally, 6.04
legal compliance, 3.15
materiality thresholds, 6.07
policy compliance on ICT, 4.11
sharing information, 6.06
Information asset
definition, 10.10
Information security policy and measures
Simplified ICT risk management framework, 10.112
Information sharing
arrangements, 14.01—14.02
governance, 5.18
Inspections
managing third-party risk, 13.13
Institution exempted pursuant to Directive 2013/36
definition, 10.36
Institution for occupational retirement provision
definition, 10.56
Insurance intermediary
ancillary intermediary, 10.54
definition, 10.53
scope of DORA, 2.02
Insurance sector
imperative need, and, 1.15
Insurance undertaking
definition, 10.51
scope of DORA, 2.02
International cooperation
managing third-party risk, 13.18
In-transit information
ICT risk management framework, 10.97
Investigations
collaboration, 7.03
communication, 7.04
competent authorities, 15.05
compliance verification, 7.09
expertise and skills, 7.12
introduction, 7.01
Lead Overseer
introduction, 7.02
powers, 7.07
managing third-party risk, 13.12
national efforts, 7.05
oversight
costs, 7.13
generally, 7.06
principles, 7.10
policy, 7.03—7.14
requirements, 7.02
rights of third-party service providers, 7.08
risk management, 7.11
systemic impacts, 7.14
technical skills and expertise, 7.12
Investment firm
definition, 10.37
scope of DORA, 2.02
Issuer of asset referenced tokens
definition, 10.60

Joint Committee
definition, 10.66

Lead Overseer
See also **Investigations**
definition, 10.65
introduction, 7.02
managing third-party risk
continuing oversight, 13.14
coordination, 13.08

Lead Overseer – *contd*
managing third-party risk – *contd*
fees, 13.17
follow-up by authorities, 13.16
inspections, 13.13
investigations, 13.12
powers, 13.09—13.10
requests for information, 13.11
role, 13.07
powers, 7.07
Learning from past disruption and events
ICT risk management framework, 10.79
Legacy ICT system
definition, 10.07
Legal compliance
emerging risk, 3.11
European Supervisory Bodies, and, 3.05
graduated impact, 3.07
ICT, for
classification, 3.14
generally, 3.12
identification, 3.14
payment incidents, 3.17
policy, 4.01—4.12
reporting incidents, 3.15
risk management, 3.13
supervisory feedback, 3.16
initiatives
new, 3.06
prior, 3.05
introduction, 3.01
national measures, 3.08
new initiatives, 3.06
payment incidents
ICT, for, 3.17
policy, 3.09
policy
emerging risk, 3.11
graduated impact, 3.07
ICT compliance, on, 4.01—4.12
introduction, 3.03
national measures, 3.08
new initiatives, 3.06
payment incidents, 3.09
prior initiatives, 3.05
regulatory framework, 3.04
responsibility, 3.10
policy on ICT compliance
continuity, 4.10
cross-border activities, 4.12
cross-sectoral influence, 4.04
graduated tests, 4.06—4.07

Legal compliance – *contd*
policy on ICT compliance – *contd*
increased attention on risk, 4.01
international requirements, 4.12
lack of effectiveness, 4.02
limited focus, 4.03
management, 4.09
monitoring, 4.11
reporting, 4.11
sector testing, 4.08
vulnerability testing, 4.05
prior initiatives, 3.05
regulatory framework, 3.04
reporting incidents
generally, 3.15
ICT compliance, of, 4.11
requirements
generally, 3.02
ICT compliance, for, 3.12—3.14
responsibility, 3.10
risk identification, 3.02
risk management framework, 3.13
strategy, 3.02
supervisory feedback, 3.16
Logging
ICT risk management framework, 10.95

Maintenance of systems
ICT risk management framework, 10.99
Simplified ICT risk management framework, 10.120
Major ICT-related incident
definition, 10.14
Major operational or security payment-related incident
definition, 10.13
Managed services
scope of DORA, 2.03
Management body
definition, 10.34
Management company
definition, 10.49
scope of DORA, 2.02
Management of third-party risk
assessment of concentration risk, 13.03
compliance, 13.19
continuing oversight, 13.14
contractual arrangements, 13.04
coordination between Lead Overseers, 13.08
definition of ICT third-party risk, 10.22

Management of third-party risk – *contd*
designation of critical ICT third-party service providers, 13.05
fees for oversight, 13.17
follow-up by competent authorities, 13.16
general principles, 13.02
harmonisation of oversight, 13.15
ICT Risk Management Framework, 12.02
inspections, 13.13
international cooperation, 13.18
introduction, 13.01
investigations, 13.12
Lead Overseer
continuing oversight, 13.14
coordination, 13.08
fees, 13.17
follow-up by authorities, 13.16
inspections, 13.13
investigations, 13.12
powers, 13.09—13.10
requests for information, 13.11
role, 13.07
oversight
continuing, 13.14
harmonisation, 13.15
Lead Overseer, 13.07—13.13
structure of the Framework, 13.06
powers of Lead Overseer
exercise of powers outside EU, 13.10
generally, 13.09
preliminary assessment of concentration risk, 13.03
principles, 13.02
requests for information, 13.11
role of Lead Overseer, 13.07
Manager of alternative investment funds
definition, 10.48
scope of DORA, 2.02
Marketing services
scope of DORA, 2.03
Medium-sized enterprise
definition, 10.68
Microenterprise
definition, 10.64

Network and information system
definition, 10.06
Network security
ICT risk management framework, 10.96
Simplified ICT risk management framework, 10.118
Non-interconnected investment firm
definition, 10.38
Notification duties
competent authorities, 15.11

Occupational retirement providers
institution for provision, 10.56
scope of DORA, 2.02
small institution for provision, 10.57
Online customer service
scope of DORA, 2.03
Operational or security payment-related incident
definition, 10.13
incident management, 11.15
Operational policies and procedures
ICT risk management framework, 10.91
Operational security
Simplified ICT risk management framework, 10.117
Outsourcing
governance, 5.14
imperative need, and, 1.25
Overall risk profile and complexity
ICT risk management framework, 10.84
Oversight of third-party risk
continuing, 13.14
harmonisation, 13.15
Lead Overseer, 13.07—13.13
structure of the Framework, 13.06

Parent undertaking
definition, 10.31
Patch management
ICT risk management framework, 10.93
Payment incidents
legal compliance
ICT, for, 3.17
policy, 3.09
Payment institution
definition, 10.39
scope of DORA, 2.02
Payment institution exempted
definition, 10.40
Payment services
imperative need, and, 1.28
scope of DORA, 2.03
Payment systems
governance, 5.48
imperative need, and, 1.06, 1.12

Penalties
administrative
between authorities, 15.03
financial cross sector exercises, 15.04
generally, 15.02
criminal, 15.07
engagement, 8.03
introduction, 8.01
policy, 8.03—8.04
requirements, 8.02
Penetration testing
generally, 12.01
threat-led, 10.21
Performance management
ICT risk management framework, 10.92
Phishing
cyber threats, and, 1.03
Physical security
ICT risk management framework, 10.101
Simplified ICT risk management framework, 10.115
Pillars
generally, 9.05
Policies
fines, 8.03—8.04
governance
See also **Governance**
generally, 5.07—5.49
ICT compliance
continuity, 4.10
cross-border activities, 4.12
cross-sectoral influence, 4.04
graduated tests, 4.06—4.07
increased attention on risk, 4.01
international requirements, 4.12
lack of effectiveness, 4.02
limited focus, 4.03
management, 4.09
monitoring, 4.11
reporting, 4.11
sector testing, 4.08
vulnerability testing, 4.05
imperative need, 1.33
investigations, 7.03—7.14
legal compliance
emerging risk, 3.11
graduated impact, 3.07
ICT compliance, on, 4.01—4.12
introduction, 3.03
national measures, 3.08
new initiatives, 3.06
payment incidents, 3.09
Policies – *contd*
legal compliance – *contd*
prior initiatives, 3.05
regulatory framework, 3.04
responsibility, 3.10
penalties and prosecutions, 8.03—8.04
Policies, procedures, protocols and tools
ICT risk management framework,10.85
Prevention of risk
ICT risk management framework, 10.75
Print services
scope of DORA, 2.03
Project management
ICT risk management framework, 10.98
Simplified ICT risk management framework, 10.121
Proportionality
general principle, 10.70
Prosecutions
engagement, 8.03
introduction, 8.01
policy, 8.03—8.04
requirements, 8.02
Protection of systems
ICT risk management framework, 10.75
Public authority
definition, 10.69

Ransomware
cyber threats, and, 1.03
Recovery procedures
ICT risk management framework
generally, 10.77—10.78
Regulation, 10.109
Register of information
governance, 5.04
regulatory reports, 6.09
Regulatory reports
bad actor motivation, 6.05
critical incidents, 6.08
divergent problems, 6.03
incidents, of
bad actor motivation, 6.05
critical incidents, 6.08
generally, 6.04
legal compliance, 3.15
materiality thresholds, 6.07
policy compliance on ICT, 4.11
sharing information, 6.06
introduction, 6.01
legal compliance, 3.15
materiality thresholds, 6.07

Regulatory reports – *contd*
policy, 6.03—6.10
register of information, 6.09
requirements, 6.02
sharing information, 6.06
skills, 6.10
Reinsurance intermediary
definition, 10.55
Reinsurance undertaking
definition, 10.52
scope of DORA, 2.02
Remedies
administrative penalties
between authorities, 15.03
financial cross sector exercises, 15.04
generally, 15.02
criminal penalties, 15.07
engagement, 8.03
introduction, 8.01
policy, 8.03—8.04
requirements, 8.02
Report on review
ICT risk management framework, 10.110
Simplified ICT risk management framework, 10.124
Reporting incidents
centralisation, 11.13
generally, 11.11
harmonisation, 11.12
Repositories
securitisation, 10.63
trade, 10.45
Requests for information
managing third-party risk, 13.11
Resilience gap
imperative need, and, 1.10
Resilience strategy
ICT risk management framework, 10.72
Resilience testing
advanced testing, 12.04
DORT-P, 12.03
general performance requirements, 12.02
ICT tools and systems, 12.03
introduction, 12.01
requirements for TLPT testers, 12.05
threat-led penetration testing (TLPT), 12.04
Response procedures
ICT risk management framework
generally, 10.77
Regulation, 10.109
Restoration of records
ICT risk management framework, 10.78
Review of disruption and events
ICT risk management framework, 10.79
Risk
imperative need, and, 1.03—1.05
Risk management
backup of records, 10.78
business continuity policy, 10.77
business impact analysis (BIA), 10.77
classification of functions, roles and responsibilities, 10.74
communication policies, 10.80
detection, 10.76
documentation of functions, roles and responsibilities, 10.74
ICT Framework
See also **ICT risk management framework**
backup, 10.78
communication, 10.80
detection, 10.76
functions, roles and responsibilities, 10.74
generally, 10.72
governance, 10.71
harmonisation, 10.81
learning from past, 10.79
protection and prevention, 10.75
Regulations, 10.83—10.110
response and recovery, 10.77
restoration, 10.78
systems, protocols and tools, 10.73
generally, 10.72
governance
generally, 10.71
responsibility, 5.02
harmonisation of tools, methods, processes and policies, 10.81
identification of functions, roles and responsibilities, 10.74
investigations, 7.11
learning from past disruption and events, 10.79
legal compliance, 3.13
prevention of risk, 10.75
protection of systems, 10.75
recovery procedures, 10.77—10.78
resilience strategy, 10.72
response procedures, 10.77
responsibility, 5.02
restoration of records, 10.78

Risk management – *contd*
review of disruption and events, 10.79
simplified framework
See also **Simplified ICT risk management framework**
generally, 10.82
legal compliance, 3.13
Regulations, 10.111—10.124
strategy, 10.72
systems, protocols and tools, 10.73
third-party risk
See also **Third-party risk management**
compliance, 13.19
continuing oversight, 13.14
contractual arrangements, 13.04
designation of critical service providers, 13.05
fees for oversight, 13.17
follow-up by competent authorities, 13.16
general principles, 13.02
harmonisation of oversight, 13.15
inspections, 13.13
international cooperation, 13.18
introduction, 13.01
investigations, 13.12
Lead Overseer, 13.07—13.10
operational coordination, 13.08
oversight, 13.06—13.17
powers of Lead Overseer, 13.09—13.10
preliminary assessment of concentration risk, 13.03
request for information, 13.11
role of Lead Overseer, 13.07
tools, methods, processes and policies, 10.81
user activity monitoring, 10.75
Rulebook
imperative need, and, 1.22

Secrecy
competent authorities, 15.09
Sectoral coverage
financial, 2.02
ICT, 2.03
introduction, 2.01
Securing information in transit
ICT risk management framework, 10.97
Securitisation repository
definition, 10.63
scope of DORA, 2.02
Security of network and information systems
definition, 10.08
Security payment-related incident
definition, 10.13
Security testing
Simplified ICT risk management framework, 10.119
Service providers
See also **Third-party service providers**
account information, 10.41
critical ICT third-party, 10.27
crowdfunding, 10.62
crypto asset, 10.59
data reporting, 10.50
ICT intra-group, 10.24
ICT third-party, 10.23
ICT third-party established in third country, 10.28
Significant cyber threat
definition, 10.17
Simplified ICT risk management framework
See also **Risk management**
access control, 10.116
acquisition of systems, 10.120
business continuity plan
components, 10.122
testing, 10.123
change management, 10.121
classification of information assets and ICT assets, 10.113
data security, 10.118
development of systems, 10.120
environmental security, 10.115
generally, 10.82
governance and organisation, 10.111
information security policy and measures, 10.112
maintenance of systems, 10.120
network security, 10.118
operations security, 10.117
physical security, 10.115
project management, 10.121
Regulation 2024/1774
generally, 10.111—10.141
text, Appendix 2
report on review, 10.124
risk management, 10.114
security testing, 10.119
system and network security, 10.118

Simplified ICT risk management framework – *contd*
systems acquisition, development and maintenance, 10.120
Small and non-interconnected investment firm
definition, 10.38
Simplified ICT Risk Management Framework, 10.82
Small enterprise
definition, 10.67
Small institution for occupational retirement provision
definition, 10.56
Spear phishing
cyber threats, and, 1.03
Standard contractual clauses
governance, 5.35
Subject-matter
general provisions, 10.02
Subsidiary
definition, 10.29
governance, 5.41
Supervision of institutions
imperative need, and, 1.35
Supervisory feedback
incident management, 11.14
System security
ICT risk management framework, 10.94
Simplified ICT risk management framework, 10.118
Systems acquisition, development and maintenance
ICT risk management framework, 10.99
Simplified ICT risk management framework, 10.120
Systems, protocols and tools
ICT risk management framework, 10.73

Testing
advanced testing, 12.04
DORT-P, 12.03
general performance requirements, 12.02
ICT tools and systems, 12.03
imperative need, and, 1.36
introduction, 12.01
legal compliance, 3.18
requirements for TLPT testers, 12.05
threat-led penetration testing (TLPT), 12.04
Third-party arrangements
governance, 5.03
Third-party risk
assessment of concentration risk, 13.03
compliance, 13.19
continuing oversight, 13.14
contractual arrangements, 13.04
coordination between Lead Overseers, 13.08
definition of ICT third-party risk, 10.22
designation of critical ICT third-party service providers, 13.05
fees for oversight, 13.17
follow-up by competent authorities, 13.16
general principles, 13.02
harmonisation of oversight, 13.15
ICT Risk Management Framework, 12.02
inspections, 13.13
international cooperation, 13.18
introduction, 13.01
investigations, 13.12
Lead Overseer
continuing oversight, 13.14
coordination, 13.08
fees, 13.17
follow-up by authorities, 13.16
inspections, 13.13
investigations, 13.12
powers, 13.09—13.10
requests for information, 13.11
role, 13.07
oversight
continuing, 13.14
harmonisation, 13.15
Lead Overseer, 13.07—13.13
structure of the Framework, 13.06
powers of Lead Overseer
exercise of powers outside EU, 13.10
generally, 13.09
preliminary assessment of concentration risk, 13.03
principles, 13.02
requests for information, 13.11
role of Lead Overseer, 13.07
Third-party service providers
See also **Service providers**
critical ICT, 10.27
ICT, 10.23
ICT established in third country, 10.28
scope of DORA
financial sector, 2.02
ICT sector, 2.03
Threat intelligence
definition, 10.19

Threat-led penetration testing (TLPT)
definition, 10.21
generally, 12.04
requirements for testers, 12.05
Threats
challenges, 1.19
'cloud' working, 1.27
co-dependency, 1.30
consolidation of risk requirements, 1.32
cost, 1.02
coverage gaps, 1.24
cyber threats, 1.02—1.06
digital operational resilience rules, 1.37
disparities, 1.23
enhanced baseline protections, 1.34
enhanced testing, 1.36
European financial body initiatives, 1.20
FinTech Action Plan, 1.31
finance activities, 1.14—1.16
gaps and vectors, 1.08
group services, 1.26
harmonisation, and, 1.21
ICT threats, 1.07
insurance sector, 1.15
international focus, 1.18
need, and, 1.08
outsourcing exposures, 1.25
payment services, 1.28
payment systems, 1.06, 1.12
pivotal reliance, 1.11
policies, 1.33
reliance and support, 1.09
resilience gap, 1.10
review of risk and systems, 1.29
Threats – *contd*
risk, 1.03—1.05
Single Rulebook, 1.22
supervision of institutions, 1.35
temporal risks, 1.05
trading, 1.13
upgrade of risk requirements, 1.32
Tools, methods, processes and policies
ICT risk management framework, 10.81
Trade repository
definition, 10.45
scope of DORA, 2.02
Trading venue
definition, 10.47
scope of DORA, 2.02
Trojans
cyber threats, and, 1.03

User activity monitoring
ICT risk management framework, 10.75

Viruses
cyber threats, and, 1.03
Vulnerability
definition, 10.20
ICT risk management framework, 10.93

Web application attacks
cyber threats, and, 1.03
Web services
scope of DORA, 2.03
Website services
scope of DORA, 2.03